ENERGY IN AMERICAN HISTORY

ENERGY IN AMERICAN HISTORY

A POLITICAL, SOCIAL, AND ENVIRONMENTAL ENCYCLOPEDIA

VOLUME 1

A–M

Jeffrey B. Webb and Christopher R. Fee, Editors

BLOOMSBURY ACADEMIC
NEW YORK • LONDON • OXFORD • NEW DELHI • SYDNEY

BLOOMSBURY ACADEMIC
Bloomsbury Publishing Inc
1385 Broadway, New York, NY 10018, USA
50 Bedford Square, London, WC1B 3DP, UK
29 Earlsfort Terrace, Dublin 2, Ireland

BLOOMSBURY, BLOOMSBURY ACADEMIC and the Diana logo
are trademarks of Bloomsbury Publishing Plc

First published in the United States of America 2024

Cover images: James Jerome Hill's first engine, the Wm. Crooks, 1908.
Library of Congress; Downtown section of Kilgore, Texas, studded with oil derricks.
Russell Lee; Nuclear power plant. Carol M. Highsmith;
Three coal miners of the Lorain Coal & Dock Company, Lorado, West Virginia

Library of Congress Cataloging-in-Publication Data
Names: Webb, Jeffrey B., editor. | Fee, Christopher R., editor.
Title: Energy in American history : a political, social, and environmental encyclopedia /
Jeffrey B. Webb and Christopher R. Fee, editors.
Description: New York : Bloomsbury Academic, 2024. | Includes bibliographical references and index. |
Contents: Volume 1. A-M – Volume 2. N-Z.
Identifiers: LCCN 2023046677 (print) | LCCN 2023046678 (ebook) |
ISBN 9798216174349 (v. 1 ; hardback) | ISBN 9798216174356 (v. 2 ; hardback) |
ISBN 9781440872143 (hardback) | ISBN 9781440872150 (ebook) | ISBN 9798216171348 (epub)
Subjects: LCSH: Energy consumption–United States–History–Encyclopedias. |
Energy development–United States–History–Encyclopedias. | Energy policy–United States–History–
Encyclopedias. | Energy industries–United States–History–Encyclopedias.
Classification: LCC HD9502.U52 E49284 2024 (print) | LCC HD9502.U52 (ebook) |
DDC 333.790973–dc23/eng/20231005
LC record available at https://lccn.loc.gov/2023046677
LC ebook record available at https://lccn.loc.gov/2023046678

ISBN: HB: 979-8-2161-7434-9 (vol. 1)
979-8-2161-7435-6 (vol. 2)
978-1-4408-7214-3 (set)
ePDF: 978-1-4408-7215-0
eBook: 979-8-2161-7134-8

Typeset by Integra Software Services Pvt. Ltd.
Printed and bound in Great Britain

CONTENTS

ALPHABETICAL LIST OF ENTRIES

ACKNOWLEDGMENTS

We would like to express our appreciation for the kind assistance and support given to us by friends and colleagues, as well as a few institutions and organizations.

The Professor Jack P. Barlow, Sr. Research and Artistic Creation Fund provided a grant for the project, and a sabbatical arranged with the Office of the Vice President for Academic Affairs and Dean of the Faculty provided time for writing and editing. Randy Neuman, Associate Director of Library Services and Assistant Professor of Library Science at HU's RichLyn Library offered timely and helpful research support.

Eric Bruce and Jeff Cartwright gave helpful direction on technical points, while Todd Martin and Jeff Clausen provided a handy sounding board. Several conversations with producer and host of "& Good Company," Sara Fiedelholtz, gave shape to some of the themes that appear in the encyclopedia. Dwight Brautigam, Tim Smith, Thom Brown, and Tyler Herber, colleagues in HU's Department of History and Political Science, helped create a supportive workplace with lots of good cheer.

Our Editorial Assistants are a talented group of people. They are Trent Yentes, Tia Robinson, Emma Fee, Phoebe Doscher, Madeleine Neiman. The project had its twists and turns and their flexibility was much valued.

Family gave way so the project could reach completion, and many thanks go to Jill, Christian, Molly, Natalie, Aaron, Allison, Emma, Chandler, and Samuel.

Thanks to Michael Millman, Patrick Hall, Kevin Downing, and Thomas Krause for their expert assistance and endless patience.

Our contributors deserve special thanks for their expertise and dedication. They weathered COVID disruptions and reorganization issues and remained committed to finishing the work. Their passion shows through many of the stories gathered in this collection and will remain with us a very dear memory.

CHRONOLOGY

1621	Sir George Yeardley arranged for a post mill on his Flowerdew Hundred Plantation near Jamestown, Virginia to harness wind power for grinding wheat and corn
1643	Construction of a fulling mill for cotton textile production on Mill River in Rowley, Massachusetts by John Pearson, utilizing waterpower for energy
1712	Nantucket ship hunting right whales killed a sperm whale; its oil made a brighter and cleaner-burning light and set off longer, more dangerous hunts for sperm whale oil
1751	Publication of Benjamin Franklin's collected letters and reports of his investigations in the field of electricity, titled *Experiments and Observations on Electricity*
1795	Oliver Evans and Thomas Ellicott published *The Young Mill-Wright and Miller's Guide*, a widely read manual for setting up and operating waterpower mills
1808	Judge Jesse Fell of Wilkes-Barre, Pennsylvania demonstrated that rock-hard anthracite coal could be burned in an open grate, raising hope for its commercial development
1820	Whaling ship *Essex* sunk by a sperm whale during a two-year voyage to the South Pacific, which inspired Melville's *Moby Dick*; depletion of sperm whales led to global hunts
	Merger of two companies to form Lehigh Coal and Navigation Company, one of the earliest firms to develop anthracite coal in the US on a commercial basis
1821	The Merrimack Manufacturing Company formed to develop the Lowell (Mass.) waterpower system, a large hydropower project powering multiple textile mills
1825	William Hart drilled a natural gas well in Fredonia, New York and piped it to local houses for illumination, becoming first US commercial natural gas distributor
1829	Peter Cooper built and demonstrated the first US steam locomotive, dubbed "Tom Thumb," which inaugurated a period of innovation in steam locomotive technology
1832	Joseph Henry's experiments in electricity and magnetism; he wrapped copper wire around poles of magnet, sent current through the wire, and boosted the magnet's strength
1840	Waterpower lumber, grain, and textile mills number more than 55,000 across the country according to the US Census, one for every 245 people
1849	Patent granted to George Corliss for his improvements on the stationary steam engine, a device that encouraged industries to replace waterpower with coal-fired steam power

1851 Whale oil production in the US peaked at 328,483 barrels, which was marketed and consumed for illumination by lamplight in American homes and workplaces

Samuel Kier began operating the first US petroleum refinery in Pittsburgh, Pennsylvania, and offered his products as pharmaceuticals and illuminants

1854 Daniel Halladay received a patent for his "Halladay Self-Governing Windmill," known as the Halladay Standard, a wind-powered device for pumping groundwater on the Plains

1859 Edwin L. Drake struck oil near Titusville, Pennsylvania, inaugurating the Pennsylvania oil boom and the domestic oil industry in the US

1866 Peter Sweeney patented a steam-powered "Rotary Rock Boring Machine" that became the basis for rotary drills used in the oil fields of Texas, Louisiana, and Oklahoma

1870 Standard Oil Company founded in Cleveland, Ohio by John D. Rockefeller and his business partners; became a key agent in the creation of petroleum industry

1871 A fleet of forty whaling ships were trapped in Arctic ice north of Point Belcher, Alaska and thirty-three were abandoned, dealing a lethal blow to the whale oil industry

1876 Thomas Edison opened his laboratory in Menlo Park, New Jersey; over the course of his life, he secured 1,093 patents for his inventions from the US Patent Office

1877 Birdsill Holly built the first district steam heating system for Lockport, New York, which served as the model for New York Steam Company's system in Manhattan

1879 Electric arc light system devised by Charles Brush illuminated Cleveland's Public Square, proving the concept of street lighting by a centralized electrical power source

California Electric Light Company founded to create a municipal electricity system for San Francisco, and would eventually grow to become utility giant PG&E

1880 The Edison Illuminating Company founded by Thomas Edison for the purpose of developing and installing city-wide electrical systems for lighting

1881 Smoke from coal-fired steam plants in factories, locomotives, and residential buildings brought Chicago to enact a smoke abatement ordinance, an early air pollution law

1882 Edison Illuminating Company opened Pearl Street Station in Manhattan, the first centralized generating plant to serve multiple buildings with electrical lighting

1883 Warren Seymour Johnson's "electric tele-thermoscope" invented, which offered users more control over interior steam heating systems and gave birth to the thermostat

1886 Westinghouse engineer William Stanley, Jr. successfully operates an alternating-current (AC) illumination system in Great Barrington, Massachusetts

1888 President Edward Johnson of the Edison Electric Light Company published *A Warning from the Edison Electric Light Company*, attacking AC in the War of the Currents

1889 The first high-voltage transmission line carried 4,000 volts of electricity between a hydroelectric plant at Willamette Falls and Portland, Oregon 16 miles away

1890 Convicted murderer William Kemmler electrocuted in New York using AC, which was used for anti-AC propaganda by Edison against Westinghouse in the War of the Currents

Alfred Thayer Mahan published *The Influence of Sea Power upon History, 1660–1783,* which argued that coal supply was crucial to US strategic interests

1892 San Francisco began its well-known electric streetcar service, following the lead of the electric Richmond Union Passenger Railway, built in Virginia four years earlier

Edward Doheny struck oil at Second Street and Glendale Boulevard in Los Angeles, which began the California oil boom of the early twentieth century

1893 Chicago World's Columbian Exposition attracts 27 million visitors to see demonstrations of new electricity technologies by Edison, Tesla, and Westinghouse

1894 Electricity enabled moving pictures to be made; Thomas Edison's *Edison Kinetoscopic Record of a Sneeze,* also known as Fred Ott's Sneeze, is the earliest known

1895 Adams Hydroelectric Generating Plant opened at Niagara Falls, using AC equipment and prompting other utilities to adopt AC, thus ending the War of the Currents

1896 Henry Ford completed work on a prototype automobile, the Quadricycle, the success of which encouraged him to continue refining his design and his ideas for mass production

1897 The first National Electrical Code published by the National Board of Fire Underwriters, creating safety standards for installation and inspection of building electrical systems

1901 Prospectors operating a drill rig on Spindletop Hill salt dome near Beaumont, Texas struck oil and produced a gusher, setting off the Texas oil boom

1902 Formation of the company that became Texaco, one of the Seven Sisters oil companies that dominated the petroleum industry in the mid-twentieth century

1903 Ford Motor Company founded in Detroit, which produced "horseless carriages" for ordinary Americans powered by gasoline-burning internal combustion engines

1904 Ida Tarbell's serialized investigative reports are published together in *The History of the Standard Oil Company*, which detailed the company's monopolistic practices

1905 Piano teacher-turned oil tycoon Emma Summers signed oil supply contracts with Los Angeles County and the City Waterworks, becoming "Oil Queen" of California

1907 Year of coal mining disasters left 3,242 dead, including 362 killed in Monongah, West Virginia and 239 at a mine explosion near Jacobs Creek, Pennsylvania

1909 St. Paul Mining Company's coal mine in Cherry, Illinois caught fire and killed 259 men and boys; twenty-one survivors lived eight days in the mine before being rescued

1910 The US established naval petroleum reserves in California and Alaska, signaling the transition from coal to oil in the US Navy and increasing demand for petroleum

1911 Standard Oil Trust found in violation of the Sherman Antitrust Act by the US Supreme Court and divided into thirty-four separate companies

Upton Machine Company founded to manufacture newly invented electric washing machines, stimulating production of electric-powered devices for the home

1913 Lincoln Highway was dedicated, connecting New York and San Francisco with over 3,000 miles of existing roads; first transcontinental road for cars and trucks

1914 Coal miners' strike against Colorado Fuel and Iron Company ends in a bloody massacre when the Colorado National Guard fires on a crowd in Ludlow, killing twenty-one

1916 The Federal-Aid Road Act enacted, which was the first federal program to assist states in building the road infrastructure to support new gasoline-powered autos

1917 US Fuel Administration created to supervise and administer coal and oil conservation policies during the First World War, including price controls and coordination of shipments

1918 The US instituted its first Daylight Saving Time during the First World War as a means of conserving coal and extending the workday into the evenings for wartime production

1922 Senate began investigation into Interior Secretary Albert Fall's suspicious granting of drilling leases on US public lands to oil executives Edward Doheny and Harry Sinclair

1927 The fifteen-millionth Ford Model T was assembled, signifying the advent of gasoline-powered automobiles as Americans' primary mode of transportation

1928 Red Line Agreement signed by Anglo-Persian Oil Company, Royal Dutch Shell Company, Compagnie Française de Pétroles, and a five-member group of US oil companies to form Turkish Petroleum Company with exclusive rights to oil in Iraq

1929 Interior Secretary Albert Fall convicted and jailed for bribery in the Teapot Dome Scandal; Harry Sinclair of Sinclair Oil and Mammoth Oil also convicted and jailed

1930 Oil glut prompted the state of Texas to give the Texas Railroad Commission authority to impose production limits to stabilize oil prices

1933 Tennessee Valley Authority Act passed to provide federal support for flood control and hydroelectric dams in the less-developed regions of the rural US South

Standard Oil of California signed a concession agreement with the government of King Ibn Saud to develop oil resources in Saudi Arabia, leading to the creation of Aramco

1935 Rural Electrification Administration created by executive order, empowered to grant loans to connect rural communities to regional power grids

Public Utility Holding Company Act signed, giving the Securities and Exchange Commission authority to monitor and break up electric utility monopolies

1936 Hoover Dam began generating electricity by hydropower as one of the New Deal's large-scale public power developments bringing energy to underserved areas

1937 Three oil tankers owned by Standard Oil Company were bombed by Japanese aircraft in Nanjing, China while evacuating civilians in the USS *Panay* incident, a prelude to war

1939 Albert Einstein wrote to President Roosevelt warning about Nazi uranium research and informed him about how atomic energy could be used to make powerful bombs

1941 FDR halted US sales of oil and gasoline to Japan in response to Japan's aggressions in China and Southeast Asia; Pearl Harbor attacks followed four months later

1942 Enrico Fermi directed the first controlled, self-sustaining nuclear chain reaction with the graphite-uranium Chicago Pile-1 underneath the University of Chicago's Stagg Field

1943 Big Inch pipeline from Texas oil fields to Pennsylvania was completed, enabling shipment of crude oil without risking German submarine attacks on oil tankers

1945 Test of atomic bomb at Trinity site in New Mexico in July, and atomic bombs were dropped on the Japanese cities of Hiroshima and Nagasaki in August

1946 President Truman signed the Atomic Energy Act, which transferred the military's Manhattan Project assets to the Atomic Energy Commission

1947 Completion of the Kerr-McGee Oil Industries, Inc.'s Kermac No. 16 oil drilling platform located eleven miles from the Louisiana coast, the world's first offshore oil drilling rig

Bell Labs scientists and inventors devised the transistor, the foundation of semiconductor technology that led to the digital revolution of the 1950s–1970s

1950 President Truman approved $1.4 billion to expand the Atomic Energy Commission's capacity to produce uranium and plutonium for nuclear weapons

1951 The Experimental Breeder Reactor No. 1 at the National Reactor Testing Station in Idaho produced electricity from a nuclear reactor for the first time

1953 President Dwight Eisenhower's "Atoms for Peace" speech calls for the use of nuclear energy in powering civilian electricity-generating plants

1954 Iran Oil Consortium Agreement gave Western oil companies rights to Iran's oil fields after US–UK initiated coup put pro-western ruler Mohammad Reza Pahlavi in power

Bell Labs demonstrated the first practical silicon solar cell, a technology that used the sun's light, rather heat to produce energy

1956 Federal-Aid Highway Act became law and established the US interstate highway system, which spurred growth in the use of gasoline-powered automobiles and trucks

1957 Roger Revelle and Hans Seuss published a scientific article showing interaction between ocean and atmosphere in absorption of carbon dioxide, pointing toward global warming

1958 Dedication of Shippingport Atomic Power Station near Pittsburgh, Pennsylvania—the first operational US civilian nuclear power plant

1959 Boeing Airplane Company's 707 jet airliner made its inaugural commercial flight in January from Los Angeles to New York, ushering in the "Jet Age"

In July, President Nixon and Soviet Premier Khrushchev faced off in Moscow in the "Kitchen Debate," surrounded by symbols of US prosperity—electrical appliances

1960 Formation of OPEC at the Baghdad Conference in Iraq, which played an important role in global oil markets and international relations in second half of the twentieth century

1961 Low-power boiling water reactor, the SL-I, blew up at Idaho National Laboratory killing three personnel, who became first US fatalities in field of nuclear energy

1966 Uniform Time Act regulated Daylight Saving Time, which Wilson and FDR imposed temporarily during the First and Second World Wars to save energy on lighting

1967 Project Gasbuggy, part of Eisenhower's "Atoms for Peace" program, detonated an atomic bomb underground in New Mexico in a test of fracturing to release natural gas

1969 Federal Coal Mine Health and Safety Act signed, which created a system of inspections and sanctions to protect coal miners from accidents, explosions, and black lung

1970 Nixon administration established the US Environmental Protection Agency to control air and water pollution, which focused attention on the coal, oil, and gas industries

Earth Day celebrated nationally to galvanize public opinion behind new environmental laws and policies designed to address air pollution and water contamination

1972 Clean Water Act created protections for US waterways and overall water quality from industrial pollutants and discharges from coal and oil operations

1973 Arab states in OPEC declared an oil embargo on the US and other states supporting Israel in the Yom Kippur War, which inflamed the Energy Crisis of the 1970s

1979 Three Mile Island (PA) Unit 2 reactor partially melted down on March 28, becoming the most serious accident in US commercial nuclear power plant operating history

Uranium spill at Church Rock (NM) on Navajo land on July 16 poisoned 80 miles of the Puerco River with 94 million gallons of radioactive uranium tailings

1981 President Ronald Reagan signed Executive Order 12287, which released oil and gas from price and allocation controls in the Emergency Petroleum Allocation Act of 1973

1982 Secretary of the Interior James Watt announced plans to step up leasing of public land to coal mining companies, and quintupled the rate under his administration

Nuclear Waste Policy Act adopted to direct Department of Energy to establish a permanent repository for radioactive waste material from nuclear plants

1983 Interior Secretary James Watt said "I have a black, a woman, two Jews and a cripple" in reference to diversity on a coal leasing panel, forcing his resignation

1987	Congress enacted a measure that identified Yucca Mountain (NV) as the only site under consideration as a permanent storage facility for nuclear waste material
1989	*Exxon Valdez* oil tanker ran aground in Alaska's Prince William Sound, spilling 10.8 million gallons of oil on pristine coastline and elevating concerns about pollution
1991	US-led military coalition forcibly evicted Iraqi troops from Kuwait in the Gulf War to prevent Iraq President Saddam Hussein from controlling Kuwaiti oil fields
1992	United Nations Rio Summit produced the UN Framework Convention on Climate Change, focused on reducing use of energy sources that produce greenhouse gases
1996	Nuclear Waste Policy Act revised the earlier act from 1987, and required the US government to set up an interim storage area for nuclear waste material
1997	Founding of Project for a New American Century, composed of war hawks who shaped aggressive US foreign policy in the wake of the September 11, 2001 terrorist attacks
	Kyoto Protocol to the UN Framework Convention on Climate Change adopted, binding signatory nations to reduce carbon dioxide emissions from oil and gas combustion
1998	Occidental Petroleum Corporation acquired Elk Hills Naval Preserve in California, divesting the US government from the extraction of oil and gas for military purposes
1999	Merger of Exxon and Mobil reunited portions of the original Standard Oil Company, which was dismantled in 1911 for violating the Sherman Antitrust Act
2000	President Bill Clinton vetoed a congressional bill that would have established Yucca Mountain (NV) as a permanent storage area for US nuclear waste material
2002	Yucca Mountain site recommended by Energy Secretary Spencer Abraham to President George Bush, who recommended it to Congress, which was approved
2005	Energy Policy Act provided incentives for expanded use of alternative fuels like biodiesel, ethanol, and hydrogen, as well as provisions for energy efficiency
2009	Energy Secretary Steven Chu, representing the Obama administration, told a Senate hearing that Yucca Mountain (NV) would not be considered for a nuclear waste facility
2010	*Deepwater Horizon* oil drilling platform exploded in the Gulf of Mexico, killing eleven and releasing 3.19 million barrels of oil into the ocean over eighty-seven days
2014	Nuclear Regulatory Commission issued report that claimed the Yucca Mountain (NV) site is a suitable location for a permanent nuclear waste storage facility
2015	CEO Don Blankenship of coal company Massey Energy sentenced to a year in federal prison for conspiring to violate mine safety laws in a 2010 mine explosion that killed twenty-nine of his employees
2016	President Barack Obama signed the Paris Agreement of 2015, which bound the US to take action to reduce carbon emissions and greenhouse gases that cause global warming
2017	Energy Secretary Rick Perry announced the Trump administration planned to proceed with Yucca Mountain (NV) designation as the US repository of nuclear waste

2020 President Donald Trump renounced the nation's participation in the Paris Agreement early in his administration, and US exit from the treaty took effect in November

2021 President Joe Biden reversed his predecessor's decision to withdraw the US from the Paris Agreement, and the US once again became a signatory to the treaty

Introduction

For nearly everyone living in the United States, life's essentials are made possible through energy, which come from fuels like coal, oil, natural gas, wind, solar, hydropower, and geothermal sources. The way our food is produced, the way our living spaces are warmed and cooled, the way our work gets done, and the way we travel are built upon a modern system of energy production, distribution, and consumption that traces its origins to the early nineteenth century. We often take for granted the existence of this system until the power goes out in a storm or blackout, or a price spike in oil causes pain at the pump. It takes a little effort to really understand that what seems to be "normal life" in the twenty-first century is the result of a series of historical developments, and none of these developments were inevitable. The progression of historical change from the age of sailing ships, whale oil lamps, and horse-drawn carriages to the age of self-driving vehicles, virtual reality media, and human space travel required a highly complex interplay of individual decisions and actions in combination with large-scale economic, technological, political, and institutional forces, all of which are the subject of this encyclopedia.

The story of energy's role in creating the foundations of modern living is really best understood as a collection of a number of different stories, and it's quite a diverse collection. It features stories about people like Thomas Edison and what happened at places like Spindletop, Texas. The stories include broad narratives like the transition from steam power to electricity and the globalization of petroleum markets. There are accounts of institutional growth, as with the consolidation of illuminating companies like General Electric and Westinghouse, and the appearance of energy-related government agencies. At the most minute level, the story of energy includes tales about corporate barons like John D. Rockefeller but also Frank Shuman, the eccentric Philadelphian who build the world's first solar energy farm in Egypt before the First World War. The history of energy in the United States features exotic locales, technological wizardry, bitter competitions, and most importantly, the energy decisions made by millions and millions of ordinary people that steered the systems by which we live, work, and travel into their present-day condition. In a way, these volumes contain many of the stories that make up the larger story of energy in American history.

THINKING BIG ABOUT ENERGY

There's no shortage of serious-minded books, magazine and newspaper articles, internet sites, cable news programming, and so on regarding energy and its role in shaping the American economy and infrastructure, environment, politics, and society. It's been a major focus of interest among people who wish to understand American growth and development since the Industrial Revolution. Long-standing concerns about greenhouse gases produced by fossil fuel combustion flared up in the 1990s, triggering a torrent of new articles and books that took a longer view of US energy history and traced out the growth of American dependence on coal, oil, and natural gas. Richard Rhodes' book, *Energy: A Human History*, and Vaclav Smil's *Energy and Civilization: A History*, both published in 2018, provide an illustration. In different ways they focus on the major energy transitions, for example the transition from wood and horse to coal and steam power, and explained the different challenges that each transition had created for the generations that experienced them. These books and many others highlighted energy transitions to offer historical context for the transition now underway from fossil fuels to a more complex mix of fossil fuels with renewables like hydroelectric power, solar and wind power, and geothermal energy.

There's a shared conviction in these recent books that energy really matters in history. One way of expressing this idea is to say that energy has had, and continues to have, "agency" in shaping historical outcomes. Here are a few examples. The discovery of oil in Texas and Oklahoma could be considered as one of the key agents that led to an influx of non-Indigenous people to this region. Likewise, the arrival of electricity to the southwest following construction of Hoover Dam and Lake Mead facilitated the expansion of cities like Los Angeles. The emergence of the Seven Sisters petroleum corporations in the 1930s through the 1950s led to changes in US foreign policy in the Middle East. None of these outcomes can be reduced to the influence of energy alone, so useful hedges like "one of the key agents" and "led to" provide acknowledgment of the complexity of historical causation. Thus, to say that "x" agent produced "y" outcome is to oversimplify the relation between cause and effect; however, one can say that energy was one important agent among a set of interlocking agents that led to these changes.

This is important to consider when undertaking a study of energy in American history. The entwined stories in these volumes suggest the profound impact that energy has had in America's larger history as a nation. One example would be the effect of the coming together of three distinct but interrelated energy developments at the end of the nineteenth and beginning of the twentieth centuries: (1) the discovery of petroleum in the United States in industrial-scale quantities; (2) the development of technologies related to internal combustion engines; and (3) the electricity-fueled mass production of automobiles offered at price points appealing to millions of Americans. The synchronous emergence of the petroleum, electricity, and automotive industries created demand for roadbuilding and thus the modern infrastructure of highways and interstates, a growing dependence on imported oil from overseas and thus pressure for greater US involvement in international affairs, and the pattern of suburbanization characteristic of post-Second World War American housing and community development.

There is an inherent danger in over-emphasizing one factor over others in a matrix of factors, such as attributing the electrification of the United States to the genius of Thomas Edison. The inventions emanating from Edison's Menlo Park laboratory mattered, but they don't tell the whole story. The historical error here is known as "reductionism," and the particular species of reductionism that appears in some literatures of energy history is called "technological determinism." Studies like *Petrocultures: Oil, Politics, Culture* (2017), written in the context of political browbeating over Western dependence on fossil fuels and the threat of uncontrollable global warming and climate change, press the issue with chapter headings like "On Petrocultures: Or, Why We Need to Understand Oil to Understand Everything Else" (Wilson 2017). The possibility of reductionism led Thomas Turnbull to reply with a critique in "Energy, History, and the Humanities: Against a New Determinism" (2021). Turnbull argued that scholars err when they attribute the massive changes in Britain during the Industrial Revolution—not just in industry but in demography, household structure, politics, imperial policy, and even "cultural transformations"—solely to the adoption of coal and steam power. He would prefer to say that energy *conditions* history, but does not *determine* it (Turnbull 2021, 246, 253).

INTERCONNECTED SYSTEMS

With this in mind, we can nevertheless appreciate the importance of energy in American history. In *Energy in the Americas: Critical Reflections on Energy and History*, the authors noted in reference to recent energy history scholarship, that "the idea that the predominant type of energy resource employed in a given country affects the quality and form of its government, its citizens' quality of life, and the development of its economy—either positively or negatively—clearly holds broad sway" (Kiddle 2021, 8). This calls for students of energy history to look for and understand important connections that integrated the various forms of energy into the social, economic, and political fabric of the nation. Such connections involve the gathering of raw materials and their processing into usable fuels together with the consumption of these fuels in various ways by end-users. Also, there's a connectedness in the way resource extraction and energy consumption impacted the natural environment and shaped the development of transportation networks, energy distribution systems, and urban environments. There are innumerable connections between energy development, public policy, and government regulation, as various issues like workers' health and safety, pollution control, consumer protection, energy availability and pricing, and market competition spilled over into politics and became matters of public concern.

A good example of this interconnectedness is the emergence of centralized steam heating in the mid-nineteenth century. Mining companies began to produce coal on an industrial scale for steam-powered railroad locomotives, providing a new kind of affordable fuel to use in generating heat. Sean Patrick Adams' *Home Fires: How Americans Kept Warm in the Nineteenth Century* made the important point that "the presence of coal itself was irrelevant without a full complement of the components that make up a mineral fuel network" (Adams 2014). It also required cheap transportation, customer familiarity with the product via marketing, and consistent, steady supply. Once acquainted with the fuel and its potential, entrepreneurs created new businesses that sold steam heat generated in coal-fired plants to customers—building owners and managers—located in their vicinity. Steam was produced at central hubs, piped under the streets to different buildings, and then carried in pipes to radiators located inside the buildings' rooms. New York City's steam heating system enabled developers and architects to create a dense concentration of soaring skyscrapers, since the buildings didn't need on-site heating systems requiring coal delivery, combustion ovens, boilers, and smokestacks. In this way, the New York Steam Company connected coal producers in Pennsylvania with steam consumers in lower Manhattan, and in the process became an agent in shaping the contours of the modern city.

Another example of interconnectedness among producers and consumers is the oil industry. Oil companies discovered petroleum in very large quantities and began extracting it on an industrial scale. This created a very affordable fuel that could be used in a variety of ways. Once conveyed by pipeline or rail tank cars to refineries, crude oil could be processed into gasoline to power vehicles equipped with newly developed internal combustion engines.

Given the availability of this resource, entrepreneurs like Henry Ford were encouraged to take the risk of mass-producing automobiles for a nationwide market. Because they were produced on a mass scale with great efficiency, automobiles could be sold at a price that made them affordable to middle-class consumers. This created a system in which crude oil extraction, petroleum transport, oil refining, automobile manufacturing, and gasoline retailing were all integrated together into a complex system of mutually reinforcing, interdependent parts. Inside these two volumes there a quite a few stories that reveal the contours of other interconnected systems, like the stories that detail the formation of the nation's electricity grid, which generates and distributes electrical power to millions and millions of energy users.

NARRATIVES OF ENERGY HISTORY

Speaking of stories, energy history contains innumerable storylines. Some of them are epic in scale and populated with large casts of characters. The epic stories, like the accounts of the great energy transitions, are sweeping and comprehensive, involving the nations' resources, people, and institutions. Energy transition narratives dovetail with the national myth of progress, which is the idea that American history is an unfolding drama of continual emancipations—from royal tyranny, from ignorance, from slavery and injustice—with new forms of energy offering freedom from harsh conditions, backbreaking toil, and the limitations of time and distance. There are other kinds of stories in the history of energy in the United States. These stories are less sweeping and more intimate. These personal narratives help us understand the genius behind technological innovation, or perhaps the human costs of unleashing the primal forces of nature. The story of energy in American history also contains morality tales. The literature abounds with parables that alternately highlight the wisdom and folly of human choices, as well as the dilemmas that accompany humanity's engagement with volatile, toxic, finite, and yet also life-giving elements of the earth.

The energy transition narratives are stories about the nation's passage from wood and horse to coal and steam, and then to petroleum and electricity, and finally to nuclear energy and renewables. These are trajectories of increasing power coefficients, measured in odd-sounding units like megawatts, BTUs, and electron volts. They offer insight into how lives were changed in response to the adoption of new energy sources. For example, the adoption of steam heating enabled people in northern regions to live more comfortably in the winter, and the adoption of electricity and incandescent lighting enabled homes to be illuminated after nightfall. But these transition narratives also feature trajectories of resource exhaustion and profound ecological disruption, which are evident in early texts like Stanley Jevons, *The Coal Question: An Inquiry Concerning the Progress of the Nation, and the Probable Exhaustion of Our Coal Mines* (1865), and later books like William R. Catton's *Overshoot: The Ecological Basis for Revolutionary Change* (1982). These books offer Malthusian prophecies of civilizational collapse, barring massive societal change in the patterns of consumption or technological and institutional adaptations that secure a path toward sustainable development. Some geologists argued that environmental changes from fossil fuel combustion over the last two centuries are so extensive that we've arrived at the dawn of a new geological era, the Anthropocene. In this account, the industrial system produced so much deforestation and atmospheric carbon dioxide that it changed the earth's habitability and its climatic patterns, leading to a massive die-off of wildlife populations and the extinction of hundreds of different species.

Narratives come in all shapes and sizes. There are large narratives, like the narratives of energy transitions and there are small narratives, like the stories of John Washington Steele and the California Spiritualist Henry L. Williams. As a young man, Steele inherited his adopted mother's oil lease royalties in the 1860s, spent his money wildly, earned the nickname "Coal-Oil Johnny," was defrauded by his business partners, and went bankrupt within a year. All of Coal-Oil Johnny's escapades were covered in sensationalized newspaper reports. His later book about his experience expressed regrets and offered up a cautionary tale about wayward living. Yet, the book also struck a very modern tone by depicting the trials of sudden fame and along with it the struggle to rebuild one's public image after a vicious media lashing. A different story involves Henry Williams, who formed a community of spiritualists on the southern coast of California and conducted séances to summon the dead. Then Summerland residents discovered oil. Within a few years oil derricks dotted the beach and out over the ocean atop extended wooden piers. Williams expressed his gratitude for the discovery since he'd become tired of the "cranks" he brought to the community, and as he said in a letter to a local banker, the influx of oil developers "will enable me to pull out nicely within the next 18 months" (Myrick 1988). These smaller, more intimate stories are more than just curiosities. They offer fine-grained perspectives on how individual people experienced the seismic forces of change in energy production.

Conflict narratives abound in energy history. Adherents of steam power put up resistance to the use of electricity in operating machinery and heating homes, workplaces, and institutional buildings. In the War of the Currents, defenders of direct current contended with proponents of alternating current to determine which system would prevail in the emergent US electricity generation and transmission system. In what might properly be called business history, smaller firms in a number of energy-related industries fought for survival as consolidation formed larger and larger corporations and trusts like Standard Oil Company. These corporations in turn fought political battles over access to oil and gas leases, as well as attempts by government to regulate the industry. Coal, oil, and natural gas operators acquired new adversaries in later decades with the advent of environmental groups like the Sierra Club and the National Resources Defense Council which opposed surface mining, offshore drilling, and hydraulic fracturing. Since the energy crisis of the 1970s, the central position of fossil fuels in the US energy supply has been the subject of ongoing, often contentious political controversy.

THE GEOPOLITICS OF CARBON ENERGY

To be sure, fossil fuels *have* occupied a central position in meeting the demand for energy in the United States over the last two centuries. Coal became the preferred fuel for powering railroad engines, steamships, industrial machinery, and heating large buildings. It also provided raw material for making coke, which served as a fuel for smelting iron and the production of steel. The energy required to produce the Industrial Revolution in Britain, the United States, and elsewhere came from the combustion of carbon in different types of coal, which runs 86 to 97 percent in anthracite, and 45 to 86 percent in bituminous coal. Within a generation, coal became a necessity in order to sustain the industrial system and extraordinary measures were taken to ensure a continuous supply. According to historian Peter Shulman in *Coal & Empire: The Birth of Energy Security in Industrial America* (2015), because of coal's importance to the nation's economic vitality Americans "came to think of sources of power, particularly fossil fuels, as being of special national significance"

(Shulman 2015, 6). This was true of oil after the turn of the twentieth century. In the course of time, sourcing these fuels became part of the "national interest," a set of objectives pursued by the US government to ensure national survival, along with protecting the borders, mustering and equipping military forces, and generating revenue to fund national defense.

When steam ships replaced sailing vessels in the merchant marine and the US Navy, coal became a strategic resource and necessitated foresight regarding coal availability on overseas voyages. Ships powered by wind could leave the shore behind, whereas steam-powered ships had to put into port for resupply of fuel. For much of the early nineteenth century, successive administrations were concerned primarily with sectional tensions and the US Civil War, but also internal expansion, which occasioned debates about Indian removal, the annexation of Texas, the US–Mexican War, and the creation of new states in the Mexican Cession of 1848. The purchase of Alaska in 1867 completed the process of continental expansion. In 1875, the United States signed a commercial treaty with the independent monarchy then governing Hawaii, which included a provision that allowed the US to lease territory on the island of Oahu for a naval base, later named Pearl Harbor. In his widely read book, *The Influence of Sea Power upon History, 1660–1783* (1890), naval officer, war college instructor, and strategist Alfred Thayer Mahan taught American readers the value of possessing islands in the Caribbean and the Western Pacific for the use of coaling stations as the nation pursued its commercial and strategic interests in distant regions. A bitter debate broke out in Washington, DC over the annexation of Hawaii in the early 1890s, but US acquisitions after the Spanish–American War (1898), which included Puerto Rico, Guam, and the Philippines, made Hawaii's annexation a foregone conclusion. For good measure, the US negotiated a lease for a naval base at Guantánamo Bay in 1903 from the government of newly independent Cuba.

The United States had become an imperial power with an overseas network of coaling stations and thus took its place alongside the other imperial powers, all of whom were dependent on coal to secure access to overseas markets and protect their territorial acquisitions. These nations proceeded with a conviction that fossil fuels were a key ingredient to national security, part and parcel of a nation's foreign policy, and a focal point of international relations. The conversion of naval fleets to oil merely reinforced these convictions. Shulman noted: "American debates around coal before World War I shaped how Americans came to think about oil, which increasingly appeared as a significant strategic fuel beginning in the 1910s" (2015, 8). The war revealed that horses and trains no longer sufficed in modern combat conditions once the motor truck demonstrated its speed and flexibility in moving troops. As historian Daniel Yergin observed, "oil and the internal combustion engine quickly transformed the battlefield" (2014). By the end of the war Allied forces utilized tens of thousands of trucks to mount offensives, bring up reinforcements, and resupply troops with munitions. Petroleum-fueled internal combustion engines also enabled the belligerents of the First World War to pioneer new kinds of weapons: attack submarines, armored tanks, fighter planes, and aerial bombers. Mechanized warfare, in Yergin's view, led to the "transformation of oil into a strategic commodity, central to international politics and critical to the fate of nations" (2014).

Despite post-war efforts at peace and disarmament, the world's statesmen agreed with the assessment about the First World War of Walter C. Teagle, president of Standard Oil Company (New Jersey), who concluded in a 1920 speech to the American Petroleum Institute:

> I will say that authorities agree on the very important part that gasoline and kindred products displayed in the final decision. From the firing of the first gun in 1914, the Allies

> held an advantage which was to prove in the end of greater value than all of Germany's preparedness, that advantage being their ability to hold open a route to America's oil fields and refineries. The importance of the tanks, motor cars and aeroplanes on land, and of the submarine, destroyer and battleship on the sea, was so completely demonstrated before the United States entered the conflict that people everywhere awoke to the extent of their dependence upon petroleum. (Teagle 1920, 3)

Certainly, the authoritarian dictators of the 1930s learned this lesson. Oil and gas fueled Nazi Germany, fascist Italy, and imperial Japan in their initial conquests, but then helped the Allied powers turn the tide on the oceans, on the Eastern and Western European fronts, and over the skies of Europe and the Far East. The Cold War, coupled with US–Soviet proxy wars in Korea and Vietnam, guaranteed that a secure supply of fossil fuels would continue to occupy an important place in considerations of US national security.

The United States expanded oil production accordingly and US companies began to invest in oil development projects in the Middle East. This began earlier with the Red Line Agreement in 1928 and continued with the formation of the Arabian American Oil Company in 1933, later known as Aramco. Domestic production in the United States increased after the war, but consumption exploded. The rate of US domestic production increased from 5.9 million barrels of oil per day to 11.6 million between 1950 and 1970; the corresponding consumption rate for the same period increased from 6.4 million barrels per day to 14.6 million. Imported oil filled the deficit. The nation imported 5.5 percent of its oil in 1950, which increased to 21.5 percent twenty years later (Lifset 2014, 27). To reduce US dependence on foreign oil, President Dwight Eisenhower enacted the Mandatory Oil Import Quota Program in 1959, which proved largely ineffective. The United States discovered its vulnerability to disruptions in oil supply in 1973 when the Arab-controlled Organization of Petroleum Exporting Countries (OPEC) imposed an oil embargo on the country and other nations supporting the state of Israel in the Yom Kippur War. In combination with several other factors, the oil embargo brought about the energy crisis of the 1970s.

Toward the end of the crisis, Jimmy Carter's State of the Union speech on January 23, 1980 addressed the Soviet invasion of Afghanistan, and added: "An attempt by any outside force to gain control of the Persian Gulf region will be regarded as an assault on the vital interests of the United States of America, and such an assault will be repelled by any means necessary, including military force" (Carter 1980). The United States applied the Carter Doctrine in the Gulf War of 1991 when Iraqi forces invaded Kuwait and seized its oil fields and the nation led a coalition of allies to end the occupation. The allied forces performed ably but provided an illustration of why the United States maintained an aggressive posture toward threats to the global supply of oil. In the First World War, US armed forces used one gallon of fuel per soldier per day. In the Gulf War, the amount rose to 4 gallons a day, and in 2006, amid combined US military operations in Iraq and Afghanistan, the figure was 16 gallons ("The World's" 2008). With the growth of India, China, and other developing economies, securing petroleum resources remained a central objective of US foreign policy, and by extension, an important factor in global geopolitics through the early decades of the twenty-first century.

In press materials touting a new policy of promoting exports of liquefied natural gas, officials from the US Department of Energy under President Donald Trump in 2019 took to calling it "freedom gas," and "molecules of US freedom" (Rueb 2019). This strange attempt to create a brand identity for American fossil fuel exports is a candid admission of how unfree, in a manner of speaking, the United States has been from the manacles of fossil fuel dependency. By linking together American ideals of freedom and liberty with the world's supply of oil and gas, they appeared to support Timothy Mitchell in his characterization of the United States as one of the industrialized world's "carbon democracies." In his book, *Carbon Democracy: Political Power in the Age of Oil* (2011), Mitchell begins with the assumption that over time, "political possibilities were opened up or narrowed down by different ways of organizing the flow and concentration of energy, and these possibilities were enhanced or limited by arrangements of people, finance, expertise and violence that were assembled in relationship to the distribution and control of energy" (Mitchell 2011, 8). This leads to his conclusion that "the leading industrialised countries" are in fact "oil states," a term usually reserved for nations with authoritarian governments warped by the "resource curse" of an overabundance of oil. He explains that "without the energy they derive from oil their current forms of political and economic life would not exist. Their citizens have developed ways of eating, travelling, housing themselves and consuming other goods and services that require very large amounts of energy from oil and other fossil fuels" (6).

A BOUNTIFUL CIVILIZATION

At a conference in 1959 hosted by Columbia University and titled "Energy and Man: A Symposium," Robert G. Dunlop gave a speech titled, "The Petroleum Revolution" which cited a recent magazine article on the topic of energy's importance to humankind. Dunlop quoted the article as follows: "The writer of a *Newsweek* roundup a few months ago may have been given to lyricism when he said: 'The whole bountiful civilization of the mid-twentieth century is petroleum and the myriad economic and scientific reactions it has stimulated or helped to make possible'" (Dunlop 1960, 26). Dunlop was Chairman and CEO of Sun Oil Company and future president of the American Petroleum Institute, so the *Newsweek* quote fitted his view of the world. According to the oil and gas industry, the United States had become a "bountiful civilization" of economic growth, consumer abundance, scientific advancement, and technological progress because of petroleum products. This doesn't go as far as Timothy Mitchell's characterization of the nation as one of many "oil states," but it does testify to a pervasive sense at mid-century that America's energy transition from coal and steam power to petroleum and electrical power fundamentally changed American society—and changed it for the better.

Dunlop might have read Thomas A. Gale's *The Wonder of the Nineteenth Century: Rock Oil in Pennsylvania and Elsewhere* (1860). The book told the story of the 1859 oil strike in Titusville by Edwin Drake, and then went on to tout the multiple uses of "rock oil," as a medication, a lubricant, a wool conditioner, a replacement for coal in powering steam engines, and a better illuminating agent than camphene or whale oil. He wrote, "our Kind Father in Heaven has caused the rock to pour us out rivers of oil and thus given us at once magnificent light for our dwellings and a source of honest wealth. The influence direct and indirect of this benefaction on our social order, will be happy, powerful, and lasting" (Gale 1860, 57). Gale's words are important here: this new source of energy is a "benefaction"—a blessing from God—and it will produce "happy" effects on the social order in America. Millions of Americans who came to enjoy homes with consistent and affordable heating, cooling, and ventilation experienced it as Gale predicted, and most US citizens embraced electrical illumination, and then all the other labor-saving appliances that electricity made possible. Henry Ford and other automobile manufacturers were successful because they made something most people wanted: self-propelled, gas-powered vehicles that offered the freedom of travel at relatively low expense.

It's possible to plumb for deeper levels to understand the change in the social order that Gale anticipated. In 1925, Mary Pattison published an essay titled, "The Abolition of Household Slavery." She was a suffragette and leader of the New Jersey State Federation of Women's Clubs. In her view, "without the modern power that electricity does and can supply, a new order of betterment would be well nigh unthinkable" and women would remain in a state of enslavement to the routines of manual domestic labor. She cited the freedom that came with the electrical vacuum, as "lifting the woman from her long and seemingly doomed relationship with dirt in the wrong place." She went on to describe how the electric washing machine, the electric cooker, the electric refrigerator, the electric dishwasher, and the electric mixer/meat grinder offered "salvation" to women, who could now "awake from what *has* been" and "demand an equality of purpose and not merely of position with the modern man of big affairs" (Pattison 1925, 125–6). Historians disagree about whether the electrification of the home resulted in fundamental changes for women, but the new uses of energy, aided by New Deal-era housing and electrification programs, "transformed the material fabric of its home life" and provided "the material instruments of mass freedom and material justice" for working and middle-class Americans (Tobey 1997, 208, 214).

These new changes had what David Nye termed "technological momentum" (Nye 1998, 4). His book, *Consuming Power: A Social History of American Energies* (1998), argues that people had the choice to stick with rail transit or buy motorcars, and to maintain traditional ways of preparing food and doing laundry after they learned about electrical appliances. However, "once people invent, assemble, market, and invest in a large social-technological system, it attains a dominant cultural position for decades or even generations." Once established, a new energy system becomes "more rigid and less responsive to social pressures," while creating new "social worlds" with "structures that underlie personal expectations and assumptions about what is normal and possible" (Nye 1998, 7). The people living in the transition to petroleum and electricity described the experience in terms of wonderment—a benefaction from God. However, as Amada Little observed in her book *Power Trip: The Story of America's Love Affair with Energy* (2009), today "energy is the thread from which our modern lives dangle, but it is an invisible thread—pumped through underwater oil pipelines, coursing through unseen cables in remove meadows, and tucked away in basement fuse boxes, just as veins are hidden beneath our skin" (Little 2009, xxv). Electricity is experienced in the same way as breathing air—people have an unacknowledged dependency on it that for the most part is appreciated only when taken away.

Energy created a bountiful civilization in the United States, enabling millions of people to live beyond the essentials and capable yet of breathtaking technological marvels. However, its relative invisibility poses a range of problems, from unseen injustices in its production and distribution to hard-to-detect environmental problems that percolate below the surface of the earth or out in the atmosphere. Energy development separated most people from the dirty work of extracting fuel from forests and getting mechanical power from draft animals. It also separated energy users from the elemental forces of nature released in combustion of fuels. According to Daniel French's study, *When They Hid the Fire: A History of Electricity and Invisible Energy in America* (2017), the light switch and the power outlet—what people experience every day as energy consumption—obscure energy's real impact on human society and on the earth and stymie efforts to make meaningful improvements in our current energy systems and practices. The goal of these volumes is to make the people, institutions, policies, and technologies that created the world in which we live more plainly evident and more comprehensible. This way, we can grasp the possibilities and challenges inherent in energy use and pursue better ways of harnessing its power for everyone's benefit.

Jeffrey B. Webb

FURTHER READING

Adams, Sean Patrick. 2014. *Home Fires: How Americans Kept Warm in the Nineteenth Century*. Baltimore: Johns Hopkins University Press.

Carter, James. 1980. "Address by President Carter on the State of the Union before a Joint Session of Congress." January 23. *Foreign Relations of the United States, 197–1980*. Vol. 1: *Foundations of Foreign Policy*. Office of the Historian. US Department of State. Washington, DC.

Dunlop, Robert G. 1960. "The Petroleum Revolution." In *Energy and Man: A Symposium*. Eds. Alan Nevins, Robert G. Dunlop, Edward Teller, Edward S. Mason, and Herbert Hoover, Jr. Pp. 24–51. New York: Appleton-Century-Crofts, Inc.

French, Daniel. 2017. *When They Hid the Fire: A History of Electricity and Invisible Energy in America*. Pittsburgh, PA: University of Pittsburgh Press.

Gale, Thomas A. 1860. *The Wonder of the Nineteenth Century: Rock Oil in Pennsylvania and Elsewhere*. Erie, PA: Sloan & Griffeth, Publishers.

Kiddle, Amelia M., ed. 2021. *Energy in the Americas: Critical Reflections on Energy and History*. Calgary, AB: University of Calgary Press.

Lifset, Robert D. 2014. "A New Understanding of the American Energy Crisis of the 1970s." *Historical Social Research—Historische Sozialforschung. Special Issue: The Energy Crises of the 1970s: Anticipations and Reactions in the Industrialized World*. Vol. 39. No. 4. Pp. 22–42.

Little, Amanda. 2009. *Power Trip: The Story of America's Love Affair with Energy*. New York: Harper Perennial.

Mitchell, Timothy. 2011. *Carbon Democracy: Political Power in the Age of Oil*. London: Verso.

Myrick, David F. 1988. "Summerland: The First Decade." *Noticias: Quarterly Magazine of the Santa Barbara Historical Society*. Vol. 34. No. 4. Pp. 64–111.

Nye, David. 1998. *Consuming Power: A Social History of American Energies*. Cambridge, MA: The MIT Press.

Painter, David S. 2012. "Oil and the American Century." *The Journal of American History*. Vol. 99. No. 1. June. Pp. 24–39.

Pattison, Mary. 1925. "The Abolition of Household Slavery." In *Giant Power: Large Scale Electrical Development as a Social Factor: The Annals of the American Academy of Political and Social Science*. Ed. Morris Llewellyn Cooke. Vol. 118. March. Pp. 124–7.

Rueb, Emily S. 2019. "'Freedom Gas': The Next American Export." *The New York Times*. May 29.

Shulman, Peter A. 2015. *Coal & Empire: The Birth of Energy Security in Industrial America*. Baltimore: Johns Hopkins University Press.

Teagle, Walter C. 1920. "The World Petroleum Problem—America." *Bulletin of the American Petroleum Institute: Addresses Delivered at General Sessions: Annual Meeting, American Petroleum Institute, Washington DC, November 17, 18, and 19, 1920*. No. 132. December 10. https://www.google.com/books/edition/Addresses_Delivered_at_General_Sessions/V31JAAAAYAAJ (accessed October 2023).

"The World's Biggest Fuel Consumer." 2008. *Forbes*. June 5. https://www.forbes.com/2008/06/05/mileage-military-vehicles-tech-logistics08-cz_ph_0605fuel.html (accessed October 2023).

Tobey, Ronald C. 1997. *Technology as Freedom: The New Deal and the Electrical Modernization of the American Home*. Berkeley, CA: University of California Press.
Turnbull, Thomas. 2021. "Energy, History, and the Humanities: Against a New Determinism." *History and Technology*. Vol. 37. No. 2. Pp. 247–92.
Wilson, Sheena, Adam Carlson, and Imre Szeman, eds. 2017. *Petrocultures: Oil, Politics, Culture*. Montreal: McGill-Queen's University Press.
Yergin, Daniel. 2014. "The First War to Run on Oil." *The Wall Street Journal*. August 14. https://www.wsj.com/articles/the-first-war-to-run-on-oil-1408045343 (accessed October 2023).

Acid Rain

The phenomenon of acid rain has been recognized in various forms since before the dawn of the Industrial Revolution. The term "acid rain" is used broadly to describe any type of precipitation (rain, snow, fog, dew, and dust) which has five to thousands of times greater acidity than natural rain, due to strong acids produced by reactions with sulfur oxides and nitrogen oxides released into the atmosphere by the combustion of fossil fuels and other processes, both anthropogenic and natural. Damages caused by acid rain began with the Industrial Revolution and became increasingly pronounced with increased fossil fuel usage after the Second World War. In the 1970s and 1980s, acid rain drew international public attention and resulted in several decades of intense debate between the power industries and independent scientists both in the United States and Europe. In the United States, the Clean Air Act Amendments of 1990 implemented a cap and trade system resulting in emission controls which significantly lowered sulfur oxide and nitrogen oxide emissions. Although a pronounced decrease in acid rain in the United States contributes to an environmental success story, acid rain from fossil fuel combustion continues to threaten sensitive ecosystems including the Great Lakes and Great Smoky Mountains regions as well as mountain regions in the northeastern United States. Public concern over acid rain has been replaced with sobering concerns over far less reversible environmental prospects from carbon dioxide emissions, which form weak acids that contribute to the acidification of the oceans, presenting the prospect of eliminating calcifying organisms (Laws 2017, 613–14). The acid rain issue, both in the United States and abroad, contributed to the development of the field of environmental science through the multidisciplinary approach needed to analyze the effects of acid rain.

As early as the 1600s, adverse effects of industrial air pollutants on people and vegetation were known, and even this early in history, taller chimneys were built in order for winds to transport these emissions to more distant places. The first recorded usage of the term "acid rain" was in a 600-page book by the English chemist Robert Angus Smith called *Air and Rain: The Beginnings of a Chemical Climatology* (1872), a culmination of studies conducted in England, Scotland, and Germany in which he linked industrial pollution to coal combustion and described acid rain damage to vegetation and materials. Smith's studies drew little attention for almost a century.

The first detailed study of precipitation chemistry in the United States, published by Macintyre and Young in 1923, focused on airborne nutrients and crop growth (Cowling 1982, 112A). In the late 1950s, Dr. Eville Gorham expanded on Smith's acid rain work in England from the previous century, but the work did not generate significant attention. In 1962, Rachel Carson used the term "poison rain" in her book *Silent Spring*, which helped generate public awareness of the atmospheric transport of pollutants. More widespread concern was generated about acid rain in the late 1960s when Dr. Svante Odén, the "father of acid rain research," published studies of the long-range transport of pollutants causing acid rain in non-industrialized regions of Scandinavia, which posed a threat to the fishing industries in his native Sweden. Results disseminated by Odén's public campaigns, which described acid rain as "chemical war," were questioned extensively by the power industries of Britain, the most significant contributors to acid rain pollution in Western Europe. A prominent US acid rain researcher influenced by Odén's discoveries and methods was Dr. Gene Likens, who noted the effects of acid rain in 1963 in the White Mountains of New Hampshire at Dartmouth College and continued studies of acid rain in the Adirondack Mountains of New York at Cornell University.

DEADLY FOG

History has shown us that in polluted areas, foggy weather conditions can turn disastrous in a matter of days when they trap pollutants close to the ground, creating acid aerosols. Depending on the mix of pollutants, acid fog can easily reach more acidic levels than acid rain—not just tens or hundreds of times more acidic than normal rain, but thousands of times more acidic, with pH levels as low as 2. Unlike raindrops, which tend to cleanse the air, acid fog can be easily inhaled. A devastating event occurred during a week in late October of 1948, in the town of Donora, Pennsylvania, which experienced a temperature inversion that trapped a layer of cold air containing pollutants from its industrial plants close to the ground, which included sulfur oxides, nitrogen oxides, and fluorine. Residents experienced breathing difficulty, houseplants began to shrivel, and by the time the five-day fog was over, twenty people were dead, and nearly half of the working-class population of Donora experienced adverse symptoms. An elevated number cardiovascular and cancer deaths from Donora were documented within the following decade (Jacobs 2018, S87). The event is commemorated by the Donora Smog Museum as the event that inspired the Clean Air Act.

Ruth E. Nalliah

Air pollution began receiving increasing attention from the US federal government in the 1950s and 1960s. Although severe smog conditions had persisted in industrial American cities in the 1800s and 1900s, conditions became more severe with increases in fossil fuel combustion after the Second World War. Events such as the deaths due to the toxic smog in Donora, Pennsylvania resulted in the first national air pollution conference convened by President Truman in 1950, in which he recognized the damage of air pollution to property and crops as well as human life. The American Association for the Advancement of Science had its first symposium on air pollution in 1954, in which it recognized the role of gaseous pollutants in addition to smoke or particulate matter. The Air Pollution Control Act of 1955 provided funds for air pollution research, followed by the Clean Air Act of 1963 which established a federal air pollution program and authorized research in pollution monitoring and control, and was expanded upon by the Air Quality Act in 1967. Continuing concerns about air pollution resulted in the Clean Air Act of 1970 mandating the construction of taller smokestacks with the idea that pollutants would be more widely dispersed and diluted. Acute concerns about the conditions of the nation's air and water led to the establishment of the US Environmental Protection Agency (EPA) under President Nixon in 1970.

Public interest in acid rain was stirred in the United States in 1974 when the *New York Times* publicized the work of a paper in *Science* by Dr. Gene Likens of Cornell and Dr. F. Herbert Bormann of Yale, in which they pointed out that the Clean Air Act of 1970 exacerbated the acid rain problem in two ways. First, soot from smokestacks had helped neutralize components causing acid rain, and the process of filtering out soot did not mitigate the release of the invisible acid-rain-causing gases such as nitrogen and sulfur oxides. Second, the requirement for taller smokestacks resulted in air currents carrying nitrogen and sulfur oxides to greater distances, making acid rain a regional problem rather than a local problem (Rensberger 1974). Public reports on the potential of acid precipitation to damage aquatic life, plant life, materials, and human health also emerged, including the leaching of nutrients from the soil. By the late 1970s it was recognized that acid rain was releasing toxic aluminum and heavy metal ions from soil and minerals into surface and ground waters in the United States as well as Scandinavia. Mitigation efforts included liming (the treatment of soil or water with alkaline substances in an effort to reduce acidity) as well as research on the breeding of acid-tolerant fish and crops.

From the mid-1970s to 1990, studies by researchers in the United States and Sweden continued during a decade and a half of intense debate with power industries over the certainty of the link between acid rain and fossil fuels. Both in Britain and the United States, government action was delayed by ever-increasing requests by the power industries for more certainty that fossil fuel combustion by-products were the source of the problem, and that emission reductions would solve the problem. Not only did US scientists collaborate with those from Sweden on research linking distant pollution sources to acid rain, but the power companies in the United States and Britain also collaborated in conducting their own monitoring and research in an effort to postpone or minimize the regulation of industrial emissions. It is reported that during the 1970s, more money was spent on emissions studies than emissions abatement (Rothschild 2019, 61).

Nevertheless, some progress was made in these years. As a result of the Clean Air Act mandating that vehicle emissions be reduced by 75 percent in all new models after 1975, the catalytic converter was introduced to US vehicles in 1975. By 1981, more advanced catalytic converters were implemented not only to reduce carbon monoxide and hydrocarbon pollution but also to convert acid rain-forming nitrogen oxides (produced by a reaction between nitrogen and oxygen from air in the combustion engine) back to nitrogen gas.

US federal government efforts aimed at acid rain in the late 1970s and into the 1980s ebbed and waned depending on the political policies of the president. The National Atmospheric Deposition Program (NADP) began in 1977, and with the Acid Precipitation Act of 1980, the Carter administration established the National Acid Precipitation Assessment Program (NAPAP), a ten-year research program on acid rain. In the early 1980s, NAPAP progress was slowed by a more cautious Reagan administration, which appointed administrators in the EPA and NAPAP who were linked to the Electric Power Research Institute (EPRI). During this period, confusion existed over which scientists, laboratories, and agencies were funded by EPRI with an objective of calling into question the certainty of the causes of acid rain and the effectiveness of air pollution abatement. Literature from the 1980s refers to the "acid rain debate," reflecting an era in which legislative action was delayed by focusing on uncertainties in the data.

International relations of the United States during this period somewhat reflected its internal policies. In the 1979 United Nations Convention on Long-Range Transboundary Air Pollution, which involved the United States, Canada, and twenty-nine European nations, the

United States put pressure on other nations to commit to continue negotiations on acid rain in order to ease Cold War tensions with the Soviet Union. After a US political climate shift on acid rain at the beginning of the Reagan administration, environmental ministers from ten nations, excluding the United States and Britain, met in Ottawa, Canada, in 1984, to declare their commitment to reduce sulfur dioxide emissions to 30 percent below 1980 levels before 1993. In 1985, the United States continued to withhold its commitment to these reductions in the United Nations Helsinki Protocol, the first international agreement requiring specific reductions. By 1986, the United States was the last industrialized nation to commit to acid rain reductions. However, in the following year rising popular concern about acid rain was beginning to turn the tide in the United States when President Reagan signed on to the United Nations Sofia Protocol to limit nitrogen oxide emissions. By the 1988 election, environmental issues were a national concern shaping the campaign promises of George H.W. Bush.

Prior to the election of George H.W. Bush, the Environmental Defense Fund began drafting a market-based solution to the acid rain problem with a cap-and-trade plan, in which companies which could not meet decreasing air pollution limits could purchase pollution allowances from companies under the limit. The cap and trade system became part of the Clean Air Act Amendments of 1990, which established the Acid Rain Program with phased-in emission reductions over a fifteen-year period: the first cap took effect in 1995 and the final cap took effect in 2010. The National Bureau of Economic Research indicated that as a result of the Acid Rain Program, air quality was improved and resulted in a 5 percent decrease in mortality risk over the first ten years (Barreca et al. 2017, 26). International agreements between the United States and Canada after the Clean Air Act Amendments of 1990 included the Air Quality Agreement of 1991 and the North American Agreement on Environmental Cooperation in 1994, which were facilitated by each country's existing domestic policies. In the early 1990s, concern over acid rain began to be overshadowed by other environmental concerns, such as ozone depletion and global warming.

From 1990 to 2017, sulfur dioxide emissions decreased by 88 percent and nitrogen dioxide emissions decreased by 50 percent according to the EPA. Dramatic decreases in acid and related depositions across the country, particularly in the East and Midwest, are displayed in animated format on the public NADP website (National Atmospheric Deposition Program 2019). However, acid rain abatement is not yet an unqualified environmental success for several reasons. First, as long as fossil fuels are in use, some damage will occur due to acid rain. Sensitive areas such as the northeastern United States have only recently begun to show signs of soil nutrient recovery after decades of depletion of the acid neutralizing capacity of soils. Yet these concerns are being replaced with a more pervasive and even less reversible phenomenon of the acidification of the oceans due to carbon dioxide emissions. Second, part of the environmental success of the acid rain program has been facilitated by a replacement of coal with natural gas obtained by hydraulic fracturing, which presents new regulatory challenges in terms of other forms of environmental contamination. Therefore, public health benefits cited from acid rain abatement must be interpreted with the perspective that environmental gains in one area can be offset with environmental risks in others.

Ruth E. Nalliah

See also: Cap and Trade System; Chicago Smoke Abatement Ordinances of 1881 and 1903; Clean Air Act of 1970; Clean Coal; Clean Power Plan of 2015

FURTHER READING

Barreca, Alan I., Matthew Neidell, and Nicholas J. Sanders. 2017. "Long-Run Pollution Exposure and Adult Mortality: Evidence from the Acid Rain Program." NBER Working Paper Series. Cambridge, MA: National Bureau of Economic Research. https://www.nber.org/system/files/working_papers/w23524/w23524.pdf (accessed October 2023).

Cowling, Ellis B. 1982. "Acid Precipitation in Historical Perspective." *Environmental Science & Technology*. Vol. 16. No. 2. Pp. 110A–123A.

Davis, Devra Lee. 2002. *When Smoke Ran Like Water: Tales of Environmental Deception and the Battle Against Pollution*. New York: Basic Books.

Jacobs, E.T., J.L. Burgess, and M.B. Abbott. 2018. "The Donora Smog Revisited: 70 Years after the Event that Inspired the Clean Air Act." *American Journal of Public Health*. Vol. 108. No. S2. Pp. S85–S88.

Laws, Edward A. 2017. *Aquatic Pollution: An Introductory Text*. 4th ed. Hoboken, NJ: John Wiley & Sons.

National Atmospheric Deposition Program. 2019. "Animated Maps." 2019. https://nadp.slh.wisc.edu/maps-data/animated-maps/ (accessed October 2023).

Nunez, Christina. 2019. "What is Acid Rain?" *National Geographic*. February 28. https://www.nationalgeographic.com/environment/global-warming/acid-rain/ (accessed October 2023).

Oreskes, Naomi, and Erik M. Conway. 2010. *Merchants of Doubt: How a Handful of Scientists Obscured the Truth on Issues from Tobacco Smoke to Global Warming*. New York: Bloomsbury Press.

Rensberger, Boyce. 1974. "Acid in Rain Found Up Sharply in East: Smoke Curb Cited." *New York Times*. June 13.

Rothschild, Rachel Emma. 2019. *Poisonous Skies: Acid Rain and the Globalization of Pollution*. Chicago: University of Chicago Press.

Roueché, Berton. 1950. "The Fog." *The New Yorker*. September 30.

US Environmental Protection Agency (EPA). 2017. "Evolution of the Clean Air Act." https://www.epa.gov/clean-air-act-overview/evolution-clean-air-act (last modified December 28, 2022).

Adair, Paul Neal "Red"

The history of energy in the United States is filled with colorful and important figures like Paul "Red" Adair (1915–2004). Although unknown to most people, Red Adair made important contributions to the development of the oil and gas industry. Through his business, The Red Adair Company, Inc., he provided support services to oil and gas drilling operations, particularly suppressing fires and controlling blowouts. The *Handbook of Texas* credits Adair with developing "many tools and strategies" for fighting fires and capping wells, and with pioneering the technology for a "semi-submersible firefighting vessel" used to control underwater fires in offshore oil and gas rigs (Taylor 2007). In the process, Adair became something of a celebrity. His career illustrates how technological and safety innovation supported the growth and expansion of the fossil fuel industry in the twentieth century.

Red Adair was born in Houston, Texas amid the early stages of the Texas Oil Boom, which is generally dated to the 1901 Spindletop strike in Beaumont. His father worked as a blacksmith but the Great Depression brought financial hardship. To help the family, Adair left high school early to work for the Southern Pacific Railroad. In 1938, Adair began his career in the oil industry at the Otis Pressure Control Company, where he developed the Athley wagon, described as "a modified bulldozer with a hydraulic winch that helps control a long (approximately 60-foot) boom assembly for clearing debris or placing explosives at the well site" (MacRae 2012). He worked at Otis until his enlistment in the US Army in 1945. Adair served in the 139th Bomb Disposal Squadron in Japan tasked with defusing bombs and executing controlled demolitions. Adair left the army at the rank of Staff Sergeant, then fought oil fires and capped blowouts for the M. M. Kinley Company for the next fourteen years. Adair then left in 1959 to begin his own company.

The Red Adair Company soon became the oil and gas industry's leading firm of its type. Its reputation expanded as a result of success in suppressing the offshore CATCO fire in 1959 and then a major fire in Algeria in 1961 when a Phillips Petroleum gas well located in the Sahara Desert blew out and burned for six months. Adair and his company moved on site, engaged in lengthy and complex preparations, and finally put out the fire with a nitroglycerin explosion (Taylor 2007). Newspapers and magazines provided coverage of Adair's work on the CATCO fire and made him something of a celebrity in their reports on the fire in Algeria, which they dubbed the "Devil's Cigarette Lighter." Adair's team with their red coveralls gave the media a useful visual, and Red burnished his reputation by providing interviews that detailed his operations. This coverage inspired the film *Hellfighters* (1968) starring John Wayne in the Red Adair role, fighting an oil rig fire in Venezuela.

Several other high-profile oil and gas well disasters gave Adair a broader platform to demonstrate the skills and technologies of his crew. *The Guardian* listed in his obituary a number of important successes, including operations in the Bay Marchand field off the Louisiana coast (1970), the Ekofisk Bravo blowout off the coast of Norway (1977), and the IXTOC blowout in the Gulf of Mexico (1979) (Reed 2004). Adair testified before the US Congress in 1977 regarding the safe operation of offshore oil drilling rigs and appeared on the *Tonight Show* (1977) and *Good Morning America* (1979, 1980) (Caruba 2016). In 1988, 165 workers and two rescuers were killed in a North Sea oil platform explosion known as the Piper Alpha disaster. Adair received much attention for suppressing the fire and for the rescue and recovery response of the MSV *Tharos*, a semi-submersible, multifunction support vessel that he had helped to design.

In 1992, Adair's company came into the media spotlight once again following the Gulf War in Kuwait. Oil wells had been set on fire and the skies filled with black smoke to thwart the Allied advance on retreating Iraqi forces. In the aftermath, Adair's company and others moved in and began suppressing the fires and capping the blowouts. They reversed the flow of Kuwait's oil pipelines to bring seawater from the Persian Gulf. Adair's firm put out 117 of the 600-plus fires, and he became the face of the effort when he testified in Washington, DC in support of requests for funding, then met with President George W. Bush to work out logistical problems attendant to the scale of the disaster. Adair's crew, clad in red overalls, provided a striking image in Werner Herzog's haunting documentary film about the oil fire disaster in Kuwait, titled *Lessons in Darkness* (1992). The film highlights the terrible environmental consequences of the oil fires but also the heroic efforts by those who attacked and suppressed them.

In some ways, the John Wayne film *Hellfires* and Herzog's *Lessons in Darkness* made Adair into a "swashbuckling 20th-century hero" as he was dubbed by one of his obituary writers (Reed 2004). A fawning autobiography appeared in 1990 that aimed to create this sort of image. Quoting Red about the experience of approaching a fire, the author described how new crew members walked to the wellhead but turned back in the face of the intense heat and ear-splitting noise. Red remarked: "I'd keep walking, not knowing exactly what was happening at the wellhead or on the floor of the drilling rig 'cause you never know until you're there and I'd say, 'I will defeat it, whatever it is. I will win.' But that a lonely walk, boy, you better believe it" (Singerman 1990). In another passage, the biographer allowed Red to downplay his bravery but nevertheless permit the label "daredevil" to be applied: "See, people call me a daredevil, but they don't understand. A daredevil's reckless, and that ain't me. The devil's down in that hole and I've seen what he can do, and I'm not darin' him at all. I'm a beware devil, that's what I am" (Singerman 1990).

Indeed, Red Adair amplified the image of hero, daredevil, and celebrity by living a life of conspicuous luxury derived from his lucrative business, which included multi-million-dollar residences, yachts, and drag racing cars. A well-known anecdote provides an illustration. In 1983, Adair bid up the prices for champion steers at the Houston Livestock Show and Rodeo. He won the bid for a steer at $140,000, which was subsequently disqualified for "show violations." Adair decided to give the money to charitable organizations (Caruba 2016). Oil made him rich, but he'd also become a generous philanthropist over the course of his life, and especially after 1993 when he sold his company and went into retirement. All told, Adair's service to the industry was substantial. He and others in his field developed the essential tools and techniques to confront, and in many cases mitigate, the hazards of drilling for oil and natural gas, not only in remote, often ecologically sensitive environments but also in the open ocean. Adair's service to industry was acknowledged with various honors, including the Walton Clark Medal Citation from the Franklin Institute, and his contributions to charity garnered awards as well before his death in 2004 at the age of eighty-nine.

Jeffrey B. Webb

See also: Caddo Oil Field; *Deepwater Horizon*; Gulf War; Roughnecks; Santa Barbara Oil Spill; Spindletop Oil Gusher; Texas Oil Boom

FURTHER READING

Caruba, Lauren. 2016. "Fighting Oil Well Fires Propelled Red Adair to Celebrity Status." Chron. June 8. https://www.chron.com/local/history/innovators-inventions/article/Fighting-oil-well-fires-propelled-Red-Adair-to-7971972.php (accessed October 2023).

MacRae, Michael. 2012. "Red Adair to the Rescue." American Society of Mechanical Engineers. https://www.asme.org/topics-resources/content/red-adair-to-the-rescue (accessed October 2023).

Reed, Christopher. 2004. "Obituary: Red Adair." *The Guardian: US Edition*. August 8. https://www.theguardian.com/news/2004/aug/09/guardianobituaries.usa (accessed October 2023).

Singerman, Philip. 1990. *An American Hero: The Red Adair Story*. Boston: Little, Brown & Co.

Taylor II, Scott T. 2007. "Adair, Paul Neal [Red]." *Handbook of Texas*. Digital edition. Texas State Historical Society. https://www.tshaonline.org/handbook (accessed October 2023).

Weaver, Bobby D. 2010. *Oilfield Trash: Life and Labor in the Oil Patch*. College Station, TX: Texas A&M University Press.

Advanced Research Projects Agency-Energy

The Advanced Research Projects Agency-Energy (ARPA-E) is a US government agency that awards funding to projects developing pioneering energy technologies—projects that are at too early a stage for private-sector investment but are seen to have the potential to radically change the US energy landscape. It is the first major government agency dedicated to disruptive energy technologies, and its promotion of research and development in energy technologies is framed as a component of future US economic prosperity, national security, and national and environmental health (ARPA-E 2019a).

ARPA-E has a piecemeal history from conception to effective launch. Its origins lie in a 2005 report by the National Academies of Sciences, Engineering, and Medicine, a US non-governmental institution that has historically served as non-partisan adviser on science and technology. The report, "Rising Above the Gathering Storm: Energizing and Employing America for a Brighter Economic Future," was created in response to a bipartisan congressional request for advice on what challenges the United States must address to remain internationally competitive and a world leader in science and technology. At the time, questions regarding the future of fossil fuels, the primary energy resource for the United States, were becoming commonplace. Concerns related to environmental degradation and rising CO_2 emissions from widespread fossil fuel production, transport, and consumption, along with oil price volatility and fears of exhausting the nonrenewable resource, were prevalent. Thus, a key issue emphasized by the report was the future of energy, and the recommendation to deal with it was the creation of an advanced research projects agency dedicated to energy.

ARPA-E was officially established when the America COMPETES (Creating Opportunities to Meaningfully Promote Excellence in Technology, Education, and Science) Act was signed into law by President George W. Bush in 2007, which was a broad policy effort to boost US governmental investment and advancement in science and technology endeavors. It was in 2009, however, that ARPA-E first got its initial funding stimulus of $400 million, with which the agency could start energy technology project investment and planning. This stimulus was received through the American Recovery and Reinvestment Act (ARRA) signed into law by President Barack Obama. ARRA was a larger stimulus package which was, in essence, a response to the financial crisis of 2008. Two of the main objectives of ARRA were to advance the alternative energy industry in the United States and invest in science research and technology—authorizing the first funding to ARPA-E would be in line with both of these objectives.

As per the National Academies' recommendation, ARPA-E was modeled on the US Department of Defense's Defense Advanced Research Projects Agency (DARPA), which was formed in 1958. DARPA is associated with major disruptive technologies such as the internet and GPS; the goal in establishing ARPA-E was that such disruptive energy technologies would be a result.

DARPA

DARPA was established as a result of the Russian Sputnik satellite. Sputnik was a major technological surprise, a problem for the United States that DARPA was to address—that the United States would never face another such surprise that could pose a threat to national security (Bonvillian and Van Atta 470). DARPA is a project-driven agency whose projects are always off-site, as it acts predominantly as a funding and managing tool. It is a flat, non-hierarchical organization where program managers serve for a limited, three-to-five year duration. DARPA projects are selected on a high-risk, high-reward basis, meaning that they have to have disruptive capability on a large scale (Executive Office of the President of the United States 7). DARPA-funded projects have led to some major success, such as Apple's desktop computing system and the internet protocol routers firm CISCO systems. In a broader sense, household names like Google and Facebook have built their businesses on the technologies and capabilities developed with DARPA funding.

Sakina Groeppmaier

Like DARPA, ARPA-E is considered a flat hierarchy with two levels, program managers (PMs) and a director, to minimize bureaucratic procedures—the director is the only sign-off needed to launch a project. PMs also typically have both academic and industry experience to accompany the research to commercialization processes of ARPA-E. PMs, research fellows, and tech-to-market advisers are hired from across the energy sector, academia, national laboratories, and industry. PMs have a three-to-five year tenure of service to the agency, meaning that rather than long-term initiatives, the agency has a portfolio of short-period endeavors. Eric Schiff, the program director, has said the ARPA-E programs are "efforts at thought leadership" (Nekuda Malik 2017, 706).

A major challenge for ARPA-E is the technology landscape. DARPA, as a military-based defense initiative, has a set launching environment of either military services, such as with its stealth technologies or GPS, or civilian sectors, such as with the internet or desktop computing. The IT revolution also provided a new frontier for DARPA technologies. ARPA-E, on the other hand, must deal with an established energy sector, and so new energy technologies must have the capability of performing at the same level or surpassing existing energy technologies that dominate the US energy landscape (Bonvillian 2011, 488). Thus, technology advancements in energy typically fall short of large-scale market adoption due to extant infrastructure and widely adopted existing technologies (Nekuda Malik 2017, 706).

By 2011, with its initial funding stimulus of $400 million, ARPA-E had awarded funding in six key energy technology areas. These include carbon capture technologies, specifically to capture 90 percent of CO_2 from coal power plants, electrofuels, like biofuels using microorganisms to convert CO_2 and water into liquid fuels, batteries for electrical energy storage in transportation to electrify the vehicular economy, grid-scale storage technologies for cost-effective balance of renewable energies with power supply fluctuations, and cooling technologies for new and retrofitted buildings to improve and increase energy efficiency (Bonvillian 2011, 483–4). These endeavors were efforts at diversifying the US makeup of major energy sources, many of which are based in fossil fuels.

Some weaknesses of ARPA-E have been connected to the rotating tenure of its project managers. Battery technology is an example. ARPA-E is aware of the generational advances of lithium battery technology, so the three-to-five year project approach would not be enough in this regard to oversee a battery technology worthy of disruption in keeping with a near-constant improvement and innovation environment (Bonvillian 2011, 496–7). Moreover, ARPA-E had funding challenges under President Donald Trump's administration with the House's 2018 Energy Appropriations Bill, which, along with the Trump administration budget plan, called for the elimination of funding to the agency altogether. Conversely, the Senate's version of the bill called for an 8 percent increase in funding to ARPA-E in 2018, when compared to 2017 (Nekuda Malik 2017, 706). So, while ARPA-E's scope is technology-driven, its existence remains positioned within the political framework of the US federal government.

Sakina Groeppmaier

See also: Bell Labs; Fuel Cell; Idaho National Energy Laboratory; US Department of Energy

FURTHER READING

Advanced Research Projects Agency – Energy (ARPA-E). 2019a. "About." ARPA-E website. https://arpa-e.energy.gov/?q=arpa-e-site-page/aboutA (accessed June 2019).

Advanced Research Projects Agency – Energy (ARPA-E). 2019b. "ARPA-E History." ARPA-E website. https://arpa-e.energy.gov/?q=arpa-e-site-page/arpa-e-history (accessed June 25, 2019).

Advanced Research Projects Agency – Energy. (ARPA-E). 2019c. "ARPA-E Budget Requests." ARPA-E website. https://arpa-e.energy.gov/?q=arpa-e-site-page/arpa-e-budget (accessed June 2019).

Blaustein, Richard. 2012. "Can Biology Transform Our Energy Future?" *BioScience*. Vol. 62. No. 2. February. Pp. 115–19. https://doi.org/10.1525/bio.2012.62.2.4 (accessed October 2023).

Bonvillian, William B. and Richard Van Atta. 2011. "ARPA-E and DARPA: Applying the DARPA Model to Energy Innovation." *The Journal of Technology Transfer*. Vol. 36. No. 5. Pp. 469– 513. https://doi.org/10.1007/s10961-011-9223-x (accessed October 2023).

Executive Office of the President of the United States. 2009. *Strategy for American Innovation: Driving towards Sustainable Growth and Quality Jobs*. United States: National Economic Council, Office of Science and Technology Policy. September 2009.

Kintisch, Eli. 2010. "Matchmaking Is Part of the Party as ARPA-E Marks Its First Birthday." *Science*. New Series 327 5971. March 12. P. 1317.

Manser, Joseph S., Joseph A. Rollin, Kristen E. Brown, and Eric A. Rohlfing. 2016. "ARPA-E: Accelerating U.S. Energy Innovation." *ACS Energy Letters*. Vol. 1. No. 5. October 18. Pp. 987–90. https://doi.org/10.1021/acsenergylett.6b00494 (accessed October 2023).

National Academy of Sciences, National Academy of Engineering, and Institute of Medicine. 2007. *Rising above the Gathering Storm: Energizing and Employing America for a Brighter Economic Future*. Washington, DC: The National Academies Press. https://doi.org/10.17226/11463 (accessed October 2023).

Nekuda Malik, Jennifer A. 2017. "ARPA-E Sees Some Success from Basic Energy Research to Societal Impact." *MRS Bulletin*. Vol. 42. No. 10 (October). Pp. 706–7. https://doi.org/10.1557/mrs.2017.221 (accessed October 2023).

Agriculture and Energy

Since the beginning of agriculture, human power has been supplemented by other sources of power to increase the efficiency of food and fiber production. Before the Industrial Revolution, agriculture relied on several sources of non-human power, such as animals, water, and wind. When Europeans migrated to the Americas, animal species were introduced which expanded animal draft power for food production and transport. Europeans also brought several technologies that had been in use for centuries in Europe to increase the efficiency of agriculture. These sources of power are still used in modern American agriculture, though they have been modified. Modern sources of power such as the internal combustion engine and electricity have substantially changed the way agriculture uses energy to power modern implements for food and fiber production.

Animals commonly associated with agricultural draft power, such as horses and oxen, were not a part of American agriculture until the Columbian Exchange. Horses were readily adopted by Native Americans and utilized by European immigrants for both transportation and agriculture. Different breeds of horses had different purposes. Larger horses of draft breeds were utilized for pulling heavy loads, such as wagons and plows. Smaller horses were more suited for pulling lighter buggies and horseback travel. Oxen were a multi-purpose animal and were used for food, pulling heavy loads, and cultivation of crop land. Donkeys and mules were also used, especially in the Southwest. Before the Columbian Exchange, indigenous peoples were known to use dogs to pull travois for transport of goods. Animals also provided fuel to heat homes, as excrement from forage-consuming animals such as bison and cattle could be used as fuel for fires when wood was not widely available.

Hydropower has been used for thousands of years as a source of mechanical energy. In the United States, farmers and artisans used paddle wheels to mill grain and lumber before steam power and electricity. Iron forges also used hydropower. Grain mills, or gristmills, were located in most towns. With mills distributed throughout the cultivated land, farmers carried their grains shorter distances for conversion from commodities to more easily utilized food ingredients. Sawmills for lumber were located on navigable bodies of water; logs were brought to the mill to be transformed into usable lumber. Iron forges utilized hydropower for the bellows to force air into the forge, thereby maintaining its temperature. Forges were used to manufacture and repair plows and other farm equipment. One aspect of hydropower that could limit availability was water flow. Not only did water need to be present, but there needed to be movement of water to turn the paddle wheel which would move the gears inside the mill. Modern hydropower is used mainly for electricity generation at dams located adjacent to large bodies of water.

Wind power has been used to power gristmills and sawmills, as well as to pump water from aquifers to the surface. Wind-powered water pumps were more common in the western United States, where groundwater was more limited and potable water had to be brought to the surface from aquifers. They were found near homes as well as to provide water for livestock. Windmills are still found in more remote areas to pump water for grazing livestock. One limitation of using wind power was the inconsistent flow of wind due to weather patterns. The use of windmills for powering gristmills, sawmills, and to provide water decreased once electricity became more commonplace in the first half of the twentieth century. Due to increased interest in renewable energy sources, wind turbines to generate electricity are becoming more widespread.

In the late nineteenth century, mechanization began to replace traditional sources of power in agriculture. Small engines powered by hand cranking of gears debuted in the 1890s. Early tractors for plowing, cultivating, and planting were powered by steam engines. While animal, water, wind, and steam power increased production over human power alone, the internal combustion engine provided a dramatic increase in the efficiency of food production. Internal combustion engines were portable, which was an advantage compared with wind and water power, faster to start than steam, and did not require energy when not being used like animals. Additionally, the land that was used to grow crops to feed the draft animals could be converted to cropland for human consumption. Gasoline-powered engines were advertised as early as 1896, and automobiles likely helped increase popularity of these engines for farmers. These engines were stationary, and provided ways for farmers to increase productivity.

The first American gasoline-powered, self-propelled traction engines were marketed by the Hart Parr company, which coined the term "tractor." These early tractors weighed around 14,000 pounds and produced thirty horsepower (NMAH 2018). Ford began to manufacture tractors, as did International Harvester. In 1918, Deere and Co., which started as a plow manufacturer, purchased the Waterloo Gasoline Engine Company and became a major player in the tractor market. In the 1930s, over 50 percent of tractors were manufactured by one of three companies: Allis-Chalmers, International Harvester, and John Deere. In 1935, International Harvester began selling a diesel-powered tractor. John Deere followed suit in 1949 (Mowitz 2019). By the 1960s, diesel was the predominant source of fuel for tractors. Tractors using fuel cells were not as popular as gasoline—or diesel-powered models. As engines advanced in power and technology, the tractor's performance did as well. Tractors were able to attach to implements and use kinetic and hydraulic power to move parts of the implements. The variety of available horsepower to fit various needs of farmers has also increased over time.

Biofuels have gained in popularity as a substitute for fossil fuels. Grains such as corn and sorghum can be fermented to produce fuel-grade ethanol, and the leftover parts of the grain are then used as a livestock feed. Crop waste and animal waste are also anaerobically fermented into methane in a contained environment, called digesters, where methane can be collected and later used similarly to natural gas. Waste oils and fats, commonly from restaurants and food production facilities, can be converted into biodiesel. While biofuels are not as widely available or frequently used as fossil fuels in agriculture, interest in production has increased.

In modern agriculture, tractors with diesel engines perform much of the work, and yet equipment powered by other fuels also aid in production. In traditional cultures, animal power is still widely used. Biofuel generation has become a new source of renewable energy as an alternative to fossil fuel use. Wind and solar energy continue to expand as sources of electricity for agriculture's diverse array of operations.

Jessica O. Baggerman

See also: Animal Power; Biofuels; Buffalo Chips; Electricity; Ford, Henry; Fuel Cell; Hydroelectric Power; Industrial Revolution; Natural Gas; Petroleum; Renewable Energy; Rural Electrification Act of 1936; Solar Power; Steam Power; Water Power; Wind Power

FURTHER READING

Fogarty, Amelia. 2018. "Five Ways the Tractor Changed American Farming." *Smithsonian Insider*. March. https://insider.si.edu/2018/03/five-facts-tractors-revolutionized-american-farming/ (accessed March 2020).

Meyer, Carrie A. 2013. "The Farm Debut of the Gasoline Engine." *Agricultural History*. Vol. 87. No. 3. Pp. 287–313.

Mowitz, Dave. 2019. "The History of Deere's Diesel Tractors." *Successful Farming*. April. https://www.agriculture.com/machinery/tractors/deeres-diesels (accessed March 2020).

National Museum of American History (NMAH). 2018. "These Tractors Show 150 Years of Farming History." https://americanhistory.si.edu/blog/these-tractors-show-150-years-farming-history (accessed October 2023).

U.S. Department of Agriculture (USDA). 2020. "Energy." U.S. Department of Agriculture Alternative Farming Systems Information Center. https://www.nal.usda.gov/afsic/energy-overview (accessed March 2020).

Alta Wind Energy Center

Alta Wind Energy Center (AWEC) is the largest wind energy project in the United States and "the second largest onshore wind farm" on earth and is owned by Terra-Gen Power (Feldman 2009; VML 2019). It is also recognized as "the Mojave wind farm, or the Tehachapi wind farm." The farm covers 3,200 acres in the foothills of California's Tehachapi Mountains, and lies near to the Tehachapi wind resource area just 2 miles away. The Alta Wind Energy Center is one of several wind farms built in the wind resource area beginning in the 1970s.

On October 19, 1973, the Organization of Petroleum Exporting Countries (OPEC) declared on oil embargo that prohibited oil export to the United States. This was in response to President Richard Nixon's decision not to tie the value of American dollar to the amount of gold owned by the US government. This led to the dollar's devaluation, and then Nixon provided Israel with military and financial aid against Egypt during the Yom Kippur War (Amadeo 2019). The resulting OPEC embargo led to an oil price increase of 350 percent (NMAH 2020). In 1973, Morris K. Udall suggested that American fossil fuel consumption should be considerably reduced before the year 2000 through the uses of windmills, water power, geothermal power, and solar energy as these do not lead to pollution (Udall 1973). He also promoted the establishment of windmill farms. President Jimmy Carter asked the nation to reduce its fossil fuel consumption in a speech to the nation on February 2, 1977 (NMAH 2020). In another speech entitled "A Crisis of Confidence" on July 15, 1979, Carter expressed his aim to reduce oil imports to the United States, fixing a quota to be controlled by an energy security agency, and to establish alternative energy resources such as a solar bank.

The main objective of the Alta Wind Energy Center is to provide clean renewable energy to the area via wind power, and thus discourage the use of carbon dioxide emitting fossil fuels. For this reason, in 2006, Alta Windpower Development, LLC signed a contract valid for more than twenty-five years to sell 1,550 megawatts of renewable energy to Southern California Edison (VML 2019). In 2008, a high-voltage transmission system called Tehachapi Renewable Transmission Project was initiated by Southern California Edison, which can deliver 4,500 megawatts of renewable energy (Feldman 2009). In July 2010, the first phase of the construction of the Alta Wind Energy Center was initiated. Units from I to V were completed in April 2011. Further phases ensued: in early 2011, the construction of Units VI and VIII were begun and then completed by the end of the year. Units VII and IX were completed in December 2012, and Units X and XI in 2013 (VML 2019).

The Alta Wind Center overcame several challenges. First, the project generated controversy over federally protected condors, which occasionally flew into wind farms. State wildlife officials issued a ruling that the condors could pass through the wind farm, leaving Alta Wind Center open to legal action in the event of the condors' decline (Woody 2012). Todd Woody proposed that radar units be deployed at wind farms in order to detect condors, which would shut down wind turbines automatically. Second, the transmission lines proved to be inadequate. This is shown by data from Iowa and Texas that demonstrate greater production and transmission of wind power than the Alta project (Feldman 2009). Third, Alta and other federally subsidized wind projects drew criticism from the industry's detractors. The earliest investors in the Alta Wind Energy Center requested more than $200 million in additional subsidies from the federal government (Doyle 2016). The center received grants of about $495 million from the US Treasury Department under the Section 1603 of the American Recovery and Reimbursement Act of 2009. The Court of Federal Claims decided that the wind farm had not made any "applicable asset acquisitions" under Section 1060. However, a federal circuit court disagreed with the Court of Federal Claims, declaring, "there is no need to show that a transaction had actual, accrued goodwill or going concern value at the time of the transaction," which defused the controversy (Kline 2018).

Despite these controversies, the Alta Wind Energy Center was projected to supply approximately 500,000 households with electricity and lead to numerous employment opportunities (Feldman 2009). The added benefit is reduction in the use of fossil fuels that cause greenhouse gas and carbon dioxide emissions, which have contributed to environmental problems associated with climate change (Jaber 2013; Schobert 2014, 627).

Fazila Derya Agis

See also: Block Island Wind Farm; Crotched Mountain Wind Farm; Energy Crisis of the 1970s; Halladay Windmill; Organization of Petroleum Exporting Countries (OPEC); Renewable Energy; Wind Power

FURTHER READING

Amadeo, Kimberly. 2019. "OPEC Oil Embargo, Its Causes, and the Effects of the Crisis: The Truth about the 1973 Arab Oil Crisis." *The Balance*. March 30. https://www.thebalance.com/opec-oil-embargo-causes-and-effects-of-the-crisis-3305806 (accessed January 15, 2020).

ArcGIS Story Maps. n.d. "Wind Farms/Alta Wind Center: A Look at Wind Energy and its Effects on the Environment, with a Focus on the Alta Wind Center." https://storymaps.arcgis.com/stories/7a7b7d8188574091992f907eafd0b42c (accessed December 2019).

Carter, Jimmy. July 15. "Energy and the National Goals—A Crisis of Confidence." https://www.americanrhetoric.com/speeches/jimmycartercrisisofconfidence.htm (accessed January 2020).

Doyle, Michael. 2016. "Investors in Huge California Wind Farm Might End up Repaying Federal Subsidies." *Impact2020*. February 11. https://www.mcclatchydc.com/news/crime/article59876101.html (accessed January 2020).

Feldman, Stacy. 2009. "Alta Wind Farm, America's Largest Wind Power Project, Blows Closer." *Insideclimate News*. July 27. https://insideclimatenews.org/news/27072009/alta-wind-farm-americas-largest-wind-power-project-blows-closer/ (accessed December 2019).

Jaber, Suaad. 2013. "Environmental Impacts of Wind Energy." *Journal of Clean Energy Technologies*. Pp. 251–4.

Kline, Craig, Adam Kobos, John Leonti and Roger Reigner. 2018. "Government Records Significant Victory in Alta Wind." *Renewable Energy Insights*. August 7. https://www.renewableinsights.com/2018/08/government-records-significant-victory-alta-wind/#page=1 (accessed January 15, 2020; URL no longer accessible).

National Museum of American History (NMAH). 2020. "Energy Crisis." Behring Center American Enterprise Exhibition. https://americanhistory.si.edu/american-enterprise-exhibition/consumer-era/energy-crisis (accessed January 2020).

Schobert, Harold H. 2014. *Energy and Society: An Introduction*. Boca Raton: CRC Press.

Udall, Morris K. 1973. "How Congress Planned to Solve the 1970s Energy Crisis." *The New Republic*. June 16. https://newrepublic.com/article/118918/how-congress-planned-solve-1970s-energy-crisis (accessed January 2020).

Verdict Media Limited (VML). 2019. "Alta Wind Energy Center (AWEC), California." *Power Technology*. https://www.power-technology.com/projects/alta-wind-energy-center-awec-california/ (accessed December 2019).

Woody, Todd. 2012. "Condor Controversy Puts Google, Other Wind Investors in Cross-Hairs." *Forbes*. January 6. https://www.forbes.com/sites/toddwoody/2012/01/06/condor-controversy-puts-google-other-wind-investors-in-cross-hairs/#3c48c1696625 (accessed January 2010).

American Petroleum Institute

The American Petroleum Institute (API) is an organization initially created to influence government policy and public opinion in the interests of the fossil fuel industry's corporations and independent operators. It began its operations in 1919 in the political context of the First World War interaction between energy company executives and the Woodrow Wilson administration and has been active in seeking to shape US energy policy—and thus US foreign policy—over the course of the twentieth and twenty-first centuries. The organization and its proponents view its efforts as beneficial to the vitality of the United States and global economies and to the everyday well-being of hundreds of millions of people. Critics charge that the API opposes policies designed to safeguard public health, ensure long-term sustainability of natural resources, and blunt the progress of anthropogenic climate change.

The API grew out of an earlier committee of industry executives assembled during the First World War to provide information about oil production to policymakers in the federal government who needed to understand the nation's oil supply and its potential productive capacity. Initially called the Petroleum Advisory Committee to the Council of National Defense, the committee renamed itself in 1918 the National Petroleum War Service Committee (NPWSC) once President Wilson created the Federal Fuel Administration. This was the agency created to manage the production and use of coal and oil to ensure adequate supply for the war effort. Under the chairmanship of A.C. Bedford, president of Standard Oil Company of New Jersey, the NPWSC provided streams of data to the Fuel Administration tracking the petroleum production of American companies. An historian of the API's origins noted: "Through this committee system, the Fuel Administration could quickly reach down into the oil industry for expertise and for the essential information needed to govern the flow of petroleum products to European battlefields. During the war the oil industry largely governed itself through its advisory committees to the Fuel Administration" (Pratt 1980, 76). Essentially, the meetings of the NPWSC encouraged the organization to imagine itself as a trade association, which the industry had not yet created in its infancy (Rich 2019).

The NPWSC reorganized as the API at the end of the First World War. At its formal founding in 1919 the API selected Thomas A. O'Donnell as president, which reflected its new identity as an agent for oil and natural gas companies. O'Donnell was one of the "big four" players in the development of California's oil and natural gas industry, a group that included Edward L. Doheny, Charles A. Canfield, and Max H. Whittier. When he first came to California, O'Donnell took a job with the Union Oil Company in Ventura County, then formed a variety of partnerships with other small oil and gas speculators until he became vice-president of both the American Petroleum Company and the American Oil Fields Company. These two companies eventually merged while controlling interests in the largest oil and gas regions in California. The company was then purchased by the corporation that became Texaco. O'Donnell's knowledge of the technical and financial aspects of oil exploration and development earned him a seat on President Wilson's wartime Fuel Conservation Board, and eventually appointment as national director of oil production for the Fuel Administration.

O'Donnell and the API took on the task of advancing the interests of the approximately 25,000 oil producers in the United States ("Fears" 1918). The API retained as one of its key functions the collection and dissemination of accurate production statistics of the nation's oil companies. The API's first secretary-general noted in a speech in 1919 that "the collection, study, and dissemination of oil statistics ought to be one of the great objectives of the American Petroleum Institute" (Pratt 1980, 78). Members of the API considered this data service to be vital for ensuring that Congress and the White House had accurate information about the industry in its deliberations on energy policy. Furthermore, industry leaders considered much of the reportage on the oil business to be misinformation spread by journalists, newspaper editors, and activists who believed that oil companies were engaging in war profiteering. By the late 1920s the API's serialized bulletins bristled with statistics on the output of wells and the production of refineries. Eventually these bulletins went beyond reports of production and refining and included data on "consumption of oil by railroads, vessels, and public utilities; imports and exports of petroleum products; the consumption of gasoline and kerosene by state; drilling activities; and receipts of California oil at Atlantic and Gulf ports" (Pratt 1980, 80).

REX TILLERSON

In 2016, President Donald Trump nominated API trustee Rex Tillerson to be the US Secretary of State, an office he held for a year until his firing. Before his short term on the cabinet, Tillerson had worked in the oil industry as an engineer, manager, and finally chairman and CEO of ExxonMobil from 2006 until 2017. Tillerson's relationship with Trump deteriorated amid reports that he questioned Trump's competence, and in a post-firing interview Tillerson described Trump as "undisciplined" and unwilling to read and learn about foreign policy issues.

Jeffrey B. Webb

These efforts were vital in establishing the API as the industry's chief clearinghouse of accurate information about petroleum production and consumption. The API also concerned itself with establishing industry standards in equipment and procedures to ensure workplace safety and to enhance operational efficiency (API 2023). However, it was concerns over taxation and government regulation that really motivated the early API leaders. There was a pervasive fear that President Wilson might move to regulate the oil and gas industry just as the federal government had done with railroads in the 1890s and early 1900s with legislation like the Hepburn Act (1906), which authorized the Interstate Commerce Commission to set freight rates. More directly, industry executives reacted strongly to a US House of Representatives bill in late 1918 that proposed to levy new "war profits and excess profits taxes" on the industry ("Fears" 1918). They claimed that in the bill, "if a producing well was brought in the Government would demand upward to 60 per cent. or more of his profit." They went on to argue that the excess profits taxes proposed in the new law would disincentivize and virtually shut down future efforts to explore and develop new oil wells ("Fears" 1918).

API president O'Donnell captured this mood of fearfulness about taxes and regulations in a speech delivered at the annual meeting of the API in Washington, DC in 1920. The speech also expressed the organization's belief regarding the fundamental importance of the petroleum industry to sustaining the world economy, and thus the modern way of life. O'Donnell said:

> There is nothing so important in our modern industrial development as petroleum. The increasing demands are greater at the present time than ever in the history of the industry. Active development of the petroleum resources of the world is important to all people everywhere. Nature, I believe, has supplied a sufficient quantity to meet the requirements. It is unbelievable that so many governments have established restrictive rules and regulations, and in those countries not yet affected there is much agitation for restrictive legislation and regulation, which will be very effective in discouraging necessary activity. A return to a 'free and open-door policy' by many governments of the world is the most important factor in an assured future supply. Unless this is done, there is no doubt that a serious shortage is confronting the world. (O'Donnell 1920, 33)

The important phrase in this passage is "restrictive legislation and regulation." O'Donnell opposed government interference with oil and natural gas company operations in the United States, and the API has pursued this objective ever since his presidency of the organization. In 1969, the API moved its offices from New York to Washington, DC. In 2018, it employed fifty-six professional lobbyists on Capitol Hill and spent $6.97 million on its lobbying effort (Open Secrets 2023). Currently, the API states its mission as follows: "API's mission is to promote safety across the industry globally and to influence public policy in support of a strong, viable U.S. oil and natural gas industry" (API 2023). To illustrate, President Joe Biden issued an executive order in 2021 to pause new oil and gas leases on federal lands and waters, which brought the API to post a lengthy document on its website objecting to the policy. The document, "Drilling Down on Federal Leasing Facts," teemed with data on oil supply and demand and projected hardship for American consumers (API 2022). The API and eleven other trade groups then filed a lawsuit in the US District Court for the Western District of Louisiana, asking for the court to intervene by blocking the new lease-restriction policy. It is important to emphasize that the API considers its mission to be much broader than influencing policy; it has been involved in many other recent initiatives to encourage energy corporations to make their workplaces safer and their operations more environmentally healthy.

Criticism of the API and its activities can be found in every historical period of its history. In 2021, a characteristic statement issued from the left-leaning opinion magazine *The Nation* pointed out that API receives millions in contributions from oil companies to fund its extensive staff of researchers, writers, lobbyists, and lawyers. It cited a report from the Royal Dutch Shell corporation that it gave API $10 million in 2020, just one year's financial outlay. That is just one of the 600 corporations that the API claims to represent, and most do not disclose amounts of their contributions to API. Its annual revenue in 2019 was nearly $240 million. *The Nation* accused Shell and other major oil companies of duplicity by projecting an image of concern over environmental degradation and climate change and at the same time secretly funneling money to API in support of its efforts to secure industry-friendly government policies: "While companies run publicity campaigns claiming to take the climate emergency seriously, the trade group works behind the scenes in Congress to stall or weaken environmental legislation" (McGreal 2021).

These corporations, which *The Nation* and environmentalists refer to as "Big Oil," rely on API to use its access to government agencies and elected officials as well as its mastery of the data on oil and gas production and consumption to make the case for continued development of oil and natural gas resources. More recently the industry lobby has presented itself as part of the solution to two major energy-related problems confronting the nation: its ever-expanding need for energy and the problem of climate change. In a media interview in 2022, Mike Sommers, president and CEO of API offered this response to the critics: "the most important environmental movement in the world is the American oil and gas industry. It is the reason why we've been able to cut greenhouse gas emissions over the course of the last decade because we've been able to discover more natural gas. And natural gas was able to compete with coal as the primary source of power in the United States. And as you said, natural gas is 50% more clean than coal" ("US …" 2022).

API negotiated the complicated terrain of energy policy in a climate of political polarization in the United States in the early twentieth century. Concerns over greenhouse gas emissions and growing domestic pressure for the adoption of renewable fuels intersected with political volatility and open violence in the Middle East, Russia, Ukraine, Africa, and other oil-producing regions. These countervailing forces offer significant ongoing challenges to an organization committed to leading the oil and gas industry into a future with fossil fuels as a key element of the global energy picture.

Jeffrey B. Webb

See also: Climate Change; Energy Crisis of the 1970s; Energy Independence; Food and Fuel Control Act of 1917; Mandatory Oil Import Quota Program; Mineral Leasing Act of 1920; National Energy Act of 1978; Oil Embargo of 1941; Peak Oil; Petroleum; Seven Sisters Oil Companies; US Fuel Administration

FURTHER READING

American Petroleum Institute (API). 2022. "Drilling Down on Federal Leasing Facts." https://www.api.org/-/media/files/policy/exploration/2022/api-factsheet-federal-leaseing-spinvsfact-final.pdf (accessed November 2023).

American Petroleum Institute (API). 2023. "About API." https://www.api.org/about (accessed October 2023).

"Fears War Tax Will End Quest for Oil." 1918. *The New York Times*. September 6. https://www.nytimes.com/1918/09/06/archives/fears-war-tax-will-end-quests-for-oil-producers-committee-reports.html (accessed October 2023).

McGreal, Chris. 2021. "How a Powerful US Lobby Group Helps Big Oil to Block Climate Action." *The Nation*. July 21. https://www.thenation.com/article/environment/oil-lobby-climate-action/ (accessed October 2023).

O'Donnell, Thomas A. 1920. "Production—the Future." Bulletin of the American Petroleum Institute: Addresses Delivered at General Sessions: Annual Meeting, American Petroleum Institute, Washington, DC, November 17, 18, and 19, 1920. No. 132. December 10. https://www.google.com/books/edition/Addresses_Delivered_at_General_Sessions/V31JAAAAYAAJ?hl=en&gbpv=1&dq=%22American+Petroleum+Institute%22&pg=PA3&printsec=frontcover (accessed October 2023).

Open Secrets. 2023. "Client Profile: American Petroleum Institute." Data for 2018. https://www.opensecrets.org/federal-lobbying/clients/lobbyists?cycle=2018&id=D000031493 (accessed October 2023).

Potter, Stephen. 1990. *The American Petroleum Institute: An Informal History, 1919–1987*. Washington, DC: The American Petroleum Institute.

Pratt, Joseph A. 1980. "Organizing Information about the Modern Oil Industry in the Formative Years of the American Petroleum Institute." *Business and Economic History*. Vol. 9. Pp. 4–86. http://www.jstor.org/stable/23702672 (accessed October 2023).

Rich, Steven. 2019. "History of the American Petroleum Institute (API)." Drillers.com. January 29. https://drillers.com/history-of-the-american-petroleum-institute-api/ (accessed October 2023).

"US Oil and Gas Industry the World's 'Most Important Environmental Movement,' Energy Exec Says." 2022. Fox Business. May 27. https://www.foxbusiness.com/energy/us-oil-gas-industry-worlds-most-important-environmental-movement-energy-exec (accessed October 2023).

American Radiator Company

In the preindustrial era, homes, workshops, churches, town halls, and other buildings were heated by wood fires in open-hearth fireplaces or enclosed metal stoves. Numerous trial-and-error experiments with stove design using baffles, ducts, and other appointments increased the efficiency and energy output of these metal stoves. However, with the advent of steam boilers during the Industrial Revolution, these heating technologies eventually gave way to centralized heating systems composed of steam boilers that circulated heated air through pipes and ducts to different endpoints, finally reaching room radiators. Radiators appeared in the mid-nineteenth century and were manufactured using industrial techniques in the 1880s, eventually dominating the market for interior heating systems. They became a common feature in the apartment and office buildings of America's growing urban spaces in the first half of the twentieth century. Among the earliest and largest commercial suppliers was the American Radiator Company, which formed in 1892 through various combinations of smaller radiator manufacturers (Wilkins 1969, 327). The history of the company and its products offer a helpful window on the changing patterns of home energy use in modern American society.

Before radiators, registers and grates located on floors and walls were used as release points for steam-heated air to enter a building's various rooms. In 1863, Joseph Nason and Robert Briggs patented a heating device composed of a set of vertical iron tubes that were designed to convey the heated air into the room and then "radiate" the heat outward, while allowing the colder, condensing air to settle in the tubes and then return to the steam boiler (Nagengast 2001). In time, the Nason–Briggs apparatus developed into the more recognizable upright, cast-iron unit with an accordion-style array of piped sections. The different firms that merged into American Radiator Company began mass-producing these units in the late 1880s and early 1890s. When the larger company formed itself in 1892, it located its headquarters in Chicago. The company took advantage of its proximity to the Chicago World's Columbian Exposition in 1893, an event that drew millions from around the world to see firsthand many of the latest advancements in energy technology. An observer described the company's booth at the Manufacturer's Building in lavish terms.

Noting that the building itself was lighted by electricity—a very new experience for most of the visitors—the writer went on to describe the American Radiator Company as "the largest makers of radiators in the world," with their radiators used exclusively in all of the World's Fair buildings ("Interesting" 1893). The booth displayed several different models in different sizes. The company offered radiators from 5 to 80 inches in length and from twenty to 40 inches high, with an average of 38 inches. The description of the products concludes with this observation about their appearance: "A feature which adds greatly to the beauty of the American radiators is their tasty ornamentation. The visitor to their exhibit is at once impressed with the fact that a radiator may be highly ornamental as well as useful" ("Interesting" 1893).

The American Radiator Company and other manufacturers of the period offered designs festooned with embossed scrollwork and floral motifs. In this way the device served more than utilitarian purposes. It might also have been a way for homeowners to express their sense of good taste, as they were doing with other elements of home décor like crown moldings, wainscotting, window treatments, furniture, carpeting and tiling, and so on. Still, radiators weren't passive decorative objects like a side table with a vase of flowers. In most homes, people interacted with their radiators. They put wet socks and gloves on them to dry and used them as warming stands for dishes brought from the oven. Owners placed pans of water on their radiators to humidify their rooms. Radiators hissed and clanged, providing a sonic backdrop to the rhythms of daily life for millions of homeowners and apartment dwellers. In larger buildings, a person in a different unit could make their presence felt when tapping on their radiator. With radiators, energy possessed a tangibility that paralleled earlier sensory experiences of humans with their crackling cooking fires and smoky kerosene lamps.

CLANGING RADIATORS

Radiators can sometimes begin vibrating and clanging, referred to as a steam or water hammer. This is the result of uncondensed water getting into the system and mixing with super-heated water vapor. The pressurized steam will dash the water against the pipes and cause the shaking and banging. Water trapped in the radiator can also prematurely cool the hot steam entering the system, creating a vacuum which rattles the pipes.

Jeffrey B. Webb

The economic disaster of the 1893 panic and depression dried up the domestic market for the company's radiators. It so happened that at the Chicago World's Fair the company made contact with several foreign visitors who rated the American radiators as better than what could be purchased in Europe. This led company secretary Clarence Mott Woolley (1863–1956) overseas to determine if English, German, and French buyers might absorb the company's surplus inventory. Within a few years the company became active in the radiator markets throughout the continent, and in 1897, the company approved the construction of manufacturing plants in several European nations beginning with Germany and France. This expansion made it necessary for the company to relocate its headquarters to New York, and in 1899 the company was reincorporated in New Jersey, with Woolley elevated to president in 1902. His obituary credits him as "one of the first two or three American industrialists to establish trading and manufacturing companies in Europe" ("Clarence" 1956).

The company grew to be so profitable that it commissioned and built the highly regarded American Radiator Building on West 40th Street in Manhattan, designed by Raymond Hood and André Fouilhoux in the Gothic and Art Deco style. Christine G. O'Malley, an architectural historian, noted that when the building opened in 1924 it "stimulated strong reactions among architectural critics and commentators and stirred imaginative interpretations of its symbolism among artists and writers" (O'Malley 2017). Woolley believed the building served to enhance the American Radiator Company's brand by attracting tourists, even from Europe, and he wrote about the building in a 1926 issue of *American Architect* magazine. O'Malley reasoned that "Woolley fully appreciated the commercial and advertising benefits of his company's distinctive skyscraper, and the powerful identification value of a skyscraper with a company or product" (O'Malley 2017). Woolley's leadership led the company to a position of market domination by the late 1920s. In 1926, the company employed 22,000 workers in plants around the United States, including nine in Buffalo, three in Detroit, and one in eleven other American cities and two in Canada. The company also operated twelve plants in England, France, Belgium, Germany, Austria, Italy, and Spain (Porter 1926, 978).

Woolley transitioned from president to chairman in 1924, and in that new role helped the company in 1929 to merge with Standard Sanitary Manufacturing Company, forming American Radiator and Standard Sanitary Corporation—commonly known as American Standard (Wilkins 1969, 346). The company persisted as an industry leader in radiator manufacturing until the appearance of new home heating technologies, particularly thermostat-controlled gas—and oil-burning furnaces with a forced-air design. These new heating systems were preferred by the millions of new homeowners who moved to the suburbs in the era after the Second World War. Even so, as of 2020 some 80 percent of residential buildings in New York City were still kept warm by free-standing radiators heated by steam (Sisson 2020).

Jeffrey B. Webb

See also: Chicago World's Columbian Exposition; Fesler, Milton A.; Gold, Stephen J.; Home Energy Efficiency; Johnson, Warren Seymour; Nason, Joseph; New York Steam Company; Pierce Steam Heating Company; Powers, William Penn

FURTHER READING

"Clarence M. Woolley, Long-Time Villager and Noted Industrialist, Dies at Age 93." 1956. *Desert Sun*. July 23. Vol. 29. No. 198.

"Interesting World's Fair Exhibits." 1893. *The Inland Architect and News Record*. Vol. 22. No. 2. P. 22.

Nagengast, Bernard. 2001. "An Early History of Comfort Heating." *The Air Conditioning, Heating and Refrigeration News*. November 6. https://www.achrnews.com/articles/87035-an-early-history-of-comfort-heating (accessed October 2023).

O'Malley, Christine G. 2017. "Radiant Heat and Glowing Lights: Raymond Hood's American Radiator Building." *Skyscraper Gothic: Medieval Style and Modernist Buildings*. Eds. Fevin D. Murphy and Lisa Reilly. Charlottesville: University of Virginia Press.

Porter, John Sherman, ed. 1926. *Moody's Manual of Investments: Industrial Securities*. New York: Moody's Investor Service.

Sisson, Patrick. 2020. "Your Old Radiator Is a Pandemic-Fighting Weapon." Bloomberg. August 5. https://www.bloomberg.com/news/articles/2020-08-05/the-curious-history-of-steam-heat-and-pandemics (accessed October 2023).

Wilkins, Mira. 1969. "An American Enterprise Abroad: American Radiator Company in Europe, 1895–1914." *Business History Review*. Vol. 43. Pp. 326–46.

An Inconvenient Truth

In 2006, the documentary film *An Inconvenient Truth* appeared in theaters, drawing a wide viewership and creating a national conversation about climate change, the film's principal subject. The conversation gained momentum due to wide media coverage of both the film itself and how celebrities and political figures responded to it. The film depicts former US Vice President Al Gore (1948–) delivering a lecture using a slide show, which he had developed over the years and given to numerous live audiences. The slideshow advances a link between planetary warming trends and various observed effects such as melting glaciers and increased CO_2 saturation in Antarctic ice cores, then suggests that these phenomena are largely due to human use of carbon-based fuels like coal and oil. The film received positive reviews and won two Academy Awards, but more importantly, persuaded many who viewed the film to accept that climate change is real and that the scientific data is conclusive. The film's "moment" in American history demonstrates the power of energy narratives like "climate crisis" to infuse and animate culture, motivate social action, and structure political dialogue.

The film originated in May 2004 when producer Laurie David attended a premier of the film *The Day After Tomorrow* (2004) and a panel discussion after the film that included Al Gore. The former vice president ran a shortened version of his slide show and David left amazed at the simplicity and persuasiveness of Gore's presentation. She gathered fellow producer Lawrence Bender and billionaire Jeffrey Skoll (also founder of Participant Media) and requested a meeting with Gore to discuss the possibility of featuring his full-length slideshow and other climate change themed material in a documentary film. Despite some misgivings, Gore agreed, and Davis Guggenheim was recruited to direct the project. Production ensued in 2004 and 2005, and the film premiered at the Sundance Film Festival in January of 2006, where it received three standing ovations. The film opened to the public on May 24 that year in New York and Los Angeles. The film has a running time of 97 minutes, and against a budget of $1.5 million, earned $49.8 million in the domestic and international box offices. Al and Tipper Gore pledged to donate their earnings to a bipartisan charity devoted to educational initiatives on global warming and climate change. The film garnered many film awards, including two for Best Documentary Feature and Best Original Song (Melissa Ethridge's "I Need to Wake Up") at the 79th Academy Awards the following year.

Many of the film's scenes show Gore speaking to a live audience in a theater in Los Angeles in front of a purpose-built, 70-foot digital screen for his slides, which had been reworked and expanded for the film. Scenes from outside the theater are added in, where Gore explains a little of his life story and particularly how he became interested in these issues. Many of the live audience slideshow segments feature Gore on camera, showing slides with scientific research on the dramatic changes in atmospheric concentrations of greenhouse gases over the last few hundred years. He stresses the ice melt of glaciers in Montana and Colorado as well as rising sea levels due to ice melt in Antarctica and Greenland. Melting sea ice, Gore explains, has changed the salinity of seawater, which might affect ocean currents. Those currents are one factor that regulates temperature and weather patterns around the world.

The film also includes material that anticipates objections to the scientific data and to the solutions proposed to halt or even reverse global warming. In all, Gore's intent is to reframe the debate on climate change from a political issue to a moral issue, asking his audience to consider their moral obligation to future generations of people who will have to deal with the consequences of poor human choices in the past and present. He makes this point at the film's conclusion:

> Each one of us is a cause of global warming, but each one of us can make choices to change that with the things we buy, the electricity we use, the cars we drive; we can make choices to bring our individual carbon emissions to zero. The solutions are in our hands, we just have to have the determination to make it happen. We have everything that we need to reduce carbon emissions, everything but political will. But in America, the will to act is a renewable resource. (IMDB)

Film critic Roger Ebert lavished praise on the film and wrote, "In 39 years, I have never written these words in a movie review, but here they are: You owe it to yourself to see this film. If you do not, and you have grandchildren, you should explain to them why you decided not to" (Ebert 2006). Studies revealed that even conservative-leaning filmgoers rated the film highly and the vast majority indicated they would recommend it to other people (Garofoli 2006). A smaller number of voices panned the film, including a *Wall Street Journal* op-ed by MIT atmospheric scientist Richard D. Lindzen who questioned the scientific consensus that Gore cites in the film, referring to it as an attempt to "intimidate the public and even scientists." He further mentioned that the human contribution to global warming cannot be determined, so the use of "scientific consensus" arguments "in promoting visions of disaster constitutes nothing so much as a bait-and-switch scam" (Lindzen 2006).

The film raised important questions about scientific research and public opinion. In the film itself, Gore says that there is "100 agreement" among scientists about global warming and quickly laments that a majority, 57 percent of people surveyed, still question whether it is an established fact. He attributes this gap between scientific research and public opinion to a disinformation campaign by the energy companies that emerged in the 1990s, which tried to depict the scientific research on global warming as still subject to an ongoing debate. This produced a number of responses in the media, including cable television programs, radio broadcasts, blog and chatroom discussions on the internet, all of which lodged charges and countercharges of using propaganda to steer policy debates about energy and the environment. Liberals accused conservatives of buying "corporate lies" designed to stop policy changes to address the problem; conservatives accused liberals of "shrill alarmism" drawn from wild claims of environmental groups and activists (Whitehouse 2016; Lindzen 2006).

It might seem that Gore's film produced a culture of debate marked by stalemate born of mutually canceling claims of misinformation, disinformation, and propaganda. But this conclusion doesn't take account of how people reported their reactions to actually seeing the movie. A survey conducted in forty-seven countries by Nielsen and Oxford University in 2007 found that two-thirds of those who saw the film "changed their mind" about global warming. More importantly, three-fourths of the viewers followed Gore's closing suggestions in the film to make different choices in their lifestyles: recycle your trash, drive a hybrid, speak up in your community (McNall 2011, 23). Partly due to his advocacy and his film, as well as its worldwide impact on public opinion, Al Gore and the Intergovernmental Panel on Climate Change were named the 2007 co-recipients of the Nobel Peace Prize.

Jeffrey B. Webb

See also: Climate Change; Global Climate Coalition; Renewable Energy; Sierra Club; Union of Concerned Scientists

FURTHER READING

Ebert, Roger. 2006. "Disaster Movie." RogerEbert.com. June 1. https://www.rogerebert.com/reviews/an-inconvenient-truth-2006 (accessed October 2023).

Garofoli, Joe. 2006. "Gore Movie Reaching the Red States, Too." *San Francisco Chronicle*. July 8. https://www.sfgate.com/politics/joegarofoli/article/Gore-movie-reaching-the-red-states-too-2493350.php (accessed October 2023).

IMDB. 2023. *An Inconvenient Truth (2006)*. https://www.imdb.com/title/tt0497116/ (accessed October 2023).

Lindzen, Richard D. 2006. "There Is No 'Consensus' on Global Warming." *Wall Street Journal*. June 26. http://epw.senate.gov/fact.cfm?party=rep&id=257863 (URL no longer accessible).

McNall, Scott G. 2011. *Rapid Climate Change: Causes, Consequences, and Solutions*. New York: Routledge.

Whitehouse, Sheldon. 2016. "Time to Wake Up: The Denial Apparatus." July 6. Sheldon Whitehouse: United States Senator for Rhode Island website. https://www.whitehouse.senate.gov/news/speeches/time-to-wake-up-the-denial-apparatus (accessed October 2023).

Animal Power

Sources of power for production of food have been required since agriculture began. Humans began domesticating various species of animals for food production, fiber sources, and power for transportation and work. Horses and cattle were not a part of New World agriculture until they were brought by Christopher Columbus's second voyage to the West Indies in 1493. The introduction of these species began to change agriculture in North America. Indigenous peoples used dogs to help with transporting people and goods until they began to use the animals brought across the continent by the settlers, soldiers, and missionaries. While dogs were useful as pack animals, especially in areas with frozen terrain, the loads they can carry are limited. The ability to haul more weight per animal was an incentive for using horses, donkeys, and cattle.

As Europeans began to settle in North America, they brought species, tools, and practices which changed agriculture. The increase in human population also increased the food requirements for an area, so intensive cultivation of food crops was needed. Animals also were important for assisting with removing felled trees for construction of buildings and increasing the area of land which could be cultivated. The most common types of draft animals were horses and oxen, or cattle trained for draft work. They can both haul freight and power the tilling of soil for crop production. However, due to the unique anatomy of each, certain tasks were more suited to a particular specie.

Oxen were used to carry heavier loads than horses, but they are slower than horses. Oxen were able to pull those loads consistently for longer period of time, making them useful in field work, such as plowing soil. They also tended to cost less than horses, making them more affordable to the majority of farms. Oxen were often part of cattle herds that were multi-purpose. Females would produce calves and milk; bulls, or intact males, were used to breed females and sometimes for draft work; and steers, or castrated males, were used for draft work. When animals were past their productive stage of life or food was scarce, owners could harvest the animals for meat. Due to the multi-purpose nature of these animals, breed used was due to preference or availability.

The horses that were introduced to North America in the early sixteenth century were lighter horses, which are more suited for transporting humans or hauling light loads, either directly on the back of the animal or in a light cart or wagon. The introduction of draft breeds from Europe during the nineteenth century changed what horses could do on the farm. Draft horses were more suited for tasks such as pulling heavy loads due to their taller height at the shoulder, stouter bone structure, increased muscularity, and shoulder conformation which was more suited to pulling when compared to light horses. Common draft breeds included Belgians, Clydedales, Percherons, and Shires. These large horses provided greater power at faster speed, making horses more common than oxen as draft animals by the end of the nineteenth century. Over time, draft horses were crossed with light horses, producing horses which were an intermediate of the two breed types (IMH 2020).

Other species used for draft animals in the United States include donkeys and mules. Due to their small size, donkeys required less feed than horses, but also could not haul the same weight. Mules are the hybrid of a male donkey bred to a female horse. As mules are infertile hybrids, they cannot reproduce, which requires both donkeys and horses to increase the number of mules. Mules were attractive to Americans, especially in the South and Southwest, as they were smaller than horses, making them suited to narrower tracks, such as trails and rows between crops. In the beginning of the twentieth century, mules were the most common draft animal in the South (Sawers 2004).

Animals provided power beyond tillage of soil and transportation of people and freight. They also were crucial in the function of mills where water was not available or flow was not consistent. These mills converted many commodity products into goods such as flour and lumber. They were also used to power bellows to maintain forge temperatures for blacksmiths to create and repair metal tools. The manure produced by the draft animals could be used for a variety of purposes, such as fertilizer for soil or fuel for fires used for heating and cooking when other materials such as wood were not readily available.

With the Industrial Revolution, internal combustion engines began to offer power that once was provided by draft animals. Replacing animals with engines meant farmers no longer had to raise extra crops to feed those animals. Furthermore, engines could provide power for many different tasks not limited to the ones performed through draft animal power. When these species were no longer required for the majority of American transport and work, the preferences for animal characteristics changed which altered the appearance of these species to more specialized types of livestock.

While mechanization replaced the majority of animals as the source of power in the United States, animals are still used as a source of transportation and draft power. There are exhibition farms which provide an example of pre-Industrial Revolution agriculture as a type of agritourism. Many livestock producers, especially in the American West, utilize horses as a source of transportation in rough terrain where automotive-based transportation cannot easily reach. Mules can also be used to haul goods in rough terrain. Animals still provide the majority of power in Amish communities, where horse-drawn buggies are used for transportation and draft horses are used for fieldwork to produce agricultural commodities. However, the use of technology and modern methods has increased over time. There are farms that use animals as a source of power, especially if these animals are being kept for other uses, and the farm wishes to minimize dependence on outside energy sources such as fossil fuels. Donkeys can also be used as guard animals for flocks of sheep. Dogs are still used throughout the United States, especially as trained animals for gathering livestock, fetching game for hunters, security and guide services, and transportation in rural areas of Alaska.

The history of animals as a source of power in the United States has changed in many ways, yet the original uses of these animals are still on display in many places. The Industrial Revolution reduced the dependence on these animals, which shifted their characteristics from multi-purpose to more specialized types that are seen today. Animals will continue to play a part in providing power in the United States, in roles that include historical reenactment, primary energy sources, and supplements to other sources of power.

Jessica O. Baggerman

See also: Agriculture and Energy; Buffalo Chips; Industrial Revolution; Waste to Energy; Whale Oil

FURTHER READING

Alberta Culture and Tourism. 2020. "Animal Power in Prehistoric Alberta." 2020. http://www.history.alberta.ca/energyheritage/energy/human-and-animal-power/animal-power-in-prehistoric-times/animal-power-in-prehistoric-alberta.aspx (accessed October 2023).

Ems, Lindsay. 2014. "Amish Workarounds: Toward a Dynamic Contextualized View of Technology Use." *Journal of Amish and Plain Anabaptist Studies*. Vol., 2. No. 1. Pp. 42–58.

Frog Chorus Farm. 2017. "Horses & Oxen: The Original Form of American Horsepower." https://www.frogchorusfarm.com/animalpower.html (accessed April 16, 2020).

International Museum of the Horse (IMH). 2020. "Draft Horse in America." http://imh.org/exhibits/current/draft-horse-in-america/ (accessed April 15, 2020).

Kauffman, Kyle D. 2011. *Encyclopedia of the Great Plains*. http://plainshumanities.unl.edu/encyclopedia/doc/egp.ag.026 (accessed April 5, 2020).

Oklahoma State University (OSU). 2015. "Breeds of Livestock." http://afs.okstate.edu/breeds/index-2.html/horses/#content (accessed April 10, 2020).

Sawers, Larry. 2004. "The Mule, the South, and Economic Progress." *Social Science History*. Vol. 28. No. 4. Pp. 667–90.

Aramco

The Arabian–American Oil Company, known as Aramco, was the corporate embodiment of the alliance between the American oil industry and the Saudi monarchy. It was born in the struggle for influence over Middle Eastern oil between the British-dominated international consortium, the Iraq Petroleum Company, which controlled Middle Eastern oil in the 1920s, and the interloping Standard Oil of California (Socal). The nucleus of Aramco was Californian-Arabian Standard Oil, a wholly owned subsidiary of Standard Oil of California which in 1933 received the oil concession in Eastern Saudi Arabia from the Saudi King Abd al-Aziz Ibn Saud (r. 1902–53). The company was largely a shell run out of Socal's corporate headquarters in San Francisco. In 1936, Texaco acquired 50 percent of the company. Texaco's marketing infrastructure provided the company ways to sell its oil. The company's early experiences in drilling in Saudi Arabia were frustrating, but in 1938 it had established a successful well. The first oil tanker sailed from Saudi Arabia in 1939. The Second World War put a strain on the operation, due to the diversion of shipping, equipment, and supplies to meet the needs of the allies and the vulnerability of the Persian Gulf to Axis forces. The company's local headquarters was bombed by the Italian air force, although it sustained little damage. The company's name was changed to Arabian–American Oil Company in 1944. In 1948 Standard Oil of New Jersey (later known as Exxon) acquired 30 percent of Aramco, and Standard Oil of New York (Mobil) acquired 10 percent, leaving Socal and Texaco with 30 percent each.

Standard Oil of New Jersey and Standard Oil of New York had been participants in the Red Line Agreement, by which a small group of American, British and French oil companies operating through the Iraq Petroleum Company had parceled out Middle Eastern oil according to fixed percentages. Since the Red Line Agreement required its parties to cooperate in all Middle Eastern oil ventures, its terms would have prevented the two companies from joining Aramco unless the other parties to the agreement had the opportunity to do so as well. Dissolution of the agreement was a necessary condition for the two American companies to enter Aramco. The exclusive Saudi arrangement with Aramco was a decisive victory for US interests over those of its main rival in the Middle East, Great Britain.

From the beginning Aramco was closely tied to the Saudi state. The Saudi monarch had made the American alliance a cornerstone of his foreign policy, even receiving a visit from US President Franklin Roosevelt in 1945. Aramco became a key intermediary between the Saudi and U.S. governments. This led Aramco to participate as a Saudi ally in territorial disputes with neighboring states such as Oman and Abu Dhabi. Given the close relationship between these states and Great Britain, this was considered a proxy American–British conflict. Aramco also participated at the behest of the Saudi states in "modernizing" technological projects not directly related to oil, such as the construction of irrigation canals. Aramco ran schools where Saudi boys were trained in the skills that the company required from its workers, and Saudis were given preference in hiring over other non-American nationals.

Saudi workers, were, however, segregated from American and other foreign workers on the job and in the associated living spaces and the hierarchy of Aramco remained American. The Saudi state and Aramco cooperated to repress worker's activism in the oil fields. The housing constructed by Aramco for its American workers attempted to reproduce the comfort and even the culture of mid-twentieth century America. Demand for American style food and the company's desire not to pay to import it meant that many Saudi farmers started growing American crops—a transformation encouraged by Aramco's agricultural experts and by the Saudi government who viewed the growth of a commercial agricultural sector as central to the country's modernization.

Aramco's key asset, of course, was its control over the largest proven oil reserves in the world in Saudi Arabia. In 1951, Aramco discovered the Safaniya field in the Persian Gulf, the largest offshore oil field in the world. In 1957, it identified the Ghawar field, the largest onshore oil field in the world. Aramco and the Saudi government in the period agreed on emphasizing high-volume production, but there were disputes over taxation. Like Western oil companies in Iraq and Iran, Aramco was coming under increasing pressure from the local government, at first for a share of profits and then for actual ownership. In 1950, Saudi concern that they were not receiving enough profit from the oil business led to the conclusion of the 50/50 agreement modeled on the agreement previously reached between American oil companies and Venezuela. This had little effect on Aramco's profitability, as it was able to deduct the amount paid to the Saudi government from its US taxes. In the 1950s, under Saudi pressure, Aramco moved its headquarters from New York to Dhahran in Saudi Arabia, a city originally founded as an oil camp.

Beginning in the 1970s, Aramco changed from an American-owned company into a Saudi-owned one. This began with the oil embargo following the 1973 Yom Kippur War, an embargo Aramco observed. Saudi Arabia acquired a 25 percent interest in Aramco in 1973, increasing to 60 percent in 1974 and complete control in 1976. In 1988 a new Saudi Company, the Saudi Arabian Oil Company, sometimes referred to as Saudi Aramco, was formed to take over Aramco's assets.

William E. Burns

See also: Carter Doctrine; Consortium Agreement of 1954; Energy Crisis of the 1970s; Getty, Jean Paul; Gulf War; Iraq War and the Project for a New American Century; Mandatory Oil Import Quota Program; Organization of Petroleum Exporting Countries (OPEC); Red Line Agreement of 1928; Texaco

FURTHER READING

Anderson, Irvine H. 1981. *Aramco, the United States, and Saudi Arabia: A Study of the Dynamics of Foreign Oil Policy, 1933–1950*. Princeton, NJ: Princeton University Press.

Kelly, J.B. 2000. *Desert Dispute: The Diplomacy of Boundary-Making in South-Eastern Arabia*. Berlin: Gerlach.

Parker, Chad H. 2015. *Making the Desert Modern: Americans, Arabs and Oil on the Saudi Frontier, 1933–1973*. Amherst: University of Massachusetts Press.

Vitalis, Robert. 2007. *America's Kingdom: Mythmaking on the Saudi Oil Frontier*. Stanford: Stanford University Press.

Argo Merchant Oil Spill

MV S.T. *Argo Merchant* was a 29,870-ton Liberian-registered oil tanker built in 1953 by Howaldtswerke in Hamburg, Germany that ran aground and sunk in 1976 southeast of Nantucket Island, Massachusetts, causing one of the largest marine oil spills in history.

Also called the *Arcturus*, *Permina Samudra III* and *Vari* during its history, the 641-foot hulled vessel had a bad accident record—five times worse than average (Winslow 1978, 223). Incidents included two other groundings in Indonesia and Sicily, a collision in Japan, and in the year of the spill off Nantucket, continuing minor oil spills and mechanical repairs. The Coast Guard considered the vessel a "suspect ship" and would have conducted a thorough inspection at its destination. In 1976, the ship-owner was Thebes Shipping Inc., a Liberian corporation. The vessel was carrying a cargo of oil owned by the S.A. Meneven subsidiary of the Venezuelan Petroleum Company, though Holborn Oil Company of Hamilton, Bermuda had agreed to sell it to Northeast Petroleum Company. The cargo insurer was Continental Insurance Company.

At about 6:00 a.m. on December 15, 1976, the *Argo Merchant* went aground on the southern end of Fishing Rip (part of the Nantucket Shoals), 29 nautical miles southeast of Nantucket Island, Massachusetts in high northwest winds, 9.8-foot seas, and 7-mile visibility. It was carrying approximately 183,000 barrels—7,700,000 US gallons or 27,566 long tons—of heavy industrial No. 6 Fuel Oil (80 percent) and cutter stock (20 percent), which had been loaded at Puerto La Cruz, Venezuela, sailing for Salem, Massachusetts. The ship was over 28 miles off its intended course. It was later established that the ship carried two unqualified crew as helmsmen, a broken gyrocompass (to find geographic direction), inadequate charts, and an inaccurate radio direction finder (to discover ship direction or bearing). Over 700 ships had mishaps in the Nantucket Shoals in the past three centuries.

Upon the ship's grounding, Captain Georgios Papadopoulos informed the US Coast Guard (USCG) and requested permission to dump his cargo to try to steady the vessel. The USCG denied the request, wanting to avoid an oil spill if possible. The captain's request was not legally necessary because he was in international waters, which begin 12 miles beyond the coastal zone, and international law permits a ship's captain to take any measures to save the ship and passengers.

The USCG and several other federal and state agencies attempted to save the *Argo Merchant* from spilling or sinking. The US First Coast Guard District invoked the Intervention Convention agreement which legally allowed the United States to take over the vessel if it presented a "grave and imminent danger" to the coastline. The rescue efforts also utilized the federal pollution fund to prevent damage. The shallow waters, windy weather conditions, and the ship's deterioration made it impossible to offload any oil or salvage the ship. Flooding had forced the shutdown of all electrical power on the ship, including the large cargo pumps and the heating coils lining the thirty cargo tanks that kept the oil at about 120 degrees

FIGURE 1: Two halves of the *Argo Merchant* foundered and sank after running aground on Nantucket Shoals off the coast of Massachusetts.

Fahrenheit or fluid enough to pump easily. But as oil cools, it thickens and when at 80 degrees it will clog the best pumps.

On the following day, with the weather worsening and preservation efforts futile, the USCG decided to evacuate the ship and its thirty-eight crew. On December 21 and 22, the vessel broke in two, the bow section split, and then capsized, dumping the remaining oil. In-situ burning of the oil to prevent dispersal was attempted twice without success.

The spilled oil could have heated 18,000 New England homes for one year. No. 6 fuel oil is very heavy and one of the least volatile petroleum products, but with toxic components partly because oil was thinned with "cutter stock" (a more volatile, lighter weight oil) to ease pumping.

Most of the spill formed large pancakes (up to 240 by 760 feet) and sheens on the sea surface, about 1–1.5 inches thick. The pancakes thickened as the oil aged, with some expanding to 10 inches thick. The cutter stock's water levels were as high as 250 parts per billion beneath the areas of fresh oil. The spill was monitored and tracked to gauge potential impacts and to help develop more accurate trajectory models for future spills. It was discovered that oil traveled about 1.1 percent of the wind speed, with sheens slower, with direction influenced by tides and currents.

Fortunately, northwesterly winds and 15-foot seas blew the 69 x 115-mile oil slick offshore. The spill moved to the south-southeast, over the continental shelf, and into the North Atlantic circulation pattern. Six thousand drift cards were deployed between the spill and the coast to give advance warning of shoreline impacts. Nantucket coastal fisheries and Cape Cod beaches were spared the worst. In 1976, there were contingency plans for cleaning up oil spills but no plans for assessing their environmental impact. Many researchers soon arrived to work on individual projects with little coordination. Scientists and technicians from fifteen different agencies and organizations—including eight federal agencies and three universities—soon were on site.

About eighty Nantucket residents voluntarily helped patrol the beaches to rescue and clean birds that came ashore alive. A 1977 NOAA study found 180 dead birds, as well as evidence of oil contamination in fish, shellfish, ichthyoplankton, and zooplankton populations in the spill area, and mortalities of developing cod and pollock embryos in eggs contaminated with oil. Scientists feared negative impacts occurring on salt marshes, shell fishing beds, and other fragile ecological areas; the breeding grounds for many marine life forms would suffer much longer than a beach being cleaned by the constant pounding of the winter seas.

Large tar balls up to 70 pounds beached in the Nantucket region during 1977, possibly coming from the vessel. Some impacts to the bottom sediments were observed in the area of the sunken bow section of the vessel. In addition to this localized area, one sediment sample taken from the area of the spill showed oil contamination.

After the incident, the Continental Insurance Company filed suit against the owner to collect $2,221,958.31—the oil's value and what it paid to the ship's owners. The company held that the tanker went aground because it was not properly equipped and maintained, thus invalidating their payout.

Thebes Shipping, Inc., of Monrovia, Liberia, the ship's owner, filed a motion under the Carriage of Goods by Sea Act (1851) to be exonerated from the accident's liability or to limit its liability to the zero value of the ship and cargo after the sinking. Both legal actions usually happened after marine accidents involving damages. It argued in US District Court in Manhattan that the *Argo Merchant* went aground because of human error by the captain.

The Liberian government's inquiry also found that human error was at fault. It revoked Papadopoulos' master's license, suspended the first mate's license for four years, and the second mate's license for nine months.

A fishing industry group headed by the Cape Cod Fishermen's Coalition filed a $60 million suit against the ship's owners and another $60 million suit against its master. The Nantucket Conservation Foundation filed a suit on behalf of the Georges Bank itself, seeking money to restore any damages caused to the area by the oil and asking for higher construction standards for oil tankers entering New England waters.

The US Senate Commerce Committee held hearings on January 11 and 12, 1977 to investigate recent oil spills in and near American waters, including the *Argo Merchant* and in the Delaware River. In 1977, the government recovered $1.1 million from TOVALOP, Tanker Owners Voluntary Agreement for Liability for Oil Pollution, of which Thebes Shipping, Inc., was a member.

The *Argo Merchant* spill aided immediate and long-term environmental protection efforts. This was somewhat because of the sinking of fifteen tankers with a million deadweight tons in 1976, the worst year in history for such accidents. The spill directly led to NOAA's development of a hazardous materials team to provide and coordinate future responses, supply needed information to the Coast Guard, and develop standard methods of assessing oil spills. NOAA now calls it the beginning of modern oil spill response.

The spill also led to the creation of the US Port and Tanker Safety Act of 1978, which set up vessel traffic services, increased supervision and control of vessels in US waters, and established an inspection program for tank vessels carrying oil and hazmat. New federal regulations required radar depth finders and pre-arrival navigation tests.

The incident also helped spur the development, adoption, and implementation (beginning in 1983) of Annex 1 of the International Convention for the Prevention of Pollution from Ships, 1973 as modified by the Protocol of 1978 (MARPOL 73/78) developed by the International Maritime organization. Annex I was the first implementation of MARPOL 73/78, an early, critically important international marine environmental convention to minimize pollution of the seas by ships. MARPOL includes provisions requiring certain oil tankers to have double hulls.

William P. Kladky

See also: *Deepwater Horizon*; Earth Day; *Exxon Valdez* Oil Spill; Oil Tankers; Santa Barbara Oil Spill; Energy Crisis of the 1970s

FURTHER READING

Goran, David. 2016. "Involved in 12 Shipping Incidents, before Running Aground with more than 7 Million Gallons of Oil." *The Vintage News*. April 8. https://www.thevintagenews.com/2016/04/08/involved-in-12-shipping-incidents-before-running-aground-with-more-than-7-million-gallons-of-oil/ (accessed October 2023).

Hall, Grey. 2011. "Argo Merchant Grounding off Nantucket Produced Lessons in Tracking Oil Spills." *Professional Mariner*. August 29. http://www.professionalmariner.com/September-2011/Argo-Merchant-grounding-off-Nantucket-produced-lessons-in-tracking-oil-spills/ (accessed October 2023).

Keefe, Patricia. 2014. "Disasters at Sea & Their Impact on Shipping Regulation." *Marine Technology Reporter*. June 20. https://www.marinetechnologynews.com/news/disasters-theirimpact-shipping-494606 (accessed October 2023).

Pletcher, Larry. 2017. *Massachusetts Disasters: True Stories of Tragedy and Survival*. Guilford, CT: Globe Pequot Press.

National Oceanic and Atmospheric Administration (NOAA). 1977. *The Argo Merchant Oil Spill: A Preliminary Scientific Report*. U.S. Department of Commerce. Washington, DC: US Government Printing Office.

NOAA. 2016. "Argo Merchant: The Birth of Modern Oil Spill Response." NOAA Office of Response and Restoration. U.S. Department of Commerce. December 14. https://response.restoration.noaa.gov/oil-and-chemical-spills/significant-incidents/argo-merchant-oil-spill/argo-merchant-birth-modern-oil (accessed October 2023).

US District Court for the Southern District of New York. 1980. "Complaint of Thebes Shipping Inc., 486 F. Supp. 436 (S.D.N.Y. 1980)." https://law.justia.com/cases/federal/district-courts/FSupp/486/436/1753837/ (accessed October 2023).

Winslow, Ron. 1978. *Hard Aground: The Story of the Argo Merchant Oil Spill*. New York: W. W. Norton & Company.

Atomic Energy Acts

The Atomic Energy Act was created in 1946 and amended in 1954 to ensure that the research and development of nuclear technology was dealt with appropriately following the Second World War. The US government transferred the wartime Manhattan Project to civilian, private enterprises overseen by the US Atomic Energy Commission.

After the use of the atomic bombs on Hiroshima and Nagasaki, the issue arose of how to deal with the Second World War-era Manhattan Project, which researched and developed the weapons. Some were convinced that such science was only for evil and that another country would drop an atomic bomb on the United States in retaliation. The US War Department and the Manhattan Project scientists were divided on how to proceed given the end of the war. General Leslie Groves, the military director of the Manhattan Project, thought that other countries would stockpile nuclear weapons if information was leaked, whereas others, such as Senator Brien McMahon of Connecticut, saw the sharing of nuclear information as a means to promote peace and technology.

The first proposed response was the May-Johnson Bill, named after the two senators who sponsored it. They proposed an independent, nine-person council to administer the research and development of nuclear weapons. The council would consist of five civilians and four military personnel, all of which would serve part time. Leslie Groves urged Senators May and Johnson to propose this legislation so that the War Department would keep control of nuclear technology, and energy with Congress. Also, military personnel were to serve as the head administrators of this committee.

The scientific committee was fearful of military control of an atomic oversight committee. Scientists also feared that the military would limit scientific inquiry, seeking to develop weapons instead of overall advances for science. Senator McMahon, one of the main opponents of this bill, argued that such legislation would push scientists away from nuclear research and would be interpreted by foreign countries that the United States condones an atomic arms race. This bill ultimately failed and would result in a Special Committee on Atomic Energy to propose a second bill.

The second proposed response was the 1946 Atomic Energy Act, also known as the McMahon Act, named after its sponsor, Senator McMahon. This bill, which was signed into law by President Truman on August 1, 1946, called for more civilian control of nuclear research and development. It also created the US Atomic Energy Commission to provide oversight for such research so that no single person, or a limited council, would control the majority of power and authority in this area.

The bill called for five full-time civilian members. It also had four divisions—research, production, engineering, and military applications. There was also a Military Liaison Committee with members of both the Department of War and Department of the Navy to appease these branches of government as well. The head of the Military Application division was also a member of the military as well.

THOUGHTS ON ATOMIC POWER

"No one can accurately predict what the ultimate result may be [of nuclear research]. It is, however, safe to say that the prospects are limitless and boundless, providing only that mankind permits the scientists the opportunity to work in peace, for peaceful ends."

Brien McMahon

"I feel impelled to speak today in a language that, in a sense, is new–one, which I, who have spent so much of my life in the military profession, would have preferred never to use. That new language is the language of atomic warfare. The atomic age has moved forward at such a pace that every citizen of the world should have some comprehension, at least in comparative terms, of the extent of this development, of the utmost significance to every one of us. Clearly, if the peoples of the world are to conduct an intelligent search for peace, they must be armed with the significant facts of today's existence" – President Dwight Eisenhower, "Atoms for Peace" speech.

Paul A. Brazinski

The bill also called for secretive measures in terms of keeping trade secrets within the United States, which caused tensions with other countries. For instance, Canada and the United Kingdom both provided technology and resources to support the Manhattan Project. In return, they signed agreements with the United States to share its nuclear advances with them. President Roosevelt signed the 1943 Quebec Agreement with Canada and the 1944 Hyde Park Agreement with the United Kingdom. However, these agreements were kept secret from Congress, as was the Manhattan Project, which resulted in Congress' overall lack of concern to respect such documents signed by the preceding president. Moreover, in the post-war era, the United States started becoming more worried about losing nuclear intelligence to the Soviet Union as Cold War tensions started to grow.

On August 30, 1954, President Eisenhower amended the 1946 bill to allow for further sharing of restricted nuclear information with civilian enterprises. The bill also gave incentives to companies that built nuclear reactors and other relevant technologies. Eisenhower also used the bill to help build nuclear power plants in foreign countries as containment measures, as with Iran and Pakistan. Further sharing of nuclear technology occurred under the 1958 US–UK Mutual Defense Agreement. In this document, both countries agreed to share nuclear weapons information for their common defense.

Overall, the Atomic Energy Acts were very important to the history of energy in the United States and the world. The 1946 bill required strict national security and secrecy, a policy other nations followed. The bill is also the reason why nuclear research and development still occurs at private enterprises in the United States with government oversight. The 1954 bill reflects the use of nuclear technology as a defensive method to deter threatening countries, as seen in the United States sharing its information to contain the Soviet Union's influence. Historians and atomic energy specialists consider Brien McMahon the father of the national nuclear policy for civilian development.

Paul A. Brazinski

See also: Dysart, Stella; Fermi, Enrico; Idaho National Laboratory; Manhattan Project; Navajo Reservation Uranium Mining; Nuclear Regulatory Commission; Nuclear Waste Policy Act of 1982; Shippingport Atomic Power Station; Steen, Charles Augustus; Three Mile Island Accident; Yucca Mountain Nuclear Waste Repository

FURTHER READING

Atomic Energy Act of 1954, Pub. L. No. 703–83, August 30, 1954, 60 Stat. 755 (1954).

Duffy, Robert. 1997. *Nuclear Politics in America: A History and Theory of Government Regulation.* Lawrence: University of Kansas Press.

Walker, J. Samuel. 2016. *Prompt and Utter Destruction: Truman and the Use of Atomic Bombs against Japan.* Chapel Hill: University of North Carolina Press.

Austin Dam

The Austin Dam, also known as the Bayless Dam, was a concrete gravity dam located in Austin, Pennsylvania, and completed in December of 1909. Commonly touted as the "dam that could not break," Austin Dam's eventual catastrophic failure on September 30, 1911 claimed the lives of more than fifty individuals. The dam's collapse was the second such deadly event in Pennsylvania within twenty-five years. It followed the collapse of the South Fork Dam, just twenty-two years earlier, on May 31, 1899, which took the lives of more than 2,000 people and became known as the Johnstown Flood. Together these events caused such significant loss of life and damage to property that they forced the Pennsylvania state government in 1913 to pass the first dam safety legislation in America.

Built as a gravity dam on Freeman Run in Potter County, Austin Dam was intended to create a reservoir of water necessary to mitigate the seasonally intermittent flow of water experienced by the Bayless Pulp and Paper Mill. Throughout the nineteenth and twentieth centuries, water power was central to paper making and continues to be used in several key steps in the complex process. Therefore, a more predictable flow provided by a dam and reservoir would ensure a more consistent yearly production process. To ensure this consistency, Austin Dam was quickly concieved and represented one of the oldest forms of dam building based on the simple premise of using its overall gravitational weight against its foundation to resist the pressure of the water flow. Once completed, the Austin Dam was comprising more than 12,000 cubic meters of cyclopean concrete stretching more than 500 feet across and approximately 50 feet tall, and "consisted of boulder-sized pieces of native sandstone rock, bound by conventional cement and concrete" (Delatte 2008, 303). Constructed on a thin layer of shale between layers of sandstone laid down during the Devonian-age Catskills Formation, the dam's rushed construction and flawed foundation foreshadowed its eventual failure.

Correspondence between the dam's design engineer T. Chalkley Hatton (1860–1951) and the dam's owner George C. Bayless (1862–1923) indicate a clear narrative of concerns about the dam's ability to drain excess water, its foundational security, and its overall construction specifications (Rich 2006, 1291). Bayless's desire for consistent production and cost-cutting measures often overrode the structural concerns of his engineer. These correspondences highlight the larger environmental conversation underway in the early decades of the twentieth century concerning dams, rivers, and human interests. Also in 1909, on the other side of the United States, John Muir and the newly created Sierra Club were in a pitched battle against the city of San Francisco, California, to deny the building of the yet-to-be named O'Shaughnessy Dam, which eventually dammed and flooded Hetch Hetchy Valley in Yosemite National Park. While the O'Shaughnessy Dam came to symbolize the larger debates between conservation and preservation across the United States, dams like the Austin Dam and others enacted these same concerns on a smaller scale.

FIGURE 2: An aerial view of the remnants of Austin Dam.

The reservoir almost overflowed in January, 1910, prompting Hatton and Bayless to make what one account described as an "absurd blunder" and use dynamite to blast a release at the top of the dam (Freiman and Schlager 1995, 211). The combination of unseasonable weather events and an earlier cost-cutting decision not to include spillways in the construction of the dam caused irreparable damage. When, on the day of September 30, 1911, a 20-foot hole appeared on the downstream side of the dam, the failure of the dam was both predictable and unsurprising.

The inevitable failure of Austin Dam was attributed to two primary factors. First, the rushed construction schedule in the winter of 1909 required the pouring and curing of concrete in below freezing temperature, which led to the formation of "cold joints." Second, the investigation revealed significant water seepage into the foundation of the dam, specifically between the strata of sandstone and shale. This seepage led to slippage between the foundation of the dam and the bedrock. As both failures occurred, the dam's structure simultaneously broke and shifted allowing the 200 million gallons of water to rush towards the town of Austin.

In an article of October 5, 1911, the *Wellsboro Gazette* described the event as "a veritable stone wall of death" flooding towards the unsuspecting town of Austin. Very little of Austin's main street remained upright or unscathed by the rush of water from Freeman Run. Most place the death toll between fifty and seventy-five, and requests for coffins went out to neighboring towns as the community searched for the missing in the days following the dam's failure. While there were no criminal charges brought or penalties assessed on Hatton, Bayless, or others in the aftermath of the deluge, the flooding of Austin and the immense death toll of the Johnstown flood finally catalyzed the state government in Harrisburg, Pennsylvania, to re-examine the role of the government in dam building and safety.

By 1913 Pennsylvania passed the first dam safety legislation in the United States. Following another dam failure in Johnstown in 1977, Pennsylvania expanded the governmental oversight and passed the state's Dam Safety and Encroachments Act (1978). The Austin Dam failure went on to instruct generations of dam engineers and inform the revisions to dam building protocols in specific geological regions. In 1987 the ruins of Austin Dam became a part of the National Park Service's National Register of Historic Places.

Lucas J. Sheaffer

See also: Cleveland East Ohio Gas Explosion; Hoover Dam; Tennessee Valley Authority; Water Power

FURTHER READING:

Delatte, Norbert J. 2008. *Beyond Failure: Forensic Case Studies for Civil Engineering*. Reston, VA: American Society of Civil Engineers.

Greene, Brian H. and Courtney A. Christ. 1998. *Pennsylvania Geology*, 29 (2/3), Summer/Fall.

Freiman, F.L., and Schlager, N. 1995. *Failed Technology: True Stories of Technological Disasters*. Vol. 2. Detroit: UXL, Gale Research.

Nuschke, Marie Kathern. 1988. *The Dam that Could Not Break: An Eye-witness Account of the 1911 Austin Flood*. Coudersport, PA: Potter Enterprise.

Rich, Thomas P. 2006. "Lessons in Social Responsibility from the Austin Dam Failure." *International Journal of Engineering Education*. Vol. 22. No. 6.

Rose, Andrew T. 2013. "Using the 1911 Austin Dam Failure Case History in Undergraduate Teaching." International Conference on Case Histories in Geotechnical Engineering.

Baltimore & Ohio Railroad

Established in 1827 by Baltimore banking scion George Brown and associates, the earliest railroad line to be chartered in the United States took its name from its terminal points, Baltimore, Maryland, in the east and the Ohio River at Wheeling, West Virginia, in the west. The Baltimore & Ohio Railroad, commonly known as the "B&O," was founded by commercial concerns in Baltimore as an attempt to enter the race to move people and merchandise to the burgeoning markets of the opening west. In this sense, the B&O was the main southern competitor to the Erie Canal, the controlling interests of which were located in New York. Ground was broken for the line on the Fourth of July, 1828, in a ceremony including a hero of the Revolutionary War. The first railroad cars for the B&O were designed by Ross Winans. He was an engineer and inventor who developed numerous technological advances for the burgeoning railroad industry; these included a locomotive wheel that was to set the standard for a century. Employed by the B&O for the opening era of the Age of Rail, Winans retired in 1860 and died in 1877, a millionaire in his own right.

The B&O proved crucial throughout the Civil War for a number of reasons, including the fact that it provided a vital lifeline from the Potomac to the Ohio. In addition, it was hardly incidental in this regard that the Washington line was the only major rail connection between the District of Columbia and the Free States during the war. This line kept the Federal Capital and camps surrounding it supplied. Moreover, although those involved with the B&O at the opening of the conflict had divided loyalties—Winans, for example, was arrested more than once for Confederate sympathies—the very importance of the line to the Union cause forced the hand of those involved and ultimately required them to throw their support behind the Federals. Thus, the B&O proved to be a thorn in the side of the Confederacy both because of its strategic value and due to its symbolic importance.

Just a dozen years after the conclusion of the Civil War, the B&O Railroad was again to be at the center of a bloody internecine struggle. In this instance, the B&O played the prime incendiary role in one of the greatest labor disputes in American history, a conflict that many readers may not realize still is commemorated annually by Labor Day, the traditional end of the American summer, and much more closely associated in our collective memories with family barbeques than with violent protests. Although the powder keg that was to explode ultimately was the result of the Panic of 1873, the spark that was to set it off can be traced directly to a letter from the desk of John W. Garrett, then the president of the railroad. Dated July 11, 1877, and written in the somewhat more formal style of the time, this document was tone-deaf to the realities of ordinary workers. Citing the bleak economic conditions in which the nation had found itself gripped for the previous few years, Garrett matter-of-factly outlined the steps that the Board of Directors were prepared to make to staunch the financial hemorrhaging of the company. This was to be accomplished, he noted, by instituting immediately an across-the-board pay cut of 10 percent for all employees earning more than a dollar a day. The somber tone of the missive was contrasted slightly with Garrett's stated belief that, as he put it, "every officer and man in the service will cheerfully recognize the necessity of the reduction, and earnestly cooperate in every measure of judicious economy" (Garrett 1877). Whether these words were rhetorical boilerplate or heartfelt conviction, they could not have been more poorly expressed.

A uniform 10 percent pay cut was represented in this letter as a reasonable and even fair way to share the economic pain, and so it may have seemed to a board full of rich and privileged men. In point of fact, however, those at the top of the organization had a far larger proportion of discretionary funds in their income than did the rank-and-file workers on the railroad. Indeed, the workers had already suffered through previous cuts, and although the buying power of their wages had dropped significantly since 1873, the cost of living had not dropped at anything approximating the same rate. Moreover, the leadership of the B&O and that of its competitors—and indeed all major related companies and industries—likewise were systematically seeking to keep labor costs minimized. In addition, labor activism was rigorously and ruthlessly hunted down and weeded out, in large part through the widespread use of paid informants, agent provocateurs, and private detectives. Therefore, since the B&O workers had at that point in time no union representation, the board must have supposed that the workers had little recourse in the face of such a policy. In this assumption that board was entirely mistaken.

When the news of the wage cut became public, railroad workers at the home base of the B&O attempted to spark resistance, but the authorities in Baltimore quelled disturbances quickly and brutally. In the long run, however, this simply meant that the riots began in earnest at the other end of the rail line. The first formal action of the strike thus began on July 16 in Martinsburg, West Virginia, when railyard workers stranded a cattle train in the summer heat, uncoupling the cars and making it difficult to move. When the police were unable to regain control of the yard, the state militia were activated. While the militia were able to move the train, they were met with active resistance from the workers and violence ensued, leaving a striker dead and a militiaman wounded. Federal troops were then deployed, and they were able to take effective control of the rail lines and the running of the trains. Unable to resist the US Army in open conflict, the strikers now began a campaign of sabotage, subterfuge, and stealth, using their knowledge of the trains and the tracks to exploit weaknesses of which the soldiers were unaware or unable to defend. In this insurgency the striking rail-workers were joined by numerous other allied tradesmen.

By the time that all was said and done, the entire B&O was affected both by the strike and the concomitant conflict. In addition, the other great railroads were swept up in the unrest, and the movement spread like wildfire across the country. Maryland troops sent to assist the West Virginia militia in quelling the uprising actually had to fight their way through brick-throwing mobs lining the streets of Baltimore on their way to complete their mission; at least ten people died in the process. When the state militia in Pittsburgh refused to quell the strikers there, the governor sent troops from Philadelphia, who used heavy arms, including cannons and a Gatling gun, subduing a large mob and killing at least twenty in the process. In retaliation, the mob raided weapons stores and utilized flaming train cars to drive the troops out of their entrenched position in the railyard; ultimately, the troops were put to flight while the city burst into flames. Meanwhile, guerrilla warfare between rioters and soldiers engulfed entire sections of Chicago.

Moreover, workers in many other trades also became involved, and as the struggle moved across the country, there is some evidence that alliances at times united workers of

FIGURE 3: A locomotive on the Baltimore and Ohio Railroad near Oakland, Maryland.

differing races that had seldom before made common cause. In all, many tens of thousands of workers joined the cause, perhaps more than 100,000. In the wake of the violence, whole neighborhoods had burned, notably in Pittsburgh, and more than 100 lives were lost. The strikers gained little in the immediate aftermath of the conflict, and the business leaders and politicians involved were largely unrepentant—and sometimes quite the opposite—considering the violence used to put down the strike and the loss of life involved. In the end, however, the strikers seem to have won the public relations war even if they lost the strike battles, and the union movement and general sympathy for the workers seemed to gain momentum as a result.

Subsequent to these cataclysmic events, the B&O returned to normal service. The railroad went bankrupt and subsequently was reorganized in the 1890s. Before that time, the railroad demonstrated the value of coal-fired steam power in transporting people, goods, and fuels throughout the American interior in the nineteenth century. It provided widespread national passenger service for several decades in the twentieth century until most of those routes were turned over to Amtrak when it was formed in the early 1970s. The B&O remained an important freight carrier, however, even after it was absorbed by the Chesapeake & Ohio Railway in 1963, and then by CSX in 1980. In 1987, the B&O ceased to exist as a distinct entity, when all the assets and routes of the B&O officially became part of the Chesapeake & Ohio, and the Baltimore & Ohio Railroad formally departed the tracks for the last time, relegated to the history books.

Christopher R. Fee

See also: Battle of Blair Mountain; Cooper, Peter; Densmore Oil Tank Car; Molly Maguires; Richmond Union Passenger Railway; Steam Power; Transcontinental Railroad

FURTHER READING

Garrett, John. 1877. "To the Officers and Employees of the Baltimore and Ohio Railroad Company." July 11. American Social History Project. Center for Media and Learning. The Graduate Center. City University of New York. https://shec.ashp.cuny.edu/items/show/686 (accessed June 24, 2021).

Kunkle, Fredrick. 2017. "Labor Day's Violent Roots: How a Worker Revolt on the B&O Railroad Left 100 People Dead." *The Washington Post*. September 4. https://www.washingtonpost.com/news/retropolis/wp/2017/09/03/labor-days-radical-roots-how-a-worker-revolt-on-the-bo-railroad-almost-became-a-revolution/ (accessed October 2023).

Sander, Kathleen Waters. 2017. *John W. Garrett and the Baltimore and Ohio Railroad*. Baltimore: Johns Hopkins University Press.

Summers, Festus P. 1993. *The Baltimore and Ohio in the Civil War*. Gettysburg, PA: Stan Clark Military Books.

West Virginia Department of Arts, Culture and History (WVDACH). 2021. "B&O Railroad Strike of 1877." *The (Martinsburg) Statesman*, July 24, 1877. https://archive.wvculture.org/history/labor/bandostrike02.html (accessed October 2023).

Bartlett Electric Cooperative

In 1935, President Franklin D. Roosevelt signed an executive order that created the Rural Electrification Administration (REA), a new federal agency charged with directing the spread of electricity to underserved rural areas of the United States. In one of its earliest initiatives, the REA extended a low-interest loan of $33,000 to the Bartlett Community Light and Power Company in Texas to enable it to string a 59-mile powerline to 110 farmhouses in the vicinity. Finally, electricity came to rural Americans in the outlying areas around Bartlett in 1936, enabling farm families to enjoy the same modern amenities as residents of cities and small towns. Soon renamed the Bartlett Electric Cooperative, this outfit represents the importance of government investment in creating the infrastructure necessary to connect every American village, hamlet, and rural community to the nationwide electrical grid. It also represents an important step in the process of universalizing the human experience with electrical power and with all the aspects of modern life that electricity had made possible by the middle of the twentieth century.

Once electrical power came to the United States in the 1880s and 1890s, private corporations began construction on centralized plants and transmission systems to serve urban and small-town customers. In places with sufficient population density, the market justified the expense of building out the infrastructure for producing and transmitting electricity. In rural areas, low population density created slim market prospects for return on investment for the for-profit utility companies. In some ways the market for electrical power left quite a few customers underserved by potential suppliers. The second director of the REA, John M. Carmody, included in his report for 1937 a description of the problem his agency was designed to solve:

> The real reason that many of the five and a half million unserved farm families have not been able to enjoy the economic and social advantages of electricity is that those private utilities that have had a monopoly control of its sale in various farm areas insisted for years that it would not be profitable to sell electricity to the farmers. Those farmers who did get it often paid the private company the cost of building the lines besides guaranteeing high minimum bills for long periods of time. Sometimes these line costs were as much as $2,000 per mile and the guarantees were for 5 years. (Carmody 1938, v)

A very wide gap opened between the standard of living of rural people and the kind of life enjoyed by city and town dwellers, who could light their home interiors at night, wash clothes in a washing machine, and keep their food chilled in an electric refrigerator. The lack of electricity became an issue of equity between these differently situated groups. FDR hoped to address these inequities as governor of New York, and then later as president. During his campaign for president in 1932, he gave a speech in Topeka, Kansas regarding the plight of farmers in the early years of the Great Depression. FDR noted the collapse of commodity prices, an epidemic of farm foreclosures, and a dearth of services like health clinics and schools that left farmers in a state of "acute distress," but he acknowledged, "You all know that better than anyone can tell you. You have felt it in your own lives and experiences" (Roosevelt 1932). In the speech he touted the work of his gubernatorial administration in New York for "enabling farmers to get necessary road improvements, telephone lines and electric power lines" and pledged to nationalize these efforts if elected president (Roosevelt 1932). He added that where the free market had failed rural consumers, his state government had encouraged the formation of cooperatives that served the interests of the farmers, and a "new system of rural credit organizations to meet the emergency created by the collapse of rural banks" (Roosevelt 1932).

When he became president, FDR invigorated US agricultural policy in a variety of areas, which resulted in such early New Deal initiatives as the Agricultural Adjustment Act, the Farm Credit Act, and the Rural Electrification Administration. The Bartlett Community Light and Power Company was first to receive an REA loan and put out its lines to new rural customers in March 1936. The company then reorganized as a member-owned cooperative after Congress enacted the Rural Electrification Act of 1936 and a Texas law authorized the operation of electric cooperatives within the state. The availability of electricity in this underserved community was experienced as a revolution. A history of the cooperative cites a *Bartlett Tribune* editorial from 1936: "Electricity comes as a willing and untiring servant to relieve those who work in the home of much tiresome labor. Rural homes need the benefits of electricity, even more than town and city homes" (Engelke 2023). The revolution spread quickly; within two years of its creation, the REA electrified the homes and farms of over 250,000 people across forty states through its program of low-interest (2.88 percent) twenty-year loans (Carmody 1938, 1, 5). By 1940, some 40 percent of rural residents were electrified, and by 1945, that number reached 90 percent (FFPC 2023, 5).

Rural electrification was particularly revolutionary because, as Carmody noted in his report, "the American farm is a combination home and factory" (Carmody 1938, v). He quoted a National Resources Committee document that identified how electricity would help to mechanize the farm and further industrialize agricultural production: "Ultimately, there will be a considerable increase in the use of automatic and semiautomatic machinery for such purposes as pumping water and operating processing machinery; an extensive use of heating devices for hotbeds and stock-watering tanks; perhaps, air-conditioning, and, possibly, substitution of electric for other power in field operations" (Carmody 1938, 2–3). Carmody affirmed that "radios, refrigerators, milk coolers, feed grinders, farm motors, poultry brooders, and other appliances are being delivered every day as newlines are energized" (Carmody 1938, vi). Pumps, chillers, incubators, milkers, and a wide variety of other devices powered by electricity promised less toil and greater efficiency, providing farmers with some of the benefits that electricity offered urban workers.

The Bartlett Electric Cooperative and other REA-funded projects ensured that with the advent of these programs, "rural life would never be the same" in the United States (FFPC 2023, 5). Electricity enabled farm families to pump water and thus have indoor plumbing, to refrigerate food and thereby avoid health hazards like hookworm. Electrified farmhouses had electric lights, sewing machines, washers and dryers, and radios. In many ways REA projects like the one in Bartlett, Texas offered a pathway for rural households to adopt the electricity-driven lifestyle rapidly becoming standard in modern American society.

Jeffrey B. Webb

See also: Agriculture and Energy; Cooke, Morris Llewellyn; Electricity; General Electric Company; Pearl Street Power Station; Rural Electrification Act of 1936; Tennessee Valley Authority

FURTHER READING

Carmody, John M. 1938. "Rural Electrification on the March." Rural Electrification Administration. Washington, DC: US Government Printing Office.

Childs, Marquis. 1952. *The Farmer Takes a Hand: The Electric Power Revolution in Rural America.* Garden City, NY: Doubleday & Co., Inc.

Engelke, Dennis. 2023. "Bartlett Electric Cooperative." Williamson County Texas History. https://williamsoncountytexashistory.org/bartlett-electric-cooperative-historical-marker-bartlett-texas/ (accessed October 2023).

Four Freedoms Park Conservancy (FFPC). 2023. "A New Deal for Farmers: Franklin D. Roosevelt and Rural America." *Hope, Recovery, Reform: The Great Depression & FDR's New Deal.* Four Freedoms Park Conservancy Resources. https://fdr4freedoms.org/wp-content/themes/fdf4fdr/DownloadablePDFs/II_HopeRecoveryReform/03_ANewDealforFarmers.pdf (accessed October 2023).

Rasmussen, Wayne D. 1983. "The New Deal Farm Programs: What They Were and Why They Survived." *American Journal of Agricultural Economics.* Vol. 65. No. 5. Pp. 1158–62.

Roosevelt, Franklin D. 1932. "Campaign Address in Topeka, Kansas on the Farm Problem." September 14. The American Presidency Project at UC Santa Barbara. https://www.presidency.ucsb.edu/documents/campaign-address-topeka-kansas-the-farm-problem (accessed October 2023).

Battle of Blair Mountain

The Battle of Blair Mountain represented the culmination of decades of growing animosity flaring into occasional violence between American workers and bosses in the coal industry. The sensational trial of the Molly Maguires in 1876 may have effectively ended the open conflict between miners and mine companies in the Pennsylvania coalfields, but it merely set the stage for the greater battles to unfold in West Virginia coal country a generation or so later. The situation had continued in the intervening decades to tilt in the favor of the employers: most West Virginia coal miners of the early twentieth century lived in so-called "company towns," built and owned by the corporation, had to pay for the use of company tools, and were paid a pittance in "company scrip," only redeemable at over-priced "company stores." Union organizing was harshly suppressed, and many miners could only keep their jobs by signing what were derisively known as "yellow dog contracts," binding pledges not to join a union. Numerous undercover operatives ensured that such pledges were kept, and the loss of a job was the least of the penalties in store for those who did not do so. Always at a simmer, the tension inherent in the company town coal-mining system boiled over into armed hostilities and finally pitched battle in 1920 and 1921, culminating in August of 1921 with the so-called Battle of Blair Mountain, sometimes noted as the most significant insurrection on American soil since the Civil War.

The first sparks that would ignite the powderkeg that was to be the Battle of Blair Mountain began to fly in the spring of 1920. The union movement was finally gaining traction in West Virginia, and in retaliation, mine owners sought to root out those workers with union sympathies, and summarily to punish harshly those with the temerity actually to join a union. This came to a head in May in Matewan, a town in Mingo County, when private detectives from the Baldwin–Felts Agency, acting on behalf of the Stone Mountain Coal Company, began evicting union miners from the company houses in which they resided. Cabell Testerman, the Mayor of Matewan, along with Sid Hatfield, the Chief of Police, were both union sympathizers, and soon raised a number of volunteers to aid them in a confrontation with the Baldwin–Felts men. Things soon turned ugly, and by the time "The Matewan Massacre" (as it came to be called) was over, seven detectives, two miners, and Mayor Testerman were all dead. Union membership surged as a result of this gunfight, a strike was called, and numerous acts of violence accompanied the introduction of non-union workers into the mines. Not incidentally, Hatfield became a local hero as a result of the Matewan Massacre, a notoriety that would end in his death in August of 1921, when Hatfield and his companion Ed Chambers were ambushed by Baldwin–Felts detectives in front of the McDowell County Courthouse in Welch, West Virginia. The Baldwin–Felts assassins reportedly acted out of frustration after Hatfield and the rest of the pro-union men involved in the Matewan Massacre were acquitted. This act of vigilante justice, however, was to light the fuse that would explode into open warfare between union and company representatives, a conflict that culminated in the Battle of Blair Mountain mere weeks later.

Led by union organizers, miners began to converge on the town of Marmet, in Kanawha County, not far from Charleston, the state capital. The miners determined to enact a protest march on Mingo County, to commemorate Hatfield's death and to call for justice to be done upon his murderers, as well as to protest the plight of those pro-union miners languishing behind bars on trumped-up charges, and ideally to rescue them or to force their release. The situation was particularly volatile, not only because passions ran high due to the assassination of Hatfield but also because the pro-union forces—estimated somewhere between 5,000 and 20,000 men (many of whom were veterans of the trenches of France in the First World War)—were heavily armed and more than prepared to fight. The military experience of the marchers was evident in the ways in which they organized themselves into units, utilized scouts, posted sentries, and even were reputed to have used passwords to protect themselves from the spies, double-agents, and provocateurs who played such crucial roles in the Coal Wars. The situation came to a head because the route to Mingo County from Marmet was through Logan County, a stronghold of the mining interests. The pro-company sheriff of that county, Don Chafin, not only determined to block the path of the marchers, but actually ordered to have built a system of breastworks and fortifications around Blair Mountain. With the route of the march effectively blocked, Chafin forced the protesters either to push forward to attack or to turn around and give up the attempt to rescue the imprisoned miners.

The marchers chose to fight. The conflict that followed had more in common with the stalemates of the fortified lines of the First World War than any labor uprising before or since. Although the union men threatened to overwhelm the anti-union forces at a number of times in a number of locations, they were consistently driven back by concentrated machine-gun fire from entrenched positions. The union men had weapons of their own, reportedly including at least one pilfered Gatling gun, and in total hundreds of thousands of rounds were discharged and an unknown number of people were killed; estimates range from a couple of dozen to a couple of hundred. Sherriff Chafin is even reputed to have hired local small aircraft to drop bombs on the miners. As the battle raged on without a clear victor, West Virginia Governor Ephraim Morgan appealed to President Warren G. Harding for federal assistance. Washington responded by dispatching 2,500 troops along with air support. This federal intervention resulted in the conclusion of the hostilities, with several hundred miners surrendering their arms and many more melting away into the hills and returning home. The aftermath of the conflict included many arrests and trials for offenses up to and including treason and murder, but in the end, although some miners were imprisoned for short sentences, there were no convictions for capital crimes, and the major consequence of the criminal prosecutions was the not inconsequential financial burden of legal defense.

Probably the most famous and well-known cinematic depiction of the West Virginia Coal Wars is the 1987 movie *Matewan,* written and directed by John Sayles, which depicts the pro-union movement in a positive light. More recently, a number of documentaries and West Virginia Public Radio programs marked a resurgence of interest in the Coal War conflict as the centenary anniversary of the most important relevant events approached. Although the efforts to unionize the mines lost ground in the immediate aftermath of the Battle of Blair Mountain, this conflict nevertheless marks an extremely important watershed moment in the history of energy and labor movements in America. The intervention of federal troops, including the innovation of air power and reconnaissance fresh from testing grounds in European battlefields, clearly tipped the scales against the pro-union forces, who were both defeated in the conflict and impoverished by the ensuing court cases. Union numbers in the region plummeted in the following years, and the funds necessary to cultivate new membership were largely eroded by legal fees and court costs. The union movement would not rise again to offer a significant challenge to the mining companies in West Virginia until the depths of the Great Depression, when federal aid again came to the rescue, this time on the side of the miners in the form of FDR's New Deal.

Christopher R. Fee

See also: Coal; Frick, Henry Clay; Harlan County War; Ludlow Massacre; Miner's and Laborer's Benevolent Association; Molly Maguires; Paint Creek Mine War; Sinclair, Upton; United Mine Workers of America

FURTHER READING

Andrews, Evan. 2016. "The Battle of Blair Mountain." *History.com.* August 25. Last Updated September 1, 2018. https://www.history.com/news/americas-largest-labor-uprising-the-battle-of-blair-mountain (accessed 26 February 2021).

Imbrogno, Douglas. 2017. "'Blood on the Mountain' Mining Documentary to Screen on Netflix." *Charleston Gazette-Mail,* April 29. https://www.wvgazettemail.com/_arts__entertainment/blood-on-the-mountain-mining-documentary-to-screen-on-netflix/article_23b325e2-5986-5e06-a345-8e01d4e7ead3.html (last updated November 21, 2017; accessed February 26, 2021).

Powell, Bob. 2018. "Sid Hatfield and Ed Chambers Shot in Welch, August 1, 1921." *West Virginia Public Broadcasting.* Posted August 1. https://www.wvpublic.org/radio/2018-08-01/sid-hatfield-and-ed-chambers-shot-in-welch-august-1-1921 (accessed March 2, 2021).

Public Broadcasting System (PBS). "The Mine Wars: The Desire for Dignity Runs Deep." *PBS: American Experience.* Aired September 3, 2019. https://www.pbs.org/wgbh/americanexperience/films/theminewars/ (accessed February 26, 2021).

Sayles, John. 1987. *Matewan.* Cinecom Pictures.

Shogan, Robert. 2004. *The Battle of Blair Mountain: The Story of America's Largest Labor Uprising.* Boulder, CO: Westview Press.

West Virginia Encyclopedia. 2019a. "Armed Miners March on Blair Mountain." *Virginia Public Broadcasting.* August 28. https://www.wvpublic.org/radio/2019-08-28/august-28-1921-armed-miners-march-on-blair-mountain (accessed March 4, 2021).

West Virginia Encyclopedia. 2019b. "August 30, 1921: John Wilburn Leads Miners against Blair Mountain." *Virginia Public Broadcasting.* August 30. https://www.wvpublic.org/radio/2019-08-30/august-30-1921-john-wilburn-leads-miners-against-blair-mountain (accessed March 4, 2021).

Bell Laboratories

Bell Laboratories, also known as "The Idea Factory," and "The Crown Jewel," was originally formed for the purpose of furthering research into Alexander Graham Bell's (1847–1922) telephone technology (ETHW 2018). As the firm grew, its research expanded into various scientific endeavors. Among the company's most famous inventions are the transistor, the laser, and the first satellite communications system.

In 1875, Alexander Graham Bell created the Bell Patent Association, along with Gardiner Greene Hubbard and Thomas Sanders. This partnership was intended to protect Bell's commercial interests in his idea for a multiple telegraph system while Bell worked on finishing his prototype. Several independent telephone companies were soon formed, including the Bell Company and the American Bell Telephone Company. In 1885, the American Telephone and Telegraph Company (AT&T) was formed as a long-distance carrier and by the end of the nineteenth century it had acquired American Bell and several other Bell companies, eventually becoming one of the world's largest monopolies (Shulman 2008, 36, 71).

AT&T owned several subsidiary companies, including the Western Electric Company, which had been founded in 1869 to manufacture telephone equipment. In 1907, Western Electric created a research department with the intent of furthering the development of telephone equipment, which resulted in new types of switchboards and the first electronic vacuum tube amplifiers (ETHW 2018).

In 1925, the research department was formally established as a separate company and named Bell Telephone Laboratories. The firm was located in downtown New York City with an initial workforce of about 4,000 scientists and engineers. In 1934, Bell Labs acquired AT&T's research department, as well as a host of additional engineers (NBL 2020a).

The first president of Bell Labs was physicist Frank B. Jewett (1879–1949), who led the firm from its inception in 1925 through 1940. Initially the company focused on developing audiovisual technologies, such as the first synchronized-sound motion picture system and the first long-distance television transmission, which were both accomplished in 1927 (NBL 2020b).

During the 1930s, Bell Labs researchers branched out into semiconductor research. Russell Ohl (1898–1987) made discoveries with silicon that would lead directly to the modern transistor, while other researchers worked on stereo sound transmission, radio astronomy, speech synthesis, and the first electrical relay digital computer (NBL 2020b).

During the 1930s and 1940s, Bell Labs worked on a wide range of projects for the war effort, including advanced radar technology, a horn-reflector antenna, and SIGSALY, a secure speech system for allied communications. Bell's commercial products included the introduction of the first mobile phone in 1946 and a proposal for a cellular phone system in 1947. These early electronic devices used glass vacuum tubes, which were heavy and large, consumed a lot of power, and were fragile. In 1945, Bell Labs formed a solid-state physics group tasked with replacing the vacuum tubes with a more durable alternative (NBL 2020b).

Mid-century saw the development of many of our modern electronic devices, including the first successful solar battery cell and a technique for mass production of integrated circuits, as well as the first computer-generated digital audio. In 1957, Bell researchers Charles Hard Townes (1915–2015) and Arthur Leonard Schawlow (1921–1999) began work on a visible light laser, which was patented in 1958 (NBL 2020b).

In the early 1960s, Bell Labs became part of a multinational agreement for a satellite-based communications system that included six ground stations. In 1961, Bell built the Andover Earth Station in Maine, one of the six ground stations needed to track the Telstar communications satellites. Telstar I was launched on July 10, 1962, from Cape Canaveral, Florida, and on July 12 it provided television viewers with the first live transatlantic show. Consumer products included the pager and the touch-tone telephone (NASA 2012).

By now Bell Labs had outgrown its downtown offices and in 1967 the headquarters was relocated to Murray Hill, New Jersey, where it occupied a 200-acre space. Construction on the massive Holmdel Complex, located in Holmdel, New Jersey, had begun in 1959 and was completed in 1962. At its height of activity, nearly 5,600 researchers worked at the complex (Christopher 2019).

In 1970, Willard S. Boyle (1924–2011) and George E. Smith (1930–) invented the charge-coupled device (CCD), an integrated circuit that turns light energy into an electrical charge. The CCD is at the heart of digital photography and can be found in cameras, cell phones, and astronomical imaging devices, including the Hubble Space Telescope's Wide Field and Planetary Camera (ETHW 2018).

Bell Labs also continued to innovate in communications research. In 1977 it introduced the first fiber optics telephone communication system, and in 1978 the first cellular phone system was put into service with an initial trial of 2,000 customers. The company also expanded its digital research, developing the C programming language in 1972 and the C++ language in 1983. During the 1980s, Bell continued to push the boundaries of digital technology, replacing older, slower analog systems, while the 1990s ushered in technologies that included a functional MRI (magnetic resonance imaging) and improved data storage devices (NBL 2020b).

THE FIRST TRANSISTOR

In December 1947, Bell researchers John Bardeen (1908–91), Walter Houser Brattain (1902–87), and William Bradford Schockley (1910–89) created the first point-contact transistor. This small lump of semiconducting material made out of germanium functioned as an amplifier and allowed a small electrical current to control a much larger current. The transistor is considered the most important invention to come out of Bell Labs, and in 1956 the inventors were jointly awarded a Nobel Prize in Physics.

Karen S. Garvin

Over the years, the behemoth AT&T had faced several antitrust suits but managed to reach agreements with the US government, until the successful antitrust case *United States v. AT&T* brought an end to its monopoly power. The case was settled in 1982 and in 1984 the company was ordered to divest itself of local telephone exchange companies, which were spun off into smaller companies, while AT&T maintained its long-distance service (Investopedia 2020).

In 1996, Lucent Technologies was formed when AT&T divested itself of Bell Lab's equipment manufacturing business. Lucent merged with Alcatel in 2006 and a year later Bell Labs merged into the fold. In 2016, Nokia acquired Alcatel-Lucent and formed Nokia Bell Labs, which continues to do innovative research, such as work on a lensless camera and quantum computing (NBL 2020b). In 2006, Alcatel-Lucent decided to sell the now-defunct Holmdel Complex to developers for an office park, but after people began petitioning to save the building it was sold in 2013 to a company that pledged to retain the building's original design as much as possible (Christopher 2019).

At one time, Bell Labs employed nearly 25,000 people (Gertner 2012b). During the past nine decades many of the company's researchers have won Nobel Prizes, and their work has produced inventions that have revolutionized communications and ushered in the digital era (NBL 2020b).

Karen S. Garvin

See also: Digital Revolution; Edison, Thomas Alva; Electricity; General Electric Company; Idaho National Energy Laboratory; Insull, Samuel; Morse, Samuel; Underwriters Laboratories

FURTHER READING

Christopher, Matthew. 2019. "Bell Labs." Abandoned America. July 23. https://www.abandonedamerica.us/bell-labs (accessed February 3, 2020).

Coll, Steve. 1988. *The Deal of the Century: The Breakup of AT&T.* New York: Simon & Shuster.

Engineering and Technology History Wiki (ETHW). 2016. "Bell Labs" August 1. https://ethw.org/Bell_Labs (accessedFebruary 9, 2020).

ETHW. 2018. "Charge-Coupled Device." May 1. https://ethw.org/Charge-Coupled_Device (accessed February 9, 2020).

Gertner, Jon. 2012a. *The Idea Factory: Bell Labs and the Great Age of American Innovation.* New York: Penguin.

Gertner, Jon. 2012b. "How Bell Labs Invented the World We Live in Today." *Time.* March 21. https://business.time.com/2012/03/21/how-bell-labs-invented-the-world-we-live-in-today/ (accessed February 9, 2020).

Investopedia. 2020. "AT&T's Successful Spinoffs." https://www.investopedia.com/ask/answers/09/att-breakup-spinoff.asp (accessed February 9, 2020).

Lindley, David. 2009. *Focus Landmarks: Birth of Modern Electronics. Physical Review Focus.* Vol. 23. No. 16. https://physics.aps.org/story/v23/st16 (accessed February 3, 2020).

National Aeronautics and Space Administration (NASA). 2012. "July 12, 1962: The Day Information Went Global." July 12. https://www.nasa.gov/topics/technology/features/telstar.html (accessed February 14, 2020; URL no longer accessible).

Nokia Bell Labs (NBL). 2020a. "History." http://www.bell-labs.com/about/history-bell-labs/ (accessed February 12, 2020).

NBL. 2020b. "Timeline." https://www.bell-labs.com/timeline/#/2020/1/closed/ (accessed February 12, 2020).

Riordan, Michael, and Lillian Hoddeson. 1998. *Crystal Fire: The Invention of the Transistor and the Birth of the Information Age.* New York: Norton.

Shulman, Seth. 2008. *The Telephone Gambit: Chasing Alexander Graham Bell's Secret.* New York: Norton.

Benedum, Michael Late

Michael Late Benedum (1869–1959) achieved vast wealth as an oil and gas developer in the first half of the twentieth century. Born in West Virginia, Benedum dropped out of school at the age of sixteen to work in a local flour mill in his hometown of Bridgeport. When he reached twenty he met John Worthington, General Superintendent of the South Penn Oil Company, on a train from Clarksburg to Parkersburg. Benedum received an offer of employment, which got him started on his long career as a prominent oil tycoon. Benedum eventually formed his own company based in Pittsburgh and took advantage of the era's many opportunities to discover and develop oil fields and gas deposits in places like Illinois, Louisiana, Texas, Mexico, Colombia, Peru, Brazil, Philippines, Turkey, and Romania. His life and very successful career as a wildcatter and businessman illustrate the kind of opportunities available to entrepreneurs in the formative period of the oil and gas industry.

Benedum's early career in milling helped to set the stage for his professional success later in life. After a two-year stint at the flour mill, working twelve-hour days for $16 a month, Benedum was hired away by a competing milling operation to become a manager, with a significant increase in salary. He was not long on the job when he was badly injured, having gotten his arm caught in a grinding wheel. This prompted another change, and he took a job selling equipment for flour mills. Benedum left the mills after his chance meeting on the Baltimore & Ohio Railroad train to Parkersburg with John Worthington, which introduced him to the field of oil and gas exploration. Worthington's firm, the South Penn Oil Company, was a subsidiary of the Standard Oil Company, the largest oil company in the United States at the time. In this new position, Benedum met with property owners where there was potential for oil, and secured lease agreements for the company to drill exploratory wells. He proved to be adept at closing deals and also ventured into the more speculative business of lease royalties. Benedum paid cash up front for the rights to property owners' future royalties on oil production in the event the exploratory wells prove to be productive.

In 1897, Benedum met his future business partner, Joseph C. Trees, who worked for Standard Oil Company. Trees—a football standout at the University of Pittsburgh—suggested that together they buy half of a one-eighth interest in an oil drilling site from the property owner at the price of $2,000. Benedum agreed and put in nearly most of their stake—$1,955—with the understanding that he'd receive three-fourths of the royalties on the back end. The deal paid off for both when the well struck; eventually the site hosted seven wells that pumped for the next twenty years. In 1900, Benedum and Trees left their jobs and formed the company known as Benedum and Trees Oil Company, based in Wheeling, West Virginia. Seven years later the company moved its business operations to Pittsburgh where it remained. For most of its history the company occupied the nineteen-story Benedum Trees Building on Fourth Avenue in the downtown district.

Benedum and Trees Oil Company became one of the most successful oil companies in the industry. Trees' particular talents lay in engineering and in the technical aspects of oil drilling, whereas Benedum brought financial acumen and a knack for securing oil and gas leases. The company's earliest wildcatting, which refers to the drilling of exploratory wells, hit deposits in West Virginia, Pennsylvania, Ohio, and Illinois and made the partners millionaires within a few years ("Benedum-Trees" 1982, 32). Its first major strike occurred in Crawford County in Southeastern Illinois along the Wabash River border with Indiana. Benedum and Trees leased 50,000 acres and hit a gusher with the Robert Athey No. 1 well. By 1907 they were able to sell the stake for more than $7 million (Miller 2001). The company followed up with a successful venture in Oklahoma before establishing the W. P. Stiles No. 1 well in 1908 in Louisiana's abundant Caddo oil field.

Within two years of the Caddo venture, Benedum and Trees followed a tip and began prospecting along the Túxpam River in Mexico, in a region dubbed "The Golden Lane" for its vast oil resources. Soon, wells known as El Alamo No. 1 and No. 2 began producing 40,000 and 75,000 barrels a day, respectively (Miller 2001). This lucrative international endeavor encouraged the company to head south to Colombia where they found oil and formed the Tropical Oil Company, which was eventually sold in 1920 to a subsidiary of the Standard Oil Company for $33 million in stock. By far the company's biggest success in wildcatting occurred in the Permian Basin in western Texas, first at Big Lake in 1924, and then in Pecos County in 1926. These operations in Pecos County eventually led to the construction of Yates 30-A, which at one point in 1929 produced 8,528 barrels of oil per hour or 204,672 barrels per day. At the time, the industry considered this a world record (Smith 2016).

Benedum achieved widespread recognition as one of the best, if not the top, oil prospector in the industry by the 1920s. Benedum hit on so many of his wells that he became known within the industry as "The Great Wildcatter." He'd even been invited by Queen Marie of Romania to explore and develop the oil resources in her country after the First World War. The city of Pittsburgh, location of a number of oil and gas company headquarters, named him "Oil Man of the Century" (Young 2021). His vast personal wealth testified to his success: at one point in the 1920s he was listed as one of the 100 richest Americans and he died in 1959 with an estate valued at $100 million. Yet, this should be put in the context of his contemporary industry tycoons, the somewhat older John D. Rockefeller (d. 1937), who in 1913 was described as having a net worth of $900 million, and the somewhat younger J. Paul Getty, who died in 1976 with an estimated net worth of $6 billion.

Half of this estate went to the Claude Worthington Benedum Foundation, which he and his wife Sarah (Lantz) Benedum founded in 1944 and named in honor of their deceased son's memory. He'd been their only child, and in 1918 succumbed to pneumonia in the Great Influenza pandemic. In his will. Benedum expressed his deep Methodist faith and his sense of duty to "extend a helping hand to the less fortunate." He wrote, "I have always felt that I have been only a trustee for such material wealth as Providence has placed in my hands" and that he had a responsibility to aid "those less fortunate than I have been" (Benedum 1957). In 2020, the foundation's assets totaled $430 million, and over its history has reportedly delivered $500 million in grants to various charitable causes in West Virginia and southwestern Pennsylvania.

Jeffrey B. Webb

See also: Caddo Oil Field; Drake, Edwin Laurentine; Getty, Jean Paul; Rockefeller, John D.; Steele, John Washington "Coal Oil Johnny"; Summers, Emma A.; Texas Oil Boom

FURTHER READING

Benedum, Michael L. 1957. "Fifth Codicil to the Last Will and Testament of Michael L. Benedum." June 15. Claude Worthington Benedum Foundation. https://benedum.org/about-us/mr-benedums-will/ (accessed October 2023).

"Benedum-Trees Properties Sold." 1982. *The Pittsburgh Press*. February 21.

Mallison, Sam T. 1953. *The Great Wildcatter*. Charleston, WV: Educational Foundation of West Virginia, Inc.

Miller, Keith L. 2001. "Benedum, Michael L." *American National Biography*. Oxford: Oxford University Press.

Smith, Julia Cauble. 2016. "Yates Oilfield." *Handbook of Texas*. Texas State Historical Association. https://www.tshaonline.org/handbook/entries/yates-oilfield (accessed October 2023).

Young, Charles. 2021. "The Lasting Legacy of Michael L. Benedum, the 'Great Wildcatter' and Generous Giver." WVNews. May 2. https://www.wvnews.com/news/wvnews/the-lasting-legacy-of-michael-l-benedum-the-great-wildcatter-and-generous-giver/article_54a885af-abba-55cd-9a4e-074e70edb768.html (accessed October 2023).

Biofuels

Biofuels are forms of energy that are derived from organic matter like plants or animal waste and in their liquid and gas forms, are known by familiar names like ethanol and methane. They differ from fossil fuels like coal, oil, and natural gas, which are extracted from deposits formed through natural geological processes. These types of fuel are considered renewable by virtue of their sources, such as grain crops, algae, hemp, wood and wood waste, and even municipal landfills. In several forms, they produce lower levels of CO_2 than their fossil fuel counterparts when burned, which on an industrial scale has made them an attractive alternative fuel source for transportation and home heating. The US Energy Information Administration (EIA) reported that in 2019, "biofuels consumption totaled 1.09 million barrels per day and accounted for 7.3 percent of total motor gasoline, distillate, and jet fuel consumption" in the United States (Shi 2020). This constitutes a small, but nevertheless important element of modern energy production and consumption.

A long history of converting plants and animal waste into fuel can be traced back to the "dawn of humanity" (Guo 2015). In prehistoric human communities, people burned charcoal and wood to cure and cook food, as well as to heat dwellings and provide a source of light. They arrayed fires to ward off predators and used primitive kilns to refine clay into pottery. In many ways these solid fuels were a linchpin in the advent of civilization as they facilitated the formation of group life typically connected with activity around the hearth (Gowlett 2016). Ancient history records its uses, and even instances of massive deforestation. In *The Acharnians*, Greek dramatist Aristophanes (448–388 BCE) includes in his cast a mob of charcoal burners from Acharnae near Athens who manufactured charcoal for sale in the region. Historians J. Donald Hughes and J.V. Thirgood described wood fuel in ancient Greece and Rome this way: "Wood and charcoal fired the kilns that hardened Greek and Roman ceramics, including pottery, bricks, and tiles; melted the metal for statues, utensils, and weapons; forced pitch out of pinewood; and reduced limestone to fertilizer" (Hughes 1982, 62). In terms of fuel for smelting, they added that for the Roman Empire, "reasonable estimates hold that a single major ancient metallurgical center would have required as much as a million acres of coppice forest to supply these needs" (Hughes 1982, 62).

This reliance on solid biofuels for heat, light, and power persisted until the Industrial Revolution. In the nineteenth century, a blend of alcohol and turpentine known as camphene enjoyed wide use as an alternative to whale oil for lamps. Distilleries in the mid-nineteenth century devoted between 30 and 80 percent of their output of alcohol for camphene production (Kovarik 1998). The popularity of ethyl alcohol as a fuel source for lighting inspired an early American pioneer of internal combustion engines, New England inventor Samuel Morey (1762–1743), to experiment with the fuel. He tinkered with new designs for steam engines and then turned to mixing water vapor with ethyl alcohol and turpentine (from pine resin) to determine their suitability as source of fuel for his new device (Kovarik 1998). In a text he wrote in 1826, he described his project this way: "Having accidentally discovered that the vapour of water and that of spirit of turpentine, when mixed with a very great proportion of atmospheric air, were highly explosive—I have been endeavouring to produce therefrom, a useful mechanical power" (Morey 1826, 104). Morey devised a "turpentine engine" to demonstrate this power, complete with a "preparing box" (carburetor) for joining the gases. He staged a successful trial using a boat that reached 8 miles an hour, and then promised "'to have the engine applied to a carriage on a railroad and when that is done, I should think I have done my part. I can but hope and trust that the ensuing winter will see the engine well applied to a carriage on a railroad'" (Getman 1936, 297). Later European developers of internal combustion engines like Germany's Nicolaus Otto designed their machines to use ethyl alcohol as a fuel as well.

It took a generation of innovation before automobiles with internal combustion engines proved to be viable on a large scale as a means of transportation, and by the early twentieth century it was petroleum, rather than a biofuels like ethyl alcohol and turpentine, that provided their source of energy. Nevertheless, European scientists and automakers had much success with adding ethyl alcohol to gasoline as an anti-knock blending agent and as an aid to higher compression; many countries required petroleum to be blended with biofuels. In the United States, Henry Ford made his early Model Ts with an adjustable carburetor that allowed it to switch between ethyl alcohol and gasoline. Ford believed the use of alcohol in automobiles would provide an enormous boost to American farmers, with whom he sympathized very deeply. He also grew concerned about US dependence on foreign oil and the eventual exhaustion of domestic petroleum reserves. In 1925, Ford told a *New York Times* reporter that "the fuel of the future is going to come from fruit like that sumach [*sic*] out by the road, or from apples, weeds, sawdust—almost anything. There is fuel in every bit of vegetable matter that can be fermented" ("Ford" 1925, 24). In the 1930s, he backed the Farm Chemurgy movement and its annual conferences, which researched and promoted alcohol as a gasoline alternative or a desirable blending agent.

E85 FLEX FUEL

There are more than 3,900 public E85 stations across forty-five states in the US, serving twenty-one million "flex fuel" vehicles. These vehicles are designed to run on either gasoline or E85, which is an ethanol-gasoline blend with 51–83 percent ethanol depending on location and time of the year. E85 is generally less expensive and burns cleaner than unblended gasoline, but has somewhat lower projected mileage per gallon.

Jeffrey B. Webb

Ford was joined in this campaign by Charles F. Kettering, vice president of research at General Motors, president of the Society of Automotive Engineers, and later founder of Delco, a parts manufacturer. Kettering's team of researchers produced studies and technical papers on ethyl alcohol as a gasoline substitute from 1919 until 1925, when General Motors collaborated with Standard Oil to create Ethyl Corporation, which steered the GM effort toward consideration of lead as an anti-knock additive with greater octane and compression capabilities. Into the 1930s, Kettering still "saw the fuel of the future as a blend of ethyl alcohol and gasoline leading to pure alcohol from cellulose as a standard fuel" (Kovarik 1998). His enthusiasm was greeted with indifference by federal officials concerned with America's fuel supply, especially at the onset of the Second World War. It also met with open hostility by the American Petroleum Institute and its member oil industry corporations. It would take another energy crisis to raise the profile of biofuels as a fossil fuel supplement, or even substitute, which came about in the Energy Crisis of the 1970s.

The OPEC oil embargo in 1973–4 exposed US dependence on foreign oil and triggered concerted efforts by government and industry to develop domestic energy resources, including biofuels. In this context, President Ford enacted fuel economy standards in the Energy Policy and Conservation Act of 1975 but did little for biofuels; President Carter formed the US Department of Energy (1977) and expanded financial incentives for ethanol production. In 1980, Congress enacted the Biomass Energy and Alcohol Fuels Act which mandated the newly created Department of Energy conduct "an accelerated research, development, and demonstration program for promoting the commercial viability of processes for the recovery of energy from municipal wastes," and the Department of Agriculture to direct timber sales from the national forest system "for use by biomass energy projects." The law prioritized funding for "any activity or project for the demonstration of technologies for the production of liquid fuels or biomass energy which substitute for petroleum or natural gas" (Biomass 1980). The number of biofuels plants expanded as a result; in 1984, the United States had 163 working ethanol plants and produced 595 million gallons of biofuel.

Biofuels production increased significantly in the wake of the 1970s energy crisis, exemplified in the creation of the "Minnesota Model." The Minnesota Department of Agriculture, hundreds of farmers, and several consulting firms collaborated on a sustained effort to secure subsidies for ethanol producers within the state. They were joined by BBI International, founded by fuel advocate and farmer Kathy Bryan (and former husband Rüdiger Graf) to promote the industry through publications like *Biomass Magazine*, *Ethanol Producer Magazine*, and *Biodiesel Magazine*. Their collective efforts, a public-private partnership, benefited the owner-operators of farms and ethanol plants while expanding the market for the growers' grain products beyond foodstuffs. Supporters argued that the model directed capital toward farmers and small operators, in contrast to large corporations, where capital is directed to shareholders and wealthy investors. In 2020, Iowa, Nebraska, and Illinois topped the list as the largest ethanol-producing states, with Minnesota placed fourth.

Energy policy in the early 2000s emerged within the context of US wars in Afghanistan and Iraq. President Bush's Energy Independence and Security Act of 2007 called for the production of biomass-based diesel fuel and an expansion in regular biofuels, with the majority to be derived from sources other than cornstarch (such as sugar or cellulose), and a federal study of the use of algae as a biomass fuel source. President Obama's American Recovery and Reinvestment Act of 2009 contained measures designed to increase production of biofuels. President Biden carried this program into his administration with financial incentives, strengthened standards, and government research grants for ethanol in the wake of Russia's invasion of the Ukraine and the corresponding disruption in oil imports. Research on biofuels is conducted at a number of major research universities, energy corporations, and at the National Bioenergy Center (established 2000) within the US Department of Energy's National Renewables Energy Laboratory.

In the US, biofuels comprised 10 percent of fuels consumed by vehicles in 2021, with 98 percent of all gasoline containing ethanol, mostly made from corn but also soybeans, sugarcane, cornstalks, waste wood chips, hemp, switchgrass, and algae. Biodiesel can be made from vegetable oil and animal fats. They offer benefits to American farmers, a way to reuse wood, grain, and plant residue, and a measure of energy independence from foreign oil. Environmentalists have mixed opinions regarding the benefits of biofuels. Greenhouse gas emissions are lower for corn ethanol than for gasoline (35 percent), and much lower for cellulosic biomass ethanol (97 percent). The use of unblended biodiesel results in a decrease of greenhouse gas emissions of 74 percent. However, the increased use of farm machinery to produce corn and other ethanol feeders, and the removal of forest cover to create new cropland increases greenhouse gases. Expanded crop production also increases the amount of water used for irrigation. Finally, the price of ethanol is subject to fluctuations in commodity prices for corn and other crops, which complicates forecasting the economies of replacing petroleum with biofuels.

Jeffrey B. Webb

See also: Agriculture and Energy; Energy Crisis of the 1970s; Energy Independence; Energy Security Act of 1980; Ford, Henry; Renewable Energy; US Department of Energy

FURTHER READING

Biomass Energy and Alcohol Fuels. 1980. Title 42, U.S. Code Chapter 96. https://uscode.house.gov/view.xhtml?path=/prelim@title42/chapter96&edition=prelim (accesed October 2023).

Fernstrum, Wendy. 2007. *High Octane: How Minnesota Led the Nation in Ethanol Development*. Minneapolis, MN: Minnesota Corn Growers Association.

"Ford Predicts Fuel from Vegetation." 1925. *New York Times*. September 20. https://www.nytimes.com/1925/09/20/archives/ford-predicts-fuel-from-vegetation-he-says-electricity-will-heat.html (accesed October 2023).

Getman, Frederick H. 1936. "Samuel Morey, a Pioneer of Science in America." *Osiris*. Vol. 1. January. Pp. 278–302.

Gowlett, J.A.J. 2016. "The Discovery of Fire by Humans: A Long and Convoluted Process." *Philosophical Transactions of the Royal Society B: Biological Sciences*. June 5. Vol. 371 (1696). 20150164.

Guo, Mingxin, Weiping Song, and Jeremy Buhain. 2015. "Bioenergy and Biofuels: History, Status, and Perspective." *Renewable and Sustainable Energy Reviews*. Vol. 42. February. Pp. 712–25.

Hughes, J. Donald and J.V. Thirgood. 1982. "Deforestation, Erosion, and Forest Management in Ancient Greece and Rome." *Journal of Forest History*. April. Vol. 26. No. 2. Pp. 60–75.

Kovarik, Bill. 1998. "Henry Ford, Charles Kettering and the Fuel of the Future." *Automotive History Review*. Spring. No. 32. Pp. 7–27.

Morey, Samuel. 1826. "An Account of a New Explosive Engine, Generating a Power that may be Substituted for that of the Steam Engine." *Journal of the Franklin Institute*. August. Vol. 2. No. 2. Pp. 115–19.

Shi, Estella and Steve Hanson. 2020. "EIA Projects U.S. Biofuel Production to Slowly Increase Through 2050." March 9. U.S. Energy Information Administration. U.S. Department of Energy. https://www.eia.gov/todayinenergy/detail.php?id=43096 (accesed October 2023).

Black Lung Disease

In the turn to the steam engine and nonrenewable fossil fuels like coal, the dawn of industrial civilization brought about changes in available energy resources and patterns of energy consumption. The nineteenth century witnessed remarkable economic growth and industrial capitalism boosted the demand for coal. In this era, two doctors on either side of the Atlantic Ocean, serving their respective coal-mining districts, conducted post-mortem exams and diagnosed miners with "black lung disease." On March 29, 1831, coal miner John Hogg explained to Dr. James C. Gregory that he was having trouble breathing and had chest pain. Twenty days after Hogg entered the infirmary, he died. Thirty years later in the heart of the Pennsylvania anthracite district, Dr. John T. Carpenter reported to his local medical society a prevalence of occupational health problems among coal miners. He described what appeared to be "the penetration of solid, carbonaceous matter into the lungs," which he observed through post-mortem examinations (Smith 1987). In Gregory and Carpenter's autopsies, they noted each coal miner's lungs were a uniform black carbonaceous color and that the inhalation of dusts and gases in the coal mines of Scotland and Pennsylvania were the source of occupational disease in the industry.

In the face of this significant health risk, the production of coal increased exponentially from the eighteenth century to the present, to the point where per capita energy consumption in industrialized societies today is five to ten times greater than in traditional preindustrial cultures. Since the cost of oxen- or horse-drawn wagons to transport freight was too high to haul large quantities of coal to mountain smelters in the late 1860s, the early coal mines were small, and seasonal operations supplied local household markets. The exploitation of mineral resources was critical not only to economic development in North America but also to industrialization across the globe. One of the most notable of these resources were the coal deposits that attracted investors and miners to the regions of Appalachia and the mountain West. In addition, a predominantly wood-powered energy regime gave way to a coal-powered regime during the process of industrialization, as coal arrived at the steel mills by rail from the mines of Pennsylvania and the Midwest. In 1850, the United States produced 8.4 million short tons of coal, but by 1900 it produced 270 million, almost one-third of world coal production. In that same year, coal provided 70 percent of the energy needs in the United States. Coal extraction grew eighty to hundredfold in the nineteenth century and another six or sevenfold in the twentieth century (McNeill and Vrtis 2017).

Beginning in the 1870s, the development of regional railroads and energy-intensive industries such as iron smelting created a relationship between railroads, coal, mining, and other industries that led to the opening of more coal mines throughout the United States. To satisfy the consumption needs of an industrializing society, mine operators dispatched recruiters to Europe, northern cities, and Southern jails looking for male workers to join the labor force in remote mountain coal mines. Many ex-slaves from the South joined former peasants from Southern Europe among the native mountaineers near the coal deposits and began extensive exploitation of the earth's coal (Smith 1987). Simultaneously, the increase in coal production also occasioned the increase in black lung disease among coal miners in a variety of states, including Pennsylvania, Kentucky, Alabama, Tennessee, and West Virginia. This accompanied major mining disasters, including mine collapses and methane explosions, making the occupation the most dangerous in the United States.

Black lung, as miners referred to it, did considerable physical and psychological harm to coal miners. They contracted a condition known as pneumoconiosis, a disease associated with the inhalation of coal dust, which acted over time to impair lung function. Pneumoconiosis is a generic term meaning "dust-containing lung," which had to be assessed and diagnosed through X-rays (Smith 1987). The progression of the disease was measured by the greater the size and number of opacities revealed on a chest film. However, coal company physicians, in the context of the reality of coal miners trying to work and live with diminished lung function, were not entirely helpful in understanding black lung disease. These physicians dubbed the widespread breathlessness, expectoration of sputum, and prolong coughing fits as a benign condition that was to be expected, thereby diverting attention from miners' respiratory distress. In so doing, they decided to diagnose the symptoms of lung disease as normal for coal miners. In the 1930s, one Pennsylvania physician informed miners not to worry about the impairment of breathing capacity (Smith 1987).

By the early 1930s, a new group of medical practitioners in mining towns became the voice for miners in matters of occupational safety and health. They appeared in the context of a growing unionization movement and greater collective bargaining strength of coal miners. The United Mine Workers of American (UMWA) reached 400,000 strong. The era of the Great Depression, the Second World War, early post-war were the most turbulent in the long history of coal mining in the United States. The UMWA President John L. Lewis (1880–1969) refused to acquiesce to the wartime no-strike pledge, and nearly half a million coal miners repeatedly shut down the entire industry. The federal government responded by seizing control of the coal mines on four occasions. In 1943 alone, over 7 million worker-days of production were lost to walkouts, which prompted President Franklin D. Roosevelt to federalize the operators' coal properties (Leavitt Walzer 1985).

These union efforts became focused on miners' health and safety. In an effort to provide coal miners with health care plans free of company control, John Lewis proposed during collective bargaining sessions in 1945 that coal companies contribute ten cents per ton to the union to provide for its members modern medical and surgical service, hospitalization, insurance, rehabilitation, and economic protection. This proposal failed, and in 1946 the union bargaining team returned to contract negotiations, putting industry-financed health care as its number one demand on the table. The coal operators refused, and miners went on strike when their contract expired. These bitter strikes led John Lewis to negotiate a commitment from the mine owners that they would be the sole contributors to a Welfare and Retirement Fund. Companies would pay a royalty to the Fund for every ton of coal extracted. By 1952, the royalty was raised from five to forty cents where it remained for the next twenty years. Initially the Fund offered union members a $100 per month retirement pension at the age of sixty-five if they had worked twenty years in the mines, a disability pension for injuries and sickness, and free medical services for miners and their dependents. Eventually, miners became the largest group of Americans for whom prepaid health care has been an entitlement for several generations. By the early 1950s Lewis' achievement attracted national attention. In return for the Welfare and Retirement Fund, the United Mine Workers agreed to accept and encourage extensive mechanization of the mining industry, which resulted in a major reduction in the labor force (Leavitt Walzer 1985).

It became apparent that companies' gains from the exchange of mechanization for fringe benefits outweighed those of the miners, and by the early 1960s, the benefits of the Fund were no longer sure. Mechanization of the mines coincided with a contraction of the coal market as oil became more and more plentiful. Appalachian coal miners who chose to remain in the region had difficulty finding employment. Those who waited experienced an increase in the demand for coal in the mid-1960s. With a resumption in greater levels of production, many older miners remembered concerns over dust levels voiced in the 1930s by physicians concerned with miners' health. This prompted the formation of the Black Lung Association, led by disabled miners and supported by a committed group of physicians and lawyers. Black lung became the symbol of the miners' hostility toward coal mine operators in 1968 and 1969, a period of renewed strikes using new methods of civil disobedience (Leavitt Walzer 1985).

In early 1969, 40,000 West Virginia miners proceeded to shut down the coal industry. Led by the Black Lung Association, and defying union leadership, thousands disrupted the state legislative session in Charleston. The strikers insisted that the coal industry be forced to maintain its long-standing agreement, that the coal miners' consent to mechanization be exchanged for employer-provided pension and health benefits. The strikers also demanded that the West Virginia legislature permit black lung to be diagnosed by several methods and not solely by X-ray. What the miners wanted was a diagnostic method to evaluate impairment of breathing capacity rather than evidence of dust accumulation in the lungs. In addition, for any miner who worked over ten years in the mines and suffered from respiratory impairment, the presumption was that they had black lung, and thus be eligible for compensation.

After three weeks of mine closure, these demands became state law in March 1969. Legal recognition of black lung as a compensable occupational disease was interpreted as a public condemnation of years of declining medical service in the region, of the unaddressed hazards of coal mining, of misplaced corporate priorities, and of the failure of the UMWA to represent the interests of its members. Finally, the debate on black lung compensation appeared in the US Congress and transformed black lung disease into an issue of national politics. This led to the creation of the Coal Mine Health and Safety Act (1969) which contained provisions requiring protection against coal dust and other particulates in the mines, and federal benefits for those who had already contracted black lung disease. Although President Richard Nixon voiced opposition, he signed the bill into law.

Mark M. Chambers

See also: Coal; Sinclair, Upton; United Mine Workers of America

FURTHER READING

Leavitt Walzer, Judith and Ronald Numbers. 1985. *Sickness and Health in America: Readings in the History of Medicine and Public Health*. Madison, WI: University of Wisconsin Press.

McNeill, John R. 2001. *Something New under the Sun: An Environmental History of the Twentieth-Century World* (The Global Century Series). New York. W. W. Norton & Company.

McNeill, John R. and George Vrtis, eds. 2017. *Mining North America: An Environmental History since 1522*. Berkeley: University of California Press.

Murchison, B. (2002). "Due Process, Black Lung, and The Shaping of Administrative Justice." *Administrative Law Review*. Vol. 54. Pp. 1025–123. http://www.jstor.org/stable/40712269 (accessed October 2023).

Sellers, Christopher C. 1997. *Hazards of the Job: From Industrial Disease to Environmental Health Science*. Chapel Hill, NC: University of North Carolina Press.

Smith, Barbara E. 1987. *Digging Our Own Graves: Coal Miners and the Struggle over Black Lung Disease*. Philadelphia, PA: Temple University Press.

Block Island Wind Farm

Block Island Wind Farm is the first operational offshore wind farm in the United States, which generates electricity for Block Island off the coast of mainland Rhode Island. The five-turbine wind farm was developed by Deepwater Wind and went online in late 2016. Although the farm produces renewable energy for tens of thousands of homes on the island, issues regarding the integrity of the cables that link the farm to the island and the mainland, as well as controversy about how the farm affects the local fishing patterns, raise some questions about its overall impact.

The power of the wind has been harnessed since the earliest generations of humankind to propel boats and run mills for grinding grain. Since the mid-nineteenth century, however, the wind has been an indispensable source of power in the United States. In 1850, the first wind engine company was started, and the Halladay Windmill was designed to capture the power of the great winds that blow across the American West (OEERE 2020). By the end of the century, wind power was being harnessed to provide electricity for households. The increasing use of wind power declined over the first half of the twentieth century, but the oil shortages of the 1970s caused the American government and public to revisit wind as a cheap and sustainable option for energy production.

The first commercial wind farms in the United States were installed in California in the 1980s. The American government began funding research for renewable energy sources and development, and thus financed many wind farms throughout the country into the mid-2000s (EIA 2019). However, wind farms must take up wide expanses of land in order to generate enough energy to be worthwhile, so the United States started to look towards the biggest source of open space and strong winds: the ocean.

Block Island is a tiny island of only about a thousand inhabitants year-round, but that number increases to nearly 20,000 during the summer months. It is very near the coast of Rhode Island, about 12 miles offshore, but until the wind farm, the island was powered solely by five diesel generators and fuel that was shipped to the island. These factors contributed to one of the highest energy costs in the nation (Bidwell 2019).

Block Island Wind Farm was conceived in 2008 when Deepwater Wind was chosen by the Rhode Island government to construct the wind farm. This decision came on the tail end of conversations and state initiatives to initiate a decrease in the use of fossil fuels and to determine the viability of an offshore wind farm. The Ocean Special Area Management Plan (Ocean SAMP) designated a thirteen-square-mile zone off of the coast as a Renewable Energy Zone, which is where the farm is located. This area was thought to be the least disruptive to commercial and personal life in the area, particularly in relation to common fishing patterns (Bidwell 2019). After the site of the farm was determined, the development of the farm officially began in tandem with Deepwater Wind. Experts in various fields related to the project, including fishermen and residents of the island, were consulted throughout the

FIGURE 4: Offshore wind turbines at Block Island Wind Farm.

development phase. The public community of Block Island and Rhode Island was also greatly engaged in the entire process, which may account for why there tended to be general support for the project (Bidwell 2019).

There were concerns with the cost of installing the wind farm, and Deepwater Wind went through multiple negotiations with the Rhode Island Public Utilities Commission and the National Grid plc, to whom Deepwater Wind sells the electricity, before agreeing upon the $300 million project. Many residents of Block Island were unhappy that the farm would not lower their energy costs, and the project had to be passed by multiple legislative bodies before it was officially approved for construction (Barrett 2010).

Construction of the thirty-megawatt farm began in mid-2015 and concluded in December of 2016. The original estimates and goals of the farm's energy production included generating 90 percent of Block Island's power, generating energy for 17,000 homes, and reducing carbon dioxide emissions by 40,000 tons per year (Schlossberg 2016). The farm also connected the island to Rhode Island's energy grid for the first time. What is not used by the island goes back into the mainland grid, contributing about 1 percent of the state's power.

Although many initial reactions to the wind farm were positive, several issues emerged and the project drew some criticism. A study published in *Frontiers in Marine Science* in November 2018 interviewed residents and local fishermen to the island to find what the perceived impacts of the wind farm were on fishing activities and general life. Many commercial fishermen were mainly concerned with the lost fishing ground due to the farm. The 13 square miles of the farm had been a productive fishery, so a valuable resource was wasted, especially during construction when the area was closed off. Even now that fishermen can navigate between the turbines, some are still concerned with running into them during conditions with poor visibility, and therefore avoid the area. Many commercial fishermen were compensated by Deepwater Wind for their losses during construction (Ten Brink 2018, 6).

An additional problem that fishermen ran into was loss of fishing ground due to the area's increased popularity with recreational fishermen. Because it became a travel destination and tourist spot, the wind farm attracted boaters, recreational anglers, and sightseers. The increased number of vessels in the water around the farm affected commercial fishermen's routes, initiating some dissatisfaction. On the other hand, a positive impact of the wind farm observed by fishermen was an increased diversity of fish due to the artificial reef created by the turbines. Fishermen reported catching greater numbers of fish and in greater varieties, including cod (Ten Brink 2018, 9).

TURBINE DETAILS

Each of the five wind turbines stands over 300 feet tall, and the individual blades extend well over 200 feet each. The turbines are also designed to withstand a Category 3 storm with winds from 111 to 129 miles per hour. The turbines were constructed partially in Louisiana, and then shipped up to Rhode Island and installed.

Emma P. Fee

Another issue that came to light in late 2019 was that the some of the cables that connect the turbines to the mainland were only buried 4 feet below the seabed. Due to shifting sand atop hard bedrock, the cables were discovered to have been exposed, posing complications for the transmission of the generated energy. Surveys were conducted over the following months to determine the severity of the situation, and it was concluded that the cables would have to be reburied. This meant that drilling would have to take place to get the cables up to 40 feet beneath the seabed to prevent further shifting. As of late 2019, the reconstruction of the exposed cables was scheduled to be completed by summer of 2021 (Shuman 2019).

Emma P. Fee

See also: Alta Wind Energy Center; Crotched Mountain Wind Farm; Halladay Windmill; Renewable Energy; Wind Power

FURTHER READING

Abel, David. 2018. "Opponents Say Block Island Wind Farms Are Causing Problems across Prime Fishing Grounds." *Boston Globe*. March. https://www.bostonglobe.com/metro/2018/03/16/plans-for-massive-offshore-wind-farms-stir-fears-among-fishermen/hzti6ZJw71WNmqFtLJepJI/story.html (accessed February 24, 2020).

American Wind Energy Association (AWEA). 2020. "1970s: Oil Prices Skyrocket and AWEA Emerges." https://www.awea.org/wind-101/history-of-wind/1970s (accessed February 24, 2020; URL no longer accessible).

Barrett, Chris and Ted Nesi. 2010. "PUC Rejects Deepwater Contract on Price." *Providence Business News*. March. https://web.archive.org/web/20221017175856/https://pbn.com/PUC-rejects-Deepwater-contract-on-price,48839/ (accessed October 2023).

Bidwell, David and Joseph Dwyer. 2019. "Chains of Trust: Energy Justice, Public Engagement, and the First Offshore Wind Farm in the United States." *ScienceDirect*. Vol. 47. Pp. 166–76.

Dennis, Brady. 2016. "The Nation's First Offshore Wind Farm is Ready to Go, Despite Critics' Blowback." *The Washington Post*. August 27. https://www.washingtonpost.com/national/health-science/the-nations-first-offshore-wind-farm-is-ready-to-go-despite-critics-blow-back/2016/08/27/7a43c6d6-693f-11e6-99bf-f0cf3a6449a6_story.html?noredirect=on (accessed February 24, 2020).

Office of Energy Efficiency and Renewable Energy (OEERE). 2020. "History of Wind Power." U.S. Department of Energy. https://www.energy.gov/eere/wind/history-us-wind-energy (accessed February 17, 2020).

Ørsted. 2020. "Our Projects in the U.S.: Block Island Wind Farm." https://us.orsted.com/Wind-projects (accessed February 24, 2020).

Schlossberg, Tatiana. 2016. "America's First Offshore Wind Farm Spins to Life." *New York Times*. December 14. https://www.nytimes.com/2016/12/14/science/wind-power-block-island.html (accessed February 17, 2020).

Shuman, Cassius. 2019. "Vessel Surveying Cables at Town Beach." *Block Island Times*. October. https://theblockislandapp.com/vessel-surveying-cables-at-town-beach/?doing_wp_cron=1699984677.2706210613250732421875 (accessed October 2023).

Ten Brink, T.S. and T. Dalton. 2018. "Perceptions of Commercial and Recreational Fishers on the Potential Ecological Impacts of the Block Island Wind Farm (US)." *Frontiers in Marine Science*. Vol. 5. No. 439. Pp. 1–13.

Thompson, Richard. 2015. "Two Louisiana Firms Playing Important Roles in Creation, Construction of Offshore Wind Farm." Nola, September 19. https://www.nola.com/news/business/article_0d0bf749-63cf-56a0-86d5-c448cc9fe035.html (accessed February 27, 2020).

U.S. Energy Information Administration (EIA). 2019. "Wind Explained: History of Wind Power." U.S. Department of Energy. https://www.eia.gov/energyexplained/wind/history-of-wind-power.php (accessed February 24, 2020).

Boeing, William Edward

The business of commercial aviation in the 1920s and 1930s attracted ambitious entrepreneurs like William Boeing (1881–1956), founder of Boeing Airplane Company (1917) and later the United Aircraft and Transport Corporation (1929), a subdivision of which became United Airlines. Boeing entered the aircraft business by manufacturing seaplanes and received a boost from the US Navy during the First World War with a defense contract to build fifty airplanes. Boeing's career corresponded with the advent of commercial aviation, which emerged as an important new sector of the US economy and fundamentally transformed the way Americans lived and traveled. This transformation was made possible by a number of factors, including rapid technological innovation and the existence of a nationwide petroleum industry to provide fuel. By the middle of the twentieth century, Boeing and United Airlines were among the industry leaders in the production of aircraft and in passenger air service.

Only a few years passed between Orville and Wilbur Wright's famous flight at Kitty Hawk, North Carolina in 1903, and William Boeing's introduction to flying machines in the Pacific Northwest. He moved to the Gray's Harbor region in Washington state when he was twenty-two, having inherited wealth from his German- and Austrian-born parents, and drawing a steady income from an iron ore investment in Minnesota. Boeing bought timber land and in 1908, moved to Seattle, where he earned income from his investments and enjoyed the sporting life. He met US Navy Captain George Conrad Westervelt at Seattle's University Club in 1910, and together they began to attend air shows; through this association Boeing developed a passion for airplanes and especially seaplanes. Boeing learned to pilot an aircraft in 1914 and within two years, he pledged to improve the design of these early seaplanes. Boeing and Westervelt worked together and built the B & W Seaplane with a bi-wing design, enclosed fuselage, and dual pontoons. Boeing started the Pacific Aero Products Company with a goal to supply the US Navy with his craft, and Boeing himself flew demonstration flights over Seattle to drum up interest in his enterprise.

In 1917, Boeing won the contract with the US Navy to build fifty patrol seaplanes, which kept him in business during the First World War. He renamed the firm Boeing Airplane Company and built the Model 2, with some of the design work completed by Wong Tsu, a Chinese aeronautical engineer and MIT graduate who performed tests in MIT's wind tunnel. After the First World War, Boeing pursued military contracts and the development of airmail planes and services. In the first instance, Boeing secured a US Army Air Service contract to build 200 Thomas-Morse MB-3A pursuit fighters, which the company built and delivered in 1922 at a price of $7,240 per plane (Boeing 2013a). Boeing's first successful attempt to build a fighter plane of its own design was the Model 15, eventually called the PW-9, which incorporated a 435-horsepower Curtiss D-12 engine that enabled it to fly faster and further than its competitors. It carried two machine guns, a 30-cal. and a.55-cal., and two 122-pound bombs. Between 1924 and 1928 the company produced 157 of these planes for both the US

Army Air Service and for the US Navy, which called it the FB-1 (Boeing 2012). The fighter established Boeing as chief rival to the Douglas Aircraft Company, another major supplier of military aircraft. The company went on to design and build the innovative P-26, nicknamed "Peashooter," which became the US Army's main fighter aircraft for several years in the mid-1930s.

JET FUEL

Modern passenger jets like the Boeing 737 or 747 use kerosene, which is a petroleum product made from crude oil in refineries. Jet fuel, classified as Jet A (for US domestic use) and Jet A-1 (for international use), must remain stable at high pressures and low temperatures. It has a higher flash point than regular gasoline, which is the temperature at which the fuel forms an ignitable combination of hydrocarbon and air, and a lower freeze point, which is the temperature at which the fuel begins to form solid crystals. Numerous chemicals are mixed with the fuel that serve as antioxidants, static suppressants, icing inhibitors, corrosion blockers, and antimicrobial agents.

Jeffrey B. Webb

Pursing other ventures, Boeing secured contracts to supply airmail carriers and delivery services. In 1925, the company designed and built the Model 40 for a US Postal Service competition to identify a replacement for its decaying squadron of converted military de Havilland DH-4s. The model failed to win the bid, but Boeing persisted and when President Calvin Coolidge allowed privatization of mail service under the Contract Air Mail Act of 1925, a redesigned Model 40A with greater carrying capacity (1,200 lbs.) earned rights to the airmail route between San Francisco and Chicago. His postal delivery service, which he called Boeing Air Transport, began in 1927 with twenty Model 40As, and importantly, also provided passenger service for two people. A later version of the plane, the Model 40C, expanded passenger capacity to four. This was Boeing's first attempt to market passenger air travel to consumers, albeit a very modest one. He told an interviewer later in this period that "'from the start of the mail operation, I looked ahead to the time … when passengers would become of primary importance'" (Winship 1998).

Having earned the mail delivery contract, Boeing set out to reincorporate his company under the name United Aircraft and Transport Corporation (UATC), signaling its intent to become a multifaceted corporation that manufactured airplanes and operated a passenger air travel service. The new company began acquiring other companies, including several other carriers and parts manufacturers like engine maker Pratt & Whitney and Hamilton-Standard Propeller. In this way Boeing followed the pattern of consolidation and vertical integration of the petroleum, steel, and automotive industries. One of its new airplanes, the Model 247 developed in 1933, is considered the first true passenger airliner. It had twin 500-horsepower prop engines, retractable landing gear, autopilot capacity, and a gyro panel for flying with instruments. The airliner could reach speeds of 200 miles per hour and fly at 25,400 feet, carrying 400 pounds of mail and ten passengers. The New York to Los Angeles transcontinental flight required twenty hours and seven stops, but this was a seven-and-a-half hour improvement on earlier aircraft (Boeing 2013b). Three different carriers flew the

Boeing 247, which numbered seventy-five in total, and exercised an early dominance at the dawn of commercial aviation (Boeing 2013b).

In the early 1930s, controversy broke out over how the Postmaster General awarded US Postal Service contracts to the major mail carriers, a group that included Boeing's United Aircraft and Transport Corporation. As a result, the Air Mail Act (1934) was passed and signed into law. The measure punished executives of the larger companies for their alleged corruption in the Air Mail scandal and initiated antitrust action to break up consolidated and vertically integrated corporations accused of monopoly behavior. The law's backers believed that manufacturing airplanes and conducting passenger airline service should be done by separate companies. On September 28, 1934, Boeing's company was severed into three separate entities: the eastern manufacturers were grouped into United Aircraft Corporation (later renamed United Technologies), the Western manufacturers left behind became known as the Boeing Airplane Company, and the passenger carriers were merged into a third corporation, United Air Lines.

Resentful and disillusioned, Boeing sold his shares of stock in his companies and resigned all of his positions. For the remaining twenty-two years of his life, Boeing pursued the kind of leisure activities available to the super-rich, including frequent yachting sessions, fly fishing, and thoroughbred racing. He built a large cattle ranch east of Seattle that he called Aldarra Farms and worked to build a reputation as a breeder of fine Herefords. The Boeing Airplane Company went on to make an enormous impact during the Second World War by converting to wartime production and building 28 percent of all the military aircraft produced by American companies. It developed the early models of the B-17 "Flying Fortress" heavy bomber in the late 1930s and went from producing 60 B-17s per month in 1942 to and astonishing 362 per month in 1944 ("Boeing Story" 2022). The company also developed and built the B-29 "Superfortress," a four-engine bomber with a pressurized cabin that permitted flights above 30,000 feet, traveling a distance of over 3,000 miles for up to 16 hours. It enabled the Allies to fly strategic bombing missions over Japan from China and the Mariana Islands toward the end of the Second World War.

After the war, the company developed the iconic Boeing 707, an airliner with four jet engines, which quickly became the dominant passenger jet in the 1960s and 1970s. It made its inaugural commercial flight in 1959 with American Airlines from Los Angeles to New York in just four hours and three minutes, ushering in what was soon termed the "Jet Age." This description of the era came about because the various configurations of the Boeing 707 could carry 144-180 passengers at a time in non-stop, coast-to-coast travel, and were delivered in such high volume that airline companies quickly scaled up air passenger service (Swopes 2019). Boeing produced 1,010 707s from 1958 to 1979, and soon expanded performance and capacity with its upgraded models, the 727, the 737, and the 747. Expanded capacity and widespread availability lowered ticket prices for ordinary consumers, who could now travel the country in a few hours' time, or even overseas, which was thought to be out of reach for all but the wealthiest Americans. Indeed, for the generation of Americans who came of age in the second half of the twentieth century, air travel became routine. In 2018, before the 2020 Covid-19 pandemic curtailed air travel, "U.S. airlines and foreign airlines serving the United States carried an all-time high of 1.0 billion systemwide (domestic and international) scheduled service passengers" (BTS 2020). Commercial aviation gave a billion individual flights to travelers in the United States in just one year alone.

Clearly, the advent of commercial aviation revolutionized the way hundreds of millions of people traveled for business, for family get-togethers, for vacations and recreation, and a variety of other purposes. Nationwide travel infrastructure like the Transcontinental Railroad and the Interstate Highway System had important impacts in their different ways. However, air travel radically compressed time and space, enabling passengers to overcome historically insurmountable distances within the span of a few hours or perhaps the length of a normal working day. This was a very new kind of lifestyle with a dramatically new kind of mobility offering new kinds of connectivity to distant places and different experiences. The advent of commercial aviation made it possible for a modern lifestyle to emerge, but only after pioneers like William Boeing created the necessary technologies and business organization to set the process in motion. None of this would have been possible without the initial development and industrialization of fuel sources to provide the energy required to operate the system on a massive scale. According to the US Department of Energy, "approximately 10 percent" of all transportation energy in the United States is consumed by the commercial aviation industry, which makes it a significant driver of the nation's overall demand for energy.

Jeffrey B. Webb

See also: Clean Air Act of 1970; Energy Policy Act of 2005; Interstate Highway System; Transcontinental Railroad

FURTHER READING

The Boeing Company (Boeing). 2012. "PW-9/FB Fighter." "Boeing History."https://web.archive.org/web/20121103010232/http://www.boeing.com/history/boeing/pw9.html (accessed October 2023).

The Boeing Company (Boeing). 2013a. "Boeing Logbook, 1920–1926." https://web.archive.org/web/20130104151846/http://www.boeing.com/history/chronology/chron02.html (accessed October 2023).

The Boeing Company (Boeing). 2013b. "Model 247." "Boeing History." https://web.archive.org/web/20130122082728/http://www.boeing.com/history/boeing/m247.html (accessed October 2023).

"The Boeing Story." The US Freedom Pavilion: The Boeing Center. The National WWII Museum Website. https://www.nationalww2museum.org/visit/museum-campus/us-freedom-pavilion/boeing-story (accessed October 2023).

Bureau of Transportation Statistics (BTS). 2020. "2018 Traffic Data for U.S Airlines and Foreign Airlines U.S. Flights." U.S. Department of Transportation. April 30. https://www.bts.dot.gov/newsroom/2018-traffic-data-us-airlines-and-foreign-airlines-us-flights (accessed October 2023).

Swopes, Bryan R. 2019. "25 January 1959." This Day in Aviation. https://www.thisdayinaviation.com/25-january-1959/ (accessed October 2023).

Winship, William. 1998. "Boeing & Douglas: A History of Customer Service." *AERO Magazine*. Vol. 1, Quarter 1. https://www.boeing.com/commercial/aeromagazine/aero_01/textonly/ps01txt.html (accessed October 2023).

Bowser, Sylvanus Freelove

According to the National Association of Convenience Stores, there are over 145,000 fueling stations in the United States, mostly convenience stores with gas pumps but also a variety of other businesses that sell fuels to car, truck, RV, and boat owners (API 2023). The gas station is one of the most readily visible buildings on the American landscape. The inventor of the first gas pump, Sylvanus Bowser (1854–1938), created a system for drawing fuel from an underground storage tank with a mechanical pump and dispensing it in measured quantities. Bowser made it possible for the first generation of automobile and truck owners to easily refuel their vehicles and provided the foundation upon which the modern business of petroleum retailing was established. As a result, generations of everyday commuters and cross-country road-trippers have made visits to a gas station an integral part of their lives.

Bowser was born before the US Civil War in a rural community north of Fort Wayne, Indiana. His family experienced great hardship and he had to leave school to help his parents put food on the table. The environment appeared to be nurturing, with thirteen children in the house and regular attendance at church. Historian Richard Pierard notes that he attended Sunday School where he participated in a Bible memorization competition and won with a total of 654 verses (Pierard 1963). He expressed deep religious convictions as a young man and by all accounts maintained those convictions throughout his life. He married in 1876 and began a career in sales but fared poorly and ultimately couldn't keep up his house payments. He continued to struggle until he hit on the idea of building a pump to help his wife draw water from their 70-foot well. The system he had in mind proved not to be suitable for water, but Bowser persisted and came to believe it would work for conveying oil and related products from their storage containers. In a period of widespread use of kerosene, oil, and "burning fuel" (camphene) for lighting, there was no good way to transfer volatile liquids from their containers to lamps and stoves. Bowser's invention offered a promising way to achieve the task cleanly and efficiently.

Bowser and brother Augustus filed for a US patent in 1886, which was granted the following year. The patent described the device as providing "improvements in liquid-storage tanks or cans which are used for the storage and for measuring when the liquids are drawn out for use—as for delivery—such liquids or fluids as kerosene-oil, burning fluid, and the light combustible products of petroleum." It went on to say that such tanks

> should be made of durable materials, should be for all practical purposes substantially fire-proof, should have convenient and durable appliances for drawing and accurately measuring the tank's contents, and in cases where the said tank or can is used for the storage of the more combustible substances hereinbefore named, which substances are more or less volatile, the said tank or can should be made gas or air tight. (Bowser 1887)

With this device, volatile liquids like "products of petroleum" could be stored safely in an airtight container and pumped out easily in quantities that could be measured with sufficient accuracy.

The patent also mentioned that his device would have wide appeal, not only to homeowners, but managers of factories and workshops, and especially owners of grocery stores and pharmacies. In the late nineteenth century, customers visited these establishments to buy kerosene or camphene to fuel their lamps. Bowser saw the need for storekeepers to have sealed, airtight kerosene and camphene tanks on site with pumps that could measure out the right quantities for the customer. Bowser had already sold one of his devices to a Fort Wayne grocer named Jake Gumpper, and a few other store owners lined up to buy them. In 1888, Bowser organized the S. F. Bowser Oil Tank & Pump Company in Fort Wayne and went on to manufacture the pumps in a variety of sizes and configurations. The company's early catalogs advertised his "Self-Measuring Gasoline Storage Pump" as well as a suite of other products for storing and handling these "volatile liquids." In addition to retailers, the company supplied machine shops, railroad sheds, maintenance facilities, power plants, shipyards, and so on. Several factory fires in the 1890s proved to be only minor setbacks, though Bowser was forced to reorganize in 1899 due to misuse of company funds by several employees.

The company's prospects improved considerably with the advent of mass production of automobiles in the first decade of the twentieth century. At first, automobiles were handmade in craft shops and could be purchased only by wealthy consumers. These early car owners could afford to have their own personal petroleum tanks and pumps installed in their garages and driveways. By 1915, once cars became affordable to people in the middle and working classes, their new owners looked for ways to fuel their vehicles that didn't require the personal expense of building an at-home fuel pumping system. They wanted to buy their gas from the local grocer or drug store. Bowser invited customers of all kinds to "Bowserize" their garage and works with the "Safe Underground Gasolene Storage System" (Bowserize 1915). The company sold the Bowser system's virtues this way: "It just can't leak. It is evaporation, leak and fire-proof. Every drop is delivered any distance into your car, full of life and power. The particular Bowser System for your Public, Private, Commercial or Works Garage is economically and easily installed. Learn about it" (Bowserize 1915). As the advertisement reveals, Bowser manufactured his pumps in a period of transition, where he sold pumps in a variety of formats to individual automobile owners, commercial retailers, and industrialized workplaces.

Bowser approached his employees in the manner of other late Victorian paternalistic industrialists. In 1908, Bowser created an Employees Relief Union which offered "sick, accident and death benefits for members at a low premium" and provided $10,000 for start-up capital (Pierard 1963). *The Automobile* magazine reported in 1916 that Bowser planned to pay his employees a dividend equal to 6 percent of their wages, an old age pension, and an insurance policy of $1,000 ("6 Per Cent" 1916). The company was then caught up in the international worker's movement in 1919; employees demanded union recognition with the threat of a strike. Bowser refused and locked out the workers. He then reopened with non-union employees and strike breakers, triggering violence that broke out sporadically over the next few months. The company survived but had been badly damaged, both financially and in terms of its standing in the industry. Bowser responded to this unrest by doubling down on paternalism. He created Bowser Loan & Trust Company to encourage thrift and saving among his employees, which included accounts for workers' newborns with $5 provided and promises of future deposits if the workers added to their children's accounts. A 1920 article about the company's newsletter and its inclusion of employee birth announcements noted, "It gives a warm, intimate, personal touch to the publication and also arouses in the minds of the readers the idea that all Bowser employees are members of a big family" (Williams 1920, 364). These benefits were balanced by the expectation that Bowser employees forego alcohol, tobacco, and dancing in clubs, and sit patiently while evangelists such as M.H. Lyon and Billy Sunday preached salvation to them on company time (Pierard 1963).

By the mid-1920s, Bowser's company regained its footing while its oil handling equipment and gasoline pumps with model names like "Red Sentry" and "Chief Sentry" became pervasive. It began to supply pumps for the new purpose-built fueling stations that rapidly blossomed across the country. The company opened offices and manufacturing plants in Toronto, London, Berlin, Paris, and Rotterdam to supply the growing international market. Its revenues reached $12 million per year, which attracted new start-ups like Wayne Oil Tank Company and Tokheim Manufacturing Company. Tokheim moved to Fort Wayne from Cedar Rapids, Iowa with its own patented, gasoline-specific pump, where it eventually came to dominate the marketplace. Together these companies earned Fort Wayne the nickname, "Gas Pump Capital of the World."

Much of the company's success would be achieved after 1922 when Bowser retired as company president. He had developed diabetes and became very ill. He later received sufficient treatment to allow him to travel to Europe, and to engage in fanatical "agitation to reorganize the church" (Pierard 1963). His behavior became so erratic that in 1937 legal proceedings were initiated over concerns of his ability to care for himself. He died in 1938 with just over $11,000 in assets, testifying to his interest in divesting himself of his oil and gas pump company, and to his generosity toward family and religious organizations (Richard 1968, 2). Part of his legacy includes the equipping of early gasoline stations, the first of which opened in 1913 according to the National Association of Convenience Stores, the national trade association for gas stations. The organization notes that at the time there were about half a million gas-powered vehicles in operation, mostly navigating dirt and gravel roads. However, in 2022 there were 270 million cars, trucks, and RVs driving some 3.94 million miles of paved streets, roads, and highways, with "approximately 38 million vehicles fueling up every day" (NACS 2022).

Jeffrey B. Webb

See also: Densmore Oil Tank Car; Interstate Highway System; Mellowes, Alfred W.; Petroleum; Sport Utility Vehicles; Standard Oil Company; Texaco; Tokheim Oil Tank & Pump Company; Whiting Refinery

FURTHER READING

"6 Per Cent Dividend for Bowser Employees." 1916. *The Automobile*. April 3.

American Petroleum Institute (API). 2023. "Service Station FAQs." API Consumer Resources. https://www.api.org/oil-and-natural-gas/consumer-information/consumer-resources/service-station-faqs (accessed October 2023).

Bowser, S.F., and Augustus Bowser. 1887. *Storage and Measuring Tank for Volatile Liquids* (US Patent No. 372,250). US Patent and Trademark Office.

"Bowserize." 1915. *American Exporter: A Monthly Journal of Foreign Trade*. October. P. 119.

Leininger, Kevin. 1981. "Bowser and His Pumps." *Fort Wayne News-Sentinel*. November 7. http://egen.fortwayne.com/ns/projects/history/scapes9.php (accessed October 2023).

National Association of Convenience Stores (NACS). 2022. "A History of Fuel Retailing." February 23. https://www.convenience.org/Topics/Fuels/The-History-of-Fuels-Retailing (accessed October 2023).

Pierard, Richard V. 1963. "Sylvanus Bowser." *Old Fort News*. Vol. 26. No. 4.

Richard, Arthur C. 1968. "Fort Wayne's Twentieth Century Industrialists: A History." Fort Wayne Quest Club. October 25.

Williams. Frank. H. 1920. "Make the Employees Read the Plant Paper by Telling about Their Babies." *American Machinist*. Vol. 53. No. 8. August 19.

Brockovich, Erin

Rising to international fame on the basis of the popular film which bore her name, Erin Brockovich (1960–) was employed as a legal secretary in Northridge, California when she was designated to do research on a pro bono case concerning drinking water contamination. Twice married and twice divorced before her rise to celebrity, Erin Brockovich was born on June 22, 1960 in Lawrence, Kansas as Erin Pattee, to a journalist mother and engineer father. In 1991, she began work at the law firm of Masry & Vititoe. The case that came to Brockovich's attention concerned claims of higher-than-ordinary levels of miscarriage and cancer in and around the town of Hinkley, California. The claimants in the case alleged that the drinking water in Hinkley contained dangerously high levels of chromium 6. Chromium 6, also known as hexavalent chromium, is produced industrially and generally is added to steel to strengthen the resultant alloy, as well as to protect it from corrosion. Contact with chromium 6 is known to be correlated with a number of serious physiological outcomes including cancer, and the respiratory system, skin, kidneys, and liver are especially vulnerable to such adverse effects. The federal guidelines for drinking water require notification for consumers if the level of chromium exceeds 0.1 mg/l or 100 ppb.

During the course of her investigations, Brockovich discovered that between 1952 and 1966, chromium 6 had been used by the Pacific Gas & Electric Company (PG&E) to protect the lining of the Hinkley natural gas pumping station cooling tower against corrosion. The wastewater from that system subsequently was drained into unlined ponds, and the chromium 6 in that wastewater thereby was able to leach into the groundwater, ultimately contaminating the drinking water of the town. Brockovich is reputed to have been remarkably dedicated to her clients and dogged in her pursuit of justice for them. Ultimately, Brockovich was responsible for bringing the total number of claimants to over six hundred. After an initial legal victory, in 1996 the claimants agreed to settle, thus staving off further court action. The settlement offer of $333 million was at that time the single greatest amount garnered in a toxic tort lawsuit. Although a climactic courtroom scene depicting the rendering of an award by a jury might have made for a more dramatic Hollywood ending, the time and money involved might not have served the claimants as well. In the end, the film version of the case certainly provided all the claimants could have desired in terms of public outcry about the matter, and consequently Brockovich clearly won a resounding victory in the court of public opinion over and above the cash settlement.

Brockovich subsequently continued legal work on cases of this sort, and after the Hinkley settlement she participated in a similar action involving the Kettleman Hills Compressor Station, located in Kings County, California, and operating along the same pipeline as the Hinkley pumping station. A decade after the first historic victory catalyzed by Brockovich, the 1,200 claimants in the Kettleman Hills case settled for $335 million. Brockovich also worked on a 2009 case concerning a high incidence of brain cancer in Cameron, Missouri,

FIGURE 5: Erin Brockovich helped win a legal settlement for victims of chromium 6 poisoning caused by energy company PG&E.

which the claimants linked to hexavalent chromium in fertilizer provided by the Prime Tanning Corporation of St. Joseph, Missouri, which produced this material as a by-product of processing leather. Brockovich has her own consulting company and has provided support to legal firms, most notably some pursuing personal injury cases involving contamination of drinking water and exposure to asbestos. Since the popularity of the movie that thrust her into the national limelight, Brockovich also has also proven to be a popular public speaker and a television personality. Moreover, in 2001 she capitalized on her newfound fame to write (with Marc Eliot) *Take It from Me: Life's a Struggle but You Can Win,* a self-help book based upon her own experiences and the challenges she faced. She has also turned her hand to fiction, writing some thrillers. More recently, in 2020 Brockovich returned to her roots in extolling the virtues of the little guy standing up to entrenched interests in order to safeguard drinking water, teaming with Suzanne Boothby to author *Superman's Not Coming: Our National Water Crisis and What We the People Can Do about It.*

The film *Erin Brockovich* (2000) clearly established its title character in the popular imagination as exactly such an advocate of ordinary people endangered and ignored by corporate interests. It starred Julia Roberts in the title role, for which Roberts won an Oscar in 2001 from the Academy of Motion Picture Arts and Sciences. The film also garnered a number of other Oscar nominations, notably for Best Picture and Best Original Screenplay, as well as various other awards and nominations. The film was clearly a crowd-pleaser and a box-office success, and Roberts was roundly praised for her performance. Although the film was based upon actual events and the eponymous heroine impressive in her own right, the true draw of the film was undoubtedly based upon Roberts' extremely sympathetic portrayal of Brockovich herself. Although the film's depiction of a brash, sexy, potty-mouthed David in battle with an immoral and unfeeling corporate Goliath captured the popular imagination, it seems to have engendered little true and abiding public outrage at situations such as those in Hinkley, which continue to be all too common. In the terms of the history of energy in the United States, the end result of the huge settlements spear-headed by Brockovich (suitably put in the terms of a fantastic "Jack the Giant-Slayer" story by the Hollywood spin on the Hinkley case) has been that such cases subsequently may have seemed a bit less quixotic to folks who feel themselves to be down-trodden by huge energy and chemical corporations. Such cases have indeed resulted in a few big wins for the little guy, although the process has proven consistently profitable for the big legal interests involved.

Christopher R. Fee

See also: California Electric Light Company; Clean Water Act; Earth Day; Natural Gas; Natural Resources Defense Council; Sierra Club; US Environmental Protection Agency; Union of Concerned Scientists

FURTHER READING

Bingham, Dennis. 2020. "Erin Brockovich: Hollywood Feminist Revisionism, after a Fashion." In *Whose Lives Are They Anyway? The Biopic as Contemporary Film Genre*. Ed. Dennis Bingham. Pp. 332–47. New Brunswick, NJ: Rutgers University Press.

Brockovich, Erin, and Suzanne Boothby. 2020. *Superman's Not Coming: Our National Water Crisis and What We the People Can Do about It*. New York: Pantheon Books.

Brockovich, Erin, and Marc Eliot. 2001. *Take It from Me: Life's a Struggle but You Can Win*. New York: McGraw Hill.

EPA (US Environmental Protection Agency). 2020. "Chromium in Drinking Water." January 21. https://www.epa.gov/sdwa/chromium-drinking-water (accessed February 22, 2021).

Forbes, J. Benjamin, and Jonathan E. Smith. 2007. "The Potential of Erin Brockovich to Introduce Organizational Behavior Topics." *Organization Management Journal*. Vol. 4. No. 3. Pp. 207–18.

McCann, Michael and William Haltom. 2008. "Ordinary Heroes vs. Failed Lawyers: Public Interest Litigation in 'Erin Brockovich' and Other Contemporary Films." *Law & Social Inquiry*. Vol. 33. No. 4. Pp. 1045–70.

Menéndez-Navarro, Alfredo. 2016. "The Vindication of Non-Expert Knowledge in the Defence of Public Health: Erin Brockovich." *Revista de Medicina y Cine*. Vol. 7. No. 2. Pp. 54–60.

Occupational Safety and Health Administration (OSHA). 2021. "Hexavalent Chromium." US Department of Labor. https://www.osha.gov/hexavalent-chromium (accessed 22 February 2021).

Soderbergh, Steven. 2000. *Erin Brockovich*. Universal Studios.

Brush, Charles Francis

In the second half of the nineteenth century, hundreds of scientists, engineers, mechanics, and tinkerers devoted themselves to extending the frontiers of energy, particularly ways to harness electricity for industrial machines, outdoor lighting, urban streetcars, building elevators, water pumps and more. Charles Brush (1849–1929) joined their number in the 1870s by improving the functionality of the generator—a machine that converts motive power to electrical power—and then improving a system of electrical arc lighting for the city of Cleveland. He formed a company to install this system in other major cities, which enabled them to switch from streetlights fueled by natural gas to lights powered by electricity. In addition to his electrical arc lighting system, Brush also devised a lead-acid battery for the storage of electricity that outperformed existing battery types. Taken together, Brush's research, experimentation, and business operations pointed in the direction of a new energy future for the United States, in large part fueled by electrical power.

Brush prepared himself for a life of work in the applied sciences by reading extensively in the physical sciences and toying with scientific instruments during his boyhood and adult years in his birthplace of Euclid, Ohio. He attended the same high school as John D. Rockefeller, Central High School in Cleveland, where Brush constructed his own arc light with electrical power supplied by a battery. He then studied at the University in Michigan where he graduated in two years with a degree in mining engineering. His interest in arc lighting continued through college and thereafter, though he began his post-graduation career in consulting as a chemist. He drew a considerable income from a venture marketing Lake Superior iron ore, and remained in Cleveland, drawn by the enormous business created by Rockefeller's Standard Oil Company of Ohio and the Cleveland Telegraph and Supply Company (CTSC). The vice president and manager of CTSP, George Stockley, provided funding for Brush to resume his research on arc lighting in hopes of perfecting the dynamo and bringing an improved model to market (Hammond 1941, 8).

Brush presented his improved dynamo to Stockley in 1876—a lighter and more efficient model than what existed on the market—and they successfully tested it with an arc lamp while connected to CTSP's power source. The problem lay with the arc lamps. These lamps worked by establishing an arc of electrical power between two closely spaced carbon rods. The arc threw off intense light and heat but burned quickly and unevenly as the carbon rods were consumed. Brush set out to rethink the design of existing arc lamps and contrived a new and improved version. It featured a double arc to extended life of the element, copper plating of the carbon rods to create a consistent stream of light, and a regulator to maintain current flow from the generator regardless of the number of lights along the circuit (Wise 1999). The development of this system took several years, during which time the directors of CTSC grew concerned about its cost to the company. Brush persisted, encouraged by winning a design competition staged in 1877 by The Franklin Institute in Philadelphia and securing patents for his generator and arc lamps in 1878.

The CTSC signed agreements with Brush to hold the rights to Brush's technology and any financial gains it should make in the marketplace. In 1879, Brush had perfected his system to the point where it was ready for sale, and so he and the company staged a highly publicized nighttime demonstration on Public Square in downtown Cleveland. Brush ran the electrical current from the CTSC building to ensure that spectators got the point: electrical current could now be sent from a centralized source through powerlines to deliver electricity to arc lights, or anything else that could be powered by electricity. The demonstration attracted thousands of onlookers who were treated to music from Gray's Band and an artillery salute. People were amazed. Wabash, Indiana ordered the system of lights to be installed on their courthouse square and in 1880 they were turned on for the first time in front of 10,000 people and representatives from nineteen other cities (Tocco 1999, 352). The Wabash *Plain Dealer* recorded the moment this way:

> People stood overwhelmed with awe, as if in the presence of the supernatural. The strange, weird light, exceeded in power only by the sun, rendered the square as light as midday. Men fell on their knees, groans were uttered at the sight and many were dumb with amazement. We contemplated the new wonder in science as lightning brought down from the heavens. (Hammond 1941, 32)

Newspaper headlines read, "'Wabash Enjoys the Distinction of Being the Only City in the World Entirely Lighted by Electricity'" (Tocco 1999, 352).

Americans witnessed for the first time a demonstration of electricity's awesome power and its potential to transform American life on a mass scale. Brush followed up with a demonstration in New York City by illuminating Broadway Avenue at night. In 1880 the CTSC reincorporated as the Brush Electric Company and installed street lighting systems in Boston, Philadelphia, Montreal, San Francisco, Buffalo, and many other cities. Brush earned royalties from the sale of these systems and his shares of stock, and soon became very wealthy. In 1884, he and his wife and three children moved into a house on Cleveland's "Millionaire's Row" on Euclid Avenue. Eventually the competition for street lighting systems caught up with Brush Electric and in 1889 in the context of patent infringement accusations, the Thomson-Houston Electric Company bought out Brush and the other company investors. He sold his stake for $75 per share valued at $3 million (Hammond 1941, 163). Within a few years, Thomas A. Edison's incandescent bulb replaced the soon-to-be obsolete system of arc lighting, and in 1892 the Thomson-Houston Electric Company became part of Edison's General Electric.

For the remainder of his life Brush continued to pursue scientific research. He built a very large, 60-foot windmill for his Euclid residence, which supplied motive energy for his generators and kept his electric light experiments running. In 1898 he claimed to discover a new gas that he called "etherion" which weighed less than other gases and moved more quickly, but his claims were discredited by subsequent scientific research. He also developed a new "kinetic" theory of gravity, but again the scientific community investigated his work and rejected it straight away. In the early twentieth century, Brush enjoyed recognition as one of the key pioneers of electricity and electrical power. Earlier, he had been awarded the French Legion of Honor (1881) and the Rumford Medal of the American Academy of Arts and Sciences (1889) for his discoveries in electricity. He received an honorary degree from The University of Michigan in 1912 and the Edison Medal of the American Institute of Electrical Engineers in 1913. The year before his death in 1929, he was given another honorary degree by The Case School of Applied Science to go with one he obtained from Western Reserve University years earlier, and he received the Franklin Medal from the Franklin Institute in Philadelphia.

Charles Brush achieved a degree of fame within in his own lifetime as an inventor, engineer, and systems designer. His electric lighting and battery storage innovations appeared within a broader context of electricity research and development that included figures like George Westinghouse, Nikola Tesla, and Thomas Edison. Together they fashioned the basic concepts and technologies that brought electricity to American homes, apartment buildings, businesses, factories, and farms into the early twentieth century. This paved the way for such staples of the modern lifestyle as indoor incandescent lighting, electrical appliances, and efficient refrigeration and air-conditioning, not to mention the fundamental transformations in business and industry facilitated by electrical power and the digital revolution of the post-war era.

Jeffrey B. Webb

See also: California Electric Light Company; Consolidated Edison Company; Edison, Thomas Alva; Electricity; Franklin, Benjamin; General Electric Company; Henry, Joseph; Insull, Samuel; Pearl Street Power Station; Tesla, Nikola; War of the Currents

FURTHER READING

Hammond, John Winthrop. 1941. *Men and Volts: The Story of General Electric*. Philadelphia: J. B. Lippencott Company.

Klein, Maury. 2010. *The Power Makers: Steam, Electricity, and the Men Who Invented Modern America*. New York: Bloomsbury Press.

Tocco, Peter. 1999. "The Night They Turned the Lights on in Wabash." *Indiana Magazine of History*. December. Vol. 95. No. 4. Pp. 350–63.

Wise, George. 1999. "Brush, Charles Francis." *American National Biography*. Oxford: Oxford University Press. https://www.anb.org/view/10.1093/anb/9780198606697.001.0001/anb-9780198606697-e-1300214 (accessed January 16, 2023).

Buffalo Chips

The Great Plains region is located between the Mississippi River and the Rocky Mountains. This area is a flat region mainly covered by prairies and grasslands. The majority of plant life in this region is grasses, with few trees. For settlers of the Great Plains, few trees and limited infrastructure for the shipping of wood products meant that the uses of available wood had to be prioritized. This often meant that wood was used for construction and structural purposes, not as the fuel source for fires used for cooking and heating. Other fuel sources used in the eastern United States, such as coal, were also limited in availability. A common fuel for fires used by both indigenous peoples of the Great Plains and settlers to the region was buffalo chips, a type of biofuel. Buffalo chips are the dried manure of American Bison.

The American Bison (*Bison bison*) is a large herbivorous animal that once freely roamed the Great Plains region of the United States. They are often referred to as American buffalo, as the original term used by European settlers to refer to these animals was buffalo. These animals are ruminants, meaning they have a stomach which is divided into four compartments: the rumen, reticulum, omasum, and abomasum. Each compartment has a distinct purpose of helping break down the fiber present in the plant matter, such as forages, that these animals consume. While mammals, including the bison, do not have the ability to produce the enzymes needed to break down the fibrous complex carbohydrates such as cellulose into smaller units to be absorbed by the gastrointestinal tract, the microorganisms that live in the rumen can. These ruminal microorganisms are a diverse population of bacteria, fungi, and protozoa that are able to secrete the enzymes needed to break down cellulose, a primary component of the fiber that gives plants structure, into smaller units the animal can absorb and use as energy. In addition to breaking down cellulose, the bacteria are able to provide protein to the host animal to use for maintenance of body tissues, growth, and reproduction by a portion of the ruminal bacteria passing to the abomasum, or the true stomach of the ruminant animal.

The ability of these bacteria to break down the plant matter is dependent on the nitrogen content of the plant matter the animal consumes. While bison are assumed to be more efficient at digesting low-quality forages than cattle, the microorganisms in the rumen of cattle require plant material to be 6 percent nitrogen to support microbial growth. Due to the growing season of the grasses commonly found on the Great Plains, the crude protein content—as determined by the nitrogen content—of the forages decreases as non-soluble fiber content increases during dormant periods such as winter. These forages which are lower in nitrogen content are less efficiently digested by the ruminal microorganisms, meaning fewer amounts of energy and protein are made available for the animal to absorb to use for normal homeostasis and possible growth or reproduction. This results in a greater amount of plant material present in the manure of the animal.

When dried, the plant material preset in the manure can be combusted for fuel. These dried piles of manure, buffalo chips, can provide a relative heating value of 0.46, compared to an overage of 0.93 of common woods used as fuel for fires (Holland 1984). Moisture content has a significant effect on the ability of buffalo chips to serve as a fuel source, meaning those who wished to use them needed to be able to access dried chips. During winter storms or rainy periods, finding dry buffalo chips could have been difficult. This often meant that people using this fuel source for heating and cooking fires needed to either be able to easily find suitably dry buffalo chips or have the ability to store the fuel in an area protected from the elements.

Just as different woods can give different flavors to foods cooked over fires, using buffalo chips as a fuel source for cooking gave a distinct flavor to foods. A common tale that has been passed down was that pepper was not needed to flavor meals cooked over buffalo chips. There was also an aversion to collecting the manure of the bison to bring into homes as a fuel source, but it was necessary due to limited wood availability while traveling and in settler's homes. Accounts also state how fewer sparks were produced by buffalo chip fires, which was advantageous if fires were built in tents or other enclosures made of flammable materials.

Unfortunately, the once abundant bison populations began to decline in the nineteenth century. In this era, interest in bison hides significantly increased, more people moved west of the Mississippi River, and the construction of railroads all contributed to declining bison populations. Interest in bison hides for the fur and leather trade increased incentives to harvest the animals for more than the meat. As more people moved west, more cattle and horses also accompanied them as sources of food and draft power. This introduced competition for the natural forages present on the Great Plains. Settlers began to construct fences to contain their herds of cattle and horses, which decreased the amount of land available for the roaming bison herds. By the end of the nineteenth century, American bison herds were decimated, almost to the point of extinction.

With the decline of bison came the decline of buffalo chips. However, increased infrastructure meant that other sources of fuel for fires became more readily available, such as coal. Settlers also looked to dried manure from cows as a fuel source similar to that of buffalo chips. There were differences between these two types of manure. Buffalo chips came from wild ruminants who ate naturally occurring forages, while cattle could be kept in confinement and fed specific feeds that supplied necessary nutrients to the animals, thereby increasing the manure's ability to burn for longer periods. By the twentieth century, other forms of energy became more widespread throughout the United States, providing the western region with electricity through petroleum, natural gas, and a variety of renewable sources.

Jessica O. Baggerman

See also: Agriculture and Energy; Biofuels; Coal; Electricity; Natural Gas; Petroleum; Rural Electrification Act of 1936

FURTHER READING

Holland, Thomas D. 1984. "A Pilot Study in the Thermal Properties of Buffalo Chips." *Plains Anthropologist*. Vol. 29. No. 4. Pp. 161–5.

Lott, Dale F., and Harry W. Greene. 2002. *American Bison: A Natural History*. Berkeley, CA: University of California Press.

Zontek, Ken. 2007. *Buffalo Nation: American Indian Efforts to Restore the Bison*. Lincoln, NE: University of Nebraska Press.

Bush, George H.W.

George H.W. Bush (1924–2018), often shortened to George Bush, was a politician and businessman who served as President of the United States from 1989 to 1993. Prior to becoming president, Bush served as vice president under President Ronald Reagan, director of the Central Intelligence Agency (CIA), chief of the liaison office to the People's Republic of China, chair of the Republican National Committee, US ambassador to the United Nations, and representative from Texas in the US House of Representatives. Prior to his political career, Bush made his fortune in the petroleum industry in Texas.

After serving as a naval aviator during the Second World War and graduating from Yale University, Bush moved his family to Texas, one of several young, well-connected entrepreneurs looking to make a fortune in the rapidly expanding oil fields of West Texas. Thanks to family connections, particularly his uncle, Wall Street financier Herbert Walker and family friend Neil Mallon, president and general director of Dresser Industries, Bush began his career working for International Derrick & Equipment Company (Ideco), a Dresser subsidiary that provided equipment to oil drillers. From 1948 to 1950, Bush worked at Ideco locations in Odessa and Midland, Texas and Bakersfield, California, moving up the ladder from general clerk to salesman. Bush returned to Midland in 1950, and with the financial support of Walker and encouragement of Mallon formed the Bush-Overby Oil Development Company with partner John Overby. Overby was an experienced locator and developer of oil production sites; his skills combined with Bush's access to capital and salesmanship produced a profitable three-year long partnership.

In March 1953, Bush and Overby co-founded a new oil company with the assistance of prominent Texas corporate attorneys J. Hugh Liedtke and William Liedtke. This new company, the Zapata Petroleum Corporation, took Bush from providing leases to other oil companies into the drilling of oil in the Permian Basin in West Texas. Hugh Liedtke became president of the new venture, with Bush serving as vice president. Over the course of the next two years, Zapata Petroleum built seventy-seven oil wells, later expanded to 130. This initial success paved the way to expanded operations, and Bush became independently wealthy.

In 1954, Bush became president of the Zapata Offshore Company, a subsidiary of Zapata Petroleum specializing in offshore drilling of wells on a contract basis for other oil distributors. The company constructed oil wells initially in the Gulf of Mexico, eventually expanding into global operations under the aegis of a new subsidiary, Seacat Zapata, which was officially registered as a British corporation. As Zapata Offshore expanded, growing tensions between Liedtke and Walker led to a split. Liedtke maintained control over the original Zapata Petroleum Corporation, while Bush and Walker spun off Zapata Offshore into an independent company in 1959. In the process of negotiating this split, Bush began a friendship with James Baker, an attorney at Baker & Botts, the law firm that negotiated the separation. While Zapata Offshore developed into a $4.5 million-a-year corporation for Bush and his partners, Zapata Petroleum merged with the Penn Oil Company in 1963, forming the massive Pennzoil Corporation.

At the same time that he took over as president of Zapata Offshore, Bush and his family moved the corporation headquarters and themselves to Houston. From there, Bush began serving on the boards of directors of other companies in the petroleum industry, as well as major industry organizations. The move to Houston led to the start of Bush's political career, where he initially became chair of the Harris County Republicans, followed by an unsuccessful campaign for the US Senate against Democratic incumbent Ralph Yarborough. Two years later, in anticipation of a run for a House seat, Bush resigned as president and chief executive officer of Zapata Offshore, and sold all of his stock in the corporation for $1.1 million. Bush was elected to the House in 1966 and served two terms representing northwest Houston. In 1970, Bush again failed to be elected to the Senate, losing to Lloyd Bentsen, who had defeated Yarborough in the Democratic primary.

After serving in a variety of roles during the presidencies of Richard Nixon and Gerald Ford, Bush ran for the Republican presidential nomination in 1980. Despite strongly criticizing the winner of that contest, Ronald Reagan, terming Reagan's economic plans as "voodoo economics," Reagan selected Bush as his running mate. Bush served as vice president for both of Reagan's terms, and with Reagan's endorsement won the Republican nomination in 1988. Bush defeated the Democratic nominee, Massachusetts Governor Michael Dukakis in a bitter, hard fought campaign.

Through his one term in the White House, Bush supported two key pieces of environmental legislation that alienated some business supporters, especially in the petroleum industry. The first consisted of a series of amendments to the Clean Air Act. Passed in 1990 with the support of the Democratically controlled Congress, the amendments significantly increased federal authority, especially in the prevention of acid rain. The act sought to decrease sulfur dioxide emissions, begin reversing the depletion of the ozone layer, reduce pollution, and increase enforcement. The act also required the sale of cleaner gasoline during the summer months to reduce pollution. The second piece of legislation was the Oil Pollution Act of 1990. Passed in the aftermath of the *Exxon Valdez* oil spill, the Act required responsible companies to reimburse federal, state, and tribal governments for the costs of oil spills, holding the companies fully liable for all costs. It also empowered the Coast Guard to enforce stricter regulations regarding oil transports and created new regulations regarding the construction of oil pipelines and offshore drilling sites. Finally, the act provided funding for the cleanup of Prince William Sound, the site of the *Exxon Valdez* spill.

In the final chapter of Bush's career of involvement with energy development and the global supply of petroleum, he created and led a UN-backed multinational coalition to expel Iraq from Kuwait after Iraq invaded in August 1990. Iraqi dictator Saddam Hussein, in deep debt after the inconclusive but bloody and expensive Iran–Iraq War (1980–8), sought to expand his oil production by seizing neighboring Kuwait and its abundant oil fields, gaining control over 20 percent of the world's oil production. Bush successfully utilized the UN to reverse this aggression, first imposing massive economic sanctions while assembling a coalition force from thirty-five nations with financial backing from Japan and based in Saudi Arabia. Beginning January 16, 1991, coalition forces bombed targets in Kuwait and Iraq. The ground invasion of Kuwait began February 23, with all Iraqi forces evicted by February 27. As allied forces moved into Iraq, the Iraqi government sought a ceasefire, which was granted on March 3. Although militarily successful, the war briefly disrupted global oil supplies, and the fires lit in Kuwaiti oil fields by the retreating Iraqis did significant environmental damage. The ensuing recession contributed to Bush's defeat by Bill Clinton in his 1992 bid for reelection.

Richard M. Filipink

See also: Acid Rain; Cheney, Richard Bruce "Dick"; Clean Air Act of 1970; *Exxon Valdez* Oil Spill; Gulf War; Halliburton Company; Iraq War and the Project for a New American Century; Petroleum; Texas Oil Boom

FURTHER READING

Allison, William Thomas. 2012. *The Gulf War, 1990–91*. New York: Palgrave MacMillan
Hahn, Peter L. 2012. *Missions Accomplished? The United States and Iraq since World War I*. New York: Oxford University Press.
Meacham, Jon. 2015. *Destiny and Power: The American Odyssey of George Herbert Walker Bush*. New York: Random House.
Naftali, Timothy. 2007. *George H.W. Bush*. New York: Times Books.
Parmet, Herbert S. 1997. *George Bush: The Life of a Lone Star Yankee*. New York: Scribner.

Caddo Oil Field

The Caddo Oil Field in Louisiana was the site of the world's first "over-water" oil well. Located near the northwestern corner of Louisiana outside of Shreveport, the revolutionary over-water well was drilled in May 1911 on top of Caddo Lake. The Caddo Oil Field's immediate benefits were the economic booms of nearby towns, as well the rapid growth of Louisiana as an oil-producing state. Longer-term, the Caddo demonstrated that drilling for oil above water was not just possible but also profitable. Today, the Caddo Oil Field is rightly remembered as the genesis for modern offshoring, as thousands of deep oil or gas wells dot the earth's oceans.

The Caddo Oil Field is situated within the broader Mid-Continent oil province. The Mid-Continent, stretching from Kansas to the Gulf of Mexico, once held the greatest amount of known oil reserves in the world. The Caddo was well-positioned for success, as the southern end of the Mid-Continent was a very productive source of oil throughout the twentieth century. Oil was first discovered in the Mid-Continent region in 1901, via the Spindletop gusher in Beaumont, Texas. This site, just 30 miles from the Texas–Louisiana border, led to urgent oil exploration in Louisiana. By August 1901, an oil field near Jennings became Louisiana's first commercial oil field, and this was followed by a 1902 discovery outside of the city of Lafayette (Cummins 2014, 317).

Due to the success of these sites in southwestern Louisiana, enterprising companies began the search for oil in the northwestern part of the state. Exploration near Caddo Lake began in 1904, and oil deposits were discovered there in 1905 (Wells 2005). By 1910, northwestern Louisiana wells were outproducing wells from southwestern Louisiana. During this time, some companies began to focus on Caddo Lake as a possible drilling site. Caddo Lake, named for the nearby Caddo Indian group, is roughly bisected by the Louisiana–Texas border. The lake itself is filled with swamps and bayous, and empties into Twelve Mile Bayou, which joins the Red River near Shreveport. In 1909, Gulf Oil Corporation won a lease from the Federal Government to drill for oil over 8,000 acres of lake bottom in the region. The lease was obtained in dramatic fashion, with approval from the Pittsburgh-based Gulf given just ninety seconds before the auction began.

In May 1911, the "Ferry No. 1" well was officially established on Caddo Lake, becoming the first over-water oil well in history. The well reached a bottomed depth of 2,185 feet and produced roughly 450 barrels per day. The drilling occurred on rigs constructed on barges floating on the lake, and additional drilling sites on Caddo Lake were soon built. Some earlier attempts at offshoring had occurred in California. However, these were land-based wells that slanted into the ocean while still physically connected to the shore, and were not true "over-water" wells (Bowman 2006).

NAMING SHREVEPORT

One theory for Caddo Lake's formation notes a giant Red River logjam as the primary culprit. Water pooled behind the natural dam known as the "Great Raft" of the Red River. Clearing this logjam spanned multiple decades throughout the nineteenth century. Henry Shreve, one of the leaders of the clearing, was honored via the naming of a nearby town: Shreveport.

Patrick D. Hagge

The Caddo Oil Field's success led to a boom of oil exploration in the northwest Louisiana region. The few Louisiana parishes near Caddo Lake accounted for 8 percent of the entire US oil production by 1922 (Cummins 2014). The same year, Louisiana ranked fourth among all oil-producing states in the country. While nearby oil extraction aided the growth of the long-established city of Shreveport, small towns closer to Caddo Lake experienced rapid prosperity, converting swampy areas into "tent cities" to house thousands of new workers. Gulf Refining Company established various businesses in the nearby town of Mooringsport, and the large influx of laborers to cities such as Vivian and Oil City led to the establishment of downtown saloons and city-wide baseball teams. These towns did not exist without conflict, as striking oil field workers led to US military occupation of oil fields during parts of 1917 and 1918.

Oil production changed the environmental landscape of Caddo Lake. In 1914, a dam was built across the Big Cypress Bayou. The dam created a larger Caddo Lake than had previously existed, thereby allowing barges better access to the growing number of over-water oil wells (Tompkins 2009). The mere existence of the pre-oil field Caddo Lake as a large, naturally occurring, non-oxbow lake is rare for the region. Several different theories exist with respect to the lake's formation. Local native Caddo groups claimed the New Madrid Earthquakes of 1811–12 created much of the lake, while others suggest a Red River logjam was the primary cause. Even today, the western portion of Caddo Lake is sometimes incorrectly advertised as "the only natural lake in Texas," even though other natural Texas lakes exist, and the Caddo shoreline has been redrawn through human interventions such as the initial 1914 dam (Tompkins 2009).

Drilling over Caddo Lake, which extended into both Texas and Louisiana, also raised legal questions of land ownership. Some of the so-called "Ferry Lakes Cases" went to the Supreme Court for final decisions. The legacy over-water wells led to additional political issues, as President Harry Truman argued that Louisiana and other Gulf States had no jurisdiction for any true "offshore" wells in 1945 (Austin 2004, 32).

The Caddo Lake area was not the only region of on-water oil development. Similar approaches to the "Ferry No. 1" well were quickly copied from Venezuelan lakes to the Caspian Sea. Due to the success of the Caddo Oil Field, investment in on-water drilling continued, even as the area of production shifted elsewhere. In 1947, the first "out-of-sight-of-land" oil well was finished off the coast of southern Louisiana, near Morgan City (Austin 2004, 1). At the same time, Caddo Oil Field's influence began to decline, as offshoring developed improved techniques resulting in deepwater drilling. During the Second World War, the Longhorn Army Ammunition Plant opened in Texas, just to the west of Caddo

Lake. In recent years, the area was designated a Superfund site, and much of the Texas land is currently part of a National Wildlife Refuge.

Regardless of its natural history and its modest technologies, the Caddo Lake Oil Field and its over-water drilling continue to hold an important place in global economic history. The modern offshore oil and gas industry owes an enormous debt to the development and success of the initial 1911 over-water oil well on Caddo Lake.

Patrick D. Hagge

See also: *Deepwater Horizon*; Gulf Oil Company; Kerr-McGee's Kermac No. 16; Santa Barbara Oil Spill; Spindletop Oil Gusher; Summerland Oil Field

FURTHER READING

Austin, Diane, Bob Carriker, Tom McGuire, Joseph Pratt, Tyler Priest, and Allan G. Pulsipher. 2004. *History of the Offshore Oil and Gas Industry in Southern Louisiana*. Washington, DC: US Department of the Interior.

Bowman, Bob. 2006. "The First 'Over Water' Oil Well." *Texas Escapes Online Magazine*. October 30. www.texasescapes.com/AllThingsHistorical/First-Over-Water-Oil-Well-BB1006.htm (accessed June 10, 2020).

Cummins, Light Townsend, Judith Kelleher Schafer, Edward F. Haas, and Michael L. Kurtz. 2014. *Louisiana: A History*. Chichester, UK: Wiley-Blackwell.

The Historic Caddo Lake Drawbridge Perpetuation Committee. 2014. "Offshore Oil Drilling on Caddo Lake." http://www.caddolakedrawbridge.com (accessed May 31, 2020).

Tompkins, Shannon. 2009. "Caddo Lake's History is the Stuff of Legend." *Houston Chronicle*. December 12. https://www.chron.com/sports/article/Tompkins-Caddo-Lake-s-history-is-the-stuff-of-1739324.php (accessed June 7, 2020).

US Fish & Wildlife Service. 2020. "Caddo Lake National Wildlife Refuge." Washington, DC: US Department of the Interior. https://www.fws.gov/refuge/Caddo_Lake/ (accessed June 8, 2020).

Wells, B.A., and K.L. Wells. 2005. "Louisiana Oil City Museum." American Oil & Gas Historical Society. https://aoghs.org/energy-education-resources/louisiana-oil-and-gas-museum/ (accessed May 31, 2020).

CAFE Standards

In 1973, Arab member states of the Organization of Petroleum Exporting Countries imposed an oil embargo against the United States in retaliation for aid given to Israel by the Nixon administration during the conflict known as the Yom Kippur War. The effects of the oil embargo reverberated through the US economy as the global price of oil increased nearly fourfold. Although the embargo ended within five months, the economic repercussions were long-lasting, and concerns arose about domestic oil production, Middle East foreign policy, US federal monetary policy, and energy independence. One of the most important results of these concerns was the establishment of federal fuel efficiency standards under the Energy Policy and Conservation Act of 1975.

The act created Corporate Average Fuel Economy (CAFE) standards, which require automakers to meet a minimum average fuel economy level, expressed in miles per gallon, for their entire fleet. CAFE standards are set and enforced by the National Highway Transportation and Safety Administration (NHTSA). The Environmental Protection Agency (EPA) establishes related greenhouse gas (GHG) emissions standards for automobiles under the authority conferred to the agency by Clean Air Act.

Initial fuel efficiency requirements took effect in 1978 and required cars to increase efficiency from 18 miles per gallon (mpg) to 27.5 mpg by 1985. Light trucks were placed in a separate category based on assumptions of their primary use being for agriculture and business. Light truck standards began in 1980 at 16 mpg and increased to 22.5 mpg by 2008. Fuel efficiency standards were not amended again until 2007 with the Energy Independence and Security Act (EISA) which affected model years 2017 and beyond. By 2025, manufacturers are required to meet a fleet average of 54.5 mpg. This includes optional equivalency improvements to air-conditioning systems to reduce GHG emissions. Actual miles per gallon is expected to settle at 49.6 mpg.

Prior to the establishment of CAFE standards, gasoline usage and miles traveled grew at the same rate. After implementation, those rates diverged. Fuel consumption fell even while miles traveled rose. Increased fuel economy resulted in an overall reduction in gas used by drivers. Based on this divergence, public policy analysts have estimated that over a forty-year span from 1975 to 2015, CAFE standards have reduced US gasoline consumption by 1.5 trillion gallons (Greene 2017, 3). A reduction in gas consumption means reduction in the amount of gas purchased by consumers. Analysis of consumer benefits of increased fuel economy show significant, long-term savings for consumers despite modest increases in new vehicle costs due to fuel economy compliance.

While consumers benefit from CAFE, manufacturers bear the initial costs. Originally, auto manufacturers relied primarily on weight reduction, engine downsizing, and improved aerodynamic design to reduce vehicle fuel consumption. Today, carmakers use an array of technological innovations to meet fuel efficiency and associated GHG emissions standards.

Despite the many changes large auto manufacturers have made to comply with increased GHG standards through the 2017 model year, they have long resisted CAFE standards (EIA, 75–118). Car manufacturers have leveraged their economic power as job providers and raised threats about global competitiveness to oppose more stringent fuel economy and GHG emission standards. However, US efficiency standards are some of the lowest among developed nations. Automakers in the United States also rank at the bottom for fuel efficiency and emissions in comparison with their global competitors. Auto manufacturing groups elsewhere have been able to meet more stringent efficiency standards and also rank at the top in auto production.

In the same way they prompted the adoption of federal fuel efficiency standards, fluctuations in oil and gas prices have played a role in maintaining the political will to increase efficiency standards. The United States is the largest consumer of petroleum, consuming just over one-fifth of the global petroleum supply. At 69 percent, transportation, by far, accounts for the largest segment of that total. Gasoline alone accounts for 45 percent of total US petroleum consumption. Unsurprisingly, the transportation sector generates the largest share of GHG emissions in the United States at 29 percent. Globally, 15 percent of CO_2 emissions come from US sources.

Greenhouse gases, particularly CO_2, are of great concern due to their heat retention properties which contribute to the greenhouse effect and resultant global warming. Global scientific consensus affirms the need to drastically reduce CO_2 and other GHG emissions in order to keep the rise in planetary warming under 2 degrees Celsius and avoid the most catastrophic consequences of climate change. Burning one gallon of fuel results in approximately 20 lbs. of tailpipe CO_2. Given the correlation between the burning of fossil fuels such as gasoline and GHG emissions, increased fuel economy standards have shown an ability to substantially reduce GHG emissions.

Whether due to concerns about effectiveness or ideological objections to government regulation, opponents of CAFE standards have argued for deregulation. They assert that compliance with government regulations, including environmental regulations, place an undue burden on businesses, particularly small businesses. Some also argue that both consumers and manufacturers will find ways around them. One example is the so-called SUV loophole wherein minivans and SUVs were classified as light trucks and therefore skirted more rigorous fuel economy requirements for passenger cars. The EISA closed the SUV exemption and raised SUV fuel economy standards to 35 mpg by 2020.

However, in light of global warming and the associated costs of adaptation, mitigation, and climate-related disaster relief, a comparison of cost burdens should be examined. Put simply, high GHG emissions from vehicles create environmental damage, and the financial outlays required to address these issues are not priced into the vehicles' cost of production. Consideration should be given to the negative market externalities associated with GHG emissions, and whether polluters should be allowed to profit without having to bear the costs of the environmental degradation associated with their products.

The 1973 OPEC oil embargo raised concerns about dependence upon foreign oil and the nation's domestic oil production capabilities. This fueled notions of establishing energy independence. US crude oil production is currently at its highest levels since the 1970s. In 2018, imports accounted for 11 percent of total US petroleum consumption. However, US imports from Arab oil producers never exceeded 15 percent of domestic consumption, even during the crisis point (Luft 2013). Oil prices are affected by forces that operate on a global level. Thus, even with increased domestic production, the prices Americans pay for fuel will still be subject to shifts in the global market. Truer energy independence will depend on the development of renewable alternative energies and a reduction in consumption of fossil fuels. All told, regulations such as CAFE standards have shown to be effective in reducing consumption, insulating consumers from price fluctuations, saving consumers money, and reducing harmful GHG emissions.

Kathryn Lisinicchia

See also: Climate Change; Energy Crisis of the 1970s; Energy Independence; Energy Policy and Conservation Act of 1975; Sport Utility Vehicles; Truck Transportation Technology; US Environmental Protection Agency

FURTHER READING

Bento, Antonio M. 2019. "Statement of Antonio M. Bento, Professor of Public Policy and Economics, Sol Price School of Public Policy and Department of Economics, University of South Carolina." US House Committee on Oversight and Reform, Subcommittee on Environment. 116th Congress. Serial No. 116–69. October 29.

Consumer Reports. 2013. "A Review of Consumer Benefits from Corporate Average Fuel Economy (CAFE) Standards." Consumer Reports, Inc. June 13.

Corbett, Michael. 2013. "Oil Shock of 1973–74." *Federal Reserve History*. Federal Reserve System. November 22.

Greene, David L. 2017. "A Trillion Gallons of Gasoline." August. On-Point 5:17. Howard L. Baker Jr. Center for Public Policy. Knoxville: The University of Tennessee.

Hathaway, Terry. 2018. "Corporate Power beyond the Political Arena: The Case of the 'Big Three' and CAFE Standards." *Business & Politics*. Vol. 20. No. 1. March. Pp. 1–37.

Luft, Gal and Anne Korin. 2013. "The Myth of U.S. Energy Dependence." *Foreign Affairs*. Council on Foreign Relations. October 15.

Myre, Greg. 2013. "The 1973 Arab Oil Embargo: The Old Rules No Longer Apply." *NPR* National Public Radio. October 16.

Siegel, Ethan. 2017. "Repealing Fuel Economy Standards to Cost American Households Nearly $1000 per Year." *Forbes*. Forbes Media, LLC. December 7.

Soren T. Anderson, et al. 2011. "Automobile Fuel Economy Standards: Impacts, Efficiency, and Alternatives." *Review of Environmental Economics and Policy*. Vol. 5. No. 1. Winter. Pp. 89–108.

US Energy Information Administration (EIA). 2019. "The 2018 Automotive Trends Report: Greenhouse Gas Emissions, Fuel Economy and Technology since 1975." U.S. Department of Energy. March 3.

Zeller Jr., Tom. 2015. "You're Really Paying more than $6 Per Gallon for That Gas." *Forbes*. Forbes Media, LLC. March 5.

California Electric Light Company

The California Electric Light Company built the first central electricity-generating station in the United States. The company was founded in 1879 by a group of businessmen in San Francisco who sought to capitalize on the new demand for electric lighting among the city's factory owners, hotel operators, and other institutional consumers. It helped to inaugurate a national trend of generating and distributing electricity from a centralized source to a network of end-users. It also demonstrated that energy production could be a profitable undertaking for entrepreneurs and investors, which shaped the early history of public utilities. Within a generation, companies like California Electric Light appeared throughout the United States and made the home consumption of electricity by ordinary Americans a relatively common experience.

In the early 1800s, most home and business interiors were illuminated by candlelight or oil-burning lamps. By mid-century, a number of cities and towns had adopted gas lighting for city streets. To fuel these streetlights, city officials built municipal gasworks, which fed the system with a flammable gas produced by coal gasification, distributed via a system of subterranean pipes. In many places, individual homeowners could pay to have the so-called "town gas" piped into their homes. This enabled millions of Americans to experience a relatively labor-free and consistently superior form of interior lighting. Historians argue these improvements dramatically increased rates of literacy among middle-class Americans. Nevertheless, gas lighting was prone to leakage, low pressure, fires, and explosions, most famously at the US Capitol Building in Washington, DC in 1898, causing extensive damage to the old north wing.

The search for a better alternative to gaslights in the streets and "town gas" in the home led to electric lamps, which had improved through the century in conjunction with innovations in electricity generation and transmission, particularly dynamos and generators. By the 1870s, inventors like Charles Brush had developed commercially viable carbon arc lamps. These devices gave off a bright, intense light from the arc of electricity that formed in the gap between two closely spaced carbon rods. When attached to a supply of electrical current, carbon arc lamps could provide consistent illumination with only periodic replacement of the burned-up carbon electrodes. The Brush arc lamp and its related technology were an important step in the direction of an integrated system that linked a centralized electricity generation to a transmission grid that extended to individual electricity consumers.

California Electric Light Company and its counterparts in other cities were important linchpins in this system. Led by George H. Roe (1852–94), the company served as the Pacific coast agent for the Brush electric arc light. Roe was a Canadian by birth who tried his hand at business in Chicago before finally arriving in San Francisco in 1875. He started a brokerage firm with W.P. Plummer, and then in 1878 an agent for Brush contacted them to help with start-up costs to begin operations on the west coast. The brokerage business collapsed and when Roe and Plummer broke up, Roe received the Brush agent's machinery. It was then that Roe formed the company and turned to the "strange science then unfolding its wonders to the world" ("George" 1894, 12). Roe hired some electricians and mechanics to improve the machinery, and they built an entirely new dynamo with a polished iron band surrounding the armature, which ultimately caused it to malfunction. Soon, however, Roe and his partners in the California Electric Light Company got the plant up and running and began selling arc lights and electricity to San Francisco consumers.

In 1879 the company built a small building behind the old Flood building on Market Street for the purpose of generating electricity for the arc lights connected to the grid. The works were housed in a wood-floored building covered in sheet iron and included the "boiler, engine, dynamos, oil-house, coal pile" and other implements. The hastily built plant was clearly a fire hazard, and it was destroyed in a blaze on April 24, 1880. The company quickly rebuilt on O'Farrell Street, but rapid expansion necessitated relocation to a larger facility on Jesse Street, then again to another, even larger building on Townshend Street. By 1890, the Townshend Street plant supplied electricity to 2,000 arc lights in San Francisco. The California Electric Light Company expanded its operations throughout the region, and within a decade of incorporation had built working plants in seventeen different cities and towns ("The Electric Light" 1890, 73). When Roe died unexpectedly in 1894, his obituary estimated his net worth at $1 million.

California Electric Light Company built the first central electricity generation station in the United States, but it was only one of a number of similar companies in other cities who were seeking to capitalize on the new technologies of electricity generation and transmission. Thomas Edison's Edison Illuminating Company built the Pearl Street Power Station in New York City in 1882 to supply electricity for 400 lamps distributed among eighty-two customers. Over the next three years, Edison Illuminating built similar grids for Shamokin, Pennsylvania (1882), Sunbury, Pennsylvania (1883), Brockton, Massachusetts (1883), Mount Carmel, Pennsylvania (1883), and Tamaqua, Pennsylvania (1885). An article in the *Western Electrician* in 1890 mentions companies like Angola Schuyler Electric Light Company (Angola, Indiana), Thompson-Houston Electric Company (Mt. Sterling, Kentucky), Burlington Electric Light & Power Company (Burlington, Iowa), New Cumberland Electric Light, Heat, and Power Company (New Cumberland, West Virginia), and the Norwalk & South Norwalk Electric Light Company (Norwalk, Connecticut) all seeking to follow California Electric Light Company's lead in electrifying their cities ("The Electric Light" 1890, 72).

The power-generation industry was subject to the same economic forces as other industries during the Industrial Revolution, especially the economies of scale to be gained from consolidation among the various competing corporations. In 1890, the California Electric Light Company merged with the Edison General Electric Company and became the Edison Light and Power Company. Two years later, Edison Light and Power merged with San Francisco Gas Light Company and assumed the new name San Francisco Gas and Electric Company. Once hydroelectric power took root along the Sierra Nevada range to supply electricity to Sacramento and other central valley cities, numerous companies began to proliferate, which then merged together to form the California Gas and Electric Company. In 1905, Roe's original company, now represented in the San Francisco Gas and Electric Company, merged with this new corporation to form Pacific Gas and Electric Company, one of the most significant public utilities in the United States in the twentieth century. In 2018, the company's market capitalization stood at $22.4 billion, with some 23,000 workers in the company's employ (PG&E 2019).

Today, Pacific Gas and Electric Company generates electricity through a combination of natural gas, nuclear, hydroelectric, and solar power, and serves 5.2 million households in the western states. The company provides the electricity that allows customers to light, cool, and heat their homes, preserve and prepare their food, power their electronic devices, and enjoy many of the other benefits of modern life. However, the company also must contend with the challenges of operating a major power company in a delicate natural environment populated by millions of people. In the 1950s and 1960s, the company dumped hundreds of millions of gallons of tainted wastewater in the ponds around Hinckley, California, which resulted in the legal action that propelled Erin Brockovich to national fame. More recently, the company's powerlines have been implicated by investigators as the cause of the major wildfires that swept through California in October 2017, as well as the November 2018 Camp Fire, which killed at least eighty-five people, with costs exceeding $16.5 billion. It stands as the most devastating wildfire in California history. Expecting massive financial liability, the company began bankruptcy proceedings under Chapter 11 in January 2019.

Jeffrey B. Webb

See also: Brockovich, Erin; Brush, Charles Francis; Coal Gasification; Consolidated Edison Company; Insull, Samuel; Pearl Street Power Station; Vulcan Street Plant

FURTHER READING

Cohn, Julie A. 2017. *The Grid: Biography of an American Technology*. Cambridge, MA: MIT Press.

Freeberg, Ernest. 2013. *The Age of Edison: Electric Light and the Invention of Modern America*. New York: Penguin Press.

"George Roe Dead." 1894. *San Francisco Call*. Vol. 77. No. 11. December. P. 12.

Harvey, Abby, Aaron Larson, and Sonal Patel. 2017. "History of Power: The Evolution of the Electric Generation Industry." *Power Magazine*. October 1. https://www.powermag.com/history-of-power-the-evolution-of-the-electric-generation-industry/ (accessed March 20, 2019).

Neufeld, John L. 2016. *Selling Power: Economics, Policy, and Electric Utilities before 1940*. Chicago: University of Chicago Press.

PG&E. 2019. *Forbes*. https://www.forbes.com/companies/pge/#3147dcd745e4 (accessed March 20, 2019).

Rhodes, Richard. 2018. *Energy: A Human History*. New York: Simon & Schuster.

"The Electric Light." 1890. *Western Electrician*. Vol. 7. No. 6. February 8. P. 72.

Winchell, Mike. 2019. *The Electric War: Edison, Tesla, Westinghouse, and the Race to Light the World*. New York: Henry Holt and Company.

Ziajka, Alan. 2014. *Lighting the City, Changing the World: A History of the Sciences at the University of San Francisco*. San Francisco: University of San Francisco.

Caltex

Among the vast economic, social, and political changes catalyzed by the onset and conclusion of the First World War, the desire for fossil fuel-based power increased dramatically. The United States provided two-thirds of the world oil production by the end of the war and, in fear of another global conflict, supercharged its oil industry throughout the 1920s (Painter 2012). A growing American infrastructure of cars, public transit, and industrial power increased the demand for oil. Opposing the "monopolistic design" of regulatory institutions over oil production, large petroleum corporations advocated for a loosening of these restrictions and even invoked the rhetoric of the "Open Door" policy applied to American trade overseas (Fitzgerald 1991). On July 31, 1928 the oil firms secured a victory in a compromise that granted five American companies a quarter share in the development of Iraq's oil fields (Fitzgerald 1991). This was known as the Red Line Agreement.

Renamed the Iraq Petroleum Company in 1929, the consortium constructed what was essentially a "cartel" based on mutual cooperation and withholding access to shares from rivals (Fitzgerald 1991). After Standard Oil of California (Socal) purchased a concession to Bahrain Island in the Middle East in 1928 and discovered its oil fields in 1932, the fragile consortium faced a serious challenge to its monopoly on oil production and pricing. In 1933, fears were realized as Socal defeated the Iraq Consortium over land rights in eastern Saudi Arabia. The Iraq Consortium responded with the acquisition and development of new oil fields throughout the Middle East, but to little avail. By 1936, the "Red Line Cartel" which consisted of Jersey Standard, Socony, and Shell attempted to buy out Socal, but their new oil competitor refused. Socal had a problem of its own, though. Despite having the Bahrain concession and the cheap crude oil that accompanied it, Socal lacked a viable system of distributing the oil to markets, which were oversaturated by its competitors. The solution came in the form of a partnership with The Texas Company which had a 10 percent share of the markets east of Suez (Fitzgerald 1991). As interests aligned, Socal gave Texas the cheap crude oil supply it needed to sustain its business in Asia, while Texas' distribution network gave Socal a market for its Bahrain concession. As a result, the two companies created the California Texas Oil Company Limited (later shortened to Caltex Corporation) which they called the "Blue Line" to oppose the Red Line oil firms (Yergin 1991).

After the venture was formed, Caltex operated through the Arabian–American Oil Company (ARAMCO). The Second World War slowed production and profits, and along with them, royalty payments to the Saudi family. As a result of these interruptions from the war, the Saudi king asked Aramco to pay $6 million in royalties in 1941. However, Aramco only agreed to $3 million, and tension ensued with the Saudi monarchy. Caltex Chairman James Moffett found a solution by asking his personal friend President Franklin D. Roosevelt to intervene. The stability of Saudi relations was imperative for the continued security of oil profits. In April 1941, Moffett and Roosevelt convened in a personal meeting that revealed the aligning corporate interests of Aramco with the government's interest in maintaining control of the Saudi oil industry. Through a calculated loophole, the United States used the Lend Lease assistance to Britain to provide money to Saudi Arabia (Stork 1973).

In 1943, in the midst of realized fears of the return of global conflict, the demand for oil increased, alongside society's dependence on the fuel. A mission to the Middle East sponsored by the US government asserted that the "center of gravity of world oil production is shifting from the Gulf-Caribbean region to the Middle East" (Painter 2012). Socal's competitive performance in the Middle East attracted the attention of the Roosevelt administration who offered to purchase the concession rights for its oil. Caltex maintained a firm grip on its oil concessions, fearing that US government involvement—which was now cooperating with Great Britain—would challenge its stake in the domestic market with cheap oil. An inability to part with property led many US oil firms into disagreements with the US government. The success of the post-war Marshall Plan depended on stability in the Middle East oil industry, but in the background, the money given to European nations brought many advantages for the United States, both economically and politically. The US government owned the debts of many European nations as a bulwark against Soviet communism.

Soon, the onset of Soviet expansion and the seeds of Cold War competition produced a paranoia among US oil firms. However, the Truman Doctrine coincided with the debt-capturing nature of the Marshall Plan and generated security for Middle Eastern oil investments. Although there is no concrete evidence that the oil companies directly participated in the creation of Truman's foreign policy plan, it was certainly a moment where the international political performance of the United States became tied to the strength and success of American oil investments in the Middle East. Texaco's chairman of the board admitted that the policy shift was unexpected but welcomed. The future of investments for Caltex now had a strong political backing to operate relatively unhindered in the Middle East as a bulwark against communism and as a foundation for European economic recovery (Wilkins 1975).

Despite these economic and political advantages and the unfolding codependence between the US government and private oil conglomerates, there were serious, long-term environmental impacts. In January 1948, US Secretary of Defense James Forrestal asserted that access to Middle East oil was imperative for the stability of the American motorcar industry. US annual per capita oil consumption was at 14.4 barrels in 1948, compared to 22.6 barrels in 2010. This federal fixation on the success of the oil industry in the Middle East led to a prioritization of cars over public transportation and energy efficiency. American dependence on oil was rapidly increasing. The US government focused on a "social and economic pattern that fostered high levels of oil use" as a way to achieve its other strategic goals (Wilkins 1975). The environmental consequences of oil dependence in the United States are tightly intertwined with its political history throughout the twentieth century and can be linked to government and corporate support of increased security and profits for oil companies such as Caltex. These environmental costs did not bear down solely on the domestic side, but had even more detrimental impacts for the Middle East. After seven "zones" opened near Turkey in 1955, two hundred exploration licenses were given to several oil companies including Caltex. The licenses covered 25 million acres of land and gave these oil companies secure access to oil (Longrigg 1954).

Environmental impacts were not the only troubling by-products of oil operations. The complex political and economic relationships between the oil corporations and governments catalyzed deeply ethical dilemmas pertaining to labor rights and worker exploitation. Indonesia was rich in oil fields, but due to the difficulties of decolonization, was plagued by political instability. The United States, and the CIA in particular, continually meddled in local political affairs, which only made politics in these regions more unstable. The father of a young, local Indonesian named Yoseph Taher witnessed the volatile unraveling of Caltex's operations in the area. In the 1950s, Taher's father went to work for Caltex with other indentured laborers known as "contract coolies" (Roosa 2020). Working in the maintenance department, he enjoyed union benefits for the first time in his life and noted that Caltex worked closely with locals. As the relationship between the Indonesian government and Caltex wavered, many government officials, including those in the communist party Partai Komunis Indonesia (PKI), began to detest the oil companies that profited from the "country's natural wealth" (Roosa 2020).

The CIA's involvement in the revolt of the Revolutionary Government of the Republic of Indonesia in 1957–8 strained the operations of Caltex. Caltex made its priorities clear in 1965 after the United States sold weapons to Malaysia. The Indonesian government rallied all the oil companies to demand that they would take "temporary control" of the oil operations (Roosa 2020). Yoseph Taher's father was told by his supervisor to rally all the workers together. They were then questioned by the police for working for Caltex and then incarcerated with many other detainees, all of whom were oil workers. In January 1966, Taher and other oil workers were "dishonorably discharged" from their employment at Caltex—the first firings of what came to be 75 percent of Caltex employees (Roosa 2020). The Indonesian problem raised important questions about the role of foreign companies during political disputes and revolutions. However, those who paid the highest price were the oil workers who lost their lives or their jobs. Caltex walked away with minimal damage to its overall economic health.

Labor exploitation and political controversy occurred elsewhere beyond Southeast Asia. In a 1976 report filed by the American Committee on Africa, officials found that US oil companies were, at the very least, complicit in the unfolding apartheid system in South Africa. The report accused oil companies of supporting racism and exploitation. These companies responded with assertions that they were contributing to the social welfare of the black population (Davis 1976). In 1975, Caltex announced a $134 million investment for its Cape Town refinery. The investment gave Caltex two-thirds of the shares of US petroleum production in South Africa. The company, moreover, declined to comment on military operations and used the South African Official Secrets Act as a way to remain apolitical. Continued operations became increasingly mechanized and automated and did not lead to an increase in employment of South Africans. In an official statement that the report classifies as "openly discriminatory," Caltex stated, "[our] employment practices are governed by South African laws, and in the event of any conflicts between these laws … the company must be guided by the former." The report concluded that the oil companies used "micro economics to obscure macro truths" (Davis 1976). Overall, Caltex's record in overseas oil development has remained a subject of persistent controversy.

Thomas David Brown

See also: Aramco; Consortium Agreement of 1954; Gulf Oil Company; Iraq War and the Project for a New American Century; Mandatory Oil Import Quota Program; Mobil Oil Corporation; Red Line Agreement of 1928; Seven Sisters Oil Companies; Texaco

FURTHER READING

Davis, Jennifer. 1976. "US Corporation Support for Apartheid – IBM & Oil Companies." Testimonies—American Committee on Africa (ACOA).

Fitzgerald, Edward Peter. 1991. "Compagnie Française des Pétroles and the Defense of the Red Line Regime in Middle Eastern Oil, 1933–36." *Business and Economic History*. Vol. 20. Pp. 117–26.

Johnson, Bobx. 2014. *Carbon Nation: Fossil Fuels in the Making of American Culture*. Lawrence, KS: University Press of Kansas.

Krane, Jim. 2019. *Energy Kingdoms: Oil and Political Survival in the Persian Gulf*. New York: Columbia University Press.

Longrigg, Stephen Hemsley. 1954. *Oil in the Middle East: Its Discovery and Development*. Royal Institute of International Affairs. New York: Oxford University Press.

Painter, David S. 2012. "Oil and the American Century." *The Journal of American History*. Vol. 99. No. 1. Pp. 24–39.

Roosa, John. 2020. "Dead Labor: Disappearances in Sumatra." In *Buried Histories: The Anticommunist Massacres of 1965–1966 in Indonesia*. Pp. 209–40. Madison, WI: University of Wisconsin Press.

Stork, Joe. 1973. "Middle East Oil and the Energy Crisis: Part 1." *MERIP Reports*. No. 20. September. Pp. 3–20. Middle East Research and Information Project, Inc.

Wilkins, Mira. 1975. "The Oil Companies in Perspective." *Daedalus*. Vol. 104. No. 4. Fall. Pp. 159–78.

Yergin, Daniel. 1991. *The Prize: The Epic Quest for Oil, Money, and Power*. New York: Simon & Schuster.

Cap and Trade System

The cap and trade system, also known as emissions trading, is a market-based approach designed to reduce global greenhouse gas (GHG) emissions. It is an emissions trading scheme, where a government sets a cap—or a limit—on all emissions. Whether set on a federal, regional, state, or municipal level, the cap applies to particular emissions by specified emitters within a jurisdiction. The concept dates back to the 1960s, when it was developed by economists Ellison Burton and William Sanjour for the US National Air Pollution Control Administration to reduce acid rain. After researching various pollution control strategies, Burton and Sanjour concluded that commodifying the right to pollute was one of the most cost-effective ways to reduce air pollution (Langwith 2011, 16). Through the Air Pollution Control Act of 1955, the US government developed a scheme based on this concept to regulate sulfur dioxide emissions from power plants, a primary contributor to acid rain, by setting a cap and allowing emitters to trade the right to emit over the limit (EPA 2019).

In any cap and trade system, emitting entities that are specified as part of the system—such as private firms—cannot exceed the cap in terms of collective emissions; rather, they must redistribute emissions, as with the cap come emissions allowances that are tradable. When setting the cap, the government issues a pre-specified amount of GHG emissions and distributes rights to emit these amounts amongst the emitting entities. For example, if the cap is set at 1 million tons of CO_2 emissions, then one million 100-ton allowances can be distributed to the emitters. These rights can then be traded between the emitters but not exceeded overall. A company that has the means to invest in emissions-reducing technologies, then, can sell emission rights they do not need to a company that does not. The cap and trade system, thus, provides financial incentives to companies not only to reduce emissions in the short term but also to develop and invest in energy-efficient and emissions-reducing technologies that be further disseminated and deployed. However, it is not always possible for all sources of GHG emissions to be addressed by a cap and trade system. Moreover, the system is not without its critics. Some scholars contend that that cap and trade systems place an unfair burden on governments to collect data and that emissions trading's market-based approach deters from uniform pollution reduction (Johnson 1999, 112–13). Environmental justice advocates have argued that these systems have a disproportionate focus on urban air quality that results in an unjust outcome concerning disadvantaged and low-income communities, as pollution in a system's jurisdiction is often shifted to lower-income communities, exacerbating socio-environmental inequality (Johnson 1999, 117–18).

The concept of cap and trade garnered increased support in the 1980s, when the US Environmental Protection Agency (EPA) and the Environmental Defense Fund (EDF) pushed for cap and trade programs to get rid of lead in fuels and regulate sulfur dioxide emissions that were causing acid rain. In 1990, Congress created a cap and trade program to address the issue. The cap, first envisioned in the 1960s, was on sulfur dioxide emissions from electric power plants. Under the program, power plants that overcomplied could sell their extra emittance allowances to power plants who undercomplied (Van Dyke 1991, 2707). The success of this program encouraged the United States to lobby for cap and trade programs on an international level, as mitigating anthropogenic climate change was becoming an important issue for the international community. The Kyoto Protocol, the landmark international agreement on climate change mitigation, incorporated cap and trade as part of its scope for participatory countries, with caps set by the United Nations Framework Convention on Climate Change (UNFCC) (Driesen 2018, 38–9). After the Kyoto Protocol and its following international climate treaty agreements, cap and trade programs became primarily concerned with carbon emissions (UN 2019). The United States never ratified the Kyoto Protocol.

In 2009, the US House of Representatives approved the American Clean Energy and Security Act (ACES), an energy bill seeking to establish a cap and trade system on a national level. The ACES would have mandated the EPA to establish two cap and trade programs, one for reducing GHG emissions and the other to reduce hydrochlorofluorocarbon (HFC) emissions by 2050 (ACESA 2009, 360–3). The ACES never entered law due to disagreement in the US Senate.

There were, however, other notable cap and trade programs implemented on a regional level. The Regional Greenhouse Gas Initiative (RGGI) was established in 2009 as a cooperation between Connecticut, Delaware, Maine, Maryland, New Hampshire, New York, Rhode Island, and Vermont to reduce CO_2 emissions in the power sector (RGGI 2019). RGGI participatory states auctioned allowances which could then be traded on a secondary market, a strategy aimed at generating additional government income. In the first phase of its program, participatory states showed an emissions reduction of 35 percent in 2016 since its launch, and electricity prices decreased by 3.4 percent in the region as well (Stutt and Shatuck 2016, 3). However, the initiative has been criticized of having little national impact, as RGGI states produce only about 7 percent of total US CO_2 emissions (Roberts 2017).

Another example is the transnational Western Climate Initiative (WCI) that was established in 2007. Combining the 2003 West Coast Global Warming Initiative between California, Oregon and Washington and the 2006 Southwest Climate Change Initiative Arizona and New Mexico, the WCI established a regional cap and trade system between the five states and grew subsequently to include Montana and Utah as well as the Canadian provinces of British Columbia, Manitoba, Ontario, and Quebec to expand its scope (WCI 2013). It set regional targets to reduce heat-trapping emissions as well as implement California's 2002 Clean Car Standard, which passed emission-reducing regulations for vehicular tailpipes in participatory states and provinces. However, Ontario—a production hub in Canada—announced its exit from the WCI in 2018.

In 2013, California implemented its own state-based cap and trade program, the California cap-and-trade program, which also produced a decrease in carbon dioxide pollution. The program required California to return to 1990 GHG emissions levels by 2020, which meant reducing GHG emissions by 15 percent overall. The first year of the program covered electricity and large industrial emitters and aimed for an emissions decline of 2 percent by 2014; the program showed that it had reached 100 percent compliance by November of that year. The California cap and trade program expanded its scope for its second phase. In 2014, it established links to the provincial cap and trade program in Quebec, Canada, and in 2015 it began including distributors of transportation, natural gas, and other fuels, with the aim to include 85 percent of California's emitters (CEPA 2015, 1–2). However, both programs were accused of being linked to increased emissions elsewhere in a process called resource shuffling, which has to do with the redistribution of emissions. This is considered to be an outgrowth of the creation of sub-national programs, which tend to increase emissions from non-participatory regions (Caron 2015, 167–9 and 188).

Sakina Groeppmaier

See also: Acid Rain; Clean Air Act of 1970; Clean Power Plan of 2015; Climate Change; US Environmental Protection Agency

FURTHER READING

ACESA (American Clean Energy and Security Act of 2009). 2009. HR 2454. US House of Representatives. 111th Congress. 1st Session. Report 111–37. Part 1. June 5.

Caron, Justin, Sebastian Rausch, and Niven Winchester. 2015. "Leakage from Sub-national Climate Policy: The Case of California's Cap-and-Trade Program." *The Energy Journal*. Vol. 36. No. 2. April. Pp. 167–90.

Center for Climate and Energy Solutions (CCES). 2011. *Climate Change 101: Understanding and Responding to Global Climate Change*. Arlington: Pew Center on Global Climate Change.

CEPA (California Environmental Protection Agency). 2015. "Overview of ARB Emissions Trading Program." Sacramento: Air Resources Board. July 15. https://ww3.arb.ca.gov/cc/capandtrade/guidance/cap_trade_overview.pdf (accessed October 2023).

Driesen, David M. 2018. "Emissions Trading versus Pollution Taxes: Playing 'Nice' with Other Instruments." *Environmental Law*. Vol. 48. No. 1. Winter. Pp. 29–80.

EPA (US Environmental Protection Agency). 2019. "Evolution of the Clean Air Act." January 3. Clean Air Act Overview. https://www.epa.gov/clean-air-act-overview/evolution-clean-air-act (accessed September 12, 2019).

Johnson, Stephen M. 1999. "Economics v. Equity: Do Market-Based Environmental Reforms Exacerbate Environmental Injustice?" *Washington & Lee Review*. Vol. 11. No. 1. Winter. Pp. 111–66.

Langwith, Jacqueline. 2011. *The Role of Government*. Farmington Hills: Greenhaven Press.

RGGI (Regional Greenhouse Gas Initiative). 2019. "Program Overview and Design." The Regional Greenhouse Gas Initiative: An Initiative of the New England and Mid-Atlantic States of the U.S. https://www.rggi.org/program-overview-and-design/elements (accessed August 15, 2019).

Roberts, David. 2017. "The Northeast's Carbon Trading System Works Quite Well. It Just Doesn't Reduce Much Carbon." *Vox*. February 28. https://www.vox.com/science-and-health/2017/2/28/14741384/rggi-explained (accessed September 12, 2019).

Stutt, Jonathan and Peter Shatuck. 2016. *Regional Greenhouse Gas Initiative Status Report: Part I: Measuring Success*. July. Boston: Acadia Center.

United Nations (UN). 2019. "International Emissions Trading." UN Framework Convention on Climate Change. https://unfccc.int/international-emissions-trading (accessed September 12, 2019).

Van Dyke, Brennan. 1991. "Emissions Trading to Reduce Acid Deposition." *Yale Law Journal*. Vol. 100. No. 8. Pp. 2707–8.

Western Climate Initiative (WCI). 2013. "History." Western Climate Initiative Website. http://westernclimateinitiative.org/index.php?option=com_content&view=article&id=29&Itemid=44 (accessed August 15, 2019).

Carrier, Willis Haviland

Willis Haviland Carrier (1876–1950) is often called "the father of air conditioning." He earned the moniker for being a key innovator and pioneer of climate-control technology and for bringing air-conditioning to the mass public. Air-conditioning as an invention is often overlooked today precisely because it is so ubiquitous. The story of temperature-controlled cooling, however, is interesting and complicated. Its creation contributed to a restructuring of American economic and social life that remains with us today.

Humans have manipulated the temperature within enclosed environments for millennia. Heat energy generated with fire, coal, steam, and other means was and remains a staple of temperature control. In the time before electricity and refrigeration ice was stored in winter to be used during the warmer months to cool rooms, melting obviously as temperatures rose but with enough stockpiled to make ice harvesting practical. Indoor cooling improved with the invention of electric fans. Some people maximized the fan's effect by putting a block of ice in front of the spinning blades for greater relief. Institutions even tried this on a mass scale to cool spaces as large as theaters. Still, all of these and other cooling measures were wasteful and insufficient.

People everywhere have suffered from heat during the summertime, especially in places where the climate is characteristically warm year-round. There have been architectural solutions to the issue, for instance with the construction of high ceilings to redirect heat upward and the installation of cross windows to maximize the breeze. These solutions grew less practical during the Industrial Revolution and increasing urbanization of the nineteenth century. Factories were dangerously hot and temperatures routinely reached triple digits, often as high as 130 to 140 degrees Fahrenheit. A new word—sweatshop—came into usage in the early 1880s to describe such working conditions. White collar workers in cramped offices had it marginally better but the heat was still unpleasant and dangerous. Crowded brick tenements offered little respite at the end of the day. Some people resorted to sleeping on rooftops and fire escapes, which sometimes led to tragedy; it was not unheard of for individuals to fall to their deaths from rolling off and hitting the pavement below. Seasonable summer temperatures were difficult to endure, but when a heat wave set in the situation grew exponentially more life-threatening. The Great Heat Wave of 1896 enveloped much of the northeastern United States and took the lives of over 1,300 individuals in New York City alone. Businesses themselves too were vulnerable because the expensive equipment used to produce manufactured goods was increasingly likely to break down as temperatures rose. This put profits as well as people in danger. These issues led scientists and engineers to consider what remedies could be done to ameliorate indoor heat.

Willis H. Carrier was born in Angola, New York, population approximately 600, on November 26, 1876. An only child, his mother died when he was eleven. The youngster toiled beside his father on the family farm, attended local schools, and tinkered with the various gadgets and equipment to be found in the scenic village just 2 miles from Lake Erie in Western New York. He majored in mechanical engineering at Cornell University and graduated in 1901. That July he went to work for the Buffalo Forge Company. Willis Carrier was a young man at the start of a new century eager to make his mark. Carrier would have known that other engineers had been designing and building crude cooling systems for some time. These were custom-designed contraptions built for wealthy Gilded Age persons and institutions. Results were mixed and solutions still elusive. In July 1902, just one year after starting at Brooklyn Forge and only twenty-five years old, Carrier founded the company's Department of Experimental Engineering. That same month the young engineer designed what one would recognize today as the first modern air conditioner.

Willis Carrier believed that a key to artificial indoor cooling was controlling humidity and he set out to accomplish just that. Effectiveness was not just a matter of decreasing the moisture in the air; instead, humidity must be lowered or raised depending upon the individual setting and circumstances. A textile mill, for instance, requires lower temperatures but relatively high humidity because yarns and cloths can become brittle and fray if they become too dry. Conversely, too much humidity in a printing plant can force equipment to stall out, warp the paper, and even interfere with the color quality in a production run. Carrier put his ideas to the test, finalizing the blueprints for the first true air conditioner on July 17, 1902 for the Sackett & Wilhelms Lithography and Printing Company of Williamsburg, Brooklyn. Soon it was installed and while there was much refinement still to be done—Carrier's whirling and gurgling cooling machine was a decidedly Rube Goldberg-like affair—it performed well and proved the efficacy of his overall theory and design. He spent the next several years further honing and installing air-conditioning systems. This included the so-named "Apparatus for Treating Air," sold to the LaCrosse (Wisconsin) National Bank in 1904 and the first spray-type conditioning unit. By the following year Carrier was named chief of the Buffalo Forge Company's Engineering Department. Meanwhile others were experimenting independently. Stuart W. Cramer, a cotton mill engineer and inventor from North Carolina, coined the term "air conditioning" in 1906. Cramer's interest in artificial cooling makes sense given that textiles were so vulnerable to fluctuations in temperature and humidity.

Carrier and six other men founded the Carrier Engineering Corporation in 1915. A turning point for the company, and air-conditioning more generally, was Carrier's 1922 development of a centrifugal refrigeration machine appropriately nicknamed "The Chiller." Carrier's primary customers in the immediately following years were department stores, hotels, industrial plants, offices in which worked the rising managerial class, government buildings in Washington DC, and movie theaters such as Paramount's spacious and majestic Rivoli. Like most American companies Carrier focused on military production after the Japanese attack on Pearl Harbor and America's entry in the Second World War, ceasing most civilian production and outfitting ships, munitions factories, and similar entities with air-conditioning.

1939 WORLD'S FAIR

The World's Fair opened in Flushing, Queens on April 30, 1939. Ford, DuPont, General Motors, and other companies built ornate pavilions to demonstrate what a "World of Tomorrow" might look like. Radio Corporation of America (RCA) demonstrated not just the newfangled medium of FM radio but one of the world's first television sets. Millions saw these wonders. There too was the Carrier Engineering Corporation, whose building was shaped like an igloo. Inside, many visitors enjoyed the pleasure of air conditioning for the first time in their lives.

Keith J. Muchowski

American society evolved when the veterans returned, married, purchased homes, and raised families. The cost of air-conditioning production had declined, allowing for the greater installation of climate-controlled cooling into the middle-class tract housing going up across the country. What had once been a luxury was becoming a necessity. It was not just to suburbs outside of large metropolitan areas to where Americans were moving. The advent of mass air conditioning opened up entire regions of the United States to migration. The sparsely populated climes of the humid Southeast and arid deserts of the Midwest were now more pleasant and comfortable given the availability of air-conditioning—and thus more habitable year-round. This migration changed the demographics not only of the warmer regions to where Americans were moving in greater numbers, but in the urban and industrial places they were leaving behind. Among other things this shift has reconfigured the number of electoral college votes and reapportionment of seats within the US House of Representatives to which states were entitled based upon the census. In 1969 one political consultant coined a new term for this demographic, social, and political phenomenon: the Sun Belt.

There have been other effects as well. Air-conditioning has had an environmental impact on the world. The electricity needed to run cooling systems is costly in energy. This is especially true during heat waves when many people are running their units, leading to blackouts and brownouts. What is more, the chemical coolants within air-conditioning deplete the ozone and, some argue, contribute to climate change. For these reasons there has been greater emphasis in recent decades on improving energy efficiency and incorporating green technologies into the industry.

Carrier was known affectionately as "The Chief" by his employees. In the almost half-century of his career Willis Haviland Carrier was given numerous awards and honorary degrees in recognition of his accomplishments. He was also a member of many professional engineering organizations. He did not live to see all of the changes he did so much to bring forth. Carrier died in New York City on October 7, 1950 at the age of seventy-three. He rests today in Buffalo's Forest Lawn Cemetery. The company he co-founded continued and prospered into the twenty-first century. After numerous mergers and acquisitions the organization exists today as Carrier Global Corporation.

Keith J. Muchowski

See also: Frigidaire; Home Energy Efficiency; Johnson, Warren Seymour; Mellowes, Alfred W.; Powers, William Penn

FURTHER READING

Arsenault, Raymond. 1984. "The End of the Long Hot Summer: The Air Conditioner and Southern Culture." *The Journal of Southern History*. Vol. 50. No. 4. Pp. 597–628.

Basile, Salvatore. 2014. *Cool: How Air Conditioning Changed Everything*. New York: Fordham University Press.

Carrier, Willis Haviland, Realto E. Cherne, and Walter A. Grant. 1950. *Modern Air-Conditioning, Heating and Ventilating*. 2nd ed. New York: Pitman Publishing Corporation.

Ingels, Margaret. 1952. *Willis Haviland Carrier, Father of Air Conditioning*. Garden City, NY: Country Life Press.

Ivins, Molly. 1999. *People of the Century: One Hundred Men and Women Who Shaped the Last One Hundred Years*. Edited by The Editors of Time-Life, Inc. CBS. New York: Simon & Schuster.

Schultz, Eric B. 2012. *Weathermakers to the World: The Story of a Company, the Standard of an Industry*. n.p.: Carrier Engineering Corp.

Carter Doctrine

The Carter Doctrine was a US foreign policy devised by US President Jimmy Carter, Zbigniew Brzezinski, the assistant to the president for national security affairs, and the National Security Council to guide strategy in the Middle East for the 1980s and beyond. Carter announced this policy on January 23, 1980, during his nationally televised State of the Union address. In his speech, he articulated a newfound US willingness to use military power to secure its national interests in the Persian Gulf region. Energy, especially oil, was at the core of the Carter Doctrine.

The Carter Doctrine began to emerge in November 1979 in response to heightened international tensions sparked by the Iran hostage crisis and the Soviet Union's subsequent invasion of Afghanistan the following month. At that time, the Iran hostage crisis had just begun and immediately became a major predicament for the Carter administration. The dilemma commenced on November 4, 1979, and would last until January 20, 1981, the day that Carter's successor, Ronald Reagan, entered office. At the time of Carter's speech, fifty-two Americans languished as hostages of radical Iranian students in what many analysts characterized as a violent reaction against US support of Mohammad Reza Pahlavi, the Shah of Iran. While this event was lingering and unresolved, Cold War tensions also heightened as the enmity between the United States and the Soviet Union escalated dramatically. The two superpowers had achieved some modest progress in the Cold War on strategic arms limitation treaties, including SALT I and II. Antagonisms rose, however, when the Soviet Union invaded Afghanistan on December 25, 1979. Carter branded this ominous development as the most troubling peril since the dawn of the Cold War. During the State of the Union, Carter announced that in response to this provocation the US Olympic team would withdraw from participation in the pending 1980 Summer Olympics scheduled for July and August in Moscow. More than sixty nations eventually joined the United States in the boycott over the Soviet–Afghan War. The Soviet Union ultimately would deploy approximately a 100,000 soldiers to Afghanistan and remain there for nearly a decade until it completed its withdrawal on February 15, 1989.

With the Carter Doctrine, the president identified three major security problems: the Soviet Union's military aggression, especially its power projection abroad; Western democracies' reliance on Middle East oil; and alarming instability in the developing world as exemplified by the Iranian Revolution led by Ayatollah Khomeini, which triggered a US domestic energy crisis in 1979. In response, Carter labeled the Persian Gulf as a region of strategic importance based on both energy and geography. This area contained roughly two-thirds of the world's oil supply and included key transit routes through the Arabian Sea, Persian Gulf, Gulf of Aden, Red Sea, Indian Ocean, and Strait of Hormuz.

Carter sought Western solidarity to thwart incitements around the Persian Gulf, triggered by the combination of such external incursions as the Soviet Union's armed hostility and such internal causes as volatility in the form of the Iranian Revolution. Carter argued that these dual dangers limited the open interchange of oil from the Middle East to global markets and transformed such economic issues as the oil trade into strategic ones that had larger geopolitical significance. Carter called for joint action by the United States and its allies to counteract these incidents and equated a threat to the Persian Gulf region, as exemplified by the Soviet invasion of Afghanistan, with peril to US vital national interests. As a result, Carter called for American readiness to use force if necessary to protect concerns there and a marked increase in defense spending to carry out such a commitment, as well as reinforcing the US military presence throughout the Indian Ocean, Persian Gulf, and northeast Africa. Carter also advocated reviving the Selective Service System and contemplated resuming a military draft.

Domestically, Carter called for a comprehensive energy policy and underscored US dependence on energy, much of it oil from the Persian Gulf region supplied by the Organization of Petroleum Exporting Countries (OPEC) amidst rapidly rising prices, emphasizing the emerging interconnectedness of international markets formed by globalization. Events halfway around the world in such places as Tehran and Kabul had a direct and at times severe impact on Americans from Baltimore to San Diego. The Carter Doctrine stoked fears that fossil fuels were finite and susceptible to significant disruptions of supply and large fluctuations in price and demonstrated the powerful sway of energy on American history. The Carter Doctrine also revealed how commingled foreign policy and domestic considerations had become, including such economic factors as rising gas prices becoming the key driver of broader debilitating inflation at that time and such domestic political calculations as resisting a reelection challenge against Carter from within his own party led by Senator Ted Kennedy (D-MA).

As evidenced by the Carter Doctrine, energy transformed from an economic issue into a security concern and had serious implications and broad reverberations on foreign policy, military deployments, and defense spending for decades, including the Iran–Iraq War beginning with the Iraqi invasion of Iran in September 1980 and lasting until August 1988, the deployment of more than 500,000 US soldiers to fight the Gulf War from 1990 to 1991, and the US goal of regime change during the Iraq War, beginning in 2003 and persisting until 2011.

William A. Taylor

See also: Aramco; Caltex; Cheney, Richard Bruce "Dick"; Energy Crisis of the 1970s; Energy Independence; Energy Policy and Conservation Act of 1975; Energy Security Act of 1980; Gulf War; Halliburton Company; Iraq War and the Project for a New American Century; Mandatory Oil Import Quota Program; National Energy Act of 1978; Organization of Petroleum Exporting Countries (OPEC); Seven Sisters Oil Companies

FURTHER READING

Bacevich, Andrew J. 2016. *America's War for the Greater Middle East: A Military History*. New York: Random House.

Da Vinha, Luis. 2016. "Structures, Processes, and Communication in the Transformation of the Carter Administration's Foreign Policy." *Journal of Policy History*. Vol. 28. No. 4. October. Pp. 624–53.

Eizenstat, Stuart E. 2018. *President Carter: The White House Years*. New York: Thomas Dunne.

Klare, Michael T. 2006/7. "Oil, Iraq, and American Foreign Policy: The Continuing Salience of the Carter Doctrine." *International Journal*. Vol. 62. No. 1. Winter. Pp. 31–42.

Moran, Daniel, and James A. Russell, eds. 2009. *Energy Security and Global Politics: The Militarization of Resource Management*. London: Routledge.

Zelizer, Julian E. 2010. *Jimmy Carter*. New York: Times.

Centralia Mine Disaster

Centralia, Illinois is the site of one of the most tragic coal mine explosions in US history. The disaster of March 25, 1947, resulted in the deaths of 111 of the 142 miners caught underground at the time of the event, with 65 of those killed in the explosion and the other 46 dead from carbon monoxide, known as the "afterdamp" (Hartley 2006, 59). The tragedy of Centralia provides an ongoing reminder to the mining industry and to society in general of the importance of following established mine safety procedures in order to minimize, or even eliminate, threats to workers. It also provides instruction on issues of response, rescue, and recovery in the event of an explosion or even dangerous conditions in coal mines.

In the 1850s, coal mining intensified in the state of Illinois, which in many places was still in a frontier condition. The town of Centralia was founded in 1853 by the Illinois Central Railroad and coal mining began in the area in order to supply the railroad with fuel for its steam locomotives. The Centralia Mining and Manufacturing Company began working in southern Illinois under the leadership of founders Ferdinand Kohl and A.M. Warner. They and a number of other investors built the company into a prosperous and influential concern. They discovered coal just south of Centralia in 1874, about 600 feet underground. The Centralia No. 1 mine opened on October 29, 1874 with a celebratory firing of a Civil War cannon, signaling hopes for the new economic development in Centralia (Hartley 2006, 25)

Immigrants supplied miners for the southern Illinois coal mining industry, and particularly in the Centralia area. Most of these immigrants arrived from Great Britain and Europe, including Germany, Italy, Poland, Spain, Austria, Hungary, Bohemia, Moravia, and Lithuania (Hartley 2006, 26). In 1905, the Bell and Zoller Coal Company of Chicago, one of the "Big Six" Illinois coal companies, bought out the owners and operated mines in the Centralia area under name of a subsidiary named the Centralia Coal Company. The company produced a reported 2,200 tons of coal per day. The town established a profitable coal mining business and along with farming and the railroad, developed through the early twentieth century as a healthy and prosperous midwestern community. In 1937, drillers struck oil near the town and by 1938, the Lake Centralia-Salem oil field came under development by large petroleum companies from Texas and Oklahoma. The town attracted thousands of Roughnecks and for a brief time obtained the character of a boomtown. The oil money brought more prosperity, which began to show in improved schools, new shops, and nightclubs.

More prosperity came during the Second World War, when mining companies were asked by President Franklin D. Roosevelt to increase production for the war effort. The expanded volume of coal reaped rewards for company investors and the mine workers received full pay, but the pace of work created safety hazards that went largely unaddressed. One of the biggest problems was managing the large volume of coal dust. The Centralia mine disaster's best historians noted: "when the mine air is saturated with dust particles, it becomes a safety hazard. A spark or a flame can ignite the highly combustible dust and touch off an explosion that roars through the tunnels and rooms, claiming everything in its path" (Hartley 2006, 30). Inspectors from the US Bureau of Mines and the Illinois Department of Mines and Minerals visited the Centralia operations very frequently, noting problems with poor ventilation, loose timbering of mine roofs, and inadequate dust management practices. It was discovered later that company officials largely brushed off the recommendations made by these inspectors: "the company ignored reports of coal dust hazards from state and federal inspectors and did little to improve mine safety" (Hartley 2006, 31).

The day of the mine disaster at Centralia was a typical workday. Miners working in different underground "rooms" in the Centralia No. 5 mine gathered coal into small carts that operated on rails and then trundled them through the mine's passages to the base of the 540-foot hoisting shaft for transport to the surface. Toward the end of every shift, a team composed of "drillers" and "shot firers" moved toward the areas where coal was actively being removed from the exposed face of the coal seam. Their job was to bore holes in the coal face and insert the explosives. On this particular day, the drillers were also serving as shot-firers. Preparations were made and then blasting commenced with 142 workers remaining in the mine's various passages, many of whom were awaiting transport to the surface at the end of the shift. The shot fired at 3:27 p.m., and the detonation touched off an explosion of accumulated coal dust, sending walls of flame down the mine's passages toward the hoisting shaft (O'Neil 2023). Those who weren't killed in the explosion were trapped in the mine and succumbed to poisoning by carbon monoxide gas. The last miner perished around 6:30 p.m., while thirty-one miners managed to make it to the surface. Reports from the scene said bodies "brought from the pit today were twisted and bruised, and clothing on some were burned," indicating they died by explosion rather than carbon monoxide poisoning (Whalen 1947).

Families rushed to the mine when news spread of the explosion. Wives, mothers, and children eagerly sought news of their loved ones, and many would have to wait long hours to learn their absent husband or son was in fact among the fatalities. Four workers from the Centralia No. 5 mine had written a letter to the governor of Illinois a year earlier, protesting the mine's hazardous conditions, and pleading, "Please save our lives." Three of those miners died in the explosion (O'Neil 2023). In the recovery, handwritten notes from the trapped miners were discovered tacked to the mine's walls saying sorrowful farewells to wives and children. One of the victims, Joe Bryant, wrote several letters, one of which read "My Dear wife good By. Name Baby Joe so you will have a Joe love all dad." When Bryant's widow gave birth to a daughter three months later—their twelfth child—she named her Joedy (Hartley 2006, 60). Photographs of shell-shocked survivors being pulled from the mine, and of relatives gasping for breath between wails of lament covered the pages of newspapers for the next several days. One headline read, "Wives Weep at Mine Entrance as they Await News of Husbands" (O'Neil 2023).

In the day or two following the explosion, recovery took place in freezing temperatures and heavy snowfall. While searching for bodies, an inspection report from the Illinois state inspector of mines, Driscoll Scanlan, was found. It was dated March 18 and 19, only a week before the explosion. Scanlans' comments highlighted several hazardous conditions at Centralia No. 5: "ventilation inadequate," "loose roof on the haulage roads," and "the mine is not adequately rock dusted" (O'Neil 2023). Rock dusting is a procedure used in mines with heavy coal dust in which pulverized limestone (or other material like dolomite, gypsum, anhydrite, or shale) is applied to the surface of the mine's tunnels and rooms. The dust is inert, meaning non-combustible, and in the event of a coal dust explosion, the pressure wave from the blast will scour the previously applied rock dust off the surface. It will then become "entrained" in the pressure wave and render inert the extant coal dust in front of the blast. The procedure is not designed to prevent coal dust explosions, but to thwart their progress throughout the mine (NIOSH 2021). If the rock dust is wet, it will "cake" onto the surface of the mine's walls and resist becoming entrained in the pressure wave of a future explosion. Thus, it must be inspected regularly to ensure its readiness to serve its purpose.

Scanlan's inspection report just prior to the explosion noted the lack of adequate rock dusting in Centralia No. 5, which might have inhibited the blast and reduced the number of fatalities. He and his supervisor Robert Medill, Director of the Illinois Department of Mines and Minerals, were important figures in the investigations and legislative hearings that were conducted in the wake of the disaster. So too were Centralia Coal Company President Homer F. McDonald and Vice President William Young. McDonald drew public censure when he was asked by a reporter about the mine's history of failed inspections and replied, "Hell, I don't know anything about a coal mine," then deflected questions to Young (O'Neil 2023). Young conceded that he had ignored or disregarded the inspection reports at a hearing that included a group of US Senators from Washington, DC, and also expressed his view that rock dusting had limited value in making mines safer (Hartley 2006, 31–2). Eventually the company paid a fine of $1,000 for various violations of mine safety regulations.

Republican Governor Dwight H. Green assembled a committee of seven to investigate the disaster and to submit a report of their findings. On April 11, 1947, the committee presented its 46-page "Report to the Governor and People of the State of Illinois." Among its other conclusions about the use of rock dust and frequency of mine inspections, the committee said: "The evidence is convincing that the public officers of the State Department of Mines and Minerals and the Members of the State Mining Board followed a weak, ineffective and indifferent policy toward enforcement of State Mining Laws for at least eighteen months with respect to this mine" ("Report" 1947, 41). The committee praised Driscoll Scanlan for his "skill, knowledge, and devotedness to his duties" and favorably noted "he had the confidence of the miners," but concluded that he should have closed the mine in spite of his belief that Director Medill, his supervisor, would have fired him if he did so ("Report" 1947, 42).

Prior to the explosion, Scanlan reportedly asked Medill for approval of the mine's closure but was denied. Allegations surfaced that Medill refused Scanlan's request because he didn't want to alienate the mine owners, whom he was courting at the time for campaign donations to the Republican Party. His position, as well as Scanlan's, were political appointments controlled by the Republican Governor Green. In 1948, Green lost his bid for reelection to Democrat Adlai Stevenson amid the fallout from the Centralia disaster, coupled with allegations that Republican-appointed state officials allowed mine owners to get away with violations of safety regulations in exchange for campaign donations. Another consequence of the event, and a similar disaster in 1951 at West Frankfurt, Illinois, was the Federal Coal Mine Safety Act of 1952, which mandated federal mine safety inspections and created federal rock dusting standards.

It is not surprising that folk singer Woody Guthrie took up the cause of the victims in three songs written on April 1, 1947 about the Centralia disaster: "Dying Miner" ("Goodbye Centralia"), "Waiting at the Gate," and "Talking Miner" ("Talking Centralia"). Guthrie wrote numerous tunes about the working class and the poor, and since the miners liked Scanlan, Guthrie did as well, as he expressed in "Waiting at the Gate": "The inspector told the boss, it was more than a year ago / You're risking these men's lives in number five / That hole's full of fumes and dust, full of high explosive gas / But the boss said we'll just have to take the chance" (Jackson 2009). At least among miners and their supporters at the time, the

Centralia mine disaster symbolized the indifference and lack of accountability on the part of mine owners and government officials that existed in the industry, which they believed required increased vigilance.

Patrice Natalie Delevante

See also: Cherry Mine Disaster; Coal; Dawson Mine Disaster; Farmington Mine Disaster; Krebs Mine Disaster; Scofield Mine Disaster; United Mine Workers of America; Upper Big Branch Mine Disaster; West Frankfort Mine Disaster

FURTHER READING

Hartley, Robert E. and David Kenney. 2006. *Death Underground: The Centralia and West Frankfort Mine Disasters*. Carbondale, IL: Southern Illinois University Press.

Jackson, Mark Allan. 2009. *Prophet Singer: The Voice and Vision of Woody Guthrie*. Jackson, MS: University Press of Mississippi.

National Institute for Occupational Safety and Health (NIOSH). 2021. "Mining Topic: Rock Dusting." January 26. Centers for Disease Control and Prevention. U.S. Department of Health & Human Services. https://www.cdc.gov/niosh/mining/topics/rockdusting.html (accessed October 2023).

O'Neil, Tim. 2023. "March 25, 1947: 'Dear Wife. Goodbye.' 111 Die in Southern Illinois Mine Disaster." *St. Louis Post-Dispatch*. March 25.

"Report to Investigate the Disaster at the Centralia Coal Company Mine Number 5." 1947. Illinois State Archives. Office of the Illinois Secretary of State. https://www.ilsos.gov/departments/archives/online_exhibits/100_documents/1947-investigate-disaster-mine5.html (accessed October 2023).

Whalen, Charles. 1947. "35 Known Dead; Little Hope for 76 Still Trapped." *Radford News Journal*. Vol. 64. No. 7. March 27.

Cheney, Richard Bruce "Dick"

Richard Bruce "Dick" Cheney (1941–), vice president of the United States from 2001 to 2009, epitomized the alliance between the petroleum industry, the Republican Party, and the federal government. Cheney's first major position in the government was as White House chief of staff to Republican President Gerald R. Ford from 1975 to the end of Ford's presidency in 1977. He was elected six times as US Representative from Wyoming, serving from 1979 to 1989. Wyoming has a powerful oil and gas industry, and as a congressman Cheney vigorously promoted its interests.

For example, in 1987 he co-sponsored a bill to open up the Arctic National Wildlife Refuge (ANWR) to drilling, a long-sought goal of both oil companies and the conservative movement. Cheney was successful as a congressman, with some seeing him as a future speaker of the house. Cheney's congressional career ended when he was nominated as secretary of defense by President George H.W. Bush after the failure of the nomination of John Tower. Cheney was an important figure shaping US policy prior to the 1991 Gulf War. He supported the decision to stop the war after the liberation of Kuwait rather than pressing on to overthrow Iraqi dictator Saddam Hussein.

After President Bush's defeat in his bid for reelection, Cheney left his secretaryship to serve as chairman of the board and chief executive officer of the Halliburton Company, which is a leading provider of oil field services. Cheney's service to Halliburton, spanning the years 1995 to 2000, was not without controversy, but it was the foundation of his private fortune. He left Halliburton to accept the role of vice-presidential candidate on the Republican ticket with George W. Bush, the son of the President Bush in whose administration Cheney had previously served.

Many historians consider Cheney the most powerful vice president in history. Although the George W. Bush administration had many connections to the oil world outside Cheney, including those of Bush himself, Cheney was frequently viewed as the oil industry's man in the administration. Cheney's most prominent energy-related role in the early days of the Bush administration was as chair of the National Energy Policy Development Group (NEPDG) informally known as the Energy Task Force or sometimes even as the "Cheney Energy Task Force." The stated mission of the group was to diminish American dependence on foreign fuels. It was a high-powered group whose other members were cabinet officials, sub-cabinet officials, and members of the White House staff. It met primarily with industry representatives, shunning labor, consumer groups, and environmentalists as well as state governments. Meetings were closed to the public. The commission was controversial due to its secrecy and its close ties with industry and industry lobbyists including Kenneth L. Lay, the head of Enron. Cheney's efforts to keep the group's deliberations secret led to a series of lawsuits where Cheney's representatives made very strong claims about the power of the executive.

The group's report, issued May 17, 2001, emphasized that the United States would remain dependent on fossil fuels for the foreseeable future while encouraging energy conservation and the development of alternative energy sources. The report recommended that the country both continue to develop its own fossil fuel resources while cultivating a diverse group of global suppliers to diminish dependence on the Middle East. It also recommended closer cooperation in North America between the United States, Canada, and Mexico, including the construction of a pipeline across Canadian territory to bring Alaskan oil to the continental United States. However, rather than turning away from the Middle East as a supplier the report recommended encouraging Middle Eastern oil producers to open up their industries for foreign, presumably American, investment. The report also recommended the renovation of old and the development of new infrastructure particularly in the area of natural gas. It also reiterated Cheney's old advocacy of oil exploration and drilling in ANWR. In order to serve future energy needs, the report claimed, fossil fuel production needed to be increased. Many of its recommendations influenced the Energy Policy Act of 2005, frequently viewed as Cheney's work. He continued to support the interests of the oil and gas industry by opposing any recognition of the severity of the climate crisis.

Like other vice presidents, Cheney brought longtime followers into office with him, many in positions related to energy and resource extraction. Randall Luthi, a Wyoming politician who had been an intern in Cheney's office when Cheney was a congressman, served as head of the Minerals Management Service in the US Department of the Interior, the agency with responsibility for offshore oil leases. In 2010, Luthi left to head the National Ocean Industries Association, a lobbying group representing offshore drillers.

The course of the Bush administration, and Cheney's role as vice president, was drastically altered by the terrorist attacks of September 11, 2001. Although Bush himself was a strong supporter of a military response directed at Iraq, a country with no connection to the 9/11 attacks, Cheney was often viewed as the "hidden hand" behind the decision for war. His support for the war was at least partially motivated by the hope of creating a Western-aligned Iraq as an alternative source of oil to Saudi Arabia. Cheney, partly due to his ties to Halliburton, a major contractor for the US occupation of Iraq, was strongly associated among opponents of the war with the idea that it was a "war for oil." His insistence on going to Baghdad and ousting Saddam Hussein was frequently attributed to the desire to control Iraqi oil resources and contrasted with the much more measured stance he had taken in the first Gulf War.

Cheney left public life at the end of the Bush administration. He largely remained quiet in retirement, although he supported his daughter, US Representative Liz Cheney (R-WY) in her opposition to Republican President Donald Trump.

William E. Burns

See also: American Petroleum Institute; Bush, George H.W.; Gulf War; Halliburton Company; Iraq War and the Project for a New American Century; Prudhoe Bay Oil Field

FURTHER READING

Gellman, Barton. 2008. *Angler: The Cheney Vice Presidency*. New York: Penguin.

Hayes, Stephen F. 2007. *Cheney: The Untold Story of America's Most Powerful and Controversial Vice-President*. New York: Harper Collins.

National Energy Policy Development Group (NEPDG). 2001. *National Energy Policy: Report of the National Energy Policy Development Group*. Washington, DC: US Government Printing Office.

Cherry Mine Disaster

Reputed to be the safest and most modern of the nation's coal mines with its electric lights throughout and firefighting equipment down below, the St. Paul Mine in Cherry, Illinois was also highly profitable, producing some 1,500 tons of coal per day and employing close to 500 men and boys. Unfortunately, the mine suffered a power outage in mid-November 1909, and while awaiting delivery of the heavy-gauge wire needed to repair it, the miners were instructed to use the old oil-based lanterns and torches, both portable and attached to the wall, so that work could continue. Disaster struck on November 13, 1909, when a coal car filled with hay for the thirty or so mules that worked in the mine caught fire. Although it began as a small fire ignored or unnoticed by workers, the blaze grew to become the third-worst mine disaster in the United States with 259 men and boys declared dead. Horrified by the disaster, the nation quickly established more stringent mine fire and safety regulations, including child labor laws, and adopted its first Workmen's Compensation Act.

In need of a steady supply of coal for its trains, the Chicago, Milwaukee, and St. Paul Railroad formed the St. Paul Coal Company, which in turn opened the St. Paul Mine about 100 miles southwest of Chicago in 1905. Named after James Cherry, the superintendent of the St. Paul Mining Company, the small community of Cherry, Illinois sat atop a huge deposit of high-grade bituminous coal. Three veins were divided by shale, clay, and rock. While the top vein was too narrow to be of any real commercial value, the second one at nearly 320 feet below ground was found to contain good quality coal that was 4 to 6 feet thick. Still further down, at about 480 feet below the surface, lay a third vein of even higher-quality "black diamonds." Altogether the Cherry deposit contained so much superior coal that the St. Paul Mine was expected to be able to run at capacity for the next half-century or more.

News of this rich deposit attracted mine workers from around the world. About 80 percent of its miners were first generation immigrants from places like Italy, Lithuania, Germany, Poland, and Wales. Unlike other mines that closed down in the summer, the St. Paul Mine provided work year-round, and it was surrounded by a quaint town that did not resemble the drab mining towns elsewhere. Cherry boasted a park, a public school, a first-class rail station, several general stores, one Catholic and one Congregationalist church, and numerous saloons. Perhaps most alluring was that, "with a tower of steel, a foundation of concrete and its engine, boiler and fan houses all made of brick and stone, the men who built it declared the Cherry Mine fireproof" (Tintori 2002, 4).

That statement was proven catastrophically false around lunch time on November 13, 1909, as a wooden coal car loaded with hay caught fire. Although it was not uncommon for a mine to have an occasional blaze, these were normally small and easy to extinguish. In the Cherry mine, however, workers had left the hay car in the second vein air shaft too close to the kerosene torches in use that day. The mixture of oxygen, accelerant, and flame quickly

FIGURE 6: People gathered at the entrance of a mine shaft in Cherry, Illinois, in the wake of a devastating fire.

turned into a high-heat conflagration billowing black smoke that pushed backward all who tried to extinguish it. Around 1:45 p.m., the signal to abandon the mine sounded, but not all the miners heard it. Especially in the deep third vein, men continued work, unaware of the dangerous situation above.

Rescue parties comprising mine staff and community volunteers went down via a work elevator as long as they could to try to save those trapped below. Thirteen men lost their lives in one final and fatal attempt to rescue their coworkers and neighbors. Over the next few hours, the Cherry Volunteer Fire Department and the Ladd Volunteer Fire Department tried to extinguish the flames, but they lacked proper equipment and experience for a fire this fierce. Mine officials refused to allow them into the mine, so the best they could do was dump water into the airshaft. At about 4:00 p.m., it appeared that the only option left was to seal the mine and deprive the fire of oxygen.

On November 14, a mining engineer with the US Geological Survey, R.Y. Williams, arrived in Cherry with firefighting equipment from the State Mine Experiment and Mine Life Saving Station. Armed with oxygen helmets and tanks, Williams and a couple of other men willing to join him made numerous brief trips into the mine to assess the situation and guide firefighting efforts and rescue plans. Calling for additional hoses, fire suppression chemicals, and special fire engines, Williams and his team of helmet men could do little more than wait. Supplies began arriving the next day along with a veteran fire chief from Chicago, but firefighters were unable to enter the mine until November 18. Two days after the firefighters entered, they were astonished to find survivors. Twenty-one men had survived eight days surrounded by toxic air with little water, and no food.

Following the rescue, expert mine professionals and politicians engaged in lengthy investigations and produced recommendations for improved mining safety practices. The Illinois legislature passed those into law, and finally in 1911, enacted a separate law that would ultimately become the Illinois Workmen's Compensation Act. On the national stage, although President Theodore Roosevelt had recommended the establishment of the US Bureau of Mines in 1907, Congress did not act until after a series of mine disasters, including the one in Cherry. On May 16, 1910, Congress passed the Organic Act, which established the US Bureau of Mines (USBM) and tasked that body with developing safer blasting materials for mines and preventing gas and dust explosions. It remained active until it was dissolved in 1996.

Dana Nichols

See also: Coal; Dawson Mine Disaster; Farmington Mine Disaster; Krebs Mine Disaster; Scofield Mine Disaster; United Mine Workers of America; Upper Big Branch Mine Disaster; West Frankfort Mine Disaster

FURTHER READING

Groves, Adam. 2022. "Cherry Mine Disaster: Introduction." Significant Illinois Fires. University of Illinois LibGuides. Illinois University Library. https://guides.library.illinois.edu/c.php?g=416856&p=2840930 (accessed July 5, 2021).

Kuk, Michael L. 2009. "A Deep and Deadly Fire: The Story of the Cherry Mine Fire Disaster." *Firehouse*. November. Pp. 110–14.

National Institute for Occupational Safety and Health (NIOSH). 2012. *History of the Mining Program*. https://www.cdc.gov/niosh/mining/content/history.html (accessed July 5, 2021).

Stout, Steve. 1979. "Tragedy in November: The Cherry Mine Disaster." *Journal of the Illinois State Historical Society*. Vol. 72. No. 1. Pp. 57–69.

Tintori, Karen. 2002. *Trapped: The 1909 Cherry Mine Disaster*. New York: Atria Books.

Chicago Smoke Abatement Ordinances of 1881 and 1903

Air pollution emerged as a major problem in the nineteenth century. The smoke from innumerable coal-fired iron furnaces, steam-powered manufacturing plants, railroad engines, and millions of coal-heated homes and other sources created a public nuisance and a health hazard that spanned the industrialized parts of Europe, the United Kingdom, and North America. Public officials engaged in political and legal efforts to control air pollution caused by coal burning as early as 1820 in England (Flick 1980, 30). By the 1870s and 1880s, smog had begun to occupy the time and attention of city officials in many American municipalities. Chicago was among the earliest cities to adopt a smoke abatement ordinance, largely because of citizen organization and action, which paved the way for smoke abatement laws in other cities. Over the next century, the US government and many states enacted clean air statutes, executive orders, and administrative regulations to respond to the atmospheric hazards created by burning fossil fuels and by the broader modern, industrialized economy.

By the 1870s, Chicago emerged as an important hub for the nation's network of railroads, and the many trains streaming into the city exacerbated smoke from steam ships crowding the Chicago River and its harbor. Historian Theodore J. Karamanski noted that "in spite of being closed in the winter, Chicago was America's busiest port" and in 1871, more ships arrived in the city than "New York, San Francisco, Philadelphia, Baltimore, Charleston, and Mobile combined" (Karamanski 2005). The growth in air pollution brought a number of Chicagoans together in 1874 to form the Citizen's Association, which sought to determine legal avenues to address the issue (Christy 1960, 126). New smoke arrived from the Joseph H. Brown Mill near Lake Calumet, built in 1875 on the city's south side. The Brown Mill began producing steel and attracted other mills to the neighborhood, which became known as "Irondale" (Bensman 2005).

In response, the Citizen's Association attempted to get a city ordinance enacted in 1880, which failed, but in the next year they succeeded with the smoke abatement sections of the Ordinance of 1881. It declared: "The emission of dense smoke from the smokestack of any boat or locomotive or from any chimney, anywhere within the City, shall be deemed and is hereby declared to be a public nuisance" (Goss 1915, 83). It empowered the Commissioner of Health and Superintendent of Police to issue fines anywhere from $5 to $50, and exempted buildings exclusively used for private residences. Between 1881 and 1884, 4,000 inspections ensued in response to smoke complaints, with 2,000 warnings issued and a number of fines levied (Goss 1915, 83). The measure was popular due to widespread favorable newspaper coverage but drew opposition from coal suppliers and industrial users. Lawsuits put the ordinance under judicial review, and it was upheld by the Illinois Supreme Court in the case of *Harmon v. City of Chicago*, 110 Ill. 400 (1884) (Zollinger 1972, 930).

The success of Chicago's Ordinance of 1881 caught the attention of concerned citizens in other communities, and similar municipal laws were adopted in Cincinnati, Cleveland, Pittsburgh, St. Louis, and St. Paul.

In 1891, the explosive industrial expansion of Chicago outpaced efforts by officials to control emissions through small fines. Prominent citizens became concerned about smog prior to welcoming visitors to Chicago for the World's Columbian Exposition in 1893 and formed the Society for the Prevention of Smoke. The organization included many prominent businessmen who lobbied for a stronger law with enforcement measures, which materialized only well after the World's Fair in the smoke abatement sections of the Ordinance of 1903. The new ordinance affirmed existing inspections and warnings while increasing fines, but also did several new and significant things. First, it established a Board of Inspectors of Steam Boilers and Steam Plants with paid staff positions titled Chief Inspector of Steam Boilers and Steam Plants, Supervising Mechanical Engineer and Deputy Inspector, and Chief Smoke Inspector. These positions were filled by engineers and technicians who were expected to dedicate themselves to the work of investigation and enforcement to a degree that public health and police officials charged with inspections under the 1881 ordinance could not. Second, the law required plans for new construction and renovation of fuel burning equipment be reviewed by the board, which issued certificates of approval. This gave the board a supervisory role over new construction in the city and power to require revisions to ensure compliance with the ordinance's emissions standards.

The Ordinance of 1903 failed to address smoke from trains and ships, which could evade inspection, so subsequent smoke abatement ordinances in 1905 and 1907 tried various remedies. The 1907 law raised the Department of Smoke Inspection to the level of a department in the city administration with a much larger staff of administrators and inspectors. Between 1907 and 1915, a smoke abatement progress report showed that "as a result of the activities of the Department of Smoke Inspection there has been an unquestioned improvement in atmospheric conditions in Chicago" (Goss 1915, 96). However, the report admitted that "visible smoke" had been substantially suppressed while chemicals in the "smokeless combustion" of fuels had yet to be identified and detected. Still, the city of Chicago was "the first in America to conduct an all-out campaign against the nuisance and health menace" of smoke from fossil fuel burning plants (Christy 1960, 130). Chicago's successive revisions of the original smoke abatement ordinance coupled with the gradual evolution of the Department of Smoke Inspection—including the expansion of its authority—provided a model for other cities to follow.

Soon, the engineers and technicians from different municipal smoke control departments formed a professional association known initially as the International Association for Prevention of Smoke. Paul P. Bird, Chief Smoke Inspector of Chicago in 1907–11, became president of the association in 1910. The association met annually where members shared reports about successful management strategies and technological innovations in their cities. The association, renamed the Smoke Prevention Association of America and finally the Air Pollution Control Association in 1950, later formulated a model smoke law for adoption by municipalities and promoted "standards relating to the methods of measuring and testing air pollution" (Christy 1960, 131). The association's reports and its professionalization of the field provided momentum for atmospheric emissions measures at the city, county, state, and federal levels. By the time the federal Clean Air Act of 1970 was enacted, 107 cities, 81 counties, and all 50 states had adopted air pollution control ordinances, statutes, or laws (Stern 1982, 44).

It is difficult to overstate the importance of the Chicago smoke abatement ordinances of 1881 and 1903, which established the key principle that governments have a responsibility to monitor and control atmospheric emissions from fossil fuel burning power plants in the interests of public health. According to David Stradling and Peter Thorsheim, "states had given cities the authority to regulate emissions, and many urban residents had come to assume that municipal governments had the obligation to improve air quality. These new expectations led to evermore complicated anti-smoke ordinances, often modeled after the Chicago law" (Stradling and Thorsheim 1999, 20). In addition, the ordinances demonstrated to later generations the effectiveness of citizen action in securing legislation to address the harmful impacts of energy production and use.

Jeffrey B. Webb

See also: Acid Rain; Chicago World's Columbian Exposition; Clean Air Act of 1970; Clean Power Plan of 2015; US Environmental Protection Agency

FURTHER READING

Bensman, David. 2005. "South Deering." *The Electronic Encyclopedia of Chicago*. Chicago: The Chicago Historical Society.

Christy, William G. 1960. "History of the Air Pollution Control Association." *Journal of the Air Pollution Control Association*. Vol. 10. No. 2. Pp. 126–74.

Flick, Carlos. 1980. "The Movement for Smoke Abatement in 19th-Century Britain." *Technology and Culture*. January. Vol. 21. No. 1. Pp. 29–50.

Goss, W.F.M. 1915. *Smoke Abatement and Electrification of Railway Terminals in Chicago: Report of the Chicago Association of Commerce, Committee of Investigation on Smoke Abatement and Electrification of Railway Terminals*. Chicago: Rand McNally & Company.

Karamanski, Theodore J. 2005. "People and the Port." *The Electronic Encyclopedia of Chicago*. Chicago: The Chicago Historical Society.

Stern, Arthur C. 1982. "History of Air Pollution Legislation in the United States." *Journal of the Air Pollution Control Association*. January. Vol. 32. No. 145. Pp. 44–61.

Stradling, David, and Peter Thorsheim. 1999. "The Smoke of Great Cities: British and American Efforts to Control Air Pollution, 1860–1914." *Environmental History*. January. Vol. 4. No. 1. Pp. 6–31.

Zollinger, Frederick H., Jr. 1972. "Local Governments and Air Pollution." *Ohio State Law Journal*. Vol. 33. No 4. Pp. 924–43.

Chicago World's Columbian Exposition

The Chicago World's Columbian Exposition was a world's fair held in Chicago in 1893. It commemorated the 400th anniversary of the arrival of Christopher Columbus in the Americas. Chicago and New York City engaged in a heated competition to host the fair. The US Congress eventually selected Chicago because, in large part, of the millions of dollars that wealthy Chicago capitalists like Marshall Field, Philip Armour, Gustavus Swift, and Cyrus H. McCormick, Jr. pledged to channel into the fair. The World's Columbian Exposition was an influential social and cultural event. It had a profound impact on many different aspects of life in the United States, not least of which was energy. The fair showcased numerous electricity-related innovations. It was illuminated at night by incandescent lamps and alternating current electricity. Thus, the fair helped increase demand for energy and demonstrated to people, on a large scale, the possibilities and benefits of electrical illumination.

Daniel Burnham (1846–1912), the director of works, and George R. Davis (1840–99), the exposition's director-general, drew some of their inspiration for the design from earlier fairs, particularly the 1889 Paris Universal Exposition, but they also looked for ways to make the Chicago exposition distinct. For many people, including Burnham, Davis, Field, Armour, Swift, McCormick, and others, the exposition became a way to demonstrate Chicago's amazing trajectory. Chicago grew exponentially in the first decades of its existence. A small town of some 4,500 souls in 1840 had become, by 1870, a city of nearly 300,000 people. The Great Chicago Fire (October 8–10, 1871) ripped through the city like a scythe. It killed 300 people, destroyed over 3 square miles of the city, and left well over a 100,000 people homeless. However, like a phoenix, Chicago was reborn from this fiery immolation and sought to prove to the world that it had indeed risen from the ashes. In 1890, the city's population had nearly tripled from the 1870 population and Chicago had truly emerged as the great metropolis of the Midwestern United States.

Burnham and his partner John Wellborn Root (1850–1891) assembled a remarkable team of architects and architects to design the exposition's buildings; a team that included Frederick Law Olmsted (1822–1903), most famous for designing New York City's Central Park. Scholars have shown that the design of the exposition was meant to capture what the designers believed to be the ideal layout of a city. Furthermore, in keeping with prevailing architectural styles, the exposition cleaved to Beaux Arts principles of design, specifically French neoclassical architecture that emphasized symmetry, balance, and splendor. The fair won the nickname "White City" because of the material (plaster of Paris and white paint) used to cover the building façades. Many people admired the White City's neoclassical architecture and believed the fair's buildings would improve the quality of architecture in US cities. Others believed that this architectural style would have a deleterious impact on US architecture. The exposition encompassed 690 acres and featured almost 200 buildings that showcased people and cultures from forty-six different countries.

CHICAGO DAY: OCTOBER 9, 1893

October 9, 1893 marked the twenty-second anniversary of the Great Chicago Fire. Thus, it became a pivotal moment in the campaign to demonstrate how Chicago had recovered and prospered after the devastating immolation. In order to boost attendance, railroad companies reduced fares, many corporations bought tickets for their employees, and businesses closed so workers could take their families to the fair. Given the day's attendance—over three-quarters of a million people—these strategies succeeded.

Evan C. Rothera

The dedication ceremonies occurred on October 21, 1892. The fairgrounds did not actually open to the public until May 1, 1893. Once opened, the fair continued until October 30, 1893. People's reasons for attending the fair varied tremendously and, once there, they no doubt found some elements more appealing than others. Many people wrote fondly about walking through the Midway, a mile-long avenue that featured a giant wheel designed by George Ferris and a number of other attractions blending education and entertainment. The famous and the elites mingled with millions of unknown and obscure people. Nikola Tesla displayed some of his inventions. Frederick Jackson Turner delivered a paper on the significance of the frontier in US history. Henry Ford admired an internal combustion engine. Over 27 million people attended the fair. On October 9, 1893, alone, which was designated as Chicago Day, the fair set a world record with a whopping attendance of more than three-quarters of a million people.

The World's Columbian Exposition featured extensive use of electricity. Many people saw the fair as one of the last episodes in the War of the Currents. White City was a coda of sorts to the famous competition between Thomas Edison, who favored direct current, and George Westinghouse, a champion of alternating current. Efforts to power the fair with electricity allowed Westinghouse Electric to demonstrate the efficacy of alternating current on a large scale. Westinghouse did not submit an initial bid. General Electric, a company formed by the merger of Edison General Electric Company and Thomson-Houston Electric, on the other hand, did submit a bid to power the fair and the planned 93,000 incandescent lamps with direct current. Given that their initial bid was rather high, General Electric lowered their bid, but Westinghouse Electric underbid them. Westinghouse could not use the Edison incandescent lamp, because the patent belonged to General Electric. Thus, Westinghouse developed a different type of lamp—the Westinghouse Sawyer-Man stopper lamp. Although one could applaud Westinghouse's ingenuity, the lamps they installed were short-lived and required a veritable platoon of workers to constantly replace them. To make matters even more difficult, Westinghouse discovered that they had severely underbid and, consequently, struggled to supply all the equipment and lighting to power the fair. Nevertheless, despite these hiccups, many people who attended the fair recalled their amazement at the dazzling effect of electricity and electric lights.

The Electrical Building at White City was one of the fair's marvels, although certainly not the only one. Visitors to this building could see a statue of Benjamin Franklin, different types of interior and exterior lighting, search lights, a seismograph, and electric incubators for chicken eggs. General Electric, Western Electric, and Westinghouse all had displays in the building. Westinghouse exhibited devices developed by Nikola Tesla including a two-phase induction motor and his "Egg of Columbus." Along with the Electrical Building, White City also featured many other exhibitions designed to highlight the industrial and manufacturing capability of the United States. These buildings and the products, tools, and inventions they displayed made the World's Columbian Exposition something well more than just another world's fair for many people. Indeed, the fair showcased not only electricity, but numerous electricity-related innovations and this helped increase demand for energy in the years following the fair.

Depictions of White City sometimes tend toward triumphal portrayals. The exposition, which was so triumphantly planned in 1890–2, occurred during the Panic of 1893, a severe economic downturn. At a time when White City offered a triumphal vision of US industrial capacity, many US industries were in freefall and people found themselves unemployed or underemployed. Mere months after the fair closed, workers at Chicago's Pullman Company, members of the American Railway Union (ARU), struck against repressive corporate policies. As the strike continued, violence mounted and Eugene V. Debs and the ARU called for a boycott of all trains carrying Pullman cars. President Grover Cleveland obtained an injunction against the strikers, although it failed to stop the strike. At that point, Cleveland sent in the US Army to stop the strikers from interfering with the trains. A Chicago company stood at the center of the strike and the subsequent violence and this was a marked contrast with the image of Chicago on display at White City. Perhaps, though, it was an image more in line with reality, in a city whose slaughterhouses would soon be immortalized—and not in a positive way—in Upton Sinclair's *The Jungle* (1906).

Furthermore, as the historian Robert W. Rydell argues, world's fairs in the Gilded Age and Progressive Era often embodied a specific set of ideas about race, nation, and empire. Expositions, Rydell contends, "offered millions of fairgoers an opportunity to reaffirm their collective national identity in an updated synthesis of progress and white supremacy" (Rydell 1984, 4). In addition, the exposition occurred at the beginning of a period historians have labeled the nadir of US race relations. Extralegal killings of African Americans occurred across the country. Many African Americans protested how the exposition tended to ignore black Americans and their achievements. Ida B. Wells and Ferdinand Barnett authored a pamphlet denouncing the absence of African Americans at the exposition. In other words, the sparkling electrified façade of the exposition tends to captures people's attention—both then and now—but divisions and ugliness hid behind that glittering exterior.

Evan C. Rothera

See also: Chicago Smoke Abatement Ordinances of 1881 and 1903; Edison, Thomas Alva; Electricity; Industrial Revolution; Insull, Samuel; Tesla, Nikola; War of the Currents; Westinghouse, George

FURTHER READING

Cronon, William. 1991. *Nature's Metropolis: Chicago and the Great West*. New York. W. W. Norton & Company, Inc.

Jonnes, Jill. 2003. *Empires of Light: Tesla, Westinghouse, and the Race to Electrify the World*. New York: Random House, Inc.

Larson, Erik. 2003. *The Devil in the White City: Murder, Magic, and Madness at the Fair that Changed America*. New York: Random House, Inc.

Rydell, Robert W. 1984. *All the World's a Fair: Visions of Empire at American International Exhibitions, 1876–1916*. Chicago: The University of Chicago Press.

Whissel, Kristen. 2008. *Picturing American Modernity: Traffic, Technology, and the Silent Cinema*. Durham: Duke University Press.

Church Rock Uranium Mill Spill

Church Rock Uranium Mill Spill, which took place in New Mexico on July 16, 1979 and became a symbol for the dangers of uranium mining (Shebala 2009), is considered the largest spill of radioactive material in US nuclear history. The spill happened three and half months after the Three Mile Island accident, and in the shade of that catastrophe Church Rock Uranium Mill spill did not receive a proper level of media coverage and public attention.

Located on what was originally Navajo reservation land, Church Rock mill was situated on privately owned land approximately 17 miles north of Gallup in the state of New Mexico. It was bordered to the north and southwest by Navajo Nation Tribal Trust lands. Church Rock was a site for extracting uranium ore from Navajo lands under leases with the Navajo Nation from 1944, when the United States started stockpiling uranium for nuclear weapons, until 1986, and operated alongside other uranium mines in this territory (EPA 2020). These mines are innocuous, with their most distinguishing features being large ponds of murky liquid, unusual in such dry terrain. Church Rock had a scattered community of Navajo families who survived by herding cattle, goats, and sheep in those lands (Wasserman 1982). After forty years of using these lands, federal officials estimate that private companies mined approximately 4 million tons of uranium ore from mines on the Navajo reservation (Jennings 2014).

In 1968 the United Nuclear Corporation launched mining operations which converted this area in the largest underground uranium mine in the United States. After initiating the technological process of extracting uranium ore, the Church Rock Mill produced more than 2 million pounds of uranium oxide per year. The waste, left from the mining process, was disposed of in three lined lagoons fortified by a human-made dam. It turned out the dam was built on geologically unsound land. According to Tommy Smith, both the United Nuclear Corporation and state and federal agencies were aware of this fact (Smith 2019).

Larry King, an underground surveyor for the United Nuclear Corporation's Church Rock Uranium mine in New Mexico, began to notice "fist-sized cracks" in the south side of the tailings dam in the early summer of 1979. The massive earthen wall of the dam held back thousands of tons of toxic water and waste, produced by the mine and the nearby mill that extracted uranium from raw ore (Gilbert 2019). However, nobody in a position of responsibility took his report seriously, and no further signs of disintegrating infrastructure were reported (Brugge 2007, 1597).

A few weeks later, at 5:30 a.m. on July 16, 1979, the dam breached and a huge amount of uranium waste and radioactive water went into the Puerco River. According to a report by the New Mexico Environmental Improvement Division, over 1,000 tons of solid radioactive mill waste and 94 million gallons of acidic, radioactive tailings solution flowed into the

Puerco River. Contaminants traveled 80 miles downstream to Navajo County, Arizona and onto the Navajo Nation, producing a level of radioactivity seven thousand times greater than that permitted in drinking water (Millard 1983, 1). The amount of radiation released in the Church Rock Uranium Mill spill was larger than the amount released at Three Mile Island, just four months prior (Cohn 2012, 132). The radioactive material was a mixture of water and mill tailings, leftover toxic contaminants from the mining process that converted mined uranium into yellow slurry, known as yellow cake. The tailings were "placed in unlined evaporation ponds at the mill site," the report says, meaning the radioactive goop that washed into the Puerco River and flowed through communities downstream was a public health hazard (Jennings 2014).

According to Judy Pasternak's *Yellow Dirt: A Poisoned Land and the Betrayal of the Navajos* (2011), the water, filled with acids from the milling process, twisted a metal culvert in the Puerco, and "sheep keeled over and died, and crops curdled along the banks. The surge of radiation was detected as far away as Sanders, Arizona, fifty miles downstream" (Pasternak 2011, 149). Surrounding residents of the mill, mostly Navajos who relied on the Puerco River as a watering source for livestock and irrigation, were not immediately aware of the toxic danger resulting from the spill (Cohn 2012).

Local Navajo people were kept in the dark about the possible consequences of the radiation spill and were not notified about radiation burns resulting in heat stroke. After the incident, high lung cancer rates were discovered among former uranium miners and local residents became aware of the accumulation of waste on tribal lands from the mines. Despite the public nature of the pollution event at Church Rock, in which massive quantities of radioactive material was discharged into the environment, the health-related consequences of uranium mining and processing were largely unknown and unacknowledged (Brugge 2002, 1410).

Just after the disaster, the United Nuclear Corporation created new drinking wells and removed 3,500 tons of sediment from the Puerco River, but this amounted to only 1 percent of the estimated total spill material. Later that year, the governor of New Mexico denied requests from the Navajo Tribal Council's Emergency Services Coordinating Committee to ask for a federal disaster area declaration. Less than five months after the spill, the Nuclear Regulatory Commission permitted the United Nuclear Corporation to resume operations at the Church Rock Mill. These activities worsened conditions in the area, leading to more extensive groundwater contamination. Finally, in 1982, the mining works were abandoned (Brugge 2007, 1595). In 1994, the US Environmental Protection Agency (EPA) belatedly mounted an investigation and cleanup at the Church Rock mine site.

In 1993, the Navajo Nation's representatives raised concerns relating to the physical hazards like shafts, pits, and debris piles and the potential exposure to uranium ore, which contained toxic materials and heavy metals. Fifteen years later, in June 2008, after completing the various studies, several federal agencies finalized a five-year plan for cleaning up the legacy effects of uranium mining on Navajo land. From 2008 through 2012, EPA spent $22 million to test and replace contaminated houses, compared with $1.5 million spent in the preceding five years. Further, agencies faced challenges in effectively engaging tribal communities, in part, because agencies have not always collaborated on their outreach efforts (Jennings 2014).

The US Government Accountability Office (GAO) provided information about the existing hazards for local residents in its May 2014 report: "the Navajo people continue to live with the environmental and health effects from mining operations: more than 500 abandoned mines are located across the reservation, some close to homes and communities, and an unknown number of homes and drinking water sources contain radioactive elements.

According to the Environmental Protection Agency (EPA) and other federal agencies, health effects—including lung cancer, bone cancer, and impaired kidney function—can result from exposure to elevated levels of uranium and other radionuclides" (GAO 2014, 7).

Despite federal agencies' efforts to reduce the highest risks to the Navajo people from uranium contamination from abandoned mines, the Navajo residents still consider that neither the federal government nor the state of New Mexico have taken sufficient steps to remediate the Church Rock spill even after forty years and have not given sufficient attention to other victims of nuclear accidents. These victims remain under the catastrophe's long shadow and must deal with poisoned livestock, ongoing health problems, and other aftereffects (Gilbert 2019). One of those aftereffects is the change in local hydrology. Before the spill, the area flowed with water only during spring rains. Currently, this area is wet year-round, dampened by water pumped from the mine shafts to keep them from flooding. This water is laced with radioactive isotopes. Navajo residents have continued to suffer health problems due to substantial increases in radioactivity found in the water, soil, and air.

Today, Church Rock remains the subject of research and debate over nuclear waste management and mitigation of radioactive environmental contaminants. Activists and Indigenous voices hope to keep the Church Rock uranium mill spill from the list of "forgotten" nuclear disasters in the United States, and to maintain the EPA's vigilance in completing the tasks of cleanup and remediation in the Navajo peoples' traditional homeland.

Inna Sukhenko

See also: Atomic Energy Acts; Energy Fuels, Inc.; Idaho National Laboratory; Navajo Reservation Uranium Mining; Nuclear Power; Nuclear Regulatory Commission; Nuclear Waste Policy Act of 1982; Yucca Mountain Nuclear Waste Repository

FURTHER READING

Brugge, Doug, and Rob Goble. 2002. "The History of Uranium Mining and the Navajo People." *American Journal of Public Health*. September. Vol. 92. No. 9. Pp. 1410–19.

Brugge, Doug, Jamie L. de Lemos, and Cat Bui. 2007. "The Sequoyah Corporation Fuels Release and the Church Rock Spill: Unpublicized Nuclear Releases in American Indian Communities." *American Journal of Public Health*. Vol. 97. No. 9. Pp. 1595–600.

Cohn, Ronald, and Jesse Russell. 2012. *Church Rock Uranium Mill Spill*. VSD.

EPA (US Environmental Protection Agency). 2020. "Navajo Nation: Cleaning Up Abandoned Uranium Mines." US Government. https://www.epa.gov/navajo-nation-uranium-cleanup (accessed May 1, 2020).

GAO (US Government Accountability Office). 2014. "Uranium Contamination: Overall Scope, Time Frame, and Cost Information Is Needed for Contamination Cleanup on the Navajo Reservation." May. GAO Publication No. GAO-14-323. Washington, DC: US Government Printing Office. https://www.gao.gov/assets/670/662964.pdf (accessed May 1, 2020).

Gilbert, Samuel. 2019. "Church Rock, America's Forgotten Nuclear Disaster, Is Still Poisoning Navajo Lands 40 Years Later." VICE. August 12. https://www.vice.com/en_us/article/ne8w4x/church-rock-americas-forgotten-nuclear-disaster-is-still-poisoning-navajo-lands-40-years-later (accessed May 2, 2020).

Jennings, Trip. 2014. "Remembering the Largest Radioactive Spill in U.S. History." *New Mexico In Depth*. July 7. http://nmindepth.com/2014/07/07/remembering-the-largest-radioactive-spill-in-u-s-history (accessed May 2, 2020).

Millard, Jere, et al. 1983. "The Church Rock Uranium Mill Tailings Spill: A Health and Environmental Assessment Summary Report." September. New Mexico Environmental Improvement Division. Health and Environment Department. US Environmental Protection Agency Records Collections. https://semspub.epa.gov/work/06/1000720.pdf (accessed May 3, 2020).

Pasternak, Judy. 2011. *Yellow Dirt: A Poisoned Land and the Betrayal of the Navajos*. New York: Free Press.

Shebala, Marley. 2009. "1979 Church Rock Spill a Symbol for Uranium Dangers." *Navajo Times*. July 23, 2009. https://navajotimes.com/news/2009/0709/072309uranium.php (accessed May 1, 2020).

Smith, Tommy. 2019. "Church Rock Uranium Mill Spill." Environment and Society Portal. The Rachel Carson Center. http://www.environmentandsociety.org/tools/keywords/church-rock-uranium-mill-spill (accessed May 3, 2020).

Wasserman, Harvey, and Norman Solomon. 1982. *Killing Our Own: The Disaster of America's Experience with Atomic Radiation, 1945–1982*. New York: Dell Publishing Co., Inc. https://ratical.org/radiation/KillingOurOwn/KOO9.html (accessed May 2, 2020).

Cist, Jacob

Born in 1782 to prominent Philadelphia publisher, businessman, and German immigrant Charles Cist, Jacob Cist (1782–1825) had a solid primary school education and became an accomplished writer and sketch artist before the age of fifteen. At this young age he entered his father's business, publishing material for the administration of President John Adams. Cist moved to Washington, DC in 1800 when the family business expanded there, as the federal capital was relocated there from its initial site in New York. At this point Cist also took a position in the US Post Office Department, a job he retained in 1801 when a new administration arrived in Washington and the Cist family printing business was shuttered.

Jacob Cist was indoctrinated early in his life in the potential and significance of the burgeoning coal industry under the watchful eye of his father and that of his uncle, Jacob Weiss, an early American proponent of coal. His father had in fact published works concerning the centrality of coal to the Industrial Revolution in England, and he and Weiss were both involved in early coal mining operations in Pennsylvania. Upon his father's death in 1805, Jacob inherited a number of shares in a mining company, although these were not particularly valuable at the time due to the company's poor management. It was when Jacob married Sarah Hollenbeck of Wilkes-Barre in 1807, however, that he really had the opportunity to invest in and to exploit the rich coal deposits of Pennsylvania. With the partnership of his rich and powerful father-in-law, Cist began to explore the possibilities inherent in anthracite, or "hard" coal, as opposed to bituminous, or "soft," coal, which then vied with charcoal and lumber as a commonly used heating resource. Although anthracite had extremely limited utility at the time, the Hollenbeck family's huge tracts of land included several tens of thousands of acres rich in this type of coal, and Cist early on made some headway in the development of industrial applications for anthracite.

An early opportunity for anthracite coal emerged with the War of 1812, and Cist was uniquely placed, prepared, and eager to exploit the opportunity. The British blockaded the mouths of the Chesapeake and the Delaware Bays, completely cutting off shipping routes to Philadelphia, which relied on deliveries of Virginia bituminous coal for a large percentage of its heating fuel. As the price of the remaining stockpiles of available soft coal skyrocketed, Cist and his business associates stepped into the marketplace with ready supplies of hard coal from nearby regions of Pennsylvania with more secure shipment routes. They pursued this opportunity aggressively by taking the financial risk of obtaining a great deal of anthracite acreage under lease in order to maximize their stock. Moreover, Cist was a central figure in the popularization of this relatively new, alternative form of fuel. He sang the praises of anthracite's cleaner-burning, fuel-efficient qualities in comparison with bituminous coal, which burns far more easily but at the cost of more soot and smoke, and considerably less heat. Cist went even further, designing a stove for burning anthracite, an entrepreneurial innovation for which he was awarded a patent. Cist also proposed and promoted numerous industrial uses for anthracite. The early success of Cist and his partners in this regard was closely aligned with the rising and falling prices of soft coal, for which markets and applications were well-established. For that reason, the profitability of the anthracite trade plummeted after the war with the British was resolved in 1815 and bituminous coal was once more readily available.

Undeterred, Cist continued to preach the gospel of anthracite after the conclusion of the War of 1812, publishing pamphlets on the topic and citing testimonials from various related industries. His expertise in this area was acknowledged by leading scientists after a major scientific journal cited him in the early 1820s as a source of samples and analysis. Cist thereafter began to be referenced as an authority in this field on a regular basis. Unfortunately for Cist, both the industrial technologies and commercial markets for anthracite were still in their nascent stages when he died in 1825. Cist was a key figure in providing a firm foundation for the burgeoning anthracite industry, however, and both his investments and investigations in this field paved the way for later entrepreneurs and scientists alike. It has been argued that innovations utilizing anthracite coal were instrumental in the American Industrial Revolution, and Jacob Cist certainly deserves special recognition in this regard.

Christopher R. Fee

See also: Coal; Cumberland Iron and Coal Company; Lakes, Arthur; Susquehanna Coal Company

FURTHER READING

Adams, Sean Patrick. 2008. "Warming the Poor and Growing Consumers: Fuel Philanthropy in the Early Republic's Urban North." *The Journal of American History*. Vol. 95. No. 1. Pp. 69–94. https://academic.oup.com/jah/article/95/1/69/781767 (accessed March 9, 2021).

Adams, Sean Patrick. 2011. "How Choice Fueled Panic: Philadelphians, Consumption, and the Panic of 1837." *Enterprise & Society*. Vol. 12. No. 4. Pp. 761–89. https://muse.jhu.edu/article/458162 (accessed March 9, 2021).

Huss, John. 2000. "Cist, Jacob (1782–1825), Anthracite Coal Pioneer, Naturalist, and Inventor." *American National Biography*. February. Oxford: Oxford University Press. https://www.anb.org/view/10.1093/anb/9780198606697.001.0001/anb-9780198606697-e-1300288 (accessed March 4, 2021).

Jones, Christopher F. 2018. "The Materiality of Energy." *Canadian Journal of History*. Vol. 53. No. 3. Pp. 378–94. https://muse.jhu.edu/article/714234 (accessed March 9, 2021).

Knies, Michael. 2001. *Coal on the Lehigh, 1790–1827: Beginnings and Growth of the Anthracite Industry in Carbon County, Pennsylvania*. Easton, PA: Canal History and Technology Press.

Powell, Benjamin. 1978. *Philadelphia's First Fuel Crisis: Jacob Cist and the Developing Market for Pennsylvania Anthracite*. University Park, PA: Pennsylvania State University Press.

Clean Air Act of 1970

The Clean Air Act of 1970 consists of a series of amendments to the original Clean Air Act of 1963. The 1970 Act significantly expanded the authority and power of the federal government to take actions to reduce air pollution. The legislation required the creation of comprehensive federal and state regulations for both industrial sources of pollution as well as vehicular sources. The newly created US Environmental Protection Agency (EPA) assumed responsibility for crafting and enforcing the federal standards while providing guidance and oversight to the states.

As the 1960s drew to a close, there was growing concern over pollution and its effects on human life and the environment. The Clean Air Act of 1963 represented the first attempt by the federal government to act on this issue. However, implementation of pollution control measures and air quality standards, especially pollution produced by automobiles and trucks, fell well short of the Act's goals. Indeed, pollution steadily worsened as the decade progressed, prompting calls for stricter enforcement and federally established standards. A subsequent attempt to impose such requirements, the Air Quality Act of 1967, was a complete failure, as the Act's provisions for the states to establish standards were never implemented. Throughout 1969 and 1970, growing public pressure for governmental action culminated in the first Earth Day, which took place on April 22, 1970. In response to this public outcry, President Richard Nixon, also pressured by the Democrat-controlled Congress, created the EPA to provide new leadership combating pollution. The EPA officially came into existence in mid-December 1970. Congress at the same time passed the Clean Air Act of 1970, which Nixon signed into law on December 30, 1970.

The act authorized the development of comprehensive federal and state regulations to limit emissions from industrial and vehicular sources. The legislation created four regulatory programs regarding stationary (industrial) pollution sources: National Ambient Air Quality Standards (NAAQS); State Implementation Plans (SIP); New Source Performance Standards (NSPS); and National Standards for Hazardous Air Pollutants (NESHAP). NAAQS established standards for how much ozone, carbon monoxide (CO), particulate matter, lead, sulfur dioxide, and nitrogen dioxide are allowed in outdoor air. For SIP, the act established a deadline of September 1, 1971 for states to submit emission standards and implementation plans for enforcing the standards, with the requirement that implementation of these plans be completed within three years. Ultimately, the implementation of state-level plans faced litigation and political hurdles, to the point the issue would have to be readdressed in subsequent legislation. NSPS entailed rules for equipment required to be installed in new and modified industrial facilities, as well as rules determining whether a facility was "new." NESHAP involved establishing maximum levels allowed in the atmosphere for 187 toxic air pollutants, defined as non-NAAQ pollutants that have a scientifically established danger to human and animal life. The goal for the NESHAP was to first regulate, then reduce then, to the extent possible, eliminate the emission of toxic substances by industrial sources. The act also set standards for aircraft emissions, including testing of aircraft by the US Department of Defense, authorized lawsuits by citizens for violation of standards, and provided greater oversight and registration of fuel additives.

Additionally, the act created substantial new standards regarding automobile emissions, including testing and certification. By model year 1975, vehicles were required to have CO and hydrocarbon (HC) emissions reduced to 90 percent less than 1970 models, though automobile manufacturers were given the option of a one-year extension for meeting the standards. Additionally, all vehicles had to be warranted to meet the new emission standards for a minimum of 50,000 miles, and to submit emission control devices for certification and testing. The act established a "light duty" category, including passenger cars, vans, pick-up trucks, and later minivans and SUVs, and a "heavy duty" category for large trucks and buses, establishing separate standards for each category. The act also required the EPA to consult with the National Academy of Sciences to conduct studies of vehicular emissions and to provide semiannual reports to both the agency and Congress.

Finally, enforcement authority was substantially expanded, granting the newly created EPA broad powers to establish and enforce standards federally and to require the states to develop standards and implementation plans. Under the legislation, the EPA determined which pollutants were a threat to public health and categorized them as either NAAQ or NESHAP. The EPA also established under the act minimum air quality standards in order to help create measurable emission standards to be enforced. The act further required the EPA to develop and publish the list of NESHAP, establishing a maximum allowable emission for each. The act required the EPA to develop standards for "new" and modified industrial facilities, taking into account both public health and the cost of implementing pollution controls, as well as the determining the best means of attaining compliance with the newly established standards. The act also mandated that the EPA implement and enforce the stricter emission standards for vehicles. In response to the act, automobile manufacturers immediately sought an extension of the deadline, which the EPA denied. The EPA's decision was later upheld by the US Court of Appeals. After negotiations, the EPA granted the one-year extension, but only after implementing interim standards that needed to be met.

The Clean Air Act of 1970 went considerably farther than its predecessor in establishing minimum air quality standards, providing federal and eventually state regulations of pollutant emissions, and in creating the foundation for long-term implementation of pollution control and health and safety measures in the United States. In particular, the 1970 act began the process of significantly reducing vehicular emissions, setting the precedent for Congress to create Corporate Average Fuel Economy (CAFE) standards for vehicle emissions in 1975, and the creation, manufacture, and installation of antipollution measures such as catalytic converters on all vehicles. The act further guaranteed the efficacy and survival of the newly created EPA, by granting the new agency significant powers and responsibilities. From oversight of the states' antipollution efforts to the creation of pollutant lists and maximum allowable atmospheric levels to the oversight of both industrial and vehicular emissions, the EPA and its first director, William Ruckelshaus, found itself leading the government's response to the public's demands for action. Over the course of the next half-century, the EPA effectively implemented the standards established by the Clean Air Act, and expanded upon them through the creation of additional acts and amendments. The Clean Air Act of 1970 served as a model of government-sponsored environmental action that helped the

United States begin the process of reducing atmospheric pollution and improving health and living standards, both domestically and globally.

Richard M. Filipink

See also: Acid Rain; CAFE Standards; Chicago Smoke Abatement Ordinances of 1881 and 1903; Clean Power Plan of 2015; Earth Day; Natural Resources Defense Council; Sierra Club; US Environmental Protection Agency

FURTHER READING

Bailey, Christopher. 1998. *Congress and Air Pollution*. Manchester: Manchester University Press.
Hoff, Joan. 1994. *Nixon Reconsidered*. New York: Basic Books.
Mintz, Joel A. 2012. *Enforcement at the EPA: High Stakes and Hard Choices*.l Rev. ed. Austin: University of Texas Press.
Rogers, Paul. 1990. "EPA History: The Clean Air Act of 1970." *E.P.A. Journal*. January/February. https://archive.epa.gov/epa/aboutepa/epa-history-clean-air-act-1970.html (accessed June 2, 2021).
Stern, Arthur C. 1982. "History of Air Pollution Legislation in the United States." *Journal of the Air Pollution Control Association*. Vol. 32. No. 1. January. Pp. 44–61. https://www.tandfonline.com/doi/pdf/10.1080/00022470.1982.10465369 (accessed June 1, 2021).

Clean Coal

Clean coal is a term with a double meaning, denoting attempts by industrial corporations to clean up the actual combustion of coal in the face of scientific and environmental concerns about its hazards, and also the discursive construction of "cleansing" the coal burning process under a different terminological banner to better allow for corporate malfeasance. Clean coal became a methodology, both as an industrial process and as a media strategy, starting in the 1980s. Much of the material work was accomplished through the US Department of Energy, which at a later date created the Clean Coal Technology & Clean Coal Power Initiative (CCPI) to test and implement clean coal technologies, but this paralleled efforts by coal mining companies, industry associations, and conservative media to respond to criticism from environmental organizations.

Clean coal programs are carried out through links between corporations and government agencies to limit pollution caused by power systems, but frequently face ardent supporters of deregulation within lobbying, conservative, and corporate sectors that have found regulation burdensome to their profit margins. Critics of clean coal programs argue that the energy lobby intentionally alters the connotations of coal burning by using the language of "clean coal" within the public sphere in order to create community-level political impetus for the United States to reject or evade emissions guidelines framed in the Kyoto Protocol, adopted in 1997, and recognized as international law in 2005.

Within recent political discourse, as evident in the contentious presidential election of 2016, the term clean coal was used, as environmentalists contend, to justify the continued use of coal supplies that pollute the environment and shorten the lives of laborers within the coal industry. Coal mining companies and coal-fueled public utilities promote the idea that coal is clean, or can become cleaner, and that carbon can simply be captured in the atmosphere through technological advances. Critics respond to these claims by suggesting that the language of clean coal is being used for political and moral cover as industries reap great profits on the backs of exploited coal miners. They further suggest that the use of the terminology of clean coal helped coal companies reestablish a positive identity within conservative culture, as they are patriotically deemed to be essential to the American way of life, despite their continued pollution and creation of other environmental hazards. The renewed support given to coal production has consequently inspired the construction of dozens of new coal plants throughout the United States in the early twenty-first century.

There are many different processes for materially cleaning the coal burning process. Early clean coal practices involved a process of desulfurization, as sulfur content is considered an impurity within most coal supplies. These original procedures created purer coal that burned with greater efficiency. The most historically pervasive coal cleaning process involved the use of smokestacks, which allowed the capture of some pollutants, which were then buried beneath the earth or used for other industrial purposes. Carbon capture, the term for the greater share of modern methods for coal cleaning, is a multivalent term for processes that include gasification to separate pollutants before combustion, the capture of exhaust gases after the energy process, and/or mixed combustion processes that limit the burning of specific materials, generally through liquefaction at early stages of the combustion process.

Furthermore, dewatering of coal supplies before burning is considered by clean coal advocates to be a clean coal process, as combustion becomes more efficient when coal is dried. Clean coal can also relate to the notion of coal washing, which operates, like some mixed combustion processes, through different chemical processes and physical methods to eliminate various impurities from coal prior to combustion. Additionally, clean coal procedures can also often involve more modern and ecologically friendly forms of gasification, which can work to prevent the release of pollutants by turning coal into gaseous substances that some consider to be relatively renewable sources of energy. A more recent turn in clean coal technology involves burning coal with heated oxygen rather than heated air, termed oxy-fuel combustion, as higher flame temperatures from oxygen reduce the amount of nitrogen released through the process.

These sometimes environmentally advantageous but unevenly applied methods, meaning the historical use of smokestacks coupled with modern processes involving carbon capture, gasification, and liquefication, can never arrest all metal pollutants or threatening gases that emerge from the coal burning process. Many of these molecules avoid detection and capture until they accumulate in the atmosphere and overheat the earth's environment. These different methods, often defined as making coal cleaner, are also usually costly processes that many energy companies attempt to avoid. Consequently, although the term clean coal was originally created to denote policies related to a reduction of emissions and pollutants that come from the burning of coal, critics contend that the concept has become a term of deception that frequently connotes cleanliness in a production scheme that can never be clean. Scientists have shown that the thermal decomposition of coal releases toxic molecules like sulfur dioxide and nitrous oxide into the atmosphere. On the basis of this knowledge, environmentalists believe the use of the term "clean coal" is a form of greenwashing that protects polluters, manipulating discourses in the media through the use of firms specializing in public relations. Greenwashing can also occur simply by passing laws that deem industrial processes once considered toxic no longer a threat to public health.

GREENWASHING

Greenwashing is the use of terms in the public sphere that are meant to convince people that business and industry are working to control pollution and to view scientifically studied green solutions as both uneconomical and socially illegitimate. These marketing manipulations, arising to great force due to the superior wealth grasped by polluters, occur with inordinate force though the use of terms like clean coal and the constant assertion of unproven dreams like carbon sequestration, or the removal of carbon from the atmosphere once it has already been released.

Andrew Kettler

The release of nitrous oxide and sulfur dioxide during the coal combustion process are widely known to produce acid rain and global warming. As such, coal companies target these two pollutants in their carbon capture processes in order to claim they are producing clean coal. However, those pollutants are only part of the broad spectrum of threatening molecules, metals, and particulates that are released as part of the combustion process, as are the associated frequent discharges of mercury, uranium, thorium, lead, and arsenic, all of which cause great risk to human health.

Whether anthracite or bituminous, coal pollution has been shown to cause cancer, autism, miscarriages, cardiovascular issues, and poor lung and brain development in children. Coal miners have much shorter life spans than the general population. Critics contend that energy companies use the term clean coal to impose an exploitative form of capitalism upon these laborers and upon the rest of society, whereby the environment becomes unhealthy for human bodies, and especially for disadvantaged groups in threatened areas like Appalachia, which are forced to suffer from pollution arising from coal mining and/or coal combustion. Throughout the history of coal mining, striking workers have risen to protest labor conditions in their mines and to obtain better pay for their families. Labor activists argue that workers have yet to come together with sufficient force to address the hidden dangers to workers' health as they continue to work in mines, live near the sources of coal pollution, consume contaminated water, and breath in coal-polluted air.

The critics of fossil fuel use contend that the Anthropocene—a fossil fuel dominated physical environment—has been introduced on the sly by the economic power of capitalism through friendly sounding terms like clean coal. Proponents of clean coal argue that the advanced technologies of carbon-scrubbing smokestacks collect sulfur and other particulates from fossil fuel combustion and produce helpful by-products like fertilizers and other useful materials. Clean coal processes remove some pollution from coal combustion and may become increasingly more efficient at removing toxins as technology advances within the power-generation sector. Nevertheless, scientists have shown that coal burning continues to change the climate by heating the atmosphere to record levels, warming the oceans, and melting the ice caps. Socially conscious environmentalists who are mindful of the medical and ecological risks of coal find it difficult to gain an audience for their views, since coal and power companies, through their media strategists and political lobbyists, produce what might be considered false perceptions about clean coal and its supposed benefits.

Andrew Kettler

See also: Acid Rain; Black Lung Disease; Climate Change; Chicago Smoke Abatement Ordinances of 1881 and 1903; Clean Air Act of 1970; Clean Power Plan of 2015; Coal

FURTHER READING

Curran, Daniel. 1993. *Dead Laws for Dead Men: The Politics of Federal Coal Mine Health and Safety Legislation*. Pittsburgh: The University of Pittsburgh Press.

Derickson, Alan. 2014. *Black Lung: Anatomy of a Public Health Disaster*. Ithaca, NY: Cornell.

Douwe, Klaes. 2010. *Clean Coal*. New York: Nova Science.

Klein, Naomi. 2007. *The Shock Doctrine: The Rise of Disaster Capitalism*. New York: Metropolitan.

Lockwood, Alan. 2012. *The Silent Epidemic: Coal and the Hidden Threat to Health*. Cambridge, MA: MIT Press.

Miller, Wayne. 2015. *Exposed: Special Issues Regarding Agent Orange, Coal Mine Dust, and Radiation Exposures*. New York: Novinka.

Clean Power Plan of 2015

The Clean Power Plan of 2015 proposed a set of greenhouse gas emissions limits for electricity-generating power plants operating in the United States. The plan consisted of standards established by the US Environmental Protection Agency (EPA) and individualized for each state, which were given flexibility to produce the reductions in emissions through different methods. The plan grew out of several decades of federal attempts to cooperate with international efforts to reduce carbon emissions. These international efforts, such as the United Nations Framework Convention on Climate Change (1992), the Kyoto Protocol (1997), and the Paris Climate Agreement (2015), envisioned a pathway to slow the rate of global warming and stave off the negative impacts of human-induced climate change. Devised under President Barack Obama, the Clean Power Plan of 2015 triggered opposition from state governments, fossil fuel interests, and political conservatives, resulting in various legal challenges and its scuttling in 2017 by the EPA under President Donald Trump. His replacement policy, the Affordable Clean Energy rule, was invalidated in early 2021 by the District of Columbia Circuit Court of Appeals, the final day of the Trump administration.

On December 7, 2009, the EPA under President Obama issued a press release that revealed the agency's determination to adopt a new and more determined policy toward the reduction of US greenhouse gas emissions. It cited a recent US Supreme Court ruling in *Massachusetts v. Environmental Protection Agency* (2007) that greenhouse gases like carbon dioxide are airborne pollutants, and thus the EPA has authority to control and regulate them under the provisions of the Clean Air Act of 1970. The press release then declared that "after a thorough examination of the scientific evidence and careful consideration of public comments," the agency concluded that "greenhouse gases (GHGs) threaten the public health and welfare of the American people" (EPA 2009). It went on to take an unequivocal position on the question of whether humans are to blame for the increase in global warming through the burning of fossil fuels and deforestation. The EPA stated explicitly that

> scientific consensus shows that as a result of human activities, GHG concentrations in the atmosphere are at record high levels and data shows that the Earth has been warming over the past 100 years, with the steepest increase in warming in recent decades. The evidence of human-induced climate change goes beyond observed increases in average surface temperatures; it includes melting ice in the Arctic, melting glaciers around the world, increasing ocean temperatures, rising sea levels, acidification of the oceans due to excess carbon dioxide, changing precipitation patterns, and changing patterns of ecosystems and wildlife. (EPA 2009)

The statement's affirmation of the scientific consensus regarding greenhouse gases, global warming, and climate change was significant, given the level of contention in the

United States over whether the scientific data was conclusive. The EPA argued that the case was proven by the science, and went on to identify the specific airborne pollutants that it believed it had authority to regulate: "EPA's endangerment finding covers emissions of six key greenhouse gases—carbon dioxide, methane, nitrous oxide, hydrofluorocarbons, perfluorocarbons and sulfur hexafluoride—that have been the subject of scrutiny and intense analysis for decades by scientists in the United States and around the world" (EPA 2009). On the basis of the "endangerment finding," the EPA and the Obama administration proceeded to create the Clean Power Plan of 2015. In general, the plan established a goal of reducing greenhouse gas emissions by US power plants to 32 percent of their 2005 levels by the year 2030. The plan also called for reductions of other greenhouse gas pollutants: sulfur dioxide to 90 percent, and emissions of nitrogen oxides to 72 percent of their 2005 levels by 2030 (EPA 2009).

The agency intended to secure these reductions by creating interim and final carbon dioxide emission performance rates for both fossil fuel-fired electric power plants and natural gas-fired "combined cycle" power plants. It sought to maximize the choices that state governments and utility companies could make to meet the lower greenhouse gas emissions rates by offering three distinct ways of measuring the state's compliance: (1) a rate-based state goal measured in pounds per megawatt hour (lb/MWh); (2) a mass-based state goal measured in total short tons of CO_2; and (3) a mass-based state goal with a new source complement measured in total short tons of CO_2. The plan called for the use of the "best system of emissions reduction" based on the particular kinds of pollutants issued by a given power plant using a particular source or sources of energy. The "building blocks" of this "best system" include (1) improving the heat rate of existing coal-fired power plants; (2) increasing electricity generation from lower-emitting existing natural gas plants while reducing generation from higher-emitting coal-fired power plants; and (3) increasing electricity generation from new zero-emitting renewable energy sources (like wind and solar).

The Clean Power Plan then proceeded to identify the "ranges of reductions that can be achieved at coal, oil and gas plants at a reasonable cost by application of each building block, taking into account how quickly and to what extent the measures encompassed by the building blocks could be used to reduce emissions," with the result that each state was given "a different goal based upon its own particular mix of affected sources" (EPA 2009). Finally, the plan extended to the states "the flexibility to select the measures it prefers in order to achieve the CO_2 emission performance rates for its affected plants or meet the equivalent statewide rate—or mass-based CO_2 goal." This could mean diversifying sources of energy, employing energy efficiency strategies, and even "emissions trading" between states. With this approach, the EPA asserted that "states will also have the ability to shape their own emissions reduction pathways over the 2022–29 period" (EPA 2009).

The EPA spent several years devising the Clean Power Plan and received 4.3 million public comments before issuing the final version. Reactions by environmental groups, utility companies, the fossil fuel industry, state governments, and other interested parties were soon in coming. Congress voted to block the plan by issuing a "Resolution of Disapproval" under the Congressional Review Act, which gave Congress power to overrule the implementation of a federal regulation. President Obama vetoed the resolution. Officials in twenty-nine states and leaders of fossil fuel companies then petitioned the US Court of Appeals for the District of Columbia Circuit to issue a stay, which would prevent the EPA from proceeding. The US Supreme Court suddenly intervened in February 2016 and ordered a halt to the plan by a 5–4 vote with conservative justices in the majority. Throughout the period of the EPA announcement, congressional debates and hearings, and court challenges, conservative groups like Americans for Prosperity and FreedomWorks contended with environmental groups like the League of Conservation Voters and EarthJustice over the plan. Conservatives claimed it would damage the economy, and environmentalists argued that delays in lowering emissions put human lives and property at risk of severe consequences from climate change.

After taking office in 2017, President Donald Trump ordered his EPA Administrator Scott Pruitt to review the Clean Power Plan. Pruitt's early departure amid scandal left his successor, Andrew Wheeler, to repeal the Obama-era policy and enact the Affordable Clean Energy rule, which eliminated the "building blocks" plan for fuel-source switching to meet lower emissions targets. It replaced this program with "new emission guidelines that will inform the state's development of standards of performance to reduce carbon dioxide (CO_2) emissions from existing coal-fired EGUs [energy generating units]—consistent with EPA's role as defined in the CAA [Clean Air Act]" (EPA 2022). This would make it easier for coal-fired power plants to meet EPA guidelines without having to switch to natural gas. States and environmental groups that favored the Clean Power Plan filed suit to stop implementation of the Affordable Clean Energy rule and won a judgment in their favor when the US Court of Appeals for the District of Columbia Circuit vacated the Trump rule, determining that it violated the Clean Air Act (Frazin 2021).

In the final chapter of the story, the US Supreme Court ruled in *West Virginia v. EPA* (2022) that in the Clean Power Plan, the Obama administration and the EPA exceeded its authority under the Clean Air Act of 1970 to control power plant emissions. The 6–3 conservative majority said in its opinion that the "EPA issued a new rule concluding that the 'best system of emission reduction' for existing coal-fired power plants included a requirement that such facilities reduce their own production of electricity, or subsidize increased generation by natural gas, wind, or solar sources." They surmised that "The question before us is whether this broader conception of EPA's authority is within the power granted to it by the Clean Air Act." To this question, the answer they gave was no, the Clean Air Act did not authorize federal imposition on the states a set of "carbon emissions caps based on a generation shifting approach." The opinion went on to note that "by design, there are no particular controls a coal plant operator can install and operate to attain the emissions limits established by the Clean Power Plan." In other words, they ruled that the agency wasn't just setting emissions limits, it was imposing rules that would have necessitated fundamental changes in how the power plants and utility companies operate. In their view the vagueness of the Clean Air Act required the administration to get "'clear congressional authorization' to regulate in that manner" (*West Virginia v. EPA* 2022).

This left the question undecided as to how far the EPA could go to curb greenhouse gas emissions in America's electricity-generating power plants. Conservative courts indicated that the EPA lacks authority under the Clean Air Act to impose "generation shifting" rules that nudge power plants toward clean-burning fuels and renewable energy sources like solar and wind power. Liberal courts considered this to be well within the scope of the Clean Air Act's provisions, which require the EPA to act in response to the "endangerment" posed by greenhouse gases and climate change. The story of the Clean Power Plan demonstrates the difficulty of reducing greenhouse gas emissions in America's electricity-generating power plants. They are part of an intricate puzzle that involves both state and federal regulatory authority as well as different types of utilities, ranging from consumer cooperatives to municipality-owned organizations to private corporations owned by shareholders. Many of these utilities own their own power plants, while others serve merely as electricity distributors.

In the event future administrations wish to assertively act to lower greenhouse gas emissions, the way forward might be difficult. According to Deborah A. Sivas, an expert in environmental law and energy policy at Stanford University, "it is hard to guess what the courts might do with all of these complex, interwoven pieces" (Jordan 2019).

Jeffrey B. Webb

See also: Cap and Trade System; Clean Air Act of 1970; Climate Change; Energy Policy Act of 2005; Global Climate Coalition; Natural Resources Defense Council; Public Utility Regulatory Policies Act of 1978; Renewable Energy; Sierra Club; Smart Grid; Union of Concerned Scientists; US Environmental Protection Agency

FURTHER READING

EPA (US Environmental Protection Agency). 2022. "Affordable Clean Energy Rule." Fact Sheet. https://www.epa.gov/sites/default/files/2019-06/documents/bser_and_eg_fact_sheet_6.18.19_final.pdf (accessed October 2023).

Frazin, Rachel. 2021. "Court Strikes Down Trump Coal Power Plant Rule." *The Hill*. January 19. https://thehill.com/policy/energy-environment/534772-court-strikes-down-trump-coal-power-plant-rule/ (accessed October 2023).

Jordan, Rob. 2019. "Goodbye, Clean Power Plan: Stanford Researchers Discuss the New Energy Rule." Stanford News Service. June 21. https://news.stanford.edu/press-releases/2019/06/21/goodbye-clean-power-plan-understanding-new-energy-rule/ (accessed October 2023).

U.S. Environmental Protection Agency (EPA). 2009. "EPA: Greenhouse Gases Threaten Public Health and the Environment." Press Release. https://www.epa.gov/archive/epapages/newsroom_archive/newsreleases/08d11a451131bca585257685005bf252.html (accessed October 2023).

West Virginia v. EPA. No. 20–1530. Argued February 28, 2022—Decided June 30, 2022.

Clean Water Act

The importance of clean, fresh water has been recognized by civilizations longer than the importance of clean air and will become even more critical in the twenty-first century. A series of mounting water problems in the United States, addressed by limited federal laws from the late 1800s through the 1960s, led to the Clean Water Act in 1972 and its subsequent amendments, supported by related laws such as the Safe Drinking Water Act in 1974. Challenges remain in safeguarding and wisely using the nation's fresh water in thermoelectric power, agriculture, manufacturing, mining, home consumption, recreation, and water transportation.

The first pumped municipal water system in the United States was established in 1762 in Bethlehem, Pennsylvania. The number of public waterworks grew to 600 by 1880, thereby increasing the availability of running water, and the problem of water pollution increased as well. Although the link between public health and water cleanliness was recognized in the late 1800s, the importance of wastewater treatment went unrecognized for decades because it was assumed that running water would purify itself. As a result, waste was piped away from populated areas rather than treated. Accordingly, the flow of the Chicago River was reversed in 1900 by the construction of the Chicago Sanitary and Ship Canal to divert Chicago's sewer discharge away from the city's Lake Michigan drinking water supply, against the objections of the downstream state of Missouri.

The Rivers and Harbors Act of 1899 is credited as being the first environmental law in the United States, although it was built on previous laws, including the Rivers and Harbors Act of 1890, which had precedent from common law of thirteenth-century England. The environmental importance of the 1899 law stems from Section 13, the Refuse Act, which prohibited the discharge of waste into navigable waters. Since the main concern of the law was regulating factors impeding navigation, sewage (including oil within the sewage) was exempt from the Refuse Act, although a broader interpretation of the term "refuse" was later used in cases such as a 1966 Supreme Court opinion, *United States v. Standard Oil Co.* in which an accidental gasoline spill was designated as a violation of the Refuse Act. As a result, interpretations of the Refuse Act were instrumental in shaping a pollution permit requirement later created by the 1972 Clean Water Act.

In the early 1900s, wastewater treatment began to be addressed on the state level, although cost-benefit analyses at the time favored drinking water treatment over sewage discharge treatment. The Public Health Service Act of 1912 was enacted to study pollution of the navigable waters of the United States, during a time when industrial pollution was not recognized as harmful. After industrial pollution increased during the First World War, investigations by the American Water Works Association in the 1920s found evidence of adverse effects of industrial pollution on water supplies. Adverse effects of nonpoint source pollution also began to be identified during this era by organizations such as the US Fish and Wildlife Service and the Izaak Walton League, and the effects of oxygen depletion were recognized and quantified from a study done on the Ohio River. The Oil Pollution Act of 1924 authorized the prohibition of vessels from releasing oil into tidal waters and authorized investigation of oil pollution's effect on commercial navigation in rivers. By 1926, the Upper Mississippi River near St. Paul and Minneapolis, with a nearly depleted fish population, was recognized as a public health hazard. The Public Works Administration, created by the New Deal in 1933, federally funded numerous wastewater treatment plants, including a much-needed treatment plant for Minneapolis-St. Paul.

The Second World War resulted in an increase in fossil fuel usage as well as a proliferation of synthetic organic compounds, including pesticides, and was a time period in which industrial pollution became the largest source of water pollution. In 1942, the Public Health Service recommended water quality standards which included upper limits for some heavy metals and organic compounds. New water pollution challenges in the post-war era included detergents, chlorinated hydrocarbons, and DDT. Over a hundred bills related to water quality had been attempted in Congress during that century before the first significant federal law controlling water pollution was passed in the form of the Federal Water Pollution Control Act of 1948. The law provided financial assistance to state and local governments but instituted no federally required guidelines.

FROM FLAMMABLE RIVERS TO FLAMMABLE TAP WATER

Rivers near major cities catching fire were not unique in the century leading up to 1970. In 1888 and 1899, Chicago River fires were community events with spectators. Other river fires cost human lives and extensive property damage. The infamous Cuyahoga River that runs through Cleveland caught fire in 1868 and at least twelve more times by 1969. *Time* magazine's publicity on the 1969 Cuyahoga River fire, which damaged two railroad bridges, helped galvanize public concern that led to environmental legislation in the early 1970s. The Buffalo River had caught fire in 1968, and the Rouge River in Detroit caught fire in 1969, shortly after the Cuyahoga. By this time, river fires had been documented in the nation for a century, and some major cities used oil dispersants on their rivers in an effort to prevent fires.

Burning rivers in the US are a thing of the past, but new water contamination sources have been emerging with increased usages of fracking. Methane in the water, which can be naturally occurring or exacerbated by fracking, can cause tap water to become flammable. The Clean Water Act took care of the flammable rivers problem in the US An emerging question is whether it can prevent a flammable tap water problem.

Ruth E. Nalliah

The Federal Water Pollution Control Act was amended by four significant laws in the 1950s and 1960s in an attempt to mediate a power balance between federal government and state control of water quality, with expansion of federal jurisdiction, federal funding, and water quality standards. Yet water quality standards under the Water Quality Act of 1965 applied only to interstate waters, affecting only one-seventh of the nation's waters. Enforcement was difficult and unwieldy in terms of linking violations of water quality standards to specific dischargers, limiting the laws' effectiveness. Rivers in Buffalo, Cleveland, and Detroit were so heavily polluted that they caught fire during the period of 1968 through 1969, and Great Lakes beach closures were common. As a result of public concern about these environmental problems and others, the EPA was created in 1970 as a more comprehensive organization to replace the Federal Water Pollution Control Administration, and the Federal Water Pollution Control Act was amended in 1972 to create what is presently known as the Clean Water Act.

The Clean Water Act consists of two broad components: authorization of federal assistance for sewage treatment plant construction (previously in the form of grants but currently in the form of loans) and regulatory requirements for industrial and municipal dischargers. A distinctive element of the Clean Water Act from previous legislation is that point source discharges are unlawful unless allowed by a permit by the National Pollutant Discharge Elimination System, which in 2016 had criteria for over 115 pollutants, including sixty-five classes of toxic substances. Thermal discharges into waterways from power plants are regulated by permits as well. Nonpoint pollution sources are regulated by the states. Two lofty goals were set in 1972 which are still not met: water quality that is both fishable and swimmable by mid-1983 and zero discharge of pollutants by 1985.

The formation of the EPA in 1970, and its regulatory actions thereafter, helped to facilitate the Great Lakes Water Quality Agreement of 1972 between the United States and Canada, based on recommendations for action by the International Joint Commission created by the Boundary Waters Treaty of 1909. The 1972 agreement resulted in limits for industrial and phosphorus pollution entering the lakes. It was updated in 1978 with a goal to rid the lakes of persistent toxic substances, and by the late 1970s and 1980s the agreement was characterized as an unprecedented success. Expanded plans and more extensive commitments were added in 1987 and 2012. Despite these many-faceted efforts, algal blooms began increasing in the 1990s in Lake Erie, where they currently create seasonal crises each year due to agricultural runoff.

The Clean Water Act of 1972 has been amended in an effort to address several types of water quality problems not yet remediated. Nonpoint sources have been estimated to represent more than 50 percent of remaining water pollution. Amendments to the 1972 Clean Water Act include the Rural Clean Water Program in 1977 to support the management of nonpoint pollution sources, while revisions in 1987 more deliberately directed states to develop nonpoint pollution control programs with federal assistance. Due to nutrient pollution runoff from agriculture and other land use, algal blooms continue to be a problem in coastal and freshwater areas in all fifty states, including significant seasonal dead zones in the Gulf of Mexico, Lake Erie, and the Chesapeake Bay.

Other Clean Water Act amendments address broad areas of water management. After the 1989 *Exxon Valdez* oil spill, the 1990 Oil Pollution Act improved contingency plans for oil spills and established liability and compensation policies. In 2014, the Water Resources Reform and Development Act helped secure national water infrastructure by authorizing new Army Corps projects and allocating funds for dam and levee safety.

Since water content is both directly and indirectly affected and required by almost every human activity, it presents such an encompassing challenge that a number of regulations in addition to those of the Clean Water Act also determine water quality. For example, the Clean Water Act does not directly regulate groundwater. Outside the domain of the Clean Water Act is the Safe Drinking Water Act of 1974, which was amended in 1986 and 1996 and provides standards for public drinking water. Examples of other statues which affect water quality include the Clean Air Act, the Resource Conservation and Recovery Act for the management of solid waste, the National Environmental Policy Act, the Mineral Policy Act, and the Federal Land Policy and Management Act. Yet gaps, ambiguities, and exemptions within these statutes create ongoing challenges for clean water.

Although coal is a dying industry, the Clean Air Act has increased demand for mining of low-sulfur coal. Mountaintop mining creates environmental and consumer water concerns with both the discharge of pollutants and the burial of river headwaters in local valleys which contribute to the water supply. The Clean Water Act regulates related water issues such as stormwater runoff and mine drainage and facilitates the availability of research on the impact of local headwaters. Nevertheless, issues with enforcement and best practices affect citizens living near mining areas, who have formed campaigns such as New Power by Kentuckians for the Commonwealth, which advocates for clean energy sources which move beyond coal.

After 2000, hydraulic fracturing (fracking) became a more widely used means of obtaining oil and gas by opening up underground fissures using high-pressure water mixtures which contain undisclosed substances likely to be toxic. Federal regulation of fracking is not well-developed. Currently, states regulate fracking, which has been banned in Maryland, New York, Vermont, and Washington. The Energy Policy Act of 2005 exempts fracking from the Underground Injection Control regulations of the Safe Drinking Water Act in a statement which has been later referred to as the Halliburton Loophole after the Halliburton Company, an energy services firm. In a 2016 report, the EPA listed concerns raised by the process of fracking for possible future focus which include exacerbation of water scarcity, discharge of inadequately treated wastewater, and various forms of water contamination from spills, well leakage, direct injection, and wastewater storage in unlined pits (EPA 2016).

The Clean Water Act has resulted in improvements to sewage treatment and the implementation of water pollution controls across the United States, although water quality challenges still abound. Challenges stem from ambiguities within the law, such as continued debates regarding which waters, such as wetlands, are exempt from the Clean Water Act. Concerns also include pollution which is not currently covered, such as emerging pollutants, and tasks which are delegated to states which have varying standards and powers of enforcement (Mulligan 2019, 15). As water resources become more precious in the future, the power of the public to shape policy may yet once again help preserve a vital resource for posterity.

Ruth E. Nalliah

See also: Church Rock Uranium Mill Spill; *Deepwater Horizon*; Energy Policy Act of 2005; *Exxon Valdez* Oil Spill; Halliburton Company; Hydraulic Fracking; Martin County Coal Slurry Spill; Santa Barbara Oil Spill; Surface Mining; US Environmental Protection Agency

FURTHER READING

Colborn, Theo, Dianne Dumanoski, and John Peterson Myers. 1996. *Our Stolen Future Are We Threatening Our Fertility, Intelligence, and Survival? A Scientific Detective Story*. New York: Dutton.

EPA (US Environmental Protection Agency). 2016. "Hydraulic Fracturing for Oil and Gas: Impacts from the Hydraulic Fracturing Water Cycle on Drinking Water Resources in the United States: Executive Summary." Office of Research and Development, Washington, DC.

EPA/600/R-16/236ES.https://cfpub.epa.gov/ncea/hfstudy/recordisplay.cfm?deid=332990 (accessed October 2023).

EPA (US Environmental Protection Agency). 2017. "History of the Clean Water Act." Last modified August 8. https://www.epa.gov/laws-regulations/history-clean-water-act (accessed October 2023).

Gatz, Laura. 2016. "Clean Water Act: A Summary of the Law." Congressional Research Service Report RL30030. https://crsreports.congress.gov/product/pdf/RL/RL30030 (accessed October 2023).

Hines, N.W. 2013. "History of the 1972 Clean Water Act: The Story behind How the 1972 Act Became the Capstone on a Decade of Extraordinary Environmental Reform." *George Washington Journal of Energy and Environmental Law*. Summer/Autumn. Pp. 80–106.

Hogue, Cheryl. 2019. "Marking 50 Years after the Cuyahoga Conflagration." *Chemical and Engineering News*. Vol. 97. No. 24. Pp. 31–4.

Keiser, David, and Joseph Shapiro. 2019. "US Water Pollution Regulation over the Last Half Century: Burning Waters to Crystal Springs?" NBER Working Paper No. w26077. https://ssrn.com/abstract=3423790 (accessed October 2023).

Lambert, Hilary A.B. 2016. "Whose Water Is It?" *American Journal of Economics and Sociology*. Vol. 75. No. 3. Pp. 681–720.

Mulligan, Stephen P. 2019. "Evolution of the Meaning of 'Waters of the United States' in the Clean Water Act." Congressional Research Service Report R44585. https://crsreports.congress.gov/product/pdf/R/R44585 (accessed October 2023).

Stets, E.G., V.J. Kelly, W.P. Broussad, III, T.E. Smith, and C.G. Crawford. 2012. "Century-Scale Perspective on Water Quality in Selected River Basins of the Conterminous United States." *U.S. Geological Survey National Water-Quality Assessment Program Scientific Investigations Report 2012–5225*. https://pubs.usgs.gov/sir/2012/5225/pdf/sir20125225.pdf (accessed October 2023).

Time. 1969. "America's Sewage System and the Price of Optimism." Vol. 94. No. 5. P. 41. http://content.time.com/time/magazine/article/0,9171,901182,00.html (accessed October 2023).

Wiseman, Hannah. 2009. "Untested Waters: The Rise of Hydraulic Fracturing in Oil and Gas Production and the Need to Revisit Regulation." *Fordham Environmental Law Review*. Vol. 20. No. 1. Pp. 115–95.

Cleveland, East Ohio Gas Explosion

At 2:40 p.m. on the afternoon of Friday, October 20, 1944, an explosion of cataclysmic proportions rocked the East Side of Cleveland, Ohio, igniting what quickly was to become the most terrifying and destructive fire in the history of that city. By the time the blaze was contained and finally extinguished over the course of the ensuing weekend, the conflagration had devastated utterly quite nearly a square mile of what was at the time the sixth largest city in the United States (Albrecht 2014). Subsequent investigations determined that the genesis of the blast was a leak from Storage Tank Number 4, which contained about 90 million cubic feet of liquefied natural gas (ECH 2023).

This tank stood in a field of large above-ground tanks located in a lot at the north end of East 61st Street, just east of East 55th Street. According to later accounts, the field of tanks was viewed by most who lived in the area as an unexceptional feature of the urban landscape. Area residents accepted the facility as safe, assuming that East Ohio Gas "knew what they were doing" (Albrecht 2014). This blasé acceptance was likely also a result of patriotic pride, considering the fact that Storage Tank Number 4 had been constructed two years before the explosion explicitly as a part of the war effort, in order to provide necessary resources for local manufacturing facilities converted to production of military supplies (ECH 2023).

A white plume emanating from the tank was spotted shortly before the explosion, and the exposure of the escaping natural gas with the oxygen in the air resulted in a volatile mixture that soon combusted. Shortly thereafter another nearby storage tank exploded, causing the eruption of "a 3,000-degree fireball into the sky, burning, sometimes vaporizing, a square mile" (Sangiacomo 2011). The explosion shot up in the air while a wall of flames moved out from the epicenter, culminating in "a tidal wave of fire" that quickly ripped through twenty blocks of the adjacent neighborhood (ECH 2023). As one witness remembers it, the initial blast shot upward through the storage tank and "blew sky high. There were three or four men on the tank when it exploded. It was horrendous" (Sangiacomo 2011). But the horrors did not end there or then, in the immediate environs of the storage tanks, or even in the ensuing blazing waves of fire. Indeed, the horror ignited additional blasts and conflagrations, some close and some surprisingly far afield. The fire spread rapidly and in unexpected ways, even to relatively distant locations, because the gas flowed down into the storm drain system. From there, the volatile material moved into the sewers, traveling quietly along the flood-water and overflow routes beneath the streets and then "exploding from time to time, ripping up pavement, damaging underground utility installations, and blowing out manhole covers" (ECH 2023).

These subterranean explosions obstructed the roadways needed by emergency vehicles. In fact, amongst many of the stark black-and-white images that record the aftermath of the blast, one particularly startling image is that of "a Cleveland fire pumper being hauled out of crater" (Albrecht 2014). Moreover, an eyewitness described the destroyed section of the city in apocalyptic terms, saying that it resembled "a war zone," and recounting horrors such as a partially destroyed body caught on a fence and a vehicle wrapped around a pole. Indeed, it was reported that the devastated neighborhood "looked like Dresden or London after a Second World War bombing raid (Sangiacomo 2011). This similarity was not lost on victims of the carnage, and fears of sabotage soon arose. Official reports do not indicate that this explosion was the result of sabotage, although it appears that "some residents initially suspected a German saboteur" (ECH 2023). Indeed, as one witness put it, as she stared in horror at the explosion, she immediately "thought that the Germans were bombing us" (Sangiacomo 2011). As residents fled the scene, survivors were evacuated and "refugees were sheltered in Willson Jr. High School on E. 55th St. where the Red Cross tried to care for approx. 680 homeless victims" (ECH 2023). Both Ohio State Guard troops and available Coast Guard units offered support to the Cleveland police in maintaining order, and various units assisted in search and rescue operations (Costello 1944).

After the smoke cleared, the extent of the devastation of the explosion became evident. The death toll eventually rose to 130, with many victims left entirely unidentifiable. The loss in property and infrastructure included the complete destruction of nearly a hundred homes and two factories in this important industrial metropolis. Well over 200 vehicles were destroyed, and many other homes, buildings, roads, and rail lines were severely damaged. The East Ohio Gas Company eventually paid millions in damages and half a million to the families of its own employees who were killed in the blast. The company remained in the vicinity and is credited with helping to rebuild some of the neighborhoods destroyed by the explosion and fire.

As a result of this catastrophe and the subsequent investigation, various safety reforms were enacted, including the implementation of new practices and guidelines for safer storage of natural gas. Drawing upon a technology that became available in the 1940s, the East Ohio Gas Company began pumping natural gas into depleted gas wells, creating vast underground storage facilities, some within 50 miles or so of the epicenter of the blast (Sangiacomo 2011). That epicenter itself was later developed into Grdina Park, a location better known for its playground and summer spray basin than for the small bronze Ohio Historical Marker that recounts the basic details of the East Ohio Gas Company Explosion. It may perhaps seem ironic that over half a century after the disaster, a landscape that had once been ripped asunder by exploding natural gas had become a city park a short drive from one of the largest caches of the resource in North America (Sangiacomo 2011).

Christopher R. Fee

See also: Hart, William Aaron; Indiana Natural Gas Boom; Natural Gas; New London School Explosion; Pittsburgh Gasometer Explosion; Project Gasbuggy; Richmond, Indiana Gas Explosions

FURTHER READING

Albrecht, Brian. 2014. "East Ohio Gas Explosion of 1944: A Day Never to be Forgotten by Those Who Witnessed It." *The Plain Dealer.* October 16.https://www.cleveland.com/metro/2014/10/east_ohio_gas_explosion_of_1944_a_day_never_to_be_forgotten_by_those_who_witnessed_it.html (accessed October 2023).

Costello, Timothy J., and George Matowitz. 1944. "East Ohio Gas Explosion, October 20, 1944: Police Response and Report." Cleveland Police Museum. Cleveland Police Historical Society. https://www.clevelandpolicemuseum.org/historical/east-ohio-gas-explosion-october-20-1944-police-response-and-report/ (accessed October 2023).

Encyclopedia of Cleveland History (ECH). 2023. "East Ohio Gas Company Explosion and Fire." Case Western Reserve University. https://case.edu/ech/articles/e/east-ohio-gas-co-explosion-and-fire (accessed February 2, 2023).

Sangiacomo, Michael, and James Ewinger. 2011. "East Ohio Gas Explosions—60 Years Later (Republished)." *The Plain Dealer.* October 17.https://www.cleveland.com/pdextra/2011/10/east_ohio_gas_explosions_--_60.html (accessed October 2023).

Climate Change

In simple terms, climate change refers to long-term shifts in prevailing weather patterns in particular geographical regions of the earth. This entails change in atmospheric factors such as temperature, humidity, rain or snowfall, atmospheric pressure, wind direction and speed, and cloudiness. Climate can also depend on proximity to large quantities of water, like oceans and glaciers, and biomass, like dense tropical vegetation, not to mention other biological and geophysical factors. Changes in climate occur naturally over time, usually considered in terms of geological eras involving hundreds of thousands and millions of years, and is dynamic, non-linear in nature. Over the twentieth and twenty-first centuries, scientists have tracked a significant increase in the pace of climate change, which they attribute to a prevailing pattern of global warming. The pace of this warming trend has in turn been attributed to greenhouse gases (particularly CO_2) produced by human activity.

The effect of increased greenhouse gases in the atmosphere on rising temperatures on the earth's surface was documented in Swedish chemist Svante Arrhenius's scientific paper from 1896, "On the Influence of Carbonic Acid in the Air upon the Temperature of the Ground" in the *Philosophical Magazine and Journal of Science*. In his paper, carbonic acid refers to the gases released by natural processes like decomposition of organic matter but also the burning of carbon substances like wood and coal. Today, chemists know Arrhenius's "carbonic acid" as CO_2. After pages of complicated chemical formulas and tables, Arrhenius found that "if the quantity of carbonic acid increases in geometric progression, the augmentation of the [surface] temperature will increase nearly in arithmetic progression" (Arrhenius 1896, 267). There are similar conclusions in other parts of the paper: "A simple calculation shows that the temperature in the arctic regions would rise about 8 or 9 degrees Celsius, if the [atmospheric] carbonic acid increased to 2.5 or 3 times its present value" (Arrhenius 1896, 268).

Arrhenius asserted that the industrial use of coal might increase the amount of CO_2 in the atmosphere: "The world's present production of coal reaches in round numbers to 500 millions of tons per annum, or 1 ton per km. of the earth's surface. Transformed into carbonic acid, this quantity would correspond to about a thousandth part of the carbonic acid in the atmosphere" (Arrhenius 1896, 270). In a passage where he speculates about a certain amount of additional carbonic acid, he claimed that this amount "is supplied to the atmosphere chiefly by "the industrial development of our time" (Arrhenius 1896, 271). Arhennius didn't exactly predict that industrialization would cause global warming, only that it would increase the levels of CO_2 in the atmosphere beyond what would otherwise be there through natural processes. It would take further research to establish the connection between industrial-scale use of carbon fuels like coal, oil, and gas and the appearance of a greenhouse effect sufficient to elevate surface temperatures on the earth—global warming.

Arrhenius discovered the basic physical laws by which volumes of gas molecules alternately accumulate and dissipate in the atmosphere and have correlating effects on changing global surface temperatures. The general acceptance of these scientific facts in the early twentieth century is well documented. What's interesting is that it didn't take much time for this knowledge to seep into the cultures of the industrialized Western societies. A remarkable document from 1912 offers a testimonial. The New Zealand *Rodney and Otamatea Times, Waitemata and Kaipara Gazette* published an article under the title, "Coal Consumption Affecting Climate." It read: "The furnaces of the world are now burning about 2 million tons of coal a year. When this is burned, uniting with oxygen, it adds about 7 million tons of carbon dioxide to the atmosphere yearly. This tends to make the air a more effective blanket for the earth and to raise its temperature. The effect may be considerable in a few centuries" ("Coal" 1912). These two connections—between rising atmospheric CO_2 levels and increased surface temperatures of the earth and between rising atmospheric CO_2 levels and industrial fossil fuel use—were established early in the twentieth century and accepted widely by the end of the Second World War.

The writer believed the effect would be seen in a few centuries. That time arrived sooner than anticipated. Consumption of all fossil fuels expanded exponentially with the post-war advent of the mass automobile market, the spread of suburban development, interstate shipping, commercial aviation, and the military build-up of air, naval, and mechanized forces in the Cold War. Every sector of the domestic economy expanded, and with it came the demand for energy. Historian Robert D. Lifset noted: "In 1950 the United States produced 5.9 million barrels of oil per day (bpd). Twenty years later US oil production peaked at 11.6 million bpd. Over that same period, US oil consumption rose from 6.4 million to 14.6 million bpd" (Lifset 2014, 27). Amid this post-war economic boom, a symposium in 1959 brought together faculty from the Columbia University School of Business and oil and gas industry executives in the American Petroleum Institute to discuss "Energy and Man." Presentations extolled the virtues of the oil and gas business and celebrated energy's role in growing and expanding the US economy and all of human civilization. Forecasts were generally upbeat about the future of oil and gas.

One of the presenters, Manhattan Project physicist Edward Teller, took the opportunity to caution the economists and executives about the potential of fossil fuels to harm the environment. In "Energy Patterns of the Future," Teller offered his audience a primer in how increased concentrations of CO_2 in the atmosphere results in global warming. He posed the question, "The carbon dioxide is invisible, it is transparent, you can't smell it, it is not dangerous to health, so why should one worry about it?" (Teller 1960, 58). He answered this way:

> Carbon dioxide has a strange property. It transmits visible light but it absorbs infrared radiation which is emitted from the earth. Its presence in the atmosphere causes a greenhouse effect in that it will allow the solar rays to enter, but it will to some extent impede the radiation from the earth into outer space. The result is that the earth will continue to heat up until a balance is re-established. (Teller 1960, 58)

As this balance is being reestablished, Teller noted

> a temperature rise corresponding to a 10 percent increase in carbon dioxide will be sufficient to melt the icecap and submerge New York. All coastal cities would be covered, and since a considerable percentage of the human race lives in coastal regions, I think that this chemical contamination is more serious than most people tend to believe. (Teller 1960, 58)

The symposium's attendees from the API's collection of oil and gas corporations probably didn't wish to hear Teller's predictions. In 1965, the White House released a report from the President's Science Advisory Committee that presented a factual, no-nonsense assessment of the increased atmospheric CO_2 produced by burning fossil fuels within the preceding forty years, and wrote "Through his worldwide industrial civilization, Man is unwittingly conducting a vast geophysical experiment," and by 2020 could anticipate CO_2 increases "sufficient to produce measurable and perhaps marked changes in climate" (PSAC 1965, 126–7). A few days after it was released, API president Frank N. Ikard brought it to the attention of the oil and gas company executives assembled for API's annual meeting, lamenting that "this report will undoubtedly fan emotions, raise fears, and bring demands for action" (Ikard 1965, 13). Ikard went on to cite the report itself as saying "the pollution from internal combustion engines is so serious, and is growing so fast, that an alternative nonpolluting means of powering automobiles, buses, and trucks is likely to become a national necessity." Ikard said that more than a hundred recommendations listed in the report would keep state and federal legislative bodies busy for generations, and thus would occupy the petroleum industry in trying to defeat them. Ikard asserted, "It takes no crystal ball to see that our involvement in government matters will intensify in the years ahead" (Ikard 1965, 12).

The API and its member corporations kept an eye on the issue and generated two internal studies that were submitted in 1968 and 1969, both of which confirmed Teller's 1959 symposium claims and the President's Science Advisory Committee's 1965 report. The energy crisis of the 1970s placed enormous pressures on the industry, but mostly pressures to increase production due the shortages created by the 1973 OPEC oil embargo. Climate change resurfaced as a concern in the 1980s, and then in 1988, the UN established the Intergovernmental Panel on Climate Change with a mandate to report on carbon emissions and climate change; its first reports appeared in 1990 and 1992 and it has issued assessment reports regularly ever since (1995, 2001, 2007, 2014, 2021). The industry's response to the IPCC was to continue working toward greater efficiency, while initiating a public relations campaign to encourage doubt about the science of global warming and climate change. In 1988, an internal memo at Exxon expressed the media strategy this way: "emphasize the uncertainty in scientific conclusions regarding the potential enhanced greenhouse effect" (Jennings 2015).

In their book from 2010, *Merchants of Doubt: How a Handful of Scientists Obscured the Truth on Issues from Tobacco Smoke to Global Warming*, science historians Naomi Oreskes and Erik M. Conway extensively documented how fossil fuel corporations and conservative foundations funded this public relations campaign, partly through "think tanks" like the Heritage Foundation and the Competitive Enterprise Institute. This program was abetted by a handful of contrarian scientists including Siegfried "Fred" Singer, Frederick Seitz, and William Nierenberg. They wrote op-ed pieces, spoke at conferences and seminars, and made themselves available for media appearances. Oreskes and Conway were critical of the media for choosing to report both the science of global warming and climate change and the well-funded propaganda of the oil industry as equal in weight in order to maintain the appearance of being "balanced" in coverage. This resulted in a misinformed public, millions of whom believed erroneously that there's an equal case for and against the scientific findings. The authors claimed this has influenced the direction of US energy policy, as liberals in the Democratic Party and conservatives in the Republican Party jousted over how to interpret the science of climate change and how to apply it to various policies regarding oil and gas leases on public lands, greenhouse gas emissions standards, funding for renewable energy research, and other concerns.

The result was a zig-zag between various policy remedies. Under Democratic President Bill Clinton the United States signed the Kyoto Protocols of 1997 in which nations pledged to reduce carbon emissions, but then never got the treaty ratified by the Senate, which would have forced US compliance. In 2001, Republican President George W. Bush repudiated the proposed Kyoto treaty. Democratic President Barack Obama's administration signed the United States into the United Nations Paris Agreement of 2015 with all of its emissions reductions targets—one of 195 nations to do so—but Republican President Donald Trump withdrew the United States from the compact in 2017. Democratic President Joe Biden then asked the UN for readmission, a request that was granted in 2021. Observers noted that this whipsaw of environmental and energy policy is the result of the science of climate change having been "politicized," and a large swath of the US population plunged into an "epistemic crisis" of not knowing which authorities they can trust on the issue. This problem was compounded in 2009 by "Climategate," which began when computer hackers stole data from the Climatic Research Unit at University of East Anglia (UK). They disseminated portions of emails out of context to expose what they alleged was a conspiracy among scientists to cook the data in order to support claims about climate change. Several investigations found no fraud, but climate deniers nevertheless damaged the credibility of the scientific community.

Despite the media static, all the major, well-established scientific associations in the United States and abroad have released statements affirming the conclusions of atmospheric research that shows (1) the earth's surface temperature has warmed at a considerable rate since the late nineteenth century; (2) the primary cause of this warming is the creation of greenhouse gas emissions from human activity; (3) persistence of this trend will increase the future likelihood of dramatic effects in various regions of the earth; and (4) the curtailment of human-produced greenhouse gas emissions can have a meaningful impact in changing this trend. In the meantime, the saturation level of atmospheric CO_2 moved from below 320 parts per million (ppm) to over 420 ppm in the period covering 1950–2020 (Lindsey 2022). There is no parallel in the geological record for this rate of increase of atmospheric CO_2, a fact which necessarily causes scientists to raise concerns over the rapidity of the earth's warming over the next few generations.

According to economist Jeffrey D. Sachs, climate change is "the toughest public policy problem that humanity has ever faced" (Sachs 2015, 394). This is because the crisis is global in scale, affecting nearly every person on the planet, and because it is difficult to get the entire world mobilized to deal with a common challenge. Another obstacle to action is that the inter-generational nature of the problem: "The people who are going to be most profoundly affected by human-induced climate change have not yet been born" (Sachs 2015, 394). Since climate change is a "slow-moving crisis," public officials are not incentivized to deal with the nature of the problem as it plays out over future decades. Finally, the warming of the earth due to human-generated activity derives in large part from burning fossil fuels, which laid the foundation for the prosperity and high standard of living that billions of people enjoy in modern industrialized societies. Significant changes—what Sachs terms a "heart transplant" in our economies to low-carbon energy—may require adjustments in lifestyle that some will find hard to accept (Sachs 2015, 395).

These adjustments will be made against a backdrop of incremental changes that began in the 1970s and have continued into the present, as power companies have drawn more and more energy from solar and wind farms, and as the automobile industry has advanced the performance and affordability of electric cars. A wide array of executive orders, bureaucratic regulations, and even federal laws served as policy "nudges" to induce climate-friendly choices among energy producers and consumers, nudges like federal tax credits, government research and development grants, and funding for renewable energy infrastructure. They are not what environmental activists demand, or what climate scientists might desire, but they show some determination to effect necessary change over the recent history of federal energy policy from the Clean Air Act of 1970 to the renewable energy-friendly Inflation Reduction Act of 2022.

Jeffrey B. Webb

See also: American Petroleum Institute; *An Inconvenient Truth*; Global Climate Coalition; Renewable Energy; Revelle, Roger R.D.; Sierra Club; Union of Concerned Scientists

FURTHER READING

Arrhenius, Svante. 1896. "On the Influence of Carbonic Acid in the Air upon the Temperature of the Ground." *Philosophical Magazine and Journal of Science*. Series 5. Vol. 41. April. Pp. 237–76.

"Coal Consumption Affecting Climate." 1912. *Rodney and Otamatea Times, Waitemata and Kaipara Gazette*. August 14. P. 7. National Library of New Zealand. https://paperspast.natlib.govt.nz/newspapers/ROTWKG19120814.2.56.5 (accessed October 2023).

Ikard, Frank N. 1965. "Meeting the Challenges of 1966." *American Petroleum Institute—Proceedings 1965*. https://www.climatefiles.com/trade-group/american-petroleum-institute/1965-api-president-meeting-the-challenges-of-1966/ (accessed October 2023).

Jennings, Katie, Dino Grandoni, and Susanne Rust. 2015. "How Exxon Went from Leader to Skeptic on Climate Change Research." *The Los Angeles Times*. October 23. https://graphics.latimes.com/exxon-research/ (accessed October 2023).

Lifset, Robert D. 2014. "A New Understanding of the American Energy Crisis of the 1970s." *Historical Social Research—Historische Sozialforschung. Special Issue: The Energy Crises of the 1970s: Anticipations and Reactions in the Industrialized World*. Vol. 39. No. 4. (150): 22– 42.

Lindsey, Rebecca. 2022. "Climate Change: Atmospheric Carbon Dioxide." National Oceanic and Atmospheric Administration. June 23. Climate.gov. https://www.climate.gov/news-features/understanding-climate/climate-change-atmospheric-carbon-dioxide (accessed October 2023).

President's Science Advisory Committee (PSAC). Environmental Pollution Panel. 1965. "Restoring the Quality of our Environment." Washington, DC: The White House. https://babel.hathitrust.org/cgi/pt?id=uc1.b4116127&seq=1 (accessed October 2023).

Sachs, Jeffrey D. 2015. *The Age of Sustainable Development*. New York: Columbia University Press.

Teller, Edward. 1960. "Energy Patterns of the Future." In *Energy and Man: A Symposium*. Eds. Alan Nevins et al. New York: Appleton-Century-Crofts, Inc.

Coal

Coal is the altered remains of prehistoric vegetation that originally accumulated in swamps and peat bogs. Vast deposits of coal originated in dried wetlands that covered most tropical land areas during the late Carboniferous (Pennsylvanian) and Permian eras. Coal is mostly carbon with variable amounts of other elements, mainly hydrogen, sulfur, oxygen, and nitrogen. Coal supplies about 25 percent of the world's primary energy and 40 percent of its electricity. Some iron, steel making, and other industrial processes burn coal, or a processed-coal material known as coke. In 2020, the world's top five coal producers were China, India, Indonesia, the United States, and Australia. Coal's extraction and combustion carries a number of health risks. In particular, coal is 60–80 percent carbon, depending on the type, and it creates carbon dioxide when burned. This gas is one of a number of gases in the atmosphere that linger and trap heat trying to escape from the earth. This is called the greenhouse effect and is one of the causes of global warming and climate change. Many industrialized nations have reduced coal usage in order to slow the process of global warming and climate change.

Coal is formed through a natural, geological process. Its formation (the first coal age) began during the Carboniferous Period, about 360 to 290 million years ago. Vast, dense forests covered the earth's surface, and over millions of years the death and decay of vegetation formed thick layers of carbonaceous material. This material accumulated and then became subject to geological processes like sedimentation and tectonic activity, which covered these layers with heavy rock, subjecting it to high pressure and temperatures. Each coal deposit's quality is determined by the types of vegetation from which the coal originated, the depths of burial, the temperatures and pressures at those depths, and the length of time the coal has been forming in the deposit. An important point to understand about coal and its uses for fuel is that "coalification" results in coals of different physical and chemical properties. As coal moves through the process of decay, turning into peat, and from that point forming into rock, it eventually reaches varying degrees of density and carbon content. Coal is classified into different types from the least carbon content to the most, beginning with low-carbon lignite, then to sub-bituminous, bituminous, and finally high-carbon (and very dense) anthracite.

The different types of coal are produced on a very long geological timeline. Initially, vegetative peat is pressed into lignite or "brown coal," which are coal-types with low organic maturity. In comparison to other coals, lignite is quite soft and its color can range from dark black to various shades of brown. Over many more millions of years, the continuing effects of temperature and pressure produce further change in the lignite, progressively increasing its organic maturity and transforming it into the range of coals known as sub-bituminous coals. Further chemical and physical changes occur until these coals became harder and blacker, forming the bituminous or hard coals. Under the right conditions, the progressive increase in the organic maturity can continue, finally forming anthracite. In addition to carbon, coals contain hydrogen, oxygen, nitrogen and varying amounts of sulfur. High-rank coals like anthracite are high in carbon and therefore heat value, but low in hydrogen and oxygen. Low-rank coals are low in carbon but high in hydrogen and oxygen content. However, each of these types of coal has commercial uses.

A coal-related material called coke is used in different industrial applications. Coke is produced from coal that is low in ash, sulfur, and phosphorus, and is created through a process known as pyrolysis. This refers to the baking of coal in an airless environment at temperatures as high as 1,000 degrees Celsius. This eliminates the volatile parts of the coal and fuses the fixed carbon and residual ash. When the process is complete, coke appears as grey, hard, and porous, with a heating value of 29.6 mega-joules per kilogram. Metallurgical coke is employed as a fuel and as a reducing agent to smelt iron ore in a blast furnace and must possess sufficient strength to endure the furnace's extreme pressures. The carbon monoxide produced by its combustion reduces hematite (an iron oxide) to iron. Petroleum coke, or "petcoke," is the solid residue obtained in oil refining, which resembles coke but contains too many impurities to be useful in metallurgical application. Some coke-making processes create by-products like coal tar, ammonia, light oils, and coal gas.

In addition to coke, chemicals have been produced from coal since the 1950s. The primary chemicals produced directly from coal include methanol, hydrogen, and carbon monoxide, and the chemical basis of many derivative chemicals, such as olefins, acetic acid, formaldehyde, ammonia, and urea. Thus, relatively inexpensive coal is used in the production of various valuable commodities. Coal can be used as a base material for producing various chemical fertilizers. A variety of chemical industries use whatever base materials are most cost-effective. Therefore, interest in using coal tends to increase in the event of higher oil and natural gas prices and during periods of high global economic growth that may strain oil and gas production. Also, production of chemicals from coal is of much higher interest in countries like South Africa, China, and India where there are abundant coal resources. The abundance of coal combined with lack of natural gas resources in China is a strong inducement for chemical producers to use coal. Coal to chemical processes require substantial quantities of water.

Two distinct methods are used in the mining of coal. The first method, surface or opencast mining, typically comes into use for coal deposits less than 200 feet underground. Large excavation machines are deployed to remove the layers of soil and rock covering the coal seam, which is called the overburden. About two-thirds of coal mining in the United States takes the form of surface mining due to its lower costs. Some forms of surface mining are called mountaintop removal due to the particular location of these deposits near the peaks of mountains (EIA 2023a). The second method is called underground mining. Typically, underground mines are accessed through mine shafts that can extend thousands of feet below the surface, and then extend for miles in horizontal tunnels off the main shaft. Mine workers are ferried to the tunnels by elevators, and then moved along horizontal tunnels by railcar. Machines do most of the work that used to be done by picks and shovels. These machines include such devices as continuous miners, mining drills and drill rigs, boring machines, longwall mining machines or shearers, and conveyers. In 2022, global coal production reached 8.1 billion metric tons (Karampela 2022).

In terms of its industrial and commercial uses, coal plays a vital role in supplying the energy needs of most industrialized nations. In the United States, 19.5 percent of electricity generation in 2022 came from coal combustion in power plants (EIA 2023b). Globally, that figure was 37 percent in 2020 (IEA 2022). Electricity "lights houses, buildings, and streets; provides domestic and industrial heat; and powers most equipment and machinery used in homes, offices and factories" (SME 2021). Coal and coke are used extensively in the production of iron, steel, and aluminum, which provide the skeletal components of the modern built environment, including the transportation systems that span the globe. Coal is also used in making cement, a central ingredient in construction, and can be converted to liquid fuels through a process called liquefaction. These coals-to-liquids fuels are used extensively in aviation (Paul 2009).

Historically, industrialized nations have struggled with the various environmental and public health effects of coal mining and coal combustion. Concerns about air pollution from coal-fired steam plants, manufacturing facilities, and steam locomotives can be traced to the mid-nineteenth century. In England, activists formed the Committee for the Consumption of Smoke at Leeds and the Association for the Prevention of Smoke in Manchester in 1842 due to the high output of chimney smoke from coal-fired steam plants. Chicago and other municipalities in the United States enacted smoke abatement ordinances in the 1880s. Coal smokestack emissions can produce a variety of cardio-pulmonary conditions and is linked to certain neurological issues as well (EPA 2022). The Great London Smog of 1952 reportedly caused the deaths of 12,000 people due to smoke inhalation from coal-fired power plants and the city's diesel-powered buses (NG 2022). This led the British Parliament to enact the Clean Air Acts of 1956 and 1968, which the United States modeled in its own Clean Air Acts in 1963 and 1970. Coal combustion also damages water resources through contamination of ground water via fly ash containment pond seepage and even major slurry spills. Finally, coal combustion was the chief source of the atmospheric sulfur dioxide that produced acid rain in the United States, leading to soil contamination and deforestation in part of the Northeast region (Weiss 2012).

Another long-standing concern about the production and consumption of coal is mine safety. In the nineteenth and early twentieth centuries, coal mines were extremely hazardous working environments for coal miners. At least 61,187 perished in coal mining accidents in the United States from 1838 to 1914, according to a 1916 report from the U.S. Bureau of Mines (Fay 1916, 7). These accidents included roof collapses in underground mines, combustion of coal dust and uncontrolled fires, explosions resulting from ignition of gases like methane, and carbon monoxide poisoning. Countless coal miners perished from a chronic condition called black lung disease, caused by inhalation of coal dust. Increased public pressure and organization of the miners by the United Mine Workers of America brought mine operations to create safer working conditions, aided by the research and oversight functions of the US Bureau of Mines. This was created in 1910 after a series of horrific mine explosions and fires in 1907–9. Many states enacted mine safety laws in the ensuing years, and in 1977 Congress enacted the Federal Mine Safety and Health Act of 1977, which created a special agency for mine safety called the Mine Safety and Health Administration to address accidents, explosions, and health issues like black lung disease.

Coal mining became safer as a result. In 2020, five miners were killed in accidents in the United States, the lowest on record (MSHA 2022). Coal continued to be an important source of energy in the United States even after the decades-long national debate over fossil fuels, global warming, and climate change from the mid-1980s into the 2010s and beyond. Research and development on renewable energy resources, coupled with numerous federal incentives to replace coal with solar, wind, hydropower, and nuclear energy, offered challenges to the coal industry in their efforts to maintain the fuel's position in the US system of energy production. Nevertheless, coal will continue to supply an important resource for a wide variety of industrial uses in the foreseeable future.

William P. Kladky

See also: Acid Rain; Centralia Mine Disaster; Chicago Smoke Abatement Ordinances of 1881 and 1903; Cist, Jacob; Clean Coal; Clean Power Plan of 2015; Coal Gasification; Coke; Colliers; Cumberland Iron and Coal Company; Industrial Revolution; Molly Maguires; Surface Mining; United Mine Workers of America; Usibelli, Emil

FURTHER READING

Fay, Albert H. 1916. "Coal Mine Fatalities in the United States, 1836–1914." Bureau of Mines. US Department of the Interior. Washington, DC: US Government Printing Office.

Freese, Carol. 2003. *Coal: A Human History*. New York: Basic Books.

International Energy Agency (IEA). 2022. "World Energy Balances: Overview." IEA, Paris. https://www.iea.org/reports/world-energy-balances-overview (accessed October 2023).

Karampela, Elli. 2022. "Global Coal Production to Grow by a Marginal 0.9% in 2022." *Mining Technology*. September 13. https://www.mining-technology.com/comment/global-coal-production/ (accessed October 2023).

Mine Safety and Health Administration (MSHA). 2022. "Coal Fatalities for 1900 through 2022." US Department of Labor. https://arlweb.msha.gov/stats/centurystats/coalstats.asp (accessed October 2023).

National Geographic (NG). 2022. "Dec 5, 1952 CE: Great Smog of 1952." Nat Geo Education Resources. May 20. https://education.nationalgeographic.org/resource/great-smog-1952/ (accessed October 2023).

Paul, A. Dilo. 2009. "A Fresh Look at Coal-Derived Liquid Fuels." *Power Magazine*. January 1. https://www.powermag.com/a-fresh-look-at-coal-derived-liquid-fuels/ (accessed October 2023).

Society for Mining, Mettalurgy, and Exploration (SME). 2021. "Coal's Importance to the World." February 21. https://www.smenet.org/What-We-Do/Technical-Briefings/Coal-s-Importance-in-the-US-and-Global-Energy-Supp (accessed October 2023).

US Energy Information Administration (EIA). 2023a. "Coal Explained: Mining and Transportation of Coal." February 16. U.S. Department of Energy. https://www.eia.gov/energyexplained/coal/mining-and-transportation.php (accessed October 2023).

US Energy Information Administration (EIA). 2023b. "What is U.S. Electricity Generation by Energy Source?" March 2. U.S. Department of Energy. https://www.eia.gov/tools/faqs/faq.php?id=427&t=3 (accessed October 2023).

US Environmental Protection Agency. 2022. "Air Pollution and Cardiovascular Disease Basics." September 12. https://www.epa.gov/air-research/air-pollution-and-cardiovascular-disease-basics (accessed October 2023).

Weiss, Marissa. 2012. "Is Acid Rain a Thing of the Past?" *Science*. June 28. https://www.science.org/content/article/acid-rain-thing-past (accessed October 2023).

Coal Gasification

Coal gasification is a chemical process whereby coal is heated in a closed, low-oxygen environment, forcing it to release a mixture of flammable gases known sometimes as coal gas, town gas, or syngas that can then be burned in ways similar to natural gas. In the early 1800s, neither natural gas nor electricity were available the way they are today, and while many modern amenities were thus missing, the most obvious was the lack of lighting. Coal gas solved this problem better than anything before it, and as coal became readily available during the Industrial Revolution, towns began building coal gasification facilities and distribution networks of pipes, connecting homes, businesses, and streetlights to this new form of energy.

In the early 1800s, most lighting was done by candles or oil lamps. In America, whale oil was especially popular for its clean-burning qualities and grew to a sprawling industry chronicled in popular novels such as Herman Melville's 1851 novel *Moby Dick*. However, it also had a high environmental cost. Most whale oil came from bowhead whales and sperm whales, and due to high levels of demand, its use led to the overfishing and depletion of some whale populations. Candles, the other main source of lighting, also posed limitations that were recorded in famous nineteenth-century literature. In Thomas Hardy's *Return of The Native*, the main character Clym goes blind trying to read by candlelight. Sports, work, and leisure were necessarily reduced or discontinued at nightfall, reducing the ability of societies to function as they do today. While electricity would eventually become the primary source of human lighting, the first step in this direction was through coal gas.

Today, humans all over the world use natural gas in homes and businesses, but these uses have only become widely viable with advances of modern technology that can efficiently extract the gas and distribute it in vast networks of pipelines and liquefied tankers. Things were much more difficult in the 1800s. Especially because of the limitations on transportation of natural gas, it was mostly consumed at or near the wellhead—where the gas comes from the earth. Because coal was much easier to extract, store, and transport than natural gas, and had become widespread during the Industrial Revolution, many towns settled on coal gas instead of natural gas.

Coal gas was a great advancement over whale oil and candles. It burned brighter, produced less soot, and could be turned up and down to control the amount of light produced (Smil 2017, 227). It could also be produced within the boundaries of a city or town and then distributed through a local network of pipes to light streetlights and lamps. Because of these advantages, many cities and towns set about building coal gasification plants in their town centers, and by the 1850s most of Western Europe and the United States had connected their gasification plants not only to streetlights, but also to commercial, government, and residential subscribers through underground distribution systems. Streetlights were especially popular, requiring a lamplighter to walk the street each evening at dusk with a small flame on a pole, lighting each of the lamps.

GASIFICATION GONE AWRY

During the first Obama administration the US Department of Energy invested heavily in an IGCC power plant in Kemper, Mississippi with the hope that it would be the first full-scale clean coal gasification facility in the world. However, the project was plagued with cost overruns and was abandoned in 2017.

Rudy Kahsar

The significance of the advent of coal gas cannot be overstated. Before this source of fuel, businesses, schools, and many forms of work and leisure could not operate after sunset. As it became widespread, huge advancements were made in industry, social life, and safety. Eventually, it became so dominant that Thomas Edison saw it as his top competitor when he sought to bring electricity to market in the 1880s (Yergin 2011, 63). By 1900, competition came instead from natural gas pipelines, built to connect fields in Texas and Oklahoma to cities and states in the Midwest. The last coal gasification facilities in the United States closed in the 1960s.

For all its benefits, coal gasification also produced a number of negative side effects. Coal gas, like all forms of fossil fuel consumption, produces greenhouse gas emissions, and while emissions were small in the 1800s, the invention and deployment of pipelines and distribution systems for gas helped usher in the new era of fossil energy. Second, while coal gas lighting was a great source of new productivity, it also perpetuated the use of open flames and flammable pipelines in and around buildings, sometimes leading to accidental fires and explosions. Furthermore, coal gas itself contains poisonous components such as carbon monoxide and hydrogen sulfide, each of which can result in death if accidentally inhaled.

Another significant and lasting environmental impact of coal gasification is the waste it produces. As a sedimentary mineral, coal contains a wide range of molecules, chemicals, and atomic constituents including heavy metals such as arsenic, mercury, and even uranium. When that coal is burned or heated to release coal gas, these heavy metals are typically left behind in a mixture of slag that contains ash, rocks, and other non-combustible materials. As modern environmental regulations on disposal were not adopted widely in the United States until the 1970s, this toxic coal slag was often dumped into fields or rivers. In fact, one of the earliest coal gasification units in the country was built on the banks of the Anacostia River in Washington, DC in order to supply coal gas and lighting to the US Capitol building. The resulting slag, dumped into the river over many years, is expected to be subject to federal environmental remediation efforts well into the 2020s.

Coal gas has been replaced by natural gas, which is used to power furnaces, stoves, water heaters, grills, refrigerators, and engines in commercial, industrial, residential, and even transportation sectors. And while coal gas is unlikely to be again used for lighting, the history of coal gasification is not over yet; scientists and engineers are still exploring new ways of using gasified coal, notably in Integrated Gasification Combined Cycle (IGCC) power plants. These plants, sometimes associated with clean coal marketing and labeling, seek to gasify coal, combust the gases in a combustion turbine, and use the waste heat to turn a steam turbine. The technology is more expensive to build than a traditional coal power plant, but it also has a higher operating efficiency and is capable of producing a pure stream of carbon dioxide that can then be sequestered (Bell 2010, 2-4).

Rudy Kahsar

See also: California Electric Light Company; Cist, Jacob; Coal; Cumberland Iron & Coal Company; Hart, William Aaron; Hydraulic Fracking; Indiana Natural Gas Boom; Industrial Revolution; Natural Gas; Whale Oil

FURTHER READING

Bell, David A., Brian F. Towler, and Maohong Fan. 2010. *Coal Gasification and its Applications*. Norwich, NY: William Andrew.

Freese, Barbara. 2016. *Coal: A Human History*. New York: Basic Books.

Nye, David E. 1999. *Consuming Power: A Social History of American Energies*. Cambridge, MA: MIT Press.

Rhodes, Richard. 2018. *Energy: A Human History*. New York: Simon & Schuster.

Smil, Vaclav. 2017. *Energy and Civilization: A History*. Cambridge, MA: MIT Press.

Yergin, Daniel. 2011. *The Quest: Energy, Security, and the Remaking of the Modern World*. New York: Penguin.

Coaling Stations

Coaling stations are depots for storing coal or—in more recent years, fuel oil—for use by civilian and naval ships. As the United States began to add coal-fired steamships to its merchant marine and Navy in the late nineteenth century, coaling stations became an object of national debate. Eventually, however, they were recognized as a necessary component of American trade and overseas expansion, and their establishment signaled what would become a growing national reliance on fossil fuels.

America's naval leaders began replacing sailing ships with coal-fired steamships in the nineteenth century, and a majority of the 671 warships in the US Navy at the end of the Civil War (1861–5) were steam-powered. However, most were decommissioned over the following decade, and those that were subsequently built were "auxiliary steamers"—sailing ships that had steam capability. Early coal-fired engines were notably inefficient, and the ships' commanders were expected to rely on sails in most circumstances and to use the ships' steam capability only in extreme situations such as combat.

During peacetime, American ships could secure coal from other countries through ordinary commercial channels. But despite the general reluctance to use coal at all, there was a belief in some quarters that the time would come when access to American-controlled coaling stations would be required overseas. However, the search for suitable locations proved difficult. On its 1844–6 circumnavigation of the globe, for instance, the USS *Constitution* was tasked with identifying promising sites for such stations, but it was not successful in doing so. Navy Commodore Matthew C. Perry (1794–1858) argued in the 1850s for the establishment of coaling stations in the Pacific Ocean, and suggested Chichi Jima in the Bonin (or Ogasawara) Islands as a potential site. However, Congress and the Department of the Navy were opposed at the time to an imperialist policy that would have involved the island's annexation, and it was occupied instead by Japan the following decade.

Despite ongoing opposition a number of public officials such as Secretary of State William H. Seward (1801–72) supported the concept of coaling stations. Seward visited the Dominican Republic in 1866 with the intention of securing an American base at Samaná Bay, and attempted during the same period to secure rights to a coaling station on the island of St. Thomas in the Danish West Indies. Secretary of the Navy William E. Chandler identified more than a dozen possible locations in an 1883 report, and in his inaugural address as President in 1889, Benjamin Harrison argued the need for conveniently located coaling stations and harbor privileges. A year later, Alfred Thayer Mahan (1840–1914) asserted in his influential book *The Influence of Sea Power upon History: 1660–1783* (1890), that the path of international preeminence lay through a strong navy and pointed out that with the introduction of steam power, the acquisition of coaling stations was a necessity.

GUANTÁNAMO BAY

Cuba and the United States negotiated a perpetual lease for the land at Guantánamo Bay in 1934, and it has remained under American control as a naval base ever since. The United States went on to establish a controversial detention camp on the base in 2002 during the "War on Terror," and despite efforts to close it, it continues in operation on a reduced basis in the early twenty-first century.

Grove Koger

The United States took control of its first overseas possession with the annexation of the tiny (and uninhabited) North Pacific atoll of Midway in 1867. Hoping to avoid the high taxes imposed by ports in the Hawaiian Islands, the Pacific Mail Steamship Company (PMSC) attempted to break a channel through the atoll's reef in order to set up its own coaling station. However, the project was a failure, and the atoll eventually became the site of a trans-Pacific telegraph cable station and seaplane base instead.

Although the nation's ambivalence toward overseas territorial expansion continued to color its actions, there was a growing realization that, as an emerging power, the United States would expand beyond North America. As a result, the country's military strategy in the Pacific Ocean during the last two decades of the nineteenth century involved identifying locations for and setting up coaling stations on foreign soil. One of the first was built at Pearl River (Pearl Harbor) on Oahu in the Kingdom of Hawaii. Land was actually leased for the station as early as 1860, but, given the Navy's emphasis on relying on sail, it initially saw little use. However, the step proved to be a prelude to the American annexation of Hawaii as the Spanish–American War (1898) drew to a close.

A few years later, in 1872, the United States established the right to build a coaling station at Pago Pago on Tutuila in the Samoan Islands, an archipelago lying about halfway between Hawaii and New Zealand. The claim was ratified by treaty six years later. Pago Pago was recognized as one of the finest harbors in the South Pacific Ocean, and the location for the station was particularly desirable since the mountains enclosing the site made it invulnerable to shelling. The Navy stockpiled 2,000 tons of coal on a rented lot in 1880, although there was no subsequent move to find land for a permanent station or to build an office to oversee the coal's dispersal. Nevertheless, the move turned out to be yet another step toward territorial expansion, with the United States taking control of several of the islands (including Tutuila) in 1900.

The American naval experience during the Spanish–American War, in which the United States defeated Spain, proved to be decisive in altering American policy in favor of expansion. It was also instrumental in swaying naval opinion in favor of establishing coaling stations and adding colliers (vessels designed to carry coal for warships) to the nation's fleets. An American fleet that had anchored in the British port of Hong Kong sailed to the Spanish colony of the Philippines, where American ships defeated the Spanish squadron in the brief Battle of Manila Bay. A smaller fleet sailing from Hawaii seized the Spanish island of Guam to the east. Subsequently, American ships and infantry units defeated Spanish forces on the other side of the world on the Caribbean island of Cuba. As was the case in the Philippines, American colliers attended the ships blockading Cuba.

In the Treaty of Paris ending the war, Spain ceded Guam, the Philippines, and the Caribbean island of Puerto Rico to the United States, with Cuba becoming an American protectorate. The large, deepwater harbor at Apra on Guam's western coast was viewed as an ideal naval base and coaling station, and both were established there in 1905. Stations and depots were also set up in several locations in the Philippines.

Cuba's new governor signed a treaty with the United States in 1903 providing for leasing territory for two coaling stations. At the time, the United States was contemplating building a canal through the Isthmus of Panama (completed in 1914), and Rear Admiral Royal B. Bradford considered it essential that a coaling station be set up in a strategic location somewhere along or near the western coast of South America. Although not precisely in that location, Guantánamo Bay, on the southeastern coast of the island, fit the perceived need well enough, and it became the Guantanamo Bay Naval Base.

Despite the nation's preliminary success in setting up coaling stations in the Pacific and the Caribbean, experience showed how difficult it was to recoal ships beyond the nation's shores. A partial solution came with the discovery of underground preserves of petroleum in such states as Ohio and Texas. Although it had been rejected by naval authorities in the past, oil generated more energy for pound than coal and was markedly easier to handle, both in port and at sea. The last American coal-burning warship, the USS *Texas*, was built in 1914. Two years later, the Navy commissioned two oil-burning ships, the USS *Nevada* and the USS *Oklahoma*. When the *Texas* itself was converted to oil in 1925, its efficiency showed a marked increase. With the transition to oil, coaling stations became more properly known as "fueling stations," although the earlier term remained in use for some time.

Grove Koger

See also: Coal; Colliers; Mahan, Alfred Thayer; Panama Canal; Petroleum; Steam Power

FURTHER READING

Bradford, Royal B. 1899. "Coaling-Stations for the Navy." *Forum* 26. February. Pp. 732–47.

Mahan, Alfred Thayer. 1890. *The Influence of Sea Power upon History, 1660–1783*. Boston: Little, Brown.

Maurer, John H. 1981. "Fuel and the Battle Fleet: Coal, Oil, and American Naval Strategy, 1898–1925." *Naval War College Review*. Vol. 34. No. 6. November–December. Pp. 69–74.

Niblack, A.P. 1904. "Colliers and Coaling Stations." *Naval Institute Proceedings*. Vol. 30. Pp. 567–76.

Shulman, Peter A. 2015. *Coal and Empire: The Birth of Energy Security in Industrial America*. Baltimore: Johns Hopkins University Press.

Coke

In the context of energy, coke is the product made from bituminous coal that has been heated to a high temperature in the absence of air. There are several processes for making coke from coal, all generally called coking, or carbonization. Properly made, coke is relatively pure carbon and thereby serves as an excellent fuel for smelting iron and other metallurgical applications. Prior to the introduction of the coking process to the iron industry, iron furnaces required charcoal (another substance that is nearly pure carbon) for smelting iron. The carbon in the charcoal or coke is necessary not only to burn, and create the heat necessary for smelting, but also for the chemical reaction of reducing the iron oxide minerals in the ore to pure iron. Acquiring the necessary charcoal required the ownership of large tracts of forest lands to supply the timber needed to make charcoal on a sustainable basis. The need for charcoal created an environmental limit to the capacity at which a furnace could operate if its owner wanted to stay in business as long as the iron ore lasted. The conversion to coke as a metallurgical fuel freed the iron industry in the nineteenth-century United States (eighteenth century in England) from that environmental limit. Without the ability to make coke from coal, the iron industries of the world could not have grown to the magnitude they have grown during the period of industrialization.

Coal has three basic components, carbon and hydrocarbon molecules, impurities such as sulfur and phosphorus, and small amounts of other minerals (called ash). When burned in the presence of air, coal combusts, leaving only the ash. When coal is heated in the absence of air, it cannot combust, because oxygen is not present. The heat volatilizes the hydrocarbons, leaving the carbon, ash, and other impurities behind. The coking of coal thereby yields three products, broadly speaking: coke (carbon, ash, and residual impurities), coal gas (manufactured gas, the hydrocarbons that remain as a gas when cooled), and coal tar (volatilized hydrocarbons that condense to a liquid when cooled). Historically, there have been two main methods of coking coal: in beehive ovens and in by-product ovens. Beehive ovens are relatively inexpensive to build, and they discharge the volatilized hydrocarbons into the atmosphere as thick smoke. By-product ovens are sealed, allowing operators to save the by-products (gas and tar) in addition to the coke.

The first commercial coking of coal in the United States took place at a manufactured gas plant in Baltimore in 1816. Its main product was the gas, used for municipal street lighting. The coke made at the plant was sold as smokeless solid fuel, but it was not a suitable metallurgical fuel because it was made from coal with too many impurities. Operators of iron furnaces (for smelting), foundries (for casting), and forges (for blacksmithing) experimented with beehive ovens to try to make suitable fuel, achieving some success in fueling foundries and forges, but they had difficulty finding a coal that was free enough of impurities to make good furnace fuel. Therefore, the US iron industry was largely dependent on charcoal for smelting until the second half of the nineteenth century. Meanwhile, the first significant move in the United States away from iron smelted with charcoal was with the introduction of anthracite coal, an excellent furnace fuel, sometimes called natural coke, mined in northeast Pennsylvania.

WASTEFUL PRACTICES

It is a matter of extreme surprise to a scientific or practical mining engineer, on first visiting the extensive coke-producing region of Pennsylvania, to see the excessive waste of the valuable products incidental to and closely allied with the process of coking coal. It is so easily remedied, and does not require an expensive series of experiments, of the efficacy of which we have abundant proof in Europe ... It behooves every manufacturer of coke to use all the economical means that science and practice are capable of devising to get the greatest possible return on the large expenditure of capital. (RW.P. Richardson. "Improved Methods of Coking Coal and the Utilization of By-Products of Combustion," *Engineering and Mining Journal*. Vol. 39 (31 January 1885). P. 71.

Fredric L. Quivik

The situation in furnace fuels in the United States began to change dramatically after 1850, when coke makers found that the Pittsburgh seam of bituminous coal in the Connellsville region of southwest Pennsylvania was a source from which to make a superior metallurgical fuel. Entrepreneurs bought coal lands and built beehive coking plants in the Connellsville region, shipped their product to Pittsburgh and elsewhere, and helped to propel Pittsburgh to become the center of the nation's iron and steel industry. In 1870, there were about 700 beehive coke ovens in the Connellsville region, and by 1880, there were more than ten times that number. Henry Clay Frick became the leading coke maker in the region. Through acquisitions, he was able to consolidate many of the area's coke companies into his H.C. Frick Coke Company. In the 1880s, Andrew Carnegie's iron and steel business was one of Frick's major customers, Carnegie became a major investor in Frick's company, and Carnegie made Frick an officer in his iron and steel enterprise. When U.S. Steel formed in 1903, the Frick Company became one of U.S. Steel's subsidiaries. The Frick Company then owned 16,000 beehive ovens, and U.S. Steel owned 30,000 nationwide. Coal fields in West Virginia and elsewhere also developed important beehive coking industries.

As Germany industrialized in the nineteenth century, it found that it had an abundance of bituminous coal, but it possessed little coal suitable for beehive coking to make metallurgical fuel. German steel makers therefore invested heavily in by-product coking, which could make an acceptable metallurgical fuel and reduce overall costs, because the coal gas could be used to fire other operations at the steel mills, and the coal tar could be sold to Germany's nascent chemical industry. This helped Germany to become the world's leading manufacturer of organic chemicals, like synthetics and pharmaceuticals, by the end of the nineteenth century. Advocates for by-product coking in the United States urged the nation's steel and coking industries to follow suit, so that the valuable resources present in the smoke emanating from the beehive ovens would not go to waste. With few exceptions, however, American coke makers were reluctant to make the switch. By-product coking plants required a much greater capital investment, and operators of iron furnaces were reluctant to commit to by-product coke. They knew that Connellsville coke and other beehive cokes were excellent, and they were unwilling to take chances with by-product coke as an inferior metallurgical fuel.

Despite furnacemen's preference for beehive coke, US steel companies began a shift to by-product coke late in the first decade of the twentieth century. As they built new steel mills, they typically built adjacent by-product coking plants to avail themselves of gas as well as coke to fuel steel mill operations. The transition was secured during the First World War, when the United States could no longer rely on Germany, as an enemy in the conflict, to supply chemicals. Thereafter, production of beehive coke went into steady decline until it virtually ceased during the Great Depression. Meanwhile, the production of by-product coke in the United States grew with the nation's steel industry. That changed in the 1970s, with passage of the Clean Air Act, under which the US Environmental Protection Agency (EPA) began imposing more restrictive regulations on the coking industry, forcing some US coking plants to close and companies to attempt redesigning others to meet regulations.

Because beehive ovens did not save the by-products of coking, the toxic smoke emanating from the coke works denuded the surrounding areas of vegetation. By-product ovens saved all the by-products for distribution and sale. After beehive coking plants were taken out of service, the disseminated pollutants gradually weathered; today there are no known beehive coking sites listed in the EPA's National Priorities List (NPL) requiring Superfund remediation. Meanwhile, by-product coking works often leaked, contaminating soils and groundwater. Processing the by-products for use or sale created wastes that were often disposed on site, further contaminating soils and groundwater. The NPL includes many former by-product-coking and manufactured-gas plants.

Fredric L. Quivik

See also: Cist, Jacob; Coal; Clean Air Act of 1970; Clean Coal; Frick, Henry Clay; Industrial Revolution; Susquehanna Company; US Environmental Protection Agency

FURTHER READING

Eavenson, Howard N. 1938. "The Pittsburgh Coal Bed—Its Early History and Development." *Transactions of the American Institute of Mining and Metallurgical Engineers*. Vol. 130.

Harkins, Scott M., Robert S. Truesdale, Ronald Hill, Paula Hoffman, and Steven Winters. 1988. "U.S. Production of Manufactured Gases: Assessment of Past Disposal Practices." Report Prepared for the US Environmental Protection Agency, Contract No. 68-01-8826 D.O. #35, February.

Historic American Engineering Record (HAER). 1994. "Connellsville Coal & Coke Region." HAER No. PA-283. Available online in the Library of Congress Digital Collections.

Tarr, Joel A. 1994. "Searching for a 'Sink' for an Industrial Waste: Iron-Making Fuels and the Environment." *Environmental History Review*. Vol. 18. Spring. Pp. 9–34.

Tarr, Joel A. 2014. "Toxic Legacy: The Environmental Impact of the Manufactured Gas Industry in the United States." *Technology and Culture*. Vol. 55. January. Pp. 107–47.

Temin, Peter. 1964. *Iron and Steel in Nineteenth-Century America: An Economic Inquiry*. Cambridge, MA: The MIT Press.

Warren, Kenneth. 2001. *Wealth, Waste, and Alienation: Growth and Decline in the Connellsville Coke Industry*. Pittsburgh: Pittsburgh University Press.

Colliers

Colliers were cargo ships built to transport coal, particularly for use by steamships, or steamers. The country's steamships initially relied on procuring coal from local suppliers at home and overseas. But as the US Navy began to commission steamships and the nation began to expand overseas in the later nineteenth century, colliers and American-controlled coaling stations, or depots, became important and eventually essential. In time of war, warships' supplies of coal had to be replenished whenever necessary. With the introduction of oil as a fuel in the early twentieth century, colliers were phased out, to be replaced by oilers. However, a number of colliers were rebuilt to serve other military purposes.

Small European ships had routinely transported coal on waterways and along coasts for centuries, but one of the first such instances in the United States involved the use of a barge in 1820. The coal was being carried from Pittsburgh, Pennsylvania, to Philadelphia, and the transport was undertaken by Pittsburgh industrialists Josiah White and Erskine Hazard.

With the introduction of coal-burning steamships, the problem of "recoaling," as the operation was known, became critical. The United States commissioned coal-burning paddle steamers to operate on the Mississippi River during the Civil War (1861–5), but it was necessary for them to sail from their designated positions to recoal at waterside facilities or in port. The earliest colliers were essentially powered barges intended to load coal onto steamships in such locations. In later years, steamships propelled by screw propellers began to replace paddle-wheelers, and it was this more efficient design that eventually prevailed. However, the necessity for recoaling did not change, as steamships continued to require enormous amounts of the fuel to operate. In fact, the US Navy was slow to replace wind-powered ships on overseas missions due to the problems involved in procuring coal from foreign sources.

In 1890, Alfred Thayer Mahan (1840–1914) argued in *The Influence of Sea Power upon History: 1660–1783,* that a strong navy was essential to international preeminence, and added that, with the introduction of steam power, it was imperative that the United States acquire an adequate number of coaling stations. Unlike nations such as Great Britain and France, however, America possessed no overseas possessions where coaling stations might be built. At the time Mahan wrote, the nation had actually begun to claim various islands in the Pacific Ocean and Caribbean Sea in strategic locations, but a different solution to supplying coal was also under development.

That solution involved colliers that could be positioned alongside battleships and load coal onto them while the battleships remained in their stations. With the approach of the Spanish–American War (1898), the Navy bought twenty such vessels, most of them from the UK and all equipped with two loading booms apiece, deploying most of them with the North Atlantic Squadron in the Caribbean area. However, they sailed slowly and were unable to transfer their coal effectively during rough weather. Even under the best of conditions, recoaling was a dirty, almost brutally difficult operation, and injuries among the crewmembers doing the work were common. Nevertheless, most of the American warships blockading the southern Cuban port of Santiago were able to recoal thanks to their presence. However, some vessels were forced to sail in small contingents 45 miles away to recoal in sheltered sites. It was during one of these episodes that the Spanish fleet succeeded in running the American blockade.

A PLAN FOILED

Due to its unreliability, the collier USS *Merrimac* was regarded as expendable, and during the Spanish–American War, Navy Rear Admiral William T. Sampson planned to block the entrance to the harbor at Santiago de Cuba by scuttling the vessel at its entrance. However, the Spanish sank the collier with shells and mines themselves. But because ocean currents twisted the *Merrimac* as it sank, the harbor entrance remained navigable and Americans ships were forced to undertake a full-scale blockade.

Grove Koger

On the other side of the world, Admiral George Dewey (1837–1917) had based the Asiatic Squadron in the British territory of Hong Kong in order to keep his ships' coal bunkers filled. He also purchased two colliers, the USS *Nanshan* and the USS *Zafiro,* in the territory, and both ships were on hand to refuel his fleet for the brief Battle of Manila Bay (May 1) in the Spanish colony of the Philippines.

Hoping to hit upon a method of what would become known as "underway replenishment," Dewey asked mechanical engineer Spencer Miller to study the possibility of transferring coal while a ship was actually sailing. Miller designed several systems whereby a battleship could tow a collier (or, depending on conditions, a collier tow a battleship) at a safe distance. An elevated cable, or "highline," was then stretched between the masts of the two vessels, after which the battleship's winches could pull a loaded trolley along the cable. Miller's designs were tested in 1899 using the battleship USS *Massachusetts* and the collier USS *Marcellus* while the two were sailing at a speed of about 5 nautical miles per hour. The system worked, but the Navy deemed the rate at which the coal could be loaded insufficient. Similar experiments at sea were carried out over the next few years, but the attempts were eventually abandoned as newly designed battleships achieved greater sailing range and the use of blockade tactics was abandoned as obsolete.

Nevertheless, the use of colliers as simple transport vessels continued. When President Theodore Roosevelt dispatched the battleships and escorts of the "Great White Fleet" around the world in 1907–9 in a display of strength, the Navy found it necessary to charter forty-nine foreign colliers to deliver coal to various ports along the way. Subsequently the Navy commissioned two new colliers and purchased three more. Unlike those that had served in the Spanish–American War, the new colliers were equipped with either four or five booms, and within a short period of time, contractors were building colliers with even more. The size and complexity of such components made colliers top-heavy, although they were designed with ballast tanks that could be filled with water after they had unloaded their cargo.

The Navy's struggle with recoaling during the Spanish–American War ultimately led it to adopt a more efficient form of fuel—oil. During the early years of the twentieth century, the discovery of vast reserves of petroleum at such sites as Spindletop Hill in eastern Texas heralded a revolutionary change in the way Americans lived, worked, and fought wars. While naval authorities had rejected oil in the past, the fact was that it generated more energy than coal and was easier to load and unload, at sea as well as in port. The US Navy commissioned one of its last coal-burning warships, the USS *Texas*, in 1914, and subsequently commissioned two oil-burning ships, the USS *Nevada* and the USS *Oklahoma*, in 1916. When the *Texas* was converted to oil less than a decade later, its efficiency increased. With what was becoming an inevitable transition to oil as fuel, colliers became known as "oilers," or, more technically, replenishment oilers or replenishment tankers, vessels designed to carry not only oil but also munitions and stores.

Over the years, colliers were frequently converted to other uses. One notable example was the collier USS *Jupiter*, which was commissioned in 1913 and which, two years later, became the first ship to transit the Panama Canal from west to east. The *Jupiter* was subsequently decommissioned in 1920, converted into an aircraft carrier, and recommissioned in 1922 as the USS *Langley*, the nation's first aircraft carrier. Another collier, the USS *Vestal*, which had been commissioned in 1909, was rebuilt and recommissioned as a repair ship in 1913; it served during the First World War, was refitted to become an oil-fired ship in 1925, and saw service again during the Second World War.

Grove Koger

See also: Coal; Coaling Stations; Mahan, Alfred Thayer; Oil Tankers; Panama Canal; Petroleum; Spindletop Oil Gusher; Steam Power

FURTHER READING

Brown, Warwick. 2010. "When Dreams Confront Reality: Replenishment at Sea in the Era of Coal." *International Journal of Naval History*. Dec. 1. https://www.ijnhonline.org/when-dreams-confront-reality-replenishment-at-sea-in-the-era-of-coal/ (accessed October 2023).

Lukacs, John A. 2018. "A Century of Replenishment at Sea." *Naval History*. June 2018. Pp. 42–7.

Maurer, John H. 1982. "Fuel and the Battle Fleet: Coal, Oil, and American Naval Strategy, 1898–1925." *Naval War College Review*. Vol. 34. No. 6. November–December. Pp. 60–77.

Miller, Marvin O. 1996. *Designing the U.S. Navy's Underway Replenishment System*. Port Hueneme, CA: Underway Replenishment Dept., Port Hueneme Division, Naval Surface Warfare Center.

Miller, Marvin O., John W. Hammett, and Terence P. Murphy. 1992. "Development of the U.S. Navy Underway Replenishment Fleet." In *Underway Replenishment of Naval Ships*. Port Hueneme, CA: Underway Replenishment Department, Port Hueneme Division, Naval Surface Warfare Center. Pp. 3–50.

Miller, Spencer. 1914. "Refueling Warships at Sea." *Transactions of the Society of Naval Architects and Marine Engineers*. Vol. 22. Pp. 157–84.

Consolidated Edison Company

Located in New York, Consolidated Edison, Inc., commonly known as Con Edison or ConEd, is one of the largest US investor-owned energy companies. The company traces its organizational lineage to 1823 with the creation of the New York Gas Light Company, which provided New York City customers with natural gas for new gas light systems. Through its two-century long history, Con Edison developed and changed alongside the development of energy from coal and steam to petroleum and electricity. Through a series of consolidations and acquisitions it became one of the nation's largest utility companies, today serving 10 million customers in New York City and Westchester County. Con Ed, a gigantic corporation with $69.06 billion in assets, $15.57 billion in revenue, and $1.66 billion in profits in 2022, operates through five subsidiaries and provides various energy-related products and services like natural gas, electricity, and steam heat. Con Edison's recent history offers a view of the technical, economic, and political challenges that power companies must confront in a changing energy environment.

In 1823, Con Edison's earliest corporate predecessor, the New York Gas Light Company, was founded by the Quaker Samuel Leggett (1782–1847) and a consortium of New York City investors, who sought to capitalize on natural gas as a replacement for illumination by whale oil and kerosene lamps. The company was given the exclusive rights to lay gas pipes in the New York City district south of Grand Street for thirty years. Leggett's residence was the first to have natural gas piped into the house for the purposes of lighting. This offered better and more consistent performance than oil lamps and candles and emerged as a popular choice for more affluent consumers. The company managed to perform well because of its ties to Tammany Hall, an informal name for the Society of St. Tammany, a social club that controlled the city's politics throughout the nineteenth century. Through their influence, the company managed to keep early competitors from becoming established in the city, guaranteeing them a secure financial future.

Eventually franchises were given to other companies to serve different parts of New York City. New York Gas Light Company served lower Manhattan, and starting in 1833 the Manhattan Gas Light Company served the city north of Grand and Canal streets. In 1855, the Harlem Gas Light Company gained access to the city customers north of 79th Street in Harlem. Metropolitan Gas Light Company received a city-wide charter in 1858 and competed with all the other companies, and in time, the New York Mutual Gas Light Company (1866) and the Municipal Gas Light Company (1876) moved into the New York market. By the early 1880s six major gas companies operated in the city, with "gas house gangs" waging turf wars to maintain their customers (HW 2023). In terms of other types of service, in 1882 the New York Steam Company began providing steam heat and power service through central plants and underground steam pipes, and the Edison Illuminating Company built the Pearl

Street Station in the same year to supply coal-fired power for electrical illumination through transmission lines around lower Manhattan.

These three distinct services—natural gas, steam heat, and electricity—formed the core of Con Edison's suite of services once a period of consolidation in utilities was completed. Certainly, the situation in the 1880s was ripe for consolidation, and his occurred in stages. First, in 1884, the New York, Manhattan, Metropolitan, Municipal, Knickerbocker, and Harlem gas companies merged to form Consolidated Gas Company (Bell 2022). In 1898, the electrical illuminating companies—including Edison Illuminating Company—were consolidated into The New York Gas & Electric Light, Heat & Power Company, which Consolidated Gas purchased the following year. In 1901, the company then merged the electrical companies it controlled into a subsidiary called The New York Edison Company. By 1910, the company controlled the majority of natural gas and electricity operations in Manhattan and portions of the Bronx through these two divisions. In 1936, the company reorganized by merging the divisions, and renamed itself the Consolidated Edison Company of New York. Con Edison acquired the New York Steam Corporation in 1959, finally encompassing most of the natural gas, steam heat, and electricity utility services in Manhattan in one corporate entity.

Con Edison embraced the full array of energy possibilities, and even applied in 1955 for a permit to open a nuclear power plant from the Atomic Energy Commission (AEC). The AEC was granted authority by the Atomic Energy Act of 1954 to issue permits to private companies to build and operate nuclear power plants. In 1962, Con Edison opened its first nuclear power plant, Indian Point 1 in Buchanan, New York, but New York state officials ordered the plant shut down in 1970 due to inadequate cooling of hot water discharges, which resulted in fish kills in the Hudson River ("At Indian Point" 1983). In 1973, the company opened Indian Point 2, and in 1976, Indian Point 3, but both were plagued with problems and forced to shut down. Indian Point 1 was closed permanently in 1974, and Nos. 2 and 3 in 2020 and 2021, but both were at the time under different owners. The company has had other issues. In 1977, the infamous New York City Blackout "gave looters and arsonists a field day," and was attributed to lightning strikes on a Con Edison electrical substation (Lescaze 1977). State courts in New York determined that the company was grossly negligent and acted with reckless and willful conduct in the affair. Steam pipe and gas leak explosions in 1989, 2007, 2009, 2014—all involving fatalities—brought further censure and public backlash.

Con Edison worked to improve its services and its public image. Concerns about carbon emissions, the greenhouse gas effect, global warming, and climate change in the 1990s turned the attention of political leaders, media, and the broader public to power companies and their use of fossil fuels. Legislation was enacted to encourage use of renewable energy sources by power companies. Beginning in the early 2000s, Con Edison responded by investing large sums, upwards of $3 billion, in solar and wind projects. As of 2020, its generation capacity using solar and wind power was 1.5 gigawatts, with three-fourths of the energy drawn from solar farms and assorted solar installations. Customers can supply Con Edison with power generated at their homes and businesses through its net metering program; from 2013 to 2022, around 32,000 of Con Edison and 8,000 of Orange & Rockland—a ConEd subsidiary—generated 375 megawatts of electricity. In 2019, Con Edison joined with other public and private electric utility companies in opposing President Donald Trump's efforts to undermine the Obama-era Clean Power Plan of 2015. The company's press release said, "the EPA's rollback of the Clean Power Plan is the wrong approach to combating climate change, and will undermine the company's own efforts to achieve meaningful reductions in greenhouse gas emissions" (CE 2019)

Con Edison pursued many initiatives to steer the company toward a cleaner system of energy generation. It made significant investments in renewable energy, including offshore wind development, created incentives to support charging stations and other electric vehicle infrastructure, reduced greenhouse gas emissions in its own operations, and sponsored home energy efficiency and solar generation programs. Yet, in 2023, Con Edison sold its subsidiary Con Edison Clean Energy Businesses to a German company for $6.8 billion, which divested the company of most of its solar, wind, and battery assets. Company officials claimed the move was intended to allow Con Edison to "invest heavily in its regulated utility operations" as it seeks to "lead New York's ambitious clean energy transition" (Blunt 2022). The move also had bottom-line implications, as the company also implemented a $1 billion stock buy-back program in the same year. With giant infrastructure maintenance costs, uncertainties in energy markets, fears of federal cutbacks in renewable energy subsidies, and the need to adopt next-generation smart grid technologies, Con Edison must prepare for multiple future energy contingencies.

William P. Kladky

See also: California Electric Light Company; Clean Power Plan of 2015; Climate Change; Digital Revolution; Electricity; Federal Power Commission; Insull, Samuel; New York City Blackout; New York Steam Company; Public Utility Regulatory Policies Act of 1978; Renewable Energy; Smart Grid

FURTHER READING

"At Indian Point, a 30-Year History of Nuclear Power, Problems and Controversy." 1983. *New York Times*. May 6. P. B5.

Axelrod, Regina. 1982. *Conflict between Energy and Urban Environment: Consolidated Edison versus the City of New York*. Washington, DC: University Press of America.

Bell, B.A., and K.L. Bell. 2022. "History of Con Edison." American Oil & Gas Historical Society. November 4. https://aoghs.org/stocks/con-edison-american-utility-company (accessed October 2023).

Blunt, Katherine. 2022. "ConEd Agrees to Sell Clean Energy Business for $6.8 Billion to RWE." *The Wall Street Journal*. October 1. https://www.wsj.com/articles/coned-agrees-to-sell-clean-energy-business-for-6-8-billion-to-rwe-11664666691 (accessed October 2023).

Con Edison (CE). 2019. "Con Edison Challenges Repeal of the Clean Power Plan." Press Release. Con Edison Media Relations. September 16. https://investor.conedison.com/news-releases/news-release-details/con-edison-challenges-repeal-clean-power-plan (accessed October 2023).

Feiner, Meryl. 2002. "Gaslights to Generators: New York's Energy History." The Cooperator of New York. September. https://cooperator.com/article/gaslights-to-generators/full (accessed October 2023).

Harlem World (HW). 2023. "Before Con Edison, There Was the Harlem Gas Light Company in Harlem, 1855–1932." *Harlem World Magazine*. https://www.harlemworldmagazine.com/before-con-edison-there-was-the-harlem-gas-light-company-in-harlem-1855-1932/ (accessed October 2023).

Lescaze, Lee and Jack Egan. 1977. "Blackout Paralyzes New York City for Day." *The Washington Post*. July 15. https://www.washingtonpost.com/archive/politics/1977/07/15/blackout-paralyzes-new-york-city-for-day/210ab366-71fb-4c66-a87f-9a15e0a6d1a8/ (accessed October 2023).

The Consortium Agreement of 1954

The Consortium Agreement of 1954, which was ratified after several years of tense, controversial negotiations concerning the ownership of Iranian oil production, is considered by most historians to be the harbinger of the political instability, military conflict, and economic collapse that plagued Iran for many decades. The Central Intelligence Agency (CIA)-sponsored *coup d'état* of Iranian Prime Minister Mohammad Mosaddegh on August 19, 1953 further complicated the negotiations and exposed several contradictions in both United States and British foreign policy. Although Mosaddegh's overthrow led to a more favorable agreement for Western oil companies such as the Anglo-Iranian Oil Company (AIOC, later renamed British Petroleum), it undermined long-term relations with Iran. The agreement served to strengthen US involvement in the Middle East in its McCarthy-era struggle against communism.

The Consortium Agreement of 1954 has often been overshadowed by the drama surrounding the overthrow of Mossadegh, but its consequences illuminate the narrow ideological perspective of the United States. Furthermore, the agreement's long-term political ramifications show how President Eisenhower unsuccessfully tried to balance the ascendancy of America's post-Second World War global economic hegemony with its commitment to decolonization, national self-determination, and liberal democracy. At the time, the CIA was run by Allen and John Foster Dulles and the overthrow of Mosaddegh was the agency's first attempt at Cold War espionage. Allen Dulles remarked of the US' predicament, "We were engaged in the defense of a way of life, and the great danger was that in defending this way of life we would find ourselves resorting to methods that endangered this way of life" (Weiner 2007, 85–6).

Several key variables emerged concerning the diplomacy that resulted in the Consortium Agreement. For the United States, securing a strong economic footing in the Middle East to meet the rising domestic demand for oil and to deter the spread of communism remained a top priority. However, the CIA's involvement in the overthrow of democratically elected Mosaddegh signaled that the spread of liberal democracy was not an urgent goal of US foreign policy. Instead, the Consortium Agreement enabled the United States and other Western oil companies, such as British Petroleum, to maintain control of Iran's oil industry. Many of Washington's allies also had imperial commitments that further entangled the United States in a conflict over national self-determination. The British government led by Prime Minister Clement Atlee was in a much different position than the United States. Revolutions for independence had spread across the British Empire and threatened British control over its economic network of colonies and therefore, its access to raw materials and resources needed for post-war industrial growth. The AIOC's involvement was one of several attempts to take advantage of a growing US economic interest in the Middle East which aimed at a continued Western presence in the area as a bulwark against the Soviet Union. In many ways the AIOC's operations symbolized "British power in the Middle East" (Heiss 1994, 512).

Although the Consortium Agreement produced a pro-American regime in Iran and the AIOC's continued dominance of Iran's oil industry, it began with Prime Minister Mohammad Mosaddegh's audit of the AIOC's shares of the industry. Mosaddegh, a political dynamo in Iran, sought economic sovereignty for his nation and, in 1949, attempted to renegotiate the terms of its agreement with the AIOC. This served to increase the revenue that Iran received from its oil industry, while preserving the foreign direct investments that temporarily bolstered its emerging political and economic stability. Mosaddegh was primarily interested in securing a path toward economic independence, free from foreign intervention, but in the context of the West's ideological crusade against communism, this was simply not an option. This was the crux of the problem concerning the ownership of Iranian oil. Despite international commitments to decolonization, the post-war global superpowers were more interested in controlling and exploiting the economies of former colonies.

In 1951, Great Britain encountered a financial crisis that further emphasized the need for the annual £100 million that came from the AIOC's revenue. However, Mosaddegh also had economic obligations to his nation and he believed that "oil revenue should benefit the Iranian people, not a foreign corporation" (Heiss 1994, 512). As a result, Mosaddegh prepared plans to nationalize the Iranian oil industry as a response to the AIOC's unwillingness to negotiate a fair settlement. In response, the AIOC offered a sham proposal that would on paper give Iranian's primary management and control of Iran's oil shares, but in practice would maintain the West's open access to those oil shares. Mosaddegh refused the proposal and as a result, the US and British governments, in cooperation with the US oil companies still claiming shares of Iran's oil, initiated an international boycott of Iranian oil. These economic sanctions undermined political and economic stability in Iran and in October 1951 resulted in the ending of diplomatic relations between Great Britain and Iran.

At this point, US interests intersected with the dispute between Tehran and London. Fearing the expansion of Soviet influence and participation in Iran's oil industry, the United States sought to broker a fair agreement between its British ally and its interests in the stability and free access of Iranian oil. However, the negotiations moved at a slow pace and resulted in noticeable economic volatility for Iran. As negotiations began to deteriorate, the United States strayed further away from diplomatic neutrality and embraced its British ally. In August 1953, the CIA sponsored a political campaign that "deposed a popular Iranian nationalist who embraced fundamental American principles and replaced him with a tyrant who despised much of what the United States stands for" (Kinzer 2008, x). The replacement of Mossadegh was a means to also replace the Anglo-Iranian oil monopoly with a consortium represented by the "Big Five" American oil companies. This gave these companies a stake in the oil reserves and solidified a "Big Five" presence in every oil-producing region in the "non-communist eastern hemisphere."

It was a critical turning point in the oil industry. The "productive center of gravity" had moved from the West to the East where it sat in the hands of "Muslim countries" holding all the "glut" of oil reserves. This reality was echoed by US foreign policy when President Dwight D. Eisenhower imposed restrictions on foreign oil imports (North 1985, 109–10). With the merging of Iran's oil industries and the Western oil companies, the Iranian agreement became "one of the most attractive contracts to the oil industry in the Middle East." Almost every oil concession in the Middle East came under the control of the seven "giant vertically integrated firms" (Stork 1973, 18). In other words, oil concessions in the Middle East switched from one monopoly to another. The only difference was in the ability of those affiliated with the consortium to protect that monopoly through a "maze of joint ownership" each with "pyramids of subsidiary and affiliated companies" who shared ownership (Stork 1973, 18).

The creation of the consortium may have marked a geographical shift in terms of where the oil was produced, but in terms of economic control and power, it signaled a decisive shift away from the British oil monopoly in Iran and into the hands of the most powerful American oil companies. Leading up to its creation, concern from the antitrust division in the US Department of Justice surfaced. However, it was in vain. In the end, the oil companies won out for a myriad of strategic reasons that outweighed the potential trade violations. In 1952, US Secretary of State Dean Acheson enunciated this contradiction when he foresaw how the antitrust suits against American oil companies might cause the deterioration of stability in the Middle East and mar Washington's reputation overseas. The State Department and the Justice Department continued to clash over how to proceed with the new consortium. Herbert Hoover, the son of the ex-President, was appointed as a petroleum adviser. His primary goal was to get Iranian oil to "flow again into the world's markets." Despite protests from trust busters, President Eisenhower called for a solution that would "protect the interests of the free world in the Near East as a vital source of petroleum supplies." Antitrust, in this case, came second to national security interests. Citing "defense" and the "fight against communism," Hoover was instructed to bring all five of the major American oil companies into Iran. Consisting of Exxon, Mobil, Socal, Texaco, Gulf, and Shell, the consortium was created almost unilaterally by American diplomacy. The National Security Council gave the final blow to the antitrust cases when they agreed to support an international consortium and decided it would not be a violation of antitrust laws (Sampson 1991, 155–7).

Fears of Arab nationalism—which forced a British withdrawal from the area—still posed a threat to executives and government officials alike. In response to this threat, the oil companies worked to create a coalition of authoritarian leaders in the region who could replace British imperial power. Even after American direct corporate and political control ended in the 1970s, the authoritarian regimes managed to stay in power and remain supportive of oil interests. The US government continued to work with these regimes, supplying arms and political support. In 1969, President Richard Nixon issued the "Nixon Doctrine" which in effect, replaced British imperial power in the Gulf by "keeping American military forces over the horizon." Between 1970 and 1979, the United States provided over "$22 billion in arms sales to Iran" which was "three-quarters of all of Iran's weapons purchases during the decade." The bypassing of antitrust laws may have brought the US government into a closer partnership with the oil companies, but at a great cost. The privileges given to oil companies in the consortium underscored decades of conflict in the Middle East and contributed to the displacement of millions of people as well as the destruction of the environment (Jones 2012, 212).

"Violence and insecurity" accompanied the rising profits of the consortium. The continued exchange of weapons for economic security led to a "full-blown arms race" in the region. Between 1975 and 1979, 56 percent of all weapons sold to the Middle East went to Iran, Iraq, and Saudi Arabia. Security transformed into insecurity as the oil producers spent more of the profits on weapons and defense. Amnesty International condemned the shah of Iran after reports revealed he had the "highest rate of death penalties in the world." "No country in the world has a worse record in human rights than Iran" remarked an Amnesty International official in 1977 (Jones 2012, 214). The oil consortium, the US government, and Iranian officials all agreed on the necessity and primacy of the stability of oil exports. The establishment of the Iranian consortium solidified the United States as the "major player in oil" and reinforced the tyranny of the "Peacock Throne of Iran" (Yergin 1991, 478). The profits of the oil industry were of more importance than democratic transition in the Middle East, human rights, and the environment. As evidenced by each political decision that led to the Consortium Agreement of 1954, the oil companies were willing to take any measures to preserve their new economic power in the region.

Thomas David Brown

See also: Aramco; Caltex; Carter Doctrine; Gulf Oil Company; Gulf War; Iraq War and the Project for a New American Century; Mandatory Oil Import Quota Program; Mobil Oil Corporation; Red Line Agreement of 1928; Seven Sisters Oil Companies; Texaco

FURTHER READING

Elm, Mostafa. 1922. *Oil, Power, and Principle: Iran's Oil Nationalization and Its Aftermath*. Syracuse: Syracuse University Press.

Heiss, Mary Ann. 1994. "The United States, Great Britain, and the Creation of the Iranian Oil Consortium, 1953–1954." *The International History Review*. Vol. 16. No. 3. August. Pp. 511–35.

Jones, Toby Craig. 2012. "America, Oil, and War in the Middle East." *The Journal of American History*. Vol. 99. No. 1. June. Pp. 208–18.

Kinzer, Stephen 2008. *All the Shah's Men: An American Coup and the Roots of the Middle East Terror*. New Jersey: Wiley.

North, F.K. 1985. "A Geologist's View of the Oil Corporate Mergers." *Energy Exploration & Exploitation*. Vol. 3. No. 2. Pp. 107–14.

Sampson, Anthony. 1991. *The Seven Sisters: The Great Oil Companies and the World They Shaped*. New York: Bantam Books.

Stork, Joe. 1973. "Middle East Oil and the Energy Crisis: Part 1." *MERIP Reports*. No. 20. September. Middle East Research and Information Project, Inc.

Weiner, Tim. 2007. *Legacy of Ashes: The History of the CIA*. New York: Doubleday.

Yergin, Daniel. 1991. *The Prize: The Epic Quest for Oil, Money, and Power*. New York: Simon & Schuster.

Cooke, Morris Llewellyn

In the first half of the twentieth century, Morris Llewellyn Cooke (1872–1960) became widely known for his expertise as a mechanical engineer, professional consultant, and administrator of government agencies and programs. He learned the techniques of reforming and directing large organizations alongside Frederick W. Taylor, whose book *Principles of Scientific Management* (1910) provided the foundation for modern managerial science and the management consulting industry. Cooke's service in municipal government and his consulting work brought him to the attention of Franklin D. Roosevelt, who appointed him as first director of the New Deal's Rural Electrification Administration. He became an advocate for the underserved, first by his efficient management of municipal utilities, and later by connecting rural communities to regional power grids. His noteworthy career in public service is part of the larger story of how energy fueled the modernization of American life.

Cooke was born into a large, prosperous family in Carlisle, Pennsylvania and graduated from Ulrich's School. He studied mechanical engineering at Lehigh University then after graduation he served as a machinist at Cramp's Shipyard in Philadelphia. He joined the US Navy during the Spanish–American War and served as assistant engineer aboard the USS *Miantonomoh* and the USS *Lancaster*. He received promotion to chief engineer on the USS *Eagle*, which performed blockade duty near Cuba. After the war, he married Eleanor Bushnell Davis, a well-born and educated child of wealthy Philadelphian parents. Cooke went into the printing business but then in 1903 he met fellow mechanical engineer Frederick W. Taylor, who brought Cooke into the work of reorganizing the American Society of Mechanical Engineers which had elected Taylor as president (Wrege 1978, 737). Cooke sat for Taylor's talks on various concepts in management of business and industry and worked with him to install Taylor's system at the Williams and Wilkins Company in Baltimore. In the 1907–9 period, Cooke wrote up much of his notes from Taylor's lectures and from his consulting work into a manuscript titled "Industrial Management," which was never published, but considered by historians to be the source for much of Taylor's own *Principles of Scientific Management* (1910) (Wrege 1978, 749).

Cooke also consulted for the Carnegie Foundation for the Advancement of Teaching, which hired him to visit eight leading universities and colleges in the United States and Canada, investigate their management systems, and report on the best methods of financial and business administration at the different institutions (Davis 1912, 55). He also seems to have been asked by President William H. Taft to provide consulting services to the White House in this period. The next stage in Cooke's career placed him in the city government of Philadelphia under Progressive reformer Rudolph L. Blankenburg. Cooke served as director of the Department of Public Works 1911–14, where he earned praise for introducing rational, efficient processes into municipal governance. He studied the city's relationship with Philadelphia Electric Company and became convinced that the utility would be better administered under public ownership. He negotiated a $1 million reduction in the city's contract with the company, which he saw as evidence that the company overcharged its customers. It led to one of his first books, *Snapping Cords: Comments on the Changing Attitude of American Cities toward the Utility Problem* (1915).

Reflecting on "the causes which retard our progress" as a nation, Cooke identified the most important as "the baneful influence constantly wielded, directly and indirectly, in almost every city in the land by the private utility interests through the support of the lowest type of political machinery and intrigue" (Cooke 1918, 232). He became frustrated that the for-profit power and lighting companies served their shareholders rather than their customers, and major portions of the nation's electricity generation and transmission system were in the hands of holding companies controlled by Wall Street financiers. He questioned the commitment of these bankers and investors to anything other than profits: "The only serious defence I have ever heard made of this method of financing is based upon a belief in the absolutism of private property, for certain it is that the capitalization of a company under this method of financing has no relation whatever to values" (Cooke 1918, 237). Cooke's engineering background, familiarity with Philadelphia's energy issues, and his systems approach to administration secured him an invitation by Pennsylvania governor Gifford Pinchot to conduct a survey of the entire state's electrical grid. His two-year study (1923–5) revealed that rural and small towns were not connected to the system because the privately owned electrical companies didn't see these areas as profitable. Cooke came to believe that the state government must undertake the electrification of its rural communities and reorganize the electricity industry in the region (McCoy 2000).

Cooke's survey of the entire state had given him a larger view of the energy landscape in the developing United States. In an edited collection of essays titled *Giant Power: Large Scale Electrical Development as a Social Factor* (1925), Cooke and his co-authors pressed issues like "The Need for Electricity on the Farm" and "Power and Working Life" in mining and industry. Several women authors contributed essays that asked questions like "What Is Giant Power For?" and asserted that electrical power would lead to "The Abolition of Household Slavery." Several pointed essays bore provocative titles like "Is Giant Power a State or Federal Utility? Should its Control be through Political Ownership or Regulation?" and "On the Regulation of Giant Power." The essays highlighted the need to address the inequities of energy development over the previous few decades as the system scaled up from small plants serving individual towns to larger networks spanning wider regions. Cooke and others came to believe that in the 1910s and 1920s, electrification benefited millions of Americans, but generally the upper-income members of the middle class more than working class and rural families (Tobey 1997, 12). In 1926, he made a national appeal for a different, more equitable model of organizing the electrical power system in the United States in a widely read essay in *The Atlantic* titled "Giant Power: An Interpretation." Essentially, the Giant Power plan argued for building power plants near fuel sources (water power, coal mines, natural gas deposits) and using a combination of central planning, state organization, and private enterprise to ensure universal access to the system (Christie 1972, 493).

In 1932, Franklin D. Roosevelt won the presidency and quickly made use of Cooke's engineering acumen, managerial expertise, and philosophical commitment to progressive reform. He appointed Cooke to several advisory boards and commissions, and then director of the Rural Electrification Administration (REA). In this role Cooke studied the technical and financial issues involved in bringing electricity to 500,000 farmers and determined that it would take about $200 million. Congress authorized $410 million in 1936 for a ten-year program of rural electrification and within two years the REA had funded 350 projects connecting 1.5 million farms in forty-five states (Malone 2008). Most of these projects entailed the funding of electricity cooperatives, which are non-profit organizations owned by the electricity consumers themselves. Historian Laurence Malone noted that the electrification of rural America was nearly complete by the 1950s, and "is considered one of the most immediate and profound successes in the history of federal policy-making for the national economy" (Malone 2008). As war loomed on the horizon, Roosevelt appointed Cooke to the Office of Production Management, which began the process of converting American industries to armaments manufacturing. During the war he served as a troubleshooter, first resolving conflicts between US petroleum companies and the Mexican government and then in 1943, leading a War Labor Board effort to mediate coal miners' strikes threatening to halt production.

In one final turn of service to the nation, Cooke chaired the Water Resources Policy Commission in 1950–1 under President Harry S. Truman, which issued a three-volume report with recommendations for harnessing the nation's water resources for energy, human consumption, irrigation, and so on. Over the course of his career, his leadership in municipal, state, and national affairs endeavored to spread the blessings of electricity to those who had been left out by the electrical power system as it was constructed in the early twentieth century. At his death in 1960, Cooke enjoyed a well-earned reputation as an engineer, technical adviser, management consultant, administrator, and vocal advocate for fair and equitable energy development in America.

Jeffrey B. Webb

See also: Agriculture and Energy; Bartlett Electric Cooperative; Electricity; Federal Power Commission; Insull, Samuel; Pearl Street Power Station; Rural Electrification Act of 1936

FURTHER READING

Christie, Jean. 1972. "Giant Power: A Progressive Proposal of the Nineteen-Twenties." *The Pennsylvania Magazine of History and Biography*. October. Vol. 96. No. 4. Pp. 480–507.

Christie, Jean. 1983. *Morris Llewellyn Cooke, Progressive Engineer*. New York: Garland Publishing.

Cooke, Morris Llewellyn. 1918. *Our Cities Awake: Notes on Municipal Activities and Administration*. Garden City, NY: Doubleday, Page and Company.

Davis, Thomas Kirby. 1912. *The Davis Family: A History of the Descendants of William Davis and His Wife, Mary Means*. Norwood, MA: The Plimpton Press.

Malone, Laurencex. 2008. "Rural Electrification Administration." EH.Net Encyclopedia, edited by Robert Whaples. March 16. http://eh.net/encyclopedia/rural-electrification-administration/ (accessed October 2023).

McCoy, Sondra Van Meter. 2000. "Cooke, Morris Llewellyn." *American National Biography*. Oxford: Oxford University Press.

Raushenbush, Hilmar Stephes, and Harry W. Laidler. 1928. *Power Control*. New York: New Republic, Inc.

Tobey, Ronald C. 1997. *Technology as Freedom: The New Deal and the Electrical Modernization of the American Home*. Berkeley: University of California Press.

Trombley, Kenneth E. 1954. *The Life and Times of a Happy Liberal: A Biography of Morris Llewellyn Cooke*. New York: Harper & Brothers.

Wrege, Charles D. and Anne Marie Stotka. 1978. "Cooke Creates a Classic: The Story behind F. W. Taylor's *Principles of Scientific Management*." *The Academy of Management Review*. October. Vol. 3. No. 4. Pp. 736–49.

The Cooke-Zevada Agreement of 1942

The Cooke-Zevada Agreement resolved a prolonged dispute between foreign oil companies operating in Mexico and the Mexican government after its decision to nationalize its oil industry in 1938. It was often portrayed through a strictly economic lens, especially from the perspective of Washington. However, its roots were inextricably embedded in the Mexican Revolution for independence. While the most pressing concern for the United States was protecting the economic interests of its nationals and maintaining international stability with its neighbors, focusing on such interests reduces the Cooke-Zevada Agreement to a one-dimensional episode about a disagreement of contract and property rights. In the context of Mexico's revolution, the Cooke-Zevada Agreement reveals an unprecedented and bold attempt to secure Mexican sovereignty, economic self-sufficiency, and independence. "La Revolucion Mexicana" was a "social, collectivist movement" entrenched in a background of fervent nationalism (Kunz 1940–4). It was not simply an economic dispute over contracts, rather it was a narrative of labor power, the ownership of Indigenous lands, and a battle between economic nationalism and foreign capital (Thomson 1939; Maurer 2011).

Although foreign investors and companies had the financial and productive means to develop Mexico's infrastructure and economy, this did not occur. A history of foreign masters produced a deeply rooted generational trauma for many Mexicans and the arrival of American and British investors and entrepreneurs evoked a justifiable reaction from Mexico. In other words, it was profoundly "emotional involving both race and nationality" (Prewett 1941). The loss of half of the national territory to the United States was still in the minds of the Mexican people and its traumatic effect was worsened by a pervasive attitude of "social superiority" from the new American and British "economic masters" (Prewett 1941). Situating the Cooke-Zevada Agreement within this social, revolutionary context demonstrates the courage and gravity of Mexico's stand-off with the foreign oil companies. Many Mexicans believed that the acquisition of Indigenous lands, hygiene, and education would bring true emancipation and sovereignty.

Within the context of the Mexican Revolution, President Lázaro Cárdenas del Río's decision to nationalize the oil industry was justifiable and ethically predictable. It was the nationalization of the oil industry that elicited a vigorous response from the foreign oil companies. Foreign investment, after all, was the main antagonist toward Mexican sovereignty in the eyes of Cardenas and his people. Oil as a natural resource is derived from an area known as the subsoil—an ambiguous space beneath the soil which produced legal controversy pertaining to the ownership rights of this portion of the land (Koppes 1982). In 1917, the Mexican Constitutional Convention passed Article 27 which stated that subsoil ownership was reserved for the state (Yergin 1991). Foreign investors, who traditionally understood land ownership as one entity marked by visible boundaries, disagreed with Mexico's legal interpretation. However, Mexico's history as a colonized nation presents a "twin heritage" that influences the scope of legal understandings (Koppes 1982). These blended traditions, one Spanish and the other Indigenous, changed the political relationship to the soil in a way that was misunderstood by foreign investors. Spanish law imposed the "reservation of mineral rights to the Crown" while Indigenous Mexicans maintained communal property ownership. Based on this historical context, it is likely that President Cardenas believed his independent nation to be the inheritor of the Crown's mineral rights. The ownership of property by the state also maintained the Indigenous tradition of communalism (Koppes 1982).

The differing opinions of how to legally interpret the ownership of land in Mexico led to controversy. Article 27 "became the center of the battle" as Mexico fought to restore its national ownership of natural resources (Yergin 1991). Although Mexico faced the struggle of legally justifying the nationalization of its oil industry, they also lacked the means to develop and market its oil without the assistance of foreign investment. What resulted was a forced codependence that, from the perspective of Cardenas, threatened Mexican sovereignty. Foreign investors were unwilling to "bear the risk and expense of development without secure contracts and the prospect of profits" (Yergin 1991). At odds with Indigenous land and labor, foreign capital pressed for certainty at the expense of the Mexican people. This particular historical quagmire raises questions about the relationship between property rights and state sovereignty within the context of international markets. Foreign investors, now supported by both the American and British governments, asserted that the property rights they secured before the revolution could not be "retroactively [seized]" by the government. In response, Mexico argued that the state never stopped owning the subsoil and that any "company property" was not owned but conceded by "the fiat of the state" (Yergin 1991). Despite its deep desire to assert its sovereignty, the Mexican government came to terms with the reality of its situation. The nation desperately needed foreign investment to assist in its "reconstruction" and the oil industry could not survive without proper marketing and development. The Mexican government reluctantly embraced an ambivalent solution that allowed the foreign corporations to continue their contracts and reserved subsoil rights to the Mexican state. On the surface level, this solution appeased both parties, but it left a deep ambiguity that could later be exploited by oil companies (Yergin 1991).

The problem of wage compensation, hours, and benefits for Mexican workers rapidly grew worse. During the 1930s, 60–70 percent of profits from oil exports went back to the United States (Koppes 1982). A majority of the employees for these companies were American or British and received generous benefits. Mexican laborers, on the contrary, were "paid half the wages of, and received poorer housing than, the foreigners" despite performing the same labor as American and British employees (Koppes 1982). Bitterness festered among Mexican workers. The developed world continued to extract its natural resources in the name of economic development, but in reality, no such development occurred for Mexicans. Article 123 of the Mexican constitution provided the means for collective bargaining, minimum wages and hours, and compensation insurance. A labor code directly related to the labor exploitation of the oil companies was enacted in 1931 to shift power back into the hands of Mexican trade unions. When such a strike did occur, it produced mixed results. The trade unions' demands presented through a collective contract exceeded the financial capacity of the companies, but the situation worsened when corporate executives refused to cooperate with the unions (Stebbins 1948).

As expected, the established terms of agreement did not protect Mexican laborers from wage exploitation. It became clear to the Mexican government that, despite its need of assistance alongside its political ambitions for national self-determination, the foreign oil companies sought only to widen the door for further profits even at the expense of its workers. President Cardenas described the situation as "comfort for the foreign personnel ... lower wages and harder, more exhausting labor for our people" (Stebbins 1948). On March 1, 1938, the Mexican Supreme Court ruled against seventeen US and British Oil companies concerning depressed wages. In an address to his nation, President Cardenas implored the "entire Nation to furnish the necessary moral and material support to face the consequence of a decision which we, of our own free will would neither have sought nor desired" (Stebbins 1948).

While it is certainly the case that the Mexican government maintained its own self-interests, which were at odds with the foreign oil companies, it was also clear that they were willing to rely on judicial institutions to resolve the conflict. The oil companies responded with a joint statement signed by Dutch-Shell-Mexican Eagle Co., Standard Oil of New Jersey, Huasteca, Sinclair Pierce Oil, Mexican Sinclair of California, and Standard of Mexico and Subsidiary Richmond Petroleum Co. They maintained that the "conditions recommended by the Commission of Experts that served as the basis of the Labor Board's decision are of such a nature that it would be impossible to comply with them." The statement further expressed the inevitability of "serious consequences for the companies, for their employees and for those dependent on the industry" (Stebbins 1948). The response from oil companies signaled their priority to maintain the Open Door policy for oil—a recycled, outworn, and ambiguous continuation of the Roosevelt Corollary to the Monroe Doctrine which was used to justify and legitimate American expansion into new markets domestically and internationally (Koppes 1982). Nationalization threatened that understanding. Secretary of the Interior Harold L. Ickes asserted that there was "no international oil policy ... except to protect the interests of our nationals" (Koppes 1982). It was abundantly clear to both the Mexican government and the oil companies that an agreement could not be reached easily.

The US government, the oil companies, and the Mexican government stumbled further into a diplomatic quagmire where each party annunciated feelings of antagonism from the opposition. From the American perspective, private property rights overshadowed all other interests and the apparent violation of such contracts most likely contributed to Washington's negative perception of Mexico. "Instability, insecurity, banditry, anarchy, a dangerous threat to the flow of a strategic resource, and welching of contracts," all pervaded the American perspective of Mexico's behavior. However, Mexico felt that the cooperation between the oil companies and Washington was a "violation of sovereignty" brought about by "Yankee imperialism" (Yergin 1991). While Washington maintained a prioritization of the economic interests of American business, more pressing foreign policy problems arose when the war in Europe escalated significantly. In 1941, President Roosevelt adopted the "Good Neighbor" policy as a way to avoid alienating a key neighbor and ally. His rationale was to preserve "hemispheric defense" in light of the mounting Nazi threat (Yergin 1991).

The implementation of the Good Neighbor Policy generated fertile ground for a new resolution. The two governments embraced the acumen of scientists to resolve the protracted dispute between the oil companies and the Mexican government. On November 19, 1941, both governments accepted the resolution to rely on two scientists to represent each nation as a way to let experts determine an agreement. Manuel J. Zevada, the undersecretary of the Department of National Economy and an engineer, represented Mexico while Morris L.

Cooke, a consulting engineer from Philadelphia, represented the United States (Pijoan 1946). The report of Cooke and Zevada found that the oil companies had "grossly overestimated the amount of money they had invested in the Mexican oil industry," and resolved the case in favor of Mexico's demands (Bermúdez 1963). On April 18, 1942, the US and Mexican governments signed the Cooke-Zevada Agreement which resulted in the Mexicans paying around $29 million in compensation to the American oil companies, including Standard Oil of New Jersey and Standard Oil Company of Southern California (OH 2023). The Mexican government paid off the compensation by 1947 and its socialized oil industry moved forward with optimism (Jayne 1997).

The Cooke-Zevada Agreement solidified a major win for the Mexican government and the nationalization of its oil industry is still considered to be "one of the greatest triumphs of the revolution" (Yergin 1991). Petrôleos Mexicanos (PEMEX) rose to international prominence as the "first and most important" nationalized oil company in the world. However, upon historical revision, many historians now contend that the short-term victory was a misdirection. Although the Good Neighbor policy worked to achieve a viable resolution to an intense controversy, historians believe that the Cooke-Zevada agreement only resolved the immediate property rights controversy and failed to address the political legitimacy of nationalization. Therefore, the agreement did not restrain capitalist exploitation in a developing nation but ensured its "long-term viability." The only real loss incurred by the Americans was its oil resources in Mexico. Mexican laborers, however, were still poor and "bound to a rigid system" of natural resource depletion (Koppes 1982). In the end, it was not the Mexican laborers that won out—it was oil.

Thomas David Brown

See also: Consortium Agreement of 1954; Cooke, Morris Llewellyn; Gulf Oil Company; Red Line Agreement of 1928; Seven Sisters Oil Companies

FURTHER READING

Bermúdez, Antonio. 1963. *The Mexican National Petroleum Industry: A Case Study in Nationalization*. Palo Alto, CA: Institute of Hispanic American and Luso-Brazilian Studies, Stanford University.

Foreign Relations of the United States: Diplomatic Papers. 1943. The American Republics, Vol. VI 412.11 Oil/161, Document 493. *The Mexican Embassy to the Department of State*. Washington, DC: Government Printing Office, 1965.

Jayne, Catherine E. 1997. *The Diplomacy of Expropriation: American and British Reactions to Mexico's Expropriation of Foreign Oil Properties, 1937–1943*. Ann Arbor, MI: ProQuest LLC.

Koppes, Clayton R. 1982. "The Good Neighbor Policy and the Nationalization of Mexican Oil: A Reinterpretation." *The Journal of American History*. Vol. 69. No. 1. June. Pp. 62–81.

Kunz, Josef L. 1940–4. "The Mexican Expropriations." *Contemporary Law Pamphlets*. No. 5.

Maurer, Noel. 2011. "The Empire Struck Back: Sanctions and Compensation in the Mexican Oil Expropriation of 1938." *The Journal of Economic History*. Vol. 71. No. 3. September. Pp. 590–615.

OH (Office of the Historian). 2023. "Mexican Expropriation of Foreign Oil, 1938." *US Milestones, 1937–1945*. Foreign Service Institute. Washington, DC: United States Department of State.

Pijoan, M. and F. Trowbridge Vom Baur. 1946. "Science as the Common Ground for Relations between Nations." *The Scientific Monthly*. Vol. 63. No. 2. August. Pp. 137–40.

Prewett, Virginia 1941. *Reportage on Mexico*. New York: E. P. Dutton & Co, Inc.
Stebbins, Marie F. 1948. *The History of the Expropriation of the American Oil Companies in Mexico*. Stockton: Department of History College of the Pacific.
Thomson, Charles A. 1939. "Results of the Lima Conference." *Foreign Policy Reports*. Vol. 15. No. 1. March 15. New York: Foreign Policy Association, Inc.
Yergin, Daniel. 1991. *The Prize: The Epic Quest for Oil, Money & Power*. New York: Simon & Schuster.

Cooper, Peter

Peter Cooper (1791–1883) was one of the greatest engineers, industrialists, and businessman of the nineteenth century. He is best known as the creator of the Tom Thumb, the first workable steam locomotive built in the United States. The application of steam energy to rail locomotion is one of the most significant human engineering accomplishments of the nineteenth century and literally changed people's sense of time and space. A journey that once lasted weeks or even months now took just days. Cooper's scientific and financial acumen made him exceptionally wealthy and he was active in the political, social, and economic affairs of the nation throughout his long life. Cooper was born two years after George Washington was sworn in as the first president of the United States and died one month before President Chester A. Arthur dedicated the Brooklyn Bridge.

Peter Cooper's ancestors came to the New World from the British Isles in the mid-seventeenth century and settled in New York's Hudson Valley. His father, John Obadiah Cooper, was born in Fishkill in 1755 and later fought the British in the American Revolution. Peter, the fifth of his nine children, was born in New York City on February 12, 1791. When Peter was young his family moved regularly between the city and country and as a boy, he received a modicum of formal education while learning practical mechanics in his father's small hat-making workshop. The youngster made what may well be one of the world's first mechanical washing machines after helping his mother with the arduous task of cleaning laundry by hand. He created his own method to make shoes for the family and as a young boy also built a wagon that he sold at a handsome profit of a few dollars. These technical and financial lessons he took forth throughout his life.

At the age of seventeen Cooper moved to New York City and for the next four years worked as an apprentice to a carriage-maker at the mechanic's shop on the corners of Chambers and Broadway. He came of legal age in 1812 and married the love of his life, Sarah Bedell of Hempstead, in December 1813. The young couple quickly began a family. Cooper tried his hand in several endeavors in New York City and Long Island. He was an inveterate tinkerer who made a number of improvements to various technologies, including a shearing-machine, an early lawnmower and, by combining a music box and other attachments to a bassinet, a rocking cradle. The period immediately following the War of 1812 was an opportune time for an enterprising young man. Six new states joined the union by 1821. The completion of the Erie Canal in 1825 opened New York to the Great Lakes and Midwest, accelerating trade and movement. Railroads were also emerging as a viable transportation technology.

Steam locomotives on rails had been utilized in Europe by the early 1800s and soon were carrying coal, ore, and other raw materials from their points of extraction to factories and consumers. By the 1820s steam locomotion was becoming a feasible form of human transport; on September 27, 1825 the first public railway, the Locomotion No. 1, began carrying passengers and goods between Stockton and Darlington in England. Americans were

> **COOPER UNION**
>
> The workplace had changed markedly during the Industrial Revolution and Peter Cooper knew that Americans needed to maintain their skills to compete in the new economy. He believed too that a venue for fostering dialogue might further peace and foster civic responsibility. In 1859 he thus founded the The Cooper Union for the Advancement of Science and Art. The following year Abraham Lincoln came to national prominence giving his Cooper Union speech. Today the Cooper Institute remains one of the world's leading educational institutions.
>
> *Keith J. Muchowski*

slower to catch on to steam rail locomotion. Even where there was rail transport in the United States the energy to pull the cars was provided by draft animals, usually horses. On February 28, 1827 investors received a charter in Maryland and founded the Baltimore & Ohio (B&O) Railroad, the first American rail company created for the commercial transportation of both freight and passengers. It would take time, however, for development of a functioning train line. What is more, the B&O's founders still believed that horse-drawn energy would be used to pull the rail cars.

In these years Cooper was running a glue factory in New York City, tinkering in his workshop, seeking additional business opportunities, and raising his growing family. In 1828 Cooper received a patent—signed by President John Quincy Adams and co-signed by Secretary of State Henry Clay—for a crank-less steam engine. That same year he purchased 3,000 acres of land in Baltimore with the intention of developing that city's harbor. When he discovered ore on his property, he founded the Canton Iron Works and began manufacturing and selling iron rails to the B&O Railroad as it continued laying its track lines. Meanwhile the first steam locomotive to operate in the United States, the Stourbridge Lion built by the Foster, Rastrick and Company of England for the Delaware and Hudson Canal Company, began service in Pennsylvania on August 8, 1829 to great excitement.

Peter Cooper's fortunes as owner of the Canton Iron Works were tied to the profits or losses of the B&O Railroad, to whom he supplied iron and whose financial backers were still uncertain about the potential and cost-effectiveness of steam rail locomotion. Shareholders' fears of bankruptcy were not unfounded. Steam energy for railroads was still of limited practicality. Speeds were slow and the rail beds often unable to support the locomotives' heavy weight. Winding turns were also an issue, with fears that rail cars pulled by steam engines would be unable to handle curves safely at accelerated speeds. In the summer of 1829, to prove the efficacy of steam rail energy, Cooper began building his own steam locomotive, one that would be light but powerful enough to handle heavy loads. He experimented in the workshop and on the B&O track lines for nearly a year creating an engine that he described decades later as "small" and "insignificant," a reference not to its lack of importance but rather to its diminutive size (Brown 1871, 109). This was the Tom Thumb.

Famously, Peter Cooper's coal-burning steam locomotive raced against a horse-drawn rail car in a run between Ellicott's Mills (today Ellicott City) and Baltimore. The historical record of when the race took place is contradictory. The most common date given by historians is August 28, 1830 while others have the race taking place on September 18. Additional sources give different dates falling within the August–September 1830 timeframe. More important than the exact date is the historical significance of the contest between the Tom Thumb and its equine challenger. Traveling at speeds of between 10 and 14 miles an hour, Cooper's machine was ahead of the gray horse until a mechanical failure forced the steam locomotive to break down. Despite the loss, railroad investors now understood the practicality of steam rail locomotives. The days of horse-drawn energy for railroads were numbered. Over the next several months the Tom Thumb—the first practical steam rail locomotive built in the United States—continued its test runs from Baltimore to Ellicott's Mills with Cooper and his engineers tinkering and improving the design and function. Because it was a prototype and not intended for permanent use, the Tom Thumb was soon dismantled. Unfortunately, there is no authoritative record today of its ultimate whereabouts.

Over the next half century, Peter Cooper went on to spectacular wealth and success. Among other things he invested in real estate and bankrolled the first transatlantic cable. He put his son Edward Cooper and son-in-law Abram Hewitt in charge of the Trenton Iron Company. The firm was instrumental in the early development and manufacture of I-beams, which in turn were used in the construction of skyscrapers. They also manufactured iron rails for the steam locomotive lines that in the middle decades of the nineteenth century began criss-crossing the different regions of the United States. Railroads were central to the Civil War effort and also the settlement of the West. At various times in his life Cooper held local elective office New York City, was active in philanthropy and political reform, the abolition of slavery, and in aiding the Union effort during the Civil War. In 1876, Cooper was nominated as the presidential candidate of the National Independent (Greenback) Party. He died on April 4, 1883 and is buried today in Brooklyn's Green-Wood Cemetery.

Keith J. Muchowski

See also: Baltimore & Ohio Railroad; Densmore Oil Tank Car; Evans, Oliver; Industrial Revolution; Richmond Union Passenger Railway; Steam Power; Transcontinental Railroad

FURTHER READING

Brown, William H. 1871. *The History of the First Locomotives in America*. New York: D. Appleton & Company.

Guérin, Polly. 2012. *The Cooper-Hewitt Dynasty of New York*. Charleston, SC: The History Press.

Gurko, Miriam. 1959. *The Lives and Times of Peter Cooper*. New York: Crowell.

Mack, Edward C. 1949. *Peter Cooper: Citizen of New York*. New York: Duell, Sloan and Pearce.

Raymond, Rossiter W. 1901. *Peter Cooper*. Boston and New York: Houghton, Mifflin & Company.

Sagle, Lawrence W. 1948. "The Tom Thumb: Little Known Facts about First Locomotive Built in America Slowly Come to Light." *The Railway and Locomotive Historical Society Bulletin*. No. 73. May. Pp. 46–53.

Corliss, George Henry

One of the key innovators in the early years of steam power was George Henry Corliss (1817–88), a native of New York who built a large steam engine manufacturing plant in Providence, Rhode Island. His patented engines sold throughout the United States, Great Britain, and Europe to textile factories, steel rolling mills, pumping stations, and a variety of other types of industries. It became the backbone of industrial production in the later decades of the nineteenth century—the machine that provided the power for other machines. Like James Watt before him, Corliss harnessed steam power in new and more productive ways to facilitate the expansion of industrial production, and therefore a massive increase in the demand for energy.

Corliss spent his childhood in the small towns of Easton and Greenwich in Washington County in rural upstate New York. He left school at fourteen to work as a clerk in a general store, then as a laborer in the William Mowry & Company textile mill. He pursued further education across the border at Castleton Seminary in Vermont, then returned home to Greenwich in 1838 to open a general store in partnership with his father. He took an interest in machinery when he discovered that the seams on his suppliers' leather boots had faulty stitching, so he tried his hand at designing a machine that could produce better results. In 1843 he patented his "sewing engine," which produced a tight saddle-stitch on the moving material as the user hand-powered the machine's awls and levers. Corliss moved with his young family to Providence seeking an investor to bring his sewing engine to market, but after taking a job as a draftsman for Fairbanks, Bancroft & Company, he dropped the idea and began experimenting with steam engines.

It's important to note that Corliss didn't invent the steam engine, which had been in use for a century and had been adapted for locomotives. Stationary steam power engines appeared in some of the cotton mills of New England in the 1840s, though waterpower was plentiful on New England's many rivers and streams, and therefore much cheaper than coal. Corliss devoted himself to understanding how the steam engine's cylinders, valves, and gears delivered power to its crankshaft and powertrain. In his shop he discovered a way to design the valves so they could be opened and closed in a variable pattern, controlled with precision by a governor, matching amounts of steam advanced to the cylinders to system's changing load requirements. The effect of this innovation was to bring greater efficiency in the use of steam through the whole process. The company reorganized as Corliss, Nightingale & Company in 1847 with Corliss as president, and over the next year moved to a new location at the Charles Street Railroad Crossing in Providence to manufacture the improved steam engine. Corliss received a patent for his design in 1849 and his company's products quickly found a market in the factories and mills around the region. Tests in England on the Corliss steam engine determined that it was much more efficient than conventional engines: "A decided economy in consumption of fuel was found to be effected by these engines, where a comparison with other engines working under the same circumstances could be made" (Inglis 1868, 191). The test suggested that the Corliss engine consumed 2.5 lbs. of coal per indicated horsepower per hour with steam pressure at 45 lbs. per inch, whereas other engines consumed up to 5 lbs. for the same level of performance (Inglis 1868, 192).

This reduction in fuel economy, coupled with the elegance and reliability of the design, gave new factory and mill owners the option of choosing steam over waterpower, and the freedom to locate their industries in centers of population rather than along rivers and streams. When the company again renamed itself as the Corliss Steam Engine Company in 1856, it had become established as a premier manufacturer of industrial steam engines. By 1863, Corliss had built 481 engines, and 450 were estimated to be in daily use (Hunter 1985, 117). Corliss engines acquired devotees among industrialists in Scotland, England, and France; in the 1867 Paris Exhibition, the Corliss engine earned a Gold Medal, awarded to less than 2 percent of exhibitors. The American Academy of Arts and Sciences awarded Corliss the Rumford Prize, given to scientists and inventors for improving human understanding of heat and light. Although the academy could confer the award annually, it only bestowed the award on four other individuals from 1796 to 1869, the year they named Corliss as recipient. The list of future winners would include Thomas Alva Edison and Enrico Fermi. Finally, the Institute of France awarded him the 1879 Montyon Prize for mechanical achievement, which was considered in the era to be among the most prestigious award of its kind.

Another highlight of Corliss' career occurred in 1876 at the International Exhibition of Arts, Manufactures, and Products of the Soil and Mine in Philadelphia. Corliss built an enormous engine specifically for the event, which stood 45 feet tall and ran at 1,400 horsepower. The unit weighed 650 tons, including its 30-foot diameter flywheel, and powered the machines in the cavernous Machinery Hall with miles of belts and shafts. President Ulysses S. Grant and Emperor Dom Pedro II of Brazil opened the Centennial Exhibition by starting the engine. A crowd of 10,000 witnessed the moment, and many attendees heard a choir of a thousand sing John Greenleaf Whittier's "Centennial Hymn," which he composed for the opening ceremony (Ujifusa 2010). Over the six months of the Philadelphia exhibition, over 9 million people passed through and witnessed firsthand the magnificence of Corliss' engine. William Dean Howells, novelist, critic, and editor of *The Atlantic Monthly*, toured Machinery Hall and related his impressions of the Corliss engine in his essay "A Sennight of the Centennial." He remarked:

> The Corliss engine does not lend itself to description; its personal acquaintance must be sought by those who would understand its vast and almost silent grandeur. It rises loftily in the centre of the huge structure, an athlete of steel and iron with not a superfluous ounce of metal on it; the mighty walking-beams plunge their pistons downward, the enormous fly-wheel revolves with hoarded power that makes all tremble, the hundred life-like details do their office with unerring intelligence. (Howells 1876, 96)

He added "wherever else the national bird is mute in one's breast, here he cannot fail to utter his pride and content" (Howells 1876, 96).

To Howells, Corliss' engine offered to exhibition goers from home and abroad a symbol of the nation's technical and mechanical genius and an icon of America's boundless energy and vision. Corliss' success brought other inventors to accuse him of patent infringement, and he filed his own lawsuits against those he thought profited off his patented work. As such, he devoted much of the later portion of his life in litigation over his intellectual property. By the time Corliss died in 1888 he held sixty-seven patents on various steam engine components, and items like a gear-cutting machine and a pumping-engine. As part of his legacy, many steam engine manufacturers received licenses from Corliss to reproduce his steam engines, which made his models among the most widespread across American industry. All told, the Corliss engine served as one of the catalysts for the shift in manufacturing from waterpower to steam power, which vastly increased the demand for coal during the Industrial Revolution.

Jeffrey B. Webb

See also: Coal; Evans, Oliver; Edison, Thomas Alva; Fermi, Enrico; Slater, Samuel; Steam Power

FURTHER READING

Hoogenboom, Olive. 2000. "Corliss, George Henry (1817–1888)." *American National Biography*. Oxford: Oxford University Press. https://www.anb.org/display/10.1093/anb/9780198606697.001.0001/anb-9780198606697-e-1300346 (accessed October 2023).

Howells, William Dean. 1876. "A Sennight of the Centennial." *The Atlantic Monthly*. Vol. 38. July. Pp. 92–107.

Hunter, Louis C. 1985. *A History of Industrial Power in the United States, 1780–1930*. Vol. 2: *Steam Power*. Charlottesville: The University Press of Virginia.

Inglis, William. 1868. "On the Corliss Expansion Valve-Gear for Stationary Engines." *Proceedings of the Institution of Mechanical Engineers*. Pp. 177–94. Birmingham: Institution of Mechanical Engineers.

Ujifusa, Steven. 2010. "The Corliss Engine." The Philly History Blog. May 18. https://blog.phillyhistory.org/index.php/2010/05/the-corliss-engine/ (accessed October 2023).

Crotched Mountain Wind Farm

On the southern ridge of New Hampshire's Crotched Mountain, the world's first "wind farm" began production of "clean," renewable energy in December 1980. Installed by developer U.S. Windpower (USW), each of the farm's twenty, intermediate-sized turbines generated up to thirty kilowatt-hours of power, the approximate average of a single household's daily use. Structural flaws in the machinery led to the closing of the venture less than a year after its opening. The wind farm itself was short-lived, yet its impact was far-reaching. The pilot project raised public awareness of wind energy potential and served as a testing ground for USW, which subsequently developed a highly successful wind farm at Altamont Pass.

Two engineers, Russell Wolfe (1925–2015) and Stanley Charren (1924–) founded the company that built the Crotched Mountain Wind Farm. Wolfe had been inspired by conversations with William Heronemus, a professor of Civil Engineering at the University of Massachusetts Amherst (UMass). In response to the 1970s oil and gas crisis, "Bill" Heronemus pioneered research into alternative energy sources. Globally acknowledged as the "father of modern wind power," he saw wind energy as a tool for combating pollution and breaking dependency on fossil fuels. Heronemus convinced Wolfe that wind could be harvested as a commercially viable, renewable, energy crop. Wolfe pitched the idea of a wind energy start-up to Charren, who then scheduled his own appointment with Heronemus. The data presented by the professor was convincing. Charren returned to Wolfe and agreed to the venture. The two friends became business partners, founding U.S. Windpower in 1974.

The Crotched Mountain Wind Farm was USW's first major project. Instead of building single, giant turbines to harvest the wind, Charren envisioned a field of medium-sized machines, grouped together, functioning as a single unit, and feeding power into an established electric service. The plan was intended to maximize production and profit. An array of turbines would continue to generate power when one of the machines had to be shut down for maintenance. Comparing the assembly to a power plant, Charren called the cluster of turbines a "windplant," but the term "wind farm," coined by Bill Heronemus, took hold in popular and trade vernacular.

To assist USW with turbine design, Charren and Wolfe turned to a pair of Heronemus' most promising students, Forest "Woody" Stoddard and Ted Van Dusen. The USW turbine was to be a derivative of the WF-1, a three-bladed, 25-kW prototype that Stoddard and Van Dusen had helped design and construct in one of Heronemus' classes. Tensions between the design specialists and management grew as the search for venture capital led to new hires, including the installation of an engineering chief that possessed no background in wind technology. Stoddard voiced concern that management's focused efforts to rush development and reduce costs would produce machines which were structurally flawed.

Identification of a suitable location for USW's wind farm posed another difficulty. Russell Wolfe and Stanley Charren had chosen Burlington, Massachusetts for the company's headquarters. The proximity to UMass and Heronemus was valuable, as was the nearness of Boston, a financial center. But the construction of a wind farm necessitated level ground, as well as reliable wind. On the eastern seaboard, houses covered most of the flatlands. Eventually, USW personnel found a potential site to the north, just beyond the Massachusetts border.

U.S. Windpower constructed the wind farm on property belonging to the Crotched Mountain Rehabilitation Center in Greenfield, New Hampshire. The facility boasted a hospital and a school for children with disabilities; it also possessed large tracts of smooth, open land. Situated on a flat shoulder of the mountain, the location appeared perfect. Reported average wind speed was 20 miles per hour, and USW turbines supposedly could function at 10 miles per hour. Established roads made the site accessible. Utility lines stood nearby for power transmission, and the Public Service Company of New Hampshire agreed to purchase the generated electricity. Stewards for the children's center were happy to trade land use for free energy.

Russell Wolfe launched a public relations blitz which had two goals. He needed to convince the citizens of Greenfield to vote in favor of rezoning the land for its new, proposed use, and he hoped to attract capital investment. Wolfe labeled the enterprise an opportunity to show charity to disabled children. He suggested that the construction of the wind farm would create jobs for the unemployed. He spoke of tax breaks for investors. And he prophesied that, one day, farmers across America would derive secondary income from cash crops of wind. The campaign produced its desired effect. The press repeated Wolfe's words, and an overwhelming number of voters in Greenfield approved rezoning.

U.S. Windpower launched construction of the Crotched Mountain Wind Farm in 1979. USW labeled the enterprise, "The Greenfield Wind Farm," but locals called the farm after the mountain on which it was located. The nickname became the accepted name. In December of 1980, twenty USW 30-kW turbines, mounted on steel tripods 60 feet in height, and sporting three fiberglass blades with a diameter of nearly 40 feet spun into operation.

A host of issues plagued the Crotched Mountain Wind Farm and led to its closure before the end of 1981. Area winds proved inconsistent, and the USW turbines did not function at 10 miles per hour, as promised. Instead, they required 13-miles-per-hour winds for minimal output and 22-miles-per-hour wind speeds for optimum power production. Unfortunately, high winds created other problems for the machines. Wind gusts and prolonged exposure caused blades to break off from the turbine assemblies. Within months, Crotched Mountain had become nothing more than a research facility for USW. The firm replaced the failing 30-kW turbines with experimental 50-kW models, called "56-50s," but the new machines also possessed structural imperfections. Less than a year after the farm's opening, U.S. Windpower dismantled the array and bulldozed the site.

Though the Crotched Mountain Wind Farm failed as a source of power for the residents of southern New Hampshire, it yielded tremendous results for the burgeoning wind industry and for USW. The press, which had played a significant role in promoting the Crotched Mountain venture and the potential of wind-generated power, devoted little coverage to the challenges the farm experienced. In growing numbers, a reading public hungry for a solution to energy crises turned to the wind. Building on knowledge gained from the project, Wolfe and Charren began constructing a wind farm in California before closing the one in New Hampshire. USW's wind farm in Altamont Pass is credited with launching the modern wind power industry, and it ushered in a period of tremendous prosperity for Charren and Wolfe's firm. U.S. Windpower relocated to the West Coast and changed its name to Kenetech, Under its new name, USW was the world's largest manufacturer of turbines throughout the 1980s.

Kregg M. Fehr

See also: Alta Wind Energy Center; Block Island Wind Farm; Brush, Charles Francis; Energy Crisis of the 1970s; Halladay Windmill; National Energy Act of 1978; Perry, Thomas Osborn; Renewable Energy; Wind Power

FURTHER READING

Asmus, Peter. 2001. *Reaping the Wind: How Mechanical Wizards, Visionaries, and Profiteers Helped Shape Our Energy Future*. Washington, DC: Island Press.

Eggleston, David M., and Forrest Stoddard. 1987. *Wind Turbine Engineering Design*. New York: Springer.

Maegaard, Preben, Anna Krenz, and Wolfgang Palz, eds. 2013. *The Rise of Modern Wind Energy: Wind Power for the World*. Singapore: Pan Stanford Publishing.

Owens, Brandon N. 2019. *The Wind Power Story: A Century of Innovation that Reshaped the Global Energy Landscape*. Piscataway, NJ: IEEE Press.

Righter, Robert W. 2008. *Wind Energy in America: A History*. Norman: University of Oklahoma Press.

Stoddard, Forrest. n.d. "The Life and Work of Bill Heronemus, Wind Engineering Pioneer." https://www.umass.edu/windenergy/about/history/heronemus (accessed February 14, 2020).

Cumberland Coal and Iron Company

The Cumberland Coal and Iron Company (CCIC), first chartered in 1842, represented an important transition in the mining, marketing, and transportation of coal. Operating in the Georges Creek Valley in Allegany County in western Maryland, it was one of the first companies to employ practices necessary to make coal a nationally used and profitable commodity. In 1852, the Maryland General Assembly, at the request of the company, adjusted the original charter to allow for the CCIC to absorb several smaller coal companies. The company not only took the lead in mining the eastern portion of the Pittsburgh Seam, colloquially referred to as "the Big Vein," but it also provided the impetus for economic growth in western Maryland north of the B&O mainline prior to the US Civil War.

Coal mining in the Allegheny Mountains dated to before the Revolutionary War. Much of it was used in local forges and furnaces. Just west of the mountains, mines on the south bank of the Monongahela River fueled homes and industries in Pittsburgh, Pennsylvania throughout the first half of the nineteenth century. Larger, national markets, however, had yet to be firmly established. The initial proliferation of mines in western Maryland coincided with expansion of new means of transportation. The Maryland Mining Company, one of those companies folded into the CCIC, was the first to operate in the Georges Creek Valley, beginning in 1828. Most of its mines lay around Frostburg, and the company built a railroad from them to Cumberland (Carback 2015, 13). That same year, construction began on the Chesapeake and Ohio Canal (C&O), although it would not reach Cumberland until 1850, seven years after the arrival of the Baltimore and Ohio Railroad (B&O).

Mine operators in the region recognized the quickly changing nature of the industry. The first company in the field was not necessarily the most well-positioned to succeed. Unprecedented amounts of capital were needed to operate profitably. The relatively small scale and modestly funded enterprises of the Jacksonian Era were no longer sufficient (Adams 2009, 200). To that end, several competitors went with the CCIC to the state legislature seeking consolidation. The resulting conglomerate had a capitalization of $5 million and its land holdings more than doubled. It also acquired a number of mines already in operation and the railroad to Cumberland constructed by the Maryland Mining Company. Some major competitors remained, but for a time the CCIC was the largest coal producer in the valley. However, the consolidation that gave it a competitive advantage would help establish an important, nationwide trend in the coal mining industry.

Demand for coal and the efforts needed to get it out of the ground and into markets meant stiff competition. Smaller, less productive, less capitalized enterprises would be pushed out or absorbed. Larger firms were also better positioned to use legal means to prevent smaller rivals or potential newcomers from buying property or developing it. National coal demand began to soar after 1850. While it would take another thirty-five years for coal consumption to surpass that of wood, use of the former consistently trended up well into the twentieth century, while wood plateaued shortly after the US Civil War and declined slowly and gradually over the last half of the nineteenth century (EIA 2011). Consolidation better equipped the CCIC to help meet this need. By 1854, it possessed the ability to send to market up to 3,000 tons per day. The company was able to use its railroad to Cumberland to rapidly transport its coal and prioritize it over the other companies' product. Until that year, it operated the only railroad in the valley.

NEW YORK CONNECTIONS

While charted and operating in Maryland, companies such as the Cumberland Coal and Iron Company were often owned by people from out of state. The CCIC, along with one its predecessors, the Maryland Mining Company, were both owned by entrepreneurs from New York. Businessmen from the Empire State frequently dominated mining and transportation companies throughout the United States during the nineteenth century, demonstrating the need for heavily capitalization to succeed.

Joseph F. Super

Getting coal to Cumberland was critical for mass marketing the product. The CCIC and some of its predecessors maintained small fleets of canal boats to transport their product east to Baltimore directly via the C&O Canal. The B&O Railroad would become both a major shipper and consumer of Appalachian coal. By 1860, coal accounted for half of that railroad's tonnage. With easy access to plentiful coal, it transitioned its engines to burn coal, rather than wood, becoming one of the first railroads to do so. This relationship also benefited the city and people of Baltimore as whole. One-third of the coal shipped back to Baltimore remained there for local use. Anthracite coal, primarily mined in northeast Pennsylvania, was the most popular in domestic uses, as it smoked less. The semi-bituminous coal of western Maryland could also be utilized in the home, but its main purpose was an industrial fuel. In the three decades after the opening of mines throughout the Georges Creek Valley, steam-powered factories, using coal to heat the boilers, multiplied rapidly in and around Baltimore (Schley 2020, 119–20). Together, these constituted one of the largest groups of employers in the city. Thus, coal helped transform not only how people lived at home but also how they traveled and how they worked.

It is perhaps these last two points that best exemplify the legacy of the Cumberland Coal and Iron Company. While the initial purpose of most railroad companies was freight hauling, trains were quickly adapted for passenger transportation. The ability to do both was further facilitated by coal itself. Likewise, to maintain profitability, coal companies required a means of rapid, mass transportation. It is no coincidence that the coal industry's success coincided with the rise of the railroad.

It was also no coincidence that coal and railroad companies were often chartered together or tried to acquire each other. For example, the B&O itself, along with some of its executives, started to purchase mines, putting further pressure on companies that relied on it to ship their own coal. Together, coal and railroads propelled America into the modern industrial age. They precipitated the dawning of a new era of business in America, one conducted on an increasingly large scale and requiring more and more financial and natural resources to sustain. It hastened the transition for rural to urban living and working.

In 1872, less than twenty years after it was rechartered to absorb other companies, the CCIC was acquired by the Consolidation Coal Company (CCC), which had been operating for less than a decade. Like the CCIC before it, the CCC recognized the benefits of consolidation. It became the largest producer in the Georges Creek Valley. Within five years, it would become a subsidiary of the B&O. Thus, the Cumberland Coal and Iron Company fell victim to its own success at pioneering practices that helped propelled coal to prominence in American life.

Joseph F. Super

See also: Baltimore and Ohio Railroad; Cist, Jacob; Coal; Coke; Industrial Revolution; Joy, Joseph Francis; Lakes, Arthur; Molly Maguires; Osgood, John Cleveland; Sinclair, Upton; Susquehanna Coal Company; Usibelli, Emil

FURTHER READING

Adams, Sean Patrick. 2009. *Old Dominion, Industrial Commonwealth: Coal Politics, and Economy in Antebellum America*. Baltimore: Johns Hopkins University Press.

Carback, Joshua T. 2015. "Public Takings by the State for Private Use: A Maryland Case Study in Georges Creek Coal & Iron Company v. New Central Coal Company (1871–1874)." *Maryland Law Review*. Vol. 75. Pp. 1–46.

EIA (US Energy Information Administration). 2011. "History of Energy Consumption in the United States, 1775–2009." https://www.eia.gov/todayinenergy/detail.php?id=10 (accessed October 2023).

Harvey, Katherine A. 1969. *The Best Dressed Miners: Life and Labor in the Maryland Coal Region, 1835–1910*. Ithaca: Cornell University Press.

Long, Priscilla. 1991. *Where the Sun Never Shines: A History of America's Bloody Coal Industry*. New York: Paragon House.

Mellander, Deane E. 1981. *Rails to the Big Vein: The Short Lines of Allegany County, Maryland: The Cumberland and Pennsylvania RR, the Georges Creek and Cumberland RR, the Cumberland and Westernport Electric*. Kensington, MD: Potomac Chapter, National Railway Historical Society.

Schley, David. 2020. *Steam City: Railroads, Urban Space, and Corporate Capitalism in Nineteenth Century Baltimore*. Chicago: University of Chicago Press.

Dakota Access Pipeline

The Dakota Access Pipeline (DAPL), in operation since June 2017, transports about 570,000 barrels of crude oil from northwestern North Dakota to the Patoka Terminal in Illinois. The 1,172-mile underground pipeline transports about 40 percent of the Bakken Formation's daily oil output in North Dakota (ETP 2020c). Since 2014, the pipeline garnered national attention as years of protest drew attention to tribal sovereignty and the environmental costs of fossil fuel infrastructure.

Owned by Energy Transfer Partners, the pipeline was billed by the company as a way of safely and efficiently transporting light sweet crude oil. After transport from the Bakken/Three Forks production area of North Dakota to Illinois, the crude oil is then transported to Gulf Coast refineries via the Energy Transfer Crude Oil Pipeline or railroad tank cars. However, buoyed by growing opposition to the Keystone XL pipeline expansion and wary of the proposed route, local opposition to DAPL grew with a focus on potential threats to water. The northern boundary of the Standing Rock Sioux Reservation, home to about 8,000 tribal members, is half a mile from the pipeline's intersection with the Missouri River, where it was dammed to form Lake Oahe reservoir in 1948. Further, about 17 million downstream users depend on the Missouri River for their drinking water. As such, members of the protest movement took on the label of Water Protectors and devised the motto, "Water Is Life".

In addition to concerns about water quality impacts, neighboring tribes joined the Standing Rock Sioux in voicing concerns about impacts to ancestral and cultural sites. In 2016, for instance, a US Army Corps of Engineers senior archaeologist identified five recorded cultural sites and thirty more within a one-mile radius of the pipeline path. Nonetheless, the Corps approved the route (Hersher 2017).

While the Federal Energy Regulatory Commission has authority to certify interstate natural gas pipelines, there is no such federal body with comprehensive jurisdiction over crude oil pipelines. Oil pipelines require the approval of state regulatory commissions in each state the pipeline enters. However, because DAPL crosses jurisdictional waters of the United States, including just over 1,000 feet beneath the Missouri river, it requires approval by the Corps of Engineers, which brings the National Environmental Policy Act (NEPA) to bear. As a result, the Standing Rock Sioux Tribe largely focused its efforts on the federal land the pipeline crosses beneath the Missouri River. The Tribe initiated litigation in federal courts in the summer of 2016, with the Cheyenne River Sioux Tribe joining later. In the courts and in public messaging, the Water Protectors movement emphasized the lack of tribal consultation as violations of NEPA and the National Historical Preservation Act (Eid 2018).

DISPLACEMENT AND DISPOSSESSION

For the Standing Rock Sioux and its tribal neighbors, the DAPL conflict was inextricably tied to a history of displacement and dishonored agreements. While the pipeline crosses about a half-mile north of the boundary of the Standing Rock Sioux Reservation, this land is Sioux territory based on the 1851 Treaty of Fort Laramie, which was effectively abrogated when Congress seized the Black Hills after the discovery of gold in 1874. While Congress offered to compensate the tribal parties of the Treaty in 1877, and in 1980 the Supreme Court ruled that fair compensation of the Black Hills was $102 million, the Sioux has never accepted payment (Zotigh 2018). Further, when the Missouri River was dammed by the Army Corps of Engineers in 1948, forming Lake Oahe, the Standing Rock and the Cheyenne River Sioux lost over 160,000 acres to the project (Lawson 1994, 50).

Keriann Conroy and Kate Clark

In December 2016, the Obama administration directed the Corps of Engineers to block permission pending a full environmental impact statement. However, the incoming Trump administration reversed course with a presidential memo in January 2017, and by early February the Corps issued an easement to allow the pipeline to cross the Missouri, arguing that there would be no significant environmental impact and thus bypassing the completion of an environmental impact statement. Legal wrangling continued to focus on whether public comment and environmental review procedures were sufficiently followed.

Despite the tribes' limited legal successes, which included months of stalled construction, the Water Protectors revived a historic movement for Indigenous sovereignty and visibility. At its peak, the protest movement included multiple encampments at sites including Rosebud, Sacred Stone, and Oceti Sakowin. In December 2016, crowds of supporters swelled to an estimated 10,000–14,000 and included religious delegations, veterans, and members from over a hundred Native American tribes (Wiles 2017; Eid 2018).

Supporters won widespread national news coverage but at a heavy cost. Between October and December 2016, law enforcement efforts to clear the camps became violent. As early as October of that year, local police from Morton County were assisted by officers from at least forty other jurisdictions from ten states, utilizing the Emergency Management Assistance Compact, generally employed in the event of a natural disaster (Erdrich 2016). The police force came with armored personnel carriers, equipped with military-grade armaments, and aided by private security forces. In a particularly heated exchange on Backwater Bridge in late November, police used tear gas, pepper spray, and rubber bullets against an estimated 400 protesters. Police use of water cannons against protesters in freezing weather caused seizures and hypothermia and resulted in at least seventeen protesters requiring hospitalization (Erdrich 2016; Hawkins 2016). A twenty-one-year-old woman nearly lost her arm after a police concussion grenade exploded near her, according to other protesters.

Police violence resulted in an upswell of support for the protesters as dramatic images and video were broadcast across the country. About a week later, some 2,000 veterans arrived on site to intervene on the Water Protectors' behalf. The organization Veterans Stand for

Standing Rock said they came in response to "assault and intimidation at the hands of a militarized police force" (Mele 2016).

After over three years of conflict, with over 750 protesters arrested, and protests and lawsuits costing DAPL's investors at least $750 million, the pipeline began operation in June 2017 (Eid 2018). Almost three years later, a federal judge ordered the Corps to undergo a full environmental review, handing the Standing Rock Sioux a legal victory in March 2020 (Kennedy 2020). Yet, since late 2019, Energy Transfer Partners has pursued a plan to nearly double the pipeline's capacity to 1.1 million barrels a day.

Kate Clark and Keriann Conroy

See also: Clean Water Act; Enbridge Pipeline System; Hydraulic Fracking; Keystone Pipeline System; Petroleum; Trans-Alaska Pipeline System

FURTHER READING

Aisch, Gregor and Rebecca K.K. Lai. 2017. "The Conflicts along 1,172 Miles of the Dakota Access Pipeline." *The New York Times*. March. https://www.nytimes.com/interactive/2016/11/23/us/dakota-access-pipeline-protest-map.html (accessed May 18, 2020).

Bearak, Max. 2016. "U.N. Officials Denounce 'Inhuman' Treatment of Native American Pipeline Protesters." *The Washington Post*. November. https://www.washingtonpost.com/news/worldviews/wp/2016/11/15/u-n-officials-denounce-inhuman-treatment-of-north-dakota-pipeline-protesters/ (accessed May 18, 2020).

Bengal, Rebecca. 2018. "What Lies beneath Lake Oahe." *Lapham's Quarterly*. July. https://www.laphamsquarterly.org/roundtable/what-lies-beneath-lake-oahe (accessed May 18, 2020).

Eid, Troy. 2018. "Beyond Dakota Access Pipeline: Energy Development and the Imperative for Meaningful Tribal Consultation." *Denver Law Review*. Vol. 95. No. 3. Pp. 593–607.

Erdrich, Louise. 2016. "Holy Rage: Lessons from Standing Rock." *The New Yorker*. December. https://www.newyorker.com/news/news-desk/holy-rage-lessons-from-standing-rock (accessed May 18, 2020).

ETP (Energy Transfer Partners). 2020a. "Asset Overview." https://cms.energytransfer.com/wp-content/uploads/2019/03/Asset_Map_March_2019.pdf (accessed May 18, 2020).

ETP (Energy Transfer Partners). 2020b. "Growth Opportunity." https://www.daplpipelinefacts.com/Updates.html (accessed May 18, 2020).

ETP (Energy Transfer Partners). 2020c. "Moving America's Energy: The Dakota Access Pipeline." https://www.daplpipelinefacts.com/ (accessed May 18, 2020).

Friedman, Lisa. 2020. "Standing Rock Sioux Tribe Wins a Victory in Dakota Access Pipeline Case." *The New York Times*. March. https://www.nytimes.com/2020/03/25/climate/dakota-access-pipeline-sioux.html (accessed May 18, 2020).

Hasselman, Jan. 2017. "DAPL Ruling: What Was Decided, What's Next." *EarthJustice*. June. https://earthjustice.org/features/dapl-ruling-what-was-decided-what-s-next (accessed May 18, 2020).

Hawkins, Derek. 2016. "Police Defend Use of Water Cannons on Dakota Access Protesters in Freezing Weather." *The Washington Post*. November. https://www.washingtonpost.com/news/morning-mix/wp/2016/11/21/police-citing-ongoing-riot-use-water-cannons-on-dakota-access-protesters-in-freezing-weather/ (accessed May 20, 2020).

Hersher, Rebecca. 2017. "Key Moments in The Dakota Access Pipeline Fight." *NPR*. February. https://www.npr.org/sections/thetwo-way/2017/02/22/514988040/key-moments-in-the-dakota-access-pipeline-fight (accessed May 18, 2020).

Kennedy, Merrit. 2020. "Judge Orders Environmental Review of Controversial Dakota Access Pipeline." *NPR*. March. https://www.npr.org/2020/03/25/821643911/judge-orders-environmental-review-of-controversial-dakota-access-pipeline (accessed May 18, 2020).

Lawson, Michael L. 1994. *Dammed Indians: The Pick-Sloan Plan and the Missouri River Sioux, 1944–1980*. Norman, OK: University of Oklahoma Press.

Mele, Christopher. 2016. "Veterans to Serve as 'Human Shields' for Dakota Pipeline Protesters." *The New York Times*. November. https://www.nytimes.com/2016/11/29/us/veterans-to-serve-as-human-shields-for-pipeline-protesters.html (accessed May 20, 2020).

O'Connell, Patrick M. 2019. "Dakota Access Pipeline Owners Want to Pump More Oil through Illinois." *Chicago Tribune*. December. https://www.chicagotribune.com/news/environment/ct-dakota-access-pipeline-expansion-illinois-20191226-cbyzry76jjd5xf5c4dllqqbkoe-story.html (accessed May 18, 2020).

Wiles, Tay. 2017. "What Standing Rock Meant for Those Who Took Part." *High Country News*. https://www.hcn.org/issues/49.1/whats-next-after-standing-rock (accessed May 20, 2020).

Zotigh, Dennis. 2018. "The 1868 Treaty of Fort Laramie, Never Honored by the United States, Goes on Public View." *Smithsonian Magazine*. October. https://www.smithsonianmag.com/blogs/national-museum-american-indian/2018/10/31/treaty-fort-laramie/ (accessed May 15, 2020).

Davenport, Thomas

Thomas Davenport (1802–51) invented an electric motor in 1834, for which he received US Patent No. 132 three years later. A blacksmith by training, Davenport also demonstrated electrical locomotion and devised an electrically powered printing press. Despite technical success, these inventions failed to attract investors, and widespread adoption of electric motors occurred only decades later. Aside from lessons about the difficulties of promoting radically new ideas, the reasons for the commercial failure of Davenport's work show how energy inventions operate within larger technical and social systems.

Born in Williamstown, Vermont, Davenport received limited formal education. His father's untimely death led to an apprenticeship with a local blacksmith in 1814. After completing seven years of training, Davenport moved to the town of Brandon and established his own smithy. He married Emily Goss (1810–62) in 1827, began raising a family, and set to work (Davenport 1851).

Davenport's interests extended beyond the mundane tasks of a small-town blacksmith. The electromagnetic work of Albany Academy professor Joseph Henry (1797–1878) attracted his attention. Conducting research into the relationships between electricity and magnetism, Henry wrapped insulated copper wire around the poles of a permanent magnet. Passing the current from a battery through that wire, he could boost the magnet's strength. In 1832, Henry made an electromagnet that could lift 1,000 pounds (King 1962).

Henry made electromagnets for practical use, one of which he sold to the Penfield and Hamond Iron Works in Crown Point, New York, where the owners used it to separate iron from crushed ore. Davenport learned of this "powerful galvanic battery" in the summer of 1833: "I had never heard of galvanism before [and] I determined to journey there and gratify my curiosity by witnessing the wonderful magnetic power … which it was stated would 'lift' a 'common blacksmith's anvil'" (Davenport 1851, 1). In December, Davenport and his brother Oliver made the twenty-five mile trip from Brandon to see this remarkable invention.

Entranced, Thomas persuaded Oliver to help buy the electromagnet, then immediately cut the wires from the battery to see how fast the magnet would respond to the interruption and restoration of power. The instantaneous action impressed Davenport: "Like a flash of lightning the thought occurred to me that here was an available power which was within the reach of man. If 3 pounds of iron and copper wire would suspend in the air 150 pounds of iron, what would three thousand pounds suspend?" (Davenport 1851, 4). He took the magnet home and unwrapped the wires while Emily recorded notes about its construction. Within a few days, he made a more powerful version.

Davenport then turned to Emily's cousin, mechanic Orange Smalley, for help (Visser 1995). Working in Smalley's shop in 1834, they set two electromagnets in a wooden ring and mounted two more electromagnets on a wheel that could rotate in the center. As the wheel rotated, a switching ring on the base sequentially conducted current from a battery to the stationary electromagnets, reversing their polarity and continuing the wheel's rotation. While

Henry made a reciprocating motor in 1831, and Moritz von Jacobi independently made a rotary electromagnetic motor in 1834, Davenport's work was a technical leap (Pope 1891).

Rotary motion is important for the efficient use of energy. The back-and-forth action of reciprocating engines makes obtaining steady power output difficult. The extra devices that level power output or convert reciprocating motion into rotary motion waste energy and reduce the efficiency of the whole machine. Directly generating rotary motion eliminates that energy loss while simplifying the machine. Davenport understood those advantages and began to work on replacing steam power with electromagnetism.

Steam engines in the early nineteenth century provided a powerful alternative to other so-called prime movers that used animal, water, or wind power. Replacing those low-energy, intermittent power sources with a higher energy, continuously running power source increased productivity. The adaptation of steam power to railroads and watercraft set off a revolution in transportation. Steam engines drove the Industrial Revolution. But like all technologies steam had its dangers, especially in the early era. Boiler explosions killed and injured many.

Davenport believed that an electrical motor would be easier to operate and far safer, providing "a valuable substitute for the murderous power of steam" (Davenport 1851, 5). Aside from safety, the need for constant attention made steam power challenging. Also, the power generated by a steam engine had to be transported to workstations by a system of shafts and belts. Electric motors held the promise of eliminating the energy losses inherent in such a system by placing power sources throughout a factory. When Smalley withdrew from the project in 1835, Davenport continued on. In late 1835, J.H. Cobb invited him to the New England Silk Company to see if an electromagnetic motor could be adapted to winding silk, but ultimately chose not to make a purchase (Davenport 1851, 19).

In December 1835, Davenport demonstrated to Boston audiences a redesigned electromagnetic motor set on a circular track. The motor turned a gear that moved a carriage around the track, demonstrating that an electric motor could propel a vehicle. The following year Davenport and his new partner Ransom Cook (1794–1881) made a motor that earned US Patent No. 132. Unfortunately, they began promoting the patent in the wake of the Panic of 1837, a sustained economic crisis that left investors wary, if still able to invest at all. Though many potential customers asked for information, they, like Cobb, did not buy motors (Schiffer 2008, 109–14).

Working in New York in late 1839, Davenport connected a reciprocating electromagnetic motor to a printing press and produced a few editions of the *Electro-Magnet and Mechanics Intelligencer* and later the *Electro Magnet*. Few subscribed and his publishing effort folded later that year (Schiffer 2008, 114). Despite his patent, testimonials from experts, and many public demonstrations, Davenport could not raise the funds he needed to commercialize his inventions. He died in 1851, still convinced of the practicality of "the silent, unseen, and inevitable power of electromagnetism" (Davenport 1851, 23).

Invention encompasses more than technical success. Davenport's inventions seem prescient, yet the fact remains that they failed to be adopted for several reasons. The direct technological problem lay in the lack of an effective power source to drive his motors, since electricity is a form—not a source—of energy. Davenport's motors needed electricity to run, but the available batteries and magneto generators were expensive and produced insufficient power. The key breakthrough came in the 1870s with the invention of dynamos that could produce substantial amounts of electrical energy.

Motors served as components in larger electrical power systems, many other parts of which needed to be invented before such systems could be practical. The so-called Second Industrial

Revolution, based on electric power, came to fruition when inventors coupled steam engines to dynamos, as seen in Thomas Edison's 1882 Pearl Street power station. Although water power played a role in electrification, steam-driven power plants fueled by coal, oil, gas, and later uranium have served as the principal power sources driving electric motors for well over a century. Rather than replacing steam power, as Davenport wished, electric motors came to depend on it.

In the larger scope, society was not yet ready to adopt electrical systems to power industry or transportation. Investors accepted steam technology and capitalized research and development. Steam advanced, safety issues receded, and the public came to accept these devices. In an era of low fuel prices and little concern for environmental costs, users deemed energy efficiency less important than equipment reliability and performance. As Schiffer points out, Davenport made prototypes, not motors whose operating costs could be easily compared to steam (Schiffer 2008, 110–12). Also, steam could be seen and felt. The intangible nature of electricity that so captivated Davenport proved too ethereal for many potential investors. Especially in the immediate aftermath of a major economic recession.

Thomas Davenport's vision and ingenuity provide a remarkable example of individual inventiveness. The failure to adopt his inventions provides an example of the limits within which inventors operate. Some limits are technical, like the lack of essential ancillary components. Other limits are social in nature. Inventors of advantageous energy technologies often face the situation where their creations either cannot meet needs as well as existing devices, or political or economic realities stall adoption. They must reach out to society to affect change.

Davenport gave public demonstrations, established a joint-stock company, and received expert endorsements as he attempted to commercialize his inventions (Schiffer 2008). He considered but did not seek government support (Pope 1891, 97). Many people then considered such funding an inappropriate use of public funds. Inventors today might receive such support or ask for interventions like tax credits to offset the short-term advantages of mature technologies they seek to replace. Or, like Davenport, they might turn to capitalists, establish companies, or seek expert validation. Regardless of their path, inventors must pay as much attention to the social structures within which they operate as they do the technical details of their ideas. Otherwise, they risk Davenport's fate—being remembered for having the right idea at the wrong time.

Harold D. Wallace, Jr.

See also: Edison, Thomas Alva; Electricity; Franklin, Benjamin; Henry, Joseph; Industrial Revolution; Morse, Samuel; Pearl Street Power Station; Stanley, William Jr.; Tesla, Nikola; War of the Currents; Westinghouse, George

FURTHER READING

Davenport, Thomas. 1851. *Autobiography of Thomas Davenport*. State of Vermont Public Records Commission. Microfilm.

King, W. James. 1962. *Development of Electrical Technology in the 19th Century*. Vol.1: *The Electrochemical Cell and the Electromagnet*. Washington, DC: Bulletin of the United States National Museum. https://archive.org/stream/bulletin228smit#page/n289/mode/2up/search/231 (accessed October 2023).

Pope, Franklin L. 1891. "The Inventors of the Electric Motor, with Special Reference to the work of Thomas Davenport." *Electrical Engineer*. Vol. 11. Pp. 1–5, 33–9, 65–71, 93–8, 125–30.

Schiffer, Michael B. 2008. *Power Struggles: Scientific Authority and the Creation of Practical Electricity before Edison*. Cambridge, MA: MIT Press.

Silliman, Benjamin. 1837–8. "Notice of the Electro-Magnetic Machine of Mr. Thomas Davenport." *American Journal of Science and Arts*. Vol. 32. Appendix. Vol. 33. Pp. 423–4.

Visser, Thomas D. 1995. "Smalley-Davenport Shop, Forestdale, Vermont." Division for Historic Preservation. Montpelier, Vermont. October 23. https://web.archive.org/web/20190202051152/http://www.uvm.edu/~histpres/SD/hist.html (accessed December 20, 2019).

Dawson Mine Disaster

At 3:10 p.m. on Wednesday, October 22, 1913, people in the coal-mining town of Dawson, New Mexico, heard a sharp crack, like a high-powered rifle, followed by a prolonged muffled roar. Then they felt the earth vibrate and saw flames shoot a 100 feet out of the entrance of Phelps Dodge Company's Stag Cañon mine No. 2. The explosion, caused by a dynamite charge that ignited coal dust in the mine, killed 263 miners and support personnel. It was a disaster of epic proportions.

The town of Dawson was located at 6,393 feet in the New Mexico highlands about 8 miles south of the Colorado–New Mexico border. Isolated at the end of a railroad branch, it was 35 miles from any town with a similar or larger population. Phelps Dodge originally purchased the Dawson property in 1905 to secure fuel for its copper smelters in Arizona, as well as coal for steam locomotives on its growing network of railroad lines. During its fifty-year history as an active Phelps Dodge property, Dawson Fuel excavated a total of ten underground mines into a continuous seam of low-sulfur coal that measured more than 5 miles long, 5 miles wide, and as much as 11 feet thick. Several hundred coke ovens located at the edge of the prosperous coal camp vented fire and smoke day and night (Schwantes 2000, 139).

The 1913 Dawson explosion was not an isolated case. In the twenty years from 1913 through 1933, 1,043 miners died in eighteen major explosions in the Rocky Mountain states. These involved some of the worst disasters ever, including the 1913 Phelps Dodge episode. But none of these tragedies led to reforms that produced any dramatic reductions in fatality rates, despite resulting in a greater awareness of the mine safety problem. The high rates of death continued in the Rocky Mountain region that ironically owed much to industrial and technological changes affecting the conditions in which the miners worked. More importantly, weaknesses in state laws and the persistence of outdated attitudes that held mine workers primarily responsible for their safety and deaths contributed to the potential of death in the mines (Whiteside 1990, 134).

At the time of the 1913 Dawson tragedy, New Mexico had a law designed to prevent disaster by requiring adequate ventilation and other safety precautions. However, the Dawson incident showed the state did not fulfill its regulatory responsibilities and, for all intents and purposes, the law was ineffective. Moreover, the law did not address, in any meaningful way, other major causes of injury and death in the mines. As terrible as the large mine explosions were, they did not account for the majority of fatalities in the industry. Historically, more mine workers died by ones and twos, in accidents involving mine hauling, electricity, and, especially, collapses of roof coal and landslides. It was these scenarios that came under increasingly more public scrutiny at the national level as a result of the burgeoning Progressive Movement (Whiteside 1989, 161).

The Progressive Movement in the 1890s to 1920s swept across the United States, when working Americans saw the impulse toward social activism and political reform across nation as a glimmer of hope. Led by middle-class, moralistic reformers, the movement was a stunningly broad and diverse effort to harness industrialization for the good of the people. Progressive crusaders broke up monopolies, regulated big business and railroads, established the Federal Reserve banking system, legislated progressive taxes, enacted food and drug safety laws, campaigned against vice and corruption, and ushered in women's suffrage and Prohibition. They carried out reforms in virtually every aspect of American life, from the boardroom to the playground. Championing human rights over property rights, progressives spoke fluently the Jeffersonian idiom of egalitarianism and lamented the "betrayal of democracy" that corporate forces had allegedly imposed on the nation. The mining industry was no exception (Southern 2005, 1).

At the federal level, it was recognized that mining was more hazardous than many other occupations, in part, because it was carried on underground. In addition to accidents in the surface industries, there were the additional and greater dangers of roof falls, not only in the working places but also along the entries the miners used in going to and from work. When compared with metal mining, coal mining presented additional danger related to the amounts of flammable and poisonous gases in the working places. To prevent or decrease accidents in coal mining was a far more complicated problem than in other industries. Machinery guards and the separation of different elements of danger were more easily arranged above ground. In surface industries, human errors might endanger only one or a few, instead of the hundreds of lives endangered by an error or a careless act that caused an explosion or a mine fire. Moreover, the difficulties of preventing accidents varied in the different states, and both miners and, during the early period, mine accidents had been treated as individual miner's carelessness. In the mid-1920s the public began placing more responsibility for mine safety on management, suggesting management was primarily responsible for providing safety-related public goods and services, training in proper mining techniques, and supervision of miners. Further, to address the issue, in 1910 Congress created the US Bureau of Mines to disseminate information about mine safety and how to improve it; however, the states were designated as the primary regulators of mine safety (Choi 1989, 133).

At the state level, however, there emerged a fundamental political reality that stymied real reform. Using their economic influence, larger employers pressed for and shaped the laws to raise their smaller rivals' costs. More directly, in the coal industry in particular, large employers practiced a defensive strategy, and narrative evidence from several states shows that coal employers heavily influenced the content and enforcement of the mining legislation. The laws with the most impact on mine accidents were ones that were generally targeted the behavior of miners as opposed to imposing limits on employers. Compliance with the laws largely relied on the goodwill of the mine owners. State enforcement budgets were limited, inspectors were poorly paid, and the courts in some states imposed few fines. The fines that were imposed were most commonly imposed on mine workers rather than mine owners and managers (Fishback 2005, 30).

From the federal perspective, the coal-mining safety movement emerged as a halting and incomplete expression of organizational change. The Bureau of Mines produced no national regulatory mine-safety legislation, not even a provision for administrative mine-safety regulations. In short, lacking coercive authority, the Bureau of Mines could function only as an educational and scientific agency with all regulatory and inspection functions remaining the responsibility of the states. Accordingly, any uniformity of safety regulation, whose promise of centralization seemed so great, proved to be an unrealistic goal for an ineffectual federal agency (Graebner 2014, 171).

On February 8, 1923, a second explosion rocked the Phelps Dodge facility at Dawson. A mine car derailed in Stag Cañon mine No. 1, sparked an electric trolley cable, and ignited coal dust. The blast killed 123 men, many of them offspring of the men who died in the 1913 explosion. Ten years later, in 1933, the New Mexico Legislature finally revised the state's coal-mining law. The new statute contained improvements in the areas of inspection and enforcement. Other regulations governed the installation of electric power lines and machinery, forbade miners to ride on coal trips, and required systematic timbering of underground roofs. Operators were to provide first-aid training and supplies and firefighting equipment. Larger mines were to train and maintain rescue teams. The new law also sought to improve coal-mine supervision by requiring examination and certification of all officials, including foremen and assistant foremen, and required supervisors to make daily inspections of all working places and see to the prompt removal of any hazards (Whiteside 1990, 153).

In New Mexico, Phelps Dodge continued operations at the Dawson facility until 1950 when, due to a reduction in demand for coal, it closed the mine and sold the whole town, buildings and all, to be carried off to other locations. A popular ghost town, today the cemetery remains Dawson's central attraction.

Brett F. Woods

See also: Cherry Mine Disaster; Coal; Farmington Mine Disaster; Krebs Mine Disaster; Scofield Mine Disaster; United Mine Workers of America; Upper Big Branch Mine Disaster; Weir, Peter; West Frankfort Mine Disaster

FURTHER READING

Choi, Pac-Kun. 1989. "Effects of Unionism and Work-related Safety on Productivity in the U.S. Bituminous Coal Mining Industry, 1898–1945." Ph.D. dissertation. University of Georgia.

Fishback, Price. 2005. *The Irony of Reform: Did Large Employers Subvert Workplace Safety Reform, 1869 to 1930?* Cambridge, MA: National Bureau of Economic Research.

Graebner, William. 2014. *Coal-Mining Safety in the Progressive Period: The Political Economy of Reform*. Lexington, KY: University Press of Kentucky.

Schwantes, Carlos A. 2000. *Vision and Enterprise: Exploring the History of Phelps Dodge Corporation*. Tucson, AZ: University of Arizona Press.

Southern, David W. 2005. *The Progressive Era and Race: Reaction and Reform, 1900–1917*. Wheeling, IL: Harlan Davidson.

Whiteside, James. 1989. "Coal Mining, Safety, and Regulation in New Mexico." *New Mexico Historical Review*. April 1989.

Whiteside, James. 1990. *Regulating Danger: The Struggle for Mine Safety in the Rocky Mountain Coal Industry*. Lincoln, NE: University of Nebraska Press.

Daylight Saving Time

Daylight Saving Time (DST) is a system of resetting clocks during for a certain period of time during the year in order to adjust to and take advantage of increased hours of daylight. In general, the practice involves rising an hour earlier and going to bed an hour earlier each day during the weeks of late spring, summer, and early fall. The result is an extra hour available for activity in the evening, after the end of the average workday, but while the sun is still up. According to its advocates, the energy savings would come with the extra hour of natural light at home in the evening, which means less energy use on lights powered by electricity.

Although touted as a means of saving energy, it has proven difficult to determine the actual amount saved, which depends on a particular area's distance from the equator as well as a number of other factors. Despite having engendered controversy and confusion over the years, DST is now routinely accepted as a familiar feature of the year's cycle by most Americans, who keep track of its basic pattern through the mnemonic phrase "spring forward, fall back."

While the idea of "saving" daylight had undoubtedly occurred to countless individuals over the centuries, the first person to share the concept in writing appears to have been American statesman and inventor Benjamin Franklin (1706–90), who served as American ambassador to France during the late 1770s and early 1780s. As he related in a light-hearted letter to the *Journal de Paris* in 1784, he had awakened early one morning to sunlight after his servant had neglected to close the shutters to his window the preceding evening. Claiming, tongue in cheek, that he had never experienced such light before noon, he went on to estimate how many candles the residents of Paris might save by rising with the sun.

Franklin did not actually suggest resetting clocks, but over the next century, other commentators did, including British builder William Willett in a 1907 pamphlet called *The Waste of Daylight.* A few communities in Canada actually experimented with the practice during the first decade of the twentieth century, but Germany and Austria-Hungary became the first countries to adopt DST, on April 30, 1916, as a means of conserving coal during the First World War. A number of other European countries followed suit. The United States itself took up DST under the terms of the Standard Time (or Calder) Act of 1918, with the change in effect from March 31 until October 27. Canada also adopted daylight saving for the summer the same year.

However, America's brief experiment with DST proved unpopular, particularly among farmers, and it was abolished in 1919, becoming a local option for more than two decades. But soon after the beginning of the Second World War, President Franklin D. Roosevelt reinstituted the program on a year-round basis as "War Time," and it remained in effect until September 30, 1945. After that date, certain states and cities, most of them in the eastern part of the country, continued to observe the practice during the summer.

Under pressure from the country's transcontinental transportation industries, which were finding it increasingly difficult to deal with an ever-changing array of local times, President

Lyndon Johnson signed the Uniform Time Act of 1966. The new law required that DST go into effect the following year at 2:00 a.m. on the last Sunday in April and end at the same hour on the last Sunday of October. The law allowed states to opt out of the program, with Arizona, Hawaii, and Michigan becoming the only three to do so, though Michigan returned to observing DST in 1973. Not surprisingly, states lying in more than one time zone found the changes required by the law particularly irksome, and a 1972 amendment allowed them to exempt those parts of the state in the different zone. Confusingly enough, however, such states were also given the option of observing DST in all the zones or none of them.

As energy shortages mounted in 1973 due to an embargo by the members of the Organization of Arab Petroleum Exporting Countries (OPEC), Congress enacted the Emergency Daylight Saving Time Energy Conservation Act. The measure was an experiment in year-round DST and went into effect on January 6, 1974. The act was amended in late 1974 to allow a return to standard time beginning October 27 of that year, with a period of DST resuming on February 23, 1975. Subsequently, the nation reverted to observing DST in the summer.

The Energy Policy Act of 2005, which remains in effect in the early twenty-first century, changed the dates for DST, beginning it at 2:00 a.m. local time on the second Sunday in March 2007 and ending it at 2:00 a.m. local time the first Sunday in November.

Since its initial inception in the United States in 1918, the merits of DST have been endlessly debated, and it has generated countless political speeches, newspaper editorials, cartoons, and letters to the editor. Members of the public long believed that it was farmers who found the system helpful. But farmers themselves pointed out that resetting clocks interfered with the natural schedules that they and their herds followed, and that it was those working uniform hours in the city, especially in the growing fields of retail sales and entertainment, who favored it. Such city-dwellers were routinely dismissed as well-to-do businessmen who merely wanted more time to play golf in the afternoon (Englishman William Willett himself, it has been pointed out, was a golfer).

DAYLIGHT SAVING IN THE NAVAJO NATION

Encompassing more than 17 million acres, the Native American territory of the Navajo Nation is larger than some states and stretches from southeastern Utah into northeastern Arizona and northwestern New Mexico. While Arizona itself does not observe DST, the Navajo Nation does. However, the Hopi Reservation, which is divided into three noncontiguous areas lying entirely within the larger Navajo Nation, follows the lead of Arizona in ignoring the system.

Grove Koger

Aside from the confusion that the program routinely engenders, many Americans complain that DST interferes with their sleep patterns and leads to sleep loss. The change also appears to increase the incidence of heart attacks in some segments of the population and complicates the use of some medical devices. However, fears of increased traffic accidents involving children walking to school or waiting for buses in the early morning hours appear to have no basis.

Determining whether DST actually promotes the conservation of energy has proven difficult. In a 1974 report to Congress, the US Department of Transportation (DOT) suggested that the results of the program were decidedly mixed. Daylight saving, the DOT said, might well lead to a slight increase in the use of heating oil, a possible reduction of 0.5 to 1 percent in the use of electricity, but no meaningful reduction in gasoline consumption. But a 2008 working paper from the National Bureau of Economic Research concluded that "extensions to DST are most likely to increase, rather than decrease, demand for residential electricity," and that "the longstanding rationale for DST is questionable" (Kotchen 2008, 23).

Whatever energy saving might have taken place at one time, changing patterns of energy use may have reduced the amount. Researchers point out that going to bed earlier may lead to greater use of air-conditioning, a consideration of significant consequence as global warming increases. In addition, greater opportunities for shopping and recreation during the extra hours of leisure in the evening, resulting in increased use of automobiles and other vehicles, may lessen the possible benefits of DST.

While practiced on a nationwide basis in the United States in the early twenty-first century, Daylight Saving Time is not observed in Arizona and Hawaii, although the system is followed in the Navajo Nation, much of which lies in the former state. It is also ignored in the overseas American territories of American Samoa, the Commonwealth of the Northern Mariana Islands, Guam, Puerto Rico, and the US Virgin Islands, as well as in some Amish communities.

Grove Koger

See also: Agriculture and Energy; Climate Change; Electricity; Energy Crisis of the 1970s; Energy Policy Act of 2005; Franklin, Benjamin; Interstate Highway System

FURTHER READING

Bartky, Ian R. 2007. *One Time Fits All: The Campaigns for Global Uniformity*. Sanford, CA: Stanford University Press.

Clark, Corrie E., and Lynn J. Cunningham. 2018. *Daylight Saving Time*. Washington, DC: Library of Congress, Congressional Research Service. https://fas.org/sgp/crs/misc/R45208.pdf (accessed June 23, 2019).

Downing, Michael. 2005. *Spring Forward: The Annual Madness of Daylight Saving Time*. Washington, DC: Shoemaker & Hoard.

Kotchen, Matthew J., and Laura E. Grant. 2008. "Does Daylight Saving Time Save Energy? Evidence from a Natural Experiment in Indiana." NBER working Paper 14429. https://www.nber.org/papers/w14429 (accessed July 1, 2019).

Pollak, Oliver B. 1981. "'Efficiency, Preparedness and Conservation': The Daylight Savings [*sic*] Time Movement." *History Today*. Vol. 31. No. 3. March. Pp. 5–9.

Prerau, David. 2005. *Seize the Daylight: The Curious and Contentious Story of Daylight Saving Time*. New York: Thunder's Mouth Press.

Deepwater Horizon

Deepwater Horizon was a 52,590 ton, mobile, very deepwater, semi-submersible offshore drilling rig owned by Transocean and constructed in 2001 by Hyundai Heavy Industries. Able to operate in water as deep as 8,000 feet, it measured 396 by 256 feet. It could drill to 30,000 feet and was one of only about 200 offshore rigs that could drill over 5,000 feet. *Deepwater Horizon* was commissioned by the R&B Falcon Corporation of Houston, Texas, which was purchased in 2000 by Transocean. The rig, like many similar vessels, was registered for tax purposes in Majuro, Republic of the Marshall Islands. It was leased to British Petroleum (BP) from 2001 to 2013 which utilized it to drill in various places for oil. It held the record for drilling the then-deepest oil well in history (2009) of 35,050 feet in the Tiber Oil Field at Keathley Canyon, about 250 miles southeast of Houston in 4,132 feet of water.

While drilling in water 5,000 feet deep in the Gulf of Mexico on April 20, 2010, *Deepwater Horizon* was destroyed by an uncontrollable blowout explosion. The explosion killed eleven crewmen and ignited a fire that could be seen 40 miles away. Attempts to extinguish the fire were futile, and on April 22, the rig sank. Uncapped, its well continued to gush oil which spread and became the largest oil spill in US waters, nearly 5 million barrels (approximately 200 million gallons) of crude oil. The rig's remains settled on the seafloor 1,300 feet under water. A subsequent investigation found that the companies involved with *Deepwater Horizon*'s operations were at fault. *Deepwater Horizon*'s explosion, coupled with other significant oil spill incidents, led to a significant tightening of US and international regulations and enforcement mechanisms for maritime oil drilling.

As oil reserves were claimed and depleted at the earth's surface, petroleum companies drilled even deeper into the earth's surface to supply the world's demand. This stimulated the development of ever-advancing technologies such as the *Deepwater Horizon*. When it exploded, it was one of the strongest and most advanced deepwater drilling mechanisms available. The rig was a Hyundai Heavy Industries' fifth-generation design that could be dynamically positioned, which refers to a computer-controlled system to automatically keep ships in position by using propellers and thrusters. Column-stabilized and able to be moved considerable distances, *Deepwater Horizon* was designed to drill wells for oil exploration below the seafloor, as well as subsequent transfer to oil tankers. It used an 18.75 inch, 15,000 psi blowout preventer, and a 21-inch outside diameter marine riser.

Deepwater Horizon—considered the jewel of Transocean's fleet—was an advance over its predecessor *Deepwater Nautilus* (built in 2000) because it could be dynamically positioned. The rig was upgraded in 2002 with the "e-drill," Perfect Point's drill monitoring system that provided Houston personnel with real-time drilling data. State-of-the-art advanced systems were utilized in all aspects of the rig's operation. This included pressure and drill monitoring technology, automated shutoff systems, and cement modeling systems. Its Halliburton-developed

FIGURE 7: In 2010, an explosion and fire destroyed the BP *Deepwater Horizon* oil drilling rig in the Gulf of Mexico.

OptiCem software cement modeling system determined safe drilling conditions by calculating real-time equivalent circulating densities using actual job volumes, rates, and fluid densities.

Hyundai Heavy Industries began construction of the *Deepwater Horizon* in 1998, laid the keel in 2000, and delivered the rig in 2001. It was initially registered in the Republic of Panama until being switched to the Marshall Islands in 2004. Transocean operated the *Deepwater Horizon* through its Steinhausen, Switzerland subsidiary Triton Asset Leasing GmbH. Transocean leased it to BP on a three-year contract for drilling in the Gulf of Mexico. Subsequently, the rental lease was renewed in 2004 for one year, in 2005 for five years, and in 2009 for 2010–13. The contract specified that BP would pay Transocean $544 million, or $496,800 daily, solely for the rig. The required crew, gear, and support vessels were estimated to cost BP an additional half a billion. As of 2010, the *Deepwater Horizon* was insured for $560 million to cover replacement cost and wreckage removal.

Deepwater Horizon was actively used by BP over 90 percent of its working life. It drilled oil wells in the Atlantis oil field, the largest field in the Gulf of Mexico, in a joint venture with BHP Billiton. Later, it drilled in the huge Thunder Horse oil field in a similar joint venture with ExxonMobil. Both fields in the Gulf about 150 miles southeast of Louisiana.

Some oil workers used to describe *Deepwater Horizon* as a "lucky" rig because of its history of oil discoveries. In 2006, it found oil in the Kaskida oil field, 250 miles southwest of New Orleans, and in 2009 in the nearby Tiber oil field. The latter well, reaching 35,055 feet below the ocean floor sitting in 4,132 feet of water, was then the deepest oil well in the world.

In 2022, the deepest well was the 2012 Exxon Neftegas Z-44 Chayvo well on the Sakhalin Shelf off the northeast coast of Sakhalin Island in eastern Russia.

The *Deepwater Horizon* had a strong safety record. In 2009 the Minerals Management Service (MMS) called the rig an industry safety model. This was significant, as the organization, since renamed Bureau of Ocean Energy Management, Regulation and Enforcement, served as the US regulatory authority for offshore oil drilling and rigs. It was never on the organization's informal problem watchlist. However, a later study found that 25 percent of the required inspections were not done, some because of extenuating circumstances. Each of the three 2010 inspections had taken two hours or less. The rig received five citations for non-compliance, four in 2002 for safety, and one in 2003 for pollution.

In early 2010, *Deepwater Horizon* began drilling its first exploratory well at the Macondo Prospect oil field in Mississippi Canyon Block 252, located roughly 41 miles southeast from the coast of Louisiana at a water depth of approximately 5,000 feet. The Macondo area had been discovered by KC Offshore in 1998. BP bought the mineral rights to drill for oil in the Macondo Prospect at a 2008 MMS lease sale. This area, known as an insular shelf, has relatively shallow water and has been the site of other finds. BP owned 65 percent of its Macondo venture along with Anadarko Petroleum at 25 percent and MOEX Offshore 2007 at 10 percent. Some of the rig's crew members nicknamed the Macondo job "the well from hell." Like many deepwater wells, it had complications. Its engineers had to adjust their operating plans as they learned more about the target geologic formations.

Deepwater Horizon was concluding its Macondo work when the destructive explosion occurred. The necessary steps to shut the well were almost complete; cement casing had been injected and was hardening. When done, the rig was move to the Tiber oil field to be a production platform, and then again to the Kaskida field to function on a semi-permanent basis. Permission had already been requested from MMS to close the Macondo site work.

At 9:45 p.m. CDT on April 20, a powerful tower of seawater shot through the marine riser through the rig and 240 feet in the air. Soon, a slushy combination of drilling mud, methane gas, and water followed. The gas part of the slushy material became fully gaseous and ignited, producing several explosions and a firestorm. The crew tried to utilize the blowout preventer and the blind shear ram, the last defense, but failed to close the now-gushing well. At the time there were 126 crew on the rig: seven BP workers, seventy-nine Transocean, and others from companies including Anadarko Petroleum, Halliburton, and M-I SWACO. Eleven of these workers were presumed killed by the initial explosion. The rig was quickly evacuated, and the US Coast Guard airlifted the injured to onshore medical facilities. *Deepwater Horizon* sank about thirty-six hours later on April 22.

About 80,000 square miles of the US Exclusive Economic Zone in the Gulf were temporarily closed to fishing. Unfortunately, and to wide public fury, the spill continued flowing into the Gulf of Mexico until July 15, 2010, when it was closed by the installation of a cap. BP used Transocean's Development Driller III to drill two relief wells that took three months to complete. Finally, the gushing well was sealed on August 4, 2010 by a "static kill," an injection of heavy fluids and cement into the wellhead at the mudline. After heavy fluids and cement were injected to permanently seal the well, it was declared dead on September 19, 2010.

Transocean received a partial insurance settlement for loss of the *Deepwater Horizon* of $401 million. It was expected that all litigation would take about twenty years to resolve. In early 2013, Transocean paid $1.4 billion for violations of the Clean Water Act. BP was fined $2.4 billion, along with possible additional penalties that could add up to $20 billion. In 2014,

Halliburton settled most of the legal claims against it by paying $1.1 billion into a trust. In 2014, US Eastern District of Louisiana District Judge Carl Barbier ruled BP was guilty of gross negligence and willful misconduct under the Clean Water Act. He assigned two-thirds of the blame to BP, 30 percent to Transocean, and 3 percent to Halliburton. The US Supreme Court denied BP's legal challenge to the compensation arrangement, which would cost BP ultimately about $7.8 billion for victim compensation. After the government ordered a half-year drilling moratorium, BP and other oil companies resumed their Gulf exploration and production.

As a result of this and other spills, the United States adopted new safety rules, accountability standards, and environmental regulations for drilling in its waters. These measures were intended to secure better environmental stewardship of the ocean, coastlines, and the Great Lakes. The new rules were purportedly the most aggressive and comprehensive reforms to offshore oil and gas regulation and oversight in history. In 2018, President Donald Trump replaced the rules directive with an executive order giving more responsibility to states for offshore oil and gas drilling, despite significant deepwater oil field accidents off the Chinese and Brazilian coasts that year.

As of 2023, BP and ExxonMobil, among others, were still drilling for oil and gas in the Gulf which had at the time fifty-nine permanent deepwater structures. However dangerous, deepwater drilling continued to expand, as along the Mediterranean and East African coasts following recent natural gas discoveries.

William P. Kladky

See also: Adair, Paul Neal "Red"; *Argo Merchant* Oil Spill; Clean Water Act; ExxonMobil Corporation; *Exxon Valdez* Oil Spill; Halliburton Company; Kerr-McGee's Kermac No. 16; Oil Tankers; Santa Barbara Oil Spill

FURTHER READING

Bureau of Safety and Environmental Enforcement (BSEE). 2019. "Gulf of Mexico Permanent Deepwater Structures: Permanent Platforms in Water Depths Greater than 1,000 feet." US Department of the Interior. September 8. https://www.data.bsee.gov/Other/DataTables/PermDeepStruc.aspx (accessed October 2023).

National Research Council of the National Academies (NRC). 2012. "Approaches for Ecosystem Services Valuation for the Gulf of Mexico after the *Deepwater Horizon* Oil Spill: Interim Report." Committee on the Effects of the *Deepwater Horizon* Mississippi Canyon-252 Oil Spill on Ecosystem Services in the Gulf of Mexico. Washington, DC: National Academies Press.

Freudenburg, William R., and Robert Graming. 2011. *Blowout in the Gulf: The BP Oil Spill Disaster and the Future of Energy in America*. Cambridge, MA: MIT Press.

Irfan, Umair. 2018. "*Deepwater Horizon* Led to New Protections for US Waters. Trump Just Repealed Them." *Vox*. June 23. https://www.vox.com/2018/6/22/17493414/trump-executive-order-deepwater-horizon-drilling-oceans (accessed October 2023).

Krauss, Clifford, and John M. Broder. 2012. "Deepwater Oil Drilling Picks Up again as BP Disaster Fades." *The New York Times*. March 4.

Leffler, William L., Richard Pattarozzi, and Gordon Sterling. 2003. *Deepwater Petroleum Exploration and Production: A Nontechnical Guide*. 2nd ed. Tulsa, OK: PennWell Corporation.

National Commission on the BP *Deepwater Horizon* Oil Spill and Offshore Drilling (NC). 2011. "Deep Water: The Gulf Oil Disaster and the Future of Offshore Drilling—Report to the President." Washington, DC: US Government Printing Office.

Safina, Carl. 2011. *A Sea in Flames: The Deepwater Horizon Oil Blowout*. New York: Crown Publishers.

Densmore Oil Tank Car

James Densmore (1820–89) and brother Amos (1825–98) hold a modest place in the story of the Pennsylvania Oil Boom and the larger development of the US oil industry in the nineteenth century. Their oil tank railcar offered a transitional means to convey crude oil from oil fields to distant refineries before the arrival of the now-familiar horizontal, tubular steel tankers seen on US freight trains. The patented Densmore Oil Tank Car solved a crucial problem of transportation in the supply chain and highlights the kind of innovation that became necessary for the fossil fuel industry to operate on a mass, nationwide scale.

The Pennsylvania Oil Boom began after Edwin L. Drake's oil strike in 1859 near Titusville, Pennsylvania. By the end of the year Drake had extracted 2,000 barrels of oil; then he dug more wells and by the end of 1860, produced 500,000 more. A multitude of other oil prospectors appeared and turned the landscape surrounding Venango County's "Oil Creek" into a petroleum exploration field dotted with hundreds of wells and oil storage tanks. Workers dragged barrels of oil by flatboats and horse-drawn wagons to the nearest railheads, littering the roads and rivers with broken barrels and untold gallons of spilled oil. Paying these workers added to the high cost of transporting the oil. Within two years, rail lines had been built to connect the Oil Creek fields to Oil City, which enabled oil transit from the region to Cleveland and New York. However, the problem of spillage persisted, since railroads simply bundled barrels of oil together on flatbed cars and subjected them to theft, uneven rail beds, and inclement weather. Several enterprising individuals tried and failed to create a bulk system for transporting oil by rail, including John Scott of Lawrenceville, Pennsylvania, John Clark of Canandaigua, New York, Samuel J. Seely of Brooklyn, and Joel F. Keeler of Pittsburgh (White 1985).

The Densmore brothers also engaged this problem in the early 1860s. James was born in Moscow, New York and his younger brother Amos in Rochester. Their parents moved the family from Rochester to land near Meadville in Crawford County, Pennsylvania to build water-powered lathes for a wooden bowl business ("The Story" 2015). James looked for his fortune in Wisconsin, serving as the manager of the Oshkosh *True Democrat* in the late 1840s, where he advocated for women's suffrage in the newly formed state. James moved around Wisconsin for other newspaper jobs, eventually buying the *Walworth County Independent* in Indiana in 1855 before returning to Pennsylvania after Drake's oil strike (Current 1947, 418). He and several of his brothers, including Amos, founded the Densmore Oil Company in Meadville. James and Amos began exploring design concepts in carrying bulk oil by rail and settled on two cylindrical wooden tanks bolted to a flat railcar. Such tanks were used by fire companies to haul water and by other producers to store wine, olive oil, vinegar, animal fats, and so on (White 1985). The Densmores found that two tanks with tight-fitting lids situated end to end on a flat railcar provided the best combination of strength and volume to accommodate a load of crude oil.

The Densmore brothers tested their vehicle in September 1865 on a trip from Oil Creek to New York, and then filed for a patent that was conferred in April 1866. Concerned the simplicity of the design would tempt imitators, they secured three more patents that year for variations on the concept. The Densmore Oil Tank Car entered production and found ready customers. In 1866–7 the car made its way through the industry, but the problems inherent in hauling heavy wooden tanks full of liquid over hundreds of miles of track could never be overcome. The loads were necessarily smallish by virtue of the design—only 3,400 gallons total in the dual tanks—with a relatively high center of gravity that encouraged wobbling. For comparison, modern oil and gasoline railcars can carry 28,000–30,000 gallons. Nevertheless, the company proved transport costs could be slashed by carrying bulk oil in large tanks rather than the standard 42-gallon barrels. Just by eliminating the barrels, the Densmore Oil Tank Car reduced transportation costs by five cents per gallon, or $170 per carload (White 1993, 366).

QWERTY

After James Densmore left the oil industry, he went into business with Christopher Latham Sholes, with whom he had partnered in Wisconsin to publish the *Telegraph*. Sholes courted Densmore to help him develop the mechanical typewriter. James noticed that the letters in early prototypes—arranged alphabetically—jammed when users typed too fast because the bars of commonly used letters were too close together. James made calculations about which letters were used most frequently, and he and brother Amos put together the famous "QWERTY" keyboard arrangement of the modern typewriter. Sholes left for other pursuits, and James, Amos, and brother Emmett created the Densmore Typewriter Company, which joined with rivals in 1893 to form the Union Typewriter Company of America.

Jeffrey B. Webb

Within a few years, oil companies and railroads encouraged innovation that led to the tubular, horizontally arranged, iron tank car. These cars originated in 1868 or 1869 with companies like J. J. Vandergrift's Star Tank Line, based in Pennsylvania. This company was acquired by Standard Oil Company in 1873 and its named changed to Union Tank Car Company, where it became part of John D. Rockefeller's expansive oil empire. In 1888, Rockefeller either owned or controlled 5,600 of the 6,100 oil tank cars in the United States, a virtual monopoly that enabled him to influence shipping prices for petroleum producers, railroads, and refinery companies ("Densmore" 2023). The iron, and later steel oil tank railcar adopted the basic concept of the Densmore Oil Tank Car but also rendered the car obsolete. In doing so, however, it secured its place in history as a link in the chain of technological development that brought the oil industry into its modern form.

Jeffrey B. Webb

See also: Drake, Edwin Laurentine; Oil Tankers; Pennsylvania Oil Boom; Rockefeller, John D.; Seaman, Elizabeth Cochrane "Nellie Bly"; Standard Oil Company; Steele, John Washington "Coal Oil Johnny"

FURTHER READING

Current, Richard N. 1947. "The First Newspaperman in Oshkosh." *The Wisconsin Magazine of History*. June. Vol. 30. No. 4. Pp. 408–22.

"Densmore Tank Cars Historical Marker." 2023. Explore PA History. Behind the Marker. https://explorepahistory.com/hmarker.php?markerId=1-A-1CC (accessed October 2023).

Pees, Samuel T., and Richard Senges. 2004. "The Densmore Brothers and America's First Successful Railway Oil Tank Car, 1865." *Oil-Industry History*. Vol. 5. No. 1. Pp. 3–17.

"The Story of James Densmore and the First Typewriter." 2016. *The Crawford Messenger*. May 15. http://crawfordpahistory.blogspot.com/2016/05/the-story-of-james-densmore-and-first.html (accessed October 2023).

White, John H. 1985. "Almost on the Right Track: The Densmore Tank Car." *Pennsylvania Heritage*. Summer Issue.

White, John H. 1993. *The American Railroad Freight Car: From the Wood-car Era to the Coming of Steel*. Baltimore: Johns Hopkins University Press.

Digital Revolution

The Digital Revolution refers to the rise of digital technologies to displace the mechanical and analogue electronic devices that shaped American life for much of the twentieth century. The impact of digital technologies on US energy use is mixed and continues to evolve. Computers and the forms of automation that they enabled have improved energy efficiency for producers and consumers while also deepening dependence on electricity. The ongoing rise of the internet has revolutionized communication and business, but it also demands large amounts of electricity to run data centers and far-flung mineral resources to build and power the proliferating electronic devices that often end up as "e-waste" in the Global South (Cubitt 2017). Much of the current importance of the Digital Revolution resides in its *potential* to inaugurate a low-carbon electric energy regime that could avert catastrophic climate change, reconfigure geopolitics, and reshape social life. The techno-utopian tendencies of Digital Revolution advocates, however, tend to elide significant challenges to its future, which include issues of privacy, energy dependence, and environmental destruction.

Although the historical roots of the Digital Revolution are long and complex, a few key technological advances in the post-war United States initiated its development. First, in 1947–8, engineers at Bell Labs invented the transistor, which enabled computers and other electronic devices to become smaller and to use much less power than analogue and vacuum tube computers. Second, several engineers in the late 1950s, including Jack Kilby of Texas Instruments, developed the integrated circuit. Small, light, and relatively inexpensive, integrated circuits dramatically increased the amount of computing power that could be located on a small chip, further enabling the miniaturization of computers and other electronic devices. Shortly thereafter, Intel co-founder Gordon Moore predicted that computing power expressed as the number of transistors on a chip would double every few years. Moore's Law, as it came to be known, held true into the early twenty-first century (O'Regan 2016, 5–7). Third, in the 1970s and 1980s, computer and software companies like Microsoft, Apple, and Oracle developed applications that encouraged the adoption of computers and electronic devices in business and everyday life. With the spread of the internet in the 1990s, the revolutionary capacities of digital technologies evolved still further.

The coming of the Digital Revolution benefited from the 1970s energy crisis, which primed American business and policymakers to pursue energy efficiency. The energy crisis punctured the illusion that the United States could wantonly burn fossil fuels to drive its economic growth and revealed the risks inherent in depending on foreign oil. So, while most Americans increased their use of electronic gadgets and fossil fueled machines after the energy crisis ended, economic pressure from higher energy prices, new energy efficiency legislation, and technological change led to gains in energy efficiency. Small computer chips improved the efficiency of car engines and regulated home heating systems to reduce waste, effectively slowing down the rate of growth in energy demand (Nye 1998, 238). Consumers bought energy-efficient appliances, insulated their homes and, for a time, preferred smaller, fuel-efficient cars.

Building on America's existing networks of electricity and telephone lines, the spread of computers also reshaped production and consumption patterns in ways that profoundly affected American workers. Improvements in global communications supported deindustrialization through the outsourcing of energy-intensive manufacturing jobs. In the wake of the energy crisis and the associated crisis of profitability in the 1970s, communication technology enabled American corporations to exploit lower wages and lower environmental standards of poorer countries. Computer software also aided the arrival of "lean production," which further devastated the working-class jobs that had been the backbone of America's post-war economic success. Nearly 12 million American workers lost their jobs between 1979 and 1984 to outsourcing and plant redesign made possible by computerization (Nye 1998, 242). Culturally, the spread of ever-smaller electronic broadcast and communication technologies reshaped how people interacted, worked, and relaxed. Thus, as David Nye notes, "electronic networks made energy systems even more central to the functioning of society than before while reducing the amount of energy needed to operate its constituent parts" (1998, 240).

Despite its fundamental role in these changes, the import of the Digital Revolution for American energy history remains largely speculative. Fossil fuels and nuclear power still dominate the nation's energy mix, including in the generation of electricity. Dependence on automobiles, electronic gadgets, communication systems, and networks has only deepened over time. Advocates for digital technologies, however, claim that they have truly revolutionary potential to foster a low-carbon energy transition. As British economist Dieter Helm notes, the spread of digital technology will increase reliance on electricity because "everything that is digital is electric" (Helm 2017, 6). As manufacturers continue to adopt robots, AI, and 3D printing, and as transportation is electrified, electricity will become the most important form of energy in the US economy, which will make the nation's economy more amenable to decarbonization (Helm 2017, 65). According to Helm, this new electric energy regime could use energy more efficiently through smart meters and broadband hubs programmed to manage household energy use for maximal efficiency (2017, 78, 81). Alphabet's now defunct Sidewalk Labs project in Toronto, which proposed to create sustainable cities in part through digital innovation, is just one example of how this narrative has been circulated by tech companies. (Sidewalk Labs 2017). But the catch, as Helm acknowledges, is that energy efficiency is a synonym for cost savings that often translate into greater demand. *How* electricity is produced is therefore crucial to the nature and future of the Digital Revolution (Helm 2017, 84).

The revolutionary potential of digital technologies to create a low-carbon energy regime depends on the development of sustainable electricity production at sufficient scale. Historically, electricity has been generated by coal—and oil-fired power plants, hydroelectric dams, and nuclear power plants, all of which cause significant environmental damage. A sustainable electric future must rely on wind and, most importantly, solar energy. The challenge of these forms of power generation is that they are intermittent—when the wind ceases to blow (or blows too hard) and the sun goes down, demand can quickly overwhelm supply. If the Digital Revolution is to break its reliance on fossil fuels and nuclear reactors, it will require significant advancements in alternative energy storage.

To date, the digitalization of American life has depended on energy stored in lithium ion batteries. These batteries have been relatively resistant to dramatic improvement, though companies like Tesla, Inc. are working aggressively to improve their capacities (Helm 2017, 72–3). Other possible storage solutions include commercializing better batteries, developing "demand dispatch" networks run by software, or improving alternatives like pumped-storage hydro power (Crabtree 2015; Fairley 2015). Other proposals for managing intermittency include long-distance transmission and distribution to overcome local weather variability. Each of these solutions face significant political, economic, and technological challenges.

Aside from achieving low-carbon sustainability, the revolutionary potential of digitalization extends to geopolitics. The United States and Europe enjoy technological advantages over other nations that put them in a position to benefit substantially from a transition to high-tech green energy grids. Indeed, many boosters see in digitalization powered by alternative energy a solution to the problem of oil dependence first raised by the 1970s energy crisis. Oil states like Russia, Saudi Arabia, and Iran would suffer as demand for fossil fuels dries up, while the United States and Europe could achieve energy independence and renewed geopolitical vigor.

Breathless predictions of a zero-carbon society based on renewable electricity, digital technology, and high-tech batteries all-too-often elide the materiality of the Digital Revolution and the real environmental and social costs that it entails. The growth of the internet and its myriad connected devices requires substantial inputs of electricity, much of which is generated by fossil fuels and nuclear power. Only significant technological advances will change this situation. Furthermore, digital technologies rely on several minerals—including lithium, aluminum, and tin—whose extraction involves ecological harm, particularly in the Global South and on Indigenous land. Some such minerals, like lithium, are also stalked by the threat of exhaustion, particularly if demand skyrockets alongside digitalization (Cubitt 2017). E-waste and the cheap manufacture of products essential to Digital Revolution, such as semiconductors, expose workers, communities, and nature to hazardous chemicals and other forms of pollution. Finally, committing to the Digital Revolution entails the mass collection and use of data, which raises serious concerns about privacy and corporate power. The Digital Revolution may have introduced substantial changes to the economic and social fabric of the United States, and it may be an important piece of the energy transition puzzle. But its many drawbacks suggest that it could also mean business as usual when it comes to pollution, resource extraction, violence, and deepening inequality.

Caleb Wellum

See also: Bell Laboratories; Electricity; Energy Crisis of the 1970s; Fuel Cell; Lithium-ion Battery; Renewable Energy; Smart Grid; Solar Power; Wind Power

FURTHER READING

Crabtree, George. 2015. "The Energy-Storage Revolution." *Nature*. Vol. 526. P. 92.

Cubitt, Sean. 2017. *Finite Media: Environmental Implications of Digital Technologies*. Durham, NC: Duke University Press.

Fairley, Peter. 2015. "Power Revolution." *Nature*. Vol. 526. Pp. 102–4.

Helm, Dieter. 2017. *Burn Out: The Endgame for Fossil Fuels*. New Haven: Yale University Press.

Nye, David. 1998. *Consuming Power: A Social History of American Energies*. Cambridge, MA: The MIT Press.

O'Regan, Gerard. 2016. *Introduction to the History of Computing*. Cham: Springer International.

Sidewalk Labs. 2017. "Building the Energy Efficient Neighborhoods of Tomorrow." https://web.archive.org/web/20200531111941/https://www.sidewalklabs.com/blog/building-the-energy-efficient-neighborhoods-of-tomorrow/ (accessed October 2023).

Drake, Edwin Laurentine

Born in Greenville, New York the son of a farming family, Edwin Laurentine Drake (1819–80) spent the early years of his life working on the family farm, first in New York and then in Vermont. As a young man Drake moved to Michigan to help on his uncle's farm, working odd jobs in the steamboat and hotel industries along the way. After stints as a clerk in Connecticut and New York City, Drake settled down with his first wife in Springfield, Massachusetts in December of 1845. For the next half-decade he worked as an express agent for the Boston & Albany Railroad, then progressed to be a conductor on the New York and New Haven line until forced due to health concerns to leave that post several years later. Drake's first wife having died in childbirth, he married his second wife, who was to bear him three children.

Living in New Haven in 1857, Drake met James M. Townsend, a fateful acquaintance who sent him to Pennsylvania in December of 1857, a journey that helped to write Drake's name into the history books under the fictitious honorific title of "Colonel," as ever afterwards Drake was known. Townsend was a Connecticut banker and an early investor in the budding oil industry, as well as founder of the Pennsylvania Rock Oil Company. Although some basic uses of petroleum had long been known, it was during this period that it became apparent that kerosene could be produced from oil as well as from coal, and the market seemed poised for a viable commercial replacement for the whale oil still widely utilized to provide light in American homes. Drake and Townsend became acquainted through the Pennsylvania Rock Oil Company, of which Drake owned a few shares. Townsend was in need of eyes on the scene in Titusville, Pennsylvania, and since Drake was in need of a job, Townsend dispatched him to oversee the company holdings in that region in December of 1857, where his letters of introduction referred to him as Colonel Drake.

Drake returned from Titusville with such a glowing assessment that shareholders in the Pennsylvania Rock Oil Company spun off a subsidiary of which Drake was immediately named the executive officer. Drake was also a shareholder in this newly formed Seneca Oil Company, a corporation that took its name from the Native Americans known for collecting and using surface-seepage petroleum scooped from atop standing water. In the spring of 1858, Drake promptly returned to Titusville with his family in tow to begin trying in earnest to drill for oil. Oil in that region of Pennsylvania was widespread and largely was discovered when it seeped to the surface, floating on top of water like scum and staining mud black. Traditional methods of collection of such petroleum included scooping the oil off the surface, as well as digging trenches in likely spots. Drake proposed to drill for oil, just as early Americans drilled for salt in proximity to salt licks and springs. Stymied by numerous technical and logistical challenges, the company struggled to find its footing in trying and uncertain economic times, and Drake might have abandoned the project had not a savior arrived in spring of 1859 in the person of William A. Smith, known to posterity as "Uncle Billy" Smith. Smith's professional savvy as a driller combined with Drake's innovation of sheathing the drill in metal piping was to lead to the establishment of a successful industrial oil well in the late summer of 1859. As the story goes, the drill crew had run the shaft down to just shy of 70 feet before breaking for the weekend; when Smith arrived to inspect the site, he found that oil had seeped to the top of the well. As word of this achievement spread, oil wells in the vicinity proliferated, although Drake himself seems to have done little to capitalize upon the new boom. Continuing to work in the area for the next few years, Drake also served for a time as a Justice of the Peace, eventually relocating in 1863 to New York City.

The rest of Drake's life was marred by ill health and bad financial decisions, and he soon found himself both unable to work and bereft of his life savings. Grateful for the role he had played in their local prosperity, however, the people of Titusville raised funds to benefit Drake and his family. Drake moved to Bethlehem, Pennsylvania in 1870, and in 1873, the Pennsylvania legislature granted him an annual stipend as recompense for his contributions to the oil industry in the Commonwealth. Drake died and was buried in Bethlehem in 1880, but twenty-one years later, funds were provided for a monument to him in Titusville and his remains were transferred there.

Rather like Jacob Cist, an early American anthracite pioneer who failed to profit personally from the industry he helped to bring to fruition, Colonel Drake was an important advocate and innovator in the development of commercial oil-well drilling who did not get rich for his efforts. However, his work laid the foundations for many oil fortunes to follow. This was primarily because he did not patent his method of protecting the oil well from dirt, gravel, sand, water, mud, and other contaminants by running a metal pipe around the drill shaft, so that the oil could flow up unimpeded and unadulterated. This method also allowed for much deeper drilling, sometimes screwing through a yard of rock a day and potentially plunging much further into the ground than traditional well-digging methods of Drake's day. This innovation—widely copied by Drake's rivals and competitors—was to prove indispensable to profitable oil drilling. The resulting rush of petroleum led both to an oil boom in Pennsylvania and to the end of the whale oil industry. A whaleship could not collect in months or years at sea what a gushing petroleum rig could produce in days or weeks from the ground. For the technical advance of the pipe-driving oil drill, in particular, Drake—though hardly a household name to most Americans—is widely celebrated in the financial history and technical publications of the oil industry to this very day.

Christopher R. Fee

See also: Benedum, Michael Late; Cist, Jacob; Densmore Oil Tank Car; Hart, William Aaron; Kier, Samuel Martin; Pennsylvania Oil Boom; Petroleum; Steele, John Washington "Coal Oil Johnny"; Sweeney, Peter; Whale Oil

FURTHER READING

Davé, Urja. 2008. "Edwin Drake and the Oil Well Drill Pipe." Pennsylvania Center for the Book. Penn State University Libraries. State College, PA. Summer.https://pabook.libraries.psu.edu/literary-cultural-heritage-map-pa/feature-articles/edwin-drake-and-oil-well-drill-pipe (accessed March 29, 2021).

"Edwin Drake." 2008. *They Made America*. WGBH History Unit. July 7. http://www.pbs.org/wgbh/theymadeamerica/whomade/drake_hi.html (accessed March 29, 2021).

Giddens, Paul H., Donald H. Kent, and Sanford W. Higginbotham. 1975. "Edwin L. Drake and the Birth of the Petroleum Industry." Harrisburg, PA: Pennsylvania Historical and Museum Commission.

Harris, Walter. 2009. "Defining Moment: Edwin Drake Strikes Oil—and Launches the Petroleum Industry, 1859." *The Financial Times Limited*. October 23. https://www.proquest.com/trade-journals/defining-moment-edwin-drake-strikes-oil-launches/docview/229285228/se-2?accountid=2694 (accessed March 22, 2021).

Lach, Edward L. Jr. 2008. "Drake, Edwin Laurentine (29 March 1819–08 November 1880)." *American National Biography*. Oxford: Oxford University Press. https://www.anb.org/view/10.1093/anb/9780198606697.001.0001/anb-9780198606697-e-1002291 (accessed March 22, 2021).

Shook, Barbara. 2009. "US Oil Industry Marks 150th Anniversary." *Oil Daily*. Energy Intelligence Group. August 27. https://www.proquest.com/trade-journals/us-oil-industry-marks-150th-anniversary/docview/199168946/se-2?accountid=2694 (accessed March 22, 2021).

Weber, D. 2010. "From 'Colonel' Drake to the Marcellus Shale Gas Play: Transmission Developments." *Pipeline & Gas Journal*. Vol. 237. No. 3. Pp. 17–21. https://search.proquest.com/docview/197490779 (accessed March 25, 2021).

Duryea, Charles and J. Frank Duryea

In 1895, brothers Charles and Frank Duryea (1869–1967) patented the first self-propelled vehicle with a gasoline-powered internal combustion engine. A year later they helped formed a company called Duryea Motor Wagon Company of Springfield, Massachusetts to manufacture and sell their automobiles, the first in the United States. The brothers won acclaim with victories in early automobile races, but soon fell into disagreements over the company's future. Charles Duryea (1861–1938) went on to form the Duryea Power Company and continued to manufacture cars until the First World War. Although the Duryea brothers were overtaken by other automakers like Henry Ford, Ransom E. Olds, William C. Durant, and David Dunbar Buick, they helped to launch the American automobile industry. Today the industry consumes energy at its manufacturing and assembly plants and by shipping parts and vehicles. The industry also requires the consumption of energy in steel, aluminum, plastics, and other industries that supply automakers with parts and materials. In addition, automobiles, trucks, and other vehicles utilize gasoline, oil, and other fuels, and thus are a major consumer of energy unto themselves. Altogether, the Duryea brothers and their contemporaries helped to birth a massive transportation revolution, with its corresponding impacts on American society, economy, culture, politics, and environment.

Like the Wright brothers Orville and Wilbur, the Duryea brothers were bicycle makers at the outset. Their family moved between a few farms in central Illinois, which gave them experience tinkering with machinery. The older brother, Charles, graduated from Gittings Seminary in 1882 and worked in bicycle shops in Peoria and St. Louis before moving with his young wife to Washington, DC. In the nation's capital, Charles worked at Herbert Owns bicycle shop and studied bike patents; soon he created his own model of a bicycle designed specifically for women. Charles then designed and built several models in his "Sylph" line, which balanced the size of the wheels more evenly and included spring suspensions. In 1888, he opened the Duryea Manufacturing Company in Washington, but then moved to New Jersey and later Massachusetts seeking investment capital and a plant to manufacture his bicycles. Frank joined Charles along the way and together they settled in Springfield, Massachusetts.

Charles contracted with Ames Manufacturing Company in Springfield, Massachusetts and the Rouse-Hazard Company in Peoria, Illinois to manufacture his bicycles. Amidst these moves, Charles and Frank learned about motor carriages powered by internal combustion engines and began to experiment with their own designs. In 1892 they secured financing and a workshop in Chicopee Falls near Springfield and Charles sketched out a design for a motor car that Frank would build. Charles returned to Peoria for business and Frank continued to work on the model. In 1893, Frank fixed his one-cylinder, four-horsepower internal combustion engine into an old horse buggy and worked out the kinks in the engine's ignition and combustion while also laboring over the transmission system that linked engine to drivetrain. The buggy was successfully tested in September 1893 in Springfield, and then went through a process of modification and further road testing to improve its performance and reliability. Over the next year, Frank built a second vehicle that developed the brothers' original concepts. Importantly, unlike their first car, this model was intended for the marketplace.

After some initial difficulty, the Duryeas lined up new investors and in 1895 formed the Duryea Motor Wagon Company. Charles also secured a patent for his "road vehicle" on June 11 of that year. To get the word out, they entered the car in the fifty-mile Chicago-to-Evanston race sponsored by the Chicago *Times-Herald*, which was held that fall on Thanksgiving Day. It advertised a hefty cash prize and attracted scores of entrants. However, only six showed up for race day because it had snowed, four cars and two motorcycles. The car built by Frank and driven by Charles won the race in 10 hours 48 minutes over the second-place car built by German automaker Karl Benz (Cohn 1944, 22). Since it was the first successfully completed automobile race in the United States, it drew national attention and Duryea's vehicle was henceforth known as "the Chicago car." The company built thirteen over 1896 while continuing to promote their product. One Duryea automobile featured in P.T. Barnum's circus during the summer, billed as "The Famous Duryea Motor-Wagon, or Motorcycle, the identical Horseless Carriage that won the great race in Chicago last November" (Cohn 1944, 101). The Duryeas also entered the London-to-Brighton race in England in the fall, which they won by an hour over the second-place finisher.

Amid frustrations in 1898 over the direction of the company, the brothers sold their stakes to their business partners and began to work independently. Charles formed Duryea Manufacturing Company in Peoria and focused on building and marketing three-wheeled, four-passenger gas-powered buggies. In 1900, he moved to Reading, Pennsylvania to form the Duryea Power Company, where he helped to design three- and four-wheeled vehicles with body types named Phaeton, Electa, Runabout, and Buggyaut. When this company folded, Charles tried his hand at several more start-ups, including a company formed in Philadelphia in 1913 that returned to the production of three-wheeled vehicles, and a brief experiment in 1920 with making trucks. Charles left the industry shortly thereafter and became a consultant and automotive writer. His brother Frank had more success in the automotive industry in partnership with J. Stevens Arms and Tool Company in the Springfield area, which made cars from 1901 to 1906 until the Stevens-Duryea Company was created to concentrate on automobile manufacturing. The company focused on upscale models and ceased production in 1915 amid adverse economic conditions in the luxury market.

Neither of the Duryeas' companies enjoyed the success of Ford Motor Company, which mastered the financial, managerial, and marketing challenges of increasing the volume of production and pricing cars so that millions of middle-income consumers could afford them. The development of a mass consumer market for automobiles fed by an equally massive industrial output would be the work of other automobile pioneers. However, the Duryeas have a place in history. In an interview for the *New York Times* marking the centennial anniversary of the Duryea Motor Wagon Company's production of thirteen cars, Richard P. Scharchburg, historian of the early automobile, noted: "'It was the first time that an automobile company was organized and produced more than one car from a single design'" (McEwen 1996). The company made a very modest start on what would become one of the most impactful industries in US history. Automobile manufacturers changed the way Americans lived, worked, and even defined their identities. The industry also transformed ordinary Americans' relationship to energy by forming a dependency on fossil fuels, with a host of complicated and long-lasting political, social, and environmental consequences.

Jeffrey B. Webb

See also: Bowser, Sylvanus Freelove; Ford, Henry; Interstate Highway System; Petroleum; Sport Utility Vehicles; Tokheim Oil Tank & Pump Company; Truck Transportation Technology; Whiting Refinery

FURTHER READING

Cohn, David L. 1944. *Combustion on Wheels: An Informal History of the Automobile Age*. Boston: Houghton Mifflin Company.

May, George W. 2000. "Duryea, Charles Edgar." *American National Biography*. Oxford: Oxford University Press. https://www.anb.org/display/10.1093/anb/9780198606697.001.0001/anb-9780198606697-e-1000484?rskey=VFOVKU&result=1 (accessed October 2023).

McEwen, Charles. 1996. "For Better or Worse, the Car Turns 100." *The New York Times*. June 9. https://www.nytimes.com/1996/06/09/automobiles/for-better-or-worse-the-car-turns-100.html (accessed October 2023).

Scharchburg, Richard P. 1993. *Carriages without Horses: J. Frank Duryea and the Birth of the American Automobile Industry*. New York: Society of Automotive Engineers.

Dysart, Stella

Stella Dysart (1878–1966) was a very lucky woman. In 1955, at the end of her rope and the end of her life, she engaged in one last opportunity to finally strike it rich. She allowed a scientist/prospector to search her land for uranium, the new mineral powering the recently launched Atomic Age. Instead of finding more of the failure that had walked with her all her life, she found that she was actually sitting on the world's largest supply of high-grade uranium. This discovered helped spark the uranium mining boom in the 1950s and 1960s in the American West.

Energy, in all its forms and sources, has played an important role in the story of humanity since before the development of the first civilizations. The amounts of energy available to a tribe, city, kingdom, republic, or empire determined what was possible for any of those states or civilizations (Rhodes 2018, 3–6). At first it was human energy, which was then followed by energy harnessed from fire, animals, water, and minerals like coal. All of these sources of energy powered the rise and fall of civilizations from Babylon to the British Empire (Rhodes 2018, 10–15). For those thousands of years, humans believed they had, for the most part, discovered the chief sources of energy available to human civilization.

But human civilization had not discovered all of the available energy sources available to be harnessed. For example, people had known of the existence of oil and natural gas since the days of the Akkadian and Babylonian Empires in Ancient Mesopotamia but had no large-scale use for them. They were considered a novelty, something to use on a small scale, and not something worth a large-scale investment or investigation. This began to change in the nineteenth century as Europeans and Americans began to explore, settle, and harness the energy of the world in new ways.

In the United States, this energy change would start in the region that would eventually become the Midwest and would change American society in ways that weren't imaginable in the late eighteenth and early nineteenth centuries. The seed of this change had its origins in Southern New York. In that region, in 1821, William Hart dug a hole. This hole, and the borehole that followed, became the first natural gas well dug on purpose in the nation. Hart used this new source of energy to power the lights, or better the lamps, of a nearby inn (Jacobs and Branden 2008, 55). Following Hart's natural gas well was the first purposed-drilled oil well in the United States, and possibly in the world. That well, drilled in 1859 by George Bissell and Edwin Drake, was located near Oil Creek near Titusville, Pennsylvania. Other wells across Western Pennsylvania, West Virginia, Ohio, and Kentucky produced oil before Bissell and Drake had drilled their well in Pennsylvania, but it was only as a by-product of looking for salt brine (Dochuk 2019, 21–5).

This well, known as the Drake well, set off a search for oil and the creation of a new industry in Pennsylvania. This new industry provided materials that could be turned into fuel, lubricant, and other things (Dochuk 2019, 25–30). A new source of energy and a new civilizational building tool had been introduced into the American system. The American oil industry spread from its cradle on Oil Creek through the neighboring states of Ohio and Indiana and down into the American Southwest, specifically Louisiana, Texas, Oklahoma, and New Mexico. By the time the American oil industry had spread to the American Southwest, it was the largest in the world. It is at this point that Stella Dysart enters the story.

One of the myths surrounding the American frontier, whether that frontier was located in Indiana, Washington State, or New Mexico, was that anyone could make it big. The frontier erases class distinctions and allows anybody, whether man or woman, to try to make it big. This is what Stella Dysart wanted to achieve. Dysart, born in Slater, Missouri in 1878, moved to New Mexico with her husband in 1923 to enter the real estate and oil businesses. The Dysarts wanted to make it big, especially Stella. Eventually, she and her two companies, the New Mexico Oil Properties Association and the Dysart Oil Company acquired 150,000 acres of land in the Ambrosia Lake area of New Mexico (Wells 2013). It seemed like she had everything necessary to make it big and move up in the world.

Over the next thirty years, Stella Dysart was a complete failure in the oil business, a complete failure as a real estate agent, and a complete failure as a criminal. Dysart drilled dry wells and sold nearly worthless pieces of property to desperate people. She and her associates committed multiple counts of conspiracy, labor law violations, and grand theft. For example, at one point, she and her associates were charged with sixty counts of conspiracy (Wells 2013). During her time in New Mexico, she acquired more criminal charges than barrels of oil or profitable pieces of land. These criminal charges drove away potential financial opportunities, and Dysart and her businesses went bankrupt. She served fifteen months in the local county jail (Wells 2013). When she got out of jail in March 1941, she was bankrupt with no real prospects. It seemed like she failed for good.

Then, at the end of her first thirty years in New Mexico, fortune, luck, favor, or a combination of the three, smiled down on her. In 1955, Dysart, who by then was seventy-eight years of age and nearly $25,000 in debt, allowed, on a whim, uranium prospector Louis Lothman onto her property to search for uranium. Lothman's search led him to discover that Stella Dysart owned the world's largest deposit of high-grade uranium (Wells 2013). Instantly she went from being a poor old woman to a very rich old woman. She had gone west in search of riches associated with America's oil industry but instead she had, by accident, found her way into the riches associated with America's, and the world's, newest energy source: uranium. She got to enjoy her newfound riches and fame until 1966 when she died.

Historians B.A. and K.L. Wells said this about her life: "there must be a little more to her story, but as someone said of Truth—'it lies hidden in a crooked well'" (Wells 2013). She went in search of oil, and like so many before her, failed horribly at it. Only a few actually made it rich by finding and developing the oil they were searching for. Stella went broke trying to find oil, only to strike it rich with uranium. Her rags to riches story is the story of celebrated Americans, both men and women, who made their mark in any number of US industries.

Jeff Hirschy

See also: Atomic Energy Acts; Church Rock Uranium Mill Spill; Navajo Reservation Uranium Mining; Nuclear Power; Nuclear Regulatory Commission; Nuclear Waste Policy Act of 1982; Steen, Charles Augustus; Yucca Mountain Nuclear Waste Repository

FURTHER READING

Armitage, Merle, and Dennis Chavez. 1959. *Stella Dysart of Ambrosia Lake: Courage, Fortitude and Uranium*. New York: Duell, Sloan, and Pearce.
Amundson, Michael A. 2004. *Yellowcake Towns: Uranium Mining Communities in the American West*. Boulder, CO: University Press of Colorado.
Dochuk, Darren. 2019. *Anointed with Oil: How Christianity and Crude Made Modern America*. New York: Basic Books.
Jacobs, Dennis Allen, and Karen Anita Branden. 2008. *From McEnergy to EcoEnergy: America's Transition to Sustainable Energy*. Pittsburgh: Dorrance Publishing.
Rhodes, Richard. 2018. *Energy: A Human History*. New York: Simon & Schuster.
Wells, B.A., and K.L. Wells. 2013. "Mrs. Dysart's Uranium Well." American Oil & Gas Historical Society. https://aoghs.org/petroleum-pioneers/uranium/ (accessed May 29, 2020).

Earth Day

Earth Day is an environmentally focused annual observance in the United States and recognized globally. It was first established on April 22, 1970, as a national agreement among the American public and government officials to take a stand on addressing environmental issues. Earth Day's origin stemmed from a build-up of social, environmental, and economic conflicts during the 1960s and 1970s. Its establishment corresponded with beginning of the modern environmental movement, and it played a role in expanding the movement. This day inspired the creation of the US Environmental Protection Agency (EPA), influenced new legislation across various environmental issues, and expanded options for the advancement of new technology and energy.

In the early 1900s, some laws and regulations were created to address certain environmental issues like air and water pollution. Rachel Carson (1907–64) began questioning the lack of environmental legislation and regulation, specifically what chemicals were being used on crops and in the environment. In her book *Silent Spring* (1962), Carson made the scientific case that the pesticide dichloro-diphenyl-trichloroethane (DDT) was a threat to human and wildlife welfare (Robertson 2017, 12). She also encouraged citizens to engage and be informed on matters that, at the time, were typically left to scientists and government officials. *Silent Spring* instilled a spirit of participatory democracy to ordinary citizens across the country and ignited a spark that unknowingly would lay a path for environmental change.

Soon after her book appeared, the United States suffered a few environmental and economic disasters. The Santa Barbara oil spill on January 28, 1969, was a key event. This spill was the result of an attempted offshore drilling platform shutoff, which lead to a mix of crude oil and gas leaching into the Santa Barbara Channel in California. Although this mixture was still leaching into the water, it was thought to have been at least contained within the channel. As it continued leaching well into February, oil and gas was found polluting the coastlines, harbors, and beaches of southern California, causing harm to the wildlife along the coast (FWPCA 1969). The second major event was the Cuyahoga River fire in Cleveland, Ohio on June 22, 1969, which was caused by a misplaced flare thrown into the debris- and oil-choked river. Fires on this river were not uncommon or unfamiliar to Clevelanders though, as it had burned more than ten times before this specific event.

What changed was the social attitudes towards these kinds of events. This shift was in part due to the Santa Barbara oil spill, Rachel Carson's impact on social awareness, and other less prominent environmental events. The "people largely saw the river a part of industrial infrastructure. In that light, a river fire seemed more normal. It is when we view a river as a natural system that a fire seems out of place" (NPS 2022). This combination of events, among many others, is what built up a social and environmental shift in the United States. With overwhelming citizen support coming into 1970, Wisconsin Senator Gaylord Nelson (1916–2005) put together the idea of a teach-in for the environment. His efforts culminated in a one-day event in which 20 million people across the United States came together to support the environment. This cemented Earth Day as an annual April 22 national observance (NPS 2023).

Earth Day was the first giant leap toward governmental and grassroot actions. The EPA was established in December of 1970, and just ten years after Earth Day was declared there were already twelve acts put into law to protect air, water, resources, conservation, and land. Throughout the 1970s and 1980s, another crisis emerged, an energy shortage. Oil prices jumped nearly 350 percent and energy became an economic crisis and environmental priority (NMAH 2021). Due to low supply, energy efficiency became a major solution for decreasing demand, and alternative types of energy were being pursed. NASA, already having experience with other forms of energy, began working with the EPA, the Department of Energy, and the Department of the State to develop more efficient and cleaner forms of energy (Dunbar 2008). NASA began pursuing solar and wind power more intently due to the crisis, but it also focused efforts on automotive pollution and hydrogen engine models. The Public Utility Regulatory Policies Act of 1978 was one attempt at promoting energy efficiency and domestic renewable energy. Soon after, the Energy Security Act of 1980 was created, which incentivized the creation and innovation of renewable energy sources like wind, solar, biomass, and geothermal. The energy crisis had placed renewable energy at the forefront for new development and was being used as a solution to help alleviate the crisis' economic effects.

Earth Day had a profound effect on the environmental movement, public conversation about energy policy, and social and cultural life in America since its inception. The environmental movement produced meaningful change in how citizens perceived the environmental problems associated with energy development and consumption. Recent Earth Day observances address a much greater range of issues that go well into and beyond the event's original focus. Every April 22, initiatives are staged throughout the country such as river cleanups, plastic waste cleanups, anti-deforestation efforts, social justice campaigns, climate change activities, green job fairs, corporate sustainability investments, and renewed advocacy. Today the event still pursues the same objective that Senator Gaylord Nelson in 1970 proclaimed, "to show the political leadership of the Nation that there was broad and deep support for the environmental movement" (Nelson 2016).

> Rachel Carson's book *The Sea around Us* was on the *New York Times* bestseller list for eighty-six weeks. It showed the interconnectedness of nature and living things. Carson's *Silent Spring* was critical to Earth Day and the environmental movement though, because it laid the foundation by making the public aware of nature's vulnerability to human intervention.
>
> *Michael T. Terronez*

Climate change has emerged as the most critical environmental issue of the early twenty-first century. The issue of climate change encompasses a wide array of subjects, the most discussed topic being greenhouse gas emissions. Within that framework, energy and transportation are largely the focus of current governmental actions addressing climate change. The US's electrical grid systems are at an all-time high for energy demand with more consumer electronic usage, growing populations to supply, and a new electric vehicle market. In response to popular concerns about climate change, as well as the work of environmental groups in pushing for changes in public policy, the demand to convert from coal and gas power and to renewable energy sources has also dramatically increased. Fortune 500 companies, large foundations and non-profit organizations, and city governments have since vowed to pursue net zero buildings, zero-carbon emission energy production and consumptions, and other energy-related goals.

The supply and demand of energy has dramatically shifted in the last several decades, and energy market volatility will be even more pronounced over the next few years. Energy trends are shaped by wars and political conflicts, as well as international trade disputes, which seem to intensify year by year. Just as in the 1970s and 1980s, political leaders and the media continue to push for US energy independence, and a reduction in the consumption of foreign oil. The future of how the United States will supply its increasing energy needs is unpredictable. What can be certain is that the widespread concerns about, and actions toward the environment can be tied to the popular awareness created by Earth Day, which is renewed annually in the United States and around the world.

Michael T. Terronez

See also: Clean Air Act of 1970; Clean Water Act; Energy Crisis of the 1970s; Energy Security Act of 1980; Natural Resources Defense Council; Public Utility Regulatory Policies Act of 1978; Santa Barbara Oil Spill; Sierra Club; Union of Concerned Scientists; US Environmental Protection Agency

FURTHER READING

Dunbar, Brian. 2008. "Glenn Responds to 1970s Energy Crisis." National Aeronautics and Space Administration. April 10. https://www.nasa.gov/centers/glenn/about/history/70s_energy.html (accessed October 2023).

FWPCA (Federal Water Pollution Control Administration). 1969. "Review of Santa Barbara Channel Oil Pollution Incident." U.S. Department of the Interior. January 8. https://nepis.epa.gov/Exe/ZyPURL.cgi?Dockey=9101SXDN.txt (accessed October 2023).

Massachusetts Institute of Technology (MIT). 2022. "Earth Day." MIT Climate Portal. Accessed July 18, 2022. https://climate.mit.edu/earthday (accessed October 2023).

NMAH (National Museum of American History). 2021. "Energy Crisis." https://americanhistory.si.edu/american-enterprise-exhibition/consumer-era/energy-crisis (accessed July 17, 2022).

Natural Resources Defense Council (NRDC). 2015. "The Story of Silent Spring." https://www.nrdc.org/stories/story-silent-spring (accessed July 21, 2022).

Nelson, Gaylord. 2016. "Earth Day '70: What It Meant." US Environmental Protection Agency, April 16. https://www.epa.gov/archive/epa/aboutepa/earth-day-70-what-it-meant.html (accessed October 2023).

NPS (National Park Service). 2022. "The 1969 Cuyahoga River Fire." US Department of the Interior. https://www.nps.gov/articles/story-of-the-fire.htm (accessed July 17, 2022).

NPS (National Park Service). 2023. "Earth Day." US Department of the Interior. https://www.nps.gov/subjects/npscelebrates/earth-day.htm (accessed October 2023).

Robertson, Margaret. 2017. *Sustainability Principles and Practice*. London: Routledge.

Edison, Thomas Alva

Perhaps the most famous inventor in American history, Thomas Alva Edison's name is associated with inventions as far-ranging as motion pictures, the phonograph, and the electrical infrastructures of the late nineteenth and early twentieth centuries. Beyond his personal scientific innovations, Edison was also the first "modern" public scientist, a business leader, marketer, and father of the modern research laboratory. Though recent revisionists have called attention to Edison's alleged patent thefts and poor treatment of his employees, his vast influence on the history of technology and American energy remains undeniable.

Thomas Edison (1847–1931) was born in Milan, Ohio in 1847 to a family of Canadian political refugees. The youngest of seven children, of whom only four survived to adulthood, the young Edison showed an early interest in mechanical and chemical experiments, even after he went to work in 1859, selling candy and newspapers to travelers on Detroit's Grand Trunk Railroad. Edison even carried out his experiments on board trains before an accidental fire briefly paused his scientific career

At the same time, the twelve-year-old Edison became almost completely deaf, a condition that would remain with him all his life. The cause is unknown, given the state of medicine in the era and the poor financial state of the Edison family at the time, with theories ranging from a childhood bout of scarlet fever to an injury to Edison's ears while working at the Grand Trunk. Given his severe struggles in school even before he went to work at the railroad and his son Charles' deafness, a congenital explanation seems likely. This was an era when being hard of hearing could have meant the end of Edison's independence, he generally treated it as a strength in his scientific research.

In 1862, Edison was trained as a telegraph operator by J.U. Mackenzie, whose son Edison had saved from a railroad accident that year. Taking advantage of this lucrative career in America's first "wired" business, Edison traveled through the United States during the 1860s, taking telegraph jobs to support his chemical and mechanical tinkering. In 1869, Edison patented his first invention—an electric voting machine.

Edison's first financial successes came not long after, from the telegraph industry specifically and electrical engineering in general. In 1869, he formed an electrical engineering firm that later merged with the Gold and Stock Telegraph Co. in 1870. Later in the decade, Edison founded the Newark Telegraph Works and the American Telegraph Works to pursue his ideas for improving telegraphy. Edison was embroiled in his first major patent lawsuit in this period when he sold his design for a quadruplex telegraph, which could send two messages simultaneously in both directions, to Atlantic and Pacific Telegraph. At the time, he was employed by Western Union, and Western Union ultimately won the subsequent lawsuit.

Perhaps this helps explain why the recently married Edison steered away from telegraph work about this time, and in 1876 opened his famous research laboratory at Menlo Park in New Jersey. Nicknamed "The Invention Factory" with its many staffers working on multiple projects, it was perhaps the first modern research laboratory in America, marking a sharp break from the "lone genius" inventors of a previous generation. In 1878, having worked for several years on an upgraded telephone transmitter, Edison produced the speaking phonograph—but the limited technology of the time meant that audio recording would remain a novelty for a decade.

> **ELECTRIC LIGHTS: NOT ALL USES ARE GOOD**
>
> Electric lights were used in 1923 to light up a cross at a KKK night rally in Roanoke, Indiana where over two thousand people reportedly were in attendance with some four hundred automobiles: "The speakers stand was arranged in front of the grandstand in the ball diamond and was built upon a truck, above which a cross that was aluminated [*sic*] by electric lights was displayed" (*Roanoke Beacon*, July 27, 1923, p. 1, c. 5).
>
> *Michael Davis*

Edison then pivoted towards electric lights and founded the Edison Electric Light Company at the end of the year. The work proved difficult, given the need to design both the bulb itself and the electrical power system that would make lighting the bulb possible. By 1879, Menlo Park was itself lit by electricity, and in 1881 with the carbonized thread problem solved, Edison's electric light factory opened in Newark. A year after that, the world's first commercial electric light system was installed in Lower Manhattan, powered by the Pearl Street Station. By 1883, more than 10,000 electric lamps were in use by more than 500 customers. Like many industrialists of Gilded Age America, Edison sought a monopoly on his product—but soon found himself faced with stiff competition from rivals like George Westinghouse in the so-called "War of the Currents." By the end of the decade, Westinghouse's alternating current had become dominant, and by the early 1890s Edison, still committed to using direct current, had largely retreated from the electrical business.

By this point Edison, a widower, had remarried and moved into a mansion in West Orange near his new laboratory with Mina Miller, his new wife, and children. In 1887, he returned to working on the phonograph, and an encounter with Eadweard Muybridge sparked Edison's interest in motion pictures. As usual, Edison was uninterested in partnership and in 1889, his employee William K.L. Dickson presented Edison with one of the first motion picture cameras, an invention Edison would soon take credit for. Then, three years later, came the Kinetoscope, a nickelodeon-style motion picture viewer.

Kinetoscope "parlors" soon spread through the nation, transforming what had been a minor project into a rapidly growing industry that was itself in the process of transformation. Theater operators were shifting from individual viewing machines to motion picture projection. Though initially reluctant to shift to projection, by 1896 Edison was marketing the Vitascope, an early projector invented by Thomas Armat and Charles Francis Jenkins, under his own name to considerable financial success.

In 1911, Edison's "brand" was organized into Thomas A. Edison, Incorporated, an business operation that sought to sustain Edison's existing markets rather than develop new technologies—with Edison himself ironically playing little role in the day-to-day operations of the company that bore his name.

In the meantime, the Edison monopoly over motion pictures, eventually broken by the federal courts in 1915, gave Edison enormous power over shaping how Americans viewed the world, with some of the first recorded "news footage" of conflicts like the Spanish–American War in 1898 having been recreated from eyewitness accounts by Edison employees. But with his monopoly broken and experiments with "talkie" pictures a failure, Edison largely abandoned the motion picture business after the First World War.

Meanwhile, having neglected the rights to the phonograph in the previous decade, Edison gradually regained them and in 1896 started the National Phonograph Company to make phonographs for home use. In 1912, the Edison phonographs adopted discs, custom-made for Edison players, and took advantage of the rising interest in the new medium. Edison's own phonograph company eventually stopped making new records at the beginning of the Great Depression, but by then it was an international business.

With the outbreak of the First World War, Edison worked as an adviser to the US government, encouraging the formation of what would become the first US naval research laboratory in 1923. In increasingly poor health, Edison began spending more time away from the office. In 1929, he made his last major public appearance at the dedication of a mockup of his Menlo Park facility in Henry Ford's Greenfield Village, Michigan. Two years later, he died at home in West Orange on October 18, 1931.

Edison was often in court in the midst of bitter patent infringement lawsuits, accused—credibly—with intellectual property theft. Nevertheless, he sustained a long career as a brilliant inventor in his own right, and became an efficient lab manager and talented brand marketer who wore the cloak of the "lone genius" of the previous century. Thomas Edison led the rapid technological development and the culture of innovation in the late nineteenth and early twentieth centuries, and in the process, defined many of the chief uses of energy and electricity in the modern world.

Michael Davis

See also: Bell Laboratories; Brush, Charles Francis; California Electric Light Company; Consolidated Edison Company; Electricity; General Electric Company; Henry, Joseph; Morse, Samuel; Pearl Street Power Station; Stanley, William Jr.; Tesla, Nikola; War of the Currents; Vulcan Street Plant; Westinghouse, George

FURTHER READING

Baldwin, Neil. 1995. *Edison: Inventing the Century*. Westport, CT: Hyperion Press.

Cep, Casey. 2019. "The Real Nature of Thomas Edison's Genius." *The New Yorker*. https://www.newyorker.com/magazine/2019/10/28/the-real-nature-of-thomas-edisons-genius (accessed October 2023).

Clark, Ronald William. 1977. *Edison: The Man who Made the Future*. London: MacDonald & Jane's.

Conot, Robert. 1979. *A Streak of Luck*. New York: Seaview Books.

Davis, L.J. 1998. *Fleet Fire: Thomas Edison and the Pioneers of the Electric Revolution*. New York: Doubleday.

Knapp, Alex. 2012. "Nikola Tesla Wasn't God and Thomas Edison Wasn't the Devil." *Forbes*. May 18. https://www.forbes.com/sites/alexknapp/2012/05/18/nikola-tesla-wasnt-god-and-thomas-edison-wasnt-the-devil/?sh=7be35b421a21 (accessed August 12, 2022).

Morus, Iwan. 2018. "Thomas Edison: Visionary, Genius or Fraud?" The Conversation. July 12. https://theconversation.com/thomas-edison-visionary-genius-or-fraud-99229 (accessed October 2023).

Electricity

Electricity is a form of energy that involves the generation and movement of charges. Electrical charges can be created naturally, as in thunderclouds, or artificially by various chemical and mechanical means. Electricity and magnetism together comprise one of the fundamental forces of nature. During the last two centuries people learned to manufacture electricity for use in a wide array of tasks. Although expensive and environmentally challenging to generate and transport, electricity is clean at the point of use and highly controllable, making it a critical foundation of modern societies.

Human awareness of electricity, in the form of lighting, arose with the species but electrical research began with less spectacular effects. Millennia ago, people observed that amber rubbed with fur created sparks and attracted feathers. Similarities between frictional static electricity and magnetic attraction caught the attention of many. William Gilbert (1544–1603) discussed both phenomena and began the modern era of electrical research in 1600 with his book *De Magnete*, coining the word "electricity" in the process. In Europe, the onset of Enlightenment empiricism spurred experimentation in many fields. Experiments required equipment, and in 1663 Otto von Guericke (1602–86) invented a static electricity generator. Hands held against a spinning globe of vitrified sulfur produced static charges more efficiently than rubbing amber or glass with fur (Heilbron 1979).

The static field around von Guericke's globe levitated pieces of paper and gave shocks. Natural philosophers learned that those effects could be transmitted through some substances but not others, later called conductors and insulators respectively. Static effects quickly dissipated, but in 1745 Ewald Georg von Kleist (1700–48) and Pieter van Musschenbroek (1692–1761) independently discovered a means of storing charges: the Leyden jar. Now called a capacitor, Leyden jars could store enough electricity to light fires and inflict painful injuries. Reporting on his "terrible experiment," Musschenbroek wrote that he would not "do it again for all the kingdom of France" (Heilbron 1979, 313).

The ability to inexpensively generate and store electricity with devices like glass globes and lead-coated jars accelerated the pace of research. Benjamin Franklin began performing electrical experiments in colonial Philadelphia in 1747 where, far from European debates, he could think freely. Curious about the new Leyden jars, he discovered that the electricity resided on the surfaces of the jar, not within the jar or the glass itself. Designing capacitors with flat glass plates rather than jars, he described charges as positive and negative rather than as two different electrical fluids. He also proposed practical (if dangerous) experiments to prove what many already believed, that lightning was an electrical phenomena.

Capacitors could store charges but discharged almost instantaneously. In 1800, Alessandro Volta (1745–1827) generated a steady current of electricity by alternating disks of metals like zinc and nickel between saltwater-soaked pads. His "pile," soon called a battery, enabled new experiments that quickly advanced electrical knowledge. Hans Christian Ørsted (1777–1851)

BURY THE LINES OR STRING THEM ON POLES?

Running power lines underground protects them from weather damage and preserves scenic vistas. However, underground lines cost about three times more than aerial lines to install, and require pumps and cooling fluids. Early cables carrying power under the East River to New York City contained oil pumped through holes, which carried away heat generated by electrical resistance. Lines on towers and poles are air-cooled and easier to maintain.

Harold D. Wallace Jr.

discovered that current flowing through a wire deflected compass needles. Michael Faraday (1791–1867) learned that an energized wire would rotate around a magnet, and that rapidly changing the direction of current flow in one coil of wire could induce a current in another coil. Joseph Henry (1797–1878) wrapped energized coils of wire around magnets and greatly amplified their magnetic properties: electromagnets (King 1962, vol. 1).

Early nineteenth-century experimentation firmly linked electricity and magnetism while codifying relationships between strength of charges, amount and properties of current flows, and the ability of those flows to perform work and transfer energy. Inventors devised practical applications like electroplating and telegraphy in the 1830s. Although batteries easily supplied low amounts of current for those early applications, battery banks quickly became impractically large. The knowledge that spinning a wire coil in a magnetic field produced a current in the coil led to electrical generators that outperformed batteries. The key breakthrough came in 1867 when several inventors independently created dynamos, enabling applications like electric lighting that required massive amounts of sustained electrical current. Inspired by new dynamos and early arc lighting installations, Thomas Edison (1847–1932) and his team at Menlo Park, New Jersey, invented a commercially practical incandescent lighting system in 1879. Demand for lighting drove electrification in the United States (King 1962, vol. 3).

Edison, inventor and entrepreneur, developed both the technical and commercial capabilities of his system. Existing lighting systems that burned manufactured gas or kerosene worked but were dangerous and required daily user maintenance. Edison's easy to control and simple to replace incandescent lamp consumed no oxygen and left no soot. Electric lighting systems offered so many advantages that demand grew quickly despite the initial expense of installing power lines. Such systems displayed what economists call network effects: the more people who participated, the lower the cost for each user. Edison and his competitors established electric lighting companies nationwide during the 1880s and 1890s, focusing on densely populated cities and towns since those offered the lowest service costs and highest potential profits.

They also sought to lower costs by cultivating other markets for electric power. Expensive equipment could not be allowed to sit idle during daylight hours, so electric companies began selling other devices. People brought electric appliances into their homes, while commercial and industrial users began installing electric motors and tools. Electricity ran elevators and water pumps in new buildings called skyscrapers. More applications resulted in economies of scale. As supplies of electrical equipment increased, prices dropped, while construction of larger, more efficient power stations lowered electricity prices.

Edison's system featured relatively small power plants that produced direct current (DC), like that obtained from batteries. Although more complicated to use, rotary generators create alternating current (AC) naturally and require additional components to make dc. DC systems held certain technical advantages but suffered from limited transmission range. Other entrepreneurs adopted AC to transmit power over long distances. George Westinghouse (1846–1914) combined several key inventions to create a practical ac system. William Stanley (1858–1916) upgraded transformers invented in Europe that raised and lowered the strength of AC current. Nikola Tesla's (1856–1942) concept of rotating magnetic fields led to a polyphase ac motor that improved system efficiency. Oliver Schallenberger's (1860–98) AC meter operated on electromagnetic induction and allowed accurate billing of users. In 1895, the Niagara Falls Power Company initiated service to Buffalo, New York, 22 miles away using a Westinghouse AC system (Hughes 1993).

Widespread adoption of electric power led to what some called the Second Industrial Revolution. Factory managers electrified plants and replaced old equipment, taking advantage of the opportunity to restructure workflows. Factories had been designed around mechanical power systems wherein shafts and belts transmitted energy from a steam engine or waterwheel to individual workstations. Accumulated energy losses along those shafts forced managers to locate workstations that required more power close to the power source, even if that meant moving products long distances between workstations. A factory with electric motors at each workstation could prioritize production flows over energy flows (Biggs 1996).

As homes and businesses electrified, service reliability became a critical issue. Utilities learned that electricity must be generated and supplied on demand since battery storage was limited and expensive. Taking power plants offline for routine maintenance grew more difficult. Also, utilities needed enough generating capacity to supply all customers at any given moment, so-called peak loads that rarely occurred but required operation of underused power plants. To address these issues, utilities built shared regional grid networks they could access at need. Starting in 1927 with the Pennsylvania-New Jersey-Maryland Interconnect (PJM), regional grids provided a cost-effective means of improving reliability. Ultimately PJM and other grids interconnected; today three grids connect the continental United States.

The increasing reliance on electricity raised basic questions of social equity. Should electric power continue as a private commodity, or should it be accessible to all? Economically, electric service is a private good. People can be excluded from receiving power and the current one user consumes is not available to another. Yet denying access to an increasingly vital service struck many as unjust, so calls grew for public ownership. Faced with poor private-sector service, some local governments took over electric systems as they had with sewerage and water systems. (Jacobson 2001). The federal government established the Federal Power Authority to provide oversight. Congress established public power systems like the Tennessee Valley Authority in economically depressed areas and passed the Public Utilities Holding Company Act to curb financial abuses that led to bankruptcies during the Great Depression.

Regardless of who owned the systems, a basic economic limitation remained. Low population density in rural America promised insufficient profits for private companies, while municipal utilities saw no reason to extend lines outside their jurisdictions. By 1932 only 10 percent of rural Americans had access to electricity; many of those made their own power with small home generators. To solve the problem, Franklin Roosevelt's New Deal established the Rural Electrification Administration (REA) in 1935, a program that provided low-cost, long-term loans to locally organized cooperatives. REA proved remarkably successful.

Though delayed by materials rationing during the Second World War, wires reached virtually all rural residents by the mid-1950s.

An economic boom followed the war, affecting all areas of the economy. Businesses expanded plants that manufactured civilian goods, while continuing to provide military equipment for the emerging Cold War. Surging housing construction combined with rapid rural electrification increased demand for electric power to operate a host of new devices like air conditioners. All three types of utilities, investor-owned, public power, and rural cooperatives, struggled to expand their systems to meet soaring energy demand. The rapid growth stressed electrical systems both technically and economically. Engineers pushed new designs too fast, creating reliability problems. Capital markets struggled to fund the expansion. Increased reliance on coal created excessive pollution that pushed some utilities to shift to cleaner-burning oil while others invested in nuclear power plants. Proliferating power lines created environmental concerns about visual pollution and fears about the health effects of electromagnetic fields (Hirsh 2003).

The shift of power generation from coal to oil halted abruptly when the Organization of Petroleum Exporting Countries (OPEC) embargoed oil shipments to nations that supported Israel in the 1973 Yom Kippur War. Oil prices soared as US drivers waited in lines to buy gasoline. Nearly 20 percent of US electric power came from oil-fired plants, so electricity prices spiked also. The immediate price spikes soon faded as did a second wave that followed the Iranian Revolution in 1979. Utilities, however, moved away from oil and never returned. Accidents at Three Mile Island in Pennsylvania and Chernobyl in the Soviet Union shook public confidence in nuclear power as well. Despite its environmental challenges most utilities returned to coal, though research and development of renewable energy sources like wind and solar surged. Deregulation of the natural gas industry set the stage for increased use of that fuel in power plants.

Even though most users connected to the grid, some industries benefited by maintaining their own power plants. To help control costs, a little noticed section of the 1978 Public Utilities Regulatory Policies Act pushed utilities to buy power from those existing non-utility generators rather than build new plants. That led some people to reconsider the nature of electricity markets, long considered natural monopolies where competition would mean wasteful duplication of expensive infrastructure. Competition in power generation seemed possible and might lead to lower costs. Deregulation separated generation from transmission in the late 1990s and encouraged new participants including marketers who pushed renewable resources. Enacted on a state-by-state basis, deregulation in some areas helped to moderate prices and encourage development of renewable resources. In other areas like California, poor market design with too little oversight led to financial disaster and blackouts.

Deregulation also fed development of automated controls as utilities sought to wheel power from one grid to another. Continental scope and massive equipment often conceals an electrical system's real fragility. Expense and heat dissipation issues limit the ability to place wires underground. Malfunctions can cascade large sections of the country into blackouts in minutes, as happened in 2003. Insufficient maintenance results in problems like overloaded lines that sag into trees and ignite fires. While vulnerable to cyber-security issues, computer control systems help operators monitor events and respond to problems in a system being called upon for ever more energy while in the midst of fundamental transformations.

The complex and fragile infrastructures that produce and transmit electrical energy are woven throughout the technological society we inhabit. As the world struggles to cope with human-induced climate change, the versatility and cleanliness of electricity is a powerful tool. We control and use electricity in amounts large and small in our daily lives, often without thought. The increased use of electric vehicles shows that process continuing today. The challenge at hand is to make the generation and transmission of electrical energy environmentally and economically sustainable.

Benjamin Franklin wrote, "When the well's dry, we know the worth of water." He could not have imagined a time when electricity would be as precious, yet we know its worth whenever the lights suddenly go out.

Harold D. Wallace, Jr.

See also: Brush, Charles Francis; Cooke, Morris Llewellyn; Edison, Thomas Alva; Energy Crisis of the 1970s; Franklin, Benjamin; Henry, Joseph; Organization of Petroleum Exporting Countries (OPEC); Public Utilities Regulatory Policies Act of 1978; Rural Electrification Act of 1936; Stanley, William Jr.; Tesla, Nikola; War of the Currents; Westinghouse, George

FURTHER READING

Biggs, Lindy. 1996. *The Rational Factory: Architecture, Technology, and Work in America's Age of Mass Production*. Baltimore: Johns Hopkins University Press.

Heilbron, John L. 1979. *Electricity in the 17th and 18th Centuries: A Study of Early Modern Physics*. Berkeley: University of California Press.

Hirsh, Richard F. 2003. *Technology and Transformation in the American Electric Utility Industry*. Cambridge: Cambridge University Press.

Hughes, Thomas P. 1993. *Networks of Power: Electrification in Western Society, 1880–1930*. Baltimore: Johns Hopkins University Press.

Jacobson, Charles 2001. *Ties that Bind: Economic and Political Dilemmas of Urban Utility Networks, 1800–1990*. Pittsburgh: University of Pittsburgh Press.

King, W. James. 1962. *The Development of Electrical Technology in the 19th Century*. Vol. 1: *The Electrochemical Cell and the Electromagnet*; Vol. 3: *The Early Arc Light and Generator*. Washington, DC: Bulletin of the United States National Museum. https://archive.org/stream/bulletin228smit#page/n289/mode/2up/search/231 (accessed October 2023).

Enbridge Pipeline System

The fossil fuels industry brought about major changes in the infrastructure of energy in the United States. The extraction of oil required derricks and pumps, which dotted the terrain in regions as diverse as Pennsylvania, Oklahoma, California, and Texas. Refineries appeared on riverfronts, shorelines, and coastal areas in Pittsburgh, Galveston, and Los Angeles. Among the more important components of this energy infrastructure are oil and gas pipelines, which convey crude oil from oil fields and offshore drilling operations to refineries to be processed into fuel. They also transport refined fuels to terminals where they can be shipped by truck to retail outlets like gas stations. They first appeared in the 1860s along with the earliest commercial development of oil in western Pennsylvania and continued to spread over the United States in the last century and a half. The Canadian-based Enbridge pipeline system is one of the largest of its kind, and it transports oil and natural gas across the US–Canadian border and throughout the United States. The company provides an important service to the industry and to the millions of users of energy, while also prompting criticism for the social and environmental problems created by the pipeline's presence on the American landscape.

Pipelines were a well-established means of oil and gas transport by the time Enbridge was chartered by the Canadian government in 1949 as the Interprovincial Pipe Line Company. One appeared in 1863, a few years after first major oil strike in Pennsylvania, when a 2-inch, 2.5-mile cast-iron pipe connected the Tarr Farm on Oil Creek to a refinery in Plumer. Several steam-powered pumps lifted the oil 500 feet of elevation over a ridgeline (Pees 2004). Independent pipeline companies like the Pennsylvania Transportation Company, Union Pipeline Company, and Empire Pipeline proliferated in the 1870s, but were eventually absorbed by the Standard Oil Company, which gave its principal owner John D. Rockefeller "practically the monopoly of the production and transportation of oil in the United States" (Montague 1902, 288). Ida Tarbell's famous "History of the Standard Oil Company," serialized in *McClure's Magazine* beginning in 1902, then appearing in book form in 1904, highlighted Rockefeller's control over the oil tanker railcars and the pipeline system as an important tool for eliminating competition at all steps in the process, from production to transportation to processing to distribution (Tarbell 1904, 1179–81).

By 1920, an estimated 40,000 miles of oil pipelines snaked throughout the country; the sinking of oil tankers by German U-boats in the Second World War induced the US government to build pipelines from Texas to the Northeast, called the "Big Inch" and "Little Inch." They were bought by Texas Eastern Transmission Corporation after the war and converted to natural gas (Castaneda 1990, 92). Homes in the Northeast were increasingly heated with natural gas, so another company, the Transcontinental Gas Pipe Line Corporation, constructed a 1,832 mile pipeline in 1948 that stretched from Hidalgo County, Texas, to New York City. At the time, it was the world's longest pipeline (Ring 1988). Construction of these extensive pipelines provided the context for the Interprovincial Pipe Line Company (IPL)—

later Enbridge—to build a pipeline in 1949–50 from the newly discovered Leduc No. 1 in the Alberta, Canada oil field to Superior, Wisconsin. The international pipeline opened its valves on October 4, 1950, and two months later crude oil finally arrived at the oil terminal in Superior (Enbridge 2023b). As it expanded, IPL made connections to Detroit (1960), Buffalo (1963), and Chicago (1968), transporting Canadian crude oil from Alberta to US refineries.

In 1998, IPL changed its name to Enbridge, Inc. after it added natural gas transmission systems to its existing oil pipelines. In the early 2000s the company bought a number of US-based oil and natural gas pipeline assets, expanding its transmission capabilities across the two North American nations. The list included Midcoast Energy Resources of Houston (2001), the Cushing Terminal and pipelines in Oklahoma (2003), the Flanagan Terminal and pipelines in Illinois (2005), and Shell Gas Transmission, described as an array of "11 natural gas transmission and gas gathering pipelines in five major offshore Gulf of Mexico corridors" (Enbridge 2023b). More recently, Enbridge bought Spectra Energy in 2016 for $28 billion, which added more transmission, storage, and distribution properties, including the aforementioned Texas Eastern Transmission Pipeline. In the process, Enbridge became one of the largest North American oil and natural gas pipeline and transmission companies by 2021, moving 30 percent of the crude oil produced in North America and transporting nearly 20 percent of the natural gas consumed in the United States (Enbridge 2023a). As of 2021, its natural gas pipelines totaled 23,850 miles, covering five Canadian provinces and thirty US states; its crude oil pipelines totaled another 17,127 miles.

Operations involving oil and natural gas transmission carry with them the risk of accidents, mechanical breakdowns, and structural deterioration, which produce terrible environmental and public health consequences. Enbridge has not been trouble-free on this account. In 2010, Line 6B in the company's Lakehead system ruptured near Marshall, Michigan, spilling over 1 million gallons of Alberta tar sands dilbit into the Kalamazoo River at peak flood stage. Dilbit (diluted bitumen) is heavy crude oil that must be diluted with chemicals in order to be transported by pipeline. The spill traveled 40 miles downriver and displaced several hundred people—the company purchased 148 houses, two mobile homes, and five empty lots where the oil had contaminated the riverbanks (Hasemyer 2016). The river closed for two years, and between 2010 and 2016, Enbridge spent $1.2 billion to clean up the spill, and another $1.6 billion to replace Line 6B. In 2016, the company settled with the US Environmental Protection Agency and the US Department of Justice for $177 million in fines and other payments (Hasemyer 2016).

In the ten-year period between 1999 and 2010, Enbridge reported 804 spills along its pipeline system, totaling 7.08 million gallons of oil, not including the Kalamazoo River spill. Some of these incidents drew organized protests, as did Enbridge's announced plans for pipeline expansion or refitting pipelines for tar sands oil. Additionally, the company drew criticism from Native American groups in the United States and Canada for violating Indigenous land sovereignty, creating environmental issues like noise and fumes, threatening water resources, deforestation, and disruption of traditional food sources (Girard 2010, iv). Added to these concerns, Enbridge and all other corporations in the fossil fuels industry faced growing pressure to address the issue of carbon dioxide, global warming, and climate change produced by the burning of fossil fuels. Not only has the company burned carbon-based fuels to conduct its operations, it provides a crucial link in the supply chain for the entire oil and gas industry. Energy companies have endured media scrutiny, legal troubles, and government regulation for much of the last century. However, with the threats posed by global warming and climate change, these pressures have multiplied.

Enbridge responded to these challenges with a series of new initiatives. It became involved with the development of new energy technologies like clean hydrogen, renewable natural gas, and carbon capture and storage. It also inaugurated a corporate strategy to achieve a set of tangible "sustainability goals." Enbridge's website describes these goals as reaching net zero emissions by 2050, hiring a more diverse workforce, and attaining "annual safety and reliability targets that drive continuous improvement towards our goal of zero incidents." Enbridge's Sustainability Report for 2021 stressed the company's commitment to refocusing its operations:

> In the face of increasing global temperatures and extreme weather events, strong action on climate change is more necessary and more urgent than ever. The global transition to a lower-emissions future is underway and Enbridge is transforming its business strategy to align with changing energy needs. We're pioneering the clean energy systems of tomorrow—while lowering our operational emissions today. (Enbridge 2022, 19)

By the early 2020s, the company had constructed twenty-three wind farms, seventeen solar energy installations, seven renewable natural gas facilities, two hydrogen facilities and ten other renewable power assets, which supplied much of electricity for the machinery that moved oil and gas in its pipelines.

Enbridge President and CEO Al Monaco expressed the predicament for energy companies in the twenty-first century: "Forecasts show that demand for energy will continue to increase as populations grow and developing nations raise their standards of living. Combined with heightened emphasis on energy security, we face the need for even more energy, and importantly, greater diversity and reliability of supply across conventional and renewable sources" (Enbridge 2022, 5). These companies reap enormous financial gains for meeting the consumer demand for more and more oil and natural gas, and they have enormous investments in legacy infrastructure from generations of fossil fuel production. However, they also recognize the economic and political hazards of conducting business as usual in a context of increasing public concern over environmental quality, public health, and the future of the earth's life-sustaining systems.

Jeffrey B. Webb

See also: American Petroleum Institute; Climate Change; Dakota Access Pipeline; Federal Power Commission; Keystone Pipeline System; Natural Gas; Petroleum; Rockefeller, John D.; Trans-Alaska Pipeline System

FURTHER READING

Castaneda, Christopher J. 1990. "The Texas-Northeast Connection: The Rise of the Post-World War II Gas Pipeline Industry." *Houston Review*. Vol. 12. Pp. 79–95.

Enbridge. 2022. "Bridge to a Cleaner Energy Future: 2021 Sustainability Report." Enbridge, Inc. https://www.enbridge.com/reports/2021-sustainability-report (accessed October 2023).

Enbridge. 2023a. "About Us." Enbridge, Inc. website. https://www.enbridge.com/about-us/ (accessed October 2023).

Enbridge. 2023b. "Our History." Enbridge, Inc. website. https://www.enbridge.com/about-us/our-history/ (accessed October 2023).

Girard, Richard. 2010. "Out on the Tar Sands Mainline: Mapping Enbridge's Web of Pipelines." The Polaris Institute. May. https://www.polarisinstitute.org/enbridge_profile (accessed October 2023).

Hasemyer, David. 2016. "Enbridge's Kalamazoo Spill Saga Ends in $177 Million Settlement." Inside Climate News. July 20. https://insideclimatenews.org/news/20072016/enbridge-saga-end-department-justice-fine-epa-kalamazoo-river-michigan-dilbit-spill/ (accessed October 2023).

Montague, Gilbert Holland. 1902. "The Rise and Supremacy of the Standard Oil Company." *The Quarterly Journal of Economics*. February. Vol. 16. No. 2. Pp. 265–92.

Pees, Samuel T. 2004. "Pipelines, Failure and Success, 1861–1864." *Oil History*. Petroleum History Institute. http://www.petroleumhistory.org/OilHistory/pages/Pipelines/failure.html (accessed October 2023).

Ring, Trudy. 1988. "Transcontinental Gas Pipe Line Corporation: 1948–1988." Houston: Transco Energy Company.

Tarbell, Ida. 1904. *The History of the Standard Oil Company*. Vol. 1. New York: McClure, Phillips & Company.

Energy Crisis of the 1970s

The energy crisis of the 1970s was a period of widespread anxiety about the availability of oil and gas and a growing panic over price spikes for all forms of energy, in part due to manipulation of the global petroleum market by the Organization of Petroleum Exporting Countries (OPEC) and a subsequent oil embargo imposed by OPEC on the United States and a few other Western nations. Other factors, both economic and geopolitical, contributed to the crisis, which had far-reaching effects in American society and culture, as well as US energy policy and its foreign relations with oil-exporting nations.

OPEC nations agreed to a number of price increases from 1970 to 1973, creating upward pressure on costs and increased volatility in the global energy market. Within such a combustible economic atmosphere, geopolitical tensions sparked distress. On October 6, 1973, Egypt and Syria launched assaults against Israeli units in the Sinai Peninsula and Golan Heights, initiating the 1973 Arab–Israeli War. The United States initially called for a ceasefire and return to the previous positions that belligerents had held in 1967, but Egypt rejected this proposition. The Soviet Union began supporting Egypt and Syria shortly after the eruption of hostilities, and the United States then reinforced Israel with military weapons and logistical supplies. In response, Arab members of OPEC launched an embargo of oil against the United States and several other countries that aided Israel in October 1973, thereby closing off oil exports to these nations, curbing their own production, and reducing global supply. The following month, US President Richard M. Nixon and Secretary of State Henry Kissinger negotiated with combatants on two interconnected fronts: they sought specifically to end the oil embargo and more generally to find a peaceful settlement to the Arab–Israeli War, including securing Israel's withdrawal from the Golan Heights and Sinai Peninsula. On January 18, 1974, diplomats signed the first Egyptian–Israeli Disengagement Agreement. As a result of this initial progress toward peace, Arab members of OPEC ended their embargo in March 1974.

The result of this explosive mix was an energy crisis. Most notably, there was an oil crunch as gasoline availability dwindled, sparking sudden and surprising scarcity of a commodity that most Americans had come to rely on and expect in steady supply. Gasoline prices spiked upward across the United States. There were also large-scale natural gas shortages and near insolvency of major publicly regulated utility companies due to heightened costs, most infamously Consolidated Edison of New York. As prices for oil and gasoline rose, so too did those for natural gas and electricity, resulting in a broad energy crisis. Long gas lines, high inflation, and economic stagnation were norms. The embargo exacerbated these conditions, but underlying systemic factors proved critical.

In 1971, the United States moved the dollar from a fixed exchange rate based on gold to a floating one based on the international market. During that same year, US domestic oil production peaked and then declined for much of the remainder of the decade. As oil production stagnated, energy consumption continued to rise by significant amounts fueled by suburbanization and motor vehicle traffic. In the summer of 1971, President Nixon ordered a price freeze, locking in gasoline and home heating oil prices. Aggravating these factors, the United States became far more reliant on imported oil than during preceding decades. In April 1973, Nixon ended the Mandatory Oil Import Program, which had capped foreign imports since its creation in 1959 by President Dwight D. Eisenhower. This change led to heightened economic unpredictability and amplified dependence on foreign oil.

By June 1973, gasoline shortages emerged. They became particularly acute by October 1973. In the face of economic turbulence and ongoing embargo, global oil prices skyrocketed, nearly quadrupling. On November 7, Nixon launched Project Independence, which aimed to stimulate US oil production and lead to national energy autonomy. By February 1974, states across the country rationed gasoline, often forcing consumers to purchase it on odd or even days depending on their license plate number. The worst of the predicament ended by May 1974, as the embargo ceased and the US public grew tired of gasoline rationing. The responses by state and federal governments varied, including the creation of a 55-miles-per-hour speed limit on national highways and calls for such alternative energy as clean coal, solar power, and wind turbines. The emergency also provided momentum toward the formation of the International Energy Agency, a long sought-after goal of the Nixon administration and led to a host of other energy policies and initiatives, including creation of the Strategic Petroleum Reserve and fuel economy standards under the Gerald R. Ford administration, among others.

Another energy crisis emerged at the end of the decade. In early 1978, Islamic fundamentalists launched a revolution against Mohammad Reza Pahlavi, shah of Iran, who subsequently fled the country on January 16, 1979. Shortly thereafter on February 11, the country became the Islamic Republic of Iran under the leadership of Ayatollah Ruhollah Khomeini. The ensuing widespread turbulence resulted in a near cessation of Iranian oil exports and contributed to another global oil dearth. In the United States, gasoline shortages and long lines quickly remerged from New York to California, while prices doubled in less than one year. In response, President Jimmy Carter called for the deregulation of oil prices, windfall profits tax, solar power, temperature limitations, and synthetic fuels. On June 30, 1980, Carter signed the Energy Security Act, a major overhaul of US energy policy aimed at addressing many of the lessons learned from the energy crisis of the 1970s.

Overall, the energy crisis of the 1970s illustrated a growing US dependence on foreign oil and increasing lack of control over energy supplies, especially volatility in international oil markets driven by events in the Middle East. The US government's efforts successfully reduced public energy consumption but only by a limited amount and for a short period of time. Shaken by the crisis, public support emerged for stricter government regulation of energy and new national policies. By the end of the 1970s, research on and use of solar energy had increased significantly. Tax incentives helped to offset the high initial costs of such alternative energy as solar power. In addition, the energy crisis of the 1970s connected energy, most visibly oil due to US reliance on imports, ever more closely with national security, morphing energy from an economic concern to a strategic one.

William A. Taylor

See also: Aramco; CAFE Standards; Carter Doctrine; Energy Independence; Energy Policy and Conservation Act of 1975; Energy Security Act of 1980; Gulf War; Iraq War and the

Project for a New American Century; Mandatory Oil Import Quota Program; National Energy Act of 1978; Organization of Petroleum Exporting Countries (OPEC); Seven Sisters Oil Companies; Strategic Petroleum Reserve

FURTHER READING

Berkowitz, Edward D. 2005. *Something Happened: A Political and Cultural Overview of the Seventies.* New York: Columbia University Press.

Horowitz, Daniel. 2004. *Jimmy Carter and the Energy Crisis of the 1970s: The "Crisis of Confidence" Speech of July 15, 1979, a Brief History with Documents*. New York: Bedford.

Jacobs, Meg. 2016. *Panic at the Pump: The Energy Crisis and the Transformation of American Politics in the 1970s*. New York: Hill and Wang.

Lifset, Robert D. 2014. "A New Understanding of the American Energy Crisis of the 1970s." *Historical Social Research*. Vol. 39. No. 4. Pp. 22–42.

Merrill, Karen R. 2007. *The Oil Crisis of 1973–1974: A Brief History with Documents*. New York: Bedford.

Vinsel, Lee Jared. 2012. "The Crusade for Credible Energy Information and Analysis in the United States, 1973–1982." *History and Technology*. Vol. 28. No. 2. June. Pp. 149–76.

Energy Fuels, Inc.

Nuclear energy is created by a process called fission, which entails the splitting of an atom and its corresponding release of energy in the form of heat. In nuclear power plants, this heat is used to boil water to create steam, and the resulting steam power drives the turbines and generators that create electricity. The fission process requires a base fuel like uranium, an element that is mined from the earth in the United States and Canada, but more importantly nations like Kazakhstan, Uzbekistan, Russia, Namibia, Niger, China, and Australia. Initially, the United States imported most of its uranium for military and civilian purposes, though domestic uranium mining appeared in the 1950s and 1960s to help supply the demand. In the early twenty-first century, Energy Fuels, Inc. emerged as the largest US supplier of uranium and also vanadium, an element used in the process of creating steel alloys. The history of the company provides a window on the problems and possibilities of nuclear energy as a carbon-free alternative to fossil fuels in an era of carbon-dioxide generated global warming and climate change.

Before the atomic age, uranium had limited uses as a coloring agent or pigment for glass and ceramics. In 1898, Marie Curie's experiments with the yellowish metal revealed its "radioactivity," a term she coined, and refining the uranium led her to the discovery of two other elements, polonium and radium. In Curie's era, scientists and medical researchers believed that radium could possibly serve as a treatment for cancer, so her discoveries sparked the search for more uranium. Curie learned of an exposed deposit near Montrose, Colorado, some of which had been brought to France for study. The uranium-laced ore, dubbed "carnotite" by French scientists, came to be seen as a desirable source for radium. In 1900, a US mining operation called Rare Metals Mining and Milling Company opened offices in Denver and began mining uranium near Naturita, Colorado. Soon more mining companies appeared on the Colorado Plateau, and eventually attracted processing plants to the region. The US uranium boom lasted until 1923, when prospectors discovered uranium in the Congo region, then under imperial control of Leopold II, King of Belgium. Congolese ore from the Shinkolobwe mine contained much higher concentrations of uranium than its American counterpart, which produced more uranium after processing and thus a greater financial return even after shipping costs.

Major advances in atomic research occurred in the 1930s. In 1932, physicists John Cockcroft and Ernest Walton, working jointly at the Cavendish Laboratory at the University of Cambridge, split a lithium atom by bombarding it with protons, turning the one lithium nucleus into two helium nuclei. In 1938, German radiochemists Otto Hahn and Fritz Strassmann split the atoms of various elements, including uranium, and discovered that the original uranium nucleus weighed more than its two subdivisions weighed together. They concluded that the mass lost in the process was converted into kinetic energy, which could be turned into heat. The term they used to describe this release of energy is "fission"

(Gosling 1999, 2). The discovery also revealed that the process of fission released neutrons that were capable of splitting other nuclei, setting off a chain reaction. If controlled, this chain reaction could produce a consistent discharge of heat, if uncontrolled, it could produce a devastating explosion. The moment heralded the creation of both the civilian nuclear power industry and the atomic bomb.

The US wartime effort to build an atomic bomb, the Manhattan Project, secured 3.4 million pounds of uranium from a stockpile at the Shinkolobwe mine in the Congo, some two-thirds of the total amount used to build the bombs that destroyed Hiroshima and Nagasaki. After the war it became clear that the United States needed to secure its uranium from domestic sources given the nuclear arms race and the global competition with the Soviet Union for vital resources. The newly created US Atomic Energy Commission acquired uranium from private mining and milling companies and processed it into fissionable material at the Hanford Site on the Columbia River in Washington and at Oak Ridge in Tennessee. The Colorado Plateau uranium mines increased production of ore from a 1948 total of 54,000 tons to 8 million tons in 1960, some twelve years later (Alvarez 2013). This kept uranium mining alive in the United States, where production peaked in 1980. Uranium mines appeared in South Dakota's Black Hills, near Spokane, Washington, and the Powder River in Wyoming. Mining companies also developed uranium sites on Navajo Nation reservation land in Arizona, New Mexico, and Utah. From 1944–89, over a thousand mines were dug on Navajo land, employing a large number of Navajo workers, which produced 4 million tons of uranium (AHF 2018).

The market for uranium began to decline once the US Department of Defense determined that it had sufficient quantities for national security purposes, and when accidents at Three Mile Island in Pennsylvania (1979) and Chernobyl in Ukraine (1986) dampened enthusiasm for civilian nuclear power. Additionally, power companies steered away from building nuclear plants due to the lengthy approval process and high costs of construction. Finally, mining companies in the United States faced stiff competition from cheaper and higher-quality uranium from Canada, Australia, and following the collapse of the Soviet Union, from Russia and former Soviet republics. Through the 1990s the US government deregulated the market for uranium and prices fell accordingly. A brief upturn in the market occurred just after 2000, when US wars in Afghanistan and Iraq threated the supply of foreign oil and revived interest in domestic nuclear power, and China and India emerged as consumers of uranium. However, the economic crisis of 2008, the Fukushima nuclear disaster in 2011, and the phase-out of nuclear power plants in Japan and Germany stifled the market for uranium once again.

IN SITU LEACH MINING

Uranium mining can be done in three ways: open pit mining, underground extraction, and a process called "in situ leach mining" or ISL. This technique entails the use of water as a dissolving agent to release uranium and other minerals from the ore. The process takes place underground where the ore is located, drawing groundwater from the site. A complexing agent and an oxidant are added to aid the process, and the water—with the minerals mixed in—is brought to the surface for separation. In the US, strict rules govern the use of ISL to prevent groundwater contamination and other environmental hazards. ISL mining predominates in uranium-rich countries like Kazakhstan and Uzbekistan, and most US operations use the ISL method (WNA 2020).

Jeffrey B. Webb

Energy Fuels, Inc., a company based in Canada, entered the market in 2006 during the temporary upturn in the market for uranium. It began by reopening and rehabilitating formerly productive mines but also exploring new sites on 55,000 acres of "highly prospective uranium and vanadium property" in the US states of Colorado, Utah, Arizona, Wyoming, Idaho, and New Mexico (EF 2009). In 2012, adverse market conditions forced the company to suspend mining operations at its Beaver, Daneros, and Pandora properties on the Colorado Plateau. In 2015 the company acquired Uranerz Energy Corporation, which operated mines in Canada, Mongolia, and the Powder River area of Wyoming, but *Business Week* described the move as "consolidating two uranium producers amid a slump in the price of the nuclear fuel" (Casey 2015). In another acquisition in 2016, the company bought Mesteña Uranium, LLC, which operated the Alta Mesa ISR Project in Brooks and Jim Hogg Counties, Texas, but then in 2022 sold the Alta Mesa ISR Project assets to enCore Energy. Not expecting expansion in the marketplace, the company banked its future on the signing of "three long-term uranium contracts with major U.S. utilities" and an agreement to sell $18.5 million of natural uranium concentrates to the US National Nuclear Security Administration to fill the strategic uranium reserve. In addition to its continued participation in a limited uranium market, the company recommitted itself to vanadium production and the development of its rare earths resources.

The press release about the strategic uranium reserve sale revealed the company's thinking about the incongruity between nuclear power's importance in converting to a clean, carbon-free energy system and the weakened state of the uranium mining and processing industry in the United States. It read:

> Today, nuclear energy provides the U.S. with roughly twenty percent of all electricity, and fifty percent of our clean, carbon-free electricity. U.S. and European nuclear industries are actively working to shift away from Russian uranium supply, but the process will be difficult and lengthy. The U.S. can rely on supply from allies like Canada, Australia and others for a large proportion of our uranium and nuclear fuel supply, but we must also restore our own capabilities. For the past several years, U.S. uranium production has been near-zero and our only uranium conversion facility has been shut-down. The Uranium Reserve is a small, but important, step toward resolving this untenable situation. (EF 2022)

The United States imports most of the uranium it uses for its civilian nuclear power plants, including 35 percent from Kazakhstan, 15 percent from Canada, 14 percent from Australia, 14 percent from Russia, and 7 percent from Namibia, with 10 percent from other countries, using 2021 figures. In that year, US power plants acquired only 5 percent of its uranium from US sources. The lack of a robust domestic uranium industry can partly be explained by the difference in grades between US resources and its competitors; the uranium content in Canada's Athabasca Basin reaches 20 percent, some one hundred times the world's average. The grade of US ore is comparatively low. However, there are other environmental, political, and social reasons for the ambivalence about nuclear power in the United States. Federal, state, and local authorities squabbled over the long-term storage of radioactive waste from nuclear power plants. Clearly, the Three Mile Island accident in 1979, which resulted in a partial meltdown and dispersion of radioactive gases, made Americans uneasy about the safety of nuclear plants. The film *Silkwood* (1983) about a whistle-blower seeking to expose unsafe practices at a plutonium processing plant followed a few years afterward and ratcheted up these anxieties.

Concerns over workers and the health of communities surrounding uranium mines, processing facilities, and nuclear power plants were, and continue to be, valid. In 1979, a uranium mill owned by United Nuclear Corporation in Church Rock, New Mexico experienced a dam breach at an evaporation pond containing water and mill tailings. Mill tailings are the contaminated remnants left behind in the mining process, in which uranium is reworked into yellow cake. The dam breach released 94 million gallons of radioactive waste into the Puerco River, spreading toxic sludge through a number of Navajo Nation communities and befouling the area's groundwater. Controversy surrounding the event led to a wider debate about the health of Navajo uranium miners and mill operators, and the toxicity of the abandoned mines and mining works left to decay on Navajo lands. In a 2019 letter to a US House subcommittee, Navajo president Jonathan Nez pointed out all the health risks of exposure to radioactive materials, and remarked, "prior to uranium mining, the Navajo people were virtually cancer-free with the lowest lung cancer rate of all Native American nations. Today, cancer is the second leading cause of mortality among the Navajo people. Cancer rates doubled on the Navajo Nation from the 1970's to the 1990's. The Navajo Nation and its people have suffered far too much from uranium's toxic legacy" (Nez 2019, 6).

Energy Fuels, Inc. began uranium mining and processing in the Navajo region long after the Church Rock uranium spill, but nevertheless must operate within a social, cultural, and political context that has been shaped by these earlier experiences. Even so, the company had some reason for optimism about the future of uranium mining and nuclear power. US Secretary of Energy Jennifer M. Granholm spoke for the federal government when she said in 2019: "The United States views nuclear energy as a pivotal technology in the global effort to lower emissions, expand economic opportunity, and ultimately combat climate change," then posted to Twitter in 2022: "Nuclear energy is clean energy and it's vital to creating good-paying jobs, supporting our energy transition, and saving our planet" (ONE 2019).

Jeffrey B. Webb

See also: Atomic Energy Acts; Church Rock Uranium Mill Spill; Fermi, Enrico; Idaho National Energy Laboratory; Manhattan Project; Navajo Reservation Uranium Mining; Nuclear Regulatory Commission; Nuclear Waste Policy Act of 1982; Three Mile Island Accident; Yucca Mountain Nuclear Waste Repository

FURTHER READING

Alvarez, Robert. 2013. "Uranium Mining and the U.S. Nuclear Weapons Program." Federation of American Scientists. November 14. https://fas.org/pir-pubs/uranium-mining-u-s-nuclear-weapons-program-3/ (accessed October 2023).

Atomic Heritage Foundation (AHF). 2018. "Uranium Mining." The National Museum of Nuclear Science & History. July 30. https://ahf.nuclearmuseum.org/ahf/history/uranium-mining/ (accessed October 2023).

Casey, Simon. 2015. "Uranium Producer Energy Fuels to Buy Miner Uranerz." Bloomberg. January 5. https://www.bloomberg.com/news/articles/2015-01-05/uranium-miner-energy-fuels-to-buy-wyoming-miner-uranerz#xj4y7vzkg (accessed October 2023).

Energy Fuels (EF). 2009. "Energy Fuels Announces Closing of Merger with Magnum Uranium Corp." News Releases. Energy Fuels Website. July 2. https://www.energyfuels.com/news-releases?item=275 (accessed October 2023).

Energy Fuels (EF). 2022. "Energy Fuels Awarded Contract to Sell $18.5 Million of Uranium to U.S. Uranium Reserve." News Releases. Energy Fuels Website. December 16. https://www.energyfuels.com/2022-12-16-Energy-Fuels-Awarded-Contract-to-Sell-18-5-Million-of-Uranium-to-U-S-Uranium-Reserve (accessed October 2023).

Gosling, F.G. 1999. *The Manhattan Project: Making the Atomic Bomb*. Washington, DC: US Department of Energy.

Nez, Johnathan and Myron Lizer. 2019. "Written Statement of the Navajo Nation." July 12. https://www.congress.gov/116/meeting/house/109694/documents/HHRG-116-II06-20190625-SD013.pdf (accessed October 2023).

"Nuclear Explained: Where Our Uranium Comes From." 2022. US Energy Information Administration. July 7. https://www.eia.gov/energyexplained/nuclear/where-our-uranium-comes-from.php (accessed October 2023).

ONE (Office of Nuclear Energy). 2019. "U.S. Secretary of Energy Jennifer Granholm and Romanian Minister of Energy Virgil Popescu Highlight New Partnership on SMRs." Press Release. November 4. US Department of Energy. https://www.energy.gov/ne/articles/us-secretary-energy-jennifer-granholm-and-romanian-minister-energy-virgil-popescu (accessed October 2023).

World Nuclear Association (WNA). 2020. "In Situ Leach Mining of Uranium." Information Library. September. https://world-nuclear.org/information-library/nuclear-fuel-cycle/mining-of-uranium/in-situ-leach-mining-of-uranium.aspx (accessed October 2023).

Energy Independence

Energy independence is a concept that originated as an explicit policy objective in an announcement by President Richard Nixon during the Energy Crisis of the 1970s. In response to the dual challenge of oil price hikes by the Organization of the Petroleum Exporting Countries (OPEC) and an embargo on crude oil deliveries to the United States by its Arab members during the Arab–Israeli war of October 1973, Nixon announced Project Independence on November 7, 1973. In his televised evening "Address to the Nation about Policies to Deal with the Energy Shortages," the president promised that by 1980 the United States would "have developed the potential to meet [its] own energy needs without depending on any foreign energy sources." This ambitious project relied on changes in consumer behavior, technological and geopolitical solutions as well as federal support of new oil explorations and alternative energy supplies. It included amongst many other proposed measures a federal 55 miles per hour speed limit on interstate highways, which became law in 1974.

The 1973 oil price crisis exposed the vulnerability of the United States to supply disruptions and price surges, but the underlying causes of US energy dependence lay much deeper and had developed decades before the 1970s. After 1945, the global center of oil production had moved from the Western hemisphere to the Middle East, but, more importantly, US energy consumption increased precipitously. Despite attempts to protect and stimulate domestic oil production by limiting foreign oil imports through the Mandatory Oil Import Program (1959–73), domestic production could not keep up with rapidly increasing demand. With the exception of the Alaskan Prudhoe oil field discovered in 1968, domestic petroleum fields were maturing, and spare production capacity disappeared. By 1972 the United States had become a net consumer of oil. Between 1974 and 1978 foreign oil imports almost doubled and for decades the United States relied on foreign supplies, increasingly from its northern neighbor Canada, who became the leading supplier in 2004 ahead of Saudi Arabia. This reliance on foreign oil slowly plateaued in the mid-2010s and in November 2019 for the first time in many decades, the United States exported more crude oil and petroleum products than it imported. Due to the so-called shale revolution, in which hydraulic fracturing and horizontal drilling facilitated oil production from shale rock formations, domestic production had picked up again. Despite these latest developments, energy independence has figured prominently in discussions on energy policy and has been embraced by Democratic and Republican administrations alike, elevating it to a bipartisan issue.

Throughout its many policy iterations since 1973, energy independence has never been clearly defined and meant different things at different times. While no government official proposed complete energy autarky, there was disagreement whether independence should mean eliminating, reducing, or managing dependence. While it was clear that energy independence entailed overcoming vulnerabilities relating to potential oil embargoes especially from OPEC or Arab producers, it was not clear whether this vulnerability pertained to both supplies and prices. Because energy independence was first launched as a policy objective in the wake of the 1973 oil price crisis and due to the significance of oil in North American high-energy societies and as an internationally traded energy carrier, the term essentially equated energy dependence with oil dependence. Overlapping with another concept that quickly gained traction in the early 1970s—energy security—it focused on establishing national independence and security in a time when interdependence best described the political and economic realities of petroleum markets and more generally a globalized economy. Arguably, it was exactly this interdependence which facilitated American dependence on potentially hostile producer nations and private oil companies. It may also explain why, contrary to the independence rhetoric, one of the many foreign policy measures which addressed US vulnerabilities and which was initiated by Secretary of State Henry Kissinger was the founding of the intergovernmental International Energy Agency (IEA) in 1974.

Energy independence has become a concept informing disparate energy policies while proposing a recognizable policy narrative which invokes the national idea of independence. When President Nixon launched Project Independence, he invoked the upcoming bicentennial and referenced both the Manhattan and Apollo projects in order to emphasize the significance of energy to the sovereignty and well-being of the country. The term's popularity can be traced through its frequent use in legislation introduced to Congress. In 1975 President Gerald Ford proposed the Energy Independence Act, which never came into law but contained demand and supply side measures, some of which, including new efficiency standards for cars and the creation of the Strategic Petroleum Reserve, were passed separately into law as part of the December 1975 Energy Policy and Conservation Act. The act also effectively established a ban on most domestic crude oil exports, which was only lifted forty years later in December 2015, after the United States had resurged as a producer of oil due to the shale revolution. Ford's successor, President Jimmy Carter, equated obtaining energy independence to "the moral equivalent of war" in his April 1977 "Address to the Nation on Energy." He resorted to a similar moral rhetoric when he gave his famous "malaise" or "crisis of confidence" speech less than two years later on July 15, 1979, in which he promised that "the generation-long growth in [American] dependence on foreign oil will be stopped dead in its tracks" and cut "by one-half by the end of the next decade." Global oil prices had more than doubled that year due to the Iranian Revolution.

The realization that Iran had now become an enemy and the Soviet invasion of Afghanistan in December 1979 led Carter to announce what was later called the Carter Doctrine in his State of the Union Address on January 23, 1980. Noting the dependence of the Western world on Middle Eastern oil and the significance of the Persian Gulf for oil shipments, he warned that the United States would resort to military means if "any outside force [were] to gain control of the Persian Gulf region." Carter, who throughout his presidency supported diversification of energy supplies away from petroleum as well as conservation efforts and who championed both solar power and coal-derived synthetic fuels (synfuels), had institutionalized energy independence in US foreign and defence policy. President Ronald Reagan terminated many of Carter's energy programs, especially the ones supporting alternative energy. He most famously took down the solar panels that his predecessor had installed on the roof of the White House. However, Reagan agreed with the energy security imperative inherent in the Carter Doctrine and so did President George H.W. Bush, who led the United States into the first Gulf War in 1991.

Throughout the 1990s energy independence remained an important narrative in energy policy circles taking on new urgency in the first decade of the twenty-first century when oil prices reached record highs of almost $150 per barrel in 2008. In his January 2006 State of the Union Address President George W. Bush had warned that "America is addicted to oil, which is often imported from unstable parts of the world." Against this backdrop of increased reliance on expensive oil imports, Congress passed the Energy Independence and Security Act of 2007, which tightened fuel efficiency standards first introduced in 1975 and provided incentives for increased biofuel production. More recently, America's newfound energy independence was celebrated by President Donald Trump as one of his administration's achievements, but he also quickly dismissed the term in favor of his vision of American energy dominance. Future presidents may return to the concept of energy dependence. However, rather than dealing with reliance on foreign oil their administrations will have to address the dependency of the United States and Americans on petroleum more generally. Climate action and decarbonization are now informing the meaning of energy independence.

Petra Dolata

See also: Bush, George H.W.; Energy Crisis of the 1970s; Energy Policy and Conservation Act of 1975; Energy Security Act of 1980; Home Energy Efficiency; Hydraulic Fracking; Iraq War and the Project for a New American Century; Mandatory Oil Import Quota Program; National Energy Act of 1978; Organization of Petroleum Exporting Countries (OPEC); Prudhoe Bay Oil Field; Strategic Petroleum Reserve

FURTHER READING

Bush, George W. 2006. "Address before a Joint Session of the Congress on the State of the Union." Online by Gerhard Peters and John T. Woolley. The American Presidency Project. https://www.presidency.ucsb.edu/node/214381 (accessed June 1, 2021).

Carter, Jimmy. 1977. "Address to the Nation on Energy." Online by Gerhard Peters and John T. Woolley. The American Presidency Project. https://www.presidency.ucsb.edu/node/243395 (accessed June 1, 2021).

Carter, Jimmy. 1979. "Address to the Nation on Energy and National Goals." Online by Gerhard Peters and John T. Woolley. The American Presidency Project. https://www.presidency.ucsb.edu/documents/address-the-nation-energy-and-national-goals-the-malaise-speech (accessed June 1, 2021).

Carter, Jimmy. 1980. "The State of the Union Address Delivered before a Joint Session of the Congress." Online by Gerhard Peters and John T. Woolley. The American Presidency Project. https://www.presidency.ucsb.edu/node/249681.

Council on Foreign Relations. n.d. "Oil Dependence and U.S. Foreign Policy, 1850–2017." https://www.cfr.org/timeline/oil-dependence-and-us-foreign-policy (accessed June 1, 2021).

Hakes, Jay E. 2008. *A Declaration of Energy Independence: How Freedom from Foreign Oil Can Improve National Security, our Economy, and the Environment*. Hoboken, NJ: J. Wiley.

Graf, Rüdiger. 2014. "Claiming Sovereignty in the Oil Crisis 'Project Independence' and Global Interdependence in the United States, 1973/74." *Historical Social Research*. Vol. 39. No. 4. Pp. 43–69.

Grossman, Peter Z. 2021. "The Four-Decade Quest for an 'Energy Independence' Policy: Chasing a Trope through Time." *Journal of Policy History*. Vol. 33. No. 1. Pp. 93–110.

Homans, Charles. 2012. "Anthropology of an Idea: 'Energy Independence.'" *Foreign Policy*. Vol. 191. Pp. 34–5.

Littlefield, Scott R. 2013. "Security, Independence, and Sustainability: Imprecise Language and the Manipulation of Energy Policy in the United States." *Energy Policy*. Vol. 52. Pp. 779–88.

Nixon, Richard. 1973. "Address to the Nation about Policies to Deal with the Energy Shortages." Online by Gerhard Peters and John T. Woolley. The American Presidency Project. https://www.presidency.ucsb.edu/node/255503 (accessed June 1, 2021).

Willrich, Mason. 1976. "Energy Independence for America." *International Affairs*. Vol. 52. No. 1. Pp. 53–66.

Energy Policy Act of 2005

Historically, the Energy Policy Act of 2005 (hereafter EPA 2005) was a continuation of previous federal energy policy acts, which started in 1920 specifically for hydropower resources. The EPA 2005 was much broader than previous continuations and set the stage for increasing penetration of renewable forms of energy into the overall US market. EPA 2005 was signed by President George W. Bush on August 8, 2005. The act was largely motivated by real world circumstances of globally rising energy prices and the growing US dependence on foreign oil. But that only provided temporary relief. By the time of EPA 2005, foreign oil imports had reached about 60 percent of US consumption. Twenty years earlier, the portion was about 30 percent. This alarming increase projected into the post-2005 future was sufficient motivation to determine strategies to curb this dependence. By 2008, new sources of production in the United States had been discovered. Along with improvements in average fuel economy that led to slightly decreased domestic consumption, the EPA 2005 helped to reduce overall net imports of foreign oil to 30 percent by 2023.

EPA 2005 was a comprehensive and broad policy act that affected virtually all areas of the energy production and delivery network. One of the major provisions of the act is improving the reliability of the delivery of electricity. EPA 2005 authorized the creation of the Electric Reliability Organization (ERO) which would report directly to the Federal Energy Regulatory Commission (FERC). The mission of the ERO was to enforce new reliability standards for bulk-power electricity transmission and to expand transmission capability in historically congested areas (mostly on the east coast). In addition, the dynamic between investor-owned utilities and the purchase of power for delivery to customers was streamlined.

The act also created a renewable fuels standard. After the act went into effect, pure gasoline was required to contain increasing amounts of ethanol or biodiesel so that renewable fuels could gain market penetration. Ultimately this manifested as E-85 fuel for most vehicles where 15 percent of the fuel volume is provided by ethanol. In addition to these renewable fuel standards, the act also included a set of tax incentives. Either production tax credits (PTC) or investment tax credits (ITC) became increasingly available as a means to encourage both domestic energy production and energy efficiency and conservation. This encouraged an increased investment in renewables with the wind energy likely benefitting the most by 2022.

Another provision of the act is a set of measures to encourage domestic energy production. The act encouraged production on federal lands by increasing access for drilling and other kinds of energy projects. In most cases, this federal land was in very remote places or in the continental shelf regions of US waters. The most controversial of these proposed lands was the Arctic National Wildlife Refuge (ANWR). House debate over the bill eventually defeated the use of ANWR as a new source of US oil production and it was not enacted into legislation. Overall, EPA 2005 was intended to increase domestic sources of energy production, improve the energy security situation in the United States, continue improvements in environmental quality, and contribute to further economic growth by opening up new kinds of industries. It also intended to improve the reliability of electricity delivery by streamlining various approval processes and restructuring FERC to have more direct authority over all aspects of the US energy market.

The comprehensive nature of EPA 2005 would come to bear on virtually all aspects of energy policy, some more significant than others. These areas include energy efficiency, renewable energy, fossil fuels, electricity generation and transmission, and energy tax policies. The first of the policy areas that the law impacted is energy efficiency. It created new federal building energy efficiency performance standards which would ultimately lead to LEED certification, which means more "green building" techniques are used to achieve energy consumption levels at least 30 percent less than extant build code. The policy added four weeks to Daylight Saving Time, which began in 2007. The idea behind this change was to decrease consumption of energy for lighting, but it hasn't been conclusively shown if any electricity is actually saved by this measure. Also in the area of energy efficiency, federal grants were made available to assist various state energy conservation projects which were meant to improve the energy efficiency of public buildings by at least 30 percent.

In terms of renewable energy, the EPA 2005 mandated that federal government operations use increasing portions of non-fossil fuel sources of energy staring from 3 percent in 2007 and increasing 7.5 percent by 2013, with continued increases after that. To a large extent, these goals were met, more due to the enacting of state renewable portfolio standards, than EPA 2005 itself. The law also established an incentive program to improve hydroelectric power production. For the most part, this led to capital improvements in extant facilities to improve their overall efficiency, rather than the construction of new power facilities. In addition, hydroelectric power is very sensitive to large-scale regional droughts. At the time EPA 2005 was enacted, overall hydro production in the US, had fallen by 20–25 percent of its production in the 1990s. Much of that decrease was due to large-scale drought in the Pacific Northwest. Indeed, EPA 2005 seemed to prioritize hydropower as a better source of emerging new renewable energy production than wind or solar. In retrospect, this appears to have been an unwise decision, as hydropower did not grow as fast as wind and other renewables following the passage of the act.

Among the more important areas of impact regarding the implementation of EPA 2005 is fossil fuel use. The act authorized the purchase oil, foreign or domestic, to fill the Strategic Petroleum Reserve to its 1-billion-barrel capacity. However, for a variety of reasons, this capacity level was never reached and the reserve maintained its capacity of 700 million barrels as of 2022. The EPA 2005 provided FERC the sole authorization to administer the approval process for operating and/or constructing new liquefied natural gas (LNG) terminals in the United States. In addition, open access requirements for new LNG facilities were relaxed to as to encourage their construction. While many of the proposed new LNG facilities were not constructed due to various environmental lawsuits, generally filed by local citizens, EPA 2005 essentially paved the way for a de facto US energy policy which relies more on importation of LNG as an energy source than it does renewables. With the post-2005 discovery of hydraulic fracking, imports of LNG are currently significantly lower than they were around that time. Additionally, production incentives were created for drilling of deep wells in the Gulf of Mexico, a policy that was implicated in the *Deepwater Horizon* oil spill in 2010. The law also incentivized extraction of natural gas from gas hydrates, often found in shale rock formations. Finally, it authorized additional funding to improve the efficiency and environmental performance, mainly through pollution allowance reductions, of the nation's coal plant infrastructure. In retrospect, this funding area may have also been unwise, as the rise of natural gas production has strongly decreased the contribution of coal facilities to the US electricity portfolio. Since 2010, approximately eighty individual coal plants have now been decommissioned.

It is worth exploring the ERA 2005's implication for electricity generation and transmission. The law gave FERC jurisdiction over more aspects of the transmission line system and bulk power delivery with the overall goal of improving the reliability of electricity delivery in general, and specifically to avoid brownouts in traditionally congested areas. After the law went into effect, the FERC could also bypass states by directly issuing permits for new transmission infrastructure and/or advanced power system upgrades to increase security and reliability. However, increasing per capita electricity use and the failure to invest in significant new transmission line infrastructure has allowed congestion events to increase most every year, regardless of the expanded jurisdiction given to FERC by EPA 2005. FERC received authority under the law to better regulate transmission rates across grid networks and to provide incentives for utilities if they could reduce transmission congestion. One mechanism for this was the use of a new pricing structure that accounted for the time of day and the regional load—effectively making the price of electricity higher (to encourage conservation) during transmission "rush-hour" times. FERC is now empowered to exercise greater control and more financial oversight of various public utility holding companies. Essentially, EPA 2005 repealed the 1935 policies in this important area. Because the infamous Enron manipulation of the energy market over the period 1997–2001 clearly showed significant vulnerabilities, EPA 2005 defined a new set of policies and significantly increased criminal fines for false price reporting. In addition, FERC was given greater control over the various financial and processing connections that are necessarily made when transmitting electricity long distances that encompass many states.

In one other important area of policy, energy tax provisions, the EPA 2005 produced modifications in the established array of tax credits to incentivize energy producers and consumers to prefer renewable energy. Indeed, a substantial number of tax incentives were created for many aspects of energy use. This included a production tax credits for renewable projects, increased depreciation periods for various kinds of electrical transmission and natural gas distribution infrastructure projects, and investment tax credits for clean coal facilities and any advanced technologies that allow for improved efficiency and reduced pollution in coal-based facilities. Furthermore, the law offered additional tax credits for residential homes that improve energy efficiency via increased use of renewables, such as solar panels on rooftops or replacing older appliances with new Energy Star rated ones. It extended tax credits for commercial building property owners to improve efficiencies in lighting, water heating, insulation and HVAC systems, while allowing the US Department of Energy (DOE) to give direct loans for innovative technologies for these conversions and other projects. Eligible projects would include renewable energy systems, advanced fossil fuel technology, efficient end-use energy technologies, and improved electrical generation, transmission and distribution technologies.

One of the criticisms aimed at EPA 2005 involved exemptions to the Safe Drinking War Act (1974). These exemptions applied to hydraulic fracking operations and to exploration activities in oil and natural gas production. In effect, these exemptions removed US Environmental Protection Agency oversight from these projects, and bypassed various regulatory requirements. For example, the exemptions disallowed EPA oversight on the use of "underground" fluids specifically used for injection into various rock formations that may contain oil and gas. This is one of the techniques used in hydraulic fracking. This was allowed into the legislation even after studies of coal beds used for methane production showed that various kinds of toxins, specifically benzenes when diesel fuel was used in the fluid mix, would be introduced to ground water. This could eventually degrade regional drinking water sources. Nonetheless, in 2004, the Environmental Protection Agency released a report that stated hydraulic fracturing fluids pose little threat to underground sources of drinking water, despite also noting in the report that very little research had actually been done to support their conclusions.

Greg Bothun

See also: Clean Power Plan of 2015; *Deepwater Horizon*; Energy Independence; Federal Power Commission; Hydraulic Fracking; Hydroelectric Power; Natural Gas; Renewable Energy; Smart Grid; US Green Building Council

FURTHER READING

Bang, Guri. 2010. "Energy Security and Climate Change Concerns: Triggers for Energy Policy Change in the United States?" *Energy Policy*. Vol. 38. No. 4 April. Pp. 1645–53.

International Energy Agency (IEA). 2021. "Energy Policy Act of 2005 (Energy Bill)." August 24. https://www.iea.org/policies/1492-energy-policy-act-of-2005-energy-bill (accessed October 2023).

Kuhn, Thomas R. 2005. "Why the Energy Policy Act is a Foundation for the Future." *The Electricity Journal*. Vol. 18. No. 10. December. Pp. 22–30.

Malmedal, Keith, Benjamin Kroposki, and Pankaj K. Sen. 2006. "The Energy Policy Act of 2005 and its Impact on Distributed Generation." IEEE Rural Electric Power Conference. Pp. 1–8.

Malmedal, Keith, Benjamin Kroposki, and Pankaj K. Sen. 2007. "Energy Policy Act of 2005 and Its Impact on Renewable Energy Applications in USA." IEEE Power Engineering Society General Meeting. Pp. 1–8.

Energy Policy and Conservation Act of 1975

The Energy Policy and Conservation Act of 1975 (EPCA) was one of the legislative responses to widespread gasoline shortages and energy instability spurred by the energy crisis of the 1970s. Major components of the EPCA included laws that revolutionized both the automotive and appliance industries through a shift towards producing more energy-efficient products. In addition, the EPCA created a national oil reserve, which would prove beneficial during times of supply shortages, while it also empowered the president to diversify the nation's energy portfolio and promote coal for electricity generation. As such, the EPCA represents the first significant attempt at comprehensive American energy policy and it gave Congress a foundation from which to amend the EPCA or establish further legislation that would attempt to achieve various social and environmental benefits, as well as enhance national energy security and independence.

By 1970, petroleum represented a significant energy source in the United States since it was used not only for electricity generation in many regions but also for home heating—especially in the northeast—as well as to meet virtually all of the nation's transportation needs. However, as the decade began, the United States experienced an energy crisis brought on by supply disruptions initiated by decreased domestic production, then followed by the OPEC oil embargo, which lasted from October 1973 until March 1974. Thus, when Gerald Ford, a Republican, assumed the US presidency in August 1974, energy policy was one of his top priorities.

Given recent events, President Ford was especially concerned about America's vulnerability to foreign energy markets. He believed the free market could naturally regulate energy supply and demand and was opposed to the price controls established by his predecessor, President Richard M. Nixon, which set a maximum price for oil. Therefore, shortly after assuming the presidency, he proposed numerous initiatives including the taxation of oil imports and the elimination of price controls, which he believed would increase domestic oil production. To many, including much of the Democrat-controlled Congress, price controls seemed like a necessary measure to keep gasoline and heating oil affordable for all Americans. Thus, after a lengthy back-and-forth, Congress offered President Ford the EPCA (Public Law 94-163) as their best compromise for his many energy policy proposals and he reluctantly signed it into law on December 22, 1975. The EPCA fell far short of Ford's call for the immediate elimination of price controls, but it did include a phase-out. More importantly, however, several components of the EPCA were in line with Ford's commitment to make the United States more energy secure by both improving the stability of supply and reducing the demand for oil.

To address energy supply issues, the EPCA confronted the painful recent memories of national gasoline shortages by creating the Strategic Petroleum Reserve (SPR). Through the provisions of the SPR, the US Department of Energy (DOE) is authorized to hold up to 714 million barrels of oil (29.988 billion US gallons) for use in emergencies, such as potential future foreign oil embargoes or domestic disasters (OCESER 2020). And, to keep more domestic oil in the United States, the EPCA established a ban on the exportation of domestic crude oil with certain exceptions to be made by the president. As a way of shifting away from such a dominant reliance on oil, the EPCA gave the federal government the authority to order power plants to burn coal instead of oil and established loan guarantees to encourage coal companies to mine new locations.

ENERGY EFFICIENCY V. ENERGY CONSERVATION

Energy efficiency means that the same amount of work or desired outcome can be achieved with less energy. An example of this is replacing a traditional incandescent lightbulb with a modern light-emitting diode (LED) lightbulb; the user achieves the same result (amount of light), but less electricity is required. Energy conservation means that someone makes a conscious effort to use less energy. An example of this is turning off the lights when they are not needed.

Curt J. Davis

The EPCA addressed national energy demand with both efficiency and conservation measures, perhaps the most notable of which relate to the nations' driving habits. As a way to improve conservation, the EPCA followed California's lead and called for every state in the nation to enact right-on-red laws, which has reduced the amount of gasoline wasted while drivers sit idling at traffic lights. Targeted at improving efficiency, the Corporate Average Fuel Economy (CAFE) standards were established to require the automobile industry to improve the future fuel efficiencies of manufacturers' fleets of cars and light trucks. In addition to addressing the efficiency of automobiles, the EPCA also created the Energy Conservation Program for Consumer Products Other Than Automobiles as the first program to set targets and measuring guidelines for energy and water efficiencies of many consumer products, such as major household appliances.

Both programs have had a significant impact on the evolution of energy efficiency for many products. Despite initial objections from the auto industry at being forced to design their products to meet government guidelines, the industry has adapted to meet consumer demand and a large segment of the auto industry has seen recent growth in the market for both hybrid (gasoline/electric) and electric vehicles since many consumers are attracted to their main selling point: high estimated miles per gallon (mpg) or mpg gasoline equivalent for electric vehicles. This presents a stark contrast with the large gas-guzzling cars of the 1970s. For other markets, such as major appliances, estimated annual electricity usage and/or cost is featured prominently on pricing labels and today "EnergyGuide" labels communicate this information to potential consumers. On average, modern refrigerators offer consumers 20 percent more storage capacity yet use only one-quarter of the amount of electricity and cost half as much as they did in 1973 (OEERE 2017).

Without the conservation and efficiency provisions of the EPCA, local air pollution in many American cities and global concentrations of greenhouse gases (GHGs) in the atmosphere could have increased much more over the past four decades. In addition to the environmental benefits of CAFE and consumer products standards, consumers have enjoyed other social benefits and are able to achieve more with a lot less energy. They can travel further with less gasoline. They can store more food in their refrigerators and spend less money while doing it. However, just as the EPCA offered policies that would reduce some pollution in the transportation sector, it also paved the way for increased air pollution and GHGs through the promotion of coal over oil for electricity generation. This represents a major social and environmental drawback of the EPCA, since—barring accidents—the mining, transport, and combustion of coal is arguably dirtier and more environmentally destructive than other combustible energy sources. Since 1975, coal use in the United States (measured in total British thermal units or BTU) reached and remained at higher levels for every year after the EPCA until 2019 when natural gas use dominated coal use nearly threefold.

Scholars offer much speculation regarding the political impacts of the EPCA, especially since it created laws that dictated how certain industries must operate. However, merely passing the EPCA in 1975 was a political milestone at a time of contentious relations between the executive and legislative branches of the government. Ford, as Nixon's vice president, became president after Nixon resigned amidst a movement for his impeachment in Congress. Thus, even though it was difficult for Ford to get Congress to agree with his ideal plan for American energy policy, the EPCA represents a model example of policy compromise and an attempt to repair the fractured relationship between the president and Congress. The one provision of the EPCA that received virtually unanimous support from all parties was the SPR, which proved to be a valuable energy safety net when it was tapped after the devastation endured by the oil-producing Gulf states after Hurricane Katrina in 2005. Since 1975, we have seen how the White House and Capitol Hill have the authority to make, amend, and annul energy policy as they see fit. Without the comprehensive energy policies of the EPCA, the United States would not have had a legislative platform from which to at least discuss and plan for America's energy security, and to deal with issues of justice, which is especially important in the age of the climate crisis.

Curt J. Davis

See also: CAFE Standards; Clean Power Plan of 2015; Energy Crisis of the 1970s; Energy Independence; Energy Security Act of 1980; Home Energy Efficiency; National Energy Act of 1978; Organization of Petroleum Exporting Countries (OPEC); Renewable Energy; Strategic Petroleum Reserve

FURTHER READING

Clark, Megan. 2014. "Why the U.S. Bans Crude Oil Exports: A Brief History." *International Business Times*. March 20. https://www.ibtimes.com/why-us-bans-crude-oil-exports-brief-history-1562689 (accessed May 15, 2020).

Energy Policy and Conservation Act (EPCA). 1975. Public Law 94-163. United States Congress. December 22. https://www.govinfo.gov/content/pkg/STATUTE-89/pdf/STATUTE-89-Pg871.pdf May 15, 2020).

Mieczkowski, Yanek. 2014. "The Toughest Thing: Gerald Ford's Struggle with Congress over Energy Policy." In *American Energy Policy in the 1970s*. Ed. Robert Lifset. Norman: University of Oklahoma Press. Pp. 19–46.

Office of Cybersecurity, Energy Security, and Emergency Response (OCESER). 2020. "About the SPR." U.S. Department of Energy. https://www.energy.gov/fe/services/petroleum-reserves/strategic-petroleum-reserve May 15, 2020).

Office of Energy Efficiency and Renewable Energy (OEERE). 2017. "Saving Energy and Money with Appliance and Equipment Standards in the United States." U.S. Department of Energy. January. https://www.energy.gov/sites/prod/files/2017/01/f34/Appliance%20and%20Equipment%20Standards%20Fact%20Sheet-011917_0.pdf (accessed May 15, 2020).

Union of Concerned Scientists. 2017. "A Brief History of US Fuel Efficiency Standards: Where We are—And Where are we Going?" December 6. https://www.ucsusa.org/resources/brief-history-us-fuel-efficiency (accessed May 15, 2020).

US Energy Information Administration (EIA). 2020. "U.S. Energy Facts Explained." https://www.eia.gov/energyexplained/us-energy-facts/ (accessed May 15, 2020).

Energy Security Act of 1980

The Energy Security Act of 1980 closed out a decade filled with energy instability and growing public distrust in the government. On June 30, 1980, President Jimmy Carter signed the Energy Security Act on the South Lawn of the White House, concluding nearly a year of continuous debate within Congress. The Energy Security Act consisted of six pieces of legislation all centered on advancing alternative sources of energy within the United States through various taxes, subsidies, and governmental programs. These bore titles such as the US Synthetic Fuels Corporation Act, Biomass Energy and Alcohol Fuels Act, Renewable Energy Resources Act, Solar Energy and Energy Conservation Act, Geothermal Energy Act, and Ocean Thermal Energy Conversion Act. Most notable was the act regarding synthetic fuels, which created the congressionally chartered US Synthetic Fuels Corporation. The purpose of the corporation was to encourage private industry to enter into domestic production of synthetic fuels, primarily from coal, oil shale, or tar sands.

Three broad trends developed in the 1970s: a growing distrust of government, rising energy prices and gasoline shortages, and inflation paired with economic stagnation. In just ten years, 1970–80, the cost of a barrel of domestic crude oil rose from $3.18 to $21.59. Additionally, domestic production of crude oil declined from 3.5 billion barrels in 1970 to 3.1 billion barrels in 1980. The United States was becoming highly reliant on foreign oil imports as a result of increased daily consumption. Additionally, the average per-gallon price of gasoline rose from $0.36 in 1970 to $1.19 in 1980. The dramatic increase of energy prices in the United States came as a result of oil embargoes placed on imports to the United States and other Western nations. These embargoes were the result of America's backing of Israel in the Arab–Israeli War. Over the course of three weeks in October 1973 war was waged between a coalition of Arab states led by Egypt and Syria against Israel over control of the Sinai Peninsula. Subsequently, the Arab-controlled Organization of Petroleum Exporting Countries (OPEC) reduced their oil production and proclaimed an embargo on oil imports to the United States for supporting Israel in the war. These actions led to an international energy crisis and the formation of infamous gas lines at stations all across the United States.

Energy consumed Carter throughout his administration, and he set forth a domestic policy agenda aimed at trying to solve some of America's energy problems. In his inaugural address Carter said, "We have learned that more is not necessarily better, that even our great nation has recognized limits, and that we can neither answer all questions nor solve all problems." The very next day he called on all Americans to turn their thermostats down to 65 degrees Fahrenheit in the day and cooler at night. Nearly four months after Carter took office, he addressed the nation during a televised speech declaring that the energy crisis of the 1970s was the moral equivalent of war, reaffirming his commitment to solving the energy crisis facing America. President Carter was attempting to bring the energy crisis onto a moral plane, one that could unite the nation and provide a sense of civic sacrifice in solving these energy issues. His rhetoric, however, did not always produce the civic engagement he was hoping for.

As an outsider in Washington, Carter's ability to gain support for legislation was limited. However, he was able to achieve some policy successes including the National Energy Act of 1978, the Crude Oil Windfall Profits Tax Act, the Energy Security Act of 1980, and perhaps most notably the creation of the US Department of Energy; the first new cabinet position in eleven years. In this context Carter strived to develop a successful national energy policy to curb the energy crisis of the 1970s, and the result was the Energy Security Act of 1980, truly the culmination of Carter's energy initiatives during his administration. The motivation for such a policy had been building over the course of his time in office, yet the legislative process was only set in motion after the Shah of Iran was overthrown in February of 1979 as a result of the Iranian Revolution. Once again energy prices skyrocketed and Americans lined up at gas stations hoping they would be able to fill up the family car that day. With a second oil crisis looming over the summer of 1979, many people began to believe that oil companies were artificially creating shortages so as to drive up prices and increase profits. In May 1979, the Associated Press and NBC News released a phone survey of 1,600 American adults showing that 37 percent believed that the energy shortages were real, 9 percent were unsure, and 54 percent thought the energy shortages were a hoax. Although small, these results showed what President Carter was up against when trying to inform Americans on the importance of reducing their energy consumption.

In light of the Three Mile Island Unit 2 nuclear power plant reactor meltdown and growing disbelief in the energy crisis and shortages facing America, President Carter was slated to give a speech on July 5th, 1979. However, without explanation he decided to cancel that speech and instead retreated to Camp David for what turned out to be a ten-day self-reflection where he invited selected guests from all walks of life to join him during his retreat. It was after those ten days that President Carter sat in the Oval Office and gave his address to the nation titled "Energy and National Goals" where Carter outlined for Americans what he believed was a "crisis of confidence." It quickly was renamed the "Malaise Speech." While speaking to nearly 65 million Americans, Carter outlined six points centered on energy security and how he aimed to reduce American dependence on foreign oil. In a sense, Carter's speech condemned the American way of life, pointing to consumerism and materialism as ideologies that got in the way of solving the energy problem. The speech was met with positive responses from the public, indicating that Americans didn't mind having their lifestyles called into question, and perhaps it was what they were looking for in President Carter all along. It was his "crisis of confidence" speech that laid the groundwork for the Energy Security Act of 1980, which became law nearly a year later.

Throughout Carter's administration, many energy policies were passed, and the work of Carter's administration resulted in reducing dependence on foreign oil. During his term, consumption of foreign oil decreased from 48 to 40 percent resulting in a reduction of 1.8 million barrels a day. The most notable measure in Carter's Energy Security Act, the Synthetic Fuels Corporation, was established to coordinate with private oil and gas companies to plan and secure funding for the construction of synthetic fuel plants in the US. Synthetic fuels are products created by converting natural gas, coal, or shale oil into gasoline and other liquid hydrocarbons. An article in the Washington Post in 1981 noted that sixty-one companies submitted proposals, mostly for coal gasification, coal liquefaction, and conversion of shale oil and tar sands into synfuels for use in transportation and other industries (Crutsinger 1981). Unfortunately, the Synthetic Fuels Corporation closed its doors only six years after its conception amid decreasing cost of foreign oil and the failure to pass the Energy Mobilization Board, which was tasked with cutting through the "red tape" to permit construction of synthetic fuel plants. The most promising aspects of the Energy Security Act of 1980 failed early on, shedding light on the difficulty of comprehensive national energy policy during those times.

Adam Gallaher

See also: Carter Doctrine; Coal Gasification; Energy Crisis of the 1970s; Energy Independence; National Energy Act of 1978; Organization of Petroleum Exporting Countries (OPEC); Peak Oil; Strategic Petroleum Reserve; Three Mile Island Accident; US Department of Energy

FURTHER READING

Crutsinger, Martin. 1981. "61 Firms Seek Subsidies for Synfuel Development." *The Washington Post.* April 2. P. D3.

Jacobs, Meg. 2016. *Panic at the Pump: The Energy Crisis and the Transformation of American Politics in the 1970s.* New York: Hill and Wang.

Mattson, Kevin. 2009. *What the Heck Are You Up To, Mr. President? Jimmy Carter, America's "Malaise," and the Speech That Should Have Changed the Country.* New York: Bloomsbury.

Priddy, Harvey Amsler. 2013. "United States Synthetic Fuels Corporation: Its Rise and Demise." Ph.D. diss., University of Texas at Austin.

Smil, Vaclav. 1983. *Biomass Energies: Resources, Links, Constraints.* New York: Plenum Press.

Miller Center. "July 15, 1979: 'Crisis of Confidence' Speech." University of Virginia. https://millercenter.org/the-presidency/presidential-speeches/july-15-1979-crisis-confidence-speech (accessed May 5, 2020).

Yergin, Daniel. 1991. *The Prize: The Epic Quest for Oil, Money, and Power.* New York: Simon & Schuster.

Yergin, Daniel. 2011. *The Quest: Energy, Security, and the Remaking of the Modern World.* New York: Penguin Press.

Evans, Oliver

Oliver Evans (1755–1819) was a mechanic and inventor who contributed to early industrialization in the United States. His two most important inventions were an automatic, or mechanized, gristmill and the high-pressure steam engine, both of which had important implications for the energy history of the United States. Evans is also important in the early history of the nation's patent system.

Evans was the fifth of twelve children born to Charles and Ann Evans at Newport, Delaware, where his father was a shoemaker, and also owned a farm. Evans apprenticed to a wheelwright at the age of seventeen. At twenty-two he began making wire, using a device he had invented to draw the wire, which was then used in making the handheld tools for carding wool. Moving to Maryland to operate a store with his brother, Evans then conceived of the idea of mechanizing all the processes involved in milling grain to make flour. He returned to Delaware in 1783 work with his brothers in perfecting the ideas involved in designing and building a completely mechanized grist mill. The milling of grain was the most important food-processing industry in the young republic at the time. Rural mills, located along streams throughout the land, employed waterpower to turn millstones for grinding grain and making flour, but the process required considerable labor to move grain and flour around the mill, to cool the flour after it had been ground, and to load the finished flour into barrels.

GROWTH OF MILLING

The total value of the flour produced in such [Evans automatic] mills had been $14 million in 1810; by 1860, that figure had increased almost 200 percent, to roughly $250 million. In that year, reckoned in terms of dollar value, flour milling was the country's leading industry, although the number of people employed in the industry was fairly small: roughly 27,000 compared, for example, to 114,000 employed in the manufacture of cotton cloth or 123,000 making boots and shoes (Cowan 1997).

Fredric Quivik

Evans' automatic mill required human labor to load grain into the mill and to move filled barrels to the loading dock, but his water-powered equipment did all the rest of the work. He devised an Archimedes screw to move grain and flour horizontally through the mill, and a bucket elevator to move material vertically. Another machine, which was wholly original to Evans, called a "hopper boy" (because it replaced the work done by a boy with that job title) raked freshly ground flour across a floor to cool it before moving it to the next step in the process. Evans' mechanized mill reduced the labor required to operate a gristmill from four men and a boy to two men. The Delaware legislature issued Evans a patent for his mill in 1786, and he soon received patent protection from Maryland, Pennsylvania, and New

Hampshire as well. When the first federal patent law passed in 1790, his was the third patent issued by the US government. In 1795, Evans published *The Young Mill-Wright and Miller's Guide*, an illustrated book of instructions, more than 200 pages, on how to build and equip a mill according to Evans' plan. Although he frequently complained to the federal government about people infringing on his patent, he eventually sold enough copies of his book that he could repay the loan for its publication. Evans' mechanized mill revolutionized milling in the United States, and that revolution in mechanized, labor-reducing production spread to Europe in a generation.

Evans moved with his wife and children in 1793 to Philadelphia, where he established a mill-supply store. Although most of his energy to date had been devoted to making a profit from his design for the mechanized mill, he had also turned some of his attention to the possibilities of harnessing steam for mechanical power. One of his early ideas was to build a steam carriage, which would be a freight wagon powered by steam rather than pulled by animals. At this time, there were some low-pressure steam engines operating in the Philadelphia area based on the ideas of James Watt in England. John Fitch's steamboat had operated on the Delaware River in the late 1780s, and at the turn of the nineteenth century the Philadelphia Waterworks was powered by giant low-pressure stationary steam engines.

Evans knew that a high-pressure steam engine could produce comparable power with a much smaller size. Refining his ideas, Evans put his first high-pressure steam engine to work at his store in 1803, grinding plaster of Paris. The next year, he received a US patent for his high-pressure steam engine. He then proposed to the Lancaster Turnpike Company, which operated a turnpike between Lancaster, PA, and Philadelphia, that it pay him to build a steam-powered wagon that would haul flour between Lancaster and Philadelphia. He also applied to the federal government to extent his patent on the mechanized mill. Both entities denied his requests, so in disgust he changed the title of the new book he was writing from *The Young Steam Engineer's Guide* to *The Abortion of the Young Steam Engineer's Guide*. Published in 1805, the book was another useful guide, but he also used it to publish the correspondence between himself and John Stephens, with whom Evans was having a technical debate about high-pressure steam engines.

After publishing *The Abortion of the Young Steam Engineer's Guide*, Evans developed the Mars Works, which housed all the shops he needed, including foundry, machine shop, blacksmith shop, and others, to build steam engines and boilers independent of outside contractors. He promoted his steam engines for use to power the machinery in factories and as well as steamboats. In *The Abortion of the Young Steam Engineer's Guide*, Evans gave special attention to the promise of using his steam engines to aid the navigation of the Mississippi River. As his business in making steam engines increased, he built another set of shops in Pittsburgh, managed by his son, George Evans, so that his steam engines did not have to be freighted over the Allegheny Mountains or shipped by sea to New Orleans to be used in the frontier areas along the Mississippi and Ohio rivers. Two years before his death, Evans wrote that his works had built more than seventy steam engines, mostly in the West but many along the Atlantic Coast, and put them into service in flour mills, sawmills, paper mills, and iron works.

The Evans steam engine was so highly regarded for steamboats that many other engine builders ignored his patent and copied his design for the high-pressure steam engine. Evans' own business in supplying engines was apparently good enough that he seems to have quit contesting others who infringed on his patent. Although very few of his steam engines were installed on boats, other engine builders and shipbuilders employed his design, so that steamboats on the Ohio, Mississippi, and Missouri rivers contributed significantly to the settling and development of the American West in the nineteenth century.

Fredric L. Quivik

See also: Cooper, Peter; Corliss, George Henry; Industrial Revolution; Lowell Waterpower System; Slater, Samuel; Steam Power; Water Power

FURTHER READING

Cowan, Ruth Schwartz. 1997. *A Social History of American Technology*. New York: Oxford University Press.

Evans, Oliver. 1990 [1795]. *The Young Millwright and Miller's Guide*. Wallingford, PA: The Oliver Evans Press.

Evans, Oliver. 1990 [1805]. *The Abortion of the Young Steam Engineer's Guide*. Wallingford, PA: The Oliver Evans Press.

Ferguson, Eugene S. 1980. *Oliver Evans: Inventive Genius of the American Industrial Revolution*. Greenville, DE: The Hagley Museum.

Hindle, Brooke, and Steven Lubar. 1986. *Engines of Change: The American Industrial Revolution, 1790–1860*. Washington, DC: Smithsonian Institution Press.

Hunter, Louis C. 1985. *A History of Industrial Power in the United States, 1780–1930*. Vol. 2: *Steam Power*. Charlottesville: The University Press of Virginia.

Hunter, Louis C. 1993. *Steamboats on the Western Rivers: An Economic and Technological History*. New York: Dover Publications Inc.

Evard, Mary E. A.W.

The history of energy contains a number of stories about its uses in food preservation and preparation, an undertaking that virtually every person has experienced in the long history of human existence. Pre-historic peoples used fire to smoke and cure meat, eventually adopting clay vessels and ovens for cooking. In ancient Greece and Rome, a baker's trade developed (Latin *pistor*) and bread was baked in wood-fired ovens and sold in the marketplace. Cast-iron stoves began to replace brick and mortar ovens in the early eighteenth century, which set off a process of innovation to make the stoves less smoky, more fuel efficient, and with greater flexibility for the user. In the 1860s, Mary Evard designed a wood- and coal-burning kitchen stove made of sheet iron that improved the performance of earlier models. Evard's Reliance Cook Stove received a patent for its distinctive features and caught the attention of the public when it was put on display. She enjoyed a brief moment of recognition before kitchen stove technology continued to evolve. Eventually, wood- and coal-burning kitchen stoves made of cast and sheet iron gave way to gas and electric ranges. For women of her generation, however, Evard's daily life was shaped by the work of preparing food using energy from wood and coal fires, and small improvements in stove design could make a meaningful difference.

Mary Evard was born in 1825 and by 1860 was living with her husband Charles Evard in the village of Leesburg, Virginia, along the Potomac River about 40 miles northwest of Washington, DC. Records list Charles' occupation as a watchmaker and Mary's as a milliner, or hat maker. Their location became a problem during the US Civil War, which was fought with great intensity along the creeks and rivers in northern Virginia. The Evards fled their home and left it abandoned for five years until the end of the war. The story of the Reliance Cook Stove begins on the day of their return to their broken-down house. Mary recalled that she was very sick and under doctor's orders not to work, but the house was "nearly demolished" and there was a need for bread. Finding nothing to cook with but an old Dutch oven, she built a fire, sat down on a log, and began to poke around in the flames. It was eight o'clock in the morning, and after morning had passed into the afternoon, her husband Charles approached and said, "Are you not going to give us dinner?" "Yes," Mary replied, "when it is noon." Charles exclaimed "Noon! It is now three o'clock" (WCC 1876, 74). Rather than tend to dinner, Mary had been thinking deeply about cooking stoves and what sort of improvements she'd like to make in their design. In the meantime, her bread came out overdone (which she blamed on poor wood), providing more motivation to make a stove that would produce consistent results.

By 1865, cooking stoves made of cast and sheet iron had already appeared in many American cities and towns. The existence of the market for these stoves owed to innovators of the 1820–60 period like John Conant, Thomas Wollson, Henry Stanley, and Philo Stewart, who adapted the free-standing cast-iron heating stove to cooking, with various modifications. This included separating the unit's fire box from its baking oven, routing combustion gases through multiple flues inside the stove to distribute the heat evenly, adding baffles and grates to slow heat loss, and attaching reservoirs and racks to boil water and keep food warm (Dwyer 1895, 360). On that day when they tried to bake bread with a Dutch oven, Evard came up with some ideas to improve the performance and functionality of these existing models, and then tried to get her son to make a wooden model of the new design. Her husband Charles grew frustrated at how long he'd been taking and sent the boy to a store to buy sheet iron. Within several weeks Charles had built a working model, although at a reduced scale.

Mary Evard applied for a patent, which was approved in 1868. In describing how her modifications made the Reliance Cook Stove different from others, the approved patent copy read:

> The oven may be subdivided by means of the vertical and horizontal partitions [F1, F2], supported respectively by grooved ridges, [f], and ledges [f1, f2], as represented in fig. 2. In this way, the entire oven may be converted into small apartments, wherein articles may be cooked separately without being affected by the flavor of other substances. These several compartments also enable different articles to be subjected to a degree of heat best adapted to the occasion, as they are respectively heated to an extent depending upon their location relatively to the fire and flues. (Evard 1868)

Evard also received two other patents at the same time, one for a "broiler apparatus" and another for a "toaster," both designed to be attached to the cook stove. With the heated cooking surface, multiple oven chambers, and the additional broiler, an entire meal could be cooked all at once. This meant that the skilled user could roast meat, bake bread, fry potatoes, and boil vegetables simultaneously. Evard prepared the stove to be displayed in 1873 at the Industrial Exhibition and Agricultural Fair in St. Joseph, Missouri (WCC 1876, 74). At the exhibition, she demonstrated the stove's features by making a meal for the judges consisting of "3 lbs. of lamb, a spring chicken, soup, several kinds of vegetables, a pound cake, and coffee" (Burr 1877, 587).

Evard's meal and her stove earned her the silver medal, the highest award available at the event. She then entered the Reliance Cook Stove into the Philadelphia Centennial Exhibition in 1876, a much bigger affair that drew travelers from foreign countries; between May and November the exhibition drew over 9 million visitors. A writer offered comment: "the Reliance Cook Stove, invented and patented by Mrs. EVARD, received much attention, not only as invention, but as a beautiful piece of work in itself, it being made of sheet iron by a jeweler, under Mrs. Evard's personal direction" (Burr 1877, 587). He went on to say that since the stove had already been used for cooking, visitors believed it was currently being manufactured and that Mary could have sold a hundred of them at the exhibition. He said in closing that the Evards intended to have the product "in the market" in 1877. However, there appears to be no record that the Reliance Cook Stove ever went into production or found its way into the kitchens of consumers.

The idea of finding better ways of using energy to cook food motivated a number of people to pioneer domestic technologies that shifted energy consumption from wood to coal, and then from coal to gas and electricity. In the nineteenth century, cooking stove patents proliferated as people found ways to improve fuel efficiency with new designs. This includes many women like Mary Evard. One researcher found the names of thirty-seven different women in US Patent Office records from 1831 to 1894 who received patents for their stove improvements and enhancements to grain dryers, toasters, broilers, and other food preparation technologies

(Stanley 1995). On the surface, their motivation could be understood as saving fuel costs. The price of wood increased in the early nineteenth century as wood became scarcer in the eastern regions of the country, and the price of coal decreased with the expansion of coal production amid the advent of steam power (Harris 2008). The newer cooking stoves could use longer-burning coal and use it with greater efficiency because of the stoves' heat-saving features. These stove innovators could also be understood as motivated by the prospect of less manual labor, with the capacity to have everything cooking at once and having to stoke the fire less frequently. If they felled, cut, split, carried, and stacked their own wood supply, then they'd save labor on that end as well.

The results of switching to coal-fired cooking stoves in American homes, especially its impact on the lives of women, were consequential. Historian Howell Harris observes: "The cooking stove types which were perfected by the early 1850s enabled the stove revolution to happen" (Harris 2008). Heating and cooking stoves inaugurated a shift in the rhythms of daily life away from the traditional open hearth to the kitchen, where it was usually warmer on cold winter days and where family could find an endless supply of hot water, what Harris (2008) calls "another ingredient of the revolution in domestic comfort." Not everyone experienced the decline of the open hearth and the shift to kitchen cooking as beneficial. According to historian Ruth Schwartz Cowan, "the impact of those stoves on the houses in which they were installed is not difficult to discern: stoves were labor-saving devices, but the labor they saved was male" (1983, 61). This is because gathering firewood for open-hearth cooking was traditionally a male activity. It fell to women, for the most part, to bring loads of coal into the house and start the stove. Furthermore, the cooking stove largely ended the practice of simple, one-pot cooking, and "probably increased the amount of time what women spent in preparing foodstuffs" because the expectation was they could now cook many different things simultaneously (Cowan 1983, 62). Finally, the early coal-burning stoves required frequent cleaning, which added to the housekeeping chores that women were expected to do already.

As more and more consumers adopted specially designed coal-fired stoves for cooking, it came to be seen within a generation or two as an essential component of the typical American household. The mass consumption of this particular kitchen appliance expanded the market for coal, and later gas and electricity, dovetailing with other transitions occurring in transportation and manufacturing. Cooking stoves also served as a wedge appliance that prepared homeowners to embrace consumer durables that came later, like washing machines, refrigerators, vacuum cleaners, dishwashers, and radios, all of which were dependent on the existence of a steady, industrial-scale supply of energy.

Jeffrey B. Webb

See also: Frigidaire; Hobart Electric Manufacturing Company; Home Energy Efficiency; KitchenAid Appliances; Mellowes, Alfred W.; Rumford Fireplace; Singer Manufacturing Company; Stewart, Philo Penfield; Upton Machine Company and Whirlpool Corporation

FURTHER READING

Burr, Samuel J., and S. De Vere Burr. 1877. "Woman's Pavilion." *Memorial of the International Exhibition*. Hartford CT: L. Stebbins.

Cowan, Ruth Schwartz. 1983. *More Work for Mother: The Ironies of Household Technology from the Open Hearth to the Microwave*. New York: Basic Books.

Dwyer, Jeremiah. 1895. "Stoves and Heating Apparatus." *One Hundred Years of American Commerce*. Ed. Chauncey M. Depew. Vol. 2. Pp. 357–64. New York: D. O. Haynes & Co.

Evard, M.E.A.W. 1868. *Cooking Stove* (U.S. Patent No. 76,315). Washington, DC: United States Patent Office.

Harris, Howell John. 2008. "Conquering Winter: U.S. Consumers and the Cast-Iron Stove." *Building Research and Information*. Vol. 36. No. 4. Pp. 337–50.

Stanley, Autumn. 1995. *Mothers and Daughters of Invention: Notes for a Revised History of Technology*. New Brunswick, NJ: Rutgers University Press.

Women's Centennial Committee (WCC). 1876. "Reliance Stove." *The New Century for Woman*. July 8. No. 9. Philadelphia: Women's Centennial Committee.

Exxon Valdez Oil Spill

A few minutes after midnight on March 24, 1989, the massive oil tanker *Exxon Valdez* hit the Bligh Reef in Alaska's Prince William Sound, spilling nearly 11 million gallons of crude oil into the ocean and onshore in one of the worst energy-related disasters in US history. The accident caused extensive environmental damage and triggered debate about the threats of oil production and transmission in Alaska and other ecologically sensitive areas. These debates eventually led to the Oil Pollution Act of 1990, an important piece of legislation that "expanded and clarified the authority of the federal government and created new oil spill prevention and preparedness requirements." The law also "strengthened existing liability provisions, providing a greater deterrent against spills" (Ramseur 2010). The accident, when coupled with the public reaction and political response, offers a window on the interplay between fossil fuel production, public concerns about the industry, and national energy policy in the United States.

The *Exxon Valdez*, owned and operated by the Exxon Corporation subsidiary Exxon Shipping Company, departed around 9:30 p.m. on Thursday, March 23 carrying 53 million gallons of crude oil drawn from the Alyeska Oil Terminal, the southern endpoint of the Trans-Alaskan Pipeline System. Heading for the port at Long Beach, California, the *Exxon Valdez* cruised for several hours and then the ship's captain, Joseph Hazelwood, left the bridge at 11:50 p.m., putting control of the ship in the hands of its third mate, Gregory Cousins. Before he left, Hazelwood received permission to leave the southbound shipping lane and enter the northbound lane to avoid ice that had broken from Columbia Glacier. The ship was to return to the southbound lane after passing the danger, but in Hazelwood's absence, Cousins maintained course and sailed beyond the northbound lane entirely, heading in the direction of an array of rocky reefs near Bligh Island in Prince William Sound. At 12:04 a.m. on March 24, the ship struck the reef and then ran aground. The final impact tore open eight of the eleven cargo tanks, gashing the entire length of the ship's hull (Skinner 1989, 3).

Within five hours, 10.8 million gallons of oil—a fifth of its total load—spilled into Prince William Sound, a pristine wilderness composed of numerous inlets, coves, and islands. The oil fouled 1,300 miles of coastline, killing a quarter of a million seabirds, 2,800 sea otters, 300 harbor seals, 250 bald eagles, and 22 killer whales. The spill disrupted salmon and herring migrations and contaminated local fisheries, leaving thousands who depended on fishing in a state of financial distress. It was revealed that Captain Hazelwood was intoxicated at the time of the incident. The third mate put in charge in his absence, Gregory Cousins, claimed to be overworked and exhausted, and lacked a special certificate required to command the ship in Prince William Sound. Compounding the problem, the *Exxon Valdez* was designed and built with a single hull, leaving it vulnerable to massive spills in the event of a hull breach. The remoteness of Prince William Sound posed a significant challenge to responders, who struggled to get oil containment equipment like skimmers and booms on the scene before the oil spread widely. A US government investigation revealed that contingency plans developed prior to the incident by the company and by federal, state, and local authorities were wholly inadequate to deal with an oil spill of this magnitude.

The national news media gave the incident extensive coverage. As the response effort reached its climax, over 11,000 personnel, 1,400 vessels, and 85 aircraft were involved, and cleanup ran from April to September, with more cleanup sessions the following four summers. Millions of Americans followed coverage provided by major newspapers, broadcast news, CNN, and weekly magazines like *U.S. News & World Report*, *Time*, and *Newsweek*, which included heartrending images of oil-soaked birds and dead sea otters. Some observers were sharply critical of Exxon's immediate response to the incident, as chairman Lawrence G. Rawl made no comment for six days and sent a "succession of lower-ranking executives" to manage the crisis, which "gave the impression that the company regarded the pollution problem as not important enough to involve top management" (Holusha 1989). Furthermore, the company ran newspaper advertisements ten days after the incident that apologized for the accident but didn't admit responsibility. Some of its other public statements tried to downplay the consequences of the spill when reports indicated the damage was extensive and likely to be long-lasting.

The disaster prompted a range of groups to file suit against Exxon, including Native American communities, commercial fishing interests, seafood processors and distributors, recreation and tourism businesses, the state of Alaska, and environmental groups like National Wildlife Federation, National Resources Defense Council, Greenpeace, National Audubon

FIGURE 8: Cleanup crews worked to rid crude oil from the shoreline of Alaska's Prince William Sound in the wake of the *Exxon Valdez* oil spill.

Society, and Sierra Club. Exxon eventually accepted responsibility for the spill and settled these lawsuits. Exxon claims that it spent $4.3 billion in "compensatory payments, cleanup payments, settlements and fines" after the *Exxon Valdez* incident (ExxonMobil 2018). Years after the oil spill, biologists discovered certain components of oil that remain long after many of its compounds break down. One of these is polycyclic aromatic hydrocarbon (PAH), which affects embryonic development in fish eggs, producing mortality, deformities, and edemas. For fish that survive, PAH weakens the strength and endurance of the heart; a herring or salmon might look healthy in every way but suffers from a heart defect that can affect longevity or reproduction (Shogren 2014).

The *Exxon Valdez* oil spill has been described as a "seminal event" in the history of the oil industry as it relates to the American people and to Washington, DC. A report issued in 2003 from the National Research Council of the National Academies of Science, Engineering, and Medicine reached this conclusion:

> Beyond the ecological damage, the *Exxon Valdez* disaster caused fundamental changes in the way the U.S. public thought about oil, the oil industry, and the transport of petroleum products by tankers. Despite continued heavy use of fossil fuels in nearly every facet of our society, 'big oil' was suddenly seen as a necessary evil, something to be feared and mistrusted. The reaction was swift and significant. (NRC 2003, 11)

One indication of this shift can be seen in the fate of a US Senate measure to open oil drilling on the Arctic coastal plain of the Arctic National Wildlife Refuge (ANWR) in Alaska, passed just ten days before the *Exxon Valdez* oil spill. Once the disaster occurred and press coverage multiplied, the measure was shelved (Shabecoff 1989). Since 1989, many attempts have been made to secure congressional approval for oil drilling in the refuge, but lingering memories of Exxon's mess in Prince William Sound produced determined opposition to those attempts. As of 2022, oil drilling opponents were successful in preventing the industry from proceeding in ANWR.

Another political response to the public outcry over the oil spill was the enactment of the Oil Pollution Act of 1990. This law built on previous Oil Pollution Acts of 1924, 1961, and 1973, closely defining areas of responsibility, liability, and enforcement in oil spill prevention and response. Among its many liability and responsibility provisions, the law also required oil companies to have their response plans reviewed and approved by the federal government, with the US Coast Guard in charge of enforcement. It also required oil tankers in US waters and ports to have double hulls and made provisions for criminal background checks and alcohol and drug testing for ship's license holders. A large section of the law contained provisions for Prince William Sound, including the creation of Prince William Sound Oil Spill Recovery Institute to study the long-term effects of oil spills. In all, the law represented an attempt to incentivize oil companies to acquire safer vessels, hire more reliable employees, prepare more effectively for oil spills, and organize to accept managerial and financial responsibility for future disasters.

After repairs, the *Exxon Valdez* carried oil in Europe, which at the time still allowed single-hulled oil tankers, under various names like *Exxon Mediterranean*, the *SeaRiver Mediterranean*, and finally the *S/R Mediterranean*. Its name changed, but not its usefulness as a symbol of human depravity and prospects for earth's demise. In the dystopian, post-apocalyptic film *Waterworld* (1995), a rusted, decaying ship emblazoned with the name *Exxon Valdez* and a portrait of captain Hazelwood in the pilothouse serves as the base of operations for a violent faction of pirates who terrorize ocean-going survivors. In 2012, the real *Exxon Valdez*, since converted to an ore carrier and renamed *Dong Fang Ocean*, and then *Oriental Nicety*, finally made it to Alang in India to be scrapped for its metal by the reclamation company Priya Blue Industries (Barley 2012). The *Exxon Valdez* may have had an obscure and unheralded end, but most agree that it had an important place in history. It embodied the basic dilemma of energy and the environment in the twentieth century: Americans want cheap and plentiful gasoline, but they also want pristine wilderness and a healthy planet.

Jeffrey B. Webb

See also: *Argo Merchant* Oil Spill; *Deepwater Horizon*; Earth Day; ExxonMobil; Natural Resources Defense Council; Oil Tankers; Prudhoe Bay Oil Field; Santa Barbara Oil Spill; Trans-Alaska Pipeline System

FURTHER READING

Barley, Shanta. 2012. "*Exxon Valdez* Laid to Rest." *Nature*. August 13. https://www.nature.com/articles/nature.2012.11141

ExxonMobil. 2018. "The Valdez Oil Spill." ExxonMobil Risk Management and Safety. September 12. https://corporate.exxonmobil.com/operations/energy-technologies/risk-management-and-safety/the-valdez-oil-spill?print=true#Overview (accessed October 2023).

Holusha, John. 1989. "Exxon's Public-Relations Problem." *New York Times*. April 21. https://www.nytimes.com/1989/04/21/business/exxon-s-public-relations-problem.html (accessed October 2023).

National Research Council (NRC). 2003. "Oil in the Sea III: Inputs, Fates, and Effects." *National Research Council of the National Academies*. Washington, DC: The National Academies Press.

Ramseur, Jonathan L. 2010. "Oil Spills in U.S. Coastal Waters: Background, Governance, and Issues for Congress." Congressional Research Service. April 30. https://www.epw.senate.gov/public/_cache/files/d/b/db4335ea-2eac-4e97-b37d-7bb90bb4b165/01AFD79733D77F24A71FEF9DAFCCB056.crs-oilspills043010.pdf (accessed October 2023).

Shabecoff, Philip. 1989. "Reaction to Alaska Spill Derails Bill to Allow Oil Drilling in Refuge." *New York Times*. April 12. https://www.nytimes.com/1989/04/12/us/reaction-to-alaska-spill-derails-bill-to-allow-oil-drilling-in-refuge.html (accessed October 2023).

Shogren, Elizabeth. 2014. "Why the *Exxon Valdez* Spill Was a Eureka Moment for Science." National Public Radio. March 22. https://www.npr.org/2014/03/22/292131305/why-the-exxon-valdez-spill-was-a-eureka-moment-for-science (accessed October 2023).

Skinner, Samuel K. and William K. Reilly. 1989. "The Exxon Valdez Oil Spill: A Report to the President." May. National Response Team. US Environmental Protection Agency.

ExxonMobil

ExxonMobil is a multinational oil and natural resources company and one of the world's largest companies by revenue. Before 1972, it was known as the Standard Oil Company of New Jersey, and in 1999 it merged with Mobil, formerly the Standard Oil Company of New York, to form ExxonMobil. ExxonMobil's primary commercial brands are Exxon, Mobil, Esso, and ExxonMobil Chemical. The Standard Oil Company of New Jersey was one of the so-called "Seven Sisters" that dominated world petroleum markets from the Second World War through the 1970s. Exxon owned businesses in each aspect of this huge industry. This included oil field production, transporting oil via pipelines, operating one of the largest global fleets of oil tankers, and managing service stations. Additionally, Exxon was involved in other forms of energy, such as natural gas, coal, nuclear fuels, chemicals, and the iron ores of copper, lead, and zinc.

In the twenty-first century, ExxonMobil was among the top six largest publicly traded US companies by market capitalization. It was the tenth most profitable company of the Fortune 500 in 2017 and had the second-largest total corporate revenue. A slight majority of its shares are owned by institutions, with its largest shareholders being the Vanguard Group (8.2 percent), BlackRock (6.6 percent), and State Street Corporation (4.8 percent). Like its parent Standard Oil from its 1870 beginning, ExxonMobil continues to be the largest oil refiner in the world, with its thirty-seven oil refineries in twenty-one countries having a combined daily refining capacity of 6.3 million barrels (1 million m3).

In 2008, ExxonMobil was responsible for roughly 3 percent of world oil production. While this ranked lower than several of the largest state-owned petroleum companies, it had a 2007 daily production of 3.921 million BOE (barrels of oil equivalent). The company has the fourteenth highest global amount of oil and gas reserves. Though it was less than 1 percent of the world total, ExxonMobil's 20 billion BOE reserves at the end of 2016 were predicted to last over fourteen years. ExxonMobil was heavily criticized for its slow and inadequate response to cleanup efforts after the 1989 *Exxon Valdez* oil spill in Alaska, one of the world's worst oil spills. It has been accused of climate change denialism in its effort to fight the scientific consensus that global warming is caused by the burning of fossil fuels. Like most global petroleum companies, ExxonMobil has also been accused of indifference toward human rights issues and having a baleful impact on developing nations. Furthermore, the company has been criticized for lobbying the US government to adopt an aggressive foreign policy in pursuit of petroleum industry interests overseas.

Both Exxon and Mobil were descendants of Standard Oil, established by John D. Rockefeller (1839–1937) and partners in 1870 as the Standard Oil Company of Ohio. Due to its various anti-competitive activities, the Standard Oil Trust was dissolved under the Sherman Antitrust Act of 1890. In 1911, the US Supreme Court split the trust into thirty-four separate companies. The two largest of these companies were Exxon's parent Jersey Standard, or the

Standard Oil Company of New Jersey, and Socony, the Standard Oil Company of New York, which later became Mobil.

When oil production proved crucial to the war effort in the First World War, with Standard Oil of New Jersey itself supplying about 25 percent of the Allies' oil, President Woodrow Wilson (1856–1924) began to favor Standard Oil in relevant policy decisions. These included his Open Door policy, referring to equal access everywhere for American capital and business, and passage of the 1920 Mineral Leasing Act. During the decades that followed, the original Standard Oil spinoffs changed their names and ownership structures and began acquiring and merging with other oil and natural resource companies. In 1948, Standard Oil of New Jersey and Socony-Vacuum joined with Texaco and the Standard Oil Company of California to form the Arabian American Oil Company (Aramco) venture in Saudi Arabia, their first significant venture in the Middle East.

In 1972, the company engaged in renaming and rebranding itself. Standard Oil of New Jersey had been marketing its gasoline at retail outlets under the names Enco and Esso. The company brought these products together under the Exxon brand and renamed itself Exxon Corporation. One of its subsidiaries, Humble Oil, became Exxon Company, U.S.A. Both Exxon and Mobil were changed as a result of the Energy Crisis of the 1970s, particularly the 1973 Arab Oil Embargo. The two companies expanded their exploration and production into the North Sea, the Gulf of Mexico, Africa, and Asia. Mobil also tried to diversify by acquiring the parent company of Montgomery Ward and Container Corporation of America, which produced paperboard packaging. In 1976, Exxon diversified by adding assets in other energy-related industries such as coal mining, which became Exxon Minerals and later ExxonMobil Coal and Minerals, the oil shale industry, and oil shale deposits. The results of these diversification efforts were mixed. For example, Exxon closed its Colony Shale Oil Project because of low oil-prices and high expenses.

Exxon and Mobil experienced prosperity in 1980s, an era of expansion in oil exploration and steadily decreasing costs of production. Then, the March 24, 1989 *Exxon Valdez* oil spill in Prince William Sound, Alaska spilled over 11 million US gallons of crude oil. Exxon was strongly criticized for its slow and light response, partly spurring passage of the US Oil Pollution Act of 1990. When the initial legal liability award of $5 billion to spill survivors was reduced to $507.5 million by the US Supreme Court in 2008, vociferous public condemnation and legal action ensued. Award distribution was attacked for proceeding too slowly.

In the 1990s, Exxon retreated from major acquisitions and became a smaller company, laying off 40 percent of its employees. It bought back shares worth $16 billion between 1983 and the mid-1990s, greatly benefiting the shareholders and the major mergers and acquisitions businesses. Institutional and individual investors, pension funds, arbitrageurs, etc., made over $100 billion from its capitalizations and stock buybacks. The story was very different for the laid-off employees and their communities.

Exxon's efforts to counter environmental criticisms took many forms, including Bern Keating's *The Gulf of Mexico* (1972), a book commissioned by Exxon Corporation. The book quotes a Louisiana State University marine biologist who said whenever the industry sinks a platform, it creates a "flourishing colony" of sea life "where it used to be just empty sea" (Keating 1972, 62). This totally misrepresented the reality, according to Rowan Jacobsen, author of *Shadows on the Gulf* (2011) because the "breeding population of snappers in the Gulf actually plunged by 97 percent since World War II," much of it lost in shrimp trawler nets and to recreational anglers near the rigs (Jacobsen 2011, 137). There are also high mercury levels in fish and shrimp living around the oil rigs, as much as twenty-five times normal levels in "produced water." This is leftover water from injection into an oil or gas reservoir to extract the mineral and from drilling mud, in spite of US Environmental Protection Agency regulation of mud dumping. Tests found that people who often ate rig-caught seafood had extremely high mercury levels (Davis 2017, 504).

In 1998, Exxon and Mobil combined into Exxon Mobil Corporation, commonly expressed as ExxonMobil. This was the largest corporate merger of its time at $73.7 billion, and created the largest oil company, and the third-largest company of any kind, in the world. As a condition of the merger, the European Commission ordered Mobil's partnership with BP dissolved, and the selling of its stake in Aral, a Germany oil company. In the early 2000s, ExxonMobil was heavily criticized, along with BP, China National Petroleum Corporation, Royal Dutch Shell, and Lukoil, for increasing oil production facilities in the Rumaila oil field and West Qurna Field after the United States and its allies invaded Iraq in 2003 and overthrew the government of Saddam Hussein. ExxonMobil alone produces 2.3 million barrels per day and reaps $967 million per year from its operations in Iraq.

The company shifted emphasis when it sold its service stations in 2008, with the Exxon and Mobil brands franchised to the new owners, and then divested of its last US coal mine the next year. The 2010 ExxonMobil purchase of XTO Energy, focused on development and production of renewable energy resources, continued this corporate redirection. Still, the company remained in the media for the wrong reasons. It was revealed that over 12 million pounds of hazardous chemicals, most of it legally discharged, went down the Mississippi in 2010 and in the years that followed. Nearly 3 million pounds came from ExxonMobil's Baton Rouge refinery, which is consistently in the US's top ten polluters list (Davis 2017, 505).

A recent investigation concluded that ExxonMobil focuses on shareholder return above any other consideration and has a cult-like corporate culture featuring secrecy, rigid conformity, aggressive exploitation of its market dominance, and a consistent pattern of public deception. It also has been shown that the company persistently attempts to undermine and block international climate agreements by debunking related science. A *Mother Jones* report in 2005 revealed that ExxonMobil had "pumped more than $8 million into more than forty think tanks, media outlets, and consumer, religious, and even civil rights groups that preach skepticism about the oncoming climate catastrophe" (Ott 2008, 230).

It also has been recognized that ExxonMobil ignores SEC regulations on how oil holdings should be counted, bombards government scientists with Freedom of Information Act requests, and deceives the public about the reality of its actions. On example is that the company would not give information about a 2015 explosion at its Torrance, California that rained ash on playgrounds and homes (Sarich 2015).

Despite this, ExxonMobil continues its business as usual because it is connected to and supported by political power at the highest level. Shortly before the United States signed the Paris climate agreement to end the 2015 COP21 United Nations summit, President Barack Obama signed a bill into law with a provision that expedites permitting of oil and gas pipelines in the United States. The Fixing America's Surface Transportation Act (FAST) has a provision that shortens environmental review time and the length of time for legal challenges. ExxonMobil, BP, Shell, America's Natural Gas Alliance (ANGA), American Petroleum Institute (API), Koch Industries, US Chamber of Commerce, and many others lobbied for the FAST Act's passage. The CEO of ExxonMobil, Rex Tillerson, served as US Secretary of

State during the first two years of the Trump administration. In 2017, it was revealed that ExxonMobil lobbyists led the effort to widen the Panama Canal as well as to deepen ports to allow them to receive bigger and heavier tankers that sit lower in the water column, such as those carrying LNG or larger shipments of oil. This included passage of the 2014 Water Resources Reform and Development Act (Horn 2017).

The future of ExxonMobil seems assured, as long as American consumers continue to demand energy in the form of petroleum, and as long as energy policy in the United States continues to equate the national interest with the economic health of oil and gas corporations and other fossil fuel extraction interests.

William P. Kladky

See also: American Petroleum Institute; Aramco; Energy Crisis of the 1970s; *Exxon Valdez* Oil Spill; Global Climate Coalition; Gulf Oil Company; Iraq War and the Project for a New American Century; Koch Brothers; Mobil Oil Corporation; Organization of Petroleum Exporting Countries (OPEC); Panama Canal; Rockefeller, John D.; Seven Sisters Oil Companies; Standard Oil Company; Texaco

FURTHER READING

Bower, Tom. 2009. *Oil: Money, Politics, and Power in the 21st Century*. New York: Grand Central Publishing.

Chayes, Sarah. 2017. "Why Read a 5-year-old Book about ExxonMobil Now? Two Words: Rex Tillerson." *Los Angeles Times*. January 27. https://www.latimes.com/books/jacketcopy/la-ca-jc-private-empire-20170127-story.html (accessed October 2023).

Coll, Steve. 2012. *Private Empire: ExxonMobil and American Power*. New York: Penguin Books.

Davis, Jack. 2017. *The Gulf: The Making of an American Sea*. New York: Liveright Publishing Corporation.

Exxon Mobil Corporation. 2014. "ExxonMobil Historical Collection, 1790–2014." Briscoe Center for American History. University of Texas at Austin. https://web.archive.org/web/20180905124041/https://legacy.lib.utexas.edu/taro/utcah/00352/cah-00352.html (accessed October 2023).

Financial Tribune (FT). 2017. "Oil Majors' Debt from Crude Collapse May Have Peaked." *Financial Tribune*. January 27. https://financialtribune.com/articles/energy/58316/oil-majors-debt-from-crude-collapse-may-have-peaked (accessed October 2023).

Henderson, Dean. 2011. "The Four Horseman behind America's Oil Wars." *Global Research*. April 26.

Horn, Steve. 2015. "Prior to Paris Climate Summit, Obama Signed Exxon-Koch Backed Bill Expediting Pipeline Permits." *DeSmogBlog*. December 15. https://www.desmogblog.com/2015/12/31/paris-climate-summit-obama-exxon-koch-bill-pipeline-permit (accessed October 2023).

Horn, Steve. 2017. "How Exxon Lobbyists Led Push to Deepen US Ports and Increase Natural Gas Exports." *Global Research*. May 19. https://www.globalresearch.ca/how-exxon-lobbyists-led-push-to-deepen-us-ports-and-increase-natural-gas-exports/5590861 (accessed October 2023).

Jacobsen, Rowan. 2011. *Shadows of the Gulf: A Journey through Our Last Great Wetland*. New York: Bloomsbury USA.

Jerving, Sara, Katie Jennings, Masako Melissa Hirsch, and Susanne Rust. 2015. "What Exxon Knew about the Earth's Melting Arctic." *Los Angeles Times*. October 9. https://graphics.latimes.com/exxon-arctic/ (accessed October 2023).

Keating, Bern. 1972. *The Gulf of Mexico*. New York: Viking Press.
Mosley, Leonard. 1973. *PowerPlay: Oil in the Middle East*. Baltimore, MD: Penguin Books.
Ott, Riki. 2008. *Not One Drop: Betrayal and Courage in the Wake of the Exxon Valdez Oil Spill*. White River Junction, VT: Chelsea Green Publishing.
Sarich, Christina. 2015. "Exxon Mobil Explosion? Complete. Media. Black Out." *Natural Society*. May 22. https://naturalsociety.com/exxon-mobile-explosion-complete-media-black-out/ (accessed October 2023).
Yergin, Daniel. 1991. *The Prize: The Epic Quest for Oil, Money, and Power*. New York: Simon & Schuster.

Farmington Mine Disaster

The coal mine explosion that occurred in Farmington, West Virginia in 1968 is one of the most significant tragedies in American history. The disaster forever changed the status of safety regulations in the mining industry. Numerous mine disasters prior to Farmington prompted passage of mine safety standards, but inspectors were given no enforcement power. Following Farmington, Congress passed the Coal Mine Safety and Health Act of 1969, which gave federal regulators authority to levy fines against mine operators for safety violations. The Farmington disaster also strengthened the power of organized labor and contributed to creation of the Occupational Safety and Health Administration (Heckathorn 1987, 92). Farmington caused horrible suffering, and the nation watched rescue efforts on live television. Although popular pressure forced politicians to pass mine safety regulations, survivors received limited compensation. Sadly, there were certain cultural dynamics within Appalachian communities that enabled circumvention of justice for the disaster victims in clear view of worldwide attention.

The Farmington coal mine, located in northern West Virginia about 30 miles south of Pittsburgh, was owned by Consolidated Coal Company (Consol), which bought it from the Jamison Coal and Coke company in 1966. Jameson had suffered an explosion that killed fifteen miners at the site in 1954. The explosion on November 20, 1968 at "Consol No 9" woke people up as far as 12 miles away. There were ninety-nine workers in the mine at the time of the explosion. Fires burned in various areas of the mine for over a week as rescue operations were underway. Twenty-one miners were eventually rescued. On November 30, the mine was sealed to starve the fire of oxygen. Of the seventy-eight miners who were killed, nineteen bodies were never recovered.

To date, the exact cause of the Farmington Mine Disaster has not been definitively determined. The most widely held theory is that a build-up of methane gas along with inadequate control of coal dust ignited the explosion. Future West Virginia Governor Joe Manchin, who lived in Farmington at the time of the disaster and lost an uncle in the explosion, states that prior to Farmington, "There was no rock dusting, (and) no controlling the mine dust, which is basically gunpowder" (Harris 2017, 73). However, federal and state regulations controlling mine dust were in effect prior to the Farmington disaster, but were not enforced (Harris 2017, 73). In 1965, mine inspectors cited Consol for unsafe electrical equipment that could spark an explosion of mounting coal dust (Stewart 2012, 35). In addition, alarms that should have warned miners of methane build-up failed to trigger an evacuation. Evidence indicates that it was common practice for the mines to remain open, even after fans designed to vent methane gases were known to be out of order. Numerous safety violations were either ignored by inspectors or left unaddressed after inspectors cited them. Regardless, no criminal charges were ever filed for the avoidable deaths of the seventy-eight miners.

FIGURE 9: Memorial and cemetery for miners lost in the Farmington coal mine explosion in 1968.

Post-disaster controversies associated with Farmington are well documented. Even though more than $10 million was spend on the recovery effort, surviving families accused Consol of being more concerned with resuming production than with finding the remaining bodies (Ship 1971, 6). A settlement agreement offering families $10,000 vaguely stipulated that Consol would work to recover the miner's bodies, "as long as a search could be done safely, reasonably, feasibly, and practically" (Stewart 2012, 204). Throughout the controversy, United Mine Workers (UMW) President Tony Boyle defended Consol, and union miners became increasingly supportive of Boyle's opponent for the union Presidency, Jock Yablonski (Stewart 2012, 143). On December 31, 1969, hitmen hired by Boyle murdered Yablonski, his wife, and his daughter in their Clarksville, Pennsylvania home. Yablonski's son, Kenneth, later represented thirty-nine widows who turned down Consol's original settlement offer. This lawsuit was eventually dismissed in state court. When Consol announced that it was shutting down its search for the missing bodies, seven widows who had agreed to the $10,000 settlement filed an additional lawsuit for breach of contract. The parties reached a settlement in 1982, in which Consul agreed to pay the remaining plaintiffs' attorney fees and give them 246 acres of land located above the mine site. In 2008, several families filed a lawsuit against Consol after learning that prior to the explosion, the company's chief electrician, Alex Kovarbasich, had disabled a ventilation fan alarm system. Federal inspector Larry L. Layne had reported this in a memo, but Layne's memo, damaging photographs, and fan charts had been withheld during previous court depositions (Ship 1971, 162–3). This lawsuit was dismissed due to the statute of limitations (AP 2018).

The absence of any criminal indictments and paltry civil settlements stemming from the Farmington disaster is well documented. What is not yet explored is the cultural context which allowed an absence of justice to occur in the plain sight of public scrutiny. Farmington occurred at a time when compensation to disaster victims was thwarted by a belief that victims were unworthy or complicit in their own demise, and that disasters were unavoidable acts of God.

Early federal disaster relief was limited to that which could be justified by the Commerce Clause. After the US Civil War, Congress began to justify relief as a humanitarian gesture (Roberts 2013, 31). Arguments for or against federal aid centered on the issue of whether or not victims were deserving. This shift first played out in debates over post-war famine relief to freed slaves. President Andrew Johnson originally vetoed the aid, and Congress debated whether or not freed slaves were undeserving by virtue of their laziness. Some argued that aid should extend to "deserving" whites who were also affected by the war. The eventual extension of relief aid to the Freedman's Bureau represents a shift from disputes about the constitutionality of disaster aid to arguments over the extent to which victims of disaster are blameless or deserving of humanitarian aid. It also marks the first time that federal disaster aid was distributed through a structured bureaucracy (Dauber 2013, 43).

Although disaster relief was an established norm by 1968, the federal government provided no aid to the victims of the Farmington disaster. The provision of such aid could easily have been justified by the Commerce Clause, or on humanitarian grounds. However, the Farmington disaster occurred during a time of discriminatory attitudes toward African Americans, immigrants, Appalachians, and women, which rendered them as low status individuals in the minds of nativist whites outside of the region.

Ronald L. Lewis documented that as early as the 1920s, West Virginia boasted a "judicial mixture" of African American coal miners comprising 33 percent of all miners (Lewis 1987, 233). The status of African Americans working in the Farmington mine was no doubt affected by the legacies of slavery, reconstruction, and racial segregation in the Jim Crow era. The Farmington disaster also occurred at a time of emerging negative labels attributed to white Appalachians. Media portrayed Appalachians appeared as negative stereotypes in popular television and film programs such as *Hee-Haw* (1969–71), *The Beverly Hillbillies* (1962–71) and *Deliverance* (1972). Negative portrayals of Appalachians were accompanied by the "culture of poverty" theory, which placed the blame of poverty on poor people's backward traits (Patterson 1981, 138).

Inasmuch as women have occupied a less than equal standing throughout American history, Appalachian women could be perceived to be stigmatized twice. The role of women in the coal fields is an understudied topic, although there has been some recognition of the influence of reform advocates such as Mary Harris "Mother" Jones (Green 2015, 141). Most accounts of coal miners' wives feature them as impoverished supporters of their struggling miner husbands. Portrayal of miners' families during Farmington disaster rescue efforts reflect this disposition. Farmington families were congregated into a small store with the media, which took advantage of their tragedies to publish images of fainting women and distraught children (Campione 2016, 9). Struggles of the female side of the coal industry is most commonly connected in the public imagination to Loretta Lynn's popular song, *Coal Miner's Daughter* (1970). Direct exploitation of coal miner women is a much less known. Evidence exists for the abuse of young girls brought to the isolated coal towns and sold into sexual slavery, which is a major undocumented crime (Kline 2017, 38).

The low status of African Americans, immigrants, Appalachians, and women coexisted within a culture where miners were at least partially complicit in their own demise. Miners sometimes contributed to explosions by sidestepping safety procedures in an effort to make a living. Safety violations circumvented by miners included inadequate cross-cuts and misuse of explosives used to eliminate stumps that remained after coal was extracted from columns. At Consol, miners were paid bonuses based on production, and workers that complained about safety violations were ostracized and given the most dangerous jobs (Stewart 2012, 30). Misuse of explosives to destroy the coal stumps contributed to an explosion that caused fifty-four deaths at Consol No. 9 in 1954. Fireboss reports indicate that prior to the 1968 disaster, inadequate stoppings contributed to compromising of ventilation. Yet, both federal and West Virginia inspectors made no ventilation findings nor any citations of the company for its dangerous "bleeding system" (Stewart 2012, 51, 115).

The perceived low status of miners and their ostensible complicity in circumventing safety procedures were accompanied by a contemporaneous belief that disasters are either natural or caused by acts of God. These coexisting contexts are less documented in the case of Farmington, due to lawsuits never making it to trial. However, their existence is well documented in analyses of the Buffalo Creek flood disaster that occurred in nearby Logan, West Virginia, just three years after Farmington. On February 26, 1972, a flood caused by the breaking of a man-made coal sludge dam killed 125 people and injured 1,121 others. Victims were again denied justice from a disaster caused by human negligence. Defendants successfully argued in court that the disaster was an act of God. Furthermore, an award-winning study by renowned sociologist Kai Erikson depicts the affected Appalachians as isolated, backward mountaineers incapable of resisting exploitation or regaining a sense of community (Erikson 1976, 250). In Farmington, Buffalo Creek, and numerous other mine disasters in the region, justice was denied because of cultural beliefs about the victims and the cause of disasters.

These beliefs are not simply outside impositions. In defending Consol against accusations of neglect in the Farmington disaster, UMW President Tony Boyle stated, "As long as we have mines, there is always this inherent danger of explosions" (Stewart 2012, 94). Similarly, one Farmington schoolteacher opined, "You have to accept the reality of God's will ... people get killed in mines as well as out of it, and none has assurance of when he will live or die" (Stewart 2012, 95). Additionally, internalized self-recognition of the low status of miners is exemplified in the often sung Appalachian folk song, "Only a Miner." Although words varied from song to song, a typical verse goes like this:

> Only a miner killed——Oh! Is that all?
> One of the timbers caved, great was the fall,
> Crushing another one shaped like his God,
> Only a miner, lad——under the sod. (Green 1972, 96)

The reference to God in this version of the song is no coincidence. The history of coal mine disasters records efforts by perpetrators and victims alike to depict the demise of low-status miners as tragedies ordained by God.

Much has changed since Farmington. Enforceable safety regulations have reduced the number of deaths in coal mines, and African Americans, Appalachians, and women have stood up against discrimination and stigmatizing stereotypes. These aspects of the 1968 Farmington

Mine Disaster stand at historical crossroads. Today, coal communities face new threats from unemployment, flooding, climate change, and environmental degradation related to an industry shift from deep mining to surface mining.

Norman R. Rose

See also: Cherry Mine Disaster; Coal; Dawson Mine Disaster; Krebs Mine Disaster; Scofield Mine Disaster; United Mine Workers of America; Upper Big Branch Mine Disaster; Weir, Peter; West Frankfort Mine Disaster

FURTHER READING

Associated Press (AP). 1970. "State Concealing Photos of Consol Mine Explosion." *Beckley Post-Herald*. November 23.

Associated Press (AP). 2018 "Court Tosses Lawsuit in the 1968 Farmington Mine Explosion." Morning Edition. West Virginia Public Broadcasting. July 26. https://wvpublic.org/court-tosses-lawsuit-in-1968-farmington-mine-explosion/ (accessed October 2023).

Campione, Bob. 2016. *Images of America: The 1968 Farmington Disaster*. Charleston, SC: Arcadia Publishing.

Dauber, Michelle. 2013. *The Sympathetic State: Disaster Relief and the Origins of the American Welfare State*. Chicago: University of Chicago Press.

Erikson, Kai. 1976. *Everything in Its Path: Destruction of Community in the Buffalo Creek Flood*. New York: Touchstone.

Ewen, Lynda, and Lewis Julia A. 1999. "Buffalo Creek Revisited: Deconstruction of Kai Erikson's Stereotypes." *Appalachian Journal*. Vol. 27. No. 1. Fall.

Green, Archie. 1972. *Only a Miner: Studies in Recorded Coal-mining Songs*. Urbana: University of Illinois Press.

Green, James. 2015. *The Devil is Here in These Hills: West Virginia's Coal Miners and Their Battle for Freedom*. New York: Atlantic Monthly Press.

Harris, Wess, ed. 2017. *Written in Blood: Courage and Corruption in the Appalachian War of Extraction*. Gay, WV: Appalachian Community Services; Oakland, CA: PM Press.

Heckathorn, Douglas D., and Steven M. Maser. 1987. "Bargaining and the Sources of Transaction Costs: The Case of Government Regulation." *Journal of Law, Economics, & Organization*. Vol. 3. No. 1. Spring.

Kline, Michelle. 2017. "The Rented Girl: A Closer look at Women in the Coalfields." In *Written in Blood: Courage and Corruption in the Appalachian War of Extraction*. Ed. Wess Harris. Oakland, California: PM Press.

Lewis, Ronald L. 1987. *Black Coal Miners in America: Race, Class, and Community Conflict, 1780–1980*. Lexington: University Press of Kentucky.

Nyden, Paul J. 2008. "Reforms Written in Miners' Blood." *Charleston Gazette*. November 23.

Patterson, James T. 1981. *America's Struggle against Poverty, 1900–1980*. Boston: Harvard University Press.

Roberts, Patrick S. 2013. *Disasters and the American State: How Politicians, Bureaucrats and the Public Prepare for the Unexpected*. New York: Cambridge University Press.

Shipp, Steve. 1971. "Body Recovery Exacting Task." *Beckley Post Herald*. July 6.

Stenberg, Ted. 2000. *Acts of God: The Unnatural History of Natural Disasters in America*. New York: Oxford University Press.

Stewart, Bonnie E. 2012. *No. 9: The Farmington Mine Disaster*. Morgantown, WV: West Virginia University Press.

Federal Power Act of 1935

The basic elements of the Federal Power Act of 1935 (FPA) were first put into legislation in 1920 as the Federal Water Power Act, which was intended to better regulate the emerging hydroelectric power market in the United States. New Deal-era lawmakers updated and revised the earlier act and in process changed its scope. The FPA has been amended many times since, with recent changes in 2005 under the provisions of the Energy Policy Act.

The historical context which motivated the changes that created the FPA in 1935 is important to understand. During the Great Depression, FDR's New Deal program created a large increase in public-sector employment through various government works projects, which included construction of hydroelectric dams like the Bonneville, Grand Coulee, and Boulder dams. These large hydroelectric facilities were designed to transmit electrical power over a widespread area that could encompass several states. In turn, this demanded clarification of the jurisdictional relationship between individual states and the federal government, as now the sale of electricity could be treated like interstate commerce.

Under the new FPA in 1935, the Federal Power Commission was renamed the Federal Energy Regulatory Commission (FERC) with the expanded role of overseeing transmission of electricity to ensure that the rates for transmission of electricity as interstate commerce would be determined in a fair, reasonable, and impartial manner. However, it would remain the jurisdiction of individual states to control the actual price of retail electricity. This dichotomy is often referred to as a "bright line" jurisdictional division, and was consistent with provisions in the Public Utility Act, also enacted in 1935, whose primary goal was to protect customers from economic exploitation by monopoly utilities. In that way, the FERC would function as an independent regulatory agency.

The FPA explicitly stated that the FERC would not be involved in overseeing the actual generation of electricity, only its interstate transport. Over the ensuing decades, the manner in which electricity is generated and transmitted evolved, which considerably blurred the original intended bright-line division. Some of this confusion was corrected through the Energy Policy Act of 2005. In essence, the operational role of the FERC became one of ensuring the transmission of electricity at fair prices and the reliability of that transmission throughout the lower forty-eight states. This was accomplished by dividing the country into regional districts for the interconnection and coordination of electricity transmission.

One "accident" of this arrangement was that Texas became isolated from sharing electricity transmission with the larger-scale US electrical grid. This Texas interconnect system resulted from a loophole that allowed the state government to avoid being subject to federal regulators. The existence of this loophole meant that if no transmitted electricity generated in Texas actually crossed state lines, then that electricity is not part of interstate commerce. In the 1930s, Texas had substantial coal, natural gas, and oil resources for power plants which easily supplied electrical power to Texas citizens. That encouraged Texas to become self-reliant and independent of the rest of the nation's policies on electricity generation and transmission. In the present day, if all of Texas lost its electricity, the nation's power grid would not be required to deliver electricity to Texas residents. This became clear in the winter of 2021 when a severe storm caused a failure in electricity generation, shutting off power to 4.5 million people, resulting in the deaths of at fifty-seven people and $195 billion in property damage (EI 2021).

The FPA worked for many decades and remains the primary legislative authority behind the federal government's efforts to sustain plentiful supplies of electricity and transmission, at reasonable prices for consumers. However, over the years, not only has US per capita electricity demand greatly increased, but patterns of electricity use have strongly shifted, particularly the requirement for more electrical usage in the American West. Indeed, in 1935, many remote areas or farms in the United States did not actually even have electricity until FDR's rural electrification program began to take effect in the 1950s. In 1960, per capita consumption of electricity in the United States was 4.04 kWh per day, when the population numbered 179 million. Forty years later, in 2000, the per capita usage rate was 13.67 kWh per day, and the US population had increased to 281 million. While the population grew by 56 percent over the forty-year period, per capita electricity consumption grew by an astonishing 338 percent. Since 2000, per capita consumption has largely become flat primarily through conservation incentives and the development of significantly more energy-efficient home appliances. This tremendous growth in per capita consumption could not have been well anticipated in 1935 but does suggest that the nature of electricity generation and distribution has significantly changed to the point where new legislation might be required to better reconcile antiquated energy policies to the modern world.

There have been two primary new methods for the generation of electricity, and its associated transmission may create the need for more legislative change. First, renewable energy is being generated in remote locations, some of which might not even have grid access. This leads to the possibility of "stranded renewables," which might include a wind energy farm in the Aleutian Islands, the development of offshore wind resources, and large solar arrays in remote desert areas. Second, power is now generated at the point of consumption in what is referred to as distributed generation (DG). A simple example of DG is an individual homeowner's use of solar panels on their land for end-use of electricity. This "off the grid" independence is increasing in many areas, and the legacy-based regulatory environment in the United States does not really address this new situation, especially when the end-user may also be able to "sell" electricity back to the local grid. This situation has been handled in a variety of ways by local utilities, with no national policy as a backdrop.

The current dilemma is best manifest by the concept of net metering. Net metering measures the difference between the amount of power produced by an end-user and the consumption of that power. Any excess, in principle, makes the electricity meter spin "backwards" as the end-user now has a surplus that can be returned to the grid. Net metering could obliterate the "bright-line" jurisdictional division as it allows retail customers to essentially become wholesale generators of electricity, albeit at very small levels. To cite a possible instance, a building on the Idaho–Oregon border could generate electricity which then crossed state lines in transmission. The question might arise, what would be the appropriate regulatory agency for this situation? This situation would not have occurred to the designers of the original FPA in 1935. In principle, this individual could be subject to both state and federal regulations, which could serve as a disincentive to practice DG in the first place. There are potential regulatory tensions in the coming years that will need to be addressed. Complicating matters even further, DG tends to produce "clean electricity," which therefore perhaps should receive a different kind of treatment than fossil fuel based electricity generation.

This evolving situation creates an opportunity for new kind of FPA for the twenty-first century. The 1935 provision in the FPA, which denies FERC any jurisdiction over facilities used for generation, has left states with total control over their choices of fuels for electricity generation. In recent years, court proceedings have highlighted the clash between state renewable energy portfolio goals and their potential effects on wholesale market prices which require federal jurisdiction. In a hypothetical case, the state of Oklahoma decides to fully build out wind infrastructure combined with energy storage for twenty-four hour, seven day a week delivery of electricity to the state's residents, while also having a substantial excess of electricity that can be exported to additional markets across state lines. This hypothetical case is moving closer to reality so there is now a real need to expand the authority of FERC in order to combine current centralized power systems with the flexibility of DG. In doing so, the nation will have a coherent and unifying federal policy environment that serves to incentivize the develop of more DG based or renewable sources of electricity and their transmission. Indeed, if plans for the generation of electricity from renewable sources must confront a difficult or unwieldy regulatory process, that disincentive will hinder the green energy movement currently underway.

Greg Bothun

See also: Cooke, Morris Llewellyn; Energy Policy Act of 2005; Federal Power Commission; Federal Water Power Act of 1920; Hoover Dam; Hydroelectric Power; Public Utility Regulatory Policies Act of 1978; Rural Electrification Act of 1936; Tennessee Valley Authority

FURTHER READING

Bothun, Greg. 2020. "Off Shore Wind Power: A Promising and Scalable Future Electricity Source." In *Complementary Resources for Tomorrow*. Ed. A. Vasel-Be-Hagh and DK Ting. EAS 2019. Springer Proceedings in Energy. Cham: Springer. https://doi.org/10.1007/978-3-030-38804-18 (accessed October 2023).

Cantelon, Philip. 2012. "The Regulatory Dilemma of the Federal Power Commission 1920–1977." *Federal History*. Vol. 4. January. Pp. 61–86.

Christiansen, Matthew R., and Joshua C. Macey. 2021. "Long Live the Federal Power Act's Bright Line." *Harvard Law Review*. Vol. 134. No. 4. February. Pp. 1361–422.

EI (Energy Institute). 2021. "The Timeline and Events of the February 2021 Texas Electric Grid Blackouts." The University of Texas at Austin. July. https://energy.utexas.edu/research/ercot-blackout-2021

Gellings, Clark W. 2016. "Value of an Integrated Grid." In *Future of Utilities—Utilities of the Future: How Technological Innovations in Distributed Energy Resources Will Reshape the Electric Power Sector*. Ed. Fereidoon P. Sioshansi. Pp. 25–50. Amsterdam: Academic Press/Elsevier.

Federal Power Commission

The Federal Power Commission (FPC) was the predecessor government agency to the current Federal Energy Regulatory Commission (FERC). The FPC was created to administer the Federal Water Power Act passed by the US Congress on June 10, 1920. The FPC *Rules and Regulations* stated that, "The commission has jurisdiction over all projects involving the construction, operation, and maintenance of dams, water conduits, reservoirs, power houses, transmission lines, or other project works for the development, transmission, and utilization of power" (FPC 1921). It was created in part to repeal section 18 of the River and Harbor Appropriation Act of 1917. The first commission included only one employee, the Executive Secretary, Oscar C. Merrill (1874–1950), who was previously the chief engineer of the US Forest Service. The chief advocate of the act was Gifford Pinchot (1865–1946), a pioneering conservationist, the first Chief of the US Forest Service, and Republican governor of Pennsylvania. He sought legislation to establish a national policy for the use and development of water power on public land. The commission, however, was not immediately an independent body.

The FPC began with a goal to streamline the process of developing hydroelectric power. In 1928, the twenty-nine employees previously assigned to the FPC from other offices became permanent employees of the commission. An act of June 23, 1930 created a five-member independent FPC. President Herbert Hoover appointed geologist George Otis Smith as the commission's first chairman. Prior to his appointment, Smith served as the director of the US Geological Survey from 1907 to 1922. In the fiscal year 1930–1, the FPC's total expenses were $1,976,074.16 with forty-five employees on the payroll besides the commissioners. By June 30, 1931, FPC had issued 223 preliminary permits and 571 licenses for major and minor projects, as defined by its *Rules and Regulations*. In 1936, regional offices were established in New York City, Atlanta, San Francisco, Denver, and Chicago.

The years leading up to the Second World War were a period of expansion for the FPC. In 1935, the agency gained rate and accounting jurisdiction over wholesale sales and transmission of interstate electric utilities when the Federal Power Act (FPA) became law under Part II of the Public Utility Act (PUA). The commission's jurisdiction expanded again in 1938 under the Natural Gas Act (NGA), granting the FPC similar jurisdiction over natural gas companies.

After the Second World War, a series of standardizations led to further growth. The Administrative Procedure Act, passed by Congress in 1946, brought the FPC under a set of common procedural standards with other federal regulatory agencies. In 1954, the US Supreme Court case *Phillips Petroleum Co. v. Wisconsin* established that all wellhead sales in interstate natural gas commerce were subject to FPC jurisdiction. Prior to this case, only pipeline resales were regulated while independent producers' sales to pipelines went unregulated. Immediately, this produced an enormous influx of applications to the FPC from producers. This led to rate regulation change, first Area Rate Regulation, approved in the Permian Basin Area Rate Cases, and later on a national basis.

THE DEPARTMENT OF ENERGY

The Department of Energy emerged in 1977 in response to the energy crises of the mid-1970s. This volatile period ushered in technological and philosophical shifts towards energy sources, use, and global energy policy. The interrelationship between national military defense and energy guided federal policy.

Elia Vargas

FPC's successor agency, FERC, was created in 1977 through the Department of Energy Organization Act (DEOA). FERC was created to be an independent regulatory commission under the US Department of Energy (DOE), also created through the DEOA in 1977. In addition to transferring jurisdiction of oil pipelines from the Interstate Commerce Commission to the FERC, it also absorbed most of the FPC's responsibilities. President Jimmy Carter appointed lawyer Charles Curtis, who had been serving as Chairman of the FPC, as the first Chairman of the FERC. Prior to 1977, as the DOE website states, "no overall energy policy existed. Government officials generally thought in terms of particular fuels, technologies, and resources rather than 'energy'" (DOE 2020). The history of the DOE derives from the heritage of national defense, specifically the Second World War-era Manhattan Project, which produced the atomic bomb. The subsequent commercial pursuit of nuclear energy enabled by the Atomic Energy Act of 1946 and the centralization of energy-related federal programs produced the DOE. US energy policy is indelibly shaped by its defense policy.

The FERC, like the FPC of 1930, is composed of up to five commissioners appointed by the US president with guidance and consent from the Senate. Its stated mission is to "assist consumers in obtaining economically efficient, safe, reliable and secure energy services at a reasonable cost through appropriate regulatory and market means, and collaborative efforts" (FERC 2018, viii). In comparison to the 1930 $1.9 million FPC budget, the FERC 2018 budget was $367 million. As required by the GPRA Modernization Act of 2010, the FERC must update its Strategic Plan every four years. The FY 2018–22 Strategic Plan, implemented by late Chairman Kevin J. McIntyre, attorney and Republican government official, focuses on addressing the significant changes to energy supply and new energy technologies. The list of FERC responsibilities, as outlined in the plan, is extensive, but it also stipulates what it does not do. For instance, it is responsible for regulating interstate transportation commerce of oil via pipeline. But, it is not responsible for the oversight of oil pipeline construction. The NGA and the FPA require that the FERC ensures safe development of new infrastructure and operations. Furthermore, the FERC oversees energy development in the private sector for economic and environmentally beneficial outcomes for the country. While it works with numerous other offices and experts to determine environmental and safety assessments, in accordance with the National Environmental Policy Act (NEPA) the FERC does not define what environmental or economic benefit means.

Returning to its inception in 1920, the FPC jurisdiction included commerce traveling on navigable waters and other waters under congressional jurisdiction, as well as public lands or reservations excepting national monuments and parks. Licenses issued under the

Federal Water Power Act were not to exceed fifty years and while it required little to no environmental protection other than safe maintenance of the project, it did require making public the information procured from its activities. In other words, the requirements for a license depended more on the efficiency and efficacy of the proposed project than the project's impact on the proposed site. Nonetheless, the goal of standardizing regulation of hydroelectric power projects began the process of US government oversight of energy commerce.

Elia Vargas

See also: Atomic Energy Acts; Federal Power Act of 1935; Federal Water Power Act of 1920; Manhattan Project; Natural Gas Act of 1938; Public Utility Regulatory Policies Act of 1978

FURTHER READING

US Department of Energy (DOE). 2020. "A Brief History of the Department of Energy." https://www.energy.gov/management/office-management/operational-management/history/brief-history-department-energy (accessed April 8, 2020).

Federal Energy Regulatory Commission (FERC). 2018. *Federal Energy Regulatory Commission Strategic Plan FY 2018–2022*. Washington, DC: US Department of Energy.

Federal Energy Regulatory Commission (FERC). 2020. "About FERC." https://www.ferc.gov/what-ferc#:~:text=What%20FERC%20Does,natural%20gas%20and%20hydropower%20projects (accessed October 2023).

Federal Power Commission (FPC). 1921. *Rules and Regulations as Amended by Order No. 11 of June 6, 1921: Governing the Administration of the Federal Water Power Act: With Copies of the Act, of Amendment Thereto, and of Orders Nos. 1 to 11, Inclusive*. Washington, DC: US Government Printing Office.

Moler, Elizabeth, David Ward, Robert C. Platt, Sherman Poland, and David Benkin. 1995. "A Salute: 75 Years for the FPC and FERC." *Energy Law Journal*. Vol. 16. No. 2. Pp. 293–7.

Pinchot, Gifford. 1945. "Long Struggle for Effective Federal Water Power Legislation." *George Washington Law Review*. Vol. 14. Pp. 9–20.

Federal Water Power Act of 1920

The Federal Water Power Act of 1920 expanded federal authority over the use of water resources for electricity generation and prepared the way for federal entry into the creation of major government hydroelectric projects. It was especially impactful in the western portion of the country. This act helped to bring order and stability to the market for electricity from hydroelectric sources, and thus continued to add to the building blocks of civilization that brought America into the modern era.

Before the twentieth century, legislation like the Federal Water Power Act was largely unneeded. The waterpower resources of the eastern portion of the United States were easy to control and adapted to serve the growing nation. This portion of the county contains many rivers, streams, and creeks for use in power generation. It also happened to have forests, coal and oil reserves, and other natural resources that enabled settlers to quickly build farms and bring the other trappings of civilization frontier areas. Larger rivers, like the Hudson, Ohio, Savannah, Tennessee, or Alabama, were all easily navigable, and easily used as a resource for agriculture or industry. Ample forests were used for a variety of purposes, and in most places the soil and animals were ready to be used to construct the sinews of a growing American civilization.

As the United States expanded westward, settlers encountered new environments that required new ways of thinking. Major rivers were few and far between, and less easily controlled than their eastern counterparts. Given the arid environment of the Great Plains, the Colorado Plateau, the desert Southwest, and much of California, natural resources were few and far between. In 1820, Stephen H. Long became the first US explorer and mapmaker to use to term "Great American Desert" to describe the region of North America that would eventually be known as the Great Plains. Unlike the eastern United States, with its abundance of rivers, forests, good soil, and large animal populations, this supposed desert, with its lack of all of those things, seemed like a wasteland that wasn't worth a person's time. This belief held as American settlers traveled through to the more supposed "productive areas" of the west looking for minerals, timber, and forage for livestock. The Great American Desert was a highway to be traveled to reach promised lands further west.

Eventually, people began to settle the Great Plains and the Colorado Plateau regions. They discovered under the prairie sod some of the best soils in the world, and in the mountain west some of the America's richest mining resources (Hahn 2016, 334–6). These settlers began to realize that to make the Great Plains and the Rocky Mountains region bloom, they had to become masters of the waters of the West.

This brought them to consider the original western land policies of the nineteenth century. Much of the arid lands in the west were under the control of the federal government as part of the US public lands system. The original idea for this land was to encourage the spread of American civilization westward through private ownership, which was legislated in the Homestead Act of 1862. Homesteaders could make a claim to 160 acres of government-surveyed land, and if they lived on it for five years and made improvements, it was theirs to keep. The policy helped move people into the west, but of some "500 million acres dispersed by the General Land Office between 1862 and 1904, only 80 million acres went to homesteaders," with the remainder being swallowed up by real estate speculators, railroad corporations, and an array of cattle, mining, and logging interests (NA 2022). When John Wesley Powell of the US Geological Survey documented the results of US land policy in the west in his *Report on the Lands of the Arid Region of the United States* (1879), he concluded that prevailing water conditions in the region made it nearly impossible for people to live like the independent land-owing farmers of the much-wetter eastern region of the country.

Powell showed that the way land and water resources were managed in the western region had to change. This included the system governing river improvement and management for the purposes of waterpower. Electrical generation through hydropower first appeared in the 1882 at Edison's Vulcan Street Plant in Appleton, Wisconsin and the new settlers in the West realized that they had to have government assistance to actually have a chance to achieve any sort of progress on this account. The water management system finally began to change as the country transitioned from the nineteenth to twentieth centuries. In 1899, Congress passed the River and Harbors Act, which banned the dumping of solid waste into rivers and streams. This was followed three years later by the Reclamation Act of 1902, which allowed for irrigation projects to be organized across the United States—particularly in the western region—and created the US Reclamation Service (later the US Bureau of Reclamation) to manage these projects. For the inhabitants of the West, the federal government, along with state administration, became master of the waters. With this mastery, farms could be built, cities could grow, and civilization—based on electricity supplied through hydropower—could have a chance to spread throughout the region.

The Federal Water Power Act of 1920 was enacted after American's entry and participation in the First World War. The war demonstrated the importance to the nation of all kinds of energy, from coal to oil and gas to electricity. The two decades before the war was a period of rapid electrification across the country as rivers were viewed by many municipalities and electrical utility companies as important sources of power. Hydroelectric projects sprang up in the eastern region. The Federal Water Power Act of 1920 created the Federal Power Commission (FPC) to supervise the generation and transmission of this new source of energy. The FPC's mandate was the following:

> To issue licenses to citizens of the United States, or to any association of such citizens, or to any corporation organized under the laws of the United States or any State thereof, or to any State or municipality for the purpose of constructing, operating, and maintaining dams, water conduits, reservoirs, power houses, transmission lines, or other project works necessary or convenient for the development and improvement of navigation and for the development, transmission, and utilization of power. (FPA 1920)

Furthermore, the mandate included language that outlined the FPC's jurisdiction and authority to "regulate commerce" across state lines or on "public lands and reservations" in the event that residents wish to utilize "surplus water or water power from any Government dam" (FPA 1920).

The onset of the Great Depression and the New Deal occasioned regional planning and construction for electrification in underserved areas, such as the hydroelectric dams of the Tennessee Valley Authority throughout the southern region, and the creation of the Bonneville, Grand Coulee, and Hoover dams and power stations in the West. This new generation capacity allowed cities, regions, and states in the south and the west the ability to grow beyond their natural environmental limits. An example of this is Las Vegas, Nevada. Just a small village for most of its history, Las Vegas was able to grow into the giant metropolis it is today because of the water provided by, and the hydroelectric power generated by, the Colorado River at the Hoover Dam (Land 2004, 49–50).

The Federal Water Power Act of 1920 was amended by the Federal Power Act of 1935, and the Federal Power Commission was turned into the five-man, independent Federal Energy Regulatory Commission (FERC), which regulated the interstate commerce in energy, particularly energy transmission, up to the present day. Overall, the commercial development of hydropower helped build the US economy and served to populate western communities, but made a profound impact on the natural environment, as entire watersheds were redesigned to suit the fresh water, irrigation, and electrical power-generation needs of a growing nation of consumers.

Jeff Hirschy

See also: Cooke, Morris Llewellyn; Electricity; Energy Policy Act of 2005; Federal Power Act of 1935; Federal Power Commission; Hoover Dam; Hydroelectric Power; Public Utility Regulatory Policies Act of 1978; Renewable Energy; Tennessee Valley Authority; Vulcan Street Plant; Water Power

FURTHER READING

Federal Power Act (FPA). 1920. 16 USCS § 791a. June 10. https://tile.loc.gov/storage-services/service/ll/uscode/uscode1940-00101/uscode1940-001016012/uscode1940-001016012.pdf (accessed May 27, 2020).

Fiege, Mark. 2012. *The Republic of Nature: An Environmental History of the United States*. Seattle: University of Washington Press.

Hahn, Steven. 2016. *A Nation without Borders: The United States and Its World in An Age of Civil Wars, 1830–1910*. New York: Viking Press.

Land, Barbara, Myrick Land, and Rocha Guy Louis. 2004. *A Short History of Las Vegas*. Reno, NV: University of Nevada Press.

McFarland, Charles K. 1966. "The Federal Government and Water Power, 1901–1913: A Legislative Study in the Nascence of Regulation." *Land Economics*. Vol. 42. No. 4. November. Pp. 441–52.

National Archives (NA). 2022. "Homestead Act (1862)." Milestone Documents. The U.S. National Archives and Records Administration. https://www.archives.gov/milestone-documents/homestead-act (accessed October 2023).

Rhodes, Richard. 2018. *Energy: A Human History*. New York: Simon & Schuster.

Fermi, Enrico

Enrico Fermi was an Italian physicist and an important member of the Manhattan Project. His work on creating the first sustainable nuclear chain reaction was critical in helping the Allied forces in the Second World War create two atomic bombs that were dropped on Japan to end the war in the Pacific. His scientific work to advance atomic and nuclear energy is an important contribution to the larger history of energy.

Fermi was born in Rome, Italy, on September 29, 1901 to Alberto and Ida de Gattis Fermi. His father was a Chief Inspector of the Ministry of Communications, and his mother was a teacher. At age fourteen, his brother Giulio died, which caused him great lament. His parents tried to console him by encouraging him to study, at which point, he became enthralled in physics. In 1918, Fermi won a scholarship to study at the Scuola Normale Superiore University in Pisa. He impressed the admissions committee so much that he was quickly elevated to the doctoral program and graduated with honors in 1922. He then won a Rockefeller Fellowship in 1923 to continue his studies in Gottingen, Germany with world renowned physicist, Max Born, who won a Nobel Prize in physics in 1954 for his research in quantum mechanics.

After earning his doctorate, Fermi was hired as a lecturer at the University of Florence in 1924, a position he held for two years. During this time, Fermi developed a new kind of statistics to account for the particles that did not follow the Pauli Exclusion Principle, which were the restrictions Wolfgang Pauli put on assigning quantum numbers to electrons in orbitals. The subatomic particles—protons, neutrons, and electrons—were not discovered before these developments in the 1920s. Fermi's new statistics, now called the Fermi-Dirac statistics, helped account for the half-integer spin of these particles, which are now called fermions in his honor. Paul A.M. Dirac independently also proposed the same new statistics as well, which is why both physicists have their names affixed to it.

FERMI ON THE TRINITY TEST

"My first impression of the explosion was the very intense flash of light, and a sensation of heat on the parts of the body that were exposed. Although I did not directly look towards the object, I had the full impression that suddenly the countryside became brighter than in full daylight" (Enrico Fermi on witnessing the Trinity Test).

Paul Brazinski

Fermi's scholarship earned him a full professorship at the University of Rome in 1926, the same city where he met his wife, Laura Capon. Fermi married Capon, the daughter of a respected Jewish family in Rome, in 1928. At the University of Rome, he investigated how to split a uranium atom and how to slow down this process. Both procedures would be required for the Manhattan Project to succeed. Fermi collaborated with other leading physicists in Italy, and was given the nickname "the Pope" for his upstanding character.

Fermi's reputation grew far and wide. Benito Mussolini gave him a position in his Accademia d'Italia, which was created to promote Italian innovation for the Fascist regime. The Accademia paid 3,000 lire a month in salary at a time when the national yearly average was around 3,100. Members were given uniforms, and called "Your Excellency" as a title of address. Only sixty members of the Italian intellectual and scientific elite were selected during Mussolini's reign. Fermi and his family grew wary of Mussolini's regime, given his wife's Jewish heritage. Fortunately for them, his work won him the Nobel Prize in Physics in 1938 for creating the first stable nuclear chain reaction, which gave them the opportunity to flee since the awards ceremony was held in Stockholm, Sweden. The family left fascist Italy and Mussolini's regime for the United States after the ceremony.

Given his scientific background, he quickly earned a professorship at Columbia University in New York, and would continue to work on his nuclear fission experiments at the University of Chicago as well. At the University of Chicago, he created the first initiated, controlled, and halted nuclear chain reaction. This prototype, called Chicago Pile-1, was constructed of piles of graphite bricks on wood and on December 2, 1942, the pile went critical, which proved that nuclear fission could be controlled. This experiment famously happened in the raquet courts underneath the football stadium at the University of Chicago. This achievement was a major advance for modern science and had implications for a wide variety of fields.

FIGURE 10: Enrico Fermi seated at the instrument panel of a particle accelerator.

In 1944, Fermi became an American citizen and was made the Associate Director of the laboratory at Lost Alamos, where the US government worked on creating the uranium-235 and plutonium bombs. Robert Oppenheimer, from the University of California-Berkeley, led the project as America's leading theoretical physicist. Together, the two men witnessed the Trinity Test, when US Army personnel dropped a uranium bomb in the isolated desert of New Mexico. The shock waves from the bomb were felt over 100 miles away and the mushroom cloud reached over 7.5 miles in height. The information from the successful Trinity Test helped influence President Truman's decisions at the Potsdam Conference on how to end the war with Japan while also taking into account the rising power of the Soviet Union.

After the war, Fermi took a professorship at Institute for Nuclear Studies (INS) at the University of Chicago, which he held until his death in 1954. At the INS, he started working on high-energy physics in areas such as pion-nucleon interaction. He died in Chicago on November 28, 1954. His wife, Laura Capon, and children, Giulio and Nella, outlived him. Fermi's legacy in the history of energy is monumental, as his research eventually led to the civilian use of nuclear energy in the post-war era. Fermi's impact on science and energy was acknowledged when element 100 in the periodic table, fermium, was named after him. Also, the US Department of Energy gives the Enrico Fermi Award to individuals who also demonstrate excellence in physics, and the Fermilab in Illinois is named in his honor.

Paul A. Brazinski

See also: Atomic Energy Acts; Church Rock Uranium Mill Spill; Energy Fuels, Inc.; Idaho National Energy Laboratory; Manhattan Project; Navajo Reservation Uranium Mining; Nuclear Power; Nuclear Regulatory Commission; Shippingport Atomic Power Station

FURTHER READING

Rhodes, Richard. 1986. *The Making of the Atomic Bomb*. New York: Simon & Schuster.

Segre, Gino, and Bettina Hoerlin. 2016. *The Pope of Physics: Enrico Fermi and the Birth of the Atomic Age*. New York: Macmillan Publishing.

Walker, J. Samuel. 1997. *Prompt and Utter Destruction: Truman and the Use of Atomic Bombs against Japan*. Chapel Hill: University of North Carolina Press.

Fesler, Milton A.

Milton Ashton Fesler (1874–1935) was part of a generation of inventors and innovators who designed new oil-burning systems for the purpose of heating office buildings, tenements, manufacturing plants, schools, hospitals, and other institutional facilities. The exponential growth of the petroleum industry in the second half of the nineteenth century inspired engineers, mechanics, and technicians to look for ways of converting coal-fueled systems to oil-burners. Oil promised greater efficiency, cost savings, and ease of use to owners of coal-burning steam heaters. Fesler invented a rotary oil burner that could provide a continuous heat source to steam- and hot-water heating boilers. The company he helped to create, Fess Rotary Oil Burner, Inc., sold the burners, but also offered installation and oil delivery services to its customers. By the mid-1920s, numerous buildings on the east coast of the United States had switched from coal to oil with Fesler-designed systems to meet their need for heating fuel.

Fesler appears in the historical record in patent #714,467 bearing the date November 25, 1902, indicating his residence as Visalia in California's Tulane County, southeast of Fresno. Not much else is known about his life before that date other than he married Nellie Nordquist on June 16, 1898 in Tulare County, and that he was twenty-eight at the time of the patent. This particular patent gave Fesler exclusive rights to a "crude-oil burner" of his own invention, which consisted of a few components including a small fire box, steam cylinder, connecting pipes, vaporizing jet, oil valve, oil regulator, and other fittings to create an oil mist. This oil mist then mixed with air in a combustion chamber where heat was generated for distribution from the furnace. Other patents followed and then in 1908, Fesler applied for a patent for a rotary oil burner, considered at the time to be a meaningful advance on existing technology. The rotary oil burner featured rotating tubes that improved the burner's performance considerably. He wrote in his patent: "It is by reason of the rapid rotary motion of these tubes that the air is drawn through the openings in the lower partition into the space between the two partitions. The oil and the air are then thrown outward with great velocity, and on account of this velocity the oil is very finely atomized and conmingled with the hot air. It is thus burned in a very effective manner" (Fesler 1912).

In 1907, Fesler formed Fess System Company in San Francisco with William C. McTarnahan as vice president and chief engineer and began selling oil burners in the marketplace (Dower 1927, 12). His rotary oil burner, finally patented in 1912, received a favorable review in 1915 at the Annual Meeting of the American Society of Heating and Ventilating Engineers in New York. H.S. Haley wrote:

> The apparatus is noiseless in operation, and is entirely automatic, being provided with no-voltage release switches, and automatic arrangement for controlling the oil supply to the burner, from the pressure in the boiler, and is so arranged that the fire cannot be extinguished by its operation. These burners are capable of operating with a clear white fire, free from smoke, within ten minutes after the fire is started, and they operate continuously without the formation of carbon in the furnace. (Haley 1915, 414)

Those features would certainly have impressed coal-fired furnace operators, who would no longer have to labor to ignite a coal fire, sweat over stoking the fire box, or bother with removing the coal ash.

In 1915, McTarnahan visited the Panama-Pacific International Exposition in San Francisco where he met west coast oil tycoon Edward L. Doheny and explained how the company's rotary oil burner worked to heat the California Building at the exposition. The meeting seems to have convinced Fesler and McTarnahan to open Fess Rotary Oil Burner, Inc. in Boston shortly thereafter, with McTarnahan as vice president and general manager ("Builders" 1927, 114). A company catalog from the period, possibly 1919, contains a powerful argument for its potential customers to replace coal with oil. Adorned with photographs of its products and services, including images of its 1,200-gallon delivery trucks, the catalog also contains pictures of many of the buildings the company had already converted to oil-burning heaters. This included Brown University in Providence, Rhode Island, Charles A. Newhall & Sons apartment buildings in Brookline, Massachusetts, Packard Motor Company plant in Boston, and the State Armory of Rhode Island. The catalog also lists over 120 schools, hospitals, libraries, churches, office buildings, newspaper press shops, and manufacturing plants in Providence and Boston that had already adopted what came to be known as the "Fess System."

One of the more interesting sections of the catalog is a collection of letters from satisfied customers who switched from coal to oil. Most testified to the cost savings, ease of use, cleanliness, and odor-free operation. The treasurer of the Holtzer-Cabot Electric Company in Boston wrote that the Fess System was installed in 1917 and had performed well in one harsh and one mild winter. He continued:

> The plant has given us most excellent service and we have no hesitancy in giving you a complete endorsement of the system. Apart from the actual fuel economy there are other important economies. (1) No banking fires is [*sic*] required and very little time is required on the part of any one to look after the operation of the system. (2) The expense of removing ashes is eliminated. (3) The flexibility of the system in meeting the extremes of our New England climate has thoroughly proven itself. (Fess *c.* 1920, 41)

In 1920, the company reorganized itself as Petroleum Heat & Power Company (PH&PC), with Fess Rotary Oil Burner operating as a subsidiary. The company's headquarters moved to Stamford, Connecticut, where Fesler filed his patent applications in the early 1920s, but maintained its Boston and Providence operations and opened an office in New York City (Grutchfield 2012).

About the reorganized company, the *Oil Trade Journal* remarked in a 1920 issue, "The company's business is to convert coalburning plants to oilburning, and it is prepared to substitute fuel oil for coal in all buildings except small private houses" ("Fuel Oil" 1920, 64). McTarnahan, now president of the PH&PC, told *Fuel Oil for Heat and Power* in 1927 that "the coming year will show an overwhelming disposition on the part of the public to get away from the use of coal, and will be marked by a national acceptance of oil as the premier fuel" (Builders 1927, 114). By 1928, Fesler was submitting patent applications for the company from the west coast once again, this time Los Angeles. He lived until the height of the Great Depression and died in 1935 at the age of sixty-one, long enough to see the transition from coal to oil in heating systems materialize in substantial and largely irreversible ways.

Jeffrey B. Webb

See also: American Radiator Company; Gold, Stephen J.; Home Energy Efficiency; Johnson, Warren Seymour; Nason, Joseph; New York Steam Company; Pierce Steam Heating Company; Powers, William Penn; Richardson & Boynton Company

FURTHER READING

"Builders of the Industry: William C. McTarnahan." 1927. *Fuel Oil for Heat and Power*. Vol. 5. No. 12. June. P. 114.

Dower, W.A.1927. "New Industries of Connecticut—No. 5: The Petroleum Heat & Power Company." *Connecticut Industry*. Vol. 5. No. 6. June. P. 12.

Fesler, Milton A. 1912. *Oil-Burner* (US Patent No. 1,026,664). Washington, DC: United States Patent Office.

Fess Rotary Oil Burner, Inc. *c*. 1920. *Oil—The Modern Fuel with the Fess System Fuel Oil Burning Equipment for Heat and Power*. Boston: Fess Rotary Oil Burner, Inc.

"Fuel Oil Tank Truck Service for Cities." 1920. *Oil Trade Journal*. January. Vol. 11. No. 1. P. 64.

Grutchfield, Walter. 2012. "Petroleum Heat & Power Co." https://www.waltergrutchfield.net/petroleum.htm (accessed October 2023).

Haley, H.S. 1915. "Crude Oil as Fuel in Low Pressure Heating Systems." *Transactions of the American Society of Heating and Ventilation Engineers* (ASHVE). Pp. 410–24. New York: ASHVE.

Food and Fuel Control Act of 1917

Also known as the Lever Act, the Food and Fuel Control Act became law on August 10, 1917 amid US entry into the First World War. The act created two new agencies, the US Food Administration and the US Fuel Administration, and gave the president broad authority to regulate both the supplies and price of food and fuel. The legislation sought to promote increased production in both the agricultural and energy sectors, authorized the federal government to ration food and fuel, sought to prevent hoarding and profiteering, and attempted to limit inflation through price regulation. The Food and Fuel Control Act successfully dealt with the challenge of balancing the needs of US and Allied militaries with the needs of the American people during the period of American participation in the war. It further established the precedent for government intervention in the energy and agricultural sectors during wartime, with implications for peacetime intervention later in the century.

After the United States entered the war in Europe, it became increasingly obvious that greater federal control of the economy was necessary to ramp up military production for the size of the armed forces necessary for what was then the most destructive war in human history. The Food and Fuel Control Act formed a key piece of that control, as it created federal regulatory agencies to oversee the two foundational sectors of the economy, agriculture and fuel. Crafted in large part in the House of Representatives by South Carolina Democrat Asbury Lever, the Act succeeded in significantly increasing food and fuel supplies for both the American and Allied armed forces through combining voluntary methods with coercive mandates.

President Woodrow Wilson appointed Herbert Hoover to lead the Food Administration, which took responsibility for encouraging, and in some cases requiring, farmers to increase production, establishing fixed prices for agricultural products, and forming rationing and conservation methods to be practiced by the general public. Through a mixture of public relations, cooperation with farm organizations, banking and commercial leaders, and high-level planning, the Food Administration cajoled willing compliance and imposed compulsory participation in the prioritizing of military food needs.

Wilson appointed Harry Garfield, president of Williams College and son of former president James Garfield, to head the Fuel Administration. In addition to price regulations, rationing, and promoting production increases primarily in coal (as well as oil and natural gas), Garfield and the Fuel Administration also asserted broad powers provided by the act to control the transportation of coal and oil and its use by industry. When railroad bottlenecks formed in mid-1917, delaying the shipment of coal to war industries and creating chaos throughout the US transportation network, Garfield ordered the temporary closure of thousands of "non-essential" factories east of the Mississippi, both to free up coal cars to break the transportation bottleneck and to limit the use of coal by non-war related industries. Despite some public outcry, the actions of the administration prevented a coal crisis in the winter of 1917–18, and lay the groundwork for greater cooperative action in 1918.

In the spring of 1918, the Fuel Administration created a comprehensive plan for streamlining the transportation of coal through extensive close cooperation between the federal government and coal companies. To achieve this improvement in distribution, the administration recruited coal company managers into temporary government service and allowed them to create a system of production and transport that met the civilian and military needs of the United States while protecting coal companies' profits. The cooperative planning brought about record coal production in 1918, and successfully prevented domestic or military shortages. Similarly, in February 1918 Garfield prioritized the distribution of fuel oil. The government announced that railroads would be the first priority, followed by the US military, Allied militaries, hospitals, and war industries, with civilian use and exports for civilian purchase at the low end of the list.

In addition to ramping up production and controlling distribution, the Fuel Administration followed the Food Administration's example in promoting voluntary cooperation with rationing goals. The Food Administration flooded magazines and newspapers with ads calling for reduced usage of wheat, growing personal vegetable gardens, and the implementation of voluntary "wheatless," "meatless," and "sweetless" days across the country to preserve foodstuffs for the military. The Fuel Administration did likewise, with Garfield calling for "heatless," "gasless," and "lightless" nights, while establishing restrictions on outdoor lighting displays. Additionally, the Fuel Administration recruited volunteers to promote conservation of fuel through public talks and school presentations. Participating schools distributed to children fuel-saving tips printed on tags to attach to their families' coal shovels. Overall, through voluntarism, incentivization, and coercion, the Food and Fuel Control Act contributed to record soft coal production, significant increases in agricultural production, and the successful provision of abundant food and fuel supplies to American and allied militaries throughout 1918.

On the downside, the abrupt end to the war in November 1918 and the subsequent expiration of the Fuel Administration in May 1919 and the Food Administration in 1920 created significant long-term economic problems for both coal and agricultural producers. Stockpiles of coal led to a decade of crisis in the industry, marked by wild price swings, bitter and sometimes violent labor struggles, and dire poverty for coal miners. Similarly, the abundance of surplus grain and livestock at home coupled with the resumption of agricultural production in Europe produced a collapse in global commodity prices, plunging farmers into economic straits well before the Great Depression of the 1930s. Additionally, Attorney General A. Mitchell Palmer utilized the act in 1919 to undermine labor unions, successfully obtaining federal court injunctions against striking coal miners and railroad workers. Palmer's actions undercut attempts by Wilson's Labor Secretary, William Wilson to prolong wartime labor-business cooperation and hastened the legislation's repeal.

The Food and Fuel Control Act succeeded in its immediate goals of supplying the military and the American people with adequate, and compared to their Allies and enemies abundant, food and fuel. It made rationing and compulsory actions more palatable to both businesses and the general public, ensuring compliance and participation by a majority of Americans, farmers, and businesses. The post-war period was less happy, with the Act used to suppress labor and its repeal leaving the economy vulnerable to the impact of wartime surpluses of coal and agricultural products.

Richard M. Filipink

See also: Agriculture and Energy; Coal; Daylight Saving Time; Strategic Petroleum Reserve; United Mineworkers of America; US Fuel Administration

FURTHER READING

Hawley, Ellis W. 1992. *The Great War and the Search for a Modern Order: A History of the American People and Their Institutions, 1917–1933*. 2nd ed. Prospect Heights, IL: Waveland Press.

Johnson, James P. 1979. *The Politics of Soft Coal: The Bituminous Industry from World War I through the New Deal*. Urbana: University of Illinois Press.

Kennedy, David M. 2004. *Over Here: The First World War and American Society*. New York: Oxford University Press.

Kostinen, Paul A.C. 1997. *Mobilizing for War: The Political Economy of American Warfare, 1865–1919*. Lawrence: University Press of Kansas.

Zieger, Robert H. 2000. *America's Great War: World War I and the American Experience*. Lanham, MD: Rowman & Littlefield.

Ford, Henry

Born during the US Civil War and raised on a farm in southeastern Michigan, Henry Ford (1863–1947) apprenticed as a machinist before his initial moves into engineering and eventually automobile design and manufacturing. He overcame significant technical, financial, and managerial challenges to make the Ford Motor Company the largest US automobile company in the early decades of the twentieth century. Ford engineered cars with simple design features and he utilized new techniques of production, which increased the speed and volume of his factories' output. The corresponding reduction in costs allowed Ford to offer automobiles at a price within reach of ordinary people. Ford's vision for building affordable vehicles for millions of middle- and working-class consumers revolutionized American society and culture. In the process, his innovations exponentially increased the demand for energy, namely the fossil fuels required to power the industry's factories and fill the tanks of the nation's colossal fleet of cars and trucks.

As a boy, Ford helped his father work the family farm with a team of horses, and he recalled the experience as one of ceaseless toil and drudgery: "My earliest recollection is that, considering the results, there was too much work on the place. That is the way I still feel about farming" (Ford 1922). When he was twelve, he happened to see a self-powered Nichols and Shepard steam engine rolling down a country lane near his farm. These engines were used to power threshing machines and sawmills, but also had a drive chain and wheels that allowed it to be mechanically moved from worksite to worksite. Ford's memoir records the experience as transformative: "From the time I saw that road engine as a boy of twelve right forward to to-day, my great interest has been in making a machine that would travel the roads" (Ford 1922). These self-propelled tractors promised to relieve some of the burden of manual labor on the farm, and self-propelled vehicles would facilitate travel without the labor of keeping, saddling, and bridling horses.

In his father's workshop Ford tried his hand at building a scale model of the Nichols and Shepard steam engine. He'd spent his early years tinkering with pocket watches and acquired a knack for the mechanical arts, so the experiment met with success. Encouraged by these experiences, Ford took on the challenge of building a copy of the so-called "Otto Engine," an early gasoline-powered, internal combustion engine designed by Nicolaus Otto in Germany. The idea was the same—an engine that could be used to power a drive shaft and thus propel a vehicle—but the technology was vastly different. Steam engines burned coal to boil water in a tank, which would then deliver pressurized steam power to its cylinders and pistons through a system of valves. Those cylinders and valves, in turn, power a drive shaft. On the other hand, internal combustion engines burned gasoline to create a series of tiny explosions inside the cylinders themselves, causing the pistons to move and in the process turn the drive shaft. This new technology eliminated the need to manage a bulky coal supply and to maintain water levels in the boiler tank.

During this period of experimentation, Ford married and left the farm to take a machinist's position at Edison Illuminating Company in Detroit, managing the operation of enormous steam engines to generate electricity for the city's new system of lighting. He quickly proved himself indispensable and earned promotions leading to chief engineer. In his spare time, Ford continued to tinker with internal combustion engines and with the other technologies required to safely convey driver and passengers in a moving vehicle: ignition systems, transmission systems, braking systems, and so on. He worked long hours with trusted friends in the brick shed in his backyard on Bagley Avenue in Detroit, and in 1896, completed the design and construction of his first full-scale, four-wheeled, internal combustion engine-driven automobile, which he called the Quadricycle. As fate would have it, Ford's rank at Edison Illuminating enabled him to meet Thomas Edison personally at an annual meeting in New York later that year, where Ford presented to Edison the designs for the Quadricycle and his future plans to manufacture them. Ford remembered that Edison exclaimed, "Young man, that's the thing. You have it. Keep at it!" The senior inventor and energy pioneer appreciated the kind of revolution Ford was proposing: "Your car is self-contained—it carries its own power-plant—no fire, no boiler, no smoke, no steam" (Ford 1922).

Encouraged by Edison's reaction, Ford began the process of organizing his own automobile company. Near the turn of the twentieth century, conventional wisdom held that automobiles were expensive playthings for the rich, or a means for status-conscious consumers to display their pretentions. Ford attracted investment from rich businessmen and bankers who adhered to this view, and his first few attempts foundered over disagreements about product development and the marketing of his vehicles. Ford also joined the competition among early car makers to design and build the fastest automobiles; his "999" and "Arrow" racers enjoyed some successes on the racing circuit. Soon these initial business frustrations and distractions gave way to a more focused effort to create a viable manufacturing operation. Ford secured sufficient financing, as well as the engineering talent, to create the Ford Motor Company in 1903, which dedicated itself to the production of inexpensive passenger automobiles, beginning with the Model A (introduced in 1902). Other models soon appeared, including the Model B (1903) with more luxurious appointments and a larger engine, and the Model N (1906), with less power and an engine-forward design but more importantly, a very affordable $500 price point. Ford sold 7,000 during its two-year production run.

Ford and his engineers drew a number of lessons from the models they created and sold in the first five years of the company's history. These lessons were brought to bear in the design, production, and marketing of the Model T, a car that appeared first in 1908 and within a decade became ubiquitous in cities, small towns, and rural areas in all parts of the country. During the Model T's development, Ford expressed his thinking this way:

> I will build a motor car for the great multitude. It will be large enough for the family, but small enough for the individual to run and care for. It will be constructed of the best materials, by the best men to be hired, after the simplest designs that modern engineering can devise. But it will be so low in price that no man making a good salary will be unable to own one—and enjoy with his family the blessing of hours of pleasure in God's great open spaces. (Ford 1922)

An affordable, reliable, elegantly engineered car that most Americans could buy. By today's standards the first Model Ts were small and underpowered: a four-cylinder, 177 cubic-inch, 20 horsepower engine with two gears (and reverse) carrying driver and passenger(s)

40–45 miles per hour with an energy consumption rate of 13–21 miles per gallon. Within a few years, Ford offered Model Ts in various formats, including an open-canopy roundabout, a touring car, a roadster, and a cargo truck. In the first four full years of production, the years 1909–12, Ford made an incredible 133,347 Model Ts, and this was before a purpose-built plant could increase his company's productive output.

That new factory, at Highland Park outside of Detroit (opened in 1910), became a kind of "modern marvel" of technological and industrial wizardry. Ford studied operations in other sectors of the economy, like the meatpacking industry, and by 1913 had adopted a moving assembly line system. Here, workers were stationed in fixed positions, each tasked with a specific job in the assembly process, while a conveyance system moved cars through the stations until the completion of the final steps in the manufacturing process. The moving assembly line system kept workers from being idle at any point in the process and allowed them to become proficient in their particular specialization. A rigorous schedule ensured an ever-increasing pace of production and maximized all of Ford's inputs: giant armies of industrial workers, mind-boggling levels of energy consumption, millions of component parts, and a bewildering array of industrial chemicals, plastics, polymers, and so on. Ford also brought all the recent developments in industrial production together at Highland Park, including the use of standardized and interchangeable parts, the mechanization and division of labor, and the integration of systems to produce a highly orchestrated, "engineered" process. In addition, Ford made his own vanadium steel and other components, thus shortening his supply chain and enabling a kind of vertical integration that other industrialists—particularly John D. Rockefeller at Standard Oil—had used to maximize efficiency. Observers coined the term "Fordism" to describe the new kind of work, which was really a new kind of society, that emerged at Highland Park.

These changes were so consequential that economists and historians began to refer to the new conditions brought about by Ford and his contemporary manufacturers as a "Second Industrial Revolution." By 1917, half of all cars in the United States were Model Ts, and by 1927, Ford's factories produced a total of 15 million of their number. This figure is significant. Ford wished to create something he called a "universal market" for automobiles, so that every person who wished to own one could actually afford it. His system of production drove down the price of Model Ts from $825 at its initial offering to $525 by 1913; at the height of its popularity in the 1920s, the Model T cost only $260. In effect, the barriers to entry had been substantially removed for the vast majority of working families in the United States. Ford further developed the universal market by organizing dealerships that eventually popped up in cities and small towns across the country. The company developed a marketing program as well. Ford remembered that the Model T was first marketed as a kind of utility—a useful, time-saving device to make life simpler and less complicated. An early advertisement read: "The investment of an exceedingly moderate sum in the purchase of a perfected, efficient, high-grade automobile would cut out anxiety and unpunctuality and provide a luxurious means of travel ever at your beck and call" (Ford 1922).

However, by the 1920s, it became clear that automobiles had become something more than just a useful time-saving tool. Cars allowed people to travel freely without regard to train schedules and routes, and without regard to the needs and demands of horses. They began to reshape the lifestyles of their owners, providing greater mobility, freedom, and even a sense of identity. Automobiles facilitated the geographical expansion of the ordinary American's range of travel and manifested itself in such important developments as the creation of the petroleum industry, massive suburbanization, and the federal interstate highway system. In his book

Republic of Drivers: A Cultural History of Automobility in America (2008) historian Cotten Seiter went as far as to say that the automobile and its attendant changes to economic, social, cultural, and political life became "essential to shaping the dominant meanings of 'America' and 'American' in the twentieth century" (Seiter 2008, 7). This growing phenomenon was clearly evident even during Henry Ford's lifetime. Because of the vision of Henry Ford and his fellow auto manufacturers, the integration of "automobility" into everyday life for Americans and for people around the world fundamentally transformed the relationship between human beings and energy. Automobility became a key factor in placing a majority of people in a state of dependence on fossil fuels and increased the magnitude of environmental degradation produced by industrialization and mass consumption.

Jeffrey B. Webb

See also: CAFE Standards; Duryea, Charles and J. Frank Duryea; Edison, Thomas Alva; Industrial Revolution; Interstate Highway System; Truck Transportation Technology

FURTHER READING

Flink, James. 1990. *The Automobile Age*. Cambridge, MA: MIT Press.

Ford, Henry, and Samuel Crowther. 1922. *My Life and Work*. Garden City, NY: Doubleday, Page & Company.

Lewis, David L., and Laurence Goldstein, eds. 1983. *The Automobile and American Culture*. Ann Arbor, MI: University of Michigan Press.

Seiter, Cotten. 2008. *Republic of Drivers: A Cultural History of Automobility in America*. Chicago: University of Chicago Press.

Snow, Richard. 2014. *I Invented the Modern Age: The Rise of Henry Ford*. New York: Scribner.

Watts, Steven. 2005. *The People's Tycoon: Henry Ford and the American Century*. New York: Vintage.

Franklin, Benjamin

Benjamin Franklin (1706–90) conducted electrical experiments and wrote extensively on the subject of electricity, which joined with the work of other contemporary scientists to advance energy-related research in the middle of the eighteenth century. His insatiable curiosity and tireless work ethic drove him to make new advances in both the conceptual understanding of electricity and its practical application. Franklin's *Experiments and Observations on Electricity* (1751) emerged as an important milestone in the development of modern scientific understanding, and influenced the work of later thinkers, such as Joseph Priestly in *The History and Present State of Electricity* (1767). He is also credited with innovations in wood stove design that produced greater efficiency in home heating.

Franklin's career as an artisan and print shop owner provided the opportunity to develop hands-on, practical skills using printing technologies of the era. Through this experience Franklin acquired a knack for applied science. Furthermore, as the publisher of the *Pennsylvania Gazette*, he became immersed in the transatlantic circulation of information and ideas. He read voraciously on a wide variety of subjects, including theology, philosophy, politics, and science, encouraged by his association with a debating club he helped to form called the Junto (1727) which Franklin later described in his autobiography as "the best school of philosophy, morality, and politics that then existed in the province." Franklin's membership in Philadelphia's Freemason lodge (1731) extended his engagement with trends in scientific and philosophical thought and offered more support for his active pursuit of intellectual improvement.

During a trip to Boston to visit family in 1743, Franklin attended seminars sponsored by the local Freemasons that featured Dr. Archibald Spencer, a Scottish-born physician and lecturer on medical and scientific topics. Franklin was awestruck by Spencer's account of Isaac Newton's theory of light as well as his demonstrations involving electricity. When Spencer came to Philadelphia for a six-month stay in 1744, Franklin acted as his agent by arranging a venue, publicizing the lectures in his *Pennsylvania Gazette*, and receiving payments from ticket-buyers at the post office (Lemay 2006, 489). Over the next year Franklin conducted his own investigations with electricity, and in 1746 he began "devoting dozens of hours every week to electrical experiments" (Lemay 2006, 321). This was made possible when Franklin's English friend John Collinson sent the Library Company of Philadelphia a glass tube called a Leyden jar along with a pamphlet detailing how German scientists had used it to gain new insights into the nature of electricity.

With the Leyden jar, which could store and release energy produced through static electricity, Franklin believed "he was making more interesting advances than those he read about from England and Europe" (Lemay 2006, 321). In 1747, Franklin wrote to Collinson:

> I never was before engaged in any study that so totally engrossed my attention and my time as this has lately done; for what with making experiments when I can be alone, and repeating them to my Friends and Acquaintance, who, from the novelty of the thing, come continually in crouds to see them, I have, during some months past, had little leisure for any thing else. (Franklin to Collinson 1747)

In the 1740s, numerous experiments with electricity were underway throughout Western Europe, Britain, and the American colonies, and observers were amazed by the sparks and loud noises produced by Leyden jars, as well as their power to set bits of metal in motion as if by some invisible force of nature. These dazzling displays aside, the basic problem remained a conceptual one. What were the basic properties of electricity, and how could these be best understood and explained?

Franklin's experiments and his published reports of these experiments made an important contribution to these basic conceptual aspects of electricity. By repeatedly charging and discharging his Leyden jar, he observed the flow of electricity, which he described as a "Stream of Electrical Effluvia" from one body to another to create a surplus on the receiving end. In effect the Leyden jar became host to an overabundance of positively charged "effluvia" drawn from the surrounding environment. Franklin conceived of the positively charged jar, now holding an accumulation of energy, as a battery. This conjecture helped to form the notion of electrical current flowing from positively charged to negatively charged objects. It should be noted that eventually, science would replace this theory with the discovery of electrons and the particle theory of electricity. Still, the idea of a unitary current of electricity flowing from positive to negatively charged objects was an important step in the advancement of scientific thinking. Another of Franklin's insights was the discovery that lightning as it occurs in nature possesses the same properties as an electrical charge produced through friction (or static electricity).

Franklin produced this insight through the oft-cited, but thinly documented kite experiment, which he described to Collinson in a letter dated from 1752. Franklin explained that "electric fire" could be drawn from the atmosphere via a kite equipped with wire, so that "as soon as any of the thunderclouds come over the kite, the pointed wire will draw the electric fire from them; and the kite, with all the twine, will be electrified; and the loose filaments of the twine will stand out every way, and be attracted by an approaching finger" (Franklin 1752). The attraction of electrically charged twine filaments to the hand is the same effect that can observed by human hair charged with static electricity. In terms of getting an electrical shock, Franklin noted that "when the rain has wet the kite and twine, so that it can conduct the electric fire freely, you will find it stream out plentifully from the key on the approach of your knuckle." Franklin's letter concludes with the observation that a vial could be used to draw off the electrical charge, which could then be made to perform in all the same ways as the Leyden jar.

The correspondence from Franklin to Collinson regarding his work was gathered together in an eighty-six-page pamphlet and published as *Experiments and Observations on Electricity, Made at Philadelphia in America, by Mr. Benjamin Franklin, and Communicated in several Letters to Mr. P. Collinson, of London, F.R.S.* (London: Printed and sold by E. Cave, at St. John's Gate, 1751). The pamphlet generated great interest and Franklin provided supplementary material for expanded versions; by 1774 Franklin's *Experiments and Observations on Electricity* had appeared in five editions and enjoyed a large international readership. His book did its part to further encourage scientific thinking as evidenced by the attention Joseph Priestly lavished on Franklin's writings in *The History and Present State of Electricity* (London: Printed for J. Dodsley, 1767). Later historians of science, such as Thomas Kuhn, credited Franklin with producing an entirely new and improved "paradigm" for understanding the fundamental principles of electricity (Kuhn 1970, 62).

Franklin's interests in natural philosophy ranged widely across fields like astronomy, meteorology, and geology, and he worked to find practical applications for his discoveries. During his experiments with the Leyden jar, Franklin wrote to Collinson that he was "Chagrin'd a little that We have hitherto been able to discover Nothing in this Way of Use to Mankind" (Franklin to Collinson 1749). Eventually his experiments resulted in the widespread adoption of the lightning rod, which saved countless buildings and lives from destruction by fire. Franklin's experiments with wood stove design, guided in some measure by reading Dutch chemist Hermann Boerhaave's *Elementa Chemiae*, resulted in what he called the Pennsylvania Fire-Place. The Franklin stove incorporated an "air-box" that drew air from outside the stove through a duct and around a collection of metal baffles to be vented back into the room as heated air. Energy efficiency was clearly Franklin's intent, as he explained in his pamphlet advertising the stove: "Since Fuel is become so expensive, and (as the Country is more clear'd and settled) will of course grow scarcer and dearer; any new Proposal for Saving the Wood, and for lessening the Charge and augmenting the Benefit of Fire, by some particular Method of Making and Managing it, may at least be thought worth Consideration" (Franklin 1744).

Benjamin Franklin left his mark on the history of energy in early America and in the United States through his experiments, his writings, and his practical inventions. Furthermore, his leadership in establishing the American Philosophical Society—an organization devoted to promoting science and technology—created momentum for further scientific investigation and discovery. Subsequent advances in energy-related research and development owed a debt to Franklin's contribution to the development of a culture of scientific inquiry, both in terms of his tangible accomplishments, and as a role model for future scientists and inventors to follow. It bears mentioning that Franklin's father was a candle maker by trade. Candles and whale oil lamps were the chief means by which people lighted interior rooms before town gas and eventually electricity. Franklin rejected his father's plan to train him in the family business, and by doing so, symbolically turned his back on a preindustrial past to face a future that would eventually be powered by electricity.

Jeffrey B. Webb

See also: Edison, Thomas Alva; Electricity; General Electric Company; Henry, Joseph; Home Energy Efficiency; Rumford Fireplace; Stewart, Philo Penfield; Tesla, Nikola; War of the Currents; Whale Oil

FURTHER READING

Cohen, I. Bernard. 1941. *Benjamin Franklin's Experiments*. Cambridge, MA: Harvard University Press.

Franklin, Benjamin. 1744. *An Account of the New Invented Pennsylvanian Fire-Places*. Philadelphia: Printed and Sold by B. Franklin. National Archives Founders Online. https://founders.archives.gov/documents/Franklin/01-02-02-0114 (accessed October 2023).

Franklin, Benjamin to Peter Collinson. 1747. March 28. National Archives Founders Online. https://founders.archives.gov/documents/Franklin/01-03-02-0055 (accessed October 2023).

Franklin, Benjamin to Peter Collinson. 1749. April 29. Benjamin Franklin Historical Society. http://www.benjamin-franklin-history.org/franklin-collison-april-29-1749/ (accessed October 2023).

Franklin, Benjamin. 1752. October 1. XCV: "A Letter of Benjamin Franklin, Esq; to Mr. Peter Collinson, F. R. S. Concerning an Electrical Kite." *Philosophical Transactions of the Royal Society*. Vol. 47. Pp. 565–7. https://royalsocietypublishing.org/doi/10.1098/rstl.1751.0096 (accessed October 2023).

Heilbron, J.L. 1979. *Electricity in the 17th and 18th Centuries: A Study of Early Modern Physics*. Berkeley: University of California Press.

Kuhn, Thomas. 1970. *The Structure of Scientific Revolutions*. 2nd ed. Chicago: University of Chicago Press.

Lemay, Leo. 2006. *The Life of Benjamin Franklin*. Vol. 2: *Printer and Publisher*. Philadelphia: University of Pennsylvania Press.

Lyons, Jonathan. 2014. *The Society for Useful Knowledge: How Benjamin Franklin and Friends Brought the Enlightenment to America*. New York: Bloomsbury Press.

Free Energy Myths

The idea of a limitless supply of energy with no need for continuing inputs—"free energy" —is persistent in American history despite its violation of the laws of physics. The myth has roots in the European Middle Ages with accounts of a "perpetual motion machine" which could run forever on an initial input of energy. Such devices violate the first or second laws of thermodynamics. Although the laws of thermodynamics were developed in the nineteenth century, they are fundamental principles embedded in nature and were incontrovertible then and now. Modern free energy promoters also emphasize the nonpolluting or "clean" nature of their technologies. Although some free energy believers are sincere, there are also many free energy proponents who are deliberately committing fraud, and the boundaries between the two groups can shift with time.

Belief in free energy is often associated with conspiratorial thinking, in which powerful energy companies or the government are charged with suppressing free energy sources or theories to protect their profits. Alternatively, energy corporations have been charged with stealing free energy technologies from their inventors to employ them in secret. Some well-known scientists, such as Nikola Tesla, are alleged to have been murdered or to have their work destroyed to suppress their research on free energy. Free energy promoters also often present themselves as opponents of the "scientific establishment" appealing to popular anti-elitism. They paint utopian visions of every household with its own free energy engine, providing endless power with no need to pay an electric company.

US PATENT OFFICE REJECTS NEWMAN'S ENGINE

"We do not doubt that a worker in this art with appellant's specification before him could construct a motor ... as shown in Fig. 6 of the drawing. Such a motor would not and could not be made to operate at an efficiency level of greater than 100% .... Such a machine is impossible. If it were possible ... some of the output energy developed could be fed back into the input and the machine would work forever without any external source of energy. Such machines are known as perpetual motion machines .... [M]achines of this type will not work. They violate either the first or the second law of thermodynamics."

(Newman v. Quigg, 1988)

Free energy claims intensified with the Industrial Revolution. The nineteenth century was a time for the development of many new power sources and types of engines, and the rapid technological progress of the era provoked interest in perpetual motion and free energy. John Gamgee, a British veterinarian and refrigeration developer, tried to sell a perpetual motion engine called the Zeromotor to President James Garfield in 1880. The Zeromotor was based on the circulation of ammonia which would expand and contract, thus driving the engine, without any outside force. The Zeromotor proved inoperable. In 1911, the US Patent Office ruled that a patent on a perpetual motion device could not be considered until a copy of the device itself be deposited at the patent office and demonstrate the ability to run by itself for a year.

Free energy is often associated with self-taught or "crank" scientists. One prominent example is Alabama's Joseph Newman, a self-educated engineer without a college degree. In 1979 he attempted to patent an electric motor, which, he claimed, produced free energy by converting some of the mass of the copper coils to energy. This was an attempt to apply Albert Einstein's mass-energy equivalence, but not one recognized by physicists. Newman engaged in a protracted struggle with the US Patent Office, the National Bureau of Standards, the courts and even the US Congress, but tests of his engine revealed that it did not put out more energy than it put in. Despite this, he, like other free energy promoters, received what was often uncritical media coverage as his engine was treated as a human interest story rather than a science story. Newman became a minor celebrity, even appearing on the Tonight Show with Johnny Carson. He attracted even more attention when he rented the New Orleans Superdome for a week to demonstrate his new technology.

Although it is technically not "free energy" and relies on generally accepted physical processes, "cold fusion" has many similarities to free energy. Cold fusion refers to a nuclear reaction taking place at close to room temperature, rather than the intense heat normally required for nuclear fusion to occur. If it could be done, it would provide a virtually limitless source of cheap energy. Cold fusion emerged into prominence on March 23, 1989, when two electrochemists working at the University of Utah, Martin Fleischman and Stanley Pons, claimed to have produced it in a small, tabletop experiment. Fleischman and Pons were not self-educated cranks but had serious academic credentials and, particularly Fleischman, previous scientific achievements to their credit. Part of the politics of the cold fusion claim within the scientific community was the support Pons and Fleischman received from other electrochemists, hoping for a boost for their relatively low-status discipline. Many of their opponents came from the high-status discipline of nuclear physics, whose preeminence Pons and Fleischman were challenging. There was also a religious dimension to the story, as many Utah Mormons viewed the cold fusion "discovery" as God's gift to the Utah economy.

Pons and Fleischman's claim attracted much interest from the media and the two appeared before a congressional committee but attempts by scientists to duplicate the results ended in failure. By the end of the year, cold fusion was discredited in the scientific community, although Fleischman and Pons never disavowed it and it has continued to be funded on a small scale. Google financed cold fusion experiments in the late 2010s, with no success.

A common claim in the contemporary free energy community is to have harnessed "zero-point energy." This energy, required by quantum theory, permeates the universe, but the idea of harnessing it is regarded by the mainstream scientific community as impossible. An even more exotic claim is that the government is hiding free energy technology derived from aliens. Claims that the US government was hiding free energy technology were part of the motivation for one of the largest hacks of government computer systems. This was carried out by the Scottish hacker Gary McKinnon in 2001 and 2002. McKinnon hacked American military and NASA computers, claiming to be looking for, among other information, the story of how the US government had suppressed free energy and anti-gravity technology reverse-engineered from alien spacecraft. Despite the efforts of the US government, he was not extradited from the United Kingdom.

William E. Burns

See also: Industrial Revolution; Nuclear Power; Tesla, Nikola; Union of Concerned Scientists

FURTHER READING

Close, Frank. 1991. *Too Hot to Handle: The Race for Cold Fusion*. Princeton: Princeton University Press.

Gardner, Martin. 2000. *Did Adam and Eve have Navels? Discourses on Reflexology, Numerology, Urine Therapy and other Dubious Subjects*. New York: W. W. Norton.

Joseph W. Newman v. Donald J. Quigg. U.S. District Court, District of Columbia. 681 F. Supp. 16 (D.D.C. 1988) 5 U.S.P.Q.2d (BNA) 1880.

Park, Robert L. 2000. *Voodoo Science: The Road from Foolishness to Fraud*. Oxford and New York: Oxford University Press.

Pigliucci, Massimo. 2018. *Nonsense on Stilts: How to Tell Science from Bunk*. Chicago: University of Chicago Press.

Tutt, Keith. 2001. *The Search for Free Energy*. London: Simon & Schuster.

Frick, Henry Clay

Henry Clay Frick (1849–1919) is one of the more notorious figures in US history. In the Gilded Age, a period generally regarded as dominated by ruthless, cutthroat, reprehensible robber barons, Frick stands out. He is usually portrayed, with significant justification, as the central villain in the Homestead Strike. However, aside from his participation in the battle for Homestead, Frick played an important role in the history of energy in the United States as an early pioneer in the coke business. Later, he led his company into a partnership with Andrew Carnegie (1835–1919), became chairman of Carnegie Steel, and served on the board of the United States Steel Corporation.

Frick was born in West Overton, Pennsylvania on December 19, 1849. His father was generally unsuccessful in business pursuits, but Frick's grandfather owned the successful Overholt whiskey distillery. As a young man of twenty-one, Frick entered into a consequential partnership. Abraham O. Tintsman, Joseph Rist, and A. S. M. Morgan formed a partnership and purchased hundreds of acres of coal land. Unlike hard anthracite coal, the soft bituminous coal on their land had little use, save in the manufacture of coke. Frick, according to many scholars, understood that the Bessemer process would increase the use of coke and joined Tintsman and Rist after Morgan dropped out of the partnership. Frick persuaded the two men to expand their operations, so the three bought more land and built ovens to turn their coal into coke. Never one to dream small, Frick reportedly vowed to be a millionaire by the time he turned thirty.

Frick received loans from the banker Thomas Mellon and formed a life-long friendship with Mellon's son Andrew. During the panic of 1873, coke prices plummeted and Frick's partners panicked. Thanks to loans from the Mellons, Frick bought out Tintsman and Rist. He never lost confidence that coke was essential to the production of steel. The Henry C. Frick Coke Company weathered the panic of 1877 and, by 1879, the year he reached thirty, Frick achieved his goal of becoming a millionaire. This was only the beginning, however. In 1881, Frick married Adelaide Child and the two honeymooned in New York City. There, Frick met Andrew Carnegie, the King of Steel, whom Frick had been observing for some time. It turned out the feeling was mutual. Carnegie invited Frick and Adelaide to dinner and, incredibly, toasted the success of a Frick/Carnegie partnership. Within a few months, the two men had established a tremendously influential partnership that benefited both men. Carnegie wanted easy access to the best coke produced in the United States and Frick planned to use Carnegie's wealth to expand his coke empire.

In some respects, Frick and Carnegie complemented each other. Both held to the same views about how to run a business. Both believed in expanding during hard time when other people cut back. However, they were also very different. Most contemporaries conceded that Frick was absorbed in business, lacked humor, and was not intellectually curious. Carnegie

ASSASSINATING FRICK

On July 23, 1892, while the battle for Homestead was raging, anarchist Alexander Berkman attempted to assassinate Frick. He shot Frick twice and stabbed him four times with a steel file. Despite the wounds, Frick helped subdue his would-be assassin and returned to work within a week. Berkman received twenty-two years in prison for attempted murder. His actions made Frick a hero in some quarters and turned public opinion definitively against the strike.

Evan C. Rothera

found him dull and, in many senses, a stereotypical US businessman. Charles M. Schwab (1862–1939), a friend of both Carnegie and Frick, acknowledged that Frick was a difficult man to understand. As Schwab wrote, Frick "was to me a curious and puzzling man. No man on earth could get close to him or fathom him. He seemed more like a machine, without emotions or impulses" (Hessen 1975, 106). Still, people of vastly different temperaments can and do work together well, so the differences between Frick and Carnegie did not necessarily doom the partnership. Indeed, Carnegie put a great deal of faith and trust in Frick and brought Frick into his company. He initially sold Frick a 2 percent interest, but that rose to 11 percent a few years later and Frick became chairman of the board. Frick superintended the creation of Carnegie Steel Company and made tremendous profits for both men.

It was in his capacity as chairman of Carnegie Steel that Frick found his name covered with both fame and infamy. The Homestead Strike proved to be a decisive moment in Frick's relationship with Carnegie, and over time the two men grew apart and actively hostile toward each other. Indeed, the divisions between them really came into the open during the Homestead Strike. Carnegie acquired the Homestead Steel Works, located on the Monongahela River in Homestead, Pennsylvania, in 1883. In the intervening decade, Homestead proved to be a problem for Carnegie because frequent disputes over wages, working hours, and contracts disrupted work at the mill. Homestead was one of the few Carnegie steel mills with a union, the Amalgamated Association of Iron and Steel Workers (AA). The AA called several strikes and proved that steelworkers could make common cause with the people of Homestead, defy the bosses, and turn back strikebreakers. In 1892, the situation exploded because the AA's contract expired on June 30, 1892. Although he proclaimed to be pro-union in public, and although he declared, again in public, not to support the use of strikebreakers, Carnegie sang a very different tune in private. He tasked Frick with destroying the union, before he left for his annual summer vacation in Scotland, because he believed it hindered production and did not represent the workers. In negotiations between Frick and the AA, the union asked for a wage increase and Frick countered with a wage decrease. Frick locked the workers out of Homestead on June 28 and June 29, 1892. The AA called a strike, the Knights of Labor supported the strike, and sympathy strikes occurred at other steel mills.

The AA and the workers determined to keep Homestead closed. Frick was equally determined to import strikebreakers, run the plant with non-union labor, and break the strike. When the sheriff and deputies posted notices directing strikers to allow strikebreakers access to the plant, the strikers ripped them down and declared they would never allow non-union workers into the plant. July 6, 1892 was the critical day. Frick hired about 300 Pinkerton detectives, armed them, and sent them on barges to Homestead (Oates 1892, 366). The Pinkertons tried to land and accounts differ as to who fired the first shots. The strikers blamed the Pinkertons and the Pinkertons blamed the crowds of striking workers and their families. Both sides took casualties, both groups established fortified positions, and fighting continued throughout the day. The AA, in an attempt to defuse the situation, called for a meeting with Frick, but Frick refused. He knew that if the situation stayed chaotic, Governor Robert E. Pattison would likely call out the state militia to restore order. The Pinkertons surrendered around 5:00 p.m. on July 6, after hours of fighting, and union officials guaranteed them safe passage out of town. In actuality, strikers overawed union officials and the town officials and forced the Pinkertons to run the gauntlet. Strikers and their supporters threw stones and clubbed some of the Pinkertons into unconsciousness. The media emphasized the awful treatment of the Pinkertons and this negative coverage helped turn popular opinion against the strikers.

Governor Pattison decided to send in the militia in on July 9. Major General George R. Snowden sympathized with Frick and Carnegie, not the strikers, and told that AA that he was now master of the situation. Thousands of soldiers surrounded the plant, displaced the strikers, and allowed officials and the strikebreakers recently hired to get to work. The strike continued and strikers appealed to Republican vice-presidential candidate Whitelaw Reid, who in turn appealed to Frick to reopen talks. Neither Reid's appeal nor an attempted assassination changed Frick's mind. The assassination attempt, in fact, made him something of a hero for many people, undermined lingering support for the AA, and heralded the final collapse of the strike. Workers began crossing the picket line, the strike failed, and the AA collapsed.

The strike's failure had lingering effects on attempts to unionize steelworkers. Carnegie sanctimoniously attempted to shift blame onto Frick, claiming that things would have gone differently if he had been in the United States. Most people, however, saw through this hypocrisy. After all, Carnegie had ordered Frick to destroy the union. The acrimony between the two men became sharper after the Homestead Strike and Carnegie eventually deposed Frick as the chairman of his company. Nevertheless, Frick played an important role in the formation of the United States Steel Corporation in 1901, which became a very larger consumer of coal and coke in the Second Industrial Revolution of the late nineteenth and early twentieth centuries. The company played an important role in shaping the industrial system itself, and thereby a factor in committing the US government to a long-term policy of support for energy-intensive industrial corporations.

Evan C. Rothera

See also: Benedum, Michael Late; Coal; Coke

FURTHER READING

Harvey, George. 1928. *Henry Clay Frick—The Man*. New York: Charles Scribner's Sons.

Hessen, Robert. 1975. *Steel Titan: The Life of Charles M. Schwab*. New York: Oxford University Press.

Krause, Paul. 1992. *The Battle for Homestead, 1880–1892: Politics, Culture, and Steel*. Pittsburgh: University of Pittsburgh Press.

Nasaw, David. 2006. *Andrew Carnegie*. New York: Penguin Group.
Oates, William C., George Ticknor Curtis, and T.V. Powderly. 1892. "The Homestead Strike." *The North American Review*. Vol. 155. No. 430. September. Pp. 355–75.
Wall, Joseph Frazier. 1970. *Andrew Carnegie*. New York: Oxford University Press.
Warren, Kenneth. 1996. *Henry Clay Frick and the Industrial Transformation of America*. Pittsburgh: University of Pittsburgh Press.

Frigidaire

Frigidaire is a line of electrical appliances that includes such devices as laundry machines, refrigerators, freezers, ranges, dishwashers, microwave ovens, dehumidifiers, and room air conditioners. The brand originated with the Guardian Refrigerator Company, which was established in 1916 in Fort Wayne, Indiana. The brand has been owned by Electrolux since 1986 and its popular refrigerators are manufactured at a plant in Dublin, Ohio (FridgeFilters 2018). Brands like Frigidaire, Whirlpool, and KitchenAid were foundational to the creation of the modern home, which featured interior electric lighting, gas and oil-fueled furnaces, central air-conditioning, and, of course, plenty of electric appliances. By mid-twentieth century, the modern home became an important component of the "American Dream" and symbolized the nation's attainment of abundance, prosperity, and material well-being.

In 1913, Fred W. Wolf of Ft. Wayne, Indiana placed a electric-powered unit on the top of an ice box, and this was the first idea related to a machine to keep foods fresh by freezing them. Then, Nathaniel B. Wales invented an electric refrigeration system in 1914 in Detroit, Michigan in 1914. But it is Alfred Mellowes who is credited with producing in 1916 the first commercially successful refrigerator (HR 2020). His company, the Guardian Refrigerator Company of Ft. Wayne, began marketing its refrigerators under the Frigidaire label, but he lacked capital to develop his operation from a small group of workers assembling machines by hand to a mechanized plant with greater production capacity. William C. Durant, owner of the General Motors Corporation, purchased the company in 1918 and gave it the name, Frigidaire Company (HR 2020).

Durant found it difficult to manufacture refrigerators in a way that made them affordable to consumers (Gasbarre 1998, 216). As such, he moved Frigidaire's operation to a General Motors subsidiary in Dayton, Ohio called Delco-Light Company and entrusted the production of refrigerators to plant known for its high-quality electric generators. In 1926, rising sales and increased consumer confidence ensured the brand's success, and General Motors made the Frigidaire Corporation a standalone subsidiary once again, this time under the leadership of president and general manager Elmer G. Biechler. Under his management, the company reduced Frigidaire's price points, making their products more competitive at the marketplace, and it began to expand its operations overseas. By the 1930s the Frigidaire became one of the standards for quality in consumer appliances.

The company manufactured not only steel refrigerators with temperature controls but also "ice-cream cabinets, refrigerated soda fountains, milk coolers, drinking fountains, room air conditioners, and display freezers for groceries" (Gasbarre 1998, 217). In the 1930s, Frigidaire added ranges, ovens, water heaters, and cloth washing and drying machines to its catalog of home appliances. In spite of the Great Depression, the company's refrigerator output topped 2.5 million in 1932, and then climbed to over 6 million by 1941 (Gasbarre 1998, 217). Like most US manufacturers, Frigidaire converted its plants to wartime production after 1941, and fabricated airplane propellers, gas tanks, hangars for bombs and a variety of other parts for the Allies' mechanized armies, navies, and air forces. After the war, the company focused on product innovation. In the 1950s, it manufactured "automatic ice-makers and auto-defrost refrigerators" alongside frost-free refrigerators (Gasbarre 1998, 217). The novelties that Frigidaire brought to the electric appliance industry paid off with greater and greater market share. The company advertised such features as "Frigi-Foam insulation, FrostProof freezing, Sheer Look styling, and the Ride-Aire accessory" (Howald 1980).

Frigidaire changed hands in 1979 when White Consolidated Industries (WCI) acquired it from General Motors, but then in 1986, WCI was bought by Electrolux, a Swedish firm (Gasbarre 1998, 217). Electrolux devised a new marking slogan for it appliance division: "Frigidaire Company ... creating a better tomorrow!" The company sold Tappan, Gibson, Kelvinator, and White-Westinghouse branded appliances and aimed at an upscale market with its UltraStyle line. Beginning in the 1970s and continuing through the next fifty

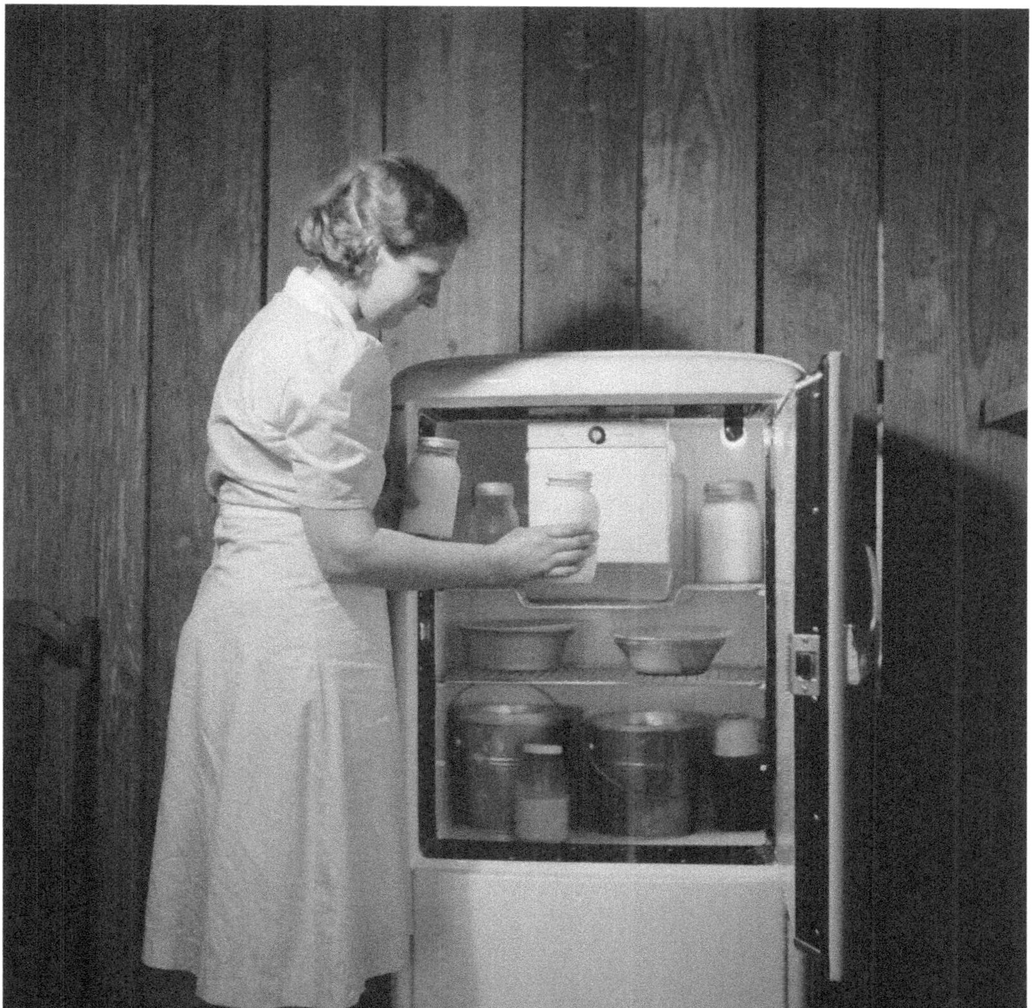

FIGURE 11: Early models of Frigidaire refrigerators revolutionized food preservation and storage.

years, Frigidaire appliances were required to comply with the energy efficiency standards provided for by the Energy Policy and Conservation Act of 1975 and subsequent legislation. The UltraStyle line of the 1990s is an example of the company's long-running effort make products more energy efficient, as it spent $500 million developing a coordinated line of 100 different appliances branded as UltraStyle that boasted energy-saving features (Gasbarre 1998, 217). Responsibility for setting energy efficiency standards for home appliances was eventually handed over to the US Department of Energy's Office of Energy Efficiency and Renewable Energy.

The Frigidaire brand of electric appliances earned numerous listings in various consumer products magazines, like *Consumer Reports* and *Good Housekeeping*. They've also garnered numerous EnergyStar awards, which are conferred by the US Environmental Protection Agency for achieving high marks in energy efficiency on some of the millions of electronic machines and devices available in the marketplace. A current model of Frigidaire refrigerator uses less electricity that two 60-watt light bulbs. The brand is still valued by consumers, but has very strong competition from brands like GE, LG, Whirlpool, Maytag, Bosch, and Samsung. The top-selling refrigerators offer some insight into the nature of the modern economy. Consumers can buy GE refrigerators from GE Appliances, which is owned by the Chinese company Haier Group Corporation. LG refrigerators are made by the South Korean company LG Electronics, and Bosch is a German brand made and sold by BSH Hausgeräte. Frigidaire, though it originated as an American-owned brand, is owned by a Swedish company, leaving Whirlpool and Maytag as the major brands that originated in the United States and still owned in large part by American investors.

The refrigerator's history is an important object in American social and cultural history. In its early stages, the appliance appealed to business owners and homeowners who needed a solution to the problem of food preservation. In the nineteenth century, Americans preserved food through canning, smoking, pickling, and fermenting. These practices are very much still in use, but most Americans buy food in grocery stores and use their refrigerators and freezers for storage. Some 99.8 percent of American homes are equipped with refrigerators, and Americans take anywhere from fifteen to twenty trips to the fridge a day (Hammond 2018). Mass production and relatively cheap energy keeps them humming. The original Guardian Frigidaire cost $775, which was equivalent to about $11,000 in 2020 adjusted for inflation. In 2020, a basic refrigerator cost about $1,500 in current dollars, which puts it in price range that makes it a household staple. Few would be willing to do without, given that the electricity costs for operating it are a mere $150 per year (2020). In the end, the refrigerator contributed to a modern lifestyle that includes a wide range of electrical devices that once were figments of the imagination, and then became real, but luxuries, and are now considered essentials.

Fazila Derya Agis

See also: Carrier, Willis Haviland; Electricity; Energy Policy Act of 2005; Energy Policy and Conservation Act of 1975; General Electric Company; Hobart Electric Manufacturing Company; Home Energy Efficiency; KitchenAid Appliances; Singer Manufacturing Company; Upton Machine Company and Whirlpool Corporation

FURTHER READING

FridgeFilters. 2018. "Frigidaire." Fridgefilters.com. https://www.fridgefilters.com/fridgepedia-frigidaire-brand.html (accessed January 24, 2020).

Gasbarre, April Dougal. 1998. "Frigidaire Home Products History." *International Directory of Company Histories*. Ed. Jay P. Pederson and Thomas Derdak. Vol. 22. Pp. 216–18. St. James, MO: St. James Press.

Hammond, Alexander. 2018. "Thanks Capitalism, Refrigerators Are Awesome!" FEE Stories. Foundation for Economic Education. January 12. https://fee.org/articles/thanks-capitalism-refrigerators-are-awesome/ (accessed October 2023).

History of Refrigeration (HR). 2020. "History of Fridges and Freezers." History of Refrigeration. http://www.historyofrefrigeration.com/refrigeration-history/history-of-fridges/ (accessed January 23, 2020).

Howald, Judith, reg. 1980. "General Motors Corporation. Frigidaire Division." Frigidaire Collection in the Alumni Historical Collection, General Motors Institute, Flint, MI.

Fuel Cells

Fuel cells generate direct current electricity by combining hydrogen and oxygen. Producing potable water and heat as waste products, they could serve as a source of sustainable energy for many applications. However, for nearly 200 years technical limitations and economic factors repeatedly blocked widespread adoption. Several non-interchangeable types now exist, each offering its own opportunities and challenges. Elegant in concept but expensive to make and use, fuel cells remain a niche technology of much promise and unfulfilled hopes.

During the decades following Alessandro Volta's invention of the battery in 1799, many researchers investigated methods of generating electricity by chemical means (King 1962). In 1838, Welsh jurist William R. Grove (1811–96) created a new type of battery and used it to reverse William Nicholson and Anthony Carlisle's electrolysis experiment. He combined hydrogen and oxygen to make water while generating electricity, demonstrating the basic concept of a fuel cell, or "gas battery" as he called it (Grove 1839, 1844). Grove combined the two experiments and in 1842, "the decomposition of water was effected by means of its composition."

Fuel cells, like batteries, typically feature two electrodes (an anode and a cathode) separated by an electrolyte. Positive electrical charges flow from one electrode to the other through the electrolyte, while negative charges flow through an external circuit and provide power. Fuel cells are grouped by the type of electrolyte, with different cell types suitable for different applications. Operating temperatures and auxiliary equipment requirements can also vary greatly. Unlike batteries, fuel cells often need a catalyst such as platinum coated on their electrodes in order to support chemical reactions (Kordesch 1996).

Grove's original gas battery used platinum electrodes with a dilute sulfuric acid electrolyte. Aside from electricity, he generated heated debate among his fellow researchers. His discovery presented "a puzzle" to a nascent scientific community still working to codify the basic laws of physics and chemistry (Ostwald 1896, 671). Did the flow of electricity come from a chemical reaction or the physical contact between different materials? Why did different materials show different reactions? Incapable of producing more than a small amount of current and requiring expensive materials, fuel cells remained a laboratory curiosity for much of the nineteenth century.

Low electrical output and high costs always raised significant barriers to the practical use of fuel cells. Makers learned to bundle individual cells into stacks to increase the power output, a pricey compromise. As people in the late nineteenth and early twentieth centuries electrified their daily lives, companies built centrally located generating stations and networks of wires to supply that power. Some electricity came from hydroelectric dams, but most stations burned coal to create steam to run generators. Growing demand for electricity attracted investors who supported research to advance steam-engine and generator designs. The development and mass production of equipment capable of generating tremendous amounts of electricity lowered the cost of electric power, spurring further demand. Researchers at the time understood that to make fuel cells practical, they needed to design units that could produce a lot of current at low cost.

Some took on the challenge, believing that fuel cells offered a way to avoid the Carnot heat-cycle that limited steam engines and thus increase the energy efficiency of generators. Ludwig Mond and Carl Langer used a hydrocarbon-containing gas as fuel. Others tried to convert coal directly into electricity, driven by concerns about finite coal supplies. One, Thomas Edison, damaged his laboratory when a fuel cell experiment exploded. In 1896, William W. Jacques announced that he had made a "carbon battery" having an 82 percent efficiency, a claim that others soon disproved. No practical devices emerged from this era but accounts of attempts to directly convert coal publicized the technology, and the term fuel cell emerged around this time (Wallace 2019, 86–7).

Most researchers to that point used various acids as electrolytes, though a few experimented with alkalis. Their cells generally operated at relatively low temperatures (below 300°C). That facilitated design but the cells required relatively pure hydrogen and oxygen to function. In the 1930s, several researchers turned to higher temperature devices more tolerant of impure gases. The work of Emil Baur and various colleagues, and of Oganes K. Davtyan, helped lay a foundation for molten carbonate and solid oxide fuel cells. Cells operating over 500°C indeed eased problems brought on by fuel contamination, at the cost of new problems like excessive degradation of internal seals. Their work brought new knowledge, but still no practical applications. Fuel cells remained a solution in search of a problem.

In the late 1930s, Francis W. Bacon (1904–92) of Britain identified a problem that seemed tailor-made for a new type of alkali cell. Submarines used diesel engines when running on the surface and banks of batteries for operating underwater. Hydrogen leaking from batteries could accumulate to explosive levels in the enclosed environment, a dangerous situation. Bacon presented his fuel cell idea to the Royal Navy, and they supported his work for a time. When Britain entered the Second World War, though, they transferred him to a higher-priority project. After the war, the introduction of nuclear power gave naval designers a more powerful alternative. Bacon continued his fuel cell work, and that later proved useful.

Fuel cells enjoyed a resurgence of public interest and funding after the Second World War for both military and civilian uses. Military users tested portable power units of various sizes: handheld devices for landing field lights, backpack-sized units for battlefield radar, and large units for encampments. Civilian applications included several ideas for fuel cell-powered cars, among other products. Union Carbide engineer Karl Kordesch test drove a fuel cell motorbike and an Austin A-40 car around Cleveland. Allis-Chalmers tested a fuel cell-powered fork lift, golf cart, and a farm tractor (Wallace 2019, 88–90).

Allis-Chalmers' tractor provides the clearest example of the problems with that era's fuel cell prototypes. The tractor's 1,008-cell stack extracted hydrogen from propane and could pull 3,000 pounds (1,360 kg). Though a successful demonstration piece, the company would have needed to invest significant resources to create a low-cost product that could compete in the market against mass-produced, gasoline-powered engines. Unlike fuel cells, farmers were familiar with and knew how to maintain gasoline engines. None of the post-war ideas for fuel cells could meet needs as economically as existing power sources like batteries and internal combustion engines. Many of the proposed civilian and military applications would have required cultural changes by users in order to succeed.

In only one area did fuel cells find a practical application. As the United States and the Soviet Union raced to reach the moon, the National Aeronautics and Space Administration (NASA) engaged in an unfamiliar activity, human space flight. They found batteries too heavy and solar cells too weak to power lunar expeditions. With virtually unlimited funding and a politically mandated deadline, NASA selected two fuel cell designs to provide astronauts with electricity and potable water. General Electric produced a cell built around a new, polymer electrolyte. Their proton exchange membrane (PEM) cell proved troublesome during Project Gemini, so NASA selected an alkali cell from Pratt & Whitney for Project Apollo. Based on Francis Bacon's research, the alkali cells worked well, and NASA later installed improved versions on their space shuttles.

On earth, fuel cells remained too expensive for most applications. Cost calculations began to change during the 1960s and, when energy prices spiked following the 1973 oil embargo, fuel cell research resurged. A new generation of prototypes and demonstrations built public enthusiasm for the technology. But again, no practical devices moved into widespread use. Energy prices receded, lessening the cost pressure on traditional energy sources. Investments in efficiency led to advances that saved energy and lowered operating costs for mature technologies. Fuel-efficient cars, for example, could leverage existing production and maintenance infrastructures. As with the fuel cell tractor, a fuel cell car would need new fuel and service infrastructures, as well as cultural changes among consumers in order to succeed.

A major challenge for fuel cells stem from their inherent nature as components within power systems. All of the components must work together: changing one usually means making physical or electrical changes to the others. Fuel cells that require pure gases, for example, must work in tandem with a reformer that can extract hydrogen from a fuel or oxygen from air. Aside from adding complexity, reformers can generate pollutants and use energy, lowing overall efficiency. Controllers and sensors (with hardware, firmware, and software) are required, and those may need to be designed from scratch. Before connecting to a grid, power inverters must change a fuel cell's direct current to alternating current. If the goal is a fuel cell for transportation, fuel storage and refueling devices must be developed.

The technical challenges are compounded by the fact that energy devices operate within social systems. Mature technologies with an existing knowledge base, familiar to many people, have an advantage over new technologies—even those that show clear advantages. Investors typically want assurance of a reasonable horizon for a return on their money. Standards and safety codes must be negotiated between public and private-sector actors. Insurers and emergency responders must plan for inevitable accidents since all devices can fail. Community engagement in energy projects is essential, as New York's Consolidated Edison learned in the 1970s, with their failed Bedford–Stuyvesant fuel cell plant.

A new push in fuel cell research during the 1990s and early 2000s led to another round of promises, tests, and prototypes—most of which quietly faded away by 2010. Some cells have entered limited use for portable and back-up power applications, and a few fuel cell vehicles are in production. Systems integration difficulties, continued high material costs, and competition from other power sources continue to block widespread adoption, however. Cost reductions coupled with significant advances in conversion efficiencies, made solar panels an attractive clean-energy option for businesses and homeowners alike. Mass production of advanced battery designs are lowering the price of energy storage. Improvements in automated control devices boost energy efficiency in existing equipment (Wallace 2019, 93–4).

Despite the problems and challenges, the reality of climate change highlights the need for clean electric power generators. The potential market for low-cost, high-output fuel cells continues to attract researchers and investors alike. To succeed, as Eisler points out, people must learn that fuel cells are not a singular technology; different cell types exhibit different challenges, run on different fuels, and have specific optimal uses (Eisler 2012, 365). The most important lesson of fuel cells may be more social than technical. Attention to the basic economics and the social prerequisites of integrating clean energy technologies into our infrastructures, may ultimately be more important than additional laboratory research.

Harold D. Wallace Jr.

See also: Advanced Research Projects Agency-Energy; Bell Laboratories; Climate Change; Digital Revolution; Energy Crisis of the 1970s; Lithium-ion Battery; Renewable Energy

FURTHER READING

Eisler, Matthew N. 2012. *Overpotential: Fuel Cells, Futurism, and the Making of a Power Panacea*. New Brunswick, NJ: Rutgers University Press.

Grove, William R. 1839. "On Voltaic Series and the Combination of Gases by Platinum." *London, Edinburgh, and Dublin Philosophical Magazine and Journal of Science*. Vol. 14. Pp. 127–30.

Grove, William R. 1844. "On the Gas Voltaic Battery." *London, Edinburgh, and Dublin Philosophical Magazine and Journal of Science*. Vol. 24. Pp. 268–78, 346–54, 422–32.

King, W. James. 1962. *Development of Electrical Technology in the 19th Century*. Vol. 1: *The Electrochemical Cell and the Electromagnet*. Washington, DC: Bulletin of the United States National Museum. https://archive.org/stream/bulletin228smit#page/n289/mode/2up/search/231 (accessed October 2023).

Kordesch, Karl, and Günter Simader.1996. *Fuel Cells and their Applications*. Weinheim, NY: VCH.

Ostwald, Wilhelm. 1980 [1896]. *Electrochemistry: History and Theory*. Trans. N.P. Date. New Delhi: Amerind Smithsonian.

Wallace, Harold D., Jr. 2019. "Fuel Cells: A Challenging History." *Substantia: An International Journal of the History of Chemistry*. Vol. 3. No. 2. Supp. 1. Pp. 83–97. https://doi.org/10.13128/Substantia-277 (accessed October 2023).

General Electric Company

Few corporations in American history rival General Electric Company (GE) in its importance to American technological, economic, and social development, or its contribution to the history of energy in the United States. Founded in 1892 in a merger between the Edison General Electric Company and the Thomson-Houston Electric Company, GE carried forward Thomas Edison's (1847–1931) innovative ambitions and entrepreneurial energy and became a force for change as millions of Americans transitioned to a modern lifestyle fueled by electricity and abounding in consumer delights. GE's success burnished the reputation of Edison, the so-called "Wizard of Menlo Park," who subsequently has been remembered as one of the most influential figures in history. Over the course of the twentieth century, GE grew its operations in energy-related enterprises like electrical devices, power-generation equipment, electricity transmission systems, home appliances, jet engines, and electric locomotive engines. It also founded the Radio Corporation of America (RCA), moved into medical technologies and healthcare, became a colossal financial services provider, and at one point owned the broadcast media and movie giant NBCUniversal. However, the corporation's downsizing in the twenty-first century occasioned recent books with titles like *Lights Out: Pride, Delusion, and the Fall of General Electric* (2020) and *Power Failure: The Rise and Fall of an American Icon* (2022).

GE's early history is tied to Thomas Edison's extraordinary career as an inventor and businessman. Born in Milan, Ohio in 1847, Edison received training as a telegraph operator at the age of fifteen and then traveled around the United States in the 1860s, taking different telegraph jobs. He took an interest in electrical engineering and in the early 1870s designed a telegraph system that could send two pairs of messages in opposite directions along the same wire. He sold the rights to this technology for a large sum and in 1876, established his historic research laboratory at New Jersey's Menlo Park. In 1878, Edison founded the Edison Electric Light Company, working at two problems simultaneously: perfecting an electric-powered, incandescent lightbulb and figuring out the electrical system needed to make it work. These issues resolved, Edison opened a factory in Newark in 1881 and began marketing electrical light systems while forming new companies along the way.

His first major project, the Pearl Street Station in New York City, opened in 1882 and contained a complete system of electrical lighting for customers within a square mile of the plant, which included steam engines for power generators feeding electricity through transmission lines to buildings in the area, and ultimately lamps containing incandescent, electric-powered lightbulbs. This system soon replaced the existing system of lighting by manufactured gas piped into homes and businesses from centralized locations. In 1889, Edison merged his different companies—Edison Lamp Company, Edison Machine Works, Bergmann & Company, and Edison Electric Light Company—into Edison General Electric Company and then purchased the Sprague Electric Railway and Motor Company. It was this version of Edison's enterprises that merged with Thomson-Houston Electric Company in 1892 to form the General Electric Company.

Since the late 1880s, Edison had been involved in a battle with Nikola Tesla over which version of electrical current—direct or alternating—would prevail in the electrical industry. Direct current (DC) had been established early, but it was limited by the single direction current could flow, making it hard to convert between low and high voltage. Tesla's alternating current (AC) reverses flow a certain number of times per second and thus can allow voltage conversion with the use of a transformer. GE submitted a bid to electrify the 1893 Chicago World's Columbian Exposition with DC but lost to George Westinghouse and Tesla's AC. Over time, user preferences for AC would create competition for the company. Edison sold his GE shares in 1894 and became a company consultant while turning his attention to new inventions. He would secure 1,093 patents over the course of his life, including patents for the phonograph, kinetograph (an early movie camera), and the alkaline storage battery. He left behind a company that had established itself as a force in the electrification of the United States and the world. In the 1890s, GE manufactured most of the components required to create, deliver, and use electrical power. These components included generators, electricity transmission equipment, electric motors for industrial use, electric light bulbs, and electric locomotives.

In the early twentieth century, GE committed itself to further innovation and the extension of electricity into the home. In 1906 the company created, and then improved, a tungsten filament for the incandescent light bulb that burned brighter, lasted longer, and didn't blacken the bulb. It sold widely, and its durability made it suitable for automobiles and trains. The company put out a very popular model of electric lamp as well as a toaster and a less well-received electric range. It also produced a commercial refrigerator, and a few years later a consumer model for homes. In 1918, GE consolidated with Hotpoint Electric Heating Company, maker of electric irons, and Hughes Electric Heating Company, maker of electric ranges, which established the company as a leader in manufacturing electrical appliances for domestic use. In many ways, GE was on the leading edge of a shift in American living standards, promoting the values of what historian Mark Rose called "comfort, convenience, and cleanliness" through its electrical lighting and its hygienic, labor-saving home appliances. The company actively promoted the use electricity in the 1920s and 1930s and informed men "in unambiguous terms of their responsibility to provide a built environment for women that was warm, well-ventilated, odor-free, and likely to protect them from disease" (Rose 1995, xv). Simply put, the company was changing how millions of Americans lived their daily lives.

GE continued to pursue ways to harness electricity along new and profitable lines. Radio emerged as an attractive new field, but "wireless" communication required a "generator to produce alternating current of high frequency" in order to span great distances. The company's engineers and technicians worked on this problem for years and by 1918, they produced a 200-kilowatt alternator that "created electromagnetic waves that leapt the oceans" (Hammond 1941, 351). In 1919, GE, Westinghouse, AT&T, and the United Fruit Company jointly formed the Radio Corporation of America (RCA), which not only manufactured radios but also built a national radio network, the National Broadcasting Company (NBC). In a similar vein, GE carried out the first television broadcast in 1928, though antitrust concerns led the company to divest itself from RCA in 1932. The company illuminated the Panama–Pacific International Exposition in 1915, using colored lighting in featured spots, which poet Edwin Markham described as "the greatest revelation of beauty that was ever seen on earth" (Hammond 1941, 364). It completed another high-profile project around the same time, the electrification of the Panama Canal, using hydroelectric generators, 1,000 electric motors, and a sophisticated system of electronic controls to operate its various locks, dams, and spillways.

LEWIS LATIMER

One of Thomas Edison's key associates was African American inventor Lewis Howard Latimer (1848–1928). Latimer was the son of runaway slaves, fought for the Union in the US Civil War, and worked for Alexander Graham Bell before joining Edison's laboratory in 1884 as a patent researcher and draftsman. Over the course of his career, he secured patents for an improved passenger rail toilet, a process for making carbon filaments for light bulbs, and an early version of the air conditioner. With Edison's encouragement, Latimer wrote one of the more important books that explained electrical power and illumination to a wide readership, titled *Incandescent Electric Lighting: A Practical Description of the Edison System* (1890).

Jeffrey B. Webb

America's growth and expansion opened markets for GE to develop cutting-edge technology to power next-generation systems. It became established as a manufacturer of advanced electric-powered locomotives before the First World War, then a provider of steam turbines with turbo-electric transmission for the first-of-its-kind USS *New Mexico*. This new class of battleship burned oil rather than coal, and GE's systems enabled it to become an "all-electric ship," with electricity powering its turrets, pumps, anchors, lights, fans, blowers, air compressors, steering mechanism, cranes, winches, refrigeration, heating, and cook stoves (Hammond 1941, 370). Early in the Second World War, GE helped to build the engine for the US Army Air Force's first experimental jet airplane, and then manufactured engines for the P-59, the US military's first production jet aircraft. In the Cold War era, GE invested in research, design, and production of jet engines, and built 30,000 J47 axial-flow engines between 1948 and 1978 for a wide variety of military aircraft. The GE-built J79 powered the F-4 Phantom II, the key US fighter aircraft in the Vietnam War, and the company manufactured 17,000 engines before the end of its production run. Entry into the business for commercial jet engines eventually followed; in 2022 GE and its partner CFM International controlled 55 percent of the jet aircraft engine market, selling to manufacturers like Boeing and Airbus.

GE's effort to sustain its leadership in energy technologies extended to hydroelectric generators and atomic and nuclear power. GE's giant generators powered Nevada's Hoover Dam electrical output beginning in 1936, and the company went on to provide generators and other electrical components for many other hydroelectric plants in the post-war era. Scientists from the company were involved in the US government's Manhattan Project at the Hanford Engineer Works facility in 1943, which processed uranium into plutonium for the atomic bomb used in the destruction of Nagasaki. After the war, GE assumed control of the facility and built five new production reactors to supply plutonium for the US nuclear weapons program, then built several research facilities to support development of propulsion systems for the US Navy's first nuclear-powered submarines. It shifted to civilian nuclear power by collaborating on the US Atomic Energy Commission's Power Reactor License No. 1 plant in Vallecitos, California, which began operating in 1957. The plant, with GE's boiling water reactor, "the first privately funded plant to supply power in megawatt amounts to the electric utility grid" (CEC 2020). Another of its boiling water reactors, the Dresden-1 (250 Mwe), was installed in 1960 at the Dresden Generating Station near Morris, Illinois.

GE remained an energy and power company, first and foremost, until the later decades of the twentieth century under Jack Welch, who from 1981 to 2001 served as Chairman and CEO. He focused on one of the company's divisions, GE Capital, which traced its history back to 1932 as a program of extending credit to consumers to buy GE home appliances. Welch steered the division into more aggressive financial pursuits including leveraged buyouts, subprime mortgages, and credit-default swaps. By 2000, half of GE's revenue came from financial services, and it was one of the US's five largest financial institutions. Another Welch acquisition, RCA, owned NBC, putting GE back into the business of broadcast television. The company then bought Universal Studios in 2004, which remade the company's image into a financial and media leviathan. However, the company's debt rendered it vulnerable to the 2008 financial crisis, when the federal government deemed GE "too big to fail" and "agreed to insure as much as $139 billion in debt for its lending subsidiary, GE Capital." From 2008 to 2014, GE Capital's revenue declined from $68.5 billion to $42.7 billion (Spross 2018) prompting Welch's successor CEO, Jeff Immelt, to sell most of its financial services assets. Under Immelt, the company also began to divest from NBCUniversal, selling off parts of the division to Comcast in 2011 and 2013. As a result of these sell offs and declining share value, GE's market capitalization shrank from $451.7 billion in 1999 to $91.55 billion in 2020, and it became mainly an industrial corporation once again, as well as a cautionary tale of corporate ambition.

Over its history, GE made light bulbs and lamps, electric power generators, home appliances, electric locomotives, jet aircraft engines, nuclear power plants, and television shows, occasionally all at the same time. The company was part of several revolutions, first bringing interior lighting to buildings once lit by kerosene and manufactured gas lamps. An exhibit of Thomas Edison's work at the Smithsonian Museum of American History noted: "The consequence was to interrupt the normal, biological rhythms of life and to alter our schedules for work and leisure. Industrial plants could operate in shifts around-the-clock, for example, and the concept of 'the city that never sleeps' became a reality" (SNMAH 2020). Then, the company helped to revolutionize American domestic life with its numerous electricity-powered appliances, giving new meaning to the idea of the "American Dream" in the typical American household. In the end, the many ways in which GE technologies and products helped the United States to transition from coal and steam power to oil and electrical power will remain one of its most important legacies.

Jeffrey B. Webb

See also: Bell Laboratories; Edison, Thomas Alva; Electricity; Hobart Electric Manufacturing Company; KitchenAid Appliances; Pearl Street Power Station; Smart Grid; Tesla, Nikola; War of the Currents

FURTHER READING

California Energy Commission (CEC). 2020. "Nuclear Power Reactors in California." California Department of Energy. March. https://www.energy.ca.gov/sites/default/files/2020-03/Nuclear_Power_Reactors_in_California_ada.pdf (accessed October 2023).

Hammond, John Winthrop. 1941. *Men and Volts: The Story of General Electric*. Philadelphia: J. B. Lippencott Company.

Morris, Edmund. 2019. *Edison*. New York: Random House.

Rose, Mark H. 1995. *Cities of Light and Heat: Domesticating Gas and Electricity in America*. University Park: Pennsylvania State University Press.

Smithsonian National Museum of American History (SNMAH). 2020. "Consequences of Edison's Lamp." *Lighting a Revolution*. Web Exhibit. May. https://americanhistory.si.edu/lighting/19thcent/consq19.htm (accessed October 2023).

Spross, Jeff. 2018. "The Fall of GE." *The New York Times*. March 19. https://theweek.com/articles/761357/fall-ge#:~:text=Ultimately%2C%20GE%20Capital%20got%20a,were%20not%20GE's%20only%20mistake (accessed October 2023).

Geothermal Power

Historically, the generation of electricity makes use of a steam turbine generator where the steam is generated by boiling water, heated by some fuel source like wood, coal, and oil. The generator itself is the device in which steam is directed at a fan blade resulting in the movement of a coils of wires around a magnet. As first discovered by Hans Christian Ørsted in the nineteenth century, this action produces electricity. Of course, if steam could be found to be naturally occurring at some location, then conceptually that would be the ideal place to install a steam turbine generator. This was first put into action in 1904 in Tuscany Italy. The initial power plant made use of dry steam fields in Larderello to produce 10 KW of power. By 1913, the harvesting of additional steam fields (powered by magma heated water a few km below the surface) had expanded to an area known as Devil's Valley to achieve a new capacity of 250 KW. Gradually additional steam plants populated the larger-scale area so that currently thirty-four individual generators now have capacity of 800 MW.

Despite this initial successful demonstration of the use of geothermal power in places where steam rising to the surface is readily available, it wasn't until the late 1950s that a second geothermal complex was built in New Zealand. This slow ramp-up to geothermal as a source for steam-generated electricity is a direct consequence of the rarity in which there are suitable locations on the earth where harvestable steam is abundantly available. Perhaps the world's best location for geothermal power is the country of Iceland, where the mid-Atlantic tectonic separation zone rises to the surface thus exposing near-constant levels of steam emanation as well as many small, but active volcanoes. The spreading velocity in Iceland is about five cm/year, roughly twice as much as the average mid-Atlantic spreading velocity.

Geothermal energy can be considered as a renewable energy source where there are locations that consistently generate steam. In other areas, like the Geysers Project in California, water must be pumped down to interact with sub-surface heat sources to produce steam. In cases like this, geothermal energy should be regarded as a mined source of energy if increasing larger amounts of water need to be injected to maintain the plant's capacity. Indeed, the Geysers Project now requires 350 injection wells to sustain its capacity 1500 MWe as generated by a combined twenty-two geothermal power planets.

As of 2020, approximately 16 GW of geothermal electrical power was available through installations in about twenty countries. In the same year, global electrical use was ~ 25,000 TWH. Continuous use of the available 16 GW would then produce 16 * 8760 (hours per year) or ~140 TWH which is about 0.5 percent of the world's total electrical production. Thus, geothermal electricity production is very much a niche application—negligible on a global scale but highly effective on some local scales such as Iceland. The development of geothermal electricity generally carries an important side benefit as the production of steam can also be co-used as a source of heating, thus further saving energy otherwise used from fossil fuels. Currently, there are seven countries whose total geothermal electrical production exceeds 1,000 MWe (1GWe). Together these countries comprise ~90 percent of world total production. Those countries and their attributes are listed below in Table 1. Column 3 of Table 1 (Eff) measures the efficiency of geothermal use in units of citizens per hundred thousand. For example, the United States has a total population of 350 million—at efficiency of 10.3, this means that the 3700 MWe of geothermally produced electricity would meet the needs of 10.3* (350 million/100,000) or 36,000 citizens.

As shown in Table 1, the leading countries in geothermal electricity production tend to also be the most populous countries leading to low individual citizen use. New Zealand citizen use is an order of magnitude higher. For some countries the source of geothermal power is highly localized as it was initially in Tuscany to active volcanic areas. Turkey and Mexico, however, represent countries with a highly distributed source of sub-surface heating locations and Turkey is currently taking the world lead in developing these distributed sources. Mexico has recently chosen not to pursue this resource. Finally, we consider the case of Iceland where geothermal electricity production has now risen to 25 percent of total electrical production. In terms of the Eff parameter in Table 1, Iceland would have value of ~2115 or another order of magnitude higher than New Zealand. Thus, where steam is abundantly available, geothermal resources should be maximized for local citizen use of electricity and heat.

While there is tremendous geothermal potential in places like the American West, most of that potential is very difficult to tap. Most of these potential sources occur in highly mountainous regions which present various access challenges. There are very few locations in which that potential rises to the surface like Old Faithful where one could simply put a steam generator on top of the geyser. To harvest this potential one must mix the hot rock with water and somehow capture and focus the steam that is being generated well below the surface. The harvest of this potential is known as Hot Dry Rock. In this scenario test wells are driven

Table 1 Top Countries for Global Geothermal Production

Country	*Production (MWe)*	*Eff*	*Comments*
USA	3700	10.3	Approximately 30 plants, located primarily in CA and NV. The production in Geyser's facility is about 40% of US total
Indonesia	2289	8.5	11 power plants distributed in thermally active areas with individual capacities of 200–350 MW
Philippines	1918	17.7	Approximately 25 plants; largest at 400 MW
Turkey	1549	18.9	Very rapid growth starting at 82 MWe in 2010 and the current value is about 20 times larger; significance source of heating for Turkish residents. Large distribution of smaller plants across Turkey
Kenya	1193	22.7	Plans for geothermal to be the leading source of clean energy for Kenya; 2010—projected 2025 growth is 596 to 1795 MWe
New Zealand	1064	217	Highly localized source in Taupo volcanic zone; 15 total plants; largest plant at 161 MWe
Mexico	1006	8.2	About 750 MWe comes from the Cerro Prieto plant in Northern Baja just across the US border. Currently Mexico has no plans for further expansion in geothermal despite having good area distributed across the country

approximately 5 km down to heated rock, which in itself is expensive. Then water is injected into those wells with the hope that steam production will emerge at another nearby well, known as the production well. Extensive tests of this approach were done in areas in New Mexico in the 1970s with the main negative result that the generated steam never reached the surface in any coherent manner. That is, generated steam simply diffused through the crust, as it already does naturally, and any attempt to drill essentially a collimated system for steam extraction simply failed.

So, while there may be strong motivation of develop this resource, harnessing geothermal energy at an increased rate will likely require very specialized and difficult kinds of new engineered infrastructure whose final cost may likely be prohibitive. This essential difficulty is reflected in the relatively slow growth rate of global geothermal electricity production. Data from the international renewable energy agency shows that in 2010 global installed capacity was ~ 10,000 GWe, which took essentially one hundred years to achieve, and in 2020 it was ~14,000 GWe. This implies a linear growth of only 400 MWe per year. For example, over this same period the linear growth in wind energy is 50,000 MWe per year and the data itself show the growth to be faster than linear.

Despite the relatively low contribution to global electricity production from geothermal, this source does have many positive features that can help to reduce future use of fossil fuels once we are better able to exploit geothermal resources with higher efficiency. There are at least four worth highlighting. First, the source is reliable. Once geothermal power can be tapped at some location, it becomes a very predictable and steady source of power and shows none of the intermittency that come with the use of wind and solar. In practice, this means that energy storage is not needed in any geothermal power plant as they have a consistent power output no matter the time of day or season. For the utility industry, the lack of fluctuations compared to other renewable sources like wind and solar makes geothermal sources very attractive for baseload power delivery.

Another positive feature is the resource's small land footprint. We can ask, how much land, as a function of technology, is needed in order to produce a given amount of power? This is determined both by the concentration of ambient energy per location and the unit size of the turbine or power-generating device. For example, the Geysers facility produces 1500 MW over an area of 117 square km leading to a figure of merit of 12 MW per sq km. Much of that area is covered with various piping needed to connect the 350 geothermal wells into a functioning transport network which would operate, at capacity twenty-four hours a day. In comparison, the Shepherds Flat Wind Farm in Oregon can produce 845 MW of electrical power through turbines distributed over 80 sq km which leads to a similar footprint factor of 10 MW per km. However, for this case the wind farm, due to the intermittent nature of wind, operates at capacity only about 30 percent of the twenty-four-hour day so the appropriate figure of merit is 3.1. The Topaz solar farm in California has a peak output, when the sun is directly overhead of the array of PV panels, of 580 MW. The average daily production is about 20 percent of the peak at a typical solar facility since the sun angle varies throughout the day and only about ten hours a day can be used. The panel arrays consume about 15 sq km of land. Thus, the figure of merit for solar would be 3.2. Hence, in general to produce the same continuous output, a geothermal plant requires four times less land area than either wind or solar.

A third positive feature of geothermal energy is its flexibility in usage. There are both utility-scale and small-scale applications for geothermal power. A typical small-scale application is the use of geothermal heat pumps for residential and commercial buildings

FIGURE 12: The Geysers geothermal field in the Mayacamas Mountains north of San Francisco in California.

which can be quite efficient. For example, the Oregon Institute of Technology in Klamath Falls Oregon was specifically built over an active thermal area ~1,500 feet below the surface. A total of twelve buildings on this campus of about 5,000 students are directly heated by geothermal which saves about $1m per year compared to commercial heating rates. Then, a fourth advantage can be identified: geothermal plants do not require much maintenance. Once built and operating the plant essentially can run by itself. In addition, there are no extra fuel requirements to power other components of the system. In addition, with simple modifications within the overall steam delivery and routing system, geothermal plants can also be a local source of hot water.

Despite these positive features, there are, of course, some obstacles and disadvantages related to geothermally generated steam for electricity. The first obstacle has been alluded to, which is the lack of suitable sites. Geothermal power plants can only be built at certain locations where reservoirs above 100 degrees centigrade are directly accessible. If excess drilling and injection of hot water to sub-surface hot rock is required to produce steam, then power plant construction at that location is generally not feasible. There is also a disadvantage to the cost structure of geothermal development. Most of the total cost package for a geothermal power plant are upfront costs as there is little post-construction maintenance costs. Much of the way a geothermal plant operates is via buried pipes and extra drilling to various hot spots and those excavation costs are large. This means on a per kilowatt-hour basis, a geothermal plant costs three–five times more to construct than an equivalent solar or wind farm. This requires a different kind of financial burden which could become an obstacle to initial construction. Finally, geothermal development results in subsidence. As a geothermal plant extracts heat and water from underground, that can alter the seismic stability of a region which can cause further land subsidence over time, especially as a geothermal reservoir nears depletion.

Greg Bothun

See also: Energy Crisis of the 1970s; Energy Security Act of 1980; Public Utility Regulatory Policies Act of 1978; Renewable Energy

FURTHER READING

Benighaus, C., and A. Bleicher. 2019. "Neither Risky Technology nor Renewable Electricity: Contested Frames in the Development of Geothermal Energy in Germany." *Energy Research and Social Science*. Vol. 47. Pp. 46–55.

Hou, Jianchao, Mengchao Cao, and Pingkuo Liu. 2018. "Development and Utilization of Geothermal Energy in China: Current Practices and Future Strategies." *Renewable Energy*. Vol. 125. Pp. 401–12.

Huang, Wenbo, Wenjiong Cao, and Fangming Jiang. 2018. "A Novel Single-Well Geothermal System for Hot Dry Rock Geothermal Energy Exploitation." *Energy/Elsevier*. Vol. 162(C). Pp. 630–44.

Huttrer, G. 2020. *Geothermal Power Production in the World 2015–2020 Update Report*. Proceedings of the World Geothermal Congress, Reykjavik, Iceland, April 26–May 2.

Melikoglu, Mehmet, 2017. "Geothermal Energy in Turkey and around the World: A Review of the Literature and an Analysis Based on Turkey's Vision 2023 Energy Targets." *Renewable and Sustainable Energy Reviews*. Vol. 76(C). Pp. 485–92.

Soltani, M. 2021. "Environmental, Economic, and Social Impacts of Geothermal Energy Systems." *Renewable and Sustainable Energy Reviews*. Vol. 140. April.

Getty, Jean Paul

During the 1950s, the "Seven Sisters" oil companies established a strong monopoly over the oil industry in the Middle East. These enormous corporations worked in concert to ensure that no other rivals would interrupt their hegemony over oil. However, in the 1950s, a "solitary millionaire from Oklahoma" challenged the entire oil industry (Sampson 1991, 168). J. Paul Getty (1892–1976), born into immense wealth after his father capitalized on the oil boom in Oklahoma during the late 1800s, became a millionaire by the age of twenty-three and secured a path to becoming the richest man in the world a few decades later (Sampson 1991).

At the end of the 1800s, the discovery of oil fields across the United States catalyzed a mass movement of eager prospectors looking to buy land. However, the displacement of sixty Indigenous tribes accompanied the rapid purchase of land for oil. It was during this time that George Franklin Getty, J. Paul Getty's father, visited Oklahoma and, upon seeing the vigor and productivity of the oil fields there, decided to join the rest of the wildcatters (Miller 1986). In May 1905, he acquired Lot 50 in Bartlesville Oklahoma which produced a 100,000 barrels a month. He also purchased a 70 percent stake in the Minnehoma Oil Company (Miller 1986). It was on August 22, 1918, that his son became a shareholder of Minnehoma. George Getty eventually became the director for Minnehoma Oil while continuing to work as a wildcatter (Miller 1986).

In 1920, Minnehoma Oil Company found the largest oil well in Oklahoma, producing up to 15,000 barrels per day. Although this discovery made son Getty an immense fortune, it came at a cost. The lack of environmental regulations combined with the brutality of the oil business reshaped the environment into an "extraordinary, hellish scene" with "huge cloud[s] of black mist swirled around ... the roaring fountain of oil" (Miller 2011, 1024). It turned the prairie into a "dirty brown color as far as the eye could see" (Miller 2011, 1024). At twenty-six, young Getty attempted to become involved in the Southern California oil industry, but soon left due to poor results. In November 1921, riding the success of Union Oil's discovery of oil just off Telegraph Road, father George Getty bought leases for four plots of land to the south. His son noted that from then on, "the name of Getty would be associated to an ever-increasing extent with California" (Miller 2011, 1179). The Getty fortune reached $15 million in 1923 around the time that Getty's father became sick. In response, he took over the business completely.

Upon the death of his father, Getty inherited the family business and the Getty fortune. He created the Sarah C. Getty Trust, a trust fund that enabled him to purchase shares of Tide Water Oil company (Pearson 1995). Although he was the sole trustee, he could not borrow any money from the trust directly. To work around this dilemma, he used the liquid assets from the trust to purchase oil shares. Getty secured a 20 percent holding from Rockefeller's Mission Corporation and finally, by 1936, used his equity to buy 25 percent of the shares of Tide Water (Pearson 1995). His shares gave him leverage over both Exxon and John D.

Rockefeller II, who also held shares in Tide Water. Getty eventually won out and established a majority hold over the company. In response to the *New York Times*, Getty remarked, "I've never felt rich because I've always been in a business where I was a moderate-sized fellow compared to Exxon, Shell, Gulf, Socal. I'm a small-sized fellow, a small-sized outfit, so I've never had delusions of grandeur" (Eder 1974, 39).

During the Second World War, Getty continued to manage the Spartan Aircraft Company, a subsidiary of Mission Corporation in Tulsa. He ran his operations from a concrete bunker out of fear of being bombed. His "eccentricities" became even more accentuated after he got a second facelift, began washing his underwear every night because of his distrust of commercial detergents, dyed his hair, and even chewed "each mouthful of food thirty-three times" (Yergin 2011, 423). By 1958, after *Fortune* magazine revealed his net worth, Getty was conducting business from the Ritz in London with a "single overworked secretary" (Sampson 1991, 142). He eschewed the entire organized oil world.

The end of the Second World War ushered in a critical shift for the geographic epicenter of the oil industry. Although Texas and other oil centers in the United States were still quite lucrative, the Middle East's oil boom attracted every oil magnate looking to keep pace with the "car economy boom" (Pearson 1995, 78). Getty missed this opportunity once before the war, but afterwards realized its full potential and reached out to the Saudi King Ibn Saud to negotiate oil concessions (Sampson 1991). With the help of geologist Paul Walton, previously the head of exploration in the Rocky Mountain Division of the Pacific Western oil company, Getty sought sole ownership of the Saudi oil concession (Yergin 2011). Getty, not tied to the political dynamics of the Seven Sisters oil consortium, obtained shares directly from King Ibn Saud for an "unprecedented royalty of 40% per barrel" (Pearson 1995, 80). In other words, Getty managed to negotiate the most lucrative deal in oil at the time. This, in part, increased Getty's notoriety and cunning, as the oil billionaire is remembered. His personal and generous relationship with King Ibn Saud led to an agreement in which Getty prepared to establish schools, houses, mosques, training programs, and free gasoline for the Saudi Army (Yergin 2011). This relationship became so close, in fact, that US Secretary of State Dean Acheson reminded the Saudi government that a private American company could not legally provide funding for another nation's army (Yergin 2011).

When Getty struck oil in the Middle East, *Fortune* magazine called it "colossal" and "history making" (Pearson 1995, 80). Although it was crude oil, Getty had refineries in the United States that could turn it into oil for use. He built a tanker fleet for shipping oil with the help of his friend, the French industrialist Commandant Paul Louis Weiller, and with a French government subsidy for the project. For the next decade, Getty's Pacific Western grew dramatically, becoming the largest producer of gasoline (Pearson 1995). In 1956, Getty changed the name of the company to Getty Oil Company. By this time, Fortune named Getty "America's richest man and its sole billionaire" (Yergin 2011, 425). Getty remarked of the statement: "If you can count your money, you don't have a billion dollars" (Yergin 2011, 425).

Getty may have established a profitable oil empire in the Middle East, but that success did not seem to influence his family life positively. In July 1973, Getty's sixteen-year-old grandson, Paul Getty III, went missing in Rome. A ransom note was sent to Getty asking for cooperation and money. Getty's response was terse as he believed the possibility that "the boy and his mother ... cooked this up to get money out of me" (Miller 2011, 5425). Eventually, when it became apparent that the situation was serious, Getty sent CIA agent Fletcher Chase to investigate. Fletcher and the Italian police found that the kidnapping was in fact real and after Getty intervened, the ransom was settled at $1 million (Miller 2011). Getty did not pay the ransom directly. Instead he loaned his son, Paul II, $850,000 at 4 percent interest to pay the ransom with the agreement that the loan would be paid back. When Paul III was rescued and the ransom paid, he tried to call his grandfather. The secretary answered: "It's young Paul calling from Rome, do you want to speak with him?" Getty replied without looking up from the newspaper he was reading: "No." (Miller 2011, 5604).

Due to Getty's celebrity status and general aversion to being in the public eye, he was often portrayed as an intelligent and successful icon. However, criticism concerning this perception arose when Getty's treatment of workers came to light. During The Depression, Getty fired all of his employees and then hired them back at lower salaries. He managed to win the loyalty of many politicians and diplomats through large campaign donations (Yergin 2011). Before the war, the FBI believed that Getty had close connections with the Nazi leaders at the time, but nothing ever came of the investigations (Yergin 2011). Getty's shale oil projects were later examined for environmental impacts. In general, the construction and operation of shale production projects caused loss of wildlife habitat, reduction in habitat quality, soil erosion, dust, fumes, and the consequences of extensive human activity. Getty spent his career building an expansive oil empire and providing jobs for people, but the environmental destruction and mistreatment of workers raises questions over the costs of Getty's growth and expansion for the sake of wealth and power.

In Getty's own words, he believed that most men were "envious and jealous" of him which he attributed to his business acumen and "so-called luck" with women (Lund 1977, 54). Disagreeing with Rockefeller's weak attempt at moral altruism with his wealth, Getty believed that "the best thing one can do for people is to provide them with jobs so that they can earn a good wage and look after themselves." He continued, "If you have to struggle for something ... you appreciate it when you get it. The current fashionable type of socialism ... encourages people to believe they are entitled to whatever they want" (Lund 1977, 54). Getty died on June 6, 1976. The J. Paul Getty Museum in Los Angeles contains his collection of priceless masterpieces. His legacy remains controversial, but it is clear that Getty Oil Company directly and dramatically shaped the oil industry in the twentieth century.

Thomas David Brown

See also: Aramco; Caltex; Consortium Agreement of 1954; Gulf Oil Company; Mandatory Oil Import Quota Program; Mobil Oil Corporation; Red Line Agreement of 1928; Seven Sisters Oil Companies; Texaco

FURTHER READING

de Chair, Somerset Struben. 1989. *Getty on Getty: A Man in a Billion*. London: Cassell.

Eder, Richard. 1974. "A Rich Isolated Old Man Views His Life—and Oil." *The New York Times*. February 6. Pp. 39, 57.

Getty, J. Paul. 1976. *As I See It: The Autobiography of J. Paul Getty*. Englewood Cliffs, NJ: Prentice Hall.

Hewins, Ralph. 1960. *The Richest American: J. Paul Getty*. New York: Dutton.

Lenzner, Robert 1986. *The Great Getty: The Life and Loves of J. Paul Getty*. New York: Crown.

Lund, Robina. 1977. *The Getty I Knew*. Kansas City: Sheed Andrews and McMeel.

Pearson, John. 1995. *Painfully Rich: J. Paul Getty and his Heirs*. London: MacMillan.
Miller, Russell. 2011. *The House of Getty*. New York: Bloomsbury Reader Edition.
Sampson, Anthony. 1991. *The Seven Sisters: The Great Oil Companies and the World They Shaped*. New York: Bantam Books.
Witzel, Morgen, ed. 2005. *The Encyclopedia of the History of American Management*. Bristol, UK: Thoemmes Continuum.
Yergin, Daniel. 2011. *The Prize: The Epic Quest for Oil, Money, and Power*. Reissue ed. New York: Free Press.

Global Climate Coalition

The Global Climate Coalition (GCC) operated from 1989 to 2001 as a non-profit advocacy organization committed to opposing political action to reduce greenhouse gas emissions, curtail global warming, and halt the progress of human-induced climate change. It represented corporations and trade groups in the fossil fuel industry who feared that the science of climate change would convince governments, and even the whole international community of nations, to force reductions in carbon emissions produced by the burning of oil and gas for energy. Major industry groups like the American Petroleum Institute (API) and companies like Phillips Petroleum financed and supported the organization in its campaigns against the Intergovernmental Panel on Climate Change reports from 1990, 1992, and 1995, as well as the provisions of the Kyoto Protocol in 1997. Environmentalists and most climate scientists refer to the GCC's media efforts as "climate denialism," an intentional campaign to sow doubt in the minds of ordinary people regarding scientific findings about changes in atmospheric gases and surface temperatures of the earth. The GCC disbanded in 2001, but the campaign it orchestrated was carried on by other like-minded, industry-funded organizations through the opening decades of the twenty-first century.

From 1989 to 1993, the GCC was a project undertaken by the National Association of Manufacturers (NAM). In a later interview with several researchers, a person described as "a senior GCC staff member" revealed the reasons for its creation. He said that the petroleum industry was caught unawares when governments agreed to a phase-out of ozone-depleting substances like chlorofluorocarbons in the Montreal Protocol of 1987, one of only two United Nations treaties to be approved by all member nations. After that experience, the NAM believed that the creation of the Intergovernmental Panel on Climate Change (IPCC) the next year, in 1988, posed an existential threat to manufacturing and fossil fuel production. The staff member recalled saying that climate change was the "mother of all issues," and required an organized effort to stop government attempts to regulate fossil fuel emissions (Levy 1999, 5). The group reconstituted itself as an independent organization in 1992, comprising the major oil and gas producers like Shell, BP, and Exxon, trade industry associations like the API and the National Coal Association, investor-owned electric utilities using fossil fuels, and corporations in the automobile, steel, chemical, and mining industries. These members paid dues to maintain a full-time staff and paid for lobbying and public opinion campaign efforts in Washington, DC.

John Shlaes, executive director of the GCC, revealed the philosophy and objectives of the organization in a 1993 statement critical of a proposed tax on carbon dioxide emissions. Shlaes claimed that "carbon taxes will have little, if any, impact on global carbon dioxide emissions," and then moved to his first point: "there is a growing debate on the veracity and reliability of the computer models that predict so-called global warming. Recent satellite and other scientific data appear to contradict model predictions" (Shlaes 1993b). This point is crucial to understanding the debate over climate change that developed from the late 1980s over the ensuing thirty years. Shlaes didn't question scientific findings about the links between increased atmospheric greenhouse gas concentrations and their link to increased fossil fuel emissions, nor did he say that scientists were wrong to conclude that the higher levels of greenhouse gases had contributed to a warming earth and a changing climate. He chose instead to focus on the computer models that forecast current trends into future periods, and to say that growing debate questioned the "veracity and reliability" of these models. While technically not wrong, the statement ignored all of what climate scientists had established as factual and true, while throwing out the phrase "growing debate" over the models without identification of who was debating them and on what grounds. The "growing debate" assertions have been and continue to be, part and parcel of the rhetorical strategy of climate denialism by the largest producers of carbon dioxide emissions and their representatives.

In a 1993 letter opening with "Dear Journalist," Shlaes invited the press to "take advantage of GCC's expertise" when covering their "angle on the climate change issue in the next year, be it economics, science or policy." He remarked, "our members are committed to ensuring a balanced, informed debate on all aspects of the climate change issue" (Shlaes 1993a). It was part of GCC's public relations strategy to suggest that journalists adopt a "balanced" approach, meaning giving equal weight to climate science and climate denialism. This would leave their readers with the impression that both positions had equal merit, scientifically speaking, thus any rash moves to cut emissions or tax carbon would be unjustified. To augment its credibility, GCC speakers, its website, and its bulletin cited material by conservative think tanks that supported their positions. For example, the GCC cited the George C. Marshall Institute in its March 1994 issue of its newsletter *Climate Watch*. The institute had issued a report saying, "there is a correlation between the rise and fall of the Earth's temperature and solar activity." Their report also noted, that "the lifetime of atmospheric carbon dioxide—a major factor in the greenhouse effect—may be closer to 10 years than to the conventional estimate of 50 years" (GCC 1994, 3).

Neither of these points undermine the scientific research linking together greenhouse gases, global warming, and climate change. Importantly, the bits pulled from the Marshall Institute report weren't even trying to claim, as the GCC's newsletter pronounced in the header, "Marshall Institute Finds No Warming." The intent of the misleading header was to have journalists simply repeat it in their reportage, thus giving the "debate" over climate change a seeming 50/50 aspect. Although this is a false equivalence, distracted readers who aren't carefully parsing these reports leave with the impression that the science of climate change is either true or false depending on what one wants to believe. It must be noted that think tanks like the Marshall Institute, the Heartland Institute, the CATO Institute, and the Competitive Enterprise Institute issued many statements and reports that are signed off by lone-wolf academics, but are not subject to peer review and do not reflect the consensus opinion of atmospheric and oceanic researchers or the major professional scientific associations like the American Association for the Advancement of Science, the American Geophysical Union, the American Meteorological Society, the American Physical Society, and the American Academy of Arts & Sciences.

The GCC achieved a temporary victory in 1997–98 by helping to prevent US participation in the Kyoto Protocol. The protocol bound its signatories to implement the emissions reductions targets in the United Nations Framework Convention on Climate Change. The United States signed the agreement, but it required Senate ratification to go into effect.

President Bill Clinton never presented it for a vote due to industry opposition and public backlash. The dust-up over US participation in Kyoto brought BP, Shell, DuPont, and Ford to withdraw from the GCC, perhaps fearing public identification with climate denialism. It didn't help their public image when environmentalists labeled the GCC a "club for polluters" (DaimlerChrysler 2000). When Texaco, GM, and DaimlerChrysler withdrew in early 2000, the GCC moved to allow only trade associations, as opposed to individual corporations, to be eligible for membership. This decline in membership and the belief that it won the Kyoto battle over government-imposed emissions reduction targets led the organization in 2001 to close down its operations.

The back-and-forth over climate change didn't go away once the GCC disappeared from the media and from US politics. Conservative advocacy groups and isolated science skeptics maintained a steady beat of climate denialism in the 2000s, leading Clinton's former vice president Al Gore to address them in his film *An Inconvenient Truth* (2006), and researchers Naomi Oreskes and Erik M. Conway to detail their campaigns in depth in *Merchants of Doubt: How a Handful of Scientists Obscured the Truth on Issues from Tobacco Smoke to Climate Change* (2010). The Union of Concerned Scientists (UCS), founded at MIT in 1969, maintained its own campaign to "fight back when powerful corporations or special interests mislead the public on science." It continued: "When special interests release bogus studies, corporations sow doubt about science, or political operatives censor, manipulate, or undermine government science, UCS is there to set the record straight with the public, the news media, and our elected officials" (UCS 2023). The organization asserted: "The consensus couldn't be clearer. Climate change is happening. It's caused primarily by the burning of oil, gas, and coal. If we do nothing, the world will become significantly less habitable" (UCS 2023).

The GCC's made appealing arguments about (1) the preference of voluntary over compulsory measures to reduce greenhouse gas emissions, (2) the economic costs attendant to making sizeable reductions in fossil fuel use, and (3) the difficulty of creating a fair international agreement on emissions reductions with such diverse systems of energy production and use throughout the world. Still, its campaign of misinformation and doubt about the science of climate change left millions of people in a state of confusion as nations proceeded to address atmospheric greenhouse gases produced by carbon-based energy production and consumption. For example, the Obama administration approved US participation in the Paris Climate Agreement of 2015, a pact among the nations to reduce carbon emissions according to "nationally determined contributions." When former president Donald Trump took office, he announced the United States would withdraw from the agreement at the first possible opportunity, which came in late 2020. When Joe Biden replaced him, one of his first acts was to sign the United States back into the agreement. This policy whiplash was the result of a partisan media environment that drew from a poisoned well of information about energy and the environment, and as a consequence, encouraged political polarization on the issue of climate change.

Jeffrey B. Webb

See also: American Petroleum Institute, *An Inconvenient Truth*; Cap and Trade System; Clean Power Plan of 2015; Climate Change; Energy Policy Act of 2005; Koch Brothers; Union of Concerned Scientists

FURTHER READING

"DaimlerChrysler Leaving Climate Coalition." 2000. *The New York Times*. January 7. https://www.nytimes.com/2000/01/07/business/daimlerchrysler-leaving-climate-coalition.html (accessed October 2023).

Dunlap, Riley E., and Peter J. Jacques. 2013. "Climate Change Denial Books and Conservative Think Tanks." *The American Behavioral Scientist*. Vol. 57. No. 6. Pp. 699–731.

Global Climate Coalition (GCC). 1994. "Marshall Institute Finds No Warming." *Climate Watch: The Bulletin of the Global Climate Coalition*. Vol. 2. No 3. March. P. 3. https://www.climatefiles.com/denial-groups/global-climate-coalition-collection/1994-climate-watch-vol-2-issue-3/ (accessed October 2023).

Levy, David L., and Sandra Rothenberg. 1999. "Corporate Strategy and Climate Change: Heterogeneity and Change in the Global Automobile Industry." Belfer Center for Science & International Affairs. October. E-99–13.

Shlaes, John. 1993a. "Dear Journalist." Global Climate Coalition. January 4. https://www.climatefiles.com/denial-groups/global-climate-coalition-collection/1993-climate-expertise-news-release/ (accessed October 2023).

Shlaes, John. 1993b. "Statement by John Shlaes, Executive Director of the Global Climate Coalition." February 2. PR Newswire Association, LLC. Farmington, MI: Gale, Cengage Learning.

Union of Concerned Scientists (UCS). 2023. "About." Union of Concerned Scientists website. https://www.ucsusa.org/about (accessed October 2023).

Gold, Stephen J.

In the age of steam, a number of inventors and innovators came to see the usefulness of steam power in a variety of applications and worked to turn this new kind of energy toward the problem of home heating. One of these inventors, Stephen J. Gold (1801–80) invented a way to warm a home with an apparatus that drew steam from a furnace and boiler and fed it through pipes to its different rooms, each equipped with a large heating chamber containing distribution plates for radiation and condensation. The device improved on earlier technology by automatically regulating the amount of steam drawn into the system, thus requiring less attention from the user. Gold wished to build a home heating system that would be less expensive, safer, and easier to use than existing models, and he accomplished this goal. Gold's device was manufactured in Connecticut and found customers throughout New England, beginning in the mid-1850s and continuing through the end of the century. It was a modest, and yet still important step in the use of energy to heat building interiors from a central location.

Gold lived in Cornwall, Connecticut as a child—one of ten in his large family—and worked there for most of his adult life. The town lies in the northwestern quadrant of the state in an area rich in iron ore, and dotted with furnaces and iron works. Gold and one of his brothers built a workshop and made wood and coal-burning cast-iron stoves for heating and cooking, as well as other iron implements. In the 1820s and 1830s, homes in New England were heated with free-standing iron stoves, or Franklin-type stoves inserted into fireplaces. Gold's shop supplied this market, but he grew interested in steam power as it spread across the region. He knew of Joseph Nason, who brought steam heating technology from England to the United States in the 1840s and installed centralized steam heating systems in large buildings and mills in Boston, Vermont, and New York. Gold developed a vision for bringing steam heat into individual homes and small businesses like his own, and he began tinkering with various steam heating components in the late 1840s and early 1850s. Gold's system borrowed from existing technology but contained a few innovations, and once its advantages over other models seemed clear, he filed for a patent. In the application, which was approved in 1854, Gold described it as "a new and useful Improvement in Apparatus for Heating Buildings" (Gold 1854, 1).

The patent continued to describe the different mechanisms and their function in the steam heating system. Gold wrote: "the object of this apparatus is the heating of buildings by radiation from broad thin chambers made [to be] the receivers and condensers of steam generated in a suitable boiler connected with the heaters." The basic operation of the system entailed moving steam heat from a boiler and furnace through a central pipe with branches to connect with heating chambers "in each apartment to be warmed"

(Gold 1854, 1). Heat "evolves" from the chambers into their respective rooms, while condensation is collected in the chambers and fed through pipes and collection boxes (cisterns) back to the boiler. Gold's added a design feature that included valve placement within the system to equalize pressure, enabling the simultaneous release of heat from the chamber and the movement of water back to the original source. Gold described this attribute of the system as "self-regulating," and believed it merited recognition as an invention. Here's his description of his breakthrough in heating technology: "This self-regulating property gives a security to the use of steam as a heater not possessed by any other apparatus, as nothing is required but to keep up the fire, and the necessary amount of steam, and no more, will be conveyed to the condensers and radiators in the several apartments to be warmed" (Gold 1854, 2).

Gold's steam heating system was intended to warm an entire house, and to do it without requiring an attendant to operate it other than keeping the firebox stoked with coal. According to an historian of steam power and steam heating, it was the first use of radiators, the first use of single pipe connections to the radiators, and "'the first attempt to make the boiler automatic'" (Stifler 1960, 28). Gold met with Yale chemistry professor Benjamin Silliman, Jr., showed him his work, and with some other investors they formed the Connecticut Steam Heating Company in New Haven to manufacture and sell Gold's system. By 1855, the company claimed to have installed it in fifty-five different manufacturing plants throughout the state. User testimonials commented favorably on its relatively low purchase price, simple design, ease of use, safety in operation, and most importantly, savings on fuel (Stifler 1960, 30). Different radiator designs appeared in the mid-to-late nineteenth century and competed with Gold's system for customers, but the company continued to produce the system into the 1890s, even offering seven options for heating chambers for different sized rooms (Lawless 2016).

Gold and inventors of his generation demonstrated new ways to harness the energy of steam beyond powering locomotives or operating textile machinery. By providing a low-cost way to heat the interior of a home, Gold's system made it possible for families in the middle and working classes to experience comfortably warm interior spaces during the cold winter months, particularly in the northern US states (Harris 2008). For Gold, his invention promised to improve his marriage and his family life. When asked later why his father invented a whole home steam heating system, Gold's son replied that his mother had weak lungs and couldn't endure the heat of a coal-fired iron stove during cold Connecticut winters. She had been wintering in the South for health reasons, and her husband's system provided a way for her to live comfortably and in good health throughout the year, and in the company of her family (Stifler 1960, 27). Steam power, coupled with innovative thinking, offered Gold a pathway out of an unhealthy family situation, while improving the lives of thousands who brought his technology into their homes and businesses.

Jeffrey B. Webb

See also: American Radiator Company; Johnson, Warren Seymour; Nason, Joseph; New York Steam Company; Pierce Steam Heating Company; Richardson & Boynton Company; Steam Power

FURTHER READING

Gold, Stephen J. 1854. "Improvement in Warming Houses by Steam" (US Patent #11,747). United States Patent Office. https://heatinghelp.com/assets/documents/145.pdf (accessed October 2023).

Harris, Howell John. 2008. "Conquering Winter: U.S. Consumers and the Cast-Iron Stove." *Building Research and Information*. Vol. 36. No. 4. Pp. 337–50.

Lawless, John. 2016. "The Complete History of Radiators: A Guide to How We've Come to Love Our Radiators." BestHeating.com. December 20. https://www.bestheating.com/info/the-complete-history-of-radiators/ (accessed October 2023).

Stifler, Susan Reed. 1960. *The Beginnings of a Century of Steam and Water Heating by the H. B. Smith Company*. Westfield, MA: The H. B. Smith Co., Inc.

Gulf Oil Company

Gulf Oil was a major global oil company based in the United States from 1901 until 1985. The eighth-largest US manufacturing company in 1941 and the ninth largest in 1979, Gulf Oil was one of the famed "Seven Sisters" oil companies that controlled global petroleum markets in the 1950s through the 1970s. Before merging with Standard Oil of California (Socal) to become Chevron, Gulf had been a large source of the Mellon family fortune with both Gulf and Mellon Financial headquartered in Pittsburgh, Pennsylvania. After 1985, Gulf Canada, Gulf's main Canadian subsidiary, was sold to Ultramar and Petro-Canada, and what became Gulf Canada Resources to Olympia & York. The Gulf brand name and several business divisions of GOC remain in operation.

Gulf now is a "new economy" business with its intellectual property assets such as brands, product specifications, and scientific expertise. Gulf Oil Limited Partnership owns the US rights to the brand and operates over 2,100 service stations and several petroleum terminals. Total S.A., a French multinational, owns the Gulf brand in Spain and Portugal. In the rest of the world, the Gulf brand is owned by Gulf Oil International (whose parent is the Hinduja Group) which operates over 500 outlets in the UK, with expansion underway to sixty countries. This company sells lubricants, car care, Gulf Nanotac Fuel Additive, Gulf branded merchandise, and fuel at its retail stations, as well as aviation fuel. It is a far cry from the dominance of Gulf Oil in fossil fuel production in the middle of the twentieth century.

Gulf Oil began in 1901 with the discovery of oil at Spindletop south of Beaumont, Texas, by former Austrian naval officer Anthony F. Lucas (1855–1921). Needing funds, he went to established oil prospectors James M. Guffey and John H. Galey, who then got financing from brothers Andrew W. and Richard K. Mellon through Pittsburgh's Mellon National Bank and Trust Company. Other investors included Mellon's Pennsylvania clients and some Texas wildcatters. They formed a joint business venture between the J.M Guffey Petroleum Company and the Gulf Refining Company in Texas, naming the company after the Gulf of Mexico, then established a modern refinery at nearby Port Arthur, Texas, to process the oil. The largest investor was William Larimer Mellon—a relative of the other Mellons—who became the company's executive manager.

Gulf expanded quickly. New oil wells were tapped in Oklahoma and sales offices opened in Houston, New Orleans, Tampa, Philadelphia, and Boston. As Spindletop's output declined, Gulf looked elsewhere for supply. In 1907, it constructed the 400-mile Glenn Pool pipeline connecting Oklahoma oil fields with its Port Arthur refinery, as part of a network of pipelines and refineries in the eastern and southern US. Mellon Bank was a frequent investor in these early projects.

In 1910, Gulf began the world's first overwater drilling operation in Louisiana. Two years later, it formed its first of many foreign ventures as the Mexican Gulf Oil Company to explore and produce petroleum there. Gulf eventually expanded its petroleum production to Venezuela, Canada, Europe, the Persian Gulf, and other regions. The company opened the world's first drive-in automobile service station in Pittsburgh in 1913. Gulf shrewdly promoted its branded product sales by selling gasoline in containers and from pumps sporting their orange disc logo. This responded to the public distrust of non-branded gasoline because of its unreliability or possible contamination.

Before the Second World War, Gulf Oil grew steadily in the United States. Like the other major oil companies, it did business in all aspects of the oil industry: exploration, production, transport, refining, and marketing. The company also ventured into petrochemicals and automobile component manufacturing. Gulf was the typical Seven Sisters company, doing big business by using political and economic muscle and connections to influence its host countries. In 1924, Gulf bought the Venezuelan–American Creole Syndicate's leases along Lake Maracaibo. Gulf was extensively involved in exploration and production operations in Kuwait, and its late 1930s joint venture Kuwait Oil Company with British Petroleum was the first oil exploration in that country.

Gulf further expanded globally after the Second World War, investing heavily in product technology while developing many specialty products, especially in the maritime and aviation engineering sectors. The company was known for its many lubricants and greases. Other commercial and technical innovations included free road maps, drilling over water at Ferry Lake, Texas, and the world's first commercial catalytic cracking unit at its Port Arthur refinery in 1951. With the other Seven Sisters, Gulf then strongly influenced oil production and prices in the developing world. It purchased filling stations in various countries, selling oil-based products produced in Canada, the Gulf of Mexico, Kuwait, and Venezuela.

The company dominated Kuwaiti oil development throughout the 1950s and 1960s, thanks to its "special relationship" with the Kuwaiti government. When in 1950 it was discovered that the Kuwait relationship was linked with "political contributions" and support for anti-democratic politics, Gulf Oil was heavily criticized.

Gulf Oil's marketing was everywhere in the 1960s, with the company as primary sponsor of NBC News special events coverage such as the US space program and a major sponsor of Walt Disney's Wonderful World of Color on NBC. It distributed its "Tourgide" road maps widely in its gas stations. Gulf was one of the oil industry leaders in pursuing various projects in the late 1960s that were in reaction to the closing of the Suez Canal after the 1967 Arab–Israeli War. For example, Gulf built deepwater terminals at Ireland's Bantry Bay and Okinawa, Japan capable of handling Ultra Large Crude Carrier (ULCC) vessels for the European and Asian markets. The loss of Gulf's Kuwaiti bonanza was a real blow to the company's financial outlook. Gulf partnered with other major energy companies, including Texaco, to build the Pembroke Catalytic Cracker refinery at Milford Haven, Wales, and the associated Mainline Pipelines fuel distribution network.

The peak of Gulf's oil development came in 1970 when it processed 1.3 million barrels (210,000 m3) of crude daily, had $6.5 billion ($41.94 billion today) in assets, and 58,000 employees worldwide. At the time, it was owned by 163,000 shareholders. Gulf was a major producer of oil, petrochemicals, plastics, and agricultural chemicals. Its subsidiary, Gulf General Atomic Inc., was involved in nuclear energy development. Throughout the 1970s, Gulf continued to pursue other sources of oil. It partnered in developing new oil fields in the North Sea and in Cabinda in Angola. Both were very expensive, though, and did not yield anything like that extracted from Kuwait.

Gulf's international dominance faded quickly after several oil-producing countries asserted their economic and political independence beginning in the 1970s. Scandals began to surface. In 1975, Gulf admitted that it had made about $5 million in illegal political contributions abroad, including $4 million to South Korean politicians. The company disguised the payments by issuing them through a Gulf Bahamas subsidiary. The same ruse funneled about $5 million to American political groups like President Nixon's 1972 re-election committee. Several senior Gulf executives were forced out, possibly precipitating what happened next.

Because global operations were struggling financially in the recession of the early 1980s, Gulf's management tried the "Big Jobber" strategic realignment in 1981. This involved selective sales of assets and concentration on those parts of the oil industry where Gulf had a competitive advantage. The company was no longer an integrated, multinational oil major. In 1980, Gulf Oil also ended its seventeen-year agreement with Holiday Inn, the world's largest lodging chain, to provide a one-stop gasoline, food, and lodging attraction for motorists. Today, there are many older Holiday Inns with the original Gulf stations on their properties: some working, some closed, but almost all with different names. It symbolizes Gulf Oil's decline from its lofty positions as a one-time enormously profitable and politically influential corporation.

In 1980, Gulf was in trouble. Its huge operations made little profit, its share price was low, and its heavy bureaucratic structure slowed down its enterprises. Its leadership seemingly was hired for their clean reputations rather than expertise, with a chairman nicknamed "Mr. Clean" and "the Boy Scout," and the only major oil company with a nun on its board of directors. Because its domestic oil and natural gas reserves were rapidly emptying (a decline of 40 percent between 1978 and 1982), Gulf increased its exploration spending to discover enough natural gas to fulfill an earlier contract. As a result, Gulf's stock market value fell below the break-up value of its assets. This meant that corporate raiders would be interested in buying the company.

In 1982, Gulf perilously joined a costly battle for ownership of Cities Service Company (Citgo) of Tulsa, Oklahoma, with T. Boone Pickens, owner of Amarillo's Mesa Petroleum and a corporate raider. Gulf outbid Pickens, bought him out, and then reneged on the whole purchase because of supposed financial irregularities. Gulf's termination of the acquisition led to over fifteen years of shareholder litigation against Gulf, and the company's successor Chevron. Gulf resisted Pickens by various means, including becoming a Delaware corporation, ending shareholders' right to cumulatively vote in order to stop Pickens from using his shares to gain control, and listening to purchase offers from Ashland Oil, General Electric, and Standard Oil of California (Socal).

Gulf chose Socal to act as its "white knight" in 1984. The whole ownership battle reportedly made the Mesa group of investors $760 million ($1,770.4 million today), and Pickens claimed that Gulf's stock price was doubled. Gulf's chairman lost his job but collected about $11 million in stock options. The merger of Gulf and Socal to create Chevron was controversial, but the Reagan administration opposed federal intervention. The Federal Trade Commission (FTC) finally approved the deal with strict conditions. This was the first time a "small operator" had succeeded in breaking apart a Fortune 500 corporation, and a "Fortune 10" corporation at that. The other major integrated oil companies were shocked.

To fulfill the FTC's antitrust requirements, Chevron sold some Gulf international businesses, some Gulf stations, and an eastern US refinery to British Petroleum (BP) and Cumberland Farms in 1985. The Gulf name was used by BP, Chevron, Cumberland Farms, and the other companies that acquired former Gulf operations until the early 1990s. All former US Gulf stations franchised by BP and Chevron now have their names.

In 2010, Gulf Oil Limited Partnership (GOLP), of Framingham, Massachusetts—two-thirds owned by Cumberland Farms—purchased the Gulf brand from Chevron and expanded nationally. Most Gulf-branded North American filling stations currently are owned by Cumberland Farms. There also are some independent companies operating under the Gulf brand, such as the American Refining Group, which is licensed by Chevron to blend and distribute Gulf-branded lubricants. Some are international, like Hinduja-owned Gulf Oil International (GOI) which owns the rights to the Gulf brand outside the US, Spain, and Portugal.

Gulf-branded lubricants are still sold worldwide through a network of licensed companies, joint ventures, and subsidiary companies. For example, Gulf is a leading lubricant brand in India. The diminished presence of the brand provides an illustration of the chaotic modern history of the oil industry, which produces a product subject to high price volatility, political convulsions in countries with large petroleum reserves, and vicious competition for control of those reserves and global energy markets by the world's great powers.

William P. Kladky

See also: American Petroleum Institute; Aramco; Energy Crisis of the 1970s; ExxonMobil; Koch Brothers; Mobil Oil Corporation; Organization of Petroleum Exporting Countries (OPEC); Seven Sisters Oil Companies; Standard Oil Company; Texaco

FURTHER READING

Chernow, Ron. 1998. *Titan: The Life of John D. Rockefeller, Sr.* New York: Vintage.

Clark, James A., and Mark Odintz. 2010. "Gulf Oil Corporation." *Handbook of Texas Online*. https://tshaonline.org/handbook/online/articles/dog02 (accessed October 2023).

Davis, Jack. 2017. *The Gulf: The Making of an American Sea*. New York: Liveright Publishing Corporation.

Downey, Morgan. 2009. *Oil 101*. Los Angeles, CA: Wooden Table Press.

Lyons, Richard D. 1975. "Gulf Oil Admits It Illegally Gave 5-Million Abroad." *The New York Times*. May 17.

Salmans, Sandra. 1984. "Gulf's Defeat and Its Lessons." *The New York Times*. March 10.

Thompson, Craig. 1951. *Since Spindletop: A Human Story of Gulf's First Half-Century*. Pittsburgh, PA: Gulf Oil.

Tirana Echo. 2018. "Gulf Oil Scandal—Mother Company Lashes Out at Albanian Partner after Fraud Scheme Leaves Customers Unprotected." *Tirana Echo*. May 7. http://www.tiranaecho.com/latest-news/gulf-oil-scandal-mother-company-lashes-out-at-albanian-partner-after-fraud-scheme-leaves-customers-unprotected/ (accessed October 2023).

University of Pittsburgh Library System (UPLS). 2019. "Gulf Oil Corporation Records." Historic Pittsburgh. https://historicpittsburgh.org/collection/gulf-oil-corporation-records (accessed October 2023).

Vassiliou, Marius S. 2009. *The A to Z of the Petroleum Industry*. Lanham, MD: Scarecrow Press.

Yergin, Daniel. 1991. *The Prize: The Epic Quest for Oil, Money, and Power*. New York: Simon & Schuster.

Gulf War

In 1990, Iraqi armed forces invaded and occupied the neighboring state of Kuwait in the Persian Gulf region under the direction of Iraq's head of state, Saddam Hussein. Iraq's aggression threatened the security of Saudi Arabia and Israel, prompting the United States and a coalition that totaled thirty-nine different nations to expel Iraq's armies by force. The war moved through different phases, starting with the Iraqi invasion itself, and then proceeding through a mobilization of coalition air and naval forces in the Gulf and ground forces in Saudi Arabia known as "Operation Desert Shield." The war's third phase entailed a massive air and ground assault of coalition forces against Iraqi positions in Kuwait and Iraq known as "Operation Desert Storm." The assault ended quickly with a complete rout of Iraqi forces and the liberation of Kuwait. The war came about due to an interplay of long-term diplomatic, strategic, and political factors. However, Hussein decided to invade Kuwait because of a breakdown of relations among OPEC nations over oil policy. The involvement of the US, UK, and other coalition nations arose from considerations of stability and security of the Middle East in the context of Western dependence on the region's oil and natural gas.

The Iraq–Iran War of 1980–8 left Iraq in a state of financial distress. The war had disrupted Iraqi oil production as drilling fell off, a pipeline closed, and the oil export terminal on the Persian Gulf at Mina al-Bakr was damaged. Its oil output fell 1 million barrels a day below its pre-war levels. Iraq needed capital to make repairs and rebuild productive capacity, but could not attract foreign companies to invest, nor could it secure loans from foreign governments. Iraq's OPEC quota at the time was just over 3 million barrels a day, but production could not be increased to reach this level. From late 1989 through mid-1990, Iraq resorted to pressuring Saudi Arabia and other OPEC nations to cut their production in order to elevate the price of oil per barrel. At several OPEC meetings over this period an agreement was reached to reduce production, but Kuwait had long favored lower oil prices and higher OPEC production quotas for long-term economic reasons. Kuwait relented and agreed to the reductions, but OPEC efforts to scale back production over the spring of 1990 were largely ineffective. In the meantime, prices for OPEC oil dropped from $20 per barrel in January of 1990 to $14 per barrel in June of that year, severely threating the stability of Iraq's economy.

In the spring and summer of 1990, the Iraqi government and the Baath Party newspaper openly insinuated that the overproducing OPEC nations were conspiring with Israel and the Western powers in a "Zionist-imperialist campaign against Iraq" (Alnasrawi 1992, 342). On July 17, the anniversary of the Iraq Revolution, Saddam Hussein used the occasion to denounce fellow Arab nations that he believed were secretly trying to undermine the Iraqi economy (Archer 1990, 41). The next day, the Iraq government filed a formal complaint with the League of Arab States that accused Kuwait and United Arab Emirates of "a planned operation to flood the oil market with excess production" in order to "cause a collapse of the Iraqi economy," which Iraq considered "an aggression no less than military aggression"

FIGURE 13: Oil well fire in Kuwait in the Gulf War.

(Alnasrawi 1992, 342–3). The memorandum also accused Kuwait of drilling under its territory in an oil field that straddled the two nations. On July 27, Saddam Hussein massed troops on the Kuwaiti border and on August 2, launched an invasion of the country. Within two days, the Iraqi army captured and killed the Kuwaiti forces that didn't escape to Saudi Arabia and Bahrain, and eventually, on August 28, Saddam Hussein announced the annexation of the country.

On the same day of Iraq's invasion of Kuwait, the UN Security Council adopted Resolution 660 which condemned the attack and demanded Iraq's immediate, unconditional withdrawal. A few days later, Resolution 661 imposed sanctions, including an embargo on trade with Iraq and Kuwait and freezing Iraqi assets. On August 7, President George H.W. Bush ordered the XVIII Airborne Corps, including the famous 82nd Airborne Division, to Saudi Arabia to dissuade Saddam Hussein from attacking further. The fear of Iraqi invasion of Saudi Arabia prompted Arab League states to vote on August 11 in favor of a resolution that read, in part, "we have decided to respond to the request by Saudi Arabia and other gulf states to deploy Arab forces to support the armed forces there to defend its lands and its regional security against any foreign attack" (Kifner 1990). Only Iraq, the Palestinian Liberation Organization, and Libya voted against the measure. In September, US Secretary of State James Baker went on an eleven-day circuit to nine countries to line up military and financial support, including Muslim-majority nations like Saudi Arabia, Egypt, Syria, and Morocco. Eventually thirty-nine nations sent military forces to join Operation Desert Shield in the Persian Gulf region. The United Nations General Assembly issued an ultimatum on November 29, which avowed the use of "all necessary means" to remove Iraqi forces from Kuwait if Saddam Hussein did not withdraw by January 15, 1991.

The United States took active and determined leadership in organizing the international community against Iraq's invasion of Kuwait. Many considerations factored into this action, not least the security of Saudi Arabia and Israel, two longtime US allies. Also, President Bush was eager to assert a principle of international law after the end of the Cold War and the collapse of the Soviet Union to not allow state aggression to go without a response. However, the oil and natural gas resources of the Middle East were fully in view as US policymakers devised their diplomatic, economic, and military response, and had been since at least the formulation in 1980 of the Carter Doctrine. With its conquest of Kuwait, Iraq controlled 20 percent of the world's known oil reserves, but more importantly it "directly menaced Saudi Arabia" and thus was in "a position to dominate—either directly or indirectly—56 percent of all proved reserves," according to one study of the conflict (Lieber 1992, 161–2). US concern over the fate of Middle East oil brought Paul Wolfowitz, US Undersecretary of Defense for Policy, to remind US Secretary of Defense Richard Cheney in a threat assessment a week before Iraq's invasion that "'the fundamental U.S. interest in the security of the Persian Gulf is oil'" (Engel 2017, 385). In the immediate wake of the Gulf War, political scientist Robert J. Lieber explained the situation facing the United States in 1990–1: "The political economy of world oil thus involves an integrated world system. All countries that import or export petroleum are linked to it. Developments occurring anywhere in the system that have a bearing on the demand or supply for oil, whether political or economic in nature, affect the overall balance of that system. Hence, when a serious disequilibrium occurs, the effects are felt globally" (Lieber 1992, 160).

By the time of the UN ultimatum's expiration, the US troops numbered 540,000 in the region of the total 750,000 in the coalition, along with massive numbers of tanks, armored vehicles, artillery, strike aircraft, bombers, fleet-based missiles, and other armaments. Saddam Hussein's refusal to withdraw brought the US Congress to issue a joint resolution effective January 14, authorizing the use of force to liberate Kuwait. On January 16, coalition forces inaugurated Operation Desert Storm, beginning with a forty-two-day aerial bombing and cruise missile campaign against Iraqi air forces and air defenses, command and communications, and military installations. Iraq responded immediately by firing Scud missiles into Israel and Saudi Arabia, hoping to trigger Israeli military intervention with the expectation that Arab troops in the coalition would refuse to fight against Iraq alongside Israelis. The ploy failed and Israel refrained from taking action. Hundreds of civilians were injured, and several died; a Scud missile hit a US military barracks in Dhahran, killing twenty-eight soldiers. The major ground offensive against Iraqi forces in Kuwait and Iraq began on February 24 and within a hundred hours the major action of the war was over with the total collapse of Iraqi military forces. The high-end estimates of Iraqi losses in the war reach toward 300,000 total killed, wounded, and captured. Thousands of civilians died in Kuwait, Saudi Arabia, and Iraq. During the war, Iraq set fire to over 600 Kuwaiti oil wells to darken the skies against coalition air attacks and to guard its retreat, fires that burned for months and created a massive environmental disaster.

The initial invasion of Kuwait sent global oil prices to $77 per barrel; after the war the price dropped to $37 and continued to drop until it reached $16 in 1994 (Sun 2022, 167). The absence of oil from Iraq and Kuwait proved to be only a minor disruption in the global oil market as other OPEC nations stepped up production and the US government authorized the release of 33.75 million barrels of oil from the Strategic Petroleum Reserve (OCESER 2023). The war stimulated anti-American sentiment among Muslim extremist groups, instigated in part by Saddam Hussein's speech in August 1990 following the placement of US troops into Saudi Arabia. Describing the US troop presence as a "humiliation" and a desecration of the holy sites of Mecca and Medina, Hussein issued a call for holy war: "'Your brothers in Iraq are determined to continue jihad without any hesitation or retreat and without any fear from the foreigner's power'" (Kifner 1990). After the war the United States kept 5,000 troops in Saudi Arabia, which became the focal point of resentment for terrorist groups across the region. The Saudi terrorist group Hezbollah Al-Hejaz targeted the US troop presence in the 1996 Khobar Tower (Saudi Arabia) bombing which killed nineteen US airmen and injured hundreds more military personnel and civilians.

The attacks by Islamic militants continued. In a fatwa issued in 1996, terrorist leader Osama bin Laden pointedly invoked the Gulf War and continued US military troop presence in Saudi Arabia as a justification for global jihad: "we are working to lift off the injustice that was inflected upon the nation by the Jewish–Crusaders alliance, especially after their occupation of the Prophet's land, praise and peace be upon him, and their desecration of land of the two holiest sites. We ask Allah to grant us victory" (Bin Laden 1996). In 1998, members of bin Ladin's al-Qaeda terrorist network bombed US embassies in Tanzania and Kenya on the anniversary of US forces moving into Saudi Arabia on August 7, 1990 during the Gulf War. After the devastating September 11, 2001 terrorist attacks on New York and Washington, DC, the 9/11 Commission concluded that the Gulf War contributed to rising militancy among Islamic radicals. Of bin Ladin, the commission report noted: "He inveighed against the presence of U.S. troops in Saudi Arabia, the home of Islam's holiest sites. He spoke of the suffering of the Iraqi people as a result of sanctions imposed after the Gulf War, and he protested U.S. support of Israel" (Commission 2004, 49). The 2,977 innocent people who died on 9/11 were victims of Islamic terrorists, but in some ways, also caught up in the perilous relationship between the United States and nations in Middle East, involving the legacies of Western imperialism, the aftermath of Cold War rivalries, US support for Israel, and US dependency on fossil fuels like oil and gas.

Jeffrey B. Webb

See also: Bush, George H.W.; Carter Doctrine; Cheney, Richard Bruce "Dick"; Consortium Agreement of 1954; Halliburton Company; Iraq War and the Project for a New American Century; Mandatory Oil Import Quota Program; Organization of Petroleum Exporting Countries (OPEC); Strategic Petroleum Reserve

FURTHER READING

Alnasrawi, Abbas. 1992. "Iraq: Economic Consequences of the 1991 Gulf War and Future Outlook." *Third World Quarterly*. Vol. 13. No. 2. Pp. 335–52.

Archer, L. et al. 1990. "The First Oil War: Implications of the Gulf Crisis in the Oil Market." Oxford Institute for Energy Studies. SP1. https://www.oxfordenergy.org/wpcms/wp-content/uploads/2010/11/SP1-TheFirstOil-WarImplicationsoftheGulfCrisisintheOilMarket-LArchereta l-1990.pdf (accessed October 2023).

Bin Ladin, Usamah Bin Muhammad. 1996. "Declaration of Jihad against the Americans Occupying the Land of the Two Holiest Sites." https://ctc.westpoint.edu/harmony-program/declaration-of-jihad-against-the-americans-occupying-the-land-of-the-two-holiest-sites-original-language-2/ (accessed November 2023).

Commission on Terrorist Attacks upon the United States. 2004. "The 9/11 Commission Report: Final Report of the National Commission on Terrorist Attacks Upon the United States (9/11 Report)." Government. National Commission on Terrorist Attacks Upon the United States. July 21.
Engel, Jeffrey A. 2017. *When the World Seemed New: George H. W. Bush and the End of the Cold War*. New York: Houghton Mifflin Harcourt.
Kifner, John. 1990. "Arab Vote to Send Troops to Help Saudis." *New York Times*. August 11.
Lieber, Robert J. 1992. "Oil and Power After the Gulf War." *International Security*. Vol. 17. No. 1. Summer. Pp. 155–76.
Office of Cybersecurity, Energy Security, and Emergency Response (OCESER). 2023. "History of SPR Releases." US Department of Energy. https://www.energy.gov/ceser/history-spr-releases#1991DesertStorm (accessed October 2023).
Sun, Yumeng. 2022. "The Impacts of Wars on Oil Prices." *Advances in Social Science, Education and Humanities Research*. Vol. 670. Pp. 167–70.

Halladay Windmill

Daniel Halladay (1826–1916) patented the first commercially viable windmill in 1854. Halladay's mills were self-governing, automatically pivoting to maintain uniform speed and to minimize the damage caused by strong winds. Originally located in Ellington, Connecticut, the Halladay Windmill Company moved to Batavia, Illinois in the mid-1850s to capitalize on migration trends. Enabling individuals and businesses to access underground water deposits, Halladay's windmills proved key to the settling of the American West. Farmers used the machines to draw water for crops and livestock, while railway companies employed the devices to supply water to their steam-powered engines.

Daniel Halladay was a trained machinist. Born in Marlboro, Vermont, Halladay took a position as a machinist apprentice in Ludlow, Massachusetts at age nineteen. Two years later, he accepted an appointment at the US armory in Harper's Ferry, Virginia, where he supervised the building and placement of machinery. In his mid-twenties he represented inventor John Ericsson (1803–89) at the 1851 Great Exhibition in London, giving demonstrations of the engineer's heat-powered, "caloric" engine in the Crystal Palace. Returning to the United States, Halladay purchased an interest in a machine shop in Ellington, Connecticut.

Daniel Halladay teamed with John Burnham, Jr. (1816–1908) to develop a marketable windmill. Burnham sold water pumps to New England farmers and was fascinated with the concept of using wind power to draw groundwater. For almost 2,000 years mills had been used to pump water, and nineteenth-century Americans were well acquainted with European windmills. But construction costs and the size of the European technologies were prohibitive for homesteaders in the United States. Moreover, windmills had to be tended, their sails turned to harness the wind, or the same power which drew water would destroy the mill. Burnham approached Halladay and asked if he could design an affordable, self-regulating windmill. Halladay replied that he could, and within a year he had completed the project. He obtained a patent for the Halladay Self-Governing Windmill, or the Halladay Standard, on August 29, 1854.

Halladay's invention introduced the blueprint for generations of American windmills, often called windpumps, as their primary purpose was to pump groundwater to the surface. The prototype Halladay Standard sported a wheel of four sails which were mounted on a single shaft. The head of the machine could swivel. A tail, or vane, kept the mill facing the wind. Centrifugal force and a simple weight and pulley system altered the pitch of the sails when wind velocities decreased or increased. Since this innovation enabled the machine to govern the wheel's speed, the Halladay Standard could maximize harvests of light winds and minimize damage from strong winds. A gearbox converted the rotary motion of the wheel into an up-and-down motion, which drew water from the ground through a long rod assembly. There were few metal components. Most of the windmill was made from wood.

Over time, the Halladay Standard evolved. Later models had four legs, instead of one. Steel and iron replaced wood as the primary building materials. A greater number of slat-like sails, or blades, were added, creating a wheel that had fewer gaps and achieving the more familiar, "classic" form of the American windmill. But the mechanics and machine design remained largely the same as those of the 1854 prototype.

After receiving the patent for the windpump, Daniel Halladay and John Burnham formed the Halladay Windmill Company and began to promote their product. Burnham served as sales agent for the firm, which was headquartered in South Coventry, Connecticut. For two years, Burnham and Halladay marketed their windmills in New England. Press reviews of the device were uniformly positive. But much of the American Northeast is filled with accessible water from streams, and sales did not reach company executives' anticipated volume. Burnham began to look for more promising markets outside the region. His attention was drawn to the Midwest.

Chicago became an agricultural and commercial hub in the 1850s. Thousands of farmers looked to the city as a center for shipping, marketing of produce, and manufacturing supply. In 1848, the first rail-transported shipment of grain from an area farm arrived in Chicago. By 1856, ten railway lines serviced the city, and thirty-eight freight trains transported goods to and from the urban center daily. That same year, Burnham moved to Chicago and began filling orders for Halladay windmills.

Business boomed. Aridity and the scarcity of surface water were primary challenges for homesteaders on the Plains. With favorable winds, a Halladay Standard could draw over a thousand gallons of water in a single day. And the machines were affordable—$50 for the mill and an additional $25 for the pump pipes. Ordering kits from Burnham, farmers assembled the windmills, tapped into the aquifers underground, and brought water to the surface for livestock, crops, and personal use. Recognizing that windpumps could provide the water necessary for steam-powered locomotives, railway magnates began purchasing the devices as well. The windmill soon became ubiquitous on the Plains, an expected feature of each homestead and each depot.

Burnham's move to Chicago increased revenues and precipitated changes for the Halladay Windmill Company. In 1857, Halladay and Burnham joined with entrepreneur and Chicago, Burlington and Quincy Railroad executive John Van Nortwick (1809–90) and reorganized the Halladay Windmill Company as the US Wind Engine & Pump Company. In 1863, the firm moved its headquarters from Connecticut to Batavia, Illinois, a town ideally situated on the northern Plains and within 50 miles of rapidly expanding Chicago. Logic dictated the move. The company avoided significant freight costs by shifting production from the East Coast to its sales center in the Midwest.

Financial success encouraged competition. By 1876, US Wind Engine & Pump had grossed $3m from the sale of Halladay Standard windpumps. Others rushed to secure a share of the market. The Chicago-Batavia area became a hotbed of innovation and expansion for the wind industry. The Eclipse Windmill Company, which generated the most sales during the last several decades of the nineteenth century, settled in Chicago. Batavia attracted six independent windmill operations, including the highly successful Aermotor Company, and became known as "The Windmill City."

Energy prices directly impacted the sale of windmills. Significant contraction occurred after the 1901 Spindletop oil discovery in Texas and the subsequent, massive expansion of the oil industry in the twentieth century. Internal combustion pumps, powered by inexpensive fossil fuels, and independent of the whims of the wind, replaced many of the Halladay-inspired windmills. A second, major contraction of the windpump market occurred after passage of the Rural Electrification Act in 1936. Popular interest in wind power returned when gas and oil prices spiked during the Energy Crisis of the 1970s.

Kregg M. Fehr

See also: Energy Crisis of the 1970s; Perry, Thomas Osborn; Rural Electrification Act of 1936; Spindletop Oil Gusher; Steam Power; Texas Oil Boom; Wind Power

FURTHER READING

Baker, T. Lindsay. 1985. *A Field Guide to American Windmills*. Norman, OK: University of Oklahoma Press.

Batavia Historical Society. 2020. "U.S. Wind Engine & Pump Company." http://www.bataviahistoricalsociety.org/exhibits-collections/companies-overview/u-s-wind-engine-pump-company/ (accessed February 28, 2020).

Carmichael, Joe M. 1949. "Water from the Wind." *The Cattleman*. Vol. 36. No. 5. October. Pp. 23–5.

Hays, Dick. 1983. *Windmills and Pumps of the Southwest*. Austin, TX: Eakin Press.

Miller, Donald L. 1996. *City of the Century: The Epic of Chicago and the Making of America*. New York: Simon & Schuster.

Webb, Walter Prescott. 1931. *The Great Plains*. Boston, MA: Ginn Press.

Halliburton Company

Halliburton Company is one of the largest energy corporations in the world. For a company with a long history in the oil and energy industries, it is easy to overlook the intricate ways in which it became the global corporate giant is known as today. Halliburton's history is controversial. Although the company is among the leading corporations in energy, its damaging impact on both the environment and on workers merits scrutiny. Furthermore, close analysis of Halliburton's history reveals that its financial growth derived from a reliance on corruption and exploitation.

Erle Palmer Halliburton entered the oil industry in 1918 after taking a low-ranking position at the Perkins Oil Well Cementing Company in California. Although most companies disregarded oil well cementing, Erle's time as a cementer provided him with skills and knowledge of the oil industry and did so at a time when those assets produced results. His time with Perkins did not last long and he was fired for "relentlessly [offering] suggestions ... on ways to improve the company" (Briody 2004, 8). Erle moved on to the Burkburnett oil fields and after some friends invested $1,000 in equipment, created the New Method Oil Well Cementing Company. He branded his cementing methods—revised and improved from his time with Perkins—as the "Halliburton process" (Briody 2004). In January 1920, however, Erle seized an opportunity to assist Skelly Oil Company with the typical problem associated with oil wells: the violent ejection of large amounts of crude oil into the air due to insecure well walls. Halliburton took advantage of having a solution to Skelly's problem and quickly restored the oil well to efficiency with his "Halliburton process." After Halliburton acquired several of the largest oil businesses as clients, he renamed his company Halliburton Oil Well Cementing Company (HOWCO) and managed to secure 3,500 shares of stock at $100 each (Briody 2004). These capital investments were crucial for Halliburton's growth and success and demonstrate how his company relied on businesses with deep pockets.

At the onset of the Great Depression, most construction and infrastructure projects came to a halt. Brown & Root, a roadbuilding business with roughly 600 employees as well as trucks and equipment, found themselves in need of obtaining new contracts despite the added difficulties of doing so during The Depression (Briody 2004). In 1932, Brown & Root, desperate for work, began working for the city of Houston transferring waste out of the city. The measures taken were extreme in some cases as Brown & Root had their men "separate the organic waste they collected, feed it to pigs, and then sell the pigs on the side" (Briody 2004). This led to legal controversy concerning municipal contracts and as one historian remarked, "public money comes with public scrutiny" (Briody 2004).

Halliburton, on the other hand, was thriving as a result of a $2 million contract for oil well cementing which gave him the opportunity to buy out his former employer, Perkins Cementing Company. The business continued to expand and weather the effects of The Depression, and by the end of the Second World War, Halliburton was a recognizable name in the oil business. Halliburton attributed the success to a personal ethic of hard work, but the trajectory of the business even after Halliburton's death suggests otherwise. In a 1949 issue of the company newsletter, *The Cementer*, Halliburton aired his views: "As the politicians have become more powerful, the operation of free enterprise and the things that we in our generation have tried to accomplish have become more difficult. If the trend continues ... the ingenuity and efforts of the next generation will be so sapped through taxation by the politicians that human progress will be reduced to the speed of a snail" (Briody 2004). The purchase of Brown & Root in 1962, however, changed all this and the company took a different direction.

In the 1990s, Halliburton acquired Dresser Industries which was owned by M.W. Kellogg. The M.W. Kellogg division of Dresser was then merged with Halliburton's subsidiary Brown & Root to form Kellogg Brown & Root (KBR). This Halliburton business maintained consistent growth over the next decades as one of its most important subsidiary companies (George 2006). In the fall of 1995, Richard "Dick" Cheney was appointed as CEO of Halliburton and oversaw the acquisition of the Logistics Civil Augmentation Program, a division of the US Army. Halliburton won what was essentially a monopoly contract on army logistics. In December 1995, President Bill Clinton authorized the military to assist Bosnia and Kosovo, two of the new, yet volatile nations formed after the collapse of Yugoslavia. Halliburton built two small, strategic cities—one in each state—with the purpose of housing troops and preparing resources for the military effort. Halliburton cashed in $2 billion from its involvement in Bosnia and Kosovo. From this moment, however, Halliburton set itself on a dangerous course, as CEO Dick Cheney tightened the relationship of his company with the US Army (Briody 2004).

Later, when Dick Cheney became vice president under President George W. Bush, his relationship with Halliburton continued to prove profitable. When President Bush authorized the invasion of Iraq in 2003, dozens of powerful corporations were awarded military contracts that transferred the role of government services to private corporations. At least seventy of the companies that received Iraq contracts donated a considerate amount of money to President Bush's election campaign (Doran 2012). Some alleged that Cheney's direct connection was the primary reason for Halliburton's lucrative contract with the military during the Iraq War. Cheney's apparent conflict of interest raised harsh criticisms and brought investigations aimed at revealing the connections between the vice president's office and his former company's contracts. Halliburton had been given a two-year, no-bid contract worth $7 billion which authorized the company to "fight oil fires" and "to pump and distribute Iraqi oil" (Doran 2012).

Controversy arose when critics realized the contract was awarded in March of 2003 before war was declared. Later, the Pentagon discovered that KBR, the subsidiary of Halliburton which oversaw operations in Iraq, overcharged the military more than $61 million for fuel in 2003. In January 2004, two Halliburton executives were found to have taken $6 million in kickbacks for sub-contracting to a Kuwaiti company providing services for US troops. A month later, the company admitted to another overcharge of $27.4 million for meals. The food services provided were not adequate for the 110,000 troops in Iraq. A military audit found "blood all over floors of refrigerators, dirty pans, dirty grills, dirty salad bars, rotting meat and vegetables" (Doran 2012). To make matters worse, Halliburton imported cheap labor from South Asia despite Iraq having a 60 percent unemployment rate at the time. They paid these migrant workers $3 per day. Meanwhile, Halliburton's stock price rose from $10 to $41 after the beginning of the Iraq War (Doran 2012). In 2006, the Pentagon terminated its contracts with Halliburton, but the damage had already been done. An investigation by the *Wall Street Journal* found that Cheney had 189,000 shares in Halliburton and 500,000 stock options while he was running for office with President George Bush. His retirement package was worth $20 million (Doran 2012). One-third of the annual profits brought in by Halliburton after 2003 came from the no-bid contracts in Iraq—worth as much as $100 billion—which proved extremely controversial amid questions surrounding the real reasons for going to war in Iraq (Bhagwat 2015).

Halliburton's financial growth and influence continued to spread globally, but the impacts of that growth were felt far beyond corporate profits. As Halliburton charged ahead in its pursuit of corporate growth, it left behind a path of environmental damage. Since the 1990s, Halliburton managed Brazil's state-owned oil company in Catu. In response to complaints about the untreated runoff of sewage and stormwater directly into the Catu River, Halliburton devised a set of "company-wide environmental standards" that pushed Halliburton's environmental management guidelines beyond the requirements of Brazilian law (Dahl 2000). Halliburton trained all of the employees at its Catu base to properly identify and treat the waste before it was released into the river. According to the 1999 report "Fostering Environmental Prosperity," Halliburton's measures proved that "good environmental practices and good business practices go hand-in-hand" (Dahl 2000). Regardless of these positive changes, which Halliburton publicized, the company's environmental record in Brazil raised concerns about the environmental costs of economic growth in developing countries, particularly through the exploitation of petroleum resources.

Despite the changes in waste management procedures at Catu, the negative environmental impacts of Halliburton's oil business were lessened, but not completely eradicated. Regrettably, this achieved legislative approval in the 2005 Energy Policy Act, which introduced new standards and protocols for fracking. The law contained language known as the "Halliburton loophole," which "exempted drilling companies from complying with the Clean Water Act" (Runnalls 2013). Halliburton wasn't culpable for the loophole since it was the company's interest to secure it, but lawmakers failed through lack of consensus on how to define hydraulic fracturing in legislative writing. The lack of attention to environmental protections demonstrates the prioritization of corporate growth over the ramifications of that growth measured in environmental destruction, labor exploitation, and anti-competitive, monopolistic practices. It is possible, therefore, that the real cost of Halliburton's presence in Catu is the dominance of global economic practices over local cultures and practices. This inattention to issues of corporate responsibility and accountability is illustrated by Halliburton's negligence in the *Deepwater Horizon* Oil Spill of January 2011 (NC 2011).

Halliburton's corruption came into clear view when it was revealed that it bribed Nigerian government officials with $180 million in exchange for energy contracts. In 1994, the company known as Tri Star (TSKJ) acquired contracts to conduct operations for a large natural gas project in Nigeria. M.W. Kellogg, which Halliburton acquired in 1998, happened to have a large sum of shares in TSKJ. Halliburton profited from these natural gas contracts with the Nigerian government and as a result, were investigated by Nigeria's Economic and Financial Crimes Commission (EFCC) (George 2006; Brock 2010). Charges against Dick Cheney in Nigeria were dropped when Halliburton agreed to pay $250 million in fines, with the company still protesting that the charges had no legal basis.

Halliburton Company is an influential corporation in the petroleum industry and is a subject of concern for those involved in conversations about climate change and American society's overreliance on fossil fuels. The company's legacy is tarnished by corruption and bribery, environmental destruction, and the exploitation of migrant laborers. However, the company has not slowed down. It continues to operate around the world as a leading corporation in the energy sector. Halliburton's legacy raises pertinent questions about the human and environmental costs of the global expansion of oil production.

Thomas David Brown

See also: American Petroleum Institute; Climate Change; *Deepwater Horizon*; Energy Policy Act of 2005; Iraq War and the Project for a New American Century

FURTHER READING

Bhagwat, Niloufer. 2015. *World Tribunal on Iraq: Making the Case against War*. Toronto: Between the Lines.

Briody, Dan. 2004. *The Halliburton Agenda: The Politics of Oil and Money*. Hoboken, NJ: John Wiley & Sons, Inc.

Brock, Joe. 2010. "Nigeria Drops Charges against Halliburton, Cheney." Reuters. December 17.

Dahl, Richard. 2000. "Global Business: Operating in the Green." *Environmental Health Perspectives*. Vol. 108. No. 5. May. Pp. 220–223.

Doran, Christopher. 2012. *Making the World Safe for Capitalism: How Iraq Threatened the US Economic Empire and had to be Destroyed*. London: Pluto Press.

George, Barbara Crutchfield and Kathleen A. Lacey. 2006. "Investigation of Halliburton Co./TSKJ's Nigerian Business Practices: Model for Analysis of the Current Anti-Corruption Environment on Foreign Corrupt Practices Act Enforcement." *The Journal of Criminal Law and Criminology*. Vol. 96. No. 2. Winter. Pp. 503–25.

Halliburton and U.S. Business Ties to Iran: Hearing before the Subcommittee on Interstate Commerce, Trade, and Tourism of the Committee on Commerce, Science, and Transportation. 2007. United States Senate. 110th Congress. 1st Session. April 30.

National Commission on the BP *Deepwater Horizon* Oil Spill and Offshore Drilling (NC). 2011. "Deep Water: The Gulf Oil Disaster and the Future of Offshore Drilling—Report to the President." Washington, DC: US Government Printing Office.

Runnalls, Jeremy. 2013. "Testing the Waters." *Corporate Knights*. Vol. 12. No. 4. November.

Weismann, Miriam F., Christopher A. Buscaglia, and Jason Peterson. 2014. "The Foreign Corrupt Practices Act: Why It Fails to Deter Bribery as a Global Market Entry Strategy." *Journal of Business Ethics*. Vol. 123. No. 4. September. Pp. 591–619.

Harlan County War

Ten years of struggle over the right to unionize, with coal companies and their deputies on one side and miners and their families on the other, earned Harlan County, Kentucky the moniker, "Bloody Harlan." From 1931–41 Harlan County resembled a war zone, with house searches and evictions, shootings and assassinations, beatings, bombings, battles, and killings. Backed by the local sheriffs, most notoriously J.H. Blair (1879–1934), the mine owners relied on the county deputizing their mine guards, granting them police powers. The struggle in Harlan epitomized the use of law enforcement to protect mine companies' interests over those living and working in the county. Faced with some of the highest rates of poverty and hunger in the country, miners and union organizers armed themselves with guns and explosives and used them in turn. Despite the repression, by the end of the decade 12,000 miners signed the first county-wide union contract with the coal operators of Harlan.

Coal lies in deep seams in Harlan, formed millions of years ago. The first commercial mining operations came to Muhlenberg County as early as 1820 and became common throughout Kentucky by 1880. Harlan was the last southeastern county in the state to develop coal fields. Bordering Virginia and close to the Tennessee line, the county contained few roads, and was mostly wooded with small farms dotting the mountainsides and narrow valleys. The demand for coal by steel mills in the Midwest and expanding rail lines opened up the mountainous county to coal extraction during the second decade of the 1900s, and coal mining in Harlan began its half-century boom (Hevener 1978).

There were some small locally owned mines, though large absentee owners including Ford, Detroit Edison, and United States Steel Corporation dominated the industry. The coal companies set up camps, some housing up to 3,000 miners, and all outfitted with company stores, homes, and script. Union organizing was met with violence from the beginning, starting with the murder of a strike leader during the first organizing drive in 1917. Coal mining remained mostly non-union throughout the 1920s due to company violence, blacklists of union members, gun thugs, and a paternalistic employment system (Taylor 2017).

With the economic crisis of the 1930s, miners turned to unionization. Wages were cut in half in 1931 (Taylor 2017), even as a local paper reported "Future for Coal Business Bright" (Portelli 2011, 183). Company stores and other local groceries were regularly raided by mobs of hungry residents. A new union drive ensued, followed by the mining companies' response of firings, evictions of miners and their families from company homes, and a growing blacklist. Still, the United Mine Workers of America (UMWA) organized over 8,000 members into the union by the end of April (Portelli 2011, 186).

Miners found some support in the county. In the town of Evarts, union miners who had been kicked out of company towns were granted the right to set up camp on the land of a pro-union property owner. The town became a center of union activity. On May 5, 1931, with union miners locked out for organizing activities, the long simmering tension broke. Passing through Evarts on the way to the Black Mountain coal camp, sheriff's deputies trucked in belongings of a non-union "scab." In what became known as the "Battle of Evarts," the deputies and miners exchanged fire in a shootout that left three deputies and at least one miner dead. The state arrested forty-three miners and organizers. Fifteen were put on trial, including several who were not even present in Evarts that day. William Hightower, district union president, was convicted of conspiracy to murder and given a life sentence even though he was talking with the sheriff while the battle raged (Hevener 1978, 75). Seven were convicted and eventually all were pardoned, the last being set free in 1941 with the conclusion of the mine wars.

The Battle of Evarts emboldened the miners, transforming the lockout of less than 2,000 miners into a full-scale strike. Within a week, 5,800 Harlan miners walked off the job. Following the Battle of Evarts, the governor sent in the National Guard and state police. What followed, including tear gassing of union meetings, raiding homes, offices, and union meetings, confiscating union literature, and shooting and killing miners and union organizers, was all organized by the sheriff. In the face of this repression, the UMWA was forced to abandon union efforts in Harlan.

THE MUSIC OF HARLAN

Two acclaimed folk singers emerged from the Harlan Mine War. The music they wrote is an important source for the social, political, and environmental aspects of energy history. Florence Reese, whose husband was a union organizer, penned the labor anthem "Which Side Are You On?" Aunt Molly Jackson, a midwife who recounted the death of children from diseases of poverty, wrote songs of struggle and toured to raise money for the union, at one point appearing before a crowd of twenty thousand in New York City.

Erik Wallenberg

The violence drew national attention. By the fall of 1931 authors Theodore Dressier and John Dos Passos, among others, came to Harlan to take testimony, later published as *Harlan Miners Speak*. The committee members were run out of town within days of their arrival. The Communist Party–backed National Miners Union (NMU) stepped into the fold, but met with little success. The union won some support, though mainly of blacklisted and unemployed miners. The NMU ran soup kitchens and provided other aid and managed to attract national publicity for the plight of the miners, but they had no winning plan to unionize.

The coal companies counted on local officials to aid their anti-union efforts, like Sheriff Blair who declared, "I did all in my power to aid the coal operators" (Hevener 1978, 16). Blair was voted out of office in 1933 and died the following year. Union miners supported avowed reformer T.R. Middleton who upon election turned out to be an even better friend to the mine operators. During his time as sheriff, Middleton acquired interests in coal companies and financial backing from the Harlan County Coal Operators' Association (HCCOA). As one historian put it, "Harlan's coal firms were not just running a business in Harlan County: they were running the county" (Hevener 1978, 22).

New Deal legislation, including the National Industrial Recovery Act (1933) opened up new opportunities to organize the miners. However, the US Supreme Court struck down the pro-union portion of the bill which resulted in union mines in Harlan plummeting from eighteen to one. Even after the 1935 Wagner Act outlawed company unions, blacklists, and yellow-dog contracts, which forced workers to sign pledges not to join unions, the Harlan mine companies continued to resist any unionizing efforts.

The county had a small number of Black miners, and the UMWA established equal pay for Black and white miners. Often, though not always segregated by crew, job, and shifts, Black and white miners regularly interacted outside of the job site (Taylor 2017, 102–4; Roye 2019). In 1935 a group of deputies kidnapped a Black coal miner and union leader named Howard Williams. Though he escaped with his life, he was unable to continue organizing in Harlan. Despite the federal legislation, miners suffered under what they called a "reign of terror." One union organizer gave a speech, "The Feudal Lords of Harlan" in which he laid out the ways in which "life and liberty have been abridged" by the "system of privately paid deputies" (Taylor 2017, 113).

It was the shooting death of a nineteen-year-old miner in his home in 1937 that finally brought the federal government into Harlan. Senator Robert La Follette Jr. convened the US Senate Civil Liberties Committee to investigate. The last of several committees that were convened over the decade, each in part recommended the abolition of the mine guard system, dismissing the sheriff, bringing in the state police, and an overhaul of the election system. The La Follette Committee determined that then-sheriff Middelton had appointed 379 deputies from the beginning of 1934 through March 1937. While 163 still held commission at the point of the investigation, the sheriff testified that only nine deputies were paid by the county while the remainder were paid by the coal operators.

This damning revelation, that the state deputized hundreds of men who were paid by the mines, exposed the extent of private–state cooperation in service to the energy industry. Miners referred to the sheriff's deputies as "gun thugs," dozens of whom were convicted felons, many of whom were recruited on their way out of jail. Through this system of intimidation and violence, the county was effectively closed to UMWA organizing in contradiction to federal law. The investigation also discovered that Sheriff Middleton had amassed a fortune during his time in office through payments in stocks and money from various coal corporations.

In the wake of the La Follette commission, an FBI investigation indicted twenty-two coal corporations, twenty-four operators, and twenty-three law officers. The trial that followed ended in a hung jury, though the mine guard system was put to an end. Hundreds celebrated, with one union leader declaring, "Today marks the end of a rule of thuggery and terrorism in Harlan County" (Taylor 2017, 168). However, violence continued to flare during subsequent contract fights, including another massacre in 1941.

"Bloody Harlan" continued to have its share of union struggles throughout the following decades, but it was not until 1973 when the violence would take on the scale of the 1930s. At the Brookside Mine, previously run by Harlan Colliers and sold to Duke Energy in 1970, the union had been beaten and made irrelevant. A new union drive starting in 1973 culminated in 1974 with violence and the shooting death of a coal miner by a new generation of mine owners' "gun thugs." In all, the Harlan County War was one instance of a larger pattern of brutal conflict that developed within the coal mining industry due to hazardous working conditions and unjust terms of employment.

Erik Wallenberg

See also: Battle of Blair Mountain; Ludlow Massacre; Molly Maguires; Paint Creek Mine War; Tommyknockers; United Mine Workers of America

FURTHER READING

Hevener, John W. 1978. *Which Side Are You On? The Harlan County Coal Miners, 1931–1939*. Chicago: University of Illinois Press.

Members of the National Committee for the Defense of Political Prisoners. 2008 [1932]. *Harlan Miners Speak: Report on Terrorism in the Kentucky Coal Fields*. Lexington: University Press of Kentucky.

Portelli, Alessandro. 2011. *They Say in Harlan County: An Oral History*. New York: Oxford University Press.

Roye, Radcliffe. 2019. "'They Will Remember Us': The Miners of Black Harlan." *The New York Review of Books*, May 3. https://www.nybooks.com/daily/2019/05/03/they-will-remember-us-the-miners-of-black-harlan/ (accessed June 28, 2021).

Taylor, Paul F. 2017 [1990]. *Bloody Harlan: The United Mine Workers of America in Harlan County, Kentucky 1931–1941*. St. Martin, OH: Commonwealth Book Company.

Titler, George J. 2015 [1972]. *Hell in Harlan*. St. Martin, OH: Commonwealth Book Company.

Hart, William Aaron

An important step in the development of energy resources for commercial use came in the 1820s with the discovery of a natural gas spring at Canadaway Creek in Fredonia, New York by local gunsmith William A. Hart (1797–1865). The spring indicated the presence of a large underground natural gas deposit, which Hart tapped by drilling at the site and then channeling the gas through pipes into homes and shops near the creek. Hart created a business out of selling the gas, establishing Fredonia as the first community in the United States to be lighted by natural gas, and his natural gas works the first known commercial enterprise in the nation to sell natural gas to consumers. Within a generation, many New England, Middle Atlantic, and Midwestern towns and cities hosted private businesses or municipal utilities that sold gas to residents and business owners. With these new systems in place, Americans could choose between older fuels for interior lighting, like whale oil or camphere (turpentine mixed with alcohol and camphor oil), and the new fuel, which burned cleaner and without interruption.

William Hart was born in 1797 to a Revolutionary War veteran who moved with his wife and family from Connecticut to Bristol in New York's Ontario County. William Hart reached the age of twenty-one and moved to nearby Fredonia in 1819, which at the time was not much more than frontier village of dirt roads and log houses. Residents had built a sawmill, a gristmill, a schoolhouse, and a few dozen homes and shops, but also a visionary building known as Cascade Hamlet for artisanal shops and living quarters. The Hamlet was built alongside Canadaway Creek to utilize waterpower for the building's machinery, and ran 150 feet in length with two wings off the main section, forming a U-shaped structure. Hart took up space in the Hamlet, which also housed a coppersmith, a blacksmith, a wagon maker, a carriage-maker, a tanner and shoemaker, a cooper, and a sculptor and painter and their families (Shepard *c.* 2011). Once established, Hart married Mary Ann Summerton of Caledonia Springs, in Sempronius in January 1821, then advertised for a journeyman to join his shop. By 1822 he had expanded his business into tin smithing and building iron stoves (Shepherd 2012).

Interestingly, the artisans in Hart's building formed the Cascade Hamlet Mechanic Society in 1823 with a constitution and bylaws and ten signatories. The bylaws forbade spiritous liquors on the premises and urged members to mentor their journeymen and apprentices toward "morality, sobriety, and industry." It also contained provisions for dividing up the storage areas and precautions for fire prevention (Shepherd *c.* 2011). In spite of this sense of community and solidarity, the Hamlet seemed to have been abandoned by 1833 and allowed to fall into ruin. By then, Hart had moved out and built his own shop in town, and began to follow other pursuits, which included securing a US patent for "Hart's Percussion Gun Lock" to replace the common flintlock firing apparatus on muskets and pistols (Andrews 1875, 475). The lock featured a sliding cover which automatically opened when cocking the hammer to allow the user to deposit a "percussion pill" into the percussion chamber. The hammer could then be released slowly, automatically sliding the cover back over the chamber, thus allowing the gun to be carried fully loaded. Pulling the trigger completely would then slide the chamber open and allow the hammer to strike the percussion pill ("In My Arms" 1955, 38). Hart also involved himself in tin, copper, and sheet iron fabrication.

While developing his firearm improvements, Hart learned about a natural gas spring bubbling on the ground on Canadaway Creek near the Cascade Hamlet. In July 1825, he and John Holmes, a student at the Fredonia Academy who roomed with the Harts, dragged an empty washtub to the site, turned it upside down on the spring, and inserted a gun barrel into a hole drilled into the tub's bottom (it should be noted that some sources give this date as 1821). After the gas accumulated in the tub, Hart lit the gun's muzzle, and the gas burned brightly and continuously (Shepherd 2012). He knew that the natural gas leaked from a deposit locked inside the shale formation beneath the creek, so he began drilling to find the source. His first two attempts failed, but on the third attempt he found the gas at 70 feet below the creek bed. He built a rough gasometer—a airtight containment tank with a valve—and housed it in a hastily built shed, then began fitting pipes from the gasometer to buildings in town. Hart charged each recipient $1.50 per year per light but gave the mill owner two free lights for the use of his property (Herrick 1949, 319).

As noted in Douglas H. Shepherd's account of Hart's career, the local paper covered Hart's achievement as the first village-wide gas light system set up on a commercial basis. The *Fredonia Censor* exclaimed in its article on August 31, 1825: "What Village can compare with Fredonia?" It went on to observe that "there is now in this village 2 stores, 2 shops and one mill that are every evening lighted up with as brilliant gas lights as are to be found in an[y] city in this or any other country." The spectacle of seven or eight buildings all brightly lit at night, all at the same time became a regional attraction: "The buildings which are now lighted have been literally thronged for several evenings past" (Shepherd 2012). In 1841, Scottish geologist Charles Lyell traveled to the United States and steamed to Fredonia to see the widely reported gas lights. In his journal he described a town with "neat white houses," six churches, and 1,200 residents. Lyell bore witness to the novel use of fossil fuel: "The streets are lighted up with natural gas, which bubbles up out of the ground, and is received into a gasometer, which I visited." He went on to describe the gas as "carburetted hydrogen" and to identify the rock formation as "a black bituminous slate" (Lyell 1845, 88).

Hart operated the gas works for several years and then sold his interests to Jesse Starr, who died in 1842 whereupon James Starr took over management. Starr raised the rate from $1.50 to $4.00 per year and seems to have operated the business until 1857 when it was incorporated as Fredonia Gas Light and Water Company to provide gas and water utility service to the whole community (Herrick 1949, 321). The new operators dug a 130-foot well in an effort to increase output and expand availability (Barris n.d.). Another gas entrepreneur, Preston Barmore, attempted to drill for gas in 1857 near the same location along Canadaway Creek. In a very early instance of fracking, he lowered 8 pounds of gunpowder 127 feet to the bottom of the well and ignited the charge. The explosion threw up a giant plume of water but also released what he described as a "plentiful supply of gas" (Barris n.d.). Fracturing rock layers to release gas trapped inside would be a feature of natural gas development through to the present day.

William Hart seems to have acquired a measure of wealth through his different enterprises. He built a nursery and "Pleasure Garden" in Fredonia that became a local attraction, promising nighttime tours with the garden illuminated, occasional "grand gala and pyrotechnical entertainment," and July 4th fireworks shows (Shepherd 2012). He lived in Fredonia until at least 1837 but then moved to Buffalo where he and his family were found in the 1850 census. They lived in a large, well-appointed home and operated a boardinghouse complete with a tearoom, restaurant, and a second Pleasure Garden with a "Circular Rail-Road." Hart seems to have traveled to Titusville, Pennsylvania sometime after the 1859 Edwin Drake oil strike to pursue business opportunities but died shortly after in 1865. He was remembered for opening natural gas resources in western New York for commercial development, and for demonstrating both the popular appeal and economic potential of city-wide natural gas lighting systems.

Jeffrey B. Webb

See also: Benedum, Michael Late; Cleveland East Ohio Gas Explosion; Coal Gasification; Hydraulic Fracking; Consolidated Edison Company; Indiana Natural Gas Boom; Natural Gas; New London School Explosion; Pittsburgh Gasometer Explosion; Richmond, Indiana Gas Explosions

FURTHER READING

Andrews, Alfred. 1875. *Genealogical History of Deacon Stephen Hart and his Descendants, 1632–1875*. Hartford, CT: The Case, Lockwood & Brainard Co.

Barris, Lois. n.d. "Fredonia Gas Light and Waterworks Company." Chautauqua County Historian. Lois and Norris Barris Collection. https://chqgov.com/county-historian/lois-and-norwood-barris?page=2 (accessed October 2023).

Herrick, John P. 1949. *Empire Oil: The Story of Oil in New York State*. New York: Dodd, Mead and Company.

"In My Arms Collection." 1955. *The American Rifleman*. Vol. 103. No. 6. P. 38.

Lyell, Charles. 1845. *Travels in North America, with Geological Observations on the United States, Canada, and Nova Scotia*. Vol 2. London: John Murray.

Shepard, Douglas H. *c*. 2011. "The Cascade Hamlet." Chautauqua County Historian. Douglas H. Shepard Collection. https://chqgov.com/county-historian/douglas-h-shepard (accessed October 2023).

Shepard, Douglas H. 2012. "The Harts and Starrs of Fredonia." Chautauqua County Historian. Douglas H. Shepard Collection. https://chqgov.com/county-historian/douglas-h-shepard (accessed October 2023).

Henry, Joseph

The American scientist Joseph Henry (1797–1878) was a pioneer in the field of electromagnetism and served as the first secretary of the Smithsonian Institution, from 1846 until his death in 1878. Henry co-discovered the principle of electromagnetic induction, in which magnetism, rather than chemical batteries, was used to produce an electric current (Freeburg 2013, 17). Electromagnetic induction's role in the production of alternating current would become vital to the fledgling electrical industry. The unit of measure for electrical inductance, the henry, is named after him.

Henry was born on December 17, 1797, in Albany, New York, to William Henry and Ann Alexander Henry, who were both Scottish immigrants. After Henry's father died, he was sent to live with his grandmother in Galway, New York. At age thirteen, Henry was briefly apprenticed as a watchmaker and silversmith but his goal was to take up acting. He might have gone on to a theater career except that he read George Gregory's book, *Lectures on Experimental Philosophy, Astronomy, and Chemistry* (1808) and became interested in science. Henry's friends persuaded him to enroll at the Albany Academy, where he received a full scholarship and attended the school from 1819 to 1822 (SIA 2019c).

In 1820, while still in school, Henry married his cousin Harriet Alexander. The couple would have four children: William Alexander, Mary Anna, Helen Louisa, and Caroline. After graduation, Henry worked briefly as an assistant engineer and in 1826 was offered a position as professor of mathematics and natural philosophy at Albany Academy (SIA 2019a). Henry combined demonstrations of scientific experiments with his lectures, and it was during his tenure at Albany that he began conducting experiments in the new field of electromagnetism. Henry's work led to some important breakthroughs, including the discovery of electromagnetic induction, which had also been discovered by English scientist Michael Faraday (1791–1867) (SIA 2019b).

YALE MAGNET

After the publication of his paper on electromagnetism in the *American Journal of Science*, Henry built a large electromagnet for the journal's editor, Benjamin Silliman, professor of chemistry at Yale. This "Yale Magnet" was able to lift 2,063 pounds and attracted more than iron—it drew a great deal of attention to Henry's work. The magnet is part of the Electricity Collection at the Smithsonian Institution Museum of American History. (SI, "Joseph Henry's Yale Magnet"; Sherman, note 8.)

Karen S. Garvin

Scientists had previously believed that electricity and magnetism were separate physical phenomena, but in April 1820 Hans Christian Ørsted (1777–1851) discovered that a compass needle would move when it was placed close to a wire carrying an electric current (Jonnes 2004, 36). This was important because it showed that a magnetic field could be created and controlled by turning an electrical current on and off (Blundell 2012, 28–30).

Øersted's magnetic field was weak, but French physicist André-Marie Ampère (1775–1836) discovered that by winding the wire into a coil shape the magnetic field could be made stronger. In 1824 English physicist William Sturgeon (1783–1850) wrapped bare copper wire around a horseshoe-shaped piece of iron and created the first working electromagnet (Blundell 2012, 31).

Henry built upon Sturgeon's work and discovered that by insulating the copper wire in silk he was able to tightly wrap many layers of wire over each other to produce a more powerful electromagnet. Throughout the 1820s Henry continued to build ever-larger electromagnets, including the twenty-one pound "Albany Magnet" capable of lifting a 750-pound weight (Sherman 2019, 2). Around 1830 he constructed the "Yale Magnet," which weighed 82.5 pounds and could lift more than a ton (SIA 2019d).

What differentiated Henry's electromagnets from others was the small power source he used. Henry's design was efficient, and his electromagnets would later be incorporated into the first electric doorbell, telephone speakers, and long-distance telegraphy. His design remains basically unchanged today.

In 1832 Henry moved to Princeton, New Jersey, where he was appointed professor in natural philosophy at the College of New Jersey, which would later become Princeton University. For a time, Henry taught astronomy, chemistry, geology, and even architecture. There was a laboratory, but the apparatus was shoddy and it was up to Henry to furnish it with the necessary equipment (SIA 2019a).

In March of 1837, Henry went to Europe, where he remained until September, visiting colleagues, touring scientific facilities, and obtaining equipment for the Princeton lab. He attended a meeting of the British Association for the Advancement of Science, and although he was impressed with the organization, Henry believed there were not yet enough competent American scientists to establish a similar organization in the United States (SIA 2019a).

By this time, Henry was becoming an important scientist in his own right. Between 1835 and 1847 he published more than thirty-five papers on a variety of topics (Weiner 1966, 1095). In December 1846 he was appointed to be the first Secretary of the newly founded Smithsonian Institution. The decision to move to Washington, DC, was a difficult one for Henry and his family, as the position would demand much of Henry's time, making it impossible for him to continue teaching (SIA 2019c).

Henry also found that the bureaucracy of office life gave him little time to continue with his experiments on electromagnetism. Determined to promote scientific research, in 1847 Henry recommended to the board of directors that the institution publish scientific articles. In 1848, the first issue of the *Smithsonian Contributions to Knowledge* was published, and a few years later Henry began distributing this and other publications through an international exchange program (Carmichael 1967, 8).

As the country's chief scientific adviser, Henry was increasingly called upon for his knowledge. In 1852, Henry was appointed to the United States Lighthouse Board, which had been established by Congress the previous year in order to select and test new technology. Henry improved fog signaling and incorporated better fuels in lighthouses; in 1871 he was appointed chairman of the lighthouse board and served in that capacity until his death (Carmichael 1967, 8). In 1863, Henry accepted the presidency of the newly established National Academy of Sciences (SIA 2019c). At the beginning of the Civil War, Henry was asked by the government to study proposals for new types of ships and weapons, a task that required him to evaluate several hundred inventions between 1860 and 1864 (Carmichael 1967, 3).

In December 1877, Henry suffered an attack brought on by kidney disease. He died on May 13, 1878, and was buried at Oak Hill Cemetery in Washington. He is remembered as one of the chief contributors to the scientific understanding of electricity, and one of the early builders of the system for harnessing electrical power.

Karen S. Garvin

See also: Brush, Charles Francis; Edison, Thomas Alva; Electricity; Morse, Samuel; Stanley, William Jr.; Tesla, Nikola; Westinghouse, George

FURTHER READING

Blundell, Stephen. 2012. *Magnetism: A Very Short Introduction*. Oxford: Oxford University Press.

Carmichael, Leonard. 1967. "Joseph Henry and the National Academy of Sciences." *Proceedings of the National Academy of Sciences*. Vol. 58. No. 1. July 15. Pp. 1–10.

Coulson, Thomas. 1950. *Joseph Henry: His Life and Work*. Princeton: Princeton University Press.

Freeburg, Ernest. 2013. *The Age of Edison: Electric Light and the Invention of Modern America*. New York: Penguin.

Jonnes, Jill. 2004. *Empires of Light: Edison, Tesla, Westinghouse, and the Race to Electrify the World*. New York: Random House.

Moyer, Albert E. 1997. *Joseph Henry: The Rise of an American Scientist*. Washington: Smithsonian Institution Scholarly Press.

Sherman, Roger. 2019. "Joseph Henry's Contributions to the Electromagnet and the Electric Motor." Smithsonian Institution Archives. https://siarchives.si.edu/history/featured-topics/henry/electromagnetism (accessed October 2023).

Smithsonian Institution Archives (SIA). 2019a. "Career as Teacher." Joseph Henry: A Life in Science. https://siarchives.si.edu/history/featured-topics/henry/career-teacher (accessed November 11, 2019).

Smithsonian Institution Archives (SIA). 2019b. "Electromagnetism." Joseph Henry: A Life in Science. https://siarchives.si.edu/history/featured-topics/henry/electromagnetism (accessed November 8, 2019).

Smithsonian Institution Archives (SIA). 2019c. "Joseph Henry A Life in Science." Joseph Henry: A Life in Science. https://siarchives.si.edu/history/featured-topics/henry/joseph-henrys-life (accessed November 8, 2019).

Smithsonian Institution Archives (SIA). 2019d. "Joseph Henry's Yale Magnet." Joseph Henry: A Life in Science. https://siarchives.si.edu/collections/siris_sic_13160 (accessed November 24, 2019).

Weiner, Charles. 1966. "Joseph Henry and the Relations between Teaching and Research." *American Journal of Physics*. Vol. 34. No. 12. December. Pp. 1093–100.

Hobart Electric Manufacturing Company

Electrical appliances appeared on the market shortly after the development of electrical power generation in the 1890s, as innovators and entrepreneurs looked for new ways profit from the clean, efficient, plentiful, and cost-effective source of energy. Hobart Electric Manufacturing Company, founded in Troy, Ohio in 1897, began with a mission to supply dynamos and electric motors for power plants, but quickly switched to manufacture electric motors for commercial coffee grinders. Over the course of the next few decades, Hobart introduced new products for use in the burgeoning food service industry, and then began marketing small electrical appliances for home use. Its widely adopted KitchenAid brand became a household staple among homeowners in the growing middle class of the post-war era. Hobart's products helped to give shape to a culture of mass consumption in the twentieth century and encouraged socially homogenizing tendencies that produced a sense of "Americanness." The company and its products contributed to the widespread diffusion of electricity use in American industries, businesses, and homes.

Company founder Clarence Charles "C.C." Hobart (1854–1932) was born in Westford, Vermont, graduated from Colgate University and the University of Iowa Law School, then passed the Ohio bar exam in 1881. He moved to Middletown, Ohio to practice law but got interested in electrical lighting systems and became superintendent of the new Edison Illuminating Company in town. He met Thomas Edison himself when the inventor visited the plant at its 1884 opening. Hobart spent his few years at Edison learning the electricity business—how dynamos and generators work, how companies can convert from steam power to electricity, how to "sell" business and factory owners on a new and unproven technology (Hobart 2005, 12–13). In 1886 Hobart struck out on his own, leasing electrical power equipment and electric lighting to paper mills in the region and by 1890, had begun manufacturing dynamos in his own plant. When a fire destroyed his factory, Hobart relocated to nearby Troy and partnered with Herbert L. Johnston, who together in 1897 founded the Hobart Electric Manufacturing Company.

Their dynamo business received a setback when electric-generating plants began to prefer equipment that worked with alternating current, and so they switched to marketing electrical motors to coffee producers. Hobart and Johnson persuaded them they could save time and money by attaching Hobart motors to their existing hand-cranked coffee grinders. This provided a good business until they could pivot to producing different kinds of electric-powered machinery for commercial and institutional food service operations. In 1905, the company introduced an electric meat chopper and then in 1906, a peanut grinder to make peanut butter. An important moment occurred in 1908 when Herbert Johnson observed a baker mixing dough with a large spoon and came up with the idea for an industrial-grade mixer. Johnson worked on the design for several years and in 1915, the company began marketing its Model A-80 mixer to restaurants, institutions, and even the US Navy, where the mixer was installed in the galleys of the USS *California*, USS *Tennessee*, and USS *South Carolina*. By the end of the First World War, Hobart equipment could be found in restaurants, grocery stores, and anywhere in the country that large-scale food processing and cooking operations were routinely conducted.

Perhaps the biggest breakthrough occurred in 1918 when Hobart began marketing a version of its "stand mixer" for light commercial and home use, the first of its products to bear the "KitchenAid" label (Kindy 2019). The initial C-10 mixer sold only in modest quantities, but Hobart hired women to sell the mixer door to door and sales picked up. As the 1920s progressed, a boom hit the US economy and electric-powered consumer goods began finding eager buyers by the millions. In 1922, Hobart redesigned the stand mixer and began to market its Model H-5 in catalogs and retail stores for $189.50, a very large sum, at the time, and found more buyers for the 1926 Model G, a less expensive, lighter, and easier to handle appliance. Hobart remained committed to controlling the market for commercial food preparation machinery by developing an electric potato peeler, an electric meat slicer, an industrial-grade dishwasher, and an improvement on its large mixer known as the M-80, which became the workhorse of the food service industry. Founder C.C. Hobart led the company through this period of expansion but died in 1932 before his company's products acquired iconic status.

The story of how KitchenAid mixers became an American icon began in the lowest point of the Great Depression. The mixer found some competition in the home appliance market with its Sunbeam rival, which was offered at a lower price point, but depressed wages, unemployment, and low consumer confidence also impacted the company's sales. In hopes of re-energizing consumer interest, Hobart hired artist and industrial designer Egmont Arens to give several of their products a makeover. Arens came up with a sleek, Art Deco-inspired design for the stand mixer that captured the aesthetic sensibility of the era. Model K mixers began to appear in the kitchens of more style-conscious consumers, and Julia Child's television cooking show, *The French Chef*, featured a blue K5SS that eventually found its way into the Smithsonian National Museum of American History with the rest of her recreated kitchen. Few electrical appliances caught the attention of ordinary Americans as did the Model K, even though it was among the priciest mixers available. The Arens-designed KitchenAid K model electric mixer was chosen in 1997 by the San Francisco Museum of Modern Art as one of twelve icons of American design. The mixer's selection for this honor was not entirely about its design features. The exhibit's curators chose items that also represented some important aspect of the collective American experience, which included blue jeans, a surfboard, the CBS logo, and a Louisville Slugger. The inclusion of the KitchenAid mixer was a recognition of the brand's ubiquity in American life and the seemingly unconscious way it became part of the daily routines of millions of people in the United States.

Some changes came to Hobart Manufacturing Company toward the end of the twentieth century. In 1981, the company became a wholly owned subsidiary of Dart & Kraft, Inc., and in 1986 the company sold the KitchenAid brand to Whirlpool, which became an industry leader in the manufacture and sale of kitchen appliances both small and large, including ovens, refrigerators, washers and dryers, and dishwashers. As of 2022, Hobart-branded products still dominated the market for commercial food preparation equipment. All told, these devices helped to normalize and domesticate electricity. In the nineteenth century, many considered electricity to be menacing and dangerous. Nathaniel Hawthorne's character Clifford Pyncheon in *The House of the Seven Gables: A Romance* (1851) exclaims: "Then there is electricity!–the demon, the angel, the mighty physical power, the all-pervading intelligence!" (Hawthorne 1851). When electricity came to the White House in 1891, the chief usher remembered that President Benjamin Harrison and his family "were actually afraid to turn the lights on and off for fear of getting a shock," and "the family were even timid about pushing the electric bell buttons to call the servants!" (Hood 1934, 7).

Within a generation, electricity came to embody other meanings, like "novelty, excitement, modernity, and heightened awareness" (Nye 1992, x). Hobart's motors, electrical equipment, and eventually its kitchen appliances aided this process, and produced a "household revolution," according to historian Ruth Schwartz Cowan. New electric-powered technologies for ironing and laundering, sweeping floors, and preparing food and cooking "mechanized" the household and thus fashioned a cleaner, healthier, and more comfortable indoor environment. At the same time, however, the household revolution raised housekeeping standards and thus increased expectations for wives and mothers (Cowan 1976, 15). By virtue of this process, the typical "middle American" household became associated with its assortment of up-to-date, electric-powered kitchen appliances.

Jeffrey B. Webb

See also: Edison, Thomas Alva; Electricity; Evard, Mary E.A.W.; Frigidaire; General Electric Company; Home Energy Efficiency; KitchenAid Appliances; Underwriters Laboratory; Upton Machine Company and Whirlpool Corporation; Westinghouse, George

FURTHER READING

Cowan, Ruth Schwartz. 1976. "The 'Industrial Revolution' in the Home: Household Technology and Social Change in the 20th Century." *Technology and Culture*. Vol. 17. No. 1. January. Pp. 1–23.

Hawthorne, Nathaniel. 1851. *The House of the Seven Gables: A Romance*. Boston: Ticknor, Reed, and Fields.

Hobart, Peter C., and Michael W. Williams. 2005. *The Industrial Hobarts: One Family's Story during the American Century*. Virginia Beach, VA: The Donning Company Publishers.

Hodges, Derek. 2023. "Hobart Company History." Katom Restaurant Supply, Inc. website. https://www.katom.com/learning-center/hobart-company-history.html#CC (accessed October 2023).

Hood, Irwin. 1934. *Forty-Two Years in the White House*. Boston: Houghton Mifflin Company.

Kindy, David. 2019. "For 100 Years, KitchenAid Has Been the Stand-Up Brand of Stand Mixers." *Smithsonian Magazine*. August 7. https://www.smithsonianmag.com/smithsonian-institution/100-years-kitchenaid-has-been-stand-brand-stand-mixers-180972838/ (accessed October 2023).

Nye, David E. 1992. *Electrifying America: Social Meanings of a New Technology, 1880–1940*. Cambridge, MA: MIT Press.

Holmes, Joseph Austin

Dr. Joseph A. Holmes (1859–1915), the first Director of the US Bureau of Mines (USBM), was born in Laurens, South Carolina. He was the eighth child of Reverend Zelotes Lee Holmes and Nancy Catherine Nickles. While attending school, he worked on a farm where he acquired an interest in plants and agriculture. He also spent a great deal of time in his father's library reading natural history books, which created a passion to study the natural sciences at Cornell University. In 1881, Holmes graduated from Cornell with a Bachelor of Agriculture, and became professor of geology and natural history at the University of North Carolina where he headed the department until 1891 and lectured there until 1903. After ten years of teaching, Holmes resigned from the professorship in 1891, and became the North Carolina Geological Survey state geologist. Shortly after Congress passed a law to establish the United States Bureau of Mines in 1910, President William H. Taft appointed Joseph Holmes to the directorship where he remained until his retirement in 1915.

In the early years of the Progressive Era, the occupational health and safety concerns of bituminous coal miners began to translate into efforts to reduce workplace dangers and redefining state mining laws. However, the roots of the USBM can be traced further back to 1865, after Senator William Morris Stewart of Nevada introduced the first bill to establish a federal mining bureau. Thereafter, Congress introduced additional bills, and at its first annual convention in 1896, the American Mining Congress proposed the establishment of a National Department of Mines in the President's cabinet (Powell 1922). More specifically, the birth of the US Bureau of Mines was related to the growing pressure to create safer explosives. During the late nineteenth century, the first blasting-related explosion disaster in the United States occurred in the Coulterville coal mine in Illinois in 1883 and resulted in ten fatalities. It was initiated by black blasting powder and propagated by coal dust. One year later, on March 13, 1884, another coal mine explosion occurred in the Laurel Mine in Virginia and resulted in 112 fatalities (Humphrey 1960).

The increasing occurrence of mine explosions and the enormous loss of human lives throughout the Progressive Era aroused public attention. Public pressure necessitated government action through federal agencies to find a solution. Before Holmes' appointment to the USBM, he served as the Director of the Department of Mines and Metallurgy at the 1904 St. Louis World's Fair Louisiana Purchase Exposition. With that experience, President Theodore Roosevelt appointed Holmes to be the chief of the US Geological Survey laboratories (USGS) to investigate mine explosions by testing fuels and structural materials in St. Louis and Pittsburgh. Following a series of coal mine explosions in December 1907, Holmes directed the study of blown-out black blasting powder shot as a cause of mine explosions, which began in 1908 as part of the Technologic Branch in the US Department of Interior's Geologic Survey (USGS) (Powell 1922).

As US coal consumption increased, the Technological Branch of the USGS was responsible for conducting this research and had two goals: to increase efficiency in fuel and mineral production and to increase mining safety. On May 22, 1908, Congress passed an appropriations bill to investigate the causes of mine explosions. Then a mine accidents division was formed and mine explosion research commenced at the Pittsburgh experiment station in November 1908. At first, explosives were tested to determine which could be safely used in coal mining. The first list of permissible explosives was published in 1909.

From 1900–10, there were 2.47 fatalities per 1,000 employed miners in the completely unionized states, 5.07 per 1,000 in those that were partially unionized, and 9.49 in the non-unionized states (Smith 1987). Accident statistics indicate that actual safety conditions underground also varied according to the extent of the presence of the growing unionization among coal miners with the United Mine Workers. These disasters severely affected coal mine workers, some who were boys as young as ten years old. Toward the end of 1907, a series of coal mine explosions killed over 600 miners. Coal miners working in the Naomi Mine of the United Coal Company near Belle Vernon, Pennsylvania experienced the first explosion on December 1, where thirty-four miners died. A coroner's jury determined that without adequate ventilation, miners died because of the accumulation of gas and dust ignited from arcing electric wires or an open light. Five days later, a series of explosions occurred at the mines at Monongah, West Virginia. Although the rescue efforts continued for several days, five miners were rescued, and 362 miners died, resulting in a makeshift outdoor morgue to accommodate the dead bodies. The Monongah explosion is the worst mine disaster in US history. The second-worst mining disaster in US history occurred on November 13, 1909, at the Cherry Coal Mine in Cherry, Illinois. Of the nearly 500 men and boys working in the mine that day, a total of 259 miners and rescuers died in the mine fire. Other miners were able to escape through the hoist shaft. All told, more than 24,000 coal miners perished in industry accidents between 1900 and 1910 (Humphrey 1960).

Following these and other tragedies, the clamor for government regulation increased and Congress responded with the Organic Act of 1910 which created the USBM in the Department of the Interior. The goal of the act was to increase health, safety, economy, and efficiency in the mining, quarrying, metallurgical, and miscellaneous mineral industries of the country. President William H. Taft appointed Dr. Joseph A. Holmes as the bureau's first director on September 3, 1910 in part due to his successful tenure with the USGS Technological Branch, but also because of his record as a compassionate mine safety advocate and his vision to make mine work safer through accident prevention, education and first aid training.

In 1910, the United States had more than 700,000 coal miners working in 15,000 coal mines, producing about 500 million tons of coal annually. Since much of the bureau's initial work was educational, it trained over 50,000 miners in first aid, mine rescue, and firefighting in its first year. When the bureau was established, the fatality rate in US coal mines was 3.91 per 1,000 miners employed. By comparison, fatality rates were 1.70 per 1,000 in England and 1.98 in Prussia. In US metal mines, the fatality rate was also above 3 per 1,000 employees. In an effort to respond to these fatality rates, Holmes and the bureau's mine safety research program focused on five specific areas: prevention of mine gas and coal dust explosions and fires, safety of explosives used in mines, electrical safety in mines, safety of mine lights and their use as gas detectors, and emergency breathing apparatus.

Under Homes' leadership, the bureau replaced the black powder used for blasting in underground coal mines with safer explosives. These carried the designation "permissible explosives" and were characterized by their flame of short duration and relatively low temperature. During his tenure, Holmes and his staff's early explosives work involved a wide range of activities including publishing information on the characteristics and chemistry of various explosives, promoting the use of "permissible explosives," reporting on tests employed to evaluate the safety of explosives, and promoting the safe and effective use of explosives. Following Homes' death, the bureau tested explosives for the US Army and Navy departments prior to and during the First World War and continued to make significant contributions to the war effort during the Second World War (Mainiero n.d.).

As first Director of the Bureau of Mines Homes set the agency's agenda and shaped its core mission. He helped the bureau to perfect new methods of preventing mine accidents, which was the central problem of the coal mining industry in this era. He established the experimental mine for testing explosions at Bruceton, Pennsylvania and organized the first national mine safety demonstration. He directed the construction of federal and state rescue stations using railroad cars as mobile safety units, and the railroad cars doubled as safety training classrooms for miners in America's coal and metal mining regions. He would not live to see the fruit of his labor. With his health declining, Holmes retired in 1915, and died on July 12 of that year at the age of fifty-five from pulmonary tuberculosis. Overall, the energy produced by coal to create the modern US economy extracted a high price in human lives. Although Holmes made an important contribution by setting the trajectory of the Bureau of Mines, mining remained a very deadly occupation until further reforms were enacted in the late 1960s and 1970s.

Mark M. Chambers

See also: Centralia Mine Disaster; Cherry Mine Disaster; Coal; Dawson Mine Disaster; Farmington Mine Disaster; Joy, Joseph Francis; Krebs Mine Disaster; Monongah Mine Disaster; Scofield Mine Disaster; Upper Big Branch Mine Disaster; West Frankfort Mine Disaster; Weir, Paul

FURTHER READING

Battle, Kemp P. 1916. "Dr. Joseph Austin Holmes at the University of North Carolina." *Journal of the Elisha Mitchell Scientific Society*. Vol. 32. No. 1. April. Pp. 20–3.

Breslin, John A. 2010. "One Hundred Years of Federal Mining Safety and Health Research." Department of Health and Human Services. Information Circular #9520. February. Pittsburgh Research Laboratory, Pittsburgh. https://www.cdc.gov/niosh/mining/UserFiles/works/pdfs/2010-128.pdf (accessed October 2023).

Coward, H.F., and G.W. Jones. 1952. "Limits of Flammability of Gases and Vapors." US Bureau of Mines. Bulletin #503. Washington, DC.

Fay, A.H. 1916. "Coal Mine Fatalities in the United States, 1870–1914." US Bureau of Mines, Bulletin #115. Washington, DC.

Humphrey, H.B. 1960. "Historical Summary of Coal-Mine Explosions in the United States, 1810-1958." Bulletin #586. Washington, DC.

Kaas, L.M., 2006. "A History of the U.S. Bureau of Mines, with Some Highlights of its Involvement in Anthracite Mining." *Thirteenth Annual Journal of The Mining History Association*. Pp. 73–92.

Mainiero, Richard J., and Harry C. Verakis. n.d. "A Century of Bureau of Mines." National Institute for Occupational Safety and Health Explosives Research. https://www.cdc.gov/niosh/mining/userfiles/works/pdfs/acobo.pdf (accessed October 2019).

Page, Arthur W. 1912. "Safety First Underground: The New Bureau of Mines and its Life Saving Campaign in the Coal Fields." In *The World's Work: A History of Our Time*. Vol. 23. March. Pp. 549–63.

Powell, Fred Wilbur. 1922. *The Bureau of Mines—its History, Activities and Organization*. Institute for Government Research. New York: D. Appleton and Company.

Smith, Barbara E. 1987. *Digging Our Own Graves: Coal Miners and the Struggle over Black Lung Disease*. Philadelphia, PA: Temple University Press.

Home Energy Efficiency

In every era of energy history in the United States, consumers have sought to conserve energy, if only just to save on fuel costs or spare the hard labor required to secure resources. Periodic fuel shortages in times such as the First and Second World Wars and the Energy Crisis of the 1970s required individual and collective efforts to curb energy use. More recently, energy efficiency has been adopted as a means to reduce the consumption of fossil fuels like oil and gasoline in recognition of how the combustion of these fuels produces carbon emissions that contribute to global warming and climate change. Energy efficiency programs have been adopted by utility companies, corporations, transportation industries, large institutions, state and municipal governments, and other large-scale entities throughout the twenty and twenty-first centuries. Americans who pay utility bills are also deeply invested in energy efficiency, and their decisions about consumption greatly affects levels of supply and demand in the energy sector of the US economy.

Before coal and oil, colonial townsmen, artisans, and farmers cut, hauled, and split wood to fuel their fireplaces, iron forges, limekilns, blacksmith shops, tallow works, and so on. This arduous job required days and weeks of work in the wood lot, or the expense of buying it from a woodcutter. Burning wood for heating and food preparation in traditional fireplaces was not particularly efficient, as "most traditional open fireplaces lose over 90 percent of the fire's heat out the chimney, and much of the heated air in the room goes with it" (EPA 2022). In 1744, Benjamin Franklin expressed some urgency about the price and availability of wood for the hearth and stove: "Wood, our common Fewel, which within these 100 Years might be had at every Man's Door, must now be fetch'd near 100 Miles to some Towns, and makes a very considerable Article in the Expence of Families" (Franklin 1744, 1–2). With that in mind, Franklin added, "since Fuel is become so expensive, and (as the Country is more clear'd and settled) will of course grow scarcer and dearer; any new Proposal for Saving the Wood, and for lessening the Charge and augmenting the Benefit of Fire, by some particular Method of Making and Managing it, may at least be thought worth Consideration." This led to the Franklin stove, which was an early heating and cooking technology developed out of concern for energy efficiency.

These trends continued into the nineteenth century, represented by inventors like Philo Penfield Stewart and Mary E.A.W. Evard who developed innovations in wood- and coal-fired cooking stoves to make them more energy efficient. The Industrial Revolution introduced coal-fired steam power, which offered a new field where mechanics and engineers could pursue fuel-saving technologies. One example is the new type of steam engine developed by George Henry Corliss, which he patented in 1849 and marketed to mills and factories to power their machinery. A test in England in 1868 found that the Corliss engine produced a "decided economy in consumption of fuel" at 2.5 lbs. of coal per indicated horsepower per hour with steam pressure at 45 lbs. per inch, whereas other engines consumed up to 5 lbs. for the same level of performance (Inglis 1868, 192). Likewise, when steam heating came to large buildings in the 1880s and 1890s, inventors like Warren Johnson and William Penn Powers devised thermostats to regulate temperatures in their different rooms. In the 1920s, Johnson's firm, Johnson Service Company, advertised that its pneumatic system of temperature and humidity control would save users up to 35 percent on fuel costs (Roberts n.d.).

The Corliss engine and the Johnson pneumatic thermostat provide illustrations of energy-efficient technology and they help to clarify the difference between energy efficiency and energy conservation. Energy conservation entails reducing consumption to preserve fuel resources, as with the promotion of "Gasless Sundays" and "Heatless Mondays" by the US Fuel Administration during the First World War to safeguard petroleum for the war effort. Similarly, the Office of Price Administration rationed gasoline, oil, coal, and wood during the Second World War as a way of reducing domestic consumption to ensure sufficient supplies for the military. Unlike energy conservation, energy efficiency "harnesses technology to help avoid or reduce energy waste" (Shinn 2018). Upgraded technologies require less energy but still provide the same benefits for the consumer in heating, lighting, or the performance of electrical appliances. In the post-war economic boom, residential housing expanded rapidly and along with it, demand for consumer durables like air conditioners, refrigerators, electric ranges, and washer and dryer units. The heating, lighting, and appliances of American homes became targets for future waves of efficiency innovations beginning with the Energy Crisis of the 1970s.

In 1973, OPEC announced an oil embargo against the United States in response to American support for Israel in the Yom Kippur War of October that year, one of the military engagements in the larger Arab–Israeli conflict. The United States was unable to increase production to offset the cessation of imported oil from OPEC nations, and fuel prices skyrocketed. During the subsequent energy crisis, federal and state governments developed strategies for reducing the consumption of petroleum. For example, the Energy Policy and Conservation Act (1975) "authorized the Federal Energy Administration to develop rationing and emergency conservation plans, to establish energy efficiency standards for household appliances, to make grants to state conservation programs, and to monitor the energy efficiency of the fifty largest energy-consuming industries" (Anders 1980, 5). In the following year, Congress enacted the Energy Conservation and Production Act (1976), which promoted energy development in several ways but also provided grants to states to "develop and implement a weatherization assistance program to increase the energy efficiency of dwellings owned or occupied by low-income persons" (ECPA 1976). This act was amended in 1979, directing the Department of Energy to set new energy efficiency standards for consumer products. Nearly a decade later, the National Appliance Energy Conservation Act (1987) set these standards directly across a range of appliances, such as clothes dryers, clothes washers, dishwashers, freezers, kitchen ovens and ranges, refrigerators, room air conditions, televisions, and water heaters.

The effects of these changes were profound, which can be seen in the case of both refrigerators and light bulbs. In the decades before the energy crisis of the 1970s, seemingly little concern for energy efficiency could be detected, as average annual energy use of refrigerators ballooned from 400 kilowatts per hour in 1947 to over 1,800 kilowatts per hour in 1974 (DiMascio 2014). Under a succession of federal policy changes aimed at increasing efficiency, appliance manufacturers implemented a variety of design innovations and by 2022, the average annual energy use of refrigerators returned to a level below 500 kilowatts per hour, near its original 1947 mark. Strikingly, this came about as refrigerators increased in volume and significantly decreased in price (DiMascio 2014). As for lightbulbs, the 1970s energy crisis also inspired technological innovation. In 1974, Sylvania developed a bulb using similar technology as energy-efficient fluorescent lights used in factories and warehouses. The company couldn't work out a way to manufacture it at scale, then in 1976 General Electric's Edward Hammer invented the compact fluorescent light bulb with a spiral design for home use. GE declined to invest in the machinery for producing the bulbs, but later manufactures refined the design and brought them into widespread use. The efficiency gains have been profound: compact fluorescent bulbs produce 50–70 lumens per watt, whereas traditional incandescent bulbs produce 10–17 per watt. Even newer technology—the LED lightbulb—produces 75–110 lumens per watt.

These particular gains in home energy efficiency have been mirrored across a wide range of appliances, but also reflected in home heating and cooling technology, and by means of other energy-saving measures like improved insulation and windows. The Energy Policy Act of 1992 contained energy efficiency measures for automobiles, power plants, and large commercial and industrial buildings, but also incentives for home energy efficiency improvements. The law included energy efficiency standards for heating, ventilation, and air-conditioning systems, commercial water heaters, and fluorescent lamps. The Energy Policy Act of 2005 and the Energy Independence and Security Act of 2007 continued in this vein with efficiency standards for new classes of consumer products and a number of other policy changes designed to reduce energy use. As of 2017, the US Department of Energy's Appliance and Equipment Standards Program, the cumulative product of these energy acts, has led to a 70 percent reduction in energy use for new clothes washers, 40 percent for new dishwashers, 50 percent for new air conditioners, and 10 percent for new furnaces as compared to 1990 levels (OEERE 2017). Alongside these changes, the US Environmental Protection Agency began its Energy Star program in 1992, which allows companies to label their products with the Energy Star label if they met the strict energy-efficiency specifications set by the agency. As of 2020, 75,000 different products for home use earned the label, and together with Energy Star participants in corporate, industrial, and building construction sectors cut back on a reported five trillion kilowatt-hours of electricity, saved $500 billion in energy costs, and secured 4 billion metric tons of reductions in greenhouse gases.

One caveat about energy efficiency has been made by economists, which is generally given expression in the term Jevons Paradox. This concept is named after an English philosopher and economist William Stanley Jevons who wrote "The Coal Question" in 1865, which posited that greater efficiency in the use of coal for fuel doesn't necessarily reduce consumption. He claimed that an industrialist who earns savings by economizing on fuel will become more profitable. This will attract more industrialists to enter the market, increasing the consumption of energy and offsetting the reduction produced by the initial efficiency gain. As a recent treatment of the Jevons Paradox noted, "the problem with efficiency gains is that we inevitably reinvest them in additional consumption" (Owen 2010). However, the current state of thinking holds that the rebound effect of increased energy consumption due to energy efficiency measures will be offset by replacing fossil fuels with renewable energy, which do not produce the same harmful environmental effects as their carbon-based counterparts. According to recent data, the residential sector accounts for 21 percent of overall energy consumption in the United States (OEERE 2023). This means that home energy efficiency will remain an important strategy for conserving natural resources, promoting energy independence, and stimulating innovation in energy-related technologies.

Jeffrey B. Webb

See also: CAFE Standards; Corliss, George Henry; Daylight Saving Time; Energy Crisis of the 1970s; Energy Policy Act of 2005; Energy Policy and Conservation Act of 1975; Evard, Mary E.A.W.; Johnson, Warren Seymour; Powers, William Penn; Smart Grid; Stewart, Philo Penfield; US Fuel Administration

FURTHER READING

Anders, Roger. 1980. "The Federal Energy Administration." US Department of Energy. Office of History and Heritage Resources. https://www.energy.gov/sites/prod/files/FEA%20History.pdf (accessed October 2023).

DiMascio, Marianne. 2014. "How Your Refrigerator Has Kept its Cool over 40 Years of Efficiency Improvements." Appliance Standards Awareness Project. September 11. https://appliance-standards.org/blog/how-your-refrigerator-has-kept-its-cool-over-40-years-efficiency-improvements (accessed October 2023).

Energy Conservation and Production Act of 1976 (ECPA). Pub. L. No. 94–385. https://www.govinfo.gov/content/pkg/COMPS-841/pdf/COMPS-841.pdf (accessed October 2023).

Franklin, Benjamin. 1744. *An Account of the New Invented Pennsylvanian Fire-Places*. Philadelphia: B. Franklin.

Inglis, William. 1868. "On the Corliss Expansion Valve-Gear for Stationary Engines." *Proceedings of the Institution of Mechanical Engineers*. Pp. 177–94. Birmingham: Institution of Mechanical Engineers.

Office of Energy Efficiency and Renewable Energy (OEERE). 2017. "Saving Energy and Money with Appliance and Equipment Standards in the United States." US Department of Energy. https://www.energy.gov/eere/buildings/articles/appliance-and-equipment-standards-fact-sheet (accessed October 2023).

Office of Energy Efficiency and Renewable Energy (OEERE). 2023. "Energy Data Facts." US Department of Energy. https://rpsc.energy.gov/energy-data-facts#:~:text=How%20much%20energy%20does%20the,of%20total%20U.S.%20energy%20consumption (accessed October 2023).

Owen, David. 2010. "The Efficiency Dilemma." *The New Yorker*. December 12.

Roberts, Brian. n.d. *Warren S. Johnson and Automatic Controls*. CIBSE Heritage Group website. http://www.hevac-heritage.org/built_environment/pioneers_revisited/johnson.pdf (accessed October 2023).

Shinn, Lora. 2018. "Energy Efficiency: The Clean Facts." National Resources Defense Council. September 20. https://www.nrdc.org/stories/energy-efficiency-clean-facts (accessed November 2023).

US Environmental Protection Agency (EPA). 2022. "Choosing the Right Fireplace or Fireplace Retrofit Device." September 8. https://www.epa.gov/burnwise/choosing-right-fireplace-or-fireplace-retrofit-device (accessed October 2023).

Hoover Dam

Hoover Dam is located in the Black Canyon of the Colorado River between the states of Nevada and Arizona. It was built to tame the notoriously wild river, improve navigation, generate hydroelectric power, and provide water for irrigation. Undertaken during the Great Depression, the dam's construction boosted Americans' confidence in their government and its ability to work with private enterprise in a time of great adversity. Hoover Dam now produces more than 4 billion kilowatt-hours of electricity annually and since its completion in 1935, it has come to be regarded as a milestone in the history American engineering.

Floods on the Colorado River were frequent and devastating. Between 1905 and 1907, for instance, the watercourse broke through an adjoining canal to create a large body of shallow water in California that became known as the Salton Sea. A 1922 report had recommended the construction of a new canal and a high dam on the river, and that same year, the Colorado River Commission, chaired by US Secretary of Commerce (and later President) Herbert Hoover, allocated a division of the river's water rights among the states in the Colorado River Basin.

Arthur P. Davis (1861–1933), director and chief engineer of the US Reclamation Service, had already proposed building a dam in Boulder Canyon, but another site, about 20 miles downriver in Black Canyon, also came under consideration. Congress passed and President Calvin Coolidge signed an act authorizing a dam in one of the two locations in late 1928, and the Black Canyon site was subsequently chosen. The act also authorized the construction of the All-American Canal linking the Colorado River with the Imperial and Coachella valleys in California.

Since no individual company was capable of undertaking such a massive project, the US Bureau of Reclamation (as the Reclamation Service had been renamed in 1923) required that interested companies work together legally as joint ventures. One such consortium was created under the name Six Companies. The firms in question were the Henry J. Kaiser Company and the Bechtel Corporation (which operated as an individual joint venture of their own as Bechtel-Kaiser), MacDonald & Kahn, the Utah Construction Company, Morrison-Knudsen, the Pacific Bridge Company, and the J.F. Shea Company. Two other joint ventures competed, but on March 11, 1931, the bureau awarded the contract to Six Companies, which had submitted a winning bid of $48,890,955. Francis "Frank" Trenholm Crowe of Morrison-Knudsen was designated superintendent.

The Great Depression, which was sparked early in the Hoover presidency by the stock market crash of October 1929, led to widespread unemployment in the United States, and as news of the ambitious project spread, thousands of workers and their families gathered in the Las Vegas area in hopes of being hired. Those who were chosen were moved to the newly established Boulder City, some 6 miles from the dam site, although a number of "tent cities" also sprang up nearby. Authorities built railway lines and a highway to link the new settlement to the construction site. Eventually, some 16,000 men worked on the project, with an average of 3,500 employed at any one time.

HARD HATS

Although hard hats made of leather and steamed canvas had been in use since the late nineteenth century, they were uncommon. It was with the building of the Hoover Dam that such gear became mandatory on a project. At constant risk from falling objects, the project's workers had learned to protect themselves by dipping their cloth hats in tar and allowing them to harden into tough shells. When the benefits became obvious, contractors ordered what were known as "hard-boiled hats" in bulk from a manufacturer.

Grove Koger

The dam in Black Canyon was built over a period of about forty-nine months, from late April 1931, shortly after the bureau gave Six Companies permission to proceed on the project, to May 29, 1935, when the last concrete was poured. Even then, the hydroelectric component of the project wasn't complete, as generators would have to be placed into service over the next several years.

The initial phase of the dam's construction had begun with workers digging four long tunnels, two on each side of the Colorado River and each of them 56 feet in diameter, to divert the river's water. Coffer dams were erected upstream and downstream of the site, and actual diversion began in mid-November 1932, leaving the dam site dry. Workers then excavated the "spoil"—the gravel and rubble that made up the riverbed—down to solid bedrock and cleared the canyon walls with jackhammers and explosives. Grout holes were drilled into the rock and filled with cement to stabilize what would be the base and sides of the dam, and the first concrete was poured on June 6, 1933—some eighteen months ahead of schedule.

To ensure that the structure would be strong enough and age without cracking, it was necessary for workers to pour the concrete in interlocking blocks that were cooled by water-filled pipes that were then filled themselves. The wet concrete was prepared in plants near the canyon and moved in large buckets running on an overhead system of cables.

Work on such a structure in such a location was difficult at best, and in many instances highly dangerous, particularly given the relentless pace set by Six Companies' managers and foremen. Several men died in rock slides, and a number of others succumbed to heatstroke during the summer months, when temperatures often reached 120 degrees Fahrenheit in Black Canyon. The trucks involved in moving debris from the diversion tunnels were routinely allowed to idle as they waited to be loaded, and the carbon monoxide they produced resulted in the deaths of several more men, although the deaths were written off as the result of pneumonia or even "natural causes." The cost in human lives has been estimated as being between 96 (the official number) and 112.

The dam was completed an astonishing two years ahead of schedule, and, after the diversion tunnels were sealed, the structure began impounding water on February 1, 1935. President Franklin D. Roosevelt formally dedicated the dam in a ceremony on September 30, 1935. Work had proceeded on the dam's power plant at the foot of the structure all the while, and the facility's first generator went into operation on October 6, 1936, when the reservoir behind the dam had filled sufficiently. The American public had followed the dam's progress closely, and its construction and successful completion during a period of economic depression and high unemployment was viewed as a triumph of American know-how and determination in the face of daunting adversity.

Before construction began, the structure had been known as Boulder Dam, despite the fact that Boulder Canyon was some 20 miles away. Subsequently it was also referred to as Hoover Dam, but the blame assigned Hoover for the Great Depression made the latter designation unpopular. It was only on April 30, 1947, that President Harry Truman signed a congressional act giving the dam the name we know today.

Hoover Dam is 726.4 feet (221.4 meters) high, 1,244 feet (379 meters) wide, 660 feet (201 meters) thick at its base, and 45 feet (13.7 meters) thick at the top. At the time of its completion, it was the largest such structure in the world. Its powerhouse currently holds seventeen main generators and produces more than 4 billion kilowatt-hours of energy in the form of hydroelectricity each year. Arizona consumes nearly 19 percent of that amount and Nevada about 23 percent, while the rest goes to California. In all, the energy generated at the dam serves some 1.3 million people. The reservoir that Hoover Dam produced is 247 square miles in extent and was named Lake Mead in honor of Dr. Elwood Mead (1858–1936), the Commissioner of the US Bureau of Reclamation between 1924 and 1936. In terms of capacity, it is the largest reservoir in the United States and holds enough water to irrigate roughly one million acres of farmland.

Hoover Dam was named a National Historic Landmark in 1985, listed by the American Society of Civil Engineers as one of the nation's Seven Modern Civil Engineering Wonders in 1994, and continues to be operated by the Bureau of Reclamation. Overall, Hoover Dam and other hydroelectric power facilities provided 6.3 percent of the total US utility-scale electricity generation in 2021, and 31.5 percent of the total utility-scale electricity generation from renewable energy sources (EIA 2022). There are considerable political and legal barriers to new hydroelectric plants, and they can be located only where land and water are available. However, they supply electricity at a lower cost to consumers without producing carbon emissions and therefore offer a "clean energy" alternative to fossil fuel burning power plants.

Grove Koger

See also: Austin Dam; Federal Water Power Act of 1920; Hydroelectric Power; Lowell Waterpower System; Slater, Samuel; Water Power

FURTHER READING

Denton, Sally. 2016. *The Profiteers: Bechtel and the Men Who Built the World*. New York: Simon & Schuster.

Dunar, Andrew J., and Dennis McBride. 1993. *Building Hoover Dam: An Oral History of the Great Depression*. New York: Twayne.

Hiltzik, Michael. 2010. *Colossus: Hoover Dam and the Making of the American Century*. New York: Free Press.

Rogers, J. David. 2010. "The Majesty of Hoover Dam." *Civil Engineering*. Vol. 80. No. 11. November 51–65.

Stevens, Joseph E. 1988. *Hoover Dam: An American Adventure*. Norman: University of Oklahoma Press.

US Energy Information Administration (EIA). 2022. "Hydropower Explained." US Department of Energy. March 16. https://www.eia.gov/energyexplained/hydropower/ (accessed October 2023).

Wiltshire, Richard L., David R. Gilbert, and Jerry R. Rogers, eds. 2014. *Hoover Dam: 75th Anniversary History Symposium*. Reston: ASCE.

Hughes, Howard R., Sr.

Howard R. Hughes, Sr. (1869–1924) was an oil prospector who invented a drill bit to combat the difficulties of accessing oil beneath hard layers of rock. The drill bit became the foundation of the Hughes Tool Company, which outfitted oil companies. Hughes's invention reduced drilling times and costs, bringing greater access to oil at a time when demand was skyrocketing. His success paved the way for future inventions and provided the inheritance that help his son, Howard Hughes, Jr., achieve international fame.

Howard Robard Hughes, Sr., was born on September 9, 1869, in Lancaster, Missouri. He was the son of Felix and Jean Hughes, and his father worked as a lawyer. After the family settled in Keokuk, Iowa, Felix Hughes was elected mayor. Howard attended the Missouri Military Academy, a private secondary school, and showed an inclination toward mechanical pursuits.

Known as "Bo," Hughes reportedly was poorly behaved as a young adult and was dismissed from multiple colleges. Along the way, he attended Harvard University from 1893 to 1895 and then studied law at the University of Iowa. Rather than complete the full program, Hughes passed the bar exam after one year and began practicing law in Keokuk.

Unsatisfied with the difficulties of the profession, Hughes soon left the firm to pursue mining, which interested him more. He worked in silver, zinc, and lead mines in various states before setting out to pursue his own fortune.

In 1901, Hughes learned of the discovery of a rich oil field at Spindletop Hill near Beaumont, Texas. He rushed to the field and purchased cheap land. He and his partners profited from reselling the land as prices rose quickly. In 1902, Hughes and partner Walter Sharp opened a contracting company to dig oil wells while also drilling some of their own on the side.

The Spindletop oil rush began the Texas oil boom that spanned the first half of the century. It was significant in leading to the formation of companies such as Gulf Oil and the Texas Fuel Oil Company (later Texaco) and broke the monopoly of Standard Oil. It also led to a major breakthrough in drilling technology. Hughes found "fishtail" drill bits too slow and limiting, bogging down expensive operations and hindering progress through hard rock formations.

In December 1902, Hughes met Allene Gano, the daughter of a Texas judge. The couple married in 1904, and had a son, Howard, Jr., in 1905. These developments forced Hughes to recognize the need to find a steady income rather than chasing oil strikes. By 1906, Hughes was determined to solve the problem of inefficient drills himself. The fishtail bit, a flat drill bit with curved pieces on either end that resembled a fishtail, was the industry standard. Hughes revolutionized drilling with a bit that featured two cones pointing toward the center, each covered with sharp teeth. It was designed to avoid the problem of rapid wear that plagued the fishtail design, speed up the drilling process, and penetrate through hard layers of rock.

Granville Humason, a millwright, stated that he sold the two-cone idea to Hughes for $150, but this story is not found in any other sources.

In 1908, Hughes built a wooden model of his drill bit and then began testing a prototype. The 166 steel cutting edges crushed the rock, a much more efficient process than scraping it with the fishtail bit. With his new invention, Hughes and Sharp were able to drill a well in Baytown, Texas, and discover oil in the Goose Creek field. Prospectors had been searching for oil in the area since 1903, and the success brought by Hughes's new drill bit helped establish one of the richest fields on the Gulf Cost.

Based on this success, he and Walter Sharp opened the Sharp-Hughes Tool Company to produce the bits. At first, they focused on renting out the bits rather than selling them. Hughes was granted two patents for his two-cone drill bit on August 10, 1909. The product was popular, and the pair was soon providing the bits to companies in several states and foreign countries. It reduced drilling time substantially, helping to reduce costs by up to 75 percent. The two-cone drill bit lasted longer, reducing the need to sharpen or replace the bit. In addition, companies were able to drill to greater depths, enabling them to access more oil before needing to dig another well or find another oil field.

Focusing on his role as the company's salesman, Hughes stopped drilling for oil. In 1912, Walter Sharp died of overexertion after fighting an oil fire. Hughes eventually bought out Sharp's portion of the business, renaming the company Hughes Tool Company. By the 1920s, Hughes was known as the richest man in the Texas oil industry. Hughes lived until 1924, continuing to work on drilling technology and sales of equipment. He amassed seventy-five patents, which enabled him to make drilling easier and more profitable for many companies around the world.

The innovation of Hughes Tool Company continued after Hughes's death, and two engineers from the company invented a tri-cone bit in 1933, which was even more successful. The company has supplied bits for oil companies for decades, and it still estimated to supply 40 percent of drill bits today (Lemann 1982).

Hughes's success was largely due to the timing of his invention of the two-cone bit. He obtained his patent the year after the Ford Motor Company introduced the Model T, and the United States was turning increasingly toward gasoline. Trains were also switching from coal to oil, driving the demand even higher, and the First World War led to a major spike in petroleum use. In 1911, the Supreme Court ordered Standard Oil to break up into smaller companies, bringing about the beginnings of Amoco, Chevron, Conoco, Exxon, and Mobil. All of these companies could immediately benefit from easier extraction of oil, allowing them to grow while supplying the needs of the automobile age.

Hughes's early experiences in the oil fields showed him that the technology of the time was insufficient for the job. His two-cone bit revolutionized drilling, reducing costs and the need for new sites. This helped see the United States, and several foreign countries, through the increased demand of oil in the twentieth century. Following Hughes's death, his son inherited the company and gained notoriety as a director, pilot, and playboy. It is important to remember that the family's fame and fortune began with Howard Hughes, Sr., and his desire to find new techniques to improve oil drilling technology.

Kevin Hogg

See also: Spindletop Oil Gusher, Texas Oil Boom; Sweeney, Peter; Weir, Paul

FURTHER READING

American Society of Mechanical Engineers (ASME). 2019. "Hughes Two-Cone Drill Bit." https://www.asme.org/wwwasmeorg/media/resourcefiles/aboutasme/who%20we%20are/engineering%20history/landmarks/246-hughes-two-cone-drill-bit-1909.pdf (accessed May 14, 2020).

Collette, Mark. 2016. "Howard Hughes Sr. Changed Oil Industry, and Houston, Forever." *Houston Chronicle*. https://www.chron.com/local/history/innovators-inventions/article/Howard-Hughes-Sr-changed-the-oil-industry-and-7958019.php (accessed May 14, 2020).

Higham, Charles. 1993. *Howard Hughes: The Secret Life*. New York: G. P. Putnam's Sons.

Lemann, Nicholas. 1982. "Texas Primer: The Hughes Drill Bit." *Texas Monthly*. https://www.texasmonthly.com/the-culture/texas-primer-the-hughes-drill-bit/ (accessed May 14, 2020).

Longden, Tom. n.d. "Howard Hughes Sr." *Des Moines Register*. https://data.desmoinesregister.com/famous-iowans/sr-hughes (accessed May 14, 2020).

Wells, Bruce A., and K.L. Wells. 2020. "Carl Baker and Howard Hughes." American Oil & Gas Historical Society. https://aoghs.org/oil-almanac/carl-baker-howard-hughes/ (accessed May 14, 2020).

Hydraulic Fracking

Hydraulic fracturing—colloquially known as "fracking"—is the process of drilling into oil and gas deposits trapped within dense strata of sand or shale and then subjecting the packed rock and soil mix to highly pressurized fluids in order to free the desired gas or oil from the surrounding encasing materials. Often the fissures in which the gas and oil are trapped are quite tiny, and the fluid pumped into the well forces them to widen considerably. Grit pumped in with the fluid keeps the fissures from re-collapsing, thus releasing the trapped reserves. According to the Geological Society of America, the first successful well in which hydraulic fracturing was utilized to maximize output was in Kansas in 1947, so it is a common misconception that fracking is a relatively recent technological innovation. That said, this method did not become extremely profitable and therefore increasingly popular and widespread for about a half a century. Historically, most of the wells which employed hydraulic fracturing were traditional vertical shafts, and thus the advantages of fracking were not optimized. During the 1990s, however, industrial engineering made some significant leaps, most notably in the development of technology that allowed for fracking to be employed in horizontal wells. This proved to be a game changer and made fracking a more attractive method as a way to tap into vast quantities of heretofore unreachable deposits of oil and gas, most notably those trapped in shale.

To understand why contemporary fracking technology can access materials that traditional wells cannot, it's important to note that traditional wells are drilled vertically into the ground, driving through soil and rock to depths of some thousands of feet. The reserves thus tapped are necessarily only those accessible from the position of the shaft at the utmost depth of the well, which often only extends a relatively short distance into the reservoir in question. The process of fracking involves designing a well that extends down to a desired depth, then thrusts horizontally into the very midst of large pools of oil or gas trapped in the rock at this depth. The volumes of fossil fuels accessible through fracking therefore can be much greater than those that can be reached through traditional vertical wells. Concurrently, in a landscape that once would have had to be punctuated by many drilling rigs in order to access similar volumes of reserves, one point of entry will suffice. Indeed, many horizontal wells may utilize the same launching point. Thus, one platform can reach reserves at quite a distance from that platform, consequently reducing the so-called "footprint" of drilling and at the same time greatly extending its reach.

Nowhere in the United States has fracking been more extensively or profitably employed than in the region containing what is known as the "Marcellus Shale." Stretching across parts of Pennsylvania, New York, Ohio, and West Virginia, this geological formation takes its name from a town in New York State. The Marcellus Shale Field is a vast sedimentary deposit created by pressure over time as organic material decomposed in a layer of mud that eventually hardened into shale. As a result of this geological process, gas was released, but for eons it has remained trapped in minute cracks and crevices spread throughout the shale. Although geologists have long known about the Marcellus Shale—and indeed, were aware of the trapped gas deposits it contained—these resources were isolated in such small quantities spread across such a huge area that there wasn't enough gas to be tapped per acre to make it profitable to extract using traditional vertical drilling methods. Thus, the Marcellus Shale did not afford a great opportunity for exploitation until the development of horizontal drilling reached a degree of sophistication and economical scale. Although the first development of such a resource in the United States was in Texas, the Marcellus deposit was one of the next regions to be the object of intense interest and investment. There are, in fact, many similar shale fields around the globe, and as the technology to utilize the trapped reservoirs of natural gas within these mineral deposits has become more refined, widespread, and cost-effective, other such reservoirs have become similarly prized.

Although natural gas is commonly believed to be a cleaner-burning and a less environmentally harmful alternative to other fossil fuels, this is not an altogether accurate perception. Although it is true that burning oil and coal produces dirtier emissions than burning natural gas, it is untrue that natural gas does not produce greenhouse gases, which are significant and alarming drivers of global warming. Furthermore, the fracking process necessary to access the reserves of gas trapped in shale creates negative environmental impacts, not least because of the vast quantities of water involved, which is highly contaminated in fracking operations. Although the industry claims that protecting groundwater is a top priority—a position long validated by the US Environmental Protection Agency (EPA)—studies have indicated that pollution of drinking water as a consequence of fracking can and does happen. Given the nature of the process, it is not hard to imagine why that might be.

In 2016, the EPA issued a report summarizing the scientific literature concerning contamination of groundwater by hydraulic fracturing. The report notes that acquiring water, mixing it with chemicals, injecting it into wells, recapturing it, and ultimately treating and disposing of such water carefully are all necessary parts of fracking, and that some level of contamination is therefore not improbable. Indeed, the EPA assessment fully acknowledged that such contamination could and indeed does takes place, outlining the scenarios in which that was likely to happen. These include times and locations when and where water levels are low and when spills of the chemicals used in the process take place. Contamination can also occur when the machinery involved develops leaks or creates spills and when chemically treated water is not properly contained or disposed of after use. The EPA report hedged, however, when it came to suggesting the likelihood or frequency of such contamination, citing incomplete data. This report therefore provided some evidence for environmentalists while concurrently providing some coverage for proponents of fracking. In sum, a fair assessment of the evidence might suggest that some or even many fracking wells do not necessarily contaminate groundwater to a significant degree. However, the size of any such problem of groundwater contamination is directly linked to the number of wells employing the technique. In other words, the huge scale-up in the rush to tap into the shale gas reserves resulted in a rapid proliferation of wells. Even if a small but significant percentage of those wells would likely cause such contamination, the problem would occur on a scale directly correlated with the scale of expansion of the practice.

The extraction of natural gas from the Marcellus Shale deposits in recent decades led to another in a series of great industrial and economic revolutions in Pennsylvania. Although fracking is not a new process, only in recent years has it become commercially viable, causing a third fossil fuel boom in the region almost overnight, following earlier coal and oil booms.

As in 1859, the region was suddenly flush in a highly valuable, easily attainable resource, and a subsequent glut caused prices to plummet for a period of time. The sudden rush to monetize this newly accessible resource raised concerns about regional impacts that echo the economic and environmental problems associated with oil's promised riches a century and a half before.

Christopher R. Fee

See also: Drake, Edwin Laurentine; Natural Gas; Pennsylvania Oil Boom; Petroleum; Project Gasbuggy

FURTHER READING

Amico, Chris, Danny DeBelius, Scott Detrow, and Matt Stiles. 2011. "Shale Play: Natural Gas Drilling in Pennsylvania." StateImpact Pennsylvania. NPR. https://web.archive.org/web/20111215205223/http://stateimpact.npr.org/pennsylvania/drilling/ (accessed October 2023).

Geological Society of America (GSA). n.d. "Hydraulic Fracturing's History and Development." GSA Critical Issue: Hydraulic Fracturing.https://rock.geosociety.org/net/documents/GSA/criticalissues/hf/GSA-HydroFracking.pdf (accessed October 2023).

US Environmental Protection Agency (EPA). 2016. "Hydraulic Fracturing for Oil and Gas: Impacts from the Hydraulic Fracturing Water Cycle on Drinking Water Resources in the United States (Final Report)." EPA/600/R-16/236F. Washington, DC. https://cfpub.epa.gov/ncea/hfstudy/recordisplay.cfm?deid=332990 (last updated February 8, 2021; accessed April 22, 2021).

Vaidyanathan, Gayathri. 2016. "Fracking Can Contaminate Drinking Water." *Scientific American*. April 4. https://www.scientificamerican.com/article/fracking-can-contaminate-drinking-water/ (accessed April 21, 2021).

Woodall, Candy. 2016. "The Rise and Fall—and Rise?—of Pa.'s Oil and Gas Industry." *The Patriot-News*. Harrisburg, Pennsylvania. March 17. https://www.pennlive.com/news/2016/03/the_rise_and_fall_and_rise_of.html (last updated January 6, 2019; accessed October 2023).

Hydroelectric Power

Humans have altered the free flow of water to suit their needs throughout history and across Eurasia, Africa, Australia, and the Americas. Mesopotamians constructed irrigation channels fed by the Euphrates and Tigris Rivers some 8,000 years ago. Ancient Egyptians built embankments on tributaries of the Nile River. Mills and millraces were also common on the rivers of Europe in the Middle Ages. In Yemen, a dam has functioned for centuries. Indigenous peoples of America such as the Paiute built aquaculture systems to raise fish and brine shrimp in small pools in the foothills of the Sierra Nevada range. Human communities have found ways of diverting, impounding, and harnessing water and hydropower for millennia.

Dams and similar water-retaining infrastructure such as embankments, diversions, channels, weirs, sluice gates, aqueducts, dikes, and canals provide a host of benefits for people. These infrastructure systems supply water to agricultural, domestic, and industrial consumers, provide recreational opportunities in their reservoirs, serve as instruments of flood control, and work as locks for raising and lowering cargo ships in canals. Considering the countless uses for damming or redirecting a river, humans are not alone in their instincts for river and waterway engineering. Beavers, most famously, build dams to control the flow of running water, and use their lodges both for protection from predators and as a winter shelter for raising their young.

In the modern era, rivers were valued as a source of power, and in the eighteenth and nineteenth century, dam spillways were a common energy source for powering lumber and flour mills. In the late nineteenth century, patents were sought and obtained in Europe and the United States for hydroturbines, paving the way for large-scale electricity generation from flowing water. Hydroelectric power, or hydropower, began to be used in 1880 in the United States with a hydro-turbine created to provide electricity service to a theater in Grand Rapids, Michigan, and soon after in Niagara, New York in 1881. Finally, on the Fox River in Appleton, Wisconsin appeared the first direct current generating power plant in 1882, which provided electric illumination for a factory and several homes. Soon after, an alternating current power plant came to Redlands, California in 1893, providing urban dwellers the means to light up their homes by hydropower-generated electricity.

Beginning in the early 1900s, larger and larger hydroelectric dams appeared all over New England, the mid-Atlantic region, and the upper Midwest. During the Great Depression, several dams were built in the tributaries of the Mississippi basin in the southern United States as part of the Tennessee Valley Authority project. This river system, the country's largest watershed, still has dozens of large hydroelectric dams. With the advent of improving technology and engineering, hydroelectric power soon became profitable, so public and private investments flourished. The intensity of hydroelectric power development in the 1930s through the 1950s brought historian Karl A. Wittfogel in *Oriental Despotism* (1957) to see patterns in history whereby agricultural societies requiring large-scale irrigation projects—ancient Egypt, China, India, pre-Columbian Peru and Mexico—tended toward mass organization of labor resources, centralization of administrative control, and ultimately more coercive political institutions. Although the large-scale hydroelectric dams built in the 1930s and through to the end of the 1960s were adopted by democratic governments, they reflected an increasing belief in the technocratic, modernist conception that man ought to gain economically by dominating nature or natural systems, which should be done under the direction and administration of highly trained policymakers, engineers, and scientists.

In this period, the largest hydropower megaproject was the Hoover Dam, with a concrete wall over 300 feet high, on the Colorado River between Arizona and Nevada. The Hoover Dam was displaced as the nation's largest by the Grand Coulee Dam with a wall over 500 feet on the Columbia River in Washington. Such projects were made possible under public works initiatives of the Roosevelt, Eisenhower, and Truman administrations when urbanization, social and geographical mobility, and technological modernization came to define the white middle class. Federal departments and agencies like the Tennessee Valley Authority, the US Army Corps of Engineers, and the US Bureau of Reclamation oversaw the construction of thousands of dams, flood control systems, and other large water projects in or near urban centers and in many cases in the far reaches of the West, putting millions of Americans to work around the country. By the late 1940s nearly a third of US electricity generation came from hydropower (BR 2016).

Throughout the twentieth century, hydropower played a significant role in the development of the US energy portfolio. The rapid increase in the rate of hydropower development in the 1930s through the 1960s tailed off, followed by a slower pace of growth. In 2022, the percentage of total energy generated hydroelectrically stood at 6 percent of the total energy production, and hydropower comprised 30 percent of so-called renewables (WPTO 2022). Hydroelectric dams are pervasive, existing in nearly every state. Over 100,000 megawatts (MW) of energy are produced by dams in the United States annually, making it the country with the second highest production of hydropower, after Canada.

DAMS AS WARFARE

Scholars such as Einbinder (2017) and Romero and Sasso (2014) show how hydropower projects are associated with violent repression of Indigenous peoples and "drag out the colonial epoch." McGee (2010) likened dams to warfare. As towering symbols of power in a rural setting, hydro projects are almost always opposed by local individuals and groups who abide by rivers since time-memorial. Daily life for Indigenous peoples depends on the watershed. Therefore, many groups have historically opposed dam construction in the face of displacement and harms to biodiversity.

Sam Orndorff

Hydropower should not be reduced to or equated with only hydroelectric dams, as dams have multiple uses. To wit, there are over 82,000 dams in the United States but only 3 percent produce energy. Although hydroelectric power is commonly equated with hydroelectric dams, dams are not the only existing option to produce this form of water-derived energy. Pumped water storage facilities, river diversions, and run-of-river installations can all generate electricity through turbines. Many of these hydropower facilities don't completely trap a river's current in a reservoir, and as such, exhibit fewer of the inherent social and ecological problems with large hydroelectric dams, defined as any dam which produces more than twenty megawatts.

Around two-thirds of the world's rivers are heavily and permanently altered by dams, many of which include hydropower-generation facilities (Lovgren 2019). Significant biodiversity losses not only in rivers but also wetlands, deltas, and estuaries are directly linked to hydroelectric power developments. The Three Gorges Dam on the Yangtze River in China is humongous, producing over 20,000 MW and resulting in the displacement of a million people. The concrete wall of the dam is so large that it slowed the turn of the earth by a fraction of a second due to the concentrated weight of its reservoir. The Yangtze River dolphin has gone extinct as a result of this mega-dam. In North America, the salmon runs that once visited every major river along the Pacific coast, stretching as far north as Alaska and as far south as Central California, have declined from dams blocking the fish's migratory journey from the sea upstream where it spawns and dies. Communities that have depended on the salmon as a food source suffer alterations to their way of life as well.

There are unavoidable ecological costs of hydropower, tangible harms to non-human populations which rely directly and indirectly upon rivers and their broader watersheds. Fish are tied to the water, so too are amphibians and reptiles. Bird species have less significant impacts because of their mobility, but they are part of food webs that include freshwater fish, reptile, and amphibian species. Hundreds of hydroelectric dams began to be removed, decommissioned, and reconsidered for their negative environmental impacts starting in the 1970s, and especially since the early 2000s. Removal projects have also intensified as more and more dams built in the 1930s–1950s hydropower boom reach the end of their fifty-year life expectancy. In fact, many dams are found to be less expensive to remove than they are to repair. Notable dam removals took place in on the Elwha River in Washington from 2011 to 2013, which were undertaken in conjunction with Indigenous Elwha Klallam leaders who have long been nourished by salmon. In the United States, some 546 large dams have been removed, while European countries like Spain, France, and England have together removed thousands (Moran 2018).

Many dams have also gone out of commission because the reservoir's eventual accumulation of sediments, in some cases weighing millions of tons, hampers the functioning of the structure. Others have burst due to engineering failures, such as in Pittsburgh in 1889, West Virginia in 1972, and Idaho in 1976, leading to catastrophe and loss of life. All hydroelectric dams go through a normal aging process as all structures do over time. However, under increasing abnormal climatic conditions, century-old infrastructure has increased risk of failure. In the extremely rainy winter of 2016–17, the Oroville Dam in Oroville, California, whose concrete curtain was built in the 1960s and measures at 770 feet tall, nearly bust, forcing nearly 200,000 people to evacuate (Moran 2018).

Additional environmental problems include habitat loss and fragmentation, pollutant accumulation, reduced dissolved oxygen as water flow stagnates in the dam, increased seismic activity due to the reservoir's mass, coastal erosion due to decreased sediment accumulation at the river mouth, and methane pollution from drowning plants in the flooded areas. Methane is a greenhouse gas that is eighty times as potent as CO_2 in its corrosive force to the atmosphere. In light of these severe ecological impacts, and as a result of social movements that have challenged hydropower, the United States has backed off from its formerly aggressive policy of building dams. Meanwhile, industrializing countries in Asia and South America have intensified hydropower.

Significant social problems arise from hydropower development. This is because hydroelectric power plants sometimes depend upon the displacement of local inhabitants and the loss of resources needed to sustain traditional lifeways when lands and natural watercourses are drowned under large reservoirs. For people directly displaced, there is no guarantee of relocation assistance, employment, or even electricity once they leave their homes in the riparian area (Einbinder 2017). Such violations have been the focus of anti-dam social and political movements in developing societies. Although hydropower has an upside as a source of renewable energy, large-scale dams create enough environmental and social disruption to render them unappealing, particularly since there are a limited number of places, geographically speaking, where such developments can be located.

Sam Orndorff

See also: Federal Power Commission; Federal Water Power Act of 1920; Hoover Dam; Renewable Energy; Sierra Club; Vulcan Street Plant; Water Power

FURTHER READING

Einbinder, Nathan. 2017. *Dams, Displacement, and Development: Perspectives from Río Negro, Guatemala*. Cham, CH: Springer International.

Everard, Mark. 2013. *The Hydropolitics of Dams: Engineering or Ecosystems?* New York: Zed Books.

Lovgren, Stefan. 2019. Two-thirds of the Longest Rivers no Longer Flow Freely—And it's Harming Us." *National Geographic*. May 8. https://www.nationalgeographic.com/environment/article/worlds-free-flowing-rivers-mapped-hydropower (accessed October 2023).

McGee, B. 2010. "Participation with a Punch: Community Referenda on Dam Projects and the Right to Free, Prior, and Informed Consent to Development." *Water Alternatives*. Vol. 3. Pp.162–84.

Moran, Emilio F., Maria C. Lopez, Nathan Moore, Norbert Müller, and David W. Hyndman. 2018. "Sustainable Hydropower in the 21st Century." *Proceedings of the National Academy of Sciences*. Vol. 115. No. 47. Pp. 11891–8.

Romero, Hugo and Jimena Sasso, 2014. "Proyectos Hídricos y Ecología Política del Desarrollo en Latinoamérica: Hacia un Marco Analítico (Hydroelectric Projects and the Political Ecology of Development in Latin America: Towards a Theoretical Framework)." *European Review of Latin American and Caribbean Studies (Revista Europea de Estudios Latinoamericanos y del Caribe)*. Vol. 97. Pp. 55–74.

US Bureau of Reclamation (BR). 2016. "Hydropower Program: The History of Hydropower Development in the United States." US Department of the Interior. https://www.usbr.gov/power/edu/history.html (accessed October 2023).

Water Power Technologies Office (WPTO). 2022. "Hydropower Basics." Office of Energy Efficiency and Renewable Energy. US Department of Energy. https://www.energy.gov/eere/water/hydropower-basics (accessed October 2023).

Idaho National Laboratory

Idaho National Laboratory (INL) is a research and development facility managed by the Battelle Energy Alliance under contract to the US Department of Energy's Office of Nuclear Energy. Located in eastern Idaho 25 miles west of the city of Idaho Falls and occupying an area of 890 square miles, the vast laboratory has passed through several changes in name and mission. Most recently, INL is regarded as the nation's lead nuclear research laboratory, but with involvement in a number of other pursuits, including the development of non-nuclear energy technology and the protection and modernization of the nation's energy infrastructure.

What would eventually become INL was established in 1949 as the National Reactor Testing Station (NRTS) by the Atomic Energy Commission, which itself had been created in 1946. Another location for the station, near Fort Peck, Montana, had also been under consideration, but the Idaho site was chosen in part due to the minimal cost to the federal government in securing the land. Much of the site had been a naval artillery maintenance facility and test range during the Second World War, while some of the remaining land was already administered by the US Bureau of Land Management. A branch of Argonne National Laboratory, known as Argonne National Laboratory-West (ANLW), was set up at INL at the same time.

The NRTS's initial mission involved the development and testing of nuclear reactor technologies for use in civilian life and defense. In pursuing those goals, it achieved a number of milestones in the history of nuclear power over the following years. The first reactor built at the station was an experimental breeder reactor that, on December 20, 1951, produced enough electricity from nuclear fission to light four 200-watt light bulbs—the first instance of turning nuclear power to peaceful purposes. The reactor, which had been designated EBR-I, was later deactivated and named a National Historic Landmark by President Lyndon B. Johnson in a 1966 ceremony.

In the early years of the nuclear era, it was impossible to know how the various components in reactors would actually be affected by the radiation being produced. The second reactor built at the NRTS, the Materials Test Reactor, was designed jointly by ANLW and Oak Ridge National Laboratory in Tennessee to determine those effects. It was brought up to full power in 1952.

A year later, in 1953, engineers in the Naval Reactors Facility at NRTS tested a Submarine Thermal Reactor (S1W) that had been designed under the supervision of Rear Admiral Hyman Rickover. In order to prove that nuclear technology was a practical means of providing propulsion and generating electricity for such craft, it had been built within an actual submarine hull and was subsequently subjected to a 100-hour test run. A reactor modeled after the S1W powered the USS *Nautilus,* the first nuclear-powered submarine in the world. In addition, sailors destined to serve on America's nuclear-powered submarines received their training using full-scale prototype reactors at the testing station. In recognition of his aggressive role in developing nuclear-powered submarines, Rickover became known as the "Father of the Nuclear Navy."

In another milestone, a boiling water nuclear reactor—BORAX-III—that had been developed by ANLW provided the nearby Idaho town of Arco with electricity for about an hour on July 17, 1955. The achievement made Arco famous as the "First City in the World to Be Lit by Atomic Power."

Work started on an Advanced Test Reactor (ATR) in 1959, but it was not until 1967 that it went into operation. Capable of revealing, in a relatively short period of time, the results of years of exposing reactor materials to radiation, it was the largest construction project in Idaho's history and has been heralded as one of the laboratory's most important achievements. The American Nuclear Society (ANS) declared the complex in which the ATR was built—the Advanced Test Reactor Complex—an ANS Nuclear Historic Landmark in May 2017, and a celebration in honor of the reactor's fiftieth anniversary was held the following month.

Any engineering facility of the size and complexity of INL is subject to accidents, and in 1961 it became the scene of a fatal one. In what was later determined to be an operator maintenance error, a low-power boiling water reactor, the SL-I, was destroyed, and the resulting explosion of steam killed three personnel working in the area.

The successor to EBR-I—EBR-II—reached criticality in November 1963. Some twenty times larger than its predecessor, it generated twenty megawatts of electrical power the following year, and from that time on supplied all of the power necessary to run ANLW until being shut down in 1994.

Since its inception in 1949, the National Reactor Testing Station had moved beyond simply building and testing nuclear reactors. In recognition of that trend, its name was changed to Idaho National Engineering Laboratory (INEL) in 1974 and its mission was broadened to include biotechnology, conservation, and renewable energy. Another change of name, to Idaho National Engineering and Environmental Laboratory (INEEL), followed in 1997, marking a move into researching responsible environmental policy. Management of the station was transferred to the US Department of Energy's Office of Nuclear Energy in July 2002, a step that emphasized INEEL's work on the development of even more advanced nuclear energy as well as nuclear energy/hydrogen co-production.

In 2004, the Space and Security Power Systems Facility became part of INEEL, a step that moved the laboratory into the nation's space exploration program. A radioisotope

BUSES

Because INL is located 25 miles from Idaho Falls, where most of its many employees live, the laboratory established a mass transit system in 1953 to carry the men and women to and from work. By 2020, the system had grown to include more than ninety buses, and as the importance of energy conservation increased, INL turned to fueling its vehicles with various mixes of petroleum and ethanol, along with liquified natural gas and mixes of petroleum diesel and biodiesel.

Grove Koger

thermoelectric generator (RTG) assembled at the laboratory powered the New Horizons space probe that flew by Pluto in 2015. The facility's engineers also designed a new RTG for NASA's Curiosity, a "rover" vehicle that landed on Mars in 2012.

INEEL had merged officially with ANLW on February 1, 2005, to become Idaho National Laboratory. Today it is one of seventeen such laboratories and is home to branches of a number of scientific governmental bodies, including the US Geological Survey, the National Oceanic and Atmospheric Administration, and the National Nuclear Security Agency's Naval Reactors Facility. It is also one of seven National Environmental Research Parks. INL operates in partnership with the Center for Advanced Energy Studies and with Boise State University, Idaho State University, the University of Idaho, and the University of Wyoming. It employs some 3,900 workers and more than 350 interns, making it the fifth-largest employer in the state of Idaho.

Since the laboratory's creation in 1949 as the NRTS, its engineers have built and tested fifty-two nuclear reactors, most of which have been decommissioned. However, four are still active as of 2020, including the ATR.

INL's headquarters, which is in Idaho Falls, arranges guided group tours of the laboratory grounds upon request. The EBR-I Historic Landmark is located some 18 miles southeast of Arco and is open to the public free of charge from the Memorial Day weekend through the Labor Day weekend from 9:00 a.m. to 5:00 p.m. For some Americans, the legacy sites of nuclear energy development on both military and civilian sides provoke a kind of nostalgia for the Atomic Age when the United States rose to become a global superpower, and citizens lived in a state of anxiety about the possibility of nuclear plant meltdowns and thermonuclear war. Besides INL, Los Alamos' Manhattan Project collection and New Mexico's Trinity Site are very popular destinations.

Grove Koger

See also: Atomic Energy Acts; Manhattan Project; Nuclear Power; Nuclear Regulatory Commission; Nuclear Waste Policy Act of 1982; US Department of Energy; Yucca Mountain Nuclear Waste Repository

FURTHER READING

Arrowrock Group. 1997. *The Idaho National Environmental and Engineering Laboratory: A Historical Context and Assessment Narrative and Inventory*. Boise, ID: The Arrowrock Group, Inc.

Idaho National Laboratory. n.d. https://inl.gov/ (accessed August 3, 2019).

McKeown, William. 2003. *Idaho Falls: The Untold Story of America's First Nuclear Accident*. Toronto: ECW Press.

Plastino, Ben J., and Diane Plastino Graves. 1998. *Coming of Age: Idaho Falls and the Idaho National Engineering Laboratory, 1949–1990*. Chelsea, MI: BookCrafters, 1998.

Stacy, Susan M. 2000. *Proving the Principle: A History of the Idaho National Engineering and Environmental Laboratory, 949–1999*. Idaho Falls, ID: Idaho Operations Office of the Dept. of Energy.

Zelus, Paul R., Joanne Tokle, and Raj Kushwaha. 1991. *Socio-Economic Impacts of the Idaho National Engineering Laboratory*. Pocatello, ID: Center for Business Research and Services, College of Business, Idaho State University.

Indiana Natural Gas Boom

East Central Indiana was once known as a primarily agricultural region, but an economic boom in the last decades of the nineteenth century was responsible for the area's transition to a regional center of the Second Industrial Revolution. This economic boom came about by the discovery of natural gas and crude oil. In 1876, George Carter and his workers were prospecting for coal by drilling near the recently incorporated town of Eaton, just north of Muncie. At a depth of 300 feet, a foul-smelling odor came out from the ground and ignited a flame reportedly more than 2 feet high (Flook 2017, 65). Carter and his workers were so startled and unsettled by the event that they quickly capped the hole and moved on in their search for coal. A decade went by before drillers found oil and natural gas in Findlay, Ohio. Word of the discovery in western Ohio traveled quickly to East Central Indiana. After hearing the news from Findlay, George Carter made the connection to what he had discovered in Eaton and quickly reopened his capped well. The gas boom in Indiana began in 1886 and within a matter of a few decades had turned to a bust, ending altogether by 1915. The production of natural gas in East Central Indiana's Trenton Oil and Gas Field peaked in 1900 and crude oil peaked four years later. Following both peaks, the drop off in production was precipitous (Flook 2017, 66).

This large hydrocarbon field was known as the Trenton Oil and Gas Field, named because the crude oil and natural gas were found in a type of sedimentary rock known as Trenton Limestone. The Trenton Field comprised around 2.5 million acres and covered twenty-eight counties across Indiana (Glass 2000, 313–15). The discovery of fossil fuels in Ohio's limestone showed that natural gas could be found in large amounts in the limestone deposits of East Central Indiana. This realization set off a mania as drillers and speculators drove up the prices of real estate ahead of the anticipated construction of drilling sites, factories, and housing.

In a span of three years, more than 200 companies were operating in East Central Indiana to remove and sell natural gas from the area's nearly 400 productive wells. By the end of the boom three decades later, around 37,000 wells had been drilled across the Trenton Field (Flook 2017, 67).

Companies relocated their manufacturing operations to Indiana during the gas boom to take advantage of inexpensive fuel and financial inducements offered to companies by cities and towns hoping to draw capital investment and spur economic growth. Hundreds of factories across this region were established during the boom period. One of the most notable companies to relocate their business to this region was the Ball Brothers Company, which produced primarily glass jars. They moved their factory operations from Buffalo, New York to Muncie in order to take advantage of cheap and readily available fuel. Glass production is a fuel-intensive industry and having easy access to inexpensive natural gas was enticing for the Ball Brothers and numerous other companies that established manufacturing concerns in the area (Glass 2000, 333).

FIGURE 14: The gas boom enabled farmers to pump water for irrigation with engines powered by natural gas.

During the Indiana gas boom, as is typical with other economic booms, there were concomitant demographic changes taking place as people moved into rapidly expanding cities and towns to find work and opportunities. Both white and African American workers came to East Central Indiana in large numbers in search of new opportunities as the region continued to industrialize. Part of this demographic change included a shift toward more factory laborers in the workforce, rather than agricultural workers. Organized labor sought to unionize workers in the glass factories, but the unions often excluded Black workers. This relegation of Black factory workers to non-union work led companies in some cases to hire them instead of white laborers, since they were able to pay lower wages and offer fewer protections (Steele 1954, 237; Blocker 1996, 315). As workers, both rural white Hoosiers and black southerners making a northward migration to Indiana, shifted from self-employed agricultural work to industrial manufacturing labor, there were significant lifestyle and cultural changes for these groups as a result. This trend can be seen more broadly among the working class in the United States during the Second Industrial Revolution.

In the three-decade timeframe of the boom-and-bust cycle it is estimated that nearly 500 billion cubic feet of natural gas from Indiana was sold and more than 500 billion cubic feet were wasted between poor drilling techniques and the lighting of ever-burning torches called flambeaux. City promoters and real estate speculators encouraged the flambeaux as an extravagant display of a strong natural gas supply. By some estimations, the flambeaux wasted around 200 cubic feet of natural gas per hour. In an 1889 report, the state geologist for Indiana, S.S. Gorby decried the wasteful flambeaux displays and called on companies to cease using them immediately (Glass 2000, 331; Flook 2017, 66–7, 73).

In response to the wasteful practice of flambeaux, the Indiana General Assembly passed laws in an effort to regulate the fossil fuel industry. In 1891, the legislative body created a Natural Gas Supervisor as well as a law that made it illegal to burn flambeaux. There was, however, a gap between the legal code and its enforcement. Lacking strong oversight, the use of flambeaux continued for several more years after it was officially outlawed.

ORIGINS OF NATURAL GAS

The oil and natural gas found in the Trenton Field was formed over millions of years by decomposing organic matter, mostly plants and, to a lesser degree, animals. The Trenton limestone in Indiana was formed hundreds of millions of years ago during the Ordovician Period, when the land, part of a supercontinent, was under a shallow tropical ocean and located much closer to the equator.

Benjamin J. Clark

By 1915, the gas boom in East Central Indiana had come to an end. Through poor management, lack of regulations, flat pricing, use of flambeaux, and piping fuel to cities outside of the Trenton Field, the fuel supply ran low, losing sufficient pressure and therefore becoming too expensive to recover remaining stocks. By some estimations, there remains 900 million barrels of crude oil still underground there, but the cost to extract it would outweigh the potential profit (Flook 2017, 65).

The gas boom and bust was a short-lived economic cycle, but the impact can still be seen today. The gas boom is essential to the story of the founding of cities and towns in East Central Indiana. The common thread of these founding stories is that the economic boom associated with the discovery of natural gas led to the social and economic transition from rural agriculture to urban industry. These significant social and economic changes brought more business, art, and culture, not to mention a large influx of people coming to find work. Even after the boom ended, some of the larger cities in East Central Indiana were able to absorb the economic bust and continue to be regionally important industrial centers well into the twentieth century. Some of the small and medium-sized towns were not as fortunate and suffered a greater economic impact. Some even reverted to agrarian economies and others were abandoned altogether. The gas boom in East Central Indiana's Trenton Field established the region as an urbanized center of the Second Industrial Revolution, which can still be seen as a legacy today. But another legacy of the boom and bust is a reminder of the limitations of fossil fuels and their larger economic and environmental impact.

Benjamin J. Clark

See also: Hart, William Aaron; Hydraulic Fracking; Mineral Leasing Act of 1920; Natural Gas; Natural Gas Act of 1938; New London School Explosion; Richmond, Indiana Gas Explosions

FURTHER READING

Blocker, Jack S. 1996. "Black Migration to Muncie, 1860–1930." *Indiana Magazine of History*. Vol. 92. No. 4. Pp. 297–320. www.jstor.org/stable/27791957 (accessed February 10, 2020).

Flook, Chris. 2017. "Waste, Ignorance, and Flambeaux: Ominous Warnings from Indiana's Oil and Gas Boom." *Oil-Industry History*. Vol. 18. No.1. Pp. 65–78.

Glass, James A. 2000. "The Gas Boom in East Central Indiana." *Indiana Magazine of History*. Vol. 96. No. 4. Pp. 313–35. www.jstor.org/stable/27792274 (accessed February 8, 2020).

Rupp, John A. 2022. "Oil and Gas—A Brief Overview of the History of the Petroleum Industry in Indiana." Indiana Geological & Water Survey. Indiana University. https://igws.indiana.edu/OilGas/(accessed March 5, 2020).

Steele, Ellsworth. 1954. "The Flint Glass Workers' Union in the Indiana Gas Belt and the Ohio Valley in the 1890s." *Indiana Magazine of History*. Vol. 50. No. 3. Pp. 229–50. https://scholarworks.iu.edu/journals/index.php/imh/article/view/8274 (accessed March 5, 2020).

Industrial Revolution

The Industrial Revolution, a term that first arose during the early nineteenth century, was not a singular event. Rather, multiple industrial revolutions occurred throughout the West from the Early Modern Era (1500–1800) until the twentieth century. Most of these revolutions in mechanical engineering and the demographics of labor involved a slow build-up of technologies necessary for larger paradigm shifts. Most scholars separate these many revolutions into two separate movements, both starting in Great Britain. There is consistent debate among scholars as to whether the Industrial Revolution, through its many waves, increased standards of living or whether Gross Domestic Product in the West would have increased without finance capitalism, increased production, and the mechanization of labor.

The first extensive stage of the Industrial Revolution began as early as the Renaissance (1400–1600) and continued past the Early Modern Era (1500–1800). This period involved the altered use of natural goods like wood, water, animals, and coal that were applied to create an escalation of production and more frequent market exchanges. This initial phase often involved the construction of towns near rivers for the application of waterpower to early textile factories that produced goods from raw cotton supplies delivered to European shores from Africa, India, the Caribbean, and the American South.

Many scholars attribute the shift from handiwork to mechanical labor as an essential aspect for defining these early stages of the Industrial Revolution. Drawing from what German sociologist Max Weber termed "the Protestant ethic," early capitalists saw their commercial pursuits as a divinely ordained mission or "calling" (*berufsmäßig* in Weber's usage) and pursued business success with spiritual fervor (Weber 1930). In their view, employment was to be undertaken with religious conviction and directed toward the common good. Wealth, social respect, and middle-class status was considered God's reward for pursuing one's calling, even in secular occupations. Supported by these discourses, the significant movement from handiwork in the home to mechanical labor in factories altered markets, communities, the commons, and domestic relationships. The first employment sector signifying a substantial shift from handiwork to factory labor probably came within the British textile industry, thriving during the late eighteenth century from the inventions of both the flying shuttle by John Kay and the spinning jenny by James Hargreaves.

The development of charcoal, coke, and steel also drove the two significant waves of what came to be called the Industrial Revolution. The first wave centered on the invention of the steam engine, which assisted the rise of coal production in the late seventeenth and early eighteenth centuries. Thomas Newcomen's invention of the steam engine was expanded upon by James Watt (1736–1819), which led to advances by Richard Trevithick. He was the first to use a steam engine that harnessed the power of steam at full pressure. This innovation facilitated the steam engine's adaptation to the two large transportation industries of the early 1800s, steam locomotives traversing the railways and steamboats conveying passengers and cargo upon the expanding canal systems of Europe and the Americas.

The Second Industrial Revolution is generally considered to have been instigated by the rise of new furnace technologies that led to the production of harder forms of iron and later steel during the nineteenth century. Prior to the innovation of the coke furnace in 1709, attributed to Abraham Darby (1678–1717), nearly all iron-making operations in the West were performed with charcoal furnaces. The charcoal furnace, because it used so much lumber for the process of making the charcoal fuel, was linked historically to rapid deforestation. Darby constructed his later coke furnaces with a combination of pit-coal technology and sand-casting, which created harder iron in a process that was the first to be profitable on a large scale.

The puddling process invented by English blacksmith Henry Cort created a much cleaner and stronger form of iron through a stirring of the liquid iron before setting the iron bars. The use of the blast furnace for the conversion of coal to coke, which created a more refined coke product for heating iron, was also altered for a more significant modern use by English metallurgist and weapon designer John Wilkinson.

The United States led the way in the production of coke for the next century, especially after the introduction of large-scale rolling mill technology by American ironmaster Colonel Isaac Meason (1743–1818). Especially in coal-rich regions like Pennsylvania, coke production drove the steel industry and the rise of the Second Industrial Revolution in North America. In the North, the switch to coke production to make iron and steel led to abundant advantages in armaments production on the eve of the US Civil War. The Confederate states, generally reliant on charcoal production for the creation of iron, were forced to use inferior weapons due, in part, to this technological lag.

Especially after the innovations of English steel magnate Henry Bessemer (1813–98), the mining of coal increased throughout North America and Europe. The Bessemer Process involved removing the initial carbon elements within iron through a process of oxidation, which then were re-added as pure carbon after the wrought iron was purified, creating softer or harder forms of iron or steel upon request. Bessemer steel was vital for the advancement of the British Empire, as new weapons of his harder and less expensive steel hit the oceans, roads, and rails of Europe and Britain's overseas territories in the decades to follow. Bessemer steel was especially essential for the expansion of railways and the use of heavier trains, exemplified by the steel rails of Cecil Rhodes' (1853–1902) aborted Cape-to-Cairo Railway. The essential timing of invention of the Bessemer Process during the Victorian Era heightened imperialism for multiple European and American powers developing their colonial empires.

THE BESSEMER PROCESS

Henry Bessemer (1813–98) invented a process for a creating less expensive forms of steel around 1856. The English inventor instituted the Bessemer Process for creating harder forms of wrought iron by blowing air through molten iron to remove impurities like silicon, manganese, and carbon, thereby creating a higher boiling temperature within the molten iron mixture. Most other processes for creating steel or wrought iron before Bessemer were also preventively expensive, as the final product would create large pig iron blooms, or lumps of material, that were so bulky that they took considerable periods of hand-forging to shape into usable iron and steel. Bessemer's invention greatly improved the quality and lowered the cost of iron and steel manufacturing, thereby instigating the Second Industrial Revolution.

Andrew Kettler

The second wave of the Industrial Revolution also involved further degradation of labor in factories and on quickening assembly lines through the development of different mass production schemes. Leading industrialists tried to monopolize their various sectors of the economy during what are often called the "Brown Decades" due to the soot covering buildings and streets from coal smoke. The plight of labor, whether of the adult working class, child labor, or industrial slaves, led to the rise of labor unions, strikes, and the ideologies of Marxism during the nineteenth century, described in *The Condition of the Working Class in England* (1844) by Friedrich Engels and expressed through the General Strike of 1842 in Great Britain.

Through these changes in labor, energy regimes, mechanical engineering, and cheaper steel production, the powers of Western Europe and the United States created greater hold upon trade networks throughout the globe, advancing colonialism into the global South. As well, the vast amount of charcoal, coal, and coke that fueled these processes caused environmental decline throughout the coal-producing regions of the Americas and Europe. Furthermore, clouds of smoke choked cities like Pittsburgh and London, often causing darkness for weeks at a time, a problem still evident in modern developing economies like China and throughout the industrializing world.

Coal was an essential ingredient in shaping the Industrial Revolution, which in turn shaped European and American politics during the nineteenth century, including the great power rivalry that began to simmer, then reach an open boil toward the end of the century. The Rhineland, a region between France and Germany, is a significant coal-producing region. The economic, social, and political pressures that led to the Franco-Prussian War (1870–1), the First World War (1914–18), and the Second World War (1939–45) were conditioned by rival German and French claims to these coal regions. They were essential to the production of coke, the resource upon which the steel-making sectors of the modern economy were built. The intricate fabric of modernity as it brought Europe, the United States, and the developed parts of Asia closer and closer to the brink was very much the interweaving of the social, economic, and political threads of industrialization spun by the many uses of coal, coke, and petroleum resources.

Andrew Kettler

See also: Coal; Coaling Stations; Coke; Frick, Henry Clay; Mahan, Alfred Thayer; Panama Canal; Petroleum; Red Line Agreement of 1928; Slater, Samuel; Steam Power; Transcontinental Railroad

FURTHER READING

Birch, Alan. 1967. *The Economic History of the British Iron and Steel Industry, 1784–1879; Essays in Industrial and Economic History with Special Reference to the Development of Technology.* London: Frank Cass.

Gordon, Robert B. 1996. *American Iron, 1607–1900.* Baltimore, MD: Johns Hopkins University Press.

Griffin, Emma. 2010. *A Short History of the British Industrial Revolution.* New York: Palgrave Macmillan.

Kornblith, Gary John. 1998. *The Industrial Revolution in America.* Boston: Houghton Mifflin.

Landes, David. 1969. *The Unbound Prometheus: Technological Change and Industrial Development in Western Europe from 1750 to the Present.* New York: Cambridge University Press.

Milward, Alan, and S.B. Saul. 1977. *The Development of the Economies of Continental Europe 1850–1914*. Cambridge, MA: Harvard University Press.

Mumford, Lewis. 1934. *Technics and Civilization*. New York: Harcourt, Brace, and Company.

Schubert, John Rudolph Theodore 1957. *History of the British Iron and Steel Industry from C. 450 B.C. to A.D.1775*. London: Routledge & K. Paul.

Weber, Max. 1930 [1905]. *The Protestant Ethic and the Spirit of Capitalism*. Trans. Talcott Parsons. New York: Charles Scribner's Sons.

Insull, Samuel

Business magnate Samuel Insull (1859–1938) pioneered the electrification of America and the creation of the regulated monopoly in electrical power. Born in London, Insull crossed the Atlantic in 1881 to work as Thomas Edison's personal secretary. The ambitious young man became more involved over the years in Edison's business enterprises, traveling much of the country to establish central-station electrical plants. In 1885, Insull made one of his first moves towards consolidation by organizing the Association of Edison Illuminating Companies, a trade association for the owners and managers of Edison generating stations and equipment manufacturers. The next year he became the manager of Edison's newly acquired manufacturing plant in Schenectady, New York.

In 1892 he moved to Chicago, where he became President of Chicago Edison, then a relatively minor player in the field of electrical generation and distribution whose territory was restricted to downtown Chicago. Chicago would be Insull's base for the rest of his career. He became a US citizen in 1896.

Like Edison, Insull strongly supported central-station electrical generation as opposed to individuals and businesses owning their own generators and controlling their own electrical supply. Under Insull's guidance, Chicago Edison (merged with Commonwealth Electric in 1907 to form Commonwealth Edison) became the dominant electrical supplier not only in the Chicago area but throughout much of the Midwest. Insull bought out many of the small electrical companies in the Chicago region to establish an effective monopoly and oversaw the construction of large new generating stations, bringing the average rate paid by Chicago electrical customers down from around 20 cents per kWh to 2.5 cents per kWh over the course of two decades. The first of these new stations was the Harrison Street Station built in 1896, making use of equipment left over from the 1893 Chicago World's Fair. However, the steam engine generation technology of the Harrison Street station quickly became obsolete, and in 1903 Insull opened the Fisk Street station, where power was generated by the new and far more efficient technology of the steam turbine. The Fisk Street station would eventually come to hold fourteen steam turbines.

Commonwealth Edison provided Chicagoans with some of the cheapest electricity in the world, and Insull vigorously promoted the use of electricity for domestic lighting and household appliances as well as industry. Insull's low rates meant that it was cheaper for businesses to buy electricity from his companies than to establish their own generating plants. Insull was a pioneer in the development of the system whereby charges for electricity varied according to demand, called "variable metering," which he saw as a way of avoiding wasteful generation of electricity that was not used under a flat-rate system.

Insull believed utilities were natural monopolies and supported state regulation. A regulated market would be more successful at attracting investment and long-term planning than a free-for-all of unregulated competition. He preferred dealing with the Illinois state government rather than corrupt and venal Chicago politicians, but also feared the Progressive movement's advocacy for municipally owned public power as opposed to private companies like Insull's. Insull also took a public role in supporting regulated central-station electricity generation in a series of addresses. Insull's model of power monopolies supported by state regulators proved highly successful in increasing profits and attracting investment.

INSULL ON MONOPOLY AND ECONOMIC EFFICIENCY

Monopoly is not a political question; and in saying that I am not only referring to the business in which I am engaged but also to any of the great industrial businesses of this country. Monopoly is an engineering question; it is a manufacturing question. It is a question of how we can get the largest possible amount of earning capacity out of the dollars of wealth that this country possesses. In my line of business I know that it is almost criminal for public officials to waste the taxpayers' money in building small electrical generating plants that we see all around the country for public lighting. What I am saying to you is exactly what I said to the capitalists who put their money into the street-railway system in Chicago—that it was money in their pockets to abandon their electrical generating stations and turn that business over to us. (From a speech delivered to the Engineers Club of Dayton, Ohio on October 6, 1914. Printed in *Public Utilities in Modern Life*, pp. 3–4)

William E. Burns

Insull expanded from his Chicago base throughout Illinois and the Midwest, pioneering electrical distribution in small town and rural America through the North Shore Electric Company, a Commonwealth Edison affiliate. At its peak, the Insull empire extended to power generation in thirty-two states, and he controlled around 10 percent of the nation's power supply. He invested in many related businesses, including major consumers of electricity such as streetcar lines. Traction companies were particularly valuable to Insull as they used electricity throughout the day when demand from homes was lower, thus helping to equalize the load on equipment and preventing electricity from going to waste. Insull consolidated Chicago's competing elevated railroad companies into a single Chicago Rapid Transit Company, the nucleus of the modern Chicago Transit Authority. Insull was also active in the natural gas business. He set up his businesses through holding companies which he controlled, often financing through bonds or non-voting stock so as not to have to share control. The first was the Middle West Utilities Company set up in 1912. Structuring his businesses through interstate holding companies also enabled Insull to evade state regulatory control when he so desired.

Although Insull initially weathered the Crash of 1929 with little difficulty, his highly leveraged businesses began to fail during the Great Depression, suffering from a steep decline in the demand for electricity and his holding companies growing debt, which eventually put Insull in the hands of the New York bankers he despised. The collapse of the "Insull Group" of companies took with it not only Insull's own fortune but that of other investors who had relied on Insull's reputation as a businessman. It should be noted that the holding companies collapsed, but the operating companies survives. He was widely vilified and was even a target of Franklin D. Roosevelt in the 1932 presidential campaign. Insull fled the country but was eventually extradited back to the United States from Turkey. He was tried for mail fraud, embezzlement and fraudulent bankruptcy. Although acquitted each time, Insull was a ruined man. He returned to Europe, where he died in Paris.

William E. Burns

See also: California Electric Light Company; Chicago World's Columbian Exposition; Consolidated Edison Company; Edison, Thomas Alva; Electricity; Federal Power Act of 1935; General Electric Company; Pearl Street Power Station; Public Utility Regulatory Policies Act of 1978; Vulcan Street Plant; War of the Currents; Westinghouse, George

FURTHER READING

Insull, Samuel. 1924. *Public Utilities in Modern Life: Selected Speeches (1914–1923)*. Chicago: Privately Printed.

Lambert, Jeremiah D. 2015. *The Power Brokers: The Struggle to Shape and Control the Electric Power Industry*. Cambridge, MA: MIT Press.

MacDonald, Forrest. 1962. *Insull: The Rise and Fall of a Billionaire Utility Tycoon*. Chicago: University of Chicago Press.

Wasik, John F. 2006. *The Merchant of Power: Samuel Insull, Thomas Edison and the Creation of the Modern Metropolis*. New York: Palgrave Macmillan.

Interstate Highway System

In the early days of the American Republic and throughout the nineteenth century, road maintenance in the United States primarily was a local or state responsibility. However, as first bicycles and then automobiles began to proliferate, interest in more centralized road-building began to grow. New Jersey became the first state to offer a state-based road-building funding program in the closing decade of the nineteenth century, after which some momentum began to build for a federal equivalent. Indeed, Congress toyed with the notion of a Federal Interstate Highway System as early as 1912, but road maintenance at that time was rudimentary and still remained almost entirely locally managed and financed, especially in vast sections of rural America that still relied mostly on dirt roads. Moreover, many rural Americans were suspicious of the notion of their tax dollars being siphoned off so that, as they supposed, city slickers could enjoy a Sunday pedal or drive.

However, farmers began to consider the potential benefits of good roads with the advent of Rural Free Delivery, which began as an experiment in the 1890s and adopted across the country on July 1, 1902, nearly forty years after free postal delivery was established in the cities. With the advent of Rural Free Delivery service, the push for better roads in the hinterlands garnered an upswell of grassroots rural support. In the same year, the American Automobile Association was formed, and this organization was at the forefront of the movement to improve and to expand long-distance roadways throughout the United States. Although some contrarian voices had long suggested that the federal government was effectively barred by the US Constitution from employing tax dollars to develop an Interstate Highway System, the 1907 US Supreme Court decision in the case of *Wilson v. Shaw* upheld the authority of Congress to construct such roadways under the umbrella of its power to regulate interstate commerce. In addition, the commercial release of the Ford Model T in 1908 brought within the reach of many Americans a versatile, rugged, and dependable mass-produced automobile. All of these factors combined to hasten and to support the movement to change the face of American highways, culminating in the Federal-Aid Road Act of 1916, which was reauthorized in 1921.

In the subsequent twenty years leading up to the Second World War, the American love affair with the automobile shifted into high gear, and the ownership and use of personal cars increased many times over. Although this burgeoning role of the automobile in American life made it abundantly clear that some sort of integrated interstate transportation system would not only prove advantageous but in fact rapidly was becoming necessary, it was unclear how best to proceed. In fact, at this point there was a lively debate concerning how best to structure a national transcontinental highway system, and what was the most practical means to pay for and to support the ongoing maintenance of such a system. Moreover, the establishment of the Pennsylvania Turnpike Commission in 1937 spurred some concern that toll roads—rather than freeways—might become the rule. Further investigations into this possibility, however, indicated that a system of long-distance freeways was more practical than an integrated nationwide tollway system.

Under the terms of the 1938 Federal Aid Highway Act, a study was mandated to assess the efficacy of a super-highway system comprising three north-south and three east-west transcontinental traffic arteries. As a part of this study, both the potential competitive and complementary roles of freeways and tollways were assessed. The resulting study published the next year found that a national toll-road system was impractical; instead, the plan recommended a series of freeways that was to provide the basic blueprint for what was to become the Interstate Highway System within a generation. However, the onset of the Second World War initially slowed the movement towards such a system, although the Federal-Aid Highway Act of 1944 effectively authorized the Federal Interstate Highway System that was to come in the next decade.

With a stroke of President Dwight D. Eisenhower's pen, the long and twisting road to nationwide highway construction began in earnest with the Federal-Aid Highway Act of 1956. Long a proponent of highway infrastructure, Eisenhower had himself experienced the travails of cross-country motoring as an officer in the First World War, during which military convoys had to face the failures of roadway infrastructure at home due to poor planning and oversight, as well as abroad due to the obvious perils of a combat zone. Under the terms of the 1956 act, the federal government was to finance 90 percent of the construction, with Title I of the act allocating 25 billion over thirteen years to construct over 40,000 miles of highways. Title II of the act was concerned with revenue generation to offset these costs. Under Title II, the Highway Trust Fund was formed, raising revenue through taxing fuel, tires, and sale and use taxes on heavy trucks. While the Highway Trust Fund legislation originally was

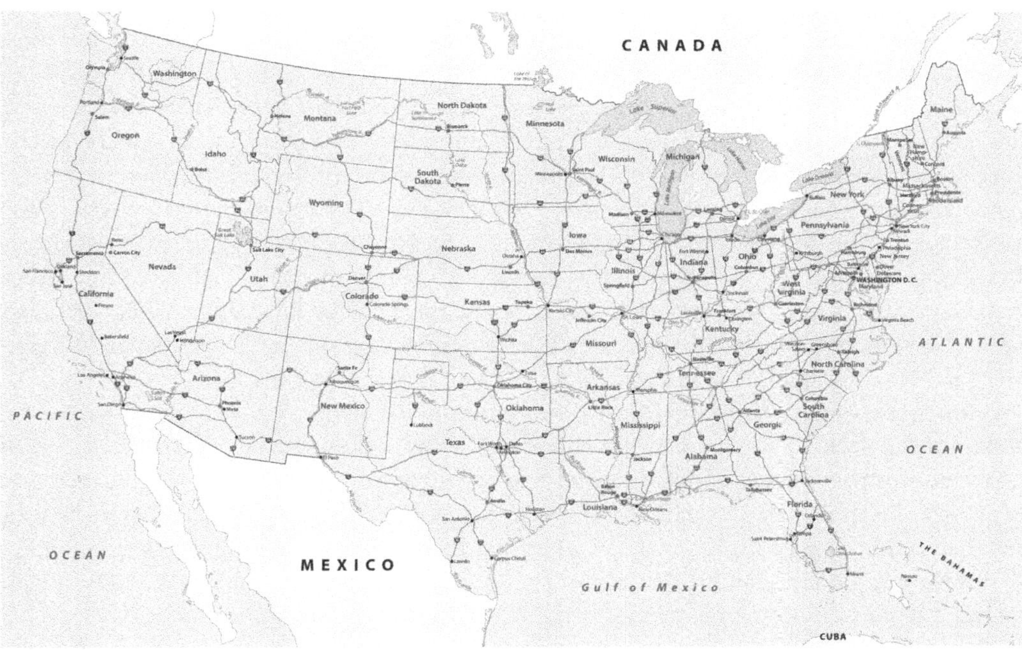

FIGURE 15: The US Interstate Highway System encouraged nationwide travel by automobiles, buses, and trucks.

supposed to expire in 1972, it has been extended numerous times by congressional action, and continues to finance road and mass transit infrastructure. Over the course of the two decades following the signing of the act, work and progress on the Interstate Highway System continued apace, and almost all of the originally planned construction was completed by the year of America's Bicentennial celebrations.

By that point over 42,000 miles of Interstate Highways had been constructed at a total cost topping $125 billion. Although there is little doubt that the Interstate Highway System achieved some of its targets and goals, an array of unpopular and sometimes perhaps unintended consequences caused an almost immediate backlash that gained momentum and popular support as the years went by and highway construction rolled on. Some of these objections and concerns were aesthetic and cultural, while others were economic and practical. The most striking aesthetic challenges raised by the construction of the Interstate Highway System were the monotony the uniform structure imposed across the nation, as well as the series of gargantuan Gordian Knots represented by freeway interchanges, vast three-dimensional, multi-layered clover-leafs that became a defining feature of the landscape of the United States during this period.

In social and cultural terms, although the original plans may have meant to foster the kind of movement of people, goods, and services that would benefit downtown areas, the construction of the Interstate Highway System largely had the opposite effect. While the promise of relatively fast transcontinental automobile travel was a boon to the American love affair with the car, it also hastened urban flight to the suburbs and exurbs, and the massive construction project itself destroyed and displaced many neighborhoods, effectively sounding a death-knell to many communities, especially those which were marginalized economically and politically. Working-class citizens, those of color, and those experiencing poverty were especially vulnerable, as plans could be redrawn to the benefit of those with more money and political influence. This process hastened segregation, and at times provided physical barriers between neighborhoods that were highly difficult to transcend by those without their own cars.

As the system sprawled across nearly every region and ecosystem across the country, critics began to note significant deleterious effects upon flora and fauna likewise displaced or disrupted. A number of manifestations of public dissatisfaction followed, and some of these engendered subsequent ameliorative measures by Congress. For instance, in 1959 there was a revolt in San Francisco against the Embarcadero Freeway. Such unrest led to the Federal-Aid Highway Act of 1962, which required cooperative planning and implementation, rather than the previous top-down approach. In addition, the Federal-Aid Highway Act of 1968 allowed for relocation assistance and wildlife protections, while in 1973 a small fraction of the Highway Trust Fund was designated to fund alternative transport for first time. In 1991, moreover, the Intermodal Surface Transportation Efficiency Act (ISTEA) allowed local communities to seek to achieve a useful balance of highway maintenance and other types of transportation infrastructure, including rail and mass transit. The military significance and utility of the Federal Interstate Highway System has not been lost on the US Department of Defense since the time of Eisenhower. In addition, the relevance of building and maintaining long-distance transcontinental roadways is of primary importance to a shipping industry that relies in large part on long-haul, or "Over the Road" (OTR), trucking.

Such vital national infrastructure priorities may seem obscure or secondary to some Americans, who since the dawn of the love affair with the car have tended to think of the freeway in terms of personal mobility and autonomous coast-to-coast travel. However, since the days of the Cold War and the rise of the American trucking industry, defense and commerce concerns have remained at the core of much federal, state, and municipal interest in maintaining and upgrading a transportation infrastructure that is well into its seventh decade.

Christopher R. Fee

See also: Bowser, Sylvanus Freelove; CAFE Standards; Ford, Henry; Duryea, Charles and J. Frank Duryea; Petroleum; Sport Utility Vehicles; Tokheim Oil Tank & Pump Company; Truck Transportation Technology

FURTHER READING

Chandra, Amitabh, and Eric Thompson. 2000. "Does Public Infrastructure Affect Economic Activity? Evidence from the Rural Interstate Highway System." *Regional Science and Urban Economics*. Vol. 30. No. 4. Pp. 457–90.

Gourdin, K.N. 2007. "Musings on the Interstate Highway System." *Defense Transportation Journal*. Vol. 63. No. 1. P. 5.

Historian of the United States Postal Service. 2013. "Rural Free Delivery." *Postal History*. August. United States Postal Service. https://about.usps.com/who/profile/history/rural-free-delivery.htm (accessed October 2023).

Lacy, Lee. 2018. "Dwight D. Eisenhower and the Birth of the Interstate Highway System." *Army Sustainment*. Vol. 50. No. 2. Pp. 64–7.

National Academies of Sciences, Engineering, and Medicine. 2019. *Renewing the National Commitment to the Interstate Highway System: A Foundation for the Future*. Washington, DC: The National Academies Press. https://doi.org/10.17226/25334 (accessed October 2023).

Perrier, Dianne. 2009. *Onramps and Overpasses: A Cultural History of Interstate Travel*. Gainesville: University Press of Florida.

Smith, J.N. 2004. "The Interstate Highway System." *World Trade*. Vol. 17. No. 5. P. 74.

Swift, Earl. 2011. *The Big Roads: The Untold Story of the Engineers, Visionaries, and Trailblazers Who Created the American Superhighways*. Boston: Houghton Mifflin Harcourt.

Tax Policy Center. 2022. "What is the Highway Trust Fund, and How is it Financed?" Key Elements of the U.S. Tax System. Urban Institute. Brookings Institution. https://www.taxpolicycenter.org/briefing-book/what-highway-trust-fund-and-how-it-financed (accessed October 2023).

Weber, Joe. 2012. "The Evolving Interstate Highway System and the Changing Geography of the United States." *Journal of Transport Geography*. Vol. 25. Pp. 70–86.

Weingroff, Richard F. 1996. "Federal Aid Road Act of 1916: Building the Foundation." *Public Roads Magazine*. Vol. 60. No. 1. Summer. https://highways.dot.gov/public-roads/summer-1996/federal-aid-road-act-1916-building-foundation (accessed October 2023).

Iraq War and the Project for the New American Century

The Iraq War, an eight-year conflict with long-standing ramifications, began with the US-led invasion of Iraq in 2003. Allegations of developing and harboring weapons of mass destruction and ties to Islamic terrorist groups were made by US President George W. Bush against President Saddam Hussein and his regime in Iraq in the years after the September 11, 2001 terrorist attacks on the United States, when terrorism linked to the Middle East had become a high priority issue for the US government. Despite resistance from the United Nations, US forces invaded Iraq with a coalition of Allied troops, including from the United Kingdom. No weapons of mass destructions were found, but the invasion resulted in toppling the Saddam regime and a long period of insecurity in Iraq. Questions concerning the motives of the invasion were prevalent, particularly in relation to the role of Iraq's massive oil reserves in US security strategy.

While the US government denied that oil was a motive for invasion, statements from prominent figures such as General John Abizaid, Commander of US Central Command from 2003 to 2017 and former Federal Reserve Chairman Alan Greenspan, both acknowledged the centrality of oil to the US invasion of Iraq (Abizaid 2007; Greenspan 2007, 463). Securing oil contracts in Iraq for US and UK corporations, such as ExxonMobil, Chevron, and British Petroleum, were also considered a motive, but one of many (Muttitt 2018, 32). An Iraq without Saddam was also considered a more amenable supplier of oil. With Hussein out of power, Iraq could increase oil production and exports as sanctions would be lifted, making more oil available for the world markets (Klare 2004, 94–105; Yergin 2011, 141–9). But while oil seemed ubiquitous in questions regarding motives, it was the unilateral decision to invade that brought attention to a US-centric geopolitical balance of power.

Prior to the Iraq War, US world leadership was a key topic for the think tank called the Project for the New American Century (PNAC). PNAC, founded in 1997 by William Kristol and Robert Kagan, was primarily concerned with how the United States would maintain its world leadership in the post-Cold War world. For PNAC, the decline in US defense spending and its connection to the potential decline in US influence abroad was of particular concern. The issue was explored at length in the PNAC report *Rebuilding America's Defenses* (2000), which argued that the United States needed to boost defense spending and invest in increasing military power to solidify global leadership (Donnelly 2000, i). While the report does not specifically refer to oil, oil and energy security in the United States are intertwined. This was demonstrated by the Energy Crisis of the 1970s, which was triggered by events in the Middle East, after which energy security became essential to national security strategy. In this regard, the report specifically pointed to "the Middle East and surrounding energy-producing region" when discussing the US role as the primary force securing the global balance of power, and, overall, international stability (Donnelly 2000, 5). The report also referred to the threats posed by Saddam Hussein and the necessity for US influence in Iraq. It argued that the CIA believed Saddam's Iraq to be hostile to the United States and either had or was developing ballistic missiles (Donnelly 2000, 51–2). PNAC argued that Iraq should not be allowed to undermine or threaten American global leadership (Donnelly 2000, 75).

Several signatories of PNAC's *Statement of Principles* became leading figures in the Bush administration and key proponents of the Iraq invasion, such as Vice President Dick Cheney, Defense Secretary Donald Rumsfeld, and envoy to Afghanistan and Iraq and later the US ambassador to Afghanistan, Zalmay Khalilzad. Other signatories included well-known intellectuals and politicians such as Paul Wolfowitz, Richard Perle, Donald Kagan, Francis Fukuyama, Elliot Abrams, and John Ellis "Jeb" Bush (Ryan 2010, 89; Albanese 2012, 72). PNAC, considered a neoconservative think tank, presented and promoted ideas that became later absorbed in US foreign policy with its invasion of Iraq during the Bush administration.

The connection between PNAC and the Iraq War is most apparent when considering the people involved. Paul Wolfowitz, a foreign policy adviser to Bush, had been concerned about Iraq and Saddam Hussein's military capabilities since the late 1970s when he worked at the Pentagon. In 1977, he warned that the United States should be strong enough to prevent Iraq from becoming a regional power, particularly as it was a significant threat to Middle Eastern oil fields (Mann 2004, 79–83). He held this stance throughout his career, lobbying for regime change in Iraq into the late 1990s (Ryan 2010, 91). Similarly, Richard Perle—chairman of

FIGURE 16: The Iraq War 2003–11 resulted in the deaths of over 4,800 US and coalition forces and over 250,000 Iraqi combatants and civilians.

the Defense Policy Board Advisory Committee from 2001 to 2003—urged Congress in 1997 to supply US air power and military supplies to the Iraqi National Congress (INC), an Iraqi political party opposing Saddam Hussein and led by Ahmed Chalabi. Chalabi would become an interim Iraqi Prime Minister in 2005, and he also served as Iraq's oil minister during the war. Zalmay Khalilzad, a former student of Wolfowitz who had a background in the oil industry and global policy research and development, wrote articles with Wolfowitz arguing for the overthrow of Saddam Hussein in 1997 (Ryan 2010, 102).

It is important to note that Khalilzad worked as a consultant for UNOCAL, a major US oil corporation now owned by Chevron, with interests in various Asian countries, and at the RAND organization, a prominent US think tank with a focus on research and analysis for both national and international policymaking. Earlier, in 1992, Khalilzad wrote *From Containment to Global Leadership*, a pamphlet arguing for the preservation of US unipolarity (Ryan 2010, 39). Along with Richard Perle, he also endorsed the INC in Congress in 1998 (Ryan 2010, 106). Donald Rumsfeld headed a commission—called the Rumsfeld Commission—that concluded that Hussein posed a ballistic threat to the United States in 1998. The Commission would have an important impact on CIA methods for missile threat analysis (Ryan 2010, 112). While these neoconservatives were in the minority during the Clinton administration, with the Republican presidency following George W. Bush's electoral win, many entered the government in leadership or consultancy positions. Ten of the PNAC founding signatories worked in or consulted with the Bush administration (Ryan 2010, 181). The attacks on the World Trade Center in 2001 emboldened support for preventative action against terrorist threats in Iraq, enabling the implementation of PNAC's foreign policy recommendations on Iraq by linking Islamic terrorism to Saddam Hussein (Ryan 2010, 183–4).

NEOCONSERVATISM

Neoconservatism is a political ideology that extends beyond traditional conservatism's focus on economics to address social and cultural stability (Kristol 1995, 37). The term was coined by Irving Kristol, the father of PNAC founder William Kristol. While neoconservatism focuses on a Realpolitik approach to foreign policy it also emphasizes democracy as an ideal and believes that American power can be used for moral purposes—this was manifested in PNAC's arguments that US action and intervention abroad would shape global politics for the better (Drury 2010, 955). Neoconservatism steadily gained supporters during the Clinton Administration with PNAC's promotion of a unipolar US strategy to maintain US global leadership. These ideas were incorporated into official US foreign policy in the post-9/11 years as notable PNAC figures gained prominence in the administration of George W. Bush. The Bush administration's report, National Security Strategy, has several similarities to PNAC's Rebuilding America's Defenses, including support for unilateral intervention in the Middle East.

Sakina Groeppmaier

PNAC was dissolved in 2006, three years into the Iraq War. The website was subsequently taken down along with many of its well-known documents, such as its *Statement of Principles* and *Rebuilding America's Defenses*, which had previously circulated online. Its influence, however, extended long beyond its life. Key PNAC figures were involved in planning regime change in Iraq long before the 9/11 attacks and the Bush presidency, and succeeded in pursuing their strategy aims of unilateral invasion once in government. The Iraq War officially ended in 2011, but the impacts of it persisted long after. Iraq continued to be plagued by instability after Saddam's downfall and terrorist groups such as the Islamic State grew in the post-war years, gaining control in much Iraqi territory. Despite an official withdrawal, the United States remained in Iraq, in part, to continue rebuilding efforts. Iraqi oil, as one of the largest world reserves of crude, remains central to global energy security and to US interests in the region.

Sakina Groeppmaier

See also: American Petroleum Institute; Bush, George H.W.; Carter Doctrine; Cheney, Richard Bruce "Dick"; Gulf War; Halliburton Company; Organization of Petroleum Exporting Countries (OPEC); Seven Sisters Oil Companies

FURTHER READING

Abizaid, John. 2007. "Courting Disaster: Fight for Oil, Water and a Healthy Planet." October 13. Roundtable at Stanford. Stanford University. https://www.youtube.com/watch?v=9sd2JseupXQ (accessed October 2023).

Albanese, Matteo. 2012. *The Concept of War in Neoconservative Thinking*. Milan: Ipoc Press.

Bookman, Jay. 2003. "The President's Real Goal in Iraq." In *The Iraq War Reader: History, Arguments, Opinions*. Eds. Micah L. Sifry and Christopher Cerf. Pp. 347–52. Touchstone: Simon & Schuster.

Donnelly, Thomas, Donald Kagan, and Gary Schmitt. 2000. "Rebuilding America's Defenses: Strategy, Forces and Resources for a New Century." Project for the New American Century. September.

Drury, Shadia B. 2010. "Neoconservatism." In *Encyclopedia of Political Theory*. Ed. Mark Bevir. P. 955. Thousand Oaks: SAGE Publications.

Fukuyama, Francis. 2006. "After Neoconservatism." *The New York Times*. February 19. https://www.nytimes.com/2006/02/19/magazine/after-neoconservatism.html (accessed August 1, 2019).

Greenspan, Alan. 2007. *The Age of Turbulence: Adventures in a New World*. New York: Penguin Books.

Klare, Michael T. 2004. *Blood and Oil: The Dangers and Consequences of America's Growing Dependency on Imported Petroleum*. London: Penguin Books.

Kristol, William. 1995. *Neoconservatism: The Autobiography of an Idea*. New York: The Free Press.

Kruse, Felix. 2014. *Oil Politics: The West and Its Desire for Energy Security since 1950*. Hamburg: Anchor Academic Publishing.

Mann, James. 2004. *Rise of the Vulcans: The History of Bush's War Cabinet*. New York: Viking.

Muttitt, Greg. 2018. "No Blood for Oil, Revisited: The Strategic Role of Oil in the 2003 Iraq War." *International Journal of Contemporary Iraqi Studies*. Vol. 13. No. 3. Pp. 319–39.

President of the United States. 2002. *The National Security Strategy of the United States of America*. September. US Department of State. https://2009-2017.state.gov/documents/organization/63562.pdf (accessed August 8, 2019).

Ryan, Maria. 2010. *Neoconservatism and the New American Century*. New York: Palgrave Macmillan.

Yergin, Daniel. 2011. *The Quest: Energy, Security, and the Remaking of the Modern World*. London: Penguin Group.

Johnson, Warren Seymour

The history of energy features innumerable technological innovations that enabled ever-greater levels of control and precision in directing its use. One of those innovations, the thermostat, emerged in the 1880s as a mechanism to regulate ambient room temperatures in steam-heated buildings. A number of inventors contributed to the development of the thermostat, but perhaps none exceeds Warren S. Johnson (1847–1911) in importance. Johnson's "electric tele-thermoscope" from 1883 enabled a room to signal automatically when it became too hot or too cold so that a damper could be moved to change the temperature, thus addressing an issue that came about with the advent of centralized steam heating systems. His company, Johnson Controls, grew into a very large corporation that designs and manufactures heating, ventilation, and cooling equipment, climate-control systems, and fire and security equipment for a wide variety of buildings. These systems became a crucial focus of attention since the 1970s as energy efficiency surfaced as a major economic and environmental concern.

Johnson's family was part of a larger migration of New Englanders to the upper middle west in the early nineteenth century. They came from Leicester, Vermont where Johnson was born, to Menomonie in northwestern Wisconsin. He largely taught himself as a child, with a focus on scientific and technological subjects, and then as a young man he worked as a printer and surveyor. Eventually Johnson went into education, first as a classroom teacher and then as principal and finally superintendent. He earned an appointment in 1876 as professor at the teacher's college in Whitewater (now University of Wisconsin-Whitewater) and soon became Professor of Natural Science. With his interests in science, Johnson investigated subjects then in vogue, which included chemistry and electricity. He kept a laboratory where he conducted experiments and tinkered with mechanical devices. Winters in northwest Wisconsin were brutal, and the steam boiler in his building had a difficult time maintaining even temperatures. When it got too cold, the janitor would manually adjust the damper in the basement, and then an hour later when it got too hot, adjustments would have to be made once again. Johnson began to work on this problem and aspired to make a control system that could signal precisely when dampers need to be adjusted to avoid wide swings in room temperatures.

The result of Johnson's study and experimentation was his electric tele-thermoscope, which received a patent in 1883. The device operated with a spring that moved very slightly with any change in room temperature, and this movement activated a set of metal pins. The pins, set on either end of an "oscillating beam," dipped left or right depending on the direction of room temperature change, and touched the surface of one of two small pans of mercury. The pans of mercury, in turn, were connected to metal rods wired electrically to a panel next to the furnace composed of pairs of electromagnets—one pair for each room. When one of the electromagnets was charged, it formed a complete circuit. Depending on which electromagnet formed the circuit, an "oscillating armature" moved to indicate "warm" or "cold" and simultaneously rang a bell. The patent wrapped up the description by narrating the action to follow: "which ever armature touches a core it will instantly ring the bell, and thus call the attention of the attendant to the fact that there has been a maximum or minimum change of temperature in one of the rooms, and the particular index moved by the armature will at once indicate which room it is and whether it is too warm or too cold." Whoever attended the furnace then opened or closed the damper to the particular room that sent the signal (Johnson 1883, 2).

By no means did the electric tele-thermoscope create a fully automated system of controls. It merely guaranteed that when the human furnace attendant adjusted the dampers according to the signals, it would create a more even level of temperature in the different rooms to be heated. Nevertheless, the response to his invention encouraged him and a business partner, William Plankinton to join with other investors in 1885 to form the Johnson Electric Service Company in Milwaukee. The company installed Johnson's system in the old city hall and the public library, drawing some public attention to their new enterprise. Johnson secured further patents for his temperature control systems, in 1885 for his "Thermal-Pneumatic Temperature-Regulator" and 1888 for his "Temperature Regulating System." Then, in 1895, Johnson patented a completely automatic temperature control system using "thermostatic fluid-pressure-controlling instruments" in the different rooms or apartments that activated fluid-pressure motors to operate the system's valves, dampers, and vents, which alternately opened and closed to regulate heat traveling into each of the different rooms. According to an intellectual property expert, it was the "first multi-zone automatic temperature control system feasible for commercial application" (Brachmann 2018).

Johnson presided over a company, renamed the Johnson Service Company, that established itself as the preeminent designer, manufacturer, and installer of temperature control systems. To be sure, competitors like the Minneapolis Heat Regulator Company, the Honeywell Heating Specialty Company, and Powers Regulator Company fought for market share and pushed the frontiers of innovation. Still, Johnson's systems were admired worldwide, and installed at such illustrious places as the US Capitol Building, the New York Stock Exchange, the Metropolitan Museum of Art, the Waldorf-Astoria Hotel, the US Military Academy, and the home of Andrew Carnegie. In 1908, the Singer Building's forty-seven-storey tower in New York was constructed using 1,200 Johnson thermostats; it was the tallest building in the world at that time. In 2008, the American Society of Mechanical Engineers (ASME) recognized Johnson's 1895 system as an "Historic Mechanical Engineering Landmark." His invention was cited as "the first reliable and economical multi-zone temperature control system," and ASME History & Heritage Committee Chair J. Lawrence Lee added that Johnson "changed the world in the late 1800s" with controls that help "companies and organizations keep their buildings comfortable and energy-efficient more than 100 years later" ("Johnson" 2008).

Johnson received over fifty patents and invented a wide range of devices including a humidistat, a pneumatic tower clock, and puncture-proof tires. He experimented with wireless telegraphy and electricity storage as well. Late in life, he took an interest in the automobile industry, securing a patent for an "auto-carriage" steam engine and leading the company to manufacture different models of vehicles, which included a steam-powered car, a fire truck, a limousine, and an ambulance. After Johnson died in 1911 of kidney disease in Los Angeles, the company sold its automotive division and focused on the technologies of temperature regulation. The company benefited from the increased popularity of air-conditioning systems in the 1920s, which required temperature control regulation systems, and the construction boom of the post-war era. Johnson purchased rival Penn Controls in 1968 and became a Fortune 500 company, then in 1974 changed its name to Johnson Controls, Inc. The acquisition of Globe-Union in 1978 made Johnson Controls the world's largest producer of batteries for cars and other vehicles, and in 1985 the company acquired Hoover Universal and Ferro Manufacturing, becoming in the process a leader in manufacturing automotive seating systems. The company employed 130,000 people worldwide at the turn of the twentieth century before divesting of some of its subsidiaries and reducing its workforce to around 100,000 in 2022, a year in which it generated $25.5 billion in revenue.

William S. Johnson's company is credited with important technological innovations in heating, cooling, and ventilation control systems that are geared toward cost savings and energy efficiency. Back in 1922, the Johnson Service Company's system for temperature and humidity control promised a fuel savings of up to 35 percent, and in 1929, the company touted a testimonial from a school official that claimed its system reduced heating costs by 62 percent. At various points in the modern history of energy in the United States, calls for greater energy efficiency have been met with innovation in the industry, which enable building owners and supervisors to regulate energy consumption with advanced sensors and digital technology. For example, calls for reductions in carbon emissions in the early 2000s led to a partnership between Johnson Controls, the Clinton Climate Initiative, management company Jones Lang LaSalle, Rocky Mountain Institute, and Empire State Building, LLC to retrofit all the Empire State Building's outdated controls. From 2008 to 2012, the group spent $20 million to update the system, adding many other energy-efficient upgrades as well, and achieved a ten-year energy savings of $40 million with a 54 percent reduction in the buildings greenhouse gas emissions (JC 2022).

Jeffrey B. Webb

See also: Henry, Joseph; Home Energy Efficiency; Nason, Joseph; Powers, William Penn; Richardson & Boynton Company; Underwriters Laboratories; US Green Building Council

FURTHER READING

Brachmann, Steve. 2018. "Warren Johnson, the Father of Thermostats and Automated Room Temperature Control." IPWatchdog.com. July 16. https://ipwatchdog.com/2018/07/16/warren-johnson-father-thermostats-room-temperature-control/id=99351/ (accessed October 2023).

Donaldson, Barry, and Bernard Nagengast. 1994. *Heat and Cold: Mastering the Great Indoors: A Selective History of Heating, Ventilation, Air-conditioning and Refrigeration from the Ancients to the 1930s*. Atlanta, GA: American Society of Heating, Refrigerating and Air-Conditioning Engineers.

Johnson Controls (JC). 2022. "Empire State Building Goes Green." Johnson Controls Insights. https://www.johnsoncontrols.com/insights/2022/feature-story/empire-state-building-goes-green (accessed October 2023).

"Johnson Controls 1895 Energy Control System Named ASME Historic Mechanical Engineering Landmark." 2008. *Engineered Systems Magazine*. July 1. https://www.esmagazine.com/articles/93382-johnson-controls-1895-energy-control-system-named-asme-historic-mechanical-engineering-landmark (accessed October 2023).

Johnson, Warren S. 1883. *Electric Tele-Thermoscope*. (US Patent #281,884). United States Patent Office. https://patentimages.storage.googleapis.com/83/96/21/7f61e638f6b543/US281884.pdf (accessed October 2023).

Roberts, Brian. n.d. *Warren S. Johnson and Automatic Controls*. CIBSE Heritage Group website.http://www.hevac-heritage.org/built_environment/pioneers_revisited/johnson.pdf (accessed October 2023).

Joy, Joseph Francis

The coal mining industry played a central role in US economic development in the era of the Industrial Revolution and the decades that followed. Despite recent declines, coal provided nearly 22 percent of the electricity produced in 2021 by US power plants (EIA 2022). Historically, the demand for coal increased in the 1890–1920 period due to the advent of electricity and the need for fuel to power electric generation plants. Mining managers and owners looked for ways to increase production and turned to mechanization. One of the most important machines to appear in this critical period was the Joy loader, the brainchild of a former miner-turned-engineer Joseph F. Joy (1883–1957). The machine replaced the traditional method of hand-loading coal, which helped coal companies meet the surge in wartime demand in the 1940s and serve the post-war economic boom of the 1950s and 1960s. The Joy loader became ubiquitous in US mining operations, and Joy's company claimed in 1954 that 72 percent of American machine-loaded coal was handled by Joy loaders ("Joy" 2012). In general, this device illustrates the impact of technological innovation in the coal industry, both in terms of expanding productive capacity and in changing the conditions of work for coal miners.

Joseph Joy was born in Cumberland in western Maryland in 1883, and at the young age of twelve began working at the local coal mines. By his mid-teens, Joy was found along the mine face, digging out the kerf—the slot under the face—along the bottom of the exposed wall, drilling holes for dynamite, blasting the face away from the coal seam, and then manually loading hunks of coal onto a coal car. This laborious process under dangerous conditions proved to be lethal: from 1839 to 1914, data shows that 53,078 workers were killed in coal mining accidents, and many more met untimely deaths due to mining-related diseases like black lung (Fay 1916, 7). As Joy came of age in mining, large-scale, single-event disasters killed 201 miners in Schofield, Utah (1900), 362 in Monongah, West Virginia (1907), and 239 at the Darr Mine in Pennsylvania (1907) (Kahle 2023). These events triggered strikes, workplace violence, and fatal clashes in places like Paint Creek, West Virginia (1912–13), Ludlow, Colorado (1913), Matewan, West Virginia (1920), and Blair Mountain, West Virginia (1921). The so-called Battle of Blair Mountain resulted in the deaths of at least 133 miners at the hands of private company security, county law enforcement, and state police (Kahle 2023).

In this context of extreme danger and violent confrontation between workers and mining companies, Joy began to experiment with machinery that could alleviate some of the toil and strain involved with extracting and moving coal. At the age of twenty he sketched a rough design for a machine that could dig and load coal while taking a correspondence course in mechanical engineering ("Joseph" 2020). In 1913, ten years later, he left the coal mines for Jeffery Manufacturing Company to become an engineer, working on a team in Pocahontas, Virginia designing cutting and loading equipment. Joy showed company officials a "gathering arm" loader that he had been developing in hopes they'd buy the rights to manufacture it, but they declined on the grounds that they thought they borrowed his idea from another machine. Joy pivoted and demonstrated his gathering arm loader for John A. Donaldson an executive with Pittsburgh Coal Company, who expressed interest. He arranged to have it fabricated and put it into service in 1916 at the company's Sommer No. 2 Mine. Donaldson was so pleased with the results that he hired Joy as a consultant and ordered five more of his machines. In this period, Joy perfected the design and received a patent in 1919 for what he termed a "Loading-Machine" (Joy 1919).

The patent claimed the machine to be an improvement on other models because it could gather coal pieces of different sizes and operated in coal mines with lower ceilings. The approved application described how the gathering mechanism included "fingers and means to cause said fingers to travel in substantially horizontal orbital paths to engage material and move it onto the conveyer, and a substantially horizontally arranged apron beyond the end of which substantially all portions of said fingers move in the gathering operation" (Joy 1919). An electric motor powered the gathering mechanism as well as the conveyor belt that moved coal over the machine to a coal car directly in the rear. The Joy loader was designed to be moved along a pair of rails that extended from the mine opening to the active mine face. Dolandson helped Joy to secure financing for the new Joy Machine Company, which signed production agreements with several manufacturing companies in Pennsylvania. The new loaders came with crawlers in order to provide more mobility, and found buyers in 1922 and 1923 throughout Pennsylvania as well as West Virginia, Illinois, and even Saskatchewan, Canada (Komatsu 2023). Joy built his own plant in Evansville, Indiana and developed new model in 1923 featuring an "articulated conveyor tail section" that made it the "forerunner of the modern loader" (Komatsu 2023).

The Evansville plant proved to be inadequate for the Joy Machine Company's purposes and so Joy moved his manufacturing operations to a plant in Franklin, Pennsylvania. Several strikes in the Pennsylvania coal fields in 1922, 1923, and 1925 disrupted the coal mining industry and forced the company to restructure its debts. This led to Joy's departure as company president. Joy and an engineering team traveled to the Soviet Union to help the mechanization of coal production in the Donetsk region, where he remained for two years until 1927, when political turmoil arose with Stalin's purge of his adversaries in the Communist Party. Joy and his team appropriated a train and made it safely to Poland. When he returned, he took up inventing, working in several different companies and even starting his own firm at one point. In these different situations, he devised improved conveyor systems, coal saws, coal cutting machines, and a safety coal drill. Finally, in 1946 he received a lifetime consulting contract with the Joy Manufacturing Company, which had reorganized in 1928 but kept his name, to devise new coal technology and mining procedures. By the time of his death in 1957, Joy had earned 190 patents for his different inventions and innovations, which the company's celebratory biography called "milestones in the history of underground mining mechanization" (Komatsu 2023).

Through a series of acquisitions, the Joy Manufacturing Company became the provider of a broad range of mining equipment which included rubber-tired shuttle cars, mining machines that combined cutting and loading, diamond drills for tunneling, mining belt conveyors, ventilation fans, electrical connectors, oil drilling tools, crushers and shredders, and other heavy tools and machinery. After forty years of frequent changes of ownership, the remnants of what was left of the original company was absorbed in 2017 into Komatsu Ltd. Joseph F. Joy's contributions to the coal industry have been long remembered. Mechanization enabled coal companies to increase production, which correspondingly lowered prices. Cheap, plentiful coal fueled the creation of the modern industrial system by means of coal-burning steam and electrical power. Mechanization eliminated some of the more odious tasks associated with coal mining, but at the same time met with resistance from some quarters in the labor force. According to historian Keith Dix, mechanization took a measure of control away from workers, who were largely treated as independent contractors in the earliest days of coal mining and loading and handed this control over to mine owners and their hired managers (Dix 1988, ix). In addition, with mechanization and the expansion of the supply of cheap coal, power plants and industries in the United States became dependent on the resource, which has made it difficult to switch to non-carbon, renewable fuels in an era concerned with the effects of carbon emissions and climate change.

Jeffrey B. Webb

See also: Battle of Blair Mountain; Black Lung Disease; Cumberland Iron and Coal Company; Dawson Mine Disaster; Industrial Revolution; Ludlow Massacre; Miner's and Laborer's Benevolent Association; Molly Maguires; Monongah Mine Disaster; Paint Creek Mine War; Scofield Mine Disaster; Sinclair, Upton; Tommyknockers; United Mine Workers of America; Weir, Paul

FURTHER READING

Dix, Keith. 1988. *What's a Coal Miner to Do? The Mechanization of Coal Mining*. Pittsburgh: University of Pittsburgh Press.

Fay, Albert H. 1916. *Coal-Mine Fatalities in the United States, 1870–1914*. Bureau of Mines, US Department of the Interior. Washington, DC: US Government Printing Office.

"Joseph Francis Joy." 2020. National Mining Hall of Fame & Museum. https://www.mininghalloffame.org/hall-of-fame/joseph-francis-joy (accessed October 2023).

Joy, Joseph Francis. 1919. "Loading-Machine" (US Patent #1,306,164). United States Patent Office. https://patentimages.storage.googleapis.com/4d/b9/51/44b180bd62a3d8/US1306064.pdf (accessed October 2023).

"Joy Loading Machine." 2012. *e-WV: The West Virginia Encyclopedia*. March 5. https://www.wvencyclopedia.org/articles/1060 (accessed October 2023).

Kahle, Trish. 2023. "Coal Mining and Labor Conflict." Yale University Energy History website. https://energyhistory.yale.edu/units/coal-mining-and-labor-conflict (accessed October 2023).

Komatsu Mining. 2023. "Joseph Francis Joy: Character, Inventor, Reformer." https://mining.komatsu/docs/default-source/non-product-documents/company/our-company/joy-history_2.pdf?sfvrsn=40 (accessed October 2023).

US Energy Information Administration (EIA). 2022. "What is U.S. Electricity Generation by Energy Source?" US Department of Energy. https://www.eia.gov/tools/faqs/faq.php?id=427&t=3 (accessed October 2023).

Kerr-McGee's Kermac No. 16

By tradition, the beginning of offshore oil drilling in the United States is dated to November 14, 1947, when Kerr-McGee Oil Industries, Inc. and Brown & Root Industrial Services completed work on Kermac No. 16, an oil drilling platform in the Gulf of Mexico nearly 11 miles from Terrebonne Parish, Louisiana. The Kermac No. 16 is considered the first commercially successful "out-of-sight-of-land" operation in order to distinguish it from earlier efforts to drill for oil over water that were connected to nearby coastal land or shoreline (Pratt 1997, 22). The company and its contractors successfully negotiated a number of technical, logistical, and weather-related challenges in order to build and operate the drilling rig in open water in a financially viable way. The Kermac No. 16 well, in conjunction with advances in the science and technology of oil exploration, encouraged other petroleum companies to venture further and further offshore and greatly expanded the volume of domestic oil production. It represented a major development in American energy history in the mid-twentieth century.

Locating oil deposits several thousand feet below the surface of the earth presented a challenge to oil prospectors before modern science and technology, to say nothing about finding oil below the seafloor. Early explorers relied on hunches and guesswork, or "adhered to superstitions which held that drilling sites be kept close to cemeteries or on the right-hand forks of creeks" (Priest 2008, 13). Generally, oil could be found on the ground near "seeps," or open springs of oil and gas, but deeper deposits required a good estimation of where oil likely could be found and drilling of expensive test wells. Oil speculators and petroleum companies turned to geology, the scientific study of the earth and its physical features and processes, to help identify where oil and gas might be found deep in the earth's layers. Geologists knew that salt domes were associated with oil and gas deposits, and used an instrument known as a torsion balance—which is sensitive to gravitational forces—to isolate likely underground salt domes that weren't visible on the landscape. Newer instruments like the gravity meter (gravimeter) improved performance, and then devices utilizing magnetism like the field balance and the magnetometer came along and further refined oil-finding techniques. Seismology offered another useful tool, which used sound waves to gauge the density of rock formations; underground salt domes allowed sound waves to travel relatively quickly, providing clues to the geologist as to their likely locations. These technologies began to prove their worth in the 1920s and 1930s.

Oil companies employed geologists or hired contracting firms like Geophysical Engineering Company, Seismos Gesellschaft, and Geophysical Research Corporation to explore the marshes, bayous, and bays of southern Louisiana and coastal Texas. They worked out how to operate their instruments on flatboats and barges and developed reflection seismology to refine their techniques of identifying deep formations likely to yield oil and gas. Drilling took place on wooden planks fastened to cypress pilings set deep in lakebeds and close offshore, or on large timber "mats" (Priest 2008, 29). The movement from land to coast to open water proceeded incrementally. At Caddo Lake in Louisiana in 1911, oil companies learned how to drill for oil over water on a stationary platform equipped with its drilling rigs and well-assembly supplies. In the late 1930s, oil was discovered offshore from Creole, Louisiana, and in 1938, Pure Oil and Superior Oil hired Brown & Root to build a platform for their drilling equipment. It was located a mile and a half offshore in 14 feet of water atop of 140 creosoted pilings driven 27 feet into the sandy ocean bed. The 180 x 320 feet structure cleared the waterline by 15 feet and required daily supply by boat from a port 10 miles away. There were no living quarters, so workers, supplies, equipment, food, and other necessaries had to be ferried one-and-a-half hours each way to work the rig. The operators built a pipeline from the platform to the mainland to transfer the oil, given the platform's relatively short distance to shore (Pratt 2014).

These types of near-shore structures prepared the way for the Kermac No. 16, an oil well that oil industry historians consider the first of its type. Located nearly 11 miles off Louisiana in 20 feet of water, the platform with its derrick could not be seen from shore. Two men in particular, Dean McGee and George Brown, conceived the project, secured a lease, and attracted investments from Phillips Petroleum Company, which garnered half interest, and Stanolind Oil Company, which bought in for three-eighths interest (Pratt 1997, 22). The dimensions of the finished platform, much smaller than the one Brown & Root built for the Creole offshore site in 1938, reflected Kerr-McGee's novel approach to operating the well. The platform measured 38 x 58 feet, large enough to accommodate the derrick, a supporting substructure, rotary table, shale shaker, drilling engines, a mud pump, tanks for water, fuel, and mud, and of course workers who were on-shift. Its small size required only sixteen steel pilings, each 140 feet long and pounded 104 feet into the ocean floor. The company could dispense with a larger and more expensive structure because it managed most of the well's operations and stored most of its supplies using several large tenders reclaimed from the Second World War-era naval salvage. The YF Naval barges were 260 feet long and 48 feet wide and hauled up to 2,300 long tons, sufficient capacity to store the mud pits, dry mud, cement, pipes and pipe racks, logging equipment, diesel fuel, drilling water, and housing for as many as forty workers (Pratt 1997, 23). Workers made daily commutes at first, but the long trip from port brought the company to institute a schedule of twelve-hour shifts on a seven-days on, seven-days off basis (Pratt 1997, 24).

These tenders were vulnerable to rough weather and choppy seas, and Kerr-McGee ran the risk of the barge knocking the platform off its pilings. To address this problem, the barge was docked alongside between three buffers made from wood pilings driven into the seabed, and could access the well by means of a landing attached to the platform. If forecasts called for bad weather, the tender could be towed to shore along with the rig's equipment and materials. The structure passed an important test when the Fort Lauderdale Hurricane rolled across the southern tip of Florida on September 19, 1947 and entered the Gulf as a Category 1 or 2 storm. The eye passed over New Orleans and brought a 9–11 feet storm surge to the coast, but the $450,000 Kermac No. 16 survived the event. Drilling had already begun a week earlier on September 9, and oil appeared on October 14; the well was fully operational on November 14. The well proved that offshore oil drilling could be done profitably and set off a rush among oil companies for leases throughout the Gulf, a list which included the California Oil Company, Humble Oil and Refining Company, Superior Oil Company, and Barnsdall Oil Company. Within two years of Kermac No. 16's construction, forty-four exploratory wells dotted eleven different oil fields in the Gulf of Mexico (BOEM 2023).

This sudden demand for leases created a conflict between federal and state governments. Prior to 1937, state governments exercised control over the seabed beyond their coastlines as a function of their police powers under the US Constitution, a situation that wasn't questioned by the federal government. Then, during the Second World War, the federal government began to assert its authority over the seabed due to national security concerns, and in a US Supreme Court ruling in 1947, the state of California's claim to ownership was invalidated. Similar rulings went against Texas and Louisiana in 1950, resulting in "a cessation of the expansion of offshore oil operations" (Corbitt 1970, 756). Congress tried to enact a law giving states ownership over a portion of the seabed adjacent to their coastlines but failed twice when President Harry Truman vetoed the measures. Finally, in 1953, Congress passed, and President Dwight Eisenhower signed the Outer Continental Shelf Lands Act. This law placed the submerged lands "lying seaward of state coastal waters (3 miles offshore)" under US jurisdiction, with mineral leases in these outer continental shelf lands to be administered by the US Department of the Interior (BOEM 2023). The federal-state dispute persisted, but the new law provided some clarity for the new offshore oil industry, which expanded through the next few decades.

This expansion owed to lessons learned from the Kermac No. 16, which operated until 1984 when it was capped, having produced 1.4 million barrels of oil and 307 million cubic feet of gas during its lifetime (Wells 2022). Companies utilized Kerr-McGee's platform and tender system but also worked to create mobile exploration and drilling platforms that could be relocated. The first, nicknamed "Mr. Charlie," began operations in 1954, and for the next thirty-two years drilled over 200 gas and oil wells along the Gulf Coast. Further innovation and development enabled mobile offshore drilling units (MODU) to drill in deeper waters. Before it was destroyed and sunk by an explosion and fire in 2010, the *Deepwater Horizon* drilled what was, at the time, the deepest oil well in history at 35,050 vertical feet in 4,132 feet of water. However, the disaster killed eleven workers and released 134 million gallons of oil in the Gulf of Mexico, making it one of the biggest oil spills in history. The US dependence on fossil fuels, particularly oil and gas, kept the industry at sea despite the many risks. In 2021, offshore drilling comprised 15 percent of the overall US domestic production of oil. Globally, offshore drilling made up nearly 30 percent of the overall volume in 2020, with onshore operations accounting for the remainder.

Jeffrey B. Webb

See also: Caddo Oil Field; *Deepwater Horizon*; Petroleum; Roughnecks; Santa Barbara Oil Spill; Summerland Oil Field

FURTHER READING

Bureau of Ocean Energy Management (BOEM). 2023. "OCS Lands Act History." US Department of the Interior. https://www.boem.gov/oil-gas-energy/leasing/ocs-lands-act-history (accessed October 2023).

Corbitt, James W. Jr. 1970. "The Federal-State Offshore Oil Dispute." *William and Mary Law Review*. Vol. 11. No. 3. Pp. 755–50.

Pratt, Joseph A., Tyler Priest, and Christopher J. Castaneda. 1997. *Offshore Pioneers: Brown & Root and the History of Offshore Oil and Gas*. Houston, TX: Gulf Publishing Company.

Pratt, Joseph A. 2014. "Offshore at 60: Remembering the Creole Field." *Offshore Magazine*. April 9. https://www.offshore-mag.com/home/article/16804683/offshore-at-60-remembering-the-creole-field (accessed October 2023).

Priest, Tyler. 2008. "Technology and Strategy of Petroleum Exploration in Coastal and Offshore Gulf of Mexico." In *History of the Offshore Oil and Gas Industry in Southern Louisiana*. Vol. 1: *Papers on the Evolving Offshore Industry*. New Orleans: US Department of the Interior, Minerals Management Service, Gulf of Mexico OCS Region. https://espis.boem.gov/final%20reports/4530.pdf (accessed October 2023).

Wells, B.A., and K.L. Wells. 2022. "Offshore Drilling History." American Oil & Gas Historical Society. https://aoghs.org/offshore-history/offshore-oil-history (accessed October 2023).

Keystone Pipeline System

The Keystone pipeline system is a system of interconnected oil pipelines linking Canadian and US crude reserves with refineries on the Gulf Coast of Texas and the Midwest. Originally proposed in 2005 by Calgary-based TransCanada Corporation, now TC Energy, it consists of four pipelines, three of which have been completed: the 2,147-mile Keystone Pipeline from Hardisty, Alberta to Patoka, Illinois, the 291-mile Keystone-Cushing line from Steele City, Nebraska to Cushing, Oklahoma, and the 487-mile Cushing Marketlink and 47-mile Houston Lateral connecting Cushing via Liberty County, Texas to Nederland, Texas and to Houston. The fourth one is Keystone XL, and the most controversial and widely known segment of the Keystone pipeline system, first proposed in 2008. Its construction has been on hold since January 20, 2021, when President Joe Biden revoked a presidential permit previously granted under the Trump administration through executive order. Like the original Keystone pipeline, this additional line, which has a larger diameter to carry more oil taking a shorter route through Montana, South Dakota and Nebraska, links Hardisty, 124 miles southeast of Alberta's provincial capital Edmonton, to Steele City in Nebraska, where it connects to an existing pipeline down to the Gulf of Mexico. Almost 1,200 miles long, it could carry up to 830,000 barrels of oil per day, mainly diluted bitumen from the Athabascan oil sands but also light shale oil from the Bakken formation in Montana and North Dakota.

Opponents of the pipeline cite environmental concerns, such as oil spills, damage to the Oglala Aquifer and increased carbon emissions from non-conventional oil sands production in Canada and shale production in the United States, as well as land issues, including the routing through Native lands and the dispossession of farming and ranching landowners as major concerns. Since 2011, opposition against the pipeline has become more vocal and protests in Washington, DC made national news, especially in February 2013, when an estimated 35,000 protesters rallied at the National Mall. In a time when climate change polarized the American public, Keystone XL came to represent the environmental destruction which carbon-intensive energy extraction brings to the natural world and to human communities, and underscores the necessity for climate action. The controversy also highlights how much pipeline construction and energy policy more generally had become politicized and polarized along partisan and ideological divisions. While the main fault lines separate environmentalists and the oil industry, discussions also pit jobs against the environment, big business against farmers and ranchers and Native communities against settler interests. These disagreements are further complicated because the pipeline crosses an international boundary, which requires approval by the State Department and a presidential permit, making the White House a highly visible political target for protesters. As a result, Keystone XL became a symbol around which support for climate change action could be rallied.

Since its conception in 2008, the Keystone XL pipeline has been subjected to multiple reviews by the State Department, which can grant a permit on the basis of national interest.

Three presidents addressed the issue, which reflects its political nature and the high stakes involved. After an August 2011 environmental impact report stated that no significant risk was to be expected if environmental guidelines were to be followed, the State Department postponed a final decision in November 2011. Four years later, President Obama finally rejected construction of the Keystone XL pipeline in November 2015, against strong Republican support for the project and after vetoing a bill passed by Congress the previous February. Donald Trump promised during his presidential campaign to approve the pipeline, a promise he kept during the first one hundred days of his presidency when he signed a presidential memorandum in his first week in office. He followed with a presidential permit on March 24, 2017. When his original permit was blocked by court, he issued a new permit in March 2019, which was later revoked by President Biden on his first day in office.

The Keystone XL controversy constitutes a more recent episode in a long history of transnational US–Canada pipeline politics bound up in energy diplomacy, not to mention transboundary environmental relations. It underlines the integrated and continental nature of the North American energy market since 1945, which has been institutionalized by the Canada–US Free Trade Agreement (CUSFTA). This agreement came into force in 1989. Since the 1970s, when the issues of energy independence and energy security became part of the policymaking process in the United States, Canada was coveted as a reliable supplier due to its energy resources. This included petroleum from the oil sands, which increasingly found its way south, thus creating a continental energy space. Both countries had complementary interests. Canada needed to ensure market access for its oil and the US petroleum buyers were guaranteed overland supplies from a friendly neighbor. The CUSFTA stipulated that Canada had to keep those deliveries at a proportional level even in times of supply crisis.

FIGURE 17: The Keystone pipeline system links oilfields in northern US and Canada to oil refineries, and has intensified political divisions over fossil fuel development and climate change.

The Keystone pipeline system was a response to the increasing importance of Canadian oil to US markets and envisaged to increase Canadian export capacity. It also made commercial sense. Gulf Coast refineries needed heavy crude oils including from the oil sands to replace diminishing heavy oil supplies from Venezuela and Mexico. When the Keystone XL pipeline application was first filed in September 2008, oil was sold at a record high of $148 per barrel, the United States was still importing more than it produced, and Canada was the biggest exporter of oil to the United States. However, by 2008 the global financial crisis had already set in, leading to an economic downturn and a drop in petroleum demand. At the same time, the so-called shale revolution began to reshape the American energy production landscape. Through the combination of hydraulic fracturing and horizontal drilling the shale revolution led to a production boom in the United States. Between 2007 and 2019, oil production more than doubled from roughly 5 million barrels per day to more than 12 million. Other events impacted the political environment in which the pipeline extension would be discussed. In 2010, the *Deepwater Horizon* accident and the Kalamazoo River oil spill, in which 900,000 barrels of oil spilled from an Enbridge pipeline, caused public outcries and directed Americans' attention toward the environmental impact of fossil fuel production and transportation. Together, these shifts led US policymakers to reconsider the desirability of importing more oil from Canada.

Defenders of the Keystone XL pipeline maintained that it would create jobs and ensure energy security. Others cautioned that most of the oil that would be pumped through the pipeline from Canada's oil sands to Gulf Coast refineries in Texas would be destined for foreign markets and only benefit oil companies but not US consumers or energy independence. In his decision to deny the permit, President Obama rejected the energy security argument, pointing out that for the first time in decades the United States was producing more oil than it bought from other countries. He also reminded Americans of the necessity to move toward cleaner energy. For the first time since the 1970s, Canadian oil supplies no longer played the role of providing energy security. The complementarity of interests of the two North American neighbors had ceased. This was a game changer for the oil sands producers and Alberta, which is a landlocked province and depends on pipelines to get oil to refineries and world markets. In order to support the Keystone XL project, the provincial government of Alberta announced a $1.1 billion equity investment and a $4.2 billion loan guarantee in late March 2020. When the Biden administration took power, these investments on behalf of the Alberta taxpayers were assumed to be most likely lost.

Petra Dolata

See also: Dakota Access Pipeline; *Deepwater Horizon*; Enbridge Pipeline System; Energy Independence; Hydraulic Fracking; Petroleum; Trans-Alaska Pipeline System

FURTHER READING

Brooks, Stephen. 2020. "Canada–United States Environmental Relations during the Trudeau-Trump Years: A Story of Divergence and Resilience. *American Review of Canadian Studies*. Vol. 50. No. 1. Pp. 48–65.

Ceccoli, Stephen. 2018. "Explaining Attitudes toward U.S. Energy Extraction: Offshore Drilling, the Keystone XL Pipeline, and Hydraulic Fracturing. *Social Science Quarterly*. Vol. 99. No. 2. Pp. 644–64.

Obama, Barack. 2015. "Remarks on the Keystone XL Pipeline Project." Online by Gerhard Peters and John T. Woolley. The American Presidency Project. https://www.presidency.ucsb.edu/node/311346 (accessed June 1, 2021).

Rioux, Jean-Sébastien, and Jennifer Winter. 2020. "Forks in the Road: Energy Policies in Canada and the US since the Shale Revolution." *American Review of Canadian Studies*. Vol. 50. No. Pp. 66–85.

Smithers, Gregory D. 2015. "Beyond the 'Ecological Indian': Environmental Politics and Traditional Ecological Knowledge in Modern North America." *Environmental History*. Vol. 20. No. 1. Pp. 83–111.

Wilson, Robert M. 2017. "Faces of the Climate Movement." *Environmental History*. Vol. 22. No. 1. Pp. 128–39.

Kier, Samuel Martin

Samuel Martin Kier (1813–74) is known by oil historians as the grandfather of the American oil industry. He was the first American to refine oil and commercialize it as an illuminant. While there were other northwestern Pennsylvanians who sold it as a medicinal substance in the early 1800s, such as Nathaniel Cary of Venango County, and the Seneca tribe took healing baths in crude oil, Kier was the first to successfully commercialize it on a large scale. His father, Thomas Kier, was a salt miner and in the mid-1840s when oil began contaminating the family salt wells in Tarentum, Pennsylvania, he began exploring its potential as a medicinal ointment. Although Kier was a business person in different fields, like salt, transportation, steel, and others, it is for his work refining oil, first for medicinal purposes, then for illumination fuel, that he is known. His interest in commoditizing oil into a profitable product were early steps towards creating the oil industry.

Kier learned of oil's medicinal potential when his wife, or his friends' wife, was prescribed "American Oil" by a doctor. The contradictory reports derive from two different accounts as noted by oil historian William R. Brice. Williamson and Daum (1959) claim it was Kier's wife, whereas A.L. Snell's *The Derrick's Hand-Book of Petroleum* (1898) references the wife of a druggist in Pittsburgh. In either case, Kier realized the medical prescription was the same substance permeating the family salt brine. At the time, the Kier spring pole salt wells were drilled up to 500 feet deep. Tarentum was a salt drilling region and the presence of petroleum in salt brine was a nuisance. Until a series of disasters that included burning rivers of flames, it was common practice to dump the salt brine oil into the canal system surrounding the region. That Kier took part in this practice is noteworthy. He had firsthand experience with the difficulty it caused the canal boats from his own investments in the industry.

WHALES AND CANDLES

Before Kier's distilled oil products, experiments with natural gas illuminated cities across the US and Europe. Kerosene, however, displaced whale oil, not natural gas. Candlepower, a measurement of luminous intensity, gets its name from high quality spermaceti candlelight, a substance from the cranium of sperm whales. It is commonly accepted that the oil industry saved whales from extinction, but due to continued industrial whaling through the twentieth century, this theory has been challenged.

Elia Vargas

Kier was one of three individuals in the 1840s and 1850s experimenting with petroleum to produce clean and smokeless fuel for artificial light as a replacement for the rapidly depleting and increasingly expensive whale oil, the common fuel for artificial light throughout industrialization. In 1846, Abraham Gesner, a Canadian physician and geologist, publicly demonstrated a new illuminant he called kerosene. After previous experimentations with crude oil, the English chemist James Young developed clean-burning lamp oil which he called *paraffine*, essentially the same refined substance as kerosene. Young obtained a British patent in 1850 and a US patent in 1852 for his process of making paraffin oil. The hydrocarbon paraffin was discovered by German chemist Karl von Reichenbach in 1830, when a waxy substance excreted from bituminous wood after being applied to heat. Burning oil for lamp fuel, however, dates at least to Persian alchemist Abu Bakr Muhammad ibn Zakariya al-Razi (*c.* 865–923). Kerosene derives from paraffin, an important part of the history of artificial illumination.

While Gesner is known as the inventor of a new artificial light source, Kier introduced commercial refining practices that expanded the oil industry. With the medicinal product "Petroleum, or Rock Oil: A Natural Remedy," he hired men to drive around Pennsylvania in brightly colored wagons to publicize the new medicine and sell it to the public. The product was advertised as "Kier's Petroleum, or Rock Oil, celebrated for its wonderful curative powers. A natural remedy! Procured from a well in Allegheny County, Pa., four hundred feet below the earth's surface. Put up and sold by Samuel M. Kier, 363 Liberty Street, Pittsburgh, Pa." ("Petroleum" 1932).

> The healthful balm, from nature's secret spring,
> The bloom of health and life to man will bring;
> As from her depths the magic fluid flows,
> To calm our sufferings and assuage our woes. (Henry 1873, 57)

Kier sold his product in half pint bottles for 50 cents each. The oil cost almost nothing since it was obtained from his own wells that extracted salt, producing two to three barrels of oil a day. However, the expense of advertising and distributing the medicinal product negated any profit. Nonetheless, Kier stoked demand for a natural remedy that promised to alleviate pain, ease suffering, cure diseases, make the lame to walk and the blind to see, and treat pretty much everything from rheumatism to gout to neuralgia.

In 1850, Kier brought a sample of petroleum to a commercial chemical lab in Philadelphia. Chemist James C. Booth, formerly an assistant to Henry D. Rogers and author of the first geological survey of Pennsylvania, recommended that Kier distill the substance and use it as an illuminant. Kier went into partnership with John T. Kirkpatrick, a Pittsburgh industrialist, and built the first still at Seventh Avenue in Pittsburgh. The still was a small cast-iron kettle with a cover and a distillation tube that had the capacity to distill one barrel of crude oil at a time. It was operating by 1851 and is known as the first petroleum refinery in the United States.

Around the same time Kier was bottling medicinal rock oil, he experimented with different distillation techniques for light fuel. But, the oil did not work with lamps designed for whale oil. To fix this, he designed a new lamp wick and eventually, by better managing the fire heating the oil and after improvements to the camphene lamp, a common illuminant of the time, he produced a distilled oil that burned with minimal smoke and odor which he named "Carbon Oil." Kier sold the oil for $1.50 a gallon. As interest in the product grew and refined petroleum light fuel proved to be superior to and cheaper than whale oil, Kier built a new five-barrel still. The next year, due to risk of fire and explosion, the City Council of Pittsburgh required the operation be moved to a less populated area. Kier relocated the refinery in Lawrenceville, just outside of Pittsburgh, where it remained for the rest of Kier's life.

Kier was an early pioneer in transforming crude oil into a commercial product. He was neither the first to sell oil nor the first to use it as medicine or an illuminant. But, his efforts to expand the commercial potential of it transformed the public's perception of the substance and normalized public consumption of it. The infrastructure that he initiated produced the conditions to expand oil production just as Drake Oil Well—the first successful US commercial well—began in Titusville, Pennsylvania in 1859. In many ways, Kier is a product of his circumstances, a business person with multiple stakes privy to the geology and geography of northwest Pennsylvania. Like many people of that region and era, economic gain overshadowed any concern for environmental impact. Nonetheless, his insistence in proving the many utilities of crude oil led to major growth in the burgeoning American oil industry.

Elia Vargas

See also: Cist, Jacob; Drake, Edwin Laurentine; Hart, William Aaron; Natural Gas; Petroleum; Pennsylvania Oil Boom; Sweeney, Peter; Whale Oil

FURTHER READING

American Manufacturer and Iron World (AMIW). 1901. *Greater Pittsburgh and Allegheny County, Past, Present, Future*. Pittsburgh: n.p.

Brice, William R. 2009. *Myth, Legend, Reality: Edwin L. Drake and the Early Oil Industry*. Oil City, PA: Oil Region Alliance.

Henry, J.T. 1873. *The Early and Later History of Petroleum, with Authentic Facts in Regard to Its Development in Western Pennsylvania*. Philadelphia: Jas. B. Rodgers Co.

McLaurin, John James. 1896. *Sketches in Crude Oil: Some Accidents and Incidents of the Petroleum Development in All Parts of the Globe*. Harrisburg, PA: n.p.

Schivelbusch, Wolfgang. 1995. *Disenchanted Night: The Industrialization of Light in the Nineteenth Century*. Berkeley: University of California Press.

"Petroleum in Days before Drake." 1932. In *Old Time Tales of Warren County*. Pp. 29–33. Meadville, PA: Press of Tribune Pub. Co.

Snell, A.L., ed. 1898. *The Derrick's Hand-Book of Petroleum: A Complete Chronological and Statistical Review of Petroleum Developments from 1859 to 1898*. Oil City, PA: Derrick Publishing Company.

Williamson, Harold F. and Arnold R. Daum. 1959. *The American Petroleum Industry: The Age of Illumination, 1859–1899*. Evanston: Northwestern University Press.

Kingston Coal Fly Ash Slurry Spill

The Kingston Fossil Plant on the Clinch River in Tennessee was the largest coal-burning power plant in the world at the time it began operations in 1955 under the Tennessee Valley Authority's (TVA) management. The plant supplied power for the nearby Oak Ridge National Laboratory, one of the nation's primary research facilities for nuclear energy. On December 22, 2008, the plant's storage ponds for coal fly ash slurry—a by-product of coal combustion—burst through a ruptured dike and contaminated stretches of the Emory and Clinch Rivers with 1.1 billion gallons of toxic waste. The spill far exceeded the volume of oil discharged from the *Exxon Valdez* in 1989 and the *Deepwater Horizon* well in 2010. The US Environmental Protection Agency (EPA) responded with tighter regulatory controls on the storage and disposal of coal fly ash, and environmental groups mounted campaigns to highlight risks of leaks and spills at similar sites around the country. The Kingston spill resulted in policy changes and a series of lawsuits, but more generally, called attention to the pollution created by coal-burning power plants and by fossil fuels in general.

In a coal-fired power plant, coal is burned to create steam, which is pressurized in order to operate turbines, which in turn spin generators that produce electrical power. Coal combustion releases gases like carbon monoxide, nitrogen dioxide, and sulfur dioxide, and creates residues known as boiler slag, bottom ash, and fly ash. According to one source, coal ash is second only to household trash as the US's largest type of waste material by volume (Ritter 2016). Some of this fly ash is recycled and used to make things like concrete and gypsum wallboard, but most of it ends up in landfills or storage ponds. The process at Kingston entailed capturing fine fly ash particulates in electrostatic containment units located inside the plant's smokestacks. These were cleansed with water and pumped into a pond to allow the ash to settle. From there, the wet ash was dredged and placed in a solid waste containment pond—or "dewatering area"—for further drying. At the time, fly ash containment and storage raised safety concerns, which were heightened in 2000 by a spill from Georgia Power's Plant Branch into Lake Sinclair, and again in 2005 by the Martins Creek Power Plant spill in Lower Mount Bethel Township, Pennsylvania. In 2007, another spill at Indiana Power and Light Company's Eagle Valley Generating Station made its way through a discharge canal into the White River. The TVA even expressed concerns about the storage ponds at Kingston in the years preceding the 2008 incident (Matheny and Robinson 2018).

Around 1:00 a.m. in the morning on December 22 of that year, a dike gave way that had been holding fly ash slurry in the dewatering area near the Kingston Fossil Plant. The breach allowed 1.1 billion gallons of fly ash slurry to inundate 300 acres of land and eventually spill into the Emory River. A dozen houses were damaged or destroyed and the spill cut a water line, a gas line, and power lines. The mud slick moved downriver causing large fish kills in the Emory, Clinch, and Tennessee Rivers. The cleanup involved removal of 3.5 million cubic yards of slurry and contaminated soil, and its transport to a landfill in Alabama, requiring 414 train loads over a span of eighteen months (Gang 2013). Years of monitoring and testing followed the initial removal. When the spill response officially ended in 2015, the TVA incurred more than $1 billion in cleanup and restoration charges. Coal ash contains a number of elements that are harmful if consumed or inhaled in excessive quantities. Initial testing by the TVA, the EPA, and the Tennessee Department of Environment and Conservation (TDEC) found somewhat elevated levels of arsenic, lead, and thallium, though an independent group that tested closer to the spill found that the governments' test results far understated the concentrations of heavy metals. They found eight different metals that exceeded EPA drinking water limits, with arsenic registering at thirty-five times the limit (Dewan 2009).

Because coal ash contains these substances, the spill posed serious health risks for residents and cleanup workers: "Short-term exposure can bring irritation of the nose and throat, dizziness, nausea, vomiting, and shortness of breath. Long-term exposure can lead to liver damage, kidney damage, cardiac arrhythmia, and a variety of cancers" (Turrentine 2019). In 2013, a group of sixty workers and their families filed a lawsuit against Jacobs Engineering Group, which served as a TVA contractor during the cleanup. Their suit alleged that the company failed to warn them about the hazards of coal ash and failed to provide protective equipment. It also alleged that the plaintiffs "developed lung and skin cancers, COPD, coronary artery disease and other serious or fatal illnesses" as a consequence of their work in the Kingston Fossil Plant cleanup (Grzincic 2022). The spill reenergized debate in the United States over whether the EPA should classify coal ash as "hazardous waste" and thus establish the agency's authority to regulate its disposal. Speaking at a 2009 congressional hearing on the issue, Ken Ladwig of the Electric Power Research Institute urged Congress not to authorize the EPA to declare coal ash hazardous waste. Ladwig offered what might be called the industry's perspective: "potentially 190 to 411 coal-fired generating units could shut down due to future costs of hazardous waste regulation of CCBs [coal combustion by-products]," putting "40,000 and 97,000 coal-fired MW [megawatts] at risk" (Ladwig 2009).

Despite the efforts of environmental groups, the EPA declined in 2014 to rule that coal ash was a hazardous waste, then proceeded to create new standards for storage and disposal of coal ash and other combustion residuals under its authority to regulate "nonhazardous waste." It required plants with leaking, unlined impoundments to begin closure and to halt new ash deposits, but those without leaks were permitted to continue operations (Clements 2020). It also offered generous extensions for plants that could demonstrate a "lack of capacity" of coal ash storage. Impoundments without liners were required to install monitoring systems but were given a two-and-a-half-year grace period before achieving compliance. Environmentalists complained the regulations did not go far enough to secure the coal ash slurry impoundments, whereas energy companies criticized them for imposing novel, and in their opinion, financially burdensome rules (Clements 2020). The question might be asked, would these regulations, if followed prior to 2008, have prevented the Kingston disaster?

A post-event investigation tried to pinpoint the source of the problem. AECOM, an infrastructure consulting firm, received a contract from the TVA to study the site and identify probable causes of the failure. They noted that fly ash had been piled up at an increasing rate, which added weight to the load in the solid waste containment area; this added weight bore down heavily on what they called "unusual slimes" at the "foundation level." The term "slimes" refers to the fine-grained sediments at the very bottom of the coal ash pile. They added, "the slimes are unusual in that they are soft, wet, had low shear strength and were susceptible to creep" (AECOM 2009, 5). They found that the coal ash exhibited no evidence of "consolidation or densification under the weight of fill placed over older ash" and so it remained "very loose and susceptible to collapse." This resulted in "static liquefaction failure," meaning that the loose wet ash began to flow "as if it were a viscous liquid." This produced an avalanche effect in which the cumulative weight of progressive ash pile failures carried the entire volume over the dike. In their words, "the failure was very sudden and dramatic, with each successive slide causing rapid movement of the failing mass, with only minimal delay between slides" (AECOM 2009, 4). The study did note that "seepage had been observed over the years" along the dike that was breached by the coal ash slide, which indicates that a more rigorous monitoring system like the one enacted by the EPA in 2015 might have alerted the TVA to potential hazards. However, it seems that the foundation problem—the "unusual slimes" at the bottom—developed over the course of decades and addressing the dike's seepage might not have been sufficient to contain the force of the slide once it had been initiated.

Under considerable pressure, the EPA released a list of the forty-four most hazardous coal ash impoundments in the United States in the year following the Kingston Fossil Plant spill (Morford 2009). This gave state governments, power plant operators, and environmental groups plenty to work with in their efforts to improve the safety of coal-fired power plants. In the end, it provided fossil fuel critics another argument for accelerating a shift from fossil fuels to renewable energy sources like solar and wind, in this instance because of the ongoing environmental hazard of surface and groundwater contamination from coal ash slurry. By the mid-2020s, the trend seemed clear. The United States obtained about 21.9 percent of its total electricity generation in 2021 from coal-fired power plants, down from 37.4 percent in 2012 (EIA 2022).

Jeffrey B. Webb

See also: Acid Rain; Church Rock Uranium Mill Spill; Clean Power Plan of 2015; Coal; Martin County Coal Slurry Spill; Tennessee Valley Authority

FURTHER READING

AECOM. 2009. "Executive Summary for Root Cause Analysis of Kingston Dredge Cell Failure." Tennessee Valley Authority. June 26. https://web.archive.org/web/20100528051649/http://www.tva.gov/kingston/rca/FINAL-062609_Executive_Summary-REV3.pdf (accessed October 2023).

Clements, Katherine. 2020. "The Coal Ash Rule Trilogy Spanning Obama, Trump, and the D.C. Circuit." Environment & Energy Law Program, Harvard University. January 28. https://eelp.law.harvard.edu/2020/01/the-coal-ash-rule-trilogy-spanning-obama-trump-and-the-d-c-circuit/#_ftnref3 (accessed October 2023).

Dewan, Shaila. 2009. "Metal Levels Found High in Tributary after Spill." *The New York Times*. January 1.

Gang, Duane W. 2013. "Kingston Coal Ash Spill: 5 Years, $1 Billion in Cleanup and No Regulations Later." *The Tennessean*. December 21. https://www.tennessean.com/story/news/2013/12/20/kingston-coal-ash-spill-5-years-1-billion-in-cleanup-and-no-regulations-later/4153801/ (accessed October 2023).

Grzincic, Barbara. 2022. "TVA Contractor Can't Ditch $3 Bln Suit by Coal-ash Cleanup Workers–6th Circ." Reuters. May 19. https://www.reuters.com/legal/government/tva-contractor-cant-ditch-3-bln-suit-by-coal-ash-cleanup-workers-6th-circ-2022-05-19/ (accessed October 2023).

Ladwig, Ken. 2009. "Written Testimony before the Subcommittee on Energy and Environment, United States House of Representatives, Washington, DC." Electric Power Research Institute. December 10. http://mydocs.epri.com/docs/CorporateDocuments/SectorPages/Portfolio/Environment/Ken%20Ladwig%20Written%20Testimony%20USHouse-E%26E%20 10Dec2009%20FINAL.pdf (accessed October 2023).

Matheny, Jim, and Grant Robinson. 2018. "Historic Disaster: 10 years after the Ash Spill." 10News Website. December 21. https://www.wbir.com/article/news/historic-disaster-10-years-after-the-ash-spill/51-3125fb4d-93bc-4dd8-9ce1-63a449fa6ff9 (accessed October 2023).

Morford, Stacy. 2009. "EPA Releases Secret List of 44 High-Risk Coal Ash Ponds." Inside Climate News. June 29. https://insideclimatenews.org/news/29062009/epa-releases-secret-list-44-high-risk-coal-ash-ponds/ (accessed October 2023).

Ritter, Stephen K. 2016. "A New Life for Coal Ash." *Chemical and Engineering News*. February 15. https://cen.acs.org/articles/94/i7/New-Life-Coal-Ash.html (accessed October 2023).

Turrentine, Jeff. 2019. "Coal Ash Is Hazardous. Coal Ash Is Waste. But According to the EPA, Coal Ash Is Not 'Hazardous Waste.'" OnEarth: Culture and Politics. Natural Resources Defense Council. https://www.nrdc.org/onearth/coal-ash-hazardous-coal-ash-waste-according-epa-coal-ash-not-hazardous-waste (accessed October 2023).

U.S. Energy Information Agency (EIA). 2022. "Electric Power Monthly: Table 1.1. Net Generation by Energy Source: Total (All Sectors), 2012–November 2022." US Department of Energy. https://www.eia.gov/electricity/monthly/epm_table_grapher.php?t=table_1_01 (accessed October 2023).

KitchenAid Appliances

Although the KitchenAid label can be found on everything from dishwashers to refrigerators, the brand originated with the first commercially available electric stand mixers. These were manufactured and sold to industrial and military customers during the First World War before being adapted and sold for domestic use. In the 1930s, competition appeared with the Mixmaster brand, which pushed the maker of KitchenAid toward innovation. Eventually, KitchenAid became a key part of the "all-electric" kitchens of the 1950s and beyond.

In 1914, the Hobart Electric Manufacturing Company of Troy, Ohio debuted the Hobart Model H, designed by Herbert L. Johnson, a harness developer turned electrical engineer. The Model H featured an eighty-quart bucket, which was clearly designed for commercial bakeries. The product soon made its way into the military; the Model H became standard equipment in the galleys of new US Navy vessels then under construction. Sales were good given the arms build-up undertaken by the United States as part of its preparedness program and the onset of German submarine warfare against Allied shipping.

As the war came to an end, Hobart's Troy Metal Products subsidiary sought to pivot to the home market by selling the H-5 KitchenAid to consumers beginning in 1919. Company lore holds that the brand name was created when a Hobart executive's wife was given the chance to test a prototype. She declared, "I don't care what you call it, but I know it's the best kitchen aid I've ever had!" (Kindy 2019). However, the company's transition back to manufacturing for domestic markets was not an easy one.

In 1920, only about a third of all American homes had access to electricity, and even fewer could afford the H-5's steep $189 price tag, which is $3,000 in 2022. But the company pressed on through the 1920s. It developed and marketed the C-10 to commercial kitchens and soda fountains under brand names like BakersAid and FountainAid. Two decades before home Tupperware parties, the company turned to a mostly female salesforce to market their product. In 1928, the G Model debuted with a smaller size more suitable for domestic households. Celebrities like Ginger Rogers, Henry Ford, and John Barrymore were all advertised as satisfied Model G customers.

Still marketed primarily at upscale households, the brand struggled in the early years of the Great Depression, particularly with the debut of the smaller, more affordable Sunbeam Mixmaster in 1930. In the 1930s, the use of electricity expanded thanks to consumer demand for electrification and the policies of the New Deal. Stand mixers like KitchenAid and models from Hamilton Beach and Sunbeam were at the forefront of this revolution as utility companies like Union Electric Light and Power in St. Louis touted the advantages of electric kitchens to prospective customers. Households eagerly adopted electrical appliances for reasons of convenience, but also to acquire the newest symbols of middle-class status. In this period, Hobart continued selling products under its own name for commercial and industrial kitchens, while KitchenAid appliances were sold to homeowners and apartment dwellers in the consumer market.

Hobart continued to manufacture models of KitchenAid electrical appliances designed and priced for modest wage-earners, but then in 1937 the company pivoted towards high culture by hiring industrial designer Egmont Arens to give KitchenAid stand mixers a stylish makeover. Arens came up with the Model K, an Art Deco "Streamline Moderne" design whose shape and interlocking bowl attachment is still used by KitchenAid mixers some eighty years later. In an age of home cooking that emphasized the technologies of speed and convenience, the KitchenAid and the "all-electric kitchen" it was part of stood for modernity, even when it remained out of the price range of many consumers.

When the Second World War began, Hobart shifted its production entirely to munitions which shuttered KitchenAid production for half a decade. Just as at the end of the First World War, however, the company was prepared for the consumer revolution to follow. Along with new models of mixer that remained backwards-compatible with older models, something not always true about KitchenAid's competitors, the brand expanded into new markets. In 1949, the KD-10 home dishwasher debuted, an offspring of Hobart's purchase of the Crescent Company some two decades earlier during the last major consumerist turn in US buying.

The brand continued to expand through the expansion of the post-war American economy, adding a KitchenAid food waste disposer, hot water dispenser, and trash compactor to the company's catalog of products. A decade later, after purchasing the Mississippi-based Chambers Corporation, Hobart took KitchenAid into the production and sale of ovens and stovetops, making it one of the largest kitchen appliance brands in America by the mid-1980s, with $150 million in sales in 1983.

In 1981, Hobart merged with Dart and Kraft to avoid a hostile takeover by a Canadian firm, and in 1985, the Whirlpool Corporation sought to purchase the KitchenAid mixer brand from Kraft. The Emerson Electric Company began manufacturing KitchenAid's dishwasher and trash compactor lines on behalf of Whirlpool. Rivals White Consolidated Industries and Magic Chef both filed antitrust lawsuits against these mergers. The Federal Trade Commission (FTC) ultimately ruled in Whirlpool's favor in 1986, which allowed the merger to proceed.

Under Whirlpool's management, KitchenAid returned to producing kitchen equipment for upper-income consumers. The company marketed to high-end appliance dealers and retailers with the goal of encouraging customers to buy an all-KitchenAid branded kitchen, complete with matching appliances, colors, and styles. This remained true even as Whirlpool divided its subsidiaries into independent units, with sales to the high-end market tripling KitchenAid's output by the end of the 1980s. By this point, the backwards compatibility of KitchenAid had turned it into an heirloom item for a new generation of consumers with mixers remembered as "Grandma's KitchenAid," a revered object. This too was part of Whirlpool's overall marketing strategy, as seen when the company took advantage of the Persian Gulf War of 1990–1 to market a family-friendly image to consumers, despite the subsequent recession.

In the decades surrounding the turn of the twentieth century, cable television, the internet, and social media bristled with food-related content like the Food Network, an entire channel of programs which first appeared in 1993. Americans responded by returning KitchenAid branded appliances to their once-lofty position in the marketplace. Celebrity chefs like Anthony Bourdain, Rachel Ray, and Gordon Ramsay built upon a longer tradition of television icons like Julia Child, who prominently featured a blue KitchenAid K5SS stand mixer as part of her show's kitchen set. Child's blue mixer has been displayed in the Smithsonian National Museum of American History. As such, the brand persisted as part of the ideal of American domesticity, as well as an important part of most individuals' connection to energy in form of home electrical appliances.

Michael Davis

See also: Evard, Mary E.A.W.; Frigidaire; Hobart Electric Manufacturing Company; Home Energy Efficiency; Underwriters Laboratory; Upton Machine Company and Whirlpool Corporation; Westinghouse, George

FURTHER READING

Kindy, David. 2019. "For 100 Years, KitchenAid Has Been the Stand-up Brand of Stand Mixers." *Smithsonian Magazine*. August 7. https://www.smithsonianmag.com/smithsonian-institution/100-years-kitchenaid-has-been-stand-brand-stand-mixers-180972838/ (accessed October 2023).

Meikle, Jeffrey L. 1997. "Material Doubts: The Consequences of Plastic." *Environmental History*. Vol. 2. No. 3. Pp. 278–300.

Möllers, Nina. 2012. "Electrifying the World: Representations of Energy and Modern Life at World's Fairs, 1893–1982." In *Past and Present Energy Societies: How Energy Connects Politics, Technologies and Cultures*. Eds. Nina Möllers and Karin Zachmann. Pp. 45–78. Bielefeld, DE: Transcript Verlag.

Nye, David E. 1992. *Electrifying America: Social Meanings of a New Technology, 1880–1940*. Cambridge, MA: MIT Press.

Woolf, Arthur G. 1987. "The Residential Adoption of Electricity in Early Twentieth-Century America." *The Energy Journal*. Vol. 8. No. 2. Pp. 19–30.

The Koch Brothers

The "Koch Brothers" is the common reference for Charles (1935–) and David (1940–2019) Koch, the proprietors of Koch Industries, the second-largest privately held company in the United States with annual revenues of $100 billion (Goldmacher 2019). Headquartered in Wichita, Kansas, Koch Industries is a multinational conglomerate, with subsidiaries involved in ranching, fertilizers, chemicals, commodities trading and investing, and most notably, the manufacturing, refining and distribution of petroleum (Fortune 2020). In the 1920s the brothers' father, Fred Koch (1900–67), with a Massachusetts Institute of Technology classmate, improved the efficiency of extracting gasoline from crude oil, then founding the company's first iteration, Winkler-Koch Engineering Company (Mayer 2016). Today, Koch Industries owns 4,000 miles of pipelines and oil refineries (SEC 2005). In the past four decades, Charles Koch, the CEO and chairman, and his brother David invested billions of dollars into US politics, donating at the local to national level in favor of policies supporting minimal social services, deregulation of industry, free trade, lower personal and corporate taxes, and climate denial.

Fred Koch invented a new process for oil refining in 1927, but due to its threat to major US oil companies, by 1929 he faced hefty lawsuits for patent infringement. After fifteen years at war with the turn-of-the-century's corporate energy behemoths, he was finally able to reach a settlement of $1.5 million. Unable to operate in the United States during this period, he looked abroad to sell his refining method. By 1930, Fred Koch secured an advanced payment agreement with Stalin's regime in the Soviet Union to train Russian engineers and facilitate the building of fifteen oil refineries under the first of Stalin's five-year plans. This initial contract set the foundations for both the Russian petroleum industry and Fred Koch's career. When Soviet officials began to copy the technology and build their own refineries for one hundred more plants, Fred Koch was hired by the USSR for technical assistance. In 1934, one year after Adolf Hitler was named chancellor of Germany, Koch's firm provided engineering plans and began constructing an enormous oil refinery in Hamburg. Completed by 1935 and able to process 1,000 tons of crude oil a day, it became the third-largest refinery in the Third Reich (Mayer 2016). Fred Koch continued to work with the Soviets and the Nazis before the onset of the Second World War, building his early fortune, and in 1932, married Mary Robinson (1907–90).

Koch and Robinson had four sons: Frederick (1933–2020), Charles, and twins, David and William (1940–). Fred and Mary Koch raised their children in Kansas, in a highly disciplinarian environment, emphasizing hard work and personal development. In young adulthood, Charles and David Koch joined their father as members of the John Birch Society, an anti-communist, archconservative group comprising right-wing businessmen from across the country who were also opposed to the 1960s American civil rights movement.

After finishing a bachelor of science in engineering and master's degrees in nuclear and chemical engineering, Charles Koch returned to Kansas in 1961 to help run the family business. In 1967, Fred Koch passed away, leaving the business to his sons. Charles Koch became chairman and CEO and the company was renamed Koch Industries, and focused primarily on refining oil, operating pipelines, and cattle ranching (Mayer 2010).

ASPEN SUMMIT OF 2010

The Koch Brothers have been singled out by environmental organizations for their role in obstructing environmental regulation. For instance, the brothers hosted the now-infamous 2010 Aspen Summit. With speakers from the American Enterprise Institute, Americans for Prosperity, George Mason University's Mercatus Center, and others involved in the climate denial movement, the summit accelerated efforts to spread climate denialism and prevent regulatory action on climate change.

Keriann Conroy and Kate Clark

In 1969, Koch industries acquired the majority share in the Pine Bend Refinery in Rosemount, Minnesota. Eight years before his death, Fred Koch had bought a one-third interest, and when the company's value increased years later it proved to be sound investment due to its geographic location. Situated near the Canadian border, it was easy to purchase inexpensive, heavy crude oil from Canada, allowing Pine Bend's profit margin to shadow others. Further, with increasing environmental regulations at the time, it became more difficult for new refineries to compete in the area. In 2012, the Pine Bend Refinery accounted for 25 percent of the 1.2 million barrels of oil the US imported from Canada's tar sands daily, with the capacity to process 330,000 barrels of crude a day (Mayer 2016). However, crude oil extracted from Canada's tar sands require immense amounts of energy compared to other crude oil, thus contributing to significantly higher amounts of greenhouse gas emissions. Large oil spills associated with the Pine Bend Refinery have resulted in over $15 million in fines (Mattera 2013). Koch Industries' role in refining up to 25 percent of Canadian oil sands later drew them into national controversy over the Keystone XL Pipeline

In 1983, after a long legal feud, Charles and David Koch bought out their brothers' shares in Koch Industries for $1.1 billion, leaving the two with 80 percent of the company's stock. Charles Koch continued as head of Koch Industries, residing in Wichita with his wife. David Koch moved to New York City, remaining the vice president of the company and CEO of its Chemical Technology Group (Mayer 2010). The brothers continued to build and expand the company in the coming decades, its growth coinciding with increased legal challenges because of stricter environmental regulation.

In the United States, Koch Industries is responsible for the processing of approximately 800,000 barrels of crude oil per day, while the corporation has been subject to multiple lawsuits. In 1995, in one of largest Clean Water Act cases in its history, the US Justice Department, the US Environmental Protection Agency, and the US Coast Guard filed a civil suit against Koch Industries for the discharge of millions of gallons of oil and 300 separate spills in Alabama, Kansas, Louisiana, Missouri, Oklahoma, and Texas. By January 2000, Koch

Industries agreed to pay $30 million for the federal environmental violations. That same year, Koch Industries was charged with a ninety-seven-count indictment for concealing data calculating the discharge of ninety-one metric tons of benzene, a highly toxic, liquid chemical compound refined from crude oil (Mattera 2013). A 2012 report from the Political Economy Research Institute at the University of Massachusetts Amherst cited Koch Industries among the top ten corporate polluters of air, land, and water in the nation.

The Koch Brothers maintained a high public profile due to their political activity, namely advancing their life-long libertarian ideology. Over the last half century, the brothers have assembled an extensive political network, hosting dozens of strategy conferences and donor summits, and shaping local, state, and national policy. In 1977, the Kochs funded the nation's first prominent libertarian think tank, the Cato Institute, donating $11 million from 1986 to 1993. Between 1998 and 2008, the brothers' foundations, their spouses, companies, and their political action committee, KochPAC, spent hundreds of millions of dollars on political campaigns and lobbying efforts. In 2004, David Koch founded Americans for Prosperity, a right-wing organization advocating for policies to weaken the public sector. The brothers' network has also funded right-wing think thanks including the Heritage Foundation, the Competitive Enterprise Institute, the National Center for Policy Analysis, and the Institute for Humane Studies. The Kochs' historically secretive political efforts became more conspicuous after 2008 with their network attacking the Obama administration and funding its opposition in the Tea Party and climate denial movements. Their considerable donations and movement-building within American politics were in the service of advancing the interests of energy corporations, particularly those involved with the production of fossil fuels.

Keriann Conroy and Kate Clark

See also: American Petroleum Institute; Benedum, Michael Late; Bush, George H.W.; Cheney, Richard Bruce "Dick"; Getty, Jean Paul; Global Climate Coalition; Halliburton Company; Rockefeller, John D.

FURTHER READING

Conway, Erik M., and Naomi Oreskes. 2010. *Merchants of Doubt: How a Handful of Scientists Obscured the Truth on Issues from Tobacco Smoke to Climate Change*. New York: Bloomsbury Press.

Doherty, Brian. 2008. *Radicals for Capitalism: A Freewheeling History of the American Libertarian Movement*. New York: PublicAffairs.

Forbes. "Charles Koch." 2020. https://www.forbes.com/profile/charles-koch/#3cb95bf657d7 (accessed May 4, 2020).

Fortune. 2020. "Koch Industries." https://fortune.com/most-important-private-companies/2016/koch-industries/ (accessed May 4, 2020).

Fred and Mary Koch Foundation (FMKF). 2023. "Who We Are." kochfamilyfoundation.org/who-we-are (accessed November 2023).

Goldmacher, Shane. 2019. "How David Koch and His Brother Shaped American Politics." *The New York Times*. August 2019. https://www.nytimes.com/2019/08/23/us/politics/david-koch-republican-politics.html (accessed May 4, 2020).

Koch, Charles G. 2015. *Good Profit: How Creating Values for Others Build One of the Most Successful Companies*. New York: Random House LLC.

Leonard, Christopher. 2019. *Kochland: The Secret History of Koch Industries and Corporate Power in America*. New York: Simon & Schuster.

Mattera, Phillip. 2013. "Koch Industries: Corporate Rap Sheet." *Corporate Research Project*. September. https://www.corp-research.org/koch_industries (accessed May 1, 2020).
Mayer, Jane. 2010. "The Koch Brothers' Covert Ops." *The New Yorker*. August. https://www.newyorker.com/magazine/2010/08/30/covert-operations (accessed May 1, 2020).
Mayer, Jane. 2016. *Dark Money*. New York: Doubleday.
Oxbow Corporation. 2020. "Who We Are." https://www.oxbow.com/About_us_Our_Company_Who_We_Are.html (accessed May 4, 2020).
Securities and Exchange Commission (SEC). 2005. "Koch Industries, Inc." https://www.sec.gov/Archives/edgar/data/41077/000119312505225697/dex996.htm (accessed May 4, 2020).
Shulman, Daniel. 2014. *Sons of Wichita: How the Koch Brothers became America's Most Powerful and Private Dynasty*. New York: Grand Central Publishing.

Krebs Mine Disaster

On January 7, 1892, an explosion in the Osage Coal and Mining Company's Mine No. 11 near Krebs, in present-day Oklahoma, killed nearly one hundred miners and injured perhaps another two hundred. It was the second in seven years at the same mine, as thirteen died in an 1885 explosion. Mine safety was a concern from the beginning of coal mining itself, but more frequent and more deadly accidents occurred as coal became the chief source of energy in the Industrial Revolution. Railroads and steam-powered machinery consumed increasing amounts of coal; in 1859, US mines produced 15.6 million tons of coal, which increased to 253.7 million forty years later (Adams 2023). This rapid expansion led to numerous mining accidents, even in the relatively undeveloped Indian Territory where the Osage Coal and Mining Company ran their operations. Mining disasters like the one near Krebs led to intense debates about mine safety, as well as union organizing activity by workers to secure safer working conditions.

The seeds of commercial coal mining were planted in Indian Territory in 1872 when entrepreneur James J. McAlester found coal on his own property, then married into the Choctaw nation to establish rights to coal deposits on Native American lands. McAlester formed the Oklahoma Mining Company and began to market coal to the railroads then working their way into the region, including the Choctaw, Oklahoma, and Gulf Railroad and the Missouri, Kansas and Texas Railway, commonly called the "Katy." The Katy came under the control of railroad tycoon Jay Gould, who was also buying up coal mining operations in Indian Territory. Eventually, McAlester merged his coal interests with the Osage Coal and Mining Company, which in 1888 became part of Gould's Katy railroad enterprise. Katy also acquired the Osage Coal and Mining Company's rival Atoka Coal and Mining Company. This flurry of acquisitions demonstrates the close connections between railroad construction and coal mining in the context of US western expansion in the late nineteenth century.

Because of this demand, coal production expanded rapidly in Indian Territory, from 150,000 tons in 1881 to more than 600,000 in 1887. Coal miners were paid by the ton, rather than by the hour or day, which encouraged a quicker pace, without careful attention to the precautions necessary given the dangers inherent in mining. Workers were exposed to slate and rock falls, roof and face collapses, railroad and haulage car injuries, and of course fires and explosions from various kinds of coal mine gases and dust. Also, without proper ventilation, workers died from asphyxiation (Corn 1983, 258). Historian Steven Sewell noted that "Oklahoma's coal mines during the early years of development had the highest death rate in the nation per million tons produced," and acquired a "reputation as the most dangerous in the United States" (1994, 97, 100). In 1887, the Atoka's Savanna mine suffered a disaster when an explosive charge set to dislodge material from the coal face detonated a much larger explosion of methane and oxygen gases, which miners called "firedamp." Six died in the blast, and then another twelve died trying to rescue their coworkers, fatally trapped in the "afterdamp"—a mixture of carbon monoxide and carbon dioxide that lingers in the wake of a fire (Sewell 1994, 98–9).

Atoka closed the Savanna mine after the 1887 disaster, but the explosion at Osage Coal and Mining Company's Krebs mine in 1892 came too close on its heels before much could be done to require stronger safety measures from mine operators. During a shift change a little after 5:00 p.m., 335 workers were in the mine, many of whom were waiting for the elevator to carry them out through the 470-foot mineshaft (Committee 1892, 7). Procedures called for a blasting pause during shift changes, but the shot-firers went early and detonated a charge. In a report from the US House of Representative Committee on Territories filed February 5, 1892, the opinion of Thomas Fleming was included. The report described him as a mining expert and former superintendent of the Krebs mine for eight years. Fleming "'said that the whole blame should be placed upon the shot-firers, who fired the blast too soon.'" The report later named the firers as John Hurley and John Williams. Fleming continued: "'A windy shot caused the catastrophe. The blast was overcharged. It should have been fired at 5:30 o'clock, after the miners had left the mine, in which case the explosion would have occurred, but only 5 or 6 men would have been killed. As it was the shot was fired at 5:07 o'clock, before the men had ascended from the mine'" (Committee 1892, 6).

The explosive charge triggered a chain reaction that combusted the accumulated "firedamp" and coal dust in the cavernous mine. The larger explosion could be heard for miles and catapulted the elevator out of the mineshaft. Over a hundred died in the explosion or from their burns, including six young boys who minded the ventilation fans (Sewell 1994, 98).

The report included many details from the location and statements from victims and rescuers. The writer observed many "heartrending scenes" and remarked, "it seems utterly impossible to describe properly any of the horrible experiences which are presented on all sides." He described a "sorrowing throng" of grieving wives, mothers, and companions searching for loved ones among the "scores of corpses and dying comrades." Added to the horrific sight, the victims' "heads, arms, legs, hands, and feet were in many instances torn from the trunks." The writer went on to say "The injured present a most pitiable sight. All were burned and many mangled by flying rocks and timbers." He then quoted survivor Peter Christie as saying, "'The dying wails and shrieks of pain of the injured were frightful. Even Dante could not picture an inferno such as I have witnessed during the last night'" (Committee 1892, 5). The report highlighted the "heroism" of Edward Morgan, who insisted on entering the mine after the explosion by himself to determine if it was safe to begin rescue operations. It also cheered the fact that "men of all nationalities are aiding in the work of rescue," including "Americans, Irishmen, Scotchmen, Polanders, Welshmen, Italians, Swedes."

However, in the report there's a mention of tension between the "white miners" and African Americans who appeared on the second day to assist in the rescue. Details are scarce, but the writer claimed that the "negroes went to Krebs and assisted in the work in only a half-hearted way, and one of their number was heard to say that it served the miners right to have been killed" which apparently enraged the white crowd. The report went on to say that "the United States deputy marshal, anticipating some such trouble, was on hand with a posse, and they drove the colored men from the place at the point of Winchesters." The end result was that "some time since the white miners refused to work with the negroes." The writer clearly believed the African Americans to be at fault, as the report included this account under the heading, "Negroes Create Trouble" (Committee 1892, 5). This should be understood in the context of race relations in Indian Territory and the Oklahoma Territory to the west. Black leaders envisioned Oklahoma as a future safe haven for freed slaves who faced racial discrimination in the eastern and southern United States. Yet, as one study found, "negroes in Indian Territory were subjected to racial discrimination by Indians as well as whites," anti-black demonstrations broke out, and in many cases Native Americans and whites joined efforts to force blacks to leave the territories (Tolson 1966, 39).

Earlier mining accidents in Indian Territory and Oklahoma Territory brought Congress to enact a law that required that coal mines meet certain standards for ventilation and appointed a mine inspector for the US territories. President Benjamin Harrison's choice for the position, Luke Bryan, didn't arrive in the region until 1894, well after the Krebs mine disaster. Mine conditions remained very unsafe in the West and throughout the rest of the nation. The rapid expansion of the coal mining industry was clear a factor. There were 35,600 coal miners in the United States in 1870, which ballooned to 395,607 thirty years later in 1899, so the number of fatalities was bound to rise (Corn 1983, 262). In the year 1870, 211 coal mine workers died in mine accidents, and somewhere between 200 and 300 died each year until 1878. Fatalities jumped higher and higher each year after that, and between 1895 and 1899, a thousand or more were killed each year in four of the five years. Over the entire thirty-year period of 1870–99, 17,645 coal mine workers perished in mine explosions and accidents (Corn 1983, 262). In just one month in 1907, dubbed "Bloody December," 703 miners died in five mine explosions (Brnich 2010). These shocking numbers testified to the massive deficiency in government regulation at the beginning of the twentieth century.

According to historian William Graebner, "the problem of industrial safety—in the nineteenth century a malingering illness to which occasional relief was administered—had by the twentieth century become an epidemic of crisis proportions, demanding immediate attention" (1976, 3). Even so, industry resistance and a general preference for state, rather than federal, level control over mine safety regulation delayed vigorous federal action in the Progressive Era. One important development was the establishment in 1910 of the US Bureau of Mines, a new federal agency with a mandate "to make diligent investigation of the methods of mining, especially in relation to the safety of miners, the use of explosives, the prevention of accidents." Further legislation requiring more frequent inspections and more stringent enforcement measures would come only after more major disasters, in the form of the Federal Coal Mine Safety Act (1952) following the December, 1951 New Orient mine explosion, and the Federal Coal Mine Health and Safety Act (1969) in the wake of the November, 1969 Farmington disaster.

Jeffrey B. Webb

See also: Centralia Mine Disaster; Cherry Mine Disaster; Dawson Mine Disaster; Farmington Mine Disaster; Monongah Mine Disaster; Scofield Mine Disaster; Upper Big Branch Mine Disaster; West Frankfort Mine Disaster

FURTHER READING

Adams, Sean Patrick. 2003. "The US Coal Industry in the Nineteenth Century." EH.Net Encyclopedia. Edited by Robert Whaples. January. https://eh.net/encyclopedia/the-us-coal-industry-in-the-nineteenth-century-2/ (accessed October 2023).

Brnich, Michael J. Jr., and Kathleen M. Kowalski-Trakofker. 2010. "Underground Coal Mine Disasters 1900-2010: Events, Responses, and a Look to the Future." The National Institute for Occupational Safety and Health (NIOSH), Centers for Disease Control and Prevention. https://www.cdc.gov/niosh/mining/userfiles/works/pdfs/ucmdn.pdf (accessed October 2023).

Corn, Jacqueline Karnell. 1983. "'Dark as a Dungeon:' Environment and Coal Miners' Health and Safety in Nineteenth Century America." *Environmental Review*. Vol. 7 No. 3. Pp. 256–68.

Committee on the Territories. 1892. "Report on Mines and Mining in the Indian Territory." US House of Representatives, 52nd Congress, 1st session. Report No. 162.

Graebner, William. 1976. *Coal-Mining Safety in the Progressive Period: The Political Economy of Reform*. Lexington, KY: The University Press of Kentucky.

Tolson, Arthur Lincoln. 1966. "The Negro in Oklahoma Territory, 1889–1907: A Study in Racial Discrimination." Ph.D. Thesis. University of Oklahoma.

Sewell, Steven L. 1994. "Development of Coal Mining in Oklahoma." *Mining History Journal*. Vol. 1. Pp. 95–103.

Lakes, Arthur

The coal, oil, and natural gas mining industries in the United States developed alongside advancements in the field of geology in the nineteenth century. Geology is the study of the earth's materials and the way those materials are structured, as well as the natural processes that act on those materials. An important geologist from the late nineteenth century is Arthur Lakes (1844–1917), an English-born naturalist, geologist, writer, teacher, and illustrator who spent a portion of his career in the 1880s and early 1890s at the Colorado School of Mines in Golden, Colorado. His career illustrates the importance of scientific thinking and expert knowledge in the utilization of natural resources for America's commercial and industrial expansion. His vast literary output provided some of the guideposts used by a generation of prospectors and developers who built the foundations of the western US fossil fuel industry.

Arthur Lakes was born in Martock, in England's southwestern county of Somerset, and spent some of his childhood in the Channel Islands. Lakes studied theology and natural science at Queen's College, Oxford University before leaving England in 1866 for Canada. He soon left New Brunswick for the American West and settled in Golden, Colorado where he helped to establish the Calvary Episcopal Church. The bishop hired Lakes to teach at Jarvis Hall, a newly established parochial school, where he began cultivating an interest in the natural history of the region. Frequent hikes with his students helped Lakes to create a collection of specimens for use in his classes. On one of these hikes, Lakes and his students discovered a large, serrated tooth that was sent to Yale University for identification, and later determined to be from a *Tyrannosaurus rex*. Yale's Othniel Charles Marsh, professor of paleontology and head of the Peabody Museum of Natural History, began a relationship with Lakes, who gathered dinosaur bones on Colorado's Front Range near Morrison for Marsh's research. The area explored by Lakes and his fossil hunters became known as "Dinosaur Ridge" for the large quantity of fossils, and the eventual identification of well-known dinosaurs like *Allosaurus*, *Apatosaurus*, *Diplodocus*, and *Stegosaurus*. In 1879, Marsh traveled to Colorado to explore the Arkansas River, and met with Lakes at Como, Wyoming, where Marsh had established another major dinosaur fossil collection site.

These associations, and his earlier teaching at Jarvis Hall, earned Lakes an appointment in 1880 as full-time professor of geology and museum curator at the Colorado School of Mines. For the next thirteen years, Lakes taught courses, continued his expeditions, and wrote extensively. One of his early pamphlets, *History and Geology of the San Juan* (1882), documented the recent history of mining in southwest Colorado's San Juan range, beginning in 1874 with A.W. Burrows' prospecting on Mineral Point Mountain. In 1885, the school's annual report to the state governor included a lengthy analysis of coal mined at Trinidad and Crested Butte written by Lakes

> to show that the school, now freed in great part from the expense of providing buildings and apparatus for students, has commenced what promises to be the most valuable portion of its legitimate work: the examination of untested mineral resources and comparatively new mineral districts of the State, thus adding each year to a stock of information that should prove useful to citizens of the State, and to capitalists residing in other portions of the country. (Annual 1886, 7–8)

This statement illustrates the importance of Lakes' geological research in Colorado, which was providing information to state leaders and potential investors outside the state about the location, quality, and extent of the region's mineral resources for the purpose of commercial development, including coal.

One of Lakes' more important publications was his *Geology of Colorado Ore Deposits* (1888), which was essentially "a rough guide or map to the prospector in search of precious metals or other economic products" within the state (Lakes 1888, 158). Though not specifically about coal, the book contains long sections identifying places where coal had been found and would likely be found later. For example, in describing one particular rock formation, Lakes wrote: "The *Laramie Cretaceous* has a thick bed of white sandstone near its base, which is utilized for building sandstone, and quarried at Trinidad, Cañon City and elsewhere. In this sandstone formation lie the principal coal seams, the largest and most worked averaging 6 to 8 feet in thickness" (157–8). In his follow up study, published as the Colorado School of Mines annual report to the governor and titled *Geology of Colorado Coal Fields* (1889), Lakes more explicitly addressed the question of where and how to find coal in the state.

In his study, Lakes encouraged prospectors to look for a specific configuration of rock layers atop "an outcrop of white or rusty sandstone," and then told them that under that, "you will find the first coal seam" (28). His concern was that miners were trying to develop very thin bands of coal that would not ultimately produce profitable mines, as he noted, "a good deal of profitless boring and shafting has been done on the plains" (28). Further, he coached his readers to look for a certain type of coal that could be processed into coke. He wrote, "costly works have been erected before now in Colorado in the neighborhood of coal mines with a view to producing coke, and the coal was found on trial not to make coke at all. In such cases a simple laboratory experiment, taking but a few minutes and costing a mere trifle, would have saved thousands of dollars" (29). Lakes took as his mission to provide the best geological information available to coal companies searching for commercially viable coal seams, and to encourage scientific analysis of deposits to measure its value at the marketplace.

Lakes left Colorado School of Mines in 1893 to become associate western editor of the *Colliery Engineer and Metal Miner* magazine with an office in Denver. The school's website notes that in that same year, the entire freshman class was suspended for playing a prank on Prof. Lakes, and many students were readmitted after they had apologized ("Timeline" 2022). It is unknown whether the two were related events but clearly the year constituted a break in his career. As magazine editor, Lakes kept his schedule of travel around the region, reporting on developments in the coal mining industry and in geology. Lakes wrote a popular book titled *Prospecting for Gold and Silver in North America*, which went into three editions (1895, 1896, 1899). He then moved to part time at *Colliery Engineer* in 1903 and continued writing for the magazine until 1912, when it closed its Denver operation. During this period, Lake served a geology consultant for the American Exploitation Company, which bought out profitable gold and silver mines, as well as limestone and gypsum quarries. An avid sketch artist and painter his whole life—he illustrated his books and articles with many of his drawings—Lakes engaged his creative inclinations later in life in British Columbia, where he retired in 1912 to be with his sons who worked locally as mining engineers.

When Arthur Lakes died in 1917, he left behind a legacy as an important figure in the history of geology and applied science. He authored over 800 books, pamphlets, and articles aimed at improving the prospecting craft in the American West, including coal mining in Colorado, New Mexico, and Wyoming. Western coal production constituted only a small portion of the overall output in the United States, but it served a critical role in supplying western and transcontinental railroads with fuel as the western region of the nation developed in the decades surrounding the turn of the twentieth century.

Jeffrey B. Webb

See also: Coal; Coke; Dawson Mine Disaster; Holmes, Joseph Austin; Ludlow Massacre; North Antelope Rochelle Mine; Osgood, John Cleveland; Scofield Mine Disaster; Transcontinental Railroad

FURTHER READING

"Annual Report of the State School of Mines." 1886. Denver: Rocky Mountain News Company.

Lakes, Arthur. 1888. *Geology of Colorado Ore Deposits*. Denver: News Printing Company.

Lakes, Arthur. 1889. *Geology of Colorado Coal Fields*. In *Annual Report of Field Work and Analyses*. Colorado School of Mines. Denver: News Printing Company.

"Timeline." 2022. Colorado School of Mines History. Colorado School of Mines website. https://libguides.mines.edu/Mines-History-Timeline/1890s (accessed October 2023).

Wolff, David A. 2014. *Industrializing the Rockies: Growth, Competition, and Turmoil in the Coalfields of Colorado and Wyoming, 1868–1914*. Boulder, CO: University Press of Colorado.

Lithium-Ion Battery

The lithium-ion battery was developed in the late 1970s and 1980s by chemists M. Stanley Whittingham, John B. Goodenough, and Akira Yoshino. These three shared the 2019 Nobel Prize in chemistry for the invention. Lithium-ion batteries were commercialized in 1991 by Sony Corporation. The lithium-ion battery boom began in the late twentieth and early twenty-first centuries when these long-lasting, rechargeable power sources enabled increased access to information technology. The rise of Li-ion batteries has coincided with the rising popularity of rechargeable electronic devices such as laptops, smartphones, camcorders, power tools, power banks, electric vehicles, and hybrid-electric vehicles. While other types of rechargeable batteries exist, ones made from lithium are comparatively lightweight, energy efficient, and cost-effective.

The chemical element lithium (Li) is a relatively abundant alkali metal that can be found in seawater, geothermal pools, igneous rocks such as pegmatite, and especially in alkali deposits on or near the earth's surface, where it can be more concentrated. Lithium has a high energy density as well as a high heat capacity. As such, lithium has been used throughout history for numerous purposes such as ceramics, rocketry, and medicine. However, since the early twenty-first century lithium production for rechargeable batteries has outstripped these other applications, with a major part of the world's lithium resources going to lithium-ion batteries.

Handheld technologies such as an iPhone may use a mere twenty grams of lithium (in one cell), while electric vehicles may use up to fifteen kilograms of the material contained in several cells. Lithium-ion batteries can be used and recharged for two to three years, which is longer than alternative rechargeable batteries and single use batteries. The fact that the batteries are lightweight makes them uniquely important. However, they can be reactive and may even catch fire, as happened with the Samsung Note 7 phone. Lithium-ion batteries are increasingly ubiquitous amidst the rise of smartphones, which estimates claim nearly half of the world's population uses. With decreasing cost and rising availability of said devices, people now enjoy increased internet connectivity and can access the web almost anywhere, anytime. Moreover, electric vehicles powered by lithium-ion batteries are oft-hailed as "green" since they reduce place point pollution.

Lithium-ion batteries continue to have a profound impact on daily life in both industrializing and industrialized regions of the world. Environmental impacts of Li-ion batteries occur most where they are extracted from earth's surface, namely in the Andes Mountains of South America and at Thacker Pass, Nevada. Electricity is needed to charge the batteries throughout use, which is done the traditional way by plugging it into the wall and drawing from the legacy electrical grid. Furthermore, lithium-ion batteries present an environmental problem upon the end of their lifetimes. Many are recycled, which is costly and complicated, but many are not, and end up in municipal landfills.

The demand for lithium has fueled rapid expansion of lithium mining from *salars* or salt-rich dried lake beds often found in mountainous areas where alkali materials accumulated over millennia. These lithium deposits are located in at least twenty countries, including Afghanistan, Argentina, Australia, Bolivia, Canada, Chile, China, Iran, Mexico, Portugal, the United States, and Zimbabwe. The "Lithium Triangle" in the aforementioned Andean region intersecting Bolivia, Argentina, and Chile contains an estimated 40 to 70 percent of global lithium resources. Many countries with lithium deposits do not have the high-technology production facilities to take lithium from powdery elemental Lithium Carbonate (Li2CO3) to a finished battery. Poorer countries produce the raw product and wealthy countries turn the commodity into a value-added product, which serves to deepen pre-existing economic and power disparities. Furthermore, the industry is dominated by oligopoly of only three companies: Albermarle Corporation, Sociedad Quimica y Minera de Chile, and FMC Corporation. Conflict over this mineral is possible, as consumer demand for lithium-ion batteries grows exponentially and surpassing $60 billion by 2024 (Dickinson 2018). The total amount of lithium resources and reserves are estimated to be 39 million tons, but the industry does not openly disclose numbers.

In the United States, there are numerous deposits of lithium, including in Arizona, California, Colorado, New Mexico, and South Dakota—which had its first mine in 1898. By 1938, the brine method had been first developed in Searles Lake, California, where a commercially viable operation began. Throughout the early to mid-twentieth century, the United States dominated lithium production. By the 1970s, lithium was still a somewhat obscure mineral, but production increased greatly by the end of the twentieth century as a result of the demand for medicine, military rockets, ceramics, and glass. By the 1980s and 1990s when rechargeable batteries increased in popularity, South American operations entered the market using cheaper brining methods. Then lithium prices fell. Key deposits in the United States have been sites of extraction, including Kings Mountain in the North and South Carolina border region, a geothermal pool near Salton Sea, California, and Great Salt Lake, Utah. However, the United States imports the vast majority of its lithium and lithium-ion batteries.

In order to produce Li-ion batteries, industrial firms first extract lithium from a brining process located at lithium deposit beds. The salt beds are pumped with water, the resulting liquid is then stored in large, shallow pools, which appear as a range of colors from red to blue. Magnesium chloride is added to the pools, and the sun evaporates the water, which becomes concentrated and isolates the lithium in the brine. Evaporation takes between twelve and twenty-four months. Large quantities of water are used in brining. Up to half a million tons of water, pumped from local aquifers via groundwater wells, may be required to yield one ton of lithium. Local hydro-geological processes are significantly impacted by lithium production, but this research is only recently emerging. The water table can also lower due to constant extraction of groundwater. This terrestrial mode of lithium production is often located in remote, arid basins such as Salar de Uyuni, Bolivia where evaporation is enhanced by clear skies, high elevation, and lack of precipitation. The brining method is now much more efficient and cheaper than the ocean-extraction and rock-mining methods of lithium production that were used in history (but still in use in Australia and China).

With Li-ion batteries, electronics can be transported away from power sources for hours or even days at a time. Information technology has been transformed by this innovation, and lithium-ion batteries have the potential to revolutionize transportation by powering electronic vehicles. Provided, that is, that the electricity used to recharge those vehicles is produced in power plants fueled by renewable energy resources like solar and wind. Spent Li-ion batteries can provide energy, but also release harmful substances into the natural environment. Recycling costs remain higher than mining for raw lithium, and as such there is little incentive to harvest metals from spent lithium-ion batteries. Future generations will confront massive amounts of electronic waste.

Sam Orndorff

See also: Digital Revolution; Electricity; Fuel Cell; Renewable Energy; Sport Utility Vehicles; Truck Transportation Technology

FURTHER READING

Bradley, Dwight C., et al. 2017. "Lithium." In *Critical Mineral Resources of the United States—Economic and Environmental Geology and Prospects for Future Supply*. Ed. Klaus J. Schulz, et al. Chapter K. US Geological Survey Professional Paper 1802. https://pubs.er.usgs.gov/publication/pp1802K (accessed October 2023).

Davis, Nicola, and Hannah Devlin. 2019. "Nobel Prize in Chemistry Awarded for Work on Lithium-ion Batteries." *The Guardian*. October 9. https://www.theguardian.com/science/2019/oct/09/nobel-prize-in-chemistry-awarded-for-work-on-lithium-ion-batteries?CMP=Share_iOSApp_Other (accessed October 2023).

Dickson, Ellsworth. 2018. "Lithium Triangle." *Resource World Magazine*. https://resourceworld.com/lithium-triangle/ (accessed October 2023).

Greenwood, Phoebe, et al. 2020. "Will Green Technology Kill Chile's Deserts?" *The Guardian*. Video. February 18. https://www.theguardian.com/global-development/video/2020/feb/18/will-green-technology-kill-chiles-deserts-video (accessed October 2023).

Lowell Waterpower System

The Lowell Waterpower System consists of 5.6 miles of canals in the city of Lowell, Massachusetts. The canals, built over the course of fifty years, powered the textile industry during the first half of the nineteenth century. Several US and British citizens, during trips to Great Britain, memorized the designs of the machines in British textile mills, since the British prohibited the export of these machines. These men carried the plans they memorized back to the United States, changed the designs as necessary, and set up factories. Initially, these factories were located in places like Pawtucket, Rhode Island and Waltham, Massachusetts, and somewhat later, in Lowell. The cluster of factories in Lowell made the city one of the most important places in the United States for mechanized textile production drawing energy from water power in the canals. Historian Patrick Malone argues that Lowell became "a model for many future efforts to harness large-scale waterpower sites in America" (2009, 5).

The story of the Lowell Waterpower System began in a sleepy settlement known as East Chelmsford. Dudley Atkins Tyng, William Coombs, Joseph Tyler, Nicholas Johnson, and Joshua Carter founded a limited liability corporation, The Proprietors of Locks and Canals on the Merrimack River, on June 27, 1792. The incorporators knew that people from New Hampshire wanted to ship goods and logs to Newburyport, Massachusetts. However, the Pawtucket Falls on the Merrimack River impeded transportation, since the river dropped 32 feet in about a mile. The proprietors saw the need for a canal at East Chelmsford. They built the Pawtucket Canal, more than a mile in length with four locks, as a highway for ships and goods to bypass the falls. The Pawtucket Canal proved especially useful, for a few years, in supplying Newburyport shipyards with logs. Unfortunately, for the proprietors, at least, a competing canal—the Middlesex Canal—soon opened. The Middlesex Canal took ten years to build (1793–1803) but, once completed, connected the Merrimack River to Boston. Thus, the Middlesex Canal stole the Pawtucket Canal's thunder. Furthermore, people praised the Middlesex Canal and studied it as they developed plans for the Erie Canal. The Pawtucket Canal, and the community of East Chelmsford, stagnated and seemed doomed to obscurity.

LORDS OF THE LOOM AND LORDS OF THE LASH

In addition to playing a critical role in the US Industrial Revolution, the Associates, the Lords of the Loom, formed a profitable alliance with slaveowners, the Lords of the Lash. Mill owners depended on slaves to grow the raw material for their mills. In turn, they sold cheap goods, called slave cloth, to masters. The Lords of the Loom generally opposed free-soil and abolitionist sentiment, largely due to commercial entanglements with slave owners.

Evan C. Rothera

External events soon intervened, however, in the form of a man named Samuel Slater (1768–1835). Born in England, Slater began working in a cotton mill at age ten. As an adult, he learned that the new United States of America hoped to develop similar machines and create a US-based textile industry, in spite of British law forbidding the export of the machines. In a move that won him fame in the United States as the "Father of the American Industrial Revolution" and infamy in Great Britain as "Slater the Traitor," Slater memorized the designs and left for New York in 1789. In the United States he joined up with Moses Brown, Smith Brown, and William Almy. After some bargaining, he adjusted the designs and built new machines for a factory that opened in 1793 in Pawtucket, Rhode Island. Eli Whitney's cotton gin significantly reduced the amount of time and labor necessary to process cotton. Consequently, southern planters began to grow more and more cotton to feed the seemingly insatiable demand of northern and British textile mills. In this way, slave labor grew the raw material to feed a new industry that would be supercharged by waterpower in Pawtucket, Waltham, Lowell, and elsewhere.

A Boston businessman and merchant named Francis Cabot Lowell (1775–1817) spent several years in Britain in the early 1810s. Lowell became intensely interested in the textile industry and like Slater before him, memorized machine designs. As the War of 1812 began, Lowell returned to the United States. Once back in Massachusetts, with the support of a group of powerful Bostonians later dubbed the Boston Associates, men such as Abbott Lawrence, Amos Lawrence, Nathan Appleton, and Patrick Tracy Jackson, Lowell founded the Boston Manufacturing Company (BMC) at Waltham, Massachusetts. He hired the gifted machinist Paul Moody and, using the designs he had memorized, they built efficient spinning and weaving machines and received a patent in 1815 for a power loom. In 1814, the BMC built its first mill beside the Charles River in Waltham. At the end of the War of 1812, Lowell lobbied for textiles to be included in the Tariff of 1816 to protect the industry against a flood of cheap British goods. Although successful, he died of pneumonia in 1817. The BMC's Waltham Mill succeeded, but the Associates knew they needed a water source that could generate more power.

Before long, the Associates realized that the sleepy settlement of East Chelmsford, situated along the roaring Merrimack River, could become the nucleus of a new factory town. In 1821, the BMC purchased the charter of the old Proprietors of Locks and Canals and formed the Merrimack Manufacturing Company (MMC). Kirk Boott became the first agent and treasurer of the company, which was initially capitalized at $600,000. The Associates rechristened the new town to honor Francis Cabot Lowell. They immediately initiated a widening and deepening project on the Pawtucket Canal in order to build additional canals off the Pawtucket Canal to run their machinery. The first of the new canals, the Merrimack Canal, powered the machinery in the MMC and opened in 1822. In the following fifteen years, the Associates built and opened five additional canals: the Hamilton (1825), Lowell (1828), Lawrence (1831), Western (1831), and Eastern Canals (1835). These canals powered additional factories and created additional income, because the Associates could sell waterpower to other companies.

Lowell began as a small factory town, but quickly grew into a larger town and then a city, with many cotton mills, all powered by the canals and the raw energy of the Merrimack River. By the 1840s, many people believed the canal system produced as much power as possible. Chief Engineer of Locks and Canals James B. Francis (1815–92) determined this was not the case. He designed the Northern Canal and the Moody Street feeder to increase the capacity of the system. Both opened in 1847, along with the Pawtucket Gatehouse. The gatehouse controlled how much water flowed from the Merrimack River into the Northern Canal. This was important because the canal stood near the Pawtucket Dam and needed protection in case of flooding. Francis also designed a gate at one of the locks on the Pawtucket Canal that could be dropped, in case of flooding, to protect the town. Most of the laborers who built the canals were Irish immigrants, many of whom had fled the potato famine. Their energy carved out canals that channeled the Merrimack River's energy into powering machinery to fuel the textile industry.

At the mill in Waltham, Francis Cabot Lowell favored the employment of women as workers, specifically women in the fifteen-to-thirty-five-year age range. The Associates also favored women workers in Lowell mills. Mill girls, or Lowell mill girls, did not receive as much money as men and this no doubt appealed to money-conscious owners. By 1840, the Lowell mills employed thousands of workers, the vast majority of them women. Women worked in the mills for many reasons, everything from seeking economic independence to escaping oppressive male relatives. Although their wages did not equal those of men, many women gained some measure of independence by working in the mills. To be sure, conditions in the mills were often dangerous and scholars debate whether factories provided a good alternative for women. Women formed the first union of working women in 1845, known as the Lowell Female Labor Reform Association. This union criticized industrialism and agitated for better conditions for workers.

The canals and the gatehouse became a Historic Civil Engineering Landmark in 1984 and a Historic Mechanical Engineering Landmark in 1985. They are currently part of Lowell National Historical Park, a site that helps visitors, through tours of some of the mills and canal boat rides, appreciate Lowell's importance in the history of the early Industrial Revolution in America, and in the history of energy in the United States more generally.

Evan C. Rothera

See also: Austin Dam; Federal Water Power Act of 1920; Hydroelectric Power; Industrial Revolution; Slater, Samuel; Vulcan Street Plant; Waterpower

FURTHER READING

Dublin, Thomas. 1979. *Women at Work: The Transformation of Community in Lowell, Massachusetts, 1826–1860*. New York: Columbia University Press.

Gross, Laurence F. 1993. *The Course of Industrial Decline: The Boott Cotton Mills of Lowell, Massachusetts, 1835–1955*. Baltimore, MD: The Johns Hopkins University Press.

Malone, Patrick M. 2009. *Waterpower in Lowell: Engineering and Industry in Nineteenth-Century America*. Baltimore, MD: The Johns Hopkins University Press.

National Park Service (NPS). 2019. "Lowell National Historic Park." https://www.nps.gov/lowe/index.htm (accessed January 31, 2020).

Sankovitch, Nina. 2017. *The Lowells of Massachusetts: An American Family*. New York: St. Martin's Press.

Stanton, Cathy. 2006. *The Lowell Experiment: Public History in a Postindustrial City*. Amherst, MA: University of Massachusetts Press.

The Ludlow Massacre

The Ludlow Massacre occurred during the morning of April 20, 1914 when members of the Colorado National Guard, under the command of the Colorado Fuel and Iron Company (CF&I), opened fire on a tent colony of 1,200 striking miners and their families. In total, the massacre claimed the lives of twenty-one individuals, including eleven children. The massacre was the bloody culmination of a fourteen-month strike that had been supported by the United Mine Workers of America.

Prior to the massacre, southern Colorado routinely found itself embroiled in bitter labor standoffs with the 1913–14 coal strike directly preceding the events of Ludlow. The strike began in September 1913 when CF&I, owned and controlled by oil baron John D. Rockefeller, refused to follow several labor laws, rebuffed worker demands for unionization, and refused to jettison the company's aggressive guard system. The miners were challenging conditions that were common for industrial workers across the nation. Back then, workers could be fired and evicted from their homes for trivial offenses. Moreover, when they were paid, their wages were converted into company scrip that was traded in at company stores that charged exorbitant prices. These conditions were exacerbated by the fact that Colorado mine workers died at a rate three-and-a-half times the national average between the years 1909 and 1913.

Once the strike commenced, CF&I kicked the miners and their families out of company owned shacks and off company land, had union organizers arrested, and rushed in strikebreakers. The United Mine Workers set up the tent community in Ludlow, Colorado to house around 10,000 men, women, and children (estimates vary) who had been ousted from their homes. Ludlow was not the only tent community constructed during the strike, but it was the largest of seven erected in the months leading up to the outbreak of violence.

The massacre can be seen as the result of CF&I and mine operator's mismanagement of the situation. Initial attempts to resolve the strike consisted of using camp guards, hiring vigilantes, and employing detectives from the Baldwin-Felts Detective Agency, which was gaining a reputation for strikebreaking. Their efforts made the situation worse by stoking violence with meagerly armed miners. The situation escalated when CF&I pressured Colorado governor Elias Ammons to deploy troops from the Colorado National Guard. Governor Ammons acquiesced in October of 1914, wherein the Colorado National Guard quashed miner activity, placing the makeshift mining communities under near-dictatorial rule in the process. Despite the strong-armed tactics, the strike dragged on. In the winter of 1914, twenty-five members of the United Mine Workers were indicted on charges of conspiring in the restraint of trade by a federal grand jury. By contrast, no charges were levied against the mine owners or strikebreaking forces they hired.

Louis Tikas, a Greek immigrant, emerged as the leader of the protesters. Leading up to the massacre, Tikas and other mine workers butted heads with company security for months, especially with national guardsman commander Karl Linderfelt. On the eve of the massacre, which happened to fall on the Greek Orthodox Easter Sunday, the strikers of Ludlow were picnicking and playing baseball. In an exchange that is part of Ludlow lore, the peaceful occasion was disrupted when five rifle-equipped gunmen stopped by some of the players and allegedly told them, “Have your fun today! We’ll have our roast tomorrow!”

On the massacre’s fated day, Linderfelt approached the tent camp to demand that Tikas release an unidentified person. At a tense meeting at the Ludlow depot, just outside the camp, Tikas insisted that the demanded person could not be found. An irate Linderfelt denounced Tikas as the strike leader and retreated back to the camp. What exactly happened next remains a mystery, but the massacre commenced when a group of Linderfelt-led guardsmen tore through the camp with machine guns and cannons. Over the next fourteen hours, tents with women and children were set ablaze and protesters attempted to seek refuge by any means necessary as the guardsmen fired on anyone they could see, including pets according to one survivor’s account. In the course of the fracas, Linderfelt found Tikas whereupon the strike leader and two other miners were taken prisoner. All three were killed while in custody.

Following the massacre, a ten-day-long series of clashes ensued, pitting National Guardsmen against riled-up miners hellbent on revenge. Fighting spread to nearby mining communities, including in Trinidad, Lynn, and Aguilar, Colorado, which claimed at least twenty-nine lives. Amid this turmoil, President Woodrow Wilson sent in the US Army to restore order.

In the days after the massacre, Colorado Governor Elias Ammons ordered a three-person board of National Guard officers to investigate the situation. The final report, filed by lawyers Major Edward J. Boughton and Captain William Danks, painted the miners in resolutely negative terms. Their report documented, with horror, the death of National Guardsman Albert Martin who “had been shot through the mouth, powder stains evidencing that a gun had been held to his lips. His head had been caved in, and his brains exuded on the ground” (quoted in DeStefanis 2006, 199). The incident was held up to show “the savage blood lust of this southern European peasantry. In this connection we find also that without exception where dying or wounded adversaries, whether soldiers or civilians, had fallen into the hands of the barbarians, they were tortured or mutilated” (quoted in DeStefanis 2006, 199). They concluded the report by chiding the coal mine owners only slightly, and then called the striking miners a “class of ignorant, lawless, and savage Southern European peasants” (quoted in DeStefanis 2006, 199).

Where the official report of the massacre treated the strikebreakers with scorn and the mine owners with kid gloves, it drew harsh criticism from newspapers around the country, who were usually business-friendly. News stories struck a tone of sympathy for the massacre’s victims and one of outrage toward mine owners and their hired troops. Such coverage of a labor conflict was unusual at the time. Despite stoking national outrage, however, little was gained from the strike. John D. Rockefeller implemented his Industrial Representation Plan that instituted a system for company-sanctioned representation that became a model for company unions. However, the aftermath of the massacre saw a further retrenchment of the struggle between unions and coal barons, which had become endemic in the coal industry.

Todd K. Platts

See also: Coal; Miner’s and Laborer’s Benevolent Association; Osgood, John Cleveland; Paint Creek Mine War; Rockefeller, John D.; United Mine Workers of America

FURTHER READING

Andrews, Thomas G. 2008. *Killing for Coal: America's Deadliest Labor War*. Cambridge, MA: Harvard University Press.

Burt, Elizabeth V. 2011. "Shocking Atrocities in Colorado: Newspapers' Responses to the Ludlow Massacre." *American Journalism*. Vol. 28. No. 3. Pp. 61–83.

DeStefanis, Anthony R. 2006. "Violence and the Colorado National Guard: Masculinity, Race, Class, and Identity in the 1913–1914 Southern Colorado Coal Strike." In *Mining Women: Gender in the Development of a Global Industry, 1670 to 2005*. Eds. Jaclyn J. Gier and Laurie Mercier. Pp. 195–212. New York: Palgrave Macmillan.

DeStefanis, Anthony R. 2012. "The Road to Ludlow: Breaking the 1913–14 Southern Colorado Coal Strike." *Journal of the Historical Society*. Vol. 12. No. 3. Pp. 341–90.

Foner, Philip S. 1980. *History of the Labor Movement in the United States*. Vol. 6: *The AFL in the Progressive Era, 1910–1915*. New York: International Publishers.

Mahan, Alfred Thayer

Alfred Thayer Mahan (1840–1914) was the preeminent theorist and intellectual of the US Navy in the late nineteenth and early twentieth-century era of coal-powered vessels, a time when the Navy was rising as a global force and the United States as an imperial state. Mahan supported the acquisition of coaling stations in the Pacific and Caribbean to support naval operations. Mahan's father was an instructor at West Point, and Mahan attended the US Naval Academy, after which he served at sea during the US Civil War and after. The US Navy decayed in the decades after the war, and Mahan advocated building a modern navy competitive with European naval power, both for the protection of the United States from foreign invasion and for the advance of American trade. He became President of the Naval War College in 1886 and retired from naval service a decade later to devote his time to research and writing.

Mahan believed that if the US Navy was going to protect American interests in international waters and overseas, it needed a network of coaling stations not under the control of any other power and it needed to exclude foreign coaling stations from its vicinity to the extent possible. When he began publishing on naval strategy, the United States had no overseas bases. The immense appetite of naval vessels for coal made it difficult for them to operate on the open ocean without a coaling facility nearby. Mahan distrusted an emphasis on speed or "coal endurance"—the ability of a ship to travel long distances before needing to recoal—because he believed that supporting a ship's fighting capabilities was a higher priority. Mahan believed that the primary mission of a successful navy was to carry out "blue-water" operations on the open ocean with large fleets rather than to support land forces or defend the country's coasts, operations in which naval forces would be closer to fuel and other resources. Coastal defense, he believed, was best left to land fortifications.

The need for coaling stations well outside US territorial waters to support fleets in the open ocean justified the expansion of the US colonial empire, particularly in the Caribbean and the Pacific in the era of the Spanish–American War, the annexation of Hawaii and the US-sponsored building of the Panama Canal. This led Mahan to support imperialism, along with his friend and admirer Theodore Roosevelt, who served as Assistant Secretary of the Navy under William McKinley before he became governor of New York, vice president, and finally president. Mahan supported the US annexation of Hawaii to provide support for Pacific operations and to prevent maritime rivals from acquiring a valuable coaling station from which to threaten the United States. He also supported US annexation of the Philippines after the Spanish–American War, as did Roosevelt.

Although Britain's Royal Navy was the dominant force on the world's oceans during Mahan's time, he did not see Britain but Germany as the main naval rival of the United States and supported cooperation between Britain and America against Germany. He further believed that British–American cooperation was fostered by their cultural similarities. This does not mean that he viewed cooperation as inevitable, and he was willing to contemplate or even plan for war with Britain. In such a conflict, the coal resources of British Columbia would enable Britain to threaten the United States as could no other European naval power. However, Mahan believed that an attack by the US Pacific Fleet on Vancouver Island might dispose of the British coal facilities at Nanaimo. It would be the task of the army to sweep into Canada and capture the British coaling facilities at Pictou, Nova Scotia on the Atlantic side, although with good fortune or a British blunder it might be possible for the US Navy to take Pictou along with the Royal Navy's port at Halifax before the army could get there. His analysis was similar to that of British naval authorities who regarded limited access to coal as a vulnerability in the western Atlantic. Mahan was also concerned with the rise of Japan as a potential rival to the United States in the Pacific.

MAHAN ON COAL AND NAVAL STRATEGY

It should be an inviolable resolution of our national policy, that no foreign state should henceforth acquire a coaling position within three thousand miles of San Francisco,—a distance which includes the Hawaiian and Galapagos islands and the coast of Central America. For fuel is the life of modern naval war; it is the food of the ship; without it the modern monsters of the deep die of inanition. Around it, therefore, cluster some of the most important considerations of naval strategy. In the Caribbean and in the Atlantic we are confronted with many a foreign coal depot, bidding us stand to our arms, even as Carthage bade Rome; but let us not acquiesce in an addition to our dangers, a further diversion of our strength, by being forestalled in the North Pacific (Mahan 1897, 26).

William E. Burns

Despite Mahan's belief in the centrality of coaling stations to naval strategy in his own time, his naval theories were not dependent on the coal age and rested on his historical studies of the conflicts between European powers during the age of sail. The principal vehicle by which his theories were disseminated were his historical studies, all devoted to the period before the introduction of steam-powered ships: *The Influence of Sea Power upon History, 1660–1783* (1890), *The Influence of Sea Power upon the French Revolution and Empire, 1793–1812* (1892), *The Life of Nelson: The Embodiment of the Sea Power of Great Britain* (1897), and *Sea Power in Relation to the War of 1812* (1905). Mahan also contributed to magazines such as the *Atlantic* and *Collier's Weekly*. Mahan, who did not particularly enjoy service at sea, even preferred sailing ships to steam ships on an aesthetic level, although he knew that the day of the sailing ship navy was gone forever. The title of his autobiography, *From Sail to Steam: Recollections of Naval Life* (1907), identifies the rise of steam power as the crucial naval transformation during his career.

Mahan's works were influential far beyond the United States, as they were widely translated and promoted by supporters of strong navies in many countries, including Great Britain, Germany, and Japan, and Mahan's ideas continued to influence naval strategy into the Second World War. However, the conversion of the US Navy from coal to more efficient oil-fueled vessels in the early twentieth century, a transformation begun in Mahan's own lifetime, made the part played by coaling stations in his strategic vision obsolete. Petroleum products like fuel oil and gasoline supplanted coal as the essential energy component of twentieth-century national security strategies devised in Washington, DC and in the capitals of the major nations of the world.

William E. Burns

See also: Coal; Coaling Stations; Colliers; Panama Canal; Steam Power; US Fuel Administration

FURTHER READING

Bourne, Kenneth, and Carl Boyd. 1968. "Captain Mahan's 'War' with Great Britain." *Proceedings of the US Naval Institute*. Vol. 94. No. 7. Pp. 71–8.

Gray, Steven. 2017. *Steam Power and Sea Power: Coal, the Royal Navy, and the British Empire, c.1870–1914*. London: Palgrave Macmillan.

Mahan, Alfred Thayer. 1897. *The Interest of America in Sea Power, Present and Future*. Boston: Little, Brown.

Puleston, W.D. 1939. *Mahan: The Life and Work of Captain Alfred Thayer Mahan, U.S.N.* New Haven: Yale University Press.

Shulman, Peter. 2015. *Coal and Empire: The Birth of Energy Security in Industrial America*. Baltimore: Johns Hopkins University Press.

Smith, Crosbie. 2018. *Coal, Steam and Ships: Engineering, Enterprise and Empire on the Nineteenth-Century Seas*. Cambridge: Cambridge University Press.

Sumida, Jon Tetsuro. 1997. *Inventing Grand Strategy and Teaching Command: The Classic Works of Alfred Thayer Mahan Reconsidered*. Baltimore: Johns Hopkins University Press.

Mandatory Oil Import Program

Between 1959 and 1973 the United States instituted the Mandatory Oil Import Program (MOIP) under which imported oil was limited for national security reasons, first to roughly 9 percent of total demand, and after 1962, to 12.2 percent of domestic production. Directed by the Oil Import Administration within the US Department of the Interior, the program regulated the importation of foreign oil—crude and unfinished oils, residual oil and refined products—into the United States, which was subdivided into five regional districts, four of them east of the Rocky Mountains. This regulatory regime was both complex and contested throughout its existence as it underwent many modifications, including exemptions for certain hemispheric producers. These import controls were shaped by competition between energy carriers, coal versus oil, within the federal administration, Justice versus State Department, and between oil companies, major corporations versus independent producers and refiners. The many controversies over the program highlight the political nature and multilevel—national, transnational, and international—dimensions of petroleum markets in the three decades after the end of the Second World War, which also occasioned the advent of a new global oil order.

In the early 1950s, the US oil industry was the most developed in the world, but countries in the Middle East, which had extensive reserves and could produce at low cost, soon became significant suppliers of crude oil shifting the geographical center of world oil production from the Western Hemisphere to the Middle East. At the same time, the post-war boom years in the United States were characterized by high oil demand from government due to the Korean War and Cold War. High industrial and consumer demand for petroleum ensured that the United States scored the highest per capita energy consumption in the world. Domestic production could not keep up with the surge in energy demand and already in 1948, the United States had become a net importer of crude oil.

The MOIP mainly targeted low-price oil imported from the Middle East by the US-based international oil majors. Since the early 1950s these imports had been on the rise and independent oil producers in Texas, Oklahoma, and California and their congressional representatives as well as the struggling coal industry in the East, who could not compete with cheap residual oil imports, called on the federal government to curtail the increasing market share of foreign oil. Already in the first half of the 1950s Congress and regulators such as the Texas Railroad Commission tried to put pressure on the majors to curb their imports of cheap Middle Eastern oil. In 1957, when nearly 12 percent of US domestic demand was met by foreign imports, a voluntary import quota program was announced. Due to lack of enforcement, the program's limited applicability to crude oil, potential antitrust implications, and the arrival of many new oil producers and refiners who lacked historical quotas, this voluntary program was replaced only two years later by the MOIP. Many of the provisions and rationales were carried over, most importantly the invocation of the national security argument to justify import quotas.

When President Eisenhower announced the Mandatory Oil Import Program in his Presidential Proclamation 3279 of March 10, 1959, discussions on oil security and import restrictions had been going on for years, if not decades. Ever since the 1930s, when domestic overproduction in Texas and cheap oil imports from Venezuela potentially jeopardized the economic viability of a domestic oil industry, there had been disagreement about how US energy security would be best achieved. Should the state help sustain a healthy domestic industry so that there would be production in times of military crisis? Should it stockpile and create strategic reserves in addition to already existing naval petroleum reserves? Or should it rely on geographical diversification and purchase foreign oil at competitive prices? Naturally, integrated major oil companies whose production was increasingly located outside the United States favoured the latter approach while small, independent producers demanded protection of their high-cost domestic production. For the Eisenhower administration there was no accepted approach that linked national security to petroleum imports, and it seems that special interests were able to sway the president to support the MOIP. As a champion of trade liberalization and supporter of the various General Agreement on Tariffs and Trade (GATT) rounds during the 1950s and early 1960s, the United States needed to resort to the one legitimate reason that allowed such far-reaching intervention into international trade, namely national security.

To ensure equity between established and new companies, between importers and refiners, and between regions, the MOIP established an intricate system of historical quotas based on previous market shares, quota exchanges to benefit domestic refiners, and sliding scales to benefit small refiners. Here, the different bureaucratic interests came into play. The Interior, Treasury, and Justice Departments often supported small producers and refiners against what they saw as an oligopoly of the major international companies or big business. However, the State Department backed the majors focusing on the strategic significance of Middle Eastern oil to supply the free Western world, especially Western Europe, during the Cold War. The program had other foreign policy repercussions and caused diplomatic tensions with Venezuela and Canada, two hemispheric producers. These were addressed when only two months into the program the first major changes to the MOIP were announced. Following diplomatic negotiations between Canada and the United States and invoking national security arguments, land-based foreign supplies were exempted. Since Mexico had no pipeline to the United States, this was mainly to allow imports from Canada, which then divided its domestic market into two separate markets east and west of Montreal, accelerating transnational supply links between Alberta and refineries in the United States and diverting some of US-bound exports from Venezuela to Eastern Canada. This hemispheric preference system was only one of many exemptions introduced over the next decade, which together with a multitude of special allocations for specific industries and regions, rendered the MOIP increasingly fragmented and inefficient.

As criticism grew, President Nixon created a Cabinet Task Force on Oil Import Control in 1969 to review the program. Its 1970 report recommended the replacement of the MOIP by tariffs. The task force questioned the national security rationale and the cost to US consumers, who enjoyed stable oil prices but at a price differential between imported and domestic oil and at the expense of adjusting to transformational long-term developments, such as increased global demand and depleting domestic reserves. By 1972, the United States had become a net consumer of oil and needed foreign oil imports. While Middle Eastern producers may have found a substitute market in Western Europe, the MOIP may have also led them to seek higher prices instead of increased production, foreshadowing the 1973 oil price crisis. As the United States had to deal with various energy crises in the 1970s, it became clear that the MOIP had only delayed the inevitable; US dependency on foreign oil had only been postponed.

Petra Dolata

See also: Consortium Agreement of 1954; Energy Crisis of the 1970s; Energy Independence; Energy Policy and Conservation Act of 1975; Organization of Petroleum Exporting Countries (OPEC)

FURTHER READING

Barber, William J. 1981. "The Eisenhower Energy Policy: Reluctant Intervention." In *Energy Policy in Perspective: Today's Problems, Yesterday's Solutions*. Ed. Craufurd D. Goodwin. Washington, DC: Brookings Institution.

Bohi, Douglas R., and Milton Russell. 1981. *Limiting Oil Imports: An Economic History and Analysis*. Baltimore: Johns Hopkins University Press.

Cicchetti, Charles J., and William J. Gillen. 1973. "The Mandatory Oil Import Quota Program: A Consideration of Economic Efficiency and Equity." *Natural Resources Journal*. Vol. 13. No. 3 Pp. 399–430.

Eisenhower, Dwight D. 1959. "Proclamation 3279: Adjusting Imports of Petroleum and Petroleum Products into the United States." Online by Gerhard Peters and John T. Woolley. The American Presidency Project. https://www.presidency.ucsb.edu/node/307795 (accessed June 1, 2021).

Nash, Gerald D. 1968. *United States Oil Policy 1890–1964*. Westport: Greenwood Press.

Nemeth, Tammy. 2002. "Consolidating the Continental Drift: American Influence on Diefenbaker's National Oil Policy." *Journal of the Canadian Historical Association*. Vol. 13. No. 1. Pp. 191–215.

United States Tariff Commission. 1973. *World Oil Developments and U.S. Oil Import Policies. A Report Prepared for the Committee on Finance, United States Senate*. Washington, DC. https://www.usitc.gov/publications/other/pub632.pdf (accessed June 1, 2021).

Vietor, Richard H. 1984. *Energy Policy in America since 1945: A Study of Business-Government Relations*. Cambridge: Cambridge University Press.

Zeiler, Thomas W. 1990. "Kennedy, Oil Imports, and the Fair Trade Doctrine." *The Business History Review*. Vol. 64. No. 2. Pp. 286–310.

Manhattan Project

The Manhattan Project was a secret American program, with the support also from Canada and the United Kingdom, to create atomic bombs during the Second World War. Led by Robert Oppenheimer and Enrico Fermi, the Manhattan Project created the first uranium-235 and plutonium-239 bombs. These bombs were dropped on Hiroshima and Nagasaki respectively at the end of the Second World War, releasing the primal force of atomic fission, one of the most powerful sources of energy ever harnessed by humankind. Albert Einstein prompted the sequence of events that led to the Manhattan Project when his colleague, Leo Szilard, a physicist working on atomic fission for the Axis powers, leaked information about the Nazi's program to make atomic weapons. With this information, Einstein wrote to President Roosevelt urging him to create such a weapon before the Nazis. In response, Roosevelt and the War Department began the top-secret Manhattan Project.

The Manhattan Project took its name from Manhattan in New York City, where the program was initially based. However, due to the instability of atomic fission and the need for secrecy, the project dispersed to several cities and regions of the United States. In many of these areas, American workers did not know exactly the nature of the project, but they knew that it was for the war effort. Overall, some 125,000 "direct staff members" contributed to the Manhattan Project, which spent $2.2 billion before the war's end (Wellerstein 2019). The chief locations for research and development on the bomb included Los Alamos, New Mexico, the Hanford Works site in Washington, the mines of Navajo Nation in the Southwest, and Oak Ridge, Tennessee, but the project involved work at several hundred different locations around the country including two dozen universities (Wellerstein 2019).

Leading physicists Robert Oppenheimer, Edward Teller, Leo Szilard, and Enrico Fermi worked on different aspects of the project from creating a working nuclear reactor at Hanford to designing the atomic bomb at a research facility at Los Alamos. In 1938, Enrico Fermi had shown that stable atomic chain reactions could occur while working in a secret lab underneath the football stadium at the University of Chicago. Beginning in 1942, the Los Alamos team worked to figure out what exact elements were needed as fuel and how to design such bombs. Eventually, they decided on uranium-235 and plutonium-239.

The Los Alamos researchers then investigated designs for the bomb. The gun-type design was used for the uranium bomb to spark its atomic reaction. This design meant that two subcritical masses were shot together forcing them to set off a nuclear chain reaction. The plutonium design used an implosion method, wherein the shockwaves would compress the mass to force a chain reaction.

The issue with uranium-235 is that it is extremely rare, occurring naturally in only 0.7 percent of all uranium on earth. Thus, the more plentiful uranium-238 was mined in the area of the Navajo Nation in the American Southwest. Thousands of workers streamed into the states of Arizona, Colorado, and New Mexico to mine this rare material for the war effort.

FIGURE 18: The Manhattan Project produced the atomic bombs exploded over the Japanese cities of Hiroshima and Nagasaki.

The uranium-238 was sent to Oak Ridge, Tennessee for enrichment in factories to become uranium-235. Oak Ridge did not exist as a city before the Manhattan Project. However, by 1945, the city population reached approximately 80,000 and used more electricity in its plants than New York City.

The first atomic bomb created by the Manhattan Project was tested at a site called "Trinity" in the deserts of New Mexico near the Los Alamos research station. The test, conducted on July 16, 1945, was successful. News of the favorable result influenced President Truman's negotiations at the Potsdam Conference and his planning for the next stage of war with Japan. President Truman warned Emperor Hirohito of Japan to surrender or suffer prompt and utter destruction, without any mention of atomic weapons. Hirohito refused, which resulted in the dropping of the uranium-235 bomb "Little Boy" on Hiroshima, Japan on August 6, 1945. The 9,000-pound bomb was dropped at 8:15 a.m. and detonated 2,000 feet above the city. Manhattan Project calculations estimated the blast to be equivalent to 12,000–15,000 tons of TNT. It created a zone of complete destruction that covered a five-square mile area. The plutonium-239 bomb, nicknamed "Fat Man," destroyed Nagasaki a few days later on August 9. On August 15, 1945, Emperor Hirohito announced Japan's unconditional surrender.

OPPENHEIMER ON TRINITY TEST

"Now I am become death, the destroyer of worlds." Oppenheimer's statement upon seeing the destruction of the Trinity Test. He is quoting the Bhagavad Gītā, a Hindu text wherein Prince Arjuna discusses the moral dilemma and despair caused by death and violence in war. He is in the midst of battle with Krishna, the Hindu god of compassion. The quote suggests Oppenheimer's moral dilemma and despair about the use of the atomic bombs.

Paul A. Brazinski

The long-term result of the atomic weapons created in the Manhattan Project go beyond the destruction of Hiroshima and Nagasaki, although the human cost of those are unfathomable. The first bomb is thought to have killed 140,000 people, half the population of the Hiroshima, and the second more than 74,000, all in a matter of minutes. Radiation poisoning killed thousands more and contaminated the environment. The atomic bombs helped to inaugurate the Cold War, in which other nations, such as the USSR, rushed to develop their own nuclear weapons. In the years following the Second World War, the number of atomic bombs and their sizes grew as research on nuclear energy advanced. The United States "won" the arms race, in a manner of speaking, with the help of physicists Edward Teller and Stanislaw Ulam, who created the basic science behind the hydrogen "super bomb."

While scientists were at work expanding the military uses of nuclear energy, not only for bombs but also nuclear-powered surface ships and submarines, others were developing technologies to adapt nuclear energy to civilian uses. The Atomic Energy Act of 1946 created the Atomic Energy Commission, which began to administer nuclear energy research at laboratories like the Argonne National Laboratory near Chicago and the National Reactor Testing Station in Idaho, later renamed the Idaho National Laboratory. These efforts contributed to the creation of the civilian nuclear power industry; the first US plant opened in 1958 at Shippingport, Pennsylvania for the commercial sale of electricity created by nuclear fission.

Nuclear accidents like the partial core meltdown at Pennsylvania's Three Mile Island plant in 1979 and the Chernobyl disaster in Ukraine in 1986 seriously dampened enthusiasm for nuclear energy in the United States, Italy, and Germany. However, other nations like France, the Netherlands, and nations in eastern and southeastern Europe embraced it as an alternative to fossil fuels. Uranium mining continued to serve the industry, but inhaling dust in and around uranium mines produced thousands of cases of lung cancer among miners and local residents. Radioactive uranium tailings can still be found near many Navajo communities, requiring costly remediation. Fierce debates broke out over the long-term disposal of nuclear waste from power plants, which remains radioactive for thousands of years. Certainly, the legacies of the Manhattan Project are among the most hotly contested issues in the history of energy.

Paul Brazinski

See also: Atomic Energy Acts; Church Rock Uranium Mill Spill; Fermi, Enrico; Idaho National Energy Laboratory; Navajo Reservation Uranium Mining; Nuclear Power; Nuclear Regulatory Commission; Nuclear Waste Policy Act of 1982; Project Gasbuggy; Shippingport Atomic Power Station; Three Mile Island Accident; Yucca Mountain Nuclear Waste Repository

FURTHER READING

Kelly, Cynthia C., ed. 2007. *The Manhattan Project: The Birth of the Atomic Bomb in the Words of its Creators, Eyewitnesses, and Historians*. New York: Black Dog & Leventhal.

Kiernan, Denise. 2013. *The Girls of the Atomic City: The Untold Story of the Women who Helped win World War II*. New York: Simon & Schuster.

Rhodes, Richard. 2012. *The Making of the Atomic Bomb*. New York: Simon & Schuster.

Walker, J. Samuel. 2016. *Prompt and Utter Destruction: Truman and the Use of Atomic Bombs against Japan*. Chapel Hill, NC: University of North Carolina Press.

Wellerstein, Alex. 2019. "Manhattan Project." *Encyclopedia of the History of Science*. Carnegie Mellon University. April. https://ethos.lps.library.cmu.edu/article/id/22/ (accessed October 2023).

Martin County Coal Slurry Spill

The history of coal mining is intertwined with the history of US economic growth and material prosperity in the nineteenth and twentieth centuries. Coal is an important part of the story of how steam power, and later electrical power, revolutionized American life and made the US standard of living one of the highest in the world. These benefits have come with many costs in terms of terrible losses of life, chronic health issues, and an array of destructive environmental impacts. An example of the hazards of coal mining is the Martin County coal slurry spill in 2000 at the Massey Energy Company coal mine near Inez, Kentucky. The spill entered two watersheds and eventually fouled the Tug Fork and Big Sandy Rivers. At the time, it measured as the largest coal slurry spill in US history.

Since 1971, the company had been putting coal waste into the Inez mine's 70-acre impoundment area. Some twenty-three years later in 1994, the impoundment's foundation gave way and poured 111 million gallons of black water into an underground mine situated at the impoundment's edge. The term "black water" refers to fine-grain coal particulates substantially diluted in water. In the wake of the 1994 incident, engineer Larry Wilson of the US Mine Safety and Health Administration (MSHA) issued a report to company officials and district MSHA staff that highlighted ongoing safety risks at the site along with "nine critical recommendations" for securing the impoundment against future leakage (Babich 2003). The company seems to have done little in response, as MSHA required no compliance and created no public record of follow up. It was discovered later that the 1994 incident identified one problem that should have been addressed, which is that the impoundment area had only 15 feet of rock and soil between its base and the location of the 1994 breach. The MSHA recommendation is that impoundments should have 150 feet of ground between their base and the nearest underground mine.

Six years later, on October 11, 2000, the impoundment broke through once again into an underground chamber inside the mine. Over 300 million gallons of wet coal slurry barreled underground for about 2 miles until it found two mine openings. From there it poured into Coldwater Fork and Wolf Creek and eventually made it way into the larger rivers along the Kentucky–West Virginia border that join with the Ohio River. Unlike the 1994 incident, this time the coal slurry was thicker in density with more coal particulates. Mercury and arsenic contained within the slurry poisoned several hundred miles of waterways and killed much of the aquatic life in the watershed's streams and rivers. Tests found "elevated levels of sulfate, sodium, ammonium, iron, manganese, arsenic, chromium, zinc, and cadmium" in groundwater and the streambed (Plumlee 2014). Some 27,000 people endured contaminated drinking water, and many years after the incident, water treatment intakes hovered only inches above sludge remaining in their water sources. Many residents resorted to consuming bottled water and continued to do so decades after the incident. One reporter noted, "the spill and the way it was handled by authorities has further eroded people's trust in both the county's water and its leaders" (George and Becker 2017).

The response by federal authorities stirred controversy. The spill occurred at the end of the presidential election cycle when a new administration under President George W. Bush came into office. Bush's appointees in MSHA were largely veterans of the coal industry. David Lauriski, Assistant Secretary of Labor and head of the MSHA, held an executive position with Energy West Mining. Deputy Assistant Secretary John Caylor worked for Amax Mining, Cyprus Minerals, and Magma Copper, and MSHA's other Deputy Assistant Secretary of Labor, John Correll, worked for Amax Mining and Peabody Coal (Babich 2003). The new heads of MSHA "dramatically narrowed" the scope of the investigation into possible company and MSHA failures prior to the incident. One member of the investigation team, Jack Spadaro, served as superintendent of the National Mine Safety and Health Academy, where MSHA staff receive their training. Spadaro and his fellow investigators uncovered the Larry Wilson MSHA report from 1994 and began to ask questions about why the coal company didn't follow the recommendations for fixing and upgrading the impoundment before 2000, or why MSHA didn't compel the company to do so. The narrowing of the investigation in early 2001 left these questions largely unexplored.

In April 2001, Spadaro resigned from the investigation team, and addressed a complaint to the Labor Department's Inspector General Gordon S. Beddell that the newly appointed heads of the investigation engaged in a "concerted effort" to "leave unreported unexamined serious defects revealed during the investigation of Martin County Coal Corporation plan submittals and the Mine Safety and Health Administration review and approval process in reference to this impoundment" (Spadaro 2001, 2). He named several people who he believed "did not want to issue any violations to the company or to thoroughly discuss this [MSHA] shortcoming" (Spadaro 2001, 1). Then, Spadaro publicly criticized a report issued by MSHA about the investigation in October 2002, and the following summer was put on administrative leave. He was forced out of his job at a later date. His case against MSHA for covering up its lax response to the 1994 incident and the agency's efforts to rig the investigation of the 2000 incident in favor of Massey Energy Company are what is known as "whistleblowing." Whistleblowers attempt to expose their supervisors' careless, unethical, or illegal actions, and sometimes face retaliation; Spadaro believed that his forced departure from MSHA was retribution for his efforts to expose MSHA's failures. Ultimately an internal study of MSHA's actions following the 1994 incident largely confirmed Spadaro's characterization of the agency's performance as inadequate, which led it to strengthen its review and inspection policies for coal slurry impoundments.

Massey Energy Company avoided criminal charges and paid relatively modest fines to the federal government. However, the state of Kentucky levied a fine of $3.25 million in penalties and damages, ordered the impoundment closed and the land reclaimed, and required the company to restore the streams and rivers in the area to meet established water quality standards. Massey also settled a civil suit out of court for $20 million. The company's public image sustained some damage with the release of the documentary film *Sludge* (2005) by director Robert Salyer, which told the story of the coal slurry spill and its aftermath. The film project was sponsored by Appalshop, originally known as the Appalachian Film Workshop, which tells stories that "support communities' efforts to achieve justice and equity and solve their own problems in their own ways" (Appalshop 2023). Massey Oil Company and other coal mining firms have been the subject of many critical books that detail the industry's mining accidents, coal slurry spills, and coal miners' health problems including Chris Hamby's *Soul Full of Coal Dust: A Fight for Breath and Justice in Appalachia* (2020), which focused on issues of economic and environmental justice for Appalachian communities suffering the detrimental effects of coal mining.

In a horrific coda to Massey Energy Company's blemished record of mine safety, its Upper Big Branch mine in West Virginia suffered an explosion in 2010 that killed twenty-nine of thirty-one miners, raising questions about CEO Don Blankenship's management of the company's operations. Blankenship resigned, and on December 3, 2015, he was sentenced to one year in federal prison for conspiring to willfully violate mine safety and health standards. Recently, the MSHA insisted that impoundments of the sort that broke at the Massey Energy's mine in Martin County—most of which are leaking—"are an integral part of mining" because they "impound waste, store water for mine use, control runoff, and prevent flooding" (MSHA 2023). The agency recognized that "faulty design, construction, or operation can lead to a failure of the dam embankment or the containment system, resulting in the release of water or liquid-borne solid waste." Finally they reassured the public that "MSHA personnel regularly inspect all dams at mining operations, investigate construction and operation issues, and conduct training in dam safety" (MSHA 2023).

Jeffrey B. Webb

See also: Coal; Kingston Coal Fly Ash Slurry Spill; Powell River Project; Surface Mining Control and Reclamation Act of 1977; Upper Big Branch Mine Disaster

FURTHER READING

Appalshop. 2023. "Our Mission." Appalshop Website. https://appalshop.org/story#mission (accessed October 2023).

Babich, Phillip. 2003. "Dirty Business: How Bush and His Coal Industry Cronies are Covering up One of the Worst Environmental Disasters in U.S. History." *Salon*. November 13. https://www.salon.com/2003/11/13/slurry_coverup/ (accessed October 2023).

George, Stephen and Benny Becker. 2017. "Troubled Waters: A Coalfield County Loses Trust in Water and Government." Louisville Public Media. January 30. https://www.lpm.org/news/2017-01-30/troubled-waters-a-coalfield-county-loses-trust-in-water-and-government (accessed October 2023).

Hamby, Chris. 2020. *Soul Full of Coal Dust: A Fight for Breath and Justice in Appalachia*. New York: Little, Brown and Company.

Mine Safety and Health Administration (MSHA). 2023. "Safety Topic: Impoundments and Dams." U.S. Department of Labor. https://www.msha.gov/safety-and-health/safety-and-health-materials/safety-topics/safety-topic-impoundments-and-dams (accessed October 2023).

Plumlee, G.S., et al. 2014. "The Environmental and Medical Geochemistry of Potentially Hazardous Materials Produced by Disasters." In *Treatise on Geochemistry*. Eds. Heinrich D. Holland and Karl K. Turekian. Vol. 11. Pp. 257–304. Amsterdam: Elsevier.

Spadaro, Jack. 2001. "Letter to Gordon S. Heddell." April 11. https://peer.org/wp-content/uploads/attachments/09_9_12_Jack_Spadaro_complaint.pdf (accessed October 2023).

Mellowes, Alfred W.

Alfred Mellowes (1879–1960) is credited with inventing the first self-contained electric refrigerator, which paved the way for the mass production of this important household appliance. But it also led to unintended environmental consequences, especially for the ozone layer and greenhouse gas emissions.

Alfred Withyman Mellowes was born April 7, 1879, in Dayton, Ohio to James and Eliza Mellowes. He graduated from Cornell University in 1906 with a degree in mechanical engineering. After college, Mellowes found work with General Electric in Schenectady, New York. By 1909, Mellowes had married Agnes Nisbet and moved back to Dayton, where he worked as an engineer at the H.W. Johns Manville Company. A few years later, Mellowes and his wife moved to Fort Wayne, Indiana where, by 1915, he was working at his home with Reuben E. Bechtold to develop what would become the first commercially viable self-contained refrigerator. In 1916, Mellowes moved to Detroit to establish a company and begin manufacturing his refrigerator.

Mellowes and Bechtold submitted a patent application filed June 10, 1916. The patent describes the invention as an improvement to the existing cooling apparatuses for refrigeration. The first household electric refrigerator was invented by Fred Wolf and sold under the brand name Domelre in 1913. This air-cooled refrigerator was made to be mounted to the top of the ice box. Though Mellowes was not the first to develop electric refrigeration, he was able to improve upon Wolf's design by making it self-contained in a casing that could be mounted to the bottom of the refrigerator unit. The apparatus Mellowes and Bechtold invented was compact, which made it more convenient for domestic use. The particular cooling apparatus they improved, the patent application notes, was a type of compressor system that is used specifically in refrigeration for grocery stores, meat shops, and soda fountains. The device used sulfur dioxide (SO_2) as its refrigerant, which can be compressed and condensed to create cooling.

The self-contained casing that Mellowes developed contained within it the machine parts, a reservoir for the refrigerant and lubricant, and the condenser. The cold temperature is created and maintained by passing the sulfur dioxide from the lower reservoir through the compressor and into the upper reservoir, where it is condensed by contact with water-cooled coils. When condensed, the sulfur dioxide falls as liquid and passes through a mineral oil lubricant, and then passes through a valve as a liquid to the expansion coils, where it absorbs heat before being returned to the suction side of the compressor. The machine allows this entire process to be done automatically and is controlled by a thermostat that detects high and low temperatures, keeping them within a range that prevents food spoilage.

The casing could be connected to the outside of a refrigerator unit and then connected to a water supply and electricity. The cooling apparatus was hermetically sealed and self-lubricating, therefore a user would ideally be able to use it for long periods without having to service the machine. The patent states that the device is portable and would be convenient for households to buy as a complete unit ready to be connected. The 1916 patent document claims that the unit could be operated for half the cost of an ice-cooled refrigerator, maintaining steadily cooler temperatures, while avoiding the messiness and inconvenience of keeping ice in the refrigerator. The inventors touted how quiet and safe their refrigerator was. The design of the machine, the patent said, prevented explosions if the flow of water to the condensing coil stopped for any reason.

MONTREAL PROTOCOL OF 1987

The use of chlorofluorocarbons in refrigeration was banned by the Montreal Protocol of 1987, an international agreement to phase out the use of CFCs. The reason for the ban is because CFCs cause the breakdown of the ozone layer, which serves as an important shield between earth and the sun's ultraviolet radiation. Without this layer of protection, which absorbs up to 99 per cent of UV radiation, life on earth would be compromised.

Benjamin J. Clark

TYPHOID EPIDEMIC OF 1903

While Alfred Mellowes was a student at Cornell University he suffered a bout of typhoid fever, becoming critically ill. A typhoid epidemic tore through Ithaca, New York, where Cornell is located. Mellowes was one of nearly three hundred Cornell students to have been struck ill with the disease. Fortunately for him, he was not among the nearly thirty students who died. The university was secretive about the outbreak, which only served to exacerbate the epidemic.

Benjamin J. Clark

In the patent, Mellowes and Bechtold were making the case for the commercial potential of their invention. However, in reality the machine was not as safe and reliable, or as profitable, as they had hoped. Even still, they had found a way to improve the way that people were able to store food and so the patent was approved and granted on August 20, 1918.

Mellowes organized the Guardian Refrigerator Company to manufacture and sell his invention. The first unit was ready to sell by August 1916. In the span of two years, the company produced only forty units. The labor-intensive production was done by hand and was therefore slow. In part because of their low output, the company struggled financially. By 1918, the company was purchased by the founder and president of General Motors, W.C. Durant, who saw potential in Mellowes's idea. After Durant and GM took ownership of Guardian Refrigerator Company, the units continued to be troublesome and had to be serviced often. Under GM's ownership the refrigerator was renamed to the well-known brand Frigidaire.

In 1919, General Motors acquired Dayton Engineering Laboratories Company (Delco), founded by Charles Kettering in 1909. In 1928, GM assigned Delco to make their Frigidaire refrigerators safer and more reliable. Kettering handed this project to Thomas Midgley, who worked with his team to develop a synthetic gas that could be used as a refrigerant instead of sulfur dioxide. The new highly stable family of gases was called chlorofluorocarbons, or CFCs. By 1930, the CFCs were being produced by DuPont Chemical under the brand name Freon. The new refrigerant made it possible to mass produce refrigerators efficiently and sell them cheaply, so that many families could afford them. Sales proved to be strong even during the Great Depression, however, sales really accelerated in the years after the Second World War, and with it grew the consumption of electricity (McNeill 2017, 140).

Before the Second World War almost half of all households in the United States had a mechanical refrigerator, but it was not until the 1950s that ownership spread more widely into Europe and across the globe, even into less wealthy and developed countries. But everything comes at a cost, including the use of CFCs and democratized use of refrigerators worldwide. The CFCs, when released into the atmosphere, cause the ozone layer to break down, reducing the planet's natural ability to protect its inhabitants (Angus 2016, 80–2).

With improvements in the refrigerator's reliability, its increased production efficiency, and more widespread electrification throughout the United States, more homes were able to purchase refrigerators, which went a long way toward keeping families' food supply from spoiling. Access to electricity jumped from 25 to 80 percent of homes between 1920 and 1929, which contributed to creating a mass market for electrically powered consumer appliances. The downside of wide refrigerator use is the amount of electricity they use. Electricity is mostly produced by burning of fossil fuels, which sends carbon into the atmosphere, contributing to global warming and climate change (Smil 2006, 40–1). Nevertheless, Mellowes's invention laid the groundwork for improved food safety and stability on a global level. Mellowes died in Milwaukee on February 1, 1960 at the age of eighty.

Benjamin J. Clark

See also: Carrier, Willis Haviland; Electricity; Energy Policy Act of 2005; Energy Policy and Conservation Act of 1975; Frigidaire; General Electric Company; Hobart Electric Manufacturing Company; Home Energy Efficiency; KitchenAid Appliances; Singer Manufacturing Company; Upton Machine Company and Whirlpool Corporation

FURTHER READING

Angus, Ian. 2016. *Facing the Anthropocene: Fossil Capitalism and the Crisis of the Earth System*. New York: Monthly Review Press.

MacKenzie, Donald A., and Judy Wajcman. 1985. *The Social Shaping of Technology: How the Refrigerator Got Its Hum*. Philadelphia: Open University Press.

McNeill, John Robert, and Peter Engelke. 2017. *The Great Acceleration: An Environmental History of the Anthropocene since 1945*. Cambridge, MA: Belknap Press of Harvard University Press.

Scarpino, Philip V. 2018. "Anthropocene World/Anthropocene Waters: A Historical Examination of Ideas and Agency." In *Rivers of the Anthropocene*. Ed. Jason M. Kelly, et al. Pp. 101–18. Oakland: University of California Press.

Smil, Vaclav. 2006. *Transforming the Twentieth Century*. Vol. 2: *Technical Innovations and Their Consequences*. New York: Oxford University Press.

Mineral Leasing Act of 1920

In the early twentieth century, Congress passed a law authorizing the federal government to issue leases—contractual arrangements—to private drilling, mining and logging companies to operate on public land. The Minerals Leasing Act of 1920 (MLA) was an attempt to balance the natural resource needs of the United States for industry, while simultaneously protecting public lands for national parks and forests as outlined by President Theodore Roosevelt. In the late nineteenth and early twentieth centuries, a number of historical developments resulted in policy changes that modified access to natural resources. First, the demand for oil rose as more and more people bought gasoline-fueled vehicles. Second, the US Navy began retrofitting warships to run on fuel oil instead of coal. Third, the federal government needed to change the way private individuals and companies gained access to the public domain. These developments resulted in changes to long-standing US mineral laws, which first appeared in the Land Ordinance of 1785 and then took more definite shape in the General Mining Act of 1872.

On the eve of the American Revolution, English common law informed the laws of the United States (Miller 1963, 506). The eighteenth-century English judge Sir William Blackstone (1723–80) described in *Commentaries on the Laws of England* (1765–1770) the age-old concept of land and mineral ownership, which would also apply to the British–American colonies. Regarding landownership, Blackstone noted, "Land hath also, in its legal signification, an indefinite extent, upwards as well as downwards ... that whoever owns the land also owns all the space upwards or downwards." In effect, there was a "direct line between the surface of any land and the center of the earth," and therefore, what lies below the ground "belongs to the owner of the surface; as is the experience in mining countries" (Miller 1963, 506–7). After the American Revolution, the new states of the American Republic continued this common law principle, equating owing land surface with owning everything beneath the surface. The concept of mineral ownership was different elsewhere. In Spain's New World possessions, colonial governors followed the "Regalia," theory of mineral ownership, in which ownership of minerals contained in the subsoil belonged to the state (Campbell 1956).

In the 1780s, the new states ceded their western land claims to the Articles of Confederation government to create a public domain, and the Confederation Congress would devise policies regarding how these lands would be distributed (Miller 1963, 507). Eventually, Congress devised a mechanism to organize these lands with the Land Ordinance of 1785. This law created a system to survey the territories into townships of 6 square miles with a section dedicated to schools, and with most of the remaining sections offered for sale. The government also wanted "one-third part of all gold, silver, lead, and copper mines sold or otherwise disposed of as Congress shall hereafter direct." This reservation followed the common English practice employed in granting land to the colonies, to which Congress adhered (Lindley 1903, 30–1).

The urgent need for revenue and policies for settlement in the western territories were the main pressures behind the Land Ordinance. Authority over the regulation of public land was explicitly written into the Constitution: "Congress shall have Power to dispose of and make all needful rules and regulations respecting the Territory or Property belonging to the United States." During the early nineteenth century, the courts repeatedly held that Congress had complete authority to dispose of public lands as it saw fit. For example, regarding the Missouri lead mines in *Gibson v. Chouteau* (1871), the Supreme Court ruled that the "Constitution vests in Congress the power of disposition and of making all needful rules and regulations ... it has the absolute right to describe the times, the conditions, and the mode of transferring this property" in public land issues. Congressional leasing of mineral lands was established policy from 1785 until 1866, with Congress providing for the leasing of lead mines discovered in the Indiana territory (1807), and for the reservation and leasing of lead mines and salt springs (1816) (Miller 1963, 508).

However, in 1845, President James Polk communicated to Congress his deep dissatisfaction with the long-standing leasing system. With over a million acres of public lands, containing lead ores and other minerals, he believed the current system of managing mineral lands was extremely flawed and unprofitable for the government. He was the first to express a desire to repeal the current system and make the land available for sale (Lindley 1903, 34). Within a few years of Polk's speech and with the discovery of gold in California in 1848, gradual changes to the federal mineral policy began. In 1866, Congress passed a law, titled Act Granting the Right of Way to Ditch and Canal Owners over Public Lands, to create a national policy regarding mineral producing public lands, and oil and gas exploitation. The Act encouraged free exploration and development on public lands by issuing patents to mining claims based on vein or lode discoveries (Miller 1963, 506).

American entrepreneur Edwin L. Drake (1819–80) accomplished the first successful drilling and commercial production of oil near Titusville, Pennsylvania in 1859. However, Congress did not connect this natural resource with public lands until after the passing of the 1866 Act. Consequently, in 1870 and 1872, Congress passed a placer mining law and a general mining law respectively, combining the 1866 and 1870 laws as one legislative act (Miller 1963, 510). The General Mining Act of 1872 allowed companies to pay a low fee to extract minerals from public land in the West. In exchange, they could eventually own the land outright and all the minerals—and profits for virtually unregulated commercial exploitation. The deposits found on federal public lands were cheaper for oil barons to access than deposits located in the Gulf of Mexico or coastal California (Miller 1963, 511).

When Congress passed the Oil Placer Act in 1897, it made public lands containing petroleum or other mineral oils "free and open to occupation, exploration, and purchase" (Ball 1915). In 1909, the US Geological Survey told the Interior Secretary that "oil companies in California were claiming oil prospects so fast—and at such low fees—that soon under the 1872 Mining Law the government will be obliged to repurchase the very oil" to run its Navy "that [previously] it has practically given away" (quoted in Western 2014). President William Howard Taft (1857–1930) believed that protecting the US Navy's fuel supply required withdrawing 3 million acres of public land with oil on it in California and Wyoming thereby keeping those lands from oil producers.

Major drilling also occurred on private or state-held land in Texas, Oklahoma, Kansas, and California. Soon the demand for oil was such that the oil companies began exploring federal public lands, focusing on California and the northern Great Plains. Considered the fifth-largest oil-producing state, California held 9 percent of the nation's oil reserves. The San

Joaquin Valley and the Los Angeles basin held crude oil rich in high-octane hydrocarbons, the best petroleum for refining into gasoline. The US government was unaware of the how many oil reserves existed in the American West. However, by 1900, oil companies like Standard Oil, and Philips Petroleum, and railroad companies like the Santa Fe and Southern Pacific, combined efforts to increase exploration and drilling in the West. In 1911, western states' oil production skyrocketed. Paul Gates, an historian of US public lands policies, noted that after 1910, "the pressure put directly on two Presidents, the Secretaries of the Interior and the Navy, and the Attorney General, as well as the congressional committees, by the oil interests was fantastic" (Gates 1968, 740).

The MLA was enacted in an attempt to forestall these pressures and to ensure greater government oversight of private mining, drilling and foresting operations on public lands. The measure established a new leasing system with guidelines on acreage and duration of the leases. To facilitate and differentiate these leases by resource, the Act divided the legal status of oil, natural gas, coal, and phosphates from that of hard rock minerals like gold, silver, copper, and lead. Guidelines were crafted to accommodate differences in how these various resources are developed. The act conferred authority to administer its provisions on the US Bureau of Land Management (BLM). Securing these lands required a claimant to prove through its lease application that the mine in question could produce large "quantities" of minerals, and that the miner spend $100 a year on land improvements and employment. The BLM would monitor the process to ensure a rational and orderly process of natural resource development. Lease holders were required to pay the government a royalty of one-eighth of the revenue they received from sale of the mineral produced from the land. The Act further apportioned the royalties, with the Reclamation Fund receiving 52.5 percent, states receiving 37.5 percent for roads and schools, and the federal treasury receiving the remaining 10 percent (Gates 1968, 744).

The MLA expanded coal mining and oil and gas prospecting on federal land but did so in a more systematic and orderly manner than the system it replaced. Gates summarized the consequences of the law this way: "The Leasing Act was the first major change in the public mining laws in more than 50 years. It was the second major change in 120 years. That the mining laws were outmoded, at least as to oil and gas, long before 1920 was a truism seemingly known to everyone except Congress" (1968, 745). The law put an end to a century of rank speculation and exploitation and contributed to both state and national wealth. With the Act, the mineral industries—including coal, oil, and natural gas—further established their importance to state and federal governments. By turns, the BLM and the Department of the Interior extended a measure of federal authority over the industrial process rapidly transforming the western regions of the country.

Mark M. Chambers

See also: Federal Water Power Act of 1920; Teapot Dome Scandal

FURTHER READING

Ball, M.W. 1915. "The Placer Law as Applied to Petroleum." *Society of Petroleum Engineers*. December 1. https://www.onepetro.org/journal-paper/SPE-915451-G (accessed November 13, 2019).

Campbell Jr., Nicholas J. 1956. "Principles of Mineral Ownership in the Civil Law and Common Law Proceedings." *Proceedings*. American Bar Association. Section of International and Comparative Law. Pp. 37–43.

Gates, Paul W. 1968. *History of Public Land Law Development*. Washington, DC: US Government Printing Office.

Hayes, Samuel. 1999. *Conservation and the Gospel of Efficiency: The Progressive Conservation Movement, 1890–1920*. Pittsburgh: University of Pittsburgh Press.

Lindley, Curtis H. 1903. *A Treatise on the American Law Relating to Mines and Mineral Lands within the Public Land States and Territories and Governing the Acquisition and Enjoyment of Mining Rights in Lands of Public Domain*. San Francisco: Bancroft-Whitney Company. https://catalog.hathitrust.org/Record/005718439 (accessed November 13, 2019).

Martin, James. 1982. "The Interrelationships of the Mineral Lands Leasing Act, The Wilderness Act, and The Endangered Species Act: A Conflict in Search of Resolution." *Environmental Law*. Vol. 12. No. 2. Pp. 363–441.

Miller, David W. 1963. "The Historical Development of the Oil and Gas Laws of the United States." 51 Calif. L. Rev. 506. P. 506. https://www.jstor.org/stable/3478968 (accessed November 2023).

Paul, Rodman Wilson. 1980. *Mining Frontiers of the Far West, 1848–1880*. Albuquerque: University of New Mexico Press.

Western, Samuel. 2014. "The Mineral Leasing Act of 1920: The Law that Changed Wyoming's Economic Destiny." Encyclopedia. Wyoming Historical Society. https://www.wyohistory.org/encyclopedia/mineral-leasing-act-1920-law-changed-wyomings-economic-destiny (accessed November 13, 2019).

Miners' and Laborers' Benevolent Association

The Miners' and Laborers' Benevolent Association of the State of Pennsylvania, as it was referred to in the 1870s, was also popularly called the Workingmen's Benevolent Association (Schlegel 1943, 246). Due to the intense demand for coal in industrial, commercial, and domestic sectors of the US economy, miners and their family members confronted unregulated exploitation. Below the earth's surface, miners suffered as they worked in poorly ventilated shafts, daily threatened by suffocation and explosions. To avoid additional expenses, coal operators created safer environments for miners only when forced to do so by public pressure or government regulation. Because of inadequate safety measures in the mines, nearly 600 miners were killed and over 1,500 became permanently disabled in the 1860s and 1870s in the Schuylkill County anthracite region (Kashatus 1987, 4–8). As coal production increased, one of America's first labor leaders, John Siney (1831–80), led miners in the county to form the forgotten Workingmen's Benevolent Association (WBA). The organization existed to represent miners as a collective group to sign collective bargaining agreements with mine operators, arbitrate disagreements with employers their employees, and, if necessary, to call strikes. It became the foundation of modern labor union organizations, which helped to secure workers' rights and improve employment conditions in the mining industry (Aurand 1966).

In the decades leading up to the US Civil War, the production of coal rose in response to the demand for fuel in steam engines and steamboats. The exploitation of mineral resources was critical not only to the US, which soon became embroiled in the war between the states, but also to the process of industrialization across the globe. In 1850, American mining operations produced 8.4 million short tons of coal, and in 1860, ten years later, the figure was considerably larger, some 20 million (McNeill 2017). Anthracite was crucial to the smelting process of pig iron and thus a crucial ingredient in the making of things like rails for railroad construction. The expansion of railroads and iron production worked in concert, and together a relationship formed between railroads, coal mining, and ore mining, a pattern that continued well into the late nineteenth century. The coal deposits of the Appalachian region attracted investors and immigrant miners wanting to exploit the abundance of the resource, which is found in plentiful quantities in Pennsylvania, Maryland, and West Virginia. The end of the US Civil War in 1865 led to a price drop for anthracite coal, and mine operators cut wages 25–35 percent. In 1868, when employers attempted to reduce wages again, John Siney and other leaders in the miner community called for workers to organize and strike (Schlegel 1943, 243–4).

John Siney was born in Ireland in 1831 to tenant farmer parents who lost their homestead in 1835 after the potato crop failed. The family uprooted and moved to Lancashire, England,

and by the age of seven, Siney was working as a bobbin boy in a cotton mill and later as an apprentice to a brick maker. At this shop, he learned the art of labor organization and helped to establish the Brick Makers' Association. After completing seven terms as the association's president, Siney immigrated to the US at the height of the war between the states. Along with other immigrants from Ireland, Scotland, and England, he settled in St. Clair, near Pottsville, Pennsylvania, a key anthracite-mining town. He found work in the coal mines, and when inflation sent the cost of living soaring during the war, he joined the strikes that became frequent as the miners pursued an increase in wages (SGPP).

BUXTON, IOWA

The Consolidation Coal Company provided coal for the Chicago and Northwestern Railroad and could not find workers to operate their mines southwestern Iowa. The company hired agents to recruit newly freed African American men in the southern states and transported them to the company town of Buxton. By 1905, African American residents numbered 2,700, in comparison with 1,991 white residents. The small hamlet thrived in a state of racial concord for a short period before coal demand sunk, and when the last mine closed in 1927 the town disappeared.

Mark M. Chambers

Siney participated in his first strike to raise wages in June 1864 (SGPP). However, lacking the organization to settle grievances in a peaceful fashion, miners occasionally resorted to violence. On more than a few occasions, they found relief by murdering unpopular bosses. Due to the importance of coal to the Union effort during the final years of the war, the War Department permanently stationed soldiers in Pottsville. Unrest continued after the war ended (Schlegel 1943). If the low wages and working conditions weren't bad enough, the use of children as laborers drove miners and their families to despair. Beginning at about age seven, young boys worked as coal breakers on large chunks of coal as they traveled along on a conveyor belt. These "breaker boys" also separated slate from coal by hand, and by the age of sixteen, joined their fathers in the mines. By 1870, 5,500 boys made up the 22,000 employees in Schuylkill County's anthracite region, with boys earning one dollar a week (Kashatus 1987, 5).

In the early years following the war, John Siney demonstrated his leadership while organizing miners at the Eagle Colliery, where he had been employed. Seeing the need for permanent increase of miner's wages and relief for the "breaker boys," he put together a plan to organize a benevolent association to provide sickness and death benefits and to build up a treasury to support miners and their families during strikes. The WBA operated similar to other mutual aid and other benevolent associations in Europe and in the early US. These associations particularly helped disadvantaged immigrant and African American laborers, but all miners were included (Scott 1990). They became institutional hubs for mining communities, designed for survival, advancement, and personal enrichment (Arnesen et al. 1998, 157–8). They organized to strengthen the workers' hand against employers. In one instance, an employer regretfully acknowledged how the membership "makes them perfectly independent and relieves them from all fear of being discharged, because when they are discharged they go right straight to" their local association (quoted in Arnesen et al. 1998). Like most mutual aid societies, Siney wanted the miners' association to pay benefits for sickness, death, and unemployment, as well as to become a vehicle for education, socializing, occupational networking, and political organizing (Lindström-Best 1988).

The WBA of St. Clair was announced in March 1868, and on April 6, seventeen members and John Siney applied to the Schuylkill County Court for a charter. Their petition said nothing of their intention to become a labor union. It ambiguously stated that the new organization was formed "in order that the stranger may find the kind of attention and fostering care of a brother when needed assistance, and be encouraged in resolutions of morality and sobriety at all times" (Schlegel 1943, 224). By July 1, 1868, the organization became a labor union just as a new state law stating that eight hours should constitute a day's work went into effect. Within a few days union leaders called for an eight-hour strike and was able to expand the WBA across the entire state by seeking delegates from the Lehigh region all the way up to Wilkes-Barre and Scranton, calling all miners to join the newly formed union (Schlegel 1943, 224).

The WBA worked to secure better terms of employment and better working conditions. The strike was the most effective means to leverage their power in relation to the coal operators. The WBA agreed to a sliding scale of wages based on the price of coal, and the operators agreed to a fixed minimum wage. This served as a formal recognition by mining companies that the association was a bargaining unit and represented the miners in their employ. Unfortunately, the price of coal declined between 1870 and 1875, but miners had secured the minimum wage. However, in their determination to maintain their profitability, coal operators not only desired to end the minimum wage policy but also to destroy the union. This set the stage for the next phase of poor management-labor relations in the region. Siney retained his leadership position, still committed to the idea of trade unionism. Eventually, he focused his goals on shortening the hours of labor, improving mine safety, and promoting arbitration as a means of resolving industrial disputes.

In 1873, Siney was involved in attempts to create a national miner's union, and accepted the presidency of the new Miner's National Association, founded in Cleveland, Ohio (Schlegel 1943, 259). Although the workers he organized in northeastern Pennsylvania wanted to retain their local association, consolidation efforts eventually resulted in the 1890 creation of the United Mine Workers of America, which went on to confront mine owners over the health hazards and exploitive labor practices of the coal mining industry in the twentieth century.

Mark M. Chambers

See also: Black Lung Disease; Cist, Jacob; Coal; Holmes, Joseph Austin; Joy, Joseph Francis; Molly Maguires; Sinclair, Upton; Susquehanna Company; Tommyknockers; United Mine Workers of America; Weir, Paul

FURTHER READING

Adams, Sean Patrick. 1998. "Different Charters, Different Paths: Corporations and Coal in Antebellum Pennsylvania and Virginia." *Business and Economic History*. Vol. 27. Fall. Pp. 78–90.

Adams, Sean Patrick. 2003. "The US Coal Industry in the Nineteenth Century." EH.Net Encyclopedia. Ed. Robert Whaples. January. https://eh.net/encyclopedia/the-us-coal-industry-in-the-nineteenth-century-2/ (accessed October 14–21, 2019).

Arnesen, Eric, Julie Greene, and Bruce Laurie eds. 1998. *Labor Histories: Class, Politics, and the Working-Class Experience*. Urbana and Chicago, IL: University of Illinois Press.
Aurand, Harold W. 1966. "The Workingmen's Benevolent Association." *Labor History*. Vol. 7. No. 1. Pp. 19–34.
Kashatus III, William C. 1987. "The Molly Maguires Fighting for Justice." *Pennsylvania Heritage*. Fall. Pp. 4–8.
Lindström-Best, Varpu. 1988. *Defiant Sisters: A Social History of Finnish Immigrant Women in Canada*. Toronto: Multicultural History Society of Ontario.
McNeill, John R., and George Vrtis, eds. 2017. *Mining North America: An Environmental History since 1522*. Berkeley, CA: University of California Press.
Paul, Rodman. 2001. *Mining Frontiers of the Far West, 1848–1880*. Albuquerque: University of New Mexico Press.
Schlegel, Marvin W. 1943. "The Workingmen's Benevolent Association: First Union of Anthracite Miners." *Pennsylvania History: A Journal of Mid-Atlantic Studies*. Vol. 10. No. 4. Pp. 243–67.
The Samuel Gompers Papers Project (SGPP). n.d. Department of History. University of Maryland. https://gompers.umd.edu/ (accessed, September 12, 2019).
Scott, Anne Firor. 1990. "Most Invisible of All: Black Women's Voluntary Associations." *The Journal of Southern History* Vol. 56. No. 1. Pp. 3–22.

Mobil Oil Corporation

Mobil, known as the Socony-Vacuum Oil Company before it became Mobil Oil Corporation, was a major American oil company that merged with Exxon in 1999 to form a parent company called ExxonMobil. Today, ExxonMobil is one of the world's largest companies by revenue. The mammoth size and political influence of the company, coupled with Americans' dependence on oil and gas, led one commentator to observe that in the absence of an effective, government-led energy policy in the United States, ExxonMobil's bottom line is "America's energy policy" (Coll 2013, 21).

Mobil was one of the so-called "Seven Sisters" that dominated the global petroleum industry from the Second World War through the 1970s. Mobil continues as a major brand name in the present day, and numerous ExxonMobil-owned but Mobil-named gas stations exist throughout the United States. Before the merger with Exxon, Mobil moved its headquarters from New York to Fairfax, Virginia, which became the combined company's headquarters until 2015 when ExxonMobil opened a new corporate campus in Spring, Texas. When independent, Mobil incorporated all aspects of oil production and product marketing, with 25 refineries and 15,000 gas stations.

Mobil's story began in 1866 with its original founding as the Vacuum Oil Company in Rochester, New York, but John D. Rockefeller (1839–1937) made it a part of his Standard Oil Company in 1879, and then in 1882, part of the Standard Oil Company and Trust. Rockefeller's corporate empire was subject to antitrust action and in 1911, courts divided it into thirty-three different business entities. Two of the larger companies were Standard Oil of New York, known as Socony, and Standard Oil of New Jersey, known as Jersey Standard. Socony later became Mobil Oil Company, and Jersey Standard later became Exxon Corporation.

In 1920, Socony registered the name "Mobiloil" as a trademark. The company proved to be a savvy promoter of its products. For example, beginning in 1928, Socony used the new media of radio to reach potential customers. It broadcasted on NBC radio a popular quarter-hour comedy program, "Soconyland Sketches," written by William Ford Manley and starring Arthur Allen and Parker Fennelly as rural New Englanders. Socony continued to sponsor the show after it switched to CBS in 1934 and was renamed "Snow Village Sketches." It concluded its run on CBS the next year, but had earned wide recognition of its brand.

In the early 1930s, the oil industry reorganized in search of wider markets. Socony merged with Vacuum Oil Company to form Socony-Vacuum in 1931. Two years later, Socony-Vacuum expanded to East Asia by partnering with Jersey Standard in a joint venture, capitalizing on its existing Indonesian oil production and refineries. The resultant company, Standard-Vacuum Oil Co. or "Stanvac," operated in fifty countries until it was disbanded in 1962. Socony-Vacuum Oil also expanded domestically. In 1935, it opened the 243-acre Mammoth Oil Port on Staten Island, New York. This facility could handle 250 million gallons of petroleum products on an annual basis and could transship oil from tankers and barges.

In 1940, the federal government won a major antitrust case in *United States v. Socony-Vacuum Oil Co.* (310 US 150), which involved the oil industry's system of price-fixing. This enforcement of antitrust action was pressed in order to stop illegal gasoline buying practices. To keep prices of gasoline from falling too low during The Depression, state governments imposed production quotas on oil companies. Many companies kept producing over their quotas, creating what was called "hot oil," or illegally produced oil. The major oil companies like Socony-Vacuum bought hot oil from smaller producers and stored it in their enormous tank farms. This gave them control over the distribution of oil to refineries, wholesale oil merchants, and gasoline retail stations, and the power they exercised at the marketplace enabled them to dictate petroleum prices. The US Supreme Court's ruling against Socony-Vacuum is considered a landmark decision in antitrust jurisprudence.

In 1955, Socony-Vacuum was renamed Socony Mobil Oil Company, and then shortened its name to Mobil Corporation in 1963. The company's emblem featured a Pegasus, or flying red horse, beneath the word Mobil. In the early 1960s, Mobil was one of the largest US sellers of gasoline, motor oils, lubricants, heating oil, and other petroleum products. Its brands were immediately recognized by consumers, with names such as Mobilgas, Mobilfuel Diesel, MobilHeat, Mobil Kerosene, Lubrite, Mobiloil, and Mobiloil Special motor oils. The company had always practiced vertical integration, combining all steps in the process of bringing crude oil out of the ground to consumers at the gasoline pump, starting with drilling and continuing through transport, storage, refining, and finally retailing. In 1960, the company diversified by founding the Mobil Chemical Company, which continues today as the ExxonMobil Chemical Company and is one of the world's largest. Along with other facilities, by 1991 it had two Texas olefins plants, a petrochemical complex at Yanbu, Saudi Arabia, and a polyethylene joint venture in Australia. By 1966, Mobil Oil's European petrol stations, oil refineries, lubricant plants, and petrochemical installations were thriving.

The 1960s was a period of increasing ecological awareness with the publication of Rachel Carson's *Silent Spring* in 1962, which documented the harmful effects of chemical pesticides on wildlife populations. Environmental activism throughout the decade culminated in the celebration of the first Earth Day in 1970, in many ways a direct, popular response to the 1969 Santa Barbara oil spill that spoiled miles of southern California coastline with sticky oil residue. Responding to environmental criticisms, Mobil began in 1970 an intensive public information campaign to promote its political and economic interests. During the 1973–74 OPEC oil embargo, it ran weekly op-ed advertisements in the *New York Times*. Afterward, it had regular advocacy ads in several major US newspapers and a biweekly column in over 500 newspapers. Mobil's $5 million campaign responded to attacks calling oil companies systematic polluters and criticized congressional proposals to break up the oil conglomerates. In response to a 1979 CBS News report suggesting that Mobil had clandestinely price-gouged and profiteered during the oil crisis, the company ran two-page ads in eight major newspapers attacking the report's accuracy and CBS' journalistic integrity.

More diversification came in the 1970s when in 1974, Mobil bought control of Marcor Inc. The company owned Container Corporation of America and Montgomery Ward & Co., which steered Mobil into very different kinds of enterprises. Although the company sold Container Corporation in 1986 and Ward in 1988, it nevertheless remained active in trying to expand its operations. In 1981, Mobil's offer of $3.4 billion to purchase Marathon was rebuffed, and Marathon was purchased for $5.9 billion by US Steel. Adding to its large Indonesian natural gas field operations and Nigerian offshore properties, Mobil signed a major oil production deal in 1980 with Kazakhstan. Then, in 1984, it bought Superior Oil

Company, and its large oil and natural gas reserves, for $5.7 billion. Mobil would become more and more involved in natural gas production in the later decades of the twentieth century, supplying industry and utility companies with fuel to power machines and generate electricity.

Mobil wrestled with another lawsuit in 1989, when the Federal Trade Commission and the attorneys general of seven US states took Mobil Chemical to court, alleging deceptive advertising and consumer fraud regarding its promotion of "Hefty" garbage bags as biodegradable. These claims turned out to be deceptive, since the biodegradable elements in the bag requires exposure to open air and direct sunlight for the process to work, whereas 90 percent of trash bags end up buried in landfills. In 1991, Mobil settled the case by paying $150,000 to six states and agreeing to "discontinue its claim of degradability until federal guidelines are developed" (Howett 1992, 430). The Hefty trash bag claims became a textbook example of how companies try to create an image of environmental concern by "green labeling" their products, which advertising professionals refer to as "greenwashing," in reference to the attempts to wash out their products' bad environmental effects with promotional trickery.

In 1991, oil prices spiked due to uncertainty surrounding the Gulf War's possible disruptions to the global oil supply. In response, the United States released oil from the Strategic Petroleum Reserve to stabilize prices. Then, the NAFTA agreement allowed low-cost oil from Mexico into the United States, further driving down the price of oil. The price of crude oil reached a low of $9.39 per barrel in 1998 and ended the year with an average price of $12.07, the lowest average annual price since 1973 (Amadeo 2022). In this context, Mobil discussed merging with British Petroleum, but in late 1998 the company agreed to be purchased by Exxon for $79.3 billion, creating the ExxonMobil Corporation. It was the largest corporation in the world at that time. Since 1999, when the acquisition was finalized, ExxonMobil has negotiated a politically volatile period characterized by serious attempts to convert power plants to non-fossil fuel energy sources like solar and wind, and to replace gasoline- and diesel-powered vehicles with battery-powered and electric-hybrid cars and trucks. Amid the uncertainty about the future of fossil fuels, the company had to contend with vexatious lawsuits involving the use of asbestos in both its products and its many facilities, such as its oil tankers and refineries.

ExxonMobil still uses the traditional Pegasus logo from the now-defunct Mobil Oil Corporation on its Mobil-branded automotive, industrial, aviation, and marine lubricant products. Also, the Mobil brand is still used by Mobil service stations and for gasoline, diesel, heating oil, kerosene, aviation fuels, and marine fuel products. ExxonMobil finds it good business to tap into the glory years of the Seven Sisters and the global dominance of US oil and gas corporations. Its diversification and branding strategies might be working, as is its bet that US consumers will still demand fossil fuels regardless of political and social changes in the last generation. ExxonMobil made $56 billion in earnings in 2022 after costs were subtracted from the company's huge $413.7 billion in revenue (Younes 2023).

William P. Kladky

See also: American Petroleum Institute; Earth Day; ExxonMobil; Gulf Oil Company; Gulf War; Koch Brothers; Organization of Petroleum Exporting Countries (OPEC); Rockefeller, John D.; Seven Sisters Oil Companies; Standard Oil Company; Strategic Petroleum Reserve; Texaco

FURTHER READING

Amadeo, Kimberly. 2022. "Oil Price History—Highs and Lows since 1970: What Makes Oil Prices So Volatile?" *The Balance*. April 13. https://www.thebalancemoney.com/oil-price-history-3306200 (accessed October 2023).

Coll, Steve. 2013. *Private Empire: ExxonMobil and American Power*. New York: Penguin Books.

Feinstein, Nick. 2013. "Learning from Past Mistakes: Future Regulation to Prevent Greenwashing." *Boston College Environmental Affairs Law Review*. Vol. 40. No. 1. Pp. 229–57.

Hancock, Jay. 1998. "Exxon, Mobil Will Merge in $79 billion Deal Standard Oil Revival Raises Environmental, Monopoly Concerns: World's Largest Energy Firm." *Baltimore Sun*. December 2. https://www.baltimoresun.com/news/bs-xpm-1998-12-02-1998336042-story.html (accessed October 2023).

Howett, Ciannat M. 1992. "The 'Green Labeling' Phenomenon: Problems and Trends in the Regulation of Environmental Product Claims." *Virginia Environmental Law Journal*. Vol. 11. No. 3. Spring. Pp. 401–61.

Lee, Suevon. 2014. "ExxonMobil-Insurer Settlements Prompt Disclosure Demand." *New York Law Journal*. March 20. https://www.law.com/ newyorklawjournal/almID/1202647584903/?slreturn=20190806181534 (accessed October 2023).

Luck, Marissa. 2019. "Exxon's Big Beaumont Petrochemical Expansion Complete." *Houston Chronicle*. July 24. https://www.chron.com/business/energy/article/Exxon-starts-big-new-Beaumont-petrochemical-plant-14119175.php (accessed October 2023).

Myerson, Allen R. 1998. "Big Oil: The Overview; Exxon and Mobil Announce $80 Billion Deal to Create World's Largest Company." *The New York Times*. December 2. https://www.nytimes.com/1998/12/02/business/big-oil-overview-exxon-mobil-announce-80-billion-deal-create-world-s-largest.html (accessed October 2023).

Spears, Mark, and Andrea Larson. 1992. *Mobil Chemical Corporation*. World Resources Institute. Washington, DC: Sustainable Enterprise Program.

United Press International (UPI). 1991. "Mobil Chemical's Beaumont Plant Capacity Boosted." UPI Archives. May 16. https://www.upi.com/Archives/1991/05/16/Mobil-Chemicals-Beaumont-plant-capacity-boosted/4692674366400/ (accessed October 2023).

Warner, Sara. 2005. *Down to the Waterline: Boundaries, Nature, and the Law in Florida*. Athens, GA: University of Georgia Press.

Younes, Lylla. 2023. "Exxon Reports Record Profits, Doubles Down on Fossil Fuels; The White House Responds with Renewed Calls to Boost Production." The Grist. February 1. 2023. https://grist.org/climate-energy/exxon-reports-record-profits-doubles-down-on-fossil-fuels (accessed October 2023).

The Molly Maguires

An evocative feature of the history and folklore of coal country throughout Appalachia, the Molly Maguires are reported to have roots stretching all the way back to the Great Potato Famine in Ireland during the 1840s. What began as a secret society dedicated to mutual protection against predatory landlords and creditors in the Old Country transformed in the coalfields of Pennsylvania into a secret labor organization thought to have been responsible for numerous acts of terrorist violence against mine owners who were deemed exploitative, as well workers considered to be allied with them. Ultimately, an undercover sting operation was purported to have infiltrated the Mollie Maguires, culminating in criminal proceedings that ended with the execution of a large number of men for murder.

The organization took its name from a legendary figure named Molly Maguire, who reputedly was a leader in the Irish underground resistance to the landlords, and who according to some reports may have died as a result. Long associated with the Ancient Order of Hibernians, which was alleged to act as a legal, public front for the dangerous and underground Mollies, the Molly Maguires seem to have become active in the United States in the 1860s, originally engaging in protests against conscription during the US Civil War. There is some evidence of a number of other covert groups of miners who organized to offer mutual aid and protection, and it is important to note that these may well have broken down largely along ethnic and religious lines. Naturally, various immigrant groups tend to congregate amongst themselves and to trust one another more implicitly, yet in this context, the fact that the Mollies were an explicitly Irish Catholic group is hardly incidental. Some recent scholarship, in fact, has suggested that the immigrant Irish miners found themselves in a stratified society with clear lines of segregation and prejudice that mirrored the Catholic/Protestant divisions in Ireland, and most especially in Ulster, the Province of Northern Ireland most tormented by sectarian fault lines.

What is known about the Molly Maguires comes mainly from a series of trials held in Pennsylvania in 1876 and 1877, which involved criminal prosecutions for a series of violent acts committed between 1862 and 1865. The trials were held in the wake of the "Long Strike" of 1875, which featured clashes between striking workers and hired security guards from Pinkerton Detective Agency. During the strike, one of the Pinkertons, James McParland, assumed the false identity of a member of the Ancient Order of Hibernians from Buffalo, New York, and was allowed into the striking workers' inner circle. His clandestine work enabled law enforcement and company officials to identify more than sixty coal miners they suspected were part of the secret Molly Maguire organization. These men were arrested in 1875, which brought the Long Strike to an end. Company officials sought vengeance, and secured indictments against the arrested miners. Numerous trials ensued in Pottsville, Pennsylvania, in which many allegations were made about Molly Maguires but with very little evidence. Particularly charged were the trials of those accused of murdering John P. Jones, a mining superintendent shot in the back for blacklisting striking workers, and police officer Benjamin Yost, who was shot while extinguishing a streetlight. Eventually, twenty-one of the miners were sentenced to death and hanged (Loy 2010).

The gripping 1876–77 Pennsylvania trials of the Molly Maguires, complete with the stunning testimony of infiltrating undercover detective James McParland, was the stuff of which true-crime writers dream. No lesser figure than Arthur Conan Doyle, in fact, was an early adapter of the material, using aspects of the story in his fourth and final Sherlock Holmes novel, *The Valley of Fear*, first published in serial form in *The Strand* from fall 1914 through spring 1915. McParland's testimony not only sent Mollies to the gallows, it also simultaneously brought an end to the worst of the violence in the Pennsylvania coalfields. In addition, McParland's undercover operation also marked the meteoric rise of a career that would take him to the mine warfare of the West, as well as on the trail of notorious figures Butch Cassidy and the Sundance Kid. Not incidentally, McParland's version of events also provided the basis for the popular American conception of the Mollies for generations.

The vision of the Molly Maguires most indelibly imprinted upon the American popular imagination, however, ultimately stems from a book by Arthur H. Lewis. Born in 1906 in Mahanoy City, Pennsylvania, in the heart of the southern portion of the Commonwealth's coal country, Lewis worked as a reporter and wrote well over a dozen books, mostly about crime. Lewis is best remembered, however, for the film version of his 1964 book *Lament for the Molly Maguires*, which he helped to adapt for the screen. Lewis worked as a reporter for the *Philadelphia Inquirer* and then as a press secretary for several Pennsylvania governors before turning his hand to freelance writing. Lewis died in Philadelphia in 1995. *The Molly Maguires* was made into a movie in 1970 by Paramount Pictures. With a screenplay by Lewis and Walter Bernstein and directed by Martin Ritt, it stars Richard Harris as undercover Pinkerton Detective James McParland, who infiltrates and betrays the Molly Maguires, and notably Jack Kehoe, who had become his close friend, and who was played by Sean Connery.

The haunting allure of the Mollies has lost none of its popular appeal over time, and the Irish Rovers recorded a *Lament for the Molly Maguires* in 2000. This song has a refrain that similarly evocates the deepest pits of hades in which a brotherhood—born in the fields of Ireland as a resistance movement against oppressive landlords—was transformed within the crucible of anthracite mine shafts into a forerunner of modern American labor movements:

> Sucking up the coal dust into your lungs,
> Underneath the hills where there is no sun
> Try to make a living on a dollar a day,
> Digging bloody coal in Pennsylvania. (Quoted in McCaffrey 1997)

These popular conceptions of the Mollies aside, in fairness, there have been those who have cast doubt on the very existence of the organized movement condemned in the Pennsylvania court proceedings and subsequently lionized in the popular imagination. It should be noted that in 1979, the state of Pennsylvania pardoned the executed John Kehoe, supposed "king" of the Molly Maguires, amid a growing legal consensus that the trials were a gross perversion of justice. Regardless, the fact remains that the legend of the Molly Maguires is undoubtedly real, compelling, and abiding, and that the genesis and development of this legend represents a very important juncture in the history of coal mining in America. The court of the day saw in the Mollies the murderous thugs of a terrorist organization; others have cast the Mollies as heroic standard-bearers of the nascent labor union movement.

Whether the truth is closer to either of these perspectives or falls somewhere in between, it is clear that the violence in and around the mines was sparked to a greater or a lesser degree by the harsh realities of life within those very mines. Indeed, it has been suggested that the Molly Maguires fired the first salvo in a developing class war within late nineteenth-century America. Thus, the legend of the Molly Maguires serves to highlight the undeniably abysmal and unsafe working conditions of the mines that fueled American industry well into the twentieth century. In addition, the Pinkerton Detective Agency rose to national prominence by helping the big mining interests to infiltrate and to destroy labor agitators. This fact underscores just how fully the deck was stacked against those workers who dared to question the justice of a system that made fortunes for the owners of mines that sapped the health, hope, and life from the miners themselves.

Christopher R. Fee

See also: Black Lung Disease; Cist, Jacob; Coal; Miner's and Laborer's Benevolent Association; Sinclair, Upton; Susquehanna Coal Company; Tommyknockers; United Mine Workers of America

FURTHER READING

Arnold, Andrew B. 2014. *Fueling the Gilded Age: Railroads, Miners, and Disorder in Pennsylvania Coal Country*. New York: New York University Press.

Bulik, Mark 2015. *The Sons of Molly Maguire: The Irish Roots of America's First Labor War*. New York: Fordham University Press.

Kenny, Kevin. 1998. *Making Sense of the Molly Maguires*. New York: Oxford University Press.

Lewis, Arthur H. 1964. *Lament for the Molly Maguires*. New York: Harcourt, Brace & World.

Loy, Matt. 2010. "The Legend of the Molly Maguires." Pennsylvania Center for the Book. Spring. https://pabook.libraries.psu.edu/literary-cultural-heritage-map-pa/feature-articles/legend-molly-maguires (accessed October 2023).

Korson, George. 2017. *Minstrels of the Mine Patch: Songs and Stories of the Anthracite Industry*. Philadelphia: University of Pennsylvania Press.

McCaffrey, Lawrence John. 1997. *The Irish Catholic Diaspora in America*. Washington, DC: Catholic University of America Press.

Mac Suibhne, Breandan 2017. *The End of Outrage: Post-Famine Adjustment in Rural Ireland*. New York: Oxford University Press.

Martin, Bill, and Phil Coulter. 1969. "The Molly Maguires." *At Home with the Dubliners*. Capitol/EMI-Columbia Records.

Millar, Will, and George Millar. 2000. "Lament for the Molly Maguires." *Upon a Shamrock Shore-Songs of Ireland and the Irish*. Geffen/Universal Music Group.

Riffenburgh, Beau. 2013. *Pinkerton's Great Detective: The Amazing Life and Times of James McParland*. New York: Viking.

Ritt, Martin, et al. 2004. *The Molly Maguires*. Distributed by Paramount.

Zaniello, Tom. 2003. *Working Stiffs, Union Maids, Reds, and Riffraff: An Expanded Guide to Films About Labor*. Ithaca, NY: Cornell University Press

Monongah Mine Disaster

The Monongah mine disaster occurred around 10:30 a.m. on December 6, 1907, when two explosions demolished the Fairmont Company's No. 6 and No. 8 mines in Monongah, West Virginia. Initial estimates of the disaster's death toll ranged from 358 to 380, but those numbers are likely underestimates as workers often took their children and other relatives into the mines for help and various off-the-record individuals also worked the mines. Though the final death tally will remain a mystery, the Monongah catastrophe stands as one of the worst mining disasters in history, and an appalling testament to the perils of coal mining.

The Monongah mines were constructed by some of the most powerful, wealthy, and influential West Virginian business leaders and politicians. John D. Rockefeller of the Standard Oil Company and various banking interests in New York and Baltimore invested in the operations as well. Ironically, just prior to the disaster, mine inspectors and miners considered the mines operated by the Fairmont Company some of the safest in the state. This is despite the fact that the mine's financial backers considered expenditures on safety too costly.

Mines No. 6 and No. 8 were relatively new, with the former opening in 1904 and the latter in 1906. Both mines were double entry slope mines. In brief, double entry slope mines have two entries driven in instead of one which allows more access for miners and materials and for easier access to coal seams by increasing the number of coal faces being mined. Slope mines utilize a sloping entrance that is driven down by an incline toward the coal bed.

Problems with the Monongah mines began almost immediately. Shortly after the mines opened, workers went on strike over issues related to payments. Wages at the mines were significantly lower than the usual rates in the surrounding area. The pay discrepancy originated from Monongah's implementation of new mining technology. The mines were among the first to use electric cutting machines, which created the new position of machine operator. The addition of electric motors and electric rail locomotives further altered prevailing job classifications and wages. The mine owners justified the lower wages by arguing the new technology made the labor of mining easier and more efficient. For the workers, wages were already low, and the seemingly minor net cut to their earnings mattered significantly. While the new technologies enhanced coal production, they had two unfortunate side effects, increased danger of explosions and greater risk to miners' health through the creation of more coal dust.

Historian Davitt McAteer pieced together the best assessment of what might have caused the explosion. According to his account, nineteen minecars were being pulled up a slope in Mine No. 6. As the cars neared the top of the incline, an iron coupling pin snapped, sending more than two tons of coal back into the mine. On the way down, the cars tore through the mine's electrical wiring. Upon thudding at the bottom of the shaft, air was shot through the ventilation system, which caused coal dust to whirl in the air and to displace methane gas. It was in this chaos that the two explosions occurred. The explosions were forceful and violent enough to be heard 8 miles away. Fire shot more than 60 feet into the sky. Debris from the explosion that horrifically contained limbs and viscera from miners fell for over fifteen minutes in the surrounding area.

As news of the explosion spread, neighbors and families rushed in to offer assistance. Efforts to rescue survivors quickly turned to exhuming bodies, many too disfigured to identify. In the following days, no less than three committees were set up deliver food and clothing to the wives, families, and dependents of the miners, many of whom lived overseas. These included the Monongah relief committee headed by Monongah Mayor W.H. Moore, the Central Relief Committee of Fairmont chaired by Fairmont Mayor W.E. Arnett, and the Union Relief Committee comprising mostly women from local churches. The committees were tasked with assisting at least 252 widows and a thousand fatherless children, who had no means of supporting themselves. It was estimated that $250,000 would be needed to provide the dependents basic assistance. The committee managed to raise just over $150,000, a sum that allowed the families to barely avoid starvation and exposure during the winter.

The day after the disaster an inquisition was launched. The official trial began on January 6, 1908, with a decision rendered on January 15. The jury concluded that the Fairmont Company was not culpable for the death and destruction caused by the explosions. Their report read,

> We ... find from the evidence that the trace of gas in these miners were slight, and not considered dangerous, and dust which was created was removed or kept watered down as far as was deemed practical and that in operating these mines the company complied with the mining laws of the State.

Despite exonerating the company, the jury made several recommendations, including "that congress make an appropriation for the establishment of a Bureau of Investigation and information to aid in the study of the various conditions under which explosions occur, and as to how they may be prevented." The Monongah mining disaster and others that occurred soon after, such as the 1908 Marianna Coal Mine Disaster and the 1909 Cherry Mine Disaster, led to the creation of the US Bureau of Mines in 1910. However, the bureau was limited to research and investigation and had no regulatory or inspection power. Creating safer conditions for coal miners would have to wait for decades, only after more terrible tragedies in one of the most dangerous sectors of energy development.

Todd K. Platts

See also: Centralia Mine Disaster; Cherry Mine Disaster; Coal; Dawson Mine Disaster; Farmington Mine Disaster; Krebs Mine Disaster; Scofield Mine Disaster; Upper Big Branch Mine Disaster; West Frankfort Mine Disaster; Weir, Paul

FURTHER READING

McAteer, Davitt. 2014. *Monongah: The Tragic Story of the 1907 Monongah Mine Disaster*. Morgantown, WV: West Virginia University Press.

Schmoll, Brett. 2013. "Masculine and Dead in the Mining Community: The Gendering of Death and the Monongah Mine Explosion of 1907." *Journal of Appalachian Studies*. Vol. 19. No. 1/2. Pp. 27–45.

Tropea, Joseph Louis. 2008. "Review: Revisiting Monongah." *Appalachian Journal*. Vol. 35. No. 4. Pp. 358–64.

Tropea, Joseph Louis. 2013. "Monongah Revisited: Sources, Body Parts, and Ethnography." *West Virginia History*. Vol. 7. No. 2. Pp. 63–91.

Tropea, Joseph Louis. 2017. "Mutilation and Metaphor: Managing the Monongah Dead." *Culture and Organization*. Vol. 23. No. 5. Pp. 341–62.

Morse, Samuel

The son of Jedidiah Morse, a Congregational minister who was also a significant early American geographer, Samuel Morse (1791–1872) was born on April 27, 1791 in Charlestown, Massachusetts. A product of Phillips Academy and Yale College, from the latter of which he graduated in 1810, Morse was passionate about painting from an early age. In addition, he also seems to have shown some interest in learning about electricity, which was just beginning to be a subject of scientific study. Although he began his post-collegiate career in publishing, he was determined to pursue his artistic interests, and in 1811 he traveled to England to study painting with Washington Allston, a leader in the American Romantic movement who was also in Britain at the time. Morse spent the entirety of the War of 1812 in England, a fact that seems to have caused him to embrace passionately his American identity in the context of a Britain with little sympathy for the United States during this conflict. Morse returned to America in 1815, where personal finances and artistic tastes required him to take up portrait painting in order to eke out a meager living. For the next decade, Morse traveled throughout New England and the eastern seaboard in pursuit of patronage for his portraits, finally establishing a base in New York City around 1825. Morse was a very talented painter, and his style, which incorporated elements of the Romantic Movement, proved popular. As a result, Morse's portraits are commonly considered amongst the best in early US history. However, it was the telegraph and its novel use of electrical power that gave him his place in history.

Morse had shown an early interest in the study of electricity, and his interest was further piqued on a sea voyage in 1832. To understand the vastly transformative effect of the development of the telegraph, it's important to remember the practical constraints of systems of communication, even as recently as two centuries ago. Although messages from ancient times might be sent by runner or horseback or carrier pigeon, such methods had obvious limitations, over and above the danger that a message be intercepted or destroyed or a messenger waylaid. The message had to be received and understood, and then a reply composed and sent, which meant in practical terms that the response time was generally roughly equal to the time required for the initial journey, which could be hours or days or weeks or longer. Direct communication between parties, moreover, was limited by the distance across which such a message might be seen or heard, meaning that one needed to be both close enough and properly positioned to be able to perceive the signal, be it a puff of smoke or a flash of light or a loud noise. Electricity offered possibilities to send messages almost instantaneously, in practical terms, and with relative security. The development of a device able to do this required first, a means to provide the necessary electrical charge, and second, an understanding of how to employ this charge in a way that could be sent easily on the one end of the message and interpreted readily on the other. The development of the battery by Alessandro Volta in 1800 answered the first need. Moreover, proof of the relationship between electric charge and magnetism by Hans Christian Ørsted in 1820 led to the development of Cooke and Wheatstone's railroad signaling system in England in the 1830s, which was an early successful attempt to answer the second need.

The story of Morse's "Eureka!" moment suggests that the idea of an electric telegraph came to him as a result of learning of the development of the electromagnet during a voyage in 1832. In point of fact, it is vital to recognize that the concept of a telegraph powered by electricity went back at least to the mid-eighteenth century, and that by the end of that century prototypes had been developed that could send messages, albeit it only over very short distances. Morse, by way of contrast, developed a working telegraph within a couple of years of conceiving his idea in 1832, and that invention led to much more widespread applications over relatively vast distances. In this regard, it is important to note that Leonard Gale introduced Morse to Joseph Henry's insight into the powers and practical applications of electromagnets, and as a result, soon Morse's telegraph could send messages over several miles rather than a few feet. Moreover, working with Alfred Vail, Morse developed the code which bears Morse's name. Made up of a sequence of long and short strokes of the telegraph key known commonly as dots and dashes, in concert with intentional pauses to mark breaks between passages of text, Morse Code provides an easily memorized and reasonably clear way to transmit alpha-numeric transmissions across telegraph wires or radio waves.

Although Morse, Gale, Vail, and other partners failed to develop enough backing to establish a European infrastructure for a telegraph system, Morse pursued an American equivalent, and in 1843 garnered congressional support, resulting in a working telegraph line from Baltimore to Washington, DC, the following year. The first message sent across that line, on May 24, 1844, comprised the later famous phrase, "What Hath God Wrought." Legal battles almost immediately ensued. Rather like Edison who followed him, various parties including former partners and competing innovators, claimed shares of or rights to Morse's signature invention. In 1854, however, the US Supreme Court decided in Morse's favor, both enshrining his name in the pantheon of American inventors and ensuring his financial future. Morse acquired a great estate overlooking the Hudson River that he called Locust Grove, and where he built a great mansion. Much of the rest of Morse's life included philanthropic pursuits, and he died April 2, 1872.

Perhaps because the half-century after his death was a period of wholesale transformation of American society through further technological advances like the telephone, radio, the automobile, and widespread electric light, Morse's significance as an inventor was somewhat diminished. Although Morse is commonly remembered by Americans as the inventor of the telegraph, that innovation is so far removed from contemporary life as to seem archaic in the extreme, and it is through the well-known code of dots and dashes that Morse remains a household name today. Even that reference is probably more of a cultural reflex than an indication of actual real-life utility, as most Americans might be hard pressed to remember any Morse Code beyond the pattern that gave the "SOS" its prominence in emergency communications. Indeed, the term "SOS" itself is most likely the single aspect of Morse's innovations that still has contemporary cultural currency. Further, it might be suggested that Morse's star fell somewhat as that of Thomas Edison ascended, although it is only fair to note in this regard that Edison himself began his career as a telegraph operator, and many of his early inventions seem to have been influenced by this experience.

In any case, a notable artist as well as one of the most important inventors during his own lifetime, Morse was also sociable and well-liked, especially in more conservative circles, and counted amongst his friends such luminaries as James Fenimore Cooper and Gilbert du

Motier, Marquis de Lafayette. His fame and wealth as a result of his most notable invention came to overshadow his talent and skill as a painter, although in recent years this trend might have reversed somewhat. Late in life, Morse used the fortune he amassed through the profits earned by the innovations for which he was credited to give generously to and be remembered as a major benefactor by numerous educational and religious institutions, as well as individual artists. Moreover, his lasting legacy as a great American inventor has also obscured many elements of his personal and political beliefs that many modern readers may find troubling, most especially his positions regarding abolition, immigration, and religious tolerance, in particular in regards to Roman Catholics and Unitarians. Though he shared in the bigotry and intolerance of his era, Morse's invention was a harbinger of a different future for Americans, a future in which electricity would thoroughly revolutionize the lives of millions of people.

Christopher R. Fee

See also: Brush, Charles Francis; Edison, Thomas Alva; Electricity; Franklin, Benjamin; Henry, Joseph; Stanley, William Jr.; Tesla, Nikola; Westinghouse, George

FURTHER READING

Botjer, George F. 2015. *Samuel F.B. Morse and the Dawn of the Age of Electricity*. Lanham, MD: Lexington Books.

Silverman, Kenneth 2003. *Lightning Man: the Accursed Life of Samuel F.B. Morse*. New York: Alfred A. Knopf.

Staiti, Paul J., and Samuel Finley Breese Morse. 1989. *Samuel F.B. Morse*. Cambridge: Cambridge University Press.

WGBH. 2004. "Samuel Morse: A Better Telegraph." They Made America. WGBH History Unit. http://www.pbs.org/wgbh/theymadeamerica/whomade/morse_hi.html (accessed October 2023).

ENERGY IN AMERICAN HISTORY

ENERGY IN AMERICAN HISTORY

A POLITICAL, SOCIAL, AND ENVIRONMENTAL ENCYCLOPEDIA

VOLUME 2

N–Z

Jeffrey B. Webb and Christopher R. Fee, Editors

BLOOMSBURY ACADEMIC
NEW YORK • LONDON • OXFORD • NEW DELHI • SYDNEY

BLOOMSBURY ACADEMIC
Bloomsbury Publishing Inc
1385 Broadway, New York, NY 10018, USA
50 Bedford Square, London, WC1B 3DP, UK
29 Earlsfort Terrace, Dublin 2, Ireland

BLOOMSBURY, BLOOMSBURY ACADEMIC and the Diana logo
are trademarks of Bloomsbury Publishing Plc

First published in the United States of America 2024

Cover images: James Jerome Hill's first engine, the Wm. Crooks, 1908. Library of Congress; Downtown section of Kilgore, Texas, studded with oil derricks. Russell Lee; Nuclear power plant. Carol M. Highsmith; Three coal miners of the Lorain Coal & Dock Company, Lorado, West Virginia

Library of Congress Cataloging-in-Publication Data
Names: Webb, Jeffrey B., editor. | Fee, Christopher R., editor.
Title: Energy in American history : a political, social, and environmental encyclopedia / Jeffrey B. Webb and Christopher R. Fee, editors.
Description: New York : Bloomsbury Academic, 2024. | Includes bibliographical references and index. | Contents: Volume 1. A-M – Volume 2. N-Z.
Identifiers: LCCN 2023046677 (print) | LCCN 2023046678 (ebook) |
ISBN 9798216174349 (v. 1 ; hardback) | ISBN 9798216174356 (v. 2 ; hardback) |
ISBN 9781440872143 (hardback) | ISBN 9781440872150 (ebook) |
ISBN 9798216171348 (epub)
Subjects: LCSH: Energy consumption–United States–History–Encyclopedias. | Energy development–United States–History–Encyclopedias. | Energy policy–United States–History–Encyclopedias. | Energy industries–United States–History–Encyclopedias.
Classification: LCC HD9502.U52 E49284 2024 (print) | LCC HD9502.U52 (ebook) |
DDC 333.790973–dc23/eng/20231005
LC record available at https://lccn.loc.gov/2023046677
LC ebook record available at https://lccn.loc.gov/2023046678

ISBN: HB: 979-8-2161-7434-9 (vol. 1)
979-8-2161-7435-6 (vol. 2)
978-1-4408-7214-3 (set)
ePDF: 978-1-4408-7215-0
eBook: 979-8-2161-7134-8

Typeset by Integra Software Services Pvt. Ltd.
Printed and bound in Great Britain

To find out more about our authors and books visit www.bloomsbury.com
and sign up for our newsletters.

CONTENTS

ALPHABETICAL LIST OF ENTRIES

Nason, Joseph

The age of steam arrived in Great Britain, Europe, and the United States in the late eighteenth and early nineteenth centuries when steam engines came into use, pumping water out of coal mines, running cotton textile machinery, and powering locomotives on the railroads. Inventors and entrepreneurs soon conceived the idea of using steam to provide heat for building interiors in colder months. Steam heating systems appeared in the United States as early as 1811 and then began to spread widely, delivering heat to government buildings, hospitals, hotels, factories, workshops, and even private homes. Joseph Nason (1815–72) was one of the early designers and manufacturers of steam heating systems, and he patented several different types of radiators that provided a more even heat distribution. Steam heating made possible a transformation in living and working conditions for a generation of mid-nineteenth-century Americans, who eagerly left behind the inefficiencies and discomforts of wood-fired heating stoves. Additionally, Nason and his cohort of innovators gave rise to new technologies of interior heating that increased demand for coal and later, fuels like oil and natural gas.

Joseph Nason left Bradford Academy in Andover, Massachusetts at the age of seventeen to work for Boston Gas Light Company. He tinkered with gas burners, and having made some upgrades on the standard model, traveled to England in 1837 to secure funding to bring it to market (Stifler 1960, 21). Instead of pursuing this initial interest, he discovered fellow Americans Jacob and Angier Marsh Perkins (father and son) at work installing heating systems in England and France and became invested in their project. In 1832, Angier developed an interior heating apparatus that utilized compressed water, heated to 400 degrees Fahrenheit, which was forced through small-diameter pipes that were routed through the building (Pierce 1995). Nason installed the Perkins system alongside Angier, and wrote to his brother-in-law in Boston, James Walworth, to say that the system would be profitable back in the United States. (Stifler 1960, 21). Together they formed Walworth & Nason in New York in 1841, which initially sold pipe and fittings, but also sought clients for the Perkins heating system. Finding fewer buyers than they thought, Walworth and Nason moved to Boston in 1842 where the company became more profitable. Part of their initial success owed to switching from hot water to exhaust steam from steam engines as their source of heat. This enabled them to quickly install the system in textile mills, which already had steam engines in use (Pierce 1995). In 1846, the company installed an apparatus at the Boston Customs House that included both heating and ventilation, the first such system to appear in the country (JWP 2014).

Walworth and Nason went separate ways in 1852 and Nason reestablished himself in New York as Joseph Nason & Company. In 1853, Nason installed a hot water heating system in the White House along the lines of the Perkins system. Through the 1850s and 1860s, Nason continued to innovate and file for patents, including different valves and fittings for his steam heating systems. Perhaps the most noteworthy is the patent he received along with Robert Briggs for a "useful improvement in tubular radiators and condensers" for steam heating (Nason 1862, 1). The prevailing view is that Nason and Brigg's 1862 radiator was the earliest built with a continuous metal tube for carrying both steam and condensation, including diaphragms or "dividing plates" inserted to control the alternate flows of steam and air. The patent remarked on this design feature: "In our invention a single pipe will answer the double purpose of supplying steam and taking off the water of condensation" (Nason 1862, 2). Moreover, Nason and Briggs designed the radiator to have a "concertinaed" array of columns featuring a series of vertical tubes bent back on themselves and anchored in a steam pedestal (Roberts 2013). Thus, it had the appearance of the now-familiar upright steam radiator common in many urban apartment buildings. Several sources credit Nason with coining the term "radiator" (Daniels 1930, 54; NCAB 1935, 150).

This invention set off a frenzy of expansion in the steam heating industry. Edward Richmond Pierce, long-time industry executive and consultant, wrote in 1911 to describe the effect: "from 1862 to 1879, the vertical-pipe wrought-iron radiator business fell into the hands of concerns of great capital and great business ability. These were the men who had the inventive power and the business capacity to make the steam-heating development in this country in those 17 years one of the business marvels of the 19th century" (Pierce 1911, 109). During this period of intense competition, operating as Nason, Dodge & Briggs, his company installed heating and ventilating systems and manufactured and sold many of Nason's inventions. This included a wide range of items such as "cast iron and malleable fittings, taper joints, angle and globe valves, balanced valves, steam traps, screw attachment to lathes, a multiple tapping machine, heating boiler and radiator," as well as "boiler draft control, hydraulic elevator and the 'Argand' gas burner" (NCAB 1935, 150). The Nason and Briggs radiator gave way to a model known as the "Bundy Loop" designed by Nelson H. Bundy in 1872, which became the most popular and widely used heating apparatus. Eventually, the American Radiator Company grew from a series of mergers and in 1892, established itself as the world's largest supplier.

Steam heating systems and radiators became increasingly familiar to office workers, apartment dwellers, church goers, schoolchildren, steamship passengers, and of course many homeowners in the early twentieth century. Although a very visible fixture in a very large number of buildings, steam heating brought the sort of comfort that largely operated in the background, particularly after the arrival of thermostatic controls. Radiators clanged and hissed, reminding users of their presence, but overall, steam heat required much less time and attention than fireplaces and wood-burning stoves. They were relatively "automatic and reliable," and because they operated mostly on a trouble-free basis, became one of the machines—like the automobile—that fully integrated itself into the daily lives of millions of Americans (Nagengast 2001). Nason wouldn't live to see the fullest expression of this transformation, since he contracted a pulmonary disease while working in England and died in 1872, having spent winters in the South over the last few years of his life directing his company through agents. Ara Marcus Daniels summed up Nason's historical significance in his 1930 essay on the history of the radiator: "Unquestionably, Mr. Nason may be considered the father, if not the grandfather, of our present systems of warming buildings as the art is practiced today" (Daniels 1930, 55).

Jeffrey B. Webb

See also: American Radiator Company; Evans, Oliver; Fesler, Milton A.; Gold, Stephen J.; Johnson, Warren Seymour; New York Steam Company; Pierce Steam Heating Company; Powers, William Penn; Richardson & Boynton Company

FURTHER READING

Daniels, Ara Marcus. 1930. "A History of the Development of the Radiator." *Domestic Engineering*. January 11.

James J. Walworth Papers (JWP). 2014. "Biographical Sketch" (James J. Walworth). Massachusetts Historical Society. https://www.masshist.org/collection-guides/view/fa0395 (accessed October 2023).

Nagengast, Bernard. 2001. "An Early History of Comfort Heating." *Air Conditioning, Heating, and Refrigeration News*. November 6. https://www.achrnews.com/articles/87035-an-early-history-of-comfort-heating (accessed October 2023).

Nason, Joseph, and Robert Briggs. 1862. *Improvement in Steam-Radiators*. (US Patent No. 34,643). United States Patent Office.

Pierce, Edmund Richmond. 1911. "A Practical Manual of Steam and Hot Water Heating: Section XLV." *Domestic Engineering*. July 29. Vol. 56. No. 5. Pp. 108–10.

Pierce, Morris A. 1995. "Urban Technological Systems Before Edison: Steam Heat and Power in Philadelphia." Documentary History of American Water-works Website. http://waterworkshistory.us/DH/1995Philadelphia.htm (accessed October 2023).

Roberts, Brian. 2013. "19th-century Radiators and Heating Systems." The Building Conservation Directory. https://www.buildingconservation.com/articles/heating-systems/heating-systems.htm (accessed October 2023).

Stifler, Susan Reed. 1960. *The Beginnings of a Century of Steam and Water Heating by the H.B. Smith Company*. Westfield, MA: H.B. Smith Company.

The National Cyclopædia of American Biography (NCAB). 1935. "Nason, Joseph." Vol. 24. P. 150. New York: James T. White & Co.

National Energy Act of 1978

During the 1970s, the United States faced an energy crisis so severe that it demanded action at the national level. President Jimmy Carter asked Congress and the American people to come together to address the challenge, and he decisively made energy policy a cornerstone of his administration. One of the most significant measures designed to provide solutions was the National Energy Act of 1978. There were three primary goals articulated in the legislation: 1) aggressive conservation of energy; 2) a transition toward the use of more fossil fuels available in the United States and less on those imported from foreign countries; and 3) investment in research and development of alternative sources of energy (DOE 1978, 1–2ff).

In the post-Second World War era, the United States had enjoyed unprecedented prosperity and industrial growth. The growth of suburban areas created a reliance on the automobile and thus greater consumer demand for oil and gas. The United States enjoyed great influence in international relations. However, by the early 1970s, shifts in the geopolitical balance, particularly regarding the Middle East, and increasing dependence on foreign oil had led to economic uncertainty. During the twentieth century, the United States had become a leader in oil production, but by 1977 was importing more than 50 percent of the oil it consumed (Richardson 1995, 62). Energy was inextricably tied to the economy and the American way of life, and any disruption in access would jeopardize the nation's future. The US government relaxed restrictions on oil trade in April of 1973, quickly increasing the importation of foreign oil to 6 million barrels per day. In October of that year, the Organization of Arab Petroleum Exporting Countries (OAPEC) imposed an oil embargo in response to US support for Israel during the Yom Kippur War, quadrupling the cost of oil per barrel and leading to a global energy crisis that would last for years. As the largest consumer of petroleum, the United States experienced grave consequences. President Richard Nixon instituted rationing to stabilize prices, which led to long lines at gas pumps. President Gerald Ford articulated a need for energy policy targeting oil independence, conservation, and efficiency. The oil embargo was lifted, but President Carter saw a duty in developing a national energy policy early in his term.

Except for passage of the Atomic Energy Act in 1954 and the initial executive and legislative responses to the energy crisis in the 1970s, there had not been a substantive or comprehensive energy policy initiated at the federal level in the post-war period. Energy production, transport, and marketing beyond that used for military purposes was controlled by the private sector and individual utility companies. However, Carter and the US Congress agreed that the oil crisis threatened national security and there was a general consensus that action was necessary. In an address to the American people on April 18, 1977, Carter warned that the energy crisis was leading the nation to catastrophe. He said, "Our decision about energy will test the character of the American people and the ability of the President and the Congress to govern this nation. This difficult effort will be the 'moral equivalent of war,' except that we will be uniting our efforts to build and not to destroy" (Mohr 1977).

After significant deliberation, the National Energy Act of 1978 was passed on October 15 and included five primary components: the National Energy Conservation Policy Act of 1978, the Powerplant and Industrial Fuel Use Act of 1978, the Public Utilities Regulatory Policy Act, the Natural Gas Policy Act of 1978, and the Energy Tax Act of 1978. It established six national energy goals to be achieved by 1985: 1) to reduce energy demand growth in the United States to not more than 2 percent annually; 2) to reduce oil imports to less than 6 million barrels per day; 3) to reduce annual gasoline consumption 10 percent from that of 1977; 4) to improve energy efficiency of heating and cooling systems in 90 percent of residential buildings, schools, and hospitals; 5) to increase coal production to at least 400 million tons over 1976 levels; and 6) to see at least 2.5 million homes using solar energy (DOE 1978, 1–2ff). In order to implement energy efficiency at the local level, the act authorized distribution of financial assistance to various states to be used by schools and health care facilities and authorized states to oversee energy audits. In addition, it expanded weatherization grants to low-income families. It also authorized monitoring of the sale and transport of natural gas and set federal price caps, with a Utility Advisory Committee to facilitate oversight and make recommendations.

GAS GUZZLER TAX

The Energy Tax Act of 1978, one component of the National Energy Act, incentivized private citizens to purchase solar, wind, or geothermal equipment to power and heat their homes by offering federal income tax credits. It also created what came to be known as the "Gas Guzzler Tax," a special tax added to the sale of automobiles with low gasoline efficiency.

Kathleen A. Tobin

Skeptics warned that goals set by Congress would be impossible to achieve and could be implemented only at a high cost to businesses and consumers. In addition, the legislation did not outline ways to expand capacity for production in drilling or refining. In addition, there was still considerable resistance to the expansion of nuclear power at the time, and solar and wind alternative technology was in very early development phases (Ikard 1978, 625–6). Ultimately, however, the nation experienced notable changes for the better. Oil imports dropped steadily from 1978 to 1985, even though they increased in subsequent years. Domestic production increased during the same time period and though it did begin to decrease after 1985. Price ceilings on intrastate sales of natural gas were eventually viewed as unnecessary and thereby eliminated. Very importantly, there was a substantial and long-lasting shift toward more energy-efficient appliances and automobiles, as well as residential and commercial building construction. Americans have not had to pay taxes on consumption, as was proposed early on, but continue to benefit from tax credits and deductions when making purchases based on efficiency (Richardson 1995, 87–8).

Kathleen A. Tobin

See also: Carter Doctrine; Coal; Energy Crisis of the 1970s; Energy Independence; Home Energy Efficiency; Natural Gas; Nuclear Power; Organization of Petroleum Exporting Countries (OPEC); Petroleum; Renewable Energy; Solar Power; Wind Power

FURTHER READING

Fehner, Terrence R. and Jack M. Holl. 1994. *Department of Energy, 1977–1994: A Summary History*. History Division. US Department of Energy. November. Washington, DC.

Hakes, Jay E. 2021. *Energy Crises: Nixon, Ford, Carter and Hard Choices in the 1970s*. Norman, OK: University of Oklahoma Press.

Ikard, Frank N. 1978. "The National Energy Act: Will It Work?" *National Resources Lawyer*. Vol. 10. No. 4. Pp. 625–31.

Lifset, Robert. 2014. *American Energy Policy in the 1970s*. Norman, OK: University of Oklahoma Press.

Mohr, Charles. 1977. "Carter Asks Strict Fuel Saving: Urges 'Moral Equivalent of War' to Bar a National Catastrophe." *The New York Times*. April 19. P. 1.

Richardson, Julia, and Robert Nordhaus. 1995. "The National Energy Act of 1978." *Natural Resources & Environment*. Vol. 10. No. 1. Pp. 62–8, 87–8.

US Department of Energy (DOE). 1978. *The National Energy Act*. Office of Public Affairs. Washington, DC.

Natural Gas

Natural gas, composed mostly of methane gas (CH_4) and other light hydrocarbons, is a fossil fuel resource found in the earth's crust. Although it was the last of the three major fossil fuels after coal and oil to reach widespread use, its importance as a fuel has increased dramatically since the start of the twenty-first century, especially in America where its favorable qualities for cooking, heating, and manufacturing have helped it rise to about 30 percent of all US primary energy consumption (Smil 2016, 80).

Natural gas was not always so widely important. When the use of fossil fuels began to accelerate during the Industrial Revolution, coal was the fuel of choice, largely because its physical properties as a solid made it easy to store, transport, and burn. By comparison, natural gas is far more difficult to harness and use: it is odorless, colorless, and gaseous under standard conditions. While these physical properties are interesting in their own right in the fields of science and engineering, they are equally important in its social history, defined largely by the struggle to deal with these physical qualities.

Perhaps the most challenging quality is that, as a gas, natural gas is 1) not very dense and 2) must be stored in a sealed container. The simplest way of dealing with these qualities is to transport it through a pipe directly from the wellhead to the consumer. The first commercial use of natural gas took place in 1821 when William Aaron Hart (1797–1865) of the Fredonia Gas Light Company of New York did just this, successfully connecting a nearby natural gas well to a pipe-based distribution and lighting system. Other American towns such as Philadelphia and Chicago followed suit, building some of America's earliest natural gas pipelines, but distribution companies were ultimately limited by the difficulties and high costs associated with the storage and transportation of natural gas from wells to consumers. Instead, cities and towns through the 1800s relied mostly on locally produced coal gas.

Safe and effective use was another barrier to widespread adoption. By the mid-1800s, coal gas had become a popular source of lighting with which natural gas could compete, but it wasn't until Robert Bunsen (1811–99) invented the Bunsen burner in 1885 that consumers gained a safe way to use natural gas for other applications such as cooking and heating. Even so, natural gas is a colorless, odorless, flammable gas that poses an obvious risk to indoor combustion. One of the greatest natural gas disasters ever occurred in 1937 when the London School of New London, Texas, having recently installed a natural gas heating system, exploded, killing approximately 294 students and teachers. The event drew international attention and brought the Texas legislature into an emergency session where it passed a law requiring sulfurous hydrocarbons, typically ethyl-mercaptan or methyl-mercaptan to be added to natural gas so that any future leaks could be smelled. The rest of the world quickly followed suit and now, as a result of these additives, commercial natural gas everywhere smells faintly of rotten eggs.

AGING INFRASTRUCTURE

Safety continues to be a top concern in the natural gas industry. In 2018, a series of residential natural gas explosions caused by old pipes led to the evacuation of 30,000 people from Boston suburbs. At the time, Massachusetts employed only two residential gas inspectors, prompting a statewide discussion around the continued maintenance, repair, and replacement of critical infrastructure.

Rudy Kahsar

Around this time, the transportation of natural gas was also improving. In the economic boom after the First World War, advances in metallurgy, pipe rolling, and welding techniques led to much-needed expansions of pipeline construction. Interstate transportation and pipelines were built to connect wellheads with consumers, and more Americans, especially in cities, came to have access. However, most conventional natural gas deposits in the United States are located in the Gulf Coast region, whereas most consumers are located in the Midwest and Northeast. Because of growing transportation and supply constraints, particularly not enough pipeline capacity, large price discrepancies began to arise between these regions. In an attempt to keep prices reasonable and regulate the prices set by interstate transmission companies, the US government passed the Natural Gas Act of 1938, the first federal regulation of the natural gas sector, putting a price ceiling on the wholesale transmission of natural gas.

However, the act did not solve the price problems, and as the use of natural gas continued to grow, shortages and price discrepancies worsened. In 1954, following a series of lawsuits, the US Supreme Court expanded the legal reach of the Natural Gas Act when it ruled in *Phillips Petroleum Co. v. Wisconsin*, that regulation of prices should extend all the way to the wellhead. Following the ruling, the price of natural gas was set by the federal government all the way from the well to the consumer. While intended to keep prices reasonable, this expansion of regulation only worsened the shortages. When the 1973 oil crisis hit, the industry and its consumers reached a breaking point. Natural gas had become plagued by low levels of production, high prices, and insufficient transportation infrastructure. In an effort to finally fix these systemic issues, the Federal Energy Regulatory Commission (FERC) took a new tactic, and with the Natural Gas Policy Act of 1978 it began deregulating wholesale natural gas markets, "unbundling" natural gas production from transportation and distribution. Continued through a series of regulatory orders in the 1980s, this regulatory transition was completed in 1992 and was largely seen as successful, bringing widespread increases in the production of natural gas, new investment in transportation infrastructure, mostly in the form of pipelines, and as a result, decreases in cost. A new era of cheap, abundant natural gas was born.

By the early 2000s, electric power utilities across the United States took advantage of this boom in natural gas and began investing heavily in natural gas generators. The trend continued easily into the 2010s when the cost of natural gas was driven even lower by the widespread adoption of hydraulic fracturing or "fracking." The use of natural gas as a form of electricity generation came at an auspicious time, coinciding with the rise of renewable energy and efforts to mitigate greenhouse gas emissions. Because of their ability to turn on and off quickly and immediately, natural gas turbines have provided an important source of dispatchable electric power-generation that has proven essential for mitigating the intermittency of renewables such as solar and wind. Furthermore, because natural gas has a higher ratio of hydrogen atoms to carbon atoms than other fossil fuels such as coal and oil, its combustion releases more water and less CO_2 per unit of energy released. As such, the transition to natural gas generators has played a significant role in helping the United States reduce its carbon emissions while keeping electricity production constant. However, while positive in the near term, some policymakers worry that the construction of so many new facilities will lead to technological lock-in and financial obligations to run these facilities twenty to thirty years into the future.

Rudy Kahsar

See also: California Electric Light Company; Coal Gasification; Energy Crisis of the 1970s; Energy Policy and Conservation Act of 1975; Federal Power Act of 1935; Hart, William Aaron; Hydraulic Fracking; Mineral Leasing Act of 1920; Natural Gas Act of 1938; New London School Explosion; Richmond Indiana Gas Explosions

FURTHER READING

Grigas, Agnia. 2017. *The New Geopolitics of Natural Gas*. Cambridge, MA: Harvard University Press.
Smil, Vaclav. 2016. *Energy Transitions: History, Requirements, Prospects*. Santa Barbara, CA: ABC-CLIO.
Smil, Vaclav. 2017. *Energy and Civilization: A History*. Cambridge, MA: MIT Press.
Towler, Brian F. 2014. *The Future of Energy*. Cambridge, MA: Academic Press.
Yergin, Daniel. 2011. *The Quest: Energy, Security, and the Remaking of the Modern World*. New York: Penguin.

Natural Gas Act of 1938

Signed into law on June 21, 1938, the Natural Gas Act (NGA) of 1938 was the federal government's first attempt at regulating the natural gas industry. As new technologies in the 1900s made it possible to safely ship natural gas between municipalities and across state lines, local governments lost the authority to regulate pricing, and transporting companies began to take advantage of this, charging higher than reasonable prices. The NGA of 1938 effectively granted control over the regulation of interstate natural gas sales to the Federal Power Commission (FPC). The FPC required that, any time there was a sale by the pipeline to a distributor, a certificate of public convenience and necessity must be obtained. Issued by the commission, these certificates set the maximum price at which natural gas could be sold. Thus, the NGA of 1938 had a major impact not only on natural gas regulation, but on US energy policy as a whole.

The beginnings of the natural gas industry in the United States can be traced to Pennsylvania where, in 1859, a former railroad conductor from New York named Edwin Drake dug a well and hit both crude oil and natural gas at a depth of about 69 feet. In order to reach this depth, he had to invent a so-called "drive pipe," a cast-iron pipe driven down to the bedrock into which drilling tools could be lowered. Designed to keep the sides of the hole from collapsing, the drive pipe allowed the steam-powered drill to penetrate the bedrock unhindered by gravelly soil above. Although other natural gas wells had been dug prior to Drake's, he was the first to utilize the drive pipe as well as the first known to successfully build a pipeline of some 5.5 miles to transport the gas from the source well to the residential village of Titusville.

Despite Drake's achievements, long-distance piping at this time was neither efficient nor safe, so natural gas usage remained very limited to a small radius around the source well. Even as technology and techniques improved and the infrastructure began to grow, natural gas was used primarily as a source of light during this time, but toward the end of the nineteenth century, electricity became the more popular means of lighting homes and cities. Producers of natural gas were forced to find other applications, and one such use came in 1885 when Robert Bunsen successfully mixed air and natural gas in the right proportions to create a flame safe for heating. Known today as the Bunsen burner, this invention sparked the development of thermostatic controls, but without an efficient and extensive web of pipelines, natural gas usage declined. In fact, natural gas deposits discovered prior to the 1920s were often vented into the air or burnt. During the 1920s, however, the United States saw significant advances in pipeline technology. Between 1927 and 1931, more than ten major transmission systems were built, each extending more than 200 miles. By 1934, sufficient pipeline had been built to supply gas in thirty-two states. Natural gas could now be used in many homes for cooking and heating, and brand new home appliances, such as gas water heaters and gas ranges, were modernizing kitchens across the pipeline.

Without regulatory measures in place, natural gas distribution companies began to engage in monopolistic practices, charging extremely high prices and garnering the attention of the Federal Trade Commission (FTC). The FTC released a report in 1935 that expressed great concern over the power of natural gas companies, and that same year, Congress passed the Public Utility Holding Company Act, which required companies engaged in retail distribution of natural gas to register with the US Securities and Exchange Commission, to comply with disclosure requirements, and to adhere to strict operational limitations. Because it did not address interstate sale, however, the US Congress subsequently passed the NGA of 1938.

After the Second World War, due to improvements in metallurgy and new welding techniques, the country underwent a pipeline construction frenzy. By 1953, almost 27 million American households were natural gas users. According to the American Gas Association's 1954 end-of-year report, the gas industry was planning to spend $4 billion over the next three years to expand even further. As a result, the NGA underwent several amendments throughout the late 1940s, the 1950s, and the early 1960s to try and regulate consumer price gouging and monopolies in this ever-growing industry.

PHILLIPS PETROLEUM V. WISCONSIN (1954)

Natural gas producers legally challenged the NGA of 1938. Phillips Petroleum argued that, since production and gathering of natural gas was exempt from federal regulation, sales between oil well owners and pipeline companies should also be exempt from regulation. Wisconsin countered that the production/gathering exemption did not apply to gas sales, but to physical movement only. The Supreme Court sided with Wisconsin and determined that the sale of natural gas, even if it occurred at the wellhead, was subject to the regulation.

Dana Nichols

By 1977, many federal agencies associated with the energy industry were consolidated into the US Department of Energy, but Congress remained adamant that an independent regulatory body was still needed. The FPC was renamed the Federal Energy Regulatory Commission (FERC) and it was charged with regulating energy prices. Governed by five commissioners appointed by the president of the United States to serve five-year terms, this agency in 2019 oversaw the delivery of approximately 28.3 trillion cubic feet of natural gas to about 77 million customers, and today it oversees a $250 billion energy industry that includes electricity, natural gas, and hydropower.

Dana Nichols

See also: Drake, Edwin Laurentine; Federal Power Act of 1935; Federal Power Commission; Natural Gas; Pennsylvania Oil Boom; US Department of Energy

FURTHER READING

American Public Gas Association (APGA). 2021. *A Brief History of Natural Gas*. https://www.apga.org/apgamainsite/aboutus/facts/history-of-natural-gas (accessed June 22, 2021).

Blanchard, Charles. 2021. *The Extraction State: A History of Natural Gas in America*. Pittsburgh, PA: University of Pittsburgh.

Dow, Fayette. 1943. "The Role of Petroleum Pipe Lines in the War." *The ANNALS of the American Academy of Political and Social Science*. Vol. 230. No. 1. November. Pp. 93–100.

US Energy Information Administration (EIA). 2020. "Natural Gas Explained: Natural Gas Pipelines." https://www.eia.gov/energyexplained/natural-gas/natural-gas-pipelines.php (accessed June 29, 2021).

US Federal Power Commission (FPC). 1939. *Opinions and Decisions of the Federal Power Commission*. Washington, DC: US Government Printing Office.

Natural Resources Defense Council

In the nineteenth century, the rise of the science of ecology and increased appreciation of nature inspired the formation of clubs and organizations with a mission to protect wilderness areas, such as the Sierra Club (1892), and to sustain animal and bird populations, such as the Audubon Society (1905). Likewise, the conservation movement of the Progressive and New Deal Eras strived to manage forests, soils, and water resources for long-term use, which partly entailed federal and state legislation and the use of government departments and agencies. By the late 1960s, the modern environmental movement appeared in response to widespread concerns about air pollution, industrial chemicals, radioactive waste, and oil spills. Activists created the first Earth Day in 1970 to promote awareness about environmental issues and to galvanize support for environmental protection. The same year, the Natural Resources Defense Council (NRDC) formed, an organization of attorneys, citizen-activists, and scientists that pursued legal and political avenues to halt environmentally destructive practices. It is widely recognized that the NRDC has made important contributions to US energy policy.

In late 1969, the NRDC came together when two different groups began to develop similar ideas about starting a legal advocacy organization for environmental causes. One group, a small network of young, like-minded law school graduates from Yale, Harvard, and Duke, were concerned about environmental problems and sought to practice public interest law. One of them, Gus Speth, thought the environment needed an organization like the NAACP, which used litigation to pursue civil rights for African Americans (Adams 2010, 15). The other group, citizen-activists from the upper Hudson River, fought against Consolidated Edison's plan to build a large pump storage power plant on Storm King Mountain in the Hudson Highlands. Calling themselves the Scenic Hudson Preservation Conference, they filed suit against the Federal Power Commission to block the power company from proceeding (Adams 2010, 18). Several lawyers involved with the Storm King Mountain effort formed the Natural Resources Defense League, thinking along the lines of the NAACP as well. Through mutual contacts they learned of one another, and also of the Ford Foundation's desire to fund legal action on environmental issues, and together they established the National Resources Defense Council with a very slight change in name and former federal prosecutor John H. Adams as the first executive director.

In its early days, the NRDC worked on a series of cases that involved provisions of the recently enacted National Environmental Policy Act of 1970 (NEPA). This law required federal agencies to perform assessments of the environmental effects of their proposed actions before proceeding. Adams remembered that "we spent hundreds of hours researching matters related to the act. We wrote papers, attended hearings, monitored regulations, and brought a score of the earliest NEPA-related lawsuits. You might almost say we 'owned'

NEPA" (Adams 2010, 31). The organization also filed suit to require the US Department of Energy (DOE) to dispose of defense-related nuclear waste according to the Resource Conservation and Recovery Act of 1976 (RCRA), which gave the US Environmental Protection Agency (EPA) regulatory control over the disposal of hazardous waste. The case centered on the DOE's claim to have sole authority over radioactive defense-related waste as a classified national security matter under the Atomic Energy Act (1954). The DOE preferred to keep its handling of nuclear waste a secret, but RCRA requirements would "subject this information to public disclosure" (Gosling 1994, 35). In 1984, the US District Court for the Eastern District of Tennessee ruled in favor of the plaintiffs, which included the NRDC, the Legal Environmental Assistance Foundation, and the Tennessee Department of Health and Environment; Judge Robert Taylor ordered the DOE to seek a RCRA permit from the EPA "with all deliberate speed" for the treatment, storage, and disposal of hazardous waste at the Oak Ridge Y-12 nuclear facility.

This case established the NRDC as a powerful advocate for full public knowledge of the nuclear waste problem in the United States, also known as the "sunshine" policy. Former NRDC director Adams remembered, we "became the most important citizen watchdog organization monitoring the federal nuclear waste program" (Adams 2010, 103). This brought the organization into the battle over the implementation of the Nuclear Waste Policy Act of 1982, which was intended to solve the problem of radioactive material from civilian nuclear power plants. The law called for the creation of a "deep geological repository" for high-level radioactive material discarded from nuclear plants, and Congress amended the law in 1987 to propose a waste repository at Yucca Mountain in Nevada for this purpose. More than three decades of political shifts and litigation, including suits by the NRDC, have stalled progress toward opening the facility.

Yet another milestone court ruling in the NRDC's favor occurred in *Chevron U.S.A., Inc. v. NRDC, Inc.* (1984), which addressed the EPA's regulatory power under the Clean Air Act of 1970. The court ruling clarified what should happen when federal agencies like EPA attempt to enforce the law, but the issue in question is not fully addressed in explicit statutory language. In what became known as "*Chevron* deference," the ruling held that if

> the court determines that Congress has not directly addressed the precise question at issue, the court does not simply impose its own construction on the statute, as would be necessary in the absence of an administrative interpretation. Rather, if the statute is silent or ambiguous with respect to the specific issue, the question for the court is whether the agency's answer is based on a permissible construction of the statute. (Chevron 1984)

One example shows how *Chevron* deference can encourage federal agencies to expand regulatory control in their different areas of jurisdiction. Under President Obama the EPA declared carbon dioxide as an "air pollutant" that "may reasonably be anticipated to endanger public health or welfare" by causing climate change. The EPA proposed stricter standards on state governments in controlling greenhouse gas emissions from power plants. This policy was framed within Obama's Clean Power Plan of 2015. After President Trump's EPA repealed the plan and President Biden's restored it, the Supreme Court—with three new Trump appointees—ruled that the plan's provision for state governments to require power plants to use "generation shifting" technology wasn't in the spirit of the Clean Air Act's language of "best system of emission reduction." In other words, the court decided that

Chevron deference to the agency's interpretation of the Clean Air Act wasn't warranted in the Clean Power Plan's provisions for lowering carbon dioxide emissions.

As the *Chevron* ruling and its later application testify, the NRDC has played a very consequential role in shaping the national debate about energy policy, as well as holding the DOE and EPA accountable in enforcing environmental laws and regulations on US petroleum, chemical, automobile, and consumer appliance industries. The EPA's problems with enforcing emissions controls under the Clean Air Act of 1970 drew the NRDC's attention during the presidency of Bill Clinton. The organization learned that diesel engine manufacturers were using "defeat devices" to evade government-mandated emissions standards. These devices, essentially software programs, "allow engines to meet EPA emission standards during testing but disable the emission control system during normal highway driving" (DOJ 1998). The NRDC wrote a letter to Clinton regarding this practice and personally met with Vice President Al Gore (Adams 2010, 181). Clinton ordered the Department of Justice (DOJ) to investigate, which uncovered fraud and deception committed by at least seven diesel engine manufacturers: Caterpillar, Inc., Cummins Engine Company, Detroit Diesel Corporation, Mack Trucks, Inc., Navistar International Transportation Corporation, Renault Vehicules Industriels, s.a., and Volvo Truck Corporation (DOJ 1998). The DOJ secured consent decrees which forced the companies to pay \$83.4 million in penalty fines, \$850 million in remediation efforts, and \$109.5 million in research and development focusing on new technologies to lower emissions. The DOJ called the fines the "largest in environmental enforcement history" (DOJ 1998).

More recently, the NRDC has been deeply involved in environmental protection, both global and local in scale. For example, the organization claims credit for shaping the Montreal Protocol of 1987, which phased out chlorofluorocarbons found in aerosol sprays and air-conditioners, which cause ozone depletion. An amendment to the protocol, known as the Kigali Agreement, provides for reductions in ozone-depleting hydrofluorocarbons and was approved in 2016 as an addition to the Montreal Protocol, then later ratified by the United States in 2022. The NDRC explained its role in the process this way: "The global agreement—backed by environmental and industry groups as well as lawmakers on both sides of the aisle—is the culmination of more than a decade of diplomacy, policymaking, and advocacy. It was shaped at every step of the way by NRDC leadership and expertise" (Lindwall 2022). On a more local level, the NRDC worked with other groups to block the construction of a Mitsubishi-sponsored salt production factory on Laguna San Ignacio on Mexico's Baja California peninsula. A NRDC criminal complaint, filed with the Mexican Attorney General's Office, alleged that a Mitsubishi saltworks elsewhere on the peninsula killed ninety-four sea turtles, in violation of Mexican law. The complaint and other legal and public pressures convinced the Mexican government and Mitsubishi to cancel the planned Laguna San Ignacio development, thus preserving a breeding ground for gray whales migrating from the Bering Sea (Campbell 2000).

The NRDC provided support for residents of Flint, Michigan when the city government switched water supply in 2014 from the Detroit's system to the Flint River, which allowed corrosive water to leach lead from pipes. This contaminated the town's drinking water at a rate one hundred times the EPA "action level" for lead. The NRDC joined with several other advocacy groups in a lawsuit to force the state and city governments to replace all leaded pipes and to monitor and treat the city's water in the future. The lawsuit was settled with the state agreeing to pay for installation of replacement service lines and to allow independent supervision of the testing process. According to the organization, "NRDC and our partners have successfully obtained multiple court orders holding Flint to its obligations under the settlement" (NRDC 2020). The organization's effort on behalf of the people of Flint was an example of its longer history of readiness to "mobilize strategic coalitions and the grassroots power of millions of citizen activists to urge elected officials to put the public interest ahead of polluting industries" and do what the law requires of them (NRDC 2023).

All told, the NRDC has featured in many legal battles, including successful campaigns to fight acid rain, leaded gasoline, the use of CFCs in aerosol cans, and mercury emissions from power plants. The organization's efforts also helped to secure efficiency standards for electrical appliances and fuel consumption in automobiles. Given the nature of its work, the NRDC has generated its share of critics, which include power companies, car and truck manufacturers, industrial trade associations, conservative think tanks, foundations, and right-leaning political action committees. However, with a membership of over 3 million, a staff of over 700, and an annual expenditure of $186.5 million in 2020, it remains an energetic and effective proponent of energy policy informed by science and oriented toward natural resource sustainability, public health, and environmental justice.

Jeffrey B. Webb

See also: Clean Air Act of 1970; Clean Power Plan of 2015; Energy Crisis of the 1970s; Nuclear Waste Policy Act of 1982; Sierra Club; Union of Concerned Scientists; US Department of Energy; US Environmental Protection Agency; Yucca Mountain Nuclear Waste Repository

FURTHER READING

Adams, John A., and Patricia Adams. 2010. *A Force for Nature: The Story of NRDC and the Fight to Save Our Planet*. San Francisco, CA: Chronicle Books.

Campbell, Duncan. 2000. "Mexico and Mitsubishi Forced to Leave Whales in Peace." *The Guardian*. March 3. https://www.theguardian.com/world/2000/mar/04/mexico (accessed October 2023).

Chevron, U.S.A., Inc., v. Natural Resources Defense Council, Inc. 467 U.S. 837, 104 S.Ct. 2778 (1984).

Gosling, F.G., and Terrence R. Fehner. 1994. "Closing the Circle: The Department of Energy and Environmental Management, 1942–1994." March. History Division, Executive Secretariat. US Department of Energy. https://www.energy.gov/management/articles/gosling-and-fehner-closing-circle (accessed October 2023).

Lindwall, Courtney. 2022. "The United States Finally Joins a Global Climate Treaty That Phases Down HFCs." December 8. *Our Stories: NRDC in Action*. National Resources Defense Council. https://www.nrdc.org/stories/united-states-finally-joins-global-climate-treaty-phases-down-hfcs (accessed October 2023).

Natural Resources Defense Council (NRDC). 2020. "Concerned Pastors for Social Action v. Khouri." "Court Battles." December 1. https://www.nrdc.org/court-battles/concerned-pastors-social-action-v-khouri-16-cv-10277-ed-mich (accessed October 2023).

National Resources Defense Council (NRDC). 2023. "How We Work." https://www.nrdc.org/how-we-work#advocacy (accessed October 2023).

US Department of Justice (DOJ). 1998. "DOJ, EPA Announce One Billion Dollar Settlement with Diesel Engine Industry for Clean Air Violations." Press release. October 22. https://www.justice.gov/archive/opa/pr/1998/October/499_enr.htm (accessed October 2023).

Navajo Reservation Uranium Mining

Uranium is used to create energy through a process called nuclear fission, in which a neutron collides with a uranium atom which splits and triggers a chain reaction, producing heat and radiation along the way. The US Atomic Energy Commission (AEC) began buying uranium in 1946 to supply nuclear energy programs for military and civilian purposes. Most of the domestic uranium ores are located and mined in the western region, particularly the Colorado Plateau states of Arizona, New Mexico, and Utah, but also central and northeast Wyoming. Estimates suggest that around 5,000 Navajos worked in mines collecting ore, and another 1,000 worked in mills that separated uranium metal from the ore. From 1944 to 1986, uranium mines and mills on Navajo land produced 30 million tons of ore from 524 sites, which aided the development of nuclear energy in the United States, but also left behind a litany of adverse human and environmental impacts. The story of Navajo reservation uranium mining in the twentieth century, in all of its complexity, contains themes of economic opportunity, but also exploitation and injustice.

Uranium mining on Navajo reservation land first appeared among the vanadium mining operations in Monument Valley, which straddles the border of Arizona and Utah. The area had long been known for its carnotite ore deposits, which contains different metals including both vanadium and uranium, and Native Americans valued it for their sand paintings because of its yellow and yellow-green pigments. With the enactment of the Indian Mineral Leasing Act of 1938, tribal councils were permitted to issue mining leases with the US Secretary of the Interior's approval. New Dealers in the Interior Department's Bureau of Indian Affairs hoped to "to ensure the Indians received the greatest return on their leases" and required that they be issued on a competitive basis (Carroll 1986, 137). On April 1, 1941, the Navajo Tribal Council issued a request for the bureau to organize lease-bidding on parcels inside reservation boundaries, and between 1942 and 1944, the bureau granted leases to four different sections of land in Monument Valley. The Vanadium Corporation of America (VCA) won bidding for three of the sections, known as Monuments No. 1, No. 2, and No. 3, and a partnership known as Carroll and Shumway secured the fourth parcel, Utah No. 1. These mining operations produced and sold vanadium, and then uranium after 1942 when the Manhattan Engineer District began buying uranium sludge at vanadium mills in Utah and Colorado for the Manhattan Project (Chenoweth 1985, 8). A history of the origins of uranium mining on Navajo land notes that the Navajo Tribe was paid $606.13 in royalties for Carroll and Shumway's Utah No. 1 yield in 1944, "the first ore mined on the Navajo Indian Reservation for which uranium was paid for" (Chenoweth 1985, 10).

The early history of VCA's Monument No. 2 is noteworthy for including Navajo Luke Yazzie in the account. Sources vary, but all agree that he knew of carnotite deposits southeast of Yazzie Mesa on the eastern side of Monument Valley. In 1942, he learned that trading post owner Harry Goulding was looking for unusual-looking rocks, so Yazzie brought Goulding to the site. Goulding then notified VCA of its location. Monument No. 2 operated from October 1943 to April 1944, then again in February and December 1945, and finally January 1946. The mine closed for a year, then resumed operations in October 1947 with some new technology—a mechanical upgrader, a concentrator, and heap leaching—and continued to 1969. An early history of the mine notes that "the Monument No. 2 Mine has produced more uranium than any other mine in Arizona" (Chenoweth 1985, 11). The mines and mills on Navajo reservation land sold its uranium to the AEC through the late 1940s and 1950s, and then after 1966 also supplied the civilian nuclear power industry. There was an element of boom and bust in uranium mining, as 650,000 pounds of uranium oxide were purchased in 1950, which ballooned to 30 million pounds in 1959 (*Begay* 1984). In the late 1960s, the AEC stopped its purchases when it determined that supplies for the US nuclear weapons program were sufficient, but commercial buying continued to sustain the greatly contracted business until 1986, when uranium mining came to an end on Navajo reservation lands (Brugge 2002).

The mines offered jobs and incomes to Navajo miners, millers, and transportation workers in the post-war era, but these economic benefits imposed a very heavy cost on the lives of the uranium miners and their families. Uranium dust, radon gas, and thorium 230 are present in underground uranium mines, and these have "chemical or radiological toxity" that greatly elevate the risk of lung cancer for miners (ACHRE 1995). Mill workers and transporters were exposed to the danger as well. Navajo workers brought dust from the mines and mills back to their homes and families, spreading contaminants throughout their communities. AEC staff members were aware of the dangers very early on. A.E. Gorman, an AEC sanitary engineer, took notes from a 1949 meeting of AEC staff and Colorado state officials, at which the "unsatisfactory conditions" of the mines were discussed, as well as "problems involving silicosis and radioactivity" (ACHRE 1995). US Public Health Service (PHS) sanitary engineer Duncan Holaday conducted radon tests in the mines, and in a 1950 memo to his supervisors he noted that while he "anticipated that the samples would show high radon concentrations, the final results were beyond all expectations." Holaday asserted that "a control program must be instituted as soon as possible in order to prevent injury to the workers" (ACHRE 1995).

The PHS circulated a report in 1952 on a "restricted" basis to federal and state officials and to mining companies. The introduction to the report said, "certain acute conditions are present in the industry which, if not rectified, may seriously affect the health of the worker." However, the agency issued a press release at the same time that asserted, "no evidence of health damage from radioactivity had been found" (ACHRE 1995). The press release might have been technically true but monitoring and testing had only been carried out for a year or two at that point, whereas lung cancer arising from exposure to radioactive material takes a number of years to become evident. The PHS and AEC continued to study the problem without forcing the mines to increase safety and health standards. According to Gorman in his notes from the aforementioned 1949 meeting, "since AEC was purchasing a very large percentage of the uranium produced, we had a moral responsibility at least to improve any unsatisfactory condition which was known to exist involving the health of workers." Compounding the problem, miners and mill workers weren't told of the possible health risks of working in the hazardous conditions of the uranium mines and milling operations (Schneider 1993).

It was not until 1968 that the federal government adopted an "in-mine radon exposure standard" of four "working level months" per year. It further required mine operators to install ventilation systems beginning in 1971, and to provide respiratory protection for workers (Shuey 2007). During this long, twenty-year delay, Navajo mine and mill workers began to experience the long-term health effects of exposure to radioactive uranium dust and radon gas. Researchers discovered the "risk of lung cancer among male Navajo uranium miners was 28 times higher than in Navajo men who never mined." Furthermore, "two-thirds of all new lung cancer cases in Navajo men between 1969 and 1993 was attributable to a single exposure—underground uranium mining" (Shuey 2007). According to one study, of the estimated five thousand Navajo uranium mine workers, 500–600 had died of lung cancer by 1990, and another 500–600 cancer victims were expected to die thereafter (Brugge 2002). Jonathan Nez, President of the Navajo Nation, noted that "prior to uranium mining, the Navajo people were virtually cancerfree with the lowest lung cancer rate of all Native American nations" (Nez 2019, 6).

The shocking rate of cancer and other health problems among former miners started to become clear in the 1970s. In 1980 and 1981 over 200 "Navajo miners who formerly worked in the underground uranium mines in Utah, Colorado, New Mexico and Arizona, both on and off the Navajo reservation, or survivors of such deceased Navajo uranium miners" filed suits against the United States seeking compensation for government failures to ensure their health and safety. The US District Court for the District of Arizona combined these cases into *Begay v. United States* (1984), with former US Secretary of the Interior Stewart Udall under Presidents Kennedy and Johnson arguing the case for the plaintiffs. The court concluded that "the weight of the evidence, including medical testimony, statistical data and historical events, leaves no doubt that there is a direct relationship between the high levels of radiation exposure suffered by the underground uranium miners and their excessive incidence of respiratory tract and lung cancer" (*Begay* 1984). Yet the court also ruled that it lacked jurisdiction in the case because the "actions of various governmental agencies complained of by plaintiffs were the result of conscious policy decisions made at high government levels based on considerations of political and national security feasibility factors" (*Begay* 1984).

The court failed to give the miners justice, but also stated that "this tragedy of the nuclear age, however, cries for redress" and suggested congressional action. After several failed attempts at passing a law in the 1980s, Congress enacted the Radiation Exposure Compensation Act of 1990 to pay victims of uranium mining, workers participating in atmospheric nuclear tests, and those exposed to radiation "downwind" from the Nevada test site. As of January 2023, 40,274 claims have been approved from this program with total compensation paid out at $2.6 billion, including distributions to 6,896 uranium miners, 1,921 uranium millers and 406 ore transporters, which includes some non-Navajo recipients (DOJ 2023). Critics protested delays in compensating widows of deceased Navajo miners due to the program's requirement that Navajo marriages be authenticated outside of tribal custom.

Public health concerns persisted so long as the mines remained open and accessible. Mining companies largely abandoned their operations as mining declined and ultimately ceased on Navajo lands. The EPA and the Navajo Nation Environmental Protection Agency identified 523 abandoned uranium mines on or near the Navajo Nation, and President Nez pointed out that the mines were "not covered, or sealed, or remediated" (Nez 2019, 1). He went on to say that generations of Navajo people were put at risk by the lack of attention to these mines:

> some common examples include an individual who as a child played in an abandoned mine or mill tailing pile, a sheep herder who watered his sheep in an un-reclaimed open pit mine, an elderly woman who for many years washed the dust-coated clothing of her

> uranium miner husband, or a family who obtained their drinking water from a stream that ran through or near a uranium mine. (Nez 2019, 2)

The EPA had been involved in cleaning up uranium industry messes on Navajo land since at least the Church Rock uranium mill spill in 1979, in which 1,000 tons of solid mill wastes and 94 million gallons of liquefied uranium tailings breached a dam in a waste disposal pond and contaminated 80 miles of the Puerco River in New Mexico with radioactive material.

The Church Rock cleanup preceded the EPA's study of abandoned Navajo uranium mines, which began in 1994 and led to a process of prioritizing disposal of mine wastes and safeguarding abandoned mines on the Navajo reservation. This included reaching settlements with companies that operated and profited from the mines. The DOJ, EPA, Navajo Nation, and other entities forged agreements with many of these companies, such as Tronox, a successor company to Kerr-McGee. After Tronox entered bankruptcy in 2009, the US government received a $5.15 billion settlement in 2014 to offset the costs of cleaning up contaminated Kerr-McGee sites across the country (Sahagun 2014). Nearly $1 billion of the amount was directed toward cleaning over fifty sites that Kerr-McGee mined on Navajo land, and the Navajo Nation received $45 million to conduct educational programming, seal off mine openings, build roads to contaminated sites, and pay for monitoring and testing activities. Other settlements involved companies like Cyprus Amax Minerals, Western Nuclear, Inc., and United Nuclear Corporation.

The story of Navajo uranium mining added a tragic chapter in the larger history of energy in the United States. Within that story, however, the Navajo organized themselves, built durable civic institutions, and found strength in solidary in their pursuit of justice. It should be said that Navajo uranium workers, though unheralded, played an important role in supporting US national security policy during the Cold War, and in building the civilian nuclear power industry. Most importantly, they forced the US government and the American people to reckon with the calamitous dangers of nuclear energy and radioactive waste, and to learn hard lessons about responsibility and accountability in the conduct of national energy policy. This includes paying close attention to public health experts and scientists who have studied, and who understand, the long-term hazards of using certain kinds of fuels to supply the American people with energy.

Jeffrey B. Webb

See also: Atomic Energy Acts; Church Rock Uranium Mill Spill; Energy Fuels, Inc.; Idaho National Laboratory; Nuclear Power; Nuclear Regulatory Commission; Nuclear Waste Policy Act of 1982; Yucca Mountain Nuclear Waste Repository

FURTHER READING

Advisory Committee on Human Radiation Experiments (ACHRE). 1995. *Final Report of the Advisory Committee on Human Radiation Experiments*. Washington, DC: US Government Printing Office.

Begay v. United States. 591 F. Supp. 991. D. Ariz. 1984. https://law.justia.com/cases/federal/district-courts/FSupp/591/991/2388751/ (accessed October 2023).

Brugge, Doug, and Rob Goble. 2002. "The History of Uranium Mining and the Navajo People." *American Journal of Public Health*. September. Vol. 92. No. 9. Pp. 1410–19.

Carroll, Peter F. 1986. "Drumming Out the Intent of the Indian Mineral Leasing Act of 1938." *Public Land & Resources Law Review*. June. Vol. 7. Pp. 135–44.

Chenoweth, W.L. 1985. "Early Vanadium-uranium Mining in Monument Valley, Apache and Navajo Counties, Arizona, and San Juan County, Utah." Arizona Geological Survey Open File Report. OFR-85-15. https://repository.arizona.edu/bitstream/handle/10150/629354/ofr_85_15.pdf?sequence=1&isAllowed=y (accessed October 2023).

Nez, Johnathan, and Myron Lizer. 2019. "Written Statement of the Navajo Nation." July 12. https://www.congress.gov/116/meeting/house/109694/documents/HHRG-116-II06-20190625-SD013.pdf (accessed October 2023).

Sahagun, Louis. 2014. "Petroleum Firm Agrees to Pay $5.15 Billion to Clean up Waste." *Los Angeles Times*. April 3. https://www.latimes.com/local/la-me-cleanup-20140404-story.html (accessed October 2023).

Schneider, Keith. 1993. "A Valley of Death for the Navajo Uranium Miners." *The New York Times*. May 3. https://www.nytimes.com/1993/05/03/us/a-valley-of-death-for-the-navajo-uranium-miners.html (accessed October 2023).

Shuey, Chris. 2007. "Uranium Exposure and Public Health in New Mexico and the Navajo Nation: A Literature Summary." Nuclear Information and Resource Service. February 27. https://www.nirs.org/wp-content/uploads/climate/background/shueyuraniummininghealthliteraturesummaryexhibitc12114.pdf (accessed October 2023).

US Department of Justice (DOJ). 2023. "Radiation Exposure Compensation System: Awards to Date 01/13/2023." https://web.archive.org/web/20230117051652/https://www.justice.gov/civil/awards-date-01132023 (accessed October 2023).

US Energy Information Administration (EIA). 2022. "What is U.S. Electricity Generation by Energy Source?" Frequently Asked Questions. US Department of Energy. https://www.eia.gov/tools/faqs/faq.php?id=427&t=3 (accessed October 2023).

New London School Explosion

The explosion that destroyed Consolidated School in New London, Texas in 1937 remains one of the most horrific energy-related disasters in US history. The blast came as a result of an electrical spark that ignited accumulated gas in the dead space between the school's foundation and basement floor. An investigation of the incident blamed a leaky gas line that connected the school's seventy-two gas heaters to a neighboring residue line owned by the Parade Gasoline Company. The explosion killed approximately 294 children, teachers, and staff and received worldwide press coverage, including the first major news report filed by Walter Cronkite of the United Press International. In its aftermath, the Texas legislature required natural gas to be odorized so that a leak could be detected, which set off a national movement to require natural gas odorization. The tragedy offers a cautionary tale regarding lack of oversight and cost-cutting in the design and construction of gas heating systems, and the safe use of combustible fuels more generally.

The school in unincorporated New London had been built just five years earlier and served schoolchildren from first through twelfth grades. It was located in northwestern Rusk County only about 11 miles from Kilgore, where oil had been discovered in 1930, drawing in thousands of workers and their families seeking employment in the oil fields. Drawing on this newfound wealth and the influx of new county residents, the school board constructed a building that at the time was one of the largest rural schools in the nation. In its planning stages, the architects called for the building to be heated with a boiler and steam radiators, which had been an established energy technology for large buildings since the mid- to late nineteenth century. The school board made a fateful decision to reject the architects' recommendation and instead install a system composed of seventy-two "gasteam" heaters. Each gasteam heater had its own gas burner and water chamber for creating steam, along with an accordion array of pipes to circulate steam and radiate the heat. The gasteam advantage over a central steam heating system or a central forced-air gas system was that each unit could be turned off and on separately, allowing individual rooms to be left cold if unused (Price 1937, 3).

The problem, however, is that it required a 2-inch gas line to enter the structure to deliver fuel to the system's branching network of gas pipes inside the building. The local provider, United Gas Company, supplied the school with gas until January 18, 1937, when the school board cancelled its $300 per month contract. The board discovered they could get the gas for free by tapping a neighboring "residue line" owned by the Parade Gasoline Company. Residue lines draw off gases like methane in the course of processing natural gas and is sometimes discarded, but in this case the residue gas was made available to the school by the company. The board hired plumbers to tap into the residue line and route the gas into the school. Two months later, on March 18 a little after 3:00 p.m., the building exploded. In his preliminary findings, investigator H. Oram Smith of the Texas Inspection Bureau noted that "'raw gas escaping from leaking lines had accumulated in a dead space between the foundation and basement floor. The gas expanded because of a drop in barometric pressure, and an electrical spark from a switch in the manual training shop had triggered the explosion'" (Steelhammer n.d., 7).

A combination of factors contributed to the catastrophe. First, there's the matter of the faulty installation of the gas pipe that leaked into the unventilated space below the structure's basement floor. Second, the space between the floor and the building's foundation was cavernous. At 65,000 cubic feet and running 254 feet in length, with two wings 136 feet in width, the space held an enormous amount of gas. Third, gas was drawn from a residue line and so it had not been odorized. Natural gas is undetectable without odorization, and so nobody in the school noticed the build-up of gas in the weeks and days before the explosion. Fourth, barometric pressure dropped during the day, allowing the gas to expand and become more potent in the event of a catalyst. Finally, the shop teacher, Limmie Raines Butler, threw a spark when he switched on an electric sander, thus providing the catalyst (Steelhammer n.d., 4). David Price, an engineer in the research division of the federal Bureau of Chemicals and Soils, was also assigned to investigate. In his report he was careful to note the importance of the change in barometric pressure. He learned that a school employee went into the area at 10:00 a.m. that day to retrieve some stored material but didn't ignite the gas when several matches were struck (Price 1937, 5).

The sound of the explosion carried for 4 miles, and the force of the blast caused the building to appear to rise and then collapse in on itself. Most of those who died were crushed or asphixiated under masses of steel, concrete, and brick. Witnesses saw a wisp of a flame over the collapsing school, but the building never caught fire. The explosion occurred only twenty to thirty minutes before students were dismissed for the day, and in fact the first through fourth graders had already gone home. The building still contained approximately 500 students and 40 staff, and a group of parents attending a PTA meeting were in the school's gymnasium some 100 feet away (Steelhammer n.d., 3). Roughnecks from the oil fields were drawn to the school by the explosion and thousands aided the rescue and recovery efforts. The force of the blast pulverized some of the victims, who could not be recognized by their panicked and grieving loved ones. This is why the count of the dead fluctuated over the ensuing days and sits at "approximately 294" according to the online exhibit at the New London Museum. The day after the explosion, *The New York Daily News* reported that 650 children had been killed, which testifies to the confusion generated by the event, its remote location from larger cities, and the difficulty of getting accurate information in this period of news reporting.

On that point, a Dallas bureau reporter for the United Press International, Walter Cronkite, made his way to the site of the disaster and filed reports over the course of four days. The news brought First Lady Eleanor Roosevelt and German Chancellor Adolf Hitler to telegram their condolences. Investigators and journalists turned up several interesting testimonials to headaches among students and teachers at the school in the days before, and day of the blast. Headaches would be a signal of gas poisoning, along with dizziness and nausea. Sadly, nobody picked up on the idea that headaches indicated a gas leak was occurring at the school. State and federal agencies launched investigations, and the governor as commander-in-chief of the Texas State Militia authorized a military court of inquiry, but nobody was charged or brought to trial for the incident (Steelhammer n.d., 7). A number of civil suits brought against the Parade Gasoline Company by parents were dismissed due to lack of evidence.

Recriminations fell on Superintendent William Chesley Shaw who resigned amid threats of violence. He wrote the following message in a letter to the newspaper:

> I do not bear any resentment again those who demanded my removal. It must be remembered that they are under an intense emotional strain, and regardless of the findings of the court of inquiry, they felt someone must be held accountable. Because of my position, I was the target. New London is and always shall remain my home. My people and my wife's people were reared in the community. Our ties of friendship date back to childhood. We could not be content anywhere else. (Brown 2012, 218)

Among the many killed in the explosion were Shaw's son Sambo, his niece Dorothy, and his nephew Marvin. They were all buried, along with more than a hundred of the victims, at the Pleasant Hill Cemetery in New London.

The event raised questions about the safety of natural gas as a source of fuel for heating and cooking. Natural gas had been piped into buildings for interior lighting for more than a century and had proven to be a safe technology. Still, another huge explosion involving natural gas and liquefied natural gas in 1944 leveled a square mile of neighborhoods in on the east side of Cleveland, killing 131 people, and another in Richmond, Indiana in 1968 destroyed the downtown area with 41 fatalities. A construction crew broke an underground gas line in St. Cloud, Minnesota in 1998, killing four. Accidents are surprisingly frequent and sometimes fatal. Using data from the US Department of Transportation's Pipeline and Hazardous Materials Safety Administration (PHMSA) annual reports, a journalist compiled a list of pipe leak incidents, explosions, injuries, and fatalities. The inquiry found that between 2010 and 2021, more than 2,700 leak events were reported, with 362 of those ending in explosions. Nearly 700 people were injured, and more than 140 killed (Sterman 2022).

The irony of the New London school explosion is that it occurred in eastern Texas, a prosperous area rich in fossil fuels like oil and natural gas. By all accounts the school district had sufficient funding to pay for fuel. However, by arranging for free gas from a residue line, school officials set in motion a chain of events that led to the destruction of the school, and tragically ended the lives of nearly 300 people. In the months that followed, the Texas state government ordered the odorization of gas lines to provide a signal to gas users of a possible leak. This policy was adopted widely in the aftermath of the New London explosion. The sulfurous odor—like rotting eggs—is unmistakable, and likely saved many lives. The American Society of Mechanical Engineers awarded the Meter-Type Gas Odorizer of 1937 the distinction of being one of the US's landmark engineering technologies. The organization noted: "By the end of World War II, natural gas had established a reputation as a safe fuel largely because of odorizers" (ASME 1992).

Jeffrey B. Webb

See also: Cleveland East Ohio Gas Explosion; Natural Gas; Pittsburgh Gasometer Explosion; Richmond, Indiana Gas Explosions; Roughnecks; Texas Oil Boom

FURTHER READING

American Society of Mechanical Engineers (ASME). 1992. "ASME Landmark #163: Meter-type Gas Odorizer." The American Society of Mechanical Engineers. https://www.asme.org/about-asme/engineering-history/landmarks/163-meter-type-gas-odorizer (accessed October 2023).

Brown, David M., and Michael Wereschagin. 2012. *Gone at 3:17: The Untold Story of the Worst School Disaster in American History*. Washington, DC: Potomac Books.

Price, David J. 1937. *Explosion at Consolidated School, New London, Tex.: Report on Explosion at Consolidated School, New London, Tex., March 18, 1937*. Washington, DC: US Government Printing Office.

Steelhammer, Robert H. Jr. n.d. "The New London School Explosion." CED Engineering. https://www.cedengineering.com/courses/the-new-london-school-explosion (accessed October 2023).

Sterman, Joce, and Bailey Williams. 2022. "Silent Threat: Gas Explosions Injured Hundreds, Killed Dozens Nationwide since 2010." InvestigateTV. July 18. https://www.wbtv.com/2022/07/18/silent-threat-gas-explosions-injured-hundreds-killed-dozens-nationwide-since-2010/ (accessed October 2023).

New York City Blackout

The New York City Blackout of 1977 began shortly after 9:30 p.m. on a hot and humid July 13 and lasted more than twenty-four hours. Earlier in the evening, a series of lightning strikes on power lines north of the city had overwhelmed the extensive grid maintained by Consolidated Edison (Con Ed), the region's electric and gas utility, and the largest in the United States (Lifset 2014, 8). Having lost their external sources of power, local generators failed, instantly blanketing the city's lively streets, buildings, and neighborhoods in darkness. Looting and violence soon erupted and continued throughout the night, at times overwhelming New York City's beleaguered police force and devastating dozens of neighborhoods and thousands of small businesses. If, as the historian David Nye argues, "the social construction of reality breaks down" when a blackout strikes, the New York City Blackout of 1977 revealed the extent to which urban social order in America had come to depend on extensive energy infrastructures (Nye 2010, 33). New Yorkers had lived through many blackouts since the introduction of urban electrification in 1882, but only the 1977 blackout unleashed such shocking social unrest. The blackout exposed America's growing and increasingly fraught dependence on mass energy inputs, as well as the social realities of mismanagement and inequality that strained the New York City's social fabric in a pivotal decade.

Although many New Yorkers responded convivially to the sudden darkness, and most did not engage in violence, the blackout is primarily remembered for the looting, arson, and rioting that broke out minutes after the lights went out. Waves of looting and property destruction beset parts of Brooklyn, Harlem, and the Upper West Side throughout the night and into the next day. A Ford Foundation study of the violence noted three waves of looters: the "criminal types" who immediately exploited the opportunity to steal, the "alienated adolescents" who followed them, and finally the everyday poor, working-class, and middle-class citizens who got swept up in the hysteria of the moment and the suspension of social order (Curvin 1979, 3–16). Looters targeted consumer goods like electronics, furniture, and even automobiles, as well as food and clothing. Thousands of people participated, including women and children who in one account picked through an A&P grocery store in Brooklyn while police officers looked on (Phillips-Fein 2017, 270–1). In more extreme cases, rioters smashed windows, set buildings on fire, and battled with police. By the time it ended, blackout rioting resulted in 1,037 fires, 204 civilian injuries, 436 police injuries, and 80 firefighter injuries (Imperato 2016, 707). New York City police arrested more than 3,700 people on July 14, the largest single day total in the history of New York City, and quickly ran out of space in which to hold them (Phillips-Fein 2017, 273).

The social chaos and hysteria of the 1977 blackout underscored the central role of energy in the maintenance of social and political order in the mid-twentieth-century United States. Between 1950 and 1975, American electricity consumption, which drew on coal, oil, hydroelectric power, and nuclear power, grew nearly sixfold, alongside the surge of fossil fuels use in transportation, heating, and other applications (EIA 2020, 141). Driving this increase was the spread of electric lighting, air-conditioning, escalators and elevators, televisions, vacuum cleaners, and many other machines and consumer goods, all of which reshaped how Americans interacted with each other and the world around them. In October 1973, the OPEC oil embargo and the energy crisis that followed demonstrated the precarious nature of such a society in the form of frustrating line-ups for gasoline, stagflation, and other intimations of national decline. The 1977 New York City Blackout affirmed the lessons of the energy crisis about dangers of energy dependence: as the structure of American life came to depend substantially on electric power, the stakes of a potential power failure grew. As David Nye notes, American social order in the 1970s relied on a range of electronic technologies to aid surveillance and the control of populations. The blackout nullified these controls and "offered release into enhanced conviviality or riot" (Nye 2010, 129).

The blackout was not solely the consequence of chance lightning strikes on an otherwise stable, high-energy network. Years of cost-cutting and mismanagement on the part of Con Ed meant that its network was unprepared to cope with an emergency. Protests by environmentalists, litigation, and adverse legislation in the 1960s and 1970s prevented Con Ed from expanding its generating capacity along the Hudson River, weakened it financially, and extended the utility's electricity supply network to include generation facilities located far outside of New York City and connected by few transmission lines (Lifset 2014, 17–18). Faced as well with declining gains in efficiency and rising consumption, Con Ed struggled to keep up with demand and to maintain its network. Cost-cutting, poor training, and mismanaged maintenance further weakened the network, which fell into disrepair and obsolescence. Con Ed's network thus failed to adapt to the lightning strikes. Its undertrained staff panicked in an out-dated control room and made critical errors that led to a system-wide blackout (Nye 2010, 119). Even though lightning strikes initiated the series of events that ended in power failure, none of the blackout's many subsequent investigators concluded that it had been a natural disaster.

Important as they are, the technical factors for the power outage are not enough to explain why *this* blackout led to the widespread looting and violence that some writers have likened to the food riots of the more distant past (Phillips-Fein 2017, 272). If growing energy consumption and grid mismanagement explain the darkness of July 13–14, 1977, the public response to it reveals the fractured social and political environment of New York City, and of America more broadly, in the 1970s. As was the case for many American cities, rising unemployment and poverty beset New York in the 1970s, diminishing city services and fostering a pervasive sense of urban decay. A rising crime rate and the loss of more than 500,000 jobs translated into the loss of nearly 1 million residents over the course of the decade, which nearly put New York City into bankruptcy as tax revenues dwindled and demand for services strained resources to breaking point. In this context, and in a national situation of stagflation and economic uncertainty, poor and working-class citizens grew frustrated with their inability to get ahead in an increasingly dysfunctional city. Many saw the blackout as an economic opportunity that had been denied them for years. As one woman told a reporter, "Poor people have been waiting for years for those lights to go out" (quoted in Phillips-Fein 2017, 276).

If the 1977 New York City Blackout reflected growing dependence on electricity and the social discontents of the 1970s, it also played a role in the rightward turn of US political culture. Conservative critics used the eruption of looting and vandalism to argue against the welfare state and to question the ability of government to address poverty. The problems of New York City and the social chaos of its "night of terror" represented for many conservatives the fundamental failure of social liberals to help the nation's poor and the necessity of restricting the role of government to stimulating job creation and maintaining law and order. The blackout was thus a critical event in America's energy history that revealed how profoundly energy had come to shape social relations and provided ammunition to the political right in the decade of its ascendancy.

Caleb Wellum

See also: Consolidated Edison Company, Electricity; Energy Crisis of the 1970s; General Electric Company; National Energy Act of 1978; Organization of Petroleum Exporting Countries (OPEC); Pearl Street Power Station; Public Utility Regulatory Policies Act of 1978; Smart Grid

FURTHER READING

Curvin, Robert, and Bruce Portner. 1979. *Blackout Looting!: New York City, July 13, 1977*. New York: Gardner Press.

Imperato, Pascal James. 2016. "Public Health Concerns Associated with the New York City Blackout of 1977." *Journal of Community Health*. Vol. 41. Pp. 707–16.

Lifset, Robert. 2014. *Power on the Hudson: Storm King Mountain and the Emergence of Modern Environmentalism*. Pittsburgh, PA: University of Pittsburgh Press.

Mahler, Jonathan. 2005. *Ladies and Gentlemen, the Bronx is Burning: 1977, Baseball, Politics, and the Battle for the Soul of a City*. New York: Picador.

Nye, David. 2010. *When the Lights Went Out: A History of Blackouts in America*. Cambridge, MA: MIT Press.

Phillips-Fein, Kim. 2017. *Fear City: New York's Fiscal Crisis and the Rise of Austerity Politics*. New York: Henry Holt and Company.

US Energy Information Administration (EIA). 2020. *Monthly Energy Review*. January. https://www.eia.gov/totalenergy/data/monthly/pdf/mer.pdf (accessed January 2020).

New York Steam Company

Among the most striking energy infrastructures in the United States is Manhattan's district steam heating system. The system traces its origins to 1881 with the formation of the New York Steam Company. Wallace C. Andrews (1833–99), company founder, envisioned a unified heating system for Manhattan, in which hundreds of large buildings would draw steam from a group of centralized stream boilers through a series of pipes located under streets and sidewalks. Once built, the steam was used principally for heating but also other purposes like hot water supply, food preparation, steam cleaning, laundering and pressing clothes, and "motive power" in industrial applications. The district steam heating system contributed to Manhattan's spatial development by encouraging density and verticality, which resulted in the city's distinctive skyline and its dynamic urban vitality. The New York Steam Company's system provided a model for other cities, and by 1918 some 397 municipal systems were in operation around the country (Pierce 2022).

Manhattan's district steam heating system doesn't own the distinction of being the first workable system of its kind in the nation. That belongs to the one built in Lockport, New York in 1877 by engineer and inventor Birdsill Holly (1820–94). Interior steam heating had established itself as a proven technology by then, and the basic elements had been improved upon. Holly attempted something new, which is delivering steam heat to multiple dwellings from a single source. He proved the concept by installing a boiler in his home on Chestnut Street in Lockport, and then routing a 1.5-inch pipe through his back yard and a neighboring property. The 490-feet pipe was buried 3 feet underground in a wooden box and insulated with asbestos, felt, and paper then encased in sawdust (NYSC 1932, 14). It appeared to work as designed and Holly got his neighbor to agree to connect his home to the system. With good results in hand, Holly founded the Holly Steam Combination Company and received a franchise from the city of Lockwood to build a larger system and solicit customers. It consisted of a small building that housed a 10 feet high, 7 feet in diameter boiler and a 30-feet-high chimney. Holly ran 2,350 feet of large main pipes from the building through his town, with smaller service pipes branching off to connect forty residences, two larger buildings, and two steam engines to the system.

Holly reincorporated as American District Steam Company in 1882, and by then had installed nineteen systems in communities around the area (Pierce 2022). His success drew the attention of Wallace C. Andrews, who made his fortune in coal mining, iron production, and railroad construction in Ohio. Andrews was a founding board member of John D. Rockefeller's Standard Oil Company and one of the business tycoons of the Gilded Age. He was fascinated with Holly's system and visited Lockport in person to observe its operation. Andrews also asked Charles E. Emery to study the system, a civil engineer with a distinguished record of service in the US Navy during the US Civil War and a budding expert in steam heating. Andrews became involved in discussions with investors about bringing Holly's system to New

York. The city's Common Council had already given a franchise to a group led by Francis B. Spinola to build the system, and Andrews bought the rights to this franchise. Another group secured a second franchise for the same purpose from the Board of Aldermen, and Andrews helped to negotiate a merger in 1881 that created the New York Steam Company. Andrews served as the company's first president, and Emery its chief engineer.

The work itself required identifying locations for the district plants, laying steam mains and service pipes, and lining up clients for the service. Andrews and Emery projected ten districts spread out over lower Manhattan, each with its own steam plant. The first plant was built on the site of the current location of the National September 11 Memorial and Museum at (formerly) 16 Cortlandt Street, which housed forty-eight boilers arranged on three floors of the facility. The distinguishing feature of the plant was its 225-foot chimney, which dominated the New York City skyline in the years prior to the appearance of the first skyscrapers. Within months the company served its first patron, the United Bank Building on the corner of Wall Street and Broadway. The building featured two elevators that were powered by steam provided by the New York Steam Company's new system (NYSC 1932, 31). By the end of 1882, the company served sixty-two customers in lower Manhattan including banks, insurance companies, manufacturers, printing companies, St. Peter's Roman Catholic Church, and a number of private residences. To power its plants, it contracted with Curtis & Blaisdell Company to provide coal from their depot on the East River at 56th and 57th Streets.

The initial phase of construction in 1881 and 1882 overlapped with the preparatory work of Edison Electric Illuminating Company for equipping the city with light and electrical power. Edison recently developed a system for generating electricity in central power stations and delivering it along a network of transmission wires to distant users in their homes, businesses, and public places. Construction on Edison's first version of the system began in 1881 on Pearl Street in the Financial District. Accounts tell of face-to-face encounters between Thomas Edison and New York Steam Company engineer Charles Emery on the streets of the city, socializing and discussing engineering problems associated with wiring and piping the city for heat, light, and electrical power (NYSC 1932, 27). These two private companies were creating the infrastructure for public utilities, which along with natural gas, telephone service, fresh water, and sanitation will be considered essential services for village, town, and city dwellers in future years. Over the next half-century, a series of mergers and acquisitions resulted in the formation of Consolidated Edison Company of New York, Inc., which took its name in 1936. Con Ed incorporated Edison's original company, an amalgamation of natural gas companies, and in 1959 the New York Steam Company. This brought some of the key essential services under the Con Ed umbrella for customers living within the region.

By then New York had become a city of skyscrapers, and the New York Steam Company played a role in that process. New "elevator" buildings built in New York after 1882 connected to the district steam heating system, enabling them to power elevators and dispense with their own coal-fired steam boilers, which also meant eliminating unsightly, smoky chimneys. These included the Times Building (1889), the Tower Building (1889), the Singer Building (1899), and the Metropolitan Life Building (1890) and its accompanying 50-storey tower (1908). In the post-First World War skyscraper boom in New York, the company supplied heat and steam power for the Chrysler Building (1930), the Western Union Building (1930), the Waldorf Astoria Hotel (1931), the General Electric Tower (1931), the Empire State Building (1931), and the Rockefeller Center (1939), in addition to dozens of other high-rise landmarks.

Architects for buildings in the 1920s–1930s Art Deco style could design their buildings without service areas for coal delivery and storage, and without rooftop accommodations for smokestacks. It allowed for compaction and the elevation of rooflines, enabling the city to maintain its walkability while increasing capacity for more residents and more businesses. Put simply, district steam heat in Manhattan was a simpler, cleaner, and more efficient way to utilize energy and in the process, facilitate building design that left a distinctive imprint on the city. According to one architectural historian: "The highly spectacular 1930s skyline was … an aesthetic consequence of the advantages of district heating" (Gallo 2003, 98).

The financial and social elite of Manhattan were quick to adopt the system as well. The system cleared their homes of smoke and dust from coal-fired steam boilers and kept dirty coal delivery trucks out of their neighborhoods. Wallace C. Andrews and his family lived in one of those mansions at 67th Street and Fifth Avenue on Central Park. Tragically, he didn't live to see the district steam heating system he worked so hard to create reach its full potential. On April 7, 1899, a little after 2:00 a.m., his house caught fire and burst into a raging inferno, trapping and killing twelve people inside. Andrews died along with his wife, his visiting sister, and her three children. Six housekeepers and nursemaids died in the house, while two other servants jumped from the house and were badly injured. Police and fire investigators determined the cause of the fire to be a natural gas explosion in the basement of the building ("Horrible" 1899).

Given the newness of district steam heating, municipal natural gas systems, and centralized electricity-generating systems, it is unsurprising that explosions like the one that killed the president of the New York Steam Company generated concerns about the safety of these new energy technologies. A letter about the Andrews mansion fire in the *Indianapolis Journal* aimed a barb at Edison's Pearl Street Station. After describing a house fire caused by an oil lamp in another recent incident, the report observed: "But there was no parlor lamp in the home of Mr. Andrews, and it is perhaps not surprising that, in view of this fire, there should be renewal of those vague comments expressing doubt as to the means now employed to secure absolute immunity from danger that may be created by the employment of the electric current for lighting purposes" ("Mystery" 1899). In the process of misidentifying the cause of the Andrews fire, the letter wondered if the quiet murmurs about the safety precautions undertaken by big energy companies like the Edison Electric Illuminating Company should be openly expressed. This testifies to the lingering uncertainties and anxieties among those who lived through the rapid energy transition that occurred at turn of the twentieth century.

The district steam heating systems devised, constructed, and maintained in Manhattan by the New York Steam Company proved to be very safe. In 1913, the Public Service Commission was granted authority to monitor the system and mandate safety improvements, which brought the company to replace its older mains and service pipes with upgraded flange-and-gasket connectors, high-rated metal pipes, and safer insulation. The system also received continual upgrades in its system controls, enabling users to better regulate building temperatures. Its demonstrable improvement in performance begat imitation, and many other cities followed suit. Between 1877 and 2020, a total of 480 district steam heating systems were built across the United States, and steam heat delivered from remote steam-generating plants remains the chief source of interior heating in 68 American towns and cities (Pierce 2022).

Jeffrey B. Webb

See also: Consolidated Edison Company; Edison, Thomas Alva; Evans, Oliver; Gold, Stephen J.; Johnson, Warren Seymour; Pearl Street Power Station; Pierce Steam Heating Company; Powers, William Penn; Steam Power

FURTHER READING

Gallo, Emmanuelle. 2003. "Skyscrapers and District Heating, an Inter-related History, 1876–1933." *Construction History*. Vol. 19. Pp. 87–106.

"Horrible Holocaust." 1899. *El Paso Daily Herald*. Vol. 19. No. 85. April 7. https://texashistory.unt.edu/ark:/67531/metapth297080/m1/1/?q=Central%20Gardens (accessed October 2023).

"Mystery of New York Fires." 1899. *Indianapolis Journal*. Vol. 49. No. 102. April 12. P. 2.

New York Steam Corporation (NYSC). 1932. *Fifty Years of New York Steam Service: The Story of the Founding and Development of a Public Utility*. New York: New York Steam Corporation.

Pierce, Morris A. 2022. "Summary of District Heating Systems in the United States, 1877–2020." Documentary History of American Water-works. February 28. http://waterworkshistory.us/DH/DHsummary.pdf (accessed October 2023).

North Antelope Rochelle Mine

The North Antelope Rochelle Mine is the world's largest coal mine in operation, and one of the economic engines of Wyoming and the American West. The mine, and the people who work it, continue a long tradition of coal mining and resource extraction in the region that stretches as far back as the 1300s and the Hopi Tribe. The Hopi used the coal they mined for producing pottery and as a fuel source (Ascarza 2014). Like the Europeans who would eventually come to their lands, the Hopi, and other tribes who had access to coal, used it as an energy source and a tool to build their civilization. In the era of exploration and discovery, Europeans determined that the tribes, their resources, and their lands should and would be exploited, which eventually fell to Americans and the US government (Cozzens 2016, 316–17).

The first commercial European coal mine in what would become the United States opened in 1701 near Richmond, Virginia (NASEM 2018). Like the Hopi, American settlers used coal to produce items and as a fuel source, but it was a secondary fuel source to their primary source, which was wood. In the aftermath of the American Revolution, wood remained the dominant fuel source. Especially in the East, the United States was covered in what seemed like limitless forests from Minnesota to Georgia (Lass 1998). But, while wood was king, the mining and production of coal was growing. Most of the coal mined from within the borders of the United States was bituminous coal. This is a soft coal that was easy to mine and easy to use. It helped power the growth of the United States, including industry, home heating, and railroads spreading across the country. Eventually, as wood became more and more scarce, and more expensive, because of deforestation and economic and population growth, coal became more and more central to the nation's economy. Eventually, this led to coal overtaking wood as the primary energy source in the 1880s. Coal held onto this status until the 1950s when it was replaced by petroleum (EIA 2013).

Coal production spread across the United States as the country expanded. Mines and the infrastructure to transport and use the coal developed where cities, factories, and other sinews of civilization developed. An example of this is Birmingham, Alabama. Birmingham, founded in the aftermath of the US Civil War, was designed to be a southern industrial city that could rival the cities of the North. It was built around all the necessary ingredients to make steel. This included coal. The city, which was quickly nicknamed the "Magic City" because of its rapid growth, began to accomplish its designated goal and expanded quickly to become an important steel producing city in the American South (McWhorter 2012, 29–31). Coal and other mineral resources made the growth of civilization possible, not only in Alabama but elsewhere that American settlers established the modern industrial system, even in the desolate West.

Wyoming, both the territory and the state, began as a sparsely settled, and still mostly unexplored, land with the possibility of substantial undiscovered mineral resources, including coal. Coal was first discovered in Wyoming in 1843, when explorer John C. Frémont discovered coal on a journey through the then unnamed area (Lightner 2020, 75). As with Birmingham, the mines and related production facilities appeared, and began the process of making the sinews of civilization. The production of coal in Wyoming began in 1867, when the Union Pacific Railroad began its march across the territory towards its rendezvous with the Central Pacific Railroad in Utah. As the railroad and its branches grew, the coal mines grew, all controlled by the Union Pacific. Because of its monopoly control, labor strife and racial violence often roiled Wyoming. In the 1870s and 1880s, coal miners attacked mine operators and those they blamed for low wages, the Chinese (Lightner 2020, 149). As long as coal was the main energy source and the railroad was the key method of transportation, the system of labor exploitation remained.

Eventually, coal's position of dominance gave way to petroleum. In the early twentieth century, automobiles and airplanes challenged passenger rail as the chief means of transportation. Ships changed from coal to oil, and electricity generation plants began a long process of switching from coal to natural gas. In Wyoming, the days of the Union Pacific Railroad's control of the coal mines was over. In time, Peabody Energy, Inc. gained control of the mines through a process of acquisition and consolidation. The company was founded as Peabody, Daniels & Company in 1883 in Chicago. The company began operations in Wyoming in 1983 when it opened the North Antelope Mine and two years later, the Rochelle Mine. In 1999, those mines were merged together to form the North Antelope Rochelle Mine. The North Antelope Rochelle Mine was and is the largest coal mine in the world, producing thermal coal for electricity generation (PEI 2021). Importantly, the mine utilizes surface mining techniques, which are controversial due to the large environmental impact they leave behind when the mining sites are not rehabilitated.

Peabody survived by supplying coal to US power plants, but coal began to fade as a source of energy due to environmental concerns surrounding coal mining sites, including contamination of surface and groundwater, as well as broader concerns about the burning of carbon-based fuels and the creation of greenhouse gases. Since the 1950s, coal has been slowly falling out of favor in the United States and around the world. In response, Peabody Energy and other coal producers have been trying to respond with messages about "clean coal" and professions of support for human rights in overseas energy exploration and development. Peabody also supports some environmental protections and regulations in order to remain relevant (PEI 2021).

While Peabody Energy operates the largest coal mine in world, which produced 85.3 million tons of coal in 2019, its battle for relevance faces steep challenges. Peabody Energy was forced to declare bankruptcy in 2016 due to decreased reliance on coal (Rucinski 2016). This has led to a steadily shrinking need for coal and for coal miners. In 2020, nearly 170 workers were laid off from the North Antelope Rochelle Mine (Erickson 2020). At one point, the North Antelope Rochelle Mine was the economic heart of northeastern Wyoming, and a driver of economic growth in the American West. Ensuring that workers, Wyoming communities, and the wider regional economy survives the end of coal will be an important part of the responsibility shared by the coal industry and by state and federal governments as the United States moves into a new energy future.

Jeff Hirschy

See also: Clean Coal; Coal; Climate Change; Dawson Mine Disaster; Ludlow Massacre; Surface Mining; Surface Mining Control and Reclamation Act of 1977; Transcontinental Railroad

FURTHER READING

Ascarza, William. 2014. "Mine Tales: State's History of Coal Mining Goes Back at Least 700 Years." *Arizona Daily Star*. May 12. https://tucson.com/news/local/mine-tales-states-history-of-coal-mining-goes-back-at-least-700-years/article_1c37a635-6143-5ab7-9f7c-b35dbaf41679.html (accessed June 4, 2020).

Cozzens, Peter. 2016. *The Earth is Weeping: The Epic Story of the Indian Wars for the American West*. New York: Alfred A. Knopf.

Erickson, Camile, and Nick Reynolds. 2020. "300 Workers Laid Off at Three Powder River Basin Mines." *Casper Star Tribune*. April 23. https://trib.com/business/energy/300-workers-laid-off-at-three-powder-river-basin-mines/article_c014e9c7-4c3f-5582-afc9-5c1b76ff5210.html (accessed June 4, 2020).

Lass, Willian E. 1998. *Minnesota: A History*. New York: W.W. Norton & Company.

Lightner Jr., Sam. 2020. *Wyoming: A History of the American West*. Cheyenne, WY: Summits and Crux.

McWhorter, Diane. 2012. *Carry Me Home: Birmingham, Alabama: The Climatic Battle of the Civil Rights Revolution*. New York: Simon & Schuster.

National Academies of Sciences, Engineering, Medicine (NASEM). 2018. "Appendix E: Coal Mining in the United States." Committee on the Study of the Control of Responsible Coal Mine Dust Exposure in Underground Mines. In *Monitoring and Sampling Approaches to Assess Underground Coal Mine Dust Explosions*. Pp. 122–9. Washington, DC: The National Academies Press.

Peabody Energy, Inc. (PEI). 2021. "North Antelope Rochelle Mine." https://www.peabodyenergy.com/Operations/U-S-Mining/Powder-River-Basin-Mining/North-Antelope-Rochelle-Mine (accessed June 4, 2020).

Rucinski, Tracy, and Tom Hals. 2016. "Leading Global Coal Miner Peabody Files for Bankruptcy." Reuters. April 13. https://www.reuters.com/article/us-peabody-energy-bankruptcy/leading-global-coal-miner-peabody-files-for-bankruptcy-idUSKCN0XA0E7 (accessed June 4, 2020).

US Energy Information Administration (EIA). 2013. "Energy Sources Have Changed throughout the History of the United States." Today in Energy. July 3. US Department of Energy. https://www.eia.gov/todayinenergy/detail.php?id=11951 (accessed June 4, 2020).

Nuclear Power

The history of nuclear power might be traced to the work of Greek natural philosopher, Democritus (570–460 BCE), who asserted that all matter was made up of small, indivisible particles, which he called *atomos*. English chemist and physicist John Dalton outlined a framework for modern atomic theory in 1803, but it was not until the 1890s that a number of European scientists began to build on one another's work in their research of radioactivity and the newly discovered radioactive elements of radium and polonium. There was a new understanding by this time that atoms themselves comprised smaller particles and were, in fact, not indivisible. In 1905, Austrian physicist Albert Einstein developed his theory of relativity, which explained the relationship between matter and energy and furthered the potential for generating power from the atom (Newton 2006, 85–6).

Atomic scientists continued their work in the early decades of the twentieth century, and intense technological competition in the development of weaponry during the Second World War drove significant advancements in nuclear research. In 1939, Einstein joined scientists Enrico Fermi and Leo Szilard in informing the US military and President Franklin D. Roosevelt of the potential for harnessing nuclear energy for military purposes. When it became clear that Germany was investing in nuclear research, the United States took action and concentrated its efforts in the Manhattan Project. Those efforts culminated in the dropping of atomic bombs on the Japanese cities of Hiroshima and Nagasaki in 1945 (Mahaffey 2009, 112).

Because of the destructive nature of atomic weapons and the exploitation of nuclear energy for use in war, the US government and atomic scientists faced challenges in transforming public opinion to acceptance of nuclear energy for peaceful purposes in the post-war period. Congress passed the Atomic Energy Act of 1946, which created the Atomic Energy Commission (AEC) to support research and regulate use of nuclear power. It would also serve to promote its use in health, industry, and energy sectors where it might generate electricity and perhaps even power vehicles one day. The 1946 legislation designated authority over all bomb making and peaceful production of nuclear power. In 1954, the Congressional Joint Committee on Atomic Energy created a legislative monopoly on all matters related to nuclear energy. The AEC and corporations produced a series of informational films to educate the public on the potential for this new energy source and to dispel fears. They included *A Is for Atom* (General Electric, 1953), *Our Friend the Atom* (Disney, 1957), and *Using Atomic Energy for Electric Power* (Popular Science, 1957).

An experimental station near Arco, Idaho generated the first electricity from nuclear energy in 1951. Then, the first nuclear power plant opened in the United States six years later. In 1960, there were seventeen reactors, and by the mid-1970s more than 100 reactors were producing 20 percent of the nation's electricity. Nuclear power was considered inexpensive and emission-free at a time when the US Environmental Protection Agency (EPA) was watching air and water pollution closely. Plant construction slowed dramatically in 1974 due to public protests and serious concerns regarding plant safety and proper disposal of waste. A number of critics had questioned the AEC's commitment to public safety when radionuclides were discovered drifting away from Nevada test sites by air, and into the 1970s there had been no satisfactory disposal of liquid waste. New methods of solidifying waste led to some optimism, but resistance to opening disposal sites appeared in various states (Cook 1982, 7–8). In 1976, California placed a moratorium on the construction of any new reactors until a national policy addressing waste was implemented. In that same year, Michigan Governor William G. Milliken vetoed a bill designed to build a waste disposal site in his state. Passage of the Nuclear Waste Policy Act of 1982 served as a major step in promoting solutions.

NUCLEAR NON-PROLIFERATION

Splitting uranium atoms is comparatively easy, making the element the most widely used in generating nuclear power; however, it is also used in the manufacture of nuclear weapons. To prevent the unregulated development of weapons, only nations that have signed on to the Nuclear Non-Proliferation Treaty (NPT) are permitted to import uranium, making it more difficult for some regions to build reactors designed to provide electricity.

Kathleen A. Tobin

The March 28, 1979 accident at the Three Mile Island nuclear generating station on the Susquehanna River near Harrisburg, Pennsylvania intensified fears and resulted in the halting of construction of any additional plants in the United States. In that incident, equipment malfunction and human error caused a partial core meltdown and release of radioactive contaminated water into the area. Plant workers were exposed to radiation and area residents fled. There were no deaths or injuries associated with the incident, but it raised serious public concerns about the ability of utility companies and the government to ensure safety. In a short time, major Hollywood production of films such as *The China Syndrome* (1979), *Silkwood* (1983), *Testament* (1983), and *The Day After* (1983) heightened public fears regarding nuclear power plant accidents and fictionalized nuclear attacks on the United States.

Nuclear research and design improvements continued, and new discussions regarding the use of nuclear power surfaced in the twenty-first century. Proponents pointed to general improvements in technology, increased safety measures, and the inability of renewable sources to meet increasing demand for energy. They saw fossil fuel conservation efforts as having had minimal success and maintained that advancements in wind and solar power production in the United States were not sufficient. Arguments for greater investment in nuclear energy included 1) its considerably low emissions of carbon and other air pollutants; 2) dependability as a concentrated source with steady output throughout each day; and 3) low cost compared to power generated by fossil fuels like oil, coal, and natural gas. Critics have expressed concern over the high capital costs associated with safe generator construction, the potential for terrorist attacks, continued potential for harm to the environment and people in case of an accident, and the low prospect for energy independence, as the majority of uranium used in generating power is sourced outside the United States (Zott 2013, 144). However, many now consider nuclear power a clean energy source free from international pressures associated with global fossil fuel markets, and a new generation sees it as a preferred source of energy. Nuclear power plants are safer, simpler, and more cost effective than in the past, and investors are securing increased capital as a shift in public opinion supports expanding nuclear capacity as key to energy in the future (Tabak 2009, 144–5).

Kathleen A. Tobin

See also: Atomic Energy Acts; Church Rock Uranium Mill Spill; Clean Power Plan of 2015; Fermi, Enrico; Idaho National Energy Laboratory; Manhattan Project; Nuclear Regulatory Commission; Nuclear Waste Policy Act of 1982; Steen, Charles Augustus; Three Mile Island Accident; Yucca Mountain Nuclear Waste Repository

FURTHER READING

Cook, Earl. 1982. "The Role of History in the Acceptance of Nuclear Power." *Social Science Quarterly*. Vol. 63. No. 1. Pp. 3–15.

Drogan, Mara. 2016. "The Nuclear Imperative: Atoms for Peace and the Development of U.S. Policy on Exporting Nuclear Power, 1953–1955." *Diplomatic History*. Vol. 40. No. 5. Pp. 948–74.

Kidd, Jerry S., and Renee A. Kidd. 2006. *Nuclear Power: The Study of Quarks and Sparks*. New York: Chelsea House.

Mahaffey, James. 2009. *Atomic Awakening: A New Look at the History and Future of Nuclear Power*. New York: Pegasus Books.

Newton, David E. 2006. *Nuclear Power*. New York: Facts On File, Inc.

Tabak, John. 2009. *Nuclear Energy*. New York: Facts On File, Inc.

Zott, Lynn M., and Helga Schier, eds. 2013. *Nuclear Power* (Opposing Viewpoints Series). Farmington Hills, MI: Greenhaven Press.

Nuclear Regulatory Commission

The US Nuclear Regulatory Commission (NRC) is an independent agency that operates to ensure the safe use of radioactive materials with the aim of protecting people and the environment. The NRC coordinates commercial nuclear power plants' functioning and the uses of nuclear materials through licensing, inspection, and enforcement of its requirements. The NRC focuses on protecting public health and safety through implementing its main regulatory functions. These include establishing standards and regulations, issuing licenses for nuclear facilities and users of nuclear materials, and inspecting facilities and users of nuclear materials to ensure compliance with the requirements. All these regulatory functions are related to the operation of nuclear power plants and the use of nuclear materials in industrial production, medicine, and scientific research (NRC 2020).

The NRC declares its mission to be licensing and regulating "the nation's civilian use of radioactive materials to provide reasonable assurance of adequate protection of public health and safety and to promote the common defense and security and to protect the environment" (NRC 2020). The scope of the mission covers three areas. First, it involves supervision of nuclear reactors in commercial facilities, commonly used for generating electric power, but also research and test reactors used for research, testing, and training. Another area is the handling of nuclear materials in medical, industrial, and academic settings and facilities that produce nuclear fuel. Finally, its scope entails the management of nuclear wastes, ranging from transportation, storage, and disposal, but also decommissioning nuclear facilities from service (NRC 2020).

Before the NRC was established by Congress in 1974, nuclear regulation was the responsibility of the Atomic Energy Commission (AEC), which was created by the Atomic Energy Act of 1946. In the Atomic Energy Act of 1954, Congress authorized the development of commercial nuclear power and made the AEC responsible for supervising civilian nuclear power facilities. The AEC's mission was to promote safety in the commercial uses of nuclear power while protecting public health, but without imposing excessive requirements that might hinder the growth of the nuclear industry. In the 1960s, an increasing number of critics charged that the AEC's regulations were insufficiently rigorous in several important areas, including radiation protection standards, reactor safety, plant siting, and environmental protection.

By the early 1970s, the AEC's regulatory programs had come under such strong attack that Congress decided to abolish the agency. Under the Atomic Energy Act of 1954, the AEC had responsibility for the development and production of nuclear weapons, while also overseeing the development and regulation of the civilian uses of nuclear materials. Supporters and critics of nuclear power agreed that these varied areas of responsibility should be assigned to different agencies. The Energy Reorganization Act of 1974 split these functions, assigning to the department now called the US Department of Energy the responsibility for the development and security of nuclear weapons and the promotion of civilian nuclear power, while assigning regulatory work to the new NRC. The new agency began its operations on January 19, 1975. It is important to note that the NRC's area of responsibility does not include regulation of defense-related nuclear facilities.

Like its predecessor AEC, the new NRC focused its attention on several issues that were essential to protecting public health and safety. As the number of plants being built and the size of nuclear power plants rapidly increased during the late 1960s and early 1970s, reactor safety became a hotly debated and enormously complex public policy issue. Concerns were expressed over a broad range of issues, including the reliability of emergency core cooling systems, pressure vessel integrity, quality assurance, and preparedness in the event of a major accident.

An accident at the Three Mile Island plant near Harrisburg, Pennsylvania on March 28, 1979 made the public aware of the possibility of radioactive contamination of areas surrounding nuclear power plants, but also revealed the weaknesses in the system of nuclear regulation then in operation. In the aftermath of the accident, the NRC placed much greater emphasis on operator training and "human factors" in plant performance. It focused on severe accidents that could occur as a result of small equipment failures, which was identified as the main issue that triggered the partial core meltdown at Three Mile Island. The agency focused on emergency planning, developing plant operating histories, and other precautionary matters.

The NRC also devoted much effort to developing policies and management strategies for disposing of high-level and low-level radioactive waste. This was a pervasive concern in the as expressed in the media and in public debate. Particularly worrisome was the possibility of the use of nuclear waste in an act of terrorism. Overall, however, the core mission of the NRC was to create the official government regulations that would guide and direct the safe use of nuclear materials for electrical power-generation in nuclear fission plants, as well as a variety of industrial, medical, and research applications.

The NRC is headed by five commissioners appointed by the president and confirmed by the Senate for five-year terms. One is designated by the president to be the chairman and official spokesperson of the commission. The commission as a collegial body that formulates policies, develops regulations governing nuclear reactor and nuclear material safety, issues orders to licensees, and adjudicates legal matters. The executive director for operations (EDO) carries out the policies and decisions of the commission and directs the activities of the program offices. The offices reporting to the EDO ensure that the commercial use of nuclear materials in the United States is safely conducted. As part of the regulatory process, the four regional offices conduct inspection, enforcement, and emergency response programs for licensees within their borders (NRC 2020).

The NRC's headquarters is located in Rockville, Maryland, and it staffs four regional offices in King of Prussia, Pennsylvania, Atlanta, Georgia, Lisle, Illinois, and Arlington, Texas. The agency's Technical Training Center in located in Chattanooga, Tennessee. The NRC also has on-site inspectors permanently stationed at each nuclear facility that it regulates (NRC 2020).

The agency endeavors to project competence, professionalism, and diligence in order to retain the confidence of the American people. Its website proclaims a commitment to "Demonstrate the Principles of Good Regulation," which it defines as independence, openness, efficiency, clarity, and reliability in the performance of its mission. NRC claims to set these principles into practice with effective, realistic, and timely regulatory actions, consistent with their organizational values and open, collaborative work environment. The agency says that the key to functioning as a responsible regulator with a very important safety and security mission is to have its values shape its regulatory activities, with a clear eye on safety and security while appropriately balancing the interests of the NRC's constituents, including the public (NRC 2020). The NRC places a high priority on openness and transparency. The agency maintains a web page, has a Public Document Room at its headquarters in Rockville, and holds public meetings throughout the United States.

Regardless of its efforts, the NRC has and will always be subject of scrutiny and public debate just by virtue of its function as the chief authority responsible for supervising and regulating the commercial use of nuclear energy. In the 1990s, the NRC was accused of failing to pursue tough regulation, denying public access to the regulatory process, and creating barriers to public participation (Byrne 1996, 160). More recently, the NRC faced censure for deeming the potential for terrorist attacks on spent fuel storage facilities "remote and speculative," and for failing to include these possibilities in the agency's required environmental assessments. One critic noted: "NRC was willing to take an obviously unauthorized shortcut to ignore the unmistakable meaning of the regulations in order to approve a license" (Lochbaum 2008). With a complicated and sensitive mission, and American public's continued wariness about nuclear energy, the NRC will have regulatory challenges in the future. This is particularly the case, given the renewed interest in weaning the United States off fossil fuels by building the next generation of nuclear power plants.

Inna Sukhenko

See also: Atomic Energy Acts; Church Rock Uranium Mill Spill; Clean Power Plan of 2015; Idaho National Laboratory; Nuclear Power; Nuclear Waste Policy Act of 1982; Project Gasbuggy; Shippingport Atomic Power Station; Steen, Charles Augustus; Three Mile Island Accident; Yucca Mountain Nuclear Waste Repository

FURTHER READING

Byrne, John, and Steven M. Hoffman. 1996. *Governing the Atom: The Politics of Risk*. Piscataway, NJ: Transaction Publishers.

Lochbaum, David. 2008. "NRC Has Failed in the Past, but There's Still Hope for its Future." *Bulletin of the Atomic Scientists*. July 11. https://thebulletin.org/roundtable_entry/nrc-has-failed-in-the-past-but-theres-still-hope-for-its-future/ (accessed March 20, 2020).

Mazuzan, George. T., and J. Samuel Walker. 1997. "Controlling the Atom: The Beginnings of Nuclear Regulation 1946–1962." (original pub. date 1984). US Nuclear Regulatory Commission. NUREG-1610. Washington, DC. https://digital.library.unt.edu/ark:/67531/metadc691308/ (accessed February 29, 2020).

US Nuclear Regulatory Commission (NRC). 2013. "Medical Use of Byproduct Material." 10 CFR Part 35. http://www.snmmi.org/IssuesAdvocacy/content.aspx?ItemNumber= (accessed February 29, 2020).

US Nuclear Regulatory Commission (NRC). 2020. "About NRC." https://www.nrc.gov/about-nrc.html (accessed February 29, 2020).

Walker, J. Samuel. 2000. *Permissible Dose: A History of Radiation Protection in the Twentieth Century*. Berkeley, CA: University of California Press.

Walker, J. Samuel. 2006. *Three Mile Island: A Nuclear Crisis in Historical Perspective*. Berkeley, CA: University of California Press.

Walker, J. Samuel. 2009. *The Road to Yucca Mountain: The Development of Radioactive Waste Policy in the United States*. Berkeley, CA: University of California Press.
Walker, J. Samuel, and George T. Mazuzan. 1992. "Containing the Atom: Nuclear Regulation in a Changing Environment, 1963–1971." US Nuclear Regulatory Commission. NUREG-1933.
Walker, J. Samuel, and Thomas R. Wellock. 2010. "A Short History of Nuclear Regulation, 1946–2009." US Nuclear Regulatory Commission. NUREG/BR-0175. https://www.nrc.gov/docs/ML1029/ML102980443.pdf (accessed February 29, 2020).
Wellock, Thomas R. 2016. "Putting the Axe to the 'Scram' Myth." US NRC Blog. February 18. US Nuclear Regulatory Commission. https://public-blog.nrc-gateway.gov/2016/02/18/refresh-putting-the-axe-to-the-scram-myth/ (accessed February 29, 2020).

Nuclear Waste Policy Act of 1982

Signed into law by President Ronald Reagan on January 3, 1983 and amended in 1987, the Nuclear Waste Policy Act of 1982 (NWPA) attempted to develop a permanent repository for the disposal of nuclear waste through the US Department of Energy (DOE). The act required the DOE to consult and cooperate with states and Indian Tribes impacted by the legislation. The 1987 amendment, called the Nuclear Waste Policy Amendments Act of 1987, further laid out a protocol for the evaluation of potential repository sites as well as guidelines to design, erect, license, conduct, and close repository sites. In particular, the act spells out selection strategies for the long-term containment of waste, the safety standards supervising this containment, the authority to construct facilities, and the surveying of potential sites. It also stipulates the grounds for approving a site for development, the documentation and containment of waste, the standards for the operation and performance of facilities, and finally, the rules of oversight, including closure, license termination, and other monitoring. No construction had taken place a half-century after the law was enacted, which illustrates the sensitive and controversial nature of nuclear energy and its environmental impacts.

The impetus for the NWPA can be traced back to the 1940s, or the beginning of nuclear power development in the United States. Initially, the generation of nuclear waste was the by-product of producing plutonium for nuclear weapons. Due to the primacy of the war effort, wastes from weapons testing were stored in steel tanks under the premise that suitable techniques for long-term management would be developed later. Little thought was given to long-term disposal of hazardous materials. Initially, it was thought that spent fuel containing radioactive elements could be reprocessed and reintroduced into the fuel cycle, but this did not occur.

By deferring the formation of a long-term waste disposal plan, policymakers left the problem for a future generation. The issue came to the fore in the 1970s when various pressures turned waste disposal into a political issue. Significant events included California's prohibition on greenlighting new reactors in 1976 until the federal government could substantiate a means of disposal for hazardous waste, and the Nuclear Regulatory Commission declaration in 1977 that "it would not continue to license reactors if it did not have reasonable confidence that the waste can and will in due course be disposed of safely" (quoted in Cotton 2006, 31). In response to these concerns, a national discussion of nuclear waste policy was initiated in 1978 by President Jimmy Carter with the appointment of the Interagency Review Group on Nuclear Waste Management. The group consisted of delegates from fourteen federal agencies, and it found a consensus on the required elements of a national policy that included the following: 1) the notion that dealing with waste management issues should not be deferred to future generations; 2) the recognition that geological disposal represented the most promising avenue for permanent disposal; 3) the selection of geologic sites should consider a variety of environments; and 4) that current storage of waste should not preempt efforts at opening the first repository. These propositions would, ultimately, be endorsed and codified with the NWPA.

The NWPA of 1982 was unique in its recognition of nuclear waste disposal as a national problem. It acknowledged that all prior efforts at dealing with waste were inadequate. The act requires consultation with states governments and Indian Tribes. This provision has made it difficult if not impossible to complete the charges set forth in the act. The selection of a site bears this out. After considering locations in Washington, Nevada, Utah, Texas, Louisiana, Mississippi, Maine, and Georgia, Yucca Mountain, Nevada was named as the only site recommended in the 1987 amendments. It was not until 2002 that a formal recommendation was forwarded. As per the act, however, the state of Nevada invoked its right to veto, which was overridden by the US Senate and House of Representatives in July 2002. A lengthy court battle ensued until 2010, when the Obama administration cut funding for the facility in the 2010 federal budget. Attempts to build a waste disposal site at Yucca Mountain have stalled but have not ceased. Significant protests emanate from state officials and Western Shoshone peoples, who consider the mountains to be sacred.

The NWPA of 1982 can be considered a policy failure insofar as no permanent waste disposal repository has been constructed pursuant to the act, and nearly all nuclear waste is stored in temporary on-site facilities.

Todd K. Platts

See also: Atomic Energy Acts; Church Rock Uranium Mill Spill; Manhattan Project; Navajo Reservation Uranium Mining; Nuclear Regulatory Commission; Nuclear Power; Steen, Charles Augustus; Three Mile Island Accident; Yucca Mountain Nuclear Waste Repository

FURTHER READING

Bella, David A., Charles D. Mosher, and Steven N. Calvo. 1988. "Technocracy and Trusts: Nuclear Waste Controversy." *Journal of Professional Issues in Engineering*. Vol. 114. No. 1. Pp. 27–39.

Brown Jr., George E. 1987. "U.S. Nuclear Waste Policy: Flawed but Feasible." *Environment*. Vol. 29. No. 8. Pp. 6–7, 25.

Clary, Bruce B. 1991–2. "The Enactment of the Nuclear Waste Policy Act of 1982: A Multiple Perspectives Explanation." *Policy Studies Review*. Vol. 10. No. 4. Pp. 90–102.

Clary, Bruce B., and Michael E. Kraft. 1988. "Impact Assessment and Policy Failure: The Nuclear Waste Policy Act of 1982." *Review of Policy Research*. Vol. 8. No. 1. Pp. 105–15.

Cotton, Thomas. 2006. "Nuclear Waste Story: Setting the Stage." In *Uncertainty Underground: Yucca Mountain and the Nation's High-Level Nuclear Waste*. Eds. Allison M. Macfarlane and Rodney C. Ewing. Pp. 29–44. Cambridge, MA: MIT Press.

Ohio Oil Boom

In the paleozoic era, 541 to 252 million years ago, marine organisms in shallow seas covering North America flourished and eventually died, accumulating in layers at the shallow seafloor. Over deep geologic time, sea levels ebbed and flowed over the region and these organic materials were converted through heat and pressure into carbon-rich coal, petroleum, and natural gas deposits beneath rock layers near the Earth's surface. Humans began extracting this fuel and burned it for heat, steam power, and electricity beginning in the mid-nineteenth century. Shortly after 1859 when the first commercial-scale extraction of oil occurred in Pennsylvania, the Ohio oil boom began in 1860 and lasted until the early 1920s, producing 23 million barrels of oil (ODNR 2007). The southeast and eastern part of the state were the sites of initial booms, while the northwest region hosted later expansions. The 1911 break-up of Cleveland-based Standard Oil Company into separate companies played a major role in ending the Ohio oil boom. However, the development of fossil fuels as raw commodities created an important legacy on Ohio's landscape, which continues to produce not only oil, coal, and natural gas but plays host to pipelines and other oil and gas infrastructure.

Prior to settlement by Euro-Americans, Ohio's rich lands and waterways played a historically significant role in agriculture, timber, game hunting, and inter-regional trade among Native Shawnee, Miami, Delaware, Potawatomi, and Cherokee nations. Before the industrial exploitation of oil, petroleum-derived products were bottled as a medicine in Ohio and Kentucky (Wells 2022). Most of the preindustrial uses of oil continued after Ohio's statehood in 1803. By the mid-1800s, livestock production, railways, technology, and fossil fuel extraction had developed in the state. The first oil well in Ohio was tapped in 1860 near Macksburg and Mecca in the eastern and northeastern parts of the state, respectively. This drilling in Ohio was concurrent with the first oil booms around the world.

Another oil strike came in the northwest portion of the state at the Trenton limestone, considered at the time to be a promising location for future exploration, which resulted in over 250 wells being dug near the Indiana border. Seventy wells were dug within Lima's city limits. In 1885, 200 barrels per day were produced there (Spencer 2008). Soon after the first wells were tapped in the southeast and east of the state, Ohio experienced a rapid increase in petroleum production, continuing into the late nineteenth century. Oil pipelines and storage tanks were built along the banks of the Ohio River, and by the 1870s, oil refineries were built by Standard Oil Company in Cleveland. Atop of Grand Lake, which is a large, shallow reservoir built on the Miami River and Ohio Canal in the 1830s and 1840s, the first over-water oil rig was built. Starting in 1891, 100 wells were installed on or near the lake by numerous operating companies, using wooden walkways and pipelines. Production declined at Grand Lake until the first few decades of the twentieth century. In those same decades, production shifted to other regions such as Texas, Oklahoma, and California.

Several towns in Ohio were built up by oil production. The Bremen-New Straitsville boom in the 1910s sustained itself for about fifteen years and helped to give the town of Bremen a make-over. Findlay, Ohio was built largely around its oil fields. Tank farms, pipelines, pumping stations, and other infrastructure gave the town its early character. Findlay was a leading oil-producing region in the state. The Marathon brand of gas and oil traces its history to this region; the original root of the company was founded in 1887 in Lima, Ohio as the Ohio Oil Company. It was purchased by Standard Oil Trust in 1889, then became independent once again when the trust was broken up in 1911 by order of the US Supreme Court under the Sherman Antitrust Act. This corresponded with the waning of the oil boom, but Ohio nevertheless retained its importance as an important state for oil refining and transportation, including pipelines and railways.

Several of the oil towns of Ohio, including Findlay, drew large numbers of immigrants, who celebrated their national identities through fairs and cultural events. They came to the United States with the promise of a better life, and largely obtained it with employment in the oil and gas industry. Their lives were made even more comfortable with the coming of electricity. On the downside, oil field workers often lived in company towns and worked for company scrip for use in company-owned stores. Labor organizations worked to coordinate demonstrations and work stoppages to secure better terms of employment and safer working conditions. In time, Ohio's place at the crossroads of railroads and highways ensured a steady stream of new migrants in the first half of the twentieth century, and with it an increase in property values. Real estate development, and even speculation, transformed the formerly agrarian regions of Ohio into industrial and transportation hubs that became linchpins in the later stages of the Industrial Revolution.

In most respects, the Ohio oil boom was over by 1915, and in 1917 Ohio dropped out of the top four oil-producing states (OHC 2014). Oil production brought wealth and prosperity to many small towns in the state, but left a legacy of an estimated nine hundred, if not thousands, of wells that were improperly plugged or simply abandoned (Olalde 2020). A small echo of the boom occurred in the mid-twentieth century when coal and natural gas reserves, rather than oil, were tapped throughout the eastern bisect of the state in the Clinton Sandstone deposit. This anticipated the arrival of hydraulic fracturing, a practice that began in Ohio in 1952 but accelerated with the development of the Marcellus and Utica/Point Pleasant Shale, which is located mostly in Pennsylvania but extends into eastern and southeastern Ohio. In the 2010s, hundreds of new oil and gas wells appeared in Ohio River Valley counties and brought another boom. In one instance, a group of around 800 property owners leased 34,000 acres for fracking operations and were given more than $200 million just for enlisting in the program (Burger 2019). Real estate values increased and schools received funding from oil and gas revenues.

Just like the earlier boom, this one came at a price for Ohio's residents and for the state's natural environment. Fracking produces brine waste, as the process requires high-powered streams of water, which returns to the surface or enters the groundwater laced with heavy metals and naturally occurring radioactive contaminants, including radon, radium-226, and radium-228. Reports indicate high rates of respiratory distress, headaches, and other health issues (Burger 2019). These issues have generated significant social resistance. After Ohio's only national forest, Wayne National Forest in the foothills of the Appalachians, was slated to be opened to intensive fracking, social and political pressure suspended the fracking plan. As scientists have begun demonstrating the increasing risk of climate change and pressure by environmental advocates continues, the state may reconsider its historic role in fossil fuel production. For states with oil and gas resources like Ohio, the dilemma is familiar: that fossil fuels are a lucrative, yet environmentally harmful mode of energy production.

Sam Orndorff

See also: Caddo Oil Field; Hydraulic Fracking; Indiana Natural Gas Boom; Pennsylvania Oil Boom; Natural Gas; Pennsylvania Oil Boom; Rockefeller, John D.; Roughnecks; Standard Oil Company; Texas Oil Boom

FURTHER READING

Burger, Beth. 2019. "Has Fracking Helped, or Harmed Eastern Ohio?" TimesReporter. USA Today Network. July 29. https://www.timesreporter.com/story/news/state/2019/07/29/has-fracking-helped-harmed-eastern/4501108007/ (accessed April 22, 2023).

Ohio Department of Natural Resources (ODNR). 2007. "Historic Oil and Gas Wells in and Adjacent to Grand Lake Saint Marys." Division of Geological Survey. September. https://ohiodnr.gov/static/documents/geology/GrandLakePoster_Vogt_2007.pdf (accessed May 30, 2021; URL is no longer accessible).

Ohio History Connections (OHC). 2014. "Oil Town Photograph." Ohio Memory. Ohio History Connections Selections. Ohio History Connections and State Library of Ohio.

Olalde, Mark. 2020. "Cleaning up after Ohio's Oil and Gas Industry Brings a Growing Price Tag." *Energy News Network*. https://energynews.us/2020/01/15/midwest/cleaning-up-after-ohios-oil-and-gas-industry-brings-a-growing-price-tag/ (accessed May 30, 2021).

Spencer, Jeff. 2008. "A Journey through Two Early Ohio Oil Booms: The Northwest Ohio and the Bremen-New Straitsville Booms." *Oil-Industry History*. Vol. 9. Pp. 59–72.

Wells, Bruce A., and K.L. Wells. 2022. "First American Oil Well." American Oil & Gas Historical Society. https://aoghs.org/petroleum-pioneers/american-oil-history (accessed April 22, 2023).

The Oil Embargo of 1941

On July 26, 1941, the US government issued an official embargo on Japan that terminated oil shipments to Japan. Four months later, on December 7, 1941, Japanese forces attacked the American naval base at Pearl Harbor and took control of the oil fields in the Indies to protect its vital supply line in Southeast Asia. The embargo left Japan with a year and a half of oil supplies and forced Japan to reassess its imperial trajectory (Anderson 1975, 201). The US decision to place the embargo on Japan was not the product of carefully calculated government policy, but was an indeterminate response to public pressure. Public opinion had held great influence on US foreign policy in many cases, but the Oil Embargo of 1941 unveiled a contradiction between US economic interests and its idealistic commitment to national self-determination and justice for humanity. This dilemma of American foreign policy captured the complexity of congressional decisions, executive power, and Washington's own mandate for an Open Door Policy in Asia. However, the embargo's ultimate failure is perhaps more rooted in the visibility and influence of lobbyists in the public sphere.

In January 1940, a treaty of commerce between the United States and Japan was terminated by the latter in response to President Roosevelt's decision to formalize US aid to China. The United States supplied a majority of Japan's vital industrial resources, such as oil, steel, and iron (Utley 1976). Japan's imperial intervention into China was a challenge to US economic interests, but the State Department remained docile in an attempt to preserve the lucrative Japanese–American trade network (Utley 1976). This posture continued into 1941 as the State Department preferred ambiguity as a way to satisfy the anti-Japanese sentiments of the country alongside its own economic interests in Asia. In fact, President Roosevelt clearly indicated to Secretary of State Cordell Hull that despite freezing Japanese assets in July 1941, it was his intention to continue oil shipments so as not to provoke Japanese aggression (Anderson 1975, 202–3). The outbreak of war in Europe nonetheless created a strategic problem for the United States, and the State Department made it abundantly clear that it was "not prepared for war on the Atlantic and the Pacific simultaneously" (Bacon 1941). An unwillingness of US allies to support an embargo without guaranteed military assistance in return from the United States further complicated the options of the State Department (Hornbeck 1941).

Tungsten, used in the manufacturing of machine tools, paint, lacquer and varnish, was a major Chinese export and subsequently fell under Japanese control in 1938. At first, American economist Eliot Janeway criticized the State Department for not containing Japanese aggression, but a year later reversed his opinion. He advocated for a "self-sufficiency" concerning materials coming from Asia as a way to preserve economic interests, while putting pressure on Japan that also would not provoke aggression (Utley 1976). It was a precarious situation. This moment of diplomatic ambivalence revealed America's contradictory desires to secure its own economic interests in Asia and at the same time defend China's interest against Japan.

The State Department's balancing act soon was shattered by an increased attentiveness of public opinion. The dissonance between the interests of the State Department and the anti-Japanese public proved to be a battleground for policymakers. Public opinion "ardently desired non-involvement" and eventually mobilized this view through the use of lobbying power (Bacon 1941). Citizens configured a myriad of local organizations driven by the "Stop Arming Japan" movement (Utley 1976, 130). These local organizations, however, were rooted in the national prowess and visibility of the American Committee for Non-Participation in Japanese Aggression, which was created during the summer of 1938. It was the largest and most powerful group of those who supported an embargo against Japan. Among its 3,000 financial contributors were powerful sponsors such as Secretary of War Henry L. Stimson, former commander of the Asiatic Fleet Admiral Harry E. Yarnell, past president of the US Chamber of Commerce Henry I. Harriman, past president of Harvard University A. Lawrence Lowell, secretary of the Presbyterian Board of Foreign Missions Robert S. Speer, and influential newspaper editor William Allen White.

The presence of such powerful men in the ranks of these lobbyist groups raises the question of how public opinion is formulated and perceived. What influence did these sponsors have on the voice of public opinion? While it is possible that they cooperated with and listened to group members, it is likely that their positions and experience held considerable sway over the committee. Regardless of their status, the influence they had on public opinion served as a strong agent in the formation of US foreign policy. This particular phenomenon certainly raised concern about the ways that the public interpreted, listened to, and followed the guidance of public officials. At a surface level, the influence that public officials had on the general populace demonstrated a fundamental ambiguity in the public relations of elected officials—representation was a multi-layered paradigm. Although a representative is an advocate of the represented, the represented people must also vocalize and mobilize their own political needs and desires. In the case of the oil embargo, however, it seems that lobbying by private organizations influenced this relationship the most. The American Committee for Non-Participation in Japanese Aggression convinced the American people that imposing economic sanctions on oil to Japan was strictly a moral decision. This invited a particular sympathy that made it easier for Congress to proceed with legislation. The suffering of China under the arm of Japanese military aggression played a vital role in shaping US public opinion and was used by many lobbyists to intensify anti-Japanese sentiments. As one pamphlet stated, "'Japan furnishes the pilot. America furnishes the airplane, gasoline, oil and bombs for the ravaging of undefended Chinese cities'" (quoted in Utley 1976, 131). However, these censures were produced with very little evidence and did not consider the influence of the army in Japanese policy compared with its position in 1919 at the Treaty of Versailles. In other words, the Japanese nation that emerged in the decade following the Treaty of Versailles posed a substantial military threat to Asia. The moral sentiments of public opinion also failed to consider the military consequences of an embargo, which came to fruition after Japan attacked the oil-producing Netherlands East Indies.

In a meeting with Secretary of State Cordell Hull in April 1940, executive secretary of the American Committee Harry B. Price sought to influence the State Department's position. Hull conceded that he was somewhat willing to enact legislation quietly. This culminated in the Hull–Pittman conference on May 12 where Secretary Hull, Senator Key Pittman, and Price convened to negotiate the terms of an embargo. As German expansion in Europe proliferated, Hull became convinced that an embargo was a reasonable option. He sent an order to Assistant Secretary Adolf A. Berle, Jr. who began writing provisions for legislation. On July 2, 1940 the bill became law and granted the Roosevelt administration the power to embargo virtually anything. This was a vast expansion of executive power. Moreover, because the legislation came from Secretary Hull, the American Committee circumvented the bureaucratic process of sending legislation through Congress. As George Gallup reported, 88 percent of American people favored the embargo. Although lobbyists advocated for an embargo on moral grounds such as the killing of Chinese women and children, the legislation was justified as "necessary to preserve a healthy American economy" (Utley 1976, 136).

Japan's imperial crusade exposed the hypocrisy of US foreign policy and further unveiled the contradiction between US economic interests in Asia and its commitment to national self-determination. The idea of the American frontier, which drove the economic, cultural, and political growth of the United States during the nineteenth century, culminated in a transcontinental empire. With no more continental space in which to fulfill this idea—and the underlying quest for economic power—the United States expanded its imperial interests into Asia with the colonization of the Philippines. When Japan entered the imperial game with considerable military tenacity and efficacy, it threatened US economic interests in Asia. However, America's expansion into Asia also provided the foundation for economic power in Japan. In other words, US imperialism cultivated the circumstances that threatened its imperial interests. Unfortunately, economic interests remained the chief concern for policymakers and especially lobbyists, who possessed a strong influence on public opinion.

The power relationships in the Pacific had indeed changed with the ascent of Japan as a viable trading partner and military power. This strategic position posed a challenging dilemma for the United States. Maintaining Japan as a trade partner provided immense economic benefit as well as access to oil in Southeast Asia, but it was also another network of power designed to keep the Open Door policy operational in China. Despite initial Japanese aggression, it was believed that treaty negotiations in tandem with the accountability of mutual economic interests would taper Japanese expansion into China. From the State Department's perspective, a war with Japan would destroy the delicate balance. The challenge was such that in order to uphold amiable Japanese relations, the United States would compromise its coveted diplomatic relationship with China. Public opinion—comprising mainly visible and vocal public sphere personalities—provided the final push for officials in Washington. When Hitler invaded France, lobbyists and radio hosts jumped at the opportunity to criticize American–Japanese relations. The promoters of embargo reinforced their position and asserted that raw materials should go to America's defense program and not to Japan. "'American mothers are not willing to send their sons to die in the Far East in order to take from the Japanese territory which they have conquered'" (quoted in Utley 1976, 132).

The oil embargo enacted against Japan, while certainly driven by public opinion as well as by the State Department's desire to avoid armed conflict with the Japanese, was also driven by economic interests connected to fossil fuel consumption. Even the American public was reluctant to intervene on behalf of the Chinese, who were experiencing atrocities at the hands of the Japanese military, unless it led to some sort of financial gain. Moral justifications and national security were underpinned by the more pressing economic matter of land use and material resources. In this regard, it is difficult to separate the social actions from the economic trepidations that guided these arguments. The response of the public was perhaps catalyzed by moral outrage, but decisions always came back to a discussion of resource management. From this perspective, Japan and the United States possessed a common interest. Oil allowed a global economy to function.

When Japan acquired the destroyed oil refineries in Balikpapan and Sumatra, which were previously owned and intentionally destroyed by Shell and Stanvac respectively, the damage was surprisingly minimal. Relying on a vast superstructure of "some four thousand oil field workers," the Japanese resurrected the oil industry in Southeast Asia and quickly reaped a surfeit of oil from the new operations. Known as the "Southern Zone," the oil-rich land of island Southeast Asia exceeded Japan's expectations for oil production. According to Daniel Yergin, "oil production in the Southern Zone had been 65.1 million barrels in 1940. In 1942, the Japanese were able to produce just 25.9 million barrels, but by 1943, they had gotten it back to 49.6 million barrels—75 percent of the 1940 level" (Yergin 1991). For perspective, the United States only produced 1.5 million barrels in 1940 (EIA 2022). This spawned a frenzied market boom in Japan. They were "victory drunk," as Yergin called it, on such rapid military and economic success in Southeast Asia (Yergin 1991). This economic momentum most certainly captured the attention of officials in Washington and was a defining factor in the decision to place an embargo on Japan. The embargo came at a cost. Possibly due to the timing or perhaps due to some amount of inevitability in Japan's economic and military expansion, the time Washington had to make a decision concerning the Japanese question in the Pacific ran out. On December 7, 1941, just four months after the embargo was enacted, Japan attacked Pearl Harbor.

If Washington had chosen not to place an embargo on Japan, its economic interests may have remained secure. However, it would have created a stronger adversary as Japan pursued its own economic interests. When the embargo was finally announced, US economic interests adapted and for a short while, it appeared that the isolationist and anti-Japanese embargoists had achieved victory. Unfortunately, the diplomatic tension created by the embargo gave a different kind of ammunition to Japan who escalated its more desperate pursuit of raw materials. Whether the embargo produced the eventual attack on Pearl Harbor or not is uncertain, but the constraints placed by the embargo did force Japan's hand. In a memorandum from an Advisor on Political Relations, Stanley Hornbeck, to the Under Secretary of State, Sumner Welles, it is clear that officials in Washington believed that "an embargo by the United States alone, while injurious to Japan's economy, would not stop her war effort" (Hornbeck 1941).

Consumption of energy and raw materials is at the heart of this particular historical narrative. It illustrates the interconnections between the social atmosphere and the consumption of energy. The Americans that participated in the formation of public opinion made it clear that the anti-Japanese embargo was about more than moral outrage. It was a deeply social and economic issue. The US State Department faced a delicate, and potentially injurious problem. Many personalities within the public sphere failed to recognize what so many officials in Washington predicted, that the embargo would lead to war. However, the public demanded an embargo without wanting to go to war. As Jonathan Utley argued, "by refusing to give the people the embargo they preferred, the Department was in fact giving them the peace they demanded" (Utley 1976, 138).

Thomas David Brown

See also: Carter Doctrine; Cooke-Zevada Agreement of 1942; Oil Tankers; Petroleum

FURTHER READING

American Committee for Non-Participation in Japanese Aggression (ACNJA). 1938. "America's Share in Japan's War Guilt." New York: Academy Press. https://palmm.digital.flvc.org/islandora/object/ucf%3A4929 (accessed October 2023).

Anderson, Irvine H. 1975. "The 1941 De Facto Embargo on Oil to Japan: A Bureaucratic Reflex." *Pacific Historical Review*. Vol. 44. No. 2. Pp. 201–31.

Bacon, Ruth. 1941. "Memorandum by Miss Ruth Bacon of the Division of Far Eastern Affairs." July 31. *Foreign Relations of the United States Diplomatic Papers: The Far East: Vol. IV*. 894.24/1587. Eds. John G. Reid, Ralph R. Goodwin, and Louis E. Gates. Washington, DC: US Government Printing Office, 1955.

Friedman, Donald J. 1968. *The Road from Isolation: The Campaign of the American Committee for Non-Participation in Japanese Aggression, 1938–1941*. Cambridge, MA: Harvard University Press.

Hornbeck, Stanley. 1941. "Memorandum by the Adviser on Political Relations (Hornbeck) to the Under Secretary of State (Welles)." January 16. *Foreign Relations of the United States Diplomatic Papers: The Far East, Vol. IV*. 711.94/1963. Eds. John G. Reid, Ralph R. Goodwin, and Louis E. Gates. Washington, DC: US Government Printing Office, 1955.

Harrington, Daniel F. 1979. "A Careless Hope: American Air Power and Japan, 1941." *Pacific Historical Review*. Vol. 48. No. 2. May. Pp. 217–38.

US Energy Information Administration (EIA). 2022. "US Field Production of Crude Oil." Washington, DC: US Department of Energy.

Utley, Jonathan G. 1976. "Diplomacy in a Democracy: The United States and Japan, 1937–1941." *World Affairs*. Vol. 139. No. 2. Fall. Pp. 130–40.

Yergin, Daniel. 1991. *The Prize: The Epic Quest for Oil, Money, and Power*. New York: Simon & Schuster.

Oil Tankers

The transport of fuels is a critically important part of the system connecting energy producers with energy consumers. Since the days of cart and horse, fuels have made their way from the site of extraction to the point of use by some means of conveyance, ranging from wagons to railroad tank cars to pipelines to trucks to steam ships. The first vessels built solely for the purpose of transporting liquids in bulk appeared in the 1870s and 1880s when steamers were designed and laid on to haul petroleum and petroleum products like kerosene. Oil transport by tanker ship became an important link in the supply chain when oil developed into a globally traded commodity in the twentieth century. Oil tankers are also a symbol. For some, they are a modern marvel, an embodiment of humankind's capacity to think big and create amazing technological wonders. For others, they are a symbol of US dependence on foreign oil, as fleets of tankers from overseas line up to unload at American ports like Long Beach and Houston. For still others, they are a symbol of energy's environmental hazards, with images of the *Argo Merchant* and *Exxon Valdez* oil spills fastened in their minds. Oil tankers are all of those things, and they serve a vital role in meeting Americans' ever-expanding demand for more and more energy.

Carrying liquid cargoes aboard ship was routine in the ancient and medieval eras. Ships transported containers full of fresh water, olive oil, wine, vinegar, honey, resins, and other goods in different types of vessels, ranging from Egyptian clay pots to Phoenician and Greek amphoras to medieval European casks and barrels (Bevan 2014, 392). However, carrying liquids in bulk is a creation of the modern era. The need for bulk cargo hauling came about with the Industrial Revolution and the requirement of resources in large enough quantities to produce at scale. Ships were converted first to bulk iron ore and coal carriers in the early nineteenth century, and then after mid-century, to oil tankers with the advent of commercial petroleum drilling. Frustrations with carrying crude oil in wooden barrels provided the impetus to innovate. Barrels were an added expense and were discarded after one use, they added additional weight, and they often leaked in transit. Beginning in 1863, the Petroleum Trading Company of Newcastle, UK, operated the *Atlantic* and the *Great Western*, two iron-hulled sailing ships, each fitted with four large tanks for carrying oil (Ratcliffe 1985, 14).

Oil tanker design shifted to steam power in 1878 when the *Zoroaster* went into operation for Ludvig and Robert Nobel, Swedish oil developers in Russian Azerbaijan who plied the vessel on the Caspian Sea. The ship measured 180 feet in length by 35 feet in width and could carry 240 gross tons of crude oil. Within ten years the number of tank steamers transporting oil on the Caspian Sea rose to thirty, and by 1898, the number multiplied to 112 (Henry 1907, vi). To unload its cargo, workers needed only to connect pumps and hoses to the steamer's tanks to transfer oil from ship to shore, a much easier and less costly method than hauling thousands of drums of oil out of a cargo hold. The economics of bulk hauling by tank steamer were very clear. In 1888, a cargo ship carrying 20,000 barrels of oil, each in their own container, paid $2,300 more in "port fees, inspection charges, loading, and other costs" than a tanker carrying the oil in bulk. Furthermore, a steamer could cross the Atlantic and return seven times in one year, as compared to three for a sailing ship (Williamson 1966, 373).

John D. Rockefeller's Standard Oil Company sent a team to Europe to acquire a fleet of tank steamers, eventually buying eighteen in all, including the *Gluckauf*, the ship considered the first modern tank steamer because it was built in 1886 specifically for the purpose of hauling crude oil and petroleum products (Henry 1907, 22). The *Gluckauf*'s cargo hold was divided by bulkheads running the length of the ship and side to side and could carry over 3,000 gross tons. It contained a pumping system to keep water from mixing with the oil, and to discharge the cargo at port, which took twelve hours (Henry 1907, 13). Rockefeller continued his exertions overseas through his company's UK subsidiary, the Anglo-American Oil Company. It formed in 1888 with the idea of controlling oil markets in the UK and Asia. A book on ocean steamships in 1891 estimated that seventy tank steamers were then in operation worldwide, and that Standard Oil owned the majority of them, either outright or through subsidiaries (Chadwick, 1891, 245). The first 3,000-barrel shipment of Spindletop oil from Texas to a Standard Oil refinery in New Jersey left Port Arthur in May 1901 in the tank steamer *Atlas*. By the end of the year, tankers mostly controlled by Standard Oil Company hauled 1.750 million barrels of oil from the Gulf to eastern US Atlantic ports.

The rapid expansion of oil production and demand for oil transport vessels stimulated innovation in oil tanker technology and design. For example, oil tankers powered by internal combustion engines appeared in the Nobel Bros. shipyard in 1903 with the *Vandale* and 1905 with the *Sarmat*, but made only modest improvement in performance on steam-powered vessels and didn't catch on (Durtnall 1913, 131). In 1910, the Royal Dutch Shell Company began operating the first diesel-fueled, ocean-going tanker *Vulcanus* and made orders for a number of others. A 1920 review of the performance of the diesel engine-powered *Artemis*, built in 1912, argued that its carrying capacity, reliability, and fuel savings made it preferable to coal-burning steam-powered tankers (Zulver 24, 1920). Diesel engines also alleviated fears that a coal-fired steam engine might throw a spark that ignites its cargo. The diesel engine could power a ship and its cargo as far on 2 tons of diesel fuel as a loaded steam-powered tanker went on 11 tons of coal. In terms of structural design, British naval architect Joseph Isherwood patented a "longitudinal girder form of framing" in 1910 that helped to prevent tanker hulls from buckling and collapsing under extreme stress. It also enabled oil tankers to grow even larger in size and carrying capacity (Solly 2021, 32).

THE *ALDEN ANDERSON* DISASTER

The oil tank steamer *Alden Anderson* blew up at port in Avon, California in the San Francisco Bay area on October 29, 1924 when a portion of the wharf collapsed, snapping electrical wires and sparking a fire. The fire ignited gasoline being pumped from the ship and spread to the ship's fuel tanks, which detonated and engulfed the ship in flames. The explosion destroyed 600 feet of wharf, a warehouse, and a barge carrying 4,000 barrels of crude oil, spreading a layer of burning oil across the harbor. The crew of thirty-six, employees of the Associated Oil Company, jumped ship and were accounted for by the next morning.

Jeffrey B. Webb

More advances in oil tanker design and technology came later, after the First and Second World Wars. Oil tankers were a part of the story of US intervention in the First World War in 1917. In 1915, a German submarine torpedoed the American tanker *Gulflight* carrying gasoline and lubricating oil to France. Three mariners were killed and President Woodrow Wilson issued a strongly worded complaint to the German government. Once the United States entered the war, largely due to unrestricted submarine warfare directed toward American shipping, Germans submarines hunted US vessels carrying coal and oil. For example, in August 1918, German U-boats attacked two oil tankers, sinking the *O.B. Jennings* and disabling the *Frederick R. Kellogg*. Between the wars, oil surfaced as an important strategic commodity when national navies switched from coal to oil and mechanized warfare developed, which included aircraft, tanks, armored personnel carriers, and motorized transport vehicles. To slow the Japanese war machine, President Franklin D. Roosevelt imposed an oil embargo in August 1941 in response to Japan's aggression in China and Southeast Asia. In response, the imperial government in Tokyo went forward with a plan to attack the US naval base at Pearl Harbor as part of a larger offensive in the Far East to capture oil fields in the Dutch East Indies.

The United States constructed a huge oil tanker fleet to support naval operations on two oceans. The US Navy's T2 tankers followed the design of civilian tankers *Mobilfuel* and *Mobilube*, which were 501.5 feet long and 68 feet wide and rated at 9,900 gross tons. The Navy's version was given a larger power plant for higher speeds. Eventually the T2 developed with a number of variations that added length and beam, increased engine power, and expanded carrying capacity. Over the course of the war, shipyards built 533 oil tankers in the T2 series (NMAH 2009). On the civilian side, US oil tankers fell victim to German U-boats once again. In early 1942, the Nazis opened a naval war against US shipping on the Atlantic called Operation Drumbeat, and a sub-operation against oil tankers in the Caribbean and along the South American coast known as Operation Neuland. Focusing on shipping near refineries and tank farms on Curaçao, Aruba, Trinidad, and British and Dutch Guiana, German U-boats wreaked havoc for weeks, destroying scores of tankers. Tankers in the Gulf waters refrained from entering the Caribbean zone out of fear of torpedo attack. One historian estimated that "roughly 95 per cent of product for the east coast of the United States—59 million gallons per day—that came from the Caribbean and the Gulf of Mexico by tanker at the end of 1941 shrank by 25 per cent as a result of the U-boat onslaught" (Bercuson 2014, 277). This was a crucial strategic problem for the Allies, as "a great part of US industrial production depended on tankers to carry oil from the Gulf of Mexico to the US east coast" (Bercuson 2014, 278). Over the entire course of the Second World War, the United States lost 148 oil tankers to enemy attacks.

By mid-1942, the Allies defeated Operation Drumbeat with new sub-hunting technologies and superior air and naval power. Production of new oil tankers continued, and when the war ended in 1945 the US government decommissioned its enormous wartime fleet of T2 vessels, which were eagerly bought up by petroleum and shipping companies. In the post-war era, "supertankers" appeared with massive increases in dead weight tonnage (dwt)—the total weight a ship can carry without riding dangerously low in the water. For comparison's sake, the Second World War-era T2 tankers could carry 16,000 dwt, whereas the *Tina Onassis* (1953), arguably the first supertanker, carried 46,080 dwt. and measured 771 feet long by nearly 72 feet wide. Five years after the *Tina Onassis* began hauling oil, supertankers were produced with 60,000 dwt, and twice the horsepower of T2-era ships. The closing of Egypt's Suez Canal in 1956 and then again in 1967 forced oil shipments heading to Europe from the Middle East to navigate around the southern tip of Africa. This enabled oil companies and shipbuilders to ignore the Suez Canal's size restrictions with new classes of carriers.

The VLCC class of oil tankers appeared (very large crude carrier), of which the *Idemitsu Maru* (1966) is considered the first. The ship was enormous, as it carried 206,006 dwt and measured 1,122 feet in length and 163 feet in width. The ULCC (ultra large crude carrier) class appeared during the energy crisis of the 1970s, with the *Seawise Giant* (1979) standing as a representative of the class. The *Seawise Giant* dwarfed the T2s from the 1940s at 564,763 dwt, 1,504 feet in length, and 225 feet in width.

The Suez Crisis of 1956 demonstrates the importance of oil tankers in the changing geopolitics of the twentieth century. For a variety of reasons, Egyptian President Gamiel Nasser nationalized the Suez Canal Company, a partly government owned, Anglo-French corporation. After diplomatic maneuvers escalated tensions, Israeli forces occupied the Sinai Peninsula and British and French paratroopers landed to take control of the canal. Backed by the Soviet Union, Nasser responded by blockading the canal with sunken ships. Meantime, Syrian forces damaged the Western-owned Iraqi Petroleum Company pipeline. Oil from the Middle East couldn't reach Europe. Daniel Yergin, historian of the geopolitics of oil, wrote, "for the most part, oil production in the Middle East had not been interrupted. The problem was, first of all, one of transportation" (Yergin 1991, 493). European and American leaders focused on shifting Europe's supply from Persian Gulf to US and South American oil fields. "Tankers were rerouted, they were shared among companies, supplies were swapped—all with the objective of moving oil in the quickest, most efficient way possible" (Yergin 1991, 493). Yergin notes that the "Oil Lift" to from the western hemispheric nations to Europe in 1956–7 met 90 percent of its need. President Nasser closed the canal a second time—for eight years—beginning in 1967 with the start of the Six-Day War, necessitating the development of the ULCC class of oil tankers to increase the efficiency of cross-ocean transport.

Concerns about the safety of oil tankers date to their origins but became more pronounced as the volume of shipping expanded, the size of tankers increased, and the amount of oil at risk in tanker hulls multiplied. The peak of oil tanker spills came in the late 1970s and early 1980s, typified by the horrific 1979 wrecks of the *Argo Merchant* off the coast of Massachusetts and the *Atlantic Empress* just east of the island of Tobago in the Caribbean. They spilled 7 million and 90 million gallons of oil respectively. Oil tanker regulations following the *Exxon Valdez* oil spill in 1989 in Alaska's Prince William Sound, especially the requirement of double-hulled construction, have considerably reduced spills from tankers. According to the International Tanker Owners Pollution Federation, the decade of the 1990s recorded 358 spills of 2,224 gallons and over, resulting in the loss of 360 million gallons of oil. For the 2000s, those numbers decreased to 181 spills of 2,224 gallons and over and 62 million gallons lost. Finally, for the 2010s, those numbers decreased again to 63 spills of 2,224 gallons and a little over 52 million gallons of oil lost (ITOPF 2023).

Oil tankers came to symbolize the hazards of US dependence on petroleum as its chief source of energy. This dependence left the United States vulnerable to the environmental effects of oil spills along America's coastlines, and vulnerable to political convulsions in regions where the United States draws much of its foreign oil. The OPEC oil embargo against Western nations that supported Israel in the Yom Kippur War in 1973 led to a spike in oil prices and the onset of the energy crisis of the 1970s. This led to the Carter Doctrine, in which President Jimmy Carter declared that the United States would use military force to protect its interests in the Persian Gulf region. Since then, US foreign policy has been shaped by political and military conflicts in the Middle East, including US involvement in the Tanker War in the 1980s, when the conflict between Iran and Iraq spilled over into attacks on oil tankers in the Persian Gulf. The United States fought the Gulf War against Iraq in 1991 over its ambition to control oil reserves in Kuwait, and then invaded Iraq in 2003 over alleged weapons of mass destruction, but also control over Iraqi oil. US Senator Chuck Hagel (later US Secretary of Defense) remarked at a Catholic University event in 2007, "People say we're not fighting for oil. Of course we are," then went on to add, "They talk about America's national interest. What the hell do you think they're talking about? We're not there for figs" (Bricker 2007). It should be noted that oil imports comprised 60 percent of oil consumed in the United States in 2005, but through various policy initiatives under Presidents Bush, Obama, Trump, and Biden had been reduced to 35 percent by 2021 (Nerurkar 2012; Elbein 2022).

Jeffrey B. Webb

See also: *Argo Merchant* Oil Spill; Carter Doctrine; Colliers; Energy Crisis of the 1970s; *Exxon Valdez* Oil Spill; Gulf War; Iraq War and the Project for a New American Century; Mandatory Oil Import Program; Organization of Petroleum Exporting Countries (OPEC); Standard Oil Company

FURTHER READING

Bercuson, David J., and Holger H. Herwig. 2014. "Long Night of the Tankers: Hitler's War Against Caribbean Oil." *Beyond Boundaries: Canadian Defence and Strategic Studies Series; 4*. Calgary, AB: University of Calgary Press.

Bevan, Andrew. 2014. "Mediterranean Containerization." *Current Anthropology*. Vol. 55. No. 4. Pp. 387–418.

Bricker, Bonnie et al. 2007. "The Costs of War for Oil." *Foreign Policy in Focus*. October 19. https://fpif.org/the_costs_of_war_for_oil/ (accessed October 2023).

Chadwick, F.E. et al. 1891. *Ocean Steamships: A Popular Account of Their Construction, Development, Management, and Appliances*. New York: Charles Scribner's Sons.

Durtnall, William P. 1913. "To the Editor." *Engineering: An Illustrated Weekly Journal*. Eds. W.H. Maw and B. Alfred Raworth. January 24. Vol. 95. Pp. 130–1. https://www.google.com/books/edition/Engineering/13G2KV-KSh8C (accessed October 2023).

Elbein, Saul. 2022. "Here's Where US Oil and Gas Supplies Come From." *The Hill*. March 8. https://thehill.com/policy/international/597389-heres-where-us-gas-supplies-come-from/ (accessed October 2023).

Henry, J.D. 1907. *Thirty-Five Years of Oil Transport: The Evolution of the Tank Steamer*. London: Bradbury, Agnew, & Co., Ld.

International Tanker Owners Pollution Federation (ITOPF). 2023. "Oil Tanker Spill Statistics 2022." https://www.itopf.org/knowledge-resources/data-statistics/statistics/ (accessed October 2023).

National Museum of American History (NMAH). 2009. "On the Water: World War II." Smithsonian National Museum of American History Behring Center Exhibit. https://americanhistory.si.edu/on-the-water/answering-call/building-ships-victory/world-war-ii (accessed October 2023).

Nerurkar, Neelesh. 2012. "U.S. Oil Imports and Exports." Congressional Research Service. April 4. https://sgp.fas.org/crs/misc/R42465.pdf (accessed October 2023).

Ratcliffe, Mike. 1985. *Liquid Gold Ships: A History of the Tanker, 1859–1984*. London: Lloyd's of London Press.

Solly, Ray. 2021. *The Development of Crude Oil Tankers: A Historical Miscellany*. Barnsley, UK: Pen & Sword Books.

Williamson, Harold F. et. al. 1966. "The American Petroleum Industry." In *Output, Employment, and Productivity in the United States after 1800*. Ed. Dorothy S. Brady. Pp. 349–404. National Bureau of Economic Research.

Yergin, Daniel. 1991. *The Prize: The Epic Quest for Oil, Money, and Power*. New York: Simon & Schuster.

Zulver, C. 1920. "Log of M.S. Artemis." *Motorship*. January. Vol. 5. P. 24. https://www.google.com/books/edition/Motorship/I_8_AQAAMAAJ (accessed October 2023).

Organization of Petroleum Exporting Countries (OPEC)

At a gathering known as the Baghdad Conference in 1960, officials from the governments of Iran, Iraq, Kuwait, Saudi Arabia, and Venezuela formed the Organization of Petroleum Exporting Countries (OPEC). Its mission was to advance the interests of its member nations by coordinating petroleum production and exports, eventually adopting a quota system. By decreasing production, OPEC could manipulate the economics of supply and demand and drive petroleum markets toward a targeted price for the commodity. Organizations that collude on production outputs to influence market prices are known as cartels, and OPEC is one of the more well-known and influential cartels in economic history. It played a well-documented role in triggering the energy crisis of the 1970s, one of the most significant events in the history of energy in the United States and continued to be a factor in global geopolitics through the beginning of the twenty-first century.

OPEC formed within the context of decolonization in the Middle East and Africa in the 1940s and 1950s. Some of the early OPEC members were formerly colonies or protectorates of Western European powers, but then secured their independence in the inter- and post-war era, including Saudi Arabia (1932), Iraq (1932), Indonesia (1949), Libya (1951), Nigeria (1960), Kuwait (1961), Qatar (1971), and the United Arab Emirates (1971). A point at issue was control of petroleum resources. The OPEC Declaratory Statement of Petroleum Policy in Member Countries (1968) noted that oil and gas were "the principal sources of their revenues and foreign exchange earnings and therefore constitute the main basis for their economic development." The statement also asserted that "the inalienable right of all countries to exercise permanent sovereignty over their natural resources in the interest of their national development is a universally recognized principle of public law and has been repeatedly reaffirmed by the General Assembly of the United Nations" (OPEC 1968).

These statements must be understood against the backdrop of the history of oil development in these regions in which Western oil companies, beginning in the 1920s, set up drilling operations, storage tank facilities, pipelines, and other infrastructure for oil and gas production. The most visible of these corporations were the Anglo-Persian Oil Company, which later became British Petroleum or BP, Standard Oil of California, Texaco, and Gulf Oil, which consolidated into Chevron, Standard Oil of New Jersey and Standard Oil Company of New York, which merged into ExxonMobil, and Royal Dutch Shell. They were collectively known as the "Seven Sisters" in recognition of their mid-twentieth century power and influence over the global trade in petroleum. In early 1959, the large oil companies slashed the price for crude oil from Venezuelan- and Middle Eastern-producing nations by 10 percent. This prompted the Arab League to organize an Arab Petroleum Congress, with Venezuela invited to attend, which raised the possibility of creating an OPEC-like organization for the purpose of united action. Then, when prices for Middle Eastern crude were reduced again in August 1960, the Baghdad Conference met a month later and formally organized OPEC.

By 1973, OPEC had grown to twelve member nations. Several political flashpoints in the 1960s and early 1970s had put the region's nations on edge, including wars fought by the US-backed Israeli government against coalitions of Arab states in the Six-Day War (1967) and the Yom Kippur War (1973). In the Six-Day War, Egyptian President Gamal Abdel Nasser closed the Suez Canal to oil shipping, and it remained blocked by sunken ships and underwater mines for the next eight years. Then, at the outset of the Yom Kippur War, the Arab states within OPEC announced an embargo on oil sales to the United States and the other nations supporting Israel. A few weeks later they announced decreases in oil production. Although other factors were involved, the embargo and cutbacks contributed to a sudden spike in oil prices, as did failure of US domestic producers to replace the deficit in oil supply. Oil with a nominal price of $3.60 per barrel in 1972 increased to $9.75 in 1974. Price increases continued along with inflation until 1980 when the price per barrel reached $37.42 (McMahon 2023). OPEC's actions contributed to an economic downturn in the US. GDP declined by 0.54 and 0.21 percent in 1974–5. The price at the pump skyrocketed and intermittent gas shortages required some states to impose a system of rationing, with fill-up days staggered based on license plate numbers. Inflation rose by margins of 6.2, 11.0, and 9.1 percent in 1973–5, and then 11.3, 13.5, and 10.3 percent in 1979–81. Finally, the Dow Jones index on the New York Stock Exchange lost 43 percent of its value over the course of 1973 and 1974.

Domestic politics went into overdrive as a result of the energy crisis of the 1970s. President Nixon's Project Independence 1980, announced in November 1973, called for a "Manhattan Project" energy self-sufficiency program including new leases for offshore oil drilling, switching oil-fired power plants to coal, building 1,000 nuclear power plants, making Daylight Saving Time permanent, setting highway speed limits to 50 miles per hour, and lowering household thermostats to 68 degrees. Nixon's successor Gerald Ford signed the Energy Reorganization Act of 1974 which created the Nuclear Regulatory Commission and the Energy Research and Development Administration, which became a cabinet-level department in 1977 with the Department of Energy Organization Act. In addition, Ford signed the Energy Policy and Conservation Act of 1975, which created the Strategic Petroleum Reserve, corporate average fuel economy standards (CAFE) for automobile manufacturers, and energy efficiency standards for electrical appliances and other consumer products. President Jimmy Carter called Americans to reduce consumption and replace energy sources with renewables, referring to the effort as the "moral equivalent of war." Congress responded with a package of laws collectively known as the National Energy Act of 1978, which encouraged natural gas production while regulating interstate pricing, created rate-making standards for public utilities, provided tax incentives for energy conservation efforts and renewable energy development, and promoted power plant switching from oil and gas to alternative sources of energy (Richardson 1995).

These dramatic changes in US domestic policy were induced by the energy crisis engendered in part by the actions of OPEC. By turns, concerted efforts to increase domestic production and reduce energy consumption in the United States, Europe, Japan, and other industrialized nations led to decreased demand for foreign oil. Americans started driving smaller, more fuel-efficient cars and insulated their homes. After the Iranian Revolution in 1979, with prospects of war between Iran and Iraq looming, panic buying set in, and the Western nations were suddenly well supplied with the oil they needed for another possible crisis. This produced a small "oil glut" that also contributed to reduced demand for OPEC's oil. This led to a drop in OPEC's share of the world's supply of oil. In 1973, OPEC provided 56 percent of the world's oil, but by 1985 that share dropped to 30 percent (Gately 1986, 242). The Iran–Iraq War created new challenges for OPEC, as it pitted two founding member nations against one another. Iraq and Iran decreased production, but this was offset by expansion of North Sea oil production, oversupply in Western nations, increasing use of alternative fuels, increased energy efficiency measures, and after 1985, increased Saudi exports, all of which put downward pressure on the price of oil, which reached $10 per barrel in July 1986.

This collapse in the oil market led OPEC to create a quota system to coordinate reductions in oil exports, which became the source of conflict among member states. Iraq left the Iran–Iraq War in 1988 in a state of financial hardship with a damaged oil infrastructure incapable of increasing output. Iraq's Saddam Hussein asked OPEC to decrease production in order to raise the price of oil so that it could secure a better yield for what oil they were able to produce. OPEC agreed, but the overall results of their attempts to decrease production were meager. This led Iraq to accuse Kuwait and the United Arab Emirates of cheating their quotas as part of a "Zionist-capitalist" plot to destroy the Iraqi economy. Iraq's invasion of Kuwait in 1990 and its seizure of Kuwait's oil fields triggered the Gulf War of 1990–1, which drew the United States, a number of Arab states, and many Western nations together in a diplomatic and military coalition to expel Iraqi forces. In many ways, President George W. Bush's leadership reflected the basic principles of the Carter Doctrine of 1980, which was framed in response to the Soviet invasion of Afghanistan, but applied to any nation seeking to dominate the region. Carter said: "An attempt by any outside force to gain control of the Persian Gulf region will be regarded as an assault on the vital interests of the United States of America, and such an assault will be repelled by any means necessary, including military force." These vital interests were shared by "those who rely on oil from the Middle East" (Carter 1980).

In the decades that followed the Gulf War, OPEC found it increasingly difficult to assert control over the global petroleum market. US military intervention in Afghanistan in 2001 and then Iraq in 2003, coupled with a dramatic increase in China's demand for oil in the 1980s, caused the price of oil to spike, and then bottom out in the financial crisis of 2008. OPEC held an emergency meeting late that year that exposed disagreements among member nations regarding the size of proposed cuts in production. Eventually an agreement was reached on a modest reduction. Oil prices increased in the early 2010s, but then US production of shale gas and oil through hydraulic fracking and horizontal drilling brought more volume to the market and dropped prices once again. Prices gyrated with the worldwide Covid-19 transportation shutdowns in 2020 and the Russian invasion of Ukraine in 2022, with corresponding sanctions on the sale of Russian oil. These conditions laid bare the conflicting goals of OPEC member states. For example, Saudi Arabia failed to secure an agreement to increase production at a contentious meeting in 2011, with Iran and Venezuela standing opposed. In 2015, OPEC nations led by Saudi Arabia met to consider production quotas for Iran as it came out from under sanctions imposed by the United States and other nations; Iran's refusal to accept production limits left OPEC without direction in a volatile oil market. The rift between Saudi Arabia and Iran continued through the 2016 OPEC meeting in Doha where Iran refused to agree to a freeze in production. Qatar left OPEC in 2019 due to Saudi Arabia's heavy-handed leadership, and Saudi Arabia openly sparred with UAE in 2021 over how to implement production cutbacks (Lawler 2021).

These tensions appeared at a time when Western consumers began to switch to electric vehicles, and renewable sources of energy like solar and wind power became more economically feasible. Lower demand in the United States and other industrialized nations for imported oil acted as a counterbalance to OPEC's ability to control global pricing for oil. To maintain its leverage, OPEC created OPEC+ in 2016, a group of ten nations that coordinate oil production with the existing thirteen members, which included Algeria, Angola, Congo, Equatorial Guinea, Gabon, Iran, Iraq, Kuwait, Libya, Nigeria, Saudi Arabia, the United Arab Emirates, and Venezuela. OPEC+ nations are also major oil producers: Azerbaijan, Bahrain, Brunei, Kazakhstan, Malaysia, Mexico, Oman, Russia, South Sudan, and Sudan. The association of these oil-producing nations may not wield the same power over global geopolitics as the original members of OPEC in the late twentieth century, but as long as petroleum remains an "important national security concern" for the United States, OPEC and its affiliates will demand strategic consideration (Lifset 2014, 38).

Jeffrey B. Webb

See also: ARAMCO; Carter Doctrine; Consortium Agreement of 1954; Energy Crisis of the 1970s; Energy Independence; Energy Policy and Conservation Act of 1975; Gulf War; Iraq War and the Project for a New American Century;. Mandatory Oil Import Quota Program; National Energy Act of 1978; Red Line Agreement of 1928; Seven Sisters Oil Companies; Strategic Petroleum Reserve

FURTHER READING

Carter, Jimmy. 1980. "Address by President Carter on the State of the Union before a Joint Session of Congress." *Foreign Relations of the United States, 1977–1980*. Vol. 1: *Foundations of Foreign Policy*. Ed. Kristin L. Ahlberg. Washington, DC: US Government Printing Office, 2014.

Gately, Dermot. 1986. "Lessons from the 1986 Oil Price Collapse." *Brookings Papers on Economic Activity*. Vol. 1986. No. 2. Pp. 237–84.

Lawler, Alex. 2021. "Factbox: A UAE Spat to 'One of the Worst Meetings': A History of OPEC and Others at Odds." Reuters. July 6. https://www.reuters.com/world/middle-east/uae-spat-one-worst-meetings-history-opec-others-odds-2021-07-06/ (accessed October 2023).

Lifset, Robert D. 2014. "A New Understanding of the American Energy Crisis of the 1970s." *Historical Social Research—Historische Sozialforschung. Special Issue: The Energy Crises of the 1970s: Anticipations and Reactions in the Industrialized World*. Vol. 39. No. 4. Pp. 22–42.

McMahon, Tim. 2023. "Historical Crude Oil Prices (Table)." InflationData.com. February 14. https://inflationdata.com/articles/inflation-adjusted-prices/historical-crude-oil-prices-table/ (accessed October 2023).

Organization of Petroleum Exporting Countries (OPEC). 1968. "Guidelines for Petroleum Policy in Member Countries." *International Legal Materials*. Vol. 7. No. 5. Pp. 1183–6.

Richard Nixon Foundation (RNF). 2016. "Nixon's Nuclear Energy Vision." October 20. https://www.nixonfoundation.org/2016/10/26948/ (accessed October 2023).

Richardson, Julia, and Robert Nordhaus. 1995. "The National Energy Act of 1978." *Natural Resources & Environment*. Vol. 10. No. 1. Summer. Pp. 62–8, 87–8.

Osgood, John Cleveland

The career of John C. Osgood (1851–1926) corresponded with the transfer of the coal-powered industrial system to Colorado and the American West. Osgood, a New York transplant by way of Iowa, became involved in railroad management, coal mining, coke production, and steel manufacturing. His primary business, the Colorado Fuel and Iron Company, provided coal for locomotives traversing the Mountain West and processed coal into coke to fuel the company's steel mills, which produced steel rails and other items for new railroad construction. Osgood's business enterprises helped to transform the Mountain West into an industrial landscape composed of resource extraction industries, materials processing plants, and extensive infrastructure. At the height of his career Osgood was "hailed as the West's leading industrial capitalist" (Scamehorn 1973, 148).

Osgood's life is recognizable as a Horatio Alger, rags-to-riches story. He and his three siblings were orphaned at a young age and were sent from their Brooklyn home to be raised by relatives in Connecticut and Rhode Island. When he was fourteen, Osgood served as an apprentice clerk in a Providence textile mill, and then at sixteen moved to New York where he took a job as a bookkeeper for a produce commission merchant (Scamehorn 1973, 133). He also took business classes at Cooper Union. One of his business associates, A.D. Moss of the Colorado Coal Company, referred Osgood to management at the Union Coal and Mining Company in Ottumwa, Iowa where he moved to work as a company cashier. After a few years at the firm, Osgood went to work in banking at First National Bank in Burlington where he learned of an investment opportunity with Whitebreast Coal and Mining Company in Lucas County, Iowa. He bought an interest in the firm and became its secretary and treasurer. He served as president starting in 1878 and salvaged an important contract for Whitebreast as supplier of coal for the Chicago, Burlington and Quincy Railroad (CB&Q). The railroad asked Osgood to travel to Colorado to investigate fuel sources for the CB&Q's new Burlington and Missouri line from Omaha to Denver, and in 1882 he made his way to the West.

Osgood was impressed by the early development of Colorado's coal resources and the wide-open field for business opportunities in the region, so he left Whitebreast and settled in Denver. He began buying coal for the Burlington and Missouri line, and by 1884 had gathered enough investors from Burlington and Uttumwa to form the Colorado Fuel Company. Over the next eight years, Osgood's company absorbed the Denver Fuel Company, Elk Mountain Fuel Company, the Huerfano Land, South Land, and Southern Colorado Coal companies, and the Grand River Coal and Coke Company. Finally in 1892, the company merged with its chief competitor, the Colorado Coal and Iron Company and renamed itself the Colorado Fuel and Iron Company. At this point, Osgood and his investors owned "69,000 acres of land, 14 operating coal mines, and four different plants housing coke ovens capable of coking 800 tons of coal a month," as well as "38 mining camps and rolling mills in Colorado, Wyoming and New Mexico along with 2,311 acres of iron ore lands" (Schreck 2023).

Osgood continued to acquire more companies such as the Trinidad Coal and Coking Company, the Canon City Coal Company, the Vulcan Fuel Company, and a controlling interest in Victor Fuel Company along with the lands leased by these companies for coal and coke exploration. Osgood put large amounts of capital into the Bessemer Works in Pueblo, a project first undertaken by the Colorado Coal and Iron Company, and which he inherited when the companies merged. The plant used its three blast furnaces and two five-ton converters to refine iron ore into pig iron, and then to steel by eliminating impurities throughout the process. It also featured bloom mills for flattening steel and shaping rails, a mill for making iron merchant bars, a cast-iron pipe foundry, and a mill for making railroad spikes. The different mills and foundries at Bessemer Works could produce 400 tons of iron, 300 tons of steel rails, and 40 tons of iron merchant bars and light rail sections every day (Scamehorn 1973, 138). However, the Panic of 1893 idled the plant, and formation of the steel trusts in the 1890s created an adverse market for the company. Financing Bessemer Works would prove to be a challenge, and eventually force Osgood from the company's leadership.

Before he left the company in 1903, however, Osgood devoted his time and effort, and quite a bit of capital to building Redstone, a community envisioned as a model for improving social and economic relations among company owners and their workers. Across the nation, the era was marked by intense conflict between the ownership class and industrial workers. Strikes were frequent in the nineteenth century as workers sought better pay, safer working conditions, shorter workdays, and other concessions from their employers. Within Osgood's lifetime, the Great Railroad Strike (1877), the Haymarket Affair (1886), the Pennsylvania Anthracite Coal Strike (1887–8), the Homestead Steel Strike (1892), and the Pullman Strike (1894) revealed massive discontent with the work arrangements in heavy industries. Various units of the Colorado Fuel and Iron Company experienced intermittent walkouts and strikes in the 1880s and 1890s, including a walkout in sympathy with the Pullman Strike. In 1901, the United Mine Workers of America organized a strike against Osgood's Colorado Fuel and Iron Company in sympathy with the company's workers in Gallup, New Mexico, which forced management to modify the system of payments based on weight.

To deflate pressures fueling labor agitation, Osgood built Redstone, a village of eighty-four houses to be rented at a modest rate to coke oven and coal mine workers and their families. They were well-designed and well-built with electricity and running water, and workers were encouraged to make improvements and beautify their lots. A company publication in 1901 described the houses as "'tasteful little cottages in different styles, prettily ornamented, comfortably arranged internally and painted in every variety of restful color'" (Schreck 2023). Osgood also arranged a kindergarten for workers' children, a school for older youth, English language training for newly arrived immigrants, library resources, and classes for adults in sewing, cooking, and various trades. The community had a clubhouse for meetings and enrichment activities, and a newsletter with a variety of material, often with pieces in Italian and German for immigrant workers. The forty-room Redstone Inn housed single men where they could relax, play games, and enjoy time off after work. Workers in the community formed a band and practiced regularly, complete with matching uniforms. A true "company town," Redstone also had a medical dispensary and a company store that accepted scrip that could be used between paychecks (Schreck 2023).

Perched on a slope above Redstone was Osgood's mansion, which he called Cleveholm Manor. The home mimicked landed estates of the English gentry with forty-two rooms, including eight bathrooms and fourteen fireplaces, as well as separate quarters for servants, a valet, a watchman, and a butler. Cleveholm Manor was decorated liberally with Tiffany glass, rare Honduran mahogany, and Persian carpets. It featured beautifully decorated rooms for entertaining, such as a billiards room and a music parlor. Taken together, Cleveholm Manor and the Redstone community reflected Osgood's ambition to live like a feudal lord, elevated above his phalanx of serfs who labored in the mines for his riches. Historians of nineteenth-century business and labor explain Osgood's company town and similar industrial towns as a form of "enlightened paternalism," or the exercise of benevolent control over subordinates to secure their labor, supposedly for the benefit of the workers themselves (ACHP 2007). According to one contemporary source, the idea was to create an interdependence between labor and management based on the employer's "parental solicitude and the employee's filial subservience" (Munsell 2009, 36).

Like most other owners and investors of industrial corporations, Osgood despised unions and worked diligently to keep them from his mines and mills. Unions were an affront to Osgood's view of proper relations between business owners and employees, which was hierarchical and paternalistic and not adversarial. A report issued in the wake of the Colorado Coalfield War of 1913–14, which included the horrific Ludlow Massacre of coal miners, mentioned Osgood's long-standing animosity toward organized labor: "Mr. Osgood repudiated the entire principle of collective bargaining, declaring that even were the United Mine Workers incorporated and financially responsible as an organization, he would refuse to deal with them" (West 1915, 38). The report went on to add that "there is no question in the world but that for years the member of the union that found his way into those mines,—take for instance the mine of Mr. Osgood,—if it was discovered that he was a member of the union, and lisped upon the subject of the union, they found a way to get rid of him" (West 1915, 54). Osgood became involved in negotiations with Colorado coal miners in the violent 1913–14 strikes as owner of Victor-American Fuel Company, but in 1904 had left the Colorado Fuel and Iron Company. What led to his departure was revenue shortfall in the company and an attempted hostile takeover, which pushed him close to bankruptcy and led him to borrow heavily from John D. Rockefeller and financier George Jay Gould. In 1903, Rockefeller put his trusted associate Frank J. Hearne in charge; Osgood stayed on the board for another year and then left the company to pursue his own business interests (Scamehorn 1973, 146).

Toward the end of his life, Osgood grappled with labor organizers and became tarnished by the brutal suppression of striking miners by the Colorado National Guard, company security personnel, and mercenaries from Baldwin-Felts Detective Agency. He also suffered through two failed marriages until finding contentment with his third wife Lucille Reid, whom he married in 1920 at the age of sixty-nine. Nevertheless, wealth had it privileges, as Osgood lived the life of a manorial baron and socialized with the business and political leaders of the nation, even hosting at different times John Rockefeller, Theodore Roosevelt, J. Pierpont Morgan, and Prince Leopold of Belgium at Cleveholm. Despite the harsh criticism that Colorado coal mine operators endured after the Ludlow Massacre, Osgood retained a long-standing reputation as a hardy, self-made man and one of the builders of modern Colorado. He was, in the words of the National Mining Hall of Fame, "the undisputed fuel king of the West" (NMHFM 2020).

Jeffrey B. Webb

See also: Battle of Blair Mountain; Coal; Coke; Cumberland Iron and Coal Company; Frick, Henry Clay; Harlan County War; Ludlow Massacre; Miner's and Laborer's Benevolent Association; Molly Maguires; North Antelope Rochelle Mine; Rockefeller, John D.; Sinclair, Upton; United Mine Workers of America

FURTHER READING

Advisory Council on Historic Preservation (ACHP). 2007. "Redstone, Colorado." ACHP Preserve America. Washington, DC. https://www.achp.gov/preserve-america/community/redstone-colorado (accessed October 2023).

Munsell, F. Darrell. 2009. *From Redstone to Ludlow: John Cleveland Osgood's Struggle against the United Mine Workers of America*. Boulder, CO: University Press of Colorado.

National Mining Hall of Fame & Museum (NMHFM). 2020. "John Cleveland Osgood." https://www.mininghalloffame.org/hall-of-fame/john-cleveland-osgood

Scamehorn, H. Lee. 1973. "John C. Osgood and the Western Steel Industry." *Arizona and the West*. Vol. 15. No. 2. Pp. 133–48.

Schreck, Christopher J. 2023. "John Cleveland Osgood: American Entrepreneur." *Colorado Fuel and Iron: Culture and Industry in Southern Colorado*. Alliance for Networking Visual Culture. https://scalar.usc.edu/works/the-colorado-fuel-and-iron-company/media/john-cleveland-osgood-american-entrepreneur (accessed October 2023).

West, George P. 1915. *Report on the Colorado Strike*. United States Commission on Industrial Relations. Chicago: Barnard & Miller, Printer.

Paint Creek Mine War

Coal provided an inexpensive source of energy in the early Industrial Revolution. Coal heated water for boilers that drove steam plants in America's early factories, and engines in early railroad locomotives. Coal-fired boilers also provided steam for operating steamboats and heating large buildings. Coal provided the base material for coke, which in turn fueled smelting furnaces to make iron and steel. None of this would have been possible without coal miners. In coal-rich West Virginia, the number of miners grew from 3,701 in 1880 to nearly 90,000 in 1917 (Lewis 2023). In the nineteenth and early twentieth centuries, mining conditions were tough and dangerous. Many miners worked twelve-hour days and risked death by explosion, fire, and mine collapse. Mining camps were located in unincorporated areas of the state, and mining companies controlled elected officials and law enforcement. They also controlled housing, schools, and shops, in some cases paying miners in company "scrip" that could only be used in company-owned stores.

In the mining communities in the Paint Creek, West Virginia area, tensions between coal miners and their employers came to a head in 1912. By national standards, West Virginia miners were paid a low wage, partly because fewer than 10 percent of West Virginia miners were unionized. As West Virginia mines expanded their operations, they hired more miners. These new employees sought unionization, which their employers refused to accept. Deterioration of workplace relations led to a nearly two-year long war in 1912–13 between miners and security guards hired by mine companies. The Paint Creek mine war in southern West Virginia eventually claimed around fifty lives, mostly due to violence but also starvation and poor living conditions. The war impelled the state government to declare martial law.

The war grew out of a strike that began on April 18, 1912. Miners at Paint Creek and Cabin Creek mine sites were making 2.5 cents less per long ton than miners in other mines. The miners demanded an increase in wages but the mine operators refused. The United Mine Workers of America (UMWA) called a strike demanding a wage increase, but also that operators accept and recognize the union, that miners have freedom of speech and the right to assembly, and that compulsory trading at the company stores be ended. The Cabin Creek miners joined the Paint Creek miners, and the UMWA hoped to spread the union into southern West Virginia. The union promised to help finance and direct the strike against the operators. During the first month, the strike was non-violent largely due to the presence of the UMWA, but that soon changed.

On May 10, the strike turned violent when the Baldwin-Felts Detective Agency arrived with 300 armed guards to break the strike, paid for by the mine operators. In early June, mine owners, frustrated with the striking miners and the union, began to evict workers from their rented homes and to bring in new workers. It was common to see daily beatings, cruelty, and deadly reprisals. Labor organizer and activist Mother Jones arrived in the midst of all the chaos and began efforts to rally the workers. Jones came through the armed guards to persuade other miners in Eskdale, West Virginia to join the strike. She also organized a secret march of 3,000 armed miners to the state capitol to speak to the governor. On July 26, miners attacked in a fight that left twelve strikers and four guards dead. After months of scattered attacks, the UMWA added 5,000 miners to the strike. The miners came from the north side of the Kanawha River. The arrival of so many new strikers added to the already overwhelming chaos, and on September 1, West Virginia Governor William E. Glasscock (1862–1925) implemented martial law. Under martial law, strikers were forced to give up their arms and ammunition. Strikers' families suffered from starvation and unsanitary conditions after they had been relocated to temporary tents at Holly Grove.

The governor decided to lift martial law on October 15 but reversed course and reimposed it on November 15. Since Glasscock only had a couple months left in office, he decided to end martial law for what miners believed was for good on January 10, 1913. Later, a retaliation attack by the Kanawha County Sheriff and a group of detectives left miner Cesco Estep dead. The attackers used machine guns and high intensity rifles from an armored train and fired into Estep's house in the Holly Grove miners settlement. Miners named this event the "Bull Moose Special." This attack was reportedly in retaliation for the February 7, 2013 Mucklow attack by miners that left at least one person dead. After the Bull Moose Special another raid on Mucklow occurred, which left at least two people dead. Martial law was implemented for the last time. Activist Mother Jones protested with a public reading of the Declaration of Independence, and was charged with inciting a riot. Later, her charges were elevated to conspiracy to commit murder. Because of the martial law declaration, trials of more than 200 civilians were held in military courts, which raised questions about civil liberties.

Things began to change for the better when the new governor Dr. Henry D. Hatfield was sworn in on March 4, 2013. Hatfield's first priority was ending martial law. He also released Mother Jones for medical treatment and made moves to find a settlement for labor dispute. He gave strikers the choice to accept what he considered to be fair and unbiased terms, or relocate elsewhere. The Paint Creek miners decided to accept Governor Hatfield's terms and signed the "Hatfield Contract" on May 1. Mother Jones was ultimately held in a makeshift prison for eighty-five days before she was pardoned by Governor Hatfield.

EXPLOITING DIFFERENCES

Coal mining brought together several different ethnic groups: recent immigrants from southern and eastern Europe, native Appalachians, and African Americans from the South. The coal mining operations were heavily dependent on labor but coal operators did not want workers to unionize. So, coal miners often exacerbated racial tension and division in coal towns.

Daniel W. Phillips III

The US Senate opened up an investigation into the treatment of miners by the mine owners. This resulted in other mine investigations on mines around the United States. The Paint Creek mine war was not the last in West Virginia. In 1921 there were two large outbreaks of violence at Matewan and Blair Mountain, the latter of which resulted in over a hundred deaths. Ten years later, the Harlan County War erupted and took the lives of five people. This pattern of labor violence in West Virginia highlighted the poor state of employer-employee relations in the coal industry in the first three decades of the twentieth century. In 1933, President Franklin D. Roosevelt enacted the National Industrial Recovery Act, which guaranteed the right of laborers to engage in collective bargaining. This resulted in a boost for the UMWA organizing efforts, the end of coal mine operators' stranglehold on labor, and improved pay and better working conditions for coal miners (EH 2023).

Daniel W. Phillips and Isiah Lamont Davis

See also: Battle of Blair Creek; Black Lung Disease; Coal; Harlan County War; Ludlow Massacre; Miner's and Laborer's Benevolent Association; Molly Maguires; United Mine Workers of America; Upton, Sinclair

FURTHER READING

Corbin, David Alan. 1981. *Life, Work, and Rebellion in the Coal Fields: The Southern West Virginia Miners, 1880–1922*. Urbana, IL: University of Illinois Press.

Corbin, David Alan, ed. 1998. *The West Virginia Mine Wars: An Anthology*. Martinsburg, WV: Appalachian Editions.

Energy History (EH). 2023. "Coal Mining and Labor Conflict." Yale University. https://energyhistory.yale.edu/units/coal-mining-and-labor-conflict (accessed October 2023).

Green, James. 2015. *The Devil is Here in These Hills: West Virginia's Coal Miners and Their Battle for Freedom*. New York: Grove.

Lee, Howard. 1969. *Bloodletting in Appalachia: The Story of West Virginia's Four Major Mine Wars and Other Thrilling Incidents of Its Coal Fields*. Morgantown, WV: West Virginia University.

Lewis, Ronald L. 2023. "Coal Industry." e-WV: The West Virginia Encyclopedia. March 8. https://www.wvencyclopedia.org/articles/1349 (accessed October 2023).

Panama Canal

The Panama Canal is an artificial waterway some 51 miles (82 kilometers) long cut through the Isthmus of Panama and linking the Atlantic and Pacific oceans. Completed by the United States in 1914, it dramatically reduced the sailing distance and time between the country's East and West coasts, cutting transportation costs and providing a significant boost to American and international shipping. In 1999, the US government turned over control to the nation of Panama, which now manages the canal's operation. Since then, the construction of a new, wider lane has expanded the canal's capacity.

The dream of cutting a canal through Central America was not a new one, and US officials had long foreseen the possibility. The country had assumed control of much of the West Coast of North America by the middle of the nineteenth century, and signed the Clayton–Bulwer Treaty with Britain in 1850, providing that neither country would have sole ownership of such a waterway or be solely responsible for its defense. A railroad crossing the Isthmus of Panama was completed in early 1855, and the Transcontinental Railroad, which linked America's coasts, in the late 1860s, but the idea of a shortened connection by water that would allow for greater amounts of goods to be shipped long distances quickly and cheaply remained attractive.

French diplomat and engineer Count Ferdinand de Lesseps (1805–94), who had developed the sea-level Suez Canal, attempted to construct a similar canal across Central America in the 1880s through the agency of the Société Civile Internationale du Canal Interocéanique de Darien. But the enormous complexity of the project, coupled with destructively heavy rains and endemic diseases, proved to be insurmountable difficulties. It is estimated that some 20,000 workers died in the attempt. The Compagnie Nouvelle du Canal de Panama took over the stalled project in 1894, but it, too, was unable to make headway.

American interest in a canal linking the Atlantic and the Pacific grew with the experience of the United States in the brief Spanish–American War in 1898. The USS *Oregon*, for instance, had taken *sixty-seven days* to sail some 12,000 miles from San Francisco around the tip of South America in order to take part in the decisive July 3 Battle of Santiago de Cuba, which itself lasted only one day. The subsequent Treaty of Paris ending the war gave the United States control of Cuba as well as ownership of another West Indian island, Puerto Rico, and the Northern Pacific islands of Guam and the Philippines. Protection of these possessions made the need for a two-ocean navy clear, prompting President Theodore Roosevelt (1858–1919) to back a proposal calling for a canal across Central America, presumably to be constructed in Nicaragua.

The Hay–Pauncefote Treaty of 1901 between the United States and Britain abrogated the terms of the earlier Clayton–Bulwer Treaty, and the Senate voted in favor of building a canal in 1902. However, Roosevelt subsequently switched his preferred site to another location, and in 1903 American and Colombian diplomats negotiated a treaty to allow construction through the Isthmus of Panama, which was then part of Colombia. When the Colombian legislature rejected the treaty's terms, however, Roosevelt dispatched gunboats to the isthmus. A revolt of Panamanians under Colombian rule erupted shortly afterward, and its leaders declared independence as the nation of Panama. The subsequent Hay–Bunau-Varilla Treaty of 1903 between the United States and Panama gave America a strip of territory—the Panama Canal Zone—10 miles (16 kilometers) wide and running roughly northwest to southeast through which to build a canal. In turn, the United States provided the new nation with an initial payment of $10 million and annual payments of $250,000 beginning nine years later.

The United States assumed control of the canal zone on May 4, 1904, and that same year bought the remaining equipment and infrastructure from Compagnie Nouvelle du Canal de Panama for $40 million. Roosevelt appointed John Findley Wallace (1852–1921) as Chief Engineer, but after acquainting himself with the myriad problems that the project would face, including the prevalence of disease, the decrepit condition of the French equipment, and the cumbersome bureaucracy he would have to work with, Wallace resigned after little more than a year.

In Wallace's place, Roosevelt appointed railroad engineer John Frank Stevens (1853–1943), who proceeded to bypass the bureaucracy that had discouraged Wallace, instead establishing direct communication with President Roosevelt. Stevens made the bold decision to postpone work on the canal itself while he built adequate housing and infrastructure for the project's workers, who had until then endured abysmally poor living and working conditions. In addition, he promised Col. William Crawford Gorgas (1854–1920), the project's Chief Sanitary Engineer, to provide whatever help he needed in order to rid the zone of yellow fever and malaria. Having learned that the diseases are spread by mosquitos, which breed in stagnant water, Gorgas initiated projects to clear the zone of the insects, and within two years' time, the diseases had been largely eradicated.

With these two projects accomplished, Stevens was finally able to proceed on the canal itself. While it had been anticipated that the waterway would be built at sea level, the engineer had come to believe that such an approach was totally impractical. Instead, he argued that a lock system was the only way to deal with Panama's rugged mountains and the flooding on the Chagres River that the region's torrential rains routinely created. The system he envisioned would involve building what became known as the Gatun Dam across the Chagres River to create a reservoir—Gatun Lake—at 85 feet (26 meters) above sea level. A channel, the Culebra (later Gaillard) Cut, would be dug through the Continental Divide to connect the reservoir to a series of locks designed to raise or lower the water level as vessels transited from or to the Pacific Ocean. Another series of locks would be built along the channel leading to the Atlantic.

AN UNOFFICIAL TRANSIT

While the first official trip through the Panama Canal was made by the SS *Ancon* on August 15, 1914, the first ship that actually passed through the completed canal was one of the Ancon's sister ships. With some 200 guests aboard, the SS *Cristobal* made a successful but unofficial test run almost two weeks before, on August 3, 1914, to test the feasibility of the system.

Grove Koger

Even with the modified design, digging the canal required removing an immense amount of dirt and rock. Before abandoning their attempt, the French had excavated some 30 million cubic yards (23 million cubic meters) of material. Now, after upgrading the railroad and using vastly improved equipment, the Americans proceeded to excavate about 170 million cubic yards (130 million cubic meters) more.

Stevens unexpectedly resigned his position in 1907 and President Roosevelt appointed Army Major George Washington Goethals as Chief Engineer. Two years later, workers began construction of the locks, each of them 110 feet (33.5 meters) wide by 1,050 feet (320 meters) long. The Culebra Cut was flooded in 1913 and the canal opened officially on August 15, 1914, two years ahead of schedule. In all, the American operation had cost about 5,600 lives. The first official transit was made on August 15 by the SS *Ancon,* while the first US Navy ship to transit was the USS *Jupiter,* which was then being used as a collier, or coal-carrying vessel.

American victory in the Spanish–American War had signaled the country's emergence as a world power, a status that the completion of the Panama Canal confirmed. Over the succeeding decades, however, the world's political climate evolved, and the end of the Second World War saw a wave of decolonization in which the European nations gave up, sometimes unwillingly, their overseas empires. Panamanian dissatisfaction with American control of the canal had grown as well, and after a period of intense domestic political controversy, the United States turned over full control of the canal to Panama itself on December 31, 1999.

In 1916, two years after the canal's completion, there were 807 transits by ship, a number that rose to 15,523 by 1970. Subsequently, the number of transits has decreased, but as the capacity of ships has increased over the same period, the number of tons involved has continued to rise. The canal has proven to be an important route for smaller (Panamax class) oil tankers passing between the oceans, while a pipeline paralleling the canal carries crude oil. Panama completed construction of a new, wider ship lane through the canal in May 2016, allowing for the passage of larger, "post-Panamax" vessels—a project that has doubled the canal's capacity.

With its completion, the Panama Canal shaved nearly 8,000 miles and approximately a month off the sea voyage between the East and West coasts of the country. It is regarded as one of the greatest engineering achievements in history and has been recognized by the American Society of Civil Engineers as one of the seven wonders of the modern world.

Grove Koger

See also: Carter Doctrine; Colliers; Oil Tankers; Petroleum; Transcontinental Railroad

FURTHER READING

Cullen, Bob. 2004. "A Man, a Plan, a Canal: Panama Rises." *Smithsonian*. March. 44–54.

Hoffman, Jon T. 2009. *The Panama Canal: An Army's Enterprise*. Washington, DC: Center of Military History, United States Army.

Khalifa, Daisy R. 2016. "Game Changer?" *Sea Power*. Vol. 59. No. 6. Pp. 46–50.

Lasso, Marixa. 2019. *Erased: The Untold Story of the Panama Canal*. Cambridge, MA: Harvard University Press.

McCullough, David. 1977. *The Path between the Seas: The Creation of the Panama Canal, 1870–1914*. New York: Simon & Schuster.

Parker, Matthew. 2007. *Panama Fever: The Epic Story of One of the Greatest Human Achievements of Al Time—The Building of the Panama Canal*. New York: Doubleday.

Peak Oil

Nothing is more essential to the world's economy than oil. It provides fuel to manufacture goods and the base element of many chemical products. It also supplies a majority of the world's energy for transportation, thereby facilitating the flow of international trade. Accordingly, concerns over oil production and consumption are of paramount concern, with peak oil representing one of the most pressing. Peak oil refers to the notion that the global production of oil will (or already has) reach its resource-limited maximum whereupon it will enter a period of irreversible decline. In other words, it is the juncture at which point half the world's oil supply has been extracted and consumed.

Sometimes dismissed as a conspiracy theory or written off as an overhyped worry, peak oil is not so much a theory as it is a geologic fact. The world has a finite supply of petroleum. Hence, the real question is not if but when peak oil will occur. Further questions and debates, though, exist over what exactly peak oil will mean. Along these lines, it is common to criticize peak oil by suggesting oil reserves are so vast that there is little cause for concern. The peak may come, but we have decades or even centuries before it does. A separate set of critics posit that peak oil will have minimal world economic effects since price mechanisms and market forces will facilitate a transition to alternative energy resources.

Peak oil was first introduced by American geologist and geophysicist Marion King Hubbert in the 1950s as a way to explain production patterns of crude oil. He argued that oil production would ultimately resemble a bell curve that would be symmetrical. The peak would occur when half of a nonrenewable resource was extracted. Today, peak oil is sometimes called Hubbert's Peak. The modern peak oil movement, however, can be traced back to the late-1990s with the publication of "The End of Cheap Oil" by petroleum geologist Colin Campbell, which he followed with *The Coming Oil Crisis* in 1997. In 2000, Campbell assembled a consortium of scientists and government officials into a group called Association for the Study of Peak Oil (ASPO) that began advocating the theory of peak oil across media outlets. In 2002, ASPO held its first conference and continues to hold annual meetings every year.

The years 2004 and 2005 witnessed the publication of a torrent of books on peak oil. These, according to Matthew Schneider-Mayerson, included *The Last Hours of Ancient Sunlight: The Fate of the World and What We Can Do Before It's Too Late* (2004), *High Noon for Natural Gas* (2004), *Out of Gas: The End of the Age of Oil* (2005), *Crude: The Story of Oil* (2004), *The Coming Oil Crisis: Oil, Jihad, and Destiny* (2004), *Crossing the Rubicon: The Decline of the American Empire at the End of the Age of Oil* (2004), *Beyond Oil: The View from Hubbert's Peak* (2004), *Blood and Oil: The Dangers and Consequences of America's Growing Oil Conspiracy* (2004), and *Powerdown: Options and Actions for A Post-Carbon World* (2004). After the publication of these and other books, peak oil became a common topic in the mainstream media from the middle to the end of the 2000s.

Adherents of peak oil argue that when peak production has occurred it will necessitate the extraction of non-conventional oils, such as tar sands oil and shale oil. These require expensive technologies and risky extraction methods such as fracking to access remaining deposits. The result will be higher production costs to access lower-quality deposits. Over time, investments will be unable to keep up with the rising extraction costs. In response, growth will slow and lead to a production decline due to changes on the energy returned on energy invested ratio (EROEI). EROEI is the ratio of usable energy extrapolated from a particular source contrasted with the amount of energy used to obtain that energy. With prospects limited to hard-to-reach reserves that will be harder to refine into usable products, the projected EROEI yield is lower.

Belief in peak oil became pronounced between 2004 and 2011. During this time, millions of Americans came to believe that an impending oil scarcity would lead to the inevitable collapse of industrial society and with it the demise of the United States. A portion of "peakists" (a sobriquet for adherents of the negative repercussions of peak oil) believe that the point of peak oil has already occurred. Matthew Schneider-Mayerson's ethnographic work suggests peakists are predominantly white, male, educated, and liberal in political philosophy. Given the movement's negative understanding of peak oil, it is sometimes referred to as the liberal apocalypse.

Three developments led to the genesis of the peak oil movement: the US invasion of Iraq in March 2003, sharp increases in the price of oil and gasoline, and growing awareness of anthropogenic climate change. The invasion and occupation of Iraq was significant because it led individuals to ponder global energy politics. After it became apparent that Iraq did not possess weapons of mass destruction, peakism became a lens to view the occupation as a resource war. Consistent with this perspective, peakists believed that petroleum depletion would lead nations into prolonged conflicts over remaining oil supplies. Conjectures over the underlying rationale for the Iraqi occupation were bolstered by the rising gasoline costs across the 2000s which saw the cost of a gallon gas increase by over 300 percent and the cost of a barrel of crude oil increase by nearly 600 percent. These price spikes were lavishly covered by television, print, and internet media, making them more noticeable.

Public awareness of climate change dates back to the late 1980s, but the success of movies *The Day After Tomorrow* (2004) and *An Inconvenient Truth* (2006) along with aftermath of Hurricane Katrina put the issue at the forefront for many Americans. In 2008, Al Gore, who had been on a speaking tour concerning climate change, and the Intergovernmental Panel on Climate Change shared the Nobel Peace Prize. As Matthew Schneider-Mayerson's research has found, the growing recognition of climate change led many to accept the peak oil idea. Whether the worst fears over peak oil turn out to be true or not, the peak oil movement can be credited for forcing Americans to consider new sources of energy while there is still sufficient oil for relatively cheap energy production.

Todd K. Platts

See also: American Petroleum Institute; *An Inconvenient Truth*; Climate Change; Cheney, Richard Bruce "Dick"; Energy Crisis of the 1970s; Energy Independence; Global Climate Coalition; Gulf War; Iraq War and the Project for a New American Century; Natural Resources Defense Council; Union of Concerned Scientists

FURTHER READING

Bardi, Ugo. 2009. "Peak Oil: The Four Stages of a New Idea." *Energy*. Vol. 34. No. 3. Pp. 323–6.

Bentley, R.W. 2016. *Introduction to Peak Oil*. New York: Springer.

Chapman, Ian. 2014. "The End of Peak Oil? Why This Topic Is Still Relevant Despite Recent Denials." *Energy Policy*. Vol. 64. Pp. 93–101.

Holland, Stephen P. 2008. "Modeling Peak Oil." *Energy Journal*. Vol. 29. No. 2. Pp. 61–79.

Schneider-Mayerson, Matthew. 2015. *Peak Oil: Apocalyptic Environmentalism and Libertarian Political Culture*. Chicago, IL: University of Chicago Press.

Pearl Street Power Station

The Pearl Street Power Station opened in Manhattan in 1882 and was the first commercial power station in the United States. The plant was constructed by Thomas Alva Edison's (1847–1931) Edison Illuminating Company for the purpose of distributing direct current (DC) electrical power for lighting and steam for heat. The plant used six coal-powered electrical generators, known as dynamos, to provide electrical service for an area that included Wall Street and several New York newspapers. The station was a first step in the creation of the nation's electricity grid, which made it possible for the vast majority of Americans to benefit from the availability of electrical power.

In late 1877, Edison had experimented with arc and incandescent light bulbs but after many failures had decided there was little commercial future for the bulbs. Then, in 1878 he witnessed arc lighting powered by a steam dynamo that was in use at a brass foundry (Jonnes 2004, 55). Arc lighting had first been demonstrated by English scientist Sir Humphry Davy (1778–1829) in the early nineteenth century, but little was done with it until the 1870s, when strong dynamos were developed that were capable of producing enough current and voltage to power the lights. Unfortunately, arc lighting was intense and tended to flicker and hum, making it an undesirable method of interior lighting (Freeberg 2013, 16, 28).

Edison realized that if he could create a less harsh lighting system and similarly power it with a dynamo, he could provide useful—and commercially successful—indoor lighting for homes and businesses (Jonnes 2004, 48). Additionally, he knew the system had to be made safe: existing arc lighting power lines used dangerously high voltages and had been the cause of several deaths (Feeberg 2013, 80).

Edison's plan was to create a system of electrical distribution based on the way gas was delivered to homes, which included an underground network of pipes, gas lamps, and a meter to calculate each customer's utility bill. But before electricity could become a viable utility to rival gas, all of the pieces needed to be invented and produced. What was needed was an inexpensive, reliable power source, glass bulbs that would not burn out quickly, and a way of directing and switching the flow of electricity so individual users could turn lights on and off without affecting other users (Freeberg 2013, 29).

In 1879, Edison produced a successful light bulb and began designing the electrical system to support it. In 1880, he installed a lighting system at his Menlo Park laboratory and formed the Edison Electric Illuminating Company for the purpose of generating and delivering electricity. This was followed in 1881 by the installation of a low-voltage DC system at a printing company and in early 1882 Edison opened the Holborn Viaduct station in London (Hausman 2008, 321).

Edison began looking for a suitable location in New York to construct a central power station. He wanted an inexpensive building that would be large enough to house the generators

ELECTRIC LIGHTING ABROAD

Even before Edison's commercial success with Pearl Street there was an international electric lighting industry. France's Société Générale d'Electricité installed an arc lighting system in Paris, which used "electric candles" designed by Russian military engineer Paul Jablochkoff. A competing German company, Siemens & Haske, set up affiliates in England and Russia, and by 1881, much of Europe had arc lighting systems, as did many Asian and South American countries (Hausman 2008, 75; Jonnes 2004, 46).

Karen S. Garvin

and yet was close to the financial district and the newspapers, although he intended to provide electrical service to both business and residential customers. In 1881, Edison purchased a large building at 255–257 Pearl Street in Manhattan for $65,000 (Jonnes 2004, 81). The location was in the First District, which included a large swath of the downtown area.

He was now ready to begin work on the central power station, and in April 1881 Edison received permission from the city of New York to dig up the streets to lay nearly 14 miles of electrical conduits (Jonnes 2004, 4, 80). Edison intended for Pearl Street to be operational before winter, but he and his team encountered many technical problems that needed to be resolved. Additionally, the installation of the wiring, 2 feet below ground level, proved to be exceedingly difficult. Much of the construction was done at night and the work stopped during the winter months because the ground froze (Jonnes 2004, 80) The copper wiring was also incredibly expensive, and Edison had to change his original design in order to reduce the amount of copper needed.

At the heart of the central power station was the dynamo. Edison built the "Jumbo" dynamo, which was modeled on a design by the German company Siemens. This massive, 27-ton electrical generator was capable of producing 100 kilowatts of power and was itself powered by steam engines fueled with coal. Edison installed six of the Jumbo dynamos at Pearl Street, which was enough to provide electrical lighting for customers within one square mile of the central station. The Jumbo dynamos produced alternating current (AC) that was then converted into what Edison believed was a safe, low-voltage direct current for distribution (Jonnes 2004, 81, 107).

Finally, Edison felt that the system was ready to go into service. The date was set for September 4, 1882, and Edison made his way to the office of J. Pierpont Morgan at the firm of Drexel, Morgan, and Company, which was one of the investors in the Pearl Street enterprise. Earlier in the day, Edison had synchronized his watch with his chief electrician, John Lieb, who would have the honors of turning on the power at exactly 3:00 p.m. (Jonnes 2004, 145). There were concerns that the system would not work, but as the lights went on in Morgan's office, any lingering doubts about the feasibility of a centralized electrical power station were extinguished.

On the first day of service, a mere eighty-five customers received electricity from the Jumbo dynamos, and Edison did not begin billing his customers until January 1883. Within a year, the number of customers rose to just over 500, but Pearl Street lost money and did not become profitable until 1884. But the central power station proved to be reliable, with only one three-hour outage, and soon every city wanted electrical service (Hausman 2008, 18).

On January 2, 1890, a fire demolished the power station and left only one of the Jumbo dynamos unscathed. The station was quickly rebuilt, and in only eleven days Edison restored power to his customers. The station continued to operate successfully, but its capacity was eclipsed by the larger power stations that were starting to come online, and in 1895 the plant was decommissioned. In 1917, a bronze commemorative plaque was installed to mark where the station had been, and the remaining Jumbo dynamo was acquired by the Henry Ford Museum in Dearborn, Michigan, where is it on display at the Greenfield Village museum.

Karen S. Garvin

See also: Brush, Charles Francis; Edison, Thomas Alva; Electricity; General Electric Company; Henry, Joseph; Stanley, William Jr.; Tesla, Nikola; Vulcan Street Plant; War of the Currents; Westinghouse, George

FURTHER READING

DeGraff, Leonard. 2013. *Edison and the Rise of Innovation*. New York: Sterling Signature.

Freeberg, Ernest. 2013. *The Age of Edison: Electric Light and the Invention of Modern America*. New York: Penguin.

Hausman, William J., Peter Hertner, and Mira Wilkins. 2008. *Global Electrification: Multinational Enterprise and International Finance in the History of Light and Power, 1878–2007*. Cambridge: Cambridge University Press.

Henry Ford Museum (HFM). 2019. "The 'Jumbo' Dynamo in Its Original Setting, Edison's Pearl Street Lighting Station, New York, New York, circa 1890." accessed December 20, 2019.

Jonnes, Jill. 2004. *Empires of Light: Edison, Tesla, Westinghouse, and the Race to Electrify the World*. New York: Random House.

Pennsylvania Oil Boom

The Pennsylvania Oil Boom was an intensive period of petroleum extraction and refining that began in 1859 and continued into the early twentieth century. During the boom years, Pennsylvania was a national center of oil production. A businessman named Edwin Drake (1819–80) tapped into an underground oil well near Titusville, PA at the start of the boom, and became the first American to successfully extract oil for industrial purposes (Wells and Wells 2016). Following these first efforts of extraction, oil as a resource proved massively influential in the industrialization of the United States as a whole, and the massive natural reserves held in the fields of Texas, Oklahoma, and California helped to power the onset of the modern era. Soon came oil and gas for owners of automobiles and an array of mechanized armaments for the world's militaries. Other states would have their turn as leaders of petroleum production, but first came Pennsylvania.

The history of oil in Pennsylvania began when the first Indigenous inhabitants made use of oil seeps, areas where liquid or gaseous oil can be found on the surface. European settlers recorded the natives as having used the oil from these sources for various ointments and tinctures. By the time of colonization, trade in oil was common, as it was touted as having certain medicinal properties and the ability to cure illnesses (Black 2010, 6). Despite this, the resource had no larger industrial purposes at the time, and the extraction of oil was, by and large, not considered worth the effort required.

This changed with the onset of the Industrial Revolution. Although coal was a leading source of energy for much of the nineteenth century, by the time Edwin Drake first traveled to the hamlet of Titusville in 1857 under the auspices of the Pennsylvania Rock Oil Company (PROC), interest in oil was also piqued by the experiments of Massachusetts chemist Samuel Kier (1813–74). Kier had founded one of the first petroleum refineries after realizing the potential of the liquid as a replacement for whale oil, which had previously been used for many of the same purposes, primarily for lamps, although petroleum would prove far more versatile (ACS 2009).

Near Titusville, Drake began drilling for oil in 1857 and continued for two years in the area that would soon be known as Oil Creek. Using a variety of methods, from digging shafts in an attempt to reach wells of oil to using the power of an old steam engine, Drake at last was able to sink a successful oil well on the morning of August 28, 1859, striking oil at a depth of 69 feet. Producing 25 barrels on the first day of extraction, the well would soon level off on around 20 barrels' worth of crude oil a day. Though insignificant by modern standards, this was a watershed for industrialists of the day, many of whom quickly moved to secure land in the area and sink wells of their own (EPC 2021).

Edwin Drake died a pauper, having failed to patent his steam-powered drill, and left with only a meager pension by the PROC, now operating under the name Seneca Oil (ACS 2009). However, his discovery had massive consequences for the industrial world as a whole, and the state in which it was made. Oil production swelled, and the countryside of Pennsylvania experienced an oil boom comparable to the gold rushes of California and the Yukon. Where once the fields of Crawford County had abounded with grain crops and livestock, there appeared an industrial sprawl of oil wells and shantytowns that crowded onto the land (Black 1998, 210). Prior to 1862, oil was floated down Oil Creek by barge and then onto the Allegheny River to Pittsburgh, where it was refined by the plants that had sprung up in the wake of Kier's discoveries. By 1862, the newly founded Oil Creek Railroad Company completed a new line connecting Titusville to the outside world, providing expanded oil transport capacity and cementing this once-sleepy hamlet's status as a true boom town.

Over the years following Drake's discovery and the ensuing frenzy in pursuit of land, Oil Creek Valley moved to the forefront of the expanding horizon of the oil industry. Major players such as John D. Rockefeller's Standard Oil Company were attracted by the promise of huge profits in an industry that seemed impossible to fail. However, it became clear that the price of oil was volatile. The initial price of a single barrel, $10, dropped to just 10 cents over the course of the 1860s. Although there were attempts among oil companies to limit output from the valley in order to maintain a minimum price of $4 a barrel, they were widely unsuccessful throughout the 1870s (Hildegarde 1959, 80). This changed by the end of the decade, when larger conglomerates, most notably Rockefeller's Standard Oil, consolidated control over the Valley. Smaller, less profitable independent producers who snatched up land in the wake of Drake's strike in 1859 ultimately sold their leases in the face of an uncertain market (EPC 2021).

This mass corporatization created the greatest excesses of the oil boom. The small operations that worked individual wells had been intimidated by the volatility of the oil market. Amid consolidation, larger companies with greater capital resources could hold strong in the face of price volatility. After the turn of the twentieth century, demand for petroleum increased with the appearance of automobiles and the conversion of naval ships from coal to oil. In 1906, the British naval vessel HMS *Dreadnought*, the first "modern" battleship, launched and triggered a worldwide naval arms race. Though powered by coal-fired steam the ship carried 1,140 barrels of oil to accelerate coal firing (Roberts 1992, 25). By 1910, the US Navy had committed to the conversion of the fleet from coal to oil, and on July 2, 1910, President William Taft established three Naval Petroleum Reserves.

Pennsylvania would pass the torch to Texas, Oklahoma, and California in terms of leadership in petroleum production. In 1891, the state produced record 58 percent of oil worldwide with 31 million barrels of oil a year. However, this represented the point at which Pennsylvania was the largest oil producer by state. In 1895, Ohio eclipsed Pennsylvania as the nation's leading producer of crude oil (Hopkins 1934, 306). By the turn of the twentieth century, discoveries of massive oil fields in Texas ultimately rendered Pennsylvania and Ohio as minor players. As an illustration of Texas' dominance, the well at Spindletop Hill, near the town of Beaumont, yielded 17 million barrels of oil a year by itself (Ramos 2001).

Throughout the twentieth century, the oil production of Pennsylvania slowly declined from its historical peak. Although demand continued to increase with the First and Second World Wars, Texas satisfied those needs, and the wars shifted the focus of the Pennsylvanian state industries towards steel production. The iron and steel industries dominated the economies of Pittsburgh and Philadelphia. Oil production dwindled as interests turned elsewhere, and in 1997, the state produced a mere 1.32 million barrels.

These numbers changed with the introduction of the controversial technology of hydraulic fracturing, or "fracking." The method, which appeared in experimental form for commercial purposes in 1947, is performed by cracking through shale with super-pressurized water to open up pockets of oil and natural gas (OFE 2009). This advance signaled a new era in Pennsylvania oil, and by 2014, the state's production had reached 6.85 million barrels of crude oil a year, a thirty-year-high. Although that count decreased to 6.56 million in 2019, these numbers still crested the average highs of the entire twentieth century (EIA 2020). All told, the Pennsylvania oil boom's place in the history of energy in the United States is secure and enduring.

Samuel B. Fee and Kathy Tyson

See also: Benedum, Michael Late; Cist, Jacob; Densmore Oil Tank Car; Drake, Edward Laurentine; Hart, William Aaron; Kier, Samuel Martin; Petroleum; Steele, John Washington "Coal Oil Johnny"; Sweeney, Peter

FURTHER READING

American Chemical Society (ACS). 2009. "Development of the Pennsylvania Oil Industry." National Historic Chemical Landmark. https://www.acs.org/education/whatischemistry/landmarks/pennsylvaniaoilindustry.html (accessed February 6, 2021).

Black, Brian. 1998. "Oil Creek as Industrial Apparatus: Re-Creating the Industrial Process through the Landscape of Pennsylvania's Oil Boom." *Environmental History*. Vol. 3. No. 2. Pp. 210–29.

Black, Brian, and Marcy Ladson. 2010. "Oil at 150: Energy Past and Future in Pennsylvania." *Pennsylvania Legacies*. Vol. 10. No. 1. Pp. 6–13.

Eno Petroleum Corporation (EPC). 2021. "Early Oil in Pennsylvania." https://www.enopetroleum.com/earlyoilpennsylvania.html (accessed February 6, 2021).

Hildegarde, Dolson. 1959. *The Great Oildorado: The Gaudy and Turbulent Years of the First Oil Rush: Pennsylvania, 1859–1880*. New York: Random.

Hopkins, G.R., and Coons, A.B. 1934. "Statistical Appendix to the Minerals Yearbook, 1932–33." US Bureau of Mines. US Department of Interior.

Office of Fossil Energy (OFE). 2009. "Modern Shale Gas Development in the United States: A Primer." National Energy Technology Laboratory. US Department of Energy. April. https://www.energy.gov/sites/prod/files/2013/03/f0/ShaleGasPrimer_Online_4-2009.pdf (accessed February 6, 2021).

Ramos, Mary. 2001. "Oil and Texas: A Cultural History." *Texas Almanac*. Texas State Historical Association. https://www.texasalmanac.com/articles/oil-and-texas-a-cultural-history (accessed February 6, 2021).

Roberts, John. 1992. *The Battleship Dreadnought: Anatomy of the Ship*. Annapolis, MD: Naval Institute Press.

US Energy Information Administration (EIA). 2020. "Pennsylvania Field Production of Crude Oil." US Department of Energy. https://www.eia.gov/dnav/pet/hist/LeafHandler.ashx?n=pet&s=mcrfppa1&f=a (accessed February 6, 2021).

Wells, B.A. and K.L. Wells. 2016. "First American Oil Well." American Oil & Gas Historical Society. https://aoghs.org/petroleum-pioneers/american-oil-history (accessed November 2023).

Perry, Thomas Osborn

Co-founder of the Aermotor Company, Thomas O. Perry (1847–1927) developed an all-metal windmill that became the favored design for the technology. Sporting concave steel blades and a back-geared pump system, it was hardier and more efficient than earlier, wooden models. During its first five years of production, Aermotor sold more than 80,000 units. The primary consumers were settlers on the Great Plains, who used the windmill to pump water for livestock, crops, and personal use.

Thomas Perry possessed an academic background in engineering. Born in Tecumseh, Michigan, Perry moved to Ann Arbor in 1885 and began studies at the University of Michigan. Graduating with a Bachelor of Arts in 1869, he served as a teacher for two years before re-entering the university to study civil and mining engineering. He completed his graduate work in 1872. As his subsequent, occupational history centered on machine design, Perry referred to himself as a mechanical engineer.

Thomas Perry's interest in wind power manifested quickly after graduation. Returning to Tecumseh, he filed his first patent application in 1873. The granted patent registered blueprints for a windmill with four vertical wings and an emphasis on protecting the device from damage caused by variable winds. Little is known of the fate of Perry's invention, but the young engineer's continuing fascination with wind power prompted him to move in 1876 to Batavia, Illinois. The base of operations for six windmill companies, Batavia was a center of production for the industry and often was referred to as "The Windmill City." Perry accepted an appointment as a draftsman with the US Wind Engine and Pump Company (USWE), which made the well-known Halladay Standard windpumps.

During his several years with USWE, Perry investigated windmill aerodynamics. Between June 1, 1882, and September 15, 1883, he conducted more than 5,000 experiments in a wind tunnel that he constructed. Inside a sealed room that measured 36 feet wide, 48 feet long, and 19 feet high, Perry used a Reynolds-Corliss steam engine to generate artificial wind. His team recorded the impact of wind velocity, barometric pressure, and temperature on sixty-one commercial and experimental wind wheels.

The findings from Thomas Perry's experiments provided the basis for his suggested modifications to windmill design. By the end of the tests, he had developed a new, metal wheel that was 87 percent more efficient than the wooden wheels commonly in use. Most of the mills of that era had numerous, closely spaced, wood slats for their blades, or sails. The aridity and high winds that characterized the Great Plains constantly wore on the wooden structures, requiring frequent repair. Other innovators had developed metal wheels, but most of these were heavy and expensive. To reduce weight and cost, Perry's wheel was made of thin, sheet steel. The blades were slightly concave to catch the wind, and there were fewer than were found on a wooden mill. The reduced number of sails produced less aerial resistance to the motion of the wheel. Perry's steel wheel turned at three times the speed of a wooden one, and would continue to turn even when wind velocity fell to 4 miles per hour. Perry further reduced cost and raised the appeal of his mill by demonstrating that a metal wheel 8 feet in diameter could pump as much water as a 10-foot, or larger, wooden wheel.

Though Perry had developed a superior windmill, his employers rejected the new design. Late in 1883, after fifteen months of testing and analysis, Perry presented his research. Shying from the costs and risks of updating its product line, the governing board of USWE chose to continue the manufacture of earlier models. No doubt disillusioned, Thomas Perry left the firm and moved to Chicago.

It was in the "Windy City," that Perry first teamed with businessman and inventor LaVerne W. Noyes (1849–1919). Known to the public for his invention of a dictionary stand, Noyes also held over fifty patents for haying tools and harvesting machinery. He likely first met Thomas Perry in Batavia, as USWE manufactured some of Noyes' farm implements. When Perry relocated to Chicago, Noyes hired him to design a self-binding harvester. The two remained in contact when Perry returned home to Tecumseh, Michigan in 1886.

Over the next two years, Perry refined the mill that he had devised in Illinois. Much of his work focused on improving durability. To ensure a low impact, constant speed of rotation, Perry located the wheel slightly off-center. Wind gusts pushed the array to the side, and a spring returned the wheel to its original position as winds abated. He further reduced mechanical stress by back-gearing his machines, using two shafts connected by a toothed, pinion wheel to create one long, fluid, water-pumping stroke for each three rotations of the windmill. By contrast, most wooden wheels were connected directly to the pump shaft, and the action of drawing water jerked and shook the mills. Accepting an invitation to view Perry's "Aermotor" windmill, Noyes made the trip to Tecumseh and immediately recognized the technology's marketing potential.

In 1888, LaVerne Noyes and other venture capitalists formed the Aermotor Company, with Thomas Perry as consulting engineer. The commercial enterprise took the name that Perry had given to his scientifically designed windmill. Competitors heaped ridicule upon the Aermotor windpump, calling it the "Mathematical Wheel," but homesteaders on the Great Plains were attracted to its durability and efficiency. Sales increased at a staggering rate. In 1888 the company moved only forty-five units, but its representatives sold 2,288 the next year, 6,268 in 1890, and 20,049 in 1891. Company executives anticipated the purchase of 60,000 Aermotors in 1892 and projected continuous expansion of sales throughout the late 1890s.

As the firm grew, Thomas Perry continued his career in windpump design, filing patents and offering expertise to Aermotor. The cleaning and oiling of a windmill's gears had proved a difficult and dangerous task for company clients. Ranch hands and members of farm families regularly climbed windmill towers to maintain the exposed machinery. Perry designed a hinged tower that could be unlocked and lowered to the ground for cleaning. Aermotor's "tilting tower" was popular with consumers until 1912, when the Elgin Wind Power & Pump Company solved the oiling dilemma by marketing a self-bathing windmill with an enclosed gearbox. Aermotor followed in 1915 with its own enclosed gear case.

Thomas Osborn Perry died in his hometown of Tecumseh on January 25, 1927, his legacy as a pioneer of the American windmill industry secure. Six years after his interment, Aermotor introduced its 702 model. The new windpump featured screw-type wheel arms and replaceable bearings, but its basic design was predicated upon the prototype mill which Perry had developed a half-century earlier. The Aermotor 702 remains in production with few modifications. Currently headquartered in San Angelo, Texas and proud of its status as the sole manufacturer of windmills in the United States, the Aermotor Company ships mills modeled on the Perry design to clients across the globe.

Kregg M. Fehr

See also: Agriculture and Energy; Alta Wind Energy Center; Block Island Wind Farm; Corliss, George Henry; Crotched Mountain Wind Farm; Halladay Windmill; Renewable Energy; Transcontinental Railroad; Wind Power

FURTHER READING

Aermotor Windmill Company (AWC). n.d. "The History of an American Icon-Aermotor Windmill." https://aermotorwindmill.com/pages/a-history-were-proud-of (accessed March 1, 2020).

Baker, T. Lindsay. 1985. *A Field Guide to American Windmills*. Norman, OK: University of Oklahoma Press.

Gillis, Christopher C. 2015. *Still Turning: A History of Aermotor Windmills*. College Station, TX: Texas A&M Press.

Ramsower, Harry C. 1917. *Equipment for the Farm and the Farmstead*. Boston, MA: Ginn Press.

Robinson, Marilyn, and Jeffery D. Schielke. 1998. *John Gustafson's Historic Batavia*. Batavia, IL: Batavia Historical Society.

Webb, Walter Prescott. 1931. *The Great Plains*. Boston, MA: Ginn Press.

Petroleum

Petroleum is a natural resource that is found in liquid form beneath the earth's crust and consists of a complex mixture of hydrocarbons. In addition, it contains non-metallic elements like oxygen, nitrogen, and sulfur. Its color is usually black or dark brown, but it has differences based on its chemical compositions. Petroleum is mostly used for fuel oil and gasoline as energy sources, but also as a raw material for many chemical products like pesticides and plastics. The oil industry classifies crude oil by its molecular characteristics and by its regional origin. For example, both West Texas Intermediate (WTI) and Brent Crude are oil benchmarks due to their light consistency, which make them easier to refine into gasoline.

In the United States, the story of petroleum is usually begun by reference to various "firsts." In 1859, Edwin Drake drilled for oil and struck a rich deposit. The area around the strike in Titusville, Pennsylvania soon became the nucleus of an oil boom that lasted for forty years. In 1901, the Spindletop oil strike inaugurated the Texas oil boom, which continued for the next sixty years. One company navigated these developments better than the others, John D. Rockefeller's Standard Oil Company, which was founded in 1870 in Cleveland, Ohio, and quickly began buying up smaller oil companies. Standard Oil also practiced vertical integration, which refers to developing operations all along the supply chain. Rockefeller's companies were involved in oil transport by railcar, oil refining into gasoline, and even gasoline distribution to retailers. His monopoly of the industry led the US Supreme Court to break up the Standard Oil Trust in 1911 under the terms of the Sherman Antitrust Act in order to restore competition to the marketplace. Rockefeller and other oil companies benefited from a favorable legal environment unique to the US, in which oil developers could acquire leases from property owners, including the US government, to extract the underground oil. Since land ownership carried with it rights to all subsoil resources, oil companies could lease these rights from property owners and trade the leases with one another.

The First and Second World Wars vaulted the oil industry to the top of US industries, as their capitalization and profitability increased from supplying the appetite of nations for fuel for their mechanized forces. Oil companies played major roles in the conflicts. In the Second World War, oil tankers supplied oil to the Allied powers for their anti-submarine campaigns on the Atlantic, their strategic bombing raids over Germany and Japan, and their massive tank and armored vehicle offensives in North Africa, Italy, France, and Germany. In the post-war era, as the Marshall Plan helped to stabilize and redevelop Western Europe, petroleum came into greater and greater demand, not only in the rebuilding economies of France, Germany, and Great Britain, but also in the United States as the American economy experienced explosive growth in the late 1940s and 1950s. As a result, petroleum emerged as a globally traded commodity.

Oil-producing nations in the Middle East benefited from these developments and began to exert their control over petroleum resources. Western companies, particularly the

"Seven Sisters," had developed oil fields in Iran, Iraq, Saudi Arabia, and elsewhere in the region. These companies included the Anglo-Persian Oil Company—later to become British Petroleum or BP—Standard Oil of California, Texaco, and Gulf Oil—later consolidated into Chevron—Standard Oil of New Jersey and Standard Oil Company of New York—which later merged into ExxonMobil, and finally, Royal Dutch Shell. These companies controlled both the production of petroleum in the Middle East and the price of oil in global markets. In response, the government of Iran seized the assets of the Anglo-Persian Oil Company (which had been renamed the Anglo-Iranian Oil Company), triggering the Iranian oil crisis of 1951–4, which ended with a Western-backed coup d'état and the reassertion of Western control over Iranian oil with the signing of the Consortium Agreement of 1954. In the 1956 Suez Crisis, the Egyptian government closed the canal to oil shipments from the Persian Gulf in an attempt to curtail Western power over regional oil resources. This effort failed, but the formation of the Organization of Petroleum Exporting Countries (OPEC), a cartel mostly composed of Middle Eastern and North African nations, in 1960 eventually gave non-Western oil-producing nations more leverage over global petroleum markets.

By the time of the energy crisis of the 1970s, which was partly due to OPEC's decision to impose an oil embargo on Western nations that supported Israel in the 1973 Yom Kippur War, it became clear that the United States and many of the industrialized nations of Western Europe had become dependent on petroleum for most of its energy needs. The dependency had become so comprehensive that it affected the way these societies developed over the previous half-century. Scholars have created the concept of "petroculture" to account for the way petroleum influenced social conflicts, political alignments, national security interests, basic infrastructure development, residential patterns, and even the shape of everyday life. Petroculture refers to the way certain forms of energy and their use influence a country's social, political, and environmental development, including their relationships with other nations. Although nations previously dependent on fossil fuels are engaged in the process of energy transition, they still bear the imprint of petroleum's importance in their emergence as modern, developed societies.

Petrocultures can be understood in a number of different aspects. First, petroleum production and consumption provide narratives in literary, social, cultural, critical, and political texts. Oil is an important source for narratives that have framed American values and in literature. Events like the major oil strikes, or the adventures of wildcatters provide dramatic elements for narratives that depict oil as new and exciting, with associated dangers. These experiences allow for the creation of tragic but thrilling storylines. Literature and film serve as means of archiving sensory and emotional values associated with North American oil cultures. For example, the 2007 film *There Will Be Blood*, directed by Paul Thomas Anderson and starring Daniel Day-Lewis as a Texas oil wildcatter was nominated for eight Academy Awards. The film was based on Upton Sinclair's novel *Oil!* (1926–7), which depicted oil tycoons of the early twentieth century, such as Edward L. Doheny of Los Angeles, in a negative light. Memoirs like *Oil Field Child* (1989) by Estha Briscoe Stowe help to sustain these narratives of lives shaped by the experiences of life in the oil fields.

Beyond literature and film, petroleum's effects in building petroculture can be understood in its effects on the economy and the natural environment. Petroleum corporations are among the most profitable and most highly capitalized businesses in the United States. They fuel economic growth and development and contribute to America's prosperity. Throughout US history, the economic power of oil companies shaped public policy, influenced land rights, and set the terms of social justice in various areas like Indigenous relations and workers' rights. Oil and gas producers, coupled with mass consumption of petroleum products like gasoline and diesel fuel, also created complicated environmental problems that necessitated major public policy responses such as the Clean Air Act (1970) and the Clean Water Act (1972). Emissions from power plants and vehicles that burn fossil fuels produce carbon dioxide, a major cause of the greenhouse effect and global warming. This issue consumed US energy policy debates in the late twentieth and early twenty-first centuries.

The idea of petroculture also serves to highlight the nature of contemporary geopolitical conflict. For example, the Gulf War of 1991 emerged out of the competing economic strategies of Iran, Iraq, Saudi Arabia, and Western fossil-fuel-dependent nations. The actions of these nations reflected the embeddedness of fossil fuels within their respective societies, which includes the nature of their economies, but also their domestic politics and public discourses. It's important to note as well that the US Department of Defense is ... "the world's largest institutional user of petroleum" (Crawford 2019, 2). Fossil-fuel resource conflicts triggered activism geared toward a "green transition" in the United States and elsewhere. Efforts have been undertaken to link together the science of alternative energy sources with new industrial initiatives—backed by various federal agencies and programs—to produce a new generation of fuels.

This raises the question of whether a green transition and a turn away from fossil fuels will produce a corresponding change in culture. The concept of petrocultures has been useful as a means of observing, assessing, and analyzing the multiple layers and impacts of petroleum and oil in not only literary texts but also in technological, economic, social, and political development. It remains to be seen how the concept will continue to benefit observers who perceive the influence of petroleum production and consumption not only in modes of cultural expression, but in the routines of everyday life in fossil-fuel-dependent societies.

The United States is both an importer and exporter of petroleum products. In 2017, the nation consumed 20 percent of the entire world's total production of petroleum (OEERE 2018). Oil ports on the Pacific, Atlantic, and Gulf coasts are busy every day, receiving cargoes of imported crude oil but also exporting gasoline and other refined products to foreign markets. The economy of petroleum production, processing, distribution, and consumption structures US relations with other countries, while fueling the nations' fleet of cars, trucks, aircraft, and ships. Over 62 percent of all petroleum in the United States is consumed in the transportation sector, with another 27 percent consumed by industry as raw material for plastics, polyurethane, solvents, and countless other consumer goods (EIA 2022).

Nikoleta Zampaki

See also: American Petroleum Institute; Aramco; Clean Air Act of 1970; Clean Water Act; Consortium Agreement of 1954; Drake, Edwin Laurentine; Energy Crisis of the 1970s; Gulf War; Iraq War and the Project for a New American Century; Organization of Petroleum Exporting Countries (OPEC); Seven Sisters Oil Companies; Spindletop Oil Gusher; Strategic Petroleum Reserve; Texas Oil Boom

FURTHER READING

Crawford, Neta C. 2019. "Pentagon Fuel Use, Climate Change, and the Costs of War." November 13. Watson Institute for International & Public Affairs. Boston University. Pp. 1–46.

Giddens, Paul H. 1938. *The Birth of the Oil Industry*. New York: The Macmillan Company.

LeMenager, Stephanie. 2012. "The Aesthetics of Petroleum, After *Oil!*" *American Literary History*. Vol. 24. No. 1. Pp. 59–86.

LeMenager, Stephanie. 2014. *Living Oil: Petroleum Culture in the American Century*. Oxford: Oxford University Press.

Office of Energy Efficiency & Renewable Energy (OEERE). 2018. "Fact of the Week #1049, October 1, 2018: The United States Consumed 20% of World Petroleum in 2017." US Department of Energy. https://www.energy.gov/eere/vehicles/articles/fotw-1049-october-1-2018-united-states-consumed-20-world-petroleum-2017 (accessed October 2023).

Szeman, Imre, and Dominic Boyer, eds. 2017. *Energy Humanities: An Anthology*, Baltimore, MD: Johns Hopkins University Press.

Szeman, Imre, Jennifer Wenzel, and Patricia Yaeger, eds. 2017. *Fueling Culture: 101 Words for Energy and Environment*. New York: Fordham University Press.

US Energy Information Administration (EIA). 2022. "Oil and Petroleum Products Explained: Use of Oil." July 1. US Department of Energy. https://www.eia.gov/energyexplained/oil-and-petroleum-products/use-of-oil.php (accessed October 2023).

Wall, Bennett H. 1988. *Growth in a Changing Environment: A History of Standard Oil Company (New Jersey) 1950–1972 and Exxon Corporation 1972–1975*. New York: McGraw Hill Book Company.

Yergin, Daniel. 1991. *The Prize: The Epic Quest for Oil, Money & Power*. New York: Simon & Schuster.

Pierce Steam Heating Company

John Bartlett Pierce (1844–1917), founder of Pierce Steam Heating Company, made important contributions to the development of steam heating for building interiors, as well as the radiators that proliferated throughout the United States in the late nineteenth and early twentieth centuries. Pierce's company and similar companies in the industry produced steam heating and ventilating systems on a mass scale, bringing cleaner, healthier air and warmer interior spaces to millions of apartment dwellers, office workers, church goers, and homeowners. This constituted nothing short of a revolution in living standards, noticed and appreciated by those who experienced the change, but taken largely for granted by later generations who didn't suffer through winters in badly heated and poorly ventilated buildings. When the Pierce Steam Heating Company merged with several other radiator companies to form American Radiator Company in 1892, the new corporation became the industry's standard for radiator design and manufacturing and made the radiator a commonplace part of everyday life.

In the present day, turning on the heat is a matter of hitting a button or flipping a switch, or even setting a thermostat and letting the system work on its own. Before these systems began to appear in the mid-nineteenth century, the interiors of buildings of all kinds were heated with wood or coal-fired stoves. This required the time and effort to build up fuel stores, load the fireboxes, tend to the fires, and clean up debris. Pioneers in centralized heating systems of the 1840s and 1850s conceived an improved way to heat buildings with coal and steam that provided better performance at lower cost, while pointing in the direction of automated modern heating and ventilation systems that use natural gas and oil-fueled furnaces. One of these pioneers in early steam heating is John Bartlett Pierce, who was born in 1844 in Embden, Maine (his birth year is stated as 1843 in several older sources). He spent his childhood at Norridgewock and graduated from Westbrook Seminary in Portland. After a brief stint with a pharmacist in Lewiston, Pierce left for Wisconsin, where he spent four years working for a lumber company. In 1868 he returned to New England to work in the hardware business, first in New Hampshire and then Ware, Massachusetts where he tried his hand at owning his own store.

The store in Ware didn't last very long, but in 1872 Pierce hired a local twenty-year old named Joseph Bond, which inaugurated a fruitful business partnership. At Ware they made and sold iron stoves and tin products along with hardware. In 1873, Pierce moved to Buffalo, New York to open a hardware store in the city. Bond joined him there, and the two took contracts to install steam-powered hot water boilers and radiators. A number of companies were already in the business of manufacturing steam heating systems and radiators, including Bartlett, Hayward & Co., Nason, Dodge & Briggs, and the A.A. Griffing Iron Co., which produced the popular Bundy Standard Radiator. The work was steady and in 1881, the two formed the Pierce Steam Heating Company in Buffalo to capitalize on the growing demand for steam heating systems in western New York. Pierce and Bond devoted much time and effort to learning how steam heating worked and how it could be improved. In 1880, they built a plant to manufacture their own boilers, known as Pierce's "wrought iron steam heater." Meanwhile they worked on an improved design for the radiator and in 1882, jointly received a US patent for the apparatus.

The partners failed to identify a foundry in Buffalo to manufacture their new radiator, so Pierce sought out the H.B. Smith Company of Westfield, Massachusetts, which was at the time manufacturing radiators designed and patented by John R. Reed (Stifler 1960, 106). Pierce spent some time observing Smith's manufacturing process, contracted with the company to fabricate the Pierce-Bond radiator, and recruited some of their "skilled radiator molders" to work at a new facility built in 1884 in Buffalo (Stifler 1960, 106). One of the Pierce Steam Heating Company's competitors, the A.A. Griffing Iron Co., provides an illustration of how steam heating and radiator companies sold their product. In their 1894–5 catalog, Griffing told its potential customers that system heating with steam was better than furnace heating because with a furnace, the air was heated to 1,200–1,500 degrees and was thus "devitalized" and robbed of its "exhilarating and tonic properties." It was also "rendered impure by carbonic oxide" and "charged with dust and fine ashes" (A.A. Griffing 1894, vi). The catalog went on to describe the beauty, ease of use, and economy of steam heating and radiators. Pierce and Bond made similar appeals and gained in market share through the 1880s and early 1890s.

However, as energy historian Bernard Nagengast describes it, "competition between manufacturers of boilers and radiators was intense" in the Gilded Age. Furthermore, "bankruptcies and consolidations were frequent," paralleling the situation in other industries like oil and natural gas production (Nagengast 2001). In 1892, Pierce and Bond merged their company with Michigan Radiator & Iron Manufacturing Company and Detroit Radiator Company to form the American Radiator Company. Bond served as the company's first president, and Pierce the vice president. The company located its headquarters in Chicago and opened sales offices in New York, Boston, Minneapolis, and Denver. The Panic of 1893 pushed the company to open sales offices overseas, and by 1897 the popularity of their radiators had convinced it to build manufacturing plants in Germany and France. The international development of its business in 1899 led the company to move its headquarters to New York. By then, the company had acquired three more plants in Bremen, Indiana, Elwood, Indiana, and Springfield, Ohio. In the late 1890s, the company also bought the St. Louis Radiator Company and Standard Radiator Company of Buffalo. By 1900, this expansion made the company the "largest manufacturer of heating equipment in the world" (ARSSC 1960, 2).

Pierce built a house in Lynnfield about 30 miles west of Boston on 800 acres of land around Suntaug Lake, 500 of which was the "Plantation of 500 Acres" granted in 1635 to John Humphrey, Deputy Governor and an original founder of Massachusetts Bay Colony. It is claimed that he delved into arboriculture and planted over 300,000 trees ("In Memorium" 1917). He continued to work at American Radiator Company until about 1908 when he retired, then passed away in 1917 at the age of seventy-four. In his will, Pierce left $1 million in American Radiator Company stock to be distributed among 400 co-workers, employees, and business associates who "demonstrated keen business ability, combined with a fine sense of honor, a high quality of integrity, and a conscientious and loyal devotion to the performance of duty." A large portion of the estate went to create the John B. Pierce Foundation to promote "research, educational, technical, or scientific work in the general field of heating, ventilating, and sanitation, for the increase of knowledge to the end that the general hygiene and comfort of human beings and their habitations may be advanced" ("In Memorium" 1917).

The foundation funds the John B. Pierce Laboratory, an independent research institution affiliated with Yale University. The lab describes itself as "a leading center for the study of physiological regulatory systems such as those that maintain body temperature, respiration, body fluids, and metabolism within healthy limits" (JBP 2020). The objectives of the foundation and its beneficiary are consistent with John B. Pierce's view that with steam heating and radiators, people could live healthier lives in cleaner, more sanitary environments. Pierce and his company played an important role in transitioning Americans from heating their interiors with coal-fired stoves to using centralized steam heating systems with radiators. The system in its entirety required a coal mining industry, infrastructure to transport coal from mines to cities, a manufacturing sector large enough to produce heating apparatus on a massive scale, and a distribution system capable of supplying the heating technology to millions of consumers. The Pierce Steam Heating Company and its rivals and successors created the fabricating, marketing, and distribution mechanisms that enabled the system to function in converting energy users to the new method of heating. By the 1930s, nearly all large buildings and most American homes had transitioned away from area heating with wood and coal stoves to centralized heating by steam, hot water, or forced air and fueled by coal, oil, or natural gas.

Jeffrey B. Webb

See also: American Radiator Company; Gold, Stephen J.; Johnson, Warren Seymour; Nason, Joseph; New York Steam Company; Powers, William Penn; Richardson & Boynton Company; Steam Power

FURTHER READING

A.A. Griffing Iron Co. 1894. *Bundy Radiators for Steam and Hot Water, also Heating Specialties*. New York: Heating Engineer Publishing Company.

John B. Pierce Laboratory (JBP). 2020. "About Us." https://jbpierce.org/about-us/ (accessed October 2023).

American Radiator & Standard Sanitary Corporation (ARSSC). 1960. "American Radiator & Standard Sanitary Corporation History." Tiffin-Seneca (Ohio) Public Library. TSPL Local History Collection. Manuscripts. https://ohiomemory.org/digital/collection/p15005coll27/id/40073 (accessed October 2023).

"In Memorium: John Bartlett Pierce, 1843–1917." 1917. HeatingHelp.com. https://heatinghelp.com/assets/262.pdf (accessed October 2023).

Nagengast, Bernard. 2001. "An Early History of Comfort Heating." *Air Conditioning, Heating, and Refrigeration News*. November 6. https://www.achrnews.com/articles/87035-an-early-history-of-comfort-heating (accessed October 2023).

Stifler, Susan Reed. 1960. *The Beginnings of a Century of Steam and Water Heating by the H. B. Smith Company*. Westfield, MA: The H. B. Smith Co., Inc.

Pittsburgh Gasometer Explosion

The Pittsburgh Gasometer Explosion of 1927, sometimes called "great gas explosion" and called by the *Pittsburgh Courier* as "one of the greatest tragedies in [Pittsburgh] history," occurred on Monday November 14 at roughly 8:45 a.m. while workers attempted to perform repairs on a large gasometer (a term for a gas storage tank) with blowtorches, which had been presumed empty. The explosion produced tremors throughout the city akin to those of an earthquake.

In the lead-up to the explosion Pittsburgh had been the site of a complex energy history. As the city industrialized, risks of explosions and the dangers involved in piping gas under high pressure into residential neighborhoods constrained natural gas adoption. By 1900, however, natural gas supplies available in the region increased due to the discovery of new well fields, the delivery of gas from West Virginia via pipeline, and the creation of compression stations and metering. Between 1897 and 1914, the number of domestic gas consumers in Pennsylvania increased from a little over 200,000 to more than 400,000, while the number of industrial consumers rose from a little over 1,000 to over 4,000. As growth continued, gas supplies had to be imported from out of state by pipeline, mostly from West Virginia. Between 1917 and 1922, the Equitable Gas Company, the largest Pittsburgh supplier, and one of the largest in nation, constructed a plant near Pittsburgh to produce gas from coal and mix it with natural gas. Eventually, the company erected three gasometers to store excess gas production.

The gasometer that exploded, said to be the largest in the world, had a roughly 5-million cubic feet of capacity. The tank shot 200 feet in the air according to witnesses. The explosion sent debris flying, which leveled buildings in the densely packed neighborhood where the gasometer stood. Damage was reported as much as 6 miles away from the explosion point. Property damage was estimated to be between $4 million and $5 million, or between $59 million and $73.7 million in inflation-adjusted dollars. In total, twenty-six individuals lost their lives, though contemporaneous accounts vary, and roughly 450 people were injured. The Salvation Army, Red Cross, and other humanitarian flooded the city in the explosion's aftermath.

Within days of the explosion, the Equitable Gas Company adopted a policy of "square dealing without quibble" as described by company President A.W. Roberts to assist in the relief effort. This was done in the spirit of humanitarianism before the legal responsibility for the catastrophe had been fixed. The decision came after a meeting of executives of the company. According to press accounts, Roberts' plan entailed immediate payment of all hospital bills of those injured, repairs to property damage suffered by 800 homeowners and tenants, and an offer to meet claims for personal injuries or loss of life. Roberts was quoted by *The Washington Post:* "Winter is coming on and our instructions are that the victims of the explosion must be restored to their former comforts. Our dealing with the people impresses us that they are fair when they know they are being dealt with fairly, and square dealing will be our principle throughout this effort to restore the losses" ("Tank-Blast" 1927, 6).

With tone deafness to prior labor catastrophes, *The New York Times* credited the gas industry for the relative rarity of such explosions. However, with the benefit of hindsight concerns over the gasometer's proximity to residential areas were arbitrated, resulting in the passing of legislation that prevented the construction of gasometers in residential areas. Today, the site of the explosion is the current location of a casino.

Todd K. Platts

See also: Cleveland, East Ohio Gas Explosion; Coal Gasification; Hart, William Aaron; Indiana Natural Gas Boom; Natural Gas; New London School Explosion; Richmond, Indiana Gas Explosions

FURTHER READING

Brotzman, W.S. 1927. "Damaging Gas Explosion at Pittsburgh, PA." *Monthly Weather Review*. November. P. 500.

Grinnell, David R. 2008. "'The Tank that Blew Up': North Side, Pittsburgh, Pa." *Western Pennsylvania History*. Summer. Pp. 8–9.

"Suffering in Wake of Blast." 1927. *Pittsburgh Courier*. November 19. Pp. 1, 8.

"Tank-Blast Victims to be Compensated 'Without Quibbling.'" 1927. *The Washington Post*. November 20. P. 6.

Tarr, Joel A., and Karen Clay. 2015. "Boom and Bust in Pittsburgh Natural Gas History: Development, Policy, and Environmental Effects, 1878–1920." *Pennsylvania Magazine of History and Biography*. Vol. 139. No. 3. Pp. 323–42.

"The Pittsburgh Gas Explosion." 1927. *The New York Times*. November 16. P. 24.

Powell River Project

The Powell River Project (PRP) Research and Education Center was founded in 1980 as a cooperative program of Virginia Polytechnic Institute and State University along with other educational institutions, environmental organizations, and natural resource industries. The 1,100-acre field site located in Wise County, Virginia was initially created to aid the coal industry with regulatory compliance. The property is owned by Energy Transfer Partners and hosts active coal mining, gas, and timber production in addition to its research and educational outreach functions. The site is used to conduct research and promote educational outreach to enhance environmental restoration and water-resource protection in coal mining regions of southwest Virginia. The Powell River Project is the longest-running program of its kind, producing research that has had a notable influence on coal mining practices in Appalachia.

The significance of the PRP arose from the federal Surface Mining Control and Reclamation Act of 1977 (SMCRA) and resultant state regulatory programs. Until the passing of SMCRA, surface mining and reclamation were governed by less rigorous and varying state programs. It was customary, at this time, for coal operators to leave mined lands in a wide range of conditions and vegetative covers. The industry also routinely compacted mine soils during site grading and hauling operations. Compacted soils did not allow for the revegetation of mined lands with native hardwood forests but instead, allowed for invasive species such as multiflora rose, autumn olive, and sericea lespedeza to flourish. The intent of SMCRA changed the scope of surface mining as it served to protect "society and the environment from the adverse effects of surface coal mining operations" to assure sound mining and reclamation practices (p. 3). One notable project at the PRP allowed for the promotion of scientifically established protocol for planting hardwoods that has prompted native Appalachian forests to regrow. This practice, known as the Forestry Reclamation Approach (FRA), expedites the growth of native Appalachian hardwoods on formally strip-mined lands by using less compaction and a mixture of soil and rock. These processes have been widely adopted by the mining industry as it is found to be both effective and cost-efficient.

Powell River Project maintains an education center where the coal industry, agencies, and the public can observe and learn about mining reclamation practices. Over the past forty years, thousands have visited the Powell River Project for various programs including K-12 groups, industry leaders, college students, researchers, and the public. Educational programs at PRP provide a hands-on experience and observation of surface mining practices and reclamation approaches developed specifically at PRP.

There are four major areas of research at the PRP including mine soil construction, mine land restoration, reforestation, and water-resource management and protection. Mine soil reconstruction is the foundation of post-mining reclamation that is essential for biological productivity and water-resource protection. Mine land restoration has changed reclamation practices and allows for native hardwood Appalachian trees to thrive, which was previously thought to be impossible. Related research programs at other locations in southwest Virginia focused on management of coal combustion residual products like fly ash and gypsum for amelioration of acidic coal refuse materials. Findings have shown that fly ash could be used as an amendment for mine soil and acidic coal refuse. This research has been recognized by the National Research Council of the National Academy of Sciences. Water-resource management and protection initiatives have been used to focus on acid mine drainage mitigation, mining-related selenium, and stream reconstruction in mined areas.

The PRP not only stands as a research and educational center but has featured many interesting land-use projects including, but not limited to, maple syrup extraction, biomass production, the reintroduction of elk populations, viticulture, beekeeping, and pasture land. This unique property has also provided a location for American Chestnut research and revitalization efforts to take place.

The PRP has supported over sixty graduate students at Virginia Tech and their research endeavors on mining reclamation research. These efforts have also been used to produce over one hundred peer-reviewed publications and over ninety conference proceedings since the mid-1990s. Collaborations between PRP and Virginia Cooperative Extension have also produced over thirty outreach publications. Overall, the PRP has utilized a unique property situated in the heart of coal country in Southwest Virginia to study the impacts of surface mining and identify methods of remediating local natural environments damaged by coal mining operations. These efforts have made notable contributions to our scientific understanding of the Forestry Reclamation Approach, an improved process for reclaiming formally strip-mined areas. The PRP has created a unique program which engages community, industry, and academics in an effort to improve surface mining approaches. By creating this synergistic approach, the PRP provides fruitful experiences for students, industry, and agencies alike by improving mining practices in Appalachia.

Aysha Bodenhamer

See also: Clean Water Act; Coal; Martin County Coal Slurry Spill; Surface Mining; Surface Mining Control and Reclamation Act of 1977

FURTHER READING

Burger, James Anthony, and Carl E. Zipper. 2019. "Restoring the Value of Forests on Reclaimed Mined Land." VTechWorks. http://hdl.handle.net/10919/54950 (accessed April 1, 2020).

Burns, Shirley Stewart. 2007. *Bringing Down the Mountains: The Impact of Mountaintop Removal on Southern West Virginia Communities*. Morgantown, WV: West Virginia University Press.

Daniels, W. Lee, Kathryn C. Haering, and John M. Galbraith. 2004. "Mine Soil Morphology and Properties in Pre-and Post-SMCRA Coal Mined Landscapes in Southwest Virginia." *Journal of the American Society of Mining and Reclamation*. June 30. Pp. 421–49. https://pdfs.semanticscholar.org/42c1/c84122069586af61e49bcb3d8eece2e94e3e.pdf (accessed April 1, 2020).

Epstein, Paul R., et al. 2011. "Full Cost Accounting for the Life Cycle of Coal." *Annals of the New York Academy of Sciences*. Vol. 1219. No. 1. Pp. 73–98.

Fox, Julia. 1999. "Mountaintop Removal in West Virginia: An Environmental Sacrifice Zone." *Organization & Environment*. Vol. 12. No. 2. Pp. 163–83.

Montrie, Chad. 2003. *To Save the Land and People: A History of Opposition to Surface Coal Mining in Appalachia*. Chapel Hill, NC: University of North Carolina Press.

Office of Surface Mining Reclamation and Enforcement. 2019. "Laws, Regulations, and Guidance." https://www.osmre.gov/lrg.shtm (accessed April 1, 2020).
Timpano, A. J., et al. 2010. "Determining Water Quality Criteria for Total Dissolved Solids in Streams of Southwestern Virginia." Powell River Project Research and Education Program Reports. Powell River Project. Pp. 71–9. https://powell735837127.files.wordpress.com/2020/04/timpano-tdssummary-2010.pdf (accessed April 1, 2020).
Tiwary, R.K. 2001. Environmental Impact of Coal Mining on Water Regime and Its Management. *Water, Air, & Soil Pollution*. Vol. 132. Pp. 185–99.
Zipper, Carl E., et al. 2011. "Restoring Forests and Associated Ecosystem Services on Appalachian Coal Surface Mines." *Environmental Management*. Vol. 47. No. 5. Pp. 751–65.

Powers, William Penn

A number of inventors and innovators contributed to making interior heating and air-conditioning an essential, but largely unnoticeable, part of daily life in the twenty-first century. Today, energy users can go about their daily routines without ever having to think about regulating the temperatures of their homes, offices, workshops, and any place they might go that has a temperature-controlled interior. This is partly the work of William Penn Powers (1842–1928), a Wisconsin born-and-bred inventor and businessman who lived and worked in the era of transition to centralized steam, hot water, and forced-air heating systems toward the end of the nineteenth century. He and his company, Powers Regulator Company, devised the earliest thermostats that allowed users to remotely control centralized building heating systems. Further technological development enabled thermostats to work automatically in response to changing room temperature and humidity levels. Although relatively small in size, Powers' thermostats represented a large step in the transition from traditional forms of interior heating to recognizably modern systems.

The story of William Penn Powers' life unfolded in Wisconsin when the state was still in the process of settlement. His parents were migrants from Vermont and New Hampshire and came to Wisconsin before the territory was admitted to statehood. His father was involved in setting up mills and inns and served as postmaster in Whitewater and Palmyra. In 1852, he was elected to the Wisconsin State Assembly and moved the family to Madison, where they remained for the next seventeen years. William Powers' memoir recounts his birth in Whitewater in 1842 and moving around the state for his father's business pursuits. When they settled in Madison, Powers had reached the age of ten and the following year began his studies at the nearby preparatory school associated with the University of Wisconsin. Two years later he began study at the university and graduated in 1860 at the age of seventeen. Powers recalled that he pursued the "full Classical Course" but found chemistry and natural philosophy particularly interesting. He experimented with electricity and built "galvanic batteries and an electrical plate machine" noting that with a Leyden jar the plate delivered "a very vigorous shock" (Powers 1924, 38). He remarked that when he left college, his mind was bent on the mechanical arts.

Over his father's objections Powers enlisted in the Union Army in August 1862, and served in the First Wisconsin Heavy Artillery at Fort Cass, one of the fortifications around Washington, DC. In 1863, he received a commission as first lieutenant and transferred to the Fourth Wisconsin Battery, then positioned near Portsmouth, Virginia. His unit remained in the area during the winter of 1863–4 then moved toward Petersburg to encircle and besiege the rebels in the city. The Fourth Wisconsin Battery helped to destroy the Petersburg and Richmond railroad, which resulted in the isolation of the capital of the Confederacy, and then supported General Benjamin Butler's May 4, 1864 assault on Ft. Darling on Drewry's Bluff outside of Richmond. Butler's army was pushed back by Confederate General P.G.T

Beauregard. Powers' letter home of May 20 speaks of the Union solders' opinion of their leadership: "we are bound to give Johnny Reb our best licks and do our biggest, but at the same time we feel a good deal like a steamboat without a helmsman, or a six-mule team without a driver. In other words, we think Butler don't amount to a hill of beans as a fighting general in the field" (Powers 1924, 71).

In October 1964, Powers contracted a lengthy sickness he called "remittent fever" and spent six weeks in a field hospital at City Point, Virginia. He decided to submit his resignation rather than try to recover sufficiently to return to active duty (Powers 1924, 75). With his Civil War service behind him, Powers married Margaret F. Knight in 1865, the person whom he'd written throughout the war, and struggled to find his footing with a troubled shingle mill but stayed solvent by patenting a wooden pump and installing it in sawmills to convey sawdust from underneath the saws to a nearby furnace. Powers further gratified his mechanical inclinations by moving to La Crosse in 1867 and installing iron pumps and tubular wells at area farms. In 1873, Powers began installing steam heating, gas fittings, and plumbing components in La Crosse, also receiving contracts for city work on sewer and water lines. It wasn't until the late 1880s that Powers began to conceive of the device that would bring him riches and a modest degree of fame.

He explained that the building he constructed in La Crosse in 1887 for his steam heating and plumbing business, a 3-storey brick structure at Fifth and Jay streets, had a hot water heating plant with a tendency to boil over into its expansion tank. During the sermon at church one Sunday, Powers' thoughts began to drift, and as he recalled, "I began a mental search for some means to prevent this." With his engineering impulses activated, he had an epiphany: "the idea occurred to me of utilizing the relative boiling points of water under different pressures to control the draught" (Powers 1924, 107). The next day he inserted a pipe with a closed end into the boiler and attached a "damper controlling diaphragm," which fixed the problem. He called it "Regulator No. 1," and it led him to wonder if he could also address the problem of an overheated office. He conjured up another device that consisted of a tube placed in the office connected to a diaphragm valve on the radiator which contained water and a small amount of "hydrocarbon" liquid with a boiling point a little lower than the desired temperature—60 degrees. A very crude thermostat, but Powers recalled that "it gave good results so long as the fluid did not escape or become absorbed in the water" (Powers 1924, 107).

Powers went on to tinker with his regular, thermostat, and diaphragm valves and came up with Regulator No. 4, a disk-shaped control system with a separation panel between the hydrocarbon liquid and the chamber for water, except that he substituted air which created a pneumatic effect. When connected to a diaphragm motor that controlled double mixing dampers on a fan heating system, the thermostat gave the user more control over interior temperatures than any other device on the market. Powers recognized that his pneumatic thermostat would attract customers big and small across the nation. Sadly, his wife Margaret passed away in 1890, and so Powers, with their four children, left La Crosse, moved to Chicago, and formed the Powers Regulator Company. His first installation was completed at First Congregational Church in Nashua, New Hampshire. He began pursuing clients for his thermostats, mostly individual homeowners at first. A breakthrough came in 1893 when he demonstrated his devices at the Chicago World's Columbian Exposition. He made contacts there that gave him entry into the New York market. He outfitted a twenty-room school on Long Island with thermostats for $2,000 and this gave him confidence to open a New York office. Powers then installed his apparatus at the Ray School in Chicago and eventually won contracts to equip other buildings in the city's school district. Powers achieved success in winning contracts for Toledo's Lucas County Courthouse and Detroit's Central High School. These larger institutions gave the Powers Regulator Company momentum in the industry, and their referrals gave it a national reach.

Powers Regulator Company would go on to install different types of thermostats in hundreds of thousands of private residences and thousands of large institutional buildings like the Minnesota State Capitol, and iconic skyscrapers like the Chrysler and Empire State buildings in Manhattan. During his career Powers' thermostats were honored with medals at the Paris Exposition in 1898 and the Pan American Exposition in Buffalo in 1902. By then, Powers had met his second wife, Louise M. Selleck, on a trip in 1893 to visit his retired father in Los Angeles; around 1910 they also retired there permanently. Before he passed away in 1928, Powers enjoyed fishing, photography, entertaining, and world travel with Louise, while mentoring his three sons Fred W., Donald J., and Robert A. Powers to assume control of his profitable business.

In 1977, Powers Regulator Company was acquired, along with its plant facilities and numerous patents by Mark Controls Corporation, which itself was acquired later by another controls company. In 2020, the major suppliers of heating, ventilation, and air-conditioning controls were Schneider Electric SE, Honeywell International, Johnson Controls International, Trane Technologies, Inc., and Siemens Automation, which in 1998 bought and retired the original Powers brand. These modern corporations built on the foundation created by William Penn Powers in the 1880s and 1890s and made a highly technical science out of the regulation of indoor temperatures in the twentieth and twenty-first centuries. These devices and their processes made energy use for home and institutional heating and cooling nearly effortless, highly efficient, and largely foolproof for the vast majority of users in the modern industrialized world.

Jeffrey B. Webb

See also: Home Energy Efficiency; Johnson, Warren Seymour; Nason, Joseph; Pierce Steam Heating Company; Underwriters Laboratories; US Green Building Council; Williams Oil-O-Matic

FURTHER READING

Donaldson, Barry, and Bernard Nagengast. 1994. *Heat & Cold: Mastering the Great Indoors: A Selective History of Heating, Ventilation, Air-conditioning and Refrigeration from the Ancients to the 1930s*. Atlanta, GA: American Society of Heating, Refrigerating and Air-Conditioning Engineers.

Lawless, John. 2016. "The Complete History of Radiators: A Guide to How We've Come to Love Our Radiators." BestHeating.com. December 20. https://www.bestheating.com/info/the-complete-history-of-radiators/ (accessed October 2023).

Nagengast, Bernard. 2001. "An Early History of Comfort Heating." *Air Conditioning, Heating, and Refrigeration News*. November 6. https://www.achrnews.com/articles/87035-an-early-history-of-comfort-heating (accessed October 2023).

Powers, William Penn. 1924. *Some Annals of the Powers Family*. Los Angeles: n.p.

Project Gasbuggy

On December 10, 1967, scientists, contractors, and staff from US government agencies and a private energy company conducted a little-known experiment to try to recover natural gas from rock layers thousands of feet below the ground. They detonated a 26-kiloton hydrogen bomb at 4,240 feet deep where they suspected natural gas might be trapped, with the idea that "fracturing" the rock would release the gas, which then could be harnessed for commercial uses. Project Gasbuggy brought together several trends in the development of energy in the post-war era. First, Americans' demand for oil and gas ballooned in the 1950s and 1960s, and officials were reluctant to meet that demand with imported fuels. Second, nuclear energy fascinated policymakers who believed the atom could be harnessed for civilian purposes. This is clear in the formation of the Atomic Energy Commission (AEC) in 1946, and President Dwight Eisenhower's famous "Atoms for Peace" speech in 1953. Third, the western states of the United States had shown promise in providing new sources of coal, oil, and natural gas, and Project Gasbuggy advocates calculated that lightly populated areas composed of Native Americans provided no barrier to experimenting with atomic energy.

Gasbuggy grew out of a program known as Project Plowshare. This came in the wake of Eisenhower's "Atoms for Peace" speech that called for the nation to pursue peacetime, civilian uses of atomic bombs. Some of the ideas for Plowshare included widening the Panama Canal, creating mountain passes for highways, and blasting to connect underground aquifers. Dozens of test explosions associated with Plowshare enabled scientists to study the release of energy and displacement of soil as well as monitoring radioactivity downwind from blast sites. Several of the major Plowshare projects were shot down before they began, or before they concluded, due to technical difficulties or long-delayed feasibility studies. Eventually, Plowshare came to an end in 1975 due to public concerns about environmental issues, namely radioactive fallout, contaminated water, and hazardous waste. Before it ended, Plowshare envisioned the use of nuclear bombs to fracture rock layers that might be trapping natural gas at otherwise inaccessible depths or locations. The fracturing test at Gasbuggy in New Mexico came first, followed by Project Rusilon (1969) and Project Rio Blanco (1973), both located in Colorado.

Fracturing is done mainly through hydraulic means, by shooting high-pressure water, sand, and chemicals into layers of rock to force open fissures that can allow gas to escape. Hydraulic fracturing is commonly known as "fracking" and has been used off and on in the United States since at least the late 1940s. Fracturing can also be accomplished with conventional explosives like gunpowder, nitroglycerin, TNT, and dynamite. Expanded use of hydraulic fracturing in untapped shale deposits led to a dramatic boom in natural gas production in the United States and Canada in the 2005–21 period, which offset increased energy demand and eased dependence on foreign sources of fuel. As for nuclear devices, the impetus for Project Gasbuggy came from the El Paso Natural Gas Company (EPNG) of New Mexico, which made an inquiry in 1958 with the Lawrence Radiation Laboratory (LRL) in California regarding the use of a nuclear device to stimulate an underground natural gas reservoir (Reeves 1971, 1). Soon after, the AEC, EPNG, LRL, and the Department of the Interior's Bureau of Mines formed a group to study the technological and engineering requirements for a test, including geological analysis of the site and the nature of the radioactivity that would result.

After a series of reviews and approvals, EPNG's contractors drilled two test wells of over 4,200 feet, GB-1 and GB-2 at the chosen site in New Mexico's Carson National Forest. Then in July 1967 they dug the final emplacement hole, known as GB-E for "Gasbuggy Emplacement." Several construction and technical problems delayed the test, which finally occurred in mid-December with the insertion into GB-E of a nuclear bomb 13 feet long and 18 inches in diameter, and its encasement in cement. The other wells were equipped with instruments and encased as well. The bomb was then detonated. Hugh F. Steen, president of EPNG, was standing 2 miles away at the control point and reported that the shock felt like a large bump in a car that "shook you all over" (UPI 1967, 20). A reporter for United Press International, one of 200 official visitors permitted to observe the explosion 5 miles away, said they felt two tremors 2.5 seconds apart, which knocked over coffee cups and rocked buses and equipment trailers (UPI 1967, 20). The bomb of 26 kilotons was nearly twice as powerful as the 15-kiloton bomb exploded in 1945 over Hiroshima.

The plan called for the explosion to vaporize rock at the bottom of the well to create a subterranean chamber, which would then be filled by a collapse of the surrounding rock to the height of 350 feet and a width of 130 feet. This collapse zone would form what the project referred to as a "chimney" that would draw natural gas from newly opened fissures at the bottom of the well. Ultimately, this chimney would be drilled once again to tap the accumulated natural gas, assuming the whole enterprise worked as expected. After the explosion, the team discovered that everything went according to form. Three days after the detonation, drilling began on the reentry well GB-ER, which came upon the chimney on January 10, 1968 at 333 feet above the detonation point. Another twenty-one days of drilling brought the reentry well to completion which was followed by months of gas sampling and radiochemistry analysis. The final stage of testing began in June and continued to November of the following year, which entailed production tests for various lengths of time and pressure values (Reeves 1971, 2).

The production tests yielded positive results. Project manager James E. Reeves, head of the AEC's Nevada Operations Office, reported that the well "produced approximately 284 MMcf [million cubic feet] of gas (213 MMcf of hydrocarbons) and, based on preliminary estimates of projected performance, should produce 900 MMcf in 20 years" (Reeves 1971, 32). Reeves further concluded that the well should "produce at least 5 times the estimated production from a conventionally completed well in the area" (Reeves 1971, 33). Overall, Project Gasbuggy cost $5.64 million, with 60 percent paid by the government and 40 percent by EPNG. The initial results justified proceeding with two other planned nuclear fracturing tests. After Project Gasbuggy came Project Rusilon, which featured a 40-kiloton bomb detonated 8,400 feet below the surface. The third, Project Rio Blanco, detonated three 33-ton devices simultaneously at depths of 5,838, 6,230, and 6,689 feet.

Initially, the project drew several protests by Native Americans living in the vicinity of the test site, but public opinion generally favored the use of nuclear bombs to develop natural gas resources. *Time* magazine ran an article in its December 22, 1967 issue with the upbeat headline, "A Good Start for Gasbuggy." However, it became clear that the output of the wells, both in terms of quality and volume, didn't justify the very high cost of preparing and conducting underground nuclear explosions. Furthermore, environmentalists claimed that natural gas released from rock layers fractured by nuclear fission came into "intimate contact with the radioactive by-products," thereby triggering "exchange reactions" that made the gas itself radioactive (Metzger 1970). The AEC claimed that flaring operations—burning off gas released into the air—would produce airborne radioactive tritium, krypton-85, and argon-37 at very low levels and pose no danger to humans. Still, cattle ranchers in the vicinity of the tests protested that their stock would eat radiation-contaminated grass, which could find its way into milk and meat meant for human consumption (Noble 2014). A month before the scheduled Project Rio Blanco explosions, *Time* magazine returned to the subject of nuclear fracturing with an April 9, 1973 article titled, "Project Dubious" ("Project" 1973).

Gasbuggy proponents responded by asserting that most radioactive by-products would be sealed in glass deep in the earth by the force of the explosion or would be drawn off with the first extraction from the well. They also claimed that any radioactivity remaining in the gas would be diluted by mixing it with gas from other, non-irradiated wells (Carlisle 1967, 222). In the end, federal officials concluded that some of the Plowshare programs, including Project Gasbuggy, were "technologically feasible," but lengthy review and approval processes, the costs of setting up the nuclear devices, serious environmental concerns, and a general lack of public support called for its termination. Nuclear energy took criticism on all fronts in the mid-1970s, sparked by the Union of Concerned Scientists' (UCS) public campaign to highlight AEC's inadequacies in licensing nuclear power plants, most notably in public hearings in 1972 and 1973 over Boston Edison Company's Pilgrim Nuclear Power Station. Articles in *Science* magazine and the *New York Times*, as well as an hour-long ABC documentary aired UCS's concerns. The lawsuit *Union of Concerned Scientists v. U.S. Atomic Energy Commission* (1974) kept the issue of nuclear plant safety in the spotlight, and public fears were confirmed by the partial reactor core meltdown in 1979 at Pennsylvania's Three Mile Island nuclear power plant. Altogether, these developments in nuclear energy soured most Americans on Eisenhower's vision of "Atoms for Peace."

Jeffrey B. Webb

See also: Atomic Energy Acts; Hydraulic Fracking; Idaho National Laboratory; Natural Gas; Nuclear Power; Nuclear Regulatory Commission; Three Mile Island Accident; Union of Concerned Scientists

FURTHER READING

Carlisle, Norman, and Jon Carlisle. 1967. "Project Gasbuggy." *Popular Mechanics*. Vol. 102. No. 3. Pp. 102–5, 222.

Kaufman, Scott. 2012. *Project Plowshare: The Peaceful Use of Nuclear Explosives in Cold War America*. Ithaca, NY: Cornell University Press.

Metzger, Peter. 1970. "Project Gasbuggy and Catch-85." *The New York Times*. February 22.

Noble, Ann Chambers. 2014. "The Wagon Wheel Project." *The Wyoming State Historical Society Encyclopedia*. November 8. https://www.wyohistory.org/encyclopedia/wagon-wheel-project (accessed October 2023).

"Project Dubious." 1973. *Time*. April 9. https://content.time.com/time/subscriber/article/0,33009,903965,00.html (accessed October 2023).

Reeves, James E. 1971. "Project Gasbuggy Manager's Report." US Atomic Energy Commission Nevada Operations Office. November. https://inis.iaea.org/collection/NCLCollectionStore/_Public/03/031/3031846.pdf (accessed October 2023).

United Press International (UPI). 1967. "Gasbuggy Explosion Successful." Camden (NJ) *Courier-Post*. December 11. P. 20.

Wells, Bruce A., and K.L. Wells. 2013. "Project Gasbuggy Tests Nuclear 'Fracking.'" American Oil & Gas Historical Society. https://aoghs.org/technology/project-gasbuggy (accessed October 2023).

Prudhoe Bay Oil Field

At 213,543 acres, the Prudhoe Bay Oil Field is the largest oil field in North America and the eighteenth largest oil field in the world. Located on Alaska's North Slope, it lies between the National Petroleum Reserve (NPR) to the west and the Arctic National Wildlife Refuge (ANWR) to the east. The field was discovered by the Humble Oil Company (now part of ExxonMobil) and the Atlantic Richfield Company (ARCO) in March 1968. To bring the oil to market, these two companies pooled their resources with six others to build the Trans-Alaska Pipeline, an 800-mile expanse of pipe stretching from Prudhoe Bay to Valdez, the farthest north, deepwater, ice-free port in the state of Alaska. Production at the field peaked at 1.5 million barrels per day in 1988 and declined to 230,000 barrels per day in 2020. Both the wealth generated by the field and its diminishing returns have prompted interest in oil exploration in nearby areas of the Arctic, including ANWR's coastal plain.

A small inlet in the Beaufort Sea on the northern coast of Alaska, Prudhoe Bay was so named by Sir John Franklin in 1826 in honor of his classmate, Captain Algernon Percy, Baron Prudhoe. Too busy searching for the Northwest Passage, Franklin failed to notice the North Slope's abundant fossil fuel resources. Subsequent nineteenth-century explorers encountered Iñupiaq hunters, who showed them naturally occurring oil seeps which saturated the tundra with liquid hydrocarbons from deep underground. After cutting oil-soaked blocks of plant matter from the tundra, the Iñupiat hauled them back to their villages where they burned them as fuel.

Although they knew of the presence of petroleum in the Arctic, late nineteenth- and early twentieth-century American oil magnates did little to advance the development of this resource. Instead, they focused their attention on more easily accessible reserves in Pennsylvania, California, and Texas. In 1923, after President Warren G. Harding designated 23 million acres of tundra as Naval Petroleum Reserve No. 4 (later renamed the National Petroleum Reserve), energy companies began exploring the Arctic in earnest. Initially, they encountered little success.

At the end of the 1950s, Congress passed the Alaska Statehood Act (1959), which contained a provision allowing the fledgling state to claim 100 million acres of unreserved federal land for the purposes of economic investment and resource development. Prompted by encouraging reports from geologists, Alaskan officials selected 1.8 million acres of land surrounding Prudhoe Bay. In 1968, Humble and ARCO, holders of some of the first leases on this parcel, drilled a test well that yielded significant results. Further study indicated that the newly discovered field was massive, containing as much as 10 billion barrels of oil. The following September, the state made more Prudhoe leases available and put them up for bid. It earned $900 million in one day.

However lucrative, the strike presented problems for Humble and ARCO, because neither company had ever attempted development in an Arctic environment where winter temperatures routinely fell to –45°C and darkness lasted for two months. They quickly adapted their drilling equipment to withstand the cold and their workers to tolerate the lack of sunlight, but then they found themselves facing another difficulty, namely bringing the oil to market. In 1968, Alaska's road and rail infrastructure ended in Fairbanks, 400 miles to the south of Prudhoe. First, Humble and ARCO considered using tankers to transport oil from the Arctic Ocean to US communities on the Atlantic and Pacific coastlines. After a few trial runs in August 1969 and 1970, they decided that this option was too financially unsustainable and too potentially disastrous for the environment. Next, they considered building an overland pipeline across the state to an ice-free, deepwater port on the Gulf of Alaska where the oil would be loaded onto tankers and taken to market. This option was the one they pursued.

In 1968, Humble and ARCO joined with six other companies—British Petroleum, Union Oil, Phillips Petroleum, Amerada Hess, Mobile Oil, and Home Oil—to form the Trans-Atlantic Pipeline System (TAPS). Two years later, they renamed the consortium the Alyeska Pipeline Service Company after an Aleut word for Alaska, which means "great land." Initially, they proposed building the pipeline over the course of two years at a cost of $900 million. These estimates proved to be incredibly optimistic and unrealistic. Because of various delays having to do with environmental compliance issues and Indigenous land claims, construction did not begin until 1975 and did not end until 1977. At a final cost of $8 billion, the Trans-Alaska Pipeline proved to be one of the most expensive, privately financed construction projects ever attempted on American soil.

On June 20, 1977, pipeline workers opened the valves to allow petroleum to flow into the pipeline for the first time. Production at Prudhoe had officially begun. Over the course of the next ten years, the field yielded ever-increasing amounts of oil, ultimately reaching a peak of 1.5 million barrels per day in 1988. Although production has declined significantly since the 1980s, the field still generates significant amounts of oil, roughly 230,000 barrels per day in 2020. Its importance also lies in the fact that it prompted the discovery of and furnished the infrastructure for several smaller satellite fields, including Point McIntyre, Kuparuk, Endicott, Milne Point, and Niakuk. As the returns from these fields have diminished, oil interests have turned their attention to other areas of the Alaskan Arctic, especially ANWR.

Primarily consisting of open tundra frequented by polar bears and caribou, ANWR has proven to be especially controversial insofar as oil exploration is concerned. Originally called the Arctic National Wildlife Range and containing 8.9 million acres, ANWR was established in 1960 by US Secretary of the Interior Fred A. Seaton. It was renamed the Arctic National Wildlife Refuge and expanded to 18 million acres by the Alaska National Interest Lands Conservation Act (ANILCA), signed by President Jimmy Carter in 1980. Importantly, ANILCA designated much of ANWR as wilderness, thereby protecting it from development in perpetuity. But it deferred making a decision about ANWR's coastal plain (also called the 1002 area), leaving it open for oil exploration in the future.

No one knows how much oil ANWR contains, because it has never been adequately studied by geologists. Current estimates range between 4.3 billion barrels and 11.8 billion barrels. Furthermore, no one knows how oil drilling in ANWR will impact wildlife, such as the Porcupine caribou herd, whose birthing grounds lie in the refuge on the shores of the Beaufort Sea. Despite these uncertainties, oil companies in search of another major strike have been eager to explore ANWR's resources. Between 1981 and 2012, congressional leaders made at least five separate attempts to pass bills opening the coastal plain to drilling. Their efforts were stymied both by legislative deadlock and by President Bill Clinton, who in 1996 vetoed the only one of these bills to pass both chambers of Congress. Adopting a different approach toward ANWR, President Barack Obama attempted to protect the coastal plain from drilling by introducing legislation designating it as wilderness. His proposal ultimately lacked enough support to pass through Congress.

The election of President Donald Trump in 2016 ushered in a new era in ANWR's history. Sensing that the political climate had shifted in favor of fossil fuel interests, Senator Lisa Murkowski (R-Alaska) added a provision to the Tax Cuts and Jobs Act of 2017 to allow oil drilling and mandate lease sales on ANWR's coastal plain. The bill was approved by Congress and was signed into law by President Trump on December 22, 2017. Nevertheless, the fate of the refuge is by no means determined. Just two years after the passage of the aforementioned legislation, several large investment banks—including Goldman Sachs, J.P. Morgan Chase, Wells Fargo, and UBS—announced their intent to end direct financing for oil drilling in the Arctic. In addition to concerns about climate change, Indigenous rights, and endangered species, many of them cited the decision to open ANWR as a motivating factor.

Jennifer Schell

See also: *Exxon Valdez* Oil Spill; ExxonMobil; Natural Resources Defense Council; Petroleum; Sierra Club; Trans-Alaska Pipeline System; Usibelli, Emil

FURTHER READING

Cohen, Stan. 1988. *The Great Alaska Pipeline*. Missoula, MT: Pictorial Histories Publishing.

Howk, Jennifer W. 2014. "Exclusion by Assimilation: Native Social Engineering in Alaska." *Harvard International Review*. Vol. 35. No. 3. Pp. 53–7.

Mufson, Steven, and Juliet Eilperin. 2019. "Trump Administration Opens Huge Reserve in Alaska to Drilling." *Wall Street Journal*. September 13. https://www.washingtonpost.com/climate-environment/trump-administration-chooses-most-expansive-approach-to-oil-gas-exploration-in-alaska-wildlife-refuge/2019/09/12/cfac63cc-d597-11e9-9610-fb56c5522e1c_story.html (accessed October 2023).

Willis, Roxanne. 2010. *Alaska's Place in the West: From the Last Frontier to the Last Great Wilderness*. Lawrence, KS: University of Kansas Press.

Yergin, Daniel. 1991. *The Prize: The Epic Quest for Oil, Money, & Power*. New York: Simon & Schuster.

Public Utility Regulatory Policies Act of 1978

The Public Utility Regulatory Policies Act (PURPA), enacted November 9, 1978, is a law created as part of the National Energy Act. It was meant to promote energy conservation, reduce the nation's dependence on conventional fossil fuels, and promote greater use of domestic energy and renewable energy. Importantly, the act required electric power companies to purchase renewable energy. The law came as a response to the energy crisis of the 1970s to encourage cogeneration, which is the joint production of electricity and heat. It also sought to create a market for power from non-utility power producers. The law aimed to develop and utilize renewable resources, while promoting market competition for electric generation.

Implemented by the Federal Energy Regulatory Commission (FERC) and the states' public service commissions for rate-regulated electric utilities, the statute imposed mandatory purchase obligations on electric utilities for power generated by cogeneration and small power production facilities. Utilities purchase energy at a price equal to the cost of the purchase of the energy from the PURPA-qualifying facility, to generate that energy on its own or purchase it from another source. States set this rate pursuant to regulations. The PURPA also encouraged increased power efficiency by ending promotional rate structures, encouraging the development of hydroelectric power, and the conservation of electric energy and natural gas (APPA 2023).

The passage of PURPA followed the 1973 oil embargo by members of the Organization of Petroleum Exporting Countries (OPEC), led by King Faisal of Saudi Arabia. The embargo targeted nations that had supported Israel during the Yom Kippur War between Israel and a group of Arab states led by Egypt and Syria. The embargo first targeted Canada, Japan, the Netherlands, Great Britain, and the United States, and was later extended to Portugal, Rhodesia, and South Africa. By the embargo's March 1974 conclusion, international oil prices had almost tripled, from $3 per barrel to nearly $12 per barrel globally, with US prices significantly higher. The price surge resulted in fuel shortages and long lines at gas stations in the United States and abroad (Rabinovich 2004).

After taking office in 1977, President Jimmy Carter pushed for energy policy changes. To reduce the country's high rates of energy consumption, he publicly campaigned for conservation. Carter also called for the United States to pursue new energy sources, including nuclear, solar, and wind power. Both approaches—energy conservation and expansion of domestic production of energy—were included in the eventual National Energy Act, which Carter signed into law in 1978. PURPA was the part of the act that addressed the electric power industry (PBS 2001).

In general, the PURPA encouraged cogeneration and renewable resources and promoted competition for electric generation along with trying to encourage electricity conservation.

The law was supervised by FERC, with state governments implementing various provisions of the law. FERC determined what constituted a qualifying facility (QF) and provided guidance on avoided costs. State public utility commissions (PUCs) were responsible for determining the avoided costs for their regulated utilities and to set the rates, terms, and conditions of power purchase contracts and operation. Avoided costs are defined in the legislation as "the incremental costs to an electric utility of electric energy or capacity or both which, but for the purchase from the qualifying facility or qualifying facilities, such utility would generate itself or purchase from another source" (PURPA n.d.).

Section 210 of the act concerns the purchase of energy from QFs by electric utilities. QFs are divided into two categories—small power production facility and cogeneration facility. A small power production facility has a capacity of 80 MW or less and its primary energy source must come from a renewable, biomass, waste, or geothermal source. A cogeneration facility is a generator that produces electricity and a second form of thermal energy (such as heat or steam) in a manner that is more efficient than producing both forms of energy separately. PURPA provides that all small power production facilities located at the same site count toward the 80 MW size limit (FERC 2023; APPA 2023).

PURPA established a requirement that electric utilities must sell power to QFs at rates that are non-discriminatory. This means that the rates must be just and reasonable and in what might be considered the "public interest." Recently, a coalition of retail customers and a solar energy advocacy group went to FERC with a challenge to a utility company's retail rates, claiming that the rates extended to customers with rooftop solar installations were in violation of QF provisions outlined in PURPA. FERC declined to act on this particular complaint, but further action in federal district court could well produce a result in favor of the QF and against the utility company in its attempt to evade PURPA regulations (APPA 2023).

In 2005, the Energy Policy Act was passed, which added section 210(m) to PURPA. This measure allows power companies to avoid the requirement of signing QF purchasing contracts if the FERC rules the QFs have access to wholesale electricity markets that are non-discriminatory. In effect, FERC holds that producing units operating at 20 MW or lower do not have "non-discriminatory access" to electricity markets, though the agency has considered lowering the operating limit from 20 MW to 1 MW among QF participants (APPA 2023).

PURPA has been an effective governmental action promoting renewable energy. Estimates suggest that the law brought on line over 12,000 MW of renewable generation capacity, excepting hydroelectric power (UCS 2002). This is partly because PURPA gave favorable terms to companies that produced electricity from renewable (non-fossil fuel) resources. For example, under the influence of PURPA, California state authorities increased wind power on the electricity grid from 10 MW in 1981 to 1,700 MW in the early 1990s.

Another result of the law was the emergence of a new class of generating facilities that receive special rate and regulatory treatment. Generating facilities in this group fall into two categories: qualifying small power-production facilities and qualifying cogeneration facilities. A small-power production facility is an electric power plant that generates less than 80 MW and uses wind, solar, or hydroelectric power as its major energy source.

According to the Union of Concerned Scientists, "the biggest beneficiary of PURPA, though, has been natural gas-fired 'cogeneration' plants, where steam is produced along with electricity" (UCS 2002). A cogeneration facility is an electric generation facility that produces both electricity and another form of energy, typically identified as thermal energy like heat or steam. This is a more efficient use of fuel than producing both forms of energy in separate facilities. PURPA required electric utilities to buy power from cogeneration plants, if that cost was less than the utility's own "avoided cost" rate to the consumer. The avoided cost rate was the additional costs that the utility would spend if it generated the required power itself or could purchase from another source. Where demand was growing, this "avoided cost" was identified as construction and fuel costs spent in the operation of a second, thermal power plant. Cogeneration plants are encouraged by the law since they utilize thermal energy that would otherwise be wasted in a single-purpose power plant that generates electricity but nothing else.

The magnitude of the law's effects varied widely among states and regions of the country because PURPA enabled states wide latitude to implement its provisions according to their peculiar conditions. Differences appeared among the states owing to the differences of availability of renewable energy sources. Where renewable power resources were available for use in generation and transmission of electricity or were available for imminent development, state regulators developed plans for their use. On the other hand, little was done in states without such resources or where the energy demand growth was slow. In several cases, prior regulation already covered the use of renewable energy resources.

After PURPA's amendment by the Energy Policy Act of 2005, Congress followed with the Hydropower Regulatory Efficiency Act of 2013. This made some changes to PURPA and Federal Power Act regulations for the development of low-output hydropower stations. These changes reduced regulatory obstacles to the construction of hydropower plants and made it easier for small-scale projects to receive prompt approval. It did so by raising license exemptions from 5,000 KW to 10,000 KW, enabling more hydropower stations to be built on an expedited schedule. At the time, the industry average length of time for securing a hydroelectric plant license was five years. Some groups within the environmental movement supported this act, such as American Rivers, because they regard small power plants as less disruptive to the environment than the megadams built in the early to mid-twentieth century. Hydropower is a significant US source of renewable energy, though it is not without its critics.

In 2020, the FERC revised its regulations of small power producers and cogenerators to adapt to the changing energy market. The new rule granted state regulatory authorities and nonregulated electric utilities the ability to require that energy rates in QF power sales contracts vary with changes in the utility's as-available avoided costs when the energy is delivered. It also granted states flexibility to allow QFs to have a fixed energy rate, and to provide that this rate can be based on projected energy prices during a QF's contract based on dates of delivery. Furthermore, it gave states authority to set "as-available" QF energy rates based on the locational marginal price (LMP) established in electric markets. To spur small power production, FERC also modified the "one-mile rule" and reduced access to power markets from 20 to 5 MW, for small power production but not cogenerators (FERC 2020).

Some aspects of PURPA have become obsolete. Many energy contracts formed in the 1980s have expired or are expiring. Deregulation helped to create a wholesale market for energy transactions. Also, most state regulatory agencies no longer force utilities to give contracts to non-utility power project developers. However, renewable energy promotion continues to be encouraged by PURPA's exemption of these projects from state and federal regulatory rules.

Hence, deregulation and the adoption of a free market model has worked by coupling new investment opportunities with government-preferred, environment-friendly renewable energy projects and technologies. While the law created a market for the development of non-utility independent power producers, some companies in the market have failed. PURPA critics have argued that power producers signed multi-year cost of electricity contracts when energy prices were high. High power prices resulted from these utilities having to honor these rates when oil prices declined (UCS 2002). As of 2023, courts continued to uphold FERC's expansive definition of "power production capacity" in its identification of qualifying facilities as it continues to work for energy efficiency and conservation (SELC 2023).

William P. Kladky

See also: Electricity; Energy Crisis of the 1970s; Energy Policy Act of 2005; Federal Power Commission; Hydroelectric Power; National Energy Act of 1978; Renewable Energy; Rural Electrification Act of 1936; Smart Grid; Union of Concerned Scientists

FURTHER READING

American Public Power Association (APPA). 2023. "The Public Utility Regulatory Policies Act of 1978." https://www.publicpower.org/policy/public-utility-regulatory-policies-act-1978#:~:text (accessed October 2023).

Bakke, Gretchen. 2016. *The Grid: The Fraying Wires between American and Our Energy Future*. New York: Bloomsbury.

Federal Energy Regulatory Commission (FERC). 2020. "FERC Modernizes PURPA Rules to Ensure Compliance, Reflect Today's Markets." July 16. RM19-15-000, AD16-16-000, Order No. 872, E-1. https://www.ferc.gov/news-events/news/ferc-modernizes-purpa-rules-ensure-compliance-reflect-todays-markets (accessed October 2023).

Federal Energy Regulatory Commission (FERC). 2023. "FERC: Qualifying Facilities (QF) FAQ." https://www.ferc.gov/about/what-ferc/frequently-asked-questions-faqs/qualifying-facilities-qf-faq (accessed October 2023).

Office of the Historian (OH). 2017. "Oil Embargo, 1973-1974." Foreign Service Institute. US Department of State. https://history.state.gov/milestones/1969-1976/oil-embargo (accessed October 2023).

Public Broadcasting System (PBS). 2001. "Public vs. Private Power: From FDR to Today." Frontline. https://www.pbs.org/wgbh/pages/frontline/shows/blackout/regulation/timeline.html (accessed October 2023).

Public Utility Regulatory Policies Act (PURPA). n.d. 18 Code of Federal Regulations §292.101(b)(6). https://www.ecfr.gov/current/title-18/chapter-I/subchapter-K/part-292/subpart-A/section-292.101 (accessed October 2023).

Rabinovich, Abraham. 2004. *The Yom Kippur War: The Epic Encounter that Transformed the Middle East*. New York: Schoken Books.

Southern Environmental Law Center (SELC). 2023. "DC Circuit Rules in Favor of Solar Energy in PURPA Eligibility Case." Press Release. February 16. https://www.southernenvironment.org/press-release/d-c-circuit-rules-in-favor-of-solar-energy-in-purpa-eligibility-case/ (accessed October 2023).

Union of Concerned Scientists (UCS). 2002. "Public Utility Regulatory Policy Act (PURPA)." https://www.ucsusa.org/resources/public-utility-regulatory-policy-act (accessed October 2023).

Red Fork Oil Gusher

The summer of 1901 heralded the discovery of the first noteworthy oil field in what is today the State of Oklahoma. The Red Fork field boomed into being on June 25, 1901, setting the stage for a great expansion of oil prospecting in the infant Mid-Continent region, which would grow into the US's—and one of the world's—most productive oil regions. This led to the growth of the nearby cattle town of Tulsa into a large city, which acquired the nickname "Oil Capital of the World." While the Red Fork's discovery laid the foundation for these relatively well-known developments, it also exemplified some of the lesser-known tensions that significantly shaped petroleum production in the western United States. The field was discovered not far from the Arkansas River, near Red Fork, Indian Territory, on land owned by Sue Bland, a Creek Indian woman. This led to conflicts between drilling companies that hoped to lease land on Native American allotments and the US Department of the Interior, which maintained restrictions upon the right of newly minted Indigenous landowners to lease or sell their property. Such circumstances accelerated white settlers' calls for statehood and exemplified how race shaped the privileges of property ownership amid the growing extraction of energy resources. Furthermore, producers in the Red Fork field struggled to find sufficient storage and pipeline capacity for the crude they did extract, problems that were only exacerbated in subsequent fields in Indian Territory and Oklahoma and that plagued the industry throughout the Mid-Continent until the 1940s.

Before 1907, the eastern half of what became the State of Oklahoma was Indian Territory, primarily home to the Five Tribes of the American Southeast, the Cherokee, Creek, Choctaw, Chickasaw, and Seminole nations. These peoples had been forcibly removed westward, across the Arkansas River, by the US government beginning in the 1830s. Once in Indian Territory, the Five Tribes quickly reestablished governing institutions and a communal land base. In 1859, a Cherokee man named Lewis Ross accidentally discovered a small oil pool near Grand Saline in the Cherokee Nation. Almost immediately, a handful of white oil drillers traveled to Indian Territory to form petroleum companies and drill prospective wells. These early oil companies in Indian Territory arose through collaboration between Native leaders and white investors and oil drillers from the United States proper. This included the Chickasaw Oil Company (1872) and a handful of other enterprises that searched parts of the Choctaw, Cherokee, and Creek nations for oil deposits throughout the 1870s and 1880s. In 1894, a meat packer from Omaha named Michael Cudahy leased around 200,000 acres from the Creek Nation and sunk a number of wells in and around the city of Muskogee. However, these drilling efforts were largely unsuccessful. Furthermore, individual Indians—who were not considered American citizens—could not legally lease specific plots of communal land to oilmen and the federal government vetoed most agreements between the Indian nations and individual prospectors.

In 1887, the federal government began the process of divvying up the communal land base in Indian Territory into 160-acre allotments to be owned by individual members of the Five Tribes. This offered a path to US citizenship for those Indians willing to become private-property owners and all surplus land would be opened to land-hungry settlers. By the turn of the twentieth century, the legal environment appeared more open to oil drilling and both white drillers and "progressive" members of the Creek Nation (Indians who supported allotment) living near Red Fork began drilling new oil wells. Exploratory wells were drilled at Red Fork—located 5 miles southeast of Tulsa—for a number of reasons. First, it was located along a large bend in the Arkansas River. "Creekology," the method of reading the landscape for evidence of oil-bearing strata that was prevalent before the development of scientific petroleum geology, held that bodies of water flowed around mineral-bearing land. Second, the Frisco Railroad passed through the area and connected Red Fork to possible refining centers. Finally, the first men to pursue drilling were local boosters who wanted Red Fork to expand and prosper above and beyond neighboring communities. When oil was struck in late June of 1901, Sue Bland, a Creek woman whose husband was part of the enterprise that drilled the initial well, requested that her allotment be located on the land where the successful well had been sunk. The Sue Bland No. 1 was a modest producer and only a small oil field was established around it. However, the Red Fork pool piqued the interest of oil companies throughout the region, not to mention the US government and the still-functioning Creek tribal government, both of which worried over what the oil discoveries meant for the ongoing process of dividing the tribe's land into individually owned plots.

Within three days, federal officials who oversaw the allotment process were investigating and reporting on the initial well and its flow of oil and gas. Pleasant Porter, chief of the Creek Nation at the time, regretted that the oil rush began before all of the nation's land had been allotted to tribal members. The possibility that large amounts of oil underlay tribal lands only complicated an already chaotic process. For oilmen, the discovery reoriented their gaze northward, away from Spindletop, Texas, where massive amounts of oil had been discovered in January. Those who attempted to enter the Red Fork field were frustrated by the federal and Indian-government restrictions they encountered. One driller who came to an agreement with a Creek family to sink a well on their allotments recalled that "pretty soon along came the Indian police, departmental sleuths, carpetbag scouts and uniformed bands of brass collars, forbidding and warning against further drilling" (Franks 1981, 22). Such frustrations over the federal oversight of Indian lands stymied the growth of the field and further fueled calls for statehood.

The US Department of the Interior began approving applications for oil leases in 1902. Although the field itself was not particularly prolific, Red Fork was the first area that drew the interest of investors from outside of Indian Territory and inaugurated the momentous growth of the nearby town of Tulsa into a vital node in the global oil industry. Tulsa's population was just over 1,300 at the turn of the twentieth century. However, the Red Fork discovery and the subsequent development of the massive Glenn Pool oil field beginning in 1905 propelled the city's growth. It quickly became the Oklahoma oil industry's premier financial center and the location of numerous oil refineries. Tulsa's population was just shy of 20,000 in 1910 and was pushing 100,000 by the 1920s. The city annexed Red Fork in 1927. Oil development around Tulsa that followed the Red Fork discovery proved vital to the financial well-being of several oil companies that are today among the largest in the world. Both the Texas (now Texaco) and Gulf companies had been recently established and were heavily invested in the Spindletop field. However, by 1905, supplies of crude in the fields on the Texas Gulf coast were rapidly dwindling. The large amounts of oil being extracted from fields around Red Fork and Tulsa necessitated the construction of pipelines connecting Indian Territory to refineries in Texas. Both the Texas Company and Gulf built long-distance pipelines that increased their assets and supplied their refineries with new sources of crude. Oil discoveries following the Red Fork success also laid the groundwork for the growth of George Getty's Minnehoma Oil Company and introduced his son, J. Paul Getty, to the oil industry.

Oklahoma was established as a state in 1907, which divested the federal government of much of its power over land use on Native allotments. This facilitated the intensification and expansion of oil drilling in what had been Indian Territory. However, increases in oil production were not always good for the oil industry. The lack of adequate storage was an ever-present problem in Oklahoma's early oil fields. Steel-tank construction had yet to be perfected, so most producers were forced to rely on wooden tanks, which proved highly susceptible to leaks when built in large sizes. Oilmen resorted to earthen pits, and by 1907, it was estimated that 5,000 barrels a day were being lost to evaporation, seepage, or fire. Overproduction caused prices to fall as low as 30 cents a barrel, too low for many smaller companies to sell profitably. Waterfowl often became mired in the earthen pits of oil and restaurant owners from boomtowns would arrive to such pits with empty buggies hoping to fill them with easily captured ducks. Cattle were sometimes victims of the pools of oil as well. Oil from Oklahoma's early fields did prove rich in gasoline, making the state's mineral resources a central part of the young but rapidly growing automobile industry.

Mark C. Boxell

See also: Caddo Oil Field; Getty, Jean Paul; Gulf Oil Company; Spindletop Oil Gusher; Summerland Oil Field; Texaco; Texas Oil Boom

FURTHER READING

Boxell, Mark C. 2021. "From Native Sovereignty to an Oilman's State: Land, Race, and Petroleum in Indian Territory and Oklahoma." *The Journal of the Gilded Age and Progressive Era*. Vol. 20. No. 2. April. Pp. 216–33.

Chang, David A. 2010. *The Color of the Land: Race, Nation, and the Politics of Landownership in Oklahoma, 1832–1929*. Chapel Hill, NC: University of North Carolina Press.

Dochuk, Darren. 2019. *Anointed with Oil: How Christianity and Crude Made Modern America*. New York: Basic Books.

Franks, Kenny A. 1984. *The Rush Begins*. Oklahoma City, OK: Oklahoma Heritage Association.

Franks, Kenny A., Paul F. Lambert, and Carl N. Tyson. 1981. *Early Oklahoma Oil: A Photographic History, 1859–1936*. College Station, TX: Texas A&M University Press.

Frehner, Brian. 2011. *Finding Oil: The Nature of Petroleum Geology, 1859–1920*. Lincoln, NE: University of Nebraska Press.

Johnson, Arthur Menzies. 1967. *Petroleum Pipelines and Public Policy, 1906–1959*. Cambridge, MA: Harvard University Press.

Rister, Carl Coke. 1949. *Oil! Titan of the Southwest*. Norman, OK: University of Oklahoma Press.

The Red Line Agreement of 1928

The Red Line Agreement, formally called the Group Agreement, was a bargain made in 1928 in the Belgian city of Ostend to between American, British, and French oil companies to limit competition and cooperatively exploit the oil resources of the Middle East. The agreement, signed on July 31, was in part a result of pressure by the US Congress to prevent European powers, mostly the British, from locking American oil companies out of the region. The four parties agreed to participate jointly in the exploitation of oil fields discovered in an area bounded by a "red line" on the map, based on the borders of the Ottoman Empire as it existed prior to the First World War. The specific line was drawn by the French and British participants along with their respective governments.

The participating American company was the Near East Development Corporation, a syndicate that included Standard Oil of New Jersey (later Exxon), the Standard Oil Company of New York (later Mobil), Gulf Oil, the Pan-American Petroleum and Transport Company, and Atlantic Refining (later Arco). In the early 1930s, the first two partners bought out the remaining three. The other major participants were the Anglo-Persian Oil Company (later British Petroleum), Royal Dutch Shell, an Anglo-Dutch company, and the French Compagnie française des pétroles (CFP). British and American companies dominated the Red Line regime; the CFP, formed after the First World War out of the German share of the original Turkish Petroleum Company (TPC), was comparatively small and weak. The revenues produced by the TPC, then an Anglo-French joint venture, would be divided equally between the four main parties, with 5 percent going to an Armenian businessman named Calouste Gulbenkian, a partner in the TPC nicknamed "Mister Five Percent."

The parties bound themselves not to seek oil resources in the area bounded by the Red Line outside the framework of the TPC—the "self-denying" clause. The self-denying clause was already part of the agreement that had formed the TPC in 1914, before the outbreak of the First World War. Despite its proclaimed support of the "Open Door" principle of free trade, the US government had no objection to the self-denying clause as a business arrangement freely entered into. The self-denying clause applied only to oil production; companies were free to run their own refining operations in the Red Line area.

The principal interest of the parties to the 1928 agreement was the Iraqi oil fields, as the oil fields of the Arabian peninsula were not yet known. The Turkish Petroleum Company was renamed the Iraqi Petroleum Company (IPC) in 1929 with its corporate headquarters in London. In binding the world's most powerful oil companies to work jointly to exploit Middle Eastern oil, the agreement was designed to stabilize markets and weaken the bargaining power of local political authorities, who would be unable to play the companies off against each other. The Red Line Agreement was part of a move away from cutthroat competition in the oil business to cartelization. The agreement was followed later in 1928 by the As-Is or Achnacarry Agreement, a price-fixing arrangement between Anglo-Persian, Royal Dutch Shell, and Standard Oil of New Jersey. American oil companies in particular viewed the British position in the Middle East as so strong that cooperation with the British was preferred over competition. For this reason, the Americans wanted as much area as possible included within the Red Line.

The weakness of the agreement is that it had no legal force outside the contractual relationship of its signatories; it did not bind and could not be enforced on non-signatories. The most important of these was Standard Oil of California, known as Socal. Socal's aggressive pursuit of oil in Bahrain and Saudi Arabia in the early 1930s posed a problem for the Red Line group. The British and American firms in the cartel responded by trying to buy Socal out, but this proved fruitless. The Second World War put more pressure on the agreement. The French share in the IPC was confiscated by the British following the fall of France in 1940 along with French resident Gulbenkian's share. The Agreement also faced opposition from the governments of the region who saw it as an imperialist enterprise depriving the peoples of the region of their rightful ownership its oil resources.

The end of the Red Line was part of a major post-war transformation in the Middle East oil regime based on an alliance between Saudi Arabia and US oil companies in the Arabian-American Oil Company, known as Aramco. The two American participants in the Agreement wished to acquire stakes in Aramco without their Agreement partners, an action forbidden by the self-denying clause. The British, realizing that American oil companies would play an increased role in the post-war oil settlement, responded by abandoning the Agreement and focusing their attention elsewhere in the region, in Iran and Kuwait. The French, who were only players in Middle East oil by virtue of their participation in the Agreement, fought stubbornly to preserve it. The French government even threatened retaliation against American oil companies operating in France—a toothless threat, given the dependence of France on Marshall Plan aid for its post-war recovery. Despite the lingering resistance of the French and Gulbenkian, the Red Line Agreement was formally dissolved in 1946. The IPC continued to exist and dominated Iraqi production into the 1960s.

William E. Burns

See also: Aramco; Caltex; Consortium Agreement of 1954; ExxonMobil; Gulf Oil Company; Mobil Oil Corporation; Organization of Petroleum Exporting Countries (OPEC); Seven Sisters Oil Companies

FURTHER READING

Black, Edwin. 2011. *British Petroleum and the Redline Agreement*. Washington, DC: Dialog Press.

Conlin, Jonathan. 2018. "From the Jaws of Defeat: France, the United States and Middle East Oil, 1940–1948." *Journal of Energy History/Revue d'Histoire de l'Énergie*. December 4. energyhistory.eu/en/node/59.

Stivers, William. 1983. "A Note on the Red Line Agreement." *Diplomatic History*. Vol. 7. Pp. 23–34.

Yergin, Daniel. 2009. *The Prize: The Epic Quest for Oil, Money and Power*. 2nd ed. New York: Free Press.

Renewable Energy

Renewable energy encompasses all sources of energy that are naturally replenished on a human timescale including sunlight, biomass, wind, tides, waves, geothermal heat, and rainwater. In the pursuit of clean, carbon-free energy, scientists and engineers have increasingly sought to capture these natural resources through a variety of techniques and technologies, typically to produce electricity. Primarily due to a surge in installed generation of wind and solar power, the United States now generates about 20 percent of its electricity from renewable energy, and as the pressure to reduce carbon emissions and mitigate climate change intensifies, this percentage is expected to continue increasing as renewable energy replaces fossil generators, typically powered by coal and natural gas.

While new forms of renewable energy such as solar photovoltaics (PV) and wind turbines have become much more widespread since the start of the twenty-first century, renewable forms of energy have been used by humans for thousands of years, primarily in the form of biomass. Anthropologists think that early human ancestors first used fire up to a million years ago and that domestication of livestock occurred about 10,000 years ago to plow fields and move goods. The first water wheels date to about 2,000 years ago, and the first windmills were built around 500 years ago. Until the Industrial Revolution, the history of energy really was a history of renewable energy. However, as the technology of the Industrial Revolution spread, the world became heavily reliant on fossil energy. The United States, in particular, was naturally blessed with extensive fossil resources and soon became a mass producer of coal, oil, and natural gas, a dominance that expanded greatly around the turn of the twentieth century.

The dominance and expansion of fossil fuels in the United States appeared to be almost unstoppable until the 1970s when conventional oil deposits peaked, and the nation suddenly became an importer of oil. External forces, rather than US production alone, influenced the price and quantity of oil in global markets. Conflict in the Middle East led to price shocks in 1973 and 1979. Simultaneously, the price of electricity more than doubled across the country as demand sputtered and environmental regulations cracked down on polluting industries, utility companies, and gasoline-powered transportation. The energy sector was squeezed in all directions. When Jimmy Carter became president in 1977, he and Congress moved quickly to pass new legislation to encourage the development of renewable energy as a clean, secure, domestically produced alternative to fossil fuels.

In the Oval Office, only two months after his inauguration, Carter gave a famous fireside chat in a mustard yellow cardigan sweater to announce a nationwide investment in renewable energy and to call on all Americans to consume less energy. He referred to the fight as the "moral equivalent of war," and made energy policy central to his administration. In 1977 he oversaw the opening of what is now the National Renewable Energy Lab (NREL) in Golden Colorado, and in 1978 he signed into law the National Energy Act (NEA) which included a number of energy-saving and renewable-energy acts. Of little interest at the time, the NEA also included the Public Utility Regulatory Policies Act of 1978 (PURPA), tacked on by a Vermont legislator interested in allowing a biomass co-gen facility to sell electricity into wholesale power markets. This seemingly insignificant act later opened the door for small non-utility generators to challenge the classic American utility model—for example, it formed the policy framework for feed-in-tariffs, a policy mechanism that greatly aided the deployment of rooftop solar in the 2000s and 2010s. Not finished yet, the Carter administration also passed the Energy Security Act of 1980, a group of six laws intended to increase production of biomass, solar, geothermal, ocean, and other renewable energies. Renewable energy had been given a jump start.

HYDROELECTRIC POWER: RENEWABLE ENERGY?

Hydroelectric power is often considered to be a renewable form of energy; however, some states such as California do not allow it to count for their climate emissions policies because they do not consider it to be sustainable. While the water in the reservoir is replenished, hydroelectric power-generation has significant biological, physical, and chemical impacts on the environment.

Rudy Kahsar

In 1980, the world's first modern wind farm was built at Crotched Mountain, New Hampshire, followed by a much larger one in 1981 at Altamont Pass, California. Investments in solar energy were similarly aggressive. Carter asserted that 20 percent of all US electricity would be solar by 2000 and even had solar panels installed on the roof of the White House. However, the price of oil collapsed in the early 1980s and governments around the world, including in the United States, turned their focus away from renewable energy and instead toward deregulation of electricity markets and fossil fuel sectors. Symbolically, the Reagan administration removed the White House solar panels in 1986, and as the price of fossil energy remained cheap during the 1990s, renewables, still quite expensive, struggled to compete.

After a lull of almost twenty years, renewable energy again began to gain a foothold around the turn of the twenty-first century. During this time, growth in oil consumption, largely from Asia, combined with new conflicts in oil-producing regions drove up the price of conventional energy. Reacting as it had in the 1970s, Congress passed a number of measures to promote renewable energy, including extensions on the Production Tax Credit (PTC) and the Investment Tax Credit (ITC), policies that designed to promote the deployment of wind and solar power, respectively. Other legislation aimed at decreasing US reliance on imports of foreign oil sought to dramatically increase the production of corn-based ethanol. Investments in renewable energy accelerated even more following the financial crisis of 2008, when the Obama administration, tasked with massive reinvestment, called for a new energy paradigm that would foster energy and climate security. Unlike the 1980s, renewable energy technology had matured, costs had come down, and as a result, the industry as a whole was ready to compete. During the 2010s the total installed capacity of wind power on the US electricity grid increased by a factor of four while the total amount of solar power increased by a factor of more than ten. Meanwhile, prices continued to decrease. In a symbol of the changing times, solar panels were re-installed on the roof of the White House in 2013. After a slow start in the 1980s and 1990s, renewable energy had finally taken a firm foothold.

Governments, scientific institutions, and investigators around the world continue to conduct research on new forms of renewable energy including ocean thermal energy, tidal energy, waste to energy, small and micro hydro facilities. Fossil-derived energy is still the primary contributor to greenhouse gas emissions in developed economies, but as the world seeks to meet emissions reductions targets, policymakers are expected to continue pushing the energy sector toward renewables. The hope is that cooking, heating and cooling, transportation, and all other forms of energy use can be powered with electricity generated by renewable energy.

Rudy Kahsar

See also: Animal Power; Biofuels; Block Island Wind Farm; Clean Power Plan of 2015; Crotched Mountain Wind Farm; Energy Crisis of the 1970s; Energy Policy and Conservation Act of 1975; Energy Security Act of 1980; Geothermal Power; Union of Concerned Scientists; Waste to Energy; Water Power; Wind Power

FURTHER READING

Lovins, Amory. 2013. *Reinventing Fire: Bold Business Solutions for the New Energy Era*. White River Junction, VT: Chelsea Green Publishing.

Rhodes, Richard. 2018. *Energy: A Human History*. New York: Simon & Schuster.

Smil, Vaclav. 2010. *Energy Transitions: History, Requirements, Prospects*. Santa Barbara, CA: ABC-CLIO.

Usher, Bruce. 2019. *Renewable Energy: A Primer for the Twenty-first Century*. New York: Columbia University Press.

Yergin, Daniel. 2011. *The Quest: Energy, Security, and the Remaking of the Modern World*. New York: Penguin.

Revelle, Roger R.D.

Roger R.D. Revelle (1909–91), a prominent researcher in the fields of oceanography and atmospheric science, was director of Scripps Institution of Oceanography from 1950 to 1964 and founding chairman of the Committee on Climate Change and the Ocean (CCCO), which was formed in 1979 by the Intergovernmental Oceanographic Commission. Beginning in the late 1950s, Revelle's research showed dramatic increases in atmospheric carbon dioxide (CO_2) since the beginning of the Industrial Revolution and concluded that this human-generated phenomenon produced by burning fossil fuels like coal, oil, and gas would result in global warming. He became established as a highly credible scientific voice on the subject of anthropogenic climate change and is considered the "grandfather of the greenhouse effect."

Revelle was born in Seattle and then moved with his parents to Southern California where he graduated in 1929 with a bachelor's degree in geology from Pomona College. He went on to earn a Ph.D. in oceanography in 1936 from the University of California, Berkeley. His doctoral research was completed at San Diego's Scripps Institution of Oceanography (SIO), which at the time was overseen by UC Berkeley's university senate (Nierenberg 1992, 119). Revelle joined the US Naval Reserve and served during the Second World War, eventually earning the rank of commander. He helped to establish the Office of Naval Research (ONR) while holding a position as chief oceanographer in the Navy's Bureau of Ships. After the war, he became head of the geophysics branch of the ONR, where he supervised the oceanographic research portion of the hydrogen bomb tests at Bikini Atoll in 1946 and 1947 (Nierenberg 1992, 119). Revelle was acknowledged as a leading oceanographer at a time when the field was just beginning to emerge, and together with Columbus Iselin of the Woods Hole Oceanographic Institution and Maurice Ewing of Columbia University, they established the field's research agenda in the post-war era (Munk 1997, 8276).

Revelle acquired his stature by directing the SIO from 1950 to 1964, where he organized and led several intensive multi-year explorations, first in the Mid-Pacific and then later in the South Pacific. He also led the formation of major scientific organizations such as the National Academy of Sciences Committee on Oceanography (NASCO), the International Geophysical Year (IGY) Panel on Oceanography, the Scientific Committee for Ocean Research (SCOR), and the International Oceanographic Commission (IOC). By means of his leadership, these organizations gave scientific research on oceanic processes a higher profile in the media and in public policy. One favorable assessment of his career noted: "Policymakers looked to him for a reasonable assessment of which scientific problems should take priority. Scientists sought his advice and support to focus research and get it funded" (Munk 1997, 8276).

In addition to his leadership in these scientific associations, Revelle produced a large volume of research on a variety of topics and issues in the scientific study of the world's oceans. His most notable work entailed studies of changing CO_2 levels in the oceans and in the atmosphere. In 1956, Charles David Keeling joined the SIO to head the IGY's program on Atmospheric Carbon

Dioxide and began documenting changes in atmospheric CO_2 through measurements at Mauna Loa and Antarctica (Munk 1997, 8276). While this data collection proceeded, Revelle and Hans Seuss published a study in 1957 titled "Carbon Dioxide Exchange Between Atmosphere and Ocean and the Question of an Increase of Atmospheric CO_2 during the Past Decades." Revelle and Suess observed that "human beings are now carrying out a large scale geophysical experiment of a kind that could not have happened in the past nor be reproduced in the future" (Revelle 1957, 19). Based on the existing studies of past CO_2 increases and corresponding increases in ocean surface temperatures, they determined that given "the probably large increase in CO_2 production by fossil fuel combustion in coming decades we conclude that a total increase of 20 to 40% in atmospheric CO_2 can be anticipated." They continued: "This should certainly be adequate to allow a determination of the effects, if any, of changes in atmospheric carbon dioxide on weather and climate throughout the earth" (Revelle 1957, 26).

Revelle was clear on the point that the Industrial Revolution contributed to rapidly increasing CO_2 concentrations in the atmosphere. Coal-burning steam plants powered locomotives, industrial machinery, and steam heating systems, as well as electricity-generating power plants. Gasoline-powered internal combustion engines fueled millions of automobiles and trucks. The use of coal, oil, and gas to supply the energy needs of industrial societies created an abundance of atmospheric carbon dioxide in a relatively short time, far beyond what nature would produce on its own, or could be absorbed readily by the world's oceans. Revelle was certain that this "large scale geophysical experiment" with the earth's oceans and atmosphere would result in climate change but did not speculate what those changes would entail. Revelle continued his research and organized and chaired a joint IOC-SCOR Committee on Climate Changes and the Ocean. This gave him an additional platform to use in calling attention to the problem of fossil fuel combustion, increased CO_2 emissions, the accumulation of greenhouse gases in the atmosphere, and the resultant effects of global warming on the earth's climate. In 1965, Revelle served on President Lyndon Johnson's Science Advisory Committee Panel on Environmental Pollution. Due to his influence, the committee's final report published later that year deemed CO_2 an "invisible pollutant," and predicted that "by the year 2000 the increase in atmospheric CO_2 will be close to 25%." It went on to conclude that "this may be sufficient to produce measurable and perhaps marked changes in climate, and will almost certainly cause significant changes in the temperature and other properties of the stratosphere" (EPP 1965, 126–7).

Revelle devoted a significant amount of time in the late 1950s to planning the creation of the University of California at San Diego (UCSD) but was passed over for the chancellorship when the new institution opened in 1960–1. He served in several advisory roles until his appointment in 1963 as Richard Saltonstall Professor of Population Policy at Harvard University, a chair he held for ten years. He returned to UCSD in 1975 as Professor of Science, Technology and Public Affairs and taught in that capacity for the next fifteen years. In 1982, he published "Carbon Dioxide and World Climate" in the August 1 issue of *Scientific American*, again calling attention to a growing environmental threat that few public officials cared to address. In 1988, however, the United Nations formed the Intergovernmental Panel on Climate Change to gather research and advise governments on climate change, largely building on the foundation created by Revelle and his cohort of oceanographers and atmospheric scientists. President George H.W. Bush awarded him the National Medal of Science in part for his "pioneering work in the areas of carbon dioxide and climate modifications," and then in 1992 signed the UN Framework Convention on Climate Change pledging US commitment to the reduction of greenhouse gas emissions (Munk 1997, 8278).

Revelle died in 1991 before he could watch the United States take more seriously the need to curtail the use of fossil fuels as the US's primary source of energy. He knew that energy politics generated great passions and fundamental conflicts, since he testified before congressional committees in the 1980s while President Ronald Reagan's appointees attempted to downplay the urgency of the problem. Oil and gas industries funded organizations like the George C. Marshall Institute (1984–2015) and the Global Climate Coalition (1989–2001) with a mission to create maximum public uncertainty about atmospheric research and the scientific consensus regarding greenhouse gases, global warming, and climate change. They were successful in pressuring President Bill Clinton to shelve the Kyoto Protocol (1997), which bound nations to adhere to carbon emissions reductions targets in the United Nations Framework Convention on Climate Change. Public opinion shifted after the release of Al Gore's film *An Inconvenient Truth* (2006) and the publication of Naomi Oreskes and Erik M. Conway's *Merchants of Doubt: How a Handful of Scientists Obscured the Truth on Issues from Tobacco Smoke to Climate Change* (2010), which exposed climate denialism as industry propaganda and made the case for scientists' claims regarding greenhouse gas emissions and global warming.

Yet, political polarization in the United States made it difficult for national energy policy to respond to Revelle's findings about fossil fuel consumption and climate change. The US presidential election cycle created a whipsaw effect when President Barack Obama approved US participation in the Paris Climate Agreement of 2015, a pact among the nations to reduce carbon emissions according to "nationally determined contributions," only to have President Donald Trump declare a US withdrawal from the agreement when he took office in 2017. Four years later, President Joe Biden reversed this decision and brought the nation back into the agreement. Supporters of a transition to non-carbon sources of energy found themselves hoping that growing public awareness, changing consumer preferences, technological innovation, and improved market conditions can succeed where political will has failed.

Jeffrey B. Webb

See also: American Petroleum Institute; *An Inconvenient Truth*; Climate Change; Global Climate Coalition; Natural Resources Defense Council; Sierra Club; Union of Concerned Scientists

FURTHER READING

Environmental Pollution Panel (EPP). 1965. *Restoring the Quality of Our Environment: Report of the Environmental Pollution Panel, President's Science Advisory Committee*. November. The White House. Washington, DC: US Government Printing Office.

Munk, Walter H. 1997. "Tribute to Roger Revelle and his Contribution to Studies of Carbon Dioxide and Climate Change." *Proceedings of the National Academy of Sciences*. Vol. 94. August. Pp. 8275–9.

Nierenberg, William A. 1992. "Roger Revelle." *Physics Today*. Vol. 45. No. 2. Pp. 119–20.

Revelle, Roger, and Hans E. Suess. 1957. "Carbon Dioxide Exchange between Atmosphere and Ocean and the Question of an Increase of Atmospheric CO_2 during the Past Decades." *Tellus*. Vol. 9. No. 1. Pp. 18–27.

Sabine, C.L., H. Ducklow, and M. Hood. 2010. "International Carbon Coordination: Roger Revelle's Legacy in the Intergovernmental Oceanographic Commission." *Oceanography*. Vol. 23. No. 3. Pp. 48–61.

Richardson & Boynton Company

Established in 1837 and originally located in Brooklyn, New York, the Richardson & Boynton Company manufactured stoves, ranges, and furnaces for home cooking and heating. Henry A. Richardson (1819–1902) partnered with inventor Nathaniel A. Boynton (1823–1900) to pioneer the mass-marketing of these appliances, enabling their use in individual family homes on a wide scale. Boynton would leave to form a competing company, Boynton & Co, in 1884, but Richardson & Boynton remained a leader in the industry, expanding its product line and developing new technologies into the twentieth century. Initially, these allowed for more efficient use of fuels such as wood and then coal, with innovations applying steam and gas being incorporated before the US Civil War and into the early twentieth century.

A convergence of social, technological, and environmental factors precipitated the rise of the stove in American life. From the colonial period through the War of 1812, the predominant means of domestic heating and cooking remained the open-hearth. While Germans and other continental European immigrant groups regularly incorporated small, stand-alone stoves into their houses, regardless of socio-economic status, those from the British Isles remained partial to the fireplace. Anglo-Americans continued to favor that form of heating for decades after the American Revolution. The drafty houses and uneven temperatures were believed to promote robust health (Adams 2014).

In the early nineteenth century, technological changes made cast iron cheaper to produce, leading to bigger, better, and relatively less expensive stoves. At the same time, large portions of the eastern seaboard, particularly in the Northeast, experienced more frequent fuel shortages, as urban growth made wood scarcer in more populated areas. Newer "closed" stoves used wood more efficiently, radiated heat more evenly, and provided better ventilation. Retailing for as little as $30, and even less in the second-hand market, their affordability allowed for middling and working-class Americans to acquire them. They could also burn coal, helping that mineral to become an increasingly important and popular domestic fuel source in larger urban areas in the late antebellum and post-Civil War periods. Wood, however, remained a major fuel source in growing communities to the west with easier access to more plentiful forests (Adams 2014).

Richardson & Boynton products highlighted not only this shift in fuels, but also another divergence between cooking and home heating devices. Revolutionary Era inventions such as the Franklin stove could be used only for heating. Antebellum stoves that could heat and be used for cooking represented a significant upgrade in both efficiency and safety (Bijker 2012, 263). However, within just a few decades the company clearly differentiated between furnaces—exclusively used for heating—and stoves, or ranges—exclusively used for cooking. This divergence helped establish markets for other applications of furnace/stove technology. Hot water heaters, steam furnaces, and laundry stoves (for flat iron pressing) were manufactured. These technological advancements coincided with coal's increasing availability and affordability throughout the country. By 1860, all major US cities were within close proximity to some coal deposit, providing Americans plentiful resources with which to fuel their increasingly technologically advanced homes. A rapidly increasing customer base, especially after the US Civil War, allowed Richardson & Boynton to establish an office in Chicago, with additional plants opened in New Jersey and upstate New York after the turn of the century.

Through various iterations of its products, the company consistently responded to various public safety concerns. Enclosed furnaces and stoves were obviously safer than an open hearth, but that did not mean they were without dangers, or at least the perception of danger. Using the appellation "Perfect" throughout its line, advertisements worked to assuage various fears, from clogs to smoky indoors to explosions. Richardson & Boynton boasted a rotating grate that would more efficiently remove ashes, a state-of-the-art ventilation system that sent all smoke outside, and minimal joint and no-bolt construction that facilitated hotter water temperatures and more steam at lower risk. Steam heat, however, never seriously challenged coal as a residential heating method, being reserved mostly for the wealthy. Trade catalogs show wood-/coal-fueled devices priced consistently and notably lower than their stream-powered counterparts throughout the company's existence.

ASSEMBLE ON SITE

Stove production methods played a key role in their availability and acceptance in America. Through the early nineteenth century, retailers assembled pre-cast pieces that had usually been manufactured at more remote blast furnaces. Technological changes, transportation improvements, and increased availability of coal allowed individual companies to manufacture products completely on site. Initially this allowed for a proliferation of designs and styles and it also helped lower the price paid by the consumer.

Joseph F. Super

Various kinds of explosion prevention proved particularly important as natural gas became a more reliable fuel source. Like coal before it, the widespread, domestic residential use of gas depended first on transmission networks. As a resource, it was plentiful, but mid-nineteenth-century means of delivering on a large scale were poor, both in terms of overall safety and consistency. Thus, it took a couple decades for gas-fired products to become widely used, even though the applied technology existed in the 1850s. Like their other "Perfect" products, Richardson & Boynton assured consumers of their gas stoves, furnaces, and heaters that there was "no chance of explosion" (RBC 1888, 8). Such developments spurred another revolution in home heating and cooking, with gas being more popular than wood and coal in the home by 1930.

The Great Depression took its toll on Richardson & Boynton, as it did on so many companies. Just one factory remained, and the company struggled to innovate and manufacture new products. Electricity was emerging as the latest fuel source, but trade publications show only coal-, steam-, and gas-powered appliances advertised. Extras like additional fireboxes, heating compartments, and boilers—essentially making the product bigger—were all the company had left to offer. It ceased operations in 1939 after declaring bankruptcy. Surviving competitors purchased some of their facilities in the early 1940s.

Joseph F. Super

See also: Coal; Franklin, Benjamin; Gold, Stephen J.; Nason, Joseph; Natural Gas; New York Steam Company; Steam Power; Pierce Steam Heating Company

FURTHER READING

Adams, Sean P. 2014. *Home Fires: How Americans Kept Warm in the Nineteenth Century*. Baltimore, MD: Johns Hopkins University Press.

Bijker, Wiebe E., Thomas Parke Hughes, T.J. Pinch, and Deborah G. Douglas. 2012. *The Social Construction of Technological Systems: New Directions in the Sociology and History of Technology*. Cambridge, MA: MIT Press.

Brewer, Priscilla. 2000. *From Fireplace to Cookstove: Technology and the Domestic Ideal in America*. Syracuse, NY: Syracuse University Press.

Harris, Howell J. 2008. "Inventing the U.S. Stove Industry, c.1815–1875: Making and Selling the First Universal Consumer Durable." *Business History Review*. Vol. 82. No. 4. Pp. 701–33.

Larkin, Jack. 1988. *The Reshaping of Everyday Life: 1790–1840*. New York: Harper Collins.

Richardson & Boynton Company (RBC). 1888. *"Perfect" Furnaces and Ranges*. New York: N.p.

Richmond Union Passenger Railway

In 1888, the first operational electric railway opened in Richmond, Virginia, with 12 miles of track. The Richmond Union Passenger Railway (UPR) was not the first effort at electrified rail in America. However, it was the first to incorporate critical design, mechanical, and electrical innovations, clearly distinguishing it from competitors and enabling it to function over varied terrain and for extended periods of time without excessive wear and tear. Many of these innovations were pioneered, adapted, or modified by inventor Frank J. Sprague (1858–1934). The UPR capitalized on the emerging availability of electricity in urban settings and led the transition away from horse, cable, and steam in rail-based public transit.

The Richmond Union Passenger Railway was not the first to utilize electricity, nor was Sprague the only one working on that technology. Several major cities in America and Europe sought to upgrade their local rail commuter systems. Efforts pre-dated the US Civil War but remained in the development stage until the 1870s. Numerous inventers, from Ernest Siemens (1816–92) to Thomas Edison (1847–1931), attempted to advance the technology that could safely and effectively apply electricity to transportation. Various cities in New England and Pennsylvania, as well as New York City, tried early versions of electric rail with mixed and limited results. Motors which worked well in the laboratory struggled to handle the practical hurdles in cities. They fared little better or even worse than horses pulling heavy loads up hill, especially in inclement weather. Attaching them to cars proved difficult, often exacerbating bumpy rides and increasing the frequency of car maintenance. Generating and transmitting electricity was so new that effectively harnessing it to the level needed to propel a loaded car over several miles caused overloads, fires, and explosions (Grant 2016, 3–4).

FRANK SPRAGUE

Even though Frank Sprague left Edison and formed a potentially rival company, the two men remained close. Edison frequently used his connections to aid Sprague. The two men disagreed on important practical aspects of electric rail, but the Wizard of Menlo Park continually advocated for Sprague and saw him as the premier innovator in the field, believing he would be the man to overcome obstacles to electrification.

Joseph F. Super

Like other early applications of electricity, the quest to bring it to trains occasioned several competing technologies and ideas, particularly about how and where the car would access the electricity. Many early efforts basically involved attaching a battery and motor to a locomotive, which would generate its own power and pull a series of passenger cars in much the same way a larger steam locomotive functioned. Safety and logistical efforts doomed these designs. Another option was to electrify the rail itself, but this presented another set of problems. The most viable option at the time, although not with its own issues, remained an overhead wire. Public perception and lack of understanding exacerbated all of these. One minor malfunction or shower of sparks was often enough to scare off investors, even with a man of Edison's renown advocating for the technology (Dalzell 2010, 79).

Those willing to take the risk often worked with razor-thin margins. In 1884, Frank Sprague left Edison's company to devote himself full time to electric rail after the company moved away from railway transit to focus on power stations. Despite being underfunded, the Sprague Electric Railway and Motor Company (SERM) quickly became a leader in the field due to Sprague's ability to find new solutions to some of the biggest problems. For example, he figured out a way to mount the motor under the passenger car and improve the overhead wire system. These enabled the car to maintain speed going uphill, prevented damage to the motor itself, and lowered the risk of cars jumping the track (Duffy 2003, 25–7).

In 1887, Sprague finally had the opportunity to take his innovations public. The previous year, investors from New York chose Richmond, Virginia, which had just one horse-drawn line, to build a state-of-the-art electrified system. Establishing the Richmond Union Passenger Railway, which was almost as poorly funded as SERM, they partnered with Sprague's company, providing him the chance to fully showcase his work. The UPR wanted its own power station and forty cars. Its twelve-mile track ran over unpaved streets and up 10 percent grades. By the spring of 1888, these obstacles had been sufficiently overcome to allow the railway to open for business and operate at a profit. Despite some continued hurdles, it was clear the age of electricity had begun. Two hundred electric railways operated across the country by 1890 (Rowsome 2013, 126). By the first years of the twentieth century, electricity completely dominated the industry.

The success of electric railways increased in relation to general advancements in electrical generation and transmission. A mix of DC and AC was used initially, but as AC grew safer and more reliable, the passenger rails covered greater distance and pulled heavier loads. Even in its earliest days, the UPR had already taken on some short-haul freight. Electricity allowed street cars to evolve beyond passenger service and rival steam locomotives for some local freight business. They could also travel well beyond the city limits, even accessing some rural areas. Many smaller cities or larger towns eventually constructed their own electric street cars.

There was another factor in the rapid expansion and adoption of electric rail. It quickly became extremely popular with the general public. Riding the streetcar was not just a quick and cheap mode of transportation. It was an experience. It allowed for an interaction and movement within urban settings that was not possible before. It also became a cultural symbol of modern urbanity and an industrial life, in both positive and negative ways. Every aspect of life was moving faster, and the electric rail helped people keep pace, even as it played a role in accelerating that existence.

The Richmond Union Passenger Railway remained in operation for over sixty years, ceasing operations in 1949 and bringing an end to electric rail service in Richmond. It was privately owned and operated for that entire time. Along with other privately held light rail companies, it succumbed to the twin pressures of public mass transit and the rising post-war popularity of the personal automobile. However, unlike the fuels it replaced, electric rail was not surpassed by something superior. Improvements were made to components and transmission but surviving mass transit systems continued to be powered by electricity. They continue to carry the legacy of the Richmond Union Passenger Railway.

Joseph F. Super

See also: Baltimore & Ohio Railroad; Edison, Thomas Alva; Electricity; Fuel Cell; Pearl Street Power Station; Transcontinental Railroad; War of the Currents

FURTHER READING

Dalzell, Frederick. 2010. *Engineering Invention: Frank J. Sprague and the U.S. Electrical Industry*. Cambridge, MA: MIT Press.

Duffy, Michael C. 2003. *Electric Railways: 1880–1990*. London: Institution of Engineering and Technology.

Grant, Roger H. 2016. *Electric Interurbans and the American People*. Bloomington, IN: Indiana University Press.

Rowsome, Jr., Frank. 2013. *The Birth of Electric Traction: The Extraordinary Life of Inventor Frank Julian Sprague*. New York: IEEE History Center Press.

Seely, Bruce E. 1994. "Back to the Future? High Speed Rail and Historical Patterns of American Transportation Development." *Railroad History*. Vol. 170. Pp. 5–14.

Richmond, Indiana Gas Explosions

On Saturday April 6, 1968 at 1:47 p.m., an explosion at the corner of 6th and Main in downtown Richmond, Indiana shocked and devastated a community. An investigation showed that the explosion was caused by a natural gas leak that originated near the basement of a gun shop, Marting Arms and Sporting Goods, from the gas company's corroded service line. Donald Marting and his wife, the shop's owners, both died in the explosion, and Mr. Marting's body was never recovered. The store had a gun firing range in the basement and speculation emerged that a gas leak in the basement of the shop, combined with people firing at the range, caused the initial explosion (Kellner 1970, 45). Seconds after the first explosion there was another, more powerful blast, caused by the black powder in the gun shop being ignited by the first explosion. Marting Arms was reduced to a pile of rubble. The explosion flipped cars upside down, sent people flying into the air, and tore victims' bodies apart. As reported in the Richmond *Palladium-Item* on April 7, forty-one people died, ranging in age from seven to seventy-two years of age, and at least 127 people were injured. Everyone who sustained an injury in the blast eventually recovered. All of the deaths from the explosion occurred in the blast or ensuing fires. The disaster resulted in a lawsuit against the Richmond Gas Company, which was found liable for the tragedy and was required to pay damages to survivors and family members of those who died. That same year, Congress passed the Natural Gas Pipeline Safety Act in order to impose regulations on the transportation of natural gas (Harper 2008).

Citizens of Richmond helped police, firefighters, and National Guard put out the fires, look for survivors, and recover body parts of those who had perished. Rescue efforts were hampered by continued hazards in the area, including gas leaks, exploding gunpowder and ammunition at Marting Arms, and raging fires throughout the business district. Witnesses reported that the scene was chaotic and looked like a war zone (Kellner 1970, 42). It took police more than five hours to restore any sort of calm to downtown Richmond. The *Palladium-Item* reported that the local hospital, Reid Memorial, was overwhelmed with people seeking treatment for injuries from the explosion. The nearby National Guard armory was used as a temporary morgue. City administration offices were moved to the armory temporarily while City Hall, which was located near the blast site, was shut down.

The day after the explosion, the *Palladium-Item* reported that sixteen people had died and the death toll was expected to rise. The newspaper called the explosion the worst catastrophe in the history of Richmond and among the worst in Indiana. Less than twenty-four hours removed from the tragedy, no one knew for certain what had caused the blast, but a gas leak was suspected as well as a secondary explosion of gunpowder at Marting Arms, both of which proved to be true. The explosion took place just two days after Martin Luther King, Jr.

was assassinated in Memphis. Some white residents reported initially thinking that the blast had been caused by Black residents in retaliation for the assassination of Dr. King. A book written about the tragedy relayed the story of Lucy Robison, a young Black woman who lived in Richmond, but who was out of town when the tragedy took place. When she heard news of the explosions, she called home to check on her children. The operator told Ms. Robison that her call could not be put through because Richmond was having a riot in response to Dr. King's assassination. Ms. Robison objected to the operator's assumption, telling the operator that it was, in fact, a gas explosion and not a riot (Kellner 1970, 120; Harper 2008).

DOWNTOWN RICHMOND

The gas explosion in Richmond, Indiana in 1968 hastened the decline of the city's downtown business district. People and commerce had already begun to move eastward to the outskirts of Richmond. This downtown decline reflected a larger national trend toward suburbanization and urban decay in the post-war years. Today, the trend can be seen in reverse, as some suburban areas decline and urban cores become more gentrified.

Benjamin J. Clark

A lawsuit found Richmond Gas Corporation to be liable for the incident. The venue for the trial was moved from Richmond to nearby Connersville. The result of the lawsuit was a settlement totaling $250,000. The gas company sought to lay blame on Marting Arms, claiming there was only a single blast that was caused by the store's gun powder. But an investigation found that the cause of the blast was leaking gas lines that were in poor condition and had not been well maintained by the gas company. In the aftermath of the explosion, it was reported that during cleanup efforts, an employee of the gas company found a length of the gas pipeline that showed beyond doubt the poor condition of the lines. This piece of evidence proved Richmond Gas Corporation's negligence. The employee refused to turn over the evidence of corroded lines to investigators. On the day of the blast people in the area reported smelling natural gas before the explosion occurred. In the weeks leading up to April 6, people reported to the gas company the strong odor of natural gas but the company did little to address the issue.

US Bureau of Mines representative Joseph M. Kutcha assisted in the investigation and authored the Bureau of Mines report, as well as a summary of the report for the local newspaper. Kutcha cited an inspection report from the Richmond Gas Corporation from just three days before the explosion that showed there were fifty-five gas leaks in the pipe infrastructure, seven of which were labeled as extremely large and posing significant hazards. The company knew that its pipes were in poor condition as early as 1959, the article reports. Some sections of iron pipe were, in 1968, already seventy years old. Kutcha's investigation concluded that the leaks prior to the explosion were significant enough that an explosion was bound to happen unless the pipes were repaired (Kutcha 1968).

Richmond was not the first city in the United States to suffer this kind of tragedy. Efforts on a national level to address pipeline integrity and safety for consumers were already underway when the explosion in Richmond occurred. In his 1967 State of the Union Address, President Lyndon Johnson called for federal pipeline safety laws. In March of that year,

Senator Magnuson introduced a bill that would become the Natural Gas Pipeline Safety Act of 1968, passed in August, just four months after the explosion in Richmond, but already well underway beforehand (Armstrong 1969, 143). The law gave power to the US Secretary of Transportation to authorize and direct safety standards that would impact the conveyance of natural gas by pipeline. Even though the legislation did not garner much attention from the public, the natural gas industry opposed the legislation and the potential regulations that would force gas companies to maintain their lines properly in order to prevent future explosions (Armstrong 1969, 152–3).

Benjamin J. Clark

See also: Cleveland, East Ohio Gas Explosion; Hart, William Aaron; Indiana Natural Gas Boom; Natural Gas; Natural Gas Act of 1938; Pittsburgh Gasometer Explosion

FURTHER READING

Armstrong, Martin F. 1969. "The Natural Gas Pipeline Safety Act of 1968." *Natural Resources Lawyer*. Vol. 2. No. 2. Pp. 142–53. www.jstor.org/stable/40921608 (accessed October 2023).

Harper, Jean, Zack Parker, and Rob Quigg. 2008. *1:47*. Web video. Directed by Jean Harper. Richmond, IN: Mahallasville Road Productions. https://www.youtube.com/watch?reload=9&v=_W-4jvlMejM&app=desktop (accessed October 2023).

Richmond Gas Corporation v. Reeves. 1973. Justia. October 31. https://law.justia.com/cases/indiana/court-of-appeals/1973/671a114-5.html (accessed October 2023).

Kellner, Esther. 1970. *Death in a Sunny Street: The Civil Defense Story of the Richmond, Indiana Disaster, April 6, 1968*. Richmond, IN: Warfel, Inc. http://cdm16066.contentdm.oclc.org/cdm/ref/collection/fulltext/id/1859 (accessed October 2023).

Kutcha, Joseph. 1968. "Kutcha Report Analyzes Safety Problems Following Downtown Blast." *Palladium-Item* (Richmond, IN). May 30. https://www.newspapers.com/image/246955209 (accessed October 2023).

Rockefeller, John D.

John D. Rockefeller (1839–1937) was an American businessman who founded the Standard Oil Corporation which established a monopoly over oil production in the United States by the 1890s. One of the first billionaires in American history, Rockefeller exemplified the ruthless robber baron stereotype of the nineteenth century, destroying or buying out all competitors, manipulating lax regulatory laws, and establishing the foundation for the nation's transition from a coal-powered to a petroleum-based economy. Later in life Rockefeller and more so his sons and grandsons established significant philanthropic initiatives, especially the Rockefeller Foundation.

Rockefeller entered the oil industry during the latter stages of the US Civil War. Prior to the war, he and his business partner, Maurice Clark, operated a produce commission business. The war significantly improved the profitability of Clark & Rockefeller, as the company was known, due to contracts to supply food to the Union Army. Looking ahead, Rockefeller recognized that the wartime produce contracts would disappear, and he sought a new profitable endeavor. Taking advantage of federal subsidies for oil production that had quadrupled the price of a barrel of oil, Clark & Rockefeller joined hundreds of other businesses and speculators entering the oil industry in 1863 with their first refinery outside of Cleveland, Ohio. Crucially, the new company, christened Andrews, Clark, and Company, implemented at Rockefeller's behest more efficient business practices. Instead of dumping wastes created by refining oil into kerosene like most oil companies of the era, Rockefeller's firm turned the by-products into salable products like petroleum jelly, enhancing the company's already significant profitability.

In February 1865, Rockefeller bought out Clark and his brothers and established the new company of Rockefeller & Andrews, which later changed to Rockefeller, Andrews, & Flagler with the addition of a new partner in 1867. By that date, the company operated two refineries, including the largest in the world at that time. As productive capacity grew, so did Rockefeller's desire for greater control. In 1870, he abolished Rockefeller, Andrews, & Flagler, and created Standard Oil of Ohio.

One of the key elements in the growth and profitability of all of Rockefeller's companies, especially Standard Oil, was Rockefeller's insistence on efficiency and reduced costs. Through a process that became known as vertical integration, Standard Oil increasingly controlled all of the steps in the production and sale of its products. The company bought wood and produced its own barrels, employed its own pipe lines, owned its own freight cars, and operated its own marketing and sales subsidiaries in addition to drilling and refining oil in Ohio and Pennsylvania. In response to the threat to their own interests, railroad companies offered bulk rates to Standard Oil, further reducing costs and allowing Rockefeller to undercut rival producers. This price war drove many smaller operators to the wall, allowing Standard Oil to acquire or bankrupt most of its competitors. By the end of the 1870s, Standard Oil refined

90 percent of the oil produced in the United States, and 80 percent produced in the world. In 1882, Rockefeller's attorneys reorganized the various holdings into the Standard Oil Trust. This new entity brought under the control of its nine-member board of trustees forty-one companies that operated 20,000 oil wells, managed 4,000 miles of pipeline, and employed 100,000 workers.

SOCIAL DARWINISM

John D. Rockefeller was a believer in Social Darwinism, which gave intellectual and moral justification for his business practices and acquisition of wealth. Rockefeller believed that monopolies were justified by "survival of the fittest." Standard Oil's dominance was a product of its superiority; its weaker competitors deserved to fail. Further, Standard's success was best for the "species" insofar as it strengthened the overall economy and the industry by weeding out the unworthy.

Richard M. Filipink

The creation of the trust brought increased criticism of both Rockefeller and the company's practices. The clear establishment of a monopoly in oil production and distribution brought public and eventually congressional scrutiny, culminating in the passage of the Sherman Antitrust Act in 1890, which forbade contracts, combinations, or conspiracies in restraint of trade or to create monopolies. The state of Ohio followed suit in establishing antitrust legislation, forcing the removal of Standard Oil of Ohio from the trust in 1892. Nevertheless, the Trust continued to expand its holdings, investing briefly in iron ore, then further expanding with the purchase of new oil fields in Ohio, Indiana, and West Virginia. As the decade progressed, Rockefeller reduced his operational control of the trust, culminating in his retirement in 1902.

In 1901, in response to the growing Progressive movement, Congress passed the Clayton Antitrust Act, tightening the regulation of monopolies and increasing opportunities for government action. With Theodore Roosevelt's accession to the presidency in September 1901, the likelihood of government action increased. In 1904, a series of articles by muckraker Ida Tarbell, published as *The History of the Standard Oil Company* further inflamed public opinion and increased calls for breaking up the trust. Rockefeller's attempts to counter Tarbell's work through public relations and pro-Standard publications largely failed. More effective in the short term was a reconsolidation of Standard Oil under friendlier corporate laws in New Jersey in 1909. At this point Standard Oil still controlled 70 percent of the nation's oil refinery business. This success was short-lived. In 1911 the Supreme Court ruled that Standard Oil Trust violated the Sherman Antitrust Act, and ordered it to be broken up into thirty-four separate companies. Rockefeller owned 25 percent of Standard Oil's stock at the time of the break-up. As part of the judgment, he retained stock in all thirty-four companies (which included the foundational companies Conoco, Esso, Mobil, and Amoco, among others). As such, Rockefeller's wealth significantly increased after the Court's decision, culminating in his attaining billionaire status within a decade.

In addition to his substantial oil holdings, in 1902–3 Rockefeller also invested in Colorado Fuel & Iron (CF&I), floating a loan to the coal and iron ore producing company in return for a minority interest in its holdings. CF&I drew national attention in 1913–14 due to a strike by the United Mine Workers of America (UMWA), begun in September 1913, demanding representation for miners in CF&I's mines. At the behest of the company, the state of Colorado called out the National Guard to protect strikebreakers, leading to clashes between the troops and the miners. These violent outbreaks culminated in the Ludlow Massacre on April 20, 1914, in which a firefight between miners and the Guard exploded into the burning of the miners' camp and the death of at least fifteen women and children. Rockefeller's son, John D. Rockefeller, Jr., testified before Congress during an investigation of the massacre, both denying responsibility and downplaying its importance.

In his retirement, Rockefeller engaged in a number of philanthropic causes, including an investment of $250 million to create the Rockefeller Foundation. The Foundation donated money to support the survivors of the Ludlow Massacre, and promote public health, medical training, and the arts. Rockefeller's legacy is the growth and development of the petroleum industry in the United States and in other nations. Out of Standard Oil grew ConocoPhillips, ExxonMobil, Chevron, and Amoco. This industry ultimately provided the foundation of the modern US economy for much of the early twentieth century. Rockefeller's enormous business empire also led to demands for greater corporate accountability and governmental regulation. Rockefeller's vast riches triggered popular reactions to the extremes of wealth and poverty in the United States, but also created a major philanthropic organization whose mission and impact continue to today.

Richard M. Filipink

See also: ExxonMobil; Ludlow Massacre; Mobil Oil Corporation; Ohio Oil Boom; Pennsylvania Oil Boom; Petroleum; Red Line Agreement of 1928; Standard Oil Company; Tarbell, Ida; United Mine Workers of America

FURTHER READING

Chernow, Ron. 1998. *Titan: The Life of John D. Rockefeller, Sr.* New York: Random House.
Hawke, David Freeman. 1980. *John D: The Founding Father of the Rockefellers.* New York: Harper & Row.
Segall, Grant. 2001. *John D. Rockefeller: Anointed with Oil.* New York: Oxford University Press.
Wiebe, Robert H. 1967. *The Search for Order 1877–1920.* New York: Hill & Wang.
Yergin, Daniel. 1991. *The Prize: The Epic Quest for Oil, Money & Power.* New York: Simon & Schuster.

Roughnecks

Roughnecks are the unskilled workers in oil field operations, mostly men who perform the actual work on the ground in the oil industry in the United States. The term roughneck first appeared in the nineteenth century in relation to traveling carnivals and other such shows. Those roughnecks, also called roustabouts, were usually very strong, somewhat brutish men, willing and able to do hard work and perform general labor, such as taking down tents, loading gear onto railcars, and performing other necessary labor needed to stage a very large traveling show. They also performed security for the performers and staff. The roughnecks and roustabouts of carnivals and circuses were those who actually enabled shows to function safely from town to town.

Eventually the terms roughnecks and roustabouts were introduced to the American oil industry. Roughneck came to refer to workers who traveled from oil field to oil field, whether in Texas, Oklahoma, or North Dakota, laboring in various capacities around the drilling rigs. As the profession grew, so did the legend of the roughnecks. While they were establishing themselves as the backbone of the industry, the roughnecks were developing a cultural image as tough, masculine men, willing and able to take on any challenge. In the song "Roughneck" from the 1963 album *Blood, Sweet, and Tears*, Johnny Cash sang: "Born to be a roughneck I'll never amount to nothin' / Pulling case and layin' pipe is hard labor. / Well I was born in a boomer shack bout a half mile from town. / Papa was a driller on a wildcat crew and my mama never was around. / I learned to cuss when I was two and fight when I was three / and by the time I was five there was no kid alive could ever get the best of me. / Born to be a roughneck."

These lyrical images of a hard-working, hard-living workforce are partly confirmed by personal memoirs, such as Bobby D. Weaver's *Oilfield Trash: Life and Labor in the Oil Patch* (2010). In an interview, Weaver recalled living in West Texas and observing the young men "with limited formal education" who came to find work: "When they first came to the patch, they were mostly young, single-type people. Most of them came from a rural background. They never had any money. Their big entertainment came when they could go to town on a Saturday and take a couple or three dollars. With that, they whooped it up if they could." He described roughnecks as men who took to hard work, men with "independent spirit" who "just wouldn't give up." He continued, "You're on a job and trying to get something done and they would figure out a way to get it handled. It might not be orthodox [laughs] but they would get it handled" (Mullins 2015).

Most work available to oil field workers occurred in rural, isolated areas with few or no amenities. Young men lived in hastily built shanties and did well to find adequate food to keep them going. Boomtowns emerged in many locations, and "managers of flimsy boarding houses along the dirt ruts of 'Main Street' charged exhausted riggers almost half a day's pay to rent a cot for twelve hours" (BM 2023). It was hard to find clean drinking water, and human waste wasn't handled in modern, sanitary ways. Typically, the air hung heavy with the stench of oil from nearby wells. Most of these temporary camps were unhealthy places where workers contracted dysentery, respiratory diseases, and other maladies. More than a few had reputations for violence, producing non-work related injuries and deaths.

Gerald Lynch's *Roughnecks, Drillers, and Tool Pushers: Thirty-Three Years in the Oil Fields* (1987) provides insight into the work routines and lifestyles of oil field workers in the mid-twentieth century. He worked for the John Champion Drilling Company in the eastern Texas field known as Corsicana and started his career as a roughneck in 1925 at the age of seventeen. The company's workers drew twelve-hour shifts, a day shift from 6:00 a.m. to 6:00 p.m., and then a night shift from 6:00 p.m. to 6:00 a.m. Lynch made $6 per shift when he began working in the oil field, and aspired to become a full-fledged "driller" who earned $12 a day (Lynch 1987, 5). At first he worked as a "boll weevil" or novice on the four-man crew, manning the drilling rig's grip ring and grief joint. The driller served as crew chief while the fireman operated the steam plant that provided power to the unit, which in his account was composed of two 90-horsepower boilers at 180 pounds per inch steam pressure. They worked for weeks to drive the bit down to 1,800 feet. Lynch remembered another "special breed of men" in the oil field, the rig builders, who constructed wooden derricks—freestanding towers to hold the drilling rig in place—that reached 84, 96, and 108 feet high. These derricks were given names like "doubles," "thribbles," and "fourbles" depending on the heights of the "stand pipes" that lined the borehole. Lynch viewed the rig builders as "exceedingly strong, ambidextrous, tough, and skillful" because "the work they did was beyond the capacity of the average able-bodied man" (Lynch 1987, 10).

In a telling passage, Lynch recalled how an ordinary laborer worked his way up the "ladder" in a drilling operation. If a roughneck wished to advance in his occupation and become a driller, he had to undergo an on-the-job training in handling the drill apparatus. Lynch wrote that "by 'feeding off' or 'holding up' on the brake, you control the amount of weight on the bit and, hence, the rate of penetration. This kept the driller standing at the brake practically all of the time, and in order to be free of the constant 'slacking off,' he usually had a favorite roughneck who 'spelled' him" (Lynch 1987, 15). This worked as a kind of apprenticeship for the roughneck who aspired to a longer career in the oil industry. Lynch continued, "since it took considerable skill and a sense of 'feel' to 'drill' without bogging'er down or 'twisting off' or just fanning, such training was a necessity." If a roughneck could get the weight right, or could acquire a feel for the task, then they could aspire to be the driller on the crew; if not, "they stayed roughnecks all their lives" (Lynch 1987, 16).

Clearly, working outdoors for long hours at strenuous tasks around dangerous machinery produced a high number of injuries and fatalities. With improvements in technology, emphasis on occupational health and safety, and greater accountability from courts and state and federal agencies, working conditions for roughnecks grew safer over time. Still, there are a multitude of ways to get injured or killed around oil wells, storage and transport areas, and offshore oil platforms given the hazardous nature of the work being performed. Workers die in falls and crashes, or from being mangled by tools or equipment. Exposure to harmful substances like benzene and hydrogen sulfide can be fatal, and fires and explosions occur all too frequently. There are high-voltage electrical hazards as well as dangers associated with handling equipment and materials under high pressure. The US Bureau of Labor Statistics monitors fatal occupational injuries in the private oil and gas extraction industries, and according to their figures, in the years 2003 through 2017 the industry suffered 1,623 fatalities (BLS 2019). In a recent article on the dangers of working in the industry, safety consultant Frank Parker said of the roughnecks, "It is a macho world. They get up in the morning and eat nails for breakfast. We need those people to do that kind of work. We've just got to find a way not to kill them" (Morris 2018).

Coal mining became safer under the pressure of unions which could use the threat of strikes to secure better working conditions through collective bargaining. Unlike workers in the coal mining industry, oil field workers were less attracted to unions. Historically unions were more successful at securing members within certain sectors of the oil industry, such as oil refineries, where there was less turnover and more stability. In the aforementioned interview with Bobby Weaver, he remembered the roughnecks he knew in the oil patch as being unenthused about organized labor: "we didn't have, we didn't need another boss. We didn't even like the one we had. [laughs] And we just visualized the union as just somebody else you had to answer to" (Mullins 2015). This squares with other evidence of an oil field culture of hardy manliness and rugged individualism. Elsewhere, Weaver expressed the mindset of the roughnecks as one of pride "that comes from the fact that few people can do what the oil-field hands do. They feel they are a cut above ordinary folk as they wander across the face of the world, proving it over and over again each time they bring in a new well." After all, "they go places and do things that ordinary folk would never attempt. They provide the world with the energy that keeps it productive" (Lynch 1987, xiv).

Jeff Hirschy

See also: Caddo Oil Field; Densmore Oil Tank Car; Enbridge Pipeline System; Hydraulic Fracking; Natural Gas; Oil Tankers; Petroleum; Prudhoe Bay Oil Field; Red Fork Oil Gusher; Spindletop Oil Gusher; Summerland Oil Field; Texas Oil Boom; Tommyknockers

FURTHER READING

Brantley, J.E. 1971. *History of Oil Well Drilling*. Houston, TX: Gulf Publishing Co.

Bullock Museum (BM). 2023. "Roughnecks." Bullock Texas State History Museum. https://www.thestoryoftexas.com/discover/campfire-stories/roughneck (accessed October 2023).

Gow, Sandy. 2005. *Roughnecks, Rock Bits, and Rigs: The Evolution of Oil Well Drilling Technology in Alberta, 1883–1970*. Calgary, AB: University of Calgary Press.

Inside Energy. n.d. "IE Questions: What's a Roughneck?" http://insideenergy.org/2014/11/29/ie-questions-whats-a-roughneck/ (accessed June 8, 2020).

Lynch, Gerald. 1987. *Roughnecks, Drillers, and Tool Pushers: Thirty-Three Years in the Oil Fields*. Austin, TX: University of Texas Press.

Lyrics. n.d. "Roughneck." https://www.lyrics.com/lyric/812726/Johnny+Cash (accessed June 18, 2020).

Morris, Jim. 2018. "Death in the Oilfields." December 21. Part 6 of Blowout: Inside America's Energy Gamble. The Center for Public Integrity. https://apps.publicintegrity.org/blowout/us-oil-worker-safety/ (accessed October 2023).

Mullins, Jesse. 2015. "The Oilfield Attitude." *The Permian Basin Petroleum Association Magazine*. May 1.

Olien, Roger M., and Diana Davids Olien. 1986. *Life in the Oil Fields*. Austin, TX: Texas Monthly Press.

US Bureau of Labor Statistics (BLS). 2019. "Injuries, Illnesses, and Fatalities: Mining, Quarrying, and Oil and Gas Extraction." US Department of Labor. https://www.bls.gov/iif/factsheets/mining-fact-sheet-2017.htm (accessed October 2023).

Weaver, Bobby D. 2010. *Oilfield Trash: Life and Labor in the Oil Patch*. College Station, TX: Texas A&M University Press.

Wikipedia. n.d. "Roughnecks." Accessed June 18, 2020. https://en.m.wikipedia.org/wiki/Roughneck (accessed October 2023).

Rumford Fireplace

The Rumford Fireplace was invented in the late 1790s. In a testament to both their efficacy and aesthetic qualities, these tall fireplaces with angular side walls that reflect heat into the room are still constructed today. Their namesake, Sir Benjamin Thompson, Count Rumford (1753–1814), successfully modified existing fireplaces to improve the draw and increase the efficiency. "Rumfordizing" a fireplace was widely popularized to improve air quality both inside and outside a home at a time when smog was a significant problem in urban centers. Furthermore, significantly less fuel was required for effective room heating.

The need for technological heating solutions to environmental and social problems caused by excess fuel consumption was apparent to many by the mid-eighteenth century, but domestic life in early America typically revolved around massive hearths and cooking fires, sustained by the vast forests across the eastern seaboard. Early on, as the degradation of these landscapes progressed, many colonial statutes were passed to limit wasteful cutting and large-scale exportation of wood products to Europe. For example, the Massachusetts Charter of 1691 levied a fine of 100 pounds for cutting a tree greater than 24 inches in diameter. William Penn required 1 acre of woods to remain standing for every 5 acres cleared in 1681. Tree-cutting regulations throughout the 1700s prohibited cutting smaller trees, as firewood shortages and rocketing fuel prices became locally common by mid-century.

The early American fireplace designs burned so much fuel in part because they were so large, but also because so much heat was lost up the chimney. The search to improve heating and cooking solutions attracted the attention of inventors and scientists, such as Benjamin Franklin (1706–90), who created the Franklin stove by 1740. Franklin's practical design transferred much more heat into the room through the insertion of a cast-iron stove into a hearth; variations on Franklin's design emerged over the following decades. However, the enclosed nature of an iron stove did not allow for the traditional, open fireplace design, nor did early iron stoves retain heat for as long as fire-brick. While Count Rumford is not as well known today as Franklin, he publicly fashioned himself in much the same way as a self-made inventor. Rumford cultivated a transatlantic reputation of his own to go along with an important, and eponymous, heating invention. Born Benjamin Thompson in Massachusetts, Rumford's life was marked by his choice to serve in the British Army during the American Revolution. Much of his adult life was then spent in Europe, including London, Bavaria, and Paris.

While in London, Rumford was struck by the smog he observed, which came from burning coal in open fireplaces. He argued for modifying existing fireplaces to create cleaner air in order to improve public health outcomes. The essay that introduced the Rumford Fireplace appeared in his 1796 book (reprinted in America in 1798). The opening lines express his motivations clearly: "The plague of a smoking Chimney is proverbial; but there are many other very great defects in open Fire-places ... and there are some of them very fatal in their consequences to health" (Rumford 1796, 297).

As to its design, the Rumford Fireplace effectively added bricks to the back of a larger, pre-existing fireplace. This reduced the size of the firebox to 12 or 13 inches front to back, while even more dramatically reducing the size of the "throat" of the chimney to as little as 4 inches. The design also specifies that the front opening of the chimney be rounded off rather than square. Together, these changes resulted in a much stronger upwards draft through dynamic pressure, which reduces backpuffing of smoke into the interior of the house when starting a fire in a cold fireplace. The sides of the firebox in a Rumford Fireplace are also reduced by adding bricks with 135 degree-angled walls, which reflect heat towards the interior of the room. The smaller opening reduced cold air drafts when not in use, and the smaller firebox necessarily burned less fuel, while managing to retain a similar heat output through greater efficiency. Because the fireplace is so much more compact yet retains much of the height and width of a traditional design, the Rumford Fireplace is readily identifiable.

The Rumford Fireplace was immediately recognized as a valuable innovation in both Europe and the United States. Thomas Jefferson (1743–1826) specified eight of them for his residence at Monticello, building both new ones as well as modifying extant fireplaces. Today, the Rumford Fireplace is still in demand by custom homebuilders and masons, and for many of the same reasons they became widely known in the 1790s.

Kyhl Lyndgaard

See also: Biofuels; Coal; Evard, Mary E.A.W.; Franklin, Benjamin; Stewart, Philo Penfield

FURTHER READING

Buckley, Jim. 1994. "Reviving the Rumford." *Journal of Light Construction*. March. Pp. 43–6.

Brown, G.I. 1999. *Count Rumford: The Extraordinary Life of a Scientific Genius*. Stroud, UK: Sutton Publishing.

Brown, Sanborn. 1979. *Benjamin Thompson, Count Rumford*. Cambridge, MA: The MIT Press.

Edgerton, Samuel Y., Jr. 1971. "Heating Stoves in Eighteenth Century Philadelphia." *Bulletin of the Association for Preservation Technology*. Vol. 3. Nos. 2/3. Pp. 15–104.

Rumford, Benjamin, Graf von. 1796. *Essays, Political, Economical, and Philosophical*. London: T. Cadell, Jr. and W. Davies.

Rural Electrification Act of 1936

The Rural Electrification Act was a law enacted by US Congress authorizing the US Department of Agriculture to provide loans to farmers to implement electric and telephone services in rural areas. The law was passed on May 20, 1936 as part of President Franklin D. Roosevelt's New Deal (McBride 2017).

In the mid-1930s, electric power was absent from 90 percent of farms due to the high cost incurred by power companies to build transmission lines out to rural areas (McBride 2017). Amid the Great Depression, Roosevelt created the Rural Electrification Administration (REA) under the Emergency Relief Appropriation Act of 1935. The REA was designed to provide direct relief to unemployed citizens, but rural populations lacked necessary electrical trade skills to utilize the funds. Further, the REA was unable to fulfill its intended purpose as a grant-making agency because private power companies were unwilling to cover expenses for extending power lines to rural America at affordable rates (Lewis 2020). Thus, through the signing of the Rural Electrification Act, the REA was able to establish policies for providing federal loans to state and local governments for large construction projects and individual homes. Repayment for these loans could extend up to twenty-five years and the interest rate remained low, while maintaining that individuals would not be held personally liable for default on a REA loan. Within a decade of its enactment, the Rural Electrification Act accounted for $466 million in loans for electric power infrastructure, 380,000 miles of power line installation, and over a million new electricity consumers. The percentage of electrified farms in the United States increased from 11 percent in 1936 to 97 percent by 1960 (Thompson 2020a).

COOPERATIVES

Rural electric cooperatives (RECs) and investor-owned utilities (IOUs) differ in many ways. RECs are not for profit, providing electricity to geographically dispersed member owners and financed by federal loans and retained earnings. Member owners serve as the governing system for RECS. IOUs are commercial, for-profit utilities financed through shareholder investment, retained earnings and the open market. Out of the 3,100 electric utilities in the United States, 200 IOUs possess a 73 percent market share. State regulatory commissions govern IOUs (University of Wisconsin Center for Cooperatives 2020).

Keriann Conroy and Kate Clark

The Rural Electrification Act has undergone more than two dozen amendments since its passage in 1936. Notable changes include placing the REA under the US Department of Agriculture (1939), liberalizing the terms of loans (1944), granting the US Secretary of the Treasury the authority to make loans, and authorizing the REA to refinance obligations owed to the Tennessee Valley Authority (1944 and 1948). Since 1962, provisions for telecommunications networks, broadband, and rural internet have been added (McBride 2007).

Though inarguably beneficial for farmers, the Rural Electrification Act was highly controversial. Drafted by US Senator George Norris (1861–1944) and US Congressman Sam Rayburn (1882–1961), the act received immense pushback from pro-business Republicans like Ford Motor Company founder Henry Ford (1963–47), who accused Norris of being a "socialist" for his support of public power (Thompson 2020b). Preference for lending under the Act was given to nonprofit farmer groups who formed rural electric cooperatives, or member owned utilities. Private power companies retaliated by building "spite lines" through proposed REA districts, building lines to profitable, rural customers while leaving the impoverished without power, and canvassing in rural places to discourage farmers and their families from joining a cooperative (Rudolph 1986, 80–3).

By 1937, the REA secured passage of the Electric Cooperative Corporation Act, a law authorizing states to facilitate the formation and operation of not-for-profit, consumer-owned electric cooperatives. Then, in 1942, cooperative leaders formed the National Rural Electric Cooperative Association (NRECA) to represent rural electric cooperative interests in Washington, DC (NRECA 2020). Presently, the NRECA represents more than 900 rural electric cooperatives, offering management and organizational oversight. Further, the organization is responsible for federal government relations for rural electric cooperatives, such as lobbying (NRECA 2020). In 2019, the NRECA spent a total of $2,450,000 in lobbying expenditures (CRP 2020).

Rural electric cooperatives are primarily responsible for the final stage of electricity delivery, known as distribution (IER 2020). Until the mid-1950s, cooperatives generated power to customers within their service areas, but due to increasing demand, cooperatives pooled purchasing power to form generation and transmission (G&T) cooperatives. In the United States, 834 electric distribution and sixty-three G&Ts serve 42 million people in forty-seven states (UWCC 2020).

Keriann Conroy and Kate Clark

See also: Agriculture and Energy; Bartlett Electric Cooperative; Cooke, Morris Llewellyn; Electricity; Federal Power Commission

FURTHER READING

Center for Responsive Politics (CRP). 2020. "Client Profile: National Rural Electric Cooperative Assn." June 6, 2020. https://www.opensecrets.org/federal-lobbying/clients/summary?cycle=2019&id=d000000153 (accessed October 2023).

Institute for Energy Research (IER). 2020. "Electricity Distribution." https://www.instituteforenergyresearch.org/electricity-distribution/ (accessed June 6, 2020).

Lewis, Joshua, and Edson Severnini. 2020. "Short- and Long-Run Impacts of Rural Electrification: Evidence from the Historical Rollout of the U.S. Power Grid." *Journal of Development Economics*. Vol. 143. Pp. 1–19.

McBride, Brandon. 2007. "USDA Rural Electrification Administration—Informational Publication 100-1." Rural Development. US Department of Agriculture. https://www.rd.usda.gov/files/UEP_IP_100-1.pdf (accessed June 8, 2020).

McBride, Brandon. 2017. "Celebrating the 80th Anniversary of the Rural Electrification Administration." US Department of Agriculture. https://www.usda.gov/media/blog/2016/05/20/celebrating-80th-anniversary-rural-electrification-administration (accessed June 6, 2020).

National Rural Electric Cooperative Association (NRECA). 2020. "History: The Story behind America's Electric Cooperatives and NRECA." https://www.electric.coop/our-organization/history/ (accessed June 6, 2020).

Rudolph, Richard, and Scott Ridley. 1986. *Power Struggle: The Hundred-Year War over Electricity*. New York: Harper & Row, Publishers.

Thompson, Lisa. 2020a. "Rural Electrification Act (1936)." The Living New Deal. Department of Geography. University of California, Berkeley. https://livingnewdeal.org/glossary/rural-electrification-act-1936/ (accessed June 6, 2020).

Thompson, Lisa. 2020b. "Rural Electrification Administration (REA) (1935)." The Living New Deal. Department of Geography. University of California, Berkeley. https://livingnewdeal.org/glossary/rural-electrification-administration-rea-1935/ (accessed June 6, 2020).

University of Wisconsin Center for Cooperatives (UWCC). 2020. "Rural Electric." https://reic.uwcc.wisc.edu/electric/ (accessed October 2023).

Santa Barbara Oil Spill

The 1969 oil spill off the coast of Santa Barbara, California remains one of the largest oil well blowouts in US history. The eleven-day spill began on January 28, 1969, roughly 6 miles offshore, and resulted in the spillage of approximately 3 million gallons of crude oil in the Santa Barbara Channel. The slick covered an expanse of 800 square miles of ocean and 35 miles of southern California coastline. In the days and weeks following the spill, newsmedia carried live coverage to the public alongside widely circulated images of oil-drenched birds and marine mammals. The disaster galvanized the modern environmental movement in the United States and prompted legislative and public action toward environmental protection, including the advent of Earth Day and a host of environmental protections.

Santa Barbara County sits atop vast reserves of petroleum deposits and has been a key site of oil extraction throughout the twentieth and twenty-first centuries. Home to the world's first offshore drilling site in 1896, the Summerland Oil Field. Seventy-three years after the birth of offshore drilling, on the morning of January 28, 1969, workers on Platform A of the Union Oil-operated Dos Cuadros Oil Field attempted to replace a drill bit in a 3,500-foot well. Union Oil had been issued a waiver by the US Geological Survey that allowed them to use shorter pipe casing than required by federal standards, which weakened the capacity of the well to prevent blowouts. With the crew's removal of a drilling tube, crude oil began to spew uncontrollably and workers were unable to install a blowout preventer. Failed attempts to plug the leak additionally prompted a series of disturbances and leaks on the ocean floor. It wasn't until February 7 that rig crews were able to plug the well using a combination of drilling mud and concrete. Researchers and private citizens, however, subsequently discovered previously undetected ruptures in the ocean floor that were continuing to leak oil from the seabed. By the end of February, seepage persisted at a dwindling rate, with smaller-scale leakages reported through the end of the year.

While the gravity of the spill was initially under-reported to the US Coast Guard by Union Oil staff, the severity of the disaster came to light on the morning of January 29. As the Coast Guard surveyed the area by helicopter, a surface slick extended for several miles in all directions from Platform A. Estimates from Union Oil's vice president initially indicated a spill rate of 5,000 gallons per day, though subsequent assessments estimated approximately 200,000 gallons of oil per day were leaking into one of the Pacific Ocean's most biologically diverse ecosystems. On February 4, one week after the blowout, a storm system began pushing the oil slick toward Santa Barbara harbor. The failure of a boom system subsequently led to the arrival of crude oil on the entire harbor, prompting the evacuation of residents. Bystanders reported foul smells from the crude oil, and over the coming days, numerous species of nonhuman animals washed up dead on the blackened beaches.

FIGURE 1: The Santa Barbara oil spill off the coast of southern California in 1969 created widespread demand for greater environmental regulation.

The disaster was met with both local and national action. Groups of concerned residents and organizations piled straw on the beaches to absorb oil, and volunteers rescued and cleaned blackened seabirds. Speaking of the community's concerted efforts to confront the spill, Thomas Storke of *The Santa Barbara News* observed: "Never in my long lifetime have I ever seen such an aroused populace at the grassroots level. This oil pollution has done something I have never seen before in Santa Barbara—it has united citizens of all political persuasions in a truly nonpartisan cause" (quoted in Clarke 2002, 160). On February 6, 1969, President Richard Nixon announced a plan to implement more stringent restrictions on offshore drilling, while legislators worked to ban it completely. Many of these struggles proved unsuccessful in court, and in August of 1969, the US Department of the Interior greenlit the construction of a new platform in the Santa Barbara Channel.

The spill prompted a flurry of media interest, with newspapers, radio, and television covering the unfolding crisis and ongoing cleanup efforts. Though Fred L. Hartley, then-president of the Union Oil Corporation, stated, "I don't like to call it a disaster, because there has been no loss of human life. I am amazed at the publicity for the loss of a few birds" (quoted in Clarke 2002, 160), accounts by journalists and photographers who documented the aftermath exposed the pervasive environmental impact of the disaster on marine life. Journalists from *Life* magazine, for example, traveled to San Miguel Island in the Santa Barbara Channel, home to flourishing colonies of elephant seals and sea lions, and reported numerous dead animals on the oil-drenched beaches (Snell 1969, 22–7). Estimates suggest that over 4,000 birds died as a result of the spill, though many estimates put the numbers higher. Amid growing awareness of the ecological devastation wrought by the disaster, middle-class environmental sensibilities took on new currency. The June 13, 1969 issue of the popular *Life* magazine featured a photo essay about the spill and arrived at more than 6 million homes. The photo essay, explains environmental scholar Stephanie LeMenager, captivated national audiences as it "remind[ed] the nation of a story no longer 'newsworthy' because it already had dragged on for five months" (2013, 41). In the aftermath of the Santa Barbara disaster, Environmental Studies programs in colleges and universities began appearing across the country, with one of the first undergraduate programs introduced at the University of California, Santa Barbara.

DEEPWATER HORIZON

In 2010, the legacy of the Santa Barbara oil spill was overshadowed again by what became the largest marine oil spill in history. On April 20, a blowout on the British Petroleum-operated *Deepwater Horizon* platform in the Gulf of Mexico caused the spillage of over 130 million gallons of crude oil over 68,000 square miles and lasted for eighty-seven days.

Delia Sarah Byrnes

The Santa Barbara oil spill capped a decade of increased public attention to industrial pollution and its ecological and public health impacts. In 1962, biologist and conservationist Rachel Carson published her landmark study on pesticides, *Silent Spring*, while 1964 marked the passage of the Wilderness Act, codifying the protection of natural spaces and enshrining a national conservation ethic. In the years following the 1969 disaster, a slew of environmental initiatives and legislation were introduced, including the California Coastal Commission, the National Environmental Policy Act (1970), the Clean Water Act (1972), the Marine Mammal Protection Act (1972), and the Endangered Species Act (1973). Additionally, the US Environmental Protection Agency began formal operations in December 1970.

Today, tar balls from the Santa Barbara oil spill continue to wash up on beaches, and there remains a fraught relationship between the US oil industry and groups seeking expanded environmental protections. This dynamic was thrust into the national spotlight twenty years later when the *Exxon Valdez* oil tanker struck the Bligh Reef in coastal Alaska on March 24, 1989, spilling nearly 11 million gallons of crude oil in Prince William Sound. In January 2018, the Trump administration opened virtually all coastal waters to oil and gas drilling, including more than 1 billion acres in the Arctic and the eastern seaboard. Industrial estimates suggest that within the next decade, over 30 percent of global oil will come from offshore wells.

Delia Sarah Byrnes

See also: *Argo Merchant* Oil Spill; Clean Water Act; *Deepwater Horizon*; Earth Day; *Exxon Valdez* Oil Spill; Natural Resources Defense Council; Sierra Club; Summerland Oil Field; US Environmental Protection Agency

FURTHER READING

Clarke, K.C., and Jeffrey J. Hemphill. 2002. "The Santa Barbara Oil Spill: A Retrospective." *Yearbook of the Association of Pacific Coast Geographers*. Vol. 64. Pp. 157–62.

Easton, Robert. 1972. *Black Tide: The Santa Barbara Oil Spill and Its Consequences*. New York: Delacorte Press.

LeMenager, Stephanie. 2013. *Living Oil: Petroleum Culture in the American Century*. New York: Oxford University Press.

Snell, David. 1969. "Iridescent Gift of Death." *Life*. Vol. 66. No. 23. Pp. 22–7.

Spezio, Teresa Sabol. 2018. *Slick Policy: Environmental and Science Policy in the Aftermath of the Santa Barbara Oil Spill*. Pittsburgh, PA: University of Pittsburgh Press.

Wheeling, Kate, and Max Ufberg. 2017. "'The Ocean is Boiling': The Complete Oral History of the 1969 Santa Barbara Oil Spill." *Pacific Standard*. https://psmag.com/news/the-ocean-is-boiling-the-complete-oral-history-of-the-1969-santa-barbara-oil-spill (accessed February 6, 2020).

Scofield Mining Disaster

On May 1, 1900, a major mine disaster took place in the mines of Pleasant Valley Coal Company in Scofield, Utah. There were warning signs of danger in the mines, including a blast that occurred weeks earlier on March 22. In terms of its significance, the Scofield mine disaster is ranked as the fourth worst in US history, and the worst ever in Utah. The explosion took the lives of 200 men that fateful day.

The town of Scofield is located 19 miles from where the Rio Grande Western Railroad crossed Utah in an area known as Pleasant Valley. The railroad company surveyed the region for coal deposits to fuel their locomotives and discovered plentiful amounts of bituminous coal. A narrow-gauge railway was built through Spanish Fork Canyon and mines were established, with Scofield serving as the site of company offices, miners' homes, and shops, including stores owned by A.H. Earll, John E. Ingles, and S.A. Henrichsen. A history of the mine disaster also notes the company store which supplied the miners with tools and dry goods (Dilley 1900, 37). By 1900 the mining lands around Scofield featured five active mines, including the Pleasant Valley Coal Company's Winter Quarters Number Four mine, where the disaster occurred.

In the two decades prior to the disaster, Mormon Bishop David Williams served as superintendent of the mines. He documented several incidents, one in 1884 when the mine caught fire and another in 1892 when a blasting operation ignited a larger coal dust explosion (Dilley 1900, 25). Closer to the May 1 explosion, one of the company's nearby mines, Castle Gate, experienced an explosion of blasting powder ignited by an electrical spark (Powell 1992). Fortunately no miners were injured or killed in the incident, but since it occurred on March 22 it served as a kind of harbinger of what would transpire some forty days later. Nevertheless, the state mine inspector Gomer Thomas would testify at an inquest after the explosion that he inspected the Winter Quarters Number Four mine on March 8 and found it in "fair condition," noting that "ventilation was good and the mine was free from gas" (Dilley 1900, 54). In other words, the previous record of mine fires and explosions raised no particular concerns about the safety of the mine in the days leading up to the explosion, and Thomas could see no warning signs that the miners' lives could be in danger.

The town residents of Scofield heard an explosion on May 1 at 10:28 a.m., which many thought was a tribute in celebration of Dewey Day, a commemoration of Admiral Dewey's victory in the Philippines over the Spanish navy in the Spanish–American War two years earlier (Powell 1992). When area residents and the mine operators realized that the mine had been consumed by a massive explosion, they began rescue operations. Burned corpses were everywhere, scattered throughout the mine's passages. Bodies bore the marks of the blast's immense power, with those near the blast site said to be "badly mutilated" (Powell 1992). Other victims died from flying debris or being thrown hundreds of feet by the force of the explosion. Tragically, a large number of fatalities came from a group of miners from the

Number Two mine. They heard the explosion and began to evacuate by taking the shortest route to the surface, which happened to be through the Number Four mine. They came close enough to the affected area that they were overcome by a mixture of toxic gases lingering around after the explosion, which included carbon dioxide, carbon monoxide, and nitrogen. Miners refer to this post-explosion cloud of poisonous air as the "afterdamp" (Powell 1992).

Two particular groups of victims came to symbolize the magnitude of the tragedy that had been visited upon the Scofield community. Nearly twenty of the victims were young boys who moved coal cars around inside the mine and opened and closed passageway doors. Another agonizing loss was inflicted on the Louma family. Seven Louma brothers and three of their children left their native country Finland to work in Utah's coal mines. All were in the Winter Quarters mine when it exploded, and only one of the brothers survived. The family patriarch, Abe Louma, had come to the United States with his wife to join them three months before the disaster, only to have to retrieve the bodies of six sons and three grandsons and bury them in American soil. The toll was heavy on the Finnish immigrant community in Carbon County. Sixty-two of the 200 miners who died were recent immigrants from Finland. On the other hand, there were also remarkable stories of survival. John Wilson had been working near the opening of the mine and the force of the explosion expelled him 820 feet through the air down the incline of the canyon. He survived but suffered a crushed skull and a stomach impalement from a stick (Powell 1992).

As with other mine explosions, the site became a place of torment and agony as grief-stricken survivors waited for news of their loved ones, and ultimately claimed their remains for burial. The 200 dead miners left behind 107 widows and 268 fatherless children (Dilley 1900, 209). Mothers with young children suddenly found themselves destitute, though the company paid for coffins and funerals, provided full pay for the month of April, cancelled debts at the company store, and gave $500 to each of the victims' families. Donations poured into the community from around Utah, from towns in the Mountain West, and from many states in the eastern portion of the country. Large funeral services were held in Scofield, one in the Finnish Lutheran tradition for the Finnish victims, and another conducted by Mormon apostles for the local LDS miners who died in the explosion. One hundred and twenty-five were buried in one corner of the Scofield cemetery while others were interred in family plots or in their distant hometown cemeteries. Newspapers throughout the country reported on the explosion and its aftermath, which included inquests into the conditions of the mine and the safety protocols followed by company officials.

The question of responsibility for the explosion sprung up quickly and gained traction. The *San Francisco Chronicle* offered a characteristic statement demanding accountability: "the disaster comes under the head of those which could with ordinary care and rational regulations have been prevented. If so, some one in authority is criminally responsible for the catastrophe and should be held accountable for it" (quoted in Dilley 1900, 193). The *Park City Record* concurred: "We hope there will be a thorough investigation as to the cause, and that the blame, if there be any placed where it belongs. The truth should be known, and the responsibility, heavy as it is, should rest on the shoulders of the guilty ones, if guilty there be" (quoted in Dilley 1900, 181). Inspired by anti-immigrant, nativist sentiments, rumors circulated that the Finnish miners were secretly bringing in extra black powder to enable them to produce more coal for increased income. Superintendent of the Mines Thomas J. Parmley appeared to give those rumors some credibility (Powell 1992).

Other culprits were named. Inspector of the Mines Gomer Thomas indicated that the company might have done more to decrease the chances of a large explosion by taking certain precautions, like coal dust suppression. Blasting coal seams to loosen fragments for removal is dangerous, but the black powder detonations are typically controlled and rarely trigger larger explosions. These rare events occur when coal dust is allowed to accumulate on a mine's walls, floors, and ceilings. It acts as a multiplier when ignited by the smaller black powder detonation, causing a chain reaction that can envelop miles of coal mine tunnels. Thomas suggested that the company might have been negligent in allowing a build-up of coal dust, which could be addressed by wet dedusting, or spraying water on the mine's interior surfaces.

A few days after the explosion, local officials held an inquest regarding one of the victims, John Hunter, to determine his official cause of death. The jurors found that "John Hunter came to his death through an explosion in Number Four mine while in the employ of the Pleasant Valley Coal Company" (quoted in Dilley 1900, 54). They weren't prepared to point the finger at anyone in particular, but Inspector Thomas testified at the inquest and said, "In my estimation the disaster was caused by a heavy shot of giant powder or loose powder exploding. The giant powder went off, caught the dust, and exploded it, being in the end nothing but a dust explosion" (quoted in Dilley 1900, 54). In not so many words, Thomas opened the possibility that the company could be blamed for allowing dust conditions to deteriorate to the point where a minor explosion could become a major explosion. A blast of excess powder without the corresponding ignition of coal dust might kill a few miners standing nearby, whereas a blast of excess powder with the addition of a secondary, and much larger, coal dust explosion would kill nearly everyone working in the mine on that day.

In the company's defense, this was only faintly understood at the time of the Scofield disaster and there were no industry-wide standards or regulatory measures to help mine operators anticipate what is an unacceptable level of coal dust accumulation. Critics also pointed out that blasting could be scheduled during shift changes when there are fewer miners in harm's way, thus putting only a few men at risk of dying in the event of a major, large-scale explosion. All told, the Scofield mine explosion shocked the nation since it was the worst mining disaster in US history up to that point (PBS 2023). However, little was done to promote mine safety until after more disasters occurred, namely the series of mine catastrophes in 1907 that killed 362 miners in Monongah, West Virginia, 239 at Jacobs Creek, Pennsylvania, and 154 at Marianna, Pennsylvania. In that one year alone, 3,242 miners' lives were taken in coal mine accidents.

Those events brought public pressure and eventually government oversight to bear on the industry in future years. Meanwhile, coal mine operators carried on with business as usual. Pleasant Valley Coal Company pressed on to meet the terms of a lucrative contract with the US Navy and quickly filled all the positions vacated by the deceased miners. The mines were up and running again in a matter of months.

Patrice Natalie Delevante

See also: Centralia Mine Disaster; Cherry Mine Disaster; Coal; Dawson Mine Disaster; Farmington Mine Disaster; Krebs Mine Disaster; Monongah Mine Disaster; Upper Big Branch Mine Disaster; West Frankfort Mine Disaster; Weir, Paul

FURTHER READING

Dilley, James W. 1900. *History of the Scofield Mine Disaster*. Provo, UT: The Skelton Pub. Co.

Powell, Allan Kent. 1973. "Tragedy at Scofield." *Utah Historical Quarterly*. Vol. 41. Spring. Pp. 182–94.

Powell, Allan Kent. 1992. *Next Time We Strike: Labor in Utah's Coal Fields, 1900–1933*. Logan, UT: Utah State University Press.

Public Broadcast System (PBS). 2023. "Mining Disaster in Scofield." 1900s Labor. America 1900: A Year in the Life of America at the Dawn of the 20th Century. American Experience. https://www.pbs.org/wgbh/americanexperience/features/1900-labor/ (accessed October 2023).

Seaman, Elizabeth Cochran "Nellie Bly"

Though she is most widely known for her career in investigative journalism, Elizabeth Cochran "Nellie Bly" Seaman is also the American entrepreneur credited with developing and manufacturing a much-needed provision for the nation's petroleum industry. As head of the Iron Clad Manufacturing Company, she was already producing milk cans, enameled kitchenware, and stackable metal garbage cans, but while touring Europe in 1904 she was inspired to create a new product. She had observed how glycerin was being efficiently and safely transported in steel containers, and she set her mind to design similar steel containers specifically for the American oil trade. She immediately began working together with company superintendent Henry Wehrhahn, and they created a few unsuccessful prototypes before patenting the iconic 55-gallon metal barrel that is still used for a wide array of purposes today.

Described in its 1905 patent as being "simple and strong in construction and effective and durable in operation," this new barrel was unlike anything the industry had used before. When commercial oil wells first appeared in the United States, prospectors had used a variety of containers they had on hand to store and transport the oil, including whiskey and wine casks of varying sizes. However, the growing industry soon saw a need to establish a standardized measure by which to sell its commodity. In 1872, the Petroleum Producers Association adopted the 42-gallon barrel as the standard measurement for oil. Anything smaller would be less profitable, and anything bigger would be too heavy and unwieldy for a person to handle. At that time, these wooden barrels were handmade by skilled craftsmen called tight coopers, and they remained the primary means for the transportation of oil until 1902 when Standard Oil Company introduced a mass-produced steel version. Cask-like in shape just like its wooden precursor, the 42-gallon steel barrel had riveted seams, and it was leak-prone and expensive to make.

Iron Clad Manufacturing's barrel sported a straight-sided and cylindrical design that was leak resistant, and thanks to two metal hoops encircling the barrel, it was strong and rigid enough to hold 55 gallons of oil, 13 gallons more than was possible before. The metal hoops not only reinforced the barrel's sides and made it strong enough to hold a larger quantity of oil, they also made the barrel easier to roll and guide. There were two problems with the new invention, however. The first was that the standardized measurement for oil did not catch up to the new container and remained 42 gallons. The other was that underground pipeline networks were springing up all over the country, reducing the need for aboveground transportation containers. As time went on, the oil industry began to invest in large tanker ships, and the 55-gallon barrel was seldom needed for the transportation of oil. Declining sales and employee fraud lead the company to bankruptcy in 1911, effectively ending Seaman's career in manufacturing.

Elizabeth Cochran had already achieved great fame in the field of journalism prior to her marriage to Robert Seaman and her subsequent foray into metal barrel production. Born in Pennsylvania in 1864, Cochran had become a so-called "girl stunt reporter" and pioneer of investigative reporting. After her response to a column in the *Pittsburgh Dispatch* caught the attention of the newspaper's editor, Cochran was offered a job writing for the *Dispatch*, and as was customary at the time for female journalists, she assumed the pseudonym "Nellie Bly," the title character of a popular Stephen Foster song. As Nellie Bly, she argued for reform of divorce laws, exposed dangerous working conditions and meager pay for factory workers, and served as a foreign correspondent in Mexico where she was threatened with arrest for criticizing then-President Porfirio Diaz's government.

Hoping to break more barriers for women reporters, she accepted a job in New York with the *New York World*. In her first attempt at stunt journalism, she feigned insanity so that she would be committed to Blackwell's Island, New York's infamous insane asylum for the poor. She had so convinced the doctors there of her insanity that they only released her when the *New York World* intervened. During her ten days there, she witnessed atrocities that included physical and mental abuse as well as overcrowding and deteriorated facilities. Her report on her experiences at Blackwell's Island helped to bring about reforms, and the state invested more money in the care and treatment of those patients.

Her most famous stunt before emerging as a prominent figure in the energy industry, however, was her attempt to travel around the world in eighty days or less. In 1889, Bly set out on her journey, hoping to prove that Jules Verne's novel *Around the World in Eighty Days* was more fact than fiction. Further, she wanted to show that a female traveling the globe alone could manage just as well, if not better, than her male counterpart. Taking with her only the dress she wore, whatever undergarments and writing instruments she could fit into one satchel, £200 in English gold and Bank of England notes, and some "American gold and paper money to use at different ports as a test to see if American money was known outside of America," Bly successfully circumnavigated the world in just seventy-two days (Bly 2014, 149). With this stunt came great fame. She toured the nation giving lectures on her trip, wrote a book titled *Around the World in 72 Days* (1890), and went on to cover major stories like the Chicago Pullman strike in favor of workers' rights. After the closure of the Iron Clad Manufacturing, Seaman went back to journalism and covered many more timely issues and events, including the First World War from Europe.

Throughout her remarkable life, Elizabeth Cochran "Nellie Bly" Seaman impacted the world in positive ways. She championed workers' rights, pushed for mental healthcare reform, and openly criticized government corruption. She not only advocated for women's rights in theoretical written treatises, she also proved by her actions that a woman could travel the world alone, run a successful manufacturing business, and design a beneficial product for the male-dominated oil industry. Although it outlived its original purpose, Seaman's 55-gallon steel barrel did not disappear into obscurity. Instead, it has become the archetype in most people's minds when they think of a steel barrel, and it is a lasting legacy of Seaman's design, durability, and ingenuity.

Dana Nichols

See also: Densmore Oil Tank Car; Drake, Edwin Laurentine; Enbridge Pipeline System; ExxonMobil; Oil Tankers; Standard Oil Company

FURTHER READING

Bly, Nellie. 2014. *Around the World in Seventy-Two Days and Other Writings*. New York: Penguin.

Norwood, Arlisha, and Mariana Brandman. 2022. "Nellie Bly." National Women's History Museum.https://www.womenshistory.org/education-resources/biographies/nellie-bly-0 (accessed October 2023).

Wells, Bruce A. 2006. "Remarkable Nellie Bly's Oil Drum." The American Oil & Gas Historical Society. https://aoghs.org/transportation/nellie-bly-oil-drum (accessed October 2023).

Wehrhahn, Henry. 1905. "Metal Barrel." US Patent No. 808,327. December 26. https://patentimages.storage.googleapis.com/19/b1/f1/e368503d765075/US808327.pdf (accessed October 2023).

Seven Sisters Oil Companies

The "Seven Sisters" is a group of multinational oil companies that dominated the oil industry in the twentieth century and continues to exercise near-autonomous control over the global production of oil today. The seven major companies, half of which are American, consist of British Petroleum (originally the Anglo-Iranian Oil Company), Royal Dutch Shell (shortened to just Shell), Standard Oil Company of California (SoCal, later Chevron), Gulf Oil, Texaco, Standard Oil Company of New Jersey (Esso, later Exxon), and Standard Oil Company of New York (Socony, later Mobil). These seven multinational corporations established an "oligopoly" on every aspect of the oil industry from production to distribution as well as to the extraction, refining, and transport of oil around the world (Ammann 2009). In many instances, these companies exercised more power than governments and nations, a phenomenon that earned them a reputation as an oil "cartel" (Sampson 1991).

In the decades leading up to the creation of Organization of the Petroleum Exporting Countries (OPEC) in 1960—a system of cooperation between oil-producing nations that helped curb the oil monopoly established by the Seven Sisters—the oil industry did not adhere to "free-market principles" (Ammann 2009). These companies maintained a system of price-fixing and were seemingly immune to "the laws of supply and demand" or the "vagaries of the stock markets" (Sampson 1991, 6). These companies were not just dominant in the oil industry, but in all the subsidiary industries associated with the production of oil including petrochemicals, coal mining, nuclear power, plastics, fertilizers, and drugs (Sampson 1991). The history of these global giants is firmly enmeshed within some of the most dramatic and impactful moments in the twentieth century where a legacy of monopoly and corporate capitalism were accompanied by environmental destruction, human rights violations, labor exploitation, and often questionable and illicit financial practices.

However, the Seven Sisters did not rise to such an international status without the legacy and inheritance of John D. Rockefeller's Standard Oil monopoly in the nineteenth and early twentieth centuries. It was Rockefeller's brand of vertical integration in the oil industry that evolved into the "defining characteristic of the modern petroleum industry" (Pratt 2012, 146). The break-up of Standard Oil ironically granted more autonomy to each of the companies that would become offspring of Standard Oil and in turn, catalyzed their growth into multinational giants. (Sampson 1991). After the First World War, fuel for industry, cars, planes, and tanks propelled the oil industry into a provider for the most important resource: energy in the form of oil and gas.

The Sherman Antitrust cases, which formalized the dissolution of Rockefeller's Standard Oil, raised an important question about the power and status of multinational corporations. However, the overlapping nature of agreements that the Seven Sisters later cultivated made it difficult to substantiate evidence against them in crimes of price Pan-American Petroleum fixing and collusion. The Seven Sisters' nearly unfettered power was emphasized in the "era of corporate domination from 1912 to 1971" (Moran 1987, 580). Their control of the oil industry can be attributed to the diplomatic role ascribed to them by Western governments throughout the twentieth century, namely to provide a steady supply of oil. The multinationals were considered to be a "buffer" and a "thin lubricating film" between producers and consumers, a key diplomatic link (Sampson 1991, 14). However, the prioritization of oil by national governments and their symbiotic relationship with these oil companies resulted in the Seven Sisters acquiring a position that went above domestic and international law. A prime example of this was the overthrow of the democratically elected leader of Iran, Mohammed Mossadegh—a mission led by the CIA and known as *Operation Ajax*. The overthrow of Mossadegh secured access to oil reserves by implementing a committed, pro-Western dictator as the leader of Iran. The resulting Consortium Agreement of 1954, made possible by the overthrow of Mossadegh, granted the Seven Sisters a 50 percent share of the nationalized Iranian oil industry (Maugeri 2006; Pratt 2012).

This was made possible, however, in the immediate post-war years under the Truman administration. In the classified National Security Council document 138/1, oil was "[recognized] as a vital source of power" (Maugeri 2006, 70). It was a sort of Open Door policy that allowed Western governments, through the position and role of the Seven Sisters, to acquire cheap oil. The Seven Sisters did not always adhere to the agreement made with the Western governments. In 1947, evidence emerged that Chevron and Texaco had overcharged the US Navy on the price of oil at $1.23 per barrel. After the reports came out, the US Federal Trade Commission investigated the Seven Sisters oil companies and in 1951, released a report titled, "The International Petroleum Cartel." The report found that, as early as 1928, the international oil trade had been "artificially restrained and manipulated" by the multinational corporations. The report also discovered that the oil companies controlled "82% of the world crude reserves, 80% of world production, and 76% of world refining capacity" (Maugeri 2006, 72). With criminal indictment likely for all seven of the major oil companies, the production of Middle Eastern oil could have collapsed. On January 12, 1953, President Truman decided to pursue civil instead of criminal litigation (Maugeri 2006). It was this crucial moment that allowed for the overthrow of Mossadegh and the continued dominance of the Seven Sisters.

The creation of the OPEC in 1960 served as a bulwark against the unrestricted control that the Seven Sisters had on the global oil industry. Nationalizations in Venezuela, Saudi Arabia, Libya, and Iran alongside the direct cooperation between the national governments of oil-producing nations replaced the middleman position that the Seven Sisters occupied (Pratt 2012). Exxon, one of the first companies to feel the effects of the creation of OPEC, searched for alternative ways to acquire cheap oil. They expanded into other industries such as new geological technologies and eventually merged with Mobil to create the largest oil company since the break-up of Standard Oil. One of the new technologies, in cooperation with geophysicists, were computers capable of producing "underground mappings" (Pratt 2012, 150). The company continued to innovate the technology to harness the power of oil and other natural resources.

These new technologies, despite the oil companies' expressed intentions to decrease environmental impacts, did not outweigh oil dependence and the underlying issue resulting from increased consumption. In other words, the only safe consumption was to reduce consumption—an impossible demand for a world that increasingly relied on oil and gas as well as plastics. The creation of the US Environmental Protection Agency (EPA) and the Occupational Safety and Health Administration (OSHA) in 1970 forced companies like

Exxon and the rest of the sisters to adhere to new demands for environmental safety. Among these regulations was the removal of lead from gasoline (Pratt 2012). Exxon, the leader of the Seven Sisters in terms of assets and output, argued against these regulations, stating that it was "not backed by good science" (Pratt 2012, 151). In 1989 the *Exxon Valdez* oil spill in Southern Alaska made Exxon into the face of all that was bad and publicly vilified about the oil companies. A year later, a deadly refinery explosion took place near New York City. Compounded with the *Exxon Valdez* spill, the company was forced to make changes and implemented the Operations Integrity Management System which was then used by the rest of the major oil companies (Pratt 2012).

The history of the Seven Sisters oil companies is firmly enmeshed in the geopolitics of the twentieth century. The impact that the provision of energy in the form of oil and gas, as well as the helpful technologies and products associated with plastics and fertilizers is undoubtedly present in the modern world. However, the harmful effects of these industries on the natural environment continues to grow in scope and scale. Regardless of these controversies and uncertainties, the Seven Sisters continue to persist as multinational giants.

Thomas David Brown

See also: Consortium Agreement of 1954; *Exxon Valdez* Oil Spill; ExxonMobil; Gulf Oil Company; Mobil Oil Corporation; Organization of Petroleum Exporting Countries (OPEC); Red Line Agreement of 1928; Rockefeller, John D.; Standard Oil Company; Tarbell, Ida; Texaco

FURTHER READING

Ammann, Daniel. 2009. *The King of Oil: The Secret Lives of Marc Rich*. New York: St. Martin's Press.

Haller, Tobias, Annja Blöchlinger, Markus John, Esther Marthaler, and Sabine Ziegler, eds. 2007. *Fossil Fuels, Oil Companies, and Indigenous Peoples: Strategies of Multinational Oil Companies, States, and Ethnic Minorities, Impact on Environment, Livelihoods, and Cultural Change*. Zürich: Lit Verlag.

Marcel, Valérie, and John V. Mitchell. 2006. *Oil Titans: National Oil Companies in the Middle East*. Washington, DC: Brookings Institution Press.

Maugeri, Leonardo. 2006. *The Age of Oil: The Mythology, History, and Future of the World's Most Controversial Resource*. Westport, CT: Praeger Publishers.

Moran, Theodore H. 1987. "Managing an Oligopoly of Would-Be Sovereigns: The Dynamics of Joint Control and Self-Control in the International Oil Industry Past, Present, and Future." *International Organization*. Vol. 41. No. 4. Autumn. Pp. 575–607.

Nore, Petter, and Terisa Turner, eds. 1980. *Oil and Class Struggle*. London: Zed Press.

Pratt, Joseph A. 2012. "Exxon and the Control of Oil." *The Journal of American History*. Vol. 99. No. 1. Pp. 145–54.

Sampson, Anthony. 1991. *The Seven Sisters: The Great Oil Companies and the World They Shaped*. New York: Viking Press.

Vernon, Raymond, ed. 1976. *The Oil Crisis*. New York: W.W. Norton & Company.

Yergin, Daniel. 1991. *The Prize: The Epic Quest for Oil, Money and Power*. New York: Simon & Schuster.

Shippingport Atomic Power Station

"Peaceful power from atomic energy is no dream of the future. That capability, already proved, is here—now—today," declared US President Dwight D. Eisenhower on December 8, 1953 at UN General Assembly. Against nuclear proliferation he declared that "this greatest of destructive forces could be developed into a great constructive force for all mankind" (Eisenhower 1960). That speech marked the beginning of Eisenhower's "Atoms for Peace" initiative, which included a call for global powers to stockpile uranium for power-generation purposes rather than for weaponization. With his "Atoms for Peace" speech he launched the first major step in the development of the civilian nuclear energy industry which emphasized "atomic energy's ability to be used for good by powering our homes and businesses" (Marano 2014). It was an initial point of "the First Wave of Nuclear Power Deployment," which encouraged nuclear power-generating reactors to be used for producing peaceful power from atomic energy to meet the people's everyday needs (Golub 2014).

Soon after the speech, Eisenhower signed the Atomic Energy Act of 1954 which allowed private ownership of nuclear reactors, leasing of nuclear fuels for private use, industrial access to classified data needed for nuclear power development, and international development of nuclear power (Golub 2014). As a direct outcome of his speech, the Atomic Energy Commission (AEC) called for bids from private enterprises to build an atomic power station in the United States. The winning bid came from the Duquesne Light Company in western Pennsylvania (Beaver 1988). Chosen for the world's first atomic electric power plant devoted exclusively to peacetime uses, the area of Shippingport was located on the Ohio River, about 25 miles northwest of Pittsburgh. On September 9, 1954 the construction of the Shippingport Atomic Power Station was launched (NPP 2020).

To design the power plant, AEC turned to Admiral Hyman G. Rickover, Chairman of the Naval Reactors Branch of the AEC, who many considered capable of successfully adapting an experimental reactor design from naval research to Shippingport. His biographer, Theodore Rockwell, highlighted the urgency of the Shippingport plant: "Commercial nuclear power was now a reality, just four and a half years after the task was assigned to Admiral Rickover. Three years later, commercial plants based on this design began to spring up across the country, and shortly after that, around the whole world" (Rockwell 2002, 197).

The construction of the Shippingport Atomic Power Station came under the responsibility of the Westinghouse Electric Company, the Duquesne Light Company, and the Bettis Atomic Power Laboratory. In their collaboration they intended to combine their visions for the first US commercial nuclear power plant and to overcome the substantial challenges presented by the application of nuclear energy during peacetime (Shirk 2009). Joining their efforts and capabilities, they launched the Westinghouse-designed pressurized water reactor (PWR) which spurred innovation in an industry that continues to gain global importance and recognition today (Marano 2014).

The groundbreaking ceremony for Shippingport took place on September 6, 1954, and construction began the following March. The plant was ready to receive the reactor vessel from Combustion Engineering in October 1956. One year later, the fuel was loaded, and the reactor prepared for testing and approaching criticality, which is the point when a reactor achieves a sustained chain reaction (Shirk 2009). The reactor distributed electricity to the Duquesne Light Company grid, which served customers in the Pittsburgh area (Golub 2014). On the day of the Shippingport Atomic Power Station's dedication, May 26, 1958, President Eisenhower delivered a speech via electronic hook up to people who gathered at the Shippingport site (Sanina 2014).

From its initial conception through construction and during most of its operating life, the Shippingport Atomic Power Station was the responsibility of Admiral H. G. Rickover, the Bettis Atomic Power Laboratory, and the Knolls Atomic Power Laboratory. The two laboratories are civilian operations funded by government contracts to research and develop nuclear power technologies for the US Navy's fleet. For Rickover and these labs, Shippingport was much more than the demonstration of the engineering feasibility of using atomic power for commercial application; the station was also established to create standards for training personnel and to apply procedures for the safe operation of civilian nuclear plants (DOE 2017, 80).

Originally developed with the intention of advancing nuclear power technology, the Shippingport Atomic Power Station was used as both a power producer and test facility (NPP 2020). Built with flexibility in mind, the power plant was able to accommodate multiple

FIGURE 2: The Shippingport Atomic Power Station in Shippingport, Pennsylvania, was dedicated in 1958 and was the world's first atomic electric power plant devoted to peacetime use.

types of reactors. It was constructed during the mid-1950s to develop and demonstrate PWR technology and to generate electricity. The first reactor at Shippingport produced 68 MW of power from 1957 until 1964. It was then replaced with a second core that pushed electrical output to approximately 100 MW. Finally, a third "light water breeder" reactor was installed in 1977 (Beaver 1988).

When Shippingport reached criticality, it became the first large-scale central station nuclear power plant with a breeder reactor, which refers to a nuclear reactor that generates more fuel than it consumes. These reactors produce large amounts of heat, which requires an elaborate cooling system. Only fifteen years earlier, these technologies had been only laboratory curiosities. Now relying upon sophisticated components and instruments, the challenge was to demonstrate the feasibility of producing useful energy from the atom for civilian application and to advance civilian power reactor technology on a large scale. In this way, Shippingport was an example for the entire nuclear industry on the phases of construction, operation, manpower, and costs of a full-scale nuclear-energy plant for producing electric power (Fleger 1955, 892).

Commercial nuclear power plants were designed to have a forty-year life span, and then decommissioned and demolished. At the end of their useful lives, the sites of nuclear power stations must be cleaned up or decontaminated (Lochbaum 2013). In October 1982, Shippingport was shut down after completion of the breeder demonstration program, and had to be decommissioned (DOE 2017). Bettis Atomic Power Laboratory ceased having any direct role in the plant when DOE accepted a competitive bid from General Electric (GE) to dismantle the facility and clean up the site. General Electric's original estimate for the cleanup was $79 million, but the final tally amounted to $98.6 million (Shirk 2009). The last of the nuclear fuel was removed from the plant on September 6, 1984, and Naval Reactors—part of the National Nuclear Security Administration—formally turned the plant over to DOE (Miller 1980). After the removal of all fuel elements, the pressure vessel was encased in an even larger steel containment vessel and removed to Hanford, Washington, and buried in a 40-foot deep trench (Shirk 2009). The deconstruction started in 1985 with the removal of the turbine and the breeder reactor auxiliary control room, which contained no radioactive contamination. This was followed by removal of more than 500 cubic yards of asbestos insulation from the piping. This was placed in polyethylene bags and transported to Hanford for disposal. Approximately 450,000 gallons of radioactive liquid waste was treated using the plant's liquid filtration system and then released into the Ohio River. Residues from the ion exchangers and filter cartridges were sealed in 55-gallon drums for removal from the site. Removal of the 56,000 linear feet of contaminated piping began in 1986 by cutting the pipes apart and shipping them overland to Hanford.

The 150-ton reactor vessel, which contained 99 percent of the radioactive contamination, was first encased in 3 inches of concrete and then sealed inside a 1-inch-thick steel casing. Additional radioactive components from the plant were embedded in concrete in the interior of the pressure vessel that was removed from the breeder pit on December 14, 1988, and placed on the *Paul Bunyan*, a barge on the Ohio River. On February 28, 1989, the *Paul Bunyan* began its voyage down the Mississippi River that eventually took it through the Panama Canal and up the Pacific Coast to Benton, Washington. After ascending the Columbia River, the material was transported overland to Hanford and buried in a forty-foot trench where radiation levels were projected to return to the normal background range within about fifty years. The remaining structures at Shippingport were demolished to a depth of 3 feet below grade level and thousands of cubic yards of additional concrete were removed. The site was graded, seeded for grass, and the land returned to Duquesne Light for unrestricted use. The cost of decommissioning the plant amounted to 12 percent of the original cost of construction, providing for the first time some real world experience for projecting decommissioning costs for future nuclear plants (Shirk 2009). After dissembling the reactor, the plant's 7-acre site on the south bank of the Ohio River was restored to a grassy knoll (Gruson 1986).

The plant's disassembly and its decommission were successful but less glorious due to environmental concerns publicized by University of Pittsburgh Professor Ernest Sternglass, who accused Shippingport executives of covering up harmful radiation levels. He discovered this in data gathered by Nuclear Utilities Services Corporation, which went unreported to government officials. Sternglass' accusations galvanized anti-nuclear power sentiment in Shippingport and elsewhere. The community and environmental groups called for a moratorium on nuclear power plants in Pennsylvania and the United States. Due to insufficient evidence the case was dismissed and the investigation closed. But in spite of the result, Sternglass' account of the scandal makes a riveting read (Sanina 2014).

Nevertheless, from 1984 to 1989, Shippingport again made history as the first nuclear plant to be decommissioned and dismantled. As a result of the successful decommissioning strategy, important precedents were set in decontamination technology and nuclear waste handling techniques. The old Shippingport site hosts a different power plant, the Beaver Valley Nuclear Generating Station, which has two Westinghouse pressurized water reactors. Beaver Valley Power Station Unit No. 1 began producing electricity in 1976 and Unit No. 2 in 1987. In US energy history, the Shippingport Atomic Power Station was the world's first full-scale atomic electric power plant devoted exclusively to peacetime uses. It operated from 1958 to 1982, generating 7.4 billion kilowatt-hours of energy in those twenty-four years. Shippingport fully accomplished the goals set forth by President Eisenhower in his Atoms for Peace speech and set the stage for the rise of commercial nuclear power in the modern era.

Inna Sukhenko

See also: Atomic Energy Acts; Clean Power Plan of 2015; Idaho National Laboratory; Nuclear Power; Nuclear Regulatory Commission; Nuclear Waste Policy Act of 1982; Project Gasbuggy; Three Mile Island Accident; Yucca Mountain Nuclear Waste Repository

FURTHER READING

Beaver, William. 1988. "Nuclear Power Goes On-Line: A History of Shippingport." *History and Technology*. Vol. 6. NoNo. 4. Pp. 257–73.

Craddock, Jack. 2016. "The Shippingport Atomic Power Station." In *Introduction to Nuclear Energy*. Stanford University. Winter 2016. http://large.stanford.edu/courses/2016/ph241/craddock1/ (accessed April 8, 2020).

Davis, Will. 2017. "Shippingport Atomic Power Station: Five Fast Facts." Nuclear Newswire. American Nuclear Society. December 2. http://ansnuclearcafe.org/2017/12/02/shippingport-atomic-power-station-five-fast-facts/#sthash.fPippCnH.dpbs (accessed April 77, 2020).

Eisenhower, Dwight D. 1960. "Address before the General Assembly of the United Nations on Peaceful Uses of Atomic Energy." *Public Papers of the Presidents of the United States,* Dwight D. Eisenhower, *1953*. Pp.813–23. Washington, DC: US Government Printing Office. https://www.iaea.org/about/history/atoms-for-peace-speech (accessed March 20, 2020).

Department of Energy (DOE). 2017. *Essential History of the Shippingport Atomic Power Station: 1957: First Large-Scale Nuclear Power Plant in America, Work of Admiral Rickover, Pressurized Water Reactor, Historic American Engineering*. N.p.: Progressive Management. https://books.apple.com/us/book/essential-history-shippingport-atomic-power-station/id1225768730 (accessed April 3, 2020).

Fleger, Philip A. 1955. "The Shippingport Atomic Power Plant." *Electrical Engineering*. Vol. 74. No. 10. October. Pp. 892–4.

Fred, Pearce. 2018. "The 60-Year Downfall of Nuclear Power in the U.S. Has Left a Huge Mess." *The Atlantic*. May 28. https://www.theatlantic.com/science/archive/2018/05/the-60-year-downfall-of-nuclear-power-in-the-us-has-left-a-huge-mess/560945/ (accessed March 25, 2020).

Golub, Sal. 2014. "Nuclear Energy: Past, Present and Future." *NRC Quarterly*. September 24. Office of Nuclear Energy. US Department of Energy. Purdue University. October 16. https://www.purdue.edu/discoverypark/energy/assets/pdfs/pdf/Golub,%20Sal_DLS%20Series.pdf (accessed March 31, 2020).

Gruson, Lindsey. 1986. "Nuclear Power Plant Dismantled." *The New York Times*. November 25. https://www.nytimes.com/1986/11/25/science/nuclear-power-plant-dismantled.html (accessed March 30, 2020).

Lochbaum, Dave. 2013. "Nuclear Plant Decommissioning." Bulletin of the Atomic Scientists. July 29. https://thebulletin.org/2013/07/nuclear-plant-decommissioning/ (accessed March 31, 2020).

Marano, Mark. 2014. "60th Anniversary of Shippingport Groundbreaking." Westinghouse. Nuclear. https://www.westinghousenuclear.com/about/news/blog/view/60th-anniversary-of-shippingport-groundbreaking (accessed March 19, 2020).

Miller R.L., and J.L. Landon. 1980. "Planning for Decommissioning of the Shippingport Atomic Power Station." In *Decontamination and Decommissioning of Nuclear Facilities*. Ed. M.M. Osterhout. Pp. 401–10. Boston, MA: Springer.

Nuclear Powers Pennsylvania (NPP). 2020. "Pennsylvania Has a Rich Nuclear Energy History." https://nuclearpowerspennsylvania.com/issue/history/ (accessed March 31, 2020).

Rockwell, Theodore. 2002. *The Rickover Effect: How One Man Made a Difference*. Lincoln, NE: iUniverse.

Sanina, Milla. 2014. "Shippingport Atomic Power Station." *Pittsburgh Post-Gazette*. June 2." https://newsinteractive.post-gazette.com/thedigs/2014/06/02/shippingport-atomic-power-station/ (accessed March 19, 2020).

Shippingport Atomic Power Station. 1957. *Atomic Energy Commission. Science*. https://www.sciencesource.com/CS.aspx?VP3=SearchResult&ITEMID=SS2402881&RW=1536&RH=754 (accessed March 20, 2020).

Shirk, Willis L. Jr. 2009. "'Atoms for Peace' in Pennsylvania." *Pennsylvania Heritage Magazine*. Vol. 35. No. 2. Spring.

Shuman, Frank

Solar energy has deep roots in US history. One of its early pioneers, Philadelphia's Frank Shuman (1862–1918), experimented with solar power in the late nineteenth century and developed a unique solar-powered steam engine. He built on this experience and in 1913 constructed a large thermal solar farm that powered water pumps to irrigate cotton fields near Egypt's Nile River. Along the way, Shuman earned a reputation as a prolific inventor with over sixty patents, and as a visionary for projecting an energy future based on renewables after the depletion of fossil fuel resources. In his view, the Nile project "proved that after our stores of oil and coal are exhausted the human race can receive unlimited power from the rays of the sun" ("American" 1916). It is doubtful that fossil fuels will disappear anytime soon, but Shuman anticipated correctly that solar energy would become more desirable as an alternative source of energy in the twenty-first century.

Shuman was born in Brooklyn during the US Civil War. His family moved to Charlottesville, Virginia because his father, who served in the Union Army, received a civil service appointment to aid in the post-war occupation. Shuman attended a local school for three years but largely educated himself prior to accepting a job at the age of eighteen as a chemist for the Victor G. Bloede Company in Parkersburg, West Virginia (Kryza 2003, 4). The company specialized in powdered dyes made from coal known as aniline, used in staining wood products. Shuman became interested in the work of his uncle Francis Shuman's Tacony Iron and Metal Company, located in the Philadelphia vicinity, which entailed the manufacture of iron members for building construction. His uncle earned a contract to supply iron plates to support the tower for the 28-ton, 37-foot bronze statue of William Penn to be placed atop the Philadelphia City Hall. Tacony Iron was asked to prepare the plates with a protective coating that didn't require constant repainting. Frank became involved with his uncle in experimenting with various methods of electroplating with copper and aluminum. With the help of a New York engineer experienced in this process, they worked out a method to encase the iron plates with aluminum atop a copper layer, which provided a perfectly weatherproofed surface (Kryza 2003, 6). This experience inspired Shuman to leave his other job and work for his uncle.

Shuman took on another challenge at Tacony Iron and Metal. New institutional buildings in Philadelphia, Baltimore, Washington DC, and other cities were designed by architects to feature cavernous interior spaces filled with natural light from large windows set in their ceilings. These skylights, sealed with plate glass, were exposed to weather, including hailstorms, heavy snowfall, and incessant spring rains. Occasional skylight failures, including injuries, begged for a solution. Shuman experimented with an industrial process of fitting thin wiring into molten glass, which gave the finished product a higher degree of break resistance while minimizing shatter effects in the case of rupture. Shuman patented his wire glass, found a ready market for the product, and identified investors willing to support him. In 1892, they formed the American Wire Glass Manufacturing Company in Tacony, and profits from the business put Shuman in the echelon of other industrial moguls of the Gilded Age. With his newfound wealth, Shuman built a home and laboratory on a 5-acre compound in Tacony with homes for other family members and began working on projects related to solar energy and steam power.

In the mid-nineteenth century, European and American scientists and engineers became fascinated with solar energy, partly as a result of the work of French mathematician Augustin Mouchout, who recovered ancient writings about solar power and in the 1860s and 1870s developed solar cooking devices, solar water pumps, and even a crude solar steam engine (Butti 1980, 64–9). His work inspired Swedish immigrant John Ericsson, known as the designer of the Civil War ironclad *The Monitor*, to build his own version of Mouchout's solar steam engine in 1870, fueled by heat from "a series of parabolic, trough-shaped solar reflectors" (Butti 1980, 77). He continued refining solar steam engines for use in pumping water and devised a workable design for sale in 1884, but which never came to market. Another English-born American, Aubrey Eneas worked on solar steam engines in the 1880s and 1890s, and his Boston-based Solar Motor Company marketed a machine along the lines of Ericsson's with an improved reflector to focus the sun's rays. By 1900, at least twenty-two patents had been filed for solar motors, and these developments received attention in journals like *Nature* and other popular scientific and technological magazines, which Shuman studied (Butti 1980, 81).

Shuman's work on solar-powered steam engines began on his Tacony property in the mid-1890s. He read about the work of another solar power researcher, Reginald Fessenden, who produced boiling water and steam pressure without the use of lenses or mirrors as thermal collectors (Kryza 2003, 9). Shuman utilized a basic "hot box" design common to solar experiments of the period, which were essentially small wooden boxes encased in glass and containing small boilers for liquids. Instead of water he used ether because of its lower boiling temperature, and then conveyed the steam to a toy steam engine borrowed from his youngest son John (Kryza 2003, 9). The device worked, and Shuman scaled up his project with hot boxes covering an area 60 by 18 feet, connected together with pipes running to a 4-horsepower steam engine attached to a water pump. He arranged for a public demonstration in 1907, the first of many, by inviting important people in Tacony and Philadelphia, even passing around handbills advertising the event as an "exhibition run of the first practical solar engine" (Butti 1980, 102).

The event achieved Shuman's objective, which was to promote his idea and attract investors. He believed the system would be a perfect fit for users closer to the equator with more days of sunshine than Philadelphia. He imagined his system "powering the nitrate industry in the deserts of Chile and the borax industry in California's Death Valley, and irrigating arid lands in the Australian Interior, Eastern India and Ceylon, and the American Southwest" (Butti 1980, 103). Shuman also considered Egypt, then under British rule, because he thought he could sell British interests on the economics of switching out coal for solar energy in their colonial operations and knew that Britain had plenty of financiers looking for the next big industrial technology that promised huge investment returns. A group of British businessmen agreed to fund his venture, and together they formed the Sun Power Company. To ensure the economic viability of his system at an industrial scale, Shuman constructed an even larger version of the machine in 1910–11 that covered a .5-acre of his property.

This expanded power plant contained a number of key improvements on the 1907 project. Inside the solar energy collectors—the hot boxes—Shuman swapped out pipes for flat copper tin plates. These tins, fixed in layered pairs, spread to the edges of their boxes and held water between the two layers. The larger surface area of the plates and thinness of the space between them boiled the water more quickly than pipes. Shuman provided better insulation for the boxes, 572 in total, and arranged them in rows with reflective glass panels placed at 120-degree angles on upper and lower edges. They were suspended 2.5 feet above ground on A-frames, which enabled them to angle perpendicular to the noonday sun and were repositioned on a regular schedule to track the perpetual changes of the sun's altitude. Suman also improved the steam engine, which had to work at relatively low temperatures and low pressure, by enlarging the cylinders and creating within them a partial vacuum, thus increasing the engine's heat and pressure values (Kryza 2003, 20). This device, described in Shuman's patent application as "a new type of low-pressure, reciprocating steam engine of great steam economy" pumped 3,000 gallons of water per minute up to 33 feet high. Shuman's British backers sent several experts to evaluate Shuman's work, A.S.E. Ackerman, Secretary of the Society of Engineers, and Charles V. Boys, a well-known British physicist.

Boys recommended some modifications, namely replacing the reflective glass panels with parabolic, trough-shaped reflectors to maximize the amount of sunlight on the hot boxes. With these tweaks, Shuman and his technicians steamed to Egypt in 1912 and arrived at Maadi, a small agricultural village about 15 miles up the Nile River from Cairo. At this location they built a solar array composed of five rows of hot boxes and parabolic reflectors each running 204 feet long, spaced at 25 feet apart, mounted on steel framing on concrete foundations. It was the largest solar array ever built. The reflector design incorporated a thermostat that triggered a tracking mechanism which angled the reflectors with the movement of the sun. Shuman's boiler consisted of a 3.5-inch zinc pipe running along the rows inside a 15-inch trough, which conveyed steam to the engine and water pump. A test of the plant in late 1912 melted the zinc pipe, which Shuman exchanged for cast iron. Finally, in July 1913, Shuman finished his work and invited dignitaries to an official opening. The system worked perfectly, pumping 6,000 gallons of Nile River water a minute to the cotton fields nearby. The additional quantity and intensity of sunlight, coupled with the parabolic reflectors, enabled the system to collect 40 percent of available solar energy, which far surpassed the performance of his Tacony models (Butti 1980, 109). Although the initial cost of the plant was double that of a coal-fired plant, it promised an annual cost savings of $2,000 on fuel. Shuman proved that solar energy could be commercially viable in providing mechanical power.

Shuman's Egyptian solar farm and steam-powered irrigation system received international news coverage, and Shuman began planning for the system to be installed in British Sudan and German South West Africa in present-day Namibia. The *New York Times* sent a reporter to Maadi and provided a description of the system, as well as Shuman's comments about solar energy's future. Shuman said, "We have proved the commercial profit of sun power in the tropics and have more particularly proved that after our stores of oil and coal are exhausted the human race can receive unlimited power from the rays of the sun" ("American" 1916). An article in the *Electrical Experimenter* in 1916 described Shuman's plant in detail and marveled at its efficiency. Inspired by what he saw, the author looked to a future without coal, oil, or natural gas: "Some day we may be able to derive all necessary light and power, for our homes at least, by means of a solar-electric plant located on the roof" ("The Utilization" 1916, 663). This dream failed to materialize because of the outbreak of the First World War, as well as the post-war success of fossil fuel companies in developing Middle Eastern oil and gas resources and controlling US and European energy markets. When the war began, Shuman returned to the United States, and passed away before the war ended in 1918.

Shuman based his career on the idea that "solar engines will ultimately furnish indirectly most of the mechanical power of the world" (Shuman 1907, 4). Furthermore, he believed that solar power, after its initial period of gestation and infancy, would one day mature into a plentiful and efficient source of renewable energy: "Sun power must go through the same long and gradual course of development that has brought other forms of mechanical power to the present high plane of efficiency, but the principle will remain fundamentally correct" (Shuman 1911). In some ways Shuman was prophetic. Research and development in the late twentieth century focused on the sun's light, rather than its thermal properties, which originally fascinated Shuman. Modern photovoltaic solar panels convert the sun's light into energy and became a promising technology for diversifying domestic energy sources amid concerns over US dependence on imported oil and natural gas and the environmental effects of fossil fuels.

Jeffrey B. Webb

See also: Renewable Energy; Public Utility Regulatory Policies Act of 1978; Solar Power; Steam Power; US Green Building Council

FURTHER READING

"American Inventor Uses Egypt's Sun for Power." 1916. *The New York Times Magazine*. July 2. https://timesmachine.nytimes.com/timesmachine/1916/07/02/104680095.html? (accessed October 2023).

Butti, Ken, and John Perlin. 1980. *A Golden Thread: 2500 Years of Solar Architecture and Technology*. Palo Alto, CA: Cheshire Books.

Kryza, Frank. 2003. *The Power of Light: The Epic Story of Man's Quest to Harness the Sun*. New York: McGraw Hill.

Shuman, Frank. 1907. *The Direct Acting Solar Engine: The Prime Mover of the Immediate Future*. Philadelphia: Review Publishing and Printing Company.

Shuman, Frank. 1911. "Power from Sunshine: A Pioneer Solar Power Plant." *Scientific American*. September 30. https://www.scientificamerican.com/article/power-from-sunshine/ (accessed October 2023).

"The Utilization of the Sun's Energy." 1916. *The Electrical Experimenter*. Vol. 3. No 11. Pp. 605–6, 662–3.

Sierra Club

The Sierra Club's traditional hallmarks of conservation and recreation have always been tightly woven with issues of energy and access. Originally a regional organization focused on their namesake Sierra Nevada mountain range that by necessity was involved with federal policy, the Sierra Club now has a large national presence. With more than 3 million members today, the Sierra Club has evolved over more than a century, making compromises and shifts in their stances on various energy projects from early hydroelectric dams to coal and gas extraction in more recent years. As one of the earliest environmental organizations, and one which has driven popular opinion through a range of rhetorical approaches, the Sierra Club has a unique profile and legacy in American society.

The Sierra Club was founded on May 28, 1892. A group of professionals from the San Francisco Bay area came together with a goal of enlarging Yosemite National Park as well as to articulate scientific and recreational approaches for the state of California. Two key figures present for the creation of the Sierra Club—men who lobbied for Yosemite—were John Muir (1838–1914) and his editor Robert Underwood Johnson (1853–1937). Fresh off the success of the 1890 founding of Yosemite, the group leaned on Muir's charismatic writing and unalloyed exuberance for mountaineering and science to increase their reach both locally and nationally. *Sierra Club Bulletin* was the organization's journal, while Muir was also publishing his writing in *The Atlantic* by 1897. In addition, the group organized excursions to Yosemite's Tuolumne Meadows starting in 1901, cannily understanding that as more people experienced the place, more people would support preserving it.

Despite an auspicious start, the challenge of preserving the vast federal lands in the West cannot be understated. The Sierra Club organized against the damming of the Hetch Hetchy Valley, in close proximity to the Yosemite Valley. The preservationists were challenging the utilitarian viewpoint, exemplified by a man Muir had previously been able to work with, Gifford Pinchot (1865–1946). Pinchot was the first chief of the US Forest Service and believed that land can be productively used for multiple purposes. Ultimately, the valley was dammed after Congress approved the project in 1913.

Such a conflict between preservation and what is often called "wise use" remained, although the Sierra Club enjoyed many successes in the first half of the twentieth century. Indeed, their work in popularizing national parks and making public lands accessible helped build hiking trails and make the case for building highways to those new recreation areas. The Sierra Club also disseminated information and sometimes pioneered new camping and climbing equipment, publishing books about places and techniques. Their ecological goals at times were eroded by their own success, and so groups such as the Wilderness Society were founded which took harder lines in favor of more strict preservationist ideals.

In 1952, David Brower (1912–2000) was named the first executive director in the Sierra Club's history. His style of leadership, coupled with a flurry of proposed hydroelectric dams in western states, pushed the Sierra Club to adopt various high-profile lobbying tactics. After a series of full-page newspaper ads against a dam at Echo Park in Colorado, the Sierra Club was threatened by the loss of their tax-exempt status. Ultimately, while the proposed Echo Park dam was defeated in 1956, a dam was built at Glen Canyon in Arizona. Brower's work included filmmaking and collaborations with photographers such as Eliot Porter (1901–90). One example of the Sierra Club's publications from this period is the coffee-table book *In Wildness Is the Preservation of the World* (1962), which sold more than 1 million copies.

The battles Brower and the Sierra Club fought in the 1950s continued in the 1960s, with a proposal to flood part of the Grand Canyon. Countering the argument that reservoirs would enhance access to remote canyons, one famous 1966 advertisement asked, "Should we also flood the Sistine Chapel so tourists can get nearer the ceiling?" Tens of thousands of letters were generated by members of the public who were influenced by the Sierra Club's campaign, and the membership rolls grew nearly as fast. Ultimately, this dam proposal was defeated, and the IRS revoked the Sierra Club's tax-exempt status. Brower's leadership was effective, but too combative for many board members, and so he resigned as executive director in 1969, just one year before the first Earth Day.

In the late 1960s and throughout the 1970s, the Sierra Club diversified its causes as its profile rapidly expanded. Sometimes the board was criticized for not publicly opposing projects, and not without reason. One controversial example was the development of the Diablo Canyon nuclear power plant in California by Pacific Gas & Electric (PG&E), the site of which was tacitly accepted by the Sierra Club when the Nipomo sand dunes where turned over by PG&E to California to become a state park.

Beyond these sorts of pragmatic choices that the Sierra Club has made periodically, the organization has been criticized on issues of equity and inclusion in more recent years, focusing on some of John Muir's earliest writings on Indigenous inhabitants of the Sierra Nevada Mountains. Others have critiqued 1970s-era statements about population control. The Sierra Club has shown some responsiveness to these concerns. For example, the group revised its historical materials and adopted an "Equitable and Just National Climate Platform" in 2019. In 2020, Executive Director Michael Brune acknowledged the harm that their at-times elite and exclusionary history and rhetoric has caused.

The Sierra Club's larger campaigns have continued to regularly focus on energy policy, with the organization's goals staying just ahead of where the public opinion has been. For example, the 2010 Beyond Coal campaign has been eclipsed by the Ready for 100 campaign, which aims to not only retire coal plants, but to rely solely on renewable energy rather than "bridge" fossil fuels such as natural gas.

With a history of evolving and staying just ahead of public opinion, the Sierra Club remains one of the largest and most influential environmental organizations in the United States. The Sierra Club continues to shape debates about land use and preservation in general, and energy and climate policy in particular. They continue to operate important publishing venues, such as *Sierra* magazine. Recent shifts to make the organization more responsive to issues of equity and the democratic process suggest that the Sierra Club is ensuring its relevance for years to come.

Kyhl Lyndgaard

See also: *An Inconvenient Truth*; California Electric Light Company; Climate Change; Earth Day; Natural Resources Defense Council; Renewable Energy; Union of Concerned Scientists; US Green Building Council

FURTHER READING

Cohen, Michael P. 1988. *The History of the Sierra Club, 1892–1970*. San Francisco, CA: Sierra Club Books.

Hays, Samuel P. 2000. *A History of Environmental Politics since 1945*. Pittsburgh, PA: University of Pittsburgh Press.

Turner, Tom. 1991. *Sierra Club: 100 Years of Protecting Nature*. New York: H. N. Abrams.

Wyss, Robert. 2016. *The Man Who Built the Sierra Club: A Life of David Brower*. New York: Columbia University Press.

Sinclair, Upton

Baltimore-born Upton Beall Sinclair Jr. (1878–1968) was an American writer, muckraker, political activist, and the 1934 Democratic Party nominee for governor of California. He wrote nearly a hundred books, plays, and nonfiction articles, and was well known and popular in the first half of the twentieth century. He won the Pulitzer Prize for Fiction in 1943. He was a novelist, but more importantly a persistent and successful journalist-crusader. Virtually all his books are novelized exposés and pleas for various social reforms. When mainstream publishers boycotted his work and refused publication, Sinclair published himself and often lost money. His books have been translated into forty-seven languages with great success in the marketplace.

The son of an itinerant liquor salesman, Sinclair wrote dime novels, jokes, and many magazine articles in boys' weekly and cheap pulp fiction magazines to pay for his tuition at the City College of New York. He wrote poetry and four unsuccessful novels before gaining employment at a socialist newspaper (Arthur 2006).

In 1906, Sinclair suddenly became very famous for his classic, powerful, muckraking novel, *The Jungle*, which exposed the very poor labor and sanitary conditions in the US meatpacking industry. The book was based on Sinclair's seven-week research in the meatpacking plants of the Chicago stockyards for the socialist newspaper *Appeal to Reason*. Its narrative fiction portrays the poverty of the working class, harsh and unhealthy living conditions, and the dire lack of needed social and economic supports. His fellow author Jack London (1876–1916) called the book "the *Uncle Tom's Cabin* of wage slavery." Five publishers rejected the work as too shocking, but the book sold 100,000 copies the first year and caused an indignant public uproar that helped—along with President Theodore Roosevelt's vigorous support—to pass the 1906 Pure Food and Drug Act and the Meat Inspection Act (Applegate 2008).

Sinclair published *The Brass Check* (1919), a muckraking investigation of the poor state of American journalism, such as the exaggerations and lies of yellow journalism and the limitations of a commercially supported "free press." The book primarily examines newspapers and the Associated Press wire service. In 1923, the first code of ethics for journalists was created. The FBI had a report on *The Brass Check* in its files by 1923. Critics at the time, and even more recently, value *The Brass Check*'s media analysis, and it has been called "muckraking at its best" and "astonishingly prescient in its critique of the coziness of big media and other corporate interests" (Klein 2006). However, when it was published most newspapers refused to review it and any reviews were hostile. *The New York Times* refused to even publish an advertisement for the book and *Time* magazine called him "a man with every gift except humor and silence" (Hicks 1943; Klein 2006).

The Brass Check was the second of the six "Dead Hand" books that Sinclair published about the failures of major American institutions to serve the public. The series includes *The*

Profits of Religion (religion), *The Goose-step* (higher education), *The Goslings* (elementary and high school education), *Mammonart* (art), and *Money Writes!* (literature).

Many of Sinclair's novels really were primarily historical works. *King Coal* (1917), *The Coal War* (published posthumously), *Oil!* (1927), and *The Flivver King: A Story of Ford-America* (1937) describe the actual working conditions of miners and workers of the coal, oil, and auto industries. For example, *The Flivver King* describes the rise of Henry Ford, his treatment of workers, and his anti-Semitic decline as *The Dearborn Independent*'s publisher.

Sinclair was an outspoken socialist and ran unsuccessfully for Congress as a nominee from the Socialist Party. He was also the Democratic Party candidate for governor of California during the Great Depression, running under the banner of the "End Poverty in California" campaign, but was defeated in the 1934 election.

Sinclair's novel *King Coal* (1917) describes the poor working conditions in the coal mining industry in the western US in the 1910s from the perspective of protagonist Hal Warner. As in his earlier works, Sinclair uses the novel to express his socialist viewpoint and details the impact of workplace conditions on the workers. Sinclair worked for over two years on *King Coal*, the first half of his massive two-episode series on the 1913–14 Colorado coal strikes. For research, he reviewed many pages of congressional committee testimony and visited Colorado three times (Arthur 2006).

Sinclair wrote *King Coal* immediately after the April 20, 1914 Ludlow massacre, where an anti-striker militia killed twenty-one miners, their wives, and children, during the Colorado Coalfield War. The workers confronted the Colorado National Guard and company security guards hired by the Colorado Fuel and Iron Company (CFI). John D. Rockefeller Jr., a CFI part-owner, was blamed for having arranged the massacre. The strike was organized by the United Mine Workers of America against poor labor conditions in the Colorado mines, and carried out by miners working for the Rocky Mountain Fuel Company and Victor-American Fuel Company.

In retaliation for the Ludlow massacre, bands of armed miners attacked dozens of anti-union establishments, destroying property and engaging in several skirmishes with the Colorado National Guard along a 225-mile front from Trinidad to Louisville. From the strike's beginning in September 1913 to intervention by federal soldiers under President Woodrow Wilson's orders on April 29, 1914, an estimated 69–199 people were killed. The coalfield war was called by historian Thomas G. Andrews the "deadliest strike in the history of the United States" (Andrews 2010).

The plot of *King Coal* is simple. Hal Warner runs away from home and becomes "Joe Smith." He gets a job in a coal mine operated by the General Fuel Company, or GFC. In their mines he makes friends with many of the workers and witnesses their exploitation at the hands of their bosses. Warner/Smith grows close to Mary Burke, a fighter for the workers' rights who has a drunken father. After taking up the workers' cause, he announces he will appeal to the bosses to become a check weigh man to measure the true amount of coal, but the GFC appoints a corrupt company check weigh man. Hal is imprisoned by the marshal, who was accused by Hal of being corrupt and unfair to the miners (Arthur 2006).

After a mine explosion, Hal contacts Percy Harrigan, an old friend whose father owns the GFC. The workers organize a strike and collectively demand their rights. Hal appeals to the United Mine Workers to back the strike, but they refuse because they think the strike is ill-timed and a waste of union resources. Hal is told to wait years for the other unions to strike, for only by pooling their efforts could the workers win. Hal tells the workers the bad news but the workers still cheer him for standing up for them. After a confrontation with his

FIGURE 3: American author Upton Sinclair based two novels on energy-related industries, including *King Coal* (1917) and *Oil!* (1927).

brother, Hal goes home and works for the cause of organized labor. Hal also concludes that he has fallen in love with Mary.

Although lauded by some, *King Coal* also has been called "not good fiction and too one-sided" a sympathetic portrayal of the miners to be considered historical. When published, it sold poorly. Sinclair's publisher turned down a sequel he had written for the same reasons. The manuscript remained unpublished during Sinclair's lifetime (Hicks 1943). After he died, the sequel was published as *The Coal War*. It dramatizes one of the most important conflicts between labor and capital and is a stark exposé of the horrible realities of an early twentieth-century miner. The novel is similar to Emile Zola's *Germinal* (1885) which novelized a crippling coal miners' strike in the 1860s northern French towns of Anzin and Denain. *Germinal* was a sensation when published and still is the best-selling Zola novel in France and internationally. Many modern translations are currently in print and widely available, and it has been filmed numerous times. Aside from Sinclair's novel, among the several books written on the coal wars and the Ludlow Massacre, Philip Duke's *A Terrible Unrest* (2014) is an especially sympathetic portrayal.

When Sinclair submitted the novel to his publishers in 1917, it was rejected as uninteresting due to its poor novelistic aspects. In 1976, it was finally published by the Colorado Associated University Press, eight years after Sinclair's death. *The Coal War*'s plot follows the continuing story of *King Coal*'s protagonist, Hal Warner. He opposes his family in the violent, bloody fight to unionize Colorado's mines. Appalled by the harsh working conditions, extremely long work hours, and low wages of the men who mine his family's mines, Warner attempts to get other privileged people to also want change. When a labor group then finally organizes a huge strike it is met with brutality by the mining companies. Hal's reform commitment puts him in extreme danger.

The phrase "King Coal" originally came from the *Fun* magazine published in March 1873 with an ominous drawing of King Coal sitting on a pile of coal sacks, watching children dying of cold and starvation. An accompanying poem warned that: "Old King Coal / Is a knowing old droll / A knowing old droll is he: / For he's paying no wages and profits they roll / In fast, at / the prices that be. / Fifty-four, fifty-five, fifty-six, go the prices / And he doesn't care / For the deep despair / Of the sons of penury" (Mathis 2018).

Despite the rather poor initial sales of Sinclair's *King Coal* novel, its publication during the muckraking period stimulated a rise in public awareness that eventually led to positive regulatory changes in the coal industry. The phrase "King Coal" has been utilized publicly to refer to coal mining, its economic dominance, or its entrepreneurs since the late nineteenth century, and always in the sense of Sinclair's criticism. When a coal magnate becomes well-known, he inevitably is called "King Coal," such as was the high-living Richard Budge, the British mining entrepreneur who owned several mines and greatly profited by the 1994 controversial privatization deal with the British government (Moore 2016).

In the 1930s, the development of oil and gas technologies diminished the demand for US coal. By 1945, the anthracite coal industry had begun to collapse. In 1970, coal became a target of the Clean Air Act and the new Environmental Protection Agency (EPA) to reduce airborne pollution. Coal was considered one of the worst pollutants because a by-product of coal combustion is sulfur dioxide ($S0_2$), which was found to cause acid rain. Consequently, from 1975 to 2002 almost all new US power plants were built to be fired by natural gas instead of coal (Martelle 2009).

While diminished, demand for coal continued and in the 1970s softer, lower-quality bituminous coal replaced anthracite as the most available. In the later 1970s, oil shortages worldwide increased the demand. With many coal regions tapped out, the demand led to the usage of surface mining to find coal. Through the decades, many efforts to reform the coal industry spoke of tackling or defeating King Coal. However, in the early 2000s, President George W. Bush's energy plan stimulated the development of hundreds of new coal-fired power plants. Since then, concerns about global warming have limited coal's resurgence.

Internationally, the coal industry is much healthier because of strong demand by the expanding economies of India and China. In the United States, far stricter federal regulation of coal mining and the EPA's efforts to limit pollutants from coal-burning power plants has kept coal production from expanding domestically. In the 2020s, coal mining has shifted from Appalachia to Wyoming and other states for reasons of availability and cost (Martelle 2009).

William P. Kladky

See also: Acid Rain; Black Lung Disease; Cist, Jacob; Clean Air Act of 1970; Coal; Cumberland Iron & Coal Company; Frick, Henry Clay; Harlan County War; Ludlow Massacre; Molly Maguires; Paint Creek Mine War; Surface Mining; United Mine Workers of America

FURTHER READING

Andrews, Thomas J. 2010. *Killing for Coal: America's Deadliest Labor War*. Cambridge, MA: Harvard University Press.

Applegate, Edd C. 2008. *Muckrakers: A Biographical Dictionary of Writers and Editors*. London: Scarecrow Press.

Arthur, Anthony. 2006. *Radical Innocent: Upton Sinclair*. New York: Random House.

Graham, John. 1976. *The Coal War*. Denver, CO: Colorado Associated University Press.

Harris, Leon. 1975. *Upton Sinclair: American Rebel*. New York: Thomas Y. Crowell Company.

Hicks, Granville. 1943. "The Survival of Upton Sinclair." *College English*. Vol. 4. No. 4. Pp. 213–20.

Klein, Julia M. 2006. "Sinclair Redux." *Columbia Journalism Review*. Vol. 45. No. 2. Pp. 58–61.

Kunitz, Stanley. 1931. *Living Authors: A Book of Biographies*. New York: H. W. Wilson Company.

Martelle, Scott. 2009. "Killing King Coal." *Sierra Magazine*. Sierra Club. March/April.

Mathis, Charles-François. 2018. "King Coal Rules: Accepting or Refusing Coal Dependency in Victorian Britain." *Revue Française de Civilisation Britannique*. Vol. 23. No. 3.

Moore, James. 2016. "Richard Budge—Dubbed 'King Coal' after Buying British Coal from the Government—Has Died Aged 69." *The Independent* (UK). July 20.

Rife, Katie. 2023. "'King Coal' Review: Appalachia Rises in Poetic, Personal Doc from Director of 'Heroin(e).'" *Indie Wire*. January 23. https://www.indiewire.com/2023/01/king-coal-documentary-review-1234802833/ (accessed October 2023).

Singer Manufacturing Company

Singer Manufacturing Company is a manufacturer of electric sewing machines that are used all around the world today. Modern Singer sewing machines function via electrical power, including a recent handheld sewing machine that works with four AA batteries (ST 2017).

Before the appearance of Singer sewing machines, Charles Wiesenthal invented double-pointed needles for sewing without using any machines in 1755. Then, in 1826 Henry Lye patented a stitching machine for leathers (Eves 2019). Four years later, Bathelemy Thimonnier invented an embroidery machine with a hooked needle that could move "downward by a cord-connected foot treadle," and then in 1846, Elias Howe created a sewing machine with "an eye-pointed needle and shuttle" (MAH 2010).

These innovations set the stage for the appearance of the Singer sewing machine. In 1850, Isaac Merritt Singer created the first straight stitch sewing machine, called Standard 1, at his shop in Boston. The next year, he formed the I.M. Singer & Company, and patented the first Singer sewing machine (SSC 2020). This "rigid-arm sewing machine" had "a table to support the cloth horizontally, instead of a feed bar" as well as "a foot treadle instead of a hand crank" (MAH 2010). Singer's patent contributed to an ongoing technological competition between different companies. Allen Benjamin Wilson developed a rotary bobbin for his sewing machines in 1850, and in 1855, he and Nathaniel Wheeler replaced shuttles with rotary hooks in their new models (Eves 2019).

Nevertheless, Singer sold the highest number of sewing machines in the world in 1855 and was awarded a prize for his machine in Paris. The company established its headquarters in New York in 1857, and then the next year it introduced its first lightweight domestic machine, known as the Grasshopper (SSC 2020). The company received twenty-two patents over the next few years, and in 1865 became an incorporated company. It started to market its "New Family" Sewing Machine when the US Civil War came to an end. Singer began to develop marketing strategies in the 1870s, for example the company started to brand its products with a red "S" girl trademark (Godley 2006, 267).

The first sewing machines were driven by a foot pedal. However, in the 1880s, Singer developed an electric sewing machine, which testing showed to be simpler and more comfortable to use than its manual counterpart. This provided the company with an advantage in the competition for market share. Beginning in 1889, Singer began to promote and sell the electric sewing machine and as a result, by 1890, the company achieved a worldwide market share of 90 percent (SSC 2020). The moment was important in the history of energy because consumers could now see how electricity could be used at home in ways other than electric lighting, which Thomas Edison had shown the world just a few years earlier. The Singer company's technological change from foot power to electric power was followed by the production of other electrical devices for the home, such as vacuum cleaners, irons, and warming pots.

In the middle of the nineteenth century, women stitched shirts by hand. Entrepreneurs had erected textile shops that produced clothing for retail markets. With the coming of electrical power, they were able to switch to electrical sewing machines, thereby establishing the practice of "sweating," or the use of the "sweatshop" mode of production in cities like New York. Women, many of whom were recent immigrants to the city, were paid very low wages to work in these factories, which brought down the price consumers paid for manufactured clothing. By the 1890s, high schools and colleges began to offer home economics programs to teach wives how to use modern technology in the home. Scholars argue that this served to integrate women into higher education, where they began to seek degrees in subjects other than home economics (Eves 2019). In this way, sewing machines powered by electricity served as a catalyst for social change.

Moreover, by 1900, many middle-class women became so familiar with their electric sewing machines that they demonstrated facility with mechanical jobs typically associated with men. Singer employed women in retail stores, at fairs, and in its advertising campaigns as models. The company manufactured toy sewing machines to be used by female children. All told, the mechanization of domestic life served to awaken middle-class women to the idea that they could earn money and that as wage earners they had rights equal to men (Eves 2019).

In the 1900s, Singer expanded its operations. It built a plant in Russia in 1902 and by 1904 was direct-marketing sewing machines in Istanbul (ST 2017). In 1905, the company bought rival sewing machine manufacturer Wheeler & Wilson, and by 1908, was large enough to justify building a skyscraper for its headquarters on Broadway in New York City (MAH 2010; SSSC 2020). The company began building and marketing other electronic consumer durables, as when it manufactured and sold vacuum cleaners after 1928.

As with most American corporations, the Stock Market Crash in 1929 and the onset of the Great Depression deeply impacted the company's profitability. Compounding the problem, women began to seek out ways of adding to the family's income. Singer experienced a decline in sales and looked for ways of reinvigorating its product line and attracting new generations of consumers. This led to the design and manufacture of the portable Featherweight 221 sewing machine, which became a company icon after it first appeared in 1933 (SSC 2020). During the Second World War, from 1939 through 1945, the company refitted its manufacturing plants and produced armaments and supplies instead of sewing machines for the war effort. In the post-war era, the company was back in the game of out-competing other companies with product innovation, and in 1952 it introduced its first zig-zag stitching machine, the Slant-o-Matic (SSC 2020).

In the 1970s, Singer entered the digital age with the 1975 model Athena 2000, a sewing machine that operated with an electronic control panel. Then, in 1978, the company produced the Touchtronic, a sewing machine with an integrated system of computerized controls. This led to innovations in pre-set stitching patterns and by the late 1980s, Singer machines automatically created monograms, embroidery patterns, and a wide variety of artistic needlework. Consumers could choose from a product line with lofty brand names like Quantum XL-5000 and Futura XL 400. In the last few decades, Singer followed other corporations into the world of the internet and mobile technology, offering an app for mobile devices called Singer Sewing Assistant. With these innovations, Singer carried forward a legacy from the nineteenth century when it first taught Americans how to make use of electricity in new and very helpful ways.

Fazila Derya Agis

See also: Davenport, Thomas; Digital Revolution; Electricity; Frigidaire; General Electric Company; Home Energy Efficiency; Industrial Revolution; KitchenAid Appliances; Underwriters Laboratories; Upton Machine Company and Whirlpool Corporation

FURTHER READING

Bissell, Don. 1999. *The First Conglomerate: 145 Years of the Singer Sewing Machine Company*. Brunswick, ME: Audenreed Press.

Eves, Jamie H., Beverly L. York, Carol Buch, and Michele Palmer. 2019. "Sewing Revolution: The Machine that Changed the World." The Mill Museum—The Windham Textile and History Museum. https://millmuseum.org/sewing-revolution/ (accessed January 30, 2020).

Godley, Andrew. 2006. "Selling the Sewing Machine around the World: Singers International Marketing Strategies, 1850–1920." *Enterprise and Society*. Vol. 7. No. 2. Pp. 266–314.

Museum of American Heritage (MAH). 2010. "Stitches in Time: 100 Years of Machines and Sewing." April 24. http://www.moah.org/stitches/ (accessed January 30, 2020).

Potkina, Irina V. 2008. "The Singer Company in Russia, 1897–1917." In *American Firms in Europe (1880–1980): Strategy, Identity, Perception and Performance*. Ed. Hubert Bonin. Pp. 283–98. Genève: Librairie Droz.

Singer Sewing Company (SSC). 2020. "History." https://www.singer.com/history (accessed January 7, 2019).

Singer Turkey (ST). 2017. "Home and History." https://www.singer.com.tr/en (accessed January 3, 2019).

Slater, Samuel

Samuel Slater (1768–1835) was an English industrialist responsible for establishing the first large-scale permanent water-powered cotton mills in the United States. Given the abundance of rivers, creeks, and streams in the Northeast, especially in New England, mills similar to Slater's were reproduced throughout the region. This resulted in not only a vibrant textile industry, which ultimately transformed America into a major industrial nation, but it also created communities of mill-working families in otherwise rural areas. In addition to bringing his knowledge of English machinery to the United States, the managerial training that Slater gained from his apprenticeship in England played a key role in the early development of the American industrial labor system.

Slater was born in Belper, a town in Derbyshire, England, and at age fourteen was apprenticed to Jedediah Strutt (1726–97), a successful textile manufacturer who employed the water-power designs of his partner, Richard Arkwright (1732–92), to power his mills. By the time he turned twenty years old, Slater had gained both the technical and managerial skills necessary to operate a water-powered textile mill. Around this time, the majority of the finer Western clothing worn in the United States was manufactured in England, even though cotton was produced in the American South. Since homespun yarn and textiles manufactured in the country were not of the same quality as those from England, American investors and merchants began offering handsome rewards for people in England to bring their knowledge of textile machinery across the Atlantic. Recognizing the need to protect the competitive advantage of its domestic textile industry, England enacted laws prohibiting the export of both machinery parts and the knowledge of their workings. Facing the threat of fines and/or imprisonment for doing so, in 1789 Slater boarded an America-bound ship disguised as a farmer to seek new opportunities with his knowledge of running textile mills.

After quickly becoming disappointed with local work prospects in New York City, Slater traveled to Rhode Island to meet with a Quaker industrialist, Moses Brown, who had posted a public flyer seeking someone to assemble recently purchased spinning machines. Slater soon entered into an arrangement with William Almy and Smith Brown (the son-in-law and nephew of Moses, respectively) and negotiated to receive a stake in the entire business in return for establishing and running his first cotton carding and spinning mill along the Blackstone River in Pawtucket, Rhode Island. The mill proved so successful that Slater eventually went into business for himself and created a small mill dynasty with his sons and brother. By the time of his death, Slater either owned or had a stake in over a dozen mills and his estate was valued at $690,000, worth about $23 million in 2023 dollars (Cowan 2018, 72).

Clearly, water power played a major role in establishing the American textile industry. Although it was a proven energy technology, since it had been used throughout colonial times to grind grains, tobacco, and other consumable items, Slater's was the first water-powered mill to operate textile machinery in America. Previously, colonists and early Americans had to spin thread using energy from the users' arms and/or legs. Without the ability to harness work from the flowing waters of rivers and streams, the American Industrial Revolution would have been slightly delayed until the development of steam engines powered by coal, which came a short time later.

Today, most factories are powered by fossil fuels and/or electricity. As such, local, state, and federal regulations, along with the price of land, labor, and supplies, determine where they are built. In Slater's time, however, the locations of water-powered mills were determined by the location of the energy source, namely moving water, which is why the mills were built along rivers in mostly rural locations. Therefore, we can observe a period-specific energy-labor tradeoff: water-powered mills were built in rural locations with ample free energy but sometimes a limited labor supply, whereas modern factories using transportable fuels can be built in or near cities where there is more available labor. Slater's first mill inspired the development of not only more mills throughout the Northeast but also more intricate systems of hydropower including the Lowell Waterpower System in Massachusetts.

PRE-INDUSTRIAL RENEWABLES

Although most people today think of renewable energy only in terms of combustible fuels and types of electricity generation, during Slater's youth, almost all energy expended on earth was considered renewable: the boat on which Slater sailed to America relied on wind and tidal energy; his mill was powered by water and was constructed with human and animal power (derived from food energy); and homes were heated in the winter with solar (sunrays) and biomass (firewood) energy.

Curt J. Davis

In addition to technology transfer, Slater created—or at least significantly inspired—a new system of labor in rural America. In his homeland, families would farm their land as their primary income and livelihood. When they were not farming, young children only worked outside of the family as apprentices, not as wage laborers. Slater knew that the success of the American mills depended on reliable workers committed to the job year-round, therefore, he hired children as wage laborers, a practice yet unknown in either England or America. Slater's practice of employing young children and eventually entire nuclear families at the textile mills became known as "Slater's system" or the "Rhode Island system." As a result, entire communities or "mill towns," complete with schools, churches, and stores, developed along rivers in rural areas, including the eponymous Slatersville located in northern Rhode Island.

Although the burgeoning American textile industry reduced reliance on imports and strengthened certain aspects of the US economy, there were clearly negative social consequences. Slater employed children as young as seven, which is now a prohibited practice in the United States on account of the creation of American labor laws designed to both establish and protect workers' rights. Although the subsequent dismal working conditions of other industrial sectors played a larger role in establishing significant labor laws, Slater's mills planted the seeds of concern for the laws we know today. Another major blemish on American history left by the early textile industry is related to the principal ingredient of clothing of that era: cotton, a chief product of the southern agrarian economy.

One cannot overlook the fact that much of the production of cotton clothing worn in the United States came as a result of slave labor on cotton plantations in the American South. Concerns over human suffering during the age of rapid industrialization caused by dismal working conditions and slavery would lead to anti-capitalist philosophic and economic movements, such as Marxism. Long before the views of European thinkers gained traction, however, some prominent Americans, such as Thomas Jefferson, had expressed concern over the transition from an agrarian to industrial society. Others, such as Alexander Hamilton, championed industrialization as the best path to achieve a powerful American economy. Despite opposing political-economic viewpoints, Slater became such a significant figure that at least one American president was impressed enough with his achievements to pay a house call to the ailing industrialist towards the end of his life.

There is an account of President Andrew Jackson visiting Slater in Pawtucket in 1833 and declaring him the "father of American manufactures." Some scholars believe that Jackson actually called him the "father of the American Industrial Revolution." Regardless of what the president actually said, Slater's accomplishments and impact on industrialization are held in high regard in American history. However, although Slater is remembered as a hero in the United States, his contemporary British referred to him as "Slater the traitor" since he was guilty of smuggling secret knowledge of the English factory system, which had been essential to maintain Britain's dominance in the textile trade. Slater is perhaps best remembered in his adopted homeland of Rhode Island, especially since there is a town that bears his name. In 1966, "Old Slater Mill," Slater's first mill in Pawtucket, Rhode Island, was listed as the first property ever to appear on the National Register of Historic Places and remains a prominent tourist attraction in the state, especially for local students.

Curt J. Davis

See also: Industrial Revolution; Lowell Waterpower System; Renewable Energy; Water Power

FURTHER READING

Bowen, Ashley. 2016. "The American Textile Industry Was Woven from Espionage." *Atlas Obscura*. January 13. https://www.atlasobscura.com/articles/the-american-textile-industry-was-woven-from-intellectual-espionage (accessed March 10, 2020).

Cowan, Ruth Schwartz, and Matthew H. Hersch. 2018. *A Social History of American Technology*. 2nd ed. New York: Oxford University Press.

Cross, Gary S., and Rick Szostak. 1995. *Technology and American Society: A History*. Englewood Cliffs, NJ: Prentice Hall.

Tucker, Barbara M. 1984. *Samuel Slater and the Origins of the American Textile Industry, 1790–1860*. Ithaca, NY: Cornell University Press.

United States National Archives (NA). "Old Slater Mill." National Register of Historic Places.https://catalog.archives.gov/id/41374777 (accessed October 7, 2020).

Woonsocket Connection. n.d. "Samuel Slater: Father of the American Industrial Revolution." http://www.woonsocket.org/slater.htm (accessed November 5, 2020).

Smart Grid

A power grid is a large system for creating and distributing electricity, which includes such components as power plants, transmission lines, substations, transformers, and service drops. It forms a complex network that connects energy producing units to energy end-users. The first power grids in the United States appeared in the 1880s, including Thomas Edison's Pearl Street Power Station, which began generating electricity in 1882 for customers in Manhattan. With successive applications of new technology, power grids developed greater sophistication over the course of the twentieth century. Finally, in the early 2000s, power grids acquired new capabilities that enabled them to calibrate electricity production to sudden shifts in consumer demand, as well as to integrate energy production from remote sites like solar-equipped roofs. "Smart grids" enable two-way communication between power plants and distant sites along the network, both in terms of the ability to generate electricity, as well as rapid communication of data to facilitate detection and reaction to demand and supply changes or disruptions. Many experts believe that smart grids are an important development in energy efficiency, while critics contend they surrender too much consumer information and individual control to energy companies and governments.

The idea of a smart grid emerged in the context of debates about deregulation of electricity markets in the 1990s. Advocates for electricity consumers hoped to restructure the industry to allow more retail and wholesale competition—to enable small producers like wind and solar farms and industrial cogeneration systems to sell their electricity to distributors and retail consumers. In 1992, the Energy Policy Act empowered the Federal Energy Regulatory Commission (FERC) to open transmission lines, so that non-utility electricity generators could sell power wholesale to distributors (Slayton 2013, 459). Concerns were raised that the electricity grid wasn't prepared to handle greater volume of energy transactions in an open market, and that increasing interactions among electricity generators, distributors, and consumers would also increase "uncertainties and the interactive complexity of the system" (Slayton 2013, 461). The Institute for Electrical and Electronics Engineers (IEEE) produced a study in 1997 that addressed the issue of how open transmission access would affect the system's reliability. The institute argued that digital technology would be required to make "'local decisions based on local measurements'" along the whole grid to prevent a major disruption. The study referred to this sort of system as Self-Managing and Reliable Transmission Grid, which is where the term SMART grid originated (Slayton 2013, 462).

As this policy debate progressed, blackouts in California in 2000–1 and in the Northeast and Midwest in 2003 alerted energy companies and policymakers to certain failures and shortcomings of the nation's power grid. The grid was once an "engineering marvel," with 9,200 electric generating units with 1 million megawatts of generating capacity, connecting the United States with electricity through 600,000 miles of transmission lines, but by the dawn of the new millennium it required what the US Department of Energy (DOE) called modernization (OE 2023a). The California blackout brought the DOE in 2003 to create the Office of Electric Transmission and Distribution and the Office of Energy Assurance, offices created to advance "technologies needed to ensure a reliable, robust, and modern U.S. electricity grid" and to "coordinate Federal response activities within the energy sector during energy emergencies" (OE 2023b). Both offices were involved in the Northeast and Midwest blackout later that year. In 2005, the two offices were combined into the Office of Electricity, which bore responsibility for spearheading the integration of smart grid elements into the existing network. Two years later, the Energy Independence and Security Act (EISA) became law, which contained a section outlining the desired outcomes of the nation's smart grid initiative.

In Title XIII of the EISA, lawmakers listed ten different smart grid characteristics, which is a starting point for understanding the concept. The section opens with an expression of the desirability of "modernization" to "maintain a reliable and secure electricity infrastructure that can meet future demand growth" (EISA 2007). First, the smart grid would have "increased use of digital information and controls technology to improve reliability, security, and efficiency of the electric grid." This would require digital monitoring and automated controls "to keep voltage magnitudes within their parameters and maintain safety and integrity across the network with a fluctuating supply," not only at the point of generation but also at substations and transformers where "new monitoring and control devices can be installed to keep the grid stable" (Petterson 2022). Second, the smart grid would also have "dynamic optimization of grid operations and resources, with full cyber-security" (EISA 2007). According to IEEE, this requires the technological capacity to manage "multi-level interaction and integration of numerous highly specialized component technologies and systems" (Amin 2018).

The EISA advanced a third characteristic of a smart grid, which is the integration of distributed resources and generation, including renewable resources. In discussions about smart grids, "distributed resources and generation" refers to the non-utility creation of energy by producers out along the grid, away from the power plants that dominated electricity generation for most of the twentieth century. This includes large corporations like Proctor & Gamble, which built a combined heat and power plant at its Mehoopany, Pennsylvania factory using on-site Marcellus Shale natural gas, and produced enough energy to power the factory and then sell its surplus power to the grid. The factory produced Bounty paper towels and napkins, Charmin toilet paper, and Pampers and Luvs diapers. This distributed generation also includes homeowners who install rooftop solar photovoltaic panels, which can produce more electricity than is used on-site. A fourth characteristic is the "development and incorporation of demand response, demand-side resources, and energy-efficiency resources," which entails increasing efficiency standards for appliances like refrigerators and freezers, central air-conditioners and heat pumps, water heaters, and clothes washers. It also includes new building codes for architects, contractors, and builders that stipulate higher energy-efficient standards.

Some of these new appliances, as well as new heating and cooling technologies, incorporate "interactive technologies that optimize the physical operation of appliances and consumer devices for metering, communications concerning grid operations and status, and distribution automation." These are the fifth and sixth characteristics of a smart grid according to the EISA. It allows the grid to communicate directly with home appliances and consumer devices to facilitate load management. Some examples of this sort of interactive technology would be "advanced electricity storage and peak-shaving technologies," "plug-in electric and hybrid electric vehicles," and "thermal storage air conditioning" (EISA 2007). The final smart grid characteristics have to do with the process of implementation, such as "providing consumers with timely information and control options," "adopting standards of communication and interoperability" of smart grid equipment, and "lowering barriers" to adoption of smart grid "technologies, practices, and services" (EISA 2007).

The DOE and smart grid advocates insist that smart grid technologies and processes facilitate a more open market for electricity, ensure reliability of the system in the event of over-demand or cyber-attack, and reduce overall energy consumption. They also downplay the potential for unwarranted surveillance and loss of control by energy users. This new technology is here to stay, though implementation will take years since the current grid incorporates a bewildering array of 6,413 power plants, including 3,273 traditional electric utilities and 1,738 non-utility power producers (CISA 2023). In its 2022 report on smart grid integration, the DOE reported that in 2020, "total capital spending on IT and OT digital technologies by US electric utilities was approximately $15 billion per year, out of which the largest portion, $8.3 billion was for smart grid technologies and systems." They added, "by 2026 these figures are projected to reach over $24.5 billion and $16.4 billion respectively" (DOE 2022, 36). Whether this will be fast enough to counteract security threats and future disruptions remains to be seen. In 2017, the DOE admitted that "cyber threats to the electricity system are increasing in sophistication, magnitude, and frequency," and "the current cyber security landscape is characterized by rapidly evolving threats and vulnerabilities, juxtaposed against the slower-moving deployment of defense measures" (DOE 2017, S-22, S-10).

Jeffrey B. Webb

See also: Advanced Research Projects Agency-Energy; CAFE Standards; Clean Power Plan of 2015; Digital Revolution; Electricity; Home Energy Efficiency; Pearl Street Power Station; Public Utility Regulatory Policies Act of 1978; Renewable Energy; Solar Power; US Department of Energy

FURTHER READING

Amin, Massoud. 2018. "Advanced Optimization to Enable Smart Grids & Resilient Interdependent Infrastructures." *IEEE Smart Grid Bulletin*. August. https://smartgrid.ieee.org/bulletins/august-2018/advanced-optimization-to-enable-smart-grids-resilient-interdependent-infrastructures (accessed October 2023).

Cybersecurity and Infrastructure Security Agency (CISA). 2023. "Energy Sector." US Department of Homeland Security. https://www.cisa.gov/topics/critical-infrastructure-security-and-resilience/critical-infrastructure-sectors/energy-sector (accessed October 2023).

Energy Independence and Security Act (EISA) 15 U.S.C. § 1301 (2007).

Office of Electricity (OE). 2023a. "Grid Modernization and the Smart Grid." US Department of Energy. https://www.energy.gov/oe/grid-modernization-and-smart-grid (accessed October 2023).

Office of Electricity (OE). 2023b. "Our History." US Department of Energy. https://www.energy.gov/oe/our-history (accessed October 2023).

Petterson, Edvard. 2022. "Caltech Research on 'Smart Grid' Explores How 100% Green Energy Can Meet Growing Demand." *Mussoula Current*. September 25. https://missoulacurrent.com/caltech-research-on-smart-grid-explores-how-100-green-energy-can-meet-growing-demand/ (accessed October 2023).

Slayton, Rebecca. 2013. "Efficient, Secure Green: Digital Utopianism and the Challenge of Making the Electrical Grid 'Smart.'" *Information & Culture*. Vol. 48. No. 4. Pp. 448–78.

US Department of Energy (DOE). 2022. *2020 Smart Grid System Report*. January. Washington, DC: US Department of Energy.

US Department of Energy (DOE). 2017. "Transforming the Nation's Electricity System: The Second Installment of the Quadrennial Energy Review: Summary for Policymakers." January. Washington, DC: US Department of Energy. https://www.energy.gov/sites/prod/files/2017/02/f34/Quadrennial%20Energy%20Review%20Summary%20for%20Policymakers.pdf (accessed October 2023).

Solar Power

Energy from the sun supports most life on earth. Humans use that energy directly by harnessing the sun's light and heat, and also indirectly by exploiting solar-derived sources like wind, biomass, and fossil fuels. Solar technologies can be as passive as a greenhouse, or as active as a power tower. Sunlight as a fuel, although plentiful and free, presents challenges of intermittent availability and low energy content. Harvesting sunlight to produce power for practical use requires complex devices, and careful technical and economic integration with larger energy infrastructures.

People have used the sun's light and heat (infrared radiation) for thousands of years. Until the development of inexpensive artificial light sources, daylight illuminated most routine activities. Savvy builders in China, the Americas, and around the Mediterranean positioned buildings to capture a maximum amount of solar heat in the winter, while minimizing exposure during the summer. Such passive use of the sun's heat extended beyond individual dwellings; architects aligned entire towns with solar energy in mind (Perlin 2013, 3–36).

Solar energy's intermittent nature constrains direct use of this resource. Unavailable at night and blocked by clouds during the day, practical uses often require storage strategies to compensate for those interruptions. Buildings made of stone exhibited one response by absorbing solar energy later released when the sun was absent. Solar's low energy content also constrains direct use. Although the sun radiates a tremendous amount of energy only a tiny fraction reaches the earth's surface, about 340 watts/m^2 (32 w/ft^2) on average (NASA 2009). Concentrating that diffuse energy with mirrors or lenses is one way to compensate. The Chinese used bronze reflectors to light fires about 3,000 years ago, and the Greeks used concentrated sunlight to ignite their Olympic torches (Perlin 2013, 37–41).

People also learned to use indirect forms of solar energy. Atmospheric heating caused by solar radiation creates blowing winds that propel watercraft and turn windmills. Wind power's energy content is erratic and it suffers from intermittent availability; users found other indirect forms of solar energy more controllable. Biomass, especially wood, absorbs energy that can be quickly released as heat and light when burned. Buried and compressed over millions of years, biomass can transform into fossil fuels such as coal and oil. Recovery and use of those solar derivatives create significant environmental challenges. However, their high energy content, ease of transport, storage, and control led to widespread adoption as societies industrialized in the eighteenth and nineteenth centuries.

Although people quickly adopted fossil fuels as the primary energy sources of the Industrial Revolution, many continued finding ways to use sunlight directly. Glass-enclosed greenhouses, known to the Romans, enjoyed a resurgence after the Renaissance as people began studying plant growth. Glass allows solar radiation into a structure to heat the interior while trapping warm air inside. Eighteenth-century natural philosophers such as Horace de Saussure conducted experiments with specially designed glass hot boxes to learn more about the nature of solar radiation. They quickly realized that such devices made effective ovens for cooking (Perlin 2013, 57–78).

CALIFORNIA SOLAR INITIATIVE

The US Department of Energy's Million Solar Roofs Initiative of 1997, inspired the California Solar Initiative (CSI) in 2005. The CSI provided rebates to encourage the purchase of photovoltaic equipment including solar panels, power inverters, and electric meters that could measure power to and from a building. This 2008 panel from a CSI installation, combined the output of many small solar cells. Programs like CSI spurred manufacturers to increase equipment supplies, thereby driving down costs.

Harold D. Wallace Jr.

Aside from passive uses, nineteenth-century inventors created novel ways to actively concentrate solar energy. Worried about finite coal supplies, John Ericsson (known for designing the US Civil War ironclad ship *Monitor*), designed a solar engine that drove a piston without steam ("Ericcson's" 1879). James Mauzey received US Patent No. 227,028 in 1880 for a solar heater with adjustable reflectors and a movable frame to track the sun. These and other inventors' devices often worked well, but their ideas failed to attract serious interest. Solar lacked the predictability and ease of control essential for practical energy use. People during this era also learned to harness electricity, a form of energy with many advantages. Adaptable and controllable, electricity proved ideal for applications large and small. Coupling generators to coal-fueled steam power produced massive amounts of convenient electrical power for industry and individuals alike.

FIGURE 4: Construction of new solar power plants surged in the 2010s in response to greater demand for electricity and government incentives promoting renewable energy sources.

While a few gave thought to using solar for large-scale electric power production, other researchers learned that some substances generate a minute electrical charge when exposed to light. Alexandre-Edmond Becquerel discovered the photovoltaic effect and demonstrated a working photocell in 1839. Willoughby Smith found photoelectric properties in the element selenium in 1873, properties that Alexander Graham Bell soon made use of by designing a photophone that transmitted speech via light. Photocells produced small amounts of direct current rather than large amounts of alternating current produced by dynamos. Few practical solar electric devices emerged during this period.

Industrialization and electrification in the United States required expensive, complex infrastructures built over the course of decades. During the early twentieth century, solar technologies filled niches in areas that lacked access to cheap electricity. Heating water with coal or wood stoves, for example, was laborious and time consuming. Several companies offered rooftop solar water heaters for homes, apartments, and commercial buildings. The heaters, black-coated water tanks set inside a glass hot box, sold well for years, but copper rationing during the Second World War slowed sales. The market never recovered despite a post-war economic boom that stimulated demand for energy throughout the country. Although users wanted more hot water for electric dishwashers and cloths washers, passive rooftop water tanks could not compete with convenient electric water heaters (Perlin 2013, 145–94).

The post-war boom did continue to spur research. MIT physicist Maria Telkes, for example, worked with architect Eleanor Raymond on Dover House, an experimental structure that used fusible salts to store solar heat (Telkes 1949). While researching the photoelectric effect at Bell Telephone Laboratories in the 1930s, Russell Ohl discovered that light would generate a current across a transition zone between two sections of a specially prepared silicon rod. The zone, called a P-N junction, is the fundamental feature of transistors and light-emitting diodes. In 1954, Ohl's colleagues, Daryl Chapin, Calvin Fuller, and Gerald Pearson, built on his discovery by designing a silicon cell that converted sunlight into electricity.

The need to design and fabricate production equipment, amortize research costs, and establish supply chains makes many technologies expensive at first. Using inexpensive silicon reduced the cost of solar cell fabrication, but finding cost-competitive markets was essential. The Bell company identified two. The expense of stringing lines delayed the advent of telephone service in many rural areas so, in 1956, Bell installed a solar-powered telephone relay in Americus, Georgia. The company then used 3,600 solar cells to generate 14 watts of power on *Telstar 1* in 1962. The first privately owned satellite, *Telstar* relayed telephone, telegraph, and television signals across the Atlantic.

Other companies identified additional markets. Bell's de facto telephone monopoly brought antitrust scrutiny from regulators, so after inventing the transistor in 1947, the company quickly licensed the technology. They followed that pattern with solar cells. One licensee, Hoffman Electronics, produced solar panels for satellites and also a line of portable transistor radios that could operate on batteries or light. A few other solar devices appeared on the market and hobbyists could purchase cells from stores like Radio Shack, but no mass market developed. The exciting idea that solar cells might offer an alternative to finite fossil fuels led to the formation of the Association for Applied Solar Energy in 1954 (Strum 1985). The excitement proved premature, however. Solar cells remained expensive and although researchers learned more about how they generated electricity, efficiencies rose slowly. Photovoltaics were used mostly in space and other remote applications through the 1960s.

New interest in renewable energy technologies emerged following the OPEC oil embargo of late 1973. The energy crisis boosted research but not all responses involved new ideas. President Jimmy Carter authorized rooftop solar water heaters for the White House. Glass jars for brewing "solar tea" reappeared on store shelves. Users simply filled the jar with water and tea bags, then placed it in the sun for an hour or so. High energy prices changed economic calculations somewhat, but prices soon declined along with the stimulus to alter energy consumption patterns. President Ronald Reagan ordered the rooftop panels taken off the White House, signaling a turn away from renewable energy. Solar still needed cost-competitive markets to support research and development.

Ironically, the oil industry provided one such market. Oil well casings passing through saline aquifers tended to corrode, a process that could be arrested by a slight electrical current. Solar panels could deliver the trickle of steady current needed to halt corrosion without the expense of running power lines to remote oil fields. The industry also needed an alternative to lead acid batteries for powering navigation beacons on offshore oil platforms. Solar panels generated electricity for years, replacing batteries that lasted only months and were dumped in the ocean when spent. Using solar offered significant cost savings in both applications, and oil companies made substantial investments (Perlin 2013).

The Electric Power Research Institute (EPRI) and the US Department of Energy (DOE) also funded solar research during the 1980s. The environmental impact of using coal or uranium to generate electricity inspired work on renewable sources for electrical generation. Efforts to directly harness solar energy took two main forms, solar thermal concentrators and massed photovoltaic "farms." DOE's Solar One power tower near Barstow, California (1981–6) reflected sunlight from many mirrors onto a tank at the tower's top. The heat generated steam that ran a turbine and an electrical generator as in a traditional power plant. Other designs used parabolic troughs to focus the sunlight. EPRI, sponsored by electric utilities, supported research on solar cells that included a 1993 project to streamline mass production of higher efficiency cells. Cells from that project powered Honda's winning entry in the 1993 World Solar Challenge car race. Commercial satellite operators and military users also increased investments in photovoltaics during this time.

Mitigation of human-produced climate change motivated work on renewable energy sources in the early 1990s, attracting investment to solar. Favorable tax structures and programs like California's Solar Initiative gave manufacturers incentive to produce more equipment, further lowering costs. Decades of solar research resulted in higher energy conversion efficiencies while manufacturing costs declined, in part by borrowing techniques from integrated circuit makers. Solar cells are made much like computer chips, by depositing very thin layers of material on silicon wafers to form microscopic circuits. Fabricators make dozens of chips on a single wafer. Mass production of solar cells and panels, especially in China, made solar cost-competitive with other forms of electric power.

Declining costs led to a solar surge in the 2010s. Many small applications that formerly used diesel generators, roadside advisory signs for example, now sport solar panels. By 2016 solar provided more new capacity to the US electric power grid than any other generating technology (EIA 2023b). Many homes now feature solar electric panels that provide electricity to users—and the power grid—on sunny days, while allowing users to take power from the grid when needed. Not everyone welcomes those installations. Some object to the visual disruption of solar panels on older buildings, while others object to covering green spaces with solar farms. One answer has been to install solar panels over existing paved spaces like parking lots, where the panels also serve to shelter cars and their drivers.

Electrical utilities raise concerns about integrating solar with existing power networks. Systems designed to reliably route power one way from generator to consumer cannot be altered quickly, either economically or technically. Electricity cannot be stored in bulk and must be generated on demand. That requires utilities to plan ahead and make expensive investments. Flooding the network with solar panels disrupts those plans. Also, electrical supply and demand must match closely in real time or the system can crash. Power engineers worry that too many sources like solar and wind will destabilize systems not designed for intermittent supply. Electrical output dropped during the 2017 solar eclipse as the moon's shadow moved across the United States, a predicted event operators could compensate for.

Solar panels produce direct current and so require a power inverter to convert that DC to the alternating current (AC) used in the electrical system. A meter that runs both ways is required to feed power into the grid. Special cut-off devices prevent current from energizing a line and endangering service personnel during system maintenance. These and other components add complexity to the electrical system and raise costs. However, advances in automated monitoring and control enable engineers to rethink how they design and operate power grids as more renewable energy, especially solar, comes online. Though producing solar cells presents environmental challenges and storage of electrical energy remains problematic, the idea of generating electricity with sunlight has become mainstream.

Upgrading energy systems in a safe and economically sound manner takes time. People have little tolerance for blackouts and politicians pay close attention. Federal action in this area is often limited by governmental structures. State public utility commissions have moved at different speeds when considering how much renewable energy to permit. Regardless of the pace, economic considerations and environmental concerns have increased adoption of solar technology. Passive and active, thermal and photovoltaic, direct use of solar energy appears poised to take a significant place in twenty-first-century energy infrastructures.

Harold D. Wallace, Jr.

See also: Public Utility Regulatory Policies Act of 1978; Renewable Energy; Shuman, Frank; Smart Grid; US Green Building Council

FURTHER READING

Abbot, Charles G. 1939. "Utilizing Heat from the Sun." *Publications of the Astronomical Society of the Pacific*. Vol. 51. No. 302. August. Pp. 197–209.

"Ericcson's Solar Engine." 1879. *Chicago Daily Tribune*. September 13.

National Aeronautics and Space Administration (NASA). 2009. "NASA Earth Observatory: Incoming Sunlight." January 14. EOS Project Science Office. NASA Goddard Space Flight Center. https://earthobservatory.nasa.gov/features/EnergyBalance/page2.php (accessed October 2023).

Perlin, John. 2013. *Let It Shine: The 6,000-Year Story of Solar Energy*. Novato, CA: New World Library.

Smith, Willoughby. 1877. "Selenium: Its Electrical Qualities, and the Effect of Light Thereon." A Paper Read before the Society of Telegraph Engineers. November 28. https://archive.org/stream/b22277687#page/n0/mode/2up (accessed October 2023).

Strum, Harvey. 1985. "The Association for Applied Solar Energy/Solar Energy Society, 1954–1970." *Technology and Culture*. Vol. 26. No. 3. Pp. 571–8.

Telkes, Maria. 1949. "A Review of Solar House Heating." *Heating and Ventilating*. Vol. 46. No. 9. Pp. 68–74.

US Energy Information Agency (EIA). 2023a. "Electricity." US Department of Energy. https://www.eia.gov/electricity (accessed October 2023).
US Energy Information Agency (EIA). 2023b. "Renewable & Alternative Fuels." US Department of Energy. https://www.eia.gov/renewable/ (accessed October 2023).

Spindletop Oil Gusher

Spindletop was an oil field located in Beaumont, Texas that oil producers began to develop in January of 1901 following the discovery of what was then the most prolific gusher in United States history. Spindletop initially proved to be a short-lived oil field and the boomtowns that sprang up around it were violent places to live and work. However, the field's development convinced petroleum companies and investors that massive deposits of crude oil existed in the South and West. Prospectors increasingly discovered profitable oil deposits in Texas, Louisiana, and Indian Territory, which merged with Oklahoma Territory and became the State of Oklahoma in 1907. These discoveries propelled the region to a position of leadership as the most important oil-producing zone in the United States, and one of the most productive petroleum areas in the world. Spindletop's copious supply of crude also convinced engineers, investors, and retailers that oil reserves were large enough to support a profitable fuel-oil market in the United States, which set Americans on a path toward dependency on petroleum for motor transport. Finally, the glut of oil found at Spindletop initiated the creation of new oil companies and the rapid growth of what were then modest operators, laying the foundation for the rise of some of the most profitable and powerful extractive corporations of the twentieth century.

Prospectors suspected that oil could be found beneath Spindletop Hill as early as the 1890s. In 1892, local businessmen created the Gladys City Oil, Gas, and Manufacturing Company in hopes of striking crude at Spindletop. Over the ensuing eight years, intermittent drilling efforts yielded little success. In October of 1900, a crew led by Anthony Lucas—one of the leading salt miners in the United States at the time—began drilling the well that would eventually hit pay dirt. On January 10, 1901, with the drill bit penetrating the earth at a depth of 1,100 feet, large amounts of mud, gas, and eventually crude oil exploded from the well at high pressure, forcing the drilling crew to flee. Speculators, prospective workers, and curious onlookers quickly flooded Beaumont as news of the strike spread. Within months, Beaumont's population grew from 10,000 to over 40,000 and land prices in the area increased prodigiously. Plots of land previously valued in the hundreds of dollars were sold for $20,000 or more and tracts as small as 1/32 of an acre were sold as oil producers sought access to the land surrounding the gusher. The field was developed with no official mode of regulation, leading to a forest of tightly packed, fire-prone derricks manned by crews that worked day and night to ensure that their companies obtained at least some of the petroleum that was quickly draining from the field due to unmitigated drilling. Indeed, while the field produced nearly 50,000 barrels a day in 1902, within two years the daily windfall fell to 10,000.

The drilling crew that sank the initial well developed new methods that quickly became common throughout the industry and greatly improved productivity. However, the first well also illustrated the ecological destruction associated with petroleum production and the subsequent rush to exploit the surrounding oil field proved wasteful and dangerous to life and property. The drilling crew that discovered the field were reportedly the first to use a slurry of water, rocks, and dirt, known as "drilling mud," to seal the wellbore. This innovation was necessitated by sandy rock formations that easily collapsed around and beneath the drill bit, preventing it from sinking further into the earth. While the drill crew displayed ingenuity when bringing in the well, it took them nine days to cap the resulting gusher. In the meantime, the tremendous amount of oil that flowed from the well—estimated at 100,000 barrels a day—cascaded onto surrounding farmland and into the local watershed, contaminating soil and water and creating a massive fire hazard. A large lake of approximately 300,000 barrels of oil accumulated as the gusher blew untamed, and soon after the well was capped sparks from a switch-engine smokestack ignited the lake. While the ensuing inferno claimed no human lives, it killed a number of livestock. Furthermore, natural gas escaping from the well asphyxiated numerous horses and cattle. As one young observer recalled in later years, "people were pretty disturbed by all that mess that was all over the face of the earth out there. They worried about the fact that it was going to kill all the fish in the creeks and interfere with agriculture" (Linsley 2002, 114). Not everyone living in the area saw black gold and industrial progress in the torrents of crude. Some directly suffered from perils that were at once both ecological and economic.

While the oil industry's introduction to the region garnered prosperity for a handful of white southerners and migrating white northerners, oil companies in the South fully embraced Jim Crow and the oil industry became one of the most racially segregated industries in the country. Oil producers refused to hire black laborers to work on drilling rigs. Such jobs represented the highest paying work in the oil field and were thus reserved for whites. Black laborers could find jobs in enterprises that were auxiliary to the direct production of oil, including as teamsters, pipeline builders, and as service workers. The oil boom greatly increased demand for such workers and, as a result, black migrants were among those who flocked to Spindletop. The large, multiracial influx of transient workers exacerbated racist violence in the area. In 1902, white men raided "South Africa"—the African American section of Beaumont that arose during the oil boom—due to the presence of black workers employed by tank-building firms in that area of the city. Whites demanded at gunpoint that such work be reserved for them. A shootout commenced with one white man wounded as a result. Black residents were routinely told not to be caught in white parts of Beaumont at night. In the Big Thicket fields near Spindletop, white vigilantes accused black construction workers of dampening wages and forcibly removed African Americans from the area.

A handful of white investors were the grandest beneficiaries of the Spindletop discovery, especially those capitalists who were best situated to create new production, pipeline, and refinery companies. The companies that emerged from the Spindletop discovery included The Texas Company (better known as Texaco), Gulf Oil (predecessor of Chevron), and Sun Oil (better known as Sunoco). The rapid growth of these companies transformed Beaumont and surrounding cities such as Port Arthur, Texas into lucrative refinery centers. The new producers and other refiners and pipeline builders that flourished during Spindletop's heyday upset Standard Oil's monopoly, which was predicated on its control of railroads and pipelines in the oil regions of Pennsylvania and Ohio. While Standard Oil eventually controlled numerous pipelines in the petroleum-rich Southwest, it never dominated the area to the extent that it controlled oil markets in the Mid-Atlantic and Northeast. Later mergers between Standard and companies that grew or originated from the Spindletop bonanza created powerful present-day multinational corporations such as Chevron and ExxonMobil.

New discoveries soon overshadowed Spindletop, but advanced drilling techniques allowed for a resurgence of production in the field during the 1920s and modest production continued into the latter decades of the twentieth century. In all, the Spindletop field produced over 150 million barrels of oil over a span of eighty-plus years. More importantly, the field contributed to American energy history by greatly increasing the understanding of just how much petroleum likely existed in the United States, especially in the Middle South and Southwest, a discovery that prompted an influx of speculation and investment in the oil industry and fueled its growing presence in said regions. This realization of prodigious oil reserves coincided with the rise of the internal combustion engine and the eventual triumph of an oil-fueled, automobile-centric economy and culture in the United States in the twentieth and twenty-first-centuries.

Mark C. Boxell

See also: Bush, George H.W.; Caltex; ExxonMobil; Getty, Jean Paul; Gulf Oil Company; Mobil Oil Corporation; Petroleum; Red Fork Oil Gusher; Rockefeller, John D.; Roughnecks; Standard Oil Company; Seven Sisters Oil Companies; Texaco

FURTHER READING

Dochuk, Darren. 2012. "Blessed by Oil, Cursed with Crude: God and Black Gold in the American Southwest." *Journal of American History*. Vol. 99. No. 1. June. Pp. 51–61.

Linsley, Judith Walker, Ellen Walker Rienstra, and Jo Ann Stiles. 2002. *Giant under the Hill: A History of the Spindletop Oil Discovery in Beaumont, Texas, 1901*. Austin, TX: Texas State Historical Association.

Olien, Diana D., and Roger M. Olien. 2002. *Oil in Texas: The Gusher Age, 1895–1945*. Austin, TX: University of Texas Press.

Rister, Carl Coke. *Oil! Titan of the Southwest*. Norman, OK: University of Oklahoma Press, 1949.

Weaver, Bobby D. 2010. *Oilfield Trash: Life and Labor in the Oil Patch*. College Station, TX: Texas A&M University Press.

Wooster, Robert, and Christine Moor Sanders. 2019. "Spindletop Oilfield." *Handbook of Texas Online*. http://www.tshaonline.org/handbook/online/articles/dos03 (accessed June 14, 2019).

Sport Utility Vehicles

The reappearance of the sport utility vehicle in the early 1980s made available a class of gas-consuming, high-emissions automobile to US and overseas consumers. SUVs have a higher wheelbase and often a two-axle drivetrain that provides four-wheel drive capability. These characteristics enable SUVs to go off-road and to be used in workplaces requiring rugged vehicles like farming, construction, and forestry. Since the late 2000s, US demand for SUVs skyrocketed. Just under 50 percent of all new cars sold in the United States in 2020 were SUVs. Globally, SUVs reached 40 percent of sales of all cars, and in the ten years between 2009 and 2019, SUVs reached 48 percent of the market for all vehicles in China. Over the four decades between 1983 and 2023, SUVs raised concerns about their poor fuel efficiency and corresponding high carbon emissions. This is particularly true in periods of pronounced US vulnerability to disruptions in oil imports as well as the emergent problem of carbon emissions, increased greenhouse gases, and climate change. Since 2004, SUVs have appeared in hybrid gas-electric and full battery-powered formats to address these concerns.

An important date in the history of SUVs is the introduction of the Jeep Wagoneer in 1963, as a replacement for the Willy's Motors Jeep station wagon. The company grew concerned about the competition growing for cars in this class after the 1961 appearance of the International Harvester Scout. A 1963 advertisement said, "Pull one simple lever and you're in 'Jeep' 4-wheel 'Drivepower.' Then there's hardly a mud hole that can bog you down. In fact, there's scarcely any driving situation that can get you down. You're free to go anywhere with the traction to pull you through" ("Evolution" 1963). The company explained the new model as a revolution in car design, and sold freedom, fun, and adventure. Yet, the vehicle also had an automatic transmission, power steering, power brakes, and optional independent front suspension, so it appealed to buyers who didn't want a vehicle that rode like a truck, as most early vehicles of this category were known. This was part of the problem with the International Harvester Scout, which limited its market appeal. The post-war baby boom also energized consumers seeking larger vehicles to transport their growing families, an issue that also compromised the relatively small Scout's marketability (Foster 2008).

Ford Motor Company claims that its Bronco, which debuted in 1965, was the first to be "called out specifically as a 'Sports-Utility Vehicle,'" thereby giving the category its name (FMC 2023). By then several other automakers had designed, manufactured, and marketed a vehicle with the Wagoneer's dimensions and features. SUVs were very successful in the 1960s and early 1970s until the energy crisis of the 1970s, when OPEC imposed an oil embargo on Western nations supporting Israel, causing oil shortages and price spikes. US automakers, which sold large vehicles with huge engines, suffered a downturn in sales as gas-guzzlers sat on dealers' lots. Customers began buying compact cars from Japan. In 1973, for example, Honda sold 38,857 Civics, which more than doubled in 1975 to 102,389 (McIntosh 2017). In the Energy Policy and Conservation Act of 1975, the federal government established the first national corporate average fuel economy standards (CAFE) for cars and light trucks (including SUVs) in the 1978 model year, which was expected to double the average fuel economy to 27.5 miles per gallon in the 1985 model year (UCS 2017).

To meet these standards, manufacturers offered smaller, more fuel-efficient cars and modified the SUV. A scaled-down version of the Jeep Cherokee, the XJ model, appeared in 1983 and won over a new generation of car buyers. However, decreases in petroleum demand in the late 1970s and early 1980s created an oil glut, and petroleum prices declined as well. Manufacturers responded with new generations of full-sized SUVs in the early 1990s, such as the GMC Yukon, Ford Explorer, and Chevrolet Suburban. Even larger SUVs soon appeared, including the Chevrolet Tahoe in 1995 and the Ford Expedition in 1997. Toyota's 4Runner and Land Cruiser, and Nissan's Pathfinder also found loyal customers in the 1990s. The turn toward larger vehicles took place in a context of suburbanization in the second half of the twentieth century. As families moved to the suburbs by the millions, travel by car became a necessity, and people spent more and more time in their vehicles. Longer commutes to work, coupled with trips to daycare, grocery stores, school functions, church, and so on encouraged suburban homeowners to choose larger vehicles for reasons of comfort but also safety. Parents with children often chose larger vehicles like SUVs and minivans because they have more capacity to absorb the energy of a collision. A 2013 study showed that in a head-to-head impact between a car and an SUV, the odds of the car driver's death are 7.6 times higher than the SUV driver ("SUVs" 2013).

In 2003, oil prices jumped, and then increased considerably until 2008. This occurred against a backdrop of growing international concern about increased CO_2 vehicle emissions. These emissions contribute to greenhouse gas build-up in the atmosphere, which is a key contributor to global warming and climate change. Together, high gas prices and CO_2 emissions brought lawmakers to consider raising federal CAFE standards in the debates over the Energy Policy Act of 2005, but the final version of the law left them untouched. In 2007, the Energy Independence and Security Act raised CAFE standards for SUVs, light trucks, and cars to a combined average of 35 miles per gallon by the 2020 model year, which projected a 10-miles-per-gallon increase in fuel economy over those thirteen years. Despite these measures, the size of many SUV models like the Ford Expedition and the Chevrolet Tahoe increased every year from 2009 to 2019 (Bomey 2019). Manufacturers offset these increases by gaining fuel economy in other models to reach the corporate average across their entire fleet of vehicles.

SUV sales remained strong into 2020 and beyond. They embody the choices Americans and people around the world have made regarding where and how to live. Developments in automotive design and technology have somewhat mitigated the impact of larger and larger vehicles. Ford introduced the Escape SUV for model year 2005, which contained a hybrid gasoline-electric motor and drivetrain that the US Environmental Protection Agency rated at 36 miles per gallon in city driving. In 2022, Honda unveiled an all-electric SUV dubbed Prologue. The vehicle still consumed electricity created in power plants, many of which use fossil fuels, but it will not produce its own carbon emissions, which is an important development in the effort to limit greenhouse gases. Clearly, more will have to be done. The largest increase in CO_2 emissions by energy sub-sector from 2010 to 2021 occurred in the power-generation sector, and SUVs placed second, producing CO_2 at a faster rate than aviation and shipping, truck transportation, and heavy industry (Cozzi 2021).

Jeffrey B. Webb

See also: CAFE Standards; Climate Change; Energy Crisis of the 1970s; Energy Policy and Conservation Act of 1975; Ford, Henry; Interstate Highway System; Truck Transportation Technology

FURTHER READING

Bomey, Nathan. 2019. "Why SUVs Are Getting Bigger and Bigger: GM, Toyota, Ford Enlarge Hefty Vehicles." *USA Today*. December 27. https://www.usatoday.com/story/money/cars/2019/12/27/suvs-gm-ford-toyota-chevrolet/4408728002/ (accessed October 2023).

Cozzi, Laura, and Apostolos Petropoulos. 2021. "Global SIV Sales Set Another Record in 2021, Setting Back Efforts to Reduce Emissions." International Energy Agency. December 21. https://www.iea.org/commentaries/global-suv-sales-set-another-record-in-2021-setting-back-efforts-to-reduce-emissions (accessed October 2023).

"Evolution Revolution." 1963. "1963 Jeep Wagoneer Ad." Classic Cars Today Online. https://www.classiccarstodayonline.com/2017/12/15/a-look-back-at-the-1963-1991-jeep-wagoneer-a-guide-to-year-to-year-changes-2/5-1963-jeep-wagoneer-ad-b/ (accessed October 2023).

Ford Motor Company (FMC). 2023. "The Ford Bronco." Ford Motor Company Website. https://corporate.ford.com/articles/history/the-ford-bronco.html (accessed October 2023).

Foster, Patrick. 2008. "1963 Jeep Wagoneer—Landmark Vehicle." *Motor Trend*. January 1. https://www.motortrend.com/features/0801-4wd-1963-jeep-wagoneer/ (accessed October 2023).

McIntosh, Jil. 2017. "Rearview Mirror: The Fuel Crisis that Changed the Industry." *Driving*. Postmedia Network Inc. February 1. https://driving.ca/auto-news/news/rearview-mirror-the-fuel-crisis-that-changed-the-industry (accessed October 2023).

"SUVs Are Safer than Cars in Front Crashes, but There is More to the Story." 2013. Consumer Reports News. May 15. https://www.consumerreports.org/cro/news/2013/05/suvs-are-safer-than-cars-in-front-crashes-but-there-is-more-to-the-story/index.htm (accessed October 2023).

Union of Concerned Scientists (UCS). 2017. "A Brief History of US Fuel Efficiency Standards." December 6. https://www.ucsusa.org/resources/brief-history-us-fuel-efficiency (accessed October 2023).

Standard Oil Company

The Standard Oil Company, first created in 1870 by John D. Rockefeller (1839–1937), Henry Flagler, and other associates, quickly became the most important American oil company, from drilling to transport to refining, and then to the retail customer. Standard Oil was so powerful, with tentacles everywhere in the United States and around the world, that the US Supreme Court declared it an illegal monopoly and in 1911 broke up the company (Yergin 2009, 90). The different pieces formed thirty-four smaller companies, and some of the offspring companies remain among the richest and most powerful corporations in the world in the early twenty-first century (Yergin 2009, 94).

The story of John D. Rockefeller's octopus of a company began in the 1850s when the US's first purpose-built oil well was drilled in Pennsylvania. That well, known as "Drake's Well," became the point of origin for the American oil industry (Yergin 2009, 11–15). From there, the industry spread across the American Midwest and into the minds of men like John D. Rockefeller. Rockefeller, a native of New York State, but a man who had come to Cleveland, Ohio to work as a bookkeeper for a produce commission company, soon realized he was sitting at the front door of the growing American oil industry. Cleveland, located on Lake Eire, and the largest city in eastern Ohio, became one of the chief centers of that industry. Refineries were built and tools produced to get the oil out of the ground, refine it, usually into kerosene in the 1850s and 1860s, then into other products as the nineteenth century turned into the twentieth (Chernow 2004, 37–70). This was the situation in the industry before the coming of John D. Rockefeller and the Standard Oil Company.

In the aftermath of the US Civil War, Rockefeller, who had made some money and served his country during the war, was brought into this growing oil industry by his brother William Rockefeller Jr. The year after the war ended, in 1866, his brother brought John and their mutual friend Henry Flagler into his refinery business and together, along with Samuel Andrews, a chemist and inventor, formed the firm Rockefeller, Andrews, and Flagler (Chernow 2004, 108–17). The company's refineries soon became the largest in the world. John, who invested the profits of the company over and over again, eventually started to want more. He wondered, why just stay in refining when one could spread out in other ways? Why not profit from all the steps in the production process from oil well to customer?

Eventually, the end came for the partnership of Rockefeller, Andrews, and Flagler when he struck out on his own and founded the Standard Oil Company in 1870. Under Rockefeller's leadership, Standard Oil went on the march slowly but surely and began the process of horizontal and vertical integration across all aspects of the oil industry in the United States. Horizontal integration is the process of buying multiple companies in the same field while vertical integration is the acquisition of operations up and down the supply chain to control all the steps in the cycle of production. Through the 1870s and into the 1880s, by means of secret deals, strong-arming, and plenty of cash, Rockefeller and his Standard Oil shareholders got what they wanted. They extended control over refineries, railroads, shipping, oil wells, tool factories, and business fronts where their kerosene and other oil products were sold to the public. The creation of the Standard Oil Trust in 1882 formalized and organized the collection of companies that had been under the command of John D. Rockefeller and the company's investors (Yergin 2009, 29). In the 1890s and 1900s, Standard Oil spread its operations into the Middle East and China. Standard Oil had become the largest company in the world and it made Rockefeller the richest man in the world at the time (Chernow 2004, 3).

But the Standard Oil Trust drew attention for its aggressive—some would say fraudulent—business practices. Investigative journalist Ida B. Tarbell examined the history of Standard Oil Company and published a book outlining how Rockefeller had managed to acquire monopoly control over the entire petroleum industry. Her book, *The History of the Standard Oil Company* (1904), became an instant classic and galvanized political support behind antitrust action against the trust. The period of the late nineteenth century became known as the Gilded Age for its extremes of wealth and poverty and the nearly unlimited power of corporations over American social and economic life (Brands 2010, 4). By the 1880s, many Americans and some political leaders decided they had to try to address these extremes. One of the tools the federal government had developed was the Sherman Antitrust Act. Passed in 1890, the act gave the government authority break up business monopolies in order to restore healthy competition to various sectors of the economy. Standard Oil was one of those monopolies now in the cross hairs of reformers (Brands 2010, 522–3). The company would soon be under assault by numerous attorneys general, government investigators, lawyers, and journalists like Ida Tarbell. All of these forces led to the downfall of Standard Oil and the humbling of a uncontrollable corporate giant.

Nearly right after the passage of the Act, the Standard Oil Trust came under assault. A lawsuit by Ohio's attorney general started the process of ending the trust. The leaders of Standard Oil morphed and twisted their Trust into various business forms until finally settling on a holding company in 1899. By the first decade of the twentieth century, Standard Oil controlled 91 percent of all oil refining in the United States and 85 percent of final sales. Standard Oil reigned supreme but it was in the crosshairs of state officials, the federal administration, Congress, and citizen action groups. After fighting off legal assault after legal assault from both private groups and the government though the deployment of small armies of lawyers and generous contributions, Standard Oil began its final legal battle with the government in 1909 when it was sued by the Taft administration. The federal government believed Standard Oil was a monopoly and meant to prove it in court. After two years of legal battles at all levels of the American judicial system, Standard Oil lost. In 1911, the US Supreme Court ordered Standard Oil separated into thirty-four separate companies under the control of different people. Standard Oil was declared an illegal monopoly and that monopoly came to an end (Yergin 2009, 93–4).

Ironically, the destruction of the Standard Oil Company made John D. Rockefeller richer. He had already retired in the 1890s, still owning nearly 25 percent of the company's stock (Segall 2001, 12). He benefited financially when everything was divided up and settled. The successor companies of Standard Oil became some of the most powerful companies in the United States. ExxonMobil, Chevron, and Marathon trace their ancestries back to the destruction of Standard Oil. All of these companies are some of the most powerful and most successful companies in the present day (Yergin 2009, 90). While John D. Rockefeller's creation died in 1911, the children and grandchildren of Standard Oil are alive and well and operating in the United States and around the world. Instead of one octopus, there are now multiple octopi across the globe influencing business, culture, and government in ways that John D. Rockefeller and his associates could have hardly ever imagined possible.

Jeff Hirschy

See also: Caltex; Drake, Edwin Laurentine; ExxonMobil; Gulf Oil Company; Mobil Oil Corporation; Petroleum; Red Line Agreement of 1928; Rockefeller, John D.; Seven Sisters Oil Companies; Tarbell, Ida; Texas Oil Boom

FURTHER READING

Brands, H.W. 2010. *American Colossus: The Triumph of American Capitalism, 1865–1900*. New York: Anchor Books.

Chernow, Ron. 2004. *Titan: The Life of John D. Rockefeller, Sr.* New York: Vintage Books.

Segall, Grant. 2001. *John D. Rockefeller: Anointed with Oil*. New York: Oxford University Press.

Tarbell, Ida B. 1904. *The History of the Standard Oil Company*. New York: McClure, Phillips & Co.

Weinberg, Steve. 2008. *Taking on the Trust: How Ida Tarbell Brought Down John D. Rockefeller and Standard Oil*. New York: W.W. Norton & Co.

Yergin, Daniel. 2009. *The Prize: The Epic Quest for Oil, Money, & Power*. New York: Free Press.

Stanley, William Jr.

The early history of electrification in the United States features numerous inventors and engineers who put together the basic components of the system that provided electrical power to the offices, workshops, factories, public buildings, and homes of Americans in the late nineteenth and early twentieth centuries. William Stanley Jr. (1858–1916) stands as one of the important figures in this history. Holder of 129 patents, Stanley developed the technology that enabled electricity generation plants to send electricity along lengthy transmission wires to their distant customers by means of transformers. These devices are a key feature of alternating current electrification because they allow for the adjustment of voltage levels as power is distributed through the system. In 2004, the Institute of Electrical and Electronics Engineers named Stanley's demonstration of transformers at Great Barrington, Massachusetts in 1886 as one of the key milestones of the history of electricity.

Stanley was born in Brooklyn a few years before the US Civil War, and in 1877, graduated from Williston Seminary (now Williston Northampton School), a boarding school in Easthampton, Massachusetts. Then he entered Yale's class of 1881 but left soon after to find work in the up-and-coming field of electricity ("Stanley" 1935). He began his career with a short tenure as an electrician in the firm of Charles T. Chester, maker of telegraph keys and fire alarms. He tried his hand at the nickel-plating business, which was also of short duration, and then took a job with the US Electric Lighting Company in New York City, a competitor of Thomas Edison in the market for incandescent lighting (Hughes 1993, 100). At US Electric, Stanley worked with inventor Hiram Maxim on electric arc and incandescent lamps and later, Edward Weston, another noted inventor and engineer. In 1882, Stanley left for Swan Electric Lighting Company in Boston. While at Swan Electric, he developed innovations in incandescent light bulbs and electric generators and received several patents. While working on an electrical installation at the Lawrenceville Works of the Union Switch and Signal Company in Pittsburgh, Stanley was brought to the attention of George Westinghouse, owner of the company (Covington 2018).

In 1884, Stanley moved to Pittsburgh to work with Westinghouse, who acquired the rights to the patents that Stanley assigned to Swan Electric. Together they engaged in an enterprise to develop an electric lighting system to compete with Charles Brush's AC arc light system, and Edison's DC incandescent lighting system. Westinghouse provided funding and Stanley began manufacturing incandescent lamps and direct-current generators to power them. In 1885, Westinghouse acquired the US rights to a primitive alternating current transformer invented in 1882 by Lucien Gaulard of France and John Gibbs of England. Briefly, the transformers in use today are essential in a larger electrical grid system because electricity is produced at a high voltage level but must be distributed to users at varied levels; a modest-sized factory might operate at 480 volts, but an ordinary single-family house operates at 120–240 volts. Transformers enable the conversion of high voltage to low voltage, as well as low to high voltage, which enable far-flung users of different amounts of electricity to be connected to a single electrical grid.

In Stanley and Westinghouse's era, direct current was preferred for safety reasons because it operated at a low voltage level. However, the natural loss of electricity along transmission lines meant that the direct current systems could service users only within a short distance of the power plant. According to one historian of the subject, "until the problem of transmission was solved, electricity was impractical for installation any distance from a generating plant." Furthermore, "Westinghouse was interested enough in alternating current to take an option on the Gaulard and Gibbs transformers developed in England" (Drew 1985, 6–7). Since alternating current frequently flips the direction of its charge flow, its voltage could be modified very easily, if provided with a mechanism designed to produce this effect.

Stanley had been engaged for several years in the study and experimentation of what he called "electromotive forces" or electromagnetism, which included investigations in electrical transmission with alternating current. After studying the transmission capabilities of the Gaulard-Gibbs device, Stanley found it unsatisfactory for commercial use by virtue of its design and began experimenting with different wiring configurations. Whereas the original had arranged the transformers in a series, Stanley rearranged them in parallel format, enabling them to "maintain constant potential" (Drew 1985, 10). As Stanley described it later, his improvement on the Gaulard-Gibbs transformer comprised "'two stationary coils insulated from each other but coupled by an iron core. This simple piece of apparatus makes possible the easy changing of an alternating current voltage'" (quoted in Drew 1985, 11). He summed up the effect of the change as follows: "'I realized that if we could make a transformer that would regulate the energy transformed by slight variations of its induced counter electromotive force in the same manner that a shuntwound motor regulated for energy transferred by variation of its rotational counter electromotive force, the problem would be beautifully solved'" (quoted in Drew 1985, 10).

Having become seriously ill in Pittsburgh due to heavy smoke from factories, Stanley moved his laboratory and his family in 1885 to Great Barrington, Massachusetts where the bucolic environment of the Berkshire Mountains restored his health. In late 1885 and early 1886, he performed his experimental work on the transformer, making use of an old mill on the Housatonic River most recently used to manufacture vulcanized rubber footwear. He installed a boiler, a restored steam engine, an alternating current generator, transmission wires, incandescent lights, and his newly designed transformers, creating a small power grid in the village. Linking the power plant located inside the mill to thirteen stores, two doctor's offices, a barbershop, the telephone exchange, and the post office, Stanley began operating the system and lighting buildings on March 6, 1886. The system was self-regulating, stepping up the generator's output from 500 to 3,000 volts and transmitting power to the center of town, then, reducing the voltage from 3,000 back to 500 for distribution to the system's different endpoints (Hughes 1993, 103). On March 20, Stanley held a public demonstration of the system, which turned into a "gala" celebration. Stanley recalled: "'The streets and stores were crowded with people, the big 150-candlepower lamps were running at about double their candlepower, and my townsmen, though very skeptical as to the dangers to be encountered when going near the lights, rejoiced with me'" (quoted in Drew 1985, 12).

Stanley had accomplished a first in the history of energy. He had demonstrated that high-voltage alternating current could be sent very long distances by means of transmission wires and transformers. Power plants could appear anywhere and could service customers hundreds of miles away. Westinghouse formed the Westinghouse Electric Company in 1886 and installed the system in Buffalo later that fall. By 1888, Westinghouse had acquired the patent rights and services of Nikola Tesla, who invented the suite of alternating current generators and motors that could power the system on a large scale. His company built 300 Westinghouse central stations around the country by 1890, powering the equivalent of 500,000 16-candlepower lamps (Hughes 1993, 105). Westinghouse and Edison became embroiled in the War of the Currents to determine whether direct current or alternating current would prevail in the electrification of the United States. Westinghouse would go on to win the contract to electrify the Chicago World's Columbian Exposition in 1893, and to build the larger portion of the giant electricity generation system in the Niagara Falls hydroelectric plant, which in 1895 became operational. The Westinghouse Electric Company, using inventions from Stanley, Tesla, and many other inventors and innovators, took the inside track in the contest to determine America's electricity future.

Stanley parted company with Westinghouse before the War of the Currents reached its climax. He felt deceived and disrespected by Westinghouse and cut ties in 1890. In the same year, he formed the Stanley Electric Manufacturing Company in Pittsfield, Massachusetts to make and sell transformers. He and his engineers invented a commercially successful alternating current induction motor and also manufactured "generators, transformers, rotary converters, motor-generators, switchboard apparatus," and other electrical components ("Consolidation" 1905, 788). In 1903, the Stanley Electric Manufacturing Company was acquired by Thomas Edison's General Electric Company, but Stanley stayed on to manage the company as a subsidiary. This arrangement continued until 1907 when General Electric consolidated the enterprise into the parent company. Stanley continued operating the Stanley Instrument Company, founded in 1897, which designed and manufactured an alternating current watt meter to measure consumers' energy usage. However, Westinghouse filed suit for patent infringement and in 1907 the company closed down.

Despite his falling out with Westinghouse, persistent litigation, and business frustrations, Stanley was recognized by other industry leaders, scientists, and engineers with the Edison Medal in 1912 for "a career of meritorious achievement in electrical science, electrical engineering, or the electrical arts" (IEEE 2021). Both Westinghouse Electric Company and General Electric Company owed a sizeable debt to Stanley for his research and development on alternating current technologies. He died four years later at the age of fifty-seven at Great Barrington, leaving behind a wife of thirty-two years and nine children.

Jeffrey B. Webb

See also: Brush, Charles Francis; California Electric Light Company; Consolidated Edison Company; Edison, Thomas Alva; Electricity; General Electric Company; Henry, Joseph; Insull, Samuel; Pearl Street Power Station; Tesla, Nikola; War of the Currents; Westinghouse, George

FURTHER READING

"Consolidation of the Stanley Electric Manufacturing Company and the General Incandescent Arc Light Company." 1905. *Electrical Review*. Vol. 46. No. 19. P. 788.

Covington, Edward J. 2018. "William Stanley, Jr." Lamptech. http://www.lamptech.co.uk/Documents/People%20-%20Stanley%20W.htm (accessed October 2023).

Drew, Bernard A., and Gerard Chapman. 1985. "William Stanley Lighted a Town and Powered an Industry." *Berkshire History*. Vol. 6. No. 1. https://berkshirehistory.org/wp-content/uploads/2018/11/Berkshire-History-Vol-VI-No-1-William-Stanley-Lighted-a-Town.pdf (accessed October 2023).

Hammond, John Winthrop. 1941. *Men and Volts: The Story of General Electric*. Philadelphia, PA: J. B. Lippincott Company.

Hughes, Thomas P. 1993. *Networks of Power: Electrification in Western Society, 1880–1930*. Baltimore, MD: Johns Hopkins University Press.

Institute of Electrical and Electronics Engineers (IEEE). 2021. "IEEE Edison Medal Recipients." https://www.ieee.org/content/dam/ieee-org/ieee/web/org/about/awards/recipients/edison-rl.pdf (accessed October 2023).

"Stanley, William." 1935. *The National Cyclopaedia of American Biography*. Vol. 24. New York: James T. White & Co. P. 394–5.

Whelan, M., Steve Rockwell, and Thomas Blalock. 2014. "William Stanley Jr.: Pioneer of the Transformer and Alternating Current (AC) Distribution." Engineering Hall of Fame. Edison Tech Center. https://edisontechcenter.org/WilliamStanley.html (accessed October 2023).

Steam Power

The modern steam engine was invented by English engineer Thomas Newcomen (1663–1729) in 1712. A steam engine can be defined as any machine that involves the use of steam to drive the mechanical work of the apparatus, usually a turbine. The various constructions of steam engines, steam turbines, and steam boilers were the leading source of energy for Western populations from the Early Modern Era (1500–1800) to the twentieth century. The steam turbine technology of the later nineteenth century is still applied to create most of the energy throughout the world's thermal power plants, whether driven by nuclear, fossil, or renewable energy sources.

The first steam engine, defined simply as using steam power to drive a turbine, was probably Heron's Aeolipyle, named after the Roman god of wind. Heron of Alexandria (10–70) invented this turbine system after reading many works of earlier scholars such as the Roman engineer Vitruvius (80–15 BCE), who had described the use of steam to create wind forces from earlier Greek sources that remain undiscovered and possibly apocryphal.

The shift from the inquiries of natural philosophers and their experiments regarding boiled water and energy to applying technologies of steam to society began during the seventeenth century. Giambattista Della Porta (1535–1615), an Italian alchemist, created a steam pressure apparatus during the early 1600s. This device included a cistern of boiled water that forced steam and water out of a tube. These improvements led to the work of French engineer Salomon de Caus, who invented a steam fountain used to raise water in a conduit. Giovanni Branca, an Italian architect, created a similarly powered steam turbine, though of greater force, that could be used to drive a series of linked wheels. This led many, including Branca, to speculate about the application of steam power to larger projects, mechanical devices, and vehicles.

French and English inventors of the seventeenth century continued to advance on these experiments of the Renaissance. Edward Somerset (1602–67), the Second Marquis of Worcester, conceivably created a large vehicle using water and steam power. This device, akin to the steam fountain of the Italians, may have involved a repetitive process that included a piston. However, it is also possible that the invention was simply an illustrated plan printed in his *Century of Inventions* (1655), rather than a physical creation. English inventor Samuel Morland, the "Master of Mechanicks" to Charles II (1630–85), increasingly applied steam power materially through inventing different pumping mechanisms. His pumps were used to drain marshes and wells through creating a vacuum that accessed liquids to be released through a pipe.

English inventor Captain Thomas Savery first published his later steam engine model in *The Miner's Friend; or, An Engine to Raise Water by Fire* (1702). Savery's engine was named in this manner due to the necessity of steam engines to remove water from mines. However, these engines lacked commercial viability, as they often overheated and caused explosions.

During the era of Savery, Denis Papin, a French mathematician, discovered how to more efficiently drive pistons using heated water. Applying these advances, Papin created the first steam digester. This was probably the first laboratory experiment that used steam power to drive a piston, although some contend the German burgomaster Otto von Guericke had created a steam digester to drive a much larger piston during the 1650s.

THOMAS NEWCOMEN

Thomas Newcomen (1663–1729) is regarded as the inventor of the first commercially viable steam engine. Newcomen was a hardware dealer, ironmonger, and the Baptist pastor of his local church in Dartmouth, Devon, England. Though he came from a family of merchants in this region of southwestern England, Newcomen chose a different career path than his ancestors. As a dealer of goods to mine owners, he sought to find a better way to remove water from ever-deepening iron and tin mines. To remove this flood water from mines, he invented a steam engine to pump liquid out of the excavations. Especially for the coal-producing English Midlands, Newcomen's invention was vital for the growth of the Industrial Revolution (1760–1840), and was an essential step forward to the invention of James Watt's (1736–1819) more advanced steam engine applied to develop steam technology for the rail locomotives of the nineteenth century.

Andrew Kettler

Newcomen, who worked with his business partner John Calley (1663–1717), invented the first commercially viable steam engine in 1712 by combining these many ancient, Italian, English, German, and French advances in steam technology. Newcomen's design for an atmospheric steam engine involved heating water to a boil beneath a piston that was encased within a cylinder. The steam released from the boiling process would raise the piston upwards. As the piston rose, a stream of heated water would be released from the cylinder at the top. The release of the heated water out of the top and the use of injected cold water in the bottom of the cylinder chilled the bottom of the chamber, creating a vacuum beneath the raised piston, allowing it to fall back into the cylinder. The force of these engines would be connected to large beams or rotative wheels that were generally applied to lift water out of mines.

Rather than in the same cylinder as the steam entered, as in Newcomen's engine, James Watt (1736–1819) devised a way to have the steam condense within a separate closed vessel. His advances led to considerable commercial applications of the steam engine in England and throughout Europe and the Americas. Following in his wake, Richard Trevithick (1771–1833) created the maximum capacity steam engine. That specific engine, developed throughout the 1790s, would be used to power the first railcar using steam in 1804.

The steam engine of American inventor George Henry Corliss (1817–88) expanded on Trevithick's engine by creating a system of multiple valves to control temperatures at different points in the process of steam production. American engineer Oliver Evans (1755–1819) applied a different version of a high-powered steam engine, discovered at the same time as Trevithick, to drive a steam-powered wagon in 1805. Later steam engines were used in the steamboat constructions of American inventor Robert Fulton (1765–1815), and the developments of rail technology and locomotive engines by English engineer George Stephenson.

Steam engines were thereafter applied to larger wagons, carriages, railways, and steamboats during the nineteenth century. Steam power also led to vast improvements in the size of naval vessels, and the speed of shipping for commercial materials and military goods. On the American frontier and within the Mississippi Valley, the steamboat became essential during the nineteenth century to move goods and slaves throughout the vast interior river system that upheld the burgeoning American economy.

The economic and naval necessities of the British and American imperialism led to increased desire for ever more powerful engines, leading to the advances of Scottish inventor William John Macquorn Rankine (1820–72), whose continued mathematical work, since called the Rankine cycle, limited the wasted energy of earlier steam engines. These improvements led to the creation of internal combustion engine during the 1850s and 1860s, attributed to both Austrian inventor Siegfried Marcus (1831–98) and Belgian engineer Étienne Lenoir (1822–1900). The emergence of the petrol engine, out of their designs, steered advances in automobile technology in the late nineteenth and early twentieth century, leading to the decline in the use of the steam engine within most sectors.

Despite the decline of the steam engine, the steam turbine remained vital to drive Western economic and industrial growth of the twentieth century. Charles Parsons (1854–1931) invented the modern steam turbine in 1884. The multiple stages of energy captured through his turbine were expanded to greater production through patents purchased by George Westinghouse (1846–1914). The low costs of energy created through the application of Parsons turbine allowed for the expansion of the industrial system to greater economic growth during the twentieth century. Steam power through turbines account for most of the energy produced within power plants in the modern world. Today, steam power from these plants, heated through diverse fossil fuel, nuclear, and renewable products, frequently leads to international conflicts over patents for mechanical equipment applied to create greater efficiency within power systems. As well, many still dream of the application of advanced steam technology, or modern steam, to smaller engines that can create steam to drive automobiles, boats, and railcars into less polluted and carbon neutral spaces of the future.

Andrew Kettler

See also: Baltimore & Ohio Railroad; Cooper, Peter; Corliss, George Henry; Evans, Oliver

FURTHER READING

Crump, Thomas. 2007. *A Brief History of the Age of Steam: The Power that Drove the Industrial Revolution*. New York: Carroll & Graf Publishers.

Dickinson, H.W. 1963. *A Short History of the Steam Engine*. London: Cass.

Dickinson, H.W., and Percy Russell. 1952. *Thomas Newcomen, Engineer: 1663–1729*. Dartmouth: Newcomen Association.

Hills, Richard Leslie. 2000. *Power from Steam: A History of the Stationary Steam Engine*. Cambridge: Cambridge University Press.

Johnson, Walter. 2013. *River of Dark Dreams: Slavery and Empire in the Cotton Kingdom*. Cambridge, MA: Harvard University Press.
Rolt, L.T.C., and J.S. Allen. 1977. *The Steam Engine of Thomas Newcomen*. Hartington: Moorland Publishing Company.
Rosen, William. 2010. *The Most Powerful Idea in the World: A Story of Steam, Industry, and Invention*. New York: Random House.
Storer, J.D. 1969. *A Simple History of the Steam Engine*. London: J. Baker.

Steele, John Washington "Coal-Oil Johnny"

Among the more curious figures in the history of energy in the United States is John Washington "Coal-Oil Johnny" Steele (1843–1920). He became an instant millionaire in the Pennsylvania oil boom of the 1860s, but his fame grew from the highly publicized way in which he managed—or mismanaged—his newfound wealth. He's not known for building an oil company or pioneering fossil fuel technology, but as a person who hit the jackpot and wasted his fortune in a six-month, self-indulgent spending spree. He became the subject of newspaper accounts and even the focal point of both a short story and a folk song. His own memoir, *Coal-Oil Johnny: Story of His Career as Told by Himself* (1902) played into the creation of the Coal-Oil Johnny legend by offering comment from the person himself on how he became known as the world's most notorious spendthrift. Altogether, the life and legend of Coal-Oil Johnny contributed to the public image of oil wealth as "easy money," and those who possessed it as men of dubious character.

John Steele and his older sister Permelia were orphaned in 1844 when John was just an infant, and they were adopted by Culbertson and Sarah McClintock, a farming couple who lived on Oil Creek in Venango County, Pennsylvania (Steele 1902, 8). Permelia died at the age of ten in 1851, and then Culbertson died in 1855 at the age of forty-five, leaving his widow to raise Steele by herself. He remembered his adopted parents fondly, writing in his memoir that "no parents could have treated children with greater care and kindness," and that their "greatest delight seemed to be doing good to others" (Steele 1902, 8). His adopted mother encouraged Steele to read and took him to church on a regular basis. When he came of age, she apprenticed him to her nephew David Haynes, a local merchant, and in 1862, John married Eleanor J. Moffitt, a young woman whose family attended their church.

Things changed for Sarah McClintock and John Steele in 1859 when Edwin Drake struck oil in nearby Titusville. Steele recalled, "it started excursions of fortune-seekers from all over Christendom to our quiet and peaceful valley" (Steele 1902, 22). His mother initially resisted, but eventually gave in and signed over leases to "a number of oil operators" who each paid $500 and one-eighth interest on royalties from the oil produced on the leased section (Miller 1941, 43). She used the money to improve her home and furnishing, including the purchase of a new stove to use for cooking instead of the fireplace. In a terrible twist, the stove flared up when she used some crude oil to stoke a fire on a cold morning in March 1864, which burned her badly enough that she died the following day (Miller 1941, 44). Her farm and the oil leases passed into Steele's hands. When he opened his mother's safe, he found $24,500 in cash, and could expect regular royalty payments into the foreseeable future.

The next year of Steele's life created the legend for which he became known. In his memoir he recalled that many of the newly rich farmers didn't know how to handle their sudden wealth and "it was the custom of the people along the creek to lose their money." Given that experience, he remembered telling a kindly person who counseled restraint, "I intended to have some fun with mine before it all got away" (Steele 1902, 42). He approached a local lawyer for advice and after a thirty-minute conversation was charged $500 as a retainer fee, which Steele naively paid. Steele bought some horses from Daniel Fowler, who recognized the young man as an easy mark. Fowler introduced him to Horace Cullom of nearby Meadville, who convinced Steel to invest $45,000 in real estate in the town. He found it hard to say no to anyone, including parents seeking money for their children's education, farmers behind on their mortgages, investors selling stock in mines, girls looking for a handout to buy new dresses (Steele 1902, 47). Steele visited Philadelphia with a new so-called friend Seth R. Slocum, who persuaded Steele to make him power of attorney. They bought new suits, visited the racetrack, drank heavily with a group of revelers, and raced around town in an expensive carriage. One of the street kids yelled, "'that's Coal-Oil Johnny and his gang!'" (Miller 1941, 46). The nickname stuck.

There were plenty more financial misadventures to come. Steele enjoyed his excursions around Philadelphia and even had his carriage painted red with a sort of "coat of arms" emblazoned on the side that featured an oil derrick, oil tanks, and a flowing oil well. He traveled with an entourage and caroused at the Girard House and the Continental Hotel. He spent part of one evening tearing up all the hats of the patrons in the Continental bar, and then bought replacement hats for everyone the next day. Steele and his crowd visited the theater and Steele befriended Low Gaylord and M.T. Skiff, producers of a struggling minstrel show. Steele bought into the production and began to fund its operations, paying for venues, travel, accommodations, and handbills to keep the show running. He traveled with the company to a number of their events, including shows throughout New Jersey and in Chicago. Steele ran up large tabs at numerous establishments, played billiards, bought a racehorse, took up boxing, and learned to play the cornet. Within the year, Steele's spending spree came to a crashing halt.

Through what Steele later called a "scheme to wrest my property from me," he lost control of his estate in 1867. The details are complicated, but put simply, his financial collapse involved dubious business agreements, legal chicanery, and outright fraud. He claimed in his memoir that he'd been "duped" by a "pestiferous devil," a reference to Dan Fowler, and come under the spell of a "hypnotic" performer, in reference to Seth Slocum. He said he was sheared like a sheep through the "machinations of those who had taken advantage of my weaknesses." This was a reference to a New York investor named William H. Wickham who was instrumental in divesting him of the McClintock farm. It eventually sold for $35,000 at a sheriff's sale to resolve a lien on overdue taxes (Miller 1941, 51). Steele declared bankruptcy in 1868 with an indebtedness over $100,000, including $19,824 to the owner of the Girard House, $5,805 to a Philadelphia jeweler, and $2,024 to a liquor distributor (Giddens 1938, 118). At this point Steele believed his "wanderings" had "disgraced" his family, and that his "home-ties" were "broken beyond repair," but he was welcomed home like the prodigal son in Jesus' famous parable: "Figuratively, the fatted calf was killed for the returning and foolish prodigal" (Steele 1902, 180, 184). He reconciled with his wife and started over as a teamster in Franklin, and then as a baggage handler at the Rouseville train depot.

Steele tried to return to an honorable life of work and family, but he couldn't shake his reputation as a self-indulgent, overspending wastrel. In some ways he had only himself to blame. During his Philadelphia escapades he played to the crowd and said he basked in the "fame that came to me" (Steele 1902, 119). He knew he was "engaged in running a little show of my own" with all of his garish displays of wealth, particularly his red-painted carriage with its odd coat of arms (Steele 1902, 120). Rumors circulated that he'd found $150,000 in the safe after his mother died, when it was fraction of that amount, and that his royalties amounted to $2,000 a day, which was a wild exaggeration that Steele did little to correct (Giddens 1938, 115). Later, he would lament that "many foolish things were attributed to me, of course, of which I was never guilty," but admitted that he was "leading a life which rendered many of the untrue surmises justifiable" (Steele 1902, 75). Though he resented the "misrepresentations of the newspaper press," he confessed he couldn't really blame his critics "through the magnifying of rumors, attributed outlandish actions to me as a spendthrift 'oil prince,'" who sported diamond pins, diamond rings, expensive gold chains, and expensive gold watches (Steele 1902, 76).

Steele realized he created a separate persona, Coal-Oil Johnny, and once it became legend through rumors and newspaper reports, he'd lost control of it. In his memoir he recalled that while living in Rouseville and trying to put his life back together, a person offered him $5,000 to give him details of his career so he could publish his story in a book. He said in his memoir, "this offer I refused, as I refused all others. I thought that possibly some day the public would be allowed to forget all about me; but it never has, and as the years roll on the accounts become more and more exaggerated" (Steele 1902, 191). In 1874, Steele and his family decided to leave Pennsylvania and start a new life in the West, beginning in Denison, Iowa where "no one in the town was aware of my identity as 'Coal-Oil Johnny'" (Steele 1902, 197). Eventually Coal-Oil Johnny caught up with him and his "place of residence soon became located, and advertised by the newspapers." He was inundated with offers by showmen to join their circuses and "hounded day and night by column after column of fabrication" as more "outlandish reports appeared in the public prints" (Steele 1902, 204–5).

In 1880, Steele and his family moved once more, this time farther west to Nebraska, where they remained for the rest of his life. Steele worked in a railroad office in Kearney and then in railyards in Louisville and Ashland. Finally, in 1902 he published his memoir to "set forth the main details of my foolish career which have been so distorted in the public prints," but also to serve as a cautionary tale to young men who might wish to live the "wild life" (Steele 1902, 211). Steele lived long enough to see Coal-Oil Johnny become the subject of a story in the collection *The Motormaniacs* (1905) by Lloyd Osbourne, who was Robert Louis Stevenson's stepson and co-author with him of three books. The legend lived on. In 1940, it was widely known enough for movie audiences to get the reference in the film *Kitty Foyle*, when actress Ginger Rogers in the titular role referred to her boyfriend as a "regular Coal-Oil Johnny," meaning spendthrift. The legend provided some colorful, if unflattering, touches to the oilman image as it became part of America's cultural heritage. Stories about wildcatters and oil tycoons became a feature of American literature and film, as in Upton Sinclair's *Oil!* (1926), which told the story of a rapacious oil tycoon and his socialist son. The book was adapted in part by Paul Thomas Anderson in his film *There Will Be Blood* (2007), for which Daniel Day-Lewis won the Academy Award for Best Actor.

Jeffrey B. Webb

See also: Drake, Edwin Laurentine; Getty, Jean Paul; Hart, William Aaron; Pennsylvania Oil Boom; Sinclair, Upton

FURTHER READING

Giddens, Paul H. 1938. *The Birth of the Oil Industry*. New York: The Macmillan Company.

Madrigal, Alexis C. 2010. "The Legend of Coal Oil Johnny, America's Great Forgotten Parable." *The Atlantic*. October 18.

Miller, Ernest C. 1941. *Oil Mania: Sketches from the Early Pennsylvania Oil Fields*. Philadelphia: Dorrance and Company Publishers.

Steele, John Washington. 1902. *Coal-Oil Johnny: Story of His Career as Told by Himself*. Franklin, PA: Samuel H. Gray.

Steen, Charles Augustus

At the end of the Second World War, US policymakers began the process of developing civilian uses for nuclear energy, which meant locating a source of uranium. Elements like uranium, plutonium, and thorium provide the base material to create and sustain fission, the nuclear chain reaction that creates intense heat to boil water for steam, which power the turbines in nuclear plants to generate electricity. One of the important figures in the early search for domestic sources of uranium is Charles "Charlie" Steen (1919–2006), a geologist who explored various regions in South America for petroleum before turning to uranium prospecting on the Colorado Plateau. After years of arduous work, he found what he was looking for in 1952 in the Lisbon Valley's anticlinal rock formations about 38 miles south-southeast of present-day Moab, Utah. Steen and a business partner created the Standard Uranium Corporation the next year.

During Steen's childhood, the family struggled with financial insecurity. His father struck it rich in oil prospecting but lost his money before he was twenty-two. In 1923, when Steen was four, his father left him, his mother, and his infant sister, which gave way to a series of stepfathers and numerous family relocations (Ringholz 2002, 3). Eventually they landed in Houston, and Steen began his studies at John Tarleton Agricultural College in Stephenville, Texas. He met his future wife at Tarleton but transferred after a year to the Texas School of Mines and Metallurgy in El Paso where he ultimately graduated in 1943 with a B.A. in geology. Steen registered for the draft and hoped to serve but was ineligible due to low weight and bad eyesight. During the war he traveled to Bolivia to work in a tin mining operation, then to Peru to survey natural gas and oil field for the Socony-Vacuum Oil Company. After the war Steen got married and tried graduate school for a year at the University of Chicago, then left to work for Standard Oil Company as a field geologist. A tangle with several of his supervisors led to his firing, and Steen realized he wasn't fitted to work for someone else.

Steen and his wife—soon to have four children—moved to Houston where Steen tried to organize investors to support him in starting an oil company. In the meantime, he began working as a self-employed contractor to pay the bills, "remodeling kitchens, adding bedroom and baths" and trying to gather start-up funds for his business. Then, he happened across an article in the December 1949 issue of *Engineering and Mining Journal* titled, "Can Uranium Mining Pay?" Since he lacked any real momentum in the Texas oil field, Steen took some inspiration from the prospect of riches in uranium mining in the four corners area of Utah, Colorado, Arizona, and New Mexico (Zoellner 2009, 134). With no money, Steen's mother mortgaged her house and gave him $1,000, and his uncle loaned him enough to buy a second-hand Jeep. Steen headed west towing a 20-foot trailer for his family to live in.

They settled in Dove Creek in southwestern Colorado and Steen fed his family venison, rabbit stew, beans, and rice, while he searched for uranium deposits in the desolate, arid landscape of the Colorado Plateau. Steen preferred to search across the border in an area of southeastern Utah known as Lisbon Valley, where sandstone rock outcroppings with synclines and anticlines buttress the valley's mesas and buttes. He'd learned that uranium ore was discovered there in 1916 and mined in 1948, but the uranium content was low, and the Atomic Energy Commission (AEC) wrote off the area as not commercially viable. Lacking the money to buy a Geiger counter, Steen fell back on what he learned in his geology classes. He learned about anticlines, which are arch-shaped folds in rock layers that sort of "dip" downward, and that uranium found on the upper portions of these arch-shaped folds would be discovered in greater concentrations further down the dips. He observed that the miners had been working outcrops along the escarpment's rim on a set of claims known as Big Buck, which overlooked the Big Indian Wash in the Lisbon Valley. He believed that the anticline pattern hinted at richer concentrations of uranium further back from the rim (Steen 2002).

Steen staked out twelve claims in 600 x 1,500 ft. rectangles, which he named for things he remembered fondly from his time in Peru: Mujer Sin Verguenza ("Shameless Woman"), Mi Corazon ("My Heart"), Besame Mucho ("Kiss Me A Lot"), Pisco (a Peruvian liquor), Fundadoro ("Founder"), Te Quiero ("I Love You"), Linda Mujer ("Beautiful Woman"), Mi Amorcita ("My Love"), Ann, Bacardi, Mi Alma ("My Soul"), and Mi Vida ("My Life") (Ringholz 2002). He left notes in tin cans on the sites and registered his claims with the San Juan County recorder on March 7, 1951. Completely broke and his wife suffering from pneumonia, Steen took his family to Tucson, Arizona where he scratched together some carpentry jobs and looked for an investment partner. Finding none, they returned to Utah in 1952 where they rented a tarpaper shack for $15 per month in Cisco, 100 miles from Steen's claims. He borrowed a derelict drilling rig from local merchant Bill McCormick and went to work. On July 6, 1952, Steen drilled a 70-foot shaft at the Mi Vida claim, which contained a 14-foot segment of dark-colored ore (NMHFM 2020). He found a friend named Buddy Cowger in Cisco who owned a Geiger counter, and his sample sent the instrument's needle jumping. It turned out to be pitchblende, an ore with high concentrations of uranium. This confirmed that his geological assessment was correct and that his investment paid off in a spectacular way.

Steen, his mother, and several associates formed the Utex (Utah-Texas) Exploration Company on October 24, 1952 to develop the mine at Mi Vida and other projects. With McCormick, Steen also formed the Standard Uranium Corporation in 1953 and a year later, they bought the Big Buck claims. To further expand their operations, Sheen and McCormick created the Uranium Reduction Company in 1955, which built the world's largest uranium ore processing mill in Moab, Utah. The mill capitalized on the expansion of uranium mining in southeast Utah, since "the Steen discovery set off an extensive rush of claim staking" in the Lisbon Valley by a range of other companies (Chenoweth 1990, 14). Historian Raye Ringholz found that "between 1946 and 1959, 309,380 claims were filed in four Utah counties," and for a time the town of Moab became known as "The Uranium Capital of the World" (Ringholz 1994). In the thirty years after Steen's discovery, the mines of the Big Indian district produced 10 million tons of ore valued at over $1 billion (NMHFM 2020).

In the 1950s and 1960s, Steen lived well on his uranium mine and mill income. He built a spacious house overlooking Moab with a swimming pool and servant's quarters, took an interest in flying and piloted his own private plane, and had his prospector boots bronzed to memorialize his Mi Vida discovery. He and his wife donated $50,000 to build a hospital in Moab and land to build schools and churches. Steen sat in the Utah State Senate for three years between 1958 and 1961, but resigned in disgust over high tax rates and his inability to secure liberalization of the state's liquor laws. Steen built a 27,000-square-foot ranch in Reno,

Nevada near the home of Lemuel "Sandy" Bowers, discoverer of Nevada's Comstock Lode. He also invested in horse breeding, a pickle plant, a marble quarry, and airplane prop factory. The Steens were known for throwing giant parties with hundreds of guests (Jensen 2009). However, the good times didn't last. The AEC declared in 1962 that its storehouse of uranium was full and would be stepping down purchases over the next eight years. In 1970, the agency stopped buying uranium altogether. Another small boom occurred in the mid-1970s when new civilian nuclear plants began buying, but then competition from foreign companies and extensive federal regulations made uranium mining for civilian power companies less profitable (Ringholz 1994).

In 1962, Steen and his partners sold Utex Exploration Company and Uranium Reduction Company to Atlas Minerals Corporation. Milling continued until 1984 and when production ceased, Atlas left behind an unlined impoundment with about 16 million tons of radioactive mill tailings and contaminated soil. The company declared bankruptcy in 1998, leaving the US Department of Energy (DOE) to take responsibility in 2001 for cleaning up the site. Tailings were removed to an "engineered disposal cell" built near Crescent Junction, Utah and the DOE began remediation on the groundwater (OEM 2019). The DOE estimated that by the end of the fiscal year in 2018, it had spent $527 million on cleanup costs at the mill and would spend up to $1.197 billion by the time the project ends in 2034 (Larson 2021, 18). Overall, the case of Steen's uranium processing plant illustrates that in many instances of energy development, initial profits accrue to private corporations, while some of the costs that weren't accounted for are borne by taxpayers through government environmental remediation programs.

Troubles mounted for Steen once the uranium boom began to subside. In 1968, he became involved in a terrible fistfight over a road rage incident near Reno, which ended in civil litigation. Also in 1968, the IRS issued tax liens totaling $3 million on Steen's assets, forcing him into bankruptcy. The mansion in Reno went up for sale to help the Steens climb out of debt (Dornan 1975). Then, in 1971, Steen suffered a severe head injury while using a coring drill at a prospective copper deposit in Colorado. No longer able to sustain his high level of energy, Steen settled for a more modest lifestyle in Moab before his death in 2006 from Alzheimer's Disease. Once worth over $130 million, his estate had dwindled considerably. Still, Steen's career was celebrated by Moab residents and by the uranium mining industry. He used his scientific understanding of the earth's geology to locate uranium deposits that weren't detected using traditional methods. He also built a successful exploration company and gave the uranium mining industry its footing, providing a secure domestic source of uranium for the civil nuclear power industry. The challenge with all aspects of nuclear power is that it produces radiation and radioactive wastes through mining, milling, and nuclear fission, all of which create serious health risks and require extensive, government-sponsored mitigation programs at very high cost.

Jeffrey B. Webb

See also: Atomic Energy Acts; Church Rock Uranium Mill Spill; Dysart, Stella; Energy Fuels, Inc.; Idaho National Laboratory; Manhattan Project; Navajo Reservation Uranium Mining; Nuclear Power; Nuclear Regulatory Commission; Nuclear Waste Policy Act of 1982; Three Mile Island Disaster; Yucca Mountain Nuclear Waste Repository

FURTHER READING

Chenoweth, William L. 1990. "Lisbon Valley, Utah's Premier Uranium Area: A Summary of Exploration and Ore Production." Utah Geological and Mineral Survey. Utah Department of Natural Resources. https://ugspub.nr.utah.gov/publications/open_file_reports/OFR-188.pdf

Dornan, Geoff. 1975. "House for Sale: $4 Million or Offer." *News-Journal* (Mansfield, OH). January 29. P. 5.

Jensen, Buckley. 2009. "Charles Steen—Uranium King of San Juan." *San Juan Record.* May 6. https://sjrnews.com/giants-san-juan/charles-steen (accessed October 2023).

Larson, Lance N. 2021. "Long-Term Federal Management of Uranium Mill Tailings: Background and Issues for Congress." Congressional Research Service. Report R45880. https://crsreports.congress.gov/product/pdf/R/R45880/4 (accessed October 2023).

National Mining Hall of Fame & Museum (NMHFM). 2020. "Charles Augustus Steen." Inductee Database. https://www.mininghalloffame.org/hall-of-fame/charles-augustus-steen (accessed October 2023).

Office of Environmental Management (OEM). 2019. "Remembering Utah's Famous Geologist Decades before Moab Cleanup." US Department of Energy. March 19. https://www.energy.gov/em/articles/remembering-utahs-famous-geologist-decades-moab-cleanup (accessed October 2023).

Ringholz, Raye C. 1994. "Uranium Mining in Utah." *Utah History Encyclopedia.* Utah Department of Cultural and Community Engagement. Utah Division of State History. https://historytogo.utah.gov/uranium-mining-utah/ (accessed October 2023).

Ringholz, Raye C. 2002. *Uranium Frenzy: Saga of the Nuclear West.* Logan, UT: Utah State University Press.

Steen, Mark. 2002. "My Old Man: The Uranium King." *The Canyon Country Zephyr.* February–March. https://www.canyoncountryzephyr.com/oldzephyr/feb-march2002/steen-part1.htm (accessed October 2023).

Zoellner, Tom. 2009. *Uranium: War, Energy, and the Rock that Shaped the World.* New York: Viking.

Stewart, Philo Penfield

Philo Penfield Stewart (1798–1868) was an American missionary, educator, philanthropist, and inventor who developed a cast-iron cooking stove that was more energy-efficient than other contemporary stoves of the early nineteenth century. His "Summer and Winter Air-Tight Cooking Stove" aimed to reduce both the amount of wood required to operate the stove, as well as the physical demands on the cook to keep the fire going. The stoves were marketed as "fuel-saving," which marked possibly the first time in American history that *energy efficiency* was promoted as a desirable feature for consumers. Although not exclusive to Stewart's designs, his stoves could be fueled with wood, as a renewable resource, as well as coal and peat, which are fossil fuels, which made them early examples of hybrid energy technologies. As a Christian missionary with a devotion to service that overshadowed any drive for personal fortune, Stewart made a significant contribution to social conceptions of energy use in America through his commitment to energy efficiency and conservation.

Stewart was born on July 6, 1798 in Connecticut near the state border with New York in the town of Sherman. At the age of ten, he was sent to Pittsford, Vermont to live with his maternal grandfather who owned a farm and several mills. Although his mother sent him away to ease the burden of raising six children after the passing of her husband, "Penfield," as he was called by his family, immediately recognized the value of moving to a place with lush pine forests, since he was fond of whitling and creating tools from wood. After arriving in Vermont, Penfield quickly began working with wood to make gifts for friends as well as to create devices meant to solve technical problems. He developed a water wheel for one of his grandfather's mills and fabricated various other tools that were used on the farm and in the mills.

After four years living with his grandfather, the young Stewart was sent to live and serve an apprenticeship with his uncle, a saddle and harness-maker, in the village of Pawlet in western Vermont. As part of his compensation for his seven-year apprenticeship, he spent three months of the year at the Pawlet Academy where he received his schooling. During these impressionable years from age fourteen to twenty-one, Stewart valued his education and became especially devoted to Christian principles through the influence of one of his teachers. At the age of twenty-three, he went to Mississippi to join a Christian mission situated near Choctaw communities. While stationed at the mission, Stewart was appreciated as an ingenious handyperson who was constantly using his hand tools to improve conditions in the kitchen and around the mission, not to mention constructing an animal-powered gristmill. It was out of a sense of necessity and utility—not the desire for monetary compensation or notoriety—that Stewart would exercise his handywork, both then and in future years.

In 1832, after years of oscillating between jobs back in the Northeast, Stewart traveled to Elyria, Ohio to join Revered John Jay Shipherd, his friend from Pawlet Academy, with whom he would establish the Oberlin Collegiate Institute, known today as Oberlin College.

Stewart noticed that the Shipherd home did not have a stove in its parlor, as the family could not afford one, and therefore built a stove out of sheet iron, thus taking his first step to establishing his name in the history of American stove-making. Although he built his first stove as a room heater, Reverend Shipherd's wife suggested adding an oven for baking, which allowed the stove to serve dual functions. Proud of his success with the stove prototype, Stewart then split his time between developing the college, and designing and patenting what he called the "Oberlin Stove." In addition to this cooking stove, he also made smaller heating stoves to be used in the students' rooms at Oberlin.

Stewart left Oberlin in 1836 and headed back east to explore new opportunities. Shortly after arriving in New York City, an unpleasant experience eating a loaf of poorly baked bread—burnt on one side and undercooked on the other—inspired him to re-examine his own stove designs to once again try to build a better stove. The resulting design allowed for more even heat distribution in the oven and became his famed "P. P. Stewart Summer and Winter Cooking Stove." Since Stewart was intent on producing a stove that would serve both the functions of ambient room heating in the winter as well as year-round cooking, he designed the stove in such a way that it could be modified seasonally by adding insulated tin coverings in the summer so that the stove did not emit as much heat into the room.

After struggling to get funds to further develop his stove in New York City, he finally secured a small amount of capital from relatives and moved to Troy, New York—then home to many of the metal foundries in the northeast region, along with Albany—to produce many iterations of the stove until he was satisfied with the design. The first foundry to produce his stove for market was Messrs. Starbuck & Co., although the company failed shortly after consummating their business arrangement. After having the parts produced by various other foundries as well as two short-lived collaborations with people who helped build and install stoves, the well-established Fuller, Warren & Co. agreed to manufacture the "Stewart Stoves" in high volume. By this time, the stove had incorporated a much larger oven and in 1859 it was patented as the "Large Oven and Air-Tight Summer and Winter Cooking Stove."

ENERGY EFFICIENCY

Colonists in New England during the seventeenth and eighteenth centuries had comparatively larger fireplaces than those in Europe since the expansive virgin forests provided ample supply of firewood. As the United States became more populated and more forests were cleared for farmland, fuelwood started to become scarcer, especially in urban areas. This created a need for improved energy efficiency where more heat energy could be extracted from less fuel (and less fuel wasted). Thus, cast-iron stoves began to replace the large and inefficient hearths in homes.

Curt J. Davis

By all accounts, Stewart was quite pleased with his stoves, since his social mission as it related to the American kitchen was to reduce the labor of tending to the fires while reducing demand for firewood. Back when he was living in New York City, Stewart was extremely poor and barely had enough money to purchase the firewood necessary to test his stove designs. Therefore, he was compelled to come up with a design in which only three sticks of wood, each roughly the size of an adult's forearm, would be enough to operate the stove. To achieve this, he designed the firebox, meaning the area inside the stove where combustion takes place, with a wider area at the top and narrower at the bottom. That way, as the wood burned it concentrated towards the bottom leaving a dense pile of hot coals. An oven chamber was placed in between the firebox and the area at the bottom where smoke exited the stove pipe thus allowing for heat to evenly circulate inside and uniformly heat what was being baked. At the top of the stove were four openings that served as burners, which could be covered to prevent smoke from escaping into the room. To add to this marvel of energy efficiency and conservation, at least when compared to the grossly inefficient fireplace hearths, a hot water reservoir surrounded the part of the stove that connected to the stove pipe, which allowed heat from the smoke to transfer to water that could be used for bathing, washing, or to be later boiled.

On December 13, 1868, Stewart succumbed to a combination of ailments including typhoid, pneumonia, and the effects of a pre-existing concussion and died at the age of seventy. He is remembered as motivated by the desire to improve the lives of others over personal fortune. In addition to being a Christian leader, fervent abolitionist—his home in New York was a part of the Underground Railroad—and passionate supporter of women's education, he was also committed to reducing the labor and energy costs of cooking. To this end, he promoted his stoves, often giving them away, knowing full well that the designs were likely to be copied by others. His friends and business associates often warned him against speaking so openly and publicly about his stove designs, but it was more important to him that more people have the opportunity to use an efficient stove than it was for him to earn a profit. In his lifetime, Stewart estimated that over 90,000 of his stoves had been produced and sold over the course of three decades. More significantly, however, by the time that Fuller, Warren and Co. went out of business in 1934, an estimated 2 million of his stoves had been produced. The environmental impact of his efficient stoves is incalculable, but they are certain to have reduced the number of trees that were cut down for firewood during the nineteenth century.

Curt J. Davis

See also: Evard, Mary E.A.; Franklin, Benjamin; Renewable Energy; Rumford Fireplace

FURTHER READING

Brewer, Priscilla J. 2000. *From Fireplace to Cookstove: Technology and the Domestic Ideal in America*. 1st ed. Syracuse, NY: Syracuse University Press.

Harris, Howell. 2015. "Philo Penfield Stewart, Inventor of the Ideal Cook Stove." January 22. http://stovehistory.blogspot.com/2015/01/philo-penfield-stewart-inventor-of.html (accessed May 31, 2021

Lopes Ramos, Ana. n.d. "A Brief History of the Kitchen." https://www.johndesmond.com/blog/design/a-brief-history-of-the-kitchen/ (accessed May 31, 2021).

Stewart, Eliza Capen. 1873. *A Worker, and Workers' Friend*. New York: n.p.

Sylvester, Nathaniel Bartlett. 1880. *History of Rensselaer Co., New York*. Philadelphia, PA: Everts and Peck.

Strategic Petroleum Reserve

The Strategic Petroleum Reserve is a US government stockpile of crude oil located near the Gulf of Mexico and available for the president to use to offset supply disruptions caused by an emergency. US policy makers originally intended the cache to counteract the negative effects of embargoes and to dissuade adversaries from exploiting them, although its scope has morphed over time. The Strategic Petroleum Reserve contains significant supplies of crude oil for utilization in a crisis and as the largest such accumulation in the world, it cost approximately $25 billion, the vast majority of which is for the oil itself. It was a direct response to the energy crisis of the 1970s.

The oil embargo from 1973 to 1974 highlighted the critical requirement for supplies and reinforced US efforts toward national storage. Arab member states of the Organization of Petroleum Exporting Countries (OPEC) stopped oil shipments to the United States in reaction to American provision of military supplies and logistical support to Israel during the 1973 Arab-Israeli War. The ensuing ban aggravated underlying economic factors and triggered the first major energy crisis of the 1970s, ushering in supply shortages, rising prices, gasoline rationing, and long lines at gas pumps. President Gerald Ford signed the Energy Policy and Conservation Act into law on December 22, 1975, which in addition to addressing such issues as production and consumption also made it a national goal to create a reserve of upward of 1 billion barrels of crude oil.

The Strategic Petroleum Reserve uses caverns mined into underground salt domes on the coast of the Gulf of Mexico to hold massive amounts of oil. Such an accommodation method is significantly less expensive than alternatives, and its location provides ready access to the main transportation routes, using a combination of land pipelines and seaborne tankers. In addition, the natural hollows provide significant environmental security due to their geological characteristics of high pressure and temperature differential. The US government procured in April 1977 the first locations and began construction on them a couple of months later. In total, there are sixty caves arrayed across four major storage sites: Bryan Mound and Big Hill in Texas and West Hackberry and Bayou Choctaw in Louisiana. Individual fissures can be massive, reaching as deep as 4,000 feet with a diameter as large as 200 feet.

The first deposits, more than 400,000 barrels of crude oil, arrived in July 1977. On December 27, 2009, the Strategic Petroleum Reserve reached its maximum capacity of more than 700 million barrels. Such a significant amount of oil potentially could offset the lack of imports for roughly six months and could impact positively the US energy market as quickly as two weeks from initiation of its use. Efforts to expand its volume to 1 billion barrels of oil began in 2005 but ended in 2011 due to waning interest.

The US president authorizes withdrawals from the Strategic Petroleum Reserve, and the Energy Policy and Conservation Act governs its overall management. While initially envisioned during the 1970s as a tool of foreign policy, the Strategic Petroleum Reserve has evolved to include potential economic disruptions and various natural disasters. In January 1991, President George H.W. Bush authorized the removal and sale of 17 million barrels of crude oil to stabilize the energy market during Operation Desert Storm. In September 2005, President George W. Bush approved the release of 11 million barrels of crude oil to counterbalance the deleterious impacts of Hurricane Katrina. In June 2011, President Barack H. Obama sanctioned the withdrawal of more than 30 million barrels of crude oil to equipoise potential interruptions on the global and domestic energy markets emanating from turmoil in Libya.

The Strategic Petroleum Reserve stocks approximately 650 million barrels of crude oil. Since its inception, the program has expanded to include the Northeast Home Heating Oil Reserve located in Connecticut, Massachusetts, and New Jersey and the Northeast Gasoline Reserve located in New York and Boston. Both of these facilities aim to aid critical sectors of the consumer market. Over the past five decades, the global energy market and the US role in it have changed dramatically. Since 2008, US oil production has increased significantly. As a result, in 2018 the United States was the top global producer of oil and one of the top ten oil exporting countries in the world. In response to these vastly changed circumstances, there has been renewed debate regarding the Strategic Petroleum Reserve, including questions about its necessity and calls for its downsizing or outright elimination. Amidst questions regarding the continued relevance of the Strategic Petroleum Reserve, US policy makers have passed legislation that requires sizeable drawdowns and consistent sales of a significant portion of its oil holdings to fund other government priorities deemed more pressing.

William A. Taylor

See also: Energy Crisis of the 1970s; Energy Independence; Energy Policy and Conservation Act of 1975; Energy Security Act of 1980; Gulf War; Halliburton Company; Iraq War and the Project for a New American Century; Organization of Petroleum Exporting Countries (OPEC); Petroleum

FURTHER READING

Beaubouef, Bruce A. 2007. *The Strategic Petroleum Reserve: U.S. Energy Security and Oil Politics, 1975–2005*. College Station, TX: Texas A&M University Press.

Blumstein, Carl, and Paul Komor. 1996. "Another Look at the Strategic Petroleum Reserve: Should Its Oil Holdings Be Privatized?" *Journal of Policy Analysis and Management*. Vol. 15. No. 2. Spring. Pp. 271–5.

Kalicki, Jan H., and David L. Goldwyn, eds. 2013. *Energy and Security: Strategies for a World in Transition*. 2nd ed. Baltimore, MD: Johns Hopkins University Press.

Pirog, Robert. 2018. *In Focus: Reconsidering the Strategic Petroleum Reserve*. Congressional Research Service. IF 10869. April 5.

US Government Accountability Office (GAO). 2018. *Strategic Petroleum Reserve: DOE (Department of Energy) Needs to Strengthen Its Approach to Planning the Future of the Emergency Stockpile, Report to Congressional Requesters*. GAO-18-477. May.

Weimer, David Leo. 1982. *The Strategic Petroleum Reserve: Planning, Implementation, and Analysis.* Santa Barbara, CA: Praeger.

Summerland Oil Field

The oil and gas industries played an important role in the development of southern California around the turn of the twentieth century. Edward L. Doherty's oil strike in 1892 in Los Angeles initiated a boom that drew prospectors to the region. In Summerland, a small beach community about 90 miles west-northwest of Los Angeles, oil and gas development began in the early 1890s and continued through the early decades of the twentieth century. Many of these wells operated offshore from wharfs. This gave the Summerland oil field a distinctive appearance with oil derricks topping the bluffs and extending through the beach and out over the coastal waters. In June 1900, oil and gas companies operated 305 wells in Summerland and had begun drilling at fifteen other well sites, while fifty-nine wells had already been abandoned (Arnold 1907, 17). These companies in Summerland and throughout Southern California helped to transform the largely agricultural countryside into an industrial landscape with oil and gas infrastructure composed of railroads, oil derricks, storage tank farms, pipelines, and refineries.

Geological reports beginning in the 1850s and continuing through the 1880s described the bituminous shales of the Summerland area as well as asphalt seeps that appeared on the ground in numerous locations in Santa Barbara County (Arnold 1907, 13). The indigenous Chumash used tar balls as a sealant for boats and baskets and the earliest European settlers utilized the material in various ways. A geological report from 1865 noted that Santa Barbara asphaltum was used by residents of San Francisco to tar their roofs and to make pavement. All indications were that oil could be found in sufficient quantities to be produced on an industrial scale. In 1866, chemist Stephen F. Peckham surveyed prospective oil deposits and wrote: "the southern portion of this State has veritable oil interests, which only need the fostering care of men of sound judgment, aided by sufficient means, to enable this section to ultimately furnish this entire Pacific coast with both illuminating and lubricating oils, at prices that will render futile all competition of eastern products" (Peckham 1882, 49).

Drilling began in the area soon to be occupied by the town of Summerland on Ortega Hill, part of a sheep farm owned by Burkhill Jacques. In 1877, Santa Barbara resident William A. Hocking discovered oil seepage at the base of Ortega Hill and received a lease to drill for oil. Hocking attempted to reach oil with hand tools but abandoned the plan and persuaded prominent Santa Barbara residents to invest in the Ortega Hill Oil Company in order to acquire a drilling rig. By the end of the year, the well reached 170 feet and produced 2 barrels a day, drawn by hand with an iron bucket (Myrick 1988, 66). The well was eventually abandoned. Two other companies attempted drilling in what became known as Oil Spring Canyon, several miles inland from the Jacques property. Neither the Santa Barbara Oil Company in 1877 nor the Occidental Petroleum and Mining Company in 1883 were successful in locating oil in commercial quantities. In 1883, Henry L. Williams bought out Burkhill Jacques and then in 1888, founded the town of Summerland with the intention

FIGURE 5: Oil derricks in the surf at Summerland, near Santa Barbara, California.

of creating an oceanside community for spiritualists. He attracted scores of people and in their meeting house they conducted séances, which were sessions that sought out visitations with the dead. Williams reopened the Ortega Hill well site in 1886 and drilled to 455 feet where he found oil sand, but it didn't appear to have commercial potential (Prutzman 1913, 408).

In 1890, a productive natural gas well opened in the village with enough output to illuminate seventeen homes (Arnold 1907, 16). Historian David F. Myrick noted that the news of the Summerland gas well traveled throughout California: "Newspaper editors in Los Angeles and San Francisco, well aware that inexpensive fuel would burgeon their cities, all but commanded that pipelines be built and that every cubic foot of gas be delivered to their communities" (Myrick 1988, 75). More excitement soon came from Williams' odd little settlement of spiritualists. In 1894, a gas well drilled by Smith L. Cole began seeping oil which he was able to recover and sell for a modest $2 per barrel. Two other wells began producing the same year, and Williams himself drilled two oil wells on the beach. Early in 1895, there were seven oil wells in operation, producing sufficient quantities to justify the expense of drilling. Reports of these successes opened the floodgates, as oil companies poured into Summerland seeking leases from property owners.

Within two years, nearly a hundred operators appeared on Ortega Hill, Oil Canyon, and the Summerland beach, which at the time was public property. With no legal barrier to entry, the beach was soon covered by oil derricks. Starting in 1896, some of these operators extended wharfs propping up their derricks over the ocean beyond low tide. A wharf built by the Southern Pacific Railroad stretched 1,230 feet and was dotted with oil derricks out to the end. These wharfs were of "the lightest piling construction, with only a suggestion of planking," and they fared poorly in winter weather (Prutzman 1913, 409). By the end of

1899, reports noted that twenty-two companies operated on twelve wharfs. Poor conditions forced the abandonment of some, and then a severe storm in 1903 put an end to the first experiment in US offshore oil drilling. Before they constructed their own wells, the oil produced in the Summerland oil field was sold as fuel for the new Southern Pacific Railroad, which had switched from coal to oil when managers discovered its availability. The rail bed bisected the oil field and made for a convenient stop-over on the train's route up and down the coast. The railroad carried some of the Summerland oil in Pacific Coast Oil Company tank cars to distant markets. The remainder of the oil was sold locally to companies like the Santa Barbara Ice Company and a sugar beet factory in Oxnard to fuel their steam boilers.

Other oil infrastructure appeared in Summerland. Williams built a 250-gallon storage tank near the railroad tracks on the east end of Ortega Hill. Then, in 1901, the California Liquid Asphalt Company built a refinery, which operated until 1910. The refinery was quite modest, with two stills and a capacity of 300 barrels, producing gasoline, kerosene, fuel oil, and asphalt (Arnold 1907, 66; Prutzman, 1913, 412). However, by the time this infrastructure was in place, Summerland's production had already peaked. Price competition with Los Angeles oil producers and a lack of adequate transportation dampened enthusiasm for Summerland projects. In 1903, the number of producing wells had dropped to 198 from 305 in 1900. As of October 1906, the number of active wells was 189. Then, in January 1912, there were just 133 in operation of a total 440 wells in the field. The rest had been abandoned (Prutzman, 1913, 412). Once there had been over a hundred different operators in Summerland, but that number dwindled by the end of 1906 to fourteen (Arnold 1907, 17).

The Summerland oil field completely shut down in 1939 and its derrick-and-wharf structures were dismantled. But then, the oil field had a second life once the technology of offshore oil drilling had been developed in the late 1940s and early 1950s by oil and gas companies in the Gulf of Mexico. Oil was discovered about a mile from shore, and two offshore oil platforms were constructed, Hilda in 1958 and Hazel in 1960, anchored to the ocean floor some 100 feet below the surface. These platforms were very productive, but Californians soured on offshore drilling in the wake of the blowout of Union Oil's Platform A in 1969, which spilled as much at 100,000 barrels of oil into the Santa Barbara Channel. The Santa Barbara oil spill galvanized the environmental movement and created political pressure to curtail offshore drilling. This pressure dissipated but gave impetus to the creation of the US Environmental Protection Agency and the enactment of the National Environmental Policy Act (1970), as well as new legislation and regulatory agencies in the state of California.

The Summerland oil field and its offshore extension left behind a legacy, albeit a complicated one. The discovery of oil and gas in sufficient quantities to justify commercial production aided the development of southern California's economy and infrastructure. Thus, the oil, gas, and railroad industries expedited the region's modernization. However, the industry left behind numerous unsealed wells, which leaked oil into California's coastal waters throughout the twentieth century. The California State Land Commission assumed responsibility for addressing the problem and noted in a 2018 report that "there are approximately 200 high priority legacy oil and gas wells" that "leak oil into the marine environment" at Summerland, "causing environmental degradation and public health and safety hazards" (CSLC 2018). The commission spent $1.2 million to seal just one of these wells. The California state legislature authorized $20 million through 2028 to continue remediation, which will not be enough.

According to California State Senator Hannah-Beth Jackson from Santa Barbara, "'The bill for the last hundred years is finally coming due, and it is sadly not being paid by those who have defiled the landscape, the seascape and the coast. It will be paid by taxpayers'" (Burns 2019).

Jeffrey B. Webb

See also: Caddo Oil Field; Kerr-McGee's Kermac No. 16; Santa Barbara Oil Spill

FURTHER READING

Arnold, Ralph. 1907. *Geology and Oil Resources of the Summerland District, Santa Barbara California*. Department of the Interior. United States Geological Survey. Bulletin No. 321. Washington, DC: Government Printing Office.

Burns, Melinda. 2019. "Offshore Oil: The Long Goodbye." *Santa Barbara Independent*. January 20. https://issuu.com/santabarbaraindependent/docs/sbi_681_01_30_19 (accessed October 2023).

California State Lands Commission (CSLC). 2018. "Report to the Legislature: SB 44—Coastal Hazards and Legacy Oil and Gas Well Removal and Remediation Program." State of California. https://www.slc.ca.gov/wp-content/uploads/2018/12/SB44_2017-18.pdf (accessed October 2023).

Myrick, David F. 1988. "Summerland: The First Decade." *Noticias: Quarterly Magazine of the Santa Barbara Historical Society*. Vol. 34. No. 4. Winter. Pp. 65–103.

Peckham, Stephen F. 1882. "Examination of the Bituminous Substances Occurring in Southern California." Pp. 49–90. In Josiah Dwight Whitney. *Economic Geology of the Coast Ranges*. Vol. 2. Cambridge, MA: John Wilson & Son, University Press, 1882.

Prutzman, Paul W. 1913. *Petroleum in Southern California*. Sacramento, CA: California State Mining Bureau.

Summers, Emma A.

Emma A. Summers (1858–1941) was known as California's "Oil Queen." Summers became a millionaire as a primary player in Los Angeles' oil market. Summers taught piano lessons, which helped to finance her oil operations; eventually her "empire" included apartments, ranches, theaters, hotels, a trolley company, art collections, mansions, a paint company, and garages. She became one of the most successful operators on the Pacific Coast during the oil boom of the early 1900s and extended her oil well investments into the Great Plains. She excelled in a predominately male venture and even confessed she never experienced gender inequality from her male counterparts because her attitude and business savvy smoothed over any concerns about her status as a female industrialist in the communities of Los Angeles and the broader Southern California region. "She performed the miracle of which few men are able. Having attained success after years of complete absorption in business, she had extricated herself from its toils and adjusted herself" (Smith 1911). She portrayed "self-reliance" and "independent thought" in proving women are capable of success in a male-dominated industry.

Summers was born in Kentucky in 1858, raised in Trenton, Tennessee, and relocated to Hickman, Kentucky when she was a child when her family moved there. Summers' father was a banker and merchant in Kentucky and her mother, Mary Elizabeth, was a "southern lady." Summers attended the prestigious New England Conservatory of Music in Boston, Massachusetts and thereafter became a popular piano teacher. She met and married Alpha C. Summers and they moved to Texas in 1879, and finally to Los Angeles in 1883 to begin a new life in California. Then the oil boom began when Edward L. Doheny (1856–1935) and Charles A. Canfield (1848–1913) struck oil on April 20, 1893, at Crown Hill at Colton Street. Doheny drilled "the first free flowing oil well in LA." (Roman 2015). He and Canfield built eighty-four wells and "a network of pipes to transport the crude oil," which was transferred "into their tankers for overseas shipments" (Roman 2015). By 1897, and thanks in part to Doheny and Canfield, Crown Hill was transformed from a residential neighborhood to one with oil drills for wildcatters with "black fever"—a person in search of black gold. When oil struck, Summers contracted black fever.

Summers attempted to find oil near where she lived on California Street on Fort Moore Hill, which is today the 101 Freeway. Summers didn't strike oil initially, but she remained committed after the first several disappointments. Soon she paid $700 for "a half interest in a well at Court and Temple streets" (Meares 2018). Because of the oil boom, migrants streamed into the city and the population ballooned overnight (Rasmussen 2018). According to researchers, Los Angeles did not initially welcome the influx of roughnecks who performed the manual labor in the oil fields, and yet homeowners eagerly sought oil on their own properties, and eventually built 300 wells of their own (Roman 2015). By the early 1900s, Summers owned fourteen wells, and her wealth increased each month, wherein she also advertised her product to railroads, hotels, and the Pacific Light and Power Company at $1.80 per barrel (Bakken 2003). She became an expert in testing oil quality, hired her own workers, bought all her tools and supplies, maintained a stable of forty working horses and their ten wagons, and built her own blacksmith works (Roman 2015).

"The genteel Summers joined her grease-spattered workers during daylight hours, directing their labors, while at night she handled the bookkeeping and gave music lessons to finance continued drilling," according to historian Cecilia Rasmussen (Rasmussen 1999). Summers taught herself the laws of supply and demand and began selling oil to major consumers all over town. Although the "Oil Queen" faced resistance from other companies, she worked independently, without taking on other investors. This left her alone to deal with cutthroat competition and lawsuits. She quickly developed business savvy as she mastered the use of oil equipment, negotiated to supply California's railroads, built up economies of scale in her operations, and kept up with her bookkeeping. While building her company, she balanced work with providing piano lessons (Roman 2015).

During 1900, she increased her enterprise by acquiring new oil sites in Long Beach and Inglewood. The oil field in Los Angeles produced half of the oil in California with 1,150 wells. At its height, Summers' company produced 50,000 barrels each month (Roman 2015). Summers' wealth, business activities, and of course her gender received extensive coverage in the Los Angeles press. A 1901 *Los Angeles Times* headline read, "Queen Emma Rules Roost: Mrs. Summers Outwits Male Competitors" (Meares 2018). When the price of oil declined from $1.80 per barrel in 1901 to 15 cents a barrel in 1903 due to an oil glut in the market, Summers diversified her operations (Roman 2015). She founded the Summers Paint Company and a blacksmith shop, and bought theaters, apartment buildings, and ranch properties in the San Fernando Valley, all financed by her oil earnings. She invested in two Los Angeles theaters, the Casino and the Broadway. "'In theaterdom they are calling Mrs. Summers the mascot of the house,'" wrote the *Los Angeles Times* in 1905. "'Whole power [*sic*] and principalities have been arrayed against the Casino in the last few months, but apparently this woman's business tact and skill, equally effective, whether in oil or amusement, has turned the tide away from the dismal strand of failure'" (quoted in Meares 2018).

Business prospects in the oil industry improved. Summers' company moved into the new Hellman Building at 4th and Spring Streets in downtown Los Angeles, a sleek new skyscraper built in 1902. In 1905, Summers signed a contract to supply 30,000 barrels of oil to Los Angeles County and another with the Los Angeles City Waterworks. These contracts made her the supplier to Los Angeles Railway Company and an array of factories and hotels in the city. She also signed contracts to provide oil to the San Pedro, Los Angeles and Salt Lake Railroad and the Redondo Railway Company. She expanded her oil portfolio to include oil reserves in Kansas. In 1911, media such as *Sunset Magazine* reported that men in the oil business frowned upon her. However, Summers responded to these claims by saying that she was well treated by men in the Los Angeles oil industry. Emma rejected the media's suggestions about gender inequality and countered that she was received among her male peers with respect. She stated, "'In my years of business experience no man has ever attempted to take advantage of me because I was a woman'" (quoted in Meares 2018). Summers gained in stature as a businesswoman when demand for oil increased in the mid-1910s due to the proliferation of new gasoline-powered automobiles and trucks, as well as the onset of the First World War and new oil contracts for military purposes (Roman 2015).

Eventually the California oil boom subsided. Summers continued with oil production through the 1920s and 1930s but was buoyed financially by her considerable investments in real estate, especially in apartment buildings—one of them known as the "Queen Apartments"—and hotels. Besides earning the title "Oil Queen," she was also known as the "Hotel Queen." For a period of time she returned to her home on Fort Moore Hill, and then later remodeled that house into the "Queen Hotel." At different times she lived in a mansion on Wiltshire Place and in the downtown Biltmore and Alexandria hotels. She finally settled at a home in Glendale. Summers died on November 27, 1941 at the age of eighty-three. She acquired a well-deserved reputation of being a successful oil company owner, hotelier, and ranch operator, all traditionally male-dominated businesses. She was "a disconcerting surprise to her masculine opponents," according to a contemporary profile by James Miller Guinn (Guinn 1915, 275). Guinn went on to attribute her success to "absolute self-reliance, independent thought and action backed by unflinching courage" (Guinn 1915, 276). Rather than conform to traditional notions of womanhood in the late nineteenth and early twentieth centuries, Summers was known to say, "'Most women, and some men, rely too much on what others tell them,'" and "I would not take even the greatest lawyers opinion unless it squared with my own convictions'" (quoted in Guinn 1915, 276).

Summers built her reputation as an astute oil developer with an impeccable reputation for sound business ethics in an occupation known for its knaves and villains. She had to contend with saboteurs and thieves who drained her storage tanks and spiked her oil wells (Meares 2018). Guinn admired her determination: "She fights her rivals with fire and sword, and with a black flag always hoisted. Then having backed them slowly but surely against the wall, she compels recognition of her demands, which are always fair and just" (1915, 276). By overcoming traditional norms of her gender and her strong-willed rivals in the oil industry, her company succeeded in providing a steady oil supply to the area's railroads, which helped to build the transportation infrastructure of Southern California, and supplying the energy needs to the factories, hotels, and shops of Los Angeles in its infant stage of development.

Patrice Natalie Delevante

See also: Benedum, Michael Late; California Electric Light Company; Caltex; Fesler, Milton A.; Petroleum; Roughnecks; Santa Barbara Oil Spill; Summerland Oil Field

FURTHER READING

Bakken, Gordon Morris, and Brenda Farrington, eds. 2003. *Encyclopedia of Women in the American West*. Thousand Oaks, CA: Sage Publications.

Division of Oil and Gas (DOG). 1961. *Summary of Operations, California Oil Fields*. Annual Report of the State Oil and Gas Supervisor. Vol. 47. California State Mining Bureau.

Guinn, James Miller. 1915. "Mrs. Emma A. Summers." *A History of California and an Extended History of Los Angeles and Environs: Biographical*. Vol. 2. Pp. 275–6. Los Angeles: Historic Record Company.

Meares, Hadley. 2018. "In the Early 20th Century, L.A.'s Oil Industry was Dominated by a Woman." *Los Angeles Magazine*. October 22.

Rasmussen, Cecelia. 1999. "The Gush of Oil was Music to 'Queen's Ears.'" *Los Angeles Times*. July 11. https://www.latimes.com/archives/la-xpm-1999-jul-11-me-54981-story.html (accessed October 2023).

Roman, James. 2015. *Chronicles of Old Los Angeles: Exploring the Devilish History of the City of the Angels*. New York: Museyon, Inc.

Smith, Bertha K. 1911. "What Women are Doing in the West: Emma A. Summers—Oil Operator." *Sunset: The Magazine of the Pacific and of all the Far West*. Vol. 27. July–December. Pp. 49–52.

Surface Mining

The term "surface mining" refers to the various types of mining that remove the foliage, soil, and rock that cover a mineral deposit rather than leaving these materials in situ as with underground mining. The term, therefore, refers to a range of different types of mining including strip mining, open-cast mining, mountaintop mining, dredging, and high-wall mining. It has also been used to refer to the initial harvesting of minerals from surface outcrops particularly in reference to preindustrial mining.

The history of surface mining stretches back hundreds of thousands of years when Paleolithic humankind began to excavate and use minerals such as stone and flint. Underground mining developed much later with evidence of its existence dating to around 40,000 BCE. In North America, Native Americans mined salt, clay, stone, turquoise, copper, chert, obsidian, and other minerals by surface mining methods (Snedeker 1990, 4). Rich mineral deposits provided an important motivation for colonizing powers and played a fundamental role in the history of the intercourse between Europe and the Americas from the outset with the search for, panning and mining of gold becoming a central goal of Christopher Columbus's (1451–1506) voyages and those of other early visitors (Waszkis 1993, 7–25). European settlers in North America quickly sought to utilize mineral deposits for use in their daily lives and within trade. Early settlers at Jamestown dredged ponds for bog iron, and later settlers in the British American colonies "dug ore out of the hillside" (Tunis 1999, 64). Blacksmiths joined early parties of settlers and efforts were made to establish an iron works near Jamestown. Iron ore was used to create pig iron that could be used to create other products or smelted by local artisans to create products directly (Tunis 1999, 64, 150). Early settlers also sought to extract and utilize resources such as sand, clay, lime, and various types of rock to produce building materials (Snedeker 1990, 4).

As had been the case following the visits of Columbus, the discovery of minerals on continental North America was spearheaded by explorers in search of precious metals. French explorers such as Philippe François Renault (1686–1755) and Antoine de la Mothe Cadillac (1658–1730) began lead mining operations in French Louisiana (modern-day Missouri) in the early eighteenth century (Boyer 2021). It was not until the nineteenth century, however, that the widescale mining of mineral deposits began. Geologist Douglas Houghton visited the Keweenaw Peninsula in 1840 and discovered copper there. His report the following year led to the first major mining boom which saw an influx of people coming to the area to mine the metal (Snedeker 1990, 4). A few years later in 1844 a surveyor called William Austin Burt and his team discovered iron outcrops of the Marquette Range further west in Michigan (Ashworth 1987, 81–3). Over the next half-century, further discoveries of iron ore were made in the region including the Menominee Range (1867), Gogebic Range (1884), Vermillion Range (1885), Mesabi Range (1890), and Cuyuna Range (1903), known collectively as the Iron Range. Initially surface mining was the primary method of mining, with shaft mining developing later. The same region also saw the extensive use of quarrying to extract rock such as sandstone which was used for building. Surface mining methodologies were also used during gold rushes. During the California Gold Rush in the mid-nineteenth century hydraulic mining, whereby a jet of water is used to remove soil and rock in order to expose mineral deposits, was widely used. This became a popular method due to the increases in efficiency and profitability that it offered; however, it also created issues as mine waste was carried downstream (Swanson 2018, 66). Despite all this, mining in the United States tended towards underground mining methodologies during the nineteenth century.

Surface mining methods became popular in the United States during the twentieth century with most surface mining operations being developed between 1930 and 1970 (Snedeker 1990, 5). This turn towards surface mining is encapsulated in a statement by Eugene P. Pfleider to the US Senate Hearing before the Subcommittee on Minerals, Materials, and Fuels in 1969. He stated that:

> In the early 1900's there were over 100 underground mines producing from the three iron ranges in Minnesota—today there are none. Practically all of our coal prior to 1930 was mined underground; today over one-third is from surface operations and that percentage is increasing. (Pfleider 1969, 103)

Indeed, by 1964, the United States produced 82 percent of its metallic ores, 77 percent of its non-metallic ores, 98 percent of its clay, stone, sand and gravel, and 35 percent of its coal by surface mining methods (Pfleider 1969, 103). At present, surface mining is also the primary method of mining coal with surface mines producing 69 percent of the US's coal

FIGURE 6: Surface mining accounts for the majority of the coal obtained in US mining operations.

production in 2010 (Kecojevic 2013, 335). This shift was driven by the greater productivity rates and reduced excavation costs of surface mining. Developments such as the invention of the steam shovel and railways, meant that by the early 1900s surface mining provided increased cost efficiency and a reduced need for manpower (Snedeker 1990, 5). In the early 1900s these innovations, as well as the development of the flotation process, also made the exploitation of other deposits such as porphyries in the southwestern United States possible, including in Nevada, Arizona, New Mexico (Snedeker 1990, 5). Surface mining, therefore, allowed companies to generate a profit from deposits that were previously thought to have provided poor prospects. At Utah's Bingham Canyon, for example, the use of steam shovels allowed the low-grade porphyric copper ore to be extracted with a high level of profitability (Waszkis 1993, 239). All major mining companies thus became engaged in surface mining. Economic factors and new technologies such as the invention of high-speed conveyor belt technology and the increasing size and flexibility of equipment have continued to fuel the adoption of surface mining methodologies (Kecojevic 2013, 335; Snedeker 1990, 6).

Despite its popularity, surface mining has created environmental problems. Amongst the issues created by surface mining are destruction of habitat and wildlife, the exacerbation of erosion, increased risk of landslides, and the pollution of waterways (Leedy 1981, 1–2). This has led to the formation of protest movements against surface mining (Montrie 2003) and strict legislation such as the Surface Mining Control and Reclamation Act (1977) which legislates the reclamation of surface coal mines following their closure.

James Harry Morris

See also: Coal; Energy Crisis of the 1970s; Energy Independence; Powell River Project; North Antelope Rochelle Mine; Surface Mining Control and Reclamation Act of 1977; Usibelli, Emil

FURTHER READING

Ashworth, William. 1987. *The Great Lakes: An Environmental History*. Detroit, MI: Wayne State University Press.

Bogue, Margaret Beattie. 2007. *Around the Shores of Lake Superior: A Guide to Historic Sites*. 2nd ed. Madison, WI: The University of Wisconsin Press.

Boyer, Mark G. 2021. *300 Years of the French in Old Mines: A Narrative History of the Oldest Village in Missouri*. Eugene, OR: Wipf & Stock.

Kecojevic, Vladislav. 2013. "Surface Mining." In *Modern American Coal Mining: Methods and Applications*. Ed. Christopher J. Bise. Pp. 335–406. Englewood, CO: Society for Mining, Metallurgy, and Exploration, Inc.

Leedy, David L., William T. Mason Jr., and Charles T. Cushwa. 1981. *Coal Surface Mining Reclamation and Fish and Wildlife Relationships in the Eastern United States*, Vol. 1: *Past Findings, the Surface Mining Law of 1977 (P.L. 95-87), Planning and Management Considerations, and Information Sources*. Kearneysville, WV: United States Department of the Interior, Fish and Wildlife Service, Eastern Energy and Land Use Team.

Montrie, Chad. 2003. *To Save the Land and People: A History of Opposition to Surface Coal Mining in Appalachia*. Chapel Hill, NC: The University of North Carolina Press.

Pfleider, Eugene P. 1969. "U.S. Mineral Policy Should Sponsor Underground Research and Development." In *National Mining and Minerals Policy, Hearing before the Subcommittee on Minerals, Materials, and Fuels of the Committee on Interior and Insular Affairs, United States*

Senate, Ninety-First Congress, First Session on S. 719, A Bill to Establish a National Mining and Minerals Policy (July 9, 1969). Edited by the Subcommittee on Minerals, Materials, and Fuels of the Committee on Interior and Insular Affairs of the United States Senate. Pp. 103–15. Washington, DC: US Government Printing Office.

Snedeker, Marianne. 1990. "History of Mining." In *Surface Mining*. 2nd ed. Ed. v Bruce A. Kennedy. Pp. 1–7. Littleton, CO: Society for Mining, Metallurgy and Exploration, Inc.

Swanson, Drew A. 2018. *Beyond the Mountains: Commodifying Appalachian Environments*. Athens, GA: University of Georgia Press.

Tunis, Edwin. 1999. *Colonial Craftsmen: And the Beginnings of American Industry*. Baltimore, MD: The Johns Hopkins University Press.

Waszkis, Helmut. 1993. *Mining the Americas: Stories and History*. Cambridge: Woodhead Publishing, Ltd.

Surface Mining Control and Reclamation Act of 1977

The Surface Mining Control and Reclamation Act of 1977 (SMCRA) is a congressional measure that sought to bring together the US Department of the Interior and the fifty state governments to better regulate surface coal mining operations and to create a system for acquiring and reclaiming abandoned mines. The SMCRA supplied a deficiency in US mining and environmental laws that were silent on the different roles of federal and state governments with respect to exhausted mining lands and derelict structures no longer in use.

The SMCRA was enacted by the 95th US Congress and was signed into law by President Jimmy Carter on August 3, 1977. In essence, SMCRA contained three components, one outlining regulations for active coal mines, a second providing for the reclaiming of abandoned mine lands, and a third creating the Office of Surface Mining Reclamation and Enforcement (OSM), an agency within the Department of the Interior. The OSM was charged with developing regulations, funding state regulatory and reclamation actions, and maintaining consistency with all state regulatory programs.

Political support for the SMCRA arose from increasing attention by investigative journalists, environmental activists, and local and state officials to the negative environmental effects of strip mining. While coal had been mined since the 1740s, surface mining became the dominant technique in the 1930s. Four states passed the first rudimentary laws to regulate the coal mining industry beginning with West Virginia in 1939. Enforcement, however proved problematic and spotty.

The Second World War produced a great demand for coal, which brought coal mining companies and state mine regulators to focus on mine safety rather than the long-term environmental consequences of strip mining, which proved to be severe. More states then enacted new laws and strengthened regulatory programs, with some of the toughest requiring mining permits or the posting of bonds to cover the costs of reclaiming the devastated land. Unfortunately, these state laws overall proved mostly unsuccessful at lessening the environmental impacts. These laws varied greatly in toughness from state to state, so mining operations tended to relocate to states with less stringent regulations. Environmental devastation worsened because surface mining became increasingly common, from 33 percent of coal from surface mines in 1963 to 60 percent ten years later. Most counties in Appalachia's coal fields had hundreds of small surface mines, and most small operators were heavily indebted and short of expertise. As of 1995, there were approximately 38,991 abandoned mine sites on land administered by the US Forest Service, with 34 percent of those mines working veins with minerals like arsenic, cadmium, copper, lead, mercury and zinc, which can cause human health and environmental impacts (USFS 2023).

The problem persisted because of politics and economics. President Gerald Ford vetoed tougher mining regulation bills in 1974 and 1975 because of fears they would hamper industry's ability to meet the nation's increasing energy demands during the energy crisis of the 1970s and also would exacerbate the inflation problem raging through the economy. After Jimmy Carter's 1976 presidential victory, the Democratic Congress passed a more stringent bill than the one vetoed by Ford, and the new president signed it into law.

The SMCRA outlined a number of regulations to govern the operations of active surface mines. In the law itself, these regulations break into categories such as standards of performance, permitting, bonding, inspection and enforcement, and finally, restrictions on land use. Congress wished to create more stringent environmental standards that mining companies must meet and empowered the OMS to establish and enforce them. Permits were required for mining operations, and these must identify pre-existing environmental conditions, details of how the operation will work on the specific site, plans for reclamation after the resource has been exhausted, provisions for fulfilling SMCRA standards of performance, and projections for post-mining land use.

Permit holders are required under SMCRA to post a bond with a large enough value to pay costs of reclaiming sites after mining, or in the event of the company's bankruptcy. Bonds are not released until relevant agency officials determine that sites have, in fact, been reclaimed as planned. The law also created a system of inspection and enforcement, complete with notification of problems to be corrected, timelines for remediation, and punishments (fines) for non-compliance. Finally, the law specifically disallowed surface mining in National Parks and wilderness areas and gave citizens the opportunity to challenge proposed surface mining operations because of local environmental concerns.

Under the law, OSM has been given authority to regulate active coal operations according to SMCRA standards and to oversee the current twenty-four states with approved regulatory programs. The agency uses a number of administrative tools to manage paperwork and communications with state regulators. Until a state or Native American tribe is judged capable of managing a regulatory program that complies with all SMCRA requirements (30 CFR Chapter VII), OSM regulates coal mining operations on their behalf. Once it does meet those requirements, it takes over the regulatory and enforcement functions, with OSM providing oversight, grant funding, and technical assistance (OSM 2019).

Title IV of the SMCRA created an Abandoned Mine Land (AML) fund to pay for the cleanup of mined lands that were abandoned before 1977. The fund is financed by taxes per ton of surface mined coal, coal mined underground, and for lignite. The OSM distributes 80 percent of proceeds from fees to states for their approved reclamation programs. The remainder OSM uses for reclamation costs of emergency cases, such as landslides, land subsidence (sinking of ground overtop mines), fires, and high-priority cleanups in states without approved programs. States with approved programs can also use AML funds to establish programs to insure homeowners against land subsidence caused by underground mining.

To support these reclamation efforts, OSM provides extensive scientific resources in technical assistance, training, and technology. It communicates the most current scientific information and technologies to the coal industry, state and tribal staff, and those responsible for SMCRA implementation. Some examples this assistance includes are communication of research on bat conservation, coal combustion residues, underground hydrology, and mine fires. The agency offers data on watersheds, water quality, mine subsidence, slope instability, and local endangered species. Training programs are provided for Unmanned Aircraft Systems, Acid Mine Drainage technologies, underground mapping, and geospatial computer software.

An example of the cooperation anticipated by SMCAR and facilitated by OSM is the Appalachian Regional Reforestation Initiative (ARRI). This is a coalition of groups, including citizens, the coal industry, and OSM staff, who work to restore forests on mined lands in the eastern portion of the United States. Currently, there are ARRI efforts involving eight state agencies, industry partners, environmental organizations, scientific researchers, and landowners. ARRI uses a forestry reclamation approach that involves tree planting to create productive forests, not only in areas with active mining operations underway but also abandoned mine lands and what are called "legacy sites" that have been previously reclaimed (OSM 2019).

Between 1978 and 2007, hundreds of SMCRA cases have been resolved with major mining operators. In one case, 500 contract mining operations were resolved in three states, with a $5 million reclamation value. Thousands of settlement agreements have been secured resulting in considerable land reclamation and millions in fees and penalties going to OSM and state regulatory agencies (Bandy 2007). By widening the window of time there are even more impressive results, at least from the OSM's own reporting. Between 1978 and 2019, SMCRA has worked in over thirty states and Native tribal lands to mitigate clogged streams, dangerous high-walls, dangerous piles and embankments, hazardous rock slides, abandoned equipment and facilities, polluted water sources, and ongoing underground mine fires. The "dangerous high-wall" projects totaled 4,015,735 over those forty-one years, which meant reduction and recontouring rock faces that towered 60–80 and sometimes 100 feet (OSM 2019, 43–4).

SMCRA has succeeded in combating emerging coal industry developments. For instance, several multi-state companies filed for bankruptcy after 2002 to evade reclamation obligations because they had mines and liabilities in one state and assets and ultimate controllers in another. Earl Bandy, Chief of the Applicant Violator System Office of OSM spoke on the law's thirtieth anniversary and its impact, noting that one operator bankruptcy with 425 SMCRA permits in five states was the largest enforcement action in history. By utilizing litigation, state regulatory action, and OSM initiatives, the violator's evasions were stopped. Bandy noted: "the States and OSM together sent a clear message that it was unacceptable to socialize reclamation liabilities," with the result that the violator paid and committed to pay reclamation efforts valued at almost $400 million (Bandy 2007).

Bandy's statement went onto summarize the reclamation successes of the law and the OSM's work since its passage. He noted that 29.5 billion tons of coal have been mined during SMCRA's history with 90 percent used to generate electrical power. Concurrently, the coal mining industry successfully reclaimed 2,238,560 acres of mined lands, with most reclamation exceeding all state and federal standards. Millions of trees have been planted for commercial forestry and wildlife habitat, and to recreate or extend the native hardwood or pine forests. Extensive wetlands, frequently part of mine drainage control, have been reclaimed and restored. Abandoned surface and underground mine lands reclaimed for farmland now have high productivity levels. Almost 240,000 acres of high-priority mine lands abandoned before 1977 have been reclaimed. Safety and environmental hazards have been eliminated on 314,108 acres. Useful buildings have been saved from collapse, sheer high walls have been turned to rolling grassland, streams where fish could not live now support thriving wildlife populations, and forests are starting to grow (Bandy 2007). The law, the OSM, and its considerable amount of funding have drawn its critics, but SMCRA's record bristles with substantial gains for local communities and for the natural environment.

The SMCRA continues to be modified to respond to regulatory and reclamation needs. In 2014, the Obama administration reformed OSM in order to enhance its environmental protection mission in regard to surface mined lands. The AML became the Abandoned Mine Land Economic Revitalization Program (AMLER), which funds abandoned mine land reclamation. The Infrastructure Investment and Jobs Act (P.L. 117–58), enacted in 2021, provided $11.3 billion for grants to states and Native American nations over the ensuing fifteen years to assist communities as they work to eliminate dangerous environmental conditions and pollution caused by past coal mining (Brown 2016).

The federal budget for OSM in 2023 was $271.2 million. The budget includes $89.6 million for environmental protection programs, $65 million for state and tribal regulatory grants, $2 million for nonprofit organizations, especially small local watershed organizations, to do projects to clean streams affected by acid-mine drainage, $24.6 million for Title V regulation of coal mining in states and tribes without approved regulatory programs, and $115 million for AMLER program grants to Appalachian states and qualifying tribes for the reclamation of abandoned mine lands and for related economic and community development activities (Means 2014; OSM 2022). SMCRA and OSM receives criticism from all sides, from coal industry promoters to local interest groups to environmental organizations, but fixing the problems created by a century of short-sighted and often malevolent coal mining practices will be neither simple nor inexpensive to accomplish.

William P. Kladky

See also: Coal; Cumberland Iron and Coal Company; Martin County Coal Slurry Spill; Mineral Leasing Act of 1920; Natural Resources Defense Council; North Antelope Rochelle Mine; Powell River Project; Sierra Club; Surface Mining; Usibelli, Emil

FURTHER READING

Bandy, Earl. 2007. "Statement of Earl Bandy, Chief, Applicant Violator System Office, OSM, US Department of Interior Committee on Natural Resources." The Surface Mining Control and Reclamation Act (SMCRA) of 1977: A 30th Anniversary Review. July 25. US Department of the Interior. https://www.doi.gov/ocl/hearings/110/SMCRA_072507 (accessed October 2023).

Brown, Dylan. 2016. "Mine Cleanup Concerns Spike as Industry Sputters." *E&E News*. March 1. https://subscriber.politicopro.com/article/eenews/1060033248 (accessed October 2023).

Means, Thomas C., and Sherrie A. Armstrong. 2014. "SMCRA: It's Back in the News and That's Not Good News for Coal," *Mining Law Monitor*. December 1. https://casetext.com/analysis/smcra-its-back-in-the-news-and-thats-not-good-news-for-coal (accessed October 2023).

Office of Surface Mining Reclamation and Enforcement (OSM). 2019. "FY 2019 Annual Report." US Department of the Interior. https://www.osmre.gov/sites/default/files/inline-files/OSMRE%20FY%202019%20Annual%20Report.pdf (accessed October 2023).

Office of Surface Mining Reclamation and Enforcement (OSM). 2022. "Press Release: President's Fiscal year 2023 Budget Includes Significant Investments in Environmental Protection and Abandoned Coal Mine Reclamation." March 28. US Department of the Interior. https://www.osmre.gov/news/presidents-fy-2023-budget (accessed October 2023).

US Forest Service (USFS). 2023. "Abandoned Mine Lands." US Department of Agriculture. https://www.fs.usda.gov/managing-land/natural-resources/geology/abandoned-mine-lands (accessed October 2023).

Susquehanna Coal Company

In the late nineteenth and early twentieth century, the Susquehanna Coal Company, a subsidiary of the Pennsylvania Railroad, mined coal in the anthracite fields of the Wyoming Valley of northeastern Pennsylvania. The company was originally incorporated in Pennsylvania in 1867 with the name the Pittston Railroad and Coal Company, and changed its name to the more-familiar Susquehanna Coal Company two years later. Another company began operations in the region somewhat earlier, called the Dauphin and Susquehanna Coal Company. The founding of the Susquehanna Coal Company was part of a post-US Civil War transformation in the anthracite fields from smaller companies and individual proprietors to large, well-financed operations connected with the region's major railroads. The company controlled 5,823 acres of coal lands along the banks of the Susquehanna, with headquarters in the city of Nanticoke.

In the late nineteenth and early twentieth century, the primary use of the anthracite coal mined by the Susquehanna Coal Company and its regional competitors was for heating homes and other buildings. Anthracite was also used in factories and other industrial processes including steelmaking. Anthracite, or "hard" coal as opposed to bituminous or "soft" coal, has the highest concentration of carbon and the fewest impurities of any variety of coal, making it the most efficient and smokeless fuel. Northeastern Pennsylvania was the only major source of anthracite in the United States and contains the largest reserves of anthracite in the world. Pennsylvania anthracite was vital for American life and industrialization in the nineteenth and early twentieth centuries. The company shipped its anthracite primarily by railroad, although about a third was shipped via the Pennsylvania Canal as late as 1884. The Pennsylvania Railroad had acquired the Pennsylvania Canal in 1867, the same year the Susquehanna Coal Company was founded. Use of canals for anthracite shipping in the Wyoming Valley mostly ended after the Susquehanna flood of 1894. In the latter part of the nineteenth century, the Susquehanna Coal Company cooperated with other anthracite companies and railroads to maintain prices for anthracite coal.

On December 18, 1885, the Company's Nanticoke No. 1 mine suffered a disaster due to a cave-in followed by a rapid influx of quicksand and water, which killed twenty-six miners. Although this was the worst mining accident in the company's history it was not the only one. The company's Luke Fidler colliery was the site of two accidents, one in October 1894 in which an explosion blamed on a careless carpenter carrying a lamp into the mine killed five people. In November 1902, another explosion at Luke Fidler killed four people.

Like other mining companies, the Susquehanna Coal Company exploited its workers ruthlessly and faced worker resistance. Boys were employed from a young age as "breakers" removing impurities from the coal. It should be added that child labor was thought to be acceptable in the earliest stages of industrialization: young girls worked for textile mills or as domestic servants. Children received little schooling in mining communities. The company

CASUALTIES OF THE 1885 DISASTER

Thomas Clifford, 14, doorboy; William Delaney, 14, driverboy; William Elkie, 19, runner; Edward Hargraves, 21, miner; John Hawk, 30, laborer; Wadislaw Jelgoshinski, 23, laborer; Oliver Kivler, 27, miner; William Kivler, 17, laborer; Frank Kivler, 32; Maux Longolki, 17, driver; Abram Lewis, 42, miner; Andrew Lowe, 25; Vincent Luke, age unknown, laborer; Edward Mathews, 20, laborer; August Matule, 45, miner; Peter Mattlewicz, age unknown, laborer; Joseph McCarty, 23, miner; John Nowach, age unknown, laborer; Abram Rubinski, age unknown, laborer; Isaac Sarver, 28, miner; John Sarver, 21, laborer; John Shutt, 28, miner; Thomas Williams, 21, laborer.

William E. Burns

controlled its workers through a "company town" system of providing housing and supply stores, thus maintaining the workers in perpetual debt to the company. It also sought to undermine worker solidarity by maintaining an ethnically and linguistically divided work force. Immigrant workers came primarily from Eastern Europe and the Middle East, joining earlier established communities of Welsh, Irish and German miners. The company took advantage of the permission afforded to mining companies by Pennsylvania Statute 228, passed in 1865, to maintain its own police force whose members carried state commissions but were paid by the companies. These "Iron and Coal Police" attacked labor organizers and troublemakers. In 1874, a night watchman named Frederik Hesser at the Hickory Ridge colliery was murdered. Two "Molly Maguires," Irish American labor activists, were charged with the killing, and one, Peter McManus, was executed for the crime.

The company experienced a small strike in Nanticoke in 1899, initially over the issue of "topping," the amount of coal the miners were required to load on each car over the level of the car itself. Ordinary miners were paid by the car, while "company men" received a daily wage. The conflict broadened to include other issues and was eventually resolved by a compromise agreement, although the company continued to refuse to recognize the United Mine Workers of America, which was trying to organize the anthracite fields. The biggest labor conflict associated with the company occurred in 1902, with a general strike by miners directed at other coal companies in the anthracite region, as well as the Susquehanna. The miners walked out on May 12, pump operators and other support personnel on June 2. The dependency of many east coast households on anthracite to heat their homes made the strike an issue of national concern as winter approached. The strike was ended on October 23 by federal mediation under President Theodore Roosevelt. The 1902 anthracite strike is often considered a turning point in the history of the labor movement in America, as it was the earliest appearance of the federal government in the role of mediator rather than strikebreaker.

The settlement of the strike accompanied economic decline in the anthracite coal fields, caused by increasing cost and effective competition from bituminous coal-based fuels such as coke, fuel briquettes, and manufactured gas. On September 26, 1913, the Pennsylvania Railroad announced plans to divest itself of its holdings in the Susquehanna Coal Company along with other anthracite mining companies, in order to avoid antitrust trouble. By 1917, the Susquehanna Coal Company left the coal mining business. The mines of the Susquehanna

Coal Company were sold to the Susquehanna Collieries Company, a subsidiary of the M.A. Hanna Company of Cleveland. The Susquehanna Coal Company is listed as dissolved in 1940 by the Pennsylvania Department of State. The company's history illustrates the larger story of the rise of the coal industry during the Industrial Revolution, along with the many workplace hazards and labor-management tensions that accompanied coal's development as an industry. It also demonstrates the industry's challenges as other forms of fuel, particularly oil and natural gas, came to dominate the nation's assortment of energy resources in the first half of the twentieth century.

William E. Burns

See also: Battle of Blair Mountain; Cist, Jacob; Coal; Cumberland Iron and Coal Company; Harlan County War; Ludlow Massacre; Molly Maguires; Paint Creek Mine War; Sinclair, Upton

FURTHER READING

Aldrich, Mark. 2018. "An Energy Transition before the Age of Oil: The Decline of Anthracite, 1900–1930." *Pennsylvania History*. Vol. 31. Pp. 1–31.

Aurand, Harold W. 2003. *Coalcracker Culture: Work and Values in Pennsylvania Anthracite, 1835–1935*. Selinsgrove, PA: Susquehanna University Press.

Blatz, Perry K. 1994. *Democratic Miners: Work and Labor Relations in the Anthracite Coal Industry, 1875–1925*. Albany, NY: SUNY Press.

Healey, Richard G. 2007. *The Pennsylvania Anthracite Coal Industry, 1860–1902: Economic Cycles, Business Decision-making and Regional Dynamics*. Scranton, PA: University of Scranton Press.

Jones, Christopher F. 2014. *Routes of Power: Energy and Modern America*. Cambridge, MA: Harvard University Press.

Sweeney, Peter

Peter Sweeney of Buffalo, and later New York City, was a prolific inventor who patented a new type of drill for oil and gas wells. It came in the wake of an oil strike in 1859 near Titusville, Pennsylvania, which commenced a wave of oil prospecting in the area and a related search for new technologies to make the process quicker and easier. Sweeney's "Rotary Rock Boring Machine" enabled operators to actually drill through layers of rock, often hundreds of feet, which was difficult to do with existing cable-tool rigs using a lift and drop method of pounding out boreholes. The rotary drill rig came into wider use after 1901 when the Spindletop oil strike in Texas led to a massive increase in US oil exploration and extraction. Improvements in rotary drills also made possible the development of offshore oil fields after the Second World War.

Very little is known about Sweeney other than the fact that he held many patents. His name appears in a patent for a rotary water pump in 1849 as a resident of Buffalo, New York. He received a patent for an improved stove the following year, and then other patents for a steam boiler and a hot-air furnace. His 1866 patent for the "Rotary Rock Boring Machine" may have been the most consequential, given how it changed the way wells were drilled for oil and gas. It consisted of a number of different components held together by a small, four-legged metal frame straddling the borehole. At the very tip of the hollow boring rod were scalloped cutter-wheels mounted on small axles in a cutter head, each bit resembling a pastry wheel for making decorative pie crust edging (Brantley 1971, 1098). A spiral flange wrapped around the outside of the boring rod raised debris out of the hole, which was aided by water or steam piped down the boring rod's hollow center. The rotation of the boring rod and cutter head was produced by a mechanism composed of screw-spindles, bevel-cog wheels, a pulley, and drive belt. The boring rod was moved up and down by means of a worm and worm-wheel.

In his patent, Sweeny identified certain advantages of his drilling rig over existing models. He noted that boring could be "continued without interruption" except for time needed to add sections to the boring rod as the borehole deepened. Also, a "clean hole is obtained" by virtue of the spiral flange which continuously discharged loose material out of the well. The rig could drill horizontally, vertically, and in "oblique" directions, and could be "used with advantage for submarine operations" (Sweeney 1866). The whole rig was connected to a steam engine, which provided the rotational power to sustain continuous drilling. This system differed greatly from the existing cable-tool drilling rigs, which dug the well by hoisting a heavy metal bit attached to a drill string and dropping it to the bottom of the borehole, pounding the rock to rubble. As one historian described it, "the heavy bit has a blunt chisel end which cracks, chips and smashes the rock by the repeated blows delivered in a measured or regular cadence" (Pees 2004). Older technologies "dug" wells for water, oil, and gas, whereas rotary bits like Sweeney's "drilled" them.

In the two-volume *A Handbook of the Petroleum Industry* from 1922, drilling equipment expert Louis C. Sands identified what he thought were the strengths and weaknesses of the two types of drilling rigs. Sands noted that the adoption of the rotary drilling system "is now almost universal in regions to which it is peculiarly adapted—Louisiana, Trinidad, and parts of Texas, Oklahoma, California, Mexico, Russia and South America." After describing its mode of operation, he observed that "instead of temporarily suspending drilling to bail out the detritus, as with cable tools, the rotary cuttings are washed out while drilling proceeds," which rendered it "conducive to great speed in drilling wells where the strata are not hard." He also commented favorably on the decreased use of casings in wells drilled by rotary rigs because "the plastering of the walls being a substitute, to a certain extent, for casing." However, he also added "the rotary is not so sensitive as cable tools to sudden changes in strata nor so responsive to the varying requirements of different conditions and regions and is, therefore, still subject to hostile criticism" (Sands 1922, 251). The rotary drilling rig's speedy and messy discharge of material from the well's bottom made it difficult for operators to "estimate the value of 'showings'" from different formations (Sands 1922, 252).

Sands gave expression to the belief in the 1920s that there was still an important place for cable-tool drilling rigs, but generally speaking, "rotary rigs soon became the preferred means of drilling for oil" in the places where oil exploration and production grew the fastest (Wells 2006). The rotary drill eventually improved with better drill bits, including the dual-cone bit patented in 1908 by Howard R. Hughes, Sr., father of famous aviation mogul and Hollywood producer Howard R. Hughes, Jr. The rotary system could perform in ways that the cable-tool system could not. The deepest cable-tool well was drilled by the New York State Natural Gas Corporation near Van Etten in New York's Chemung County, reaching a depth of 11,145 feet. The project was completed in 1953 after two years and five months of drilling over a five-year period ("70th" 2010). By contrast, ConocoPhillips completed a well in Alaska in 2019 with a rotary drilling system that plunged to a depth of 14,370 feet, and then turned horizontally for another 18,098 feet—impossible for cable-tool rigs—bringing its total length to 32,468 feet (Sullivan 2019).

Sweeney's invention cut a new path for the development of oil and gas well drilling technology, but apparently he moved on to other pursuits. It's possible that he was one of the two men named Peter Sweeney from New York City who served in New York regiments during the US Civil War, one of which enlisted in the 99th Infantry in 1861 at age thirty, and the other in the 10th Infantry in 1864 at the age of thirty-six. After his 1866 "Rotary Rock Boring Machine" patent, his inventions from the 1870s through the 1890s involved a nozzle for water pipes, lubricating compounds, a vegetable felt, a lantern, a method for treating hides, and an apparatus for lubricating streetcar axles. Although an obscure figure, his career provides an illustration of the important role played by individual inventors and innovators in the expansion of the oil and gas industries in the Industrial Revolution's later stages.

Jeffrey B. Webb

See also: Drake, Edwin Laurentine; Hughes, Howard R., Sr.; Kerr-McGee's Kermac No. 16; Roughnecks; Spindletop Oil Gusher

FURTHER READING

"70th Anniversary Retrospective." 2010. *Drilling Contractor*. Magazine of the International Association of Drilling Contractors. https://drillingcontractor.org/70th-anniversary-retrospective-2-5450 (accessed October 2023).

Brantley, John Edward. 1971. *History of Oil Well Drilling*. Houston, TX: Gulf Publishing Company.

Pees, Samuel T. 2004. "Cable-Tool Drilling." Oil History. Petroleum History Institute. https://www.petroleumhistory.org/OilHistory/pages/Cable/cable.html (accessed October 2023).

Sands, Louis C. 1922. "Oil-Field Development and Petroleum Production." In *A Handbook of the Petroleum Industry*. 2 Vols. Ed. David T. Day. Pp. 201–320. New York: John Wiley & Sons, Inc.

Sullivan, Patty. 2019. "Longest Rotary Well in Alaska for the 17th Time." *Spirit Now*. December 18. ConocoPhillips. https://www.conocophillips.com/spiritnow/story/longest-rotary-well-in-alaska-for-the-17th-time (accessed October 2023).

Sweeney, Peter. 1866. *Improvement in Rock-Drills*. (US Patent #51,902). United States Patent Office.

Wells, Bruce W., and K.L. Wells. 2006. ""Making Hole—Drilling Technology." American Oil & Gas Historical Society. https://aoghs.org/technology/oil-well-drilling-technology (accessed October 2023).

Tarbell, Ida

Ida Tarbell (1857–1944) was an investigative journalist and author of the pioneering work, *The History of the Standard Oil Company* (1904). This bestseller, which first appeared as a series of nineteen articles in *McClure's Magazine*, exposed unethical and corrupt business practices used by the Standard Oil Company to monopolize and control the oil industry. Tarbell's exposé contributed to the dissolution of the Standard Oil Trust and cemented her reputation as a reformer or "muckraker" in the Progressive Era of American history. Tarbell's legacy includes her pioneering works in the field of investigative journalism, as well as the dismantling of Standard Oil which resulted in the creation of many of the major oil companies of the present era.

Ida Minerva Tarbell was born on November 5, 1857 in Hatch Hollow, Erie County, Pennsylvania, to Esther McCullough and Franklin Tarbell. In 1859, oil was discovered about 40 miles south of Hatch Hollow, at the Drake Well near Titusville. This discovery triggered the first oil drilling boom in the United States, and Franklin Tarbell sensed an opportunity in the need for oil storage tanks. He crafted tanks from wood, and within a short time developed a successful oil tank business. Demand for oil was high, and in this decade, the use of oil for illumination by ordinary people had expanded in multiple ways. In the mid-1850s, an analysis from Benjamin Silliman, Jr. (1816–85), a chemist at Yale University, had determined the viability of crude oil to be used as an illuminant. Additionally, paraffin, distilled from petroleum, enabled the mass production of inexpensive candles. As demand for oil increased, Franklin Tarbell set his sights on expanding to oil production and refinement.

In 1860, the family moved to a community south of Titusville at Rouseville, situated near Oil Creek and an area known as Pithole, which was flush with oil. With the Pennsylvania oil rush in full swing, thousands rushed in to drill wells. As a child, Ida witnessed firsthand the human toll of the boom and bust that accompanied oil production work. This was very dangerous work. Drilling operations were destructive and deadly, the wooden drilling rigs were prone to catching fire if sparked, and gaping pits of oil dotted the landscape. As Ida later recalled, "All about us rose derricks, squatted engine houses and tanks; the earth about them was streaked and damp with the dumping of the pumps ... every bit of grass in the vicinity was coated with black grease and left to die ... Tar and oil stained everything" (Tarbell 1939). The following year an explosion killed and wounded a number of oil workers, and Ida witnessed her mother attend to the charred body of a family friend (Brady 1989).

In 1870, after a downturn in the oil business, the Tarbells moved to Titusville. Ida's father, along with other independent oil businessmen, relied on the railroads to transport their products. Increasingly, corporations, including the Standard Oil Company run by John D. Rockefeller (1839–1937), began to place pressure on independents. In late 1871, when Ida was fourteen, a secret alliance, known to members as the South Improvement Company (SIC), was formed between the railroads and a group of refiners, including Rockefeller. Their goal was to increase the price of oil by squeezing out non-member refiners and paying rebates to SIC members. The secret deal, leaked to the press, infuriated independent oilmen and newspapers called the clash "the oil war." As Ida recalled later, "At the news all Oildom rushed into the streets ... On every lip there was but one word, and that was 'conspiracy'" (Tarbell 1904). As a result, Ida's father, along with many other independents, saw their businesses and finances decimated.

PITHOLE

Pithole, or Pithole City, was home to the world's first pipeline, was the first city "to be fully illuminated by petroleum," and is notoriously known as "the oiltown that vanished as quickly as it appeared" (DWMP 2023). In 1865, the population reached 15,000, and businesses, brothels, and a newspaper thrived. In 1866, after oil prices plummeted—and after seventeen deadly fires—the population dropped to under 2,000. In 1877 the city was dissolved.

Michelle Elise Houle

Ida graduated from high school in 1875, and in 1876 became one of the first women admitted into Allegheny College, where she pursued a degree in biology. Upon graduation, she accepted a teaching assignment, but left this role dissatisfied with the working conditions. Her next role, in 1883, was as a writer and editor for *The Chautauquan*, a magazine published by the Methodist Church. In this role she wrote, translated articles from French, and eventually became involved in all aspects of publishing. In 1891, Ida made the decision to leave her position and move to France to become a freelance writer. In Paris she studied at the Sorbonne, researched a figure from the French Revolution—Madame Manon de Roland—and built a reputation as a hard-worker. She sold a few articles to publishing syndicates, and eventually the caliber of her work attracted notice.

In 1892, Samuel McClure, founder of *McClure's Magazine*, flew to Paris to convince Ida to write for his magazine. She accepted, and between 1894 and 1896 contributed two well-received series of biographical articles on Napoleon and Abraham Lincoln. These successes positively impacted both the magazine circulation and Tarbell's reputation as a writer. In 1899, she moved to New York City, and in 1901 turned her biographer's eye to John D. Rockefeller, the man at the center of Standard Oil.

By 1882, Rockefeller had acquired a large number of smaller oil-producing and refining companies and consolidated these companies into the Standard Oil Trust, and "by the 1890s, nearly every household lamp in the U.S. was lit by kerosene refined and sold by Rockefeller's Standard Oil Company" (CRF 2019). By 1899, the Standard Oil Trust had reorganized and expanded in such a manner that Rockefeller's company monopolized the oil industry in the United States.

In her study of Rockefeller and how he built the Standard Oil empire, Ida conducted thorough, methodical, and extensive investigative research, digging through libraries, business records, and case histories. In January 1902, through the help of Mark Twain (1835–1910), Tarbell secured a series of interviews with Henry H. Rogers, an executive of Standard Oil. Rogers, perhaps thinking Tarbell planned to write a flattering profile, provided candid insights into practices at Standard Oil. These interviews, which occurred over the course of two years, revealed corrupt dealings, including the development of illegal agreements with railroad companies to manipulate pricing and secure questionable rebates. Tarbell wrote nineteen articles on Standard Oil which ran in *McClure's Magazine* from November 1902 to October 1904; these articles eventually formed her 1904 book, *The History of the Standard Oil Company*.

Tarbell's exposé came during a time in US history, known as the Progressive Era roughly 1890–1920, when magazines informed public sentiment and inspired activism against social issues such as chronic poverty, unsafe working conditions, and the undue influence of trusts. *The History of the Standard Oil Company*, and the outcry it inspired, are largely seen as hastening the dissolution of Standard Oil. In 1909, the US Justice Department filed suit against Standard Oil for violating the Sherman Antitrust Act, and in May 1911, the US Supreme Court ruled in favor of dissolving the Standard Oil Trust. The Standard Oil Company was split into thirty-four successor companies, several of which are still in business, including ExxonMobil, Marathon Oil Company, and Chevron Corporation.

In subsequent years, Tarbell continued writing, lecturing, and traveling for speaking engagements. Tarbell died on January 6, 1944. Today, she is considered a pioneer in the field of investigative journalism.

Michelle Elise Houle

See also: Drake, Edwin Laurentine; ExxonMobil; Mobil Oil Corporation; Ohio Oil Boom; Pennsylvania Oil Boom; Red Line Agreement of 1928; Rockefeller, John D.; Standard Oil Company

FURTHER READING

Brady, Kathleen. 1989. *Ida Tarbell: Portrait of a Muckraker*. Pittsburgh, PA: University of Pittsburgh Press.

Catte, Elizabeth. 2018. "Ida Tarbell and the Spirit of Reform." *Belt Magazine*. October 5. https://beltmag.com/ida-tarbell-standard-oil-spirit-reform (accessed May 18, 2021).

Constitutional Rights Foundation (CRF). 2019. "Ida Tarbell and the Muckrakers." *The Bill of Rights in Action*. Vol. 34. No. 3. Spring.

Drake Well Museum and Park (DWMP). 2023. "Historic Pithole City." Pennsylvania Historical and Museum Commission. https://www.drakewell.org/plan-your-visit/what-to-see-and-do/pithole (accessed November 2023).

Godden, Judith. 2020. *Citizen Reporters: S. S. McClure, Ida Tarbell, and the Magazine that Rewrote America*. New York: Ecco Press.

King, Gilbert. 2012. "The Woman Who Took on the Tycoon." *Smithsonian Magazine*. July 5. https://www.smithsonianmag.com/history/the-woman-who-took-on-the-tycoon-651396/ (accessed June 4, 2021).

Tarbell, Ida M. 1904. *The History of the Standard Oil Company*. New York: McClure, Phillips & Co.

Tarbell, Ida M. 1939. *All in the Day's Work*. New York: Macmillan Company.

Teapot Dome Scandal

The Teapot Dome Scandal marked the first significant political bribery scandal in the United States and the first arrest of a member of the cabinet while serving office. US Secretary of the Interior Albert B. Fall (1861–1944) ultimately violated national security and tainted public trust in governmental leaders when he accepted a bribe from wealthy oil company owners to drill on federally protected land. Edward L. Doheny (1856–1935) and Harry Ford Sinclair (1876–1956) were exposed for drilling in the teapot-shaped outcrop of Naval Petroleum Reserves in Wyoming, called the Teapot Dome, as well as California's Elk Hills and Buena Vista Hills—areas otherwise left undrilled unless there was an emergency. The scandal uncovered both President Warren G. Harding's and Fall's missteps in granting federal oversight of the US Navy petroleum reserves to the US Department of the Interior. The US Senate continues to investigate government corruption as a result of this series of events.

Since 1909, the US Navy had been converting ships running on coal into vessels powered by oil. In preparation for a global mission, the Navy chose to shift to a fuel source more reliable than coal, which faced weight limitations and slowed down their process with coaling stations. The switch to petroleum occurred under the administration of President William H. Taft, and before long, the Navy began to be concerned at the indefinite supply of petroleum. The oil demand had grown by the end of the First World War, resulting in a nationwide oil production of 450 million barrels by the year 1920 (CRF 2009). Congress, as a result, designated naval oil reserves, or likely locations of oil deposits, that would be set aside from drilling unless the country faced a national emergency. One such location in Natrona County, Wyoming—known as Teapot Dome—stood out for its atypical rock formation in the area. This dome-shaped reserve held oil underneath layers of rock with the top, concave-shaped layer. In line with the law, oilmen in the West avoided drilling in federally reserved areas, though debates ensued about how the protection of natural resources might potentially harm the economic interests of the oil industry (McCartney 2008).

When Harding assumed the presidency, however, his newly appointed Interior Secretary Albert Fall considered granting drilling leases in federally protected areas in violation of the law. Harding, a Republican, initiated a development-centered administration that believed permits should be leased liberally to the oil industry. His decision to appoint Fall, a New Mexico senator and rancher, in 1921, was an indication of his preferences for leasing naval oil reserves. Despite Prohibition, both men played poker and drank whiskey, illusrating a camaraderie between the cabinet secretary and president (McCartney 2008). Shortly after taking the position, Fall convinced Harding to transfer oversight of the Naval Petroleum Reserves from the US Navy to the US Department of the Interior under the argument that his department was "better able" to protect reserves set apart for emergencies (Roberts 2014). After assuming control over the Naval Petroleum Reserves, Fall began to make secret deals with prominent oilmen.

FIGURE 7: Edward Doheny (left), owner of Pan American Petroleum & Transport, was implicated in the Teapot Dome bribery scheme that tainted the Harding administration and led to a prison sentence for former Secretary of the Interior Albert Fall; Doheny inspired the lead characters in Upton Sinclair's novel *Oil!* (1926) and the film *There Will be Blood* (2007).

Meanwhile, Edward Doheny and Harry Sinclair, two wealthy oil industry moguls, began negotiations with Fall to secure leases in the naval reserves for drilling. Both men proved themselves to be successful in developing oil fields and meeting contract obligations. In addition, they both donated money in support of Harding's campaign. Doheny, owner of the Pan American Petroleum and Transport Company, first drilled in Los Angeles in 1893, and by 1916, he had expanded to Mexico (CRF 2009). Sinclair, meanwhile, garnered his fortune by leasing oil reserves in Kansas and Oklahoma for his corporation Mammoth Oil Company, and by 1920 had begun a pursuit of oil in Columbia and Venezuela (CRF 2009). They sought support from Fall for opening the naval oil reserves, and in exchange Fall took bribes from them and permitted drilling in Teapot Dome area.

In the years before Fall granted leases to Doheny and Sinclair, he opposed the conservation policies of Presidents Theodore Roosevelt, William Taft, and Woodrow Wilson. On the contrary, Fall was in favor of allowing government land to be used for private profit (CRF 2009). Fall, a friend of Doheny, assured the oil baron as soon as he had control over the Teapot Dome area that he could lease the naval reserves through the president without consulting the US Navy (CRF 2009). On their part, naval officials were wary about the turnover of the administration and feared for the security of the oil under Fall and Harding.

The three reserved oil sites—Teapot Dome and California's Elk Hills and Buena Vista Hills—were worth millions of dollars in oil. Instead of permitting public leases for the oil industry, Fall made secret negotiations with Doheny and Sinclair and the men returned minor favors to the government, including building an oil storage facility at the Pearl Harbor naval base and constructing a pipeline from Wyoming to Kansas City (McCartney 2008). In November of 1921, Doheny made a deal with Fall to provide a $100,000 loan in exchange for the lease of the California reserves. Doheny's oil companies were responsible for the Pearl Harbor facility, which was expected to bring in $1 million in profit for the royalties paid from drilling in the reserves (CRF 2009). Sinclair, on the other hand, negotiated a twenty-year-term lease with Fall to extract oil and gas from the Teapot Dome reserve, which went into effect in April 1922. Similarly, Sinclair offered Fall bonds and "loans" totaling almost $300,000 and helped Fall pay back taxes he had owed since 1912 (CRF 2009).

SEND IN THE MARINES

Around the time the *Wall Street Journal* released their story uncovering the scandal, the publishers of the *Denver Post* heard tell of Fall and Harding's confrontation with oilman James G. Darden who had claimed first dibs on the Teapot Dome site. In order to prevent Darden from drilling, Fall convinced Harding to dispatch the US Marines. The *Denver Post* threatened further publication about the incident, but ended up, along with another oilman on Darden's side, being paid $1 million by Sinclair, who may, in part, have been pressured to pay off the press by Harding himself.

Phoebe M. Doscher

By April of 1922, Democratic Wyoming Governor Leslie Miller began to notice trucks with the Sinclair logo bringing in drilling equipment to the Teapot Dome reserve. She consulted with US Democratic Senator John B. Kendrick about the activity at the site and he brought the matter to a Senate investigating committee (Roberts 2014). On April 14, 1922, the *Wall*

Street Journal unveiled a front-page story about the affair and Kendrick launched a criminal probe in the US Senate. In the aftermath, Fall faced an outcry from the oil industry, as many company owners and investors questioned why competitive bidding on the reserves had not been offered. Harding continued to support Fall's actions even in the face of an uproar from Congress. In fact, the president remained so devoted to his Interior Secretary that when Fall announced his resignation in early 1923, Harding offered him a position on the US Supreme Court (CRF 2009).

Senate hearings over the scandal began in October of 1923, following Fall's resignation in January of that year, leaving him time to relocate to his ranch in New Mexico and continue making oil deals for Sinclair and Doheny in the Soviet Union and Mexico (McCartney 2008). At that time, Harding had embarked on a cross-country tour, and after returning from Alaska, died in August 1923, avoiding impeachment just as the scandal unfolded. At first, Fall claimed he kept the lease agreements secret in an attempt to protect the locations of the federal reserves and prevent oilmen from draining them. When the hearing commenced, Fall refused to testify and the Senate resolved that the leases involved "fraud and corruption." Calls were issued to President Calvin Coolidge to take necessary actions to persecute and cancel the leases (CRF 2009). In the end, Fall was sent to federal prison in the fall of 1929 and fined $100,000, becoming the first cabinet-level official to serve jail time for crimes committed while in office (Roberts 2014). Sinclair and Doheny were acquitted of charges of bribery and criminal conspiracy, but Sinclair faced six and a half months in prison for contempt of court.

The US Supreme Court voided the leases on the Wyoming and California reserves in 1927. During the Second World War, oil drilling occurred on the Elk Hills site, and then during the energy crisis of the 1970s, the naval oil reserves were tapped. President Bill Clinton sold Elk Hills in 1995, which was eventually taken over by Occidental Petroleum Company. The Teapot Dome reserve faced a competitive bidding process and in 2015, was bought by Stranded Oil Resources Corporation for $45.2 million. The Harding administration entered the historical record with its image tainted by corruption, having put federal energy policy in the service of oil industry corporations.

Phoebe M. Doscher

See also: Energy Crisis of the 1970s; Food and Fuel Control Act of 1917; Mahan, Alfred Thayer; Mineral Leasing Act of 1920; Petroleum; Strategic Petroleum Reserve; US Fuel Administration

FURTHER READING

Constitutional Rights Foundation (CRF). 2009. *Bill of Rights in Action*. Vol. 24. No. 4. https://www.crf-usa.org/bill-of-rights-in-action/bria-24-4-the-teapot-dome-scandal.html (accessed October 2023).

Davis, Margaret Leslie. 1998. *Dark Side of Fortune: Triumph and Scandal in the Life of Edward L. Doheny*. Berkeley, CA: University of California Press.

McCartney, Laton. 2008. *The Teapot Dome Scandal, How Big Oil Bought the Harding White House and Tried to Steal the Country*. New York: Random House.

Noggle, Burl. 1965. *Teapot Dome: Oil and Politics in the 1920's*. New York: W.W. Norton & Company, Inc.

Roberts, Phil. 2014. "The Teapot Dome Scandal." WyoHistory.org. The Wyoming State Historical Society. November 8. https://www.wyohistory.org/encyclopedia/teapot-dome-scandal (accessed October 2023).

Stratton, David H. 1998. *Tempest over Teapot Dome: The Story of Albert B. Fall*. Norman, OK: University of Oklahoma Press.

US Senate. 1924. *Hearings before the Committee on Public Lands and Surveys, United States Senate, Pursuant to S. Res. 282, S. Res. 294, and S. Res. 434, Sixty-Seventh Congress, Senate Resolutions Providing for an Investigation of the Subject of Leases Upon Naval Oil Reserves, and S. Res. 147, Sixty-Eighth Congress, Providing for an Investigation of the Subject of Leases Upon Naval Oil Reserves*. 3 Vols. Washington, DC: US Government Printing Office.

Tennessee Valley Authority

The Tennessee Valley Authority (TVA) was created on May 18, 1933 via a congressional charter. As a federally owned and operated corporation, the TVA operates like a private company and receives no taxpayer funding. The TVA was initially tasked with providing electricity, flood control, fertilizer manufacturing, and economic development to the Tennessee Valley, a region especially impacted by the Great Depression. Still operating today, TVA's service region includes most of Tennessee, parts of Alabama, Mississippi, and Kentucky, and small portions of Georgia, North Carolina, and Virginia. Initially, the TVA was headquartered in Muscle Shoals, Alabama, but later moved operations to Knoxville, Tennessee, where it remains today.

At its inception, the TVA was responsible for providing, for the first time, electricity to rural residents of its service area in the 1930s while also employing thousands of previously unemployed workers. Presently, the company supplies power to roughly 10 million people through means such as nuclear, coal, natural gas, hydroelectric, and renewable energy. The TVA also engages with flood control with its various hydroelectric dams.

Almost immediately, private business challenged the constitutionality of the TVA. Across several lawsuits they alleged that government ownership of utilities prevented private companies from entering the market. On occasion, lower courts enjoined the TVA from building facilities and distributing power. However, the US Supreme Court ruled the TVA had a right to produce, distribute, and market power in *Tennessee Elec. Power Co. v. TVA* (1939).

Though the TVA was founded in 1933, the agency has its roots in 1916. In that year, Congress authorized then-president Woodrow Wilson to build munitions-grade nitrate plants and a hydroelectric support facility on the Tennessee River at Muscle Shoals, Alabama as part of a war preparedness effort. The initiative was underwritten by the belief that privately owned power companies were charging excessive rates for power and that they used unfair operating practices at the expense of consumers. The Republican administrations of Warren Harding, Calvin Coolidge, and Herbert Hoover, however, opposed a government-run utility. The TVA survived across these years through the efforts of progressive Republican Senator George Norris. Norris demanded the federal government harness the resources and facilities in Muscle Shoals for the benefit of the people living the Tennessee River Valley. Norris was able to pass two bills on the initiative, one in 1928 and the other in 1931, but both received presidential vetoes. The impasse over the use of the Tennessee River Valley ended with the election Franklin D. Roosevelt, who affirmed Norris' vision and implemented the TVA mere months into his presidency.

Roosevelt appointed three men to head-up the TVA: Arthur E. Morgan, president of Antioch College in Ohio and an experienced dam builder, Harcourt Morgan (no relation), president of the University of Tennessee and distinguished agriculturist, and David E. Lilienthal, utilities

FIGURE 8: The Tennessee Valley Authority provided electricity by means of hydroelectric dams, which included the construction in 1942 of the Fort Loudon Dam in Tennessee.

lawyer and leader of the Wisconsin Public Service Commission. Roosevelt, however, did not give this group clearly specified goals, only vague charges of planning, conservation, and natural resource development. To confound matters, Morgan, Morgan, and Lilienthal had equal power and different ideas for planning and administration of the TVA. Arthur Morgan wanted to prioritize planning and initiatives to alleviate poverty. He also wanted electric rates set at levels comparable to private industry. Lilienthal desired public ownership and for the TVA to compete with private power companies. Harcourt Morgan opposed the central planning advocated by Arthur Morgan and wound up allying with Lilienthal, which meant, for the first years of its existence, the TVA promoted dam construction for flood control and power-generation.

Growth of the TVA was phenomenal. The agency developed a network of forty-two dams across seven states. By the 1940s, the TVA began constructing steam-generating facilities. During the Second World War the TVA began a hydropower construction program to provide electricity for aluminum plants that were instrumental in building airplanes, weapons, and other essential war materials. This effort led to the employment of some twenty-eight thousand workers.

At the conclusion of the war, the TVA completed a 650-mile navigation channel the length of the Tennessee River and had become the nation's largest electricity supplier. Demand for electricity in the region exceeded the capacity of the agency's resources, however. Because of this, Congress authorized TVA to issue bonds to fund the construction of coal-fired plants that would make use of the extensive coal reserves of the region in 1959. Also in 1959, the TVA became self-financing. In the 1960s, it started to run at a profit and became so self-sufficient that it issued payments to states and counties in place of taxes.

During the 1970s, a nationwide oil crisis led to a fivefold increase in the cost of the TVA's electricity. In the 1980s the TVA cut its costs significantly, which included laying off a significant portion of its workforce. This trend continued into the 1990s and the TVA began to accrue more debt, which stood at roughly $22 million in 2019. A significant change occurred in 2005 when Congress passed legislation to re-organize its board from three full-time members to nine part-time members. Into the 2010s, the TVA partnered with the US Environmental Protection Agency in a pledge to reduce carbon emissions and pollution, an effort that has involved the closure of several coal-fired plants.

Steven Neuse argues that, from its beginnings, the TVA has embraced five principles: 1) unified development; 2) decentralized administration; 3) citizen participation in TVA decisions; 4) social responsibility; and 5) policy making free of political considerations. Unified development involves commitment to the development of the people in the region and an operational strategy that cooperation across agencies. Decentralized administration has encouraged independent action, professional commitment and discretion, and a greater willingness to cooperate with interests in the valley. Because operations are local, the agency is seen as being more attuned to the needs of those in its service region and hence more responsive to those needs. Citizen participation has been the most problematic of TVA's principles. TVA has mostly served as a steward. TVA has not always lived up to its ideal of social responsibility, but it has routinely participated in development projects which have emphasized job skills training, educational programs, and community revitalization. The principle of policy making free of political considerations can be witnessed with TVA's recent decision to go against President Donald Trump's wishes when it closed two coal plants.

Todd K. Platts

See also: Bartlett Electric Cooperative; Cooke, Morris Llewellyn; Electricity; Federal Power Act of 1935; Federal Power Commission; Hoover Dam; Hydroelectric Power; Rural Electrification Act of 1936

FURTHER READING

Ansar, Atif. 2018. "The Fate of Ideals in the Real World: A Long View on Philip Selznick's Classic on the Tennessee Valley Authority (TVA)." *International Journal of Project Management*. Vol. 36. No. 2. Pp. 385–95.

Cebul, Brent. 2018. "Creative Competition: Georgia Power, the Tennessee Valley Authority, and the Creation of a Rural Consumer Economy, 1934–1955." *Journal of American History*. Vol. 105. No. 1. Pp. 45–70.

Hargrove, Erwin C. 1994. *Prisoners of Myth: The Leadership of the Tennessee Valley Authority, 1933–1940*. Princeton, NJ: Princeton University Press.

Morgan, Arthur E. 1935. "Social Methods of the Tennessee Valley Authority." *Journal of Educational Sociology*. Vol. 8. No. 5. Pp. 261–5.

Neuse, Steven M. 2004. "Tennessee Valley Authority (TVA)." *Encyclopedia of the Great Depression*. Ed. Robert S. McElvaine. Pp. 972–9. New York: Palgrave Macmillan.

O'Neill, Karen M. 2002. "Why the TVA Remains Unique: Interest Groups and the Defeat of New Deal River Planning." *Rural Sociology*. Vol. 67. No. 2. Pp. 163–82.

Tesla, Nikola

From electrical engineering pioneer to pop culture hero, Nikola Tesla's stock has risen in the twentieth and twenty-first centuries. Though best known in his own lifetime as the inventor of alternating current and the source of increasingly unlikely scientific speculations, Tesla (1856–1943) has been reimagined in the modern era as a martyr to the power of capitalism, an unworldly scientist outsmarted by the "villainous" Thomas Edison, and a pulp-fiction-mad scientist on par with Victor Frankenstein or Marvel's Tony Stark (aka Iron Man). In death, Tesla gained the fame and popularity that so often eluded him in life.

Born on July 10, 1856, Tesla appeared amid the tangle of nationalities in nineteenth-century southeastern Europe. His family were Serbs, with his father Miltunin a Serbian Orthodox priest and his mother Djuka the daughter of another. Smilijan, his birthplace, was in Lika-Krbava County, a part of the Croatian Military Frontier, part of the historic Kingdom of Croatia in territory administered by the Hungarian half of the Austro-Hungarian Empire. When he attended gymnasium in the city of Karlovec in 1870, the language of instruction was in German, as was usual in the region.

Though a successful student, Tesla struggled as a young adult, nearly dying of cholera shortly after his 1873 graduation. This is an indication of the rural nature of Tesla's home and upbringing, since cholera was long since understood by European medical science. Tesla fled into the countryside in 1874 to avoid the Austro-Hungarian military draft. A year later he was in Graz, Austria, attending what then was the Imperial-Royal Technical College. He was by all accounts an impressive student but left after his third year in 1878 without graduating. Returning home after a plea from his ill father, he eventually left Gospic in Croatia in 1880 to study at Charles-Ferdinand University in Prague. But this was a failure too; he arrived too late in the year to enroll and anyway had never taken the Greek and Czech that were required parts of the curriculum.

Tesla headed for Budapest a year later, finding work with the Budapest Telephone Exchange and making connections with Tivadar Puskás (1844–93), the eastern European telephone pioneer and agent of Thomas Edison in Europe. Puskás made Tesla the company's chief electrician, then in 1884 dispatched him to Paris to work for the Continental Edison Company. CEC was then in the process of bringing electricity to greater Paris, and Tesla personally worked to install electric lighting systems in the suburb of Ivry-sur-Seine. But Third Republic France, not particularly friendly to immigrants, proved too small a place for Tesla. Later that same year, his manager Charles Batchelor (1845–1910) returned to the United States to manage the Edison Machine Works on the Lower East Side of Manhattan. Tesla followed him in June 1884.

In terms of Tesla's relationship with the larger organization, the move was unsatisfactory. He worked under Edison for six months, only meeting Edison himself a handful of times. The work was demanding and unrewarding and he was crammed into a tenement on the

Lower East Side. Tesla felt cheated by several offers of bonuses that had never materialized. Stories about why Tesla left Edison's employ are legion, with Tesla himself claiming that either Edison or Batchelor, depending on when he told the story, went back on a promise of a cash bonus equal to more than $1.5 million in today's currency if a particular problem was solved. Most researchers doubt this account, since the figure would have been larger than the company's capital at the time. In Tesla's diary for the end of 1884, he wrote simply "Good by [*sic*] to the Edison Machine Works!" (quoted in Carlson 2015, 73).

Tesla struggled at first as an independent agent, writing years later that in 1885 and 1886, "my high education in various branches of science, mechanics and literature seemed to me like a mockery" (quoted in Perko 2022, 71). But with the help of powerful patrons, he founded the Tesla Electric Company in 1887 and soon established a business relationship with George Westinghouse (1846–1914) whose company licensed Tesla's AC induction motor. This device became the first cheap, mass-produced AC electric motor. The license, and Westinghouse's generous consulting fees to Tesla made him a wealthy man. This was particularly true after Westinghouse bought out Tesla's royalties for $216,000 in 1892, a sum equal to more than $6 million in 2020.

With his wealth established, Tesla devoted much of his time and resources to developing new technologies that he could patent and bring to market. In 1891, the same year he became a naturalized citizen of the United States, he patented the most famous invention that bears his name, the Tesla coil. In the interim, he traveled the country as a popular spokesman for science, becoming widely recognized for his impressive showmanship and ability to captivate audiences during public lectures and demonstrations. He conducted numerous experiments with mechanical oscillators and generators, electrical discharge tubes, and early X-ray imaging. He even built a wireless-controlled boat, which was considered a groundbreaking achievement at the time and attracted the attention of many wealthy patrons and celebrities like Samuel Clemens, whose pen name was Mark Twain.

Throughout the 1890s, Tesla focused his attention on developing wireless lighting and worldwide wireless electric power distribution. He conducted a series of high-voltage, high-frequency power experiments in both New York and Colorado Springs, which he believed could revolutionize the way people accessed and used electricity. In 1893, years before Marconi's first tests of wireless radio transmission, Tesla made bold predictions about the possibility of wireless communication using his devices, and he worked tirelessly to turn these ideas into a practical reality. His most ambitious project was the Wardenclyffe Tower, an intercontinental wireless communication and power transmitter that might have transformed the way people accessed and used electricity around the world. But despite years of effort and intense lobbying of his new financial patron J.P. Morgan, Tesla's work came to a halt in 1905 as his funding—and his emotional state—collapsed.

Tesla spent much of the rest of his life in difficult circumstances. Though he demonstrated more inventions, such as a bladeless turbine in 1906 that is still used in luxury car speedometers and similar settings, financial success continued to elude him. In 1915, he sued the Marconi Company for patent infringement over the wireless, losing that claim but winning some patents thanks to a later case in 1943 not long before his death. Still, he was deprived of the title of inventor of the radio.

In 1915 there were rumors he was to be awarded the Nobel Prize, almost certainly false ones based on the records of the Nobel committee. Throughout this period, he lived in a variety of hotels in New York City, running up unpaid bills and then moving along, making a hobby of feeding the pigeons in Central Park and other parts of the city. He enjoyed a brief resurgence of fame in the 1930s after a journalist friend organized his seventy-fifth birthday party in 1931, attracting national attention after a series of grandiose claims about his future scientific discoveries during future parties.

In 1934, the Westinghouse Company began paying Tesla a yearly stipend for "consulting," embarrassed by the poor conditions in which their former star inventor lived. In 1937 he was hit by a car while crossing a street in Manhattan late one night to feed his pigeons. On January 7, 1943, a maid at the Hotel New Yorker discovered his body two days after he put up a Do Not Disturb sign. Dr. John G. Trump, an electrical engineer with the National Defense Research Committee of the Office of Scientific Research and Development, evaluated his papers and concluded: "His thoughts and efforts during at least the past 15 years were primarily of a speculative, philosophical, and somewhat promotional character often concerned with the production and wireless transmission of power; but did not include new, sound, workable principles or methods for realizing such results" (quoted in Cheney 1999, 160).

Perhaps befitting a man who lived so much in his imagination, Tesla after death has enjoyed the lasting success he never found in life. From the pages of Brian Clevinger's *Atomic Robo* to a major David Bowie-performed role in 2006's *The Prestige*, popular culture in the twentieth century has made Tesla a secular saint, often casting him as the hero pitted against the sinister forces of Thomas Edison. But Tesla was more than a pop culture figure; he was a brilliant self-promoter and self-made immigrant genius, a man of many cultures whose inventions are used and remembered today across the world.

Michael Davis

See also: Consolidated Edison Company; Davenport, Thomas; Edison, Thomas Alva; Electricity; General Electric Company; Henry, Joseph; Insull, Samuel; Pearl Street Power Station; Stanley, William Jr.; War of the Currents; Westinghouse, George

FURTHER READING

Carlson, W. Bernard. 2015. *Tesla: Inventor of the Electrical Age*. Princeton, NJ: Princeton University Press.

Cheney, Margaret, and Robert Uth. 1999. *Tesla: Master of Lighting*. New York: Barnes and Noble Books.

Cooper, Christopher. 2015. *The Truth about Tesla: The Myth of the Lone Genius in the History of Innovation*. New York: Race Point Publishing.

Dommermuth-Costa, Carol. 1994. *Nikola Tesla: A Spark of Genius*. Minneapolis, MN: Learner Publications Company.

Jonnes, Jill. 2003. *Empires of Light: Edison, Tesla, Westinghouse, and the Race to Electrify the World*. New York: Random House.

O'Neill, John J. 1944. *Prodigal Genius: The Life of Nikola Tesla*. New York: Ives Washburn.

Perko, Marko, and Stephen M. Stahl. 2022. *Tesla: His Tremendous and Troubled Life*. Lanham, MD: Prometheus.

Texaco

Texaco was created in 1902, and Texaco, Inc. is currently an American oil and gasoline brand owned and operated by the Chevron Corporation. Texaco was an independent company until 2001 when its refining operations were purchased by the Chevron Corporation, and most of its gas station franchises were purchased by Shell USA, a subsidiary of Shell plc.

In its heyday from the mid-1940s to the 1970s, Texaco was one of the so-called "Seven Sisters" which dominated the global petroleum industry. The brand became familiar to gasoline customers in the United States from graphics with the logo of a white star in a red circle, the lone star of Texas, and the advertising slogan, "You can trust your car to the man who wears the star." The slogan appeared on highly respected shows like NBC's Texaco Star Theater and Huntley-Brinkley Report (Pollard 2016). Despite its ownership by Chevron, the Texaco brand maintains its loyalty among customers in the United States, Latin America, and West Africa. Petrol users in the UK still support about 980 Texaco-branded service stations.

Texaco traces its origins to the earliest moments of the Texas oil boom. When the Spindletop Oil Gusher burst on January 10, 1901, hundreds of men poured into Beaumont, Texas seeking their fortune in oil. One of the early arrivals, Joseph S. "Buckskin Joe" Cullinan, was a Standard Oil Company employee in Pennsylvania, and believed the nearly 200 oil drilling companies producing around 100,000 barrels of oil per day needed a buyer to help get their crude oil to distant refineries. Cullinan received investment backing from New Yorker Arnold Schlaet and founded the Texas Fuel Company, and soon reorganized with a group of other investors as The Texas Company. The company intended to serve as a middleman, buying crude from drilling companies and selling it to refineries. Then Cullinan began a drilling company called Producers Oil Company to extend his reach into oil field development, but financial considerations led the two companies to merge, and the company moved forward as The Texas Company (RFB 2023). In its early years the company built a pipeline from Spindletop to the Gulf of Mexico city of Port Arthur to supply Louisiana sugar planters the oil they used to fuel their boilers. It also began drilling northwest of Spindletop at Sour Lake, Texas, and then in Oklahoma and Louisiana.

Within its first ten years The Texas Company became wildly successful, with assets in 1913 worth $60 million. In this period of its infancy, the company trademarked the brand "Texaco" in 1906, which was the abbreviation the company's New York office used in telegram communications. It also began to market its products under the Texaco brand and developed the first version of its logo, this one with a green "T" overlaid on a red star. A big change in the company's business model occurred with the arrival of mass-produced automobiles with internal combustion engines fueled by gasoline. In 1911, the company opened its first retail gasoline station in Brooklyn, New York, and by 1916, had established fifty-seven service stations across the United States (RFB 2023). The automobile industry enabled the company to leave behind its earlier identity as a supplier of fuel oil for railroad engines and factories and illuminating oil for large institutional customers.

After the First World War, automobile production exploded in volume, and a new sector, aviation, increased demand for petroleum products. In the late 1920s the company developed Texaco Aviation Gasoline in response to this demand, and in 1932 introduced its Fire Chief brand of high-octane gasoline for fire company vehicles and other specialized equipment. The company also acquired the Indiana Refining Company and its high-selling brand Havoline Wax Free Motor Oil. In 1938, The Texas Company began to market Sky Chief premium grade gasoline. Although the company grew exponentially in the 1910s and 1920s, it suffered along with most US corporations the disruptions of the Stock Market Crash of 1929 and the onset of the Great Depression. These new fuels were attempts to give new life to the brand and win over new customers. Then, the company revived along with other energy-related corporations when the Second World War began and the federal government arrived with massive contracts for petroleum products to fuel the global Allied war effort.

The Texas Company, since reorganized in Delaware as The Texas Corporation, with The Texas Company operating as a subsidiary, had already anticipated the globalization of the market for petroleum. The company muscled its way into oil fields around the world, making deals with local strongmen in Colombia in 1936 when it bought the 1-million-acre Barco oil concession in a joint development venture with Socony-Vacuum Corporation. The resulting three-year project drilled wells, constructed a 247-foot suspension bridge, and built a pipeline across mountains and through uncharted swamps and jungles. An estimated eight employees of the oil companies were killed by Motilone Indians defending their territory ("U.S. Business" 1939). Also in 1936, The Texas Company formed a joint marketing venture with Standard Oil Company of California (Socal) named California Texas Oil Company Limited (shortened to Caltex Corporation in 1968) in which the venture would draw petroleum products from Socal's Bahrain refinery and Arabian oil fields and market them through The Texas Company's channels in Asia, East Africa, and Australia. Caltex went on to pursue expansion in other international operations through the end of the century.

These efforts to globalize production and marketing brought unwanted media attention and political trouble to the company in the years leading up to the Second World War. The Texas Company assisted fascists in Spain and Adolf Hitler's Nazi regime in the 1930s. The company's Chairman of the Board Torkild Rieber arranged to provide General Francisco Franco, an ally of Adolf Hitler, with 3.5 million tons of oil on credit. Historian Adam Hochschild discovered that Reiber's assistance amounted to $20 million, or $325 million in 2016 dollars. Rieber also provided Franco's regime with intelligence on shipments of oil to Republican forces so they could be targeted for attack. Gen. Franco made Reiber a Knight of the Grand Cross of the Order of Isabella the Catholic for his help in defeating Republican forces in the Spanish Civil War (Hochschild 2016a). After the Nazi blitzkrieg swarmed over Poland, Rieber traveled to Germany, met with Herman Göring at his country estate, toured key industrial sites, and made various business arrangements (Hochschild 2016b). After the fall of France, Rieber and executives from IT&T, General Motors, and Ford Motor Company met with German agent Gerhardt Alois Westrick at a party staged at the Manhattan Waldorf Astoria hotel on June 26, 1940, a meeting designed to encourage American businesses to support German ambitions in Europe (Moss 2003, 248–9).

Rieber acted as a go-between, delivering in person a message that Göring received from Hitler to President Roosevelt, inviting the United States to support a Nazi-dominated European Union. Roosevelt dismissed the suggestion (Stephenson 1999). Rieber was ultimately forced to resign as The Texas Company's board chairman on August 12, 1940 when the *New York Herald Tribune* reported that British intelligence documented his involvement in supplying oil and intelligence to Gen. Franco as well as his association with German agents. Since supplying belligerents with credit and armaments was a violation of the Neutrality Acts enacted between 1935 and 1937, the company was fined $22,000. Rieber claimed that his activities were simply "'good business'" and that his resignation came "'in view of the harm that might be done to the company by reason of the unfair and unjust criticism which appeared recently in the news'" (quoted in "Torkild" 1968). Other accusations arose over The Texas Company's connections to German military and intelligence officials, which might explain why Texaco ranked very low—ninety-third—among US corporations in military production contracts.

After the War ended, the company purchased the Trinidad Oil Company in 1956 and the Seaboard Oil Company in 1958, providing the company with further oil reserves in South America. After The Texas Company changed its corporate name to Texaco, Inc. in 1959, it continued its international expansion, buying a majority interest in West German oil company Deutsch Erdol A.G. in 1966, and then reorganizing Caltex in 1967 by taking over one-half of the group's interest in twelve European countries that imported oil from its Saudi Arabian wells (RFB 2023). By the end of the 1960s, Texaco was stitched firmly into the domestic and global markets for petroleum products. It had become the largest selling US gasoline brand, and the only company that sold its brand in all fifty US states.

Beginning in the 1970s, Texaco navigated the complicated economics of the Clean Air Act of 1970 and the energy crisis of the 1970, as well as the complicated politics of oil development in unstable Central and South American, Middle Eastern, and South Asian nations. After petroleum companies began adding lead to gasoline as an anti-knock agent, environmental concerns about air pollution led Congress to pass the Clean Air Act of 1970 and to create the US Environmental Protection Agency to establish limits on the quantity of lead that companies could add to gasoline. Eventually leaded gasoline was banned for vehicles beginning in model year 1975 (EIA 2022). In 1974, Texaco introduced an innovative fuel as the first regular-octane lead-free gasoline.

The energy crisis of the 1970s proved to be a greater challenge. The combined effects of the OPEC Oil Embargo of 1973, federal responses to the embargo, and the nationalization of overseas US assets by hostile foreign governments led to a drop in Texaco's net income from $1.6 billion in 1974 to $830.6 million in 1975. Texaco lost its share in Aramco when Saudi Arabia began to nationalize the company, beginning in 1972 and completing the process in 1980. Libya took over Texaco's Texas Overseas Petroleum Company in 1973–4, and then the Iranian Revolution of 1979 disrupted Texaco's Caltex operation, which divested part of its assets to the government of Bahrain (RFB 2023). Texaco reduced its number of retail filling stations in the United States from 35,500 in 1974 to 27,000 in 1980, and closed six refineries by 1982.

Then, on November 20, 1980, the Lake Peigneur-Jefferson Island giant sinkhole disaster occurred. Texaco's faulty oil rig drilling pierced an actively mined salt dome, releasing 3.5 billion gallons of oil, which caused the Delcambre Canal to flow backward. The flood submerged barges and sent trapped air hundreds of feet high, leaving the oil rigs, buildings, salt-filled barges, and other equipment at the bottom of a ruined salt mine. Because of its errors, Texaco paid $45 million to the salt mine company and millions more to affected landowners (KLFY 2020). Around this time, accusations surfaced that Texaco had provided support for a Colombian narco-paramilitary organization known as Muerte a Secuestradores to protect the company's interests in the South American nation, which committed various atrocities against community leaders, elected officials, Communist sympathizers, and farmers who opposed the regime in power (Santina 1998–9). As these claims began to surface, Texaco lost a $10.53 billion judgment in court on November 19, 1985, when Pennzoil's legal team convinced a jury that Texaco interfered with Pennzoil's contract to buy Getty Oil. Texaco eventually paid $3 billion, and in 1987, was forced into bankruptcy proceedings.

Another lawsuit, filed in 1993, led to significant losses for the company. Texaco was found to have released 16 million gallons of crude oil and 18.5 billion gallons of toxic water into the Amazon watershed and around its Ecuadorean offshore drilling sites in the early 1960s through the early 1990s. Texaco paid $40 million to clean up the sites, but fought the lawsuit, which ballooned into a class action suit in an Ecuadorean court signed onto by 30,000 Ecuadoreans citing a wave of cancers, miscarriages, and birth defects as a result of the environmental pollution. After years of litigation, much of it coming after Chevron's acquisition of Texaco in 2001, the Ecuadorean court ruled against the company and handed down a judgment with a fine of $18 billion in damages. The number was subsequently reduced to $9.5 billion, but the company pulled its assets out of the country and avoided paying the fine. Still, Chevron—Texaco's new owner—paid $400 million in legal fees to fight the case (Simon 2022). Before its acquisition by Chevron, Texaco paid $176 million to settle class action racial discrimination lawsuits filed by black employees at the company, with *Roberts v. Texaco* the largest racial discrimination lawsuit settlement to that point in US history. Texaco's public relations disaster worsened when tapes were released of meetings with company executives using offensive language about Black employees and planning to destroy incriminating evidence (Mulligan 1996).

Chevron benefited from recent developments in global oil and gas markets. During the Covid pandemic, demand dropped as people stopped flying and driving. Once the pandemic restrictions were lifted, demand spiked, aided by Russia's invasion of Ukraine when nations lined up to boycott Russian oil. This placed greater demand on US production, and Chevron took advantage with its assets in the Permian Shale Basin. In 2022, the company earned record profits of $36.5 billion on revenues of $235.72 billion, which actually disappointed forecasters who expected a better fourth quarter performance (Valle 2023). In 2022, Chevron ranked second to ExxonMobil as the US's richest petroleum corporation.

William P. Kladky

See also: Aramco; Caltex; Consortium Agreement of 1954; Energy Crisis of the 1970s; Energy Policy and Conservation Act of 1975; ExxonMobil; Getty, Jean Paul; Gulf Oil Company; Koch Brothers; Mobil Oil Corporation; Organization of Petroleum Exporting Countries (OPEC); Petroleum; Seven Sisters Oil Companies; Standard Oil Company; Texas Oil Boom

FURTHER READING

Hochschild, Adam. 2016a. "How Texaco Helped Franco Win the Spanish Civil War." *Mother Jones*. March 29.

Hochschild, Adam. 2016b. "The Untold Story of the Texaco Oil Tycoon Who Loved Fascism." *The Nation*. March 21. https://www.thenation.com/article/archive/the-untold-story-of-the-texaco-oil-tycoon-who-loved-fascism/ (accessed October 2023).

KLFY. 2020. "40th Anniversary of Salt Mine Breach Creating Louisiana's Deepest Lake." November 24. https://www.klfy.com/local/iberia-parish/40th-anniversary-of-salt-mine-breach-creating-louisiana-deepest-lake (accessed October 2023).

Moss, Norman. 2003. *Nineteen Weeks: America, Britain, and the Fateful Summer of 1940*. New York: Houghton Mifflin.

Mulligan, Thomas S., and Chris Kraul. 1996. "Texaco Settles Race Bias Suit for $176 Million." November 16. *Los Angeles Times*. https://www.latimes.com/archives/la-xpm-1996-11-16-mn-65290-story.html (accessed October 2023).

Pollard, Garland. 2016. "Texaco Still a Strong Brand." BrandlandUSA. https://www.brandlandusa.com/2016/01/17/texaco-still-a-strong-brand/ (accessed October 2023).

Reference for Business (RFB). 2023. "Texaco, Inc." Advameg, Inc. https://www.referenceforbusiness.com/history2/40/Texaco-Inc.html (accessed October 2023).

Santina, Peter. 1998–9. "Army of Terror: The Legacy of US-Backed Human Rights Abuses in Colombia." *Harvard International Review*. Vol. 21. No. 1. Winter. Pp. 40–3.

Simon, Morgan. 2022. "Courts are not a Weapon: How Corporations Like Chevron Use the Law to Get Their Way." *Forbes*. May 26. https://www.forbes.com/sites/morgansimon/2022/05/26/courts-are-not-a-weapon-how-corporations-like-chevron-use-the-law-to-get-their-way/ (accessed October 2023).

Stephenson, William S., ed. 1999. *British Security Coordination: The Secret History of British Intelligence in the Americas, 1940–1945*. Mt. Prospect, IL: Fromm International.

"Torkild Rieber Is Dead at 86; Seaman Rose to Head Texaco." 1968. *The New York Times*. August 11. https://timesmachine.nytimes.com/timesmachine/1968/08/11/296386762.html?pageNumber=72 (accessed October 2023).

"U.S. Business Opens the Great New Barco Oil Fields in Colombia." 1939. *Life*. Vol. 7. No. 20. November 13. Pp. 15–19.

US Energy Information Administration (EIA). 2022. "Gasoline Explained: Gasoline and the Environment." December 20. US Department of Energy. https://www.eia.gov/energyexplained/gasoline/gasoline-and-the-environment-leaded-gasoline.php (accessed October 2023).

Valle, Sabrina. 2023. "Chevron Annual Profit Hits Record but Q4 Miss Hits Shares." Reuters. January 27. https://www.reuters.com/business/energy/chevron-annual-profit-doubles-record-365-bln-misses-estimates-2023-01-27 (accessed October 2023).

Texas Oil Boom

On January 10, 1901, a gusher on Sour Spring Mound near Beaumont, Texas inaugurated the Texas oil boom, a period of rapid exploration and development during the early twentieth century. With the discovery of vast petroleum reserves in and around southeastern Texas, oil was poised to become a fuel for mass consumption. The industrial frenzy across the state subsequently heralded the Oil Age as petroleum and its by-products became foundational to both American and global modern life. One of the most rapid economic booms in US history, oil-led development in southeast Texas quickly spread, and by the mid-twentieth century Texas had become one of the most populous states in the Union. At the center of its dynamic oil industry was Houston, which remains one of the largest and most diverse oil and gas industries in the world.

At the turn of the twentieth century, Texas was primarily a ranching and agricultural state. As the prospect of oil swept into the region in the 1890s, it quickly became the site of rapid industrialization. In the decade prior to the discovery near Beaumont, various companies had tried to find oil in the region, which had many of the salt domes suspected to house petroleum. In 1899, amateur geologist and businessperson Pattillo Higgins enlisted mining engineer Anthony F. Lucas to search for oil around the Sour Spring Mound, which was subsequently dubbed "Spindletop." After nearly two years, they finally struck black gold over 1,000 feet below the ground. The new well they developed at Spindletop produced approximately 100,000 barrels of crude oil per day and ushered in the modern drilling industry. Investors flocked to the region and speculation swiftly turned Beaumont into a boomtown.

As operations grew, financial consolidation and acquisition altered the industrial landscape of Texas. Ownership of oil interests changed hands as smaller companies were absorbed by regional and national corporations. The Lucas-Higgins operations at Spindletop, for example, were acquired by J.M. Guffey and eventually absorbed into the Gulf Coast Oil Company. Decades later, this company was purchased by the California-based Chevron. With the influx of capital from out-of-state investors and businesses, industry and civic leaders in Texas grew wary of losing political and economic power to outsiders. Consequently, beginning in 1906, the Texas Attorney General introduced a series of antitrust lawsuits aimed at weakening the hold of out-of-state corporations. One of the prime targets of this campaign was the industry titan Standard Oil, established in 1870 by John D. Rockefeller (1839–1937).

In the early years of the boom, the industry was driven by small and independent producers. Even Texas governor James S. Hogg became an investor after the Spindletop discovery. In the coming decades, salt dome exploration expanded across the state and oil infrastructure quickly sprang up across southeastern Texas, with refineries and pipelines connecting the state. In addition to corporate investment and development, the Texas oil boom ushered in an era of "wildcatters," entrepreneurial prospectors who purchased vast tracts of land in hopes of discovering oil. Rural areas in North Texas and the Permian Basin also saw a rapid influx of oil field workers, investors, and prospectors. Yet like many economic booms, the Texas oil boom led to subsequent busts for many regions in the state as smaller reserves of oil dried up and populations shrunk. In 1914, the Houston Ship Channel was completed, linking the Port of Houston to the Gulf of Mexico. The Ship Channel further cemented the city's status as the center of the Texas oil boom as refineries and other related operations sprang up along the channel. Commercial centers in Texas flourished as a result of the influx of capital, with Houston growing by over 500 percent in the first three decades of the twentieth century. By the 1930s, drilling had expanded into the offshore, further contributing to the burgeoning oil development across Texas and neighboring states such as Louisiana. Yet with rapid expansion came environmental costs. Due in part to the extensive refining and production industries centered around Houston, the city quickly became a hotbed of industrial pollution.

By the Great Depression, Texas was one of the few states whose economy continued to expand due to the high demand for petroleum. The oil boom had a ripple effect, extending to heavy industries such as lumber, concrete, steel, automobile, and chemical production. Much of the state's wealth and power was linked to a handful of businessmen who maintained a firm hold on both industry and politics. The "Big Four" included Hugh Roy Cullen (1881–1957), Sid Richardson (1891–1959), Clint Murchison, Sr. (1895–1969), and H. L. Hunt (1889–1974), all of whom were oil magnates and political power brokers in the 1920s and 1930s and maintained close ties with senior government, including President Lyndon Johnson. In his study of the Big Four's influence, author Bryan Burrough underscores "Texas Oil's contribution to America's rightward shift" in subsequent decades (Burrough 2009, xiii).

The Texas oil boom also extended to cultural development, particularly in urban centers. The influx of wealth and investment in Houston contributed to its status as a cultural hub as institutions such as the University of Houston, the Museum of Fine Arts, and the Houston Zoo opened their doors. Similarly, the discovery of the East Texas oil field propelled Dallas to the financial center of the state's petroleum industry in the early 1930s. Meanwhile, the discovery of oil on university-owned land in West Texas rapidly increased the revenues of the University of Texas at Austin, which remains one of the wealthiest public universities in the nation.

The widespread influence of the Texas oil boom has shaped many facets of modern American life. The emergence of car culture as a result of the state's access to cheap gasoline, for example, also led to Texas's pioneering spatial arrangements, from urban sprawl to freeway expansion. Additionally, the spectacle of wealth generated by the region's petroleum industry gained a firm hold in the popular imagination, as did ideas about a distinct Texan identity (Burrough 2009, xi). Novels like Edna Ferber's Pulitzer Prize-winning *Giant* (1952) and its film adaptation of the same name four years later further catapulted the iconic figure of the Texas oil baron into popular culture, as did the long-running prime-time drama *Dallas* (1978–91), which revolved around a feuding Texas oil family.

THE BOOM IN LITERATURE

In addition to popular film and television, literature about the Texas oil boom captured the American imagination. Winifred Sanford (1890–1983) of Wichita Falls, Texas, was one of the first literary voices to tackle the state's oil industry and the cultural consequences of the boom. Her stories appear in the posthumous collection *Windfall*.

Delia Sara Byrnes

During the global oil crises of the 1970s, petroleum prices rose dramatically. Since Texas remained one the world's top producers of petroleum, the state benefited significantly during this era, even as recessions hobbled other American industries. As the nation doubled down on efforts to produce oil domestically rather than relying on overseas sources, Texas and the broader Gulf Coast region found themselves amid a second great oil boom. In the twenty-first century, Texas and the broader Gulf Coast region remain one of the nation's top producers of petroleum and greenhouse gas emissions.

Delia Sara Byrnes

See also: Caltex; ExxonMobil; Gulf Oil Company; Mobil Oil Company; Petroleum; Rockefeller, John D.; Seven Sisters Oil Companies; Spindletop Oil Gusher; Standard Oil Company; Sweeney, Peter; Texaco

FURTHER READING

Burrough, Bryan. 2009. *The Big Rich: The Rise and Fall of the Greatest Texas Oil Fortunes*. New York: Penguin Books.

Melosi, Martin V., and Joseph A. Pratt. 2007. *Energy Metropolis: An Environmental History of Houston and the Gulf Coast*. Pittsburgh: University of Pittsburgh Press.

Olien, Roger. 1982. *Oil Booms: Social Change in Five Texas Towns*. Lincoln, NE: University of Nebraska Press.

Sanford, Winifred. 1988. *Windfall and Other Stories*. Dallas: Southern Methodist University Press.

Tarbell, Ida. 1904. *The History of the Standard Oil Company*. New York: McClure, Philips and Company.

Wright, Lawrence. 2017. "The Dark Bounty of Texas Oil." https://www.newyorker.com/magazine/2018/01/01/the-dark-bounty-of-texas-oil (accessed October 2023).

Three Mile Island Accident

On 28 March 1979, the Unit 2 Reactor of the Three Mile Island nuclear power plant suffered a partial meltdown. Located in the midst of the Susquehanna River and easily within sight of Harrisburg International Airport, "TMI," as it is known locally in South Central Pennsylvania, is around a bend in the river from the capital of Pennsylvania. It is thus no surprise that this calamity—which occurred just over a 100 miles from Washington, DC, within close proximity to all of the major population centers of the Eastern Seaboard—caused widespread panic and dominated the national news for some time. It resulted in the large-scale voluntary evacuation of nearly 150,000 people. The accident was the most significant nuclear power plant accident in US history and led to a severe public backlash against the nuclear power industry.

The Three Mile Island meltdown began around four in the morning, when the pumps that moved water between the reactor's heat exchanger and the steam-generator failed. These pumps provided the circulatory system that removed heat from the reactor core and used it to generate steam to spin turbines and generate electricity. When the pumps failed to operate properly, a couple of other systems cut out automatically. First, the generator turbine that produces electricity shut down, and shortly thereafter, so did the reactor itself, as control rods were inserted to stop the chain reaction. Since the secondary water was not circulating and taking away heat, the temperature remained high even after the control rods were put in. As pressure in the system began to build up as a result of this shutdown, a pressure-release valve opened. Although this valve was designed to close automatically once the proper pressure level had been regained, in this case the valve became stuck in the open position. The gauges in the control room indicated that the valve had closed, however, and thus the plant operators ignored the alarms that indicated that steam was rushing out of the stuck valve, causing the coolant level covering the reactor core to drop precipitously. Unfortunately, there was no water-level gauge to indicate this drop, as under normal conditions, the pressure vessel surrounding the core was always full of water; thus, if the pressure gauge reading indicated that the pressure was within the normal range, the core therefore was believed to be completely covered with water.

This, however, proved to be a disastrous operating assumption, as at this point the plant personnel took a number of steps based on false readings and erroneous assessments. Human error, in fact, was to be the crucial factor that resulted in the uncovering of the core. Because the pressure release valve was stuck open, the pressure in the system fell to such a low point that the coolant pumps began to vibrate, and therefore the staff turned them off. Concurrently, the emergency coolant water rushing into the system was shut off because of the mistaken belief that it would soon flood the pressurizer entirely. Both the normal coolant circulatory system and the emergency back-up coolant water system were thus intentionally shut down because the staff of the plant drastically misunderstood the situation. As more water boiled off and escaped as steam through the open valve the reactor became uncovered,

FIGURE 9: The Three Mile Island Nuclear Generating Station was a nuclear power plant at the Lake Frederic reservoir on the Susquehanna River near Harrisburg, Pennsylvania.

and the core became exposed as a result, and this caused the meltdown of the Unit 2 Reactor at the Three Mile Island Nuclear Power Plant. Thus, the events at Three Mile Island were the result of a combination of factors, a "perfect storm," as it were. These contributing elements included some engineering and design flaws, elements of equipment failure, and compounding operator error. The direct consequences of this meltdown included some release of radioactivity, although luckily this release was relatively small scale. The hydrogen bubble that was generated from interaction of steam with the fuel-rod cladding caused a lot of concern that there would be an explosion, and in fact there was apparently an explosion within the reactor vessel. To everyone's relief, the hydrogen gas dissipated eventually and the reactor vessel's integrity was never compromised.

Although many studies have concluded that the release of radioactivity as a result of the accident did not result in widespread and significant health risks, one study by the Penn State College of Medicine at Hershey in 2017 posited a correlation between the TMI incident and thyroid cancer. With that notable exception, there is as yet little other conclusive evidence to suggest that the meltdown at Three Mile Island resulted in widespread or long-lasting radioactive damage to people, animals, or property in the area, although ever since, people in the region have blamed the incident for a range of medical maladies. In any case, the nature of the event, coupled with the public reaction to it, did indeed have some discernible long-term policy effects. The most obvious of these included more careful training of nuclear workers, more clearly established nuclear safety protocols, and more federal oversight of the nuclear industry. However, although the incident at TMI is generally thought responsible for stopping all new nuclear development for the next forty years, it is important to note that many existing plants continued past their designed lifespans, and that nuclear output actually grew significantly. Although many plans for new plants were cancelled in the wake of the TMI meltdown, others in later stages of development were completed. Indeed, because of extended plant lifespans and the completion of building units that were already underway before 1979, nuclear electricity generation increased from around 250 billion kWhr/yr around 1980 to 806 billion kWhr/yr around 2007. Moreover, a number of other factors also contributed to the decline of nuclear power in the United States. As a result of the accident, the emergency response system in place to deal with potential disasters was adjusted, and the general professional consensus is that the nuclear power industry became much safer as a result of the governmental and industrial reactions to the crisis.

A fact that was apparent to a great number of Americans at the time but is less so today is that a film entitled *The China Syndrome* that depicted a nuclear meltdown had opened at movie theaters across the country just eight days before the TMI catastrophe, on March 16. Starring iconic Hollywood actors Michael Douglas, Jane Fonda, and Jack Lemmon, the film enjoyed a great deal of popular success but also incited a firestorm of controversy, bringing into the limelight and putting at odds the anti-nuclear activists who supported the movie and the nuclear power industry which reviled it. Indeed, *The New York Times* even ran a piece on March 18 which pitted these various perspectives against one another, attempting to give equal weight to those who saw the film as unnecessarily alarmist and those who praised its accuracy. In retrospect, however, this piece helps to underscore just how terrifyingly prescient the movie was to seem just ten days later.

Most notable of all, however, is the fact that the film infamously contained a chilling line that seemed little short of clairvoyant as the Three Mile Island crisis unfolded. In response to a reporter's query, an expert indicated that a large-scale nuclear accident could make an area the size of Pennsylvania forever unfit for human beings. Although undoubtedly coincidental, this passage seemed in retrospect to presage the Three Mile Island accident, and this offhand remark in the fictional representation of a California meltdown was totally unnerving in the context of the actual event occurring in real time in Pennsylvania. Indeed, because the production company was very wary of being criticized for profiting from the events at Three Mile Island, that particular line was edited from the version of the film shown in some theaters. Interestingly, however, some involved in the making of the film claimed that they had hurried to produce the movie before a nuclear accident that they were convinced would soon follow, a perspective reported by Michael Douglas in an interview with *People* magazine the month after the Three Mile Island Accident.

Although many Americans who remember that moment well might have assumed that Three Mile Island was shuttered decades ago, this was not at all the case. In fact, the final operating reactor at Three Mile Island was retired on September 20, 2019. In the years leading up to the shutdown, nuclear power plants in Pennsylvania had been having increasing trouble competing with other energy sources. Three Mile Island, having especially limited capacity due to the accident forty years before, had long been especially vulnerable in this regard. Although this might seem to have ended the saga, controversy continues to surround this and other closings of nuclear power plants, especially given the lack of a coherent national policy regarding the treatment and storage of spent radioactive material. It is also worth noting that—as reviled as TMI became because of the partial meltdown in 1979—the power plant was an important local employer. Several hundred workers lost their jobs when it shut down in 2019, creating a local backlash to the closing that might have come as a shock to the national audience captivated by the accident four decades ago.

Christopher R. Fee

See also: Atomic Energy Acts; Clean Power Plan of 2015; Idaho National Laboratory; Nuclear Power; Nuclear Regulatory Commission; Nuclear Waste Policy Act of 1982; Shippingport Atomic Power Station; Yucca Mountain Nuclear Waste Repository

FURTHER READING

Burnham, David. 1979. "Nuclear Experts Debate 'The China Syndrome.'" *The New York Times*. March 18.

Sholtis, Brett. 2019. "As Three Mile Island Stops Producing Electricity, One Community Braces for Change." WITF. September 20. https://www.witf.org/2019/09/20/as-three-mile-island-stops-producing-electricity-one-local-community-braces-for-change/ (accessed October 2023).

Solovey, Matt. 2017. "Possible Correlation Shown between TMI Nuclear Accident and Thyroid Cancers." Research: Health and Medicine. Pennsylvania State University News. May 31. https://news.psu.edu/story/469874/2017/05/31/research/possible-correlation-shown-between-tmi-nuclear-accident-and-thyroid (accessed October 2023).

Southwick, Ron. 2019. "Three Mile Island Accident was Eerily Foreshadowed by a Hollywood Blockbuster Days Before." PennLive. March 17. https://www.pennlive.com/news/2019/03/the-three-mile-island-accident-followed-a-hollywood-blockbuster.html (accessed October 2023).

US Energy Information Administration (EIA). 2017. "Today in Energy: Most U.S. Nuclear Power Plants Were Built between 1970 and 1990." US Department of Energy. April 27. https://www.eia.gov/todayinenergy/detail.php?id=30972 (accessed October 2023).

US Energy Information Administration (EIA). 2022. "Electricity Explained: Electricity in the United States." US Department of Energy. July 15. https://www.eia.gov/energyexplained/electricity/electricity-in-the-us.php (accessed October 2023).

US Nuclear Regulatory Commission (NRC). 2022. "Backgrounder on the Three Mile Island Accident." November 15. https://www.nrc.gov/reading-rm/doc-collections/fact-sheets/3mile-isle.html (accessed October 2023).

Tokheim Oil Tank & Pump Company

A number of factors led to the explosive growth of the US economy in the late nineteenth century, including a culture of entrepreneurship and a legal environment conducive to business formation. Availability of land and investment capital, and an increase in immigration, contributed as well. The economy expanded in all sectors, including agriculture, industry, and finance. The energy sector benefited from this expansion, but also served as a catalyst for further growth in the American economy and infrastructure by the beginning of the twentieth century. The Tokheim Oil Tank & Pump Company, founded in 1902, was one of tens of thousands of energy-related businesses that appeared in the half-century between 1870 and 1920, which extracted fossil fuels, or designed or manufactured devices that produced, stored, transported, dispensed, or consumed these fuels. Tokheim offers a small window on the impact of energy-related development in American economic and social history.

The Tokheim Oil & Pump Company traces its origins to the 1890s and the arrival of its founder, John J. Tokheim (1871–1941) to the United States. He emigrated from Odda, Norway in 1887 as a sixteen year old and joined an older brother who had left in 1880 and settled near Thor, Iowa. After a few years of work as a sheet metal apprentice, accompanied by self-study and a half-year business course in Des Moines, Tokheim moved to Chicago in 1895 to work as a tinsmith in a factory. He stayed there for six months, during which time he met and married his future wife Senva Eide, before returning to Thor to open a combined tin shop, machine shop, and hardware store ("Time" 2016). Tokheim dispensed kerosene to customers to use for lighting and heating. He felt there must be a better way to deliver fuel to customers than pumping it out of 55-gallon drums into measuring cans. In 1898, he used his metal-working experiences and skills to fabricate a storage tank to be buried underground, containing fuel drawn by a pump of his own making.

This innovation led to a patent approved in 1900 for his "Measuring-Pump," which enabled the user to draw fuel from an underground tank by means of a traditional water pump handle into a domed, glass container with markings for measurement, which was then dispensed from the container by means of a spigot (Tokheim 1900). Tokheim's invention pleased consumers because it worked fairly cleanly and offered precision in calculating the product's volume and price. Acting entrepreneurially, Tokheim decided to shift from retail to manufacturing, and organized the Tokheim Manufacturing Company with capital from a number of investors. The company located in an abandoned factory in Cedar Rapids, Iowa and began looking for customers. The periodical *The Iron Age* from June 19, 1902 provides a view of how Tokheim marketed his device to hardware store owners: the pump "can be set in any convenient location in the store, as it is not necessary to set the pump on the tank nor directly over the tank in the basement, as it will draw oil, it is explained, 1,000 feet from any angle if desired." The magazine blurb went on to say that the merchant can "place the oil tank underground at a fire proof distance from the building, where the oil supply is out of the frost in the winter and out of the sun in summer and always convenient for filling" ("Tokheim" 1902, 89).

The advertisement made a special effort to promote the measuring dome, made of "heavy flint glass." The pitch went this way: "the manufacturers explain that it computes a gallon or any fraction of a gallon, from 1 cent's worth up, at any price, money value, in plain sight of the merchant and the customer" ("Tokheim" 1902, 89). It ended by asserting that Tokheim's pump was recommended by insurance companies and city fire departments. The company had created an industry standard of dispensing fuel in underground tanks via surface-level measuring pumps, and quickly mobilized to dominate the market for hardware and grocery installations once "horseless carriages" began to appear nationwide. Tokheim kept receiving patents for improved versions of his measuring pump, but then in 1910 several of his larger shareholders staged a hostile takeover of the company. Tokheim was forced out in 1911, losing his Cedar Rapids factory, his patents, and access to the market he created for gasoline pumps (Cejka 2009).

Tokheim was a dedicated if frustrated energy innovator and entrepreneur. He formed a new enterprise called Vac Liquid Equipment Company with two of his patents, making and selling devices for dispensing cider and vinegar in bulk. He would go on and manufacture the Triune Electric Gasoline Pump, one of the earliest electric pumps with a metered discharge, and the Triune Electric Filtered Gasoline Pump, which featured a flow meter and a wet-hose discharge nozzle (Hinckley 2005, 238). Reclaiming his name in 1915, he rebranded as The Tokheim Company and made a successful business of producing pumps and gauges for a variety of applications until 1941, when he died after an extended illness at the age of sixty-nine (Anderson 2002). Most of his early patents and the Tokheim brand were taken in the 1910 purchase of his company by banker Ralph F. Diserens and manufacturer Matthew B. Muxen of the Wayne Pump and Tank Company, both of Ft. Wayne, Indiana. In 1918, the Tokheim Manufacturing Company brought in more investors from Ft. Wayne, and its operations were moved there from Cedar Rapids. It became known as The Tokheim Oil Tank & Pump Company, and in 1953 shortened its name to The Tokheim Corporation (Anderson 2002).

After its move and name change in 1918, The Tokheim Oil Tank & Pump Company competed with the S.F. Bowser & Company, also based in Ft. Wayne. By then, American automobile manufacturers had mastered the techniques of mass production and cars proliferated. Between 1909 and 1912, the Ford Motor Company manufactured 133,347 Model Ts, and then another 2 million more by 1918. In the earliest years of the automobile, owners had to install their own tanks and pumps at home or hope to find a local grocery or hardware store that had adopted a fuel dispensing system. In December 1913, the Gulf Refining Company opened the first service station at Baum Boulevard and St. Clair Street in Pittsburgh. The historical marker at the site describes the station as "the first drive-in facility designed and built to provide gasoline, oils, and lubricants to the motoring public." Further, it claims that "its success led to construction of thousands of gas stations by different oil companies across the nation" ("1st" 2000). These thousands of new service stations opened by the oil companies were customers for Tokheim and Bowser gasoline pumps. In this way all the different facets of the US energy production, energy distribution, and energy consumption were brought together in an integrated system.

The company introduced new models quite frequently, and a few constituted meaningful improvements in the user experience. In 1918, it marketed the Victory Visible, which enabled buyers to see their 5 gallons of gas before it was pumped into their car's gas tank, which inspired confidence they were getting the right amount, and that the gas contained no impurities. Starting in the 1920s, it offered a series of "clock-face" pump models that displayed the amount dispensed on a meter in the round shape of a wall clock. These were widely sold and in some models were given an Art Deco design flourish. In 1934, Tokheim began selling its first computing pumps, which provided a numeral display of the customer's purchase, in terms of both gallons and gallon-fractions and dollars and cents. One historian noted that this was "one of the first pumps to provide equal protection to both the motorist and the service station attendant," which made it a "brilliant merchandising concept" (Derdak 2019). The Stationliter came along in 1935, which contained a built-in light for use at night, and in 1956 the Tokheim Twin allowed two users to use the pump at the same time from opposite sides. The gas pump became an abundant feature of the built environment of the United States in the twentieth century.

The Tokheim Corporation and its competitors upgraded their models to take advantage of new technologies, including gas/ethanol capability, automatic cut-offs, digital readouts, and credit card readers. It enjoyed a brief moment as the largest company in the petroleum dispenser business when in 1996 it acquired French manufacturer Sofitam and reached 37 percent market share. However, financial adversity forced the company to declare bankruptcy in 2000 and several more times in the ensuing decade. In 2016, the company was acquired by Dover Corporation and became part of its OPW Fueling Components, Inc. subsidiary. Time will tell regarding the future of gasoline pumps. In 2019, RS Automotive of Takoma Park, Maryland became the first US gas station to convert to an electric vehicle-charging station, aided by a $786,000 grant from the Maryland state government and the Electric Vehicle Institute of Baltimore (Hagemann 2019).

Jeffrey B. Webb

See also: Bowser, Sylvanus Freelove; Densmore Oil Tank Car; Interstate Highway System; Mellowes, Alfred W.; Petroleum; Sport Utility Vehicles; Whiting Refinery

FURTHER READING

"1st Drive-In Filling Station." 2000. Pennsylvania Historical Marker Program. Pennsylvania Historical and Museum Commission. Commonwealth of Pennsylvania. https://share.phmc.pa.gov/server/api/reports/marker/stream/?keyword=filling%20station (accessed October 2023).

Anderson, Scott. 2002. "The Gas Pump Showcase." *Petroleum Collectibles Monthly*. November. https://www.pcmpublishing.com/articles/27.html (accessed October 2023).

Cejka, Ann. 2009. "Tokheim, John J." *The Biographical Dictionary of Iowa*. The University of Iowa Libraries. The University of Iowa. http://uipress.lib.uiowa.edu/bdi/DetailsPage.aspx?id=380 (accessed October 2023).

Derdak, Thomas. 2019. "Tokheim Corporation." International Directory of Company Histories. https://www.encyclopedia.com/books/politics-and-business-magazines/tokheim-corporation (accessed October 2023).

Hagemann, Hannah. 2019. "Gas Station Converts to Electric Charging Station and Speeds Ahead of Curve." WBUR National Public Radio News. October 26. https://www.wbur.org/npr/773446805/gas-station-converts-to-electric-charging-station-and-speeds-ahead-of-curve (accessed October 2023).

Hinckley, Jim, and Jon G. Robinson. 2005. *The Big Book of Car Culture: The Armchair Guide to Automotive Americana*. Minneapolis: Motorbooks International.

Jakle, John A., and Keith A. Sculle. 1994. *The Gas Station in America*. Baltimore, MD: Johns Hopkins University Press.

"Time Machine: The Tokheim Co. Company Provided Vacuum Pumps and Air Compressors to Garages, and Equipment for Gas Stations and Dry Cleaners." 2016. *The Gazette* (Cedar Rapids, IA). March 7. https://www.thegazette.com/news/time-machine-the-tokheim-co-company-provided-vacuum-pumps-and-air-compressors-to-garages-and-equi/ (accessed October 2023).

"The Tokheim Measuring Pump." 1902. *The Iron Age*. Vol. 69. June 19. Radnor, PA: Chilton Company.

Tokheim, John J. 1900. *Measuring-Pump*. (United States Patent #640-336). United States Patent Office.

Tommyknockers

"Tommyknockers," often known simply as "knockers"—generally pronounced and sometimes spelled "knackers"—are subterranean sprites who immigrated to the United States in the imaginations of Cornish miners. Said to live in the mines that they haunt, Tommyknockers can be benign or even helpful when properly propitiated, most often with choice morsels of food. Like other Little People, however, Tommyknockers are wont to be mischievous, and when offended or ignored they have been known to be downright malicious. A fascinating aspect of traditional Cornish lore in their own right, in addition, Tommyknockers are a significant and interesting facet of US energy history because the spread of this folklore both tracks and highlights the importance of the influx of Cornish miners with whom stories of the Tommyknockers traveled.

Described in most of the traditional Cornish sources as diminutive, gray-bearded and wrinkly old men who made characteristic noises in the mines, Tommyknockers were said to be generally more playful than spiteful. Occasionally, the sprites did favors for good-hearted and respectful miners, sometimes by warning them of impending cave-ins. Tommyknockers were especially good to the generous, while they often punished the selfish or bad-natured. Both bad luck and physical maladies such as rheumatism or arthritis might be attributed to the Tommyknockers, especially if the miner who fell victim had a reputation for greed, a lack of respect for the spirits, or other bad habits. An interesting aspect of Cornish Tommyknocker lore was an old and pervasive belief that these little people were the spirits of Jewish slaves who had been forced by the Romans to mine for tin in ancient Cornwall. A number of traditional Cornish mining terms seem related to this belief, as is the notion that the Tommyknockers remained quiet on the Jewish Sabbath, amongst other holidays. Alternatively, some other sources suggest that the Tommyknockers were actually the vestigial population of pre-Celtic Britain forced underground by the invasion of the island by Celtic peoples, although this origin seems less well-attested in the modern period.

Along these lines, however, the Tommyknockers of Cornwall and Devon seem to have been first cousins of the *Coblynau* in Wales, another important early mining region of the United Kingdom. Indeed, wherever miners left the open air, light, and life of the upper world in the pre-modern and early-modern world, they seem to have developed stories about the Little People who were there when they arrived. This may have been especially common in British mining communities specifically because of how much ancient lore of the British Isles and Ireland focuses upon previous races of inhabitants forced to live underground after the ancestors of the present peoples arrived. Much of this lore seems to have merged old stories of early conflicts between those ancestors and those they absorbed or displaced with the commonplace physical presence of *tumuli,* as ancient "barrows" or burial mounds are technically known. Many of the most prominent of these barrows had entry passages and sometimes even doors, which helps to explain why the notion of other races of beings living within those mounds seems to have been quite widely accepted. It is possible that such notions were ready-made to help to explain the surreal experience of a working life underground, especially given the extremely volatile and hazardous nature of such work.

As the folklore concerning Tommyknockers as the spirits of ancient miners enslaved by the Romans make clear, from the dawn of history Cornwall was a region of great underground wealth, and Cornish miners seem to have long enjoyed a reputation as particularly skilled. In the modern age, this reputation seems to have led to the disproportionate representation of miners from Cornwall emigrating to the United States. This trend was exacerbated and accelerated by a concurrent decline in the mining industry in Cornwall itself, a decline which bottomed out with a crash in the copper market in 1866 and the rapid diminishment of the tin industry just four years later. On the other side of the Atlantic, meanwhile, the California Gold Rush of 1849 heralded numerous rapidly expanding opportunities for miners in the following decades. Meanwhile, many Cornish miners who had earlier emigrated to Latin America moved north towards these North American opportunities in English-speaking America as a number of South American mining ventures failed. These and other economic and political factors combined to make the United States an attractive destination for Cornish miners, who found their experience and expertise valued, offering wages, opportunities, and advancement impossible at home. Cornishmen were widely called "Cousin Jack" in America, purportedly because they were always quick to ask the foreman to save a job for Cousin Jack, who was an able miner. It has also been suggested that this trend was the result of the archaic practice, common amongst the Cornish of the time, to refer to one another as "cousin"; "Jack" was also one of the most popular men's names in Cornwall.

There have been reports in the twentieth century of modern American twists on the old Cornish Tommyknocker folkloric tradition, specifically in terms of stories told to children of modern miners about knocking sounds emanating up from beneath their houses. Sometimes these stories were purportedly designed to explain away noises that might otherwise lead to awkward questions about activities in the basement. Whatever the cause of such noises or the reasons for the storytelling, it is clear that by that point the original British folklore about Little People in the mine-shafts had been coopted into a bedtime story in some American mining communities.

Because of the large number of Cornish miners who immigrated to America, the Tommyknocker became a particularly widespread and well-known aspect of mining lore. That said, it is important to note that such folklore about a race of magical underground creatures who came into contact with surface-dwellers in the mines is hardly limited to Cornwall or the United States. Although the German Kobold is perhaps one of the better-known variants, these examples represent a widespread phenomenon reported throughout Europe and Asia, as well as in South America. In addition, it is interesting that Stephen King took the name of the Cornish variety of mineshaft sprite for the name of his 1987 novel, which was adapted for television in 1993. Utilizing his trademark talent at rendering everyday experiences and childhood memories into grist for the horror mill, King grounded his novel about an ancient buried spaceship unearthed in the New England woods within a passage of what he presented as a commonly known nursey rhyme. It is important to note, however, that the actual place and time of the origin of the verse he cites are not entirely clear. King is reported to have based the malevolence within the ship upon his interpretation of Cornish lore, understanding Tommyknockers to be either ravenous subterranean monsters or the forlorn spirits of buried miners, ever knocking from below in the hope of obtaining sustenance and rescue. Certainly, the mysterious forces at work in King's novel emerge from the bowels of the earth with resonating vibrations that seem to bring gifts that quickly turn into curses.

While some might well suggest that the notion of the little people of the mines is only well-remembered today because of Stephen King's appropriation of their name, students of myth, legend, and folklore might assert that it is the other way around. Stephen King is highly successful and wildly popular precisely because he taps so fully and seemingly effortlessly into the pre-existing but often slumbering angels and demons of the collective imaginations of Americans. Few would dispute that the history of energy in the United States was built in large measure on a foundation of coal, and coal miners have since the beginning of their craft plumbed the darkest corners beneath the earth and returned with folklore that reflects analogous corners of the human psyche. Tommyknockers thus represent important and abiding aspects of the history of energy in America, as well as reflecting the collective anxieties and fears of those who created that history with their perceptive hearts and minds in addition to their strong backs and hands.

Christopher R. Fee

See also: Cist, Jacob; Coal; Miner's and Laborer's Benevolent Association; Molly Maguires; Sinclair, Upton; Susquehanna Company; United Mine Workers of America

FURTHER READING

"Cornish Mining in North America." 2020. *The Spread of Cornish Mining around the Globe*. October 16. https://www.cornishmining.org.uk/about/mining-in-cornwall-and-west-devon/mining-around-the-globe (accessed February 888, 2021).

Gorner, Peter. 1987. "King Forgoes Horror for Gore in 'The Tommyknockers.'" *Chicago Tribune*. November 22. https://www.chicagotribune.com/news/ct-xpm-1987-11-22-8703280115-story.html (accessed February 12, 2021).

"Immigration and Emigration: I'm Alright Jack." n.d. *Legacies: UK History Local to You (Cornwall)* http://www.bbc.co.uk/legacies/immig_emig/england/cornwall/article_1.shtml (accessed February 8, 2021).

James, Ronald M. 1992. "Knockers, Knackers, and Ghosts: Immigrant Folklore in the Western Mines." *Western Folklore*. Vol. 51. No. 2. Pp. 153–77.

Jessen, Kenneth. 2012. "Colorado History: Cornish Miners Brought Cousin Jacks to Colorado." *Reporter Herald*. Loveland, CO. November 23.https://www.reporterherald.com/2019/11/23/colorado-history-cornish-miners-brought-cousin-jacks-to-colorado/ (accessed February 8, 2021).

Kit, Borys. 2018. "Universal Wins Stephen King's 'Tommyknockers' Bidding War." *The Hollywood Reporter*. April 20. https://www.hollywoodreporter.com/heat-vision/univeral-wins-stephen-kings-tommyknockers-bidding-war-1104737 (accessed February 12, 2021).

McNary, Dave. 2018. "Stephen King's 'The Tommyknockers' in Works as Movie from James Wan, Roy Lee." *Variety*. March 29. https://variety.com/2018/film/news/stephen-king-tommyknockers-movie-1202739627/ (accessed February 12, 2021).

Trimble, Marshall. 2016. "Cornish Miners in the West." *True West Magazine*. March 4. https://truewestmagazine.com/cornish-miners-in-the-west/ (accessed February 8, 2021).

Trans-Alaska Pipeline System

The Trans-Alaska Pipeline System (TAPS) is an 800-mile pipeline, which transports raw crude oil from the fields at Prudhoe Bay to the Alaskan port of Valdez, where it is loaded onto tankers and shipped to refineries around the world. Inspired by the discovery of oil in northern Alaska in 1968, TAPS was built between 1974 and 1977 at a cost of $8 billion by a consortium of petroleum companies. Despite the initial expense, the pipeline has yielded a significant return on investment. In total, it has brought 18 billion barrels of Alaska's otherwise inaccessible Arctic oil to market. When production at Prudhoe peaked in 1988, TAPS carried as much as 2 million barrels of oil per day. At present, the amount has decreased to just 600,000 barrels per day. Nevertheless, the pipeline remains integral to Alaska's energy infrastructure insofar as it still generates billions of dollars in revenue each year for the state and for the oil industry.

Oil exploration in Arctic Alaska began in earnest in the 1920s when President Warren G. Harding created Naval Petroleum Reserve No. 4 (later renamed the National Petroleum Reserve), a 23-million-acre expanse of tundra stretching from the Brooks Range to the Arctic Ocean. Although their initial efforts proved fruitless, oil companies remained undaunted, increasing their forays into the Arctic over time. Finally, in 1968, the Humble Oil Company and the Atlantic Richfield Company (ARCO) discovered a gigantic oil deposit on state-owned land near Prudhoe Bay, an inlet in the Beaufort Sea situated between the National Petroleum Reserve (NPR) and Arctic National Wildlife Refuge (ANWR). Geologists initially estimated the size of the field at 10 billion barrels of oil.

Though they were keen on development, Humble and ARCO recognized that Alaska lacked the infrastructure to bring Arctic oil to market safely and easily. After exploring a number of options, one of which involved navigating oil-laden tankers through the Northwest Passage, they decided to build an overland pipeline across Alaska from north to south. To alleviate construction costs, they joined forces with six other companies—British Petroleum, Union Oil, Phillips Petroleum, Amerada Hess, Mobile Oil, and Home Oil (Canada)—to form the Trans-Atlantic Pipeline System, later renamed Alyeska after an Aleut word for Alaska meaning "great land." During the initial planning stages, Alyeska considered several possible paths and terminuses. After taking into account a number of geographic and economic factors, they decided in favor of the shortest but most challenging route, beginning in Prudhoe and ending in Valdez, the northernmost, ice-free, deepwater port in the United States.

Eager to begin construction, Alyeska set their engineers to work designing a pipeline capable of transporting massive amounts of unrefined crude oil without incident across 800 miles of rugged wilderness. After receiving some of the necessary government permits, they began to amass the manpower and materials needed to build the pipeline. In 1969, they purchased 550,000 tons of 48-inch steel pipe from Japan at the relatively low cost of $100 million and shipped it to Alaska. They also positioned equipment and established camps along the proposed route for their workers.

Preparations soon ground to a halt, however, because several important social and environmental issues had yet to be resolved. One problem was that Alyeska planned to build the pipeline on land claimed by Alaska Natives as their own, land that had been "frozen" in 1966 by US Secretary of the Interior Stewart Udall to prevent any transfer of ownership until the matter was resolved. Rapidly mobilizing, Alaska Natives formed the Alaska Federation of Natives (AFN) to protect their interests and rights. Lawsuits were filed and permits were rescinded. To expedite what promised to be a protracted series of negotiations, the state created the Land Claims Task Force, which included representatives from Alaska Native communities as well as various government officials. Their efforts resulted in the Alaska Native Claims Settlement Act (ANCSA), passed by Congress and signed into law by President Richard Nixon in 1971. In accordance with this legislation, the federal government transferred $962.5 million and 44 million acres of land to Alaska's Indigenous inhabitants. Thus, one of the major obstacles to the building of TAPS was removed.

Construction on the pipeline did not begin immediately, however. In the time that it took to resolve the land claims, environmentalists mobilized. They filed numerous lawsuits and demanded the completion of an environmental impact statement (EIS), as required by the 1969 National Environmental Policy Act (NEPA). Completed in 1970, the EIS proved to be inadequate because it failed to consider alternate routes or potential spills. It also neglected to take into account the impact of the pipeline on permafrost integrity, wildlife behavior, and oceanic ecosystems. As a result, the US Department of the Interior re-reviewed the project, expanding their initial report to nine volumes, containing 3,550 pages of material. While this EIS satisfied NEPA requirements, the pipeline project remained stalled in the courts until 1973, when the US Supreme Court transferred the matter to Congress. Motivated by the Middle East oil embargo, Congress quickly passed the Trans-Alaska Pipeline Authorization Act, signed by President Nixon on November 16, 1973.

Importantly, the lengthy permitting process forced Alyeska's engineers to design a more ecologically responsible pipeline. They decided to elevate large portions of TAPS so that heat caused by the friction of the flowing oil would not thaw the permafrost. They created wildlife corridors for migrating caribou by refrigerating some sections of pipe and burying them below ground. They designed bridges, capable of withstanding variable ice conditions, to carry the line safely across large rivers, and they devised special posts, capable of significant flexion, to enable the line to absorb the force of earthquakes. They also included in the design a series of regularly spaced gate and check valves to stop the flow of oil in case of an accident.

TAPS construction officially began on March 27, 1975 and ended on May 31, 1977. In addition to the line, Alyeska built a series of pump stations and communication towers to keep oil flowing and monitor potential problems. At the terminus in Valdez, they installed infrastructure capable of storing large amounts of oil and loading it onto deepwater tanker ships. All of this activity created a boomtown atmosphere in Alaska, attracting an influx of people and money into pipeline towns, such as Fairbanks and Valdez, as well as more distant cities, such as Anchorage. The project furnished jobs for as many as 70,000 people—most of whom left the state as soon as the pipeline was finished—and increased crime in many Alaskan communities. Nevertheless, it also generated untold wealth for a fledgling state with few other significant sources of income. Although they spent much of this money on immediate needs, Alaskans sought to preserve the remainder for future generations, by creating the Alaska Permanent Fund and the Alaska Permanent Fund Corporation to oversee its management.

Between 1977 and 2019, TAPS transported 18 billion barrels of oil from the fields at Prudhoe to market. Although production has declined steadily since 1988, the pipeline still conveys enough oil—approximately 600,000 barrels per day—to remain both relevant and profitable. Importantly, the pipeline has not caused any large-scale environmental disasters along its overland route. A few incidents have occurred, however. In February 1978, Philip Martin Olson of Fairbanks detonated an explosive device underneath TAPS, causing a rupture through which flowed 14,000 barrels of oil, and in March 2006, the failure of a corroded pipe at the Prudhoe Bay field caused 6,000 barrels of oil to seep onto the tundra.

More significant environmental problems have occurred at the terminus in Valdez. On March 29, 1989, the *Exxon Valdez* ran aground on Bligh Reef, spilling 257,000 barrels of crude oil into Prince William Sound. Incredibly difficult to mitigate, the incident proved catastrophic for wildlife, killing thousands of sea otters and shore birds, as well as hundreds of harbor seals and bald eagles. It also caused the collapse of the local Pacific herring fishery. Although no disasters on that scale have occurred since the 1980s, the port has been prone to hundreds of minor incidents, including one in April 2020 in which a series of mechanical failures caused oily water to spill into the ocean for two weeks before it could be stopped.

Jennifer Schell

See also: Dakota Access Pipeline; Enbridge Pipeline System; *Exxon Valdez* Oil Spill; Federal Power Commission; Keystone Pipeline System; Prudhoe Bay Oil Field; Usibelli, Emil

FURTHER READING

Cohen, Stan. 1988. *The Great Alaska Pipeline*. Missoula, MT: Pictorial Histories Publishing.

Cole, Dermot. 1997. *Amazing Pipeline Stories: How Building the Trans-Alaska Pipeline Transformed Life in America's Last Frontier*. Fairbanks, AK: Epicenter Press.

"Facts and Figures." 2020. *Alaska Oil and Gas Association*. https://web.archive.org/web/20110313173329/http://www.aoga.org/facts-and-figures/ (accessed October 2023).

Howk, Jennifer W. 2014. "Exclusion by Assimilation: Native Social Engineering in Alaska." *Harvard International Review*. Vol. 35. No. 3. Pp. 53–7.

Yergin, Daniel. 1991. *The Prize: The Epic Quest for Oil, Money & Power*. New York: Simon & Schuster.

Willis, Roxanne. 2010. *Alaska's Place in the West: From the Last Frontier to the Last Great Wilderness*. Lawrence, KS: University of Kansas Press.

Transcontinental Railroad

The Transcontinental Railroad was a rail line connecting existing lines in the eastern United States with California. Built between 1863 and 1869 under the terms of the Pacific Railroad Act of 1862 and subsequent acts, it resulted in a network that was initially 1,776 miles long, stretching from Council Bluffs, Iowa, across the Great American Desert and the Sierra Nevada Mountains, to Sacramento, California. Also known as the Pacific Railroad and the Overland Route, the Transcontinental Railroad accelerated the settlement of the lands west of the Mississippi River, contributing to the growth of agriculture and mining and producing a significant expansion of commerce. Its completion led within two decades to what historians regard as the closing of the American frontier.

A few rudimentary railroads had been built in colonial America and in the early days of the newly independent country, but the first common carrier seems to have been the Baltimore and Ohio Railroad, which was chartered in 1827 and opened in 1830. Over the next few years, thousands more miles of rail were laid down east of the Mississippi River. In 1845, merchant Asa Whitney (1797–1872) proposed a plan to Congress for subsidizing a railroad from the Mississippi to the West Coast, and went on to publish a book, *A Project for a Railroad to the Pacific* (1849). The California Gold Rush had begun a year before, and California itself became a state in 1850. When silver was discovered in Nevada in the late 1850s, even more miners were attracted to the region.

At the time, there were three ways of reaching the West Coast. The first was by ship around South America, a long and dangerous trip that could be expected to take about six months. Another route—by ship to disease-ridden Panama, through its jungles and mountains via the Panama Railroad (opened in 1855), and by ship again to California—would take about two months. The third route, by wagon through North America's deserts and western mountains, would take four to six months. In the minds of many, the need for a fast, dependable connection had become acute. Anticipating that such a connection would be built, Theodore D. Judah (1826–63), Chief Engineer of the Sacramento Valley Railroad, began surveying possible routes through California's formidable Sierra Nevada Mountains.

Construction of a transcontinental line was delayed for a time by sectionalism between the northern and southern states, with each region arguing the desirability of building the line through its territory. However, the argument ended with the start of the US Civil War in 1861, and without having to consider the South's position, Congress passed and President Abraham Lincoln signed the Pacific Railroad Act the following year. The document chartered the Central Pacific Railroad Company, which had been incorporated in 1861, to begin building eastward from Sacramento, California, and created the Union Pacific Railroad, which it directed to start building westward from the Nebraska Territory. The two lines were to coordinate their plans in order to meet at some unspecified location.

The Pacific Railroad Act gave the companies ample compensation for their costs while stimulating competition between the two. It provided for issuing federal bonds to a company for each mile of rail it laid, with their denomination determined by the difficulty of the terrain being crossed. Each company would also receive 200 feet of right-of-way on each side of its tracks, along with alternate sections (square miles) of adjoining land totaling 6,400 acres for each mile of rail laid. After a campaign by railroad managers that involved bribes of cash and bonds, the grant of land was doubled in 1864 and the companies were given control of all the natural resources lying along their lines.

Central Pacific's workers began construction in late October 1863, but progress slowed as the line passed through the Sierra Nevada Mountains, and by early December 1866, they had managed to lay less than 100 miles of track. Their path forward would take them through Donner Pass, which Judah had determined to be the most practical route eleven years before. They completed 1,659-foot Tunnel No. 6, the so-called Summit Tunnel, in late August 1867, and eventually dug a total of fifteen tunnels through the range. In addition, the Central Pacific built about 40 miles of snow sheds in order to keep its line open during blizzards.

Meanwhile, officials of the Union Pacific had studied the possible routes that their section of the Transcontinental Railroad would follow. With the assistance of Peter A. Dey, Chief Engineer Grenville Dodge (1831–1916) eventually chose a course along the Platte River in the Nebraska Territory, across the Continental Divide at South Pass and on to Green River, both of which were in the Wyoming Territory. President Lincoln had fixed the beginning of the line at Council Bluffs, Iowa, on the eastern bank of the Missouri River, but Union Pacific actually started laying rails from Omaha, Nebraska, on the western bank.

AN IMPERFECT CEREMONY

Unused to handling heavy hammers, both Stanford and Durant actually missed their ceremonial spikes and instead struck the rails, leaving it to more practiced hands to tap the precious spikes gently into place. The Union Pacific's official photographer, Colonel Charles R. Savage, was on hand to record the ceremony, but he dropped the glass plate showing Stanford's clumsy swing and it shattered on the ground.

Grove Koger

The Central Pacific had hired some fifty Chinese emigrants on a trial basis in early 1865 but recognizing their willingness to work long and grueling hours, the company proceeded to add more. Eventually about 80 percent of the company's workers were Chinese. Thanks to their dedication and perseverance, the Central Pacific's line reached the border of the Utah Territory in 1868. Most of Union Pacific's workers were Irish, German, and Italian immigrants, many of whom had learned to lay track during the US Civil War. While their route passed over relatively easy terrain, they were forced to deal routinely with raids by the Native Americans whose land they were crossing. Eventually, as the two lines entered the Utah Territory, both companies hired members of the Church of Jesus Christ of Latter-day Saints, or Mormons, as well.

FIGURE 10: Completed in 1869, the Transcontinental Railroad enabled passengers and cargo to traverse the continent during the era of steam-powered locomotives.

On May 10, 1869, workers for the Union Pacific and the Central Pacific finally approached each other at Promontory Summit, Utah, 53 miles west of Ogden. With two locomotives—coal-burning Union Pacific No. 119 and Central Pacific's wood-burning *Jupiter*—facing each other, Central Pacific President Leland Stanford and Union Pacific Vice President Thomas C. Durant prepared to drive spikes of precious metal into place before an audience of some 1,500 spectators. The first trains to complete the run over the connected tracks reached Sacramento five days later.

In the final analysis, workers for the Union Pacific had laid 1,086 miles of track, while those for the Central Pacific, having faced more formidable working conditions, managed only 690 miles. In what was to be the Transcontinental Railroad's final link to the Pacific Ocean, a line connecting Sacramento and the shore of San Francisco Bay was completed in November 1869. Yet another link was added in 1872, when, at the railroad's eastern terminus, Union Pacific completed the Missouri River Bridge connecting Omaha with Council Bluffs. Until that time, passengers and cargo had to be ferried across the river.

The completion of the Transcontinental Railroad marked a revolutionary transition in the nation's commercial growth from a reliance on ferry, stagecoach, and wagon train. What once would have taken months could now be accomplished in a week, and at much lower cost. The railroad created a series of new settlements along its course, encouraging the already burgeoning westward movement and bringing jobs and commerce in its wake. It is regarded as one of the greatest engineering achievements in the history of the nation.

Today, the point at Promontory Summit where the Central Pacific and the Union Pacific met is maintained by the National Park Service as the Golden Spike Historical Park. In the years since the Transcontinental Railroad's completion, numerous sections have been rerouted, although Amtrak's *California Zephyr* still runs over part of the original route. The famous Summit Tunnel was replaced in 1997 by a 10,322-foot tunnel, "The Big Hole," about a mile south of Donner Pass.

Grove Koger

See also: Baltimore & Ohio Railroad; Coal; Cooper, Peter; Halladay Windmill; Krebs Mine Disaster; Richmond Union Passenger Railway; Steam Power

FURTHER READING

Ambrose, Stephen E. 2000. *Nothing like It in the World: The Men Who Built the Transcontinental Railroad, 1863–1869*. New York: Simon & Schuster

Bain, David Haward. 1999. *Empire Express: Building the First Transcontinental Railroad*. New York: Viking.

Borneman, Walter R. 2010. *Rival Rails: The Race to Build American's Greatest Transcontinental Railroad*. New York: Random House.

Chang, Gordon H. 2019. *Ghosts of Gold Mountain: The Epic Story of the Chinese Who Built the Transcontinental Railroad*. Boston: Houghton Mifflin Harcourt.

White, Richard. 2011. *Railroaded: The Transcontinentals and the Making of Modern America*. New York: Norton.

Williams, John Hoyt. 1988. *A Great and Shining Road: The Epic Story of the Transcontinental Railroad*. New York: Times Books.

Truck Transportation Technology

For as long as people have inhabited North America, they have shipped cargo over land, using a wide variety of conveyances. Native Americans pulled their travois by human power and later, horses; European colonists built carts and wagons to haul freight. In the nineteenth century, railroads offered much greater capacity and speed, and became the preferred technology for shipping goods throughout the American interior. At the turn of the twentieth century, "motor trucks" began rolling off assembly lines and introduced cargo transport by means of gasoline-powered, and later diesel-powered, internal combustion engines. It wasn't long until the Interstate Highway System appeared and made semitrailer truck a fixture on American bypasses and toll roads. In the twenty-first century, the explosion of e-commerce through online retailers like Amazon and Walmart increased consumer demand for over-the-road trucking. While energy-saving technology had been integrated into the nation's fleet of trucks, the increase in shipping resulted in greater consumption of fossil fuels and increased emissions of greenhouse gases that contribute to climate change. In turn, this has stimulated further research in next-generation technologies to reach emissions reduction goals.

Several figures are credited with conceiving the semitrailer, referring to a trailer that doesn't have a front axle. Alexander Winton was an automobile manufacturer in Cleveland, Ohio. He built a single-axle flatbed trailer in 1898 and hitched it to a motor car so he could deliver another of his newly built cars to a customer. The trailer was large and strong enough to haul a car, but only one at a time. The combination of semitrailer and car had the appearance of a two-wheeled cart drawn by a horse. The other figure, August Charles Fruehauf, was a blacksmith and carriage-maker in Detroit, Michigan. In 1914, he built a trailer upon request that could be attached to a Ford Model T in order to haul a boat to upper Michigan. Fruehauf's work pleased the boat's owner, who ordered another to haul lumber. This success encouraged him to start the Fruehauf Trailer Company in 1918 and begin manufacturing them for a growing market. Even as early as 1918 the market was large enough for trailer companies to organize an industrial association known as the Trailer Manufacturer's Association of America, based in New York ("Trailer" 1918).

For the time being, railroads carried freight over long distances, and heavy trucks served the need for haulage around worksites in industries like construction, mining, oil and gas drilling, logging, and quarrying. Commercial-grade trucks were built in Europe by Benz & Cie. and Adolph Saurer AG, and in New York City, the Mack Brothers Motor Car Company entered the truck manufacturing business. Having built city buses beginning in 1900, Mack moved to Allentown, Pennsylvania in 1905 and in 1911, became part of International Motor Truck Company along with Saurer's US division. The Mack brand came of age in the First World War when Allied forces used the Mack AC model extensively and gave the truck its

"Bulldog" motif. The Four Wheel Drive Corporation's Model B went into widespread use in Allied operations as well. These heavy trucks stirred interest in their cargo-hauling and towing capabilities and increased demand for models in this class in the following decades.

The war turned out to be a catalyst for the cargo truck manufacturing, transportation, and road construction industries. Historian Richard F. Weingroff noted that since "the railroads were unable to keep up with military shipping, the fledgling trucking industry seized its opportunity to secure interstate shipping." Most of the interior roads in the United States were still composed of dirt and gravel. Weingroff continued: "As a result, the roads that the states did not have the resources to improve were deteriorating under the unexpected weight of the loaded trucks" (Weingroff 1996). The Federal-Aid Road Act of 1916 provided a very modest $5 million for road improvement, but then in 1919 Thomas H. MacDonald, who had worked extensively in state highway planning and construction, became head of the US Bureau of Public Roads. MacDonald and other state officials developed the bill that became the Federal Highway Act of 1921, which created a system of "federal-aid highways" meant to be "interstate in character" (Weingroff 1996). Again, the funding was modest, but the principle of federal highway planning and construction had been established. Weingroff concluded: "The 1920s were a 'golden age' for road building," and "federal-aid projects totaling 16,500 km were completed at a cost of $189 million" in 1922 alone. This constituted a threefold increase in roadbuilding over all the construction done since the 1916 federal-aid program began (Weingroff 1996).

This infrastructure was crucial to the emergence of a transportation industry that included semitrailer trucks hauling cargoes on US highways. However, this industry also required some technological innovation, since heavy trucks had developed mainly to perform short-haul tasks around worksites where they used solid rubber tires. One of the innovators in this period was Roy Chapin, president of the Hudson Motor Car Company. He helped organize the Lincoln Highway Association, founded in 1913 "to procure the establishment of a continuous improved highway from the Atlantic to the Pacific, open to lawful traffic of all description without toll charges" (Weingroff 2017). In addition to promoting highway construction, Chapin worked with the US government during the First World War to develop pneumatic tires for trucks to enable them to travel longer distances. As roads improved, semitrailer trucks would have to abandon solid rubber tires in order to make longer journeys tolerable. Another innovator, Francis W. Davis, engineered a power steering system in 1926 for heavy vehicles at the Pierce-Arrow Motor Car Company. In the same period, the company also adopted a system similar to today's power brakes by adding a vacuum assist to their hydraulic brakes.

The numbers bear out this expansion. In 1925, 2.4 million motor trucks were registered across the country, and five years of increases pushed the registration number in 1930 to 3.4 million (George 1936, 250). Responding to the "magnitude of interstate motor transportation" and the "increasing urgency of problems of public safety on the highways," Congress enacted a law amending the Interstate Commerce Act known as the Motor Carrier Act of 1935 (George 1936, 251). This law defined a motor vehicle as "any vehicle, machine, tractor, trailer, or semitrailer propelled or drawn by mechanical power and used upon the highways in the transportation of passengers or property." It also defined a "common carrier" by motor vehicle as a "person who or which undertakes, whether directly or by a lease or any other arrangement, to transport passengers or property, or any class or classes of property, for the general public in interstate or foreign commerce by motor vehicle for compensation, whether over regular or irregular routes." The intent of the law was to bring companies and proprietors operating semitrailer trucks under federal regulation, and thereby protect railroad companies who were undermined by the expansion of truck transportation.

The use of semitrailer trucks for interstate shipping expanded greatly after the Second World War due to increased consumer demand, which was unleashed after years of privation during the Great Depression and the conversion of industry to wartime production. President Dwight Eisenhower signed the Federal-Aid Highway Act of 1956, which created the Interstate Highway System and gave further impetus to long-distance shipping by truck. The act transformed the landscape and intensified patterns of American mobility. Another important development in the 1950s was the "containerization" of cargo transport by Malcolm P. McLean, owner of a trucking company in North Carolina. He started out as a driver and endured long hours of waiting at port while shipping crates were unloaded from other trucks and hoisted into ships' cargo holds. He thought it would be more efficient to mount standard-sized containers on semitrailers that could be hoisted in their entirety onto ships and stacked in a way as to remain secure and stable. He bought the Pan-Atlantic Steamship Company and renamed it SeaLand Industries, refitted the ships to carry standardized containers (8' × 8' × 35'), then had his semitrailers converted as well. The idea of containerization was to use seaports as hubs, with semitrailer trucks serving these hubs within localized ambits. The maiden voyage of the containerized oil tanker *Ideal X* in 1956 carried fifty-six of McLean's boxes from Port Newark, New Jersey to Houston (Mayo 2005).

McLean had invented containerization and advanced the field of logistics. A few of the new technologies that made semitrailer trucks more efficient and more versatile appeared in the interwar and post-war eras. On the trailer side, mechanical refrigeration arrived in the late 1930s and enabled carriers to transport a wider variety of cargoes. In terms of the cab, the Kenworth Motor Truck Company utilized a diesel engine manufactured by the Cummins Engine Company in its 1933 production model, which created greater fuel efficiency with a fuel that was cheaper to refine. Diesel engines offered more torque, superior reliability, and a longer lifespan. Other companies like Peterbilt, White, and Mack followed suit and made the diesel engine the standard power plant for semitrailer trucks. However, diesel engines of the era produced higher levels of particulate matter, sulfur, oxides of nitrogen, hydrocarbons, carbon monoxide, and carbon dioxide. By the 1960s, air pollution had become an important matter of public concern and led to a series of laws beginning in the 1950s and culminating in the Clean Air Act of 1970.

Congress included in the 1970 law a justification for its provisions: "the growth in the amount and complexity of air pollution brought about by urbanization, industrial development, and the increasing use of motor vehicles, has resulted in mounting dangers to the public health and welfare, including injury to agricultural crops and livestock, damage to and the deterioration of property, and hazards to air and ground transportation." The Clean Air Act of 1970 created a regulatory system for establishing and enforcing emissions standards for motor vehicles, including heavy trucks beginning in 1974. These standards were raised in subsequent additions to the Clean Air Acts of 1990 and 1997, and the US Environmental Protection Agency (EPA) and the National Highway Traffic Safety Administration (NHTSA) worked to establish and increase greenhouse gas and fuel economy standards for heavy-duty trucks through the 2000–20 period. The industry responded to these requirements with lower-sulfur diesel fuel and the use of catalytic converters, which were required after the 2007 model year.

Ironically, new technology put diesel engine manufacturers in legal jeopardy with the US Department of Justice (DOJ) in the mid-1990s over EPA emissions standards. They created "defeat devices" for their engines, which were essentially computerized controls, to "allow engines to meet EPA emission standards during testing but disable the emission control system during normal highway driving" (DOJ 1998). A DOJ investigation found that seven manufacturers—Caterpillar, Cummins, Detroit Diesel, Mack, Navistar International, Renault, and Volvo—engaged in a pattern of fraud and deception. The companies signed consent decrees that required them to pay fines that officials called the "largest in environmental enforcement history" (DOJ 1998). Nevertheless, new technologies have revolutionized the fleet, both in terms of lowering emissions and increasing fuel efficiency, but also in systems management with satellite technology and computer tracking. Advanced sensors provide information about the vehicles' performance and operating conditions, and developments in aerodynamics and composite materials like carbon fiber contribute to decreased drag and lighter weight.

The explosion in e-commerce in the early twenty-first century increased the volume of freight trips. The founding of Amazon in 1994 offers a point of reference. One report noted that "when the company was founded, an average of about one freight trip per day was taken on U.S. roads for every 10 Americans; by 2017, it had more than doubled to 2.5 trips per day." The report went on to say that this was "a phenomenon that experts directly attribute to the rise of online retail" (Wilson 2021). The concern is increased carbon emissions that result in climate change, since the combustion of 1 liter of diesel fuel commonly used by semitrailer trucks releases about 13 percent more carbon dioxide than the same amount of gasoline (ICCT 2019). To bring carbon emissions from truck transportation to an end, some manufacturers experimented with battery-electric technology. In 2022, Tesla delivered Semi, its all-electric semitrailer truck, to PepsiCo, and in 2023, Freightliner handed over the eCascadia, to United Parcel Service. These zero-emissions vehicles signaled the advent of a new era of technological development in a key, energy-consuming industry.

Jeffrey B. Webb

See also: CAFE Standards; Clean Air Act of 1970; Energy Crisis of the 1970s; Energy Policy and Conservation Act of 1975; Interstate Highway System; US Environmental Protection Agency

FURTHER READING

Clean Air Amendments of 1970. 91–604, §1, Dec. 31, 1970, 84 Stat. 1676.

George, John J. 1936. "Federal Motor Carrier Act of 1935." *Cornell Law Review*. Vol. 21. No. 2. Pp. 249–75.

International Council on Clean Transportation (ICCT). 2019. "Gasoline v. Diesel: Comparing CO2 Emission Levels of a Modern Medium Size Car Model under Laboratory and On-road Testing Conditions. May. https://theicct.org/wp-content/uploads/2022/01/Gas-_v-_Diesel_-CO2_emissions_-EN_-Fact-_Sheet-2019_05_07_0.pdf (accessed October 2023).

Mayo, Anthony J. Nitin Nohria. 2005. "The Truck Driver Who Reinvented Shipping." Working Knowledge. Harvard Business School. October 3. https://hbswk.hbs.edu/item/the-truck-driver-who-reinvented-shipping (accessed October 2023).

Motor Carrier Act. 1935. Public Law no. 255 (74th Congress) (Senate 1629) approved August 9, 1935.

"Trailer Manufacturers Organize." 1918. *The American Exporter*. Vol. 84. P. 158.

US Department of Justice (DOJ). 1998. "DOJ, EPA Announce One Billion Dollar Settlement with Diesel Engine Industry for Clean Air Violations." Press Release. October 22. https://www.justice.gov/archive/opa/pr/1998/October/499_enr.htm (accessed October 2023).

Weingroff, Richard F. 1996. "From 1916 to 1939: The Federal-State Partnership at Work." *Public Roads*. Vol. 60. No. 1. Summer. https://highways.dot.gov/public-roads/summer-1996/1916-1939-federal-state-partnership-work (accessed October 2023).

Weingroff, Richard F. 2017. "The Lincoln Highway." Highway History. Federal Highway Administration. US Department of Transportation. https://www.fhwa.dot.gov/infrastructure/lincoln.cfm (accessed October 2023).

Wilson, Kea. 2021. "A Look Back at Bezos's Dirty Legacy on U.S. Roadways." Streetsblog USA. February 5. https://usa.streetsblog.org/2021/02/05/a-look-back-at-bezos-bloody-polluting-legacy-on-u-s-roadways/ (accessed October 2023).

Underwriters Laboratories

The rapid development of new technologies in the nineteenth century outpaced the ability of industry and government to ensure their safety. In particular, new electrical systems appeared and, in some instances, triggered fires due to poorly insulated wires and other issues. In response, the Underwriter's Electrical Bureau was established in 1894 to test electrical components to ensure their resistance to spark and fire. Eventually, the mission of the bureau expanded, and in 1901 it became Underwriters Laboratories (UL). The UL's tests and reports on a bewildering number of items, ranging from building materials to industrial equipment to consumer goods, gradually increased confidence in these new technologies and paved the way for the nation's modernization. This change in Americans' attitudes toward technology is an important facet of the history of energy in the United States.

The Underwriter's Electrical Bureau, predecessor to UL, was founded by MIT electrical engineering student William Henry Merrill (1868–1923). After graduation in 1889, Merrill became an inspector of electrical installations for the Boston Board of Fire Underwriters. The board inspected wiring out of concern for fires, having experienced one on Thanksgiving Day in 1889 alleged to have been caused by electrical telegraph circuits. The fire destroyed a six-floor building and killed five firefighters (Fratus 2021). Electricity had been proven safe, but enough fires occurred with new electrical installations to induce caution in the public mind. An observer in London believed this concern was unwarranted but noted that the number of fatalities in the United States was "deplorable and sufficient to excite alarm" (Page 1890, 158). He went on to say that the electrical accidents had been exaggerated, that "some of those narratives are most sensational, not to say ridiculous." He took the opportunity to blame lax regulation in the United States, that "there is little public control in such matters in New York city" in contrast to England (Page 1890, 158). Indeed, most Americans didn't understand how electricity worked and unwarranted fears were pervasive. An example of this lack of understanding, coupled with overhyped supposed perils, is the publication of Alexander Watt's *The Earth in Danger!* (1875). He expressed alarm that railroads were channeling "electric fluid" through their rails and into the ground, and posed the question, "is it not reasonable to infer that where the earth's surface becomes surcharged, it must, in time, give way, and an eruption take place in the form of an electrical earthquake?" (Watt 1875, 8).

Against this backdrop of ignorance and wariness, Merrill became involved in one of the serious, if now lost, debates in the nation: was the new technology of electricity safe? Merrill was summoned to Chicago in 1893 to inspect electrical wiring and circuitry at the World's Columbian Exposition, particularly the Electrical Building. Keep in mind that Chicago had its own devastating fire in 1871, and many smaller fires since that time. The event featured a large-scale demonstration of the alternating current system of Nikola Tesla and Westinghouse Electric Company, with twelve 1,000-horsepower AC generators operating 100,000 lights arranged around the so-called White City. Merrill set up an operation at the fair and ran through inspections of the fire alarm system, fire extinguishers, and all the electrical components that powered lights and machinery. Two fires raged at the fair, one in the Cold-Storage Building on July 10, 1893, and the other on January 8, 1894 that began in the Casino and spread to a number of other buildings. Sixteen lives were lost in the first, including fifteen Chicago firefighters, and one in the second, also a firefighter. News reports claimed that the fire alarms in the Casino Building failed, and both fires were attributed to arsonists.

Merrill had found his life's work. With financial support from the Chicago Board of Fire Underwriters and the Western Insurance Association Electrical Bureau, Merrill managed the Underwriter's Electrical Bureau in Chicago. Historian Ross Cheit's book, *Setting Safety Standards: Regulation in the Public and Private Sectors* (1990) noted that "the original idea was to provide information to insurance companies on the fire risks attendant to various electrical equipment" (Cheit 1990, 94). The outfit was renamed Underwriters Laboratories in 1898; when the UL was incorporated in 1901, Henry Clay Eddy became president with Merrill as manager. In 1896–7, Merrill was an important member of the committee that created the first National Electrical Code (1897). He also served as secretary-treasurer of the National Fire Protection Association (1903–9) and then became its president (1910–12). During the First World War, Merrill chaired the Fire Prevention Section of the War Industries Board.

This distinguished career had its beginnings in the Chicago offices of the UL where Merrill and his staff painstakingly tested wires, switches, and sockets, as well as the fireproof qualities of the insulation for these components. In 1898, UL published its first list of tested and certified electrical parts and devices and after incorporation, offered its services to manufacturers. Cheit described the early UL process as follows: "A manufacturer would submit its product to UL for testing, pay a testing fee, and receive permission to display the UL label (also for a fee) if the product was approved" (Cheit 1990, 94). The UL label service was respected because it wasn't tied to industry and maintained a separate identity as an objective, scientific organization committed to public health and safety.

The UL label service, which first appeared in 1905, was important. Merrill's career overlapped with a national reckoning over the old doctrine of "caveat emptor," meaning "let the buyer beware." The nineteenth century was a period of laissez-faire economic policy as customers took their chances with a variety of products including items like pharmaceuticals, building materials, steam boilers, gas lamps, and electric lights. A variety of voices ranging from muckraking journalists to settlement house workers to new professional societies like the American Medical Association began to demand state and federal legislation guaranteeing the safety of consumer products, which resulted in the Pure Food and Drug Act (1906) and the Meat Inspection Act (1906). UL joined these efforts to ensure product safety and increase consumer confidence. In 1906, buildings that had been inspected and consumer products that had been tested were given the UL Mark, a small, visible symbol to show the building owner or manufacturer had gone through the trouble of having a third party with training and expertise provide a rigorous review and give its stamp of approval.

After the terrible Iroquois Theatre fire in New York in late 1903, UL produced its first set of product standards, in this instance the standard for "Tin Clad Fire Doors." The fire killed 600 people, among them many women and children, and set UL on to testing and labeling fire extinguishers and developing standards for a wide variety of equipment used in fire protection. Over the next century, UL developed standards for over 1,500 classes of products. They grew with the evolution of technology in the twentieth century, moving from electric refrigerators to home air-conditioning units and then on to television sets, Xerox copiers, and personal computers. Some examples of currently available standards are "Manual Signaling Boxes for Fire Alarm Systems," "Industrial Control Panels," "Energy Storage Systems and Equipment," "Steel Aboveground Tanks for Flammable and Combustible Liquids," and "Lithium Batteries." Recently, UL advertised testing services for unmanned aerial vehicles, Bluetooth devices, photovoltaic cells, and battery enclosures for battery-electric vehicles. Eventually those types of products will have UL-developed standards that manufacturers can use to meet widely accepted criteria for product safety.

UL underwent a few changes that reflected its expanded suite of services and increasingly larger, international reach. In 1916, UL finally became an independent entity and Merrill became president. In the same year, UL opened an inspection office in London to test British products exported to the United States, which began a long process of internationalization of UL operations. One historian summed up its growth this way: "By the 1920s, UL had established a nationwide network of clients, with regional labs to serve them. The lab had around 200 engineers and 'inside' employees, 250 outside inspectors, 55,000 square feet in Chicago, labs on both coasts, a Canadian organization, offices in 141 cities, and a 'connection in London'" (Knowles 2011). In 1936, UL incorporated as a nonprofit organization in Delaware, clarifying its status as an independent, third-party testing service working in the public interest. The organization's last link to the insurance industry had been severed. Then, in 1952, UL bought 153 acres of land in Northbrook, Illinois with the intent to build a larger facility. Another company milestone occurred in 1979 when UL moved to Northbrook, where its current headquarters and main center of operations are located.

In 2022, UL reorganized into three divisions. Two of the three—UL Research Institutes and UL Standards and Engagement—remained non-for-profit entities, and the other—UL Solutions—became a for-profit corporation. The traditional UL testing, inspecting, and certification services moved to the for-profit entity. This was partly due to competition from other testing and licensing organizations like CSA Group, Intertek Testing Services, Nemko, SolarPTL, and SGS. The US Department of Labor's Occupational Safety and Health Administration lists twenty other organizations in its "Nationally Recognized Testing Laboratory Program" besides UL Solutions. Ross Cheit's assessment of UL still stands: "UL continues to be viewed as the most independent of the private standards-setters. UL's reputation is excellent" (Cheit 1990, 95). Over its history, UL did much to encourage public acceptance of electrical appliances like toasters and microwave ovens as safe from fire and shock hazards. In doing so, the public embraced electricity itself as a tremendous benefit to humanity.

Jeffrey B. Webb

See also: Chicago World's Columbian Exposition; Electricity; Tesla, Nikola; War of the Currents; Westinghouse, George

FURTHER READING

Bezane, Norm. 1994. *This Inventive Century, 1894–1994: The Incredible Journey of Underwriters Laboratories*. Northbrook, IL: Underwriters Laboratories.

Cheit, Ross E. 1990. *Setting Safety Standards: Regulation in the Public and Private Sectors*. Berkeley, CA: University of California Press.

"Electrical Men of the Times: William H. Merrill." 1911. *Popular Electricity*. Vol. 4. No. 7. Pp. 636–7.

Fratus, Matt. 2021. "The Massive Thanksgiving Day Fire of 1889 that Killed 5 Boston Firefighters." *Coffee or Die Magazine*. November 24. https://coffeeordie.com/thanksgiving-day-fire-boston/ (accessed October 2023).

Knowles, Scott Gabriel. 2011. *The Disaster Experts: Mastering Risk in Modern America*. Philadelphia: University of Pennsylvania Press.

Page, S. Flood. 1890. "Fire Dangers." *The Electrical Engineer*. Vol. 5. February 21.

Watt, Alexander. 1875. *The Earth in Danger*. London: E.W. Allen and C.H. Clarke.

Union of Concerned Scientists

The Union of Concerned Scientists (UCS) is a nonprofit organization that has helped shape US policy on energy, climate change, nuclear weapons, and many other issues for roughly five decades. Founded in 1969 at the height of the Vietnam War, the organization began after students and faculty at the Massachusetts Institute of Technology (MIT) organized walkouts to protest the heavy investment of civilian scientific knowledge toward developing military technology. Their statement, drafted by UCS founders Kurt Gottfried and Henry Kendall, launched the organization by calling for scientific research to be directed toward solving pressing environmental and social problems (UCS 1968).

UCS first gained widespread attention on energy issues in 1971 when congressional testimony by the organization's independent technical experts raised concerns over nuclear power safety. In 1977, a UCS analysis showed that the Nuclear Regulatory Commission had dramatically understated the probability of an accident at some sixteen nuclear facilities of similar design (UCS 1977). UCS called for the government to shut down the facilities, including the Three Mile Island nuclear power plant in Harrisburg, Pennsylvania. No immediate action was taken, but not long after the report was released, the Three Mile Island plant experienced a partial meltdown in 1979. This event is considered the most serious nuclear accident in the United States to date.

UCS's prescient warning helped build the group's reputation and the organization soon expanded to offer independent technical expertise on a wider array of issues, including the prospects for renewable energy sources such as wind and solar power. In 1979, the organization published *Energy Strategies: Toward a Solar Future*, a book that assessed world energy needs, surveyed renewable and nonrenewable resources, and discussed future energy policy (UCS 1979). UCS continued to bring public attention to the prospects for renewable energy and clean vehicle technology with several key analyses. In 1991, UCS produced a report, *America's Energy Choices*, that debunked prevailing assumptions by showing that renewables could contribute significantly to the nation's energy mix (UCS 1991a). The organization also issued a report that year entitled *Steering a New Course* demonstrating how renewable sources of energy could alleviate pollution resulting from the nation's heavy reliance on fossil fuels (UCS 1991b).

The UCS report *Powering the Midwest* was published in 1993; at the time, 74 percent of the electricity produced in that region came from burning coal (UCS 1993). The report laid the foundation for the organization's future work on clean energy at both the federal and local level by outlining how states could take advantage of energy deregulation to insist that their power be sourced from renewables. It used a geographic modeling system to identify wind power opportunities in twelve states and estimated the costs of connecting wind farms to the transmission grid. UCS field organizers met with state legislators, environmental activists, and farmers to build support for renewable energy and showed how siting wind turbines on farms could create jobs and boost local economies.

These efforts, soon followed by a book co-authored by UCS staff member Nancy Cole, *Renewables are Ready* (1995), helped establish the viability of renewable energy sources in the United States. At this time, UCS began to focus on the absence of a policy mechanism to help accelerate the transition to clean energy. Shortly after the release of the organization's Midwest report, Nancy Rader, an energy consultant who headed the California Wind Energy Association, came up with a strategy she called the Renewable Portfolio Standard (RPS). The idea was that states could require utilities to supply a certain percentage of their electricity from renewable sources by a specific date. States could set their own levels of ambition by determining their own deadlines and targets and utilities could meet the requirements however they chose. The strategy offered a powerful policy tool through which states could help transition to renewable sources of energy. UCS soon began to promote the idea of using these state standards across the nation, referring to them as RPS or Renewable Electricity Standards (RES), and the organization began a number of specific efforts to persuade individual states to adopt them.

By many measures, the standards had a major impact. As of 2020, a total of thirty states, Puerto Rico and Washington, DC had adopted RES policies and the approach is widely credited as effective in building renewable energy capacity, boosting the emerging clean energy sector, and reducing global warming emissions (NCSL 2021). According to one 2018 study, roughly half of all growth in US renewable electricity generation and capacity since 2000 is associated with state RES policies (LBNL 2018). Similarly, the standards have helped drive down the cost of wind and solar by at least 70 percent over the last decade, as US wind capacity more than tripled and solar power boasted an average annual growth rate of 50 percent (Lazard 2020; LBNL 2020).

Over the years, UCS's combination of research and outreach have proven pivotal in accelerating the shift to renewable energy sources and building momentum. In 2020, 80 percent of the nation's new electrical generating capacity came from renewable sources, inspiring further confidence that a rapid transition to renewable energy is possible (WM 2021). New wind and solar facilities are now cheaper to build than new fossil fuel plants in many regions of the country, even without subsidies (Lazard 2020).

Over the past decade, UCS continued to lead the way on clean energy, demonstrating how the electric grid can accommodate even higher levels of renewables, and emphasizing the importance of energy storage and updating the power grid. UCS began to tackle this issue directly in its 2013 report, *Ramping up Renewables: Energy You Can Count On*, showing how tools such as better forecasting of renewable energy generation, stronger transmission connections between states and regions, and a mix of renewable energy technologies could help address these issues to achieve reliability even with a higher percentage of renewable energy (UCS 2013).

Today, UCS continues to press the case for clean energy and a modern electricity grid. The organization is also working to address systemic injustices in the US electricity system to ensure that all communities, and especially low-income communities and communities of color that have been historically disproportionately burdened by the impacts of fossil fuels, directly benefit from and participate in the clean energy transition. At the federal level, UCS promotes national energy standards, energy storage, and tax credits and investments that stimulate innovation and accelerate the equitable deployment of renewable energy. With commitments from eight states, more than a hundred cities, and many companies and institutions to make the swift transition to generating 100 percent of their electricity from clean or renewable sources, momentum is building toward a sustainable energy economy

(SC 2021). Forthcoming UCS analysis aims to tackle some of the remaining technical hurdles and systemic equity issues involved in making this transition possible, as well as showcasing the feasibility and necessity of moving to 100 percent clean energy and quantifying the many benefits of doing so for policy makers and the public alike.

Jiayu Liang and Seth Shulman

See also: Earth Day; Energy Security Act of 1980; Natural Resources Defense Council; Nuclear Power; Nuclear Regulatory Commission; Renewable Energy; Sierra Club; Smart Grid; Solar Power; Three Mile Island Accident; Wind Power

FURTHER READING

Cole, Nancy, and P.J. Skerrett. 1995. *Renewables are Ready: People Creating Renewable Energy Solutions*. White River Junction, VT: Chelsea Green Pub. Co.

Lawrence Berkeley National Laboratory (LBNL). 2018. *U.S. Renewable Portfolio Standards 2018 Annual Status Report*. Berkeley, CA: Lawrence Berkeley National Laboratory. https://emp.lbl.gov/publications/us-renewables-portfolio-standards-1 (accessed June 30, 2020).

Lawrence Berkeley National Laboratory (LBNL). 2020. *Utility-Scale Solar Data Update: 2020 Edition*. Berkeley, CA: Lawrence Berkeley National Laboratory. https://emp.lbl.gov/utility-scale-solar (accessed April 10, 2021).

Lazard. 2020. *Levelized Cost of Energy*. Analysis-Version 14.0. October 2020. https://www.lazard.com/research-insights/levelized-cost-of-energy-levelized-cost-of-storage-and-levelized-cost-of-hydrogen-2020/#:~:text=Lazard's%20latest%20annual%20Levelized%20Cost,build%20basis%2C%20continue%20to%20maintain (accessed October 2023).

National Conference of State Legislatures (NCSL). 2021. *State Renewable Portfolio Standards and Goals*. Denver, CO: National Conference of State Legislatures. https://www.ncsl.org/aboutus/ncslservice/ncsl-contact.aspx (accessed April 13, 2021).

Sierra Club (SC). 2021. "Ready for 100." https://www.sierraclub.org/climate-and-energy/map#:~:text=The%20Sierra%20Club's%20Ready%20For,energy%20by%20the%20year%202050 (accessed October 2023).

Union of Concerned Scientists (UCS). 1968. "MIT Faculty Statement." https://ucsusa.org/about/history/founding-document-1968-mit-faculty-statement (accessed June 30, 2020).

Union of Concerned Scientists (UCS). 1977. *The Risks of Nuclear Power Reactors: A Review of the NRC Reactor Safety Study WASH-1400*. Cambridge, MA: Union of Concerned Scientists.

Union of Concerned Scientists (UCS). 1979. *U.S. Energy Strategies: Toward a Solar Future: Report of the Union of Concerned Scientists' Energy Study*. With Daniel F. Ford. Cambridge, MA: Ballinger Pub. Co.

Union of Concerned Scientists (UCS). 1991a. *America's Energy Choices: Investing in a Strong Economy and a Clean Environment*: Cambridge, MA: Union of Concerned Scientists.

Union of Concerned Scientists (UCS). 1991b. *Steering a New Course: Transportation, Energy, and the Environment*. With Deborah Gordon. Washington, DC: Island Press.

Union of Concerned Scientists (UCS). 1993. *Powering the Midwest: Renewable Electricity for the Economy and the Environment*. With Michael Brower. Cambridge, MA: Union of Concerned Scientists.

Union of Concerned Scientists (UCS). 2013. *Ramping Up Renewables: Energy You Can Count On*. https://www.ucsusa.org/resources/ramping-renewables-0 (accessed June 22, 2020).

Wood Mackenzie (WM). 2021. *US Solar Market Insight 2020 Year-in-Review*. https://www.woodmac.com/research/products/power-and-renewables/us-solar-market-insight (accessed April 7, 2021).

United Mine Workers of America

The United Mine Workers of America (UMWA) was founded in Columbus, Ohio in January 1890 as part of a merger of the National Progressive Union of Miners and Mine Laborers and the National Trade Association Assembly No. 135 of the Knights of Labor. The union initially represented the interests of coal miners, but has since come to also represent healthcare workers, trucker drivers, manufacturing workers, and public employees in the United States and Canada. In addition to advocating for workers' rights, the union has advocated for better roads, schools, and universal healthcare. At its peak, the UMWA was one of the largest and most powerful labor unions in North America.

From its inception, the UMWA adopted a three-prong strategy to labor relations: improving mine safety, curating worker independence from owners and company stores, and equipping miners with collective bargaining power. This strategy helped the union to achieve many notable achievements, including eight-hour working day (1898), collective-bargaining rights (1933), health and retirement benefits (1946), and federal coal mine safety and health standards (1969). The UMWA became significant and notable for actively, though imperfectly, working against racism, organizing workers without regard for craft, and using the legal system and politics to procure and defend worker gains in the workplace.

Many prominent labor leaders came from the UMWA such as John Mitchell (1870–1919), John L. Lewis (1880–1969), Mary "Mother" Jones (1837–1930), William B. Wilson (1862–1934), John Brophy (1883–1963), William Green (1873–1952), Philip Murray (1886–1952), and Richard Trumka (1949–).

The founding of the UMWA traces back to an era of poor working conditions experienced by coal miners. In the early years of the coal industry, miners enjoyed a lot of autonomy in hours worked and amount of coal mined, which became an issue between miners and mine owners. Spats over autonomy, hours of work, and compensation served as the catalysts for the genesis of unions. Miners often lived in company-owned and isolated towns. They lived in company houses, bought goods at company stores, were paid in script rather than cash, and were often cheated in wages. In this situation, miners realized that they had to unite for their well-being. Unions were formed to improve work conditions, living conditions, and pay. The UMWA was the end result of organizing at ever-high levels, beginning with local units and proceeding through regional and finally national organizations

Leadership of the UMWA has been historically centralized through their president, where it has experienced strong leadership, but also significant corruption. Early presidents of the UMWA served short terms: John B. Rae (1890–92), John McBride (1892–5), Phil Penna (1895–6), and Michael Ratchford (1897–8). John Mitchell (1870–1919), who was president from 1898 to 1907, was the first to serve for an extended period of time. Under Mitchell's watch, the UMWA expanded from the United States to Canada, collective bargaining became institutionalized and modeled by other industries, and the union won an eight-hour workday. For twenty-years after Mitchell stepped down, the union dealt with bitter internal feuding and disputes with mine operators.

In 1919, John L. Lewis became acting president of the union and was elected president in 1920, a position he maintained until 1960. As president, Lewis attempted consolidate all power in the national office. Lewis violated the UWMA's constitution by jettisoning his opponents from the union and elevating his supporters to the presidency of the union's districts. During the 1920s and 1930s Lewis struggled to keep the union from falling apart. Across the country, a surplus of energy capacity occurred, which coincided with declining demand for coal. This led to layoffs among miners and forced the union to accept wage reductions. Though Lewis supported President Herbert Hoover's elections in 1928 and 1932, Lewis worked with president-elect Franklin D. Roosevelt to implement Section 7a in the 1933 National Industrial Recovery Act (NIRA) which gave unions the right to organize. Seen as a crooked leader, Lewis was challenged by John Brophy, president of District 2 of the UMWA. Lewis defeated Brophy in a questionable election. Brophy was Lewis's last major opposition until Lewis's retirement in 1960. In 1946, Lewis was compelled to create the UMWA Welfare and Retirement Fund, a benefit that coal companies refused to grant. The government also implemented safety codes that the operators had to accept once control of the mines was returned to them.

Lewis so dominated the union that there was no strong leadership to succeed him after he left office. In 1960, Lewis was replaced by long-time vice president Thomas Kennedy who had an unremarkable tenure before passing away in 1963. Kennedy's successor, Tony Boyle, served from 1963 to 1972 and his term was characterized by violence, bribery, and manipulation. Boyle was challenged by Jock Yablonski in 1969. After winning a corrupt election, Boyle had Yablonski murdered. In 1969, Boyle's presidency secured one crowning achievement, the passing of the Coal Mine Health and Safety Act. This law addressed hazardous mining practices and provided compensation for miners with black lung disease.

In 1972 Arnold Miller, a supporter of Yablonski, unseated Boyle for the presidency. Under his leadership, the union declined dramatically in power, in part because of a significant drop in the demand for coal. Miller attempted to reform the UMWA in terms of collective bargaining and issues of health and safety. However, internal disputes prompted him to step down in 1972 to be replaced by vice president Sam Church. Church's tenure, however, was short-lived, as Richard Trumka took the reins of the UMWA from 1982 to 1995.

Trumka assumed control of the presidency at a difficult time. The Reagan administration was no friend of labor, the coal demand dropped once more, and non-union mine workers grew, all of which made union negotiations all the more daunting. In 1995, Trumka left the UMWA to become secretary-treasurer of the American Federation of Labor. In 1995, Cecil Roberts became the UMWA's president. Despite a long-term reduction in union miners, Roberts made several noteworthy achievements, including wage and pension increases. Roberts also made climate change a significant issue for the union and its members.

Through its imperfect history the UMWA has demonstrably improved the lives of workers in one of the most dangerous occupations. The union has been a leader in advocating for workers' rights and improved health and safety through collective bargaining.

Todd K. Platts

See also: Battle of Blair Mountain; Cooke, Morris Llewellyn; Harlan County War; Ludlow Massacre; Miner's and Laborer's Benevolent Association; Molly Maguires; Osgood, John Cleveland; Paint Creek Mine War

FURTHER READING

Baratz, Morton S. 1983. *The Union and the Coal Industry*. New Haven, CT: Yale University Press.

Hill, Herbert. 1988. "Myth-Making as Labor History: Herbert Gutman and the United Mine Workers of America." *Politics, Culture, and Society*. Vol. 2. No. 2. Pp. 132–200.

Laslett, John M., ed. 1996. *The United Mine Workers of America: A Model of Industrial Solidarity?* State College, PA: Penn State University Press.

Montgomery, David. 1987. *The Fall of the House of Labor: The Workplace, the State, and American Labor Activism, 1865–1925*. New York: Cambridge University Press.

Upper Big Branch Mine Disaster

On April 5, 2010, Massey Energy's Upper Big Branch (UBB) coal mine in Raleigh County, West Virginia suffered an explosion, killing twenty-nine of the thirty-one workers inside. It was the largest mine disaster in the United States since the Farmington, West Virginia mine disaster in 1968. The disaster garnered much attention as investigators, regulatory agencies, company lawyers, special-interest groups, and the media all argued the cause of the explosion. As a result of the criminal investigation that followed, two Massey officials received prison sentences. The disaster followed a period of declining injuries and fatalities in coal mining but served as a terrible reminder of the industry's bloody record of death, disease, and violence in the United States.

The Mine Safety and Health Administration (MSHA) reported that the Upper Big Branch mine disaster was caused by a spark from a longwall shear, which ignited a pocket of methane gas. MSHA stated that sparks are not uncommon in coal mining operations, but mechanical controls are designed to stop emergent threats. In the case of UBB, mechanical and safety failures were to blame for the explosion. The water spray system was not functional and air flow was inadequate in the mine. Combined with an accumulation of methane gas and coal dust, this "perfect storm" produced a blast that could be heard as much as 7 miles away.

Other investigations echoed sentiments that UBB was caused by the failure to implement basic safety practices. Five separate state, federal, and independent investigations were conducted, and they largely agreed with the MSHA assessment that "the physical conditions that led to the explosion were the result of a series of basic safety violations at UBB and were entirely preventable. PCC/Massey disregarded the resulting hazards" (MSHA 2014, 2). The United Mine Workers of America conducted its own investigation and accused Massey Energy of "industrial homicide" due to its reckless negligence (Thomas 2012, 260).

US Secretary of Labor Hilda L. Solis requested a review of MSHA's enforcement actions to determine if more could have been done to secure the coal company's compliance with mine safety regulations. An independent assessment panel studied MSHA's inspections and reports and concluded, "If MSHA had engaged in a timely enforcement of the Mine Act and applicable standards and regulations, it would have lessened the chances of—and possibly could have prevented—the UBB explosion" (IAP 2012, 9). In other words, if MSHA had fully enforced mine safety regulations at UBB, the mine would have closed, therefore preventing the explosion.

The controversy that enshrouded the UBB disaster originated in the mine's safety record. Massey Energy Co., once the fourth largest coal company in the world, was known for amassing record levels of safety and environmental violations under the leadership of CEO, Donald Blankenship. In the years prior to the explosion, the UBB mine, owned and operated by Performance Coal Company, a subsidiary of Massey Energy, incurred more than 1,100 safety violations. In fact, MSHA ordered parts of UBB to close at least sixty times for safety violations prior to the explosion (Young 2010). Anecdotally, many miners expressed concern about working at the UBB mine. Despite these repeated violations, Blankenship remained adamant that the UBB mine disaster was caused by MSHA and their implementation of a faulty ventilation plan.

Less than a year after the UBB explosion, Blankenship announced his retirement, and Massey Energy changed ownership. The company gave Blankenship a $12 million severance package upon leaving, and on January 31, 2011, Alpha Natural Resources announced its intentions to buy Massey Energy for $7.1 billion. Alpha Natural Resources subsequently closed the UBB mine in 2012.

BLACK LUNG

While the explosion at Upper Big Branch was traumatic, studies based on twenty-four of the victims at UBB showed cause for even more concern—black lung. Lung samples from these miners showed that 71 percent had developed black lung, a preventable occupational lung disease. These findings reveal that miners experienced high levels of coal dust exposure while working at UBB mine.

Aysha Bodenhamer

Blankenship was later indicted for conspiracy to violate mine safety standards and conspiracy to impede federal mine safety officials. Blankenship was convicted in 2015 on a misdemeanor charge of conspiring to violate federal mine safety laws. He served a year in federal prison and a halfway house, making it the first time a coal mine operator was criminally charged for a coal miner's death. Acting US Attorney Carol Casto remarked, "putting the former chief executive officer of a major corporation in prison sends a message that violating mine safety laws is a serious crime, and those who break those laws will be held accountable" (SDWV 2016). Gary May, UBB mine superintendent, was also sentenced to twenty-one months in prison for conspiracy to impede the function of MSHA.

The Upper Big Branch Mining Memorial was built in 2012 to honor the fallen victims at UBB. The 48 by 9 feet tall American black granite monument sits at the center of the memorial plaza in Whitesville, West Virginia. The memorial portrays a silhouette of twenty-nine life-sized miners with an inscription that reads: "Come to me all you who labor and I will give you rest." This memorial joined many others in West Virginia, such as the memorial in Mannington to the 78 who died in the 1968 Farmington Mine No. 9 explosion, the memorial in Lumberport to the 22 who died in the 1963 Clinchfield Mine No. 2 explosion in Dola, and the memorial in Monongah to the 361 souls lost in the explosion of Fairmont Mines Nos. 6 and 8 in 1907. Taken together, they symbolize the appalling cost paid in human lives for the energy wrought from coal mining in West Virginia and throughout the world.

Aysha Bodenhamer

See also: Centralia Mine Disaster; Cherry Mine Disaster; Coal; Dawson Mine Disaster; Farmington Mine Disaster; Krebs Mine Disaster; Monongah Mine Disaster; Paint Creek Mine War; Scofield Mine Disaster; United Mine Workers of America; West Frankfurt Mine Disaster

FURTHER READING

Independent Assessment Panel (IAP). 2012. "An Independent Panel Assessment of an Internal Review of MSHA Enforcement Actions at the Upper Big Branch Mine South." Mine Safety and Health Administration. US Department of Labor. March 22. https://arlweb.msha.gov/performancecoal/NIOSH/Independent%20Assessment%20Panel%20Report%20w_Errata.pdf (accessed April 19, 2020).

Lilly, Jessica. 2015. "Inside Appalachia: Blankenship, Upper Big Branch, and Mine Safety." Morehead State Public Radio. September 25. https://www.wmky.org/post/inside-appalachia-blankenship-upper-big-branch-and-mine-safety (accessed April 29, 2020).

Mine Safety and Health Administration (MSHA). 2014. "Report of Investigation, Fatal Underground Mine Explosion, April 5, 2010, Upper Big Branch Mine-South, Performance Coal Company, Montcoal, Raleigh County, West Virginia." ID 46-08436. US Department of Labor. https://www.msha.gov/sites/default/files/Data_Reports/Fatals/Coal/Upper%20Big%20Branch/FTL10c0331noappx_0.pdf (accessed October 2023).

Southern District of West Virginia (SDWV). 2016. "Blankenship Sentenced to a Year in Federal Prison." US Department of Justice. April 6. https://www.justice.gov/usao-sdwv/pr/blankenship-sentenced-year-federal-prison (accessed October 2023).

Thomas, Erin Ann. 2012. *Coal in Our Veins: A Personal Journey*. Logan, UT: Utah State University Press.

Ward, Ken Jr. 2014. "Miners Say Upper Big Branch Mine Cheated on Dust Sampling." Center for Public Integrity. July 8. https://publicintegrity.org/inequality-poverty-opportunity/workers-rights/miners-say-upper-big-branch-mine-cheated-on-dust-sampling/ (accessed April 19, 2020).

Young, Jeff. 2010. "The Story behind the Upper Big Branch Mine Disaster." The World. Public Radio Exchange (PRX). April 13. https://www.pri.org/stories/2010-04-13/story-behind-upper-big-branch-mine-disaster (accessed April 16, 2020).

Upton Machine Company and Whirlpool Corporation

The history of energy contains numerous accounts of technologies that transformed the daily lives of millions of ordinary people. Electrical appliances are among those technologies, and washing machines rank highly on the list. Prior to electricity, laundry required hours of toil using a washboard and a tub, often with a hand-cranked wringer attachment. With the appearance of electric washing machines, and particularly their mass production, the routines of domestic life began to change. The Upton Machine Company and its successor, the Whirlpool Corporation, made the electric washing machine a fixture in the American household and further solidified electrical power as a mainstay in the life of the nation. They opened the gateway for a revolution in how energy was consumed in the twentieth century.

In the late 1890s, an owner of a washing tub could buy a small electric motor and attach it to an agitator and to the tub's double-roll wringer mechanism. Perhaps as early as 1905, washing machines built with an integrated electric motor were manufactured and sold. The earliest patent issued for a specially designed electrical washing machine dates to 1907 (Maxwell 2009, 10). In the same year, at the age of twenty-one, Louis Upton (1886–1952) went to work for Commonwealth Edison in Chicago, where he saw the awesome power of electricity and began to envision new ways to harness its potential. He soon became interested in washing machines and happened to be contacted by a hardware store owner in South Bend, Indiana, about the possibility of going into business together to manufacture one that had just been patented, albeit a manual, not electric device. Upton invested $500 in the enterprise, but it failed almost immediately. His partner, recognizing Upton's loss, offered him the patent on the machine, which Upton accepted. He showed the washing machine to his uncle, Emory Upton in Benton Harbor, Michigan, to see if it could be converted to electrical power. The uncle was a "wise and clever mechanic" and made it work ("Louis" 1952).

Still at Commonwealth Edison, Upton connected with an affiliate, Federal Electric Company in Chicago, which sold electrical devices. He convinced the company to take 100 units to be sold for $85 and set up shop in St. Joseph, Michigan. Upton and his brother Frederick built and delivered the washers, which ultimately proved deficient due to the use of iron gearing. Upton changed to steel gears and Federal Electric agreed to 200 more units. Upton and his brother then established Upton Machine Company in 1911 in St. Joseph with six employees, drawing financial backing from Lowell C. Bassford. When Federal Electric decided in 1916 to make their own electric washers, Upton grew desperate, but secured a deal with Sears, Roebuck and Company to take on twenty-five units a month. This provided a steady income for the company while consumers were adjusting to the general idea of electric washing machines. Clearly, many Americans were still concerned about the wisdom of connecting electrical power to a device full of water. The Upton Machine Company continued to make improvements and eventually overcame these misgivings.

In the early 1920s, sales increased, and Upton's company created a closer working relationship with Sears. In 1925, they made an agreement for Upton to move its products from the catalog to Sears' eighty retail outlets, with Upton being the sole provider of Sears' washing machines. Upton put salesmen inside the stores to train Sears employees on the machines' merits. This produced a boom for the company; sales increased from 25,000 in 1925 to 125,000 in 1928. In 1929, Upton merged on an equitable basis with another washing machine manufacturer, the Nineteen Hundred Washing Machine Company, and took the name Nineteen Hundred Corporation, with Upton as vice president. By the end of the decade, 70 percent of American homes were wired for electricity—90 percent in urban areas—and were potential buyers for the new combined company's washing machines (Strand 2008, 162). In 1933, the company's president resigned, and Upton took his place. Despite years of economic privation in the Great Depression, the company's sales continued to improve. Upton closed Nineteen Hundred's Binghamton, New York plant in 1939 and moved all operations to St. Joseph to consolidate production. The company's plant then closed in early 1942 to refit for wartime production. While Upton served on the War Productions Board, his company manufactured a range of parts for aircraft, bombs, gun mounts and sights, vehicle engines and transmissions, and many other items.

Upton's company left the Second World War as the largest manufacturer of washing machines. After the war it unveiled a new brand, Whirlpool. The Whirlpool brand, and another known as Kenmore, met a consumer market that experienced constriction through years of depression and war and was primed for dramatic expansion. The G.I. Bill provided veterans with education benefits and low-interest home loans with no down payment. The National Archives noted that 4.3 million home loans were granted by 1955 through the program with a face value of $33 billion. Records show that veterans bought 20 percent of new homes several decades after the war (NARA 2022). The blizzard of new home construction vastly expanded demand for home appliances like washing machines, electric dryers (first introduced in 1924), refrigerators, electric ranges, vacuum cleaners, and air-conditioners.

Nineteen Hundred Corporation was a beneficiary of these economic and social developments with the post-war introduction of Whirlpool and Kenmore brand automatic washing machines. By 1950, these brands and other products brought $78 million in sales, and by 1960, that figure reached $440 million. The company had 3,463 employees in 1950, and ten years later had expanded its workforce to 14,600 (Eliasohn 2001). This large volume of sales prompted Upton and company directors and executives to associate the company with the Whirlpool brand, and in 1950 it became the Whirlpool Corporation. Soon after, in 1955, Whirlpool merged with Minneapolis-based Seeger Refrigerator Company. Founded in 1906, Seeger was an important manufacturer of refrigerators and freezers. This expanded Whirlpool's line of products and extended its reach in the American home from the laundry room to the kitchen. Upton never got to see the merger, as he died of a cerebral hemorrhage in 1952 while riding in a car to a business meeting.

In 1959, Whirlpool became part of Cold War history as the backdrop to the 'Kitchen Debate' between Vice President Richard Nixon and Soviet Premier Nikita Khrushchev. The occasion for the debate was the American National Exhibition in Moscow, in which about

450 American corporations contributed to the various exhibits, including brands like Levi's, Pepsi-Cola, Kodak, Ford Thunderbird, Disney, RCA, Betty Crocker, and Whirlpool. One of the exhibits, the RCA/Whirlpool Miracle Kitchen, featured futuristic appliances arranged around a control panel with an elegantly styled American woman pushing buttons to activate the appliances. The exhibit proclaimed: "'Household chores in the future will be gone for the American housewife at the touch of a button or the wave of a hand'" (Delloye 2019). Standing in front of the Miracle Kitchen, Nixon told Khrushchev, "'What we want to do, is make life more easy for our housewives.'" Khrushchev retorted, "'Your capitalistic attitude toward women does not occur under Communism'" (Delloye 2019). The two figures continued jawing about the differences between the United States and the Soviet Union, and between life under capitalism and life under communism, largely surrounded by Whirlpool appliances on display in three other "typical" American kitchens.

This shows that by mid-century, the possession of a suite of Whirlpool appliances was considered part of what it meant to attain the "American Dream." Culturally speaking, electrical appliances symbolized prosperity and abundance, ingenuity and technological know-how, and ideas about progress and improvement. America's rise to great power status in the post-war era corresponded with Whirlpool's rise to become the industry's leader in providing these symbols. Over the remainder of the century, Whirlpool grew by acquisition of other appliance manufacturers like Philips N.V. and InSinkErator, while expanding overseas production in ten other countries. It marketed recognizable brands like Whirlpool, KitchenAid, Amana, Maytag, and Hotpoint, as well as German brand Bauknecht, Brazilian brand Brastemp, and Italian brand Indesit (Snyder 2008, xvi). Whirlpool's research and development program included responses to the Energy Policy and Conservation Act of 1975 and its successor legislation, which outlined energy efficiency standards for appliances. Since 2001, Whirlpool appliances garnered numerous Energy Star awards, conferred by the US Environmental Protection Agency (EPA) on products that meet EPA energy efficiency specifications.

In 2021, the company claimed revenues of $22 billion with 69,000 employees across fifty-four manufacturing and technology research centers. The next year, Whirlpool earned a place on *Fortune*'s list of the world's most respected companies, ranked third on *Newsweek*'s list of most responsible companies, and ranked fifth on the *Wall Street Journal*'s Management 250, earning praise for its commitment to net-zero emissions and net-zero waste to landfill ("Whirlpool" 2023). Whirlpool remained committed to innovation and corporate responsibility, endeavoring to make an impact on American manufacturing and on American society in general. It's part of a legacy that began with its core product in 1911, the electric washing machine, which historian Stephen van Dulken named as one of a hundred "inventions that shaped the world" in the twentieth century (van Dulken 2002).

Jeffrey B. Webb

See also: Carrier, Willis Haviland; Electricity; Energy Policy Act of 2005; Energy Policy and Conservation Act of 1975; Frigidaire; General Electric Company; Hobart Electric Manufacturing Company; Home Energy Efficiency; KitchenAid Appliances; Singer Manufacturing Company; Westinghouse, George

FURTHER READING

Delloye, Tate. 2019. "Dick vs. Nik: The Infamous Cold War 'Kitchen Debate.'" DailyMail.com. June 22. https://www.dailymail.co.uk/news/article-7160173/60th-anniversary-Kitchen-Debate-summer-Nixon-sold-American.html (accessed October 2023).

Eliasohn, Michael. 2001. "Whirlpool Celebrates 90 Years of Appliance-making." *The Herald-Palladium*. November 25. https://www.heraldpalladium.com/whirlpool-celebrates-90-years-of-appliance-making/article_d535edcf-8661-557f-9dc5-5ddc6cb1e0d4.html (accessed October 2023).

"Louis C. Upton's Determination and Vision Overcame All Obstacles." 1952. *The News-Palladium* (Benton Harbor, MI). October 10. P. 15.

Maxwell, Lee. 2009. "Who Invented the Electric Washing Machine?" Lee Maxwell Washing Machine Museum. February 19. https://www.oldewash.com/ (accessed October 2023).

Snyder, Nancy Tennant, and Deborah L. Duarte. 2008. *Unleashing Innovation: How Whirlpool Transformed an Industry*. San Francisco: Jossey-Bass.

Strand, Ginger. 2008. *Inventing Niagara: Beauty, Power, and Lies*. New York: Simon & Schuster.

US National Archives and Records Administration (NARA). 2022. "Serviceman's Readjustment Act of 1944." Milestone Documents. https://www.archives.gov/milestone-documents/servicemens-readjustment-act (accessed October 2023).

van Dulken, Stephen. 2002. *Inventing the 20th Century: 100 Inventions that Shaped the World from the Airplane to the Zipper*. New York: NYU Press.

"Whirlpool Corporation Celebrates 2022 Environmental, Social and Governance Achievements." 2023. 3BL CSRwire. January 9. https://www.csrwire.com/press_releases/763911-whirlpool-corporation-celebrates-2022-environmental-social-and-governance (accessed October 2023).

US Department of Energy

The US Department of Energy has its origins in the Manhattan Project of the 1940s, where scientists harnessed nuclear power in the creation of the atomic bomb. The nature of developing this new energy technology warranted federal oversight and support, which expanded the role of the government in the field of energy. In the post-war period, discussions regarding the use of atomic energy for military and civilian purposes followed, resulting in the creation of the Atomic Energy Commission (AEC) in 1946. This placed the development of nuclear energy clearly under government control. The AEC concentrated its efforts on military uses of nuclear energy through the early 1950s, and the Atomic Energy Act of 1954 opened the door to additional AEC regulation and support. This allowed for more extensive research in non-military uses of the atom, including the construction of nuclear power plants in subsequent decades.

Events of the 1970s challenged the federal government to further examine its responsibility regarding energy. In 1973, the Organization of Petroleum Exporting Countries (OPEC) quadrupled the price of oil over a period of a few months and the Organization of Arab Petroleum Exporting Countries (OAPEC) instituted an embargo and cut production, severely affecting the United States. By this time, the nation had become increasingly dependent on foreign oil and subject to geopolitical instability, endangering energy supply and national security. This energy crisis, in conjunction with concerns over nuclear safety and the common good, led to new expectations for a sound energy policy with federal oversight. Other oil-producing countries of the Western world responded to varying degrees, and the US government viewed the crisis as has having such serious political and economic implications for the nation that it took unprecedented steps (Bösch 2014, 8–9).

President Richard Nixon proposed a Department of Energy and Natural Resources in 1973 in response to the nation's energy problem, but his efforts were not approved by Congress. In November of the same year, he appealed to the American people to conserve at home. In 1974, the newly created Federal Energy Office—quickly renamed the Federal Energy Administration—took greater steps to influence policy related to petroleum products and their regulation. As shortages continued, Americans expected more effective solutions from the federal government in the form of renewable energy research and a stronger attempt at securing energy independence. At the same time, nuclear energy research continued. Through the leadership of President Carter and extensive deliberations in Congress, the US Department of Energy (DOE) was created.

On October 1, 1977, the DOE became the twelfth federal cabinet-level agency. It was charged with creating comprehensive policy related to research, production, regulation, conservation, and pricing. Before the crisis of 1973, the United States had benefited from decades of easy and affordable access to energy and until the development of atomic energy in the 1940s, private development and control of energy resources was accepted as standard operation, except when monopolies might jeopardize fair prices to customers. Any policy making related to energy was generally superseded by the authority of other agencies or conservation during wartime. However, the nation's energy history had entered a new phase. Assistant to President Carter James R. Schlesinger initiated energy agency reorganization soon after Carter's inauguration. With experience as AEC chairman, Secretary of Defense, and Director of the Central Intelligence Agency, Schlesinger demonstrated an understanding of and expectation for the federal government's role, and when appointed as the first US Secretary of Energy he quickly became known as the nation's "energy czar." Carter did not promise energy independence with the creation of the DOE, but said when reducing energy consumption, developing alternative energy sources, and practicing conservation, the nation could see a notable difference in dependence by 1985 (Holl 1982, 4–5).

US SECRETARIES OF ENERGY

James Schlesinger, 1977–9 (Carter)
Charles Duncan, 1979–81 (Carter)
James B. Edwards, 1981–2 (Reagan)
Donald P. Hodel, 1982–5 (Reagan)
John S. Herrington, 1985–9 (Reagan)
Admiral James Watkins, 1989–93 (Bush, G.)
Hazel R. O'Leary, 1993–7 (Clinton)
Frederico Peña, 1997–8 (Clinton)
Bill Richardson, 1998–2001 (Clinton)
Spencer Abraham, 2001–5 (Bush, G.W.)
Samuel W. Bodman, 2005–9 (Bush, G.W.)
Steven Chu, 2009–13 (Obama)
Ernest Moniz, 2013–17 (Obama)
Rick Perry, 2017–19 (Trump)
Dan Brouillette, 2019–21 (Trump)
Jennifer M. Granholm, 2021– (Biden)

Kathleen A. Tobin

Under the Regan administration and a more conservative Congress in the 1980s, new policies favored a free market, including that related to fossil fuels and other energy supplies. The new administration attempted to reduce government control, questioned the benefits of a national energy policy, and sought to dismantle the DOE. It cut funding for the department, particularly in the areas of research and development of new technologies and conservation programs. It shifted responsibilities and expanded the role of the Department of Commerce in supporting petroleum corporations. President George H.W. Bush's ties to the oil industry also shaped federal policy. However, the DOE remained in place during the Reagan-Bush era and subsequent administrations (Katz 1984, 153–69).

The US Department of Energy did not act in isolation. Rather, it often coordinated efforts with the Department of the Interior, the Environmental Protection Agency, the Nuclear Regulatory Commission, and the Synthetic Fuels Corporation, as well as various congressional committees and state-level agencies. At stake were an adequate resources, regulation, environmental and economic impact, and international military developments (Kash 1984, 239–55). It is important to remember that a primary reason for the creation of the DOE was to decrease dependence on foreign oil and stabilize energy flow through periods of geopolitical tensions. At the same time, it developed a close partnership with the Department of Defense in order to protect foreign resources and guard sites of production and refining on American soil in the case of military or terrorist attacks.

In the twenty-first century, the DOE has sought to balance federal roles and energy needs with an emphasis on sustainability through research and development in clean energy, including solar, wind, water, geothermal, biofuels, and nuclear. It strives to meet challenges in developing new hydrogen and fuel cell technology, as well as energy storage and waste disposal to keep the nation safe.

Kathleen A. Tobin

See also: Energy Crisis of the 1970s; Energy Independence; Energy Policy and Conservation Act of 1975; Energy Security Act of 1980; Manhattan Project; National Energy Act of 1978; Organization of Petroleum Exporting Countries (OPEC); US Environmental Protection Agency

FURTHER READING

Bösch, Frank, and Rüdiger Graf. 2014. "Reacting to Anticipations: Energy Crises and Energy Policy in the 1970s." *Historical Social Research*. Vol. 39. No. 4. Pp. 7–21.

Fehner, Terrence R., and Jack M. Holl. 1994. *Department of Energy 1977–1994: A Summary History*. Washington, DC: History Division, US Department of Energy.

Holl, Jack M. 1982. *The United States Department of Energy: A History*. Washington, DC: History Division, US Department of Energy.

Kash, Don E., and Robert W. Rycroft. 1984. *U.S. Energy Policy: Crisis and Complacency*. Norman, OK: University of Oklahoma Press.

Katz, James Everett. 1984. *Congress and National Energy Policy*. London: Transaction Books.

Ladislaw, Sarah, and Nikos Tsafos. 2020. "The Age of Energy Dominance." In *Race to the Top: Case for a New U.S. International Energy Policy*. Center for Strategic and International Studies (CSIS). http://www.jstor.org/stable/resrep29326.5 (accessed October 2023).

Lifset, Robert, ed. 2014. *Energy Policy in the 1970s*. Norman, OK: University of Oklahoma Press.

Office of Legacy Management (OLM). "DOE History." US Department of Energy. https://www.energy.gov/lm/doe-history (accessed October 2023).

US Environmental Protection Agency

The US Environmental Protection Agency (EPA) is an independent federal agency first established by the Nixon administration and Congress in 1970. Its creation was part of wider efforts by President Richard Nixon to promote legislative and administrative environmental protection efforts, including regulating pollution and energy usage, increasing energy efficiency, protecting animals from toxic substances, and safeguarding human health. It was founded the same year as the Council on Environmental Quality (CEQ) and the passage of the National Environmental Policy and Clean Air Acts, as well as Earth Day. It consolidated many of the organizations and agencies formed during the Johnson administration (1963–9) and inspired the creation of similar agencies on a state level. The EPA has not only reduced redundancy and overlap within federal responsibilities by providing a central agency devoted to environmental protection, but has remained a powerful, and overall successful, regulatory governmental force.

During the 1960s, a series of publications and events alerted Americans to the increasing threat that humans, industry especially, posed to the environment. Publications like Rachel Carson's *Silent Spring* (1962) arguably kick-started this move towards greater environmental awareness, highlighting the dangers of pesticides and nuclear weapons to both humans and animals. Throughout the decade, and into the 1970s, disasters like the Santa Barbara Oil Spill (1969), which killed thousands of birds and marine life, emphasized the deleterious effects of nonrenewable energy on the environment, while the oil crisis of 1973, among other things, highlighted the need to seek alternative energy sources. The *Earthrise* photograph, taken during Apollo 8 (1968), allowed people to see a "whole earth," awakening many to the idea that their planet was small, beautiful, and fragile. In general, people began to believe that earth's resources were not only finite, but that its lands and animals needed protection.

In 1970, President Nixon kicked off the "decade of the environment" with Earth Day (Daynes 2010, 10). The decade of the 1970s was devoted to environmentalism, with increased environmental legislation and activism. Nixon argued that it was the "birthright of every American" to have clean air and water and open natural spaces (Daynes 2010, 69). While some scholars have debated just how committed he was to environmental causes, the formation of agencies like the EPA and the CEQ gave the environment its own designated place within the government.

From the beginning, conflicts from within and out of the EPA challenged their commitment to environmental protection. Because pollution, waste, and energy usage were largely by-products of industry, and in dire need of regulation to protect the environment, much of the EPA's history also comprises conflicts between industry and environmental interests. More "environmentally friendly" administrations accepted or even bolstered EPA's cause, while those with greater concerns in protecting corporate interests or who were even openly hostile to environmental concerns often weakened environmental protections in favor of economic and industrial growth.

EPA AND PUBLIC HEALTH

While the Environmental Protection Agency was originally founded to protect the environment, from early on the EPA focused heavily on human and public health, especially cancer prevention from environmental causes. This is partly due to most of its founding employees coming from other federal agencies and having expertise in other areas, such as health and agriculture, rather than the environment.

Caitlin Fendley

For example, environmental protection suffered under the Reagan administration (1981–9), which encouraged development and economic growth over environmentalism. Staunchly anti-environmentalist, Reagan focused on rolling back regulations to support business and industry and focused on economic growth and development rather than environmental initiatives. His New Federalism, which transferred a large share of the domestic responsibilities from federal to local and state governments, meant that environmental protections in the 1980s "were decentralized and defunded" (Daynes 2010, 174). Budget cuts to the EPA were part of this. Further, Reagan ignored scientific expertise when it misaligned with his political beliefs or efforts to drive economic growth and development and sought a revision by the EPA of hundreds of environmental regulations which did not fit the values of his administration.

At the heart of this approach to the EPA, then, was a dedicated effort to protect corporate interests over the need to better regulate energy and industry and their pollutants for environmental purposes. However, initiatives like Energy Star, introduced in 1992 under the Clinton administration (1993–2001), reflected a desire to effectively utilize the EPA to promote both global and domestic environmental concerns and balance consumer, industry, business, and environmental interests. Defined as "a voluntary labeling program designed to identify and promote energy-efficient products," Energy Star sought to reduce carbon emissions and energy consumption while promoting such products more easily to consumers (Brown 2002, 505).

Other energy-related bills included the Energy Independence and Security Act of 2007, passed during the Bush administration (2001–9), which was part of wider efforts to cut American gasoline consumption by one-fifth within the ensuing decade. While President George W. Bush sought to increase America's energy efficiency and energy security in more environmentally friendly ways, he also weakened the authority of the EPA and other agencies, like the CEQ, by appointing administrators with conflicted interests in energy and industry and sought to generally undermine and create skepticism towards environmental and climate change initiatives.

Proposals to cut emissions and energy usage and to promote efficiency continued under the Obama administration (2009–17). On August 3, 2015, President Obama announced the Clean Power Plan (CPP), first outlined by Obama and the EPA a couple years prior. He emphasized in his speech that human-made climate change not only caused premature death and health problems among Americans but threatened national security. Despite power plants causing about one-third of the country's carbon pollution, there "have never been federal limits on the amount of carbon power plants can dump into the air," which highlighted a need to reduce emissions, regulate energy usage, and generate more clean energy. And, like other proposals introduced with the EPA in prior years, he noted that "special interests"—those with financial stake in nonrenewable energy—would aggressively challenge this plan (Obama 2015).

But shortly after President Trump (2017–21) entered office, the EPA announced a replacement of the CPP with the Affordable Clean Energy Rule which would relax emissions and regulation standards for power plants. The EPA argued that they did not have the authority to implement the CPP, while figures like New Jersey Governor Phil Murphy believed this change of plans reflected a desire to "put polluters and corporations above the American public," making it easier for polluting power plants to avoid regulations (OAG 2018). Further, Murphy believed that these attacks on the CPP went against what was good for the New Jersey people, echoing statements by politicians like Nixon who stated that Americans had a "birthright" to clean air and water and other environmental protections. Such legislative whiplash reflects continued conflicts between energy and other corporations and the need and efforts to regulate and streamline their pollutants to protect human health and the environment.

Caitlin Fendley

See also: Clean Power Plan of 2015; Earth Day; Energy Policy and Conservation Act of 1975; National Energy Act of 1978; Natural Resources Defense Council; Sierra Club

FURTHER READING

Brown, R., C. Webber, and J.G. Koomey. 2002. "Status and Future Directions of the ENERGY STAR Program." *Energy*. Vol. 27. Pp. 505–20. https://doi.org/10.1016/S0360-5442(02)00004-X (accessed July 4, 2021).

Daynes, Byron W., and Glen Sussman. 2010. *White House Politics and the Environment: Franklin D. Roosevelt to George W. Bush*. College Station, TX: Texas A&M University Press.

Flippen, J. Brooks. 2000. *Nixon and the Environment*. Albuquerque, NM: University of New Mexico Press.

Obama, Barack. 2015. "Remarks by the President in Announcing the Clean Power Plan." Office of the Press Secretary. The White House. https://obamawhitehouse.archives.gov/the-press-office/2015/08/03/remarks-president-announcing-clean-power-plan (accessed July 4, 2021).

Office of the Attorney General of New Jersey (OAG). 2018. "Top NJ Officials Urge EPA Not to Abandon Clean Power Plan: Call EPA's New Proposed Energy Rule Unwise, Dangerous." Office of the Governor. State of New Jersey. October 31. https://www.nj.gov/governor/news/news/562018/approved/20181031d.shtml (accessed July 4, 2021).

Russell, Edmund P. 1997. "Lost among the Parts Per Billion: Ecological Protection at the United States Environmental Protection Agency, 1970–1993." *Environmental History*. Vol. 2. No. 1. Pp. 29–51.

US Environmental Protection Agency (EPA). 2021. "Proposal: Affordable Clean Energy (ACE) Rule." https://www.epa.gov/stationary-sources-air-pollution/proposal-affordable-clean-energy-ace-rule (accessed July 4, 2021).

US Fuel Administration

The US Fuel Administration (USFA) operated as an executive branch agency between 1917 and 1919. Industrialization and urbanization placed unprecedented stresses on US energy infrastructures, especially affecting coal. Those stresses, exacerbated by US entry into the First World War, brought the nation's first energy crisis and resulted in establishment of the USFA. The agency functioned through state-level subsidiaries and in conjunction with other federal agencies to promote conservation and energy efficiency by regulating fuel prices, rationalizing energy production and transportation systems, and providing technical information. Success varied depending on the program undertaken, and on people's willingness to comply with government directives.

The United States has always been home to a citizenry wary of centralized authority. Even in times of national crisis, many resist government mandates as an intrusion on personal freedom. That characteristic rarely impacted energy issues during the first century of the nation's existence since people used localized sources such as water, wood, animals, and human labor. Federal involvement with energy mainly consisted of purchasing supplies for government use and granting patents to inventors. That situation began to change during the latter nineteenth century as the United States industrialized and developed national markets. Driven by Progressives intent on reducing cronyism and inefficiency in governments, federal reorganization began in the 1880s. That reorganization included creating a professional civil service and regulatory bodies like the Interstate Commerce Commission (Campbell 1995).

Industrial energy requirements grew too great for localized resources to meet. Water power, subject to flow variation and dependent on geography, was too confining a resource. Easily harvested wood stocks, either used directly or processed into charcoal, took too long to renew. Given the early state of US crude oil production, industrialists turned to plentiful coal deposits to meet their energy needs. Available in several forms or processed into coke, coal could be mined relatively easily and transported by the railroads that also powered their locomotives with the fuel. Additional coal demand came as naval and maritime applications shifted from wind to steam power. On land and sea people preferred coal over wood due to higher energy content and convenience in use.

The growth of large cities and towns also increased coal consumption. Many urbanites burned manufactured gas, and electrification gave them another energy option starting in the 1880s. The expense of gas and electric service, however, led many people to adopt coal for space and water heating, and for cooking. Manufacturing gas or generating electricity created yet more demand for coal. As electrification accelerated during the 1890s some electric light and power companies built hydroelectric stations, but most ran their generators with coal-fired steam engines (Nye 1998).

At the dawn of the twentieth century, industrialization, urbanization, electrification, and transportation, all depended on regular coal supplies. Soaring demand for the fuel raised costs, and stressed coal production and transportation infrastructures. Relations between coal miners and mine owners, never harmonious, descended into violence as miners sought to unionize and owners sought to expand profits. By 1914, strikes became predictable; railroads and electric utilities learned to stockpile coal as miners' contracts approached expiration.

Railroad dysfunction created even more significant complications. Lines often carried coal in all-purpose cars intermixed with other freight cars, snarling traffic in rail yards and delaying deliveries. Railroads did not generally run dedicated, coal-only trains until 1957 (Gordon 1978, 94–7). Railroad systems poached each other's rolling stock and some customers used railcars for storage, practices that led some lines to embargo shipments over state borders. Lines were loath to purchase new specially designed coal cars only to watch them disappear. Railroads' practice of giving coal, a low-profit commodity, low priority in scheduling compounded transportation problems, as did labor unrest on the rails.

By 1915, military orders from European combatants drove industrial demand for coal even higher. Supplies failed to keep pace with demand due to labor unrest and railroad dysfunction. People worried about a "coal famine" as prices steadily climbed. In the winter of 1915–16 some electric power stations measured their coal reserves in hours. Despite an official policy of neutrality, President Woodrow Wilson began a program of national preparedness. Federal officials viewed the coal famine with alarm. They faced the real prospect that US involvement in the war might find the US Navy unable to steam, industry shuttered, and people freezing in the cities.

US entry into the First World War in April 1917 brought the crisis to a head, and federal authorities enacted several measures over the following months. In August, using authority granted under the Food and Fuel Control Act (Lever Act), Wilson established the US Fuel Administration to deal with energy supplies. He named former Princeton colleague Harry A. Garfield (1863–1942) as administrator, and delegated authority to intervene in the nation's energy infrastructures. While coal was USFA's most important charge and occupied most of their attention, the agency also exercised authority over other energy sources including wood, oil, natural gas, gasoline, and kerosene. Only the severity of the problems and the perceived temporary nature of a war emergency made such a political intervention into the US economy seem acceptable (LD 1919).

Even so, Garfield and his team faced resistance and moved with political sensitivity as they tried to impose order on the nation's energy supply. Their immediate need to compensate for a presidential "stumble" provides a case in point. In June, Wilson imposed coal prices lower than those voluntarily agreed to by the coal industry; that compromised USFA's position in subsequent labor negotiations (Cuff 1978, 46). Garfield reported that they spent "the first three months ... reconciling differences that had arisen between operators and mine workers" (Garfield 1918). Although they could legally force cooperation, Wilson's personal and political preferences ran toward voluntary compliance based on appeals to patriotism and rational self-interest. Such voluntarism proved difficult to obtain as many individuals and businesses would not put aside their own interests.

USFA established state-level subsidiaries to encourage cooperation and account for local conditions and markets, usually naming local leaders to coordinate and customize general policies. Those subsidiaries included special districts for New England, Pittsburgh and its surrounding counties, and Cuba (LD 1919, 34–6). The state administrators organized committees representing counties, as well as cities with 2,500 or more residents. Garfield could pay for staff, but requested they engage volunteers wherever possible. By December

1917, USFA in Washington, DC employed 391 people supported by fourteen volunteers, and employed 304 people supported by 2,584 volunteers in the USFA field offices (Mitchell 1920).

While negotiating to obtain cooperation from private individuals and businesses, the USFA also maneuvered around public sector agencies at all levels. The Federal Trade Commission (FTC) already maintained a section to monitor the coal industry and did not welcome encroachment. Relations with the FTC became such that Wilson ultimately transferred their entire coal section to the USFA. The War Industries Board (WIB) dealt with supplies of raw materials and set production priorities that USFA had to work into fuel rationing plans.

In December 1917, railroad chaos forced Wilson to nationalize the system under the US Railroad Administration (USRA). Coal's importance to the railroads called for USFA and USRA collaboration, a sometimes contentious activity. To help break the gridlock, Garfield authorized a system of coal production zones, specifying geographic areas that given mines could supply. That increased railcar availability and saved coal by reducing transport mileage, but the zones also interfered with commercial relations and profitable railroad practices. When USRA Administrator William McAdoo supported railroads' objections to the zones, Wilson stepped in to support Garfield's plan (Cuff 1978, 47).

Not all intermural interactions were so contentious. When industry resisted WIB's prioritization decisions, Garfield restricted the amount of coal that low priority industries could receive. USFA issued booklets written by the Bureau of Mines that taught coal conservation and energy efficiency in steam plant operations. In November 1917, USFA restricted fuel used for outdoor advertising and lighting, a move welcomed by the railroads. The utilities responded by giving local governments electric signs that spread patriotic messages and kept electricity sales flowing. USFA could do little to counteract such evasions since Congress exempted local governments from agency regulations. The restrictions went largely unheeded and in December, Garfield ordered the nation to make Sunday and Tuesday evenings "lightless nights."

The order underscored the seriousness of the railroad situation. Military supplies that could reach coastal ports remained dockside because ships could not get coal. Also, "the country has passed through the most severe winter of record for 50 years. From the first week of December until well along into February, the demands for coal for domestic purposes were unprecedented" (Garfield 1918). To meet the emergency, Garfield ordered a nationwide five-day business shutdown in late January so coal shipments could reach cities and ports without competition from other freight. He reported that 480 ships refueled and sailed for Europe as a result. The adoption of daylight savings time in late March eased the lighting restrictions, but the continued failure of voluntary cutbacks led to re-imposition of lightless nights in July.

While attendant to political sensitivities, Garfield and his staff relied heavily on experts and professionals in crafting their policies. This reflected a respect for specialized training and knowledge at odds with populist views of democracy. Government decision makers needed cooperation and information, and set aside worries about conflicts of interest. Some of the expertise came from industry executives, but much information came from professional engineers who wrote information sheets, advised consumers, and gave talks that promoted energy conservation. In the era of scientific management that looked for the one best way to accomplish a task, the engineers promoted small, incremental steps that would bring major fuel savings. While they hoped to continue those steps, the relatively brief US involvement in the war, a period of eighteen months, gave scant time to develop, much less implement, longer-range energy efficiency plans.

Coal problems continued after the Armistice in November 1918, keeping the USFA in operation until June 1919 to avoid an abrupt transition. Prewar animosity returned to labor relations in the coalfields. A November 1919 strike brought the USFA back for one month, until replaced by the Bituminous Coal Commission. Railroad troubles also resumed with the end of the zones. Commercial and residential consumers, fearing a return of the coal famine, engaged in panic buying that brought a market boom and bust in late 1920 (Montague 1922, 757). However, as the 1920s progressed, energy concerns receded along with federal energy intervention.

Evaluating the USFA's success in achieving their goals is difficult and subject to interpretation based on value judgments about government economic interventions. Post-war reports from the state administrators tell a mixed story; some reported excellent compliance resulting in much fuel saved, others reported more resistance and few savings. Not all states implemented every USFA policy, and not all local authorities enforced federal mandates on friends and neighbors. Asking for voluntary cooperation with agency programs often failed, but mandatory regulations often fared little better.

The history of USFA offers lessons for policy makers and energy advocates alike. A political culture within the United States that values individual liberty above all and distrusts authority makes collective action difficult. Especially when plentiful energy supplies and the ability to use them as one saw fit became "an inalienable American right" (Nye 1998, 250–1). Even in times of national crisis, some people simply refused to cooperate for the common good. Private sector actors gave priority to personal or business interests, while public sector actors sought to prevent mission encroachment. To succeed, proposals that mandate energy policies or technologies must be carefully structured, crafted in collaboration with affected stakeholders, and offer clear benefits.

Harold D. Wallace Jr.

See also: Coal; Daylight Saving Time; Federal Power Act of 1935; Federal Power Commission; Food and Fuel Control Act of 1917; Oil Embargo of 1941; Strategic Petroleum Reserve

FURTHER READING

Campbell, Ballard C. 1995. *The Growth of American Government: Governance from the Cleveland Era to the Present*. Bloomington, IN: Indiana University Press.

Cuff, Robert. 1978. "Harry Garfield, the Fuel Administration, and the Search for a Cooperative Order during World War I." *American Quarterly*. Vol. 30. No. 1. Spring. Pp. 39–53. https://www.jstor.org/stable/2712278 (accessed October 2023).

Garfield, Harry A. 1918. "The Fuel Question." *Scientific American*. Vol. 118. No. 14. April 6. Pp. 307, 328–30. https://www.jstor.org/stable/10.2307/26031239 (accessed October 2023).

Gordon, Richard L. 1978. *Coal in the U.S. Energy Market: History and Prospects*. Lexington, MA: Lexington Books.

Legal Division (LD). 1919. *General Orders, Regulations and Rulings of the United States Fuel Administration, Including the Acts of Congress, Executive Orders, and Proclamations of the President Pursuant to Which the United States Fuel Administration was Created and is Acting*. United States Fuel Administration. Washington, Government Printing Office.

Mitchell, Lawrence. 1920. *Final Report of the Business Manager to H. A. Garfield*. Washington, DC: US Government Printing Office.

Montague, Gilbert H. 1922. "Trade Associations and the Government." *North American Review*. Vol. 215. No. 799. Pp. 751–60. https://www.jstor.org/stable/25121057 (accessed October 2023).

National Archives and Records Administration (NARA). n.d. Records of the U.S. Fuel Administration, 1917–20. Record Group 67. https://www.archives.gov/research/guide-fed-records/groups/067.html (accessed October 2023).

Nye, David. 1998. *Consuming Power: A Social History of American Energies*. Cambridge, MA: MIT Press.

U.S. Green Building Council

In the late twentieth century, concerns about climate change mounted and inspired a group of architects, building contractors, engineers, government officials, policy experts, and non-profit leaders to form the U.S. Green Building Council (GBC). The organization first met in 1993 with a mission to "transform how buildings and communities are designed, built and operated, enabling an environmentally and socially responsible, healthy, and prosperous environment that improves the quality of life for all" (GBC 2016). They developed the LEED certification program, starting in 2000, which encouraged builders to meet high standards of energy efficiency, employ water conservation strategies, incorporate local and regional sources of energy, utilize materials that are renewable, recyclable, locally sourced, and non-toxic, and finally, integrate natural site features into building design and function. LEED certification addressed concerns about sustainability, which refers to the ongoing ability of the earth to carry on the natural processes that support human life. The GBC represented a serious effort to change past habits of energy use, as people and organizations failed to adequately account for how their habits might result in future resource exhaustion, ecological degradation, and chronic human health problems.

Events in the late 1980s and early 1990s brought increased awareness to environmental issues, particularly the problem of climate change. In 1988, NASA climatologist James Hansen testified in a hearing of the US Senate Committee on Energy and Natural Resources that "the greenhouse effect has been detected and it is changing our climate now" (Hansen 1988, 40). Later that year, the United Nations endorsed the formation of the Intergovernmental Panel on Climate Change, which compiled scientific reports about climate change and consulted with governments on energy and environmental policy. Then, in 1989, the *Exxon Valdez* oil spill dramatized the environmental hazards of fossil fuels. A comprehensive Clean Air Act of 1990 received much debate, which was followed in 1992 by the UN's Earth Summit in Rio Janeiro. The Earth Summit produced the Framework Convention on Climate Change, which the United States didn't sign. However, it created a large, global conversation about the need to reduce greenhouse gas emissions from power plants, industry, transportation, and other sources to halt the progress of global warming.

The early beginnings of GBC and LEED can be traced to a meeting of the American Institute of Architects (AIA) in 1989 when Kansas City architect Bob Berkebile tried to get the organization's board of directors to establish a committee to identify ways the AIA could advance environmentally mindful design and construction practices. When they declined, Berkebile and like-minded architects proceeded to win a vote at the ensuing annual meeting to form the AIA Committee on the Environment (Barth 2018). The committee, with Berkebile as chair, joined efforts with the US Environmental Protection Agency (EPA) to review environmental standards in building design, and consulted with administration officials in 1993 to help make the White House a model for energy efficiency (Barth 2018). The Berkebile's committee received funding from the EPA and hoped to become an independent organization guided by the best possible scientific research. However, corporations wished to become involved through large donations, threatening the group's detachment and objectivity. A meeting was arranged that brought together architects from Berkebile's committee and leaders of green initiatives within industry, and the result was the creation of a separate organization, the GBC, cofounded by Mike Italiano, David Gottfried, and Rick Fedrizzi.

Gottfried worked in real estate and became interested in sustainable development. He later served as head of Reset360, Regenerative Ventures, and Regen Network and authored *Explosion Green: One Man's Journey to Green the World's Largest Industry* (2014). He also held an executive role at Blue Planet Systems, a company that made synthetic limestone aggregate by sequestering and mineralizing carbon dioxide from power plants and other sources. Fedrizzi worked as an environmental marketing officer for Carrier Global Corporation and became chairman and CEO of the International WELL Building Institute. He published *Greenthink: How Profit Can Save the Planet* (2015), which argued that economic and environmental concerns can and should be harmonized. Italiano was educated in physical geography and received a law degree before becoming CEO of Market Transformation to Sustainability and Capital Markets Partnership. They worked with a committed group of professionals committed to reorienting the design and construction industry toward greener buildings. Robert K. Watson, senior scientist at the Natural Resources Defense Council (NRDC) and J.D. Polk, founder of Solar Cells, Inc. offered initial counsel in devising the LEED certification standards.

LEED stands for Leadership in Energy and Environmental Design. After years of developing certification criteria, the GBC began working on LEED certification projects like the Philip Merrill Environmental Center on the Chesapeake Bay near Annapolis, Maryland. The building, which houses the headquarters of the Chesapeake Bay Foundation and conducts educational programs on the site, received highest, "Platinum" level certification in 2000. The process leading to certification brought together the foundation, SmithGroup—an architectural firm familiar with LEED requirements—and a project team. A description of the certification noted the design and build features that helped the project meet the criteria. The building's "solar array reduced grid energy use by about one-third, and its rainwater collection system and composting toilets reduced water use by 90% compared to a typical office building" (Stanley 2020). The design maximized availability of sunlight, which illuminated the interior and reduced electricity use. The architectural plan called for siting the facility on a creek next to the bay, which enabled staff to make organic connections between its core mission and its physical surroundings.

Between 2000 and 2020, GBC certified 3,800 buildings at the Platinum level, and many others at the Certified, Silver, and Gold levels. The certification worked by means of earning a total amount of points for various design and build features that met the LEED criteria. Over time, the system grew from one certification to an array of possible certifications that project directors could choose from, such as design and construction, interior design and construction, or building operations and maintenance. In 2008, GBC created a separate organization, the Green Building Certification Institute (GBCI), the purpose of which was to provide third-party, independent oversight of LEED certifications. The GBCI also supervised a separate program that targeted architects and developers with credentialing in LEED project supervision. Depending on the amount of coursework and level of exam, participants in the program could receive certification as a LEED Green Associate, LEED Accredited Professional, or LEED Accredited Professional with Specialty. These two tracks, project certification and professional credentialing, were intended to work hand in glove, as LEED Accredited Professionals provided guidance to architects and developers seeking LEED certification for their building projects. In 2014, GBCI renamed itself Green Business Certification, Inc. and began to oversee certification programs offered by other organizations with missions similar to the GBC, including the Global Real Estate Sustainability Benchmark, International WELL Building Institute, and Perfect Power Institute.

The appearance of these other building certification programs reflected some disagreement among key figures in the green building movement about how to approach the problem of "greening" of the built environment. For some, reducing energy use and therefore carbon emissions through LEED principles wasn't sufficient to bend the curve on greenhouse gas production and its global warming effects. In 2010, the International Living Future Institute began an alternative certification program called Living Building Challenge. The organization promoted what it called "living buildings," which are: (1) "regenerative buildings that connect occupants to light, air, food, nature, and community," (2) "self-sufficient and remain within the resource limits of their site," and (3) "create a positive impact on the human and natural systems that interact with them" (ILFI 2022). Under this program, building project could be certified only if they benefited the health of people and the natural environment, as opposed to merely harming it less than other building projects. Buildings had to produce more energy than they consumed and must produce a net-positive water use and net-positive waste production (Barth 2018).

In October 2022, the GBC announced that it had reached 100,000 LEED-certified projects (Holmes 2022). Although it still had its critics, the program became a catalyst for research and development in new construction materials, solar energy technologies, air quality monitoring devices, smart window glass, and advanced lighting control systems. As such, it pushed a very large industry in a more environmentally oriented direction than it otherwise might have been inclined to go. The GBC could not solve the problem of greenhouse gas emissions and climate change on its own, but it created a helpful tool among the many other tools that the environmental movement could use to shape consumer preferences, influence the revision of building codes, and direct the public conversation about energy conservation.

Jeffrey B. Webb

See also: Climate Change; Geothermal Energy; Home Energy Efficiency; Johnson, Warren Seymour; Natural Resources Defense Council; Powers, William Penn; Sierra Club; Solar Power

FURTHER READING

Barth, Brian. 2018. "Is LEED Tough Enough for the Climate-Change Era?" City Lab: Environment. Bloomberg. https://www.bloomberg.com/news/articles/2018-06-05/reconsidering-leed-buildings-in-the-era-of-climate-change (accessed October 2023).

Hansen, James. 1988. "Statement of Dr. James Hansen, Director, NASA Goddard Institute for Space Studies." *Hearing before the Committee on Energy and Natural Resources, United States Senate, One Hundredth Congress, First Session on the Greenhouse Effect and Global Climate Change, June 23, 1988*. Part 2. Pp. 39–80. Washington, DC: US Government Printing Office.

Holmes, Selina. 2022. "LEED Hits 100,000 Certified Projects." U.S. Green Building Council. October 10. https://www.usgbc.org/articles/leed-hits-100000-certified-projects (accessed October 2023).

International Living Future Institute (ILFI). 2022. "Living Building Challenge." https://living-future.org/lbc/ (accessed October 2023).

Stanley, Sarah. 2020. "On Earth Day, a Look Back at the First LEED Platinum Building." U.S. Green Building Council. April 22. https://www.usgbc.org/articles/earth-day-look-back-first-leed-platinum-building (accessed October 2023).

U.S. Green Building Council (GBC). 2016. "2017–2019 Strategic Plan." https://www.usgbc.org/about/mission-vision (accessed October 2023).

Usibelli, Emil

The life and career of Emil Usibelli (1893–1964) offers a perspective on a number of important developments in energy history, but also other aspects of the broader history of the United States. Usibelli's family emigrated from Italy to the United States between 1880 and 1920, which is an important era in the history of immigration in America. The family settled in the Pacific Northwest, where Emil worked as a logger and coal miner, and eventually he moved to Alaska to pursue opportunities in the coal mining industry. His mine, Usibelli Coal Mine, Inc. (UCM), played a small role in the larger twentieth-century development of energy resources in Alaska. The company's primary method, surface mining, produced coal in sufficient quantities to achieve profitability, but raised concerns about its environmental impacts. Surface mining's advantages are lower costs of production and safter working conditions for miners, but it can contaminate local streams and underground aquifers. UCM's management passed from Usibelli to his son, and then to his grandson, and entered the twenty-first century as a successful and respected company, though not completely free of controversy due to the nature of the industry.

Usibelli's birthplace, La Val in Alta Baldia, is located in the Dolomites in far northeastern Italy. He migrated to the United States in 1907 at the age of fourteen with his mother and siblings, joining his father in Washington state who had settled there two years earlier. Usibelli went to work in local coal mines and in a Canadian silver mine, and built railcars alongside his brother for the Pacific Car and Foundry in Seattle. He then bought into the Renton Fuel Company, a coal storage operation, which fared poorly due to the Great Depression (Green 2000). In 1935, Usibelli made his way to Alaska where he worked for several coal mining companies until a serious mining injury prompted him to take up logging. In 1943, the US Army Air Corps hired him to survey coal prospects near Suntrana on the Healey River at the northeast edge of present-day Denali National Park. Usbelli and a partner secured a lease and a one-year contract to supply 10,000 tons of coal to Ladd Field, an airbase used to service aircraft on their way to the Aleutian Islands for operations against the Japanese, or the Soviet Union under the Lend-Lease program.

Usibelli became known among the coal mine operators in the Nenana coalfield for utilizing surface mining techniques. He used a bulldozer to remove some of the overburden atop the coal seam, as well as hydraulic stripping, which applies pressurized water to move loose rock and gravel. He bought out his partner in 1948 and established UCM, which continued development on the Suntrana site. Eventually he cut a horizontal shaft called an "adit" and began traditional underground mining. Usibelli adopted the latest mining technologies and mechanized his operation, including use of a continuous miner and a mechanical loader. Still, Usibelli's preference was for surface mining, which had proven to be the most cost-effective way of extracting mineral from his location. The Alaska Mining Hall of Fame tribute to Usibelli notes that "by the late 1950s, coal from UCM's surface operations exceeded coal output from all of the company's underground competitors" (Green 2000).

UCM experienced all the customary troubles that mining operations suffered throughout the history of the industry, including tension between management and labor, accidents resulting in horrific injuries and fatalities, and by-products from coal mining that create noxious environmental hazards. In his official report for 1952, Alaska Commissioner of Mines Phil Holdsworth noted that "the Usibelli Coal Mine, Inc. continued its strip mining on a large scale and was the largest single producer in the Territory, capable of 1,600 tons a day" (Holdsworth 1953, 30). He went on to describe how workplace relations had soured at the mine: "This operation was plagued with labor difficulties and an extended shutdown due to picketing in May, and early June of 1952 was marked by mob violence and destruction of company property" (Holdsworth 1953, 30). This was part of a national trend, as a 1952 report from the US Bureau of Labor Statistics outlined regarding work stoppages. The report's lede made this observation: "More man-days of idleness (59,100,000) resulted directly from work stoppages in 1952 than in any year except 1946, when 116,000,000 man-days were reported. The total of 3,540,000 workers involved in work stoppages beginning in the year was the third highest on record, exceeded only in 1919 and 1946" (USBLS 1953, 1).

Much of that involved manufacturing, particularly work stoppages in steel mills, but coal miners were well-represented. In October, 270,000 bituminous coal miners went on strike throughout the country, some involving violence like the UCM mine incident. These tensions between Usibelli and his employees were part and parcel of coal mining's history, as were accidents and fatalities. In 1954, Holdsworth reported that a UCM bulldozer operator named Ernest C. Rivers was killed while "bulldozing loose material away from underneath a highwall of overburden 40 feet high" (Holdsworth 1955, 71). He continued by noting that an overhanging piece of sandstone weighing 4 tons broke away and crushed Rivers in his bulldozer. Tragically, this was the second such incident within the span of a few months, with the other worker injured badly by falling rock. Holdsworth was blunt in his assessment of UCM's lax safety protocols: "The unsafe practices of working under a highwall with overhanging material and operating a tractor without an adequate overhead canopy for protection, were the causes of this accident" (Holdsworth 1955, 71). Lamentably, another UCM miner died in 1961, this time in an underground mine collapse, which brought the company to shift entirely to surface mining (Mitchell 2020, 11).

Although considered safer than working in underground mines, surface mining contained its own health and safety risks. In terms of UCM's early environmental record, not much is known, or at least documented. In 1957, UCM was involved in litigation over dumping overburden into the Healey River. A rival operator, the Suntrana Mining Company, filed suit in 1957 asking $30,000 in damages and requesting a restraining order against UCM and another company because their actions flooded the river and made the Suntrana mine vulnerable to inundation. Suntrana received a favorable ruling from the court and Usibelli was forced to desist from its dumping practices (Mitchell 2020, 11). But that issue was connected to Suntrana's sense of having been wronged, rather than concerns about damage to the environment. Surface mining creates mounds of loose dirt and rock that erode into local watercourses, which produces excess siltation. Furthermore, exposed rock in the surface mine is subject to weathering and leaching. Metals like chromium, nickel, copper, zinc, and cadmium can leach into nearby streams and underground aquifers, contaminating drinking water and habitat for aquatic life (EPA 2022). The enactment of the Clean Water Act of 1972 was partly the result of these environmental concerns about mining and water quality.

Deforestation also came to be understood as a serious environmental problem. It contributes to loss of wildlife habitat, and the environmental movement of the 1960s raised alarm about the number of species extinctions that had occurred as a result of overharvesting timber. Surface mining can disrupt routes that some terrestrial animal species require for reproduction. Under criticism for its strip mining practices, UCM began a program in 1972 that experimented with grasses and fertilizers to determine which combination might work best for rehabilitating derelict mining lands. In 1973, the company reseeded 1,600 acres by low-flying aircraft, and a federal report noted that "the reclamation project was evaluated by the State of Alaska" and "adjudged successful" (ERDA 1976, 34). When Usibelli died at an accident at his own mine in 1964, control of the company passed to his son Joseph Usibelli, and then in 1987 his grandson Joseph Usibelli, Jr. assumed leadership of UCM. The management philosophy of the company developed with successive generations of Usibellis, a kind of evolution that corresponded with increased concerns about the health and safety of miners and the environmental hazards of mining practices. Joseph Usibelli, the founder's son, "initiated the modernization of the mine's equipment, introduced new mining techniques, and implemented a successful land reclamation program" (Horton 2022).

This modern equipment includes the Bucyrus Erie 1300W walking dragline, nicknamed "Ace in the Hole." The disassembled machine, acquired in 1977, required twenty-six railcars and forty trucks to transport it to Alaska, and then eleven months to reassemble. Ace in the Hole boasts a 225-foot mast and a 325-foot boom, with dragline buckets that move up to 42 cubic feet of overburden (Buchsbaum 2009). Giant Orenstein & Koppel hydraulic excavators with backhoes and front shovels move the coal to specialized Caterpillar mining trucks for hauling to the crusher, and then on to the tipple for loading onto railcars. Currently UCM produces 1–1.5 million tons of coal per year and supplies six power plants in Alaska as the state's only provider of coal. The company also ships coal overseas to South Korea, Japan, and Chile. Its coal became a sought-after fuel in the early 2000s because of its low sulfur content, a feature highlighted by advocates of the emergent "clean coal" program for reducing pollutants from power plants.

In 2022, company president Joseph Usibelli, Jr. was named University of Alaska Fairbanks College of Business and Security Management's 2022 Business Leader of the Year, specifically for the company's "solid record for environmental stewardship" and "more than 1,000 consecutive days of operations without a single employee injury resulting in lost work time" (King 2022). The award seemed to signify that under his leadership, the company became more attuned to Americans' concerns about coal mining, namely its risks to mine workers and to the environment as well. Yet, in 2011, the EPA fined UCM $60,000 for "unpermitted discharges" between 2007 and 2010 into the Nenana River and Hoseanna, Sanderson, and Francis Creeks (EPA 2011). It seems the company "discharged storm water or mine drainage into surface waters when berms of settling ponds or other containment structures were overwhelmed or breached during intense storm events in the Healy area" (McKee 2011).

Fred Wallis, company vice president, argued that the discharges were just dirty rainwater, that the breaches were not intentional, and the company had turned itself in for allowing the unpermitted discharges. Kirby Spangler, vice president of the environmental organization Castle Mountain Coalition, said "'this is just another outrageous example of Usibelli Coal Company's disrespect for the environment and the community. Despite the myths that Usibelli is somehow different, the record shows that they behave just like any other coal company'" (McKee 2011). This illustrates the confounding situation of the coal mining industry as consumers demand more and more electricity, but wish to have it at near-zero risk to coal miners' well-being, and to the health of our natural surroundings.

Jeffrey B. Webb

See also: Clean Coal; Coal; Cumberland Iron and Coal Company; Martin County Coal Slurry Spill; North Antelope Rochelle Mine; Sinclair, Upton; Surface Mining; Surface Mining Control and Reclamation Act of 1977

FURTHER READING

Buchsbaum, Lee. 2009. "Alaska's Usibelli Coal: Three Generations and Counting." *Coal Age*. November 12. https://www.coalage.com/features/alaskas-usibelli-coal-three-generations-and-counting/ (accessed October 2023).

Energy Research and Development Administration (ERDA). 1976. "Fossil Energy Update." Office of Public Affairs. Technical Information Center. June. https://www.google.com/books/edition/Fossil_Energy_Update/AMLIIl2ApFEC?hl=en&gbpv=1 (accessed October 2023).

Green, Charles B., and Becki Phipps. 2000. "Emil Usibelli (1893–1964)." Alaska Mining Hall of Fame Foundation. https://alaskamininghalloffame.org/inductees/usibelli.php (accessed October 2023).

Holdsworth, Phil R. 1953. "Report of the Commissioner of Mines for the Biennium Ended December 31, 1952." Territory of Alaska. Department of Mines.

Holdsworth, Phil R. 1955. "Report of the Commissioner of Mines for the Biennium Ended December 31, 1954." Territory of Alaska. Department of Mines.

Horton, Jameka Lache. 2022. "Joseph Usibelli Sr., Chairman of the Board of Directors of Usibelli Coal Mine, Dies at Age 83." Gray Media Group, Inc. May 15. https://www.webcenterfairbanks.com/2022/05/15/joseph-usibelli-sr-chairman-board-directors-usibelli-coal-mine-dead-83/ (accessed October 2023).

King, Gabriel. 2022. "UAF Honors Usibelli as Business Leader of the Year." *Alaska Business*. December 1. https://www.akbizmag.com/industry/education/uaf-honors-usibelli-as-business-leader-of-the-year/ (accessed November 2023).

McKee, K.T. 2011. "EPA Fines Usibelli $60K." *Mat-Su Valley Frontiersman*. January 25. https://www.frontiersman.com/news/epa-fines-usibelli-60k/article_6cefe4ef-c2df-55c2-9c76-46e7529268f5.html (accessed October 2023).

Mitchell, Beverly Hall. 2020. "Healy History." DiscoverDenali.org. https://discoverdenali.org/wp-content/uploads/2020/10/Healy-History.pdf (accessed October 2023).

US Bureau of Labor Statistics (USBLS). "Analysis of Work Stoppages in 1952." 1953. US Department of Labor. Bulletin #1136. https://www.bls.gov/wsp/publications/annual-summaries/pdf/work-stoppages-1952.pdf (accessed October 2023).

US Environmental Protection Agency (EPA). 2011. "Usibelli Coal Mine, near Healy, Alaska, Agrees to Pay $60,000 EPA Penalty for Clean Water Act Violations." January 20. https://www.epa.gov/archive/epapages/newsroom_archive/newsreleases/e8887310a95a422b8525781e006943c9.html (accessed October 2023).

US Environmental Protection Agency (EPA). 2022. "Abandoned Mine Drainage." December 22. https://www.epa.gov/nps/abandoned-mine-drainage (accessed October 2023).

Vulcan Street Plant

The Vulcan Street Plant in Appleton, Wisconsin, was the first waterpower facility to generate electricity using the Edison system. It went into service in 1882, riding two important trajectories of energy history in the United States: electrification and the development of turbines for efficiently deriving mechanical power from flowing water.

Rural mills in the United States had operated on waterpower since the colonial period using overshot or undershot waterwheels. The introduction of turbines in the first half of the nineteenth century greatly improved the efficiency with which mills could extract energy from flowing and falling water. The scientific analysis of efficient turbine design made great strides in the 1840s through the work of James Francis, who worked for the Proprietors of Locks and Canals at the textile-milling center of Lowell, Massachusetts. Over the next few decades, other innovators also developed improved designs to compete for efficiency with the Francis turbine. America's growing industries used such turbines to provide mechanical power for milling flour, sawing lumber, making paper, driving machine shops, and numerous other applications. One such enterprise that was using turbines to drive its machinery in 1880 was the Appleton Paper and Pulp Company.

At about the same time, innovators were introducing new electrical technologies to the American economy. Samuel Morse introduced his telegraph in 1844, Alexander Graham Bell received a US patent for his electric telephone in 1876, and in 1877, Charles Brush received a US patent for his dynamo for converting mechanical power to electrical energy. His dynamo was driven by coal-fired steam. Brush's intent was to design a generator for electric current to supply arc lights that was simpler and easier to maintain than European models that were available. He went on to develop an arc lighting system that by 1881 had been installed for public lighting in numerous US municipalities. Arc lamps could produce a very bright light—too bright for some applications—by means of an electric arc that jumped between two carbon electrodes.

At the same time, Thomas Edison was working on improving the incandescent light bulb. His success with the incandescent bulb was accompanied by a complete lighting system that he introduced in New York City in 1882. The system is best known for the lights bulbs that illuminated streets and interiors of businesses in the Pearl Street neighborhood, but it also featured dynamos, a network for distributing electric current, and the accessories needed to supply customers and charge them for the electricity they used. The dynamos in Edison's Pearl Street generating station were also driven by coal-fired steam. In the years prior to activating his Pearl Street Power Station, Edison also created the Edison Electric Light Company to own his various patents and to sell franchises for his lighting systems that others might want to install elsewhere.

The Edison organization incorporated the Western Edison Electric Light Company in 1882 with rights to develop Edison systems in Illinois, Wisconsin, and Iowa. Some

Appleton businessmen, led by Henry J. Rogers of Appleton Paper and Pulp, invited a Western Edison engineer to their city to explain the system. A month later, the Appleton promoters ordered two Edison dynamos and had one of them installed in the water-powered Vulcan paper mill. By September 1882, the Edison system was supplying current to incandescent lights in the mill as well as in Rogers' nearby mansion. There was one problem, however; the turbine that drove the dynamo also powered the equipment in the mill. Fluctuations in the load the equipment placed on the turbine caused its speed to vary, which in turn caused brightness of the lights to change. The owners of the mill therefore decided to build a small shack nearby to house the second dynamo so that it could be powered by its own turbine, which drew water from a power canal and then discharged into a tailrace on the Fox River. The head for the turbine was only 10 feet. By the next year, 1883, the Vulcan Street Plant was supplying electricity to lights in a hotel, at least four residences, a blast furnace, and about six paper mills. This made the Vulcan Street Plant the first Edison-system central station to be driven by waterpower in the United States.

The Vulcan Street Plant was not, however, the first hydroelectric lighting plant in the nation. That distinction belongs to a plant in Grand Rapids, Michigan, which went into service in 1880, supplying electricity to a Brush system that lighted a hotel, a factory, and several retail establishments.

The Vulcan Street Plant and the Vulcan mill were destroyed by fire in 1891. The Wisconsin Michigan Power Company, a successor to the enterprise that built the Vulcan Street Plant, built a replica of the plant on Appleton's South Oneida Street in 1932. The replica was relocated to a site near the original location of the Vulcan Street Plant in 1987. In 1977, the American Society of Mechanical Engineers, the American Society of Civil Engineers, and the Institute of Electrical and Electronics Engineers designated the Vulcan Street Plant a National Engineering Landmark.

The first dynamo installed at Appleton had produced electricity in what was essentially an isolated plant, a generating station that supplied electric current to its owner. The Vulcan Street Plant was a central station, a generating station that supplied electricity to a variety of customers who paid the operator of the plant for the current they used. Over the next couple decades, as electrification spread throughout the United States, debate raged in the industry as to whether isolated plants or central stations would provide the most economical service. Eventually, central stations, owned by large private and public utilities, and much larger than the Vulcan Street Plant, came to be the nation's dominant model. Meanwhile, hydroelectric generating stations, again much larger than the Vulcan Street Plant, grew to be important sources of electricity for both light and power, especially in the mountain regions of the American West and in the southeastern United States, where rivers were conducive to reliable hydroelectric generation.

Fredric L. Quivik

See also: Austin Dam; Brush, Charles Francis; California Electric Light Company; Davenport, Thomas; Edison, Thomas Alva; Electricity; Federal Water Power Act of 1920; Henry, Joseph; Hoover Dam; Hydroelectric Power; Lowell Waterpower System; Morse, Samuel; Pearl Street Power Station; Slater, Samuel

FURTHER READING

Allerhand, Adam. 2020. "Hydroelectric Power: The First 30 Years." *IEEE Power & Energy Magazine*. September/October. Pp. 76–87.

ASCE, ASME, and IEEE. 1977. "Vulcan Street Plant." National Historic Landmark Dedication Booklet. September 15.

Hughes, Thomas P. 1983. *Networks of Power: Electrification in Western Society*. Baltimore, MD: Johns Hopkins University Press

Kellogg, Louise P. 1922. "The Electric Light System at Appleton." *The Wisconsin Magazine of History*. Vol. 6. December. Pp. 189–94.

War of the Currents

In the 1880s and 1890s, two teams of inventors and entrepreneurs contended for dominance in building the US system of electricity generation and transmission. Thomas Edison, the "Wizard of Menlo Park" and head of Edison Illuminating Company, led his team against George Westinghouse, head of Westinghouse Electric and Manufacturing Company. Through a series of mergers and patent acquisitions, the two teams advanced rival systems for delivering electricity from centralized generating stations through transmission wires out to a network of customers. Edison's direct current (DC) system and Westinghouse's alternating current (AC) system each offered to put electricity to work for millions of Americans in innumerable ways. In the end, the alternating current system gained the advantage, but the company Edison founded, General Electric Company, became one of the nation's most successful and important energy technology corporations. In recent years, DC power enjoyed a resurgence in technologies like computers, electric vehicles, LEDs, and solar cells.

By the time of Edison and Westinghouse, the basic properties of electricity and the means of controlling electrical current had been worked out by a number of scientists and tinkerers. For example, Italian Alessandro Volta invented a battery that could store and release an electrical charge, and Englishman Michael Faraday invented early versions of electrical motors and dynamos. Using an improved dynamo created by Belgian Zénobe Gramme, Russian Pavel Yablochkov illuminated the streets of Paris in 1878 at the Exposition Universelle with sixty-four electric arc lights. It is important to note that the Yablochkov system utilized alternating current, which operates at a high voltage level and powers the arc lights at a high level of heat and intensity. Thus, the arc light system using AC—without transformers stepping down the voltage—could work only for street lighting or illuminating very large indoor spaces like factories or railway stations. Nevertheless, the Yablochkov system became a worldwide sensation and set off the movement to create electricity-powered illumination systems in the United States.

Many American communities had built lighting systems using natural gas piped from centralized locations into homes, workplaces, and institutional buildings. The new electric lighting system offered new possibilities, and electricity innovators like Charles Brush began installing experimental arc lighting systems, starting in Cleveland in 1879 and Wabash, Indiana the following year. A successful demonstration on Broadway in New York led Brush and some investors to form the Brush Electric Company in 1880 and the installation of street lighting systems in Boston, Philadelphia, Montreal, San Francisco, Buffalo, and others. Meantime, Thomas Edison had been working in the same vein but using slightly different technologies.

He pioneered a new type of incandescent light bulb, powered by electricity, that was safer and longer lasting than its predecessors. Edison utilized DC power in his experiments, which ran at a lower voltage than AC current in order to avoid overheating the delicate carbon fibers he'd been using in his experiments. Edison aimed to illuminate interior spaces, and so his incandescent carbon-filament lamps burned at a lower level of intensity and heat value. Edison installed his system at his laboratory in Menlo Park in 1879, then two years later, on lower Manhattan's Pearl Street. Finally in 1884, he formed Consolidated Edison Company to install his electrical illuminating system in other cities and towns.

Edison's path would collide with George Westinghouse in the coming years. Westinghouse had entered the electricity business in 1882 with his Union Switch and Signal Company, which used the rails of a railroad track to conduct electricity for controlling signals and switches. He observed the operations of Consolidated Edison and took an interest in forming his own illuminating company. He hired two talented individuals, mechanical engineer H.M. Byllesby and electrician William Stanley, Jr. to develop the technology, formed Westinghouse Electric Company, and began installing DC systems similar to Edison's. In 1885, Westinghouse learned about electrification in Europe involving AC current. This type of current is different in that DC current flows only in one direction, while AC current alternates between forward and reverse directions, sixty times per second in North America. If it could be made to work, a system of electricity generation and transmission using AC could potentially have a much farther reach because it operates at a higher voltage than DC power. But this current would have to be stepped up and then stepped down with AC transformers in order to deliver electricity safely into homes connected to the grid. Westinghouse bought the US rights to a primitive AC transformer invented by Lucien Gaulard and John Dixon Gibbs, and William Stanley produced a modified version that would serve Westinghouse's purposes. In 1886, Stanly successfully illuminated Great Barrington, Massachusetts with an AC electricity generation and transmission system.

Westinghouse acquired engineer Nikola Tesla's patents for several AC components that rendered AC even more efficient, and for a time employed Tesla at his company. This led to stunning commercial success. By 1887, Westinghouse already had half as many electricity-generating stations as Edison's company, but by 1891, those numbers were 323 for Westinghouse, and 202 for Edison. It should be noted that in that year, Thomson-Houston Electric Company (founded 1882) led the way with 666 generating stations (including numerous DC arc light systems), and Brush Electric Company registered 199 stations ("Electric" 1891, 110). The late 1880s featured intense competition among these companies and others, like United States Illuminating Company and Waterhouse Electric Light Company, to secure contracts to illuminate American cities, which energy historians typically consider the start of the War of the Currents.

A good starting point in understanding the war is the publication in 1888 of *A Warning from the Edison Electric Light Company*, by President Edward H. Johnson. The eighty-three-page pamphlet cautioned against adopting Westinghouse's system because of myriad lawsuits accusing the company of patent infringement. If Westinghouse lost those suits, the company's equipment would be rendered illegal. It also accused Westinghouse executives and salesmen of "absurd and unsupported claims" about cost and performance. Finally, it highlighted tragic accidents using Westinghouse's alternating current system. The pamphlet said: "Since the destructive effect, either upon life or property, is enormously enhanced even by the interruption of an ordinary current traversing it, it follows that the complete *reversal* of the current causes it to assume the form of a real danger" (Johnson 1888, 21). Quoting a letter to Johnson from William T.M. Mottram of New Orleans, the text said plainly that the Westinghouse "alternating current has killed two men," lit a house on fire, and went down repeatedly, causing power outages (Johnson 1888, 53–4). Johnson made a point to include

FIGURE 11: The War of the Currents unleashed campaigns by advocates of direct current and alternating current, each trying to discredit the other. This cartoon from 1888 depicts alternating current as "An Unrestrained Demon" electrocuting pedestrians, playing on public fears about electricity's potential dangers.

an anecdote about a horse on Staten Island that was electrocuted by a telephone wire that had broken and crossed with an AC electric light wire.

Edison's animus toward the AC system and Westinghouse's use of it is well-documented. He seems to have been behind the 1888 campaign of engineer Harold Pitney Brown to discredit the system by lobbying the New York Board of Electrical Control to place severe limits on AC installations in the city. Brown also staged a public demonstration in which he shocked a stray dog with 1,000 volts of DC current, which the dog survived, then shocked it with 330 volts of AC, which killed it. A few days later he killed three more dogs with 300 volts of AC to show that the DC current hadn't weakened the dog before killing it with AC in the first demonstration. At the time, the state of New York was exploring whether AC or DC current should be used in the first-of-its-kind execution of death row inmate William Kemmler. Brown accepted an offer to consult with the committee assembled to recommend a system for the purpose. Brown set up experiments at Edison Electric Light's West Orange laboratory, where he shocked four calves and a horse to death with AC current. The committee approved the AC method, and newspapers covering the execution in 1890 associated electrocution—death by AC current—with Westinghouse.

Eventually, Edison himself voiced his concerns in a late 1889 *North American Review* essay titled, "The Dangers of Electric Lighting." He said, rather bluntly, "'My personal desire would be to prohibit entirely the use of alternating currents. They are as unnecessary as they are dangerous'" ("Mr. Edison" 1889, 289). The anti-AC campaign of 1888–90 hovered in the background as the electric lighting companies bid for electrification contracts throughout the country. This intense competition brought the Edison Electric Company to merge with Thomson-Houston Electric Company in 1892, which had bought out the Brush Electric Company three years earlier. The combination was orchestrated by financier J.P. Morgan and took the name General Electric Company. Edison was left with a minority stake in the company and receded from leadership. Also in 1892, a bidding competition held to provide electrical illumination for the Chicago World's Columbian Exhibition pitted General Electric against Westinghouse and other companies. Westinghouse won the bid and gained a massive publicity advantage, as 100,000 electric lights illuminated the fair using Tesla's "polyphase system of alternating current power generation and transmission," enchanting the 27 million visitors who toured the exhibition (Jonnes 2004, 296).

The next, and last, true battle in the War of Currents occurred in the planning and construction of the Niagara Falls power tunnel. Two companies formed to build a tunnel and hydroelectric power stations at Niagara Falls, the Niagara Falls Power Company and the Cataract Construction Corporation, with significant investments from Gilded Age financial titans John Astor, J.P. Morgan, and William Vanderbilt. An initial round of competitive bidding to build the generation and transmission system produced no feasible plan, which included bids from both General Electric and Westinghouse. Having visited the Chicago World's Columbian Exposition and seen Nikola Tesla's "universal AC power system, with its AC generator, transformers, transmission lines, working induction motors, synchronous motor, and Westinghouse-invented rotary converter that supplied direct current for the railway motor," the Niagara investors and company officials agreed to hire Westinghouse to build the system at Powerhouse #1, known as the Adams Hydroelectric Generating Plant (Jonnes 2004, 296). General Electric, by this time shed of its anti-AC hostility due to Edison's departure from company leadership, received contracts to build the transformers and transmission lines.

With AC current featured at Niagara when it opened in 1895, the War of the Currents largely ended. The Institute of Electrical and Electronics Engineers designated the Adams plant a "milestone" technology in the history of electricity. Since "it was the first time that power was distributed to an entire region over a long-distance network of high voltage transmission lines," the hydroelectric plant and its system of transmission lines became "the birthplace of a new electric utility industry" (IEEE 1990). The importance of the war consists in its clarification of the electricity standard for the US electricity grid, although power plants producing DC current continued to operate through the twentieth and twenty-first centuries.

Simply put, AC came to dominate because its higher voltage enabled longer transmissions via transformers, enabling power companies to reach more customers. DC continues to be the mode used for many new technologies, particular solar panels, personal computers, and batteries for electric vehicles because internal circuits of these systems can only work with power moving in a single direction.

The War of the Currents is one of the more important narratives in the history of energy in the United States. It is the focus of books like *The Age of Edison: Electric Light and the Invention of Modern America* (2014), *Tesla vs Edison: The Life-Long Feud that Electrified the World* (2016), and *The Electric War: Edison, Tesla, Westinghouse, and the Race to Light the World* (2019). It also served as the subject of an historical film, *The Current War* (2017), starring Benedict Cumberbatch as Edison and Nicholas Hoult as Tesla and directed by Alfonso Gomez-Rejon. The film kept the narrative alive in American culture and testified to its enduring relevance. Since the electricity grid connects to most of the people living in the United States, it is one of the few products of human ingenuity that is nearly universal in scope.

Jeffrey B. Webb

See also: Brush, Charles Francis; California Electric Light Company; Chicago World's Columbian Exposition; Consolidated Edison Company; Edison, Thomas Alva; Electricity; Franklin, Benjamin; General Electric Company; Henry, Joseph; Insull, Samuel; Pearl Street Power Station; Smart Grid; Stanley, William Jr.; Westinghouse, George

FURTHER READING

Baldwin, Neil. 1995. *Edison: Inventing the Century*. Westport. CT: Hyperion.

Davis, L.J. 1998. *Fleet Fire: Thomas Edison and the Pioneers of the Electric Revolution*. New York: Doubleday.

"Electric Light and Electric Railway Statistics." 1891. *The Electrical World*. Vol 17. No. 7. February 14.

Institute of Electrical and Electronics Engineers (IEEE). 1990. "Adams Hydroelectric Generating Plant, 1895." IEEE Milestones Program. https://ethw.org/Milestones:Adams_Hydroelectric_Generating_Plant,_1895 (accessed October 2023).

Johnson, Edward H. 1888. *A Warning from the Edison Electric Light Company*. The Edison Electric Light Company, N.p.

Jonnes, Jill. 2004. *Empires of Light: Edison, Tesla, Westinghouse, and the Race to Electrify the World*. New York: Random House.

"Mr. Edison on Low Currents." 1889. *The Electrical World*. Vol. 14. No. 18. November 2. PO. 289.

Waste to Energy

Since the time humans burned buffalo chips to make fire, waste has been used to create energy. Beginning in the 1970s, municipal sanitation departments in the United States incinerated trash to create energy, using the heat created by incineration to fire steam plants that power generators to produce electricity. Five were built in 1970–80, and then fifty more from 1981 to 1990. New construction fell off after 1990 amid concerns about emissions of mercury and dioxins from the plants, and their locations near poor and disadvantaged communities (Baptista 2019). The United States produces a modest amount of its overall energy from burning trash, and much less than other modern, industrialized nations. Another method of producing energy from waste is by capturing and treating methane that seeps from animal manure and other biomass material, including wood pulp, agricultural residue, and municipal green wastes. Since 2000, the US government has encouraged the development of waste to energy programs—particularly biomass—in legislation like the Biomass Research and Development Act of 2000, the Energy Policy Act of 2005, and the Energy Independence and Security Act of 2007.

According to the US Environmental Protection Agency (EPA), Americans generated an estimated 292.4 million tons of municipal solid waste in 2018, the most recent year for which figures are available. At the time, this was calculated to be 4.9 pounds of trash per person, per day. About half of this garbage ended up in landfills, and of the remainder, the EPA calculated that 69 million tons were recycled, 25 million were composed, 17.7 million constituted food waste "managed by other methods," and 35 million "were combusted with energy recovery" (EPA 2022). The last figure is noteworthy: all told, Americans converted 11.8 percent of their 2018 trash into energy through combustion in the seventy-five plants still in operation. The energy produced through combustion in municipal incinerators makes up a very small fraction (0.1 percent) of the total amount of energy created in the United States by all methods. A recent report on municipal incineration noted that its current lowly state is the result of "a volatile revenue model, aging plants, high operation and maintenance costs, and growing public interest in reducing waste, promoting environmental justice and combating climate change" (Baptista 2019).

This contrasts with the experience in other nations with a stronger commitment to using waste to energy to supply energy needs. For example, Sweden operates thirty-five waste-to-energy plants for its 10.4 million people, which produce 10 percent of the nation's energy (Yee 2018). Strict laws enacted in the mid-2000s banned organic and combustible refuse in landfills, producing a social transformation in the way people dispense with the trash in their homes and apartments. Journalist Amy Yee found data from the Swedish waste management association Avfall Sverige which showed that from 1975 to 2016, the average amount of trash sent to landfills declined from 430 to 6.6 pounds per person, and that trash sent to recycling rose from 40 to 357 pounds per person. Avfall Sverige estimated that the trash incineration program yields enough energy to meet the "heating demand of 1.25 million apartments and electricity for 680,000 homes" (Yee 2018). This output derived from the Swedish government's change in waste management and waste-to-energy policy, but also reflects long-term planning that designed centralized steam heating systems for urban areas that in most cases are heated in the winter by steam produced from incinerating trash. Recently, Avfall Sverige reported that less than 1 percent of Sweden's trash goes to landfills.

Japan offers another example of a successful waste to energy system. According to the Japanese Ministry of the Environment, only 1.1 percent of the entire volume of waste generated in Japan in 2015 was sent to landfills (Dobrowolski 2021). This is the result of policy and planning since the 1960s, given Japan's relative lack of available space for landfills. As of 2022, some 380 incineration plants in Japan, out of a 1,000 total, have the capacity to generate electricity from the combustion of waste. The Japanese government, and many observers of Japanese culture, cite the idea of *mottainai* as an important contributor to the success of the Japanese waste-to-energy system. The term means "a sense of regret towards creating waste," which is traceable to Shinto beliefs that encourage an appreciation for nature and a respect for the resources that are provided by the natural environment (Jaramillo 2020). The results obtained in Japan from recycling solid waste and generating usable electricity have made it a global leader. In 2021, the Japanese company JFE Engineering Corporation announced the construction of a plant in Vietnam that will "incinerate 500 tons of municipal solid waste and industrial solid waste per day, with a power output of 11.6 MW and an expected annual power generation of 91,872 MWh" after its 2024 completion (JFE 2021).

The relative strength of the waste-to-energy programs in Sweden and Japan compared to the United States is the result of deliberate policies devised in response to these nations' industrial, geographical, and environmental conditions. As in the case of Japan, cultural affinities can also reinforce a vigorous policy of energy recovery mandated by the government, administered by municipalities, and carried out by private corporations. In the United States the relative abundance of land for landfills, relatively cheap energy, and a different kind of culture, a culture of consumerism, create obstacles for a more effective waste-to-energy program. According to Giles Slade in his book, *Made to Break: Technology and Obsolescence in America* (2007), "not only did we invent disposable products, ranging from diapers to cameras to contact lenses, but we invented the very concept of disposability itself, as a necessary precursor to our rejection of tradition and promotion of progress and change" (Slade 2007, 4). The American idea of "disposability" lies in tension with Japanese notions of *mottainai*, which results in different results between the two nations in focused, sustained efforts to convert waste to energy.

Besides combustion of municipal solid waste, energy can be produced through animal wastes or drawn from existing landfills. Manure from domestic livestock like cows and pigs produces usable methane gas, though it must be captured by an anerobic digester. This is an airtight container in which manure is dumped and subjected to bacterial action. Micro-organisms break down the organic material in the manure and create methane. From this point, the methane can be piped away and burned just like coal or natural gas to heat water, generate steam, drive rotors inside turbines, and finally power the generators that produce electricity. It is possible to do the same with pipes inserted into landfills. In 1994, the EPA created the Landfill Methane Outreach Program in order to encourage landfill operators to add methane capture to their operations. One of these, the Rumpke Sanitary Landfill in Colerain Township near Cincinnati, Ohio, operates the world's largest landfill gas-to-power pipeline. Montauk Renewables, an energy company, built the gas collection system at the landfill and operates the plants that convert the methane into usable natural gas. According to Rumpke officials, the landfill produces enough fuel to supply 30,000 homes with their natural gas needs (Rumpke 2022).

Through a system of low-interest loans and tax credits, the US government has incentivized waste-to-energy projects, including municipal solid waste incinerators that generate heat for electricity, and biomass facilities that capture natural gas for both heat and power. Additionally, scientists at the US Department of Energy's National Renewable Energy Laboratory conduct advanced research on pyrolysis, the process of decomposition of biomass to produce heat, which will aid the development of future biomass technologies. These federal supports for waste-to-energy help to maintain the current economic viability of these operations and provide direction to an industry that reduces landfill usage, provides a domestic source of sustainable energy, and offsets the need for energy from fossil sources which produce carbon dioxide emissions.

Jeffrey B. Webb

See also: Agriculture and Energy; Biofuels; Buffalo Chips; Energy Policy Act of 2005; Geothermal Power; Renewable Energy

FURTHER READING

Baptista, Ana. 2019. "Is Burning Trash a Good Way to Dispose of It? Waste Incineration in Charts." PBS NewsHour. June 23. https://www.pbs.org/newshour/science/is-burning-trash-a-good-way-to-dispose-of-it-waste-incineration-in-charts (accessed October 2023).

Dobrowolski, Piotr. 2021. "Waste to Energy: Lessons from Japan." Waste Management World. WEKA Industrie Medien GmbH. https://waste-management-world.com/waste-to-energy/waste-to-energy-lessons-from-japan/ (accessed October 2023).

Jaramillo, Jorge. 2020. "Is Japan's High Recycling Rate Enough?" *Earth Island Journal*. August 14. https://www.earthisland.org/journal/index.php/articles/entry/japans-high-recycling-rate-plastic/ (accessed October 2023).

JFE Engineering Corporation. 2021. "Participating in a Large-Scale Waste to Energy Project in Vietnam." December 16. https://www.jfe-eng.co.jp/en/news/2021/20211216.html (accessed October 2023).

Rumpke Waste & Recycling. 2022. "A Refreshed Outlook on Waste Management." *The Cincinnati Inquirer*. October 18.

Slade, Giles. 2007. *Made to Break: Technology and Obsolescence in America*. Cambridge, MA: Harvard University Press.

US Environmental Protection Agency (EPA). 2022. "National Overview: Facts and Figures on Materials, Wastes and Recycling." Facts and Figures about Materials, Waste and Recycling. https://www.epa.gov/facts-and-figures-about-materials-waste-and-recycling/national-overview-facts-and-figures-materials (accessed October 2023).

Yee, Amy. 2018. "In Sweden, Trash Heats Homes, Powers Buses and Fuels Taxi Fleets." *The New York Times*. September 21. https://www.nytimes.com/2018/09/21/climate/sweden-garbage-used-for-fuel.html (accessed October 2023).

Water Power

Water power is power extracted from the energy of rapidly moving water. America's European colonists brought a variety of technologies with them from the Old World, and were quick to take advantage of their new home's water resources. Mills were built to grind grain into flour for baking, for instance, to saw trees into planks, and to crush plants into fiber to be made into cloth. As settlers penetrated drier areas of the continent where irrigation was necessary for growing crops, they sometimes built water-raising wheels on the banks of streams and canals. In time, inventors learned to generate electricity from the power of moving water, and the nation entered a new era.

Settlers along the eastern seaboard of North America found far more streams and rivers than they were used to in the British Isles and the Low Countries, and so took advantage of the situation by setting up watermills alongside them. A mill was a nucleus for a community, and its presence drew people as well as other enterprises. As a result, colonists eventually built tens of thousands of the structures in their new home. Several locations are credited with being the site of the first watermill erected in the American colonies, including Bethlehem, Pennsylvania, on the bank of the Lehigh River, and Dorchester, Massachusetts, on the bank of the Neponset River.

Watermills took five principal forms. In the first type, the horizontal (or Norse, or tub) mill, a paddle wheel lay on its side at the edge of the stream, while in the second type, an undershot (or stream shot) mill, a vertical wheel was mounted above the stream. In overshot and backshot wheels, water-powered vertical wheels by striking their long, shallow troughs or "buckets" at the top and briefly filling them, deriving energy from both the speed of the water and its weight. In these two designs, the only important differences were the direction in which their buckets pointed and in which they moved.

A compromise between the undershot and overshot, the breast (or breastshot) wheel, was frequently employed. In this design, water struck the wheel's buckets at about the height of the axle, and although such wheels were less efficient than overshot and backshot varieties, they were capable of handling greater rates of flow and so generated a good deal of power. For this reason, they became the most common waterwheels in the country. In each case, a combination of shafts and joints connected to the wheel's axle conveyed the power.

A stream needed to drop at least 10 feet to propel an overshot wheel effectively, so if the terrain were not steep enough, a dam would be built to create a mill pond and a narrow channel, or mill race, dug to increase the flow and pressure. The bank of a deep, swiftly flowing river was an ideal location for an undershot wheel, while a narrow channel was a good location along which to site a horizontal waterwheel. This last design was the easiest and cheapest to build, although it was able to generate the least amount of power.

In cases where there was sufficient tidal range, settlers built tide mills in combination with small reservoirs alongside estuaries to take advantage of the periodic ebb and flow of water.

Such mills were constructed in suitable locations up and down the eastern seaboard. One of the last surviving tide mills in the United States was the Perkins Mill. Built in 1749 on the shore of a tidal channel of Maine's Kennebunk River, it remained in operation until 1939.

Watermills could be put to a wide range of essential uses, and farmers gladly traveled dozens of miles to have their raw materials processed by a mill. To grind enough wheat or corn by hand to feed a family required several hours of hard work every day, for instance, and the rough flour or meal that such primitive methods produced made poor bread. In contrast, a gristmill, as it was known, could grind multiple bushels per hour. In cases in which the grain would be fed to cattle, a chopping-mill ground the grain more roughly. Where apples were grown, cider mills crushed the fruit for beverages. Where cotton was grown, cotton mills designed to card and spin the mature plants' bolls sprang up. It is believed that the first such mills in the colonies were built in Beverly, Massachusetts, in 1789 and Pawtucket, Rhode Island, a year later. Cotton seeds themselves could then be pressed for cottonseed oil, as could flax seeds to produce linseed oil. The miller typically collected a quarter of the milled material as payment.

Besides having an abundance of streams, much of eastern North America was heavily wooded, and settlers built water-powered sawmills to saw timber for lumber, shingle mills to cut shingles, and bark mills to grind select bark and roots into a powder to be used in tanning hides. Within a short period of time, the colonists were able to begin exporting timber to Europe, much of which was less heavily wooded.

Watermills could also be instrumental in the manufacture of textiles, a process that involved several steps, including fulling, or cleaning and thickening the fibers that would make up the cloth. The first such mill in the English colonies appears to have been built in 1643 on Mill River in Rowley, Massachusetts, by John Pearson. In 1820, the mill complex and community of nearby Lowell grew into a major center for textile production, and the industry would soon become the most important in the United States.

BREAKTHROUGH

Lester Allan Pelton is said to have devised his turbine thanks to a simple accident. He was studying the operation of a waterwheel when a piece of the mechanism slipped. The result was that rather than bouncing back from the paddle or bucket, which wasted much of its energy, the water swirled to the side—a pattern that increased the speed of the rotating wheel.

Grove Koger

Because watermills played a central role in community life, enterprising publishers printed manuals explaining their components and outlining the duties of those working in them. One of the most popular was *The Young Mill-wright and Miller's Guide* by Oliver Evans and Thomas Ellicott. Published for the first time in 1795, it eventually ran through more than a dozen editions, with the last appearing in 1860.

Over the course of the colonial period and the first century of American independence, watermills provided much of the power the growing population needed in order to survive and prosper. They also contributed to the country's industrial revolution—its transition from an agricultural society to a manufacturing and commercial one. By the time the US census was taken in 1840, there were more than 55,000 mills—one for every 245 people.

In the latter decades of the nineteenth century, however, an important improvement to the waterwheel, the water turbine, gained ascendancy. There have been a number of differing turbine designs, but one of the best known, the Pelton Wheel, was introduced by American millwright and inventor Lester Allan Pelton (1829–1908) in the 1870s. The Pelton Wheel was mounted with pairs of spoon-shaped buckets, and the water was directed onto the vane dividing them, thus splitting it before deflecting it out and back. This simple design was particularly efficient in a fast-flowing stream or in conjunction with a nozzle, and doubled the efficiency of the more familiar waterwheels then in use. Other turbines were enclosed in a casing or could operate completely under water, making them safer from floating debris and from the ice that might form on the surface during winter.

Within a few decades of the introduction of turbines, however, an even greater innovation, hydroelectric power, began to replace older methods of generating power from water. It is believed that the first hydroelectric plants in the United States came online in 1882. The new technology continued to rely on turbines, however, and in 1887 an enterprising miner attached a dynamo to a Pelton Wheel to generate the first hydroelectricity in the Sierra Nevada Mountains—where Pelton himself had perfected his turbine. Subsequently, hydroelectric power became a key source of energy in the United States over the course of the twentieth century, and it remains so in the early decades of the twenty-first.

Grove Koger

See also: Agriculture and Energy; Austin Dam; Hydroelectric Power; Industrial Revolution; Lowell Waterpower System; Renewable Energy; Slater, Samuel

FURTHER READING

Hasse, Larry. 1984. "Watermills in the South: Rural Institutions Working against Modernization." *Agricultural History*. Symposium on the History of Rural Life in America. Vol. 58. No. 3. Pp. 280–95.

Howell, Charles. 1975. "Colonial Watermills in the Wooden Age." In *America's Wooden Age: Aspects of Its Early Technology*. Ed. Brooke Hindle. 120–59. Tarrytown, NY: Sleepy Hollow Restorations.

Hunter, Louis C. 1979. *A History of Industrial Power in the United States, 1780–1930*, Vol. 1: *Waterpower in the Century of the Steam Engine.* Charlottesville, VA: Published for the Eleutherian Mills-Hagley Foundation by the University Press of Virginia.

Laland, Patricia. 2001. "The Legacy of Water Mills." *Early American Life*. Vol. 32. No. 1. Pp. 38–44.

Malone, Patrick M. 2009. *Waterpower in Lowell: Engineering and Industry in Nineteenth-Century America*. Baltimore, MD: Johns Hopkins University Press.

Reynolds, Terry S. 1983. *Stronger than a Hundred Men: A History of the Vertical Water Wheel.* Baltimore, MD: Johns Hopkins University Press.

Weir, Paul

The coal industry changed considerably from the late nineteenth through the mid-twentieth century. Coal production expanded rapidly to supply the growing railroad and steel industries. Mining corporations became larger through mergers and acquisitions, and they grew in capitalization (Nelson 1959, 41). As mines deepened, they became more mechanized, utilizing pumping, ventilation, and conveyance systems. Always a very dangerous industry, terrible explosions and accidents around the turn of the twentieth century sparked conflict between management and labor, unionization, and federal intervention. These trends were reshaping the industry when Paul Weir (1894–1972) entered the field as a mining engineer, later to become an influential consultant on issues of mine development and operations, mining technology, and mine safety. His career reflects the growing professionalization of industrial management and the improvement of the coal industry's record on workers' health and safety.

In 1918, Paul Weir graduated with a B.S. in engineering from Pennsylvania State University and served in the US Army Engineers at the end of the First World War. He taught mining engineering at Case Institute of Technology in the vicinity of Cleveland, Ohio for a year and then took a position as chief engineer of Bell and Zoller Coal Company in Illinois. He was promoted to general superintendent in 1923, then to vice president in 1926, where he remained for the next ten years. Weir also served as vice president of Crescent Coal Company over that same period. In 1936, Weir left to start his own business, the Paul Weir Company, described at the time as a "Mining Engineering Service, specializing in the modernization and management of coal mining properties, offering engineering, production, and preparation service" ("News" 1935–6, 374). He and his staff engineers and geologists offered consulting to mining companies, utilities, railroads, financial institutions, and government agencies.

When Weir entered the field in 1918, coal mining had just suffered some of the worst tragedies in its history. Taking a long view, there were 61,187 fatalities in coal mining accidents in the United States from 1838 to 1914, according to a 1916 report from the US Bureau of Mines, which almost certainly understates the real number (Fay 1916, 7). But then, in 1907, the Monongah mine explosion in West Virginia killed 362 miners, the worst mining disaster in US history. Before the end of the year 3,242 lives were taken in mining disasters, including 239 at an explosion at Jacobs Creek, Pennsylvania and 154 at another blast at Marianna, Pennsylvania. In 1909, 259 miners died in an explosion at Cherry, Illinois. President Theodore Roosevelt had proposed the creation of a US Bureau of Mines in 1907 to study and develop blasting materials and techniques that could be used amid flammable mine gases and coal dust, and of course to prevent future incidents. After the Cherry disaster, Congress finally acted in 1910 with legislation authorizing the agency.

The new agency had its work cut out for it, as mining accidents continued apace: the Banner mine explosion in Alabama (1911) killed 128, the Price-Pancoast Colliery fire in

Pennsylvania (1911) killed 72, the Dawson, New Mexico explosion (1913) killed 263, and the Eccles, West Virginia mine explosion (1914) killed 180 miners, including five boys under the age of fourteen. Paul Weir entered the profession in 1920 when the industry was searching for solutions to the problems of mine safety. In 1921, Weir was listed as a member of the editorial advisory board of *The Coal Industry* magazine, demonstrating his early connections to industry leaders. He also appears in the historical record in a 1922 advertisement for mechanical conveyor belts by Stephenson-Adamson Manufacturing Company as the winner of a friendly coal-conveying race between two mines in Illinois. Weir ran the system at Bell and Zoller's Zeigler No. 1 and over twenty-seven days of the contest, the machine conveyed 164,109 tons of coal out of the mines. The combined output of both mines over that period filled 6,520 railcars, stretching 60 miles long. Weir helped the conveyor company with an endorsement: "The entire system has given excellent service and is ready for another race any time" (SA 1922, 12). In 1923, Weir was promoted from chief engineer to general superintendent of his company, and at that point he had responsibility for the safety of 2,500 employees producing 17,500 tons of coal per day (NMHFM 2020).

Weir became involved in the American Institute of Mining and Metallurgical Engineers, which held regular professional meetings and published a journal. This association brought him into regular contact with other mining engineers and mine owners, and articles in the journal maintained a steady beat of updates on mining operations throughout the country, particularly regarding mechanization and scientific management techniques. As a representative of the institute, he spoke at the 1936 annual meeting of the American Wood-Preservers Association about the uses of creosoted timber in mining. But in his comments he wanted to give his audience "a description of a really modern mine." He went on to say that

> today an ever increasing number of engineers are employed as superintendents and foreman. The larger companies have technical staffs of mining, electrical, mechanical, and civil engineers, as well as chemical engineers. The point I want to make is that there is more and more a tendency in coal mining to seek out facts and then to arrive at a course of action based on facts rather than to continue in the traditional ways of our grandfathers. (Weir 1936, 335)

This modernization of management extended to mechanization as well. He informed his audience that "the familiar expression 'untouched by hands' can now be applied truthfully to the product of the most modern mines." He continued, "the operations performed in the process of removing coal are cutting, drilling and shooting, and then loading into cars from 4 to 5 tons capacity. Each operation is accomplished by different mechanical and electrical machines operated by crews who are expert on that particular machine." In the comments that followed Weir's speech, A.R. Joyce said "we are accustomed to think of the railroads and the public utilities as having efficient engineering organizations. It is now evident that the leading coal companies have equally efficient engineering organizations" (Weir 1936, 337–8). With Wier and his generation of engineers in charge of the mines, the era of pick and shovel in the coal industry had come to an end.

One of the key achievements of Weir's career came after he left Bell and Zoller and formed the Paul Weir Company. He became involved in research and development of the so-called "Cardox system," an attempt to address the risks of blasting with black powder in underground mines filled with methane gas and coal dust. It is mentioned in the mining journals as early as 1932, and its operation was described in a 1955 coal report from Illinois:

> Its energy comes from the expansion of carbon dioxide in a hollow steel shell. The shell is pushed to the end of a drill hole. It is electrically detonated. At a certain predetermined pressure, the energy is liberated and the coal, previously mined, is broken similar to that from an explosive except at lesser unit pressure, requiring over double the number of drill holes per working face. (Schull 1955, 61)

In his discussion of the earliest experiments with Cardox, coal mine safety engineer J.E. Jones praised the technology for partially solving a problem dating back half a century: "safety and efficiency are analogous terms in all industrial progress. Possibly in no other field than that of blasting have these two been of such fundamental importance" (Jones 1932, 56). Weir would heartily agree.

Weir spent the remainder of his career as an active member of the profession. He served on the Illinois state board of mines, reported on coal mining prospects, consulted with water departments and power companies, dabbled in magnesium mining, and testified before boards and committees on best mining practices, which were directed at protecting the interests of mining companies. He was honored with selection to a mission to the UK with US coal executives during the Second World War, and in 1956 was awarded with an honorary life membership in the UK Institute of Mining Engineers. Weir earned the Erskine Ramsay Gold Metal from the American Institute of Mining, Metallurgy, and Petroleum Engineers (1949), the highest award given for lifetime contributions to the coal mining industry. When he passed away in 1972, he could see the fruits of his work in promoting the mechanization of mining and devising safer coal mine operating procedures. In 1920, when Weir began his career, 2,272 miners died in mining accidents; in the year he died, the number had dwindled to 156. A century after he began his career—2020—that number was five, the lowest number in US history (MSHA 2022).

Jeffrey B. Webb

See also: Centralia Mine Disaster; Cherry Mine Disaster; Coal; Dawson Mine Disaster; Farmington Mine Disaster; Holmes, Joseph Austin; Joy, Joseph Francis; Krebs Mine Disaster; Monongah Mine Disaster; Scofield Mine Disaster; Upper Big Branch Mine Disaster; West Frankfort Mine Disaster

FURTHER READING

Eliasberg, Vera F. 1966. "Some Aspects of Development in the Coal Mining Industry, 1839–1918." In *Output, Employment, and Productivity in the United States after 1800*. Ed. Dorothy S. Brady. Pp. 405–39. Cambridge, MA: National Bureau of Economic Research.

Fay, Albert H. 1916. "Coal Mine Fatalities in the United States, 1836–1914." Bureau of Mines. US Department of the Interior. Washington, DC: US Government Printing Office.

Jones, J.E. 1932. "Safety in Blasting Coal—Cardox." *Proceedings of the Illinois Mining Institute*. Pp. 56–9. Champaign, IL: The Geo. D. Louden Printing Co.

Mine Safety and Health Administration (MSHA). 2022. "Coal Fatalities for 1900 through 2022." US Department of Labor. https://arlweb.msha.gov/stats/centurystats/coalstats.asp (accessed October 2023).

National Mining Hall of Fame and Museum (NMHFM). 2020. "Paul Weir (1874–1972)." Inductee #151. Induction Year 1999. https://www.mininghalloffame.org/hall-of-fame/paul-weir (accessed October 2023).

Nelson, Ralph L. 1959. "The Merger Movement from 1895 to 1920." In *Merger Movements in American Industry, 1895–1956*. Ed. Ralph L. Nelson. Pp. 33–70. Princeton: Princeton University Press.

"News Notes." 1935–6. *The Explosives Engineer*. Vol. 13–4. P. 374.

Schull, Ben H. 1955. "Explosives Used in Mining Coal." *A Compilation of the Reports of the Mining Industry of Illinois, from Earliest Records to 1954*. Department of Mines and Minerals. State of Illinois. Springfield, IL: State of Illinois.

Stephenson-Adamson Manufacturing Company (SA). 1922. "Establishing a World's Record." *The Labor Saver: Promoting Advanced Conveyor Practice*. No. 115. January.

Weir, Paul. 1936. "Treated Timber Requirements from the Viewpoint of the Coal Mine Operator." *Proceedings of the Thirty-Second Annual Meeting of the American Wood-Preservers' Association*. Washington, DC: American Wood-Preservers' Association.

West Frankfort Mine Disaster

On December 21, 1951, an explosion in the Orient No. 2 coal mine in West Frankfort, Illinois killed 119 men and injured five others. The mine, located in the southern coal mining region of the state, was one of the area's major employers and was owned by the Chicago, Wilmington & Franklin Coal Corporation. It was the worst mining disaster in the United States since 1928, and affected a major industry that employed around a half-million workers.

As the population of West Frankfort was only 11,251 at the time, nearly everyone was touched by the tragedy, including grade schoolers who remembered their own losses or the suffering of classmates. Since the disaster occurred amid holiday preparations, many residents declared that they could never celebrate Christmas again. The incident received national attention from the wire services, newspapers, and magazines like *Time* and *Life*.

In its report on the explosion, the US Bureau of Mines called the disaster "avoidable." As a result of previous mine safety problems, culminating in the West Frankfort catastrophe, Congress enacted the Federal Coal Mine Safety Act of 1952.

Commercial coal mining began in Illinois in 1810, and eventually coal seams were discovered and developed in seventy-six different Illinois counties. More than 7,400 coal mines appeared throughout Illinois during the years that coal dominated the US energy supply, whereas fewer than thirty were in operation as of 2022. The Orient No. 2 coal mine was located 3 miles northwest of West Frankfort and 70 miles southeast of St. Louis. It covered an area equal to 12 square miles, and when it opened in 1922 it turned into a highly productive enterprise. Its daily output was 9,500 tons of coal in its initial phase of development, and at one point it logged a then-record 15,152 tons of coal in one eight-hour shift.

At the time of the disaster, Orient No. 2 was known as a safe mine—modern, mechanized, and efficient. However, accidents were not unknown. Miners had been killed in explosions before in comparatively small incidents. Nine days before the incident, the mine had a seven-day inspection, and was checked again by a certified examiner at 6:00 p.m. after the day shift came off duty. Although inspectors had previously classified the mine as "gassy" and required "rock dusting to alleviate combustible coal dust in the mine," the mine continued to operate with acceptable levels of gas (ILMines 2022).

With each miner having his metal fire-check tag punched with his number and headlamp, the night shift descended into the mine in a clanging, creaking, steel cage operated by mechanical pulleys until all 257 workers had arrived. The mantrips, or shuttles, left the shaft bottom about 6:25 p.m., reaching the working sections 550 feet below the surface some twenty–thirty minutes later. This was the last scheduled shift before the Christmas vacation ("Disasters" 1951; Ratay n.d.).

At 7:40 p.m., an explosion ripped through the mine tunnels. The alarm could not be sounded because the switchboard power had failed. The blast sent a shock wave that filled the tunnel with dust. The night mine manager was on the surface when power went off

FIGURE 12: Mine safety engineers installed rock dust traps in US coal mines to prevent the spread of mine explosions, since combustible coal dust was found to be a contributing factor in the 1951 West Frankfort, Illinois mine disaster.

in the mine and smoke and dust came up the shaft. When the power came on after about five minutes, he telephoned all the sections on the mine's south side to bring the men to the surface immediately but could only reach two of the north sections. He then called the company officials (Ankeny 1951).

The rescuers faced a dangerous task. The explosion had twisted miles of track and ripped them from their bed. Most heavy loading machines and steel pit cars, each weighing several tons, were overturned. Miles of telephone and power lines mostly were out. Fire was smoldering in the blasted entries, with some of the 12 × 12 framing timbers having been snapped like twigs. The force of the explosion extended for more than a mile inside the mine's passageways. Despite the conditions, 113 men got to the surface after the explosion. Most of the missing men were working some 2 miles from the elevator shaft down the wrecked entries.

The rescue effort started immediately with about 500 men from surrounding towns in southern Illinois, including the brothers, sons, and fathers of trapped miners. Initial explorations were made by asbestos-clothed apparatus crews who built temporary stoppings (barricades) to restore ventilation in the carbon-monoxide-filled, black, smoky tunnels (Ratay n.d.). Wearing gas masks, and depending on their miners' cap lamps for light, the rescue teams traveled 2–3 miles through the tunnels and carried out the bodies one by one. At times, the rescuers scrambled and crawled 2 miles to carry bodies to the shuttles.

Cave-ins made the work even more hazardous. Many of the rescue workers were temporarily overcome by gas, emerging from the mine gasping and coughing (Ankeny 1951).

As the bodies were recovered from the mine, they were taken to the West Frankfort junior high school auditorium, a temporary morgue for the dead. Grieving family members watched as the tarps covering the bodies were individually pulled back until each body was recognized and identified. Almost all of the bodies bore marks from being thrown against the walls or machinery, as well as charred skin and clothing. Expert observers said there could not have been enough oxygen left to support a fire after the mine explosion consumed all of it in the tunnels. Medical evidence indicated that most of the men died almost instantly (Ratay n.d.).

All bodies were recovered by 2:00 p.m. on December 26, three days after the blast. The 119 men who died left 301 dependents, which included 109 widows, 175 children under 18, and 17 other family dependents. The average age of the deceased men was 40.9 years, with the youngest 19 and the oldest 64. The burying of the dead began Christmas Eve when eighteen funerals were held with twenty-four on Christmas Day and the remainder on December 26.

The day after the explosion, the *St. Louis Post-Dispatch* charged that the mine's management had ignored federal mine inspectors' recommendation that abandoned mine workings should either be sealed or ventilated, and that the air used for ventilating them should not be distributed to the rest of the mine. Mine Superintendent John R. Foster hotly insisted that "these are [both] strictly controversial matters" ("Disasters" 1951).

The *United Mine Workers Journal* from 15 January 1952 reported that a team of six federal experts concluded that the roof caving in the abandoned areas of the mine, plus the partial short-circuiting of the air current from an opening of a ventilating door, caused a "large body of gas" to push out of the abandoned area into the active working section. The single ventilating door, open for shuttles and locomotives to move through, also allowed the cloud of gas to go through. Investigators said it was evident that a moving column of gas, rather than a standing body of gas, was ignited.

All working sections affected by the explosion were ventilated by air that had passed by the entrances to abandoned workings. Three of these old ends were caving just previous to the explosion, releasing gas. A day shift gas watchman was assigned to watch one of these places. At the time of the explosion a train of empty cars was standing in the main ventilating door at a location in the mine known as 3 and 4 south at 27 east north west. This took air pressure off the abandoned entries and let gas come out onto the active workings where it was ignited, probably in an area that contained electrical equipment near the junction of 3 south off 27 east north west and No. 3 stub entry off 3 south, using conventional designations of mine locations. The flame was propagated by coal dust and by gas from other worked-out and abandoned areas. The rock dusting methods used to suppress dust build-up had proven inadequate.

Two shuttle cars in poor condition were the first ignition source the body of gas contacted, as reports indicated. It was unknown whether the cars were in operation. Two electric drills, also in poor condition, were the second source reached by the gas. Further spread of the explosion stopped when it reached areas where it could expand into open workings and where enough rock dust had been applied to stop flame propagation.

After first blaming miners' smoking for igniting the gas and dust, Illinois Director of Mines Walter Eadie—finding no evidence that cigarettes were the ignition—said that the explosion was caused by a spark from a moving electric locomotive or by the accumulation of methane gas. Federal inspectors had previously criticized some methods used to control methane, but the company had ignored the recommendations. James Westfield, a US Bureau of Miners official, called the disaster "somebody's carelessness and an absolutely avoidable accident." The inspectors found thirty-one violations of the federal mine safety code, mostly minor, but some were "serious hazards similar to those that had caused heavy loss of life or destruction of property" (quoted in Jones n.d.). US Representative Melvin Price said shortly after the explosion:

> Federal inspectors could only recommend that these safety violations be corrected. Had the Federal law the teeth it required and a bill which I have pending in this Congress, H.R. 268, will give to it, the mine operators would have been compelled to comply with the inspector's recommendation or be subject to strong penalty, and if the inspector found imminent danger the legislation provides authority to close the mine. (quoted in Ratay n.d.)

The next year after the explosion, the accumulation of mine disasters, including local ones like the Cherry Mine Disaster in Cherry, Illinois (1909) and the Centralia Mine Disaster in Centralia, Illinois (1947) finally forced Congress to act. In 1952, President Harry S. Truman signed the Federal Coal Mine Safety Act. United Mine Workers President John L. Lewis' (1880–1969) advocacy was crucial. The act authorized mine inspectors to require any mine employing over fifteen men to comply with mine safety provisions. The federal government could now shut down any mines that it deemed potentially dangerous and mine inspectors could now enforce the laws on any mine not found to meet the act's safety standards. As a direct result, mines became better ventilated to control methane gas; floating coal dust was more controlled by dusting the mine walls with limestone. There has been but one mine disaster in southern Illinois since the law's enactment.

William P. Kladky

See also: Centralia Mine Disaster; Cherry Mine Disaster; Coal; Dawson Mine Disaster; Farmington Mine Disaster; Krebs Mine Disaster; Scofield Mine Disaster; United Mine Workers of America; Upper Big Branch Mine Disaster; Weir, Paul

FURTHER READING

Ankeny, M.J. et al. 1951. *Reports Dated 12/21/1951 Orient No. 2 Mine*. US Bureau of Mines. US Department of the Interior. https://usminedisasters.miningquiz.com/saxsewell/orient_1951.pdf (accessed October 2023).

"Disasters: This is a Bad One." 1951. *Time*. December 31.

Hartley, Robert, and David Kenney. 2006. *Death Underground: The Centralia and West Frankfort Mine Disasters*. Carbondale, IL: Southern Illinois University Press.

ILMines. 2022. "Mine Index 0366: Orient Number Two Coal Company, Orient No. 2 Mine." ILMines Wiki. April 1. https://ilmineswiki.web.illinois.edu/index.php/0366 (accessed October 2023).

Jones, Ashley. n.d. "The New Orient Coal Mine Disaster of 1951." City of West Frankfort. https://www.westfrankfort-il.com/mine-disaster-of-1951 (accessed October 2023).

Ratay, Desiree Southern. n.d. "The Orient No. 2 Coal Mine Explosion." *The Evansville Boneyard: A Journal of History, Opinions, Adventures, and Ideas*. http://evansvilleboneyard.org/orient.htm (accessed October 2023).

US Mine Rescue Association. 1951. "Chicago, Wilmington and Franklin Coal Co., Orient No. 2 Mine Explosion." Mine Disasters in the United States. https://usminedisasters.miningquiz.com/saxsewell/orient.htm (accessed October 2023).

"West Frankfort, IL Coal Mine Gas Explosion, Dec 1951." 1951. *Waterloo Daily Courier*. December 23.

Westinghouse, George

The American engineer and inventor George Westinghouse (1846–1914) created more than sixty industrial companies during his lifetime, including the Westinghouse Electric and Manufacturing Company and the Westinghouse Air Brake Company. His many patents included one for a railroad safety air brake, improvements to railway signaling and switching apparatus, and an alternating current electric meter. Westinghouse was instrumental in promoting the adoption of alternating current (AC) for electrical distribution.

George Westinghouse Jr. was born in Central Bridge, New York, to George Westinghouse Sr. and Emeline Vedder Westinghouse. The family moved to Schenectady, where his father opened a shop that manufactured threshing machines. Westinghouse worked in the shop for several years until enlisting in the military during the Civil War. He served briefly in the army as a cavalryman and then became an assistant engineer in the Navy before being discharged in 1865 (Jonnes 2004, 120).

After the war, Westinghouse attended college for a short time, but after receiving his first patent, which was for a rotary steam engine, he dropped out to devote his time to working on inventions. More inventions soon followed, including a device to put derailed trains back on track and one that prevented trains from derailing at track junctions (LOC 2020).

In 1867, Westinghouse courted and married Marguerite Erskine Walker, and they would have one son, George Westinghouse III. Westinghouse was a private man and left very little in the way of private correspondence (Skrabec 2007, 2).

In April 1869, Westinghouse invented one of his most useful and important creations: a safety air brake for trains that allowed the engineer to simultaneously apply the brakes on every car and bring the train to a safe halt. Previously, each car had needed its own brakeman to manually apply brakes, but because of problems with timing that often resulted in accidents (Jonnes 2004, 118; LOC 2020).

Westinghouse astutely recognized that his air brake could be profitable, and in July 1869 he organized the Westinghouse Air Brake Company for the purpose of manufacturing his improved air brakes. He eventually expanded his business into Canada and Europe. Having lost income on some of his earlier patents after the railway companies had made small improvements to them, Westinghouse became protective of his financial interests and threatened lawsuits against anyone who would try to circumvent his patents (Jonnes 2004, 118).

The ambitious Westinghouse soon expanded his business interests to include railroad signaling. Early railroad signals used oil lamps, but they were not very reliable. In 1872, electrical engineer William Robinson (1840–1921) had invented a track circuit that used the steel rail to conduct electricity for railway signals. In 1881, Westinghouse began buying patents on electrical signaling equipment, which he improved and modified, as well as producing his own creations (Jonnes 2004, 119). In 1882, he formed the Union Switch and Signal Company, locating it in Swissvale, Pennsylvania, just outside of Pittsburg.

The electrical railway signaling equipment was Westinghouse's introduction to electricity, which he realized might offer him a way to expand his business interests even further. Westinghouse was aware of Thomas Edison's (1847–1931) Pearl Street Power Station, which delivered direct current (DC) power to parts of downtown Manhattan, but the DC central power station was severely limited in the number of customers it could handle. Westinghouse thought he could do better. In 1884, he hired mechanical engineer H.M. Byllesby (1859–1924) and electrician William Stanley Jr. (1858–1916) and formed the Westinghouse Electric Company. Westinghouse showcased his DC power system at the Philadelphia Electric Exhibit and prepared to go into the business of providing electric power (Jonnes 2004, 120).

RAILWAY AIR BRAKES

The Westinghouse Air Brake Company was formed in 1869 to manufacture railway safety air brakes. Initially located in Pittsburg, in 1889 the company moved to Wilmerding, Pennsylvania, and by 1905 employed 3,000 workers. It offered a nine-hour workday, housing, welfare, and other employee benefits (LOC 2023). Westinghouse continued to improve the air brake, introducing an automatic air brake in 1872 and a quick action triple valve in 1887 (LOC 2023).

Karen S. Garvin

And then in 1885, Westinghouse read about an alternating current (AC) system that was on exhibit in London. Intrigued with AC's potential to economically provide electricity over long distances, Westinghouse sent one of his employees to investigate and by November had received a Gaulard-Gibbs transformer. However, the apparatus was poorly soldered and was rebuilt by Reginald Belfield at Westinghouse's Garrison Alley Works in Pittsburg. The resulting new transformer was a complete redesign that allowed for the creation of much higher voltages (Jonnes 2004, 130–3).

In January 1886 Westinghouse incorporated the Westinghouse Electric Company. Stanley and Belfield were sent to Barrington, Massachusetts, where they set up a complete AC power system that used a 500-volt generator and a step-up/step-down transformer. On March 20 the town was lit up in the "Great Barrington Electrification," proving that AC could be safely used to provide electricity to a large number of customers.

In 1888, Westinghouse obtained rights to the patents for Nikola Tesla's (1856–1943) polyphase alternating current system, which used several voltage sources to produce an efficient way of distributing AC power. He even managed to hire Tesla. In May 1890, Westinghouse received a patent for an alternating current electric meter.

By the late 1880s there were competing electric systems: alternating current and direct current. Proponents of DC, including Edison, argued that AC was unsafe because its high voltage had already caused several deaths, including the electrocution of lineman John Feeks, which had created an ugly public spectacle (Freeberg 2013, 181). In turn, Westinghouse and Tesla denounced Edison's DC system, thus unleashing a bitter rivalry between the two camps that became known as the War of the Currents.

In 1891 the *Electrical World* magazine reported just over 200 Edison DC power stations in use, while there were nearly 1,000 AC power stations in use (Jonnes 2004, 287). Continuing the AC trend, Westinghouse received the contract to light the 1893 Chicago World's Columbian Exposition, and also that year contracted with the Cataract Construction Company to provide generators for a hydroelectric power plant on the Niagara River.

By 1904, Westinghouse's business interests included a wide array of companies, including the Westinghouse Machine Company, the Pittsburg Meter Company, the American Brake Company, and several businesses in England, France, Germany, and Russia. However, the 1907 Bankers' Panic resulted in Westinghouse losing control of his companies, and by 1911 he withdrew from active business life.

Shortly thereafter, Westinghouse's health began to decline, and he was confined to a wheelchair. He died on March 12, 1914, and was buried at Woodlawn Cemetery, then later moved to Arlington National Cemetery. He and his contemporaries left behind the legacy of electrification of the United States, with a power grid based on centralized electricity-generating stations, transmission lines, substations, and transformers linking together cities, towns, and rural communities across the nation.

Karen S. Garvin

See also: Brush, Charles Francis; Davenport, Thomas; Edison, Thomas Alva; Electricity; Henry, Joseph; Pearl Street Power Station; Stanley, William Jr.; Tesla, Nikola; War of the Currents

FURTHER READING

Freeberg, Ernest. 2013. *The Age of Edison: Electric Light and the Invention of Modern America*. New York: Penguin.

Hausman, William J., Peter Hertner, and Mira Wilkins. 2008. *Global Electrification: Multinational Enterprise and International Finance in the History of Light and Power, 1878–2007*. Cambridge: Cambridge University Press, 2008.

Jonnes, Jill. 2004. *Empires of Light: Edison, Tesla, Westinghouse, and the Race to Electrify the World*. New York: Random House.

Library of Congress (LOC). 2023. "Collection: Inside an American Factory: Films of the Westinghouse Works, 1904." https://www.loc.gov/collections/films-of-westinghouse-works-1904/ (accessed November 2023).

Skrabec, Quentin R. 2007. *George Westinghouse: Gentle Genius*. New York: Algora Publishing.

Whale Oil

Whale oil is fat rendered from blubber, bones, and other whale by-products. It played a crucial role in the history of American industrialization. Until the 1850s when it was replaced by kerosene, which is refined petroleum, whale oil was the primary source of illumination as lamp fuel, and a lubricant when treated with sulfur. Although the first records of whaling date to Scandinavia in 10,000 BCE, whale oil became the first commercial oil fuel, beginning in 1690 off the coast of Nantucket, Massachusetts and Long Island, New York. Other uses included the manufacturing of varnish, leather, linoleum, and rough cloth. An overlooked energy source, the importance of whale oil throughout industrialization cannot be overstated. The whaling industry was a brutal and cataclysmic assault on the global population of whales and their ecosystems, which nearly resulted in their extinction.

Whale oil is an umbrella term that describes different commercialized illuminating and lubricating substances rendered from whale by-products. Spermaceti was the most highly prized of these products, a liquid wax found in the head of sperm whales, originally thought to be semen. Spermaceti has a high melting point of about 50°C and provided a clean bright light with minimal odor. The photometric unit candlepower, defined by the UK Metropolitan Gas Act of 1860, is based on the light quality of spermaceti candles. Sperm oil, used for lubrication at high temperatures, came from the blubber of sperm whales. It was also used as a high-quality indoor light in public, private homes, and lighthouses. "Train oil," deriving from the Dutch word "traan," meaning tear or drop, principally came from right whales, bowhead whales, humpback whales, and occasionally blue whales. Apart from the sperm whale, these baleen whales were preferred to toothed whales because their oil contained more useful properties.

Baleen whale oil was more useful in chemicals and applications because it is primarily made up of triglycerides. Toothed whale oil was primarily made up of wax-like properties. The sperm whale, however, prized for both spermaceti and sperm oil were hunted aggressively. A large sperm whale contained up to 3 tons of sperm oil. Historians argue that sperm whales were the first animal or mineral oil to be commercially viable. In Massachusetts, New York, Connecticut, and Rhode Island, 45,000 barrels of sperm oil a year were produced between 1770 to 1775. A standard barrel of whale oil contained thirty US gallons.

During the nineteenth century, the United States dominated the whaling industry, peaking in 1846 with 735 of 900 global whaling ships operating out of US ports. At the time, whaling was the fifth largest US industry. Starting in 1830, known as the golden age of American whaling, the following thirty years would see unprecedented profits, industry domination, and transformation. From 1842–6, New England whalers captured and killed 20,000 whales—$1.1 million worth of whale oil. In 1844, 17,500 whalers went to sea. In 1853 alone, 8,000 whales were slaughtered. In the first half of the nineteenth century, only 10 percent of whaling ventures returned with a loss. In 1851, sperm oil sold for nearly

$40 per barrel. At the time, an average sperm whale contained 1,890 gallons of oil, equaling 63 barrels, making each whale worth $2,520. The peak of whale oil production came in 1851 at 328,483 barrels.

Oftentimes, the oil was distilled in makeshift refineries right on the ships. The sweltering, foul conditions of whaling ships were described in detail by Herman Melville in *Moby-Dick* (1851), a fictionalized account of the whaling business, but nevertheless a reference valued by many historians. Whaling trips were forty-two- to forty-eight-month enterprises; it was economical to process the whales on board and discard the waste back into the ocean.

Land refineries contained large iron vats that could hold up to 1,000 gallons of oil. Blubber could produce 50–80 percent oil by weight, bones 10–70 percent, and meat 2–8 percent. The fatty acids for soaps and fatty alcohols for cosmetics and detergents were separated by neutralizing whale oil fats in alkalis. These would be heated to 100 degrees Celsius for 6-to-10 hours until all the water burned off. Whale oil is not soluble in water; once the water had been removed, it would not rejoin. This process purified the oils, which varied in color from yellow-brown to clear. The last phase of refining required chilling the oil for 10-to-14 days at zero degrees Celsius. During this process the oil would congeal into small pellets, which were placed in 2-to-4-gallon canvas bags and put under 1,000–2,000 pounds of pressure per square inch. The subsequent oil that flowed out was crystal clear.

At the same time the whale industry was peaking, the commercial potential of crude oil had been discovered. In 1846, Abraham Gesner, a Canadian physician and geologist, publicly demonstrated a new illuminant he called kerosene. The English chemist James Young obtained a British patent in 1850 and a US patent in 1852 for his process of making *paraffine oil*. In 1851, Samuel Kier (1813–74) began operating the first US petroleum refinery, in Pittsburgh, Pennsylvania. The hydrocarbon paraffin was discovered by German chemist Karl von Reichenbach in 1830. Kerosene derives from paraffin and as the illuminating potential of the distilled petroleum by-product was popularized, streamlined, and commodified, it challenged the increasingly expensive whaling industry. Kerosene was a cheaper, cleaner, and less odorous artificial light fuel.

WICK DESIGN

The wick, argues historian of technology Wolfgang Schivelbusch, represents the first revolution in artificial lighting, by separating the fuel source from the site of combustion. The Argand lamp, invented in 1783 by chemist Francois Ami Argand, was a philosophical transformation of combustion. Instead of a solid wick, it utilized a hollow wick for greater oxygen flow. It was the standard whale oil lamp until it was replaced by kerosene lamps in the 1850s.

Elia Vargas

Whaling was increasingly an expensive and difficult undertaking. In 1870, John D. Rockefeller formed the Standard Oil Company to standardize kerosene quality for consistently safe and reliable domestic use. The whaling industry was irreversibly changed in 1871 when thirty-three whaling boats were crushed in ice north of Point Belcher, Alaska. The catastrophic event resulted from the pursuit of ever more difficult hunting grounds amidst more expensive overhead and decreasing profits. The fleet stayed one day too long and the ships that were not destroyed were intentionally grounded. In total, $1,600,000 was lost. By 1876, the 735-ship American fleet had dropped to thirty-nine. At its height, in 1856, whale oil reached $1.77 a gallon, but in 1896, it sold for just 40 cents. By comparison, Kerosene sold for 59 cents a gallon in 1865 and only 7 cents per gallon in 1895.

During the nineteenth century, it is estimated that nearly 236,000 whales were killed. In the twentieth century whale oil's application broadened. Developments in chemistry produced edible whale oil products, such as margarine. Whale oil was a vital ingredient in the manufacturing of nitroglycerin for explosives in the First and Second World Wars. In 1986, the International Whaling Commission banned whaling in numerous countries, including the United States. Despite the environmental and species risk, a few countries, including Iceland and Japan, have recently revived whaling.

Elia Vargas

See also: Biofuels; Colliers; Keir, Samuel Martin; Oil Tankers; Panama Canal; Rockefeller, John D.

FURTHER READING

Brice, William R. 2009. *Myth, Legend, Reality: Edwin L. Drake and the Early Oil Industry*. 1st ed. Oil City, PA: Oil Region Alliance.

Coleman, James L. 1995. "The American Whale Oil Industry: A Look Back to the Future of the American Petroleum Industry?" *Nonrenewable Resources*. Vol. 4. No. 3. Pp. 273–88.

Davis, Lance E. 1997. *In Pursuit of Leviathan: Technology, Institutions, Productivity, and Profits in American Whaling, 1816–1906*. Chicago: University of Chicago Press.

Melville, Herman. 2018. *Moby-Dick*. Ed. Hershel Parker. A Norton Critical Edition. New York; London: W.W. Norton & Company, Inc.

Schivelbusch, Wolfgang. 1995. *Disenchanted Night: The Industrialization of Light in the Nineteenth Century*. Berkeley, CA: University of California Press.

Tønnessen, Johan Nicolay, and Arne Odd Johnsen. 1982. *The History of Modern Whaling*. Berkeley, CA: University of California Press.

Whiting Refinery

In a secret deal during the late nineteenth century, the Standard Oil Company acquired approximately 300 acres of property in a marshy area along the southern tip of Lake Michigan at what was known as Whiting's rail stop. The refinery envisioned there would eventually become one of largest producers in the world and key to international petroleum history. In 1889, oil workers arrived from Cleveland with plans to build a plant designed to refine crude oil from Lima, Ohio. Ohio was becoming the largest supplier of oil, but newly discovered crude was not as clean as that from Pennsylvania and far less desirable. However, Standard Oil founder John D. Rockefeller was determined to make it profitable. It was being pumped into Chicago, where it was used as a low-grade industrial oil and lubricant, but it was high in sulfur and created a terrible stench in the refining process. Constructing a refinery downwind from the residents of Chicago, who could prove to be a strong customer base, seemed to satisfy Rockefeller. One million Chicagoans needed paraffin for candles, kerosene for lamps, and a high-quality axle grease for carriages. This was the westernmost refinery of the time and it would help to open the Midwest to industrial and modern agricultural development (Babcock 1939, 1).

The company had a tremendous impact on what would become the city of Whiting. Within a few years, the natural area surrounding what had been a simple train stop saw the filling of marsh and leveling of sand dunes, the building of houses and the draw of workers from across the region and Eastern Europe. Rockefeller's accumulation of wealth and devotion to philanthropy made a visible impact on the city to the northwest, including the founding of the University of Chicago, and the Whiting refinery became even more profitable. His son, John D. Rockefeller II, carried on the tradition in Whiting and through the Standard Oil Company funded neighborhood activities and the building of the Whiting Community Center in 1923. The community center housed an auditorium, bowling alley, swimming pool, gymnasiums, and meeting rooms to be used by the residents of Whiting, many of whom were employed by the refinery. Not all were enamored with the Rockefellers, however, and Journalist Ida M. Tarbell exposed company corruption and monopolistic business practices in her work, *The History of the Standard Oil Company* (1904).

COMPETITION

In coming through the oil crisis during the late 1970s, Whiting competed with Texas City, Texas in refining the most barrels of oil. As part of British Petroleum (BP) in the twenty-first century, Whiting remained the largest refinery in the Midwest and BP's largest in the world, with the capacity to process 440,000 barrels each day.

Kathleen A. Tobin

During the second decade of the twentieth century, output at the Whiting refinery increased significantly. The number of automobiles in the United States increased from under 1 million in 1912 to more than 6 million in 1918. The demand for gasoline, motor oil, and lubricants were high in the Midwest. In addition, Standard Oil of Indiana expanded its marketing territory and developed plans for a system of company-owned and operated service stations with personnel training headquartered in Chicago. This put added pressure on Whiting to increase production. When the United States entered the First World War, the Whiting refinery became a member of the National Petroleum War Service Committee and was a major supplier of wartime petroleum products. Whiting was also the first in the petroleum industry to create a safety department in 1918 (Giddens 1955).

As a major supplier, the Whiting refinery was tied to the global economy and was forced to slow production during the Great Depression. The company sought to keep as many employees working as possible, transferring some to construction and repair jobs and redistributing workers to part time (Giddens 1955, 468–9). The outbreak of the Second World War increased demand and the refinery once again worked with government controls under the Petroleum Industry War Council. In addition, the Selective Service was pulling workers away to join military forces. A new supply of crude from the Texas Gulf incentivized the refinery to further modernize and increase research and development. New wartime products included aviation fuel and toluene, which was used in explosives. By 1945, Whiting had produced 29.5 million gallons of toluene, enough for almost 0.5-million tons of bombs (Giddens 1955, 615--19).

Post-war production in Whiting remained high as the refinery became the fourth largest in the nation. This was due primarily to the demand for gasoline in what was quickly becoming an American age of prosperity enhanced by an automobile culture and the development of the Interstate Highway System. Safety was a top concern at the refinery, but in early morning hours of August 27, 1955, there was a terrible explosion and fire. Workers were starting what was then the nation's largest hydroformer, a 26-storey unit that converted low-octane fuel to high-octane. The process ignited a fire that quickly spread over more than 40 acres of the refinery and melted storage tanks. Residents described the explosion as sounding like the end of the world, and smoke was seen for hundreds of miles. Thousands were sent in to build sand dikes to contain the fire (Grossman 2015).

During the 1970s, Whiting increased refining of US oil to meet the nation's desire for oil independence and it benefited from the opening of the Trans-Alaska Pipeline in 1977. The plant underwent a transition in branding in the late twentieth century, as Standard Oil became officially recognized as the American Oil Company (Amoco) and merged with British Petroleum (BP). Since 2001, the refinery has operated under BP. In 2012, BP invested $14 billion to modernize the refinery, update equipment, install pollution controls, and expand capacity for refining Western Canadian tar sands oil. Environmentalists and nearby residents remain vigilant and regularly seek assistance from the US Environmental Protection Agency, Indiana Department of Environmental Management, and US Department of Justice as concerns regarding air pollution, fire potential, and the discharge of waste into Lake Michigan, the primary source of drinking water in Northwest Indiana, continue (Wlasiuk 2014, 706–7).

Kathleen A. Tobin

See also: Ford, Henry; Interstate Highway System; Kier, Samuel Martin; Ohio Oil Boom; Petroleum; Rockefeller, John D.; Standard Oil Company; Tarbell, Ida; Trans-Alaska Pipeline System

FURTHER READING

Babcock, F. Laurence. 1939. *The First Fifty, 1889–1939*. Chicago: Standard Oil Company (Indiana).

Giddens, Paul H. 1955. *Standard Oil Company (Indiana): Oil Pioneers of the Middle West*. New York: Appleton-Century-Crofts.

Grossman, Ron. 2015. "1955 Standard Oil Refinery Blast Sounded like End of the World." *Chicago Tribune*. August 27. https://www.chicagotribune.com/opinion/commentary/ct-whiting-refinery-explosion-standard-oil-bp-gas-prices-flashback-0823-jm-20150821-story.html (accessed October 22, 2022).

McKinlay, Archibald. 2003. *Oil and Water: A Pictorial History of Whiting, Indiana*. Virginia Beach, VA: The Donning Co. Publishing.

Whiting-Robersdale Historical Society (WRHS). 2015. *One Minute after Sunrise: The Story of the 1955 Whiting Refinery Fire* (film). Whiting, Indiana.

Tarbell, Ida M. 1904. *The History of the Standard Oil Company*. New York: McClure, Phillips & Co.

Wlasiuk, Jonathan. 2014. "A Company Town on Common Waters: Standard Oil in the Calumet." *Environmental History*. Vol. 19. No. 4. Pp. 687–713.

Seiter, Cotton. 2008. *Republic of Drivers: A Cultural History of Automobility in America*. Chicago: University of Chicago Press.

Williams Oil-O-Matic

The Williams Oil-O-Matic oil burner and thermostat was manufactured from the 1920s through the 1950s by the Williams Oil-O-Matic Heating Company of Bloomington, Illinois. It was patented by Walter W. Williams in 1932, who invented the device believing that heating with oil should be as easy as possible. The Oil-O-Matic was one of the first electrically operated liquid-fuel-burning devices, driven by electric motors, able to be connected to electric-light circuits, and thermostatically controlled.

The Oil-O-Matic invention was a great advance in home heating technology and helped facilitate the transition of households from using coal to burning oil to heat their homes. It made oil heating automatic, much more dependable, and consistent. It was heating "without work or worry." Its lower noise level was advertised as "hushed heat." The homeowner could set a temperature with the thermostat and the Oil-O-Matic would provide the right amount of oil, atomize the oil for combustion, keep the flame with a fan, and increase the heat in the combustion chamber. The heat could then be pushed through ducts, thereby warming the whole house. By 1929, the company also sold its Oil-O-Matic Junior for smaller homes and developed one that used "low cost" fuel oil (WOA 1929).

Thermostats in virtually every twenty-first century home are the result of more than a century of innovation, industrial design, and engineering. It appears to be an everyday object in almost every home, but the process of creating the thermostat required technological know-how and trial-and-error experimentation. In the late nineteenth century, most American households heated their homes with manually operated coal furnaces that necessitated a coal storage area in the basement and lighting and stoking a coal-fired furnace. In 1886, Albert Butz had patented a "damper-flapper" (eventually a vent/flue damper) system that enabled homeowners to set a primitive-type thermostat to a certain temperature, which then would open a damper to the furnace to stoke the coal fire for increased heat to be distributed throughout the house. Subsequent inventions equipped the thermostats to utilize gas lines, to use electricity for some functions, to turn on at a set time, to include heating and cooling in one energy system, and finally to connect to the internet.

At first, crude oil had been distilled and refined to yield kerosene for lanterns and other substances for lubricants. Burning oil, rather than coal, to heat building interiors occurred to many people but it required innovation to turn users away from their energy practices and embrace new ones. At the time, most homes were heated with steam from boilers attached to coal furnaces. An oil burner for home heating was invented by Milton A. Fesler in 1903 to capitalize on energy created by the discovery of oil in California. Multiple patents by various individuals and companies followed, including a new device patented by William H. Wafer, also in 1903 (GES 2019).

The Oil-O-Matic heater was first constructed in the auto garage and showroom of Charles Urban Williams (1867–1953) at 207 E. Washington Street in Bloomington.

Williams was an itinerant photographer who had a lucrative business photographing flamboyant evangelist preacher Billy Sunday (Gridley 2016). Williams tried other commercial ventures, like the picture postcard business and later a successful auto dealership located at the same location. He and his son Walter adapted the auto garage to produce the early versions of the Oil-O-Matic. Initially, they reused oil from cars serviced at the dealership (Gridley 2016).

Fortunately, Williams' invention quickly began selling widely and very well. The Oil-O-Matic largely flourished because of the coal shortage caused by the First World War and continuing for some time afterward. With all of the sales, the company could then afford to have constructed a handsome brick factory at Bell and Hannah Streets on Bloomington's south side. The enlarged space enabled the manufacture of more units. Their oil burners also fortuitously were popular overseas, with many homes and businesses benefiting. Aiding the marketing effort, the Oil-O-Matic also was installed in various well-known buildings like the King David Hotel in Jerusalem and Westminster Abbey in London (Kemp 2009). Williams kept expanding his heating business by patenting and selling other inventions such as the Ice-O-Matic, a compressor-operated refrigerator for the home (Spencer 2020).

Oil-O-Matic sales rose and fell dramatically in the mid-1920s and through the 1930s due to the consumer frenzy of the Roaring 20s, the Stock Market Crash of 1929, and the prolonged Great Depression. However, fortunes drastically improved in the early 1940s. In 1944, the company, now headed by William A. Matheson, won its first war-related contract. Oil-O-Matic was one of three companies hired to produce a hydraulically controlled automatic antiaircraft firing mechanism. During the war, Oil-O-Matic worked on a multitude of military contracts that required their expertise in precision machine work. For instance, the company manufactured hydraulic control devices, called "oil gears," for aiming anti-aircraft guns, smoke screen generators for the US Navy, and various parts of the Boeing B-29 Superfortress bomber. The company's plant became the largest in the Twin Cities of Bloomington-Normal (Kemp 2009).

Once the United States entered the war, Oil-O-Matic shifted completely to war production. By May 1942, the plant produced on a twenty-four-hour, seven-day-a-week schedule, with no holiday shutdowns. Factory workers did a standard forty-eight-hour week, with time-and-a-half for over eight hours a day or forty hours a week. All of the eventual 2,800 workers agreed to a 10 percent payroll deduction for war bonds. Like other companies during the Second World War, Oil-O-Matic trained women for work in their machine shops. Eventually some 300 or more women were employed, as well as a number of African Americans (Kemp 2009).

In 1945 the company merged with the Eureka Company of Detroit, a Detroit-based maker of vacuum cleaners since 1909, and was renamed Eureka-Williams Corporation. Walter W. Williams was the principal stockholder of the company at this time ("Merger" 1945). Williams and Eureka then started a $350,000 advertising campaign to support its intensive sales training and merchandising program. Some 70-80 percent of the ads were run in daily newspapers in cities serviced by enfranchised dealers of the products ("New" 1945).

After dropping the name Williams, Eureka became one of the best-selling vacuum cleaner manufacturers of North America. In 1973, Eureka-Williams purchased 38 acres of land in north Normal and built a warehouse and motor department building. The Eureka-Williams Corporation was purchased by AB Electrolux of Sweden and in 1974 changed its name to the Eureka Company. Around this time, a 5,000-square-foot addition was built at the Bloomington plant and a 210,000-square-foot warehouse plant in Normal. The company built a plant in Juarez, Mexico in 1981, and two years later a large plant-warehouse in El Paso.

The Normal plant finally was closed in 2004, ending production in Bloomington. In 2004, the Eureka Company name was discontinued and the company became Electrolux Home Products. Electrolux then closed its Minnesota plants, and along with it the manufacture of the Oil-O-Matic (MCMH 2012).

Early advertisements offer a window on American society as it was passing through the major interior heating energy transition from to coal to oil and natural gas. The Oil-O-Matic and related company products were sold to the public through licensed dealers, some hardware stores, electrical shops, department stores, utility companies, and by franchised dealers who dealt only in that manufacturer's products. The advertisements touted the way it could save its owner money—fuel costs, upkeep costs, cleaning bills, doctors' bills, and time due to the labor of refilling a coal furnace. They also encouraged wives to persuade their husbands to convert to heating with oil in order to maintain domestic harmony, appealing to gender and family roles that were in the process of changing through the early to mid-twentieth century.

The advertisements for the Oil-O-Matic were creative and spoke to the family dynamics of the early twentieth century. A typical ad that can still be found circulating on the internet is headed, "Men may buy the coal, but women pay for it," and stresses coal's dirtiness, "drudgery," and inefficiencies (Amazon 2023). Often, ads were in the popular Art Deco style, like a 1930s ad showing a delighted housewife in an evening gown looking at her new heater. The ad "Men can be so stubborn about a thing like oil heat" was run in *National Geographic* and other magazines. Another black and white Williams Oil-O-Matic oil burner ad read, "Lazy? We call him smart ... he's now enjoying heat without work or worry." The company also distributed booklets, such as a 1925 "New Facts About Oil Heating" Williams Oil-O-Matic Company circular, which begins: "Bitter cold dawn—Every room delightfully warm." This multi-page booklet was colored and illustrated profusely with cute, family-friendly drawings.

Some 87 percent of homes that use heating oil today were built before 1990 (LTI 2023). Most of the domestic oil burners now on the market use basically the same principles of the Oil-O-Matic, but the majority of residential homes are actually heated with utility gas or electricity. Only 9 percent of homes used fuel oil for heating in 2000, though the percentage was much higher in the New England states of Maine, Vermont, New Hampshire, and Connecticut (USCB 2000). As for the Williams Oil-O-Matic, its photographs, illustrations, and advertisements are displayed in many museums in the United States such as the Metropolitan Museum of New York and the Smithsonian National Museum of American History.

The reason museums preserve these artifacts is because they provide a window on a time of great change in American society. The Oil-O-Matic was a significant technological advance that enabled many homes beginning in the 1930s and 1940s to convert from coal-fire to oil-fire heat. Still, late adopters burned coal in furnaces well into the 1940s, either out of habit or the financial hurdles of conversion to heating oil. The US Census of 1940 revealed that 75 percent of homes were still heated by coal or wood, with 55 percent burning coal/coke and 23 percent burning wood. With products like the Oil-O-Matic getting better and cheaper over time and sold through slick advertising and marketing, a conversion finally came, as those numbers of coal and wood burners dwindled in the census of 1970 to 2.9 percent and 1.3 percent, respectively.

William P. Kladky

See also: Home Energy Efficiency; Johnson, Warren Seymour; Nason, Joseph; Powers, William Penn; Richardson & Boynton Company

FURTHER READING

Amazon. 2023. "1926 Oil-O-Matic Oil Home Heater—Coal Furnaces Are Dirty—Original Magazine Ad." https://www.amazon.com/Matic-Heater-Furnaces-Original-Magazine/dp/B06XJDHCC8 (accessed October 2023).

Gridley, Rochelle. 2016. "Charles U. Williams, 1867–1953." 100 Years Ago in the Pentagraph. February 28. https://rgridley.wixsite.com/mclean-100-years-ago/post/2016/02/27/charles-u-williams-1867-1953 (accessed October 2023).

Griffith Energy Services (GES). 2019. "Home Heating Oil: An Overview of Its History and How It Heats Your Home." September 14. https://www.griffithenergyservices.com/articles/home-heating-oil-an-overview-of-its-history-and-how-it-heats-your-home (accessed October 2023).

Kemp, Bill. 2009. "Williams Oil-O-Matic Plant Beat Plowshares into Swords." *The Pentagraph*. August 29. https://pantagraph.com/news/local/williams-oil-o-matic-plant-beat-plowshares-into-swords/article_5b025a3e-94e5-11de-83e0-001cc4c03286.html (accessed October 2023).

Levco Tech, Inc. (LTI). 2023. "Heating Oil—A Brief History." https://www.levcooil.com/blog/heating-oil-a-brief-history (accessed October 2023).

McLean County Museum of History (MCMH). 2012. "Eureka Williams Electrolux." MCMH Bloomington, Illinois. https://mchistory.org/research/finding-aids/eureka-williams-electrolux (accessed October 2023).

"Merger Votes to Come." 1945. *The New York Times*. May 6.

"New Ads for Oil-O-Matic." 1945. *The New York Times*. August 2.

Spencer, Jeff A. 2020. "C. U. Williams (1867–1953): Petroleum Postcards to Oil-o-Matic Burners." *Oil-Industry History*. Vol. 21. Petroleum History Institute.

US Census Bureau (USCB). 2000. "Historical Census of Housing Tables: House Heating Fuel." US Department of Commerce. https://www.census.gov/data/tables/time-series/dec/coh-fuels.html (accessed October 2023).

Williams Oil-O-Matic (WOA). 1929. "A Fur Coat for Your Home." 1929 Williams Oil-O-Matic heating systems original vintage advertisement. Ad Classix. https://www.adclassix.com/a3/29williamsfurnace.htm (accessed October 2023).

Wind Power

Wind power is power derived from the energy of moving air, or wind. The Europeans who colonized the eastern shores of North America relied on the wind to propel the ships that carried them and their cargo, and they continued to do so in ascending the continent's rivers and in establishing trade with Europe and the islands of the West Indies. While they harnessed energy from the region's many rivers and streams with watermills in order to grind grain, saw wood, and so on, they also built windmills for the same purposes where conditions warranted. Windmills came into their own as Americans moved westward across the drier regions of the continent where they were needed to pump water. Today wind-generated electricity provides an increasing percentage of the nation's energy needs.

By the time European colonists reached the eastern shores of North America, shipbuilding was already a highly sophisticated technology, and the ships themselves were complex machines with a myriad working parts, large and small. For instance, the *Mayflower*, on which the Pilgrims sailed in 1620, was a three-masted, three-decked ship about 100 feet long and 25 feet wide capable of holding some 180 tons of cargo. It carried over a hundred passengers and a crew of about thirty, while armed with cannons of several sizes. Despite the ship's relative sophistication, however, it was not necessarily suited to a transatlantic voyage, as its high stern made it difficult to steer into the westerly winds it encountered on its outward voyage.

As time passed, Americans built a variety of ships suited for particular tasks, from carrying passengers to waging war, and from fishing and whaling to transporting cargo across the Atlantic and up and down the continent's coasts. Depending on their size and task, ships might be fitted with one mast or as many as seven, with sails arranged in a variety of patterns. The most sophisticated examples were the nineteenth-century China clippers that carried tea from China and were capable of speeds of up to 16 nautical miles per hour, making them the fastest commercial sailing vessels ever launched. Over the course of the nation's history, individuals with the skills and/or income also built and sailed small ships for pleasure, and the practice continues into the twenty-first century.

Windmills were in some ways the land-bound equivalents of sailing ships. They were common in many parts of Europe, and colonists from England, France, and the Netherlands built numerous examples in their new home. The structures came in two general designs. The first, the post mill, was mounted on a massive, vertical post (often reinforced with cross-trees) and needed to be turned in its entirety to face the wind. It is believed that the first windmill in British North America was a post mill built for Sir George Yeardley on his Flowerdew Hundred Plantation near Jamestown, Virginia, in 1621 to grind wheat and corn.

The second major type of windmill was the tower mill, built primarily of brick or stone or masonry, in which it was necessary to turn only the mill's cap into the wind. The structure of tower mills meant that the miller's family could live on the mill's lower floors. A variation on the tower mill, the smock mill, was often erected where the ground was unstable or otherwise unable to support a heavier structure. Built primarily from wood, smock mills were named for their resemblance to the garment worn by workers and often used for draining wet ground.

In a windmill, the force of the wind turned what were known as blades, or sails, which in turn rotated the windshaft, or axle, to which they were attached. The axle itself was connected to a brake wheel that turned the millstones at the base of the mill. Typical mills had four sails, and while as many as eight were possible, it was essential that the sail assembly always face directly into the wind in order to maintain the structure's stability. The earliest sails consisted of wooden frames covered with cloth, and while they were simple to make, it was necessary for the miller to disengage the mill's mechanism in order to furl the cloth. Later sail designs incorporated shutters, and eventually such shutters could be opened and closed while the mill remained in operation. A consistent wind speed of 15–25 miles an hour was generally necessary in order for a mill to be practical. Thanks to their strength, tower mills were able to handle wider and taller sails, a factor that increased the energy that they could generate.

Although most common in the eastern United States, windmills were eventually built in many locations throughout the country, and many remained in use until after the close of the US Civil War. However, as settlers moved across the Great Plains and into the Southwest, they were forced to rely on windmills for a different purpose—to pump water from aquifers, which are subterranean deposits of water, in order to irrigate their crops, sustain their herds, and provide for the requirements of advancing railroads. This situation brought about a series of revolutionary changes in mill design.

In 1854, Vermont-born machinist Daniel Halladay (1826–1916) patented the first commercially successful water-pumping windmill, the Halladay Standard—a model that turned automatically to face the wind and that featured multiple self-furling sails, which is important if the wind reached destructive strength. Shortly afterward, Halladay and two partners established what would become the Halladay Wind Mill Company, which was subsequently purchased by the US Wind Engine and Pump Company. It was while working for the latter firm that engineer Thomas Osborn Perry (1847–1927) developed a significantly more efficient design for windmill blades. But when his employers rejected his innovation, Perry joined forces with inventor and entrepreneur LaVerne W. Noyes (1849–1919) in 1888 to found the highly successful Aermotor Windmill Company. Thanks to this series of advances, more 600,000 water-pumping windmills dotted the United States by the 1930s, and they had become familiar landmarks.

JUMBO

One of the most unusual American windmills was the jumbo. The mill resembled an overshot waterwheel in form, generally being set up near the ground and having a horizontal axle and four to eight blades. A farmer could build a jumbo windmill from materials such as scrap lumber, flattened metal cans, and feed sacks, and its simplicity and low cost made the design a popular choice in the Midwest for pumping water for small gardens or powering simple machines.

Grove Koger

By then, however, yet another change was on the way. In the late 1880s, Ohio inventor Charles F. Brush (1849–1929) built an enormous 80,000-pound automatically operated wind turbine in his back yard. Believed to be the first large wind-to-electricity turbine in the world, it featured a 12-kilowatt dynamo and operated for more than twenty years. Within a short time, manufacturers had begun marketing versions that were small enough to be practical for farms. But as electrical utilities expanded service to the country's more isolated areas under the terms of the Rural Electrification Act of 1936, their use declined.

As concern about the problems such as climate change associated with fossil fuels has spread, however, research into renewable energy has grown rapidly. In turn, electricity-generating wind turbines have increased dramatically in size and numbers, with a prototype of one of the largest installed in 2018 at the UL Advanced Wind Turbine Test Facility at West Texas A&M University. Developed by Goldwind Americas, the turbine is 426.5 feet high at its hub, which is the center of its blade assembly, and its three blades rotate in a circle 446.2 feet in diameter.

America's first "wind farm," or group of wind turbines, was built in New Hampshire's Crotched Mountain in the early 1980s. A wind farm that went into operation in 2016 off the coast of Rhode Island, the Block Island Wind Farm, is the first commercial offshore wind farm in the country. Presently, California's Alta Wind Energy Center is the largest such facility in the country. In late 2023, there were 72,731 wind turbines on wind farms in forty-three states, with California's Alta Wind Energy Center being the largest such facility. The previous year, wind turbines generated over ten percent of the country's energy—a figure that is expected to grow to twenty percent by 2030.

While wind turbines appear to be a solution to many of the problems created by burning fossil fuels, critics point to the threat that they and the power lines and towers associated with them pose to birds and bats. However, the number of fatalities caused by turbines appears low in comparison with other human-related interactions with such animals.

Grove Koger

See also: Agriculture and Energy; Alta Wind Energy Center; Block Island Wind Farm; Climate Change; Crotched Mountain Wind Farm; Electricity; Halladay Windmill; Industrial Revolution; Perry, Thomas Osborn; Renewable Energy; Rural Electrification Act of 1936

FURTHER READING

Baker, T. Lindsay. 1985. *A Field Guide to American Windmills*. Norman, OK: University of Oklahoma Press.

Chapelle, Howard Irving. 1935. *The History of American Sailing Ships*. New York: Norton.

Jordan, Terry G. 1973. "Evolution of the American Windmill: A Study in Diffusion and Modification." *Pioneer America*. Vol. 5. No. 2. Pp. 3–12.

Noble, Allen G. 1992. "Windmills in American Agriculture." *Material Culture*. Special Farm Windmills and Domestic Tankhouse Issue. Vol. 24. No. 1. Pp. 1–12.

Office of Energy Efficiency and Renewable Energy (OEERE). 2015. *Wind Vision: A New Era for Wind Power in the United States*. Office of Scientific and Technical Information. US Department of Energy. https://www.nrel.gov/docs/fy15osti/63197-2.pdf (accessed December 24, 2019).

Righter, Robert W. 2011. *Windfall: Wind Energy in America Today*. Norman, OK: University of Oklahoma Press.

Yucca Mountain Nuclear Waste Repository

Located about 100 miles northwest of Las Vegas, Nevada, the Yucca Mountain Nuclear Waste Repository is undoubtedly one of the most controversial sites in the history of energy in the United States. In a world hungry for ever more electricity but also desperate to control carbon emissions, nuclear energy offers certain undeniable advantages. Perhaps most notable amongst these is the fact that the energy directly produced by a nuclear power plant is carbon neutral. The mining and refining of uranium ore, the construction of the power plants themselves, and the ground transportation of materials involved, produce greenhouse gases, but not the electricity generation itself. Moreover, completed nuclear power plants can continue to produce energy free of carbon emissions for decades once they go online. The unfortunate flipside is that these plants produce radioactive waste, this waste grows over time, this waste is highly dangerous, and this material remains exceptionally hazardous for generations. To be fair, other forms of energy also produce waste products that are quite problematic, and often vastly larger, but they tend to appear less sinister in the popular imagination. As nuclear power plants became increasingly common, the problem of what to do with the resulting nuclear waste became much more pressing. In 1982, Congress passed the Nuclear Waste Policy Act, which required the construction of two repositories purpose-built to store nuclear waste safely, one in the East of the United States, and one in the West.

Although many government projects traditionally have been perceived as attractive job-creating and economy-stimulating pork-barrel projects for politicians, the Nuclear Waste Policy Act, as we shall see, soon engendered a classic NIMBY ("Not In My Backyard") reaction. While proponents—and even opponents—of nuclear energy saw the clear and pressing need to dispose of and to store nuclear waste safely, few people would wish to have such a repository anywhere near their own homes. In 1983, a number of sites in half a dozen states had been identified as possible contenders, and the next year the US Department of Energy (DOE) issued specific site guidelines. By 1986, when the handful of remaining contenders were winnowed down to three finalists in Texas, Washington State, and Nevada, there was no longer any plan to build a repository in the East. The resulting choice of Yucca Mountain set the stage for decades of political wrangling, largely leaving unresolved the issues of safe storage of nuclear waste that Congress attempted to address in the original 1982 legislation.

Ultimately, Yucca Mountain was chosen as the site for the National Nuclear Waste Repository for a number of reasons that seemed to fulfill safety criteria. It is located within a 1,500-foot high rocky hill 100 miles from the nearest population center in Las Vegas, it is in the midst of inhospitable desert, and it is surrounded by federal land. Moreover, the site is largely isolated physically by various geographical features, namely the surface water within its basin is isolated from other water sources, seemingly eliminating the possibility of the contamination of public water supplies via surface water. It should be noted, however, that the groundwater deep within the rock beneath Yucca Mountain flows southward and westward out of the immediate area, passing through the Amargosa Valley, potentially compromising agricultural and Native American water sources. Most of this groundwater eventually emerges and returns to the atmosphere in Death Valley, some 50 miles away.

Moreover, technical and logistical elements, while undoubtedly crucial and emphasized during the selection process, were never the only factors involved in the decision. In truth, everything to do with the process of choosing and pursuing a site for a nuclear waste repository, including the determination upon Yucca Mountain, the ensuing years of debate and controversy, the eventual mothballing of the project, and more recent political promises regarding the site, all had strong political overtones. To cite perhaps the most contentious example, in 1987 when Yucca Mountain in Nevada was chosen, the contenders in Washington State and Texas were eliminated and Congress voted to stop the selection process and to finalize the choice of the site. It appeared to some observers that it was no coincidence that the Speaker of the House of Representatives, Jim Wright, was from Texas, and Tom Foley, the House Majority Leader, was from Washington State. Indeed, not many Nevadans believe in coincidence, at least not when it comes to nuclear waste, which explains in some measure why over three decades later it is still commonplace in the Silver State to refer to the 1987 Amendment to the Nuclear Waste Policy Act of 1982 as the "Screw Nevada Bill."

The next year the DOE began hearings on what is called "site characterization," an in-depth analysis of the history, composition, and suitability of the site for its proposed purpose. This process is meant to be exhaustive and should include analysis of key factors such as geology, hydrology, and susceptibility to seismic activity, as well as the structural and engineering parameters necessary to provide the safe and stable construction of the proposed facility on the potential site. One of the key outcomes of the site characterization at Yucca Mountain was the publication of a "Site Characterization Plan" by the DOE in 1988. One of the core recommendations of this plan was the design and construction of what was termed an "Exploratory Studies Facility." This facility in effect was to be test shafts meant to explore and test the site above, below, and on the level of proposed storage of hazardous waste in order to examine and ideally to prove the site's suitability for this purpose. The surface grading for this project began in 1993, and the next year the actual boring into the mountain began. As early as that same year, however, opponents of the project claimed that some aspects of the ongoing construction seemed more appropriate for and in line with Waste Repository design than Exploratory Facility construction. In 1995, the tunneling machinery encountered loose unstable layers, and by the next year it was clear that the site at Yucca Mountain was less than ideal for its intended purpose. Thermal testing proceeded in 1997, however, although the site was not prepared to accept waste by the stipulated deadline of January 1998. Lawsuits followed in the wake of this breach of contract with nuclear power providers, a situation exacerbated by the fact that Congress refused to approve temporary storage legislation. That same year, DOE issued a Yucca Mountain Viability Assessment that indicated that an official recommendation to proceed with the Repository could not be rendered until additional work had been completed on the site. Meanwhile the site was determined to remain viable for the planned purpose.

The more than twenty years since the late 1990s have been consumed with political and legal wrangling; Democratic administrations worked against the opening of the Repository, while their Republican counterparts were more supportive. Bill Clinton, for example, was prepared to veto legislation in favor of Yucca Mountain on multiple occasions, while President Obama convened the 2010 Blue Ribbon Commission on America's Nuclear Future, a board of fifteen experts, which eventually determined that Congress should create a body specifically to deal with spent nuclear fuel. The Obama administration attempted but ultimately failed to shutter the project. The Bush and then the Trump administrations, by way of contrast, managed to keep the project alive, if only on life-support. Nevadans of all political stripes, meanwhile, tended to oppose the project. Notable in this regard were long-time Nevada Democratic Senator Harry Reid and even Brian Sandoval, the Republican Governor of the State from 2011 to 2019, who was not incidentally a former State Attorney General (2003–5). There seemed to be no silver bullet to end the continuing political wrangling over the permanent storage of nuclear waste material at Yucca Mountain.

The political, legal, environmental, and regulatory issues surrounding the Yucca Mountain Repository are thorny and long-lasting, and cannot be resolved easily. Procedural problems with the choice of site, the imperfections of the site itself, and the lack of viable alternatives were, and continue to be, obstacles to a resolution. The unfortunate reality is, however, that the squabbling over this issue led to lost funds and wasted time, while no real progress has been made in the establishment of a centralized safe storage facility for nuclear waste in the United States. The end result is that spent nuclear fuel is stored at well over a hundred sites throughout most of the fifty states, and perhaps more than half the American population lives under 100 miles from such nuclear waste. The NIMBY controversy over Yucca Mountain has therefore guaranteed that the problem of nuclear waste is effectively in all of our back yards.

Christopher R. Fee

See also: Atomic Energy Acts; Church Rock Uranium Mill Spill; Energy Independence; Idaho National Laboratory; Natural Resources Defense Council; Navajo Reservation Uranium Mining; Nuclear Power; Nuclear Regulatory Commission; Shippingport Atomic Power Station; Three Mile Island Disaster; Union of Concerned Scientists

FURTHER READING

Belcher, Wayne R., John S. Stuckless, and Scott C. James. 2012. "The Saturated Zone Hydrology of Yucca Mountain and the Surrounding Area, Southern Nevada and Adjacent Areas of California, USA." In *GSA Memoirs: Hydrology and Geochemistry of Yucca Mountain and Vicinity, Southern Nevada and California*. Ed. John S. Stuckless. Boulder, CO: Geological Society of America. https://pubs.geoscienceworld.org/books/book/211/chapter/3794479/The-saturated-zone-hydrology-of-Yucca-Mountain (accessed 1 February 2021).

Conca, Jim. 2020. "Guest Opinion: Yucca Mountain is Not the Best Place for Nuclear Waste." *Tri-City Herald* (Kennewick, WA). February 13. https://www.tri-cityherald.com/opinion/opn-columns-blogs/article240247301.html (accessed 1 February 2021).

Ferguson, Bob. 2021. "Yucca Mountain Nuclear Waste Repository." Office of the Attorney General. State of Washington. https://www.atg.wa.gov/yucca-mountain-nuclear-waste-repository (accessed 1 February 2021).

Ford, Aaron D. 2021. "The Fight against Yucca Mountain." Office of the Attorney General. State of Nevada. https://ag.nv.gov/Hot_Topics/Issue/Yucca/ (accessed 1 February 2021).

Halstead, Bob. 2020. "Where I Stand: Nevada is Winning the War, but Yucca Mountain is Not Dead." *Las Vegas Sun* (Henderson, NV). August 23. https://lasvegassun.com/news/2020/aug/23/nevada-is-winning-the-war-but-yucca-mountain-is-no/ (accessed 1 February 2021).

Lupiani, Joyce. 2018. "History of Yucca Mountain: 1982-2018." KTNV Las Vegas. ABC 13. May 10. https://www.ktnv.com/news/history-of-yucca-mountain-1982-2018 (accessed 1 February 2021).

Nevada Commission on Nuclear Projects (NCNP). 2019. "Report and Recommendations of the Nevada Commission on Nuclear Projects." State of Nevada. November. https://www.yuccamountain.org/pdf/2019-nwpo-report-to-commission.pdf (accessed 1 February 2021).

US Environmental Protection Agency (EPA). 2020. "What are the Characteristics of Yucca Mountain?" April 10. https://www.epa.gov/radiation/what-are-characteristics-yucca-mountain (accessed 1 February 2021).

US Geological Survey (USGS). 2021a. "U.S. Geological Survey Involvement at Yucca Mountain." US Department of the Interior. https://nevada.usgs.gov/doe_nv/yucca_mountain.html (accessed 1 February 2021).

US Geological Survey (USGS). 2021b. "Yucca Mountain as a Radioactive Waste Repository." Circular #1184. US Department of the Interior. https://pubs.usgs.gov/circ/1184/pdf/c1184.pdf (accessed 1 February 2021).

US Nuclear Regulatory Commission (NRC). 2018. "Backgrounder on Licensing Yucca Mountain." June 18. https://www.nrc.gov/reading-rm/doc-collections/fact-sheets/yucca-license-review.html (accessed 1 February 2021).

US Nuclear Regulatory Commission (NRC). 2019. "Backgrounder on Radioactive Waste." July 23. https://www.nrc.gov/reading-rm/doc-collections/fact-sheets/radwaste.html (accessed 1 February 2021).

US Nuclear Regulatory Commission (NRC). 2012. "Progress Report #16, Chapter 7: Exploratory Studies Facility Design and Construction." November 17. https://www.nrc.gov/docs/ML0037/ML003773043.pdf (accessed 1 February 2021).

CHRONOLOGY

1621 Sir George Yeardley arranged for a post mill on his Flowerdew Hundred Plantation near Jamestown, Virginia to harness wind power for grinding wheat and corn

1643 Construction of a fulling mill for cotton textile production on Mill River in Rowley, Massachusetts by John Pearson, utilizing waterpower for energy

1712 Nantucket ship hunting right whales killed a sperm whale; its oil made a brighter and cleaner-burning light and set off longer, more dangerous hunts for sperm whale oil

1751 Publication of Benjamin Franklin's collected letters and reports of his investigations in the field of electricity, titled *Experiments and Observations on Electricity*

1795 Oliver Evans and Thomas Ellicott published *The Young Mill-Wright and Miller's Guide*, a widely read manual for setting up and operating waterpower mills

1808 Judge Jesse Fell of Wilkes-Barre, Pennsylvania demonstrated that rock-hard anthracite coal could be burned in an open grate, raising hope for its commercial development

1820 Whaling ship *Essex* sunk by a sperm whale during a two-year voyage to the South Pacific, which inspired Melville's *Moby-Dick*; depletion of sperm whales led to global hunts

Merger of two companies to form Lehigh Coal and Navigation Company, one of the earliest firms to develop anthracite coal in the US on a commercial basis

1821 The Merrimack Manufacturing Company formed to develop the Lowell (Mass.) waterpower system, a large hydropower project powering multiple textile mills

1825 William Hart drilled a natural gas well in Fredonia, New York and piped it to local houses for illumination, becoming first US commercial natural gas distributor

1829 Peter Cooper built and demonstrated the first US steam locomotive, dubbed "Tom Thumb," which inaugurated a period of innovation in steam locomotive technology

1832 Joseph Henry's experiments in electricity and magnetism; he wrapped copper wire around poles of magnet, sent current through the wire, and boosted the magnet's strength

1840 Waterpower lumber, grain, and textile mills number more than 55,000 across the country according to the US Census, one for every 245 people

1849 Patent granted to George Corliss for his improvements on the stationary steam engine, a device that encouraged industries to replace waterpower with coal-fired steam power

1851 Whale oil production in the US peaked at 328,483 barrels, which was marketed and consumed for illumination by lamplight in American homes and workplaces

Samuel Kier began operating the first US petroleum refinery in Pittsburgh, Pennsylvania, and offered his products as pharmaceuticals and illuminants

1854 Daniel Halladay received a patent for his "Halladay Self-Governing Windmill," known as the Halladay Standard, a wind-powered device for pumping groundwater on the Plains

1859 Edwin L. Drake struck oil near Titusville, Pennsylvania, inaugurating the Pennsylvania oil boom and the domestic oil industry in the US

1866 Peter Sweeney patented a steam-powered "Rotary Rock Boring Machine" that became the basis for rotary drills used in the oil fields of Texas, Louisiana, and Oklahoma

1870 Standard Oil Company founded in Cleveland, Ohio by John D. Rockefeller and his business partners; became a key agent in the creation of petroleum industry

1871 A fleet of forty whaling ships were trapped in Arctic ice north of Point Belcher, Alaska and thirty-three were abandoned, dealing a lethal blow to the whale oil industry

1876 Thomas Edison opened his laboratory in Menlo Park, New Jersey; over the course of his life, he secured 1,093 patents for his inventions from the US Patent Office

1877 Birdsill Holly built the first district steam heating system for Lockport, New York, which served as the model for New York Steam Company's system in Manhattan

1879 Electric arc light system devised by Charles Brush illuminated Cleveland's Public Square, proving the concept of street lighting by a centralized electrical power source

California Electric Light Company founded to create a municipal electricity system for San Francisco, and would eventually grow to become utility giant PG&E

1880 The Edison Illuminating Company founded by Thomas Edison for the purpose of developing and installing city-wide electrical systems for lighting

1881 Smoke from coal-fired steam plants in factories, locomotives, and residential buildings brought Chicago to enact a smoke abatement ordinance, an early air pollution law

1882 Edison Illuminating Company opened Pearl Street Station in Manhattan, the first centralized generating plant to serve multiple buildings with electrical lighting

1883 Warren Seymour Johnson's "electric tele-thermoscope" invented, which offered users more control over interior steam heating systems and gave birth to the thermostat

1886 Westinghouse engineer William Stanley, Jr. successfully operates an alternating-current (AC) illumination system in Great Barrington, Massachusetts

1888 President Edward Johnson of the Edison Electric Light Company published *A Warning from the Edison Electric Light Company*, attacking AC in the War of the Currents

1889 The first high-voltage transmission line carried 4,000 volts of electricity between a hydroelectric plant at Willamette Falls and Portland, Oregon 16 miles away

1890 Convicted murderer William Kemmler electrocuted in New York using AC, which was used for anti-AC propaganda by Edison against Westinghouse in the War of the Currents

Alfred Thayer Mahan published *The Influence of Sea Power upon History, 1660–1783,* which argued that coal supply was crucial to US strategic interests

1892 San Francisco began its well-known electric streetcar service, following the lead of the electric Richmond Union Passenger Railway, built in Virginia four years earlier

Edward Doheny struck oil at Second Street and Glendale Boulevard in Los Angeles, which began the California oil boom of the early twentieth century

1893 Chicago World's Columbian Exposition attracts 27 million visitors to see demonstrations of new electricity technologies by Edison, Tesla, and Westinghouse

1894 Electricity enabled moving pictures to be made; Thomas Edison's *Edison Kinetoscopic Record of a Sneeze,* also known as Fred Ott's Sneeze, is the earliest known

1895 Adams Hydroelectric Generating Plant opened at Niagara Falls, using AC equipment and prompting other utilities to adopt AC, thus ending the War of the Currents

1896 Henry Ford completed work on a prototype automobile, the Quadricycle, the success of which encouraged him to continue refining his design and his ideas for mass production

1897 The first National Electrical Code published by the National Board of Fire Underwriters, creating safety standards for installation and inspection of building electrical systems

1901 Prospectors operating a drill rig on Spindletop Hill salt dome near Beaumont, Texas struck oil and produced a gusher, setting off the Texas oil boom

1902 Formation of the company that became Texaco, one of the Seven Sisters oil companies that dominated the petroleum industry in the mid-twentieth century

1903 Ford Motor Company founded in Detroit, which produced "horseless carriages" for ordinary Americans powered by gasoline-burning internal combustion engines

1904 Ida Tarbell's serialized investigative reports are published together in *The History of the Standard Oil Company*, which detailed the company's monopolistic practices

1905 Piano teacher-turned oil tycoon Emma Summers signed oil supply contracts with Los Angeles County and the City Waterworks, becoming "Oil Queen" of California

1907 Year of coal mining disasters left 3,242 dead, including 362 killed in Monongah, West Virginia and 239 at a mine explosion near Jacobs Creek, Pennsylvania

1909 St. Paul Mining Company's coal mine in Cherry, Illinois caught fire and killed 259 men and boys; twenty-one survivors lived eight days in the mine before being rescued

1910 The US established Naval Petroleum Reserves in California and Alaska, signaling the transition from coal to oil in the US Navy and increasing demand for petroleum

1911 Standard Oil Trust found in violation of the Sherman Antitrust Act by the US Supreme Court and divided into thirty-four separate companies

Upton Machine Company founded to manufacture newly invented electric washing machines, stimulating production of electric-powered devices for the home

1913 Lincoln Highway was dedicated, connecting New York and San Francisco with over 3,000 miles of existing roads; first transcontinental road for cars and trucks

1914 Coal miners' strike against Colorado Fuel and Iron Company ends in a bloody massacre when the Colorado National Guard fires on a crowd in Ludlow, killing twenty-one

1916 The Federal-Aid Road Act enacted, which was the first federal program to assist states in building the road infrastructure to support new gasoline-powered autos

1917 US Fuel Administration created to supervise and administer coal and oil conservation policies during the First World War, including price controls and coordination of shipments

1918 The US instituted its first Daylight Saving Time during the First World War as a means of conserving coal and extending the workday into the evenings for wartime production

1922 Senate began investigation into Interior Secretary Albert Fall's suspicious granting of drilling leases on US public lands to oil executives Edward Doheny and Harry Sinclair

1927 The 15-millionth Ford Model T was assembled, signifying the advent of gasoline-powered automobiles as Americans' primary mode of transportation

1928 Red Line Agreement signed by Anglo-Persian Oil Company, Royal Dutch Shell Company, Compagnie Française de Pétroles, and a five-member group of US oil companies to form Turkish Petroleum Company with exclusive rights to oil in Iraq

1929 Interior Secretary Albert Fall convicted and jailed for bribery in the Teapot Dome Scandal; Harry Sinclair of Sinclair Oil and Mammoth Oil also convicted and jailed

1930 Oil glut prompted the state of Texas to give the Texas Railroad Commission authority to impose production limits to stabilize oil prices

1933 Tennessee Valley Authority Act passed to provide federal support for flood control and hydroelectric dams in the less-developed regions of the rural US South

Standard Oil of California signed a concession agreement with the government of King Ibn Saud to develop oil resources in Saudi Arabia, leading to the creation of Aramco

1935 Rural Electrification Administration created by executive order, empowered to grant loans to connect rural communities to regional power grids

Public Utility Holding Company Act signed, giving the Securities and Exchange Commission authority to monitor and break up electric utility monopolies

1936 Hoover Dam began generating electricity by hydropower as one of the New Deal's large-scale public power developments bringing energy to underserved areas

1937 Three oil tankers owned by Standard Oil Company were bombed by Japanese aircraft in Nanjing, China while evacuating civilians in the USS *Panay* incident, a prelude to war

1939 Albert Einstein wrote to President Roosevelt warning about Nazi uranium research and informed him about how atomic energy could be used to make powerful bombs

1941 FDR halted US sales of oil and gasoline to Japan in response to Japan's aggressions in China and Southeast Asia; Pearl Harbor attacks followed four months later

1942 Enrico Fermi directed the first controlled, self-sustaining nuclear chain reaction with the graphite-uranium Chicago Pile-1 underneath the University of Chicago's Stagg Field

1943 Big Inch pipeline from Texas oil fields to Pennsylvania was completed, enabling shipment of crude oil without risking German submarine attacks on oil tankers

1945 Test of atomic bomb at Trinity site in New Mexico in July, and atomic bombs were dropped on the Japanese cities of Hiroshima and Nagasaki in August

1946 President Truman signed the Atomic Energy Act, which transferred the military's Manhattan Project assets to the Atomic Energy Commission

1947 Completion of the Kerr-McGee Oil Industries, Inc.'s Kermac No. 16 oil drilling platform located 11 miles from the Louisiana coast, the world's first offshore oil drilling rig

Bell Labs scientists and inventors devised the transistor, the foundation of semiconductor technology that led to the digital revolution of the 1950s–1970s

1950 President Truman approved $1.4 billion to expand the Atomic Energy Commission's capacity to produce uranium and plutonium for nuclear weapons

1951 The Experimental Breeder Reactor No. 1 at the National Reactor Testing Station in Idaho produced electricity from a nuclear reactor for the first time

1953 President Dwight Eisenhower's "Atoms for Peace" speech calls for the use of nuclear energy in powering civilian electricity-generating plants

1954 Iran Oil Consortium Agreement gave Western oil companies rights to Iran's oil fields after US–UK initiated coup put pro-Western ruler Mohammad Reza Pahlavi in power

Bell Labs demonstrated the first practical silicon solar cell, a technology that used the sun's light, rather heat to produce energy

1956 Federal-Aid Highway Act became law and established the US interstate highway system, which spurred growth in the use of gasoline-powered automobiles and trucks

1957 Roger Revelle and Hans Seuss published a scientific article showing interaction between ocean and atmosphere in absorption of carbon dioxide, pointing toward global warming

1958 Dedication of Shippingport Atomic Power Station near Pittsburgh, Pennsylvania—the first operational US civilian nuclear power plant

1959 Boeing Airplane Company's 707 jet airliner made its inaugural commercial flight in January from Los Angeles to New York, ushering in the "Jet Age"

In July, President Nixon and Soviet Premier Khrushchev faced off in Moscow in the "Kitchen Debate," surrounded by symbols of US prosperity—electrical appliances

1960 Formation of OPEC at the Baghdad Conference in Iraq, which played an important role in global oil markets and international relations in second half of the twentieth century

1961 Low-power boiling water reactor, the SL-I, blew up at Idaho National Laboratory killing three personnel, who became first US fatalities in field of nuclear energy

1966 Uniform Time Act regulated Daylight Saving Time, which Wilson and FDR imposed temporarily during the First and Second World Wars to save energy on lighting

1967 Project Gasbuggy, part of Eisenhower's "Atoms for Peace" program, detonated an atomic bomb underground in New Mexico in a test of fracturing to release natural gas

1969 Federal Coal Mine Health and Safety Act signed, which created a system of inspections and sanctions to protect coal miners from accidents, explosions, and black lung

1970 Nixon administration established the US Environmental Protection Agency to control air and water pollution, which focused attention on the coal, oil, and gas industries

Earth Day celebrated nationally to galvanize public opinion behind new environmental laws and policies designed to address air pollution and water contamination

1972 Clean Water Act created protections for US waterways and overall water quality from industrial pollutants and discharges from coal and oil operations

1973 Arab states in OPEC declared an oil embargo on the US and other states supporting Israel in the Yom Kippur War, which inflamed the energy crisis of the 1970s

1979 Three Mile Island (PA) Unit 2 reactor partially melted down on March 28, becoming the most serious accident in US commercial nuclear power plant operating history

Uranium spill at Church Rock (NM) on Navajo land on July 16 poisoned 80 miles of the Puerco River with 94 million gallons of radioactive uranium tailings

1981 President Ronald Reagan signed Executive Order 12287, which released oil and gas from price and allocation controls in the Emergency Petroleum Allocation Act of 1973

1982 Secretary of the Interior James Watt announced plans to step up leasing of public land to coal mining companies, and quintupled the rate under his administration

Nuclear Waste Policy Act adopted to direct Department of Energy to establish a permanent repository for radioactive waste material from nuclear plants

1983 Interior Secretary James Watt said "I have a black, a woman, two Jews and a cripple" in reference to diversity on a coal leasing panel, forcing his resignation

1987 Congress enacted a measure that identified Yucca Mountain (NV) as the only site under consideration as a permanent storage facility for nuclear waste material

1989 *Exxon Valdez* oil tanker ran aground in Alaska's Prince William Sound, spilling 10.8 million gallons of oil on pristine coastline and elevating concerns about pollution

1991 US-led military coalition forcibly evicted Iraqi troops from Kuwait in the Gulf War to prevent Iraq President Saddam Hussein from controlling Kuwaiti oil fields

1992 United Nations Rio Summit produced the UN Framework Convention on Climate Change, focused on reducing use of energy sources that produce greenhouse gases

1996 Nuclear Waste Policy Act revised the earlier act from 1987, and required the US government to set up an interim storage area for nuclear waste material

1997 Founding of Project for a New American Century, composed of war hawks who shaped aggressive US foreign policy in the wake of the September 11, 2001 terrorist attacks

Kyoto Protocol to the UN Framework Convention on Climate Change adopted, binding signatory nations to reduce carbon dioxide emissions from oil and gas combustion

1998 Occidental Petroleum Corporation acquired Elk Hills Naval Preserve in California, divesting the US government from the extraction of oil and gas for military purposes

1999 Merger of Exxon and Mobil reunited portions of the original Standard Oil Company, which was dismantled in 1911 for violating the Sherman Antitrust Act

2000 President Bill Clinton vetoed a congressional bill that would have established Yucca Mountain (NV) as a permanent storage area for US nuclear waste material

2002 Yucca Mountain site recommended by Energy Secretary Spencer Abraham to President George Bush, who recommended it to Congress, which was approved

2005 Energy Policy Act provided incentives for expanded use of alternative fuels like biodiesel, ethanol, and hydrogen, as well as provisions for energy efficiency

2009 Energy Secretary Steven Chu, representing the Obama administration, told a Senate hearing that Yucca Mountain (NV) would not be considered for a nuclear waste facility

2010 *Deepwater Horizon* oil drilling platform exploded in the Gulf of Mexico, killing eleven and releasing 3.19 million barrels of oil into the ocean over eighty-seven days

2014 Nuclear Regulatory Commission issued report that claimed the Yucca Mountain (NV) site is a suitable location for a permanent nuclear waste storage facility

2015 CEO Don Blankenship of coal company Massey Energy sentenced to a year in federal prison for conspiring to violate mine safety laws in a 2010 mine explosion that killed twenty-nine of his employees

2016 President Barack Obama signed the Paris Agreement of 2015, which bound the US to take action to reduce carbon emissions and greenhouse gases that cause global warming

2017 Energy Secretary Rick Perry announced the Trump administration planned to proceed with Yucca Mountain (NV) designation as the US repository of nuclear waste

2020 President Donald Trump renounced the nation's participation in the Paris Agreement early in his administration, and US exit from the treaty took effect in November

2021 President Joe Biden reversed his predecessor's decision to withdraw the US from the Paris Agreement, and the US once again became a signatory to the treaty

CHRONOLOGICAL LIST OF PRIMARY DOCUMENTS

Henry David Thoreau, Except from *Walden*, 1856

Excerpt from *A Warning from The Edison Electric Light Co.*, 1888

Excerpt from a Report on the Krebs Mine Explosion, 1892

Theodore Roosevelt, Excerpt from *An Autobiography* on the Coal Panic of 1902

Ida M. Tarbell, Excerpt from *The History of The Standard Oil Company*, 1904

Henry Adams, Excerpt from "The Dynamo and the Virgin" in *The Education of Henry Adams*, written in 1907 and published in 1918

"The Constantly Increasing Use of the Motor Truck," 1915

"Electricity Solves Servant Problem," 1917

George Otis Smith, Excerpt from "A World View of the Oil Supply," 1920

Henry Ford, Excerpt from *My Life and Work*, 1922

Automobile Fatality, 1922

Mary Pattison, "The Abolition of Household Slavery," 1925

Franklin D. Roosevelt, "Address at the Dedication of Boulder Dam," 1935

Dwight D. Eisenhower, Excerpt from Atoms for Peace Speech, 1953

Jimmy Carter, "Address to the Nation on Energy," 1977

Dr. James Hansen, Testimony before the U.S. Senate Committee on Energy and Natural Resources Hearing on the Greenhouse Effect and Global Climate Change, 1988

PRIMARY DOCUMENTS

1. HENRY DAVID THOREAU, EXCERPT FROM *WALDEN*, 1856

As I sit at my window this summer afternoon, hawks are circling about my clearing; the tantivy of wild pigeons, flying by twos and threes athwart my view, or perching restless on the white-pine boughs behind my house, gives a voice to the air; a fishhawk dimples the glassy surface of the pond and brings up a fish; a mink steals out of the marsh before my door and seizes a frog by the shore; the sedge is bending under the weight of the reed-birds flitting hither and thither; and for the last half hour I have heard the rattle of railroad cars, now dying away and then reviving like the beat of a partridge, conveying travellers from Boston to the country. For I did not live so out of the world as that boy who, as I hear, was put out to a farmer in the east part of the town, but ere long ran away and came home again, quite down at the heel and homesick. He had never seen such a dull and out-of-the-way place; the folks were all gone off; why, you couldn't even hear the whistle! I doubt if there is such a place in Massachusetts now:—

> "In truth, our village has become a butt
> For one of those fleet railroad shafts, and o'er
> Our peaceful plain its soothing sound is—Concord."

The Fitchburg Railroad touches the pond about a hundred rods south of where I dwell. I usually go to the village along its causeway, and am, as it were, related to society by this link. The men on the freight trains, who go over the whole length of the road, bow to me as to an old acquaintance, they pass me so often, and apparently they take me for an employee; and so I am. I too would fain be a track-repairer somewhere in the orbit of the earth.

The whistle of the locomotive penetrates my woods summer and winter, sounding like the scream of a hawk sailing over some farmer's yard, informing me that many restless city merchants are arriving within the circle of the town, or adventurous country traders from the other side. As they come under one horizon, they shout their warning to get off the track to the other, heard sometimes through the circles of two towns. Here come your groceries, country; your rations, countrymen! Nor is there any man so independent on his farm that he can say them nay. And here's your pay for them! screams the countryman's whistle; timber like long battering rams going twenty miles an hour against the city's walls, and chairs enough to seat all the weary and heavy laden that dwell within them. With such huge and lumbering civility the country hands a chair to the city. All the Indian huckleberry hills are stripped, all the cranberry meadows are raked into the city. Up comes the cotton, down goes the woven cloth; up comes the silk, down goes the woollen; up come the books, but down goes the wit that writes them.

When I meet the engine with its train of cars moving off with planetary motion,—or, rather, like a comet, for the beholder knows not if with that velocity and with that direction it will ever revisit this system, since its orbit does not look like a returning curve,—with its steam cloud like a banner streaming behind in golden and silver wreaths, like many a downy cloud which I have seen, high in the heavens, unfolding its masses to the light,—as if this travelling demigod, this cloud-compeller, would ere long take the sunset sky for the livery of his train; when I hear the iron horse make the hills echo with his snort like thunder, shaking the earth with his feet, and breathing fire and smoke from his nostrils, (what kind of winged horse or fiery dragon they will put into the new Mythology I don't know), it seems as if the earth had got a race now worthy to inhabit it. If all were as it seems, and men made the elements their servants for noble ends! If the cloud that hangs over the engine were the perspiration of heroic deeds, or as beneficent as that which floats over the farmer's fields, then the elements and Nature herself would cheerfully accompany men on their errands and be their escort.

I watch the passage of the morning cars with the same feeling that I do the rising of the sun, which is hardly more regular. Their train of clouds stretching far behind and rising higher and higher, going to heaven while the cars are going to Boston, conceals the sun for a minute and casts my distant field into the shade, a celestial train beside which the petty train of cars which hugs the earth is but the barb of the spear. The stabler of the iron horse was up early this winter morning by the light of the stars amid the mountains, to fodder and harness his steed. Fire, too, was awakened thus early to put the vital heat in him and get him off. If the enterprise were as innocent as it is early! If the snow lies deep, they strap on his snow-shoes, and with the giant plow, plow a furrow from the mountains to the seaboard, in which the cars, like a following drill-barrow, sprinkle all the restless men and floating merchandise in the country for seed. All day the fire-steed flies over the country, stopping only that his master may rest, and I am awakened by his tramp and defiant snort at midnight, when in some remote glen in the woods he fronts the elements incased in ice and snow; and he will reach his stall only with the morning star, to start once more on his travels without rest or slumber. Or perchance, at evening, I hear him in his stable blowing off the superfluous energy of the day, that he may calm his nerves and cool his liver and brain for a few hours of iron slumber. If the enterprise were as heroic and commanding as it is protracted and unwearied!

Far through unfrequented woods on the confines of towns, where once only the hunter penetrated by day, in the darkest night dart these bright saloons without the knowledge of their inhabitants; this moment stopping at some brilliant station-house in town or city, where a social crowd is gathered, the next in the Dismal Swamp, scaring the owl and fox. The startings and arrivals of the cars are now the epochs in the village day. They go and come with such regularity and precision, and their whistle can be heard so far, that the farmers set their clocks by them, and thus one well conducted institution regulates a whole country. Have not men improved somewhat in punctuality since the railroad was invented? Do they not talk and think faster in the depot than they did in the stage-office? There is something electrifying in the atmosphere of the former place. I have been astonished at the miracles it has wrought; that some of my neighbors, who, I should have prophesied, once for all, would never get to Boston by so prompt a conveyance, are on hand when the bell rings. To do things "railroad fashion" is now the by-word; and it is worth the while to be warned so often and so sincerely by any power to get off its track. There is no stopping to read the riot act, no firing over the heads of the mob, in this case. We have constructed a fate, an Atropos, that never turns aside. (Let that be the name of your engine.) Men are advertised that at a certain hour and minute these bolts will be shot toward particular points of the compass; yet it interferes with no man's business, and the children go to school on the other track. We live the steadier for it. We are all educated thus to be sons of Tell. The air is full of invisible bolts. Every path but your own is the path of fate. Keep on your own track, then.

What recommends commerce to me is its enterprise and bravery. It does not clasp its hands and pray to Jupiter. I see these men every day go about their business with more or less courage and content, doing more even than they suspect, and perchance better employed than they could have consciously devised. I am less affected by their heroism who stood up for half an hour in the front line at Buena Vista, than by the steady and cheerful valor of the men who inhabit the snow-plough for their winter quarters; who have not merely the three-o'-clock in the morning courage, which Bonaparte thought was the rarest, but whose courage does not go to rest so early, who go to sleep only when the storm sleeps or the sinews of their iron steed are frozen. On this morning of the Great Snow, perchance, which is still raging and chilling men's blood, I hear the muffled tone of their engine bell from out the fog bank of their chilled breath, which announces that the cars *are coming*, without long delay, notwithstanding the veto of a New England north-east snow storm, and I behold the ploughmen covered with snow and rime, their heads peering, above the mould-board which is turning down other than daisies and the nests of field-mice, like bowlders of the Sierra Nevada, that occupy an outside place in the universe.

Commerce is unexpectedly confident and serene, alert, adventurous, and unwearied. It is very natural in its methods withal, far more so than many fantastic enterprises and sentimental experiments, and hence its singular success. I am refreshed and expanded when the freight train rattles past me, and I smell the stores which go dispensing their odors all the way from Long Wharf to Lake Champlain, reminding me of foreign parts, of coral reefs, and Indian oceans, and tropical climes, and the extent of the globe. I feel more like a citizen of the world at the sight of the palm-leaf which will cover so many flaxen New England heads the next summer, the Manilla hemp and cocoa-nut husks, the old junk, gunny bags, scrap iron, and rusty nails. This carload of torn sails is more legible and interesting now than if they should be wrought into paper and printed books. Who can write so graphically the history of the storms they have weathered as these rents have done? They are proof-sheets which need no correction. Here goes lumber from the Maine woods, which did not go out to sea in the last freshet, risen four dollars on the thousand because of what did go out or was split up; pine, spruce, cedar,—first, second, third, and fourth qualities, so lately all of one quality, to wave over the bear, and moose, and caribou. Next rolls Thomaston lime, a prime lot, which will get far among the hills before it gets slacked. These rags in bales, of all hues and qualities, the lowest condition to which cotton and linen descend, the final result of dress,—of patterns which are now no longer cried up, unless it be in Milwaukie, as those splendid articles, English, French, or American prints, ginghams, muslins, &c., gathered from all quarters both of fashion and poverty, going to become paper of one color or a few shades only, on which forsooth will be written tales of real life, high and low, and founded on fact! This closed car smells of salt fish, the strong New England and commercial scent, reminding me of the Grand Banks and the fisheries. Who has not seen a salt fish, thoroughly cured for this world, so that nothing can spoil it, and putting the perseverance of the saints to the blush? with which you may sweep or pave the streets, and split your kindlings, and the teamster shelter himself and his lading against sun wind and rain behind it,—and the trader, as a Concord trader once did, hang it up by his door for a sign when he commences business, until at last his oldest customer cannot tell surely whether it be animal, vegetable, or mineral, and yet it shall be as pure as a snowflake, and if it be put into a pot and boiled, will come out an excellent dun fish for a

Saturday's dinner. Next Spanish hides, with the tails still preserving their twist and the angle of elevation they had when the oxen that wore them were careering over the pampas of the Spanish main,—a type of all obstinacy, and evincing how almost hopeless and incurable are all constitutional vices. I confess, that practically speaking, when I have learned a man's real disposition, I have no hopes of changing it for the better or worse in this state of existence. As the Orientals say, "A cur's tail may be warmed, and pressed, and bound round with ligatures, and after a twelve years' labor bestowed upon it, still it will retain its natural form." The only effectual cure for such inveteracies as these tails exhibit is to make glue of them, which I believe is what is usually done with them, and then they will stay put and stick. Here is a hogshead of molasses or of brandy directed to John Smith, Cuttingsville, Vermont, some trader among the Green Mountains, who imports for the farmers near his clearing, and now perchance stands over his bulk-head and thinks of the last arrivals on the coast, how they may affect the price for him, telling his customers this moment, as he has told them twenty times before this morning, that he expects some by the next train of prime quality. It is advertised in the *Cuttingsville Times*.

While these things go up other things come down. Warned by the whizzing sound, I look up from my book and see some tall pine, hewn on far northern hills, which has winged its way over the Green Mountains and the Connecticut, shot like an arrow through the township within ten minutes, and scarce another eye beholds it; going

"to be the mast
Of some great ammiral."

And hark! here comes the cattle train bearing the cattle of a thousand hills, sheepcots, stables, and cow-yards in the air, drovers with their sticks, and shepherd boys in the midst of their flocks, all but the mountain pastures, whirled along like leaves blown from the mountains by the September gales. The air is filled with the bleating of calves and sheep, and the hustling of oxen, as if a pastoral valley were going by. When the old bell-wether at the head rattles his bell, the mountains do indeed skip like rams and the little hills like lambs. A carload of drovers, too, in the midst, on a level with their droves now, their vocation gone, but still clinging to their useless sticks as their badge of office. But their dogs, where are they? It is a stampede to them; they are quite thrown out; they have lost the scent. Methinks I hear them barking behind the Peterboro' Hills, or panting up the western slope of the Green Mountains. They will not be in at the death. Their vocation, too, is gone. Their fidelity and sagacity are below par now. They will slink back to their kennels in disgrace, or perchance run wild and strike a league with the wolf and the fox. So is your pastoral life whirled past and away. But the bell rings, and I must get off the track and let the cars go by;—

What's the railroad to me?
I never go to see
Where it ends.
It fills a few hollows,
And makes banks for the swallows,
It sets the sand a-blowing,
And the blackberries a-growing,

but I cross it like a cart-path in the woods. I will not have my eyes put out and my ears spoiled by its smoke and steam and hissing.

Source: Thoreau, Henry David. *Walden; or, Life in the Woods.* Boston: Ticknor & Fields, 1854.

2. EXCERPT FROM *A WARNING FROM THE EDISON ELECTRIC LIGHT CO.*, 1888

Some Dangers of the Alternating System

Dr. Otto Moses, the apostle of the alternating system, made the following statement in August last, before the National Electric Light Association, at its session in Boston:

"A friend of mine was testing a 400 light 1050 volt alternating dynamo fully loaded only a few days ago, and going towards the machine, his foot slipped and he fell quite close to it; in his confusion he quickly reached out his hands and unfortunately placed them directly upon the poles of the dynamo. He said from where he fell to the walls behind him was about fifteen feet, and it seemed to him as if that dynamo was suddenly converted into an electrical gun, and he got shot across the room until the velocity of his movement was interfered with by the wall."

At the same meeting, W. R. Kimball of Boston, electrical expert, said:

"The question of the insulation of high potential wires is one which appeals to every part of the electric light station, whether he be lineman or manager. In the one case, it is his own life and limb that are involved; and in the other case it is property. And yet there is danger in carrying high potential wires into cellars and basements".

"The question of the insulation between the primary and the secondary of the inductive coil is governed by a variety of causes. Where converters are placed out of doors moisture will get in. No matter how careful the wires may be placed, the current will be affected. This bold expedient of grounding the inside wire has been brought to the attention of this Convention and the public by some of the electrical papers. It seems to me that it opens a field for discussion. The question naturally arises in the minds of insurance men whether running electrical wires down to the ground is not an unheard of thing".

One of the prominent exponents of the Westinghouse methods also said at the same session:

"In Pittsburgh, where we were running lights in a rather poor neighborhood, we found it cheaper to run secondary mains, attaching our lights in the houses from the secondary current, using fifty or one hundred volts as we pleased. In other parts of the town, where they were using fifteen or twenty lights in each house, we found it better to carry the converters into the building or fasten them as close as possible on the outside wall, so as to enable us to use the fifty-volt lamps exclusively. In the case of hotels, we would run a high-pressure wire down the centre of the corridor, and place converters at each group".

In marked contrast with this confidence inspired by ignorance and recklessness, we find that a year ago the eminent European electrical firm of Siemens & Halske, in a pamphlet issued by them on alternating currents, gave an alarm of no uncertain sound. The fact should be borne in mind that they were really the inventors and the builders of the best alternating machinery which has ever been offered to the public, that the product of their mammoth factory has been widely used for a long series of years, and they have discontinued building this apparatus as being dangerous. They conclude in these words:

"SO FAR LEGISLATION HAS NOT CONCERNED ITSELF WITH THE DANGERS OF THIS SYSTEM, BUT SOONER OR LATER WILL BE COMPELLED TO DO SO."

Recent advices show that action has since been taken to prohibit the use of high-tension alternating currents. It is also noteworthy that in the United States the insurance companies have been independently led, because of actual burning out of converters, and explosion of their metal cases, to absolutely prohibit their placement in buildings.

This restriction has recently been enforced, even in cases where underground services had been introduced and the converters placed on the walls of cellars. No more forcible commentary can be imagined of the distrust felt by the underwriters in subjecting their risks to the hazards of high—pressure currents, than the rule issued November 1, 1887, by the Boston Board of Fire Underwriters:

"Converters on alternating circuits must be outside of buildings, and must be placed high enough from the roof to prevent possible injury to firemen."

Within a few days of this issue (November 4, 1887) the New England Insurance Exchange, at a meeting of representatives of all the electric light companies doing business in the Eastern States, called to consider this subject, gave notice that they should under no circumstances allow converters to be placed within the walls of buildings.

In Philadelphia, the only city where these silent dynamos are thus tolerated inside the walls of buildings under any intelligent supervision, Inspector McDevitt of the Insurance Patrol confines them strictly to cellars, and states distinctly that they will be obliged to go to the street the moment any one of them explodes or sets a fire.

In Chicago, City Inspector Haskins absolutely prohibits the use of any alternating current system or other high—pressure makeshift for incandescent lighting.

[Extracts from the *Daily States* (New Orleans), Sept. 23, 1887.]

Electric Wire Dangers. How Linemen are Injured or Killed. The Alternating Current as Contrasted with the Low Tension Direct Current.

Several accidents have happened of late to linemen of electric light companies, who have been knocked senseless by coming in contact with wires while in the performance of their duties. Tuesday last a lineman in the employ of the Edison Light Company was knocked from a pole at the corner of Canal and Carondelet Streets by receiving a shock from a wire charged with the alternating high-tension current from the Westinghouse machines used by the Brush Electric Light Company.

The accident was the second serious occurrence in this city from the Westinghouse alternating current. Fortunately it has not so far turned out to be fatal as did the accident of a month ago, which occurred as follow: The unfortunate man who was killed was at work on a pole pulling up a dead arc wire, when his foot slipped and he fell across the wires carrying the alternating current, which wires had been bared of insulation in order to tie them in firmly to the insulators. The man was suspended by the wires, and the current passed through his body from the inside of one thigh to the upper ribs on the other side, the flesh being burned to the bone in both places. It was probably five minutes before they could switch off the current from him and by that time he was stone dead.

Two serious accidents, one being fatal from the alternating current in the course of five weeks, render it necessary to call attention to this new element of danger in the streets, and to consider what precautions should be taken. The alternating system is new in this country, and very little experience has been had with it compared with the arc system. However, this experience has shown that this current is quite as dangerous, if not more so, than the arc current, which has killed so many men. There are two reasons for this: first—the full pressure of current (1,000 to 1,200 volts) is on every pole line circuit; second—the wires running parallel with one an other only a short distance apart, it is very easy to obtain a shock; in fact it is very difficult for a man working on a pole to avoid receiving a shock sufficient to knock him from a pole, and should he be suspended and unable to free himself, as occurred in the fatal accident referred to, the shock quickly proves fatal.

The effects of an alternating shock merely from leakage are graphically described in the records of the convention before referred to. Mr. Smith of the Westinghouse Company detailed the prostration of a veteran lineman who was unable to release himself, became black in the face, was treated for asphyxia, and was so severely burned that his hand was opened by the attending surgeon. Those who went to his assistance were painfully shocked in spite of careful protection to their own persons.

Not alone is this current dangerous to station employees. The "New York World" of December 12, 1887, has the following account of the death of a horse: Killed by Electricity. A Horse Touches a Telephone Wire on Staten Island and Drops Dead.

"A singular accident resulting in the death of a horse belonging to C.F. Gaellis, a cracker dealer, at Mariners' Harbor, S. I., occurred this morning at 4:30 o'clock. Mr. Gaellis sends his wagon with a double team to this city early every Monday morning.

While his driver, Christian Klengel, was passing in front or near the residence of Dr. W.C. Walsh at Port Richmond, S.I., one of the horses became entangled in a telephone wire which was dangling in the street, being broken, and in a twinkling the horse, valued at $250, was dead.

Policeman Finan, who was nearby, attempted to remove the horse from the middle of the street to the gutter, when he received a severe electric shock which knocked him senseless. He soon recovered.

Some time during the night one of the telephone wires broke, and, falling across the electric light wire, became charged with electricity, and when the horse was entangled, the circuit to the ground was complete. Hence the accident".

NEW ORLEANS, La., November 29th, 1887.
E. H. JOHNSON, Esq.,
Prest. Edison Electric Light Company, New York.

DEAR SIR: As New Orleans is with one exception the largest and most important station now supplying incandescent lights on the Westinghouse Alternating system, you will doubtless be interested to hear some account of its operation during the eight months of its existence.

Their record during this period has been a continual series of mishaps. They have suffered damages and interruptions from almost every possible cause, viz.: engines, dynamos, line wires and converters.

The alternating current has killed two men and has injured several others. One of these accidents has resulted in a lawsuit for $25,000 damages, and it is rumored that another suit is contemplated on behalf of the relatives of one of the men killed. This was a telephone lineman and was at the time stringing wires in the ordinary way. The telephone company have applied to the courts for an injunction against the Brush company using a Westinghouse alternating system to prevent them from running their wires in proximity to telephone wires or poles.

Some time ago one of their high-tension alternating circuits dropped on to a tin roof and set the woodwork underneath on fire. The fire department were called out and had considerable difficulty in extinguishing the flames. The short circuit burnt out a 1,300 light armature, whereupon the dynamo man threw another machine into circuit, and a second armature burned out.

About ten days ago they knocked out a cylinder head and broke the cross-head of one of their large Corliss engines, carrying a 1,300 light and a 650 light dynamo. Having no reserve, all the lights supplied by these dynamos were out a week, their customers having to resort to gas, candles or kerosene. After four days they got their engine repaired and started again. Shortly after starting one of the 1,300 light armatures burned out from no apparent cause. Putting in the only spare armature they had they ran all right for about twelve hours, when the second armature burned out in the same way.

This caused another delay of three days, and made a total to date of four armatures burnt out.

On a recent Saturday evening a pulley came off one of the 1,300 light machines, putting a theatre, among the rest, in darkness for half an hour.

Until their dynamos were fairly loaded they ran with a fair amount of satisfaction except during thunderstorms, during which the lightning played havoc with the converters, burning out from three to seven every time.

In addition to the above they have had a large number of mishaps of which I have not heard the details.

Naturally their customers are all very much dissatisfied, and it is a very common thing to see the Westinghouse lights helped out by gas, or arc lights burning at the same time.

They light up the prominent clubs, and unfortunately for them they are all supplied by the circuit which was disabled for a week through the breaking down of the engine and the burning out of the two armatures.

The operation of the Westinghouse system has been disastrous financially to the local Brush company. Previous to commencing with it they were in a sound financial condition.

Now they are nearly bankrupt and are at their wits' end to know how to raise money to go on. Their $100 stock is unsalable at twenty five; in fact a block was recently sold at twenty-two. A gentleman whom I know has a large amount of stock which he could have sold a year ago at $85, and he would now be glad to get $30. The daily paper for Jan. 13, 1887, quotes Brush stock at $73 "asked," to day's paper gives $35 "asked" and $20 offered. On the other hand the recent breakdown of the Westinghouse system has caused gas stock to go up five points within a week.

Yours very truly,
WM. T. M. MOTTRAM.

Source: Johnson, Edward H. *A Warning from the Edison Electric Light Company*. The Edison Electric Light Company, 1888.

3. EXCERPT FROM A REPORT ON THE KREBS MINE EXPLOSION, 1892

Mourning at the M'Alester, Ind. T. mines–Sixty-seven wounded and fourteen missing—Sixty-five coffins ordered—Edward Morgan's heroism—The cause of the explosion.

McAlester, Ind. T., January 9

The sister cities of South McAlester, McAlester, and Krebs to-day presented the appearance of deepest mourning. The court, which has been in session at South McAlester, was adjourned by Judge Shackelford yesterday morning and was not reconvened to-day. All business places are closed and are draped in mourning. The sole topic is the terrible mine explosion which has befallen the community.

The list of the dead, as far as can be ascertained, numbers fifty-one, with fourteen missing, and sixty-seven injured. The scenes at Krebs to-day were awful. The explosion has rendered hundreds of homes desolate. Your correspondent visited as many of them as possible and can only say that one line will describe the misery of all. The same heartrending scenes may be witnessed in each successive house. Every hovel is an improvised hospital, with beds and floors strewn with the injured.

"For God's sake, give me a mattress," wailed one unfortunate wretch who had lain upon the hard floor for forty-eight hours.

"We are doing our utmost to relieve their sufferings," said General Surgeon E. N. Allen, of the Choctaw Railroad, "but the medical force has been inadequate. Why, last night at 5 o'clock I personally attended injured men who had been brought to the surface twenty hours before and had lain all that time without medical attention, all simply because all the available physicians and surgeons, though working to their utmost capacity, could not reach them before." The injured present a most pitiable sight. All were burned and many mangled by flying rocks and timbers.

Stories of the Rescued

"I have experienced all the tortures of hell," said Peter Christie, who escaped by climbing through a tunnel to shaft 7, which adjoined the doomed No. 11.

"I was thrown 20 feet through the air over two cars. I jumped up and started through the air tunnel, seeking to escape. My injuries soon exhausted me, and I fell and was quickly trampled over by the fleeing miners, all bruising my body as you can see. I gained strength enough to raise a pick, and threatened the others who would have stepped upon me. Then, gaining additional strength, I got up and groped my way to the entrance and climbed out. On my way I encountered scores of dead and dying comrades. Some of the latter were undergoing every agonizing contortion imaginable. One man whose clothes were burning from his body appeared so lifelike in posture that I went to his assistance only to discover that he was dead. The dying wails and shrieks of pain of the injured were frightful. Even Dante could not picture an inferno such as I have witnessed during the last night. One man was kicked to death in my sight by the frightened mules, whose heels he was unable to escape. I can not half tell the terrors of last night".

Another victim said: "I have been a fool. I have known of the threatened danger in shaft 11, but remained at work thinking that the danger was at least not immediate. Now, in consequence, I am a physical wreck, perhaps permanently incapable of work, while in the past year I have made three hundred and sixty-five resolutions not to enter that shaft again."

The neighborhood of the disaster was comparatively quiet to-day. Sorrowing friends and relatives seemed to have exhausted themselves and sought much-needed rest in their homes. Many tales of both horror and valor are brought to light. One corpse was brought to the surface to-day clasping tightly in its stiffened arms the detached arm of a comrade, and throughout the entire day that once vigorous member of a swarthy human laid upon the slab unrecognized and adding additional terror to the hearts of the sorrowing throng, who seemed to hope that they would find familiar faces amongst the dead. One widowed mother lost both sons who were her only means of support. A blind father lost one son, while his remaining son is fatally injured, depriving him of his only means of support. A bride of two weeks mourns the loss of her idol. It seems utterly impossible to describe properly any of the horrible experiences which are presented on all sides. Wives distracted by seeking absent husbands, mothers seeking sons who are their only means of support, and sweethearts seeking those who soon were to have been their all in this world, it can easily be understood that columns should be devoted to an accurate description of such pathetic scenes.

Edward Morgan's Heroism

Even deeds of heroism, which are numerous, can not be recounted in detail, though they certainly deserve it. Conspicuous, however, is the act of Edward Morgan, who was the first man to enter the yawning maw of the death hole. Other miners volunteered to accompany him, but were urged back by him.

"It is useless to expose an unnecessary number of lives to sacrifice," said he. "I will go down and ascertain the danger, and you can follow if it is safe." Fortunately it was safe, and the volunteers have worked nobly in the rescue of their imprisoned brothers. The different secret organizations have assumed charge of the funeral arrangements. Special engines were dispatched by the Choctaw and M. K. and T. railways last night for an extra supply of coffins, but many corpses remain unprepared for burial because the supply of caskets and shrouds were early exhausted. Sixty-five coffins have been ordered by the company alone, while local undertakers have sent for another carload.

Negroes Create Trouble

Men of all nationalities are aiding in the work of rescue. Americans, Irishmen, Scotchmen, Polanders, Welshmen, Italians, Swedes; all but negroes are at the work. Some time since the white miners refused to work with the negroes. This morning a number of the negroes went to Krebs and assisted in the work in only a half-hearted way, and one of their number was heard to say that it served the miners right to have been killed. The word was passed from month to mouth, and the indignation and fury of the miners knew no bounds. It seemed as though another horror would be added to the scene, but the United States deputy marshal, anticipating some such trouble, was on hand with a posse, and they drove the colored men from the place at the point of Winchesters.

It was almost impossible to recognize any resemblance to the human form in the bodies of many of those rescued. Heads, arms, legs, hands, and feet were in many instances torn from the trunks. The pit clothes were either partially or entirely burned away, and in several cases the flames had roasted almost all the flesh on the body. The dead were taken to a blacksmith shop near the main shaft, where a morgue had been improvised, and the living to their homes. The crowd vacillated between the shaft and the blacksmith shop all day. The latter place was constantly crowded with people searching to find those whom they knew must be either dead or badly hurt.

Each article of clothing and the contents of the pockets were closely scrutinized, and any distinguishable mark of nature whereby the body could be identified was eagerly searched for. A number of dismembered limbs are lying in the morgue waiting identification. They were fitted to many bodies with the arms and legs missing, but no identification could be made. Yesterday afternoon when the work of relief began carload after carload of earth was removed from the mine, loosened by the explosion, and quantities of rock and slate were also taken out. There are probably ten more bodies under the earth and rock remaining.

A Horrible Sight

A most horrible sight met the rescuing parties as the bottom of the shaft was reached. Here a head, there a hand or leg protruded from the mass of fallen rock. A number of burned lamps, caps, and dinner buckets completed the desolation of the scene. The bodies were removed with all possible care, but this did not prevent an arm or a leg, almost severed from the body, from being completely torn off when taken from under the wreckage.

The force of the explosion tore the mine all to pieces. It closed up the galleries, tore down the barricades, which kept the air from circulating freely through the unused portion of the mine, thus cutting off all air from the galleries in use and left them, as was supposed, wholly untenable. None escaped except those brought up from the entrance or by shaft No.7.

This morning the relief party of the Krebs miners was compelled, after forty-eight hours' steady labor, to stop work. The party was completely exhausted. The relief party is headed by Young Cameron, boss of the mine at Lehigh. The men are doing excellent work under his direction. Three carloads of mules were in the mine when the explosion occurred, and strange to say only two of the animals were hurt. The boss driver, Tom Kane, was killed.

The frenzied brutes committed great damage to the mine in their efforts to find an outlet.

The Shot-Firers to Blame

Thomas Fleming, a mining expert and for eight years superintendent of the mine, but now general manager of the Southwestern Coal and Improvement Company, was interviewed this morning in regard to the explosion. He said that the whole blame should be placed upon the shot-firers, who fired the blast too soon. A windy shot caused the catastrophe. The blast was overcharged. It should have been fired at 5:30 o'clock, after the miners had left the mine, in which case the explosion would have occurred, but only 5 or 6 men would have been killed. As it was the shot was fired at 5:07 o'clock, before the men had ascended from the mine.

Source: Committee on the Territories. "Report on Mines and Mining in the Indian Territory." US House of Representatives, 52nd Congress, 1st session. Report No. 162, 1892.

4. THEODORE ROOSEVELT, EXCERPT FROM *AN AUTOBIOGRAPHY* ON THE COAL PANIC OF 1902

So great was that public interest in the Coal Strike of 1902, so deeply and strongly did I feel the wave of indignation which swept over the whole country that had I not succeeded in my efforts to induce the operators to listen to reason, I should reluctantly but none the less decisively have taken a step which would have brought down upon my head the execrations of many of "the captains of industry," as well as of sundry "respectable" newspapers who dutifully take their cue from them. As a man should be judged by his intentions as well as by his actions, I will give here the story of the intervention that never happened.

While the coal operators were exulting over the fact that they had "turned down" the miners and the president, there arose in all parts of the country an outburst of wrath so universal that even so naturally conservative a man as Grover Cleveland wrote to me, expressing his sympathy with the course I was following, his indignation at the conduct of the operators, and his hope that I would devise some method of effective action. In my own mind I was already planning effective action; but it was of a very drastic character, and I did not wish to take it until the failure of all other expedients had rendered it necessary. Above all, I did not wish to talk about it until and unless I actually acted. I had definitely determined that somehow or other act I would, that somehow or other the coal famine should be broken. To accomplish this end it was necessary that the mines should be run, and, if I could get no voluntary agreement between the contending sides, that an Arbitration Commission should be appointed which would command such public confidence as to enable me, without too much difficulty, to enforce its terms upon both parties. Ex-President Cleveland's letter not merely gratified me, but gave me the chance to secure him as head of the Arbitration Commission. I at once wrote him, stating that I would very probably have to appoint an Arbitration Commission or Investigating Commission to look into the matter and decide on the rights of the case, whether or not the operators asked for or agreed to abide by the decisions of such a Commission; and that I would ask him to accept the chief place on the Commission. He answered that he would do so. I picked out several first-class men for other positions on the Commission.

Meanwhile the Governor of Pennsylvania had all the Pennsylvania militia in the anthracite region, although without any effect upon the resumption of mining. The method of action upon which I had determined in the last resort was to get the Governor of Pennsylvania to ask me to keep order. Then I would put in the army under the command of some first-rate general. I would instruct this general to keep absolute order, taking any steps whatever that was necessary to prevent interference by the strikers or their sympathizers with men who wanted to work. I would also instruct him to dispossess the operators and run the mines as a receiver until such time as the Commission might make its report, and until I, as President, might issue further orders in view of this report. I had to find a man who possessed the necessary good sense, judgment, and nerve to act in such event. He was ready to hand in the person of Major-General Schofield. I sent for him, telling him that if I had to make use of him it would be because the crisis was only less serious than that of the Civil War, that the action taken would be practically a war measure, and that if I sent him he must act in a purely military capacity under me as commander-in-chief, paying no heed to any authority, judicial or otherwise, except mine. He was a fine fellow—a most respectable-looking old boy, with side whiskers and a black skull-cap, without any of the outward aspect of the conventional military dictator; but in both nerve and judgment he was all right, and he answered quietly that if I gave the order he would take possession of the mines, and would guarantee to open them and to run them without permitting any interference either by the owners or the strikers or anybody else, so long as I told him to stay. I then saw Senator Quay, who, like every other responsible man in high position, was greatly wrought up over the condition of things. I told him that he need be under no alarm as to the problem not being solved, that I was going to make another effort to get the operators and miners to come together, but that I would solve the problem in any event and get coal; that, however, I did not wish to tell him anything of the details of my intention, but merely to have him arrange that whenever I gave the word the Governor of Pennsylvania should request me to intervene; that when this was done I would be responsible for all that followed, and would guarantee that the coal famine would end forthwith. The Senator made no inquiry or comment, and merely told me that he in his turn would guarantee that the Governor would request my intervention the minute I asked that the request be made.

These negotiations were concluded with the utmost secrecy, General Schofield being the only man who knew exactly what my plan was, and Senator Quay, two members of my Cabinet, and ex-President Cleveland and the other men whom I proposed to put on the Commission, the only other men who knew that I had a plan. As I have above outlined, my efforts to bring about an agreement between the operators and miners were finally successful. I was glad not to have to take possession of the mines on my own initiative by means of General Schofield and the regulars. I was all ready to act, and would have done so without the slightest hesitation or a moment's delay if the negotiations had fallen through. And my action would have been entirely effective. But it is never well to take drastic action if the result can be achieved with equal efficiency in less drastic fashion; and, although this was a minor consideration, I was personally saved a good deal of future trouble by being able to avoid this drastic action. At the time I should have been almost unanimously supported. With the famine upon them the people would not have tolerated any conduct that would have thwarted what I was doing. Probably no man in Congress, and no man in the Pennsylvania State Legislature, would have raised his voice against me. Although there would have been plenty of muttering, nothing would have been done to interfere with the solution of the problem which I had devised, until the solution was accomplished and the problem ceased to be a problem. Once this was done, and when people were no longer afraid of a coal famine, and began to forget that they ever had been afraid of it, and to be indifferent as regards the consequences to those who put an end to it, then my enemies would have plucked up heart and begun a campaign against me. I doubt if they could have accomplished much anyway, for the only effective remedy against me would have been impeachment, and that they would not have ventured to try.

They would doubtless have acted precisely as they acted as regards the acquisition of the Panama Canal Zone in 1903, and the stoppage of the panic of 1907 by my action in the Tennessee Coal and Iron Company matter. Nothing could have made the American people surrender the canal zone. But after it was an accomplished fact, and the canal was under way, then they settled down to comfortable acceptance of the accomplished fact, and as their own interests were no longer in jeopardy, they paid no heed to the men who attacked me because of what I had done—and also continue to attack me, although they are exceedingly careful not to propose to right the "wrong," in the only proper way if it really was a wrong, by replacing the old Republic of Panama under the tyranny of Colombia and giving Colombia sole or joint ownership of the canal itself. In the case of the panic of 1907 (as in the case of Panama), what I did was not only done openly, but depended for its effect upon being done and with the widest advertisement. Nobody in Congress ventured to make an objection at the time. No serious leader outside made any objection. The one concern of everybody was to stop the panic, and everybody was overjoyed that I was willing to take the responsibility of stopping it upon my own shoulders. But a few months afterward, the panic was a thing of the past. People forgot the frightful condition of alarm in which they had been. They no longer had a personal interest in preventing any interference with the stoppage of the panic. Then the men who had not dared to raise their voices until all danger was past came bravely forth from their hiding places and denounced the action which had saved them. They had kept a hushed silence when there was danger; they made clamorous outcry when there was safety in doing so.

Just the same course would have been followed in connection with the Anthracite Coal Strike if I had been obliged to act in the fashion I intended to act had I failed to secure a voluntary agreement between the miners and the operators. Even as it was, my action was remembered with rancor by the heads of the great moneyed interests; and as time went by was assailed with constantly increasing vigor by the newspapers these men controlled. Had I been forced to take possession of the mines, these men and the politicians hostile to me would have waited until the popular alarm was over and the popular needs met, just as they waited in the case of the Tennessee Coal and Iron Company; and then they would have attacked me precisely as they did attack me as regards the Tennessee Coal and Iron Company.

Of course, in labor controversies it was not always possible to champion the cause of the workers, because in many cases strikes were called which were utterly unwarranted and were fought by methods which cannot be too harshly condemned. No straightforward man can believe, and no fearless man will assert, that a trade union is always right. That man is an unworthy public servant who by speech or silence, by direct statement or cowardly evasion, invariably throws the weight of his influence on the side of the trade union, whether it is right or wrong. It has occasionally been my duty to give utterance to the feelings of all right thinking men by expressing the most emphatic disapproval of unwise or even immoral notions by representatives of labor. The man is no true democrat, and if an American, is unworthy of the traditions of his country who, in problems calling for the exercise of a moral judgment, fails to take his stand on conduct and not on class. There are good and bad wage-workers just as there are good and bad employers, and good and bad men of small means and of large means alike.

But a willingness to do equal and exact justice to all citizens, irrespective of race, creed, section or economic interest and position, does not imply a failure to recognize the enormous economic, political and moral possibilities of the trade union. Just as democratic government cannot be condemned because of errors and even crimes committed by men democratically elected, so trade-unionism must not be condemned because of errors or crimes of occasional trade-union leaders. The problem lies deeper. While we must repress all illegalities and discourage all immoralities, whether of labor organizations or of corporations, we must recognize the fact that to-day the organization of labor into trade unions and federations is necessary, is beneficent, and is one of the greatest possible agencies in the attainment of a true industrial, as well as a true political, democracy in the United States.

Source: Roosevelt, Theodore. *An Autobiography*. New York: The Macmillan Company, 1913.

5. IDA M. TARBELL, EXCERPT FROM *THE HISTORY OF THE STANDARD OIL COMPANY*, 1904

[John D. Rockefeller] had the powerful imagination to see what might be done with the oil business if it could be centered in his hands—the intelligence to analyse the problem into its elements and to find the key to control. He had the essential element of all great achievement, a steadfastness to a purpose once conceived which nothing can crush. The Oil Regions might rage, call him a conspirator, and all those who sold him oil, traitors; the railroads might withdraw their contracts and the Legislature annul his charter; undisturbed and unresting he kept at his great purpose. Even if his nature had not been such as to forbid him to abandon an enterprise in which he saw promise of vast profits, even if he had not had a mind which, stopped by a wall, burrows under or creeps around, he would nevertheless have been forced to desperate efforts to keep up his business. He had increased his refining capacity in Cleveland to 10,000 barrels on the strength of the South Improvement Company contracts. These contracts were annulled, and in their place was one signed by officials of all the oil-shipping roads refusing rebates to everybody. His geographical position was such that it cost him under these new contracts fifty cents more to get oil from the wells to New York than it did his rivals on the creek. True, he had many counterbalancing advantages—a growing Western market almost entirely in his hands, lake traffic, close proximity to all sorts of accessories to his manufacturing, but this contract put him on a level with his rivals. By his size he should have better terms than they. What did he do?

He got a rebate. Seven years later Mr. Rockefeller's partner, H. M. Flagler, was called before a commission of the Ohio State Legislature appointed to investigate railroads. He was asked for the former contracts between his company and the railroads, and among others he presented one showing that from "the first of April until the middle of November, 1872," their East-bound rate was $1.25, twenty-five cents less than that set by the agreement of March 25th, between the oil men and the railroads. The discrepancy between the date Mr. Flagler gives for this contract and that of Mr. Vanderbilt's telegram to Mr. Hasson stating that his road had no contract with the Standard Oil Company, April 6, and of Mr. Rockefeller's own telegram stating he had no contracts with the railroads, April 8, the writer is unable to explain. How had Mr. Rockefeller been able to get this rebate? Simply as he had always done—by virtue of the quantity he shipped. He was able to say to Mr. Vanderbilt, I can make a contract to ship sixty carloads of oil a day over your road—nearly 4,800 barrels; I cannot give this to you regularly unless you will make me a concession; and Mr. Vanderbilt made the concession while he was signing the contract with the oil men. Of course the rate was secret, and Mr. Rockefeller probably understood now, as he had not two months before, how essential it was that he keep it secret. His task was more difficult now, for he had an enemy active, clamorous, contemptuous, whose suspicions had reached that acute point where they could believe nothing but evil of him—the producers and independent refiners of the Oil Regions. It was utterly impossible that he should ever silence this enemy, for their points of view were diametrically opposed.

They believed in independent effort—every man for himself and fair play for all. They wanted competition, loved open fight. They considered that all business should be done openly; that the railways were bound as public carriers to give equal rates; that any combination which favoured one firm or one locality at the expense of another was unjust and illegal. This belief long held by many of the oil men had been crystallised by the uprising into a common sentiment. It had become the moral code of the region.

Mr. Rockefeller's point of view was different. He believed that the "good of all" was in a combination which would control the business as the South Improvement Company proposed to control it. Such a combination would end at once all the abuses the business suffered. As rebates and special rates were essential to this control, he favoured them. Of course Mr. Rockefeller must have known that the railroad was a common carrier, and that the common law forbade discrimination. But he knew that the railroads had not obeyed the laws governing them, that they had regularly granted special rates and rebates to those who had large amounts of freight. That is, you were able to bargain with the railroads as you did with a man carrying on a strictly private business depending in no way on a public franchise. Moreover, Mr. Rockefeller probably believed that, in spite of the agreements, if he did not get rebates somebody else would; that they were for the wariest, the shrewdest, the most persistent. If somebody was to get rebates, why not he? This point of view was no uncommon one. Many men held it and felt a sort of scorn, as practical men always do for theorists, when it was contended that the shipper was as wrong in taking rates as the railroads in granting them.

Thus, on one hand there was an exaggerated sense of personal independence, on the other a firm belief in combination; on one hand a determination to root out the vicious system of rebates practised by the railway, on the other a determination to keep it alive and profit by it. Those theories which the body of oil men held as vital and fundamental Mr. Rockefeller and his associates either did not comprehend or were deaf to. This lack of comprehension by many men of what seems to other men to be the most obvious principles of justice is not rare. Many men who are widely known as good, share it. Mr. Rockefeller was "good." There was no more faithful Baptist in Cleveland than he. Every enterprise of that church he had supported liberally from his youth. He gave to its poor. He visited its sick. He wept with its suffering. Moreover, he gave unostentatiously to many outside charities of whose worthiness he was satisfied. He was simple and frugal in his habits. He never went to the theatre, never drank wine. He gave much time to the training of his children, seeking to develop in them his own habits of economy and of charity. Yet he was willing to strain every nerve to obtain for himself special and unjust privileges from the railroads which were bound to ruin every man in the oil business not sharing them with him. He was willing to array himself against the combined better sentiment of a whole industry, to oppose a popular movement aimed at righting an injustice, so revolting to one's sense of fair play as that of railroad discriminations.

Religious emotion and sentiments of charity, propriety and self-denial seem to have taken the place in him of notions of justice and regard for the rights of others.

Unhampered, then, by any ethical consideration, undismayed by the clamour of the Oil Regions, believing firmly as ever that relief for the disorders in the oil business lay in combining and controlling the entire refining interest, this man of vast patience and foresight took up his work. That work now was to carry out some kind of a scheme which would limit the output of refined oil. He had put his competitors in Cleveland out of the way. He had secured special privileges in transportation, but there were still too many refineries at work to make it possible to put up the price of oil four cents a gallon. It was certain, too, that no scheme could be worked to do that unless the Oil Regions could be mollified. That now was Mr. Rockefeller's most important business. Just how he began is not known. It is only certain that the day after the newspapers of the Oil Regions printed the report of the Congressional Committee on Commerce denouncing the South Improvement Company as "one of the most gigantic and dangerous conspiracies ever attempted," and declaring that if it had not been checked in time it "would have resulted in the absorption and arbitrary control of trade in all the great interests of the country." Mr. Rockefeller and several other members of the South Improvement Company appeared in the Oil Regions. They had come, they explained, to present a new plan of co-operation, and to show the oil men that it was to their interest to go into it. Whether they would be able to obtain by persuasion what they had failed to obtain by assault was now an interesting uncertainty.

Source: Tarbell, Ida M. *The History of the Standard Oil Company*. New York: McClure, Phillips & Co., 1904.

6. HENRY ADAMS, EXCERPT FROM "THE DYNAMO AND THE VIRGIN" IN *THE EDUCATION OF HENRY ADAMS*, WRITTEN IN 1907 AND PUBLISHED IN 1918

Until the Great [Paris] Exposition of 1900 closed its doors in November, Adams haunted it, aching to absorb knowledge, and helpless to find it. He would have liked to know how much of it could have been grasped by the best-informed man in the world. While he was thus meditating chaos, Langley came by, and showed it to him. At Langley's behest, the Exhibition dropped its superfluous rags and stripped itself to the skin, for Langley knew what to study, and why, and how; while Adams might as well have stood outside in the night, staring at the Milky Way. Yet Langley said nothing new, and taught nothing that one might not have learned from Lord Bacon, three hundred years before; but though one should have known the "Advancement of Science" as well as one knew the "Comedy of Errors," the literary knowledge counted for nothing until some teacher should show how to apply it. Bacon took a vast deal of trouble in teaching King James I and his subjects, American or other, towards the year 1620, that true science was the development or economy of forces; yet an elderly American in 1900 knew neither the formula nor the forces; or even so much as to say to himself that his historical business in the Exposition concerned only the economies or developments of force since 1893, when he began the study at Chicago [World's Columbian Exposition].

Nothing in education is so astonishing as the amount of ignorance it accumulates in the form of inert facts. Adams had looked at most of the accumulations of art in the storehouses called Art Museums; yet he did not know how to look at the art exhibits of 1900. He had studied Karl Marx and his doctrines of history with profound attention, yet he could not apply them at Paris. Langley, with the ease of a great master of experiment, threw out of the field every exhibit that did not reveal a new application of force, and naturally threw out, to begin with, almost the whole art exhibit. Equally, he ignored almost the whole industrial exhibit. He led his pupil directly to the forces. His chief interest was in new motors to make his airship feasible, and he taught Adams the astonishing complexities of the new Daimler motor, and of the automobile, which, since 1893, had become a nightmare at a hundred kilometres an hour, almost as destructive as the electric tram which was only ten years older; and threatening to become as terrible as the locomotive steam engine itself, which was almost exactly Adams's own age.

Then he showed his scholar the great hall of dynamos, and explained how little he knew about electricity or force of any kind, even of his own special sun, which spouted heat in inconceivable volume, but which, as far as he knew, might spout less or more, at any time, for all the certainty he felt in it. To him, the dynamo itself was but an ingenious channel for conveying somewhere the heat latent in a few tons of poor coal hidden in a dirty engine-house carefully kept out of sight; but to Adams the dynamo became a symbol of infinity. As he grew accustomed to the great gallery of machines, he began to feel the forty-foot dynamos as a moral force, much as the early Christians felt the Cross. The planet itself seemed less impressive, in its old-fashioned, deliberate, annual or daily revolution, than this huge wheel, revolving within arm's length at some vertiginous speed, and barely murmuring–scarcely humming an audible warning to stand a hair's-breadth further for respect of power–while it would not wake the baby lying close against its frame. Before the end, one began to pray to it; inherited instinct taught the natural expression of man before silent and infinite force. Among the thousand symbols of ultimate energy the dynamo was not so human as some, but it was the most expressive.

Yet the dynamo, next to the steam engine, was the most familiar of exhibits. For Adams's objects its value lay chiefly in its occult mechanism. Between the dynamo in the gallery of machines and the engine-house outside, the break of continuity amounted to abysmal fracture for a historian's objects. No more relation could he discover between the steam and the electric current than between the Cross and the cathedral. The forces were interchangeable if not reversible, but he could see only an absolute fiat in electricity as in faith. Langley could not help him. Indeed, Langley seemed to be worried by the same trouble, for he constantly repeated that the new forces were anarchical, and especially that he was not responsible for the new rays, that were little short of parricidal in their wicked spirit towards science. His own rays, with which he had doubled the solar spectrum, were altogether harmless and beneficent; but Radium denied its God–or, what was to Langley the same thing, denied the truths of his Science. The force was wholly new.

A historian who asked only to learn enough to be as futile as Langley or Kelvin, made rapid progress under this teaching, and mixed himself up in the tangle of ideas until he achieved a sort of Paradise of ignorance vastly consoling to his fatigued senses. He wrapped himself in vibrations and rays which were new, and he would have hugged Marconi and Branly had he met them, as he hugged the dynamo; while he lost his arithmetic in trying to figure out the equation between the discoveries and the economies of force. The economies, like the discoveries, were absolute, supersensual, occult; incapable of expression in horse-power. What mathematical equivalent could he suggest as the value of a Branly coherer? Frozen air, or the electric furnace, had some scale of measurement, no doubt, if somebody could invent a thermometer adequate to the purpose; but X-rays had played no part whatever in man's consciousness, and the atom itself had figured only as a fiction of thought. In these seven years man had translated himself into a new universe which had no common scale of measurement with the old. He had entered a supersensual world, in which he could measure nothing except by chance collisions of movements imperceptible to his senses, perhaps even imperceptible to his instruments, but perceptible to each other, and so to some known ray at the end of the scale. Langley seemed prepared for anything, even for an indeterminable number of universes interfused–physics stark mad in metaphysics.

Historians undertake to arrange sequences,–called stories, or histories–assuming in silence a relation of cause and effect. These assumptions, hidden in the depths of dusty libraries, have been astounding, but commonly unconscious and childlike; so much so, that if any captious critic were to drag them to light, historians would probably reply, with one voice, that they had never supposed themselves required to know what they were talking about. Adams, for one, had toiled in vain to find out what he meant. He had even published a dozen volumes of American history for no other purpose than to satisfy himself whether, by severest process of stating, with the least possible comment, such facts as seemed sure, in such order as seemed rigorously consequent, he could fix for a familiar moment a necessary sequence of human movement. The result had satisfied him as little as at Harvard College. Where he saw sequence, other men saw something quite different, and no one saw the same unit of measure. He cared little about his experiments and less about his statesmen, who seemed to him quite as ignorant as himself and, as a rule, no more honest; but he insisted on a relation of sequence, and if he could not reach it by one method, he would try as many methods as science knew. Satisfied that the sequence of men led to nothing and that the sequence of their society could lead no further, while the mere sequence of time was artificial, and the sequence of thought was chaos, he turned at last to the sequence of force; and thus it happened that, after ten years' pursuit, he found himself lying in the Gallery of Machines at the Great Exposition of 1900, his historical neck broken by the sudden irruption of forces totally new.

Source: Adams, Henry. *The Education of Henry Adams.* Boston: Houghton Mifflin Company, 1918.

7. "THE CONSTANTLY INCREASING USE OF THE MOTOR TRUCK," 1915

Horse and Wagon Method of Transportation Steadily Giving Way to the Power Propelled Vehicle—More than 300 Different Lines of Business Have Adopted It.

The reason for the notable popularity of motor trucks is obvious. They have become an economic necessity through an extended and severe course of experience and demonstration. The truck is practical in that it will go anywhere a horse and wagon could be driven and in much less time. Its efficiency is another factor which has had much to so with its success. Not a few cases are on record where one truck has taken the place of ten horses and five wagons in the transportation of merchandise. Instances where six horses and three wagons have been replaced are, of course, more numerous, and it is safe to say that there is hardly a truck in operation today that has not done away with at least four horses and two wagons. These figures relate to the heavy motor truck of 2, 4 or 6 ton capacity. The lighter vehicles with a capacity of 1/2, 3/4 and one ton, while operating in another sphere of work, have been found just as satisfactory and efficient, and many of the great department stores are using them almost exclusively. While the number of horses and wagons displaces is not as great per vehicle, it is not unusual to find business concerns whose lines of merchandise are of comparatively light character, which have done away with three to five on-horse wagons since the introduction of the power vehicle. The economy secured by the truck is another important feature of its use. It cannot only be operated at a smaller expenditure than necessary where horses and wagons do the same amount of work, but it further enhances the profits of its owner in that it enables him to secure and take care of new business in that the power vehicle works faster than any horse and wagon outfit could, and performs a given amount of work in less time than has heretofore been possible.

With these facts in mind it is readily seen that the field of use for the large motor truck and light motor delivery wagon is practically unlimited. It is estimated that more than three hundred different lines of business are now using the power vehicle, and practically every sort of merchandise is being transported by it.

That the motor truck will in the near future entirely eliminate the horse from the large contracting business is the view of the general manager of a prominent concern in this line which has been handling the work connected with the building of the great Catskill Aqueduct tunnel in New York City. This company found that there was no department of the work which could have been profitably done with horses and wagons. From 20 to 25 per cent. on the cost of disposal has been saved by the use of the trucks, and there has also been a great economy in the delivery of material. All of the trucks used on this tunnel work are equipped with heavy platform bodies which receive a dump bucket with a capacity of 4 cubic yards. By the use of thee buckets the truck is never idle, a full load being ready for it on its return from the dumping place every trip. The records kept of some of the trucks show that they have traveled as high as 1,592 miles in one month, with a total daily travel as high as 96 miles, or 24 round trips from the tunnel to the dumping place.

American ingenuity has devised a noteworthy array of practical labor-saving devices in connection with these dumping bodies for motor trucks. Dumping bodies are provided that can be operated by hand or by the power of the engine; bodies that tip up at the rear or dump from the side; bodies that dump one compartment at a time while the others remain loaded for customers further along the route. One design is operated by compressed air, another by the pressure of oil against a plunger in a cylinder. There is a dump body that revolves on a turntable so that it can be tilted to the rear or to either side, as may be necessary. Several types can be operated by the driver without leaving his seat, and quite a few have a hinged tail gate that automatically lifts and distributes crushed stone or a similar load in a layer of desired thickness on the road as the truck progresses slowly along under absolute control of the driver. To motor wagon users who are always on the alert to reduce operating costs to the minimum, in connection with the handling of loose material in bulk, these dumping bodies have fully demonstrated their utility and efficiency in numerous instances.

A great deal of interurban traffic is now handled by motor trucks that a year or two ago was the work of steam and trolley roads, and the movement is increasing steadily as its economies are understood and appreciated. Shipping by rail from one city to another, say a distance of fifteen to twenty-five miles, means the handling three times the goods—namely, by truck to the freight station in one city, then by train and by trick against for delivery in another city. On the other hand, motor trucks running between points so situated take on their load at the shipper's platform and deliver directly at the door of the customer in the other town. Not only does this method effect a material saving in actual time of transit, but it is decidedly less expensive. Transportation lines of this nature are rapidly increasing in number and importance in various sections of the United States.

For planting his field, harvesting his crops, threshing his grain, the enterprising and up-to-date farmer has learned to substitute steam power for horse whenever possible, and he is even using a mechanical device to milk his cows. It was accordingly natural that the motor truck should appeal to him as a means of getting to and from town in quick time in cases of emergency, especially in the planting and threshing season, and in any kind of weather. A farmer living twenty miles from market who can make a daily trip with a minimum of strain and spend his nights comfortably in bed has an obvious advantage over his neighbor who drives a horse and may spend the entire night on the road in delivering his product. If he has a large crop of grain which must be hauled a great distance, and invests in one of the trucks, carrying perhaps three or four times as much as he could with a span of horses, it needs no elaborate figuring to arrive at the saving in time and energy. The speedy transpiration of fruit, garden truck and livestock is a big question wherever efficient farming is being done, notably near the large cities, where the call for quick delivery is most imperative. In many of the states during the fruit season of the past two years, the motor truck has been thoroughly tried out and has given a convincing demonstration of its utility. Greater ease and lower cost in transportation have in every case resulted from the adoption of this method of delivery. Motor transportation companies are also recognizing more and more the business possibilities of going out to get the fruit in communities where the farmer is not thus equipped. In many of the fruit regions of the country there is now a well defined and constantly spreading movement to substitute the motor truck for the horse and wagon.

The principal objection which business men have made to the motor truck thus far has been that of excessive wear. The merchant who still clings to horse and wagon methods of delivering his goods, when approached on the subject of buying a motor truck, sometimes alludes to the fact that perhaps his neighbor's truck lasted only a couple of years. It is pointed out that careless or ignorant drivers have insisted on speeding the vehicle unnecessarily and thus racking it to pieces in a comparatively short period of time. This objection has, however, been surmounted by the introduction of a simple mechanical arrangement, a governor by which the speed of the truck can be limited to suit the ideas of the owner. The governor is set and sealed so that it cannot be adjusted or tampered with without detection. It effectually prevents the racing of the car, inasmuch as the supply of fuel is automatically terminated when the motor reaches the stipulated speed.

The field for the use of the motor truck is practically unlimited. Trucks are now delivering all sorts of merchandise, and even the huge boiler and locomotive can be transported by it. The truck has demonstrated its worth no less in the business of contracting, where several tons of crushed stone or concrete or structural iron constitute a load, than in the delivery of flowers, where half a dozen ten-pound boxes are carried on a trip.

Source: *The American Exporter*. Vol. 77. 1915. Pp. 66–8.

8. "ELECTRICITY SOLVES SERVANT PROBLEM," 1917

Electricity Solves Servant Problem

At a club meeting held recently one of the lady member said, "Why should I bother with a servant when I have all the electrical appliances that make it easy for me to do all my own work? Electricity has solved the servant problem for me. There is no drudgery in my home. Everything is simple and easy. Nothing could induce me to have a servant in the home again." There were a large number of women at the meeting who were doing the same thing yet two or three years ago they were worried about the servant problem. It is typical of the attitude of the many practical and efficient housewives. They have found the way out of their difficulty, especially since the scarcity of servants, and particularly of dependable servants, became so great.

The extent to which electrical appliances for the home are replacing servants can be realized when it is known that during 1916 the sales of this class of merchandise exceeded the sales for 1915 by more than 100 percent. This modernizing influence does not only extend to the city home, but to thousands of rural community houses which are being electrically equipped equal to any in the cities. The woman whose duty it is to manage the house knows the saving in time and labor that can be easily effected in a modern home.

In the home where the housewife does her own laundry work will be found the electric washer and the electric flatiron, both of which have been responsible for the changed attitude towards the weekly washing. With these two appliances the housewife no longer dreads to do her own laundry work, but prefers that to having her garments improperly laundered outside the home.

Of course cleaning and cooking are the major duties of the housewife, and in the development of devices for these purposes great progress has been made during the last years. The electric vacuum cleaner is one of the greatest labor-saving devices for the home that has ever been offered to the women of the world.

For cooking and incidental purposes a well selected assortment includes the electric range, disk stove, grill with ovenette attachment, percolator, plate warmer, chafing dish, tea kettle, toaster, eff boiler, waffle iron, fireless cooker, warming oven, drink mixer, dish-washing machine, fan for dish-drying, the power unit for stirring and turning the coffee-mill, grinder and freezer, and exhaust fan and ozonator to remove all kitchen odors.

For the woman who uses a sewing machine an electric-motor attachment will save time and conserve energy and health.

The home seeker is beginning to demand a house or apartment properly constructed and wired so that all these electric devices may be used. It is no longer sufficient to have light sockets only. The demand is for side wall and floor outlets where these appliances can be quickly and conveniently attached. This influence is being felt by builders and landlords, and they are constructing and reconstructing their buildings in line with the most modern improvements.

The strongest appeal to the housewife has been the saving of time and labor. Every woman desire to manage her home just as efficiently as the business man manages his factory or store. She realizes the need for economy and efficiency, especially in times like these.

Source: "Electricity Solves Servant Problem." *Electrical Review*. Vol. 71. No. 10. September 8, 1917. P. 413.

9. GEORGE OTIS SMITH, EXCERPT FROM "A WORLD VIEW OF THE OIL SUPPLY," 1920

Open Door Policy Advocated

Our present knowledge of the facts of world supply and demand is amply sufficient to warrant us in continuing to advocate the open door policy. Much can be gained for all nations by pooling the world's resources of so essential a raw material as petroleum. With about 60 per cent. of the world's future supply concentrated in two regions, while by far the greater part of the demand arises outside those oil-rich regions, there must be a world commerce in oil. The United States has given to all comers, whatever their nationality, opportunity to acquire oil lands within its territory, and the new leasing law puts no limit upon foreign participation in operating the public oil lands unless there is an absence of reciprocal treatment. Of course, any nation realizes that the adoption of the open door policy need not involve throwing away the key.

Not only has the United States been generous in welcoming foreign capital to our domestic oil fields, but it has been prodigal in marketing the products of the American wells and refineries. Whatever our motive has been in winning so large a share of the world's oil trade, the record of the past fully justifies the United States in asking for reciprocity in the future from all other nations.

By taking the world view we realize that international trade rests upon the unequal distribution of raw materials among the nations, as well as on differences in their industrial productivity and consumptive needs. Commerce between two nations, like an exchange of products between two men, can benefit both participants if commerce is not carried on as a war. The nation that is weak in resources may be tempted to think in terms of unfair trade practices, but the richer and stronger nations can surely afford to be idealistic in planning their industrial and commercial policies. Unfair tactics in interstate business are now forbidden by our laws, and Federal commissions enforce the laws, and it seems to me that the most important function of great organizations like the American Iron and Steel Institute and the American Petroleum Institute is to enforce among their constituent corporations this rule of "live and let live." That kind of regard of the stronger for the rights of the weaker makes for industrial peace and health. It is now recognized as good business to promote fair competition between merchants or manufacturers here at home; it should also be good business to carry the same spirit into world trade.

Government Backing of Foreign Development

There is urgent need of pioneering the world for oil to meet the needs of this generation, but there is no warrant for regarding this advance into new fields as beginning a contest whose aim is world conquest. The present need of the United States for oil from abroad can be met only by world-wide exploration, development and operation by American companies backed up by our government, and we should expect other nations that are embarrassed by a similar or even greater discrepancy between consumption and production to adopt the same policy.

The natural trend of a far-flung search for oil must be toward the frontier countries of the world, which have not yet been able to develop their own resources, and this introduces new international relationships. On this subject of national rights I may quote from a letter of the Secretary of the Interior addressed last June to a Senate committee to the effect that in any legislation intended to strengthen the position of American oil companies in foreign exploration there should be full recognition of national rights, and no language should be used that could be misunderstood and made the occasion of any anti-American feeling. "Our government," said Secretary Payne, "would surely recognize the preferential right of another nation to the products of its own territory in time of need and under conditions of equitable compensation to our nationals, whatever their possessory rights."

However great our own exigencies, then, we may set down this principle: The rights of the company that discovers and develops a foreign oil supply are subject to national rights and even a mandatory is created to develop the weaker nation, not to exploit it. If the nations of the world shall join to bring about a changed order, one that expresses the spirit of peace rather than of war, there can be no place in the international scheme for special partners or preferred stock, even though the Argonauts of today, in their search for a flood of oil, are seeking a treasure of far greater value than any golden fleece.

The first thought in either a national or a world program for oil is to stimulate production; "more oil needed" describes the symptom felt by every nation, and new and larger supplies of oil is the remedy sought. Taking the long view as well as the broad view, however, we are forced to admit the equal need of checking consumption. A world policy, if it is to safeguard the future, must draw up a program that will favor thrift in the use of the oil currently produced, and in that program also there must be a joining of the nations in continued effort for the common good. When the world runs short of oil all nations will suffer, regardless of the geographic location of the remaining wells. America has led in teaching the world to use petroleum, whether in lamp or automobile or tractor, and it should be America's special duty to teach the world to use petroleum most efficiently. No longer is there any need to make a market for oil; the task is to find the oil to supply the demand already created.

Source: Smith, George Otis. "A World View of the Oil Supply." In *Addresses Delivered at General Sessions, Annual Meeting American Petroleum Institute, Washington, DC November 17, 18, 19, 1920*. Pp. 8–12. Washington, DC: American Petroleum Institute, 1920.

10. HENRY FORD, EXCERPT FROM *MY LIFE AND WORK*, 1922

In 1879—that is, about four years after I first saw that Nichols-Shepard machine—I managed to get a chance to run one and when my apprenticeship was over. I worked with a local representative of the Westinghouse Company of Schenectady as an expert in the setting up and repair of their road engines. The engine they put out was much the same as the Nichols-Shepard engine excepting that the engine was up in front, the boiler in the rear, and the power was applied to the back wheels by a belt. They could make twelve miles an hour on the road even though the self-propelling feature was only an incident of the construction. They were sometimes used as tractors to pull heavy loads and, if the owner also happened to be in the threshing-machine business, he hitched his threshing machine and other paraphernalia to the engine in moving from farm to farm. What bothered me was the weight and the cost. They weighed a couple of tons and were far too expensive to be owned by other than a farmer with a great deal of land. They were mostly employed by people who went into threshing as a business or who had sawmills or some other line that required portable power.

Even before that time I had the idea of making some kind of a light steam car that would take the place of horses—more especially, however, as a tractor to attend to the excessively hard labour of ploughing. It occurred to me, as I remember somewhat vaguely, that precisely the same idea might be applied to a carriage or a wagon on the road. A horseless carriage was a common idea. People had been talking about carriages without horses for many years back—in fact, ever since the steam engine was invented—but the idea of the carriage at first did not seem so practical to me as the idea of an engine to do the harder farm work, and of all the work on the farm ploughing was the hardest. Our roads were poor and we had not the habit of getting around. One of the most remarkable features of the automobile on the farm is the way that it has broadened the farmer's life. We simply took for granted that unless the errand were urgent we would not go to town, and I think we rarely made more than a trip a week. In bad weather we did not go even that often.

Being a full-fledged machinist and with a very fair workshop on the farm it was not difficult for me to build a steam wagon or tractor. In the building of it came the idea that perhaps it might be made for road use. I felt perfectly certain that horses, considering all the bother of attending them and the expense of feeding, did not earn their keep. The obvious thing to do was to design and build a steam engine that would be light enough to run an ordinary wagon or to pull a plough. I thought it more important first to develop the tractor. To lift farm drudgery off flesh and blood and lay it on steel and motors has been my most constant ambition. It was circumstances that took me first into the actual manufacture of road cars. I found eventually that people were more interested in something that would travel on the road than in something that would do the work on the farms. In fact, I doubt that the light farm tractor could have been introduced on the farm had not the farmer had his eyes opened slowly but surely by the automobile. But that is getting ahead of the story. I thought the farmer would be more interested in the tractor.

I built a steam car that ran. It had a kerosene-heated boiler and it developed plenty of power and a neat control–which is so easy with a steam throttle. But the boiler was dangerous. To get the requisite power without too big and heavy a power plant required that the engine work under high pressure; sitting on a high-pressure steam boiler is not altogether pleasant. To make it even reasonably safe required an excess of weight that nullified the economy of the high pressure. For two years I kept experimenting with various sorts of boilers–the engine and control problems were simple enough–and then I definitely abandoned the whole idea of running a road vehicle by steam. I knew that in England they had what amounted to locomotives running on the roads hauling lines of trailers and also there was no difficulty in designing a big steam tractor for use on a large farm. But ours were not then English roads; they would have stalled or racked to pieces the strongest and heaviest road tractor. And anyway the manufacturing of a big tractor which only a few wealthy farmers could buy did not seem to me worth while.

But I did not give up the idea of a horseless carriage. The work with the Westinghouse representative only served to confirm the opinion I had formed that steam was not suitable for light vehicles. That is why I stayed only a year with that company. There was nothing more that the big steam tractors and engines could teach me and I did not want to waste time on something that would lead nowhere. A few years before—it was while I was an apprentice—I read in the *World of Science*, an English publication, of the "silent gas engine" which was then coming out in England. I think it was the Otto engine. It ran with illuminating gas, had a single large cylinder, and the power impulses being thus intermittent required an extremely heavy fly-wheel. As far as weight was concerned it gave nothing like the power per pound of metal that a steam engine gave, and the use of illuminating gas seemed to dismiss it as even a possibility for road use. It was interesting to me only as all machinery was interesting. I followed in the English and American magazines which we got in the shop the development of the engine and most particularly the hints of the possible replacement of the illuminating gas fuel by a gas formed by the vaporization of gasoline. The idea of gas engines was by no means new, but this was the first time that a really serious effort had been made to put them on the market. They were received with interest rather than enthusiasm and I do not recall any one who thought that the internal combustion engine could ever have more than a limited use. All the wise people demonstrated conclusively that the engine could not compete with steam. They never thought that it might carve out a career for itself. That is the way with wise people—they are so wise and practical that they always know to a dot just why something cannot be done; they always know the limitations. That is why I never employ an expert in full bloom. If ever I wanted to kill opposition by unfair means I would endow the opposition with experts. They would have so much good advice that I could be sure they would do little work.

The gas engine interested me and I followed its progress, but only from curiosity, until about 1885 or 1886 when, the steam engine being discarded as the motive power for the carriage that I intended some day to build, I had to look around for another sort of motive power. In 1885 I repaired an Otto engine at the Eagle Iron Works in Detroit. No one in town knew anything about them. There was a rumour that I did and, although I had never before been in contact with one, I undertook and carried through the job. That gave me a chance to study the new engine at first hand and in 1887 I built one on the Otto four-cycle model just to see if I understood the principles. "Four cycle" means that the piston traverses the cylinder four times to get one power impulse. The first stroke draws in the gas, the second compresses it, the third is the explosion or power stroke, while the fourth stroke exhausts the waste gas. The little model worked well enough; it had a 1-inch bore and a 3-inch stroke, operated with gasoline, and while it did not develop much power, it was slightly lighter in proportion than the engines being offered commercially. I gave it away later to a young man who wanted it for something or other and whose name I have forgotten; it was eventually destroyed. That was the beginning of the work with the internal combustion engine.

Source: Ford, Henry, and Samuel Crowther. *My Life and Work*. Garden City, NY: Doubleday, Page & Company, 1922.

11. AUTOMOBILE FATALITY, 1922

Another life was sacrificed in an auto accident on Sunday, the victim this time being William Fessler, aged twenty-four years, of 2304 West Lehman Street, West Lebanon, better known to his friends as "Freddie" Fessler. He sustained fatal injuries when he was thrown from a Ford runabout on the running board of which he was standing while going with others to Ebenezer shortly before noon. The original party was made up at Twenty-second and Lehman Streets, West Lebanon, and consisted only of three. A car belonging to Adam Zerbe, hostler at the West Lebanon hotel was impressed into use. It is said that the younger men had several times taken Zerbe's car and as he didn't seem to mind It, the machine was taken on this occasion without the trouble of asking his permission It Is alleged. The trio had taken a ride, and were homeward bound along the Tunnel Hill road, when they reached the bridge at the Snavely fruit farm, near Westmont station, they met Fessler and several others who had walked out to that point for a bit of fresh country air. As the distance back to West Lebanon was not great, the hikers were invited to ride along back home. As they reached the school house at Pansy Hill, it was suggested that the gasoline that was used on the trip should be replaced, so instead of turning down toward West Lebanon, they turned northward toward Ebenezer. The car had passed the turn of the road at the Ebenezer Dam, and was climbing the hill toward the store where gasoline is sold, when a horse-drawn vehicle suddenly came down the hill from the other direction. With the heavy load in the auto it was necessary to make some speed to climb the hill, and a quick turnout was necessary when the other vehicle approached. In making this turn a smash-up seemed eminent, and it is said that Fessler in fear of the menacing danger, jumped and was thrown violently against a pole, head striking first, his brains dashed out. Walter Petry, who is said to have been driving the car, and his companions gave Fessler such first aid as they knew, but it was apparent from the first that he was badly hurt, so the Good Samaritan ambulance was summoned. Driver Pat Kale had a record run to the hospital, but Fessler breathed his last before the ambulance arrived at its destination. The fatality created a considerable sensation at West Lebanon, as well as elsewhere. It was rendered additionally sad by reason of the fact that Fessler was the principal help of his blind brother, Charles Fessler, who conducts a small restaurant and confectionary store at West Lebanon. William had been employed at the furnace plant near West Lebanon, but for a long time past had been helping his blind brother in the management of the restaurant. Besides the blind brother, and their mother, Mrs. Catherine Fessler, the deceased leaves another brother, Howard of West Lebanon, and four sisters, Lillian, wife of Noah Kline; Minnie, wife of Charles Fields, Ida, wife of Samuel Smith, and Katie, at home. Dr. A. W. Shultz;, the county coroner, investigated the case on Sunday and this morning. He ran up against the same number of conflicting statements as did reporters. He was told that the machine was a two-seated Ford and that only two or three were riding on the running board, seven being seated within. His information was to the effect that the machine was running at high speed, and that Fessler was pitched off in the whirl of a sudden turn of the machine. He viewed the place of the accident and found that Fessler was first thrown against a rural mall-box post which was broken off by the force of the impact, and Fessler's head and the mail box struck the tree with great violence at the same time, the box post and the tree having been but 2 feet apart. An examination of the body also showed that one side of the head had been scalped, and the front of the head stove in. The brains of the victim protruded from the opening. The machine had been in use less than half an hour, the coroner was told. The coroner was told that Petry the driver of the car does not have a license to drive an auto vehicle. As the material facts are all known, Coroner Shultz stated that he would not put the county to the expense of an inquest.

Source: *Lebanon Semi-Weekly News*. June 26, 1922. Pp. 1, 8.

12. MARY PATTISON, "THE ABOLITION OF HOUSEHOLD SLAVERY," 1925

The "Macedonian" cry of the home woman is at last reaching the ear of the engineer and inventor as well as the manufacturer and electrician and in fact is being picked up by the artis, the musician and the educator. Even the expert business man is listening to the call for better home conditions on his way to "larger" things—though in truth there is nothing larger nor more important in the nation's welfare than the twenty million homes—around which all other industries center. The National Better homes Movement is a sign of the realization of this. Officered by the best that Washington can supply, and sponsored by the General Federation of Clubs, it bids fair to become a permanent feature of wide significance in home progress. But without the modern power that electricity does and can supply, a new order of betterment would be well nigh unthinkable. Already our first move in the morning may be at the call of an electrically regulated clock. Much of our toilet is performed by the tune of this power. We eat breakfast entirely prepared by it. And whether we clean the house, wash the clothes, prepare the vegetables, nurse the sick, or cut the grass, electricity in its application is our constant companion through the day—yes, even on into the night, with lights and music and the dance. Its actual use is unquestioned—its future possibilities as yet undreamed.

Emancipation of the Housewife

Perhaps the one machine most widely welcomed and universally adopted is the vacuum cleaner. Woman has been a dirt eraser for so many ages with no relief in sight and no hope of anything better than beginning again at the moment of finishing, that one wonders whether the romance of dirt has not kept pace with the degradation of its daily influence and perhaps finally won out in the ultimation of the cleaner. For of all the modern electrical home machines in daily use this one pays a smaller interest on the money invested than do most of the others, yet it has a gigantic value in lifting the woman from her long and seemingly doomed relationship with dirt in the wrong place. Dust or dirt in the right place seems to be the medium of the creative process. All growth, beauty and civilization are dependent upon it—the world is unthinkable without it. But on the best chair or the living room floor we feel it has no part and should be carefully removed. The machine that removes it, sucks it right out of the house altogether, costs in the neighborhood of $75 and is used in the average home about two hours a week. The old broom had at least a half day record. About the same intelligence is needed in the operation of each, although the cleaner requires far more thought and care to keep it in fitness and can be as successfully handled in a dinner or calling costume as with apron and cap.

Another great transformer of household drudgery is the electric washing machine. This is about as popular as the vacuum cleaner and really does a heaver and more irksome task in a surprisingly acceptable fashion, requiring only about one-fifth of the time and no particular skill or strength. The average washer woman is now rated at between $4–$5 a day and is quite a scarce entity at that. So that this machine together with the ironer pays rather a high rate on the investment—in lieu of the uncertainty of the public laundry—even though the machine does service but for a few hours a week.

The biggest modern aid to the household as we find it is the electric cooker, notwithstanding the many curses heaped upon it. This it is that transforms the old order of "woman's work never being done" to the new and magical one of "touch the button and we'll do the rest." Better food, better cooking and better conditions general result from the wise use of this device. With an automatic starter and cut-off the cost in current covers only just what is used with no waste and no wasteful attention. When we think of the old coal range and stove with the kitchen fire constantly on one's mind, it is wonderful that the woman of many cares ever did get beyond its black and heavy influence. The little electric cooker can be plugged into a lamp socket, filled to the brim and left to start and stop itself with right royal results; costing no more in current than the price of 2.5 kilowatt-hours with nothing for attention and no dreaded pots and pans to wash after the best mean you ever ate is over.

Then to the dishwasher—a device that makes as nothing the most generally disliked task of all the household list! It is finally perfected to do the work as well or better than by hand—as well because it makes them over 95 per cent clean and better because it does it in three minutes instead of thirty, protecting the dishes from breakage or nicking and then polishing and sterilizing them on the way with no effects of greasy or dirty water to contend with.

In many cases the electric refrigerator is an investment worthy of its price. In some cases not. That it is a huge convenience and comfort to have food kept at an even temperature goes without saying. No moisture and no waste, no iceman and no ice compartment to clean. At the same time no home-made ice cream with oodles of ice to waste. But one must needs sacrifice something in the gaining of something else. The refrigerator is here to stay and take its important part in the well-equipped home of the future thus doing away with the iceman and the iceman's tracks.

Speaking of tracks, the electric scrubbing machine is another modern power device of untold value. It cleans and polishes floors, scrubs the porches, as well as the kitchen, and washes and cleanse both rugs and carpets. Costing $150.00 and practically lasting a lifetime, it pays a high interest on the investment even though used but a small portion of the year. To keep floors in good condition is the economical way to have waxed floors. Frequent treatment with an abundance of heavy rubbing is all they require for years and nothing but a power polisher makes this practical in these days of high hand labor costs. Hence a machine that one might imagine only of occasional value becomes an invaluable possession where floor space warrants any such service, if we rate it by the year and not by the infrequent usings.

Another little Giant Power possession of the greatest sort of value is the universal motor for all kitchen purposes, such as grinding meal and flour, making bread and cake, grating cheese or chocolate, milling coffee and spice, beating cream and eggs, polishing silver and brass, freezing ices or shelling peas, cutting beans or peeling potatoes—it does them all and more equally well. It is a veritable "motor of all work," taking the place of both man and maid and leaving rest, not fatigue, in its wake, and so constructed as to use any size and kind of vessel or pan that can be turned with a rod or a pin. The whole outfit costs less than $100 and can be made to return 300 per cent the first year, even in the average small family. Of course where conditions have brought the kitchen to the primal simplicity of a gas jet and a can opener with a delicatessen near by, it may not be the place for this sort of motor. But where health and care in food preparation is considered it is one of the best big tools. It brings one nearer to nature and nature's best than the most fastidious shop and therefore to the way we should, but do not eat.

These are but a few of the larger power household devices now in use in the one-family home. Many more there are and many more there will be as soon as the average woman can be made to think in terms of mechanics and not hand housework, in business methods not personal ones and in social and cultural motives and not self-sacrifice and self-degenerating tradition.

Rise of a New Era

Thought goes before action. One must think out one's salvation if one would be saved, yet most people want their thinking done for them—canned fashion. Giant business like Giant Power has marvelous advantages but it also has its paralyzing effect. It tells you want to have and how to have it and supplies what the thoughtless demand. If the good public could only put in its request for the well considered benefits it could and should have we might all be controlling the heating of our houses with a turn button instead of a coal shovel; living in an atmosphere of electrically driven engines, sootless and smokeless; enjoying heavenly music of a wireless order and going to college over the radio even though we are fifty or more years of age. Indeed, greater things than these shall be done when the dear women of the home awake from what *has* been, and when they demand an equality of purpose and merely of position with the modern man of big affairs.

To curl and dry one's hair with electricity, to warm one's fingers and toes, to make some waffles for luncheon and percolate coffee at night is all very well, but it does not go far enough. There must be some big fundamental changes in this home of ours if it would be the social unit it gives promise of being. It might at lease be brought up to the standard of the best factory and office system and of course go far ahead in its own individual charm.

These changes are first largely mechanical and electrical. They have to do with the management and methods of home making—not with the psychological or personal results, although they make clear the way for these while furnishing the leisure and inclination to develop and enjoy them. The cry of the home honored woman to be released from the dish pan, the tub and the kitchen range is answered. It is now a matter of how far she will do on the new road and what amount of culture she can and will take on in the performance of the common task. From a musical standpoint she can move as far as time, tune and rhythm can be made to play upon her daily routine. Artistically we find every effort being brought to bear upon the home to give it the atmosphere it deserves. More and more beautiful things and effects are rapidly being incorporated. The artist is awake to this need and the woman is moving slowly in the wake of such suggestion.

The old idea of domestic service has gone. The new one of domestic independence is here. One of the chief differences is that while the dainty lady of the past had but to express her wish to have the work accomplished, she must needs now be the manager and accomplisher in one. A certain leisure was granted her by right in which to pursue the more cultural arts. The same leisure must now be earned by self-effort with the arts and culture as a part of the job. Ignorant help and mechanical progress are unthinkable in combination. Shall we then cling to the dish pan, the broom, and the washboard for our own isolated selfish end because we can perhaps still hold on to the servant that goes with those things? Or shall we move apace with our social and industrial lights and help to usher in a new order of service—trained, intelligent and scientific—by first working out the problem for ourselves? Giant Power is ours! We need but connect the wire of progress and touch the button of independence to prove to ourselves and each other that education and culture lie in mastering the technique of the *common* task. All the helps in the world are of no use to those who will not help themselves. The surprise of the feminine life will be when it is discovered collectively and personally that you can get out of housework all you have the brains to put into it.

Source: Pattison, Mary. "The Abolition of Household Slavery." In *The Annals of the American Academy of Political and Social Science*. Vol. 118: *Giant Power: Large Scale Electrical Development as a Social Factor*. March, 1925. Pp. 124–7.

13. FRANKLIN D. ROOSEVELT, "ADDRESS AT THE DEDICATION OF BOULDER DAM," 1935

Senator Pittman, Secretary Ickes, Governors of the Colorado's States, and you especially who have built Boulder Dam:

This morning I came, I saw and I was conquered, as everyone would be who sees for the first time this great feat of mankind.

Ten years ago the place where we are gathered was an unpeopled, forbidding desert. In the bottom of a gloomy canyon, whose precipitous walls rose to a height of more than 1,000 feet, flowed a turbulent, dangerous river. The mountains on either side of the canyon were difficult of access with neither road nor trail, and their rocks were protected by neither trees nor grass from the blazing heat of the sun. The site of Boulder City was a cactus-covered waste. The transformation wrought here in these years is a twentieth-century marvel.

We are here to celebrate the completion of the greatest dam in the world, rising 726 feet above the bedrock of the river and altering the geography of a whole region; we are here to see the creation of the largest artificial lake in the world—115 miles long, holding enough water, for example, to cover the State of Connecticut to a depth of ten feet; and we are here to see nearing completion a power house which will contain the largest generators and turbines yet installed in this country, machinery that can continuously supply nearly two million horsepower of electric energy.

All these dimensions are superlative. They represent and embody the accumulated engineering knowledge and experience of centuries; and when we behold them it is fitting that we pay tribute to the genius of their designers. We recognize also the energy, resourcefulness and zeal of the builders, who, under the greatest physical obstacles, have pushed this work forward to completion two years in advance of the contract requirements. But especially, we express our gratitude to the thousands of workers who gave brain and brawn to this great work of construction.

Beautiful and great as this structure is, it must also be considered in its relationship to the agricultural and industrial development and in its contribution to the health and comfort of the people of America who live in the Southwest.

To divert and distribute the waters of an arid region, so that there shall be security of rights and efficiency in service, is one of the greatest problems of law and of administration to be found in any government. The farms, the cities, the people who live along the many thousands of miles of this river and its tributaries—all of them depend upon the conservation, the regulation, and the equitable division of its ever-changing water supply. What has been accomplished on the Colorado in working out such a scheme of distribution is inspiring to the whole country. Through the cooperation of the States whose people depend upon this river, and of the Federal Government which is concerned in the general welfare, there is being constructed a system of distributive works and of laws and practices which will insure to the millions of people who now dwell in this basin, and the millions of others who will come to dwell here in future generations, a just, safe and permanent system of water rights. In devising these policies and the means for putting them into practice the Bureau of Reclamation of the Federal Government has taken, and is destined to take in the future, a leading and helpful part. The Bureau has been the instrument which gave effect to the legislation introduced in Congress by Senator Hiram Johnson and Congressman Phil Swing.

We know that, as an unregulated river, the Colorado added little of value to the region this dam serves. When in flood the river was a threatening torrent. In the dry months of the year it shrank to a trickling stream. For a generation the people of Imperial Valley had lived in the shadow of disaster from this river which provided their livelihood, and which is the foundation of their hopes for themselves and their children. Every spring they awaited with dread the coming of a flood, and at the end of nearly every summer they feared a shortage of water would destroy their crops.

The gates of these great diversion tunnels were closed here at Boulder Dam last February. In June a great flood came down the river. It came roaring down the canyons of the Colorado, through Grand Canyon, Iceberg and Boulder Canyons, but it was caught and safely held behind Boulder Dam.

Last year a drought of unprecedented severity was visited upon the West. The watershed of this Colorado River did not escape. In July the canals of the Imperial Valley went dry.

Crop losses in that Valley alone totaled $10 million that summer. Had Boulder Dam been completed one year earlier, this loss would have been prevented, because the spring flood would have been stored to furnish a steady water supply for the long dry summer and fall.

Across the San Jacinto Mountains southwest of Boulder Dam, the cities of Southern California are constructing an aqueduct to cost $220 million which they have raised, for the purpose of carrying the regulated waters of the Colorado River to the Pacific Coast 259 miles away.

Across the desert and mountains to the west and south run great electric transmission lines by which factory motors, street and household lights and irrigation pumps will be operated in Southern Arizona and California. Part of this power will be used in pumping the water through the aqueduct to supplement the domestic supplies of Los Angeles and surrounding cities.

Navigation of the river from Boulder Dam to the Grand Canyon has been made possible, a 115-mile stretch that has been traversed less than half a dozen times in history. An immense new park has been created for the enjoyment of all our people.

At what cost was this done? Boulder Dam and the power houses together cost a total of $108 million all of which will be repaid with interest in fifty years under the contracts for sale of the power. Under these contracts, already completed, not only will the cost be repaid, but the way is opened for the provision of needed light and power to the consumer at reduced rates. In the expenditure of the price of Boulder Dam during the depression years work was provided for 4,000 men, most of them heads of families, and many thousands more were enabled to earn a livelihood through manufacture of materials and machinery.

And this picture is true on different scales in regard to the thousands of projects undertaken by the Federal Government, by the States and by the counties and municipalities in recent years. The overwhelming majority of them are of definite and permanent usefulness.

Throughout our national history we have had a great program of public improvements, and in these past two years all that we have done has been to accelerate that program. We know, too, that the reason for this speeding up was the need of giving relief to several million men and women whose earning capacity had been destroyed by the complexities and lack of thought of the economic system of the past generation.

No sensible person is foolish enough to draw hard and fast classifications as to usefulness or need. Obviously, for instance, this great Boulder Dam warrants universal approval because it will prevent floods and flood damage, because it will irrigate thousands of acres of tillable land and because it will generate electricity to turn the wheels of many factories and illuminate countless homes. But can we say that a five-foot brushwood dam across the head waters of an arroyo, and costing only a millionth part of Boulder Dam, is an undesirable project or a waste of money? Can we say that the great brick high school, costing $2 million is a useful expenditure but that a little wooden school house project, costing five or ten thousand dollars, is a wasteful extravagance? Is it fair to approve a huge city boulevard and, at the same time, disapprove the improvement of a muddy farm-to-market road?

While we do all of this, we give actual work to the unemployed and at the same time we add to the wealth and assets of the Nation. These efforts meet with the approval of the people of the Nation.

In a little over two years this great national work has accomplished much. We have helped mankind by the works themselves and, at the same time, we have created the necessary purchasing power to throw in the clutch to start the wheels of what we call private industry.

Such expenditures on all of these works, great and small, flow out to many beneficiaries; they revive other and more remote industries and businesses. Money is put in circulation. Credit is expanded and the financial and industrial mechanism of America is stimulated to more and more activity. Labor makes wealth. The use of materials makes wealth. To employ workers and materials when private employment has failed is to translate into great national possessions the energy that otherwise would be wasted. Boulder Dam is a splendid symbol of that principle. The mighty waters of the Colorado were running unused to the sea. Today we translate them into a great national possession.

I might go further and suggest to you that use begets use. Such works as this serve as a means of making useful other national possessions. Vast deposits of precious metals are scattered within a short distance of where we stand today. They await the development of cheap power.

These great Government power projects will affect not only the development of agriculture and industry and mining in the sections that they serve, but they will also prove useful yardsticks to measure the cost of power throughout the United States. It is my belief that the Government should proceed to lay down the first yardstick from this great power plant in the form of a State power line, assisted in its financing by the Government, and tapping the wonderful natural resources of Southern Nevada. Doubtless the same policy of financial assistance to State authorities can be followed in the development of Nevada's sister State, Arizona, on the other side of the river.

With it all, with work proceeding in every one of the more than 3,000 counties m the United States, and of a vastly greater number of local divisions of Government, the actual credit of Government agencies is on a stronger and safer basis than at any time in the past six years. Many States have actually improved their financial position in the past two years. Municipal tax receipts are being paid when the taxes fall due, and tax arrearages are steadily declining.

It is a simple fact that Government spending is already beginning to show definite signs of its effect on consumer spending; that the putting of people to work by the Government has put other people to work through private employment, and that in two years and a half we have come to the point today where private industry must bear the principal responsibility of keeping the processes of greater employment moving forward with accelerated speed.

The people of the United States are proud of Boulder Dam. With the exception of the few who are narrow visioned, people everywhere on the Atlantic Seaboard, people in the Middle West and the Northwest, people in the South, must surely recognize that the national benefits which will be derived from the completion of this project will make themselves felt in every one of the forty-eight States. They know that poverty or distress in a community 2,000 miles away may affect them, and equally that prosperity and higher standards of living across a whole continent will help them back home.

Today marks the official completion and dedication of Boulder Dam, the first of four great Government regional units. This is an engineering victory of the first order—another great achievement of American resourcefulness, American skill and determination.

That is why I have the right once more to congratulate you who have built Boulder Dam and on behalf of the Nation to say to you, "Well done."

Source: Roosevelt, Franklin D. "Address at the Dedication of Boulder Dam." September 30. Gerhard Peters and John T. Woolley. The American Presidency Project, 1935.

14. DWIGHT D. EISENHOWER, EXCERPT FROM ATOMS FOR PEACE SPEECH, 1953

The United States knows that if the fearful trend of atomic military build-up can be reversed, this greatest of destructive forces can be developed into a great boon, for the benefit of all mankind. The United States knows that peaceful power from atomic energy is no dream of the future. The capability, already proved, is here today. Who can doubt that, if the entire body of the world's scientists and engineers had adequate amounts of fissionable material with which to test and develop their ideas, this capability would rapidly be transformed into universal, efficient and economic usage?

To hasten the day when fear of the atom will begin to disappear from the minds the people and the governments of the East and West, there are certain steps that can be taken now.

I therefore make the following proposal.

The governments principally involved, to the extent permitted by elementary prudence, should begin now and continue to make joint contributions from their stockpiles of normal uranium and fissionable materials to an international atomic energy agency. We would expect that such an agency would be set up under the aegis of the United Nations. The ratios of contributions, the procedures and other details would properly be within the scope of the "private conversations" I referred to earlier.

The United States is prepared to undertake these explorations in good faith. Any partner of the United States acting in the same good faith will find the United States a not unreasonable or ungenerous associate.

Undoubtedly, initial and early contributions to this plan would be small in quantity. However, the proposal has the great virtue that it can be undertaken without the irritations and mutual suspicions incident to any attempt to set up a completely acceptable system of world-wide inspection and control.

The atomic energy agency could be made responsible for the impounding, storage and protection of the contributed fissionable and other materials. The ingenuity of our scientists will provide special safe conditions under which such a bank of fissionable material can be made essentially immune to surprise seizure.

The more important responsibility of this atomic energy agency would be to devise methods whereby this fissionable material would be allocated to serve the peaceful pursuits of mankind. Experts would be mobilized to apply atomic energy to the needs of agriculture, medicine and other peaceful activities. A special purpose would be to provide abundant electrical energy in the power-starved areas of the world.

Thus the contributing Powers would be dedicating some of their strength to serve the needs rather than the fears of mankind.

The United States would be more than willing—it would be proud to take up with others "principally involved" the development of plans whereby such peaceful use of atomic energy would be expedited.

Of those "principally involved" the Soviet Union must, of course, be one.

I would be prepared to submit to the Congress of the United States, and with every expectation of approval, any such plan that would, first, encourage world-wide investigation into the most effective peacetime uses of fissionable material, and with the certainty that the investigators had all the material needed for the conducting of all experiments that were appropriate; second, begin to diminish the potential destructive power of the world's atomic stockpiles; third, allow all peoples of all nations to see that, in this enlightened age, the great Powers of the earth, both of the East and of the West, are interested in human aspirations first rather than in building up the armaments of war; fourth, open up a new channel for peaceful discussion and initiative at least a new approach to the many difficult problems that must be solved in both private and public conversations if the world is to shake off the inertia imposed by fear and is to make positive progress towards peace.

Against the dark background of the atomic bomb, the United States does not wish to present merely strength but also the desire and the hope for peace. The coming months will be fraught with fateful decisions. In this Assembly, in the capitals and military headquarters of the world, in the hearts of men everywhere, be they governed or governors, may they be the decisions which will lead this world out of fear and into peace.

To the making of these fateful decisions, the United States pledges before you, and therefore before the world, its determination to help solve the fearful atomic dilemma—to devote its entire heart and mind to finding the way by which the miraculous inventiveness of man shall not be dedicated to his death, but consecrated to his life.

I again thank representatives for the great honour they have done me in inviting me to appear before them and in listening to me so graciously.

Source: Eisenhower, Dwight D. "Address by Mr. Dwight D. Eisenhower, President of the United States of America, to the 470th Plenary Meeting of the United Nations General Assembly." December 8, 1953. International Atomic Energy Agency.

15. JIMMY CARTER, "ADDRESS TO THE NATION ON ENERGY," 1977

Good evening.

Tonight I want to have an unpleasant talk with you about a problem that is unprecedented in our history. With the exception of preventing war, this is the greatest challenge that our country will face during our lifetime.

The energy crisis has not yet overwhelmed us, but it will if we do not act quickly. It's a problem that we will not be able to solve in the next few years, and it's likely to get progressively worse through the rest of this century.

We must not be selfish or timid if we hope to have a decent world for our children and our grandchildren. We simply must balance our demand for energy with our rapidly shrinking resources. By acting now we can control our future instead of letting the future control us.

Two days from now, I will present to the Congress my energy proposals. Its Members will be my partners, and they have already given me a great deal of valuable advice.

Many of these proposals will be unpopular. Some will cause you to put up with inconveniences and to make sacrifices. The most important thing about these proposals is that the alternative may be a national catastrophe. Further delay can affect our strength and our power as a nation.

Our decision about energy will test the character of the American people and the ability of the President and the Congress to govern this Nation. This difficult effort will be the "moral equivalent of war," except that we will be uniting our efforts to build and not to destroy.

Now, I know that some of you may doubt that we face real energy shortages. The 1973 gas lines are gone, and with this springtime weather, our homes are warm again. But our energy problem is worse tonight than it was in 1973 or a few weeks ago in the dead of winter. It's worse because more waste has occurred and more time has passed by without our planning for the future. And it will get worse every day until we act.

The oil and natural gas that we rely on for 75 percent of our energy are simply running out. In spite of increased effort, domestic production has been dropping steadily at about 6 percent a year. Imports have doubled in the last 5 years. Our Nation's economic and political independence is becoming increasingly vulnerable. Unless profound changes are made to lower oil consumption, we now believe that early in the 1980's the world will be demanding more oil than it can produce.

The world now uses about 60 million barrels of oil a day, and demand increases each year about 5 percent. This means that just to stay even we need the production of a new Texas every year, an Alaskan North Slope every 9 months, or a new Saudi Arabia every 3 years. Obviously, this cannot continue.

We must look back into history to understand our energy problem. Twice in the last several hundred years, there has been a transition in the way people use energy.

The first was about 200 years ago, when we changed away from wood–which had provided about 90 percent of all fuel—to coal, which was much more efficient. This change became the basis of the Industrial Revolution.

The second change took. place in this century, with the growing use of oil and natural gas. They were more convenient and cheaper than coal, and the supply seemed to be almost without limit. They made possible the age of automobile and airplane travel. Nearly everyone who is alive today grew up during this period, and we have never known anything different.

Because we are now running out of gas and oil, we must prepare quickly for a third change—to strict conservation and to the renewed use of coal and to permanent renewable energy sources like solar power.

The world has not prepared for the future. During the 1950's, people used twice as much oil as during the 1940's. During the 1960's, we used twice as much as during the 1950's. And in each of those decades, more oil was consumed than in all of man's previous history combined.

World consumption of oil is still going up. If it were possible to keep it rising during the 1970's and 1980's by 5 percent a year, as it has in the past, we could use up all the proven reserves of oil in the entire world by the end of the next decade.

I know that many of you have suspected that some supplies of oil and gas are being withheld from the market. You may be right, but suspicions about the oil companies cannot change the fact that we are running out of petroleum.

All of us have heard about the large oil fields on Alaska's North Slope. In a few years, when the North Slope is producing fully, its total output will be just about equal to 2 years' increase in our own Nation's energy demand.

Each new inventory of world oil reserves has been more disturbing than the last. World oil production can probably keep going up for another 6 or 8 years. But sometime in the 1980's, it can't go up any more. Demand will overtake production. We have no choice about that.

But we do have a choice about how we will spend the next few years. Each American uses the energy equivalent of 60 barrels of oil per person each year. Ours is the most wasteful nation on earth. We waste more energy than we import. With about the same standard of living, we use twice as much energy per person as do other countries like Germany, Japan, and Sweden.

One choice, of course, is to continue doing what we've been doing before. We can drift along for a few more years.

Our consumption of oil would keep going up every year. Our cars would continue to be too large and inefficient. Three-quarters of them would carry only one person—the driver—while our public transportation system continues to decline. We can delay insulating our homes, and they will continue to lose about 50 percent of their heat in waste. We can continue using scarce oil and natural gas to generate electricity and continue wasting two-thirds of their fuel value in the process.

If we do not act, then by 1985 we will be using 33 percent more energy than we use today.

We can't substantially increase our domestic production, so we would need to import twice as much oil as we do now. Supplies will be uncertain. The cost will keep going up. Six years ago, we paid $3.7 billion for imported oil. Last year we spent $36 billion for imported oil—nearly 10 times as much. And this year we may spend $45 billion.

Unless we act, we will spend more than $550 billion for imported oil by 1985—more than $2,500 for every man, woman, and child in America. Along with that money that we transport overseas, we will continue losing American jobs and become increasingly vulnerable to supply interruptions.

Now we have a choice. But if we wait, we will constantly live in fear of embargoes. We could endanger our freedom as a sovereign nation to act in foreign affairs. Within 10 years, we would not be able to import enough oil from any country, at any acceptable price.

If we wait and do not act, then our factories will not be able to keep our people on the job with reduced supplies of fuel.

Too few of our utility companies will have switched to coal, which is our most abundant energy source. We will not be ready to keep our transportation system running with smaller and more efficient cars and a better network of buses, trains, and public transportation.

We will feel mounting pressure to plunder the environment. We will have to have a crash program to build more nuclear plants, strip mine and bum more coal, and drill more offshore wells than if we begin to conserve right now.

Inflation will soar; production will go down; people will lose their jobs. Intense competition for oil will build up among nations and also among the different regions within our own country. This has already started.

If we fail to act soon, we will face an economic, social, and political crisis that will threaten our free institutions. But we still have another choice. We can begin to prepare right now. We can decide to act while there is still time. That is the concept of the energy policy that we will present on Wednesday.

Our national energy plan is based on 10 fundamental principles. The first principle is that we can have an effective and comprehensive energy policy only if the Government takes responsibility for it and if the people understand the seriousness of the challenge and are willing to make sacrifices.

The second principle is that healthy economic growth must continue. Only by saving energy can we maintain our standard of living and keep our people at work. An effective conservation program will create hundreds of thousands of new jobs.

The third principle is that we must protect the environment. Our energy problems have the same cause as our environmental problems-wasteful use of resources. Conservation helps us solve both problems at once.

The fourth principle is that we must reduce our vulnerability to potentially devastating embargoes. We can protect ourselves from uncertain supplies by reducing our demand for oil, by making the most of our abundant resources such as coal, and by developing a strategic petroleum reserve.

The fifth principle is that we must be fair. Our solutions must ask equal sacrifices from every region, every class of people, and every interest group. Industry will have to do its part to conserve just as consumers will. The energy producers deserve fair treatment, but we will not let the oil companies profiteer.

The sixth principle, and the cornerstone of our policy, is to reduce demand through conservation. Our emphasis on conservation is a clear difference between this plan and others which merely encouraged crash production efforts. Conservation is the quickest, cheapest, most practical source of energy. Conservation is the only way that we can buy a barrel of oil for about $2. It costs about $13 to waste it.

The seventh principle is that prices should generally reflect the true replacement cost of energy. We are only cheating ourselves if we make energy artificially cheap and use more than we can really afford.

The eighth principle is that Government policies must be predictable and certain. Both consumers and producers need policies they can count on so they can plan ahead. This is one reason that I'm working with the Congress to create a new Department of Energy to replace more than 50 different agencies that now have some control over energy.

The ninth principle is that we must conserve the fuels that are scarcest and make the most of those that are plentiful. We can't continue to use oil and gas for 75 percent of our consumption, as we do now, when they only make up 7 percent of our domestic reserves. We need to shift to plentiful coal, while taking care to protect the environment, and to apply stricter safety standards to nuclear energy.

The tenth and last principle is that we must start now to develop the new, unconventional sources of energy that we will rely on in the next century.

Now, these 10 principles have guided the development of the policy that I will describe to you and the Congress on Wednesday night.

Our energy plan will also include a number of specific goals to measure our progress toward a stable energy system. These are the goals that we set for 1985:

—to reduce the annual growth rate in our energy demand to less than 2 percent;
—to reduce gasoline consumption by 10 percent below its current level;
—to cut in half the portion of U.S. oil which is imported–from a potential level of 16 million barrels to 6 million barrels a day;
—to establish a strategic petroleum reserve of one billion barrels, more than a 6-months supply;
—to increase our coal production by about two-thirds to more than one billion tons a year;
—to insulate 90 percent of American homes and all new buildings;
—to use solar energy in more than 2 1/2 million houses.

We will monitor our progress toward these goals year by year. Our plan will call for strict conservation measures if we fall behind. I can't tell you that these measures will be easy, nor will they be popular. But I think most of you realize that a policy which does not ask for changes or sacrifices would not be an effective policy at this late date.

This plan is essential to protect our jobs, our environment, our standard of living, and our future. Whether this plan truly makes a difference will not be decided now here in Washington but in every town and every factory, in every home and on every highway and every farm.

I believe that this can be a positive challenge. There is something especially American in the kinds of changes that we have to make. We've always been proud, through our history, of being efficient people. We've always been proud of our ingenuity, our skill at answering questions. Now we need efficiency and ingenuity more than ever.

We've always been proud of our leadership in the world. And now we have a chance again to give the world a positive example.

We've always been proud of our vision of the future. We've always wanted to give our children and our grandchildren a world richer in possibilities than we have had ourselves. They are the ones that we must provide for now. They are the ones who will suffer most if we don't act.

I've given you some of the principles of the plan. I'm sure that each of you will find something you don't like about the specifics of our proposal. It will demand that we make sacrifices and changes in every life. To some degree, the sacrifices will be painful—but so is any meaningful sacrifice. It will lead to some higher costs and to some greater inconvenience for everyone. But the sacrifices can be gradual, realistic, and they are necessary. Above all, they will be fair. No one will gain an unfair advantage through this plan. No one will be asked to bear an unfair burden.

We will monitor the accuracy of data from the oil and natural gas companies for the first time, so that we will always know their true production, supplies, reserves, and profits. Those citizens who insist on driving large, unnecessarily powerful cars must expect to pay more for that luxury.

We can be sure that all the special interest groups in the country will attack the part of this plan that affects them directly. They will say that sacrifice is fine as long as other people do it, but that their sacrifice is unreasonable or unfair or harmful to the country. If they succeed with this approach, then the burden on the ordinary citizen, who is not organized into an interest group, would be crushing.

There should be only one test for this program—whether it will help our country. Other generations of Americans have faced and mastered great challenges. I have faith that meeting this challenge will make our own lives even richer. If you will join me so that we can work together with patriotism and courage, we will again prove that our great Nation can lead the world into an age of peace, independence, and freedom.

Thank you very much, and good night.

Source: Carter, Jimmy. "Address to the Nation on Energy." April 18, 1977. Gerhard Peters and John T. Woolley. The American Presidency Project.

16. DR. JAMES HANSON, TESTIMONY BEFORE THE US SENATE COMMITTEE ON ENERGY AND NATURAL RESOURCES HEARING ON THE GREENHOUSE EFFECT AND GLOBAL CLIMATE CHANGE, 1988

Hearing Before the Committee on Energy and Natural Resources, United States Senate, One Hundredth Congress, First Session on the Greenhouse Effect and Global Climate Change, June 23, 1988, Part 2.

Statement of Dr. James Hansen, Director, NASA Goddard Institute for Space Studies

Mr. Chairman and committee members, thank you for the opportunity to present the results of my research on the greenhouse effect which has been carried out with my colleagues at the NASA Goddard Institute for Space Studies.

I would like to draw three main conclusions. Number one, the earth is warmer in 1988 than at any time in the history of instrumental measurements. Number two, the global warming is now large enough that we can ascribe with a high degree of confidence a cause and effect relationship to the greenhouse effect. And number three, our computer climate simulations indicate that the greenhouse effect is already large enough to begin to effect the probability of extreme events such as summer heat waves.

My first viewgraph, which I would like to ask Suki to put up if he would, shows the global temperature over the period of instrumental records which is about 100 years. The present temperature is the highest in the period of record. The rate of warming in the past 25 years, as you can see on the right, is the highest on record. The four warmest years, as the Senator mentioned, have all been in the 1980s. And 1988 so far is so much warmer than 1987, that barring a remarkable and improbable cooling, 1988 will the warmest year on the record.

Now let me turn to my second point which is causal association of the greenhouse effect and the global warming. Causal association requires first that the warming be larger than natural climate variability and, second that the magnitude and nature of the warming be consistent with the greenhouse mechanism. These points are both addressed in my second viewgraph. The observed warming during the past 30 years, which is the period when we have accurate measurements of atmospheric composition, is shown by the heavy black line in this graph. The warming is almost 0.4 degrees centigrade by 1987 relative to climatology, which is defined as the 30-year mean, 1950 to 1980 and, in fact, the warming is more than 0.4 degrees centigrade in 1988. The probability of a chance warming of that magnitude is about 1 percent. So, with 99 percent confidence we can state that the warming during this time period is a real warming trend.

The other curves in this figure are the results of global climate model calculations for three scenarios of atmospheric trace gas growth. We have considered several scenarios because there are uncertainties in the exact trace gas growth in the past and especially in the future. We have considered cases ranging from business as usual, which is scenario A, to draconian emission cuts, scenario C, which would totally eliminate net trace gas growth by the year 2000.

The main point to be made here is that the expected global warming is of the same magnitude as the observed warming. Since there is only a 1 percent chance of an accidental warming of this magnitude, the agreement with the expected greenhouse effect is of considerable significance. Moreover, if you look at the next level of detail in the global temperature change, there are clear signs of the greenhouse effect. Observational data suggests a cooling in the stratosphere while the ground is warming. The data suggest somewhat more warming over land and sea ice regions than over open ocean, more warming at high latitudes than at low latitudes, and more warming in the winter than in the summer. In all of these cases, the signal is at best just beginning to emerge, and we need more data. Some of these details, such as the northern hemisphere high latitude temperature trends, do not look exactly like the greenhouse effect, but that is expected. There are certainly other climate factors involved in addition to the greenhouse effect.

Altogether the evidence that the earth is warming by an amount which is too large to be a chance fluctuation and the similarity of the warming to that expected from the greenhouse effect represents a very strong case. In my opinion, that the greenhouse effect has been detected, and it is changing our climate now.

Then my third point. Finally, I would like to address the question of whether the greenhouse effect is already large enough to affect the probability of extreme events, such as summer heat waves. As shown in my next viewgraph, we have used the temperature changes computed in our global climate model to estimate the impact of the greenhouse effect on the frequency of hot summers in Washington, DC and Omaha, Nebraska. A hot summer is defined as the hottest one-third of the summers in the 1950 to 1980 period, which is the period the Weather Bureau uses for defining climatology. So, in that period the probability of having a hot summer was 33 percent, but by the 1990s, you can see that the greenhouse effect has increased the probability of a hot summer to somewhere between 55 percent and 70 percent in Washington according to our climate model simulations. In the late 1980s, the probability of a hot summer would be somewhat less than that. You can interpolate to a value of something like 40 to 60 percent.

I believe that this change in the frequency of hot summers is large enough to be noticeable to the average person. So, we have already reached a point that the greenhouse effect is important. It may also have important implications other than for creature comforts.

My last viewgraph shows global maps of temperature anomalies for a particular month, July, for several different years between 1986 and 2029, as computed with our global climate model for the intermediate trace gas scenario B. As shown by the graphs on the left where yellow and red colors represent areas that are warmer than climatology and blue areas represent areas that are colder than climatology, at the present time in the 1980s the greenhouse warming is smaller than the natural variability of the local temperature. So, in any given month, there is almost as much area that is cooler than normal as there is warmer than normal. A few decades in the future, as shown on the right, it is warm almost everywhere.

However, the point that I would like to make is that in the late 1980s and in the 1990s we notice a clear tendency in our model for greater than average warming in the southeast United States and the Midwest. In our model this result seems to arise because the Atlantic Ocean of the coast of the United States warms more slowly than the land. This leads to high pressure along the east coast and circulation of warm air north into the Midwest or southeast. There is only a tendency for this phenomenon. It is certainly not going to happen every, and climate models are certainly an imperfect tool at this time. However, we conclude that there is evidence that the greenhouse effect increases the likelihood of heat wave drought situations in the southeast and Midwest United States even though we cannot blame a specific drought on the greenhouse effect.

Therefore, I believe that it is not a good idea to use the period 1950 to 1980 for which climatology is normally defined as an indication of how frequently droughts will occur in the future. If our model is approximately correct, such situations may be more common in the next 10 to 15 years than they were in the period 1950 to 1980.

Finally, I would like to stress that there is a need for improving these global climate models, and there is a need for global observations if we're going to obtain a full understanding of these phenomena.

That concludes my statement, and I'd be glad to answer questions if you'd like.

Source: *Hearing before the Committee on Energy and Natural Resources, United States Senate, One Hundredth Congress, First Session on the Greenhouse Effect and Global Climate Change, June 23, 1988, Part 2.* Pp. 39–41. Washington, DC: US Government Printing Office.

CONTRIBUTORS

Fazila Derya Agis, Ph.D., is an independent scholar and Instructor of English at the University of the People and previously a research associate at the Hadassah-Brandeis Institute at Brandeis University.

Jessica O. Baggerman, Ph.D., is an Assistant Professor in the Department of Agricultural Studies at Huntington University.

Aysha Bodenhamer, Ph.D., is an Assistant Professor in the Department of Sociology at Radford University.

Gregory Bothun, Ph.D., is a Professor in the Department of Physics at the University of Oregon.

Mark C. Boxell, Ph.D., is an Assistant Professor in the Department of History at the University of Nebraska Omaha.

Paul A. Brazinski, Ph.D., is an Upper School History Faculty Member and Administrative Master at Woodberry Forest School.

Thomas David Brown, M.A., is a Ph.D. candidate in the Department of History at Northern Illinois University.

William E. Burns, Ph.D., is the author of *The Scientific Revolution in Global Perspective* and *An Age of Wonders: Prodigies, Politics and Providence in England, 1657– 1727.*

Delia Sarah Byrnes, Ph.D., is an Assistant Professor in the Department of Environmental Science and Sustainability at Allegheny College.

Mark M. Chambers, Ph.D., is a Lecturer in History at Stony Brook University and author of *Gray Gold: Lead Mining and Its Impact on the Natural and Cultural Environment, 1700–1840.*

Benjamin J. Clark is a Ph.D. student at Indiana University Purdue University Indianapolis, and Researcher at the IUPUI Arts & Humanities Institute.

Kate Clark, Ph.D., is an Assistant Professor of Environment & Sustainability at Western Colorado University.

Keriann Conroy, M.E.M., is a Research Associate at Energy and Policy Institute in Colorado.

Curt J. Davis, Ph.D., is a Global Development, Education, and Energy Specialist and Consultant in Delaware.

Isiah Lamont Davis holds a B.A. in Criminal Justice Administration from Campbellsville University.

Michael Davis, Ph.D., is an Assistant Professor of History at Hampton University.

Patrice Natalie Delevante, M.A., is an independent scholar, published author, songwriter, and poet in South Carolina.

Petra Dolata, Ph.D., is an Associate Professor in the Department of History at the University of Calgary and author of *The German Coal Crisis in the National and Transatlantic Context* and convener of Energy in Society for Calgary Institute for the Humanities.

Phoebe M. Doscher holds a B.A. in English with a writing concentration from Gettysburg College; she is a content production editor at Medscape and a freelance writer.

Emma P. Fee holds a B.A. in English from Gettysburg College; she works with the Quaker Voluntary Service and ACHIEVEability in Philadelphia, PA.

Samuel B. Fee is at Gettysburg College in Gettysburg, PA.

Kregg M. Fehr, Ph.D., is a Professor of History at Lubbock Christian University, specializing in the field of History of Science and Technology.

Caitlin Fendley, M.A., is a Ph.D. candidate in the Department of History at Purdue University.

Richard M. Filipink, Ph.D., is a Professor in the Department of History at Western Illinois University and author of *Dwight Eisenhower and American Foreign Policy during the 1960s: An American Lion in Winter.*

Adam Gallaher is a Ph.D. Candidate in the Department of Geography at the University of Connecticut.

Karen S. Garvin, M.A., is an independent scholar who contributes to an open access textbook on the history of applied science and technology, and who has written on a wide variety of subjects in the history of science and technology.

Sakina Groeppmaier is a Ph.D. candidate at Amerika-Institut, Ludwig-Maximilians-Universität München.

Patrick D. Hagge, Ph.D., is an Associate Professor in the Department of Geography at Arkansas Tech University.

Jeff Hirschy, Ph.D., is an Assistant Professor in the School of Library and Information Science at the University of Southern Mississippi.

Kevin Hogg, M.A., teaches Law and English at Mount Baker Secondary School in Cranbrook, British Columbia.

Michelle Elise Houle, M.Ed., is an independent scholar, educator, and consultant in California.

Rudy Kahsar, Ph.D., is Manager of the Strategic Team at the Rocky Mountain Institute in Colorado.

Andrew Kettler, Ph.D., is an Assistant Professor of History at University of South Carolina Union and author of *The Smell of Slavery: Olfactory Racism in the Early Modern World.*

William P. Kladky, Ph.D., is a Lecturer at the College of Notre Dame of Maryland and a contributor to the Digital Encyclopedia of George Washington.

Grove Koger is an independent scholar with a Master of Librarianship degree from the University of Washington iSchool.

Jiayu Liang holds a B.A. in Communication of Science and Technology from Vanderbilt University and is a Stabile Reporting Fellow at the Columbia Journalism School.

Kathryn Lisinicchia, M.Ed., is Northeast Indiana Resiliency Coordinator for Earth Charter Indiana.

Kyhl Lyndgaard, Ph.D., is Director of First Year Seminar and Writing Centers at St. John's University in Minnesota and author of *Captivity Literature and the Environment Nineteenth-Century American Cross-Cultural Collaborations.*

James Harry Morris, Ph.D., is an Assistant Professor at Waseda Institute for Advanced Study at Waseda University in Japan.

Keith J. Muchowski, M.L.S., M.A., is an Instruction/Reference Librarian and Associate Professor at New York City College of Technology (CUNY).

Ruth E. Nalliah, Ph.D., is a Professor in the Department of Chemistry at Huntington University.

Dana Nichols, Ph.D., is Vice Chancellor of Academic Affairs at the University System of Georgia.

Sam Orndorff, M.A., is a Ph.D. candidate in Geography with the Joint Doctoral Program of San Diego State University and University of California, Santa Barbara.

Daniel W. Phillips III, Ph.D., is an Associate Professor of Criminal Justice at Campbellsville University.

Todd K. Platts, Ph.D., is a Professor of Sociology at Piedmont Virginia Community College.

Fredric L. Quivik, Ph.D., is a Professor of History in the Department of Social Sciences at Michigan Technological University.

Norman R. Rose, Ph.D., is an Assistant Professor in the Department of Sociology and Criminal Justice at Kent State University.

Evan C. Rothera, Ph.D, is an Assistant Professor of History at the University of Arkansas—Fort Smith and author of *Civil Wars and Reconstructions in the Americas: The United States, Mexico, and Argentina, 1860–1880.*

Jennifer Schell, Ph.D., is a Professor in the Department of English at the University of Alaska Fairbanks.

Lucas J. Sheaffer, Ph.D., is Chair of Liberal Arts and Associate Professor at the Rocky Mountain College of Art + Design.

Seth Shulman is co-author of *Cooler Smarter: Practical Steps for Low-Carbon Living*, author of *The Telephone Gambit: Chasing Alexander Graham Bell's Secret*, and editorial director at Union of Concerned Scientists.

Inna Sukhenko, Ph.D., is a Research Fellow of the Helsinki Environmental Humanities Hub at the University of Helsinki in Finland.

Joseph F. Super, Ph.D., is an Assistant Professor of History at Liberty University Online.

William A. Taylor, Ph.D., is an Associate Professor of Security Studies at Angelo State University and author of *Military Service and American Democracy: From World War II to the Iraq and Afghanistan Wars.*

Michael T. Terronez is a Neighborhood Planner within the Neighborhood Planning and Activation workgroup for the Community Development Division of the City of Fort Wayne in Indiana.

Kathleen A. Tobin, Ph.D., is a Professor of History at Purdue University Northwest and author of *Politics and Population Control: A Documentary History.*

Kathy Tyson holds a B.A. from Franklin & Marshall College. She studied Secondary Education at Arcadia University and Applied Behavior Analysis at Penn State, and is an educator at Biglerville High School in Biglerville, PA.

Elia Vargas, Ph.D., is a Lecturer at California State University Monterey Bay.

Harold D. Wallace, Jr., Ph.D., is a Curator at the National Museum of American History of the Smithsonian Institution.

Erik Wallenberg is a Ph.D. candidate in History at the Graduate Center, City University of New York and Acquisitions Editor at *Science for the People.*

Caleb Wellum, Ph.D., is an Assistant Professor of U.S. History at the University of Toronto, Mississauga, editor of *Energy Humanities*, and contributor to *Solarities: Seeking Energy Justice* and *After Oil.*

Brett F. Woods, Ph.D., is a Professor of History at the American Public University System and author of *James Monroe Diplomatic Correspondence: Paris, 1794–1796.*

Nikoleta Zampaki, Ph.D., is a post-doc Researcher at the Faculty of Philology of the National and Kapodistrian University of Athens in Greece and associate and managing editor of *Journal of Ecohumanism.*

BIBLIOGRAPHY

Ackland, Len. 1999. *Making a Real Killing: Rocky Flats and the Nuclear West*. Albuquerque, NM: University of New Mexico Press.

Adams, Sean P. 2014. *Home Fires: How Americans Kept Warm in the Nineteenth Century*. Baltimore, MD: Johns Hopkins University Press.

Alnasrawi, Abbas. 1992. "Iraq: Economic Consequences of the 1991 Gulf War and Future Outlook." *Third World Quarterly*. Vol. 13. No. 2. Pp. 335–52.

Anderson, Irvine. 1981. *Aramco, the United States, and Saudi Arabia: A Study of the Dynamics of Foreign Oil Policy, 1933–1950*. Princeton, NJ: Princeton University Press.

Andrews, Thomas G. 2008. *Killing for Coal: America's Deadliest Labor War*. Cambridge, MA: Harvard University Press.

Angus, Ian. 2016. *Facing the Anthropocene: Fossil Capitalism and the Crisis of the Earth System*. New York: Monthly Review Press.

Arrhenius, Svante. 1896. "On the Influence of Carbonic Acid in the Air upon the Temperature of the Ground." *Philosophical Magazine and Journal of Science*. Series 5. Vol. 41. April. Pp. 237–76.

Asmus, Peter. 2001. *Reaping the Wind: How Mechanical Wizards, Visionaries, and Profiteers Helped Shape Our Energy Future*. Washington, DC: Island Press.

Aurand, Harold W. 2003. *Coalcracker Culture: Work and Values in Pennsylvania Anthracite, 1835–1935*. Selinsgrove, PA: Susquehanna University Press.

Baker, T. Lindsay. 1985. *A Field Guide to American Windmills*. Norman, OK: University of Oklahoma Press.

Bakke, Gretchen. 2017. *The Grid: The Fraying Wires between Americans and our Energy Future*. New York: Bloomsbury.

Barrett, Ross, and Daniel Worden, eds. 2014. *Oil Culture*. Minneapolis, MN: University of Minnesota Press.

Basile, Salvatore. 2014. *Cool: How Air Conditioning Changed Everything*. New York: Fordham University Press.

Bell, David A., Brian F. Towler, and Maohong Fan. 2010. *Coal Gasification and its Applications*. Norwich, NY: William Andrew.

Bell, Shannon E. 2016. *Fighting King Coal: The Challenges to Micromobilization in Central Applachia*. Cambridge, MA: MIT Press.

Bentley, R.W. 2016. *Introduction to Peak Oil*. New York: Springer.

Bijker, Wiebe, E., Thomas Parke Hughes, T.J. Pinch, and Deborah G. Douglas. 2012. *The Social Construction of Technological Systems: New Directions in the Sociology and History of Technology*. Cambridge, MA: MIT Press.

Black, Brian C. 2003. *Petrolia: The Landscape of America's First Oil Boom*. Baltimore, MD: Johns Hopkins University Press.

Black, Brian C. 2014. *Crude Reality: Petroleum in World History*. Lanham, MD: Rowman & Littlefield Publishers, Inc.

Blatz, Perry K. 1994. *Democratic Miners: Work and Labor Relations in the Anthracite Coal Industry, 1875–1925*. Albany, NY: SUNY Press.

Blume, Steven W. 2017. *Electric Power System Basics for the Nonelectrical Professional*. Piscataway, NJ: IEEE Press-Wiley.

Bower, Tom. 2009. *Oil: Money, Politics, and Power in the 21st Century*. New York: Grand Central Publishing.

Bowman, Andy. 2021. *The West Texas Power Plant That Saved the World: Energy, Capitalism, and Climate Change*. Lubbock, TX: Texas Tech University Press.

Brantley, J.E. 1971. *History of Oil Well Drilling*. Houston, TX: Gulf Publishing Co.

Brewer, Priscilla. 2000. *From Fireplace to Cookstove: Technology and the Domestic Ideal in America*. Syracuse, NY: Syracuse University Press.

Brower, Michael. 1994. *Cool Energy: Renewable Solutions to Environmental Problems*. Cambridge, MA: MIT Press.

Brown, Kate. 2013. *Plutopia: Nuclear Families, Atomic Cities, and the Great Soviet and American Plutonium Disasters*. Oxford: Oxford University Press.

Burns, Shirley Stewart. 2007. *Bringing Down the Mountains: The Impact of Mountaintop Removal on Southern West Virginia Communities*. Morgantown, WV: West Virginia University Press.

Burrough, Brian. 2009. *The Big Rich: The Rise and Fall of the Greatest Texas Oil Fortunes*. New York: Penguin Books.

Byrne, John, and Steven M. Hoffman. 1996. *Governing the Atom: The Politics of Risk*. Piscataway, NJ: Transaction Publishers.

Campbell, John. 1988. *Collapse of an Industry: Nuclear Power and the Contradictions of U.S. Policy*. Ithaca, NY: Cornell University Press.

Caron, Justin, Sebastian Rausch, and Niven Winchester. 2015. "Leakage from Sub-national Climate Policy: The Case of California's Cap-and-Trade Program." *The Energy Journal*. Vol. 36. No. 2. April. Pp. 167–90.

Castaneda, Christopher. 1999. *Invisible Fuel: Manufactured and Natural Gas in America, 1800–2000*. Woodbridge, CT: Twayne Publishers.

Cater, Casey P. 2019. *Regenerating Dixie: Electric Energy and the Modern South*. Pittsburgh, PA: University of Pittsburgh Press.

Chapelle, Howard Irving. 1935. *The History of American Sailing Ships*. New York: Norton.

Childs, Marquis. 1952. *The Farmer Takes a Hand: The Electric Power Revolution in Rural America*. Garden City, NY: Doubleday & Co., Inc.

Cohn, Julie A. 2017. *The Grid: Biography of an American Technology*. Cambridge, MA: MIT Press.

Cooper, Andrew. 2011. *The Oil Kings: How the U.S., Iran, and Saudi Arabia Changed the Balance of Power in the Middle East*. New York: Simon & Schuster.

Cowan, Ruth Schwartz. 1983. *More Work for Mother: The Ironies of Household Technology from the Open Hearth to the Microwave*. New York: Basic Books.

Cowan, Ruth Schwartz. 1997. *A Social History of American Technology*. New York: Oxford University Press.

Crosby, Alfred W. 2006. *Children of the Sun: A History of Humanity's Unappeasable Appetite for Energy*. New York: W.W. Norton & Co.

Crump, Thomas. 2007. *A Brief History of the Age of Steam: The Power that Drove the Industrial Revolution*. New York: Carroll & Graf Publishers.

Cummins, Light Townsend, Judith Kelleher Schafer, Edward F. Haas, and Michael L. Kurtz. 2014. *Louisiana: A History*. Chichester, UK: Wiley-Blackwell.

Dalzell, Frederick. 2010. *Engineering Invention: Frank J. Sprague and the U.S. Electrical Industry*. Cambridge, MA: MIT Press.

Davenport, Thomas. 1851. *Autobiography of Thomas Davenport*. State of Vermont Public Records Commission. Microfilm.

Davis, Devra Lee. 2002. *When Smoke Ran like Water: Tales of Environmental Deception and the Battle against Pollution*. New York: Basic Books.

Davis, Lance E. 1997. *In Pursuit of Leviathan: Technology, Institutions, Productivity, and Profits in American Whaling, 1816–1906*. Chicago, IL: University of Chicago Press.

Davis, Margaret Leslie. 1998. *Dark Side of Fortune: Triumph and Scandal in the Life of Edward L. Doheny*. Berkeley, CA: University of California Press.

DeGraff, Leonard. 2013. *Edison and the Rise of Innovation*. New York: Sterling Signature.

Dewey, Scott Hamilton. 2000. *Don't Breathe the Air: Air Pollution and U.S. Environmental Politics, 1945–1970*. College Station, TX: Texas A&M Press.

Dix, Keith. 1988. *What's a Coal Miner to Do? The Mechanization of Coal Mining*. Pittsburgh, PA: University of Pittsburgh Press.

Dochuk, Darren. 2019. *Anointed with Oil: How Christianity and Crude Made Modern America*. New York: Basic Books.

Donaldson, Barry, and Bernard Nagengast. 1994. *Heat & Cold: Mastering the Great Indoors: A Selective History of Heating, Ventilation, Air-conditioning and Refrigeration from the Ancients to the 1930s*. Atlanta, GA: American Society of Heating, Refrigerating and Air-Conditioning Engineers.
Erikson, Kai. 1976. *Everything in Its Path: Destruction of Community in the Buffalo Creek Flood*. New York: Touchstone.
Fitzgerald, Edward Peter. 1991. "Compagnie Française des Pétroles and the Defense of the Red Line Regime in Middle Eastern Oil, 1933–36." *Business and Economic History*. Vol. 20. Pp. 117–26.
Flink, James. 1990. *The Automobile Age*. Cambridge, MA: MIT Press.
Forbes, Robert James. 1958. *Studies in Early Petroleum History*. Leiden: E.J. Brill.
Freeberg, Ernest. 2013. *The Age of Edison: Electric Light and the Invention of Modern America*. New York: Penguin Books.
Freese, Carol. 2003. *Coal: A Human History*. New York: Basic Books.
Frehner, Brian. 2011. *Finding Oil: The Nature of Petroleum Geology, 1859–1920*. Lincoln, NE: University of Nebraska Press.
French, David. 2017. *When They Hid the Fire: A History of Electricity and Invisible Energy in America*. Pittsburgh, PA: University of Pittsburgh Press.
Gates, Paul W. 1968. *History of Public Land Law Development*. Washington, DC: US Government Printing Office.
Gertner, Jon. 2012. *The Idea Factory: Bell Labs and the Great Age of American Innovation*. New York: Penguin.
Giddens, Paul H. 1938. *The Birth of the Oil Industry*. New York: The Macmillan Company.
Giddens, Paul H. 1955. *Standard Oil Company (Indiana): Oil Pioneers of the Middle West*. New York: Appleton-Century-Crofts.
Gordon, Richard L. 1978. *Coal in the U.S. Energy Market: History and Prospects*. Lexington, MA: Lexington Books.
Gow, Sandy. 2005. *Roughnecks, Rock Bits, and Rigs: The Evolution of Oil Well Drilling Technology in Alberta, 1883–1970*. Calgary, AB: University of Calgary Press.
Graebner, William. 2014. *Coal-Mining Safety in the Progressive Period: The Political Economy of Reform*. Lexington, KY: University Press of Kentucky.
Grant, Roger H. 2016. *Electric Interurbans and the American People*. Bloomington, IN: Indiana University Press.
Greenberger, Martin. 1983. *Caught Unawares: The Energy Decade in Retrospect*. Cambridge, MA: Ballinger Publishing Company.
Grigas, Agnia. 2017. *The New Geopolitics of Natural Gas*. Cambridge, MA: Harvard University Press.
Hakes, Jay E. 2021. *Energy Crises: Nixon, Ford, Carter and Hard Choices in the 1970s*. Norman, OK: University of Oklahoma Press.
Hammond, John Winthrop. 1941. *Men and Volts: The Story of General Electric*. Philadelphia, PA: J. B. Lippencott Company.
Harris, Howell J. 2008. "Inventing the U.S. Stove Industry, c.1815–1875: Making and Selling the First Universal Consumer Durable." *Business History Review*. Vol. 82. No. 4. Pp. 701–33.
Harris, Wess, ed. 2017. *Written in Blood: Courage and Corruption in the Appalachian War of Extraction*. Gay, WV: Appalachian Community Services; Oakland, CA: PM Press.
Hausman, William J., Peter Hertner, and Mira Wilkins. 2008. *Global Electrification: Multinational Enterprise and International Finance in the History of Light and Power, 1878–2007*. Cambridge: Cambridge University Press.
Heilbron, John L. 1979. *Electricity in the 17th and 18th Centuries: A Study of Early Modern Physics*. Berkeley, CA: University of California Press.
Herring, Horace, and Steve Sorrell, eds. 2009. *Energy Efficiency and Sustainable Consumption: The Rebound Effect*. New York: Palgrave Macmillan.
Hills, Richard Leslie. 2000. *Power from Steam: A History of the Stationary Steam Engine*. Cambridge: Cambridge University Press.
Hindle, Brooke, and Steven Lubar. 1986. *Engines of Change: The American Industrial Revolution, 1790–1860*. Washington, DC: Smithsonian Institution Press.

Hinton, Diana Davids, and Roger M. Olien. 2002. *Oil in Texas: The Gusher Age, 1895–1945*. Austin, TX: University of Texas Press.

Hirsh, Richard F. 1999. *Power Loss: The Origins of Deregulation and Restructuring in the American Electric Utility System*. Cambridge, MA: MIT Press.

Hirsh, Richard F. 2003. *Technology and Transformation in the American Electric Utility Industry*. Cambridge: Cambridge University Press.

Hobart, Peter C., and Michael W. Williams. 2005. *The Industrial Hobarts: One Family's Story through the American Century*. Virginia Beach, VA: The Donning Company Publishers.

Huber, Matthew T. 2013. *Lifeblood: Oil, Freedom, and the Forces of Capital*. Minneapolis, MN: University of Minnesota Press.

Hughes, Thomas P. 1993. *Networks of Power: Electrification in Western Society, 1880–1930*. Baltimore, MD: Johns Hopkins University Press.

Hunter, Louis C. 1979. *A History of Industrial Power in the United States, 1780–1930*. Vol. 1: *Waterpower in the Century of the Steam Engine*. Charlottesville, VA: Published for the Eleutherian Mills-Hagley Foundation by the University Press of Virginia.

Hunter, Louis C. 1993. *Steamboats on the Western Rivers: An Economic and Technological History*. New York: Dover Publications, Inc.

Inman, Mason. 2016. *The Oracle of Oil: A Maverick Geologist's Quest for a Sustainable Future*. New York: W.W. Norton & Co.

Jaber, Suaad. 2013. "Environmental Impacts of Wind Energy." *Journal of Clean Energy Technologies*. Vol. 1. No. 3. Pp. 251–4.

Jacobs, Dennis Allen, and Karen Anita Branden. 2008. *From McEnergy to EcoEnergy: America's Transition to Sustainable Energy*. Pittsburgh, PA: Dorrance Publishing.

Jacobs, Meg. 2016. *Panic at the Pump: The Energy Crisis and the Transformation of American Politics in the 1970s*. New York: Hill and Wang.

Jacobson, Charles. 2001. *Ties That Bind: Economic and Political Dilemmas of Urban Utility Networks, 1800–1990*. Pittsburgh, PA: University of Pittsburgh Press.

Jensen, W.G. 1968. "The Importance of Energy in the First and Second World Wars." *Historical Journal*. Vol. 11. No. 3. Pp. 538–54.

Johnson, Arthur Menzies. 1967. *Petroleum Pipelines and Public Policy, 1906–1959*. Cambridge, MA: Harvard University Press.

Johnson, Bob. 2014. *Carbon Nation: Fossil Fuels in the Making of American Culture*. Lawrence, KS: University Press of Kansas.

Johnson, James P. 1979. *The Politics of Soft Coal: The Bituminous Industry from World War I through the New Deal*. Urbana, IL: University of Illinois Press.

Jones, Christopher F. 2014. *Routes of Power: Energy and Modern America*. Cambridge, MA: Harvard University Press.

Jones, Toby Craig. 2012. "America, Oil, and War in the Middle East." *Journal of American History*. Vol. 99. No. 4. Pp. 208–18.

Jonnes, Jill. 2003. *Empires of Light: Edison, Tesla, Westinghouse, and the Race to Electrify the World*. New York: Random House.

Kash, Don E., and Robert W. Rycroft. 1984. *U.S. Energy Policy: Crisis and Complacency*. Norman, OK: University of Oklahoma Press.

Kaufman, Scott. 2012. *Project Plowshare: The Peaceful Use of Nuclear Explosives in Cold War America*. Ithaca, NY: Cornell University Press.

Kidd, Jerry S., and Renee A. Kidd. 2006. *Nuclear Power: The Study of Quarks and Sparks*. New York: Chelsea House.

Klein, Maury. 2010. *The Power Makers: Steam, Electricity, and the Men Who Invented Modern America*. New York: Bloomsbury Press.

Kovarik, Bill. 1998. "Henry Ford, Charles Kettering and the Fuel of the Future." *Automotive History Review*. No. 32. Spring. Pp. 7–27.

Kuletz, Valerie L. 1998. *The Tainted Desert: Environmental and Social Ruin in the American West*. New York: Routledge.

Lambert, Jeremiah D. 2015. *The Power Brokers: The Struggle to Shape and Control the Electric Power Industry*. Cambridge, MA: MIT Press.

Leggett, Jeremy K. 1999. *The Carbon War: Global Warming and the End of the Oil Era*. New York: Penguin Books.

Lewis, David L., and Laurence Goldstein, eds. 1983. *The Automobile and American Culture*. Ann Arbor, MI: University of Michigan Press.

Lifset, Robert. 2014. *American Energy Policy in the 1970s*. Norman, OK: University of Oklahoma Press.

Lifset, Robert. 2014. *Power on the Hudson: Storm King Mountain & The Emergence of Modern American Environmentalism*. Pittsburgh, PA: University of Pittsburgh Press.

Lockwood, Alan. 2012. *The Silent Epidemic: Coal and the Hidden Threat to Health*. Cambridge, MA: MIT Press.

Long, Priscilla. 1991. *Where the Sun Never Shines: A History of America's Bloody Coal Industry*. New York: Paragon House.

Longrigg, Stephen Hemsley. 1954. *Oil in the Middle East: Its Discovery and Development*. Royal Institute of International Affairs. New York: Oxford University Press.

Lynch, Gerald. 1987. *Roughnecks, Drillers, and Tool Pushers: Thirty-Three Years in the Oil Fields*. Austin, TX: University of Texas Press.

MacKenzie, Donald A., and Judy Wajcman. 1985. *The Social Shaping of Technology: How the Refrigerator Got Its Hum*. Philadelphia, PA: Open University Press.

Mahaffey, James. 2009. *Atomic Awakening: A New Look at the History and Future of Nuclear Power*. New York: Pegasus Books.

Mahan, Alfred Thayer. 1897. *The Interest of America in Sea Power, Present and Future*. Boston: Little, Brown.

Malone, Patrick M. 2009. *Waterpower in Lowell: Engineering and Industry in Nineteenth-Century America*. Baltimore, MD: The Johns Hopkins University Press.

Marcel, Valérie, and John V. Mitchell. 2006. *Oil Titans: National Oil Companies in the Middle East*. Washington, DC: Brookings Institution Press.

Maugeri, Leonardo. 2006. *The Age of Oil: The Mythology, History, and Future of the World's Most Controversial Resource*. Westport, CT: Praeger Publishers.

McNall, Scott G. 2011. *Rapid Climate Change: Causes, Consequences, and Solutions*. New York: Routledge.

McNeill, John R. 2001. *Something New under the Sun: An Environmental History of the Twentieth-Century World*. New York: W.W. Norton & Company.

McNeill, John R., and George Vrtis, eds. 2017. *Mining North America: An Environmental History since 1522*. Berkeley, CA: University of California Press.

Melosi, Martin V. 1985. *Coping with Abundance: Energy and Environment in Industrial America*. New York: Alfred A. Knopf.

Melosi, Martin V., and Joseph A. Pratt. 2007. *Energy Metropolis: An Environmental History of Houston and the Gulf Coast*. Pittsburgh, PA: University of Pittsburgh Press.

Merrill, Karen R. 2007. *The Oil Crisis of 1973–1974: A Brief History with Documents*. New York: Bedford.

Miller, Russell. 2011. *The House of Getty*. New York: Bloomsbury Reader Edition.

Miner, H. Craig. 1993. *Wolf Creek Station: Kansas Gas and Electric Company in the Nuclear Era*. Columbus, OH: Ohio State University Press.

Mitchell, Timothy. 2011. *Carbon Democracy: Political Power in the Age of Oil*. New York: Verso Press.

Mom, Gijs. 2004. *The Electric Vehicle: Technology and Expectations in the Automobile Age*. Baltimore, MD: Johns Hopkins University Press.

Montrie, Chad. 2003. *To Save the Land and People: A History of Opposition to Surface Coal Mining in Appalachia*. Chapel Hill, NC: University of North Carolina Press.

Moran, Daniel, and James A. Russell, eds. 2009. *Energy Security and Global Politics: The Militarization of Resource Management*. London: Routledge.

Morrison, B.M. 1982. "Household Energy Consumption, 1900–1980: A Quantitative History." In *Energy and Transport: Historical Perspectives on Policy Issues*. Eds. A.H. Daniels and M. Rose. Pp. 201–33. New York: SAGE Publications.

Moyer, Reed. 1964. *Competition in the Midwestern Coal Industry*. Cambridge, MA: Harvard University Press.

Nash, Gerald D. 1968. *United States Oil Policy, 1890–1964*. Pittsburgh, PA: University of Pittsburgh Press.

Nebeker, Frederik. 2009. *Dawn of the Electronic Age: Electrical Technologies in the Shaping of the Modern World, 1914 to 1945*. Piscataway, NJ: Wiley-IEEE Press.

Needham, Andrew. 2014. *Power Lines: Phoenix and the Making of the Modern Southwest*. Princeton, NJ: Princeton University Press.

Neufeld, John L. 2016. *Selling Power: Economics, Policy, and Electric Utilities before 1940*. Chicago, IL: University of Chicago Press.

Noggle, Burl. 1965. *Teapot Dome: Oil and Politics in the 1920's*. New York: W.W. Norton & Company, Inc.

Nye, David E. 1992. *Electrifying America: Social Meanings of a New Technology, 1880–1940*. Cambridge, MA: MIT Press.

Nye, David E. 1998. *Consuming Power: A Social History of American Energies*. Cambridge, MA: MIT Press.

Olien, Roger. 1982. *Oil Booms: Social Change in Five Texas Towns*. Lincoln, NE: University of Nebraska Press.

Olien, Diana D., and Roger M. Olien. 2002. *Oil in Texas: The Gusher Age, 1895–1945*. Austin, TX: University of Texas Press.

Olien, Roger M., and Diana Davids Hinton. 2000. *Oil & Ideology: The Cultural Creation of the American Petroleum Industry*. Chapel Hill, NC: University of North Carolina Press.

Oreskes, Naomi, and Erik M. Conway. 2010. *Merchants of Doubt: How a Handful of Scientists Obscured the Truth on Issues from Tobacco Smoke to Global Warming*. New York: Bloomsbury Press.

Ortiz, I.A., and B.M. Morrison. 1983. "Energy and Home Economics: An 80 Year History." *Journal of Home Economics*. Vol. 75. No. 3. Pp. 40–7.

Osif, Bonnie A., Anthony J. Baratta, and Thomas W. Conkling. 2004. *TMI 25 Years Later: The Three Mile Island Nuclear Power Plant Accident and Its Impact*. University Park, PA: Penn State Press.

Owens, Brandon N. 2019. *The Wind Power Story: A Century of Innovation that Reshaped the Global Energy Landscape*. Piscataway, NJ: IEEE Press.

Page, Brian, and Richard Walker. 1991. "From Settlement to Fordism: The Agro-Industrial Revolution in the American Midwest." *Economic Geography*. October. Vol. 67. No. 4. Pp. 281–315.

Painter, David S. 2012. "Oil and the American Century." *The Journal of American History*. Oil in American History. Vol. 99. No. 1. June. Pp. 24–39.

Parker, Chad H. 2015. *Making the Desert Modern: Americans, Arabs and Oil on the Saudi Frontier, 1933–1973*. Amherst, MA: University of Massachusetts Press.

Pasternak, Judy. 2010. *Yellow Dirt: An American Story of a Poisoned Land and a People Betrayed*. New York: Free Press.

Penna, Anthony N. 2020. *A History of Energy Flows: From Human Labor to Renewable Power*. New York: Routledge.

Perlin, John. 2013. *Let It Shine: The 6,000-Year Story of Solar Energy*. Novato, CA: New World Library.

Perrier, Dianne. 2009. *Onramps and Overpasses: A Cultural History of Interstate Travel*. Gainesville, FL: University Press of Florida.

Platt, Harold A. 1991. *The Electric City: Energy and the Growth of the Chicago Area, 1880–1930*. Chicago, IL: University of Chicago Press.

Pope, Franklin L. 1891. "The Inventors of the Electric Motor, with Special Reference to the Work of Thomas Davenport." *Electrical Engineer*. Vol. 11. Pp. 1–5, 33–9, 65–71, 93–8, 125–30.

Potter, Stephen. 1990. *The American Petroleum Institute: An Informal History, 1919–1987*. Washington, DC: The American Petroleum Institute.

Rees, Jonathan. 2013. *Refrigeration Nation: A History of Ice, Appliances, and Enterprise in America*. Baltimore, MD: Johns Hopkins University Press.

Reynolds, Terry S. 1983. *Stronger than a Hundred Men: A History of the Vertical Water Wheel*. Baltimore, MD: Johns Hopkins University Press.

Rhodes, Richard. 2018. *Energy: A Human History*. New York: Simon & Schuster.
Righter, Robert W. 1996. *Wind Energy in America: A History*. Norman, OK: University of Oklahoma Press.
Righter, Robert W. 2008. *Wind Energy in America: A History*. Norman, OK: University of Oklahoma Press.
Ringholz, Raye C. 2002. *Uranium Frenzy: Saga of the Nuclear West*. Logan, UT: Utah State University Press.
Riordan, Michael, and Lillian Hoddeson. 1998. *Crystal Fire: The Invention of the Transistor and the Birth of the Information Age*. New York: Norton.
Rister, Carl Coke. 1949. *Oil! Titan of the Southwest*. Norman, OK: University of Oklahoma Press.
Roosa, John. 2020. "Dead Labor: Disappearances in Sumatra." In *Buried Histories: The Anticommunist Massacres of 1965–1966 in Indonesia*. Pp. 209–240. Madison, WI: University of Wisconsin Press.
Rose, Mark H. 1995. *Cities of Light and Heat: Domesticating Gas and Electricity in America*. University Park, PA: Pennsylvania State University Press.
Rosen, William. 2010. *The Most Powerful Idea in the World: A Story of Steam, Industry, and Invention*. New York: Random House.
Rothschild, Rachel Emma. 2019. *Poisonous Skies: Acid Rain and the Globalization of Pollution*. Chicago, IL: University of Chicago Press.
Rowsome, Jr., Frank. 2013. *The Birth of Electric Traction: The Extraordinary Life of Inventor Frank Julian Sprague*. New York: IEEE History Center Press.
Rudolph, Richard, and Scott Ridley. 1986. *Power Struggle: The Hundred-Year War over Electricity*. New York: Harper & Row.
Sabol Spezio, Teresa. 2018. *Slick Policy: Environmental and Science Policy in the Aftermath of the Santa Barbara Oil Spill*. Pittsburgh, PA: University of Pittsburgh Press.
Sachs, Jeffrey D. 2015. *The Age of Sustainable Development*. New York: Columbia University Press.
Sampson, Anthony. 1991. *The Seven Sisters: The Great Oil Companies and the World They Shaped*. New York: Viking Press.
Sawers, Larry. 2004. "The Mule, the South, and Economic Progress." *Social Science History*. Vol. 28. No. 4. Pp. 667–90.
Scamehorn, Lee. 2002. *High Altitude Energy: A History of Fossil Fuels in Colorado*. Boulder, CO: University Press of Colorado.
Schiffer, Michael B. 2008. *Power Struggles: Scientific Authority and the Creation of Practical Electricity before Edison*. Cambridge, MA: MIT Press.
Schivelbusch, Wolfgang. 1995. *Disenchanted Night: The Industrialization of Light in the Nineteenth Century*. Berkeley, CA: University of California Press.
Schneider-Mayerson, Matthew. 2015. *Peak Oil: Apocalyptic Environmentalism and Libertarian Political Culture*. Chicago, IL: University of Chicago Press.
Schobert, Harold H. 2014. *Energy and Society: An Introduction*. Boca Raton, FL: CRC Press.
Schurr, Sam H., and Bruce C. Netschert. 1960. *Energy in the American Economy, 1850–1975: An Economic Study of Its History and Prospects*. Baltimore, MD: Johns Hopkins University Press.
Segall, Grant. 2001. *John D. Rockefeller: Anointed with Oil*. New York: Oxford University Press.
Seiter, Cotten. 2008. *Republic of Drivers: A Cultural History of Automobility in America*. Chicago, IL: University of Chicago Press.
Shulman, Peter. 2015. *Coal and Empire: The Birth of Energy Security in Industrial America*. Baltimore, MD: Johns Hopkins University Press.
Sieferle, Rolf P. 1990. "The Energy System: A Basic Concept of Environmental History." In *The Silent Countdown*. Eds. P. Brimblecombe and C. Pfister. Pp. 9–20. New York: Springer.
Smil, Vaclav. 1994. *Energy in World History*. Boulder, CO: Westview Press.
Smil, Vaclav. 2006. *Transforming the Twentieth Century*. Vol. 2: *Technical Innovations and Their Consequences*. New York: Oxford University Press.
Smil, Vaclav. 2017. *Energy and Civilization: A History*. Cambridge, MA: MIT Press.
Smith, Barbara E. 1987. *Digging Our Own Graves: Coal Miners and the Struggle over Black Lung Disease*. Philadelphia, PA: Temple University Press.
Stotz, Louis. 1938. *History of the Gas Industry*. New York: Stettiner Bros.

Stradling, David. 1999. *Smokestacks and Progressives: Environmentalists, Engineers, and Air Quality in America, 1881–1951*. Baltimore, MD: Johns Hopkins University Press.

Swift, Earl. 2011. *The Big Roads: The Untold Story of the Engineers, Visionaries, and Trailblazers Who Created the American Superhighways*. Boston, MA: Houghton Mifflin Harcourt.

Tarbell, Ida. 1904. *The History of the Standard Oil Company*. New York: McClure, Philips and Company.

Teller, Edward. 1960. "Energy Patterns of the Future." In *Energy and Man: A Symposium*. Eds. Alan Nevis et al. Pp. 53–72. New York: Appleton-Century-Crofts, Inc.

Theriot, Jason P. 2014. *American Energy, Imperiled Coast: Oil and Gas Development in Louisiana's Wetlands*. Baton Rouge, LA: LSU Press.

Tobey, Ronald C. 1997. *Technology as Freedom: The New Deal and the Electrical Modernization of the American Home*. Berkeley, CA: University of California Press.

Towler, Brian F. 2014. *The Future of Energy*. Cambridge, MA: Academic Press.

Usher, Bruce. 2019. *Renewable Energy: A Primer for the Twenty-first Century*. New York: Columbia University Press.

Vernon, Raymond, ed. 1976. *The Oil Crisis*. New York: W.W. Norton & Company.

Vietor, Richard H.K. 1984. *Energy Policy in America since 1945*. Cambridge: Cambridge University Press.

Vitalis, Robert. 2007. *America's Kingdom: Mythmaking on the Saudi Oil Frontier*. Stanford, CA: Stanford University Press.

Voyles, Traci Brynne. 2015. *Wastelanding: Legacies of Uranium Mining in Navajo Country*. Minneapolis, MN: University of Minnesota Press.

Walker, J. Samuel. 2000. *Permissible Dose: A History of Radiation Protection in the Twentieth Century*. Berkeley, CA: University of California Press.

Walker, J. Samuel. 2006. *Three Mile Island: A Nuclear Crisis in Historical Perspective*. Berkeley, CA: University of California Press.

Walker, J. Samuel. 2009. *The Road to Yucca Mountain: The Development of Radioactive Waste Policy in the United States*. Berkeley, CA: University of California Press.

Wall, Bennett H. 1988. *Growth in a Changing Environment: A History of Standard Oil Company (New Jersey) 1950–1972 and Exxon Corporation 1972–1975*. New York: McGraw Hill Book Company.

Weaver, Bobby D. 2013. *Oilfield Trash: Life and Labor in the Oil Patch*. College Station, TX: Texas A&M University Press.

Wellock, Thomas Raymond. 1998. *Critical Masses: Opposition to Nuclear Power in California, 1958–1978*. Madison, WI: University of Wisconsin Press.

Wight, David M. 2021. *Oil Money: Middle East Petrodollars and the Transformation of US Empire, 1967–1988*. Ithaca, NY: Cornell University Press.

Wilkins, Mira. 1975. "The Oil Companies in Perspective." *Daedalus*. Vol. 104. No. 4. Fall. Pp. 159–78.

Williams, James C. 1997. *Energy and the Making of Modern California*. Akron, OH: University of Akron Press.

Williamson, Harold, Ralph L. Andreano, Arnold R. Daum, and Gilbert C. Klose. 1963. *The American Petroleum Industry: 1899–1959, The Age of Energy*. Evanston, IL: Northwestern University Press.

Wilson, Sheena, Adam Carlson, and Imre Szeman, eds. 2017. *Petrocultures: Oil, Politics, Culture*. Montreal & Kingston: McGill-Queen's University Press.

Winchell, Mike. 2019. *The Electric War: Edison, Tesla, Westinghouse, and the Race to Light the World*. New York: Henry Holt and Company.

Woolf, Arthur G. 1987. "The Residential Adoption of Electricity in Early Twentieth-Century America." *The Energy Journal*. Vol. 8. No. 2. Pp. 19–30.

Yergin, Daniel. 1991. *The Prize: The Epic Quest for Oil, Money & Power*. New York: Simon & Schuster.

Yergin, Daniel. 2009. *The Prize: The Epic Quest for Oil, Money & Power*. Reissue ed. New York: Free Press.

Yergin, Daniel. 2011. *The Quest: Energy, Security, and the Remaking of the Modern World*. New York: Penguin.

Zaretsky, Natasha. 2018. *Radiation Nation: Three Mile Island and the Political Transformation of the 1970s*. New York: Columbia University Press.

Zoellner, Tom. 2009. *Uranium: War, Energy, and the Rock that Shaped the World*. New York: Viking.

Zott, Lynn M., and Helga Schier, eds. 2013. *Nuclear Power*. Opposing Viewpoints Series. Farmington Hills, MI: Greenhaven Press.

Zuckerman, Gregory. 2013. *The Frackers: The Outrageous Inside Story of the New Billionaire Wildcatters*. New York: Portfolio/Penguin.

INDEX

ABOUT THE EDITORS

Jeffrey B. Webb, Ph.D., is Professor of American History at Huntington University, Huntington, IN. He is coeditor of two ABC-CLIO reference works, the award-winning *Conspiracies and Conspiracy Theories in American History*, 2 vols. (2019) and *American Myths, Legends, and Tall Tales: An Encyclopedia of American Folklore*, 3 vols. (2016). He is a member of the International Association for the Study of Environment, Space, and Place and his research in the field of environmental history is published in the association's international, peer-reviewed journal, *Environment, Space, Place*.

Christopher R. Fee, Ph.D., is Graeff Professor of English at Gettysburg College, Gettysburg, PA. He is coeditor of two ABC-CLIO reference works, the award-winning *Conspiracies and Conspiracy Theories in American History*, 2 vols. (2019) as well as *American Myths, Legends, and Tall Tales: An Encyclopedia of American Folklore*, 3 vols. (2016). Fee is also author of *Arthur: God & Hero in Avalon* (Reaktion 2019); *The Goddess: Myths of the Great Mother* (Reaktion 2016); *Mythology in the Middle Ages: Heroic Tales of Monsters, Magic, and Might* (Praeger 2011); and *Gods, Heroes, and Kings: The Battle for Mythic Britain* (Oxford 2001).